P9-DVI-469

Oxford
Italian
Mini Dictionary

FOURTH EDITION

Italian–English
English–Italian

Italiano–Inglese
Inglese–Italiano

Handwritten notes:

Fer
Fec + a
Fatto

nd,
m
ti
gu/le
Ci
vi
gli

Ref   Dir.

Si: 10/12
Si: li/re

Piu di
Piu che sono
Io mi sono
seduta

OXFORD
UNIVERSITY PRESS

OXFORD

UNIVERSITY PRESS

Great Clarendon Street, Oxford OX2 6DP

Oxford University Press is a department of the University of Oxford.
It furthers the University's objective of excellence in research, scholarship,
and education by publishing worldwide in

Oxford New York

Auckland Cape Town Dar es Salaam Hong Kong Karachi Kuala Lumpur
Madrid Melbourne Mexico City Nairobi New Delhi Shanghai Taipei
Toronto

With offices in

Argentina Austria Brazil Chile Czech Republic France Greece
Guatemala Hungary Italy Japan Poland Portugal
Singapore South Korea Switzerland Thailand Turkey Ukraine Vietnam

Oxford is a registered trade mark of Oxford University Press
in the UK and in certain other countries

British Library Cataloguing in Publication Data
Data available

Library of Congress Cataloging in Publication Data
Data available

ISBN 978-0-19-956682-2 (special edition)
ISBN 978-0-19-953434-0

10 9 8 7 6 5 4 3 2 1

Typeset by Interactive Sciences Ltd, Gloucester
Printed and bound in Italy
by L.E.G.O.S.p.A, Lavis (TN)

masculine or feminine	*mf*	maschile o femminile
military	*Mil*	militare
music	*Mus*	musica
noun	*n*	sostantivo
nautical	*Naut*	nautica
pejorative	*pej*	peggiorativo
personal	*pers*	personale
photography	*Phot*	fotografia
physics	*Phys*	fisica
plural	*pl*	plurale
politics	*Pol*	politica
possessive	*poss*	possessivo
past participle	*pp*	participio passato
prefix	*pref*	prefisso
preposition	*prep*	preposizione
present tense	*pres*	presente
pronoun	*pron*	pronome
psychology	*Psych*	psicologia
past tense	*pt*	tempo passato
someone	*qcno*	qualcuno
something	*qcsa*	qualcosa
rail	*Rail*	ferrovia
reflexive	*refl*	riflessivo
religion	*Relig*	religione
relative pronoun	*rel pron*	pronome relativo
somebody	*sb*	qualcuno
school	*Sch*	scuola
singular	*sg*	singolare
something	*sth*	qualcosa
technical	*Techn*	tecnico
telephone	*Teleph*	telefono
theatrical	*Theat*	teatrale
television	*TV*	televisione
typography	*Typ*	tipografia
university	*Univ*	università
auxiliary verb	*v aux*	verbo ausiliare
intransitive verb	*vi*	verbo intransitivo
reflexive verb	*vr*	verbo riflessivo
transitive verb	*vt*	verbo transitivo
transitive and intransitive verb	*vt/i*	verbo transitivo e intransitivo
vulgar	*vulg*	volgare
familiar	▯	familiare
slang	▣	gergo
cultural equivalent	≈	equivalenza culturale

Imperfecto

	essere	(I) (P)
avo ei	Ero	il → i
v e	Eri	la → le
vemo	Era	
vate	Eravemo	
vano	Eravate	
	Ereno	

Potere = to be able

posso
puoi
puo
possiamo
potere
possono

PP ho potuto
imp poteva

Volere = to want

voglio
vuoi
vuole
vogliamo
vogliamo

PP = ho voluto
imp voleva

Dovere = to must

devo
devi
deve
dobbiamo
davere
devono

PP = ho davuto
imp = davevo

Sapere = to know

so
sa
sa
sappiamo
sapete
sanno

PP = seputo

Contents/Indice

Fourth edition/Quarta edizione
Editors/Redazione
Joanna Rubery, Loredana Riu, Pat
Bulhosen

Third Edition/Terza edizione
Editors/Redazione
Nicholas Rollin, Francesca Logi

Second Edition/Seconda edizione
Editors/Redazione
Debora Mazza, Donatella Boi, Sonia
Tinagli-Baxter, Peter Terrell, Jane
Goldie, Francesca Logi, Carla Zipoli

First Edition/Prima edizione
Editor/Redazione
Joyce Andrews

Phrasefinder/Trovafrasi
Colin McIntosh, Francesca Logi
Loredana Riu, Neil and Roswitha
Morris

Proprietary terms

This dictionary includes some words which are or are asserted to be, proprietary names or trademarks. Their inclusion does not imply that they have acquired for legal purposes a non-proprietary or general significance, nor is any other judgement implied concerning their legal status. In cases where the editor has some evidence that a word is used as proprietary name or trade mark this is indicated by the symbol (®), but no judgement concerning the legal status of such words is made or implied thereby.

Marchi registrati

Questo dizionario include alcune parole che sono o vengono considerate marchi registrati. La loro presenza non implica che abbiano acquisito legalmente un significato generale, né si suggerisce alcun altro giudizio riguardo il loro stato giuridico. Qualora il redattore abbia trovato testimonianza dell'uso di una parola come marchio registrato, quest'ultima è stata contrassegnata dal simbolo ®, ma nessun giudizio riguardo lo stato giuridico di tale parola viene espresso o suggerito in tal modo.

Preface/Prefazione

This new edition of the *Oxford Italian Mini Dictionary* has been updated to reflect the changes in English and Italian since the last edition in 2005. Notable additions include terms from the spheres of computing, business and communications, that have become common in modern life. The *Phrasefinder* section has been expanded to provide more useful expressions needed for everyday communication. The section is arranged thematically and covers nine key topics: *going places, keeping in touch, food and drink, places to stay, shopping and money, sport and leisure, good timing, health and beauty* and *weights and measures*.

Questa nuova edizione del *Mini Dizionario Oxford* è stata aggiornata per riflettere i cambiamenti avvenuti nell'inglese e nell'italiano dopo la scorsa edizione del 2005. Tra le voci aggiunte si segnalano in particolare termini del settore informatico, commerciale e delle comunicazioni divenuti ricorrenti nella lingua di tutti i giorni. La sezione *Trovafrasi* è stata infine ampliata per dare maggior spazio alle espressioni necessarie alla comunicazione quotidiana. Tale sezione è presentata per tema e copre nove aree chiave: *in viaggio, comunicazioni, mangiare e bere, dove alloggiare, spese e soldi, sport e tempo libero, l'ora giusta, salute e bellezza,* e *pesi e misure*.

Introduzione

Allo scopo di fornire il maggior numero possibile di informazioni riguardo all'inglese e all'italiano, questo dizionario ricorre ad alcune convenzioni per sfruttare al meglio lo spazio disponibile.

All'interno della voce un trattino ondulato ~ è utilizzato al posto del lemma.

Qualora il lemma contenga una barra verticale |, il trattino ondulato sostituisce solo la parte del lemma che precede la barra. Ad es.: **dark|en** *vt* oscurare. **~ness** *n* buio **m** (la seconda parola in neretto va letta **darkness**).

Vengono forniti indicatori per indirizzare l'utente verso la traduzione del senso voluto di una parola. I tipi di indicatori sono:

- etichette semantiche, indicanti lo specifico settore d'uso di una parola o di un senso (commercio, informatica, fotografia ecc.);
- indicatori di significato, ad es.: **redazione** *f* (ufficio) editorial office; (di testi) editing;
- soggetti tipici di verbi, ad es.: **trovarsi** *vr* (luogo:) be;
- complementi oggetti tipici di verbi, collocati dopo la traduzione del verbo stesso, ad es.: **superare** *vt* overtake (veicolo); pass (esame);
- sostantivi che ricorrono tipicamete con certi aggettivi, ad es.: **solare** *adj* (energia, raggi) solar; (crema) sun.

Il pallino nero indica che la stessa parola viene tradotta come una diversa parte del discorso, ad es.: **calcolatore** *adj* ... ● *m* ...

La pronuncia inglese è trascritta usando l'Alfabeto Fonetico Internazionale (vedi pag. viii).

L'accento tonico nelle parole italiane è indicato dal segno ' collocato davanti alla sillaba accentata.

Le parentesi quadre racchiudono parti di espressioni che possono essere omesse senza alterazioni di significato.

Introduction

In order to give the maximum information about English and Italian in the space available, this new dictionary uses certain space-saving conventions.

A swung dash ~ is used to replace the headword within the entry.

Where the headword contains a vertical bar | the swung dash replaces only the part of the headword that comes before the |. For example:

efficien | te *adj* efficient. **~za** *f* efficiency (the second bold word reads efficienza).

Indicators are provided to guide the user to the best translation for a specific sense of a word. Types of indicator are:

- field labels, which indicate a general area of usage (commercial, computing, photography etc);

- sense indicators, eg: **bore** *n* (of gun) calibro *m*; (person) seccatore, -trice *mf*;

- typical subjects of verbs, eg: **bond** *vt* (glue:) attaccare;

- typical objects of verbs, placed after the translation of the verb, eg: **boost** *vt* stimolare (sales); sollevare (morale);

- nouns that typically go together with certain adjectives, eg: **rich** *adj* ricco; (food) pesante;

A bullet point means that a headword has changed its part of speech within an entry, eg: **partition** *n* ... ● *vt* ...

English pronunciation is given for the Italian user in the International Phonetic Alphabet (see p viii).

Italian stress is shown by a ' placed in front of the stressed syllable in a word.

Square brackets are used around parts of an expression which can be omitted without altering its sense.

Pronuncia inglese

Simboli fonetici

Vocali e dittonghi

iː	see	ɔː	saw	eɪ	page	ɔɪ	join
ɪ	sit	ʊ	put	əʊ	home	ɪə	near
e	ten	uː	too	aɪ	five	eə	hair
æ	hat	ʌ	cup	aɪə	fire	ʊə	poor
ɑː	arm	ɜː	fur	aʊ	now		
ɒ	got	ə	ago	aʊə	flour		

Consonanti

p	pen	tʃ	chin	s	so	n	no
b	bad	dʒ	June	z	zoo	ŋ	sing
t	tea	f	fall	ʃ	she	l	leg
d	dip	v	voice	ʒ	measure	r	red
k	cat	θ	thin	h	how	j	yes
g	got	ð	then	m	man	w	wet

Note: ' precede la sillaba accentata.

Pronunciation of Italian

Vowels

a is broad like *a* in *father*: **casa**

e has two sounds: closed like *ey* in *they*: **sera**; open like *e* in *egg*: **sette**

i is like *ee* in *feet*: **venire**

o 1. closed like *o* in *show*: **croma**. 2. open like *o* in *dog*: **bocca**.

u is like *oo* in *moon*: **luna**

When two or more vowels come together each vowel is pronounced separately: **buono; baia**.

Consonants

b, d, f, l, m, n, p, t, v are pronounced as in English. When these are double, they are pronounced as separate sounds: **bello**.

c before **a, o** or **u** and before consonants is like *k* in *king*: **cane**.
Before **e** or **i** it is like *ch* in *church*: **cena**.

ch is also like *k* in *king*: **chiesa**

g before **a, o** or **u** is hard like *g* in *got*: **gufo**.
Before **e** or **i** it is like *j* in *jelly*: **gentile**.

gh is like *g* in *gun*: **ghiaccio**.

gl when followed by **a, e, o** and **u** is like *gl* in *glass*: **gloria**.

gli is like *lli* in *million*: **figlio**.

gn is like *ni* in *onion*: **bagno**.

h is silent.

ng is like *ng* in *finger*: **ringraziare**.

r is pronounced distinctly.

s between two vowels is like *s* in *rose*: **riso**. at the beginning of a word it is like *s* in *soap*: **sapone**.

sc before **e** or **i** is like *sh* in *shell*: **scienza**.

z sounds like *ts* within a word: **fazione**; like *dz* at the beginning: **zoo**.

Stress is shown by the sign ' printed before the stressed syllable.

Aa

a (ad *before vowel*) *prep* to; (*stato in luogo, tempo, età*) at; (*con mese, città*) in; (*mezzo, modo*) by; **dire qcsa a qcno** tell sb sth; **alle tre** at three o'clock; **a vent'anni** at the age of twenty; **a Natale** at Christmas; **a dicembre** in December; **ero al cinema** I was at the cinema; **vivo a Londra** I live in London; **a due a due** two by two; **a piedi** on o by foot; **maglia a maniche lunghe** long-sleeved sweater; **casa a tre piani** house with three floors; **giocare a tennis** play tennis; **50 km all'ora** 50 km an hour; **4 euro al chilo** 4 euros a kilo; **al mattino/alla sera** in the morning/evening; **a venti chilometri/due ore da qui** twenty kilometres/two hours away

a'bate *m* abbot

abbacchi'ato *adj* downhearted

ab'bacchio *m* [young] lamb

abbagli'ante *adj* dazzling ● *m* headlight, high beam

abbagli'are *vt* dazzle. **ab'baglio** *m* blunder; **prendere un ~** make a blunder

abbai'are *vi* bark

abba'ino *m* dormer window

abbando'na|re *vt* abandon; leave (*luogo*); give up (*piani ecc*). **~rsi** *vr* let oneself go; **~rsi a** give oneself up to (*ricordi ecc*). **~to** *adj* abandoned. **abban'dono** *m* abandoning; *fig* abandon; (*stato*) neglect

abbas'samento *m* (*di temperatura, prezzi ecc*) drop

abbas'sar|e *vt* lower; turn down (radio, tv); **~e i fari** dip the headlights. **~si** *vr* stoop; (sole ecc:) sink; *fig* demean oneself

ab'basso *adv* below ● *int* down with

abba'stanza *adv* enough; (*alquanto*) quite

abbat'ter|e *vt* demolish; shoot down (aereo); put down (animale); topple (regime); (fig: demoralizzare) dishearten. **~si** *vr* (cadere) fall; *fig* be discouraged

abbatti'mento *m* (morale) despondency

abbat'tuto *adj* despondent

abba'zia *f* abbey

abbel'lir|e *vt* embellish. **~si** *vr* adorn oneself

abbeve'ra|re *vt* water. **~'toio** *m* drinking trough

abbi'ente *adj* well-to-do

abbiglia'mento *m* clothes *pl*; (industria) clothing industry

abbigli'ar|e *vt* dress. **~si** *vr* dress up

abbina'mento *m* combining

abbi'nare *vt* combine; match (colori)

abbindo'lare *vt* cheat

abbocca'mento *m* interview; (conversazione) talk

abboc'care *vi* bite; (tubi:) join; *fig* swallow the bait

abboc'cato *adj* (vino) fairly sweet

abbof'farsi *vt* stuff oneself

abbona'mento *m* subscription; (ferroviario ecc) season-ticket; **fare l'~** take out a subscription

abbo'na|re *vt* make a subscriber. **~rsi** *vr* subscribe (a to); take out a season-ticket (a for) (teatro, stadio)

∼to, -a mf subscriber

abbon'dan|te adj abundant; (quantità) copious; (nevicata) heavy; (vestiario) roomy. **∼te di** abounding in. **∼te'mente** adv (mangiare) copiously. **∼za** f abundance

abbon'dare vi abound

abbor'da|bile adj (persona) approachable; (prezzo) reasonable. **∼ggio** m (Mil) boarding. **∼re** vt board (nave); approach (persona); (Ⅰ: attaccar bottone a) chat up; tackle (compito ecc)

abbotto'na|re vt button up. **∼tura** f [row of] buttons. **∼to** adj fig tight-lipped

abboz'zare vt sketch [out]; **∼ un sorriso** give a hint of a smile. **ab'bozzo** m sketch

abbracci'are vt embrace; take up (professione); fig include. **ab'braccio** m hug

abbrevi'a|re vt shorten; (ridurre) curtail; abbreviate (parola). **∼zi'one** f abbreviation

abbron'zante m sun-tan lotion

abbron'za|re vt bronze; tan (pelle). **∼rsi** vr get a tan. **∼to** adj tanned. **∼tura** f [sun-]tan

abbrusto'lire vt toast; roast (caffè ecc)

abbruti'mento m brutalization. **abbru'tire** vt brutalize. **abbru'tirsi** vr become brutalized

abbuf'far|si vr Ⅰ stuff oneself. **∼ta** f blowout

abbuo'nare vt reduce

abbu'ono m allowance; Sport handicap

abdi'ca|re vi abdicate. **∼zi'one** f abdication

aber'rante adj aberrant

a'bete m fir

abi'etto adj despicable

'abi|le adj able; (idoneo) fit; (astuto) clever. **∼ità** f inv ability; (idoneità) fit-

ness; (astuzia) cleverness. **∼'mente** adv ably; (con astuzia) cleverly

abili'ta|re vt qualify. **∼to** adj qualified. **∼zi'one** f qualification; (titolo) diploma

abis'sale adj abysmal. **a'bisso** m abyss

abi'tabile adj inhabitable

abi'tacolo m (Auto) passenger compartment

abi'tante mf inhabitant

abi'ta|re vi live. **∼to** adj inhabited **● m** built-up area. **∼zi'one** f house

'abito m (da donna) dress; (da uomo) suit. **∼ da cerimonia/da sera** formal/evening dress

abitu'al|e adj usual. **∼'mente** adv usually

abitu'are vt accustom. **∼si a** vr get used to

abitu'dinario, -a adj of fixed habits **● mf** person of fixed habits

abi'tudine f habit; **d'∼** usually; **per ∼** out of habit; **avere l'∼ di fare qcsa** be in the habit of doing sth

abnegazi'one f self-sacrifice

ab'norme adj abnormal

abo'li|re vt abolish; repeal (legge). **∼zi'one** f abolition; repeal

abomi'nevole adj abominable

abor'rire vt abhor

abor'ti|re vi miscarry; (volontariamente) have an abortion; fig fail. **∼vo** adj abortive. **a'borto** m miscarriage; (volontario) abortion. **∼sta** adj pro-choice

abrasi'one f abrasion. **abra'sivo** adj & m abrasive

abro'ga|re vt repeal. **∼zi'one** f repeal

'abside f apse

abu'lia f apathy. **a'bulico** adj apathetic

abu's|are vi **∼ di** abuse; overindulge in (alcol); (approfittare di) take advantage of; (*violentare*) rape. **~ivo** *adj* illegal

a'buso *m* abuse. **~ di confidenza** breach of confidence

a.C. *abbr* (avanti Cristo) BC

'acca *f* 🔲 **non ho capito un'~** I understood damn all

acca'demi|a *f* academy. A~**a di Belle Arti** Academy of Fine Arts. **~co, -a** *adj* academic ● *mf* academician

acca'd|ere *vi* happen; accada quel che accada come what may. **~uto** *m* event

accalappi'are *vt* catch; *fig* allure

accal'carsi *vr* crowd

accal'da|rsi *vr* get overheated; *fig* get excited. **~to** *adj* overheated

accalo'rarsi *vr* get excited

accampa'mento *m* camp. **accam'pare** *vt fig* put forth. **accam'parsi** *vr* camp

accani'mento *m* tenacity; (*odio*) rage

acca'ni|rsi *vr* persist; (*infierire*) rage. **~to** *adj* persistent; (*odio*) fierce; *fig* inveterate

ac'canto *adv* near; **~ a** *prep* next to

accanto'nare *vt* set aside; (*Mil*) billet

accaparra'mento *m* hoarding; (*Comm*) cornering

accapar'ra|re *vt* hoard. **~rsi** *vr* grab; corner (mercato). **~'tore, ~'trice** *mf* hoarder

accapigli'arsi *vr* scuffle; (*litigare*) squabble

accappa'toio *m* bathrobe; (*per spiaggia*) beachrobe

accappo'nare *vt* fare **~ la pelle a** qcno make sb's flesh creep

accarez'zare *vt* caress; *fig* cherish

accartocci'ar|e *vt* scrunch up. **~si** *vr* curl up

acca'sarsi *vr* get married

accasci'arsi *vr* flop down; *fig*

lose heart

accata'stare *vt* pile up

accatti'vante *adj* beguiling

accatti'varsi *vr* **~ le simpatie/la stima/l'affetto di** qcno gain sb's sympathy/respect/affection

accat'tonaggio *m* begging. **accat'tone, -a** *mf* beggar

accaval'la|re *vt* cross (gambe). **~si** *vr* pile up; *fig* overlap

acce'cante *adj* (luce) blinding

acce'care *vt* blind ● *vi* go blind

ac'cedere *vi* **~ a** enter; (*acconsentire*) comply with

accele'ra|re *vi* accelerate ● *vt* accelerate. **~to** *adj* rapid. **~'tore** *m* accelerator. **~zi'one** *f* acceleration

ac'cender|e *vt* light; turn on (luce, TV ecc); *fig* inflame; ha da **~e?** have you got a light?. **~si** *vr* catch fire; (*illuminarsi*) light up; (TV ecc.) turn on; *fig* become inflamed

accendi'gas *m inv* gas lighter; (*su cucina*) automatic ignition

accen'dino *m* lighter

accendi'sigari *m* cigar-lighter

accen'nare *vt* indicate; hum (melodia) ● *vi* **~ a** beckon to; *fig* hint at; (*far l'atto di*) make as if to; accenna a piovere it looks like rain. **ac'cenno** *m* gesture; (*con il capo*) nod; *fig* hint

accensi'one *f* lighting; (*di motore*) ignition

accen'ta|re *vt* accent; (*con accento tonico*) stress. **~zi'one** *f* accentuation. **ac'cento** *m* accent; (*tonico*) stress

accentra'mento *m* centralizing

accen'trare *vt* centralize

accentu'a|re *vt* accentuate. **~rsi** *vr* become more noticeable. **~to** *adj* marked

accerchia'mento *m* surrounding

accerchi'are *vt* surround

accerta'mento *m* check

accer'tare *vt* ascertain; (*controllare*) check; assess (reddito)

a

ac'ceso adj lighted; (radio, TV ecc) on; (colore) bright

acces'sibile adj accessible; (persona) approachable; (spesa) reasonable

ac'cesso m access; (Med: di rabbia) fit; vietato l'~ no entry

acces'sorio adj accessory; (secondario) of secondary importance ● m accessory; **accessori** pl (rifiniture) fittings

ac'cetta f hatchet

accet'tabile adj acceptable

accet'tare vt accept; (aderire a) agree to

accettazi'one f acceptance; (luogo) reception. ~e [bagagli] check-in. [banco] ~ check-in [desk]

ac'cetto adj agreeable; **essere bene** ~ be very welcome

accezi'one f meaning

acchiap'pare vt catch

acchito m di primo ~ at first

acciac'care vt crush; fig prostrate. ~to, -a adj essere ~to ache all over. **acci'acco** m infirmity; **acciacchi** pl aches and pains

acciaie'ria f steelworks

acci'aio m steel; ~ inossidabile stainless steel

acciden'ta|le adj accidental. ~l'mente adv accidentally. ~to adj (terreno) uneven

acci'dente m accident; (Med) stroke; **non capisce un** ~ 🆇 he doesn't understand a damn thing. **acci'denti!** int damn!

accigli'a|rsi vr frown. ~to adj frowning

ac'cingersi vr ~ a be about to

acci'picchia int good Lord!

acciuf'fare vt catch

acci'uga f anchovy

accla'ma|re vt applaud; (eleggere) acclaim. ~zi'one f applause

acclima'ta|re vt acclimatize. ~si vr get acclimatized

ac'clu|dere vt enclose. ~so adj enclosed

accocco'larsi vr squat

accogli'en|te adj welcoming; (confortevole) cosy. ~za f welcome

ac'cogliere vt receive; (con piacere) welcome; (contenere) hold

accol'larsi vt take on (responsabilità, debiti, doveri). **accol'lato** adj high-necked

accoltel'lare vt knife

accomia'tar|e vt dismiss. ~si vr take one's leave (da of)

accomo'dante adj accommodating

accomo'dar|e vt (riparare) mend; (disporre) arrange. ~si vr make oneself at home; **si accomodi!** come in!; (si sieda) take a seat!

accompagna'mento m accompaniment; (seguito) retinue

accompa'gna|re vt accompany; ~re qcno a casa see sb home; ~re qcno alla porta show sb out. ~'tore, ~'trice mf companion; (di comitiva) escort; (Mus) accompanist

accomu'nare vt pool

acconci'a|re vt arrange. ~'tura f hair-style; (ornamento) head-dress

accondiscen'den|te adj too obliging. ~za f excessive desire to please

accondi'scendere vi ~ a condescend; comply with (desiderio); (acconsentire) consent to

acconsen'tire vi consent

acconten'tar|e vt satisfy. ~si vr be content (di with)

ac'conto m deposit; **in** ~ on account; **lasciare un** ~ leave a deposit

accop'pare vt 🆇 bump off

accoppia'mento m coupling; (di animali) mating

accoppi'a|re vt couple; mate (animali). ~rsi vr pair off; mate. ~ta f (scommessa) bet on two horses for first *and second place*

acco'rato *adj* sorrowful

accorci'ar|e *vt* shorten. **~si** *vr* get shorter

accor'dar|e *vt* concede; match (colori ecc); (Mus) tune. **~si** *vr* agree

ac'cordo *m* agreement; (Mus) chord; (armonia) harmony; andare d'~ get on well; d'~! agreed!; essere d'~ agree; prendere accordi con qcno make arrangements with sb

ac'corgersi *vr* ~ di notice; (capire) realize

accorgi'mento *m* shrewdness; (espediente) device

ac'correre *vi* hasten

accor'tezza *f* (previdenza) forethought

ac'corto *adj* shrewd; mal ~ incautious

acco'stamento *m* combination

acco'star|e *vt* draw close to; approach (persona); set ajar (porta ecc). **~si** *vr* ~si a come near to

accovacci'a|rsi *vr* crouch

accoz'zaglia *f* jumble; (di persone) mob

accoz'zare *vt* ~ colori mix colours that clash

accredita'mento *m* credit; ~ tramite bancogiro Bank Giro Credit

accredi'tare *vt* confirm (notizia); (Comm) credit

ac'cresc|ere *vt* increase. **~ersi** *vr* grow larger. **~i'tivo** *adj* augmentative

accucci'arsi *vr* (cane:) lie down; (persona:) crouch

accu'dire *vi* ~ a attend to

accumu'la|re *vt* accumulate. **~rsi** *vr* accumulate. **~'tore** *m* accumulator; (Auto) battery. **~zi'one** *f* accumulation.

accura'tezza *f* care

accu'rato *adj* careful

ac'cusa *f* accusation; (Jur) charge; essere in stato di ~ have been charged; la Pubblica A~ the public prosecutor

accu'sa|re *vt* accuse; (Jur) charge; complain of (dolore); **~re** ricevuta di acknowledge receipt of. **~to, -a** *mf* accused. **~'tore** *m* prosecutor

a'cerbo *adj* sharp; (non maturo) unripe

'acero *m* maple

a'cerrimo *adj* implacable

a'ceto *m* vinegar

ace'tone *m* nail-polish remover

A.C.I. *abbr* (Automobile Club d'Italia) Italian Automobile Association

acidità *f* acidity. ~ di stomaco acid stomach

'acido *adj* acid; (persona) sour ● *m* acid

a'cidulo *adj* slightly sour

'acino *m* berry; (chicco) grape

'acne *f* acne

'acqua *f* water; fare ~ leak; ~ in bocca! fig mum's the word!. ~ corrente running water. ~ dolce fresh water. ~ minerale mineral water. ~ minerale gassata fizzy mineral water. ~ naturale still mineral water. ~ potabile drinking water. ~ salata salt water. ~ tonica tonic water

acqua'forte *f* etching

ac'quaio *m* sink

acquama'rina *adj* aquamarine

acqua'rello *m* = ACQUERELLO

ac'quario *m* aquarium; (Astr) Aquarius

acqua'santa *f* holy water

acqua'scooter *m inv* water-scooter

ac'quatico *adj* aquatic

acquat'tarsi *vr* crouch

acqua'vite *f* brandy

acquaz'zone *m* downpour

acque'dotto *m* aqueduct

'acqueo *adj* vapore ~

water vapour

acque'rello m water-colour

acqui'rente mf purchaser

acqui'si|re vt acquire. ~to adj acquired. ~zi'one f attainment

acqui'st|are vt purchase; (ottenere) acquire. ac'quisto m purchase; uscire per ~i go shopping; fare ~i shop

acqui'trino m marsh

acquo'lina f far venire l'~ in bocca a qcno make sb's mouth water

ac'quoso adj watery

'acre adj acrid; (al gusto) sour; fig harsh

a'crilico m acrylic

a'croba|ta mf acrobat. ~'zia f acrobatics pl

a'cronimo m acronym

acu'ir|e vt sharpen. ~si vr become more intense

a'culeo m sting; (Bot) prickle

acumi'nato adj pointed

a'custic|a f acoustics pl. ~o adj acoustic

acu'tezza f acuteness

acutiz'zarsi vr become worse

a'cuto adj sharp; (suono) shrill; (freddo, odore) intense; (Gram, Math, Med) acute ●m (Mus) high note

ad prep = a (davanti a vocale)

adagi'ar|e vt lay down. ~si vr lie down

a'dagio adv slowly ●m (Mus) adagio; (proverbio) adage

adattabi'lità f adaptability

adatta'mento m adaptation; avere spirito di ~ be adaptable

adat'ta|re vt adapt; (aggiustare) fit. ~rsi vr adapt. ~tore m adaptor. a'datto adj suitable (a for); (giusto) right

addebita'mento m debit. ~ diretto direct debit

addebi'tare vt debit; ascribe (colpa)

ad'debito m charge

addensa'mento m thickening; (di persone) gathering

adden'sar|e vt thicken. ~si vr thicken; (affollarsi) gather

adden'tare vt bite

adden'trarsi vr penetrate

ad'dentro adv deeply; essere ~ in be in on

addestra'mento m training

adde'strar|e vt train. ~si vr train

ad'detto, -a adj assigned ●mf employee; (diplomatico) attaché. ~ stampa press officer

addiaccio m dormire all'~ sleep in the open

addi'etro adv (indietro) back; (nel passato) before

ad'dio m & int goodbye. ~ al celibato stag party

addi'rittura adv (perfino) even; (assolutamente) absolutely; ~! really!

ad'dirsi vr ~ a suit

addi'tare vt point at; (in mezzo a un gruppo) point out; fig point to

addi'tivo adj & m additive

addizio'nal|e adj additional. ~'mente adv additionally

addizio'nare vt add [up]. addizi'one f addition

addob'bare vt decorate. ad'dobbo m decoration

addol'cir|e vt sweeten; tone down (colore); fig soften. ~si vr fig mellow

addolo'ra|re vt grieve. ~si vr be upset (per by). ~to adj distressed

ad'dom|e m abdomen. ~i'nale adj abdominal; [muscoli] addominali pl abdominals

addomesti'ca|re vt tame. ~'tore m tamer

addormen'ta|re vt put to sleep. ~rsi vr go to sleep. ~to adj asleep; fig slow addos'sar|e vt ~e a (appoggiare) lean against; (attribuire) lay on. ~si vr (ammassarsi) crowd; shoulder (responsabilità ecc)

ad'dosso adv on; ~ a prep on; (molto vicino) right next to; mettere gli occhi ~ a qcno/qcsa hanker after sb/sth; non mettermi le mani ~! keep your hands off me!; stare ~ a qcno fig be on sb's back

ad'durre vt produce (prova, documento); give (pretesto, esempio)

adegua'mento m adjustment

adegu'a|re vt adjust. ~rsi vr conform. ~to adj adequate; (conforme) consistent

a'dempi|ere vt fulfil. ~'mento m fulfilment

ade'noidi fpl adenoids

ade'ren|te adj adhesive; (vestito) tight. ~m follower. ~za f adhesion. ~ze pl connections

ade'rire vi ~ a adhere to; support (petizione); agree to (richiesta)

adesca'mento m (Jur) soliciting

ade'scare vt bait; fig entice

adesi'one f adhesion; fig agreement

ade'sivo adj adhesive ● m sticker; (Auto) bumper sticker

a'desso adv now; (poco fa) just now; (tra poco) any moment now; da ~ in poi from now on; per ~ for the moment

adia'cente adj adjacent; ~ a next to

adi'bire vt ~ a put to use as

'adipe m adipose tissue

adi'ra|rsi vr get irate. ~to adj irate

a'dire vt resort to; ~ le vie legali take legal proceedings

'adito m dare ~ a give rise to

adocchi'are vt eye; (con desiderio) covet

adole'scen|te adj & mf adolescent. ~za f adolescence. ~zi'ale adj

adolescent

adom'brar|e vt darken; fig veil. ~si vr (offendersi) take offence

adope'rar|e vt use. ~si vr take trouble

ado'rabile adj adorable

ado'ra|re vt adore. ~zi'one f adoration

ador'nare vt adorn

adot'ta|re vt adopt. ~ivo adj adoptive. adozi'one f adoption

adrena'lina f adrenalin

adri'atico adj Adriatic ● m l'A~ the Adriatic

adu'la|re vt flatter. ~tore, ~trice mf flatterer. ~zi'one f flattery

adulte'ra|re vt adulterate. ~to adj adulterated

adul'terio m adultery. a'dultero, -a adj adulterous ● m adulterer ● f adulteress

a'dulto, -a adj & mf adult; (maturo) mature

adu'nanza f assembly

adu'na|re vt gather. ~ta f (Mil) parade

a'dunco adj hooked

ae'rare vt air (stanza)

'aereo adj aerial; (dell'aviazione) air; attrib ● m aeroplane, plane

ae'robic|a f aerobics. ~o adj aerobic

aerodi'namic|a f aerodynamics sg. ~o adj aerodynamic

aero'nautic|a f aeronautics sg; (Mil) Air Force. ~o adj aeronautical

aero'plano m aeroplane

aero'porto m airport

aero'scalo m cargo and servicing area

aero'sol m inv aerosol

'afa f sultriness

af'fabil|e adj affable. ~ità f affability

affaccen'da|rsi vr busy oneself (a

affacci'ar|si vr show oneself; ~ alla finestra appear at the window

affa'ma|re vt starve [out]. ~**to** adj starving

affan'na|re vt leave breathless. ~**rsi** vr busy oneself; (agitarsi) get worked up. ~**to** adj breathless; dal respiro ~**to** wheezy. af'fanno m breathlessness; fig worry

af'fare m matter; (Comm) deal; (occasione) bargain; affari pl business; non sono affari tuoi it's none of your business. af'fa'rista mf wheeler-dealer

affasci'nante adj fascinating; (persona, sorriso) bewitching

affasci'nare vt bewitch; fig charm

affati'camento m fatigue

affati'ca|re vt tire; (sfinire) exhaust. ~**rsi** vr tire oneself out; (affannarsi) strive

af'fatto adv completely; non... ~ not... at all; niente ~! not at all!

affer'ma|re vt affirm; (sostenere) assert. ~**rsi** vr establish oneself

affermativa'mente adv in the affirmative

afferma'tivo adj affirmative

affermazi'one f assertion; (successo) achievement

affer'rar|e vt seize; catch (oggetto); (capire) grasp; ~ **al volo** fig be quick on the uptake. ~**si** vr ~**si a** grasp at

affet'ta|re vt slice; (ostentare) affect. ~**to** adj sliced; (maniere) affected ● m cold meat.

affet'tivo adj affective; rapporto ~ emotional tie

af'fetto¹ m affection

af'fetto² adj ~ **da** suffering from

affettuosità f inv (gesto) affectionate gesture

affettu'oso adj affectionate

affezio'nar|si vr ~**rsi a** grow fond of. ~**to** adj devoted (a to)

affian'car|e vt put side by side; (Mil) flank; fig support. ~**si** vr come side by side; fig stand together; ~**si a** qcno fig help sb out

affiata'mento m harmony

affia'ta|rsi vr get on well together. ~**to** adj close-knit; una coppia ~**ta** a very close couple

affib'bi'are vt ~ **qcsa a qcno** saddle sb with sth; ~ **un pugno a qcno** let fly at sb

affi'dabil|e adj dependable. ~**ità** f dependability

affida'mento m (Jur: dei minori) custody; fare ~ **su qcno** rely on sb; non dare ~ not inspire confidence

affi'dar|e vt entrust. ~**si** vr ~**si a** rely on

affievo'lirsi vr grow weak

af'figgere vt affix

affi'lare vt sharpen

affili'ar|e vt affiliate. ~**si** vr become affiliated

affi'nare vt sharpen; (perfezionare) refine

affinché conj so that, in order that

af'fine adj similar. ~**ità** f affinity

affiora'mento m emergence; (Naut) surfacing

affio'rare vi emerge; fig come to light

af'fisso m bill; (Gram) affix

affitta'camere m inv landlord ●f inv landlady

affit'tare vt rent; 'af'fittasi' 'for rent'

af'fitt|o m rent; contratto d'~**o** lease; dare in ~**o** let; prendere in ~**o** rent. ~**u'ario, -a** mf (Jur) lessee

af'figger|e vt torment; fig vt distress oneself

af'fli|tto adj distressed. ~**zi'one** f distress; fig affliction

afflosci'arsi vr become floppy; (accasciarsi) flop down; (morale:) decline

afflu'en|te adj & m tributary. ~**za** f

flow; (di gente) crowd

afflu'ire vi flow; fig pour in

af'flusso m influx

affo'gare vt/i drown; (Culin) poach; ~re in fig be swamped with. ~to adj (persona) drowned; (uova) poached. ~to al caffè m ice cream with hot espresso poured over it

affol'lare vt, ~rsi vr crowd. ~to adj crowded

affonda'mento m sinking

affon'dare vt/i sink

affossa'mento m pothole

affran'care vt redeem (bene); stamp (lettera); free (schiavo). ~rsi vr free oneself. ~trice f franking machine. ~tura f stamping; (di spedizione) postage

af'franto adj prostrated; (esausto) worn out

af'fresco m fresco

affret'tare vt speed up. ~rsi vr hurry. ~ta'mente adv hastily. ~to adj hasty

affron'tare vt face; confront (nemico); meet (spese). ~si vr clash

af'fronto m affront, insult; fare un ~ a qcno insult sb

affumi'care vt fill with smoke; (Culin) smoke. ~to adj (prosciutto, formaggio) smoked

affuso'lare vt taper [off]. ~to adj tapering

afo'risma m aphorism

a'foso adj sultry

'Africa f Africa. afri'cano, -a agg & mf African

afrodi'siaco adj & m aphrodisiac

a'genda f diary

a'gente m agent; agenti pl atmosferici atmospheric agents. ~ di cambio stockbroker. ~ di polizia police officer

agen'zia f agency; (filiale) branch office; (di banca) branch. ~ di viaggi

travel agency. ~ immobiliare estate agency

agevo'lare vt facilitate. ~zi'one f facilitation

a'gevol|e adj easy; (strada) smooth. ~'mente adv easily

aggan'ciare vt hook up; (Rail) couple. ~si vr (vestito:) hook up

ag'geggio m gadget

agget'tivo m adjective

agghiacci'ante adj terrifying

agghiacci'are vt fig ~ qcno make sb's blood run cold. ~si vr freeze

agghin'dar|e vt [T] dress up. ~rsi vr [T] doll oneself up. ~to adj dressed up

aggiorna'mento m up-date

aggior'na|re vt (rinviare) postpone; (mettere a giorno) bring up to date. ~rsi vr get up to date. ~to adj up-to-date; (versione) updated

aggi'rar|e vt surround; (fig: ingannare) trick. ~si vr hang about; ~si su (discorso ecc:) be about; (somma:) be around

aggiudi'car|e vt award; (all'asta) knock down. ~si vr win

aggi'un|gere vt add. ~ta f addition. ~'tivo adj supplementary. ~to adj added • adj & m (assistente) assistant

aggiu'star|e vt mend; (sistemare) settle; ([T]: mettere a posto) fix. ~si vr adapt; (mettersi in ordine) tidy oneself up; (decidere) sort things out; (tempo:) clear up

agglomera'mento m conglomeration

agglome'rato m built-up area

aggrap'par|e vt grasp. ~si vr ~si a cling to

aggra'vante (Jur) f aggravation • adj aggravating

aggra'var|e vt (peggiorare) make worse; increase (pena); (appesantire)

a

weigh down. **~si** vr worsen

aggrazi'ato adj graceful

aggre'dire vt attack

aggre'ga|re vt add; (associare a un gruppo ecc) admit. **~rsi** vr **~rsi a** join. **~to** a group ● em aggregate; (di case) block

aggressi'one f aggression; (atto) attack

aggres's|ivo adj aggressive. **~ività** f aggressiveness. **~ore** m aggressor

aggrin'zare, aggrin'zire vt wrinkle

aggrot'tare vt **~ le ciglia/la fronte** frown

aggrovigli'a|re vt tangle. **~rsi** vr get entangled; fig get complicated. **~to** adj entangled; fig confused

agguan'tare vt catch

aggu'ato m ambush; (tranello) trap; **stare in ~** lie in wait

agguer'rito adj fierce

agia'tezza f comfort

agi'ato adj (persona) well off; (vita) comfortable

a'gibil|e adj (palazzo) fit for human habitation. **~ità** f fitness for human habitation

'agile adj agile. **~ità** f agility

'agio m ease; **mettersi a proprio ~** make oneself at home

a'gire vi act; (comportarsi) behave; (funzionare) work; **~ su** affect

agi'ta|re vt shake; wave (mano); (fig: turbare) trouble. **~rsi** vr toss about; (essere inquieto) be restless; (mare:) get rough. **~to** adj restless; (mare) rough. **~tore, ~trice** mf (persona) agitator. **~zi'one** f agitation; **mettere in ~zione** qcno make sb worried

'agli = **A** + **GLI**

'aglio m garlic

a'gnello m lamb

agno'lotti mpl ravioli sg

a'gnostico, -a adj & mf agnostic

'ago m needle

ago'ni|a f agony. **~z'zare** vi be on one's deathbed

ago'nistic|a f competition. **~o** adj competitive

agopun'tura f acupuncture

a'gosto m August

a'grari|a f agriculture. **~o** adj agricultural ● em landowner

a'gricol|o adj agricultural. **~tore** m farmer. **~tura** f agriculture

agri'foglio m holly

agritu'rismo m farm holidays, agro-tourism

Agriturismo In the 1980s many farmers began to supplement their falling incomes by offering tourists an authentic experience of the Italian countryside. *Agriturismo* is now a very popular form of tourism in Italy. Guests can learn traditional skills and crafts, such as cooking and wine-making, all of which helps to preserve a threatened way of life.

'agro adj sour

agroalimen'tare adj food attrib

agro'dolce adj bitter-sweet; (Culin) sweet-and-sour; **in ~** sweet and sour

agrono'mia f agronomy

a'grume m citrus fruit; (pianta) citrus tree

aguz'za|re vt sharpen; **~ le orecchie** prick up one's ears; **~ la vista** look hard

aguz'zino m slave-driver; (carceriere) jailer

ahimè int alas

'ai = **A** + **I**

'aia f threshing-floor

'Aia f **L'~** The Hague

Aids mf Aids

ai'rone m heron

ai'tante adj sturdy

aiu'ola f flower-bed

aiu'tante mf assistant ● m (Mil) adjutant. **~ di campo** aide-de-camp

aiu'tare vt help

ai'uto m help, aid; (assistente) assistant

aiz'zare vt incite; **~ contro** set on

al = A+IL

'ala f wing; **fare ~** make way

ala'bastro m alabaster

'alacre adj brisk

a'lano m Great Dane

'alba f dawn

Alba'nia f Albania. **a.~ese** adj & mf Albanian

albeggi'are vi dawn

albe'ra|to adj wooded; (viale) tree-lined. **~tura** f (Naut) masts pl. **albe-'rello** m sapling

al'bergo m hotel. **~o diurno** hotel where rooms are rented during the daytime. **~a'tore**, **~a'trice** mf hotel-keeper. **~hi'ero** adj hotel attrib

'albero m tree; (Naut) mast; (Mech) shaft. **~ genealogico** family tree. **~ maestro** (Naut) mainmast. **~ di Natale** Christmas tree

albi'cocc|a f apricot. **~o** m apricot-tree

al'bino m albino

'albo m register; (libro ecc) album; (per avvisi) notice board

'album m album. **~ da disegno** sketch-book

al'bume m albumen

'alce m elk

'alcol m alcohol; (Med) spirit; (liquori forti) spirits pl; **darsi al'~** take to drink. **al'colici** mpl alcoholic drinks. **al'colico** adj alcoholic. **alco'lismo** m alcoholism. **~iz'zato**, **-a** adj & mf alcoholic

alco'test® m inv Breathalyser®

al'cova f alcove

al'cun, **al'cuno** adj & pron any; **non ha ~ amico** he hasn't any/no friends. **alcuni** pl some, a few; **~i suoi amici** some of his friends

alea'torio adj unpredictable

a'letta f (Mech) fin

alfa'betico adj alphabetical

alfabetizzazi'one f **~ della popolazione** teaching people to read and write

alfa'beto m alphabet

alfi'ere m (negli scacchi) bishop

al'fine adv eventually, in the end

'alga f seaweed

'algebra f algebra

Alge'ri|a f Algeria. **a.~no**, **-a** agg & mf Algerian

ali'ante m glider

'alibi m inv alibi

alie'na|re vt alienate. **~rsi** vr become estranged; **~rsi le simpatie di qcno** lose sb's good will. **~to**, **-a** adj alienated ● mf lunatic

a'lieno, **-a** mf alien ● adj **è ~ da invidia** envy is foreign to him

alimen'ta|re vt feed; fig foment ● adj food attrib; (abitudine) dietary ● m **~ri** pl food-stuffs. **~'tore** m power unit. **~zi'one** f feeding

Alimentari Alimentari are food shops offering a range of products, from groceries, fruit, and vegetables to prepared foods like cheeses, cured hams, and salamis. Some even bake their own bread. An alimentari will also usually prepare panini (filled rolls) using their own ingredients. Small villages which have no other shops usually have an alimentari.

ali'mento m food; **alimenti** pl food; (Jur) alimony

a'liquota f share; (di imposta) rate

ali'scafo m hydrofoil

'alito m breath

'alla = A + LA

allaccia'mento m connection

allacci'ar|e vt fasten (cintura); lace up (scarpe); do up (vestito); (collegare) connect; form (amicizia). ~**si** vr do up, fasten

allaga'mento m flooding

alla'gar|e vt flood. ~**si** vr become flooded

allampa'nato adj lanky

allarga'mento m widening

allar'gar|e vt widen; open (braccia, gambe); let out (vestito ecc); fig extend. ~**si** vr widen

allar'mante adj alarming

allar'ma|re vt alarm. ~**to** adj panicky

al'larme m alarm; dare l'~ raise the alarm; falso ~ fig false alarm. ~ **aereo** air raid warning

allar'mis|mo m alarmism. ~**ta** mf alarmist

allatta'mento m (di animale) suckling; (di neonato) feeding

allat'tare vt suckle (animale); feed (neonato)

'alle = A + LE

alle'a|nza f alliance. ~**to**, -**a** adj allied ● mf ally

alle'are vt unite. ~**si** vr form an alliance

alle'gare[1] vt (Jur) allege

alle'gare[2] vt (acciudere) enclose; set on edge (denti). ~**to** adj enclosed ● m enclosure; (Comput) attachment; in ~**to** attached. ~**zi'one** f (Jur) allegation

alleg'gerir|e vt lighten; fig alleviate. ~**si** vr become lighter; (vestirsi leggero) put on lighter clothes

allego'ria f allegory. **alle'gorico** adj allegorical

allegra'mente adv breezily

alle'gria f gaiety

al'legro adj cheerful; (colore) bright; (brillo) tipsy ● m (Mus) allegro

alle'luia int hallelujah!

allena'mento m training

alle'na|re vt, ~**rsi** vr train. ~**tore**, ~**trice** mf trainer, coach

allen'tar|e vt loosen; fig relax. ~**si** vr become loose; (Mech) work loose

aller'gia f allergy. **al'lergico** adj allergic

all'erta f stare a ~ be alert

allesti'mento m preparation. ~ **scenico** (Theat) set

alle'stire vt prepare; stage (spettacolo); (Naut) fit out

allet'tante adj alluring

allet'tare vt entice

alleva'mento m breeding; (processo) bringing up; (luogo) farm; (per piante) nursery; **pollo di** ~ battery chicken

alle'vare vt bring up (bambini); breed (animali); grow (piante)

allevi'are vt alleviate; fig lighten

alli'bito adj astounded

allibra'tore m bookmaker

allie'tar|e vt gladden. ~**si** vr rejoice

alli'evo, -**a** mf pupil ● m (Mil) cadet

alliga'tore m alligator

allinea'mento m alignment

alline'ar|e vt line up; (Typ) align; Fin adjust. ~**si** vr fall into line

'allo = A + LO

al'locco m Zool tawny owl

al'lodola f [sky]lark

alloggi'are vt put up; (casa:) provide accommodation for; (Mil) billet ● vi stay; (Mil) be billeted. **al'loggio** m apartment; (Mil) billet

allontana'mento m removal

allonta'nar|e vt move away; (licenziare) dismiss; avert (pericolo). ~**si** vr go away

al'lora adv then; (a quel tempo) at that time; (in tal caso) in that case;

d'∼ in poi from then on; e ∼? what now?; (e con ciò?) so what?; fino ∼ until then

al'loro m laurel; (Culin) bay

'alluce m big toe

alluci'na|nte adj 🔲 incredible; sostanza ∼nte hallucinogen. ∼to, -a mf 🔲 space cadet. ∼zi'one f hallucination

allucino'geno adj (sostanza) hallucinatory

al'ludere vi ∼ a allude to

allu'minio m aluminium

allun'gar|e vt lengthen; stretch [out] (gamba); extend (tavolo); (diluire) dilute; ∼e il collo crane one's neck. ∼e le mani su qcno touch sb up. ∼e il passo quicken one's step. ∼si vr grow longer; (crescere) grow taller; (sdraiarsi) lie down

allusi'one f allusion

allu'sivo adj allusive

alluvio'nale adj alluvial

alluvi'one f flood

al'meno adv at least; [se] ∼ venisse il sole! if only the sun would come out!

a'logeno m halogen ● adj lampada alogena halogen lamp

a'lone m halo

'Alpi fpl le ∼ the Alps

alpi'nis|mo m mountaineering. ∼ta mf mountaineer

al'pino adj Alpine ● m (Mil) gli alpini the Alpine troops

al'quanto adj a certain amount of ● adv rather

alt int stop

alta'lena f swing; (tavola in bilico) see-saw

altale'nare vi fig vacillate

alta'mente adv highly

al'tare m altar

alta'rino m scoprire gli altarini di qcno reveal sb's guilty secrets

alte'ra|re vt alter; adulterate (vino); (falsificare) falsify. ∼rsi vr be altered; (cibo:) go bad; (merci:) deteriorate; (arrabbiarsi) get angry. ∼to adj (vino) adulterated. ∼zi'one f alteration; (di vino) adulteration

al'terco m altercation

alter'nanza f alternation

alter'na|re vt, ∼rsi vr alternate. ∼'tiva f alternative. ∼'tivo adj alternate. ∼to adj alternating. ∼'tore m (Electr) alternator

al'terno adj alternate; a giorni ∼i every other day

al'tezza f height; (profondità) depth; (suono) pitch; (di tessuto) width; (titolo) Highness; essere all'∼ di be on a level with; fig be up to

altezzosa|'mente adv haughtily. ∼ità f haughtiness

altez'zoso adj haughty

al'ticcio adj tipsy, merry

altipi'ano m plateau

alti'tudine f altitude

'alto adj high; (di statura) tall; (profondo) deep; (suono) high-pitched; (tessuto) wide; (voce) northern; a notte alta in the middle of the night; avere degli alti e bassi have some ups and downs; ad alta fedeltà high-fidelity; a voce alta, ad alta voce in a loud voice; (leggere) aloud; essere in ∼ mare be on the high seas. alta finanza f high finance. alta moda f high fashion. alta tensione f high voltage ● adv high; in ∼ at the top; (guardare:) up; mani in ∼! hands up!

alto'forno m blast-furnace

altolà int halt there!

altolo'cato adj highly placed

altopar'lante m loudspeaker

altopi'ano m plateau

altret'tanto adj & pron as much; (pl) as many ● adv likewise; buona fortuna! – grazie, ∼ good luck! – thank you, the same to you

a

altri'menti *adv* otherwise

'altro *adj* other; un ∼, un'altra another; l'altr'anno last year; domani l'∼ the day after tomorrow; l'ho visto l'∼ giorno I saw him the other day ●*pron* other [one]; un ∼, un'altra another [one]; ne vuoi dell'∼? would you like some more?; l'un l'∼ one another; nessun ∼ nobody else; gli altri (la gente) other people. ●*m* something else; non fa ∼ che lavorare he does nothing but work; desidera ∼? (*in negozio*) anything else?; più che ∼, sono stanco I'm tired more than anything; se non ∼ at least; senz'∼ certainly; tra l'∼ what's more; ∼ che! and how!

altro'eri *m* l'∼ the day before yesterday

al'tronde *adv* d'∼ on the other hand

al'trove *adv* elsewhere

al'trui *adj* other people's ●*m* other people's belongings *pl*

al'tura *f* high ground; (*Naut*) deep sea

a'lunno, -a *mf* pupil

alve'are *m* hive

al'za|re *vt* lift; (*costruire*) build; (*Naut*) hoist; ∼re le spalle shrug one's shoulders. ∼**rsi** *vr* rise; (*in piedi*) stand up; (*da letto*) get up; ∼**rsi in piedi** get to one's feet. ∼**ta** *f* lifting; (*aumento*) rise; (*da letto*) getting up; (*Archit*) elevation. ∼**to** *adj* up

a'mabile *adj* lovable; (*vino*) sweet

a'maca *f* hammock

amalga'ma|re *vt*, ∼**si** *vr* amalgamate

a'mante *adj* ∼ di fond of ●*m* lover ●*f* mistress, lover

a'ma|re *vt* love; like (*musica, ecc.*). ∼**to, -a** *adj* loved ●*mf* beloved

ama'rena *f* sour black cherry

ama'retto *m* macaroon

ama'rezza *f* bitterness;

(*dolore*) sorrow

a'maro *adj* bitter ●*m* bitterness; (*liquore*) bitters *pl*

ama'rognolo *adj* rather bitter

ama'tore, -'trice *mf* lover

ambascia'|ta *f* embassy; (*messaggio*) message. ∼**tore**, ∼**trice** *m* ambassador ●*f* ambassadress

ambe'due *adj* & *pron* both

ambien'ta|le *adj* environmental. ∼**lista** *adj* & *mf* environmentalist

ambien'tar|e *vt* acclimatize; set (*personaggio, film ecc.*). ∼**si** *vr* get acclimatized

ambi'ente *m* environment; (*stanza*) room; *fig* milieu

ambigu'ità *f inv* ambiguity; (*di persona*) shadiness

am'biguo *adj* ambiguous; (*persona*) shady

am'bire *vi* ∼ a aspire to

'ambito *m* sphere

ambiva'len|te *adj* ambivalent. ∼**za** *f* ambivalence

ambizi'o|ne *f* ambition. ∼**so** *adj* ambitious

ambu'lante *adj* wandering; venditore ∼ hawker

ambu'lanza *f* ambulance

ambula'torio *m* (*di medico*) surgery; (*di ospedale*) out-patients'

a'meba *f* amoeba

a'meno *adj* pleasant

A'merica *f* America. ∼ **del Sud** South America. **ameri'cano, -a** *agg* & *mf* American

ami'anto *m* asbestos

ami'chevole *adj* friendly

ami'cizia *f* friendship; fare ∼ con qcno make friends with sb; amicizie *pl* (*amici*) friends

a'mico, -a *mf* friend; ∼ del cuore bosom friend

'amido *m* starch

ammac'ca|re *vt* dent; bruise

(frutto). **~rsi** vr (metallo:) get dented; (frutto:) bruise. **~to** adj dented; (frutto:) bruised. **~tura** f dent; (livido) bruise

ammae'stra|re vt (istruire) teach; train (animale). **~to** adj trained

ammai'nare vt lower (bandiera); furl (vele)

amma'la|rsi vr fall ill. **~to, -a** adj ill • mf sick person; (paziente) patient

ammali'are vt bewitch

am'manco m deficit

ammanet'tare vt handcuff

ammani'cato adj essere ~ have connections

amma'raggio m splashdown

amma'rare vi put down on the sea; (nave spaziale:) splash down

ammas'sar|e vt amass. **~si** vr crowd together. **am'masso** m mass; (mucchio) pile

ammat'tire vi go mad

ammaz'zar|e vt kill. **~si** vr (suicidarsi) kill oneself; (rimanere ucciso) be killed

am'menda f amends pl; (multa) fine; fare ~ **di** qcsa make amends for sth

am'messo pp di ammettere • conj ~ **che** supposing that

am'mettere vt admit; (riconoscere) acknowledge; (supporre) suppose

ammic'care vi wink

ammini'stra|re vt administer; (gestire) run. **~tivo** adj administrative. **~tore, ~trice** m administrator; (di azienda) manager; (di società) director. **~tore delegato** managing director. **~zi'one** f administration; **fatti di ordinaria ~zione** fig routine matters

ammi'ragli|o m admiral. **~'ato** m admiralty

ammi'ra|re vt admire. **~to** adj restare/essere **~to** be full of admiration. **~tore, ~trice** mf admirer. **~zi'one** f admiration. **ammi'revole**

adj admirable

ammis'sibile adj admissible

ammissi'one f admission; (approvazione) acknowledgement

ammobili'a|re vt furnish. **~to** adj furnished

am'modo adj proper • adv properly

am'mollo m in ~ soaking

ammo'niaca f ammonia

ammoni'mento m warning; (di rimprovero) admonishment

ammo'ni|re vt warn; (rimproverare) admonish. **~tore** adj admonishing. **~zi'one** f Sport warning

ammon'tare vi ~ a amount to • m amount

ammonticchi'are vt heap up

ammorbi'dente m (per panni) softener

ammorbi'dir|e vt, **~si** vr soften

ammorta'mento m (Comm) amortization

ammor'tare vt pay off (spesa); (Comm) amortize (debito)

ammortiz'za|re vt (Comm) = AM-MORTARE; (Mech) damp. **~tore** m shock-absorber

ammosci'ar|e vt make flabby. **~si** vi get flabby

ammucchi'a|re vt, **~rsi** vr pile up. **~ta** f (🔲: orgia) orgy

ammuf'fi|re vi go mouldy. **~to** adj mouldy

ammutina'mento m mutiny

ammuti'narsi vr mutiny

ammuto'lire vi be struck dumb

amni'stia f amnesty

'amo m hook; fig bait

a'more m love; fare l'~ make love; per l'amor di Dio/del cielo! for heaven's sake!; andare d'~ e d'accordo get on like a house on fire; amor proprio self-respect; è un ~ (persona) he/she is a darling; per ~ di for the sake of; amori pl love affairs. **~ggi'are** vi flirt.

a

amo'revole adj loving

a'morfo adj shapeless; (fig) grey

amo'roso adj loving; (sguardo ecc) amorous; (lettera, relazione) love

ampi'ezza f (di esperienza) breadth; (di stanza) spaciousness; (di gonna) fullness; (importanza) scale

'ampio adj ample; (esperienza) wide; (stanza) spacious; (vestito) loose; (gonna) full; (pantaloni) baggy

am'plesso m embrace

amplia'mento m (di casa, porto) enlargement; (di strada) widening

ampli'are vt broaden (conoscenze)

amplifi'ca|re vt amplify; fig magnify. ~'tore m amplifier. ~zi'one f amplification

am'polla f cruet

ampu'ta|re vt amputate. ~zi'one f amputation

amu'leto m amulet

anabbagli'ante adj (Auto) dipped ●mpl anabbaglianti dipped headlights

anacro'nis|mo m anachronism. ~tico adj anachronistic

a'nagrafe f (ufficio) register office; (registro) register of births, marriages and deaths

ana'grafico adj dati mpl ana-grafici personal data

ana'gramma m anagram

anal'colico adj non-alcoholic ●m soft drink, non-alcoholic drink

analfa'be|ta adj & mf illiterate. ~'tismo m illiteracy

anal'gesico m painkiller

a'nalisi f inv analysis; (Med) test. ~ grammaticale/del periodo/logica parsing. ~ del sangue blood test

ana'li|sta mf analyst. ~tico adj analytical. ~z'zare vt analyse; (Med) test

anal'lergico adj hypoallergenic

analo'gia f analogy. a'nalogo adj analogous

'ananas m inv pineapple

anar'chi|a f anarchy. a'narchico, -a adj anarchic ●mf anarchist. ~smo m anarchism

A.N.A.S. f abbr (Azienda Nazionale Autonoma delle Strade) national road maintenance authority

anato'mia f anatomy. ana'tomico adj anatomical; (sedia) contoured

a'natra f duck

ana'troccolo m duckling

'anca f hip; (di animale) flank

ance'strale adj ancestral

'anche conj also, too; (persino) even; ~ se even if

anchilo'sato adj fig stiff

an'cora adv still, yet; (di nuovo) again; (di più) some more; ~ una volta once more

'anco|ra² f anchor; gettare l'~ra drop anchor. ~'raggio m anchorage. ~'rare vt anchor

anda'mento m (del mercato, degli affari) trend

an'dante adj (corrente) current; (di poco valore) cheap ●m (Mus) andante

an'da|re m (funzionare) work; ~ via (partire) leave; (macchia:) come out; ~ [bene] (confarsi) suit; (taglia:) fit; ti va bene alle tre? does three o'clock suit you?; non mi va di mangiare I don't feel like eating; ~ di fretta be in a hurry; ~ fiero di be proud of; ~ di moda be in fashion; va per i 20 anni he's nearly 20; ma va! [là]! come on!; come va? how are things?; ~ a male go off; ~ a fuoco go up in flames; va spedito [entro] stamattina it must be sent this morning; ne va del mio lavoro my job is at stake; come è andata a finire? how did it turn out?; cosa vai dicendo? what are you talking about?. ~rsene go away; (morire) pass away ●m going; a lungo ~re eventually

'andito m passage

an'drone m entrance

a'nneddoto m anecdote

ane'lare vt ~ a long for. **a'nelito** m longing

a'nello m ring; (di catena) link

ane'mia f anaemia. **a'nemico** adj anaemic

a'nemone m anemone

aneste'sia f anaesthesia; (sostanza) anaesthetic. **~'sta** mf anaesthetist. **ane'stetico** adj & m anaesthetic

an'fibi mpl (stivali) army boots

an'fibio m (animale) amphibian ● adj amphibious

anfite'atro m amphitheatre

'anfora f amphora

an'fratto m ravine

an'gelico adj angelic

'angelo m angel. ~ **custode** guardian angel

angli'cano adj Anglican.

angli'smo m Anglicism

an'glofilo, -a adj & mf Anglophile

an'glofono, -a mf English-speaker

anglo'sassone adj & mf Anglo-Saxon

ango'lare adj angular. **~zi'one** f angle shot

'angolo m corner; (Math) angle. ~ **[di] cottura** kitchenette

ango'loso adj angular

an'goscia f anguish. ~**'are** vt torment. ~**'ato** adj agonized. ~**'oso** adj (disperato) anguished; (che dà angoscia) distressing

angu'illa f eel

an'guria f water-melon

an'gustia f (ansia) anxiety; (penuria) poverty. ~**'are** vt distress. ~**'arsi** vi be very worried (**per** about)

an'gusto adj narrow

'anice m anise; (Culin) aniseed; (liquore) anisette

an'dride f ~ **carbonica** carbon dioxide

'anima f soul; non c'era ~ **viva** there was not a soul about; all'~! good grief!; un' ~ **in pena** a soul in torment. ~ **gemella** soul mate

ani'male adj & m animal; ~**li domestici** pl pets. ~**'lesco** adj animal

ani'mare vt give life to; (ravvivare) enliven; (incoraggiare) encourage. ~**rsi** vr come to life; (accalorarsi) become animated. ~**to** adj animate; (discussione) animated; (paese) lively. ~**'tore**, ~**'trice** mf leading spirit; Cinema animator. ~**zi'one** f animation

'animo m (mente) mind; (indole) disposition; (cuore) heart; **perdersi d'~** lose heart; **farsi ~** take heart. ~**sità** f animosity

ani'moso adj brave; (ostile) hostile

'anitra f = ANATRA

annac'quare vt water down. ~**to** adj watered down

annaffi'are vt water. ~**'toio** m watering-can

an'nali mpl annals

anna'spare vi flounder

an'nata f year; (importo annuale) annual amount; (di vino) vintage

annebbia'mento m fog build-up; fig clouding

annebbi'are vt cloud (vista, mente). ~**si** vr become foggy; (vista, mente) grow dim

annega'mento m drowning

anne'gare vt/i drown

anne'rire vt/i blacken. ~**si** vr become black

annessi'one f (di nazione) annexation

an'nesso pp di annettere ● adj attached; (stato) annexed

an'nettere vt add; (accludere) enclose; annex (stato)

annichi'lire vt annihilate

anni'darsi vr nest

annienta'mento m annihilation

annien'tar|e vt annihilate. **∼si** vr abase oneself

anniver'sario adj & m anniversary. **∼ di matrimonio** wedding anniversary

'anno m year; **Buon A∼!** Happy New Year!; **quanti anni ha?** how old are you?; **Tommaso ha dieci anni** Thomas is ten [years old]. **∼ bisestile** leap year

anno'dar|e vt knot; do up (cintura); fig form. **∼si** vr become knotted

annoi'a|re vt bore; (recare fastidio) annoy. **∼rsi** vr get bored; (condizione) be bored. **∼to** adj bored

anno'tare vt note down; annotate (testo). **∼zi'one** f note

annove'rare vt number

annu'a|le adj annual, yearly. **∼rio** m year-book

annu'ire vi nod; (acconsentire) agree

annulla'mento m annulment; (di appuntamento) cancellation

annul'lar|e vt annul; cancel (appuntamento); (togliere efficacia a) undo; disallow (gol); (distruggere) destroy. **∼si** vr cancel each other out

annunci'a|re vt announce; (preannunciare) foretell. **∼'tore, ∼'trice** mf announcer. **A∼zi'one** f Annunciation

an'nuncio m announcement; (pubblicitario) advertisement; (notizia) news. **annunci** pl **economici** classified advertisements

'annuo adj annual, yearly

annu'sare vt sniff

annuvo'lar|e vt cloud. **∼si** vr cloud over

'ano m anus

a'nomalo adj anomalous

anoni'mato m **mantenere l'∼** remain anonymous

a'nonimo, -a adj anonymous ● mf (pittore, scrittore) anonymous painter/writer

ano'ressico, -a mf anorexic

anor'mal|e adj abnormal ● mf deviant. **∼ità** f inv abnormality

'ansa f handle; (di fiume) bend

an'sare vi pant

'ansia, ansi'età f anxiety; **stare/essere in ∼ per** be anxious about

ansi'oso adj anxious

antago'nis|mo m antagonism. **∼ta** mf antagonist

an'tartico adj & m Antarctic

antece'dente adj preceding ● m precedent

ante'fatto m prior event

ante'guerra adj pre-war ● m pre-war period

ante'nato, -a mf ancestor

an'tenna f (Radio, TV) aerial; (di animale) antenna; (Naut) yard. **∼ parabolica** satellite dish

ante'porre vt put before

ante'prima f preview; **vedere qcsa in ∼** have a sneak preview of sth

anteri'ore adj front attrib; (nel tempo) previous

antia'ereo adj anti-aircraft attrib

antial'lergico adj hypoallergenic

antia'tomico adj **rifugio ∼** fallout shelter

antibi'otico adj & m antibiotic

anti'caglia f (oggetto) piece of old junk

antica'mente adv long ago

anti'camera f ante-room; **far ∼** be kept waiting

antichità f inv antiquity; (oggetto) antique

antici'clone m anticyclone

antici'pa|re vt advance; (Comm) pay in advance; (prevedere) anticipate; (prevenire) forestall ● vi be early. **∼ta'mente** adv in advance. **∼zi'one** f anticipation; (notizia) advance news

an'ticipo m advance; (caparra) deposit; **in** ∼ early; *(nel lavoro)* ahead of schedule

an'tico *adj* ancient; *(mobile ecc)* antique; *(vecchio)* old; **all'antica** old-fashioned ● *mpl* **gli antichi** the ancients

anticoncezio'nale *adj* & *m* contraceptive

anticonfor'mis|mo *m* unconventionality. ∼**ta** *mf* nonconformist. ∼**tico** *adj* unconventional

anticonge'lante *adj* & *m* antifreeze

anticostituzio'nale *adj* unconstitutional

anti'crimine *adj inv* (squadra) crime *attrib*

antidemo'cratico *adj* undemocratic

antidolo'rifico *m* painkiller

an'tidoto *m* antidote

anti'droga *adj inv* (campagna) anti-drugs; (squadra) drug *attrib*

antie'stetico *adj* ugly

antifa'scismo *m* anti-fascism

antifa'scista *adj* & *mf* anti-fascist

anti'furto *m* anti-theft device; *(allarme)* alarm ● *adj inv* (sistema) anti-theft

anti'gelo *m* antifreeze; *(parabrezza)* defroster

antigi'enico *adj* unhygienic

An'tille *fpl* **le** ∼ the West Indies

an'tilope *f* antelope

antin'cendio *adj inv* **allarme** ∼ fire alarm; **porta** ∼ fire door

anti'nebbia *m inv* (Auto) [faro] ∼ foglamp

antinfiamma'torio *adj* & *m* anti-inflammatory

antinucle'are *adj* anti-nuclear

antio'rario *adj* anti-clockwise

anti'pasto *m* hors d'oeuvre

an'tipodi *mpl* antipodes; **essere agli** ∼ *fig* be poles apart

antiquari'ato *m* antique trade

anti'quario, -a *mf* antique dealer

anti'quato *adj* antiquated

anti'ruggine *adj inv* rust-inhibitor

anti'rughe *adj inv* anti-wrinkle *attrib*

anti'scippo *adj inv* theft-proof

anti'settico *adj* & *m* antiseptic

antisoci'ale *adj* anti-social

antista'minico *m* antihistamine

anti'stante *a prep* in front of

anti'tarlo *m inv* woodworm treatment

antiterro'ristico *adj* antiterrorist *attrib*

an'titesi *f inv* antithesis

'antivirus *m inv* virus checker

antolo'gia *f* anthology

'antro *m* cavern

antropolo'gia *f* anthropology. **antro'pologo, -a** *mf* anthropologist

anu'lare *m* ring-finger

'anzi *conj* in fact; *(o meglio)* or better still; *(al contrario)* on the contrary

anzianità *f* old age; *(di servizio)* seniority

anzi'ano, -a *adj* elderly; *(di grado)* senior ● *mf* elderly person

anziché *conj* rather than

anzi'tempo *adv* prematurely

anzi'tutto *adv* first of all

a'orta *f* aorta

apar'titico *adj* unaligned

apa'tia *f* apathy. **a'patico** *adj* apathetic

'ape *f* bee; **nido di api** honeycomb

aperi'tivo *m* aperitif

aperta'mente *adv* openly

a'perto *adj* open; **all'aria aperta** in the open air; **all'**∼ open-air.

aper'tura *f* opening; *(inizio)* beginning; *(ampiezza)* spread; *(di arco)* span; *(Pol)* overtures *pl*; *(Phot)* aperture; ∼ **mentale** openness

'apice *m* apex

apicol'tura f beekeeping

ap'nea f immersione in ~ free diving

a'polide adj stateless ● mf stateless person

a'postolo m apostle

apostro'fare vt (mettere un apostrofo a) write with an apostrophe; reprimand (persona)

a'postrofo m apostrophe

appaga'mento m fulfilment

appa'ga|re vt satisfy. ~rsi vr ~rsi di be satisfied with

appa'iare vt pair; mate (animali)

appallotto'lare vt roll into a ball

appalta'tore m contractor

ap'palto m contract; dare in ~ contract

appan'naggio m (in denaro) annuity; fig prerogative

appan'nar|e vt mist (vetro); dim (vista). ~si vr mist over; (vista:) grow dim

appa'rato m apparatus; (pompa) display

apparecchi'a|re vt prepare ● vi lay the table. ~'tura f (impianti) equipment

appa'recchio m apparatus; (congegno) device; (radio, tv ecc) set; (aeroplano) aircraft. ~ acustico hearing aid

appa'ren|te adj apparent. ~temente adv apparently. ~za f appearance; in ~za apparently

appa'ri|re vi appear; (sembrare) look. ~scente adj striking; pej gaudy. ~zi'one f apparition

apparta'mento m apartment

appar'ta|rsi vr withdraw. ~to adj secluded

apparte'nenza f membership

apparte'nere vi belong

appassio'nante adj (storia, argomento) exciting

appassio'na|re vt excite; (commuovere) move. ~rsi vr ~rsi a become excited by. ~to adj passionate; ~to di (entusiastico) fond of

appas'sir|e vi wither. ~si vr fade

appel'larsi vr ~ a appeal to

ap'pello m appeal; (chiamata per nome) rollcall; (esami) exam session; fare l'~ call the roll

ap'pena adv just; (a fatica) hardly ● conj [non] ~ as soon as

ap'pendere vt hang [up]

appen'dice f appendix. appendi'cite f appendicitis

Appen'nini mpl gli ~ the Appennines

appesan'tir|e vt weigh down. ~si vr become heavy

ap'peso pp di appendere adj hanging; (impiccato) hanged

appe'ti|to m appetite; aver ~ be hungry; buon ~to! enjoy your meal!. ~toso adj appetizing; fig tempting

appezza'mento m plot of land

appia'nar|e vt level; fig smooth over. ~si vr improve

appiat'tir|e vt flatten. ~si vr flatten oneself

appic'care vt ~ il fuoco a set fire to

appicci'car|e vt stick; ~ a (fig: appioppare) palm off on ● vi be sticky. ~si vr stick; (cose:) stick together; ~si a qcno fig stick to sb like glue

appicci'caticcio adj sticky; fig clingy

appicci'coso adj sticky; fig clingy

appie'dato adj sono ~ I don't have the car; sono rimasto ~ I was stranded

appi'eno adv fully

appigli'arsi vr ~ a get hold of; fig stick to. ap'piglio m fingerhold; (per piedi) foothold; fig pretext

appiop'pare vt ~ a palm off on; (①: dare) give

appiso'larsi vr doze off

applau'dire vt/i applaud. ap'plauso m applause

appli'cabile adj applicable

appli'ca|re vt apply; enforce (legge ecc). ~**rsi** vr apply oneself. ~**tore** m applicator. ~**zi'one** f application; (di legge) enforcement

appoggi'ar|e vt lean (a against); (mettere) put; (sostenere) back. ~**si a** lean against; fig rely on. ap'poggio m support

appollai'arsi vr fig perch

ap'porre vt affix

appor'tare vt bring; (causare) cause. ap'porto m contribution

apposita'mente adv especially

ap'posito adj proper

ap'posta adv on purpose; (espressamente) specially

apposta'mento m ambush; (caccia) lying in wait

appo'star|e vt post (soldati). ~**si** vr lie in wait

ap'prend|ere vt understand; (imparare) learn. ~i'mento m learning

appren'di|sta mf apprentice. ~**stato** m apprenticeship

apprensi'one f apprehension; essere in ~ per be anxious about. appren'sivo adj apprehensive

ap'presso adv & prep (vicino) near; (dietro) behind; come ~ as follows

appre'star|e vt prepare. ~**si** vr get ready

apprez'zabile adj appreciable. ~**mento** m appreciation; (giudizio) opinion

apprez'za|re vt appreciate. ~**to** adj appreciated

ap'proccio m approach

appro'dare vi land; ~ **a** fig come to; non ~ **a nulla** come to nothing. ap'prodo m landing; (luogo) landing-stage

approfit'tare vi take advantage

(di of), profit (di by). ~**tore**, ~**trice** mf chancer

approfondi'mento m deepening; di ~ fig (esame) further

approfon'di|re vt deepen. ~**rsi** vr (divario) widen. ~**to** adj (studio, ricerca) in-depth

appropri'a|rsi vr (essere adatto a) suit; ~**rsi** di take possession of. ~**to** adj appropriate. ~**zi'one** f (Jur) appropriation. ~**zione indebita** (Jur) embezzlement

approssi'ma|re vt ~**re per eccesso/difetto** round up/down. ~**rsi** vr draw near. ~**tiva'mente** adv approximately. ~**tivo** adj approximate. ~**zi'one** f approximation

appro'va|re vt approve of; approve (legge). ~**zi'one** f approval

approvvigiona'mento m supplying; approvvigionamenti pl provisions

approvvigio'nar|e vt supply. ~**si** vr stock up

appunta'mento m appointment; fissare un ~ make an appointment; darsi ~ decide to meet

appun'tar|e vt (annotare) take notes; (fissare) fix; (con spillo) pin; (appuntire) sharpen. ~**si su** (teoria:) be based on

appun'tire vt sharpen. ~**to** adj (mento) pointed

ap'punto¹ m note; (piccola critica) niggle

ap'punto² adv exactly; per l'~! exactly!; stavo ~ dicendo... I was just saying...

appu'rare vt verify

a'pribile adj that can be opened

apribot'tiglie m inv bottle-opener

a'prile m April; il primo d'~ April Fools' Day

a'prir|e vt open; turn on (acqua ecc); (con chiave) unlock; open up (ferita ecc). ~**si** vr open; (spaccarsi) split; (confidarsi) confide (con in)

apri'scatole *f inv* tin-opener

a **aqua'planing** *m* andare in ∼ aquaplane

'aquila *f* eagle; non è un'∼al he is no genius!. ∼**lino** *adj* aquiline

aqui'lone *m* (*giocattolo*) kite

ara'besco *m* arabesque; *hum* scribble

A'rabia Sau'dita *f* l'∼ Saudi Arabia

'arabo, -a *adj* Arab; (*lingua*) Arabic • *mf* Arab • *m* (*lingua*) Arabic

a'rachide *f* peanut

ara'gosta *f* lobster

a'ran|cia *f* orange. ∼**ata** *f* orangeade. ∼**o** *m* orange-tree; (*colore*) orange. ∼**one** *adj & m* orange

a'ra|re *vt* plough. ∼**tro** *m* plough

ara'tura *f* ploughing

a'razzo *m* tapestry

arbi'trar|e *vt* arbitrate in; *Sport* referee. ∼**ietà** *f* arbitrariness. ∼**io** *adj* arbitrary

ar'bitrio *m* will; è un ∼ it's very high-handed

'arbitro *m* arbiter; *Sport* referee; (*nel baseball*) umpire

ar'busto *m* shrub

'arca *f* ark; (*cassa*) chest

ar'ca|ico *adj* archaic. ∼**ismo** *m* archaism

arc'angelo *m* archangel

ar'cata *f* arch; (*serie di archi*) arcade

archeolo'gia *f* archaeology. ∼**o'logico** *adj* archaeological. ∼**ologo, -a** *mf* archaeologist

ar'chetto *m* (*Mus*) bow

architet'tare *vt fig* devise; cosa state architettando? *fig* what are you plotting?

archi'tet|to *m* architect. ∼**tonico** *adj* architectural. ∼**tura** *f* architecture

archivi'are *vt* file; (*Jur*) close

ar'chivio *m* archives *pl*; (*Comput*) file

archi'vista *mf* filing clerk

ar'cigno *adj* grim

arci'pelago *m* archipelago

arci'vescovo *m* archbishop

'arco *m* arch; (*Math*) arc; (*Mus, arma*) bow; nell'∼ di una giornata/due mesi in the space of a day/two months

arcoba'leno *m* rainbow

arcu'a|re *vt* bend. ∼**rsi** *vr* bend. ∼**to** *adj* bent, curved

ar'dente *adj* burning; *fig* ardent. ∼'**mente** *adv* ardently

'ardere *vt/i* burn

ar'desia *f* slate

ar'di|re *vi* dare. ∼**to** *adj* daring; (*coraggioso*) bold; (*sfacciato*) impudent

ar'dore *m* (*calore*) heat; *fig* ardour

'arduo *adj* arduous; (*ripido*) steep

'area *f* area. ∼ **di rigore** (*nel calcio*) penalty area. ∼ **di servizio** service area

a'rena *f* arena

are'narsi *vr* run aground; *fig*: (*trattative*) reach deadlock; **mi sono arenato** I'm stuck

'argano *m* winch

argen'tato *adj* silver-plated

argente'ria *f* silver[ware]

ar'gento *m* silver

ar'gil|la *f* clay. ∼**loso** *adj* (*terreno*) clayey

argi'nare *vt* embank; *fig* hold in check, contain

'argine *m* embankment; (*diga*) dike

argomen'tare *vi* argue

argo'mento *m* argument; (*motivo*) reason; (*soggetto*) subject

argu'ire *vt* deduce

ar'gu|to *adj* witty. ∼**zia** *f* wit; (*battuta*) witticism

'aria *f* air; (*aspetto*) appearance; (*Mus*) tune; andare all'∼ *fig* come to nothing; avere l'∼... look...; corrente d'∼ draught; mandare all'∼ qcsa

23

fig ruin sth

aridità f aridity, dryness

'arido adj arid

arieggi'a|re vt air. ~**to** adj airy

ari'ete m ram. A~ (Astr) Aries

ari'etta f (brezza) breeze

a'ringa f herring

ari'oso adj (locale) light and airy

aristo'cra|tico, -a adj aristocratic • mf aristocrat. ~**zia** f aristocracy

arit'metica f arithmetic

arlec'chino m Harlequin; fig buffoon

'arma f weapon; **armi** pl arms; (forze armate) [armed] forces; **chiamare alle armi** call up; **sotto le armi** in the army; **alle prime armi** fig inexperienced. ~ **da fuoco** firearm. **armi** mpl **di distruzione di massa** weapons of mass destruction.

armadi'etto m locker, cupboard

ar'madio m cupboard; (guardaroba) wardrobe

armamen'tario m tools pl; fig paraphernalia

arma'mento m armament; (Naut) fitting out

ar'ma|re vt arm; (equipaggiare) fit out; (Archit) reinforce. ~**rsi** vr arm oneself (**di** with). ~**ta** f army; (flotta) fleet. ~**tore** m shipowner. ~**tura** f framework; (impalcatura) scaffolding; (di guerriero) armour

armeggi'are vi fig manoeuvre

armi'stizio m armistice

armo'ni|a f harmony. **ar'monica** f ~ [**a bocca**] mouth organ. **ar'monico** adj harmonic. ~**oso** adj harmonious

armoniz'zare vt harmonize • vi match. (colori) match

ar'nese m tool; (oggetto) thing; (congegno) gadget; **male in** ~ in bad condition

'arnia f beehive

a'roma m aroma; **aromi** pl herbs.

~**tera'pia** f aromatherapy

aro'matico adj aromatic

aromatiz'zare vt flavour

'arpa f harp

ar'peggio m arpeggio

'arpia f harpy

arpi'one m hook; (pesca) harpoon

arrabat'tarsi vr do all one can

arrabbi'a|rsi vr get angry. ~**to** adj angry. ~**tura** f rage; **prendersi una** ~**tura** fly into a rage

arraf'fare vt grab

arrampi'ca|rsi vr climb [up]. ~**ta** f climb. ~**tore, ~trice** mf climber. ~**tore sociale** social climber

arran'care vi limp, hobble

arrangia'mento m arrangement

arrangi'ar|e vt arrange. ~**si** vr manage; ~**si alla meglio** get by; **arrangiati!** get on with it!

arra'parsi vr 🅃 get randy

arre'care vt bring; (causare) cause

arreda'mento m interior decoration; (l'arredare) furnishing; (mobili ecc) furnishings

arre'da|re vt furnish. ~**tore, ~trice** mf interior designer. **ar'redo** m furnishings pl

ar'rendersi vr surrender

arren'devo|le adj (persona) yielding. ~**lezza** f softness

arre'sta|re vt arrest; (fermare) stop. ~**si** vr halt. **ar'resto** m stop; (Med, Jur) arrest; **la dichiaro in [stato d']** **arresto** I arrest you; **sono in arresto** you are under arrest; **mandato di arresto** warrant. **arresti domiciliari** (Jur) house arrest

arre'tra|re vt/i withdraw; pull back (giocatore); ~**to** (paese ecc) backward; (mese) rear; **numero** ~**to** (di rivista) back number; **del lavoro** ~**to** a backlog of work • m (di stipendio) back pay

arre'trati mpl arrears

arricchi'mento m enrichment

arric'chi|re vt enrich. ~**rsi** vr get

rich. ~to. -a *mf* nouveau riche

arricci'are *vt* curl; ~ il naso turn up one's nose

ar'ringa *f* harangue; (*Jur*) closing address

arrischi'a|rsi *vr* dare. ~to *adj* risky; (*imprudente*) rash

arri'va|re *vi* arrive. ~re a (*raggiungere*) reach; (*ridursi*) be reduced to. ~to, -a *adj* successful; ben ~to! welcome! ●*mf* successful person

arrive'derci *int* goodbye; ~ a domani see you tomorrow

arri'vis|mo *m* social climbing; (*nel lavoro*) careerism. ~ta *mf* social climber; (*nel lavoro*) careerist

ar'rivo *m* arrival; Sport finish

arro'gan|te *adj* arrogant. ~za *f* arrogance

arro'garsi *vr* ~ il diritto di fare qcsa take it upon oneself to do sth

arrossa'mento *m* reddening

arros'sar|e *vt* make red (occhi). ~si *vr* go red

arros'sire *vi* blush, go red

arros'stire *vt* roast; toast (pane); (ai ferri) grill. ar'rosto *adj & m* roast

arroto'lare *vt* roll up

arroton'dar|e *vt* make round; (*Math ecc*) round off. ~si *vr* become round; (*persona*:) get plump

arrovel'larsi *vr* ~ il cervello rack one's brains

arroven'ta|re *vt* make red-hot. ~rsi *vr* become red-hot. ~to *adj* red-hot

arruf'fa|re *vt* ruffle; *fig* confuse. ~to *adj* (*capelli*) ruffled

arruffiana|rsi *vr* ~ qcno *fig* butter sb up

arruggini'r|e *vt* rust. ~rsi *vr* go rusty; *fig* (*fisicamente*) stiffen up; (*conoscenze*:) go rusty. ~to *adj* rusty

arruola'mento *m* enlistment

arruo'lar|e *vt/i*, ~si *vr* enlist

arse'nale *m* arsenal; (*cantiere*)

[*naval*] dockyard

ar'senico *m* arsenic

'arso *pp di* ardere ●*adj* burnt; (*arido*) dry. ar'sura *f* burning heat; (*sete*) parching thirst

'arte *f* art; (*abilità*) craftsmanship; le belle arti the fine arts. arti figurative figurative arts

arte'fa|re *vt* adulterate (vino); disguise (voce). ~tto *adj* fake; (*vino*) adulterated

ar'tefice *mf* craftsman; craftswoman; *fig* author

ar'teria *f* artery. ~ [stradale] arterial road

arterioscle'rosi *f* arteriosclerosis

'artico *adj & m* Arctic

artico'la|re *adj* articular ●*vt* articulate; (*suddividere*) divide. ~rsi *vr* fig ~rsi in consist of. ~to *adj* (*Auto*) articulated; *fig* well-constructed. ~zi'one *f* (*Anat*) articulation

ar'ticolo *m* article. ~ di fondo leader

artifici'ale *adj* artificial

arti'fici|o *m* artifice; (*affettazione*) affectation. ~'oso *adj* artful; (*affettato*) affected

artigia'nal|e *adj* made by hand; *hum* amateurish. ~'mente *adv* with craftsmanship; *hum* amateurishly

artigia'na|to *m* craftsmanship; (*ceto*) craftsmen *pl.* ~'ano, -a *m* craftsman ●*f* craftswoman

artigli'ere *m* artilleryman. ~e'ria *f* artillery

ar'tiglio *m* claw; *fig* clutch

ar'tis|ta *mf* artist. ~ica'mente *adv* artistically. ~ico *adj* artistic

'arto *m* limb

ar'trite *f* arthritis

ar'trosi *f* rheumatism

arzigogo'lato *adj* bizarre

ar'zillo *adj* sprightly

a'scella *f* armpit

ascen'den|te *adj* ascending ●*m*

(*antenato*) ancestor; (*influenza*) ascendancy; (*Astr*) ascendant

ascensi'one f ascent; l'A~ the Ascension

ascen'sore m lift, elevator Am

a'scesa f ascent; (*al trono*) accession; (*al potere*) rise

a'scesso m abscess

a'sceta mf ascetic

'ascia f axe

asciugabian'cheria m inv (*stenditoio*) clothes horse

asciugaca'pelli m inv hair dryer

asciuga'mano m towel

asciu'gar|e vt dry. ~si vr dry oneself; (*diventare asciutto*) dry up

asci'utto adj dry; (*magro*) wiry; (*risposta*) curt; essere all'~ fig be hard up

ascol'tar|e vt listen to ● vi listen. ~tore, ~trice mf listener

a'scolto m listening; dare ~ a listen to; mettersi in ~ Radio tune in

asfal'tare vt asphalt

a'sfalto m asphalt

asfis'si|a f asphyxia. ~'ante adj oppressive; fig (*persona*) annoying. ~'are vt asphyxiate; fig annoy

'Asia f Asia. asi'atico, -a agg & mf Asian

a'silo m shelter; (*d'infanzia*) nursery school. ~ nido day nursery. ~ politico political asylum

asim'metrico adj asymmetrical

'asino m donkey; (*fig: persona stupida*) ass

'asma f asthma. a'smatico adj asthmatic

asoci'ale adj asocial

'asola f buttonhole

'sparagi mpl asparagus sg

a'sparago m asparagus spear

asperità f inv harshness; (*di terreno*) roughness

aspet'ta|re vt wait for; (*prevedere*) expect; ~re un bambino be expecting [a baby]; fare ~re qcno keep sb waiting ● vi wait. ~rsi vr expect. ~'tiva f expectation

a'spetto[1] m appearance; (*di problema*) aspect; di bell'~ good-looking

a'spetto[2] m sala f d'~ waiting room

aspi'rante adj aspiring; (*pompa*) suction attrib ● m/f (*a un posto*) applicant; (*al trono*) aspirant; gli aspiranti al titolo the contenders for the title

aspira'polvere m inv vacuum cleaner

aspi'ra|re vt inhale; (*Mech*) suck in ● vi ~re a aspire to. ~'tore m extractor fan. ~zi'one f inhalation; (*Mech*) suction; (*ambizione*) ambition

aspi'rina f aspirin

aspor'tare vt take away

aspra'mente adv (*duramente*) severely

a'sprezza f (*al gusto*) sourness; (*di clima*) severity; (*di suono*) harshness; (*di odore*) pungency

'aspro adj (*al gusto*) sour; (*clima*) severe; (*suono, parole*) harsh; (*odore*) pungent; (*litigio*) bitter

assag'gia|re vt taste. ~'gini mpl (*Culin*) samples. as'saggio m tasting; (*piccola quantità*) taste

as'sai adv very; (*moltissimo*) very much; (*abbastanza*) enough

assa'li|re vt attack. ~'tore, ~'trice mf assailant

as'salto m attack; prendere d'~ storm (*città*); fig mob (*persona*); hold up (*banca*)

assapo'rare vt savour

assassi'nare vt murder, assassinate

assas'sin|io m murder, assassination. ~o, -a adj murderous ● m murderer ● f murderess

'asse f board ● m (*Techn*) axle; (*Math*) axis. ~ da stiro ironing board

assecon'dare vt satisfy; (*favorire*) support

assedi'are vt besiege. **as'sedio** m siege

assegna'mento m allotment; **fare ~u** rely on

asse'gna|re vt allot; award (*premio*). **~tario** mf recipient. **~zi'one** f (*di alloggio, borsa di studio*) allocation; (*di premio*) award

as'segno m allowance; (*bancario*) cheque; **contro ~** cash on delivery. **~ circolare** bank draft. **assegni** pl **familiari** family allowance. **~ non trasferibile** non-transferable cheque.

assem'blea f assembly; (*adunanza*) gathering

assembra'mento m gathering

assen'nato adj sensible

assen'tarsi vr go away; (*da stanza*) leave the room

as'sen|te adj absent; (*distratto*) absent-minded ● mf absentee. **~te'ismo** m absenteeism. **~te'ista** mf frequent absentee. **~za** f absence; (*mancanza*) lack

asse'ri|re vt assert. **~tivo** adj assertive. **~zi'one** f assertion

assesso'rato m department

asses'sore m councillor

assesta'mento m settlement

asse'sta|re vt arrange; **~ un colpo** deal a blow. **~si** vr settle oneself

asse'tato adj parched

as'setto m order; (*Aeron, Naut*) trim

assicu'ra|re vt assure; (*Comm*) insure; register (*posta*); (*fissare*) secure; (*accertare*) ensure. **~rsi** vr (*con contratto*) insure oneself; (*legarsi*) fasten oneself; **~rsi che** make sure that. **~tivo** adj insurance attrib. **~tore, ~trice** mf insurance agent ● adj insurance attrib. **~zi'one** f assurance; (*contratto*) insurance

assidera'mento m exposure. **as'side'rato** adj (*Med*) suffering from exposure; Ⓣ frozen

assidu'a'mente adv assiduously. **~ità** f assiduity

as'siduo adj assiduous; (*cliente*) regular

assil'lante adj (*persona, pensiero*) nagging

assil'lare vt pester

as'sillo m worry

assimi'la|re vt assimilate. **~zi'one** f assimilation

as'sise fpl assizes; Corte d'A~ Court of Assize[s]

assi'sten|te mf assistant. **~te so'ciale** social worker. **~te di volo** flight attendant. **~za** f assistance; (*presenza*) presence. **~za sociale** social work

assistenzi'a|le adj welfare attrib. **~lismo** m welfare

as'sistere vt assist; (*curare*) nurse ● vi **~ a** (*essere presente*) be present at; watch (*spettacolo ecc*)

'asso m ace; **piantare in ~** leave in the lurch

associ'a|re vt join; (*collegare*) associate. **~rsi** vr join forces; (*Comm*) enter into partnership. **~rsi a** join. **~zi'one** f association

assogget'tar|e vt subject. **~si** vr submit

asso'lato adj sunny

assol'dare vt recruit

as'solo m (*Mus*) solo

as'solto pp di **assolvere**

assoluta'mente adv absolutely

assolu'tismo m absolutism

asso'lu|to adj absolute. **~zi'one** f acquittal; (*Relig*) absolution

as'solvere vt perform (*compito*); (*Jur*) acquit; (*Relig*) absolve

assomigli'ar|e vi **~e a** resemble. **~si** vr resemble each other

assom'marsi vr combine; ~ a qcsa add to sth

asso'nanza f assonance

asson'nato adj drowsy

assor'pirsi vr doze off

assor'bente adj & m absorbent. ~ igienico sanitary towel

assor'bire vt absorb

assor'da|re vt deafen. ~nte adj deafening

assorti'mento m assortment

assor'ti|re vt match (colori). ~to adj assorted; (colori, persone) matched

as'sorto adj engrossed

assottigli'ar|e vt make thin; (aguzzare) sharpen; (ridurre) reduce. ~si vr grow thin; (finanze): be whittled away

assue'fa|re vt accustom. ~rsi vr ~rsi a get used to. ~tto adj (a caffè, aspirina) immune to the effects; (a droga) addicted. ~zi'one f (a caffè, aspirina) immunity to the effects; (a droga) addiction

as'sumere vt assume; take on (impiegato); ~ informazioni make inquiries

as'sunto pp di **assumere** ● m task. **assunzi'one** f (di impiegato) employment

assurdità f inv absurdity; ~ pl nonsense

as'surdo adj absurd

'asta f pole; (Mech) bar; (Comm) auction; a mezz'~ at half-mast

a'stemio adj abstemious

aste'n|ersi vr abstain (da from). ~si'one f abstention

aste'nuto, -a mf abstainer

aste'risco m asterisk

astig'ma|tico adj astigmatic. ~'tismo m astigmatism

'astio m rancour; avere ~o contro qcno bear sb a grudge. ~'oso adj resentful

a'stratto adj abstract

astrin'gente adj & m astringent

'astro m star

astro|lo'gia f astrology. a'strologo, -a mf astrologer

astro'nauta mf astronaut

astro'nave f spaceship

astr|ono'mia f astronomy. ~o'nomico adj astronomical. a'stronomo m astronomer

astrusità f abstruseness

a'stuccio m case

a'stu|to adj shrewd; (furbo) cunning. ~zia f shrewdness; (azione) trick

ate'ismo m atheism

A'tene f Athens

'ateo, -a adj & mf atheist

a'tipico adj atypical

at'lant|e m atlas. l'A~ico adj Atlantic; l' (Oceano) A~ico the Atlantic [Ocean]

at'let|a mf athlete. ~ica f athletics sg. ~ica leggera track and field events. ~ica pesante weight-lifting, boxing, wrestling, etc. ~ico adj athletic

atmo|'sfer|a f atmosphere. ~ico adj atmospheric

a'tomic|a f atom bomb. ~o adj atomic

'atomo m atom

'atrio m entrance hall

a'troc|e adj atrocious; (terrible) dreadful. ~ità f inv atrocity

atrofiz'zarsi vr atrophy

attaccabot'toni mf inv [crashing] bore

attacca'brighe mf inv troublemaker

attacca'mento m attachment

attacca'panni m inv [coat-]hanger; (a muro) clothes hook

attac'car|e vt attach; (legare) tie; (appendere) hang; (cucire) sew on; (contagiare) pass on; (assalire) attack; (iniziare) start ● vi stick; (diffondersi) catch

a

on. ~**si** vr cling; (affezionarsi) become attached; (litigare) quarrel

attacca'ticcio adj sticky

at'tacco m attack; (punto d'unione) junction

attar'darsi vr stay late; (indugiare) linger

attec'chire vi take; (moda ecc:) catch on

atteggia'mento m attitude

atteggi'ar|e vt assume. ~**si** vr ~**si** a pose as

attem'pato adj elderly

at'tender|e vt wait for ● vi ~**e** a attend to. ~**si** vr expect

atten'dibil|e adj reliable. ~**ità** f reliability

atte'nersi vr ~ a stick to

atten'tamente adv attentively

atten'ta|re vi ~**re** a make an attempt on. ~**to** m act of violence; (contro politico ecc) assassination attempt. ~**tore**, ~**trice** mf (a scopo politico) terrorist

at'tento adj attentive; (accurato) careful; ~! look out!; **stare** ~ pay attention

attenu'ante f extenuating circumstance

attenu'a|re vt attenuate; (minimizzare) minimize; subdue (colori ecc); calm (dolore); soften (colpo). ~**rsi** vr diminish. ~**zione** f lessening

attenzi'one f attention; ~! watch out!

atter'raggio m landing. ~**re** vt knock down ● vi land

atter'rir|e vt terrorize. ~**si** vr be terrified

at'tes|a f waiting; (aspettativa) expectation; **in** ~**a di** waiting for. ~**o** pp di **attendere**

atte'sta|re vt state; (certificare) certify. ~**to** m certificate. ~**zi'one** f certificate; (dichiarazione) declaration

'attico m attic

at'tiguo adj adjacent

attil'lato adj (vestito) close-fitting

'attimo m moment

atti'nente adj ~ a pertaining to

at'tingere vt draw; fig obtain

atti'rare vt attract

atti'tudine f (disposizione) aptitude; (atteggiamento) attitude

atti'v|are vt activate. ~**ismo** m activism. ~**ista** mf activist. **attività** f inv activity; (Comm) assets pl. ~**o** adj active; (Comm) productive ● m assets pl

attiz'za|re vt poke; fig stir up. ~**toio** m poker

'atto m act; (azione) action; (Comm, Jur) deed; (certificato) certificate; **atti** pl (di società ecc) proceedings; **mettere in** ~ put into effect

at'tonito adj astonished

attorcigli'ar|e vt twist. ~**si** vr get twisted

at'tore m actor

attorni'ar|e vt surround. ~**si** vr ~**si di** surround oneself with

at'torno adv around, about ● prep ~ a around, about

attrac'care vt/i dock

attra'ente adj attractive

at'tra|rre vt attract. ~**rsi** vr be attracted to each other. ~**t'tiva** f charm

attraversa'mento m crossing. ~ **pedonale** crossing, crosswalk Am

attraver'sare vt cross; (passare) through

attra'verso prep through; (obliquamente) across

attrazi'on|e f attraction. ~**i** pl turistiche tourist attractions

attrez'za|re vt equip; (Naut) rig. ~**rsi** vr kit oneself out; ~**tura** f equipment; (Naut) rigging

at'trezzo m tool; **attrezzi** pl equipment; Sport appliances pl; (Theat) props pl

attribu'ir|e vt attribute. ~**si** vr

ascribe to oneself; **~si il merito di** claim credit for

attri'bu|to m attribute. **~zi'one** f attribution

at'trice f actress

at'trito m friction

attu'abile adj feasible

attu'al|e adj present; (di attualità) topical; (effettivo) actual. **~ità** f topicality; (avvenimento) news; **programma di ~ità** current affairs programme. **~iz'zare** vt update. **~'mente** adv at present

attu'a|re vt carry out. **~rsi** vr be realized. **~zi'one** f carrying out

attu'tire vt deaden; **~ il colpo** soften the blow

au'dac|e adj audacious;. **~ia** f boldness; (insolenza) audacity

'audience f inv (telespettatori) audience

'audio m audio

audiovi'sivo adj audiovisual

audi'torio m auditorium

audizi'one f audition; (Jur) hearing

'auge m height; **essere in ~ be** popular

augu'rar|e vt wish. **~si** vr hope. **au'gurio** m wish; (presagio) omen; **auguri!** all the best!; (a Natale) Happy Christmas!; **tanti auguri** best wishes

'aula f classroom; (università) lecture-hall; (sala) hall. **~ magna** (in università) great hall. **~ del tribunale** courtroom

aumen'tare vt/i increase. **au'mento** m increase; (di stipendio) [pay] rise

au'reola f halo

au'rora f dawn

auscul'tare vt (Med) auscultate

ausili'are adj & mf auxiliary

auspi'cabile adj **è ~ che...** it is to be hoped that...

auspi'care vt hope for

au'spicio m omen; **auspici** (pl: pro-

tezione) auspices

austerità f austerity

au'stero adj austere.

Au'strali|a f Australia. **a~'ano, -a** adj & mf Australian

'Austria f Austria. **au'striaco, -a** agg & mf Austrian

autar'chia f autarchy. **au'tarchico** adj autarchic

autenti'c|are vt authenticate. **~ità** f authenticity

au'tentico adj authentic; (vero) true

au'tista m driver

'auto+ pref self +; **auto-**

autoabbron'zante m self-tan ● adj self-tanning

autoambu'lanza f ambulance

autoartico'lato m articulated lorry

autobio|gra'fia f autobiography. **~'grafico** adj autobiographical

auto'botte f tanker

'autobus m inv bus

auto'carro m lorry

autocommiserazi'one f self-pity

autoconcessio'nario m car dealer

auto'critica f self-criticism

autodi'fesa f self-defence

auto'gol m inv own goal

au'tografo adj & m autograph

autolesio'nis|mo m fig self-destruction. **~tico** adj self-destructive

auto'linea f bus line

au'toma m robot

automatica'mente adv automatically

auto'matico adj automatic ● m (bottone) press-stud; (fucile) automatic

automatiz'za|re vt automate. **~zi'one** f automation

auto'mezzo m motor vehicle

auto'mobi|le f [motor] car. ∼**lismo** m motoring. ∼**lista** mf motorist. ∼**listico** adj (industria) automobile attrib

autonoma'mente adv autonomously

autono'mia f autonomy; (Auto) range; (di laptop, cellulare) battery life. **au'tonomo** adj autonomous

auto'psia f autopsy

auto'radio f inv car radio; (veicolo) radio car

au'tore, -'trice mf author; (di pinti) painter; (di furto ecc) perpetrator; **quadro d'**∼ genuine master

auto'revo|le adj authoritative; (che ha influenza) influential. ∼**lezza** f authority

autori'carica f mobile phone tariff where users' accounts are credited depending on usage

autori'messa f garage

autori'tà f inv authority. ∼**tario** adj autocratic. ∼**ta'rismo** m authoritarianism

autori'tratto m self-portrait

autoriz'za|re vt authorize. ∼**zi'one** f authorization

auto'scontro m inv bumper car

autoscu'ola f driving school

auto'stop m hitch-hiking; **fare l'**∼ hitch-hike. ∼**pista** f hitch-hiker

auto'strada f motorway

autostra'dale adj motorway attrib

autosuffici'en|te adj self-sufficient. ∼**za** f self-sufficiency

autotrasporta'|tore, -'trice mf haulier, carrier

auto'treno m articulated lorry

autove'icolo m motor vehicle

Auto'velox m inv speed camera

autovet'tura f motor vehicle

autun'nale adj autumnal

au'tunno m autumn

aval'lare vt endorse

a'vallo m endorsement

avam'braccio m forearm

avangu'ardia f vanguard; fig avant-garde; **essere all'**∼ be in the forefront

a'vanti adv (in avanti) forward; (davanti) in front; (prima) before; ∼**!** (entrate) come in!; (suvvia) come on!; (su semaforo) cross now; **va'** ∼**!** go ahead!; **andare** ∼ (precedere) go ahead; (orologio): be fast; ∼ **e indietro** backwards and forwards ● adj before ● prep ∼ **a** before; (in presenza di) in the presence of

avanti'eri adv the day before yesterday

avanza'mento m progress; (promozione) promotion

avan'za|re vi advance; (progredire) progress; (essere d'avanzo) be left [over] ● vt advance; (superare) surpass; (promuovere) promote. ∼**rsi** vr advance; (avvicinarsi) approach. ∼**ta** f advance. ∼**to** adj advanced; (nella notte) late; **in età** ∼**ta** elderly. **a'vanzo** m remainder; (Comm) surplus; **avanzi** pl (rovine) remains; (di cibo) left-overs

ava'ri|a f (di motore) engine failure. ∼**ato** adj (frutta, verdura) rotten; (carne) tainted

ava'rizia f avarice. **a'varo, -a** adj stingy ● mf miser

a'vena f oats pl

---

a'vere

Si può usare have o have got per parlare di ciò che si possiede. have got non si usa nell'inglese americano.

● vt have; (ottenere) get; (indossare) wear; (provare) feel; **ho trent'anni** I'm thirty; **ha avuto il posto** he got the job; ∼ **fame/freddo** be hungry/cold; **ho mal di denti** I've got toothache; **cos'ha a che fare con lui?** what has it got to do with him?; **~ da fare** be busy; **che hai?** what's the matter with you?; **nei hai per molto?** will you be long?; **quanti ne abbiamo oggi?** what date is it today?; **avercela con qcno** have it in for sb

● v aux have; **non l'ho visto** I haven't seen him; **le hai visto?** have you seen him?; **l'ho visto ieri** I saw him yesterday

● m **averi** pl wealth sg

avia'tore m flyer, aviator. **~zi'one** f aviation; (Mil) Air Force

avidità f avidness. **'avido** adj avid

avio'getto m jet

'avo, -a mf ancestor

avo'cado m inv avocado

a'vorio m ivory

Avv. abbr avvocato

avva'lersi vr avail oneself (**di** of)

avval'mento m depression

avvalo'rare vt bear out (tesi); endorse (documento); (accrescere) enhance

avvam'pare vi flare up; (arrossire) blush

avvantaggi'ar|e vt favour. **~si** vr ~**si di** benefit from; (approfittare) take advantage of

avve'd|ersi vr (accorgersi) notice; (capire) realize. **~uto** adj shrewd

avvelena'mento m poisoning

avvele'na|re vt poison. **~rsi** vr poison oneself. **~to** adj poisoned

avve'nente adj attractive

avveni'mento m event

avve'nire[1] vi happen; (aver luogo) take place

avve'ni|re[2] m future. **~'ristico** adj futuristic

avven'ta|rsi vr fling oneself. **~to** adj (decisione) rash

av'vento m advent; (Relig) Advent

avven'tore m regular customer

avven'tu|ra f adventure; (amorosa) affair; **d'~** (film) adventure attrib. **~rarsi** vr venture. **~ri'ero, -a** m adventurer ● f adventur-ess. **~roso** adj adventurous

avve'ra|bile adj (previsione) that may come true. **~rsi** vr come true

av'verbio m adverb

avver'sar|e vt oppose. **~io, -a** adj opposing ● mf opponent

avversi|'one f aversion. **~tà** f inv adversity

av'verso adj (sfavorevole) adverse; (contrario) averse

avver'tenza f (cura) care; (avvertimento) warning; (avviso) notice; (premessa) foreword; **avvertenze** pl (istruzioni) instructions

avverti'mento m warning

avver'tire vt warn; (informare) inform; (sentire) feel

avvez'zar|e vt accustom. **~si** vr accustom oneself. **av'vezzo** adj avvezzo a used to

avvia'mento m starting; (Comm) goodwill

avvi'a|re vt start. **~rsi** vr set out. **~to** adj under way; **bene ~to** thriving

avvicenda'mento m (in agricoltura) rotation; (nel lavoro) replacement

avvicen'darsi vr alternate

avvicina'mento m approach

avvici'nar|e vt bring near; approach (persona). **~si** vr approach; **~si a** approach

avvi'lente adj demoralizing; (umiliante) humiliating

avvili'mento m despondency; (degradazione) degradation

avvi'li|re vt dishearten; (degradare) degrade. **~rsi** vr lose heart; (degradarsi) degrade oneself. **~to** adj disheartened; (degradato) degraded

avvilup'par|e vt envelop. **~si** vr

wrap oneself up; (aggrovigliarsi) get entangled

avvinaz'zato adj drunk

avvin'cente adj (libro ecc) enthralling. **av'vincere** vt enthral

avvinghi'ar|e vt clutch. **~si** vr cling

av'vio m start-up; dare l'~ a qcsa get sth under way; prendere l'~ get under way

avvi'sare vt inform; (mettere in guardia) warn

av'viso m notice; (annuncio) announcement; (avvertimento) warning; (pubblicitario) advertisement; **a mio ~ di garanzia** (Jur) notification that one is to be the subject of a legal enquiry

avvi'stare vt catch sight of

avvi'tare vt screw in; screw down (coperchio)

avviz'zire vi wither

avvo'cato m lawyer; fig advocate. **~tura** f legal profession

av'volgere vt wrap [up]. **~si** vr wrap oneself up

avvol'gibile m roller blind

avvol'toio m vulture

aza'lea f azalea

azi'en|da f business. **~ agricola** farm. **~ di soggiorno** tourist bureau. **~'dale** adj (politica) corporate; (giornale) in-house

aziona'mento m operation

azio'nare vt operate

azio'nario adj share attrib

azi'one f action; Fin share; **d'~** (romanzo, film) action[-packed]. **azio'nista** mf shareholder

a'zoto m nitrogen

azzan'nare vt seize with its teeth; sink its teeth into (gamba)

azzar'd|are vt risk. **~arsi** vr dare. **~ato** adj risky; (precipitoso) rash. **az'zardo** m hazard; **gioco d'azzardo** game of chance

azzec'care vt hit; (indovinare) guess

azzuf'farsi vr come to blows

az'zur|ro adj & m blue; **il principe ~** Prince Charming. **~rognolo** adj bluish

Bb

bab'beo adj foolish ● m idiot

'babbo m fam dad, daddy. **B~** Natale Father Christmas

bab'buccia f slipper

babbu'ino m baboon

ba'bordo m (Naut) port side

baby'sitter mf inv baby-sitter; **fare la ~** babysit

ba'cato adj wormeaten

'bacca f berry

bacca'là m inv dried salted cod

bac'cano m din

bac'cello m pod

bac'chetta f rod; (magica) wand; (di direttore d'orchestra) baton; (di tamburo) drumstick

ba'checa f showcase; (in ufficio) notice board. **~ elettronica** (Comput) bulletin board

bacia'mano m kiss on the hand; **fare il ~ a qcno** kiss sb's hand

baci'ar|e vt kiss. **~si** vr kiss [each other]

ba'cillo m bacillus

baci'nella f basin

ba'cino m basin; (Anat) pelvis; (di porto) dock; (di minerali) field

'bacio m kiss

'baco m worm. **~ da seta** silkworm

ba'cucco adj **un vecchio ~** a senile old man

'bada f **tenere qcno a ~** keep sb at bay

ba'**dante** *mf* carer
ba'**dare** *vi* take care (a of); (*fare attenzione*) look out; **bada ai fatti tuoi!** mind your own business!
ba'**dia** *f* abbey
ba'**dile** *m* shovel
'**badminton** *m* badminton
'**baffi** *mpl* moustache *sg*; (*di animale*) whiskers; **mi fa un baffo** I don't give a damn; **ridere sotto i ~** laugh up one's sleeve
baf'**futo** *adj* moustached
ba'**gagli** *mpl* baggage. **~'aio** *m* (*Rail*) baggage car; (*Auto*) boot
ba'**gaglio** *m* baggage; **un ~** a piece of baggage. **~ a mano** hand baggage
baggia'**nata** *f* **non dire baggianate** don't talk nonsense
bagli'**ore** *m* glare; (*improvviso*) flash; (*fig: di speranza*) glimmer
ba'**gnante** *mf* bather
ba'**gna|re** *vt* wet; (*inzuppare*) soak; (*immergere*) dip; (*innaffiare*) water; (*mare:*) wash; (*fiume:*) flow through. **~rsi** *vr* get wet; (*al mare ecc*) bathe
ba'**gnato** *adj* wet
ba'**gnino, -a** *mf* life guard
'**bagno** *m* bath; (*stanza*) bathroom; (*gabinetto*) toilet; (*in casa*) toilet; (*al mare*) bathe; **bagni** *pl* (*stabilimento*) lido; **fare il ~** have a bath; (*nel mare ecc*) [have a] swim; **andare in ~** go to the toilet; **mettere a ~** soak. **~ turco** Turkish bath
bagnoma'**ria** *m* bain marie
bagnoschi'**uma** *m inv* bubble bath
'**baia** *f* bay
baio'**netta** *f* bayonet
'**baita** *f* mountain chalet
bala'**ustra, balaus'trata** *f* balustrade
balbet'**t|are** *vt/i* stammer; (*bambino:*) babble. **~io** *m* stammering; babble

bal'**buzi|e** *f* stutter. **~'ente** *adj* stuttering ● *mf* stutterer
Bal'**can|i** *mpl* Balkans. **b~ico** *adj* Balkan
balco'**nata** *f* (*Theat*) balcony
balcon'**cino** *m* **reggiseno a ~** underwired bra
bal'**cone** *m* balcony
baldac'**chino** *m* canopy; **letto a ~** four-poster bed
bal'**dan|za** *f* boldness. **~'zoso** *adj* bold
bal'**doria** *f* revelry; **far ~** have a riotous time
ba'**lena** *f* whale
bale'**nare** *vi* lighten; *fig* flash; **mi è balenata un'idea** I've just had an idea
bale'**niera** *f* whaler
ba'**leno** *m* **in un ~** in a flash
ba'**lera** *f* dance hall
ba'**lia** *f* **in ~ di** at the mercy of
'**balla** *f* bale; (▢: *frottola*) tall story
bal'**labile** *adj* good for dancing to
bal'**la|re** *vi* dance. **~ta** *f* ballad
balla'**toio** *m* (*nelle scale*) landing
balle'**rino, -a** *mf* dancer; (*classico*) ballet dancer; **ballerina** (*classica*) ballet dancer, ballerina
bal'**letto** *m* ballet
'**ballo** *m* dance; (*il ballare*) dancing; **sala da ~** ballroom; **essere in ~** (*lavoro, vita:*) be at stake; (*persona:*) be committed; **tirare qcno in ~** involve sb
ballonzo'**lare** *vi* skip about
ballot'**taggio** *m* second count (*of votes*)
balne'**a|re** *adj* bathing *attrib*. **sta-gione ~** swimming season. **sta-zione ~** seaside resort. **~zi'one** *f* è **vietata la ~zione** no swimming
ba'**lordo** *adj* foolish; (*stordito*) stunned; **tempo ~** nasty weather
'**balsamo** *m* balsam; (*per capelli*) conditioner; (*lenimento*) remedy

'baltico adj Baltic. **il** [mar] **B~ the Baltic** [Sea]

balu'ardo m bulwark

'balza f crag; (di abito) flounce

bal'zano adj (idea) weird

bal'zare vi bounce; (saltare) jump; ~ **in piedi** leap to one's feet. **'balzo** m bounce; (salto) jump; **prendere la palla al balzo** seize an opportunity

bam'bagia f cotton wool

bambi'nata f childish thing to do/say

bam'bi|no, -a mf child; (appena nato) baby; **avere un ~no** have a baby. **~'none, -a** mf pej big or overgrown child

bam'boccio m chubby child; (sciocco) simpleton; (fantoccio) rag doll

'bambo|la f doll. **~'lotto** m male doll

bambù m bamboo.

ba'nal|e adj banal; **~ità** f inv banality; **~iz'zare** vt trivialize

ba'nan|a f banana. **~o** m banana-tree

'banca f bank. **~ [di] dati** databank

banca'rella f stall

ban'cario, -a adj banking attrib; **trasferimento ~** bank transfer ● mf bank employee

banca'rotta f bankruptcy; **fare ~** go bankrupt

banchet'tare vi banquet. **ban'chetto** m banquet

banchi'ere m banker

ban'china f (Naut) quay; (in stazione) platform; (di strada) path; **~ non transitabile** soft verge

ban'chisa f floe

'banco m (di scuola) desk; (di negozio) counter; (di officina) bench; (di gioco, banca) bank; (di mercato) stall; (degli imputati) dock; **sotto ~** under the counter; **medicinale da ~** over the counter medicines. **~ informazioni** information desk. **~ di nebbia**

fog bank

'bancomat® m inv cashpoint, ATM; (carta) bank card

ban'cone m counter; (in bar) bar

banco'nota f banknote, bill Am; **banco'note** pl paper currency

'banda f band; (di delinquenti) gang. **~ d'atterraggio** landing strip. **~ larga** broad band. **~ rumorosa** rumble strip

banderu'ola f weathercock; (Naut) pennant

bandi'e|ra f flag. **~'rina** f (nel calcio) corner flag. **~'rine** pl bunting sg

ban'di|re vt banish; (pubblicare) publish; fig dispense with (formalità, complimenti). **~to** m bandit. **~tore** m (di asta) auctioneer

'bando m proclamation; **~ di concorso** job advertisement (published in an official gazette for a job for which a competitive examination has to be taken)

bar m inv bar

> ### i
> **Bar** In Italy a bar is first and foremost a place where coffee is drunk, although alcoholic and soft drinks are also served. Italians tend to drink their coffee standing up at the bar, and there is usually an additional charge for sitting at a table.

'bara f coffin

ba'rac|ca f hut; (catapecchia) hovel; **mandare avanti la ~ca** keep the ship afloat. **~'cato** m person living in a makeshift shelter. **~'chino** m (di gelati, giornali) kiosk; Radio CB radio. **~'cone** m (roulotte) circus caravan; (in luna park) booth. **~'copoli** f inv shanty town

bara'onda f chaos

ba'rare vi cheat

'baratro m chasm

barat'tare vt barter. **ba'ratto** m barter

ba'rattolo m jar; (di latta) tin

'barba f beard; (🔲: noia) bore; **farsi la ~** shave; **è una ~** (noia) it's boring

barbabi'etola f beetroot. **~ da zucchero** sugar-beet

bar'barico adj barbaric. **bar'barie** f barbarity. **'barbaro** adj barbarous ● m barbarian

'barbecue m inv barbecue

barbi'ere m barber; (negozio) barber's

barbi'turico m barbiturate

bar'bone m (vagabondo) vagrant; (cane) poodle

bar'boso adj 🔲 boring

barbu'gliare vi mumble

bar'buto adj bearded

'barca f boat. **~ a motore** motorboat. **~ da pesca** fishing boat. **~ a remi** rowing boat. **~ di salvataggio** lifeboat. **~ a vela** sailing boat. **~i'olo** m boatman

barcame'narsi vr manage

barcol'lare vi stagger

bar'cone m barge; (di ponte) pontoon

bar'dare vt harness. **~si** vr hum dress up

ba'rella f stretcher. **~li'ere** m stretcher-bearer

'Barents: **il mare di ~** the Barents Sea

bari'centro m centre of gravity

ba'rile m barrel. **•'lotto** m fig tub of lard

ba'rista m barman ● f barmaid

ba'ritono m baritone

bar'lume m glimmer; **un ~ di speranza** a glimmer of hope

'barman m inv barman

'baro m cardsharper

ba'rocco adj & m baroque

ba'rometro m barometer

ba'rone m baron; **i baroni** fig the top brass. **baro'nessa** f baroness

'barra f bar; (lineetta) oblique; (Naut) tiller. **~ spazio** (Comput) space bar. **~ strumenti** (Comput) tool bar

bar'rare vt block off (strada)

barri'ca|re vt barricade. **~ta** f barricade

barri'era f barrier; (stradale) roadblock; (Geol) reef. **~ razziale** colour bar

barri're vi trumpet. **~to** m trumpeting

barzel'letta f joke; **~ sporca** o **spinta** dirty joke

basa'mento m base

ba'sar|e vt base. **~si** vr **~si su** be based on; **mi baso su ciò che ho visto** I'm going on [the basis of] what I saw

'basco, -a mf & adj Basque ● m (copricapo) beret

'base f basis; (fondamento) foundation; (Mil) base; (Pol) rank and file; **a ~ di** containing; **in ~ a** on the basis of. **~ dati** database

'baseball m baseball

ba'setta f sideburn

basi'lare adj basic

ba'silica f basilica

ba'silico m basil

ba'sista m grass roots politician; (di un crimine) mastermind

'basket m basketball

bas'sezza f lowness; (di statura) shortness; (viltà) vileness

bas'sista mf bassist

'basso adj low; (di statura) short; (acqua) shallow; (televisione) quiet; (vile) despicable; **parlare a bassa voce** speak in a low voice; **la bassa Italia** southern Italy ● m lower part; (Mus) bass. **guardare in ~** look down

basso'fondo m (pl bassifondi) shallows pl; **bassifondi** pl (quartieri) *poveri)* slums

bassorili'evo m bas-relief

bas'sotto m dachshund

ba'stardo, -a adj bastard; *(di animale)* mongrel ●mf bastard; *(animale)* mongrel

ba'stare vi be enough; *(durare)* last; **basta!** that's enough!; **basta che** *(purché)* provided that; **basta così** that's enough; **basta così?** is that enough?; *(in negozio)* anything else?; **basta andare alla posta** you only have to go to the post office

Basti'an con'trario m contrary old so-and-so

basti'one m bastion

basto'nare vt beat

baston'cino m ski pole. ~ **di pesce** fish finger, fish stick Am

ba'stone m stick; *(da golf)* club; *(da passeggio)* walking stick

ba'tosta f blow

bat'tagli|a f battle; *(lotta)* fight. ~**re** vi battle; fig fight

bat'taglio m *(di campana)* clapper; *(di porta)* knocker

battagli'one m battalion

bat'tello m boat; *(motonave)* steamer

bat'tente m *(di porta)* wing; *(di finestra)* shutter; *(battaglio)* knocker

'batter|e vt beat; *(percorrere)* scour; thresh *(grano)*; break *(record)* ●vi *(bussare, urtare)* knock; *(cuore)* beat; *(ali ecc)* flap; Tennis serve; ~**a macchina** type; ~**le palpebre** blink; ~**le mani** clap [one's hands]; ~**le ore** strike the hours. ~**si** vr fight

bat'teri mpl bacteria

batte'ria f battery; *(Mus)* drums pl

bat'terio m bacterium. ~**logico** adj bacteriological

batte'rista mf drummer

bat'tesimo m baptism

battez'zare vt baptize

battiba'leno m in un ~ in a flash

batti'becco m squabble

batticu'ore m palpitation; **mi venne il** ~ I was scared

bat'tiglia f water's edge

batti'mano m applause

batti'panni m inv carpetbeater

batti'stero m baptistery

batti'strada m inv outrider; *(di pneumatico)* tread; Sport pacesetter

battitap'peto m inv carpet sweeper

'battito m *[heart]*beat; *(alle tempie)* throbbing; *(di orologio)* ticking; *(della pioggia)* beating

bat'tuta f beat; *(colpo)* knock; *(spiritosaggine)* wisecrack; *(osservazione)* remark; *(Mus)* bar; Tennis service; *(Theat)* cue; *(dattilografia)* stroke

ba'tuffolo m flock

ba'ule m trunk

'bava f dribble; *(di cane ecc)* slobber; **aver la** ~ **alla bocca** foam at the mouth

bava'glino m bib

ba'vaglio m gag

'bavero m collar

ba'zar m inv bazaar

baz'zecola f trifle

bazzi'care vt/i haunt

be'arsi vr delight *(di* in*)*

beati'tudine f bliss. **be'ato** adj blissful; *(Relig)* blessed; **beato te!** lucky you!

beauty-'case m inv toilet bag

bebè m inv baby

bec'caccia f woodcock

bec'ca|re vt peck; fig catch. ~**rsi** vr *(litigare)* quarrel. ~**ta** f peck

beccheggi'are vi pitch

bec'chino m grave-digger

'bec|co m beak; *(di caffettiera ecc)* spout. ~**cuccio** m spout

be'fana f Epiphany; *(donna brutta)* old witch

Befana La Befana, whose name is derived from *Epifania* (Epiphany), is an old woman who is said to visit children on 6 January, bringing presents and sweets. *Befana* is also the name for the Epiphany holiday and usually signals the end of the Christmas celebrations and the return to school.

'**beffa** f hoax; farsi beffe di qcno mock sb. bef'fardo *adj* derisory; (persona) mocking

bef'far|e *vt* mock. ∼si *vr* ∼si di make fun of

'**bega** f quarrel; è una bella ∼ it's really annoying

beige *adj* & *m* beige

be'la|re *vi* bleat. ∼to *m* bleating

'**belga** *adj* & *mf* Belgian

'**Belgio** *m* Belgium

'**bella** f (in carte, Sport) decider

bel'lezza f beauty; che ∼! how lovely!; chiudere/finire in ∼ end on a high note

bell|ico *adj war attrib.* ∼'coso *adj* warlike. ∼ge'rante *adj* & *mf* belligerent

'**bello** *adj* nice; (di aspetto) beautiful; (uomo) handsome; (moralmente) good; cosa fai di ∼ stasera? what are you up to tonight?; oggi fa ∼ it's a nice day; una bella cifra a lot; un bel piatto di pasta a big plate of pasta; nel bel mezzo right in the middle; un bel niente absolutely nothing; bell'e fatto over and done with; bell'amico! [a] fine friend he is/you are!; questa è bella! that's a good one!; scamparla bella have a narrow escape ●*m* (bellezza) beauty; (innamorato) sweetheart; sul più ∼ at the crucial moment; il ∼ è che... the funny thing is that...

'**belva** f wild beast

be'**molle** *m* (Mus) flat

ben ▷BENE

benché *conj* though, although

'**benda** f bandage; (per occhi) blindfold. ben'dare *vt* bandage; blindfold (occhi)

'**bene** *adv* well; ben ∼ thoroughly; ∼! good!; star ∼ (di salute) suit; (vestito, stile:) suit; (finanziariamente) be well off; non sta ∼ (non è educato) it's not nice; sta/va ∼! all right!; ti sta ∼! [it] serves you right!; ti auguro ogni ∼ I wish you well; di ∼ in meglio better and better; fare ∼ (aver ragione) do the right thing; fare ∼ a (cibo:) be good for; una persona per ∼ a good person; per ∼ (fare) properly; è ben difficile it's very difficult; come tu ben sai as you well know; lo credo ∼! I can well believe it! ●*m* good; per il tuo ∼ for your own good; beni *mpl* (averi) property *sg*; un ∼ di famiglia a family heirloom

bene'detto *adj* blessed

bene'di|re *vt* bless. ∼zi'one f blessing

benedu'cato *adj* well-mannered

benefat'tore, -'trice *mf* benefactor *mf* benefactress

benefi'care *vt* help

benefi'cenza f charity

benefici'ar|e *vi* ∼e di profit by. ∼io, -a *adj* & *mf* beneficiary. bene'ficio *m* benefit. be'nefico *adj* beneficial; (di beneficenza) charitable

bene'placito *m* approval

be'nessere *m* well-being

bene'stante *adj* well-off ●*mf* well-off person

bene'stare *m* consent

be'nevolo *adj* benevolent

ben'fatto *adj* well-made

'**beni** *mpl* property *sg*; Fin assets; ∼ di consumo consumer goods

benia'mino *m* favourite

be'nigno *adj* kindly; (Med) benign

beninfor'mato adj well-informed

benintenzio'nato, -a adj well-meaning • mf well-meaning person

benin'teso adv of course

benpen'sante adj selfrighteous

benser'vito m dare il ~ a qcno fire sb

bensì conj but rather

benve'nuto adj & m welcome

ben'visto adj essere ~ go down well (da with)

benvo'lere vt farsi ~ da qcno win sb's affection; prendere qcno in ~ take a liking to sb; essere benvoluto da tutti to be well-liked by everyone

ben'zina f petrol, gas Am; far ~ get petrol. ~ verde unleaded petrol. benzi'naio, -a mf petrol station attendant

'bere vt drink; (assorbire) absorb; fig swallow • m drinking; (bevande) drinks pl

berga'motto m bergamot

ber'lina f (Auto) saloon

Ber'lino m Berlin

ber'muda mpl (pantaloni) Bermuda shorts

ber'noccolo m bump; (disposizione) flair

ber'retto m beret, cap

bersagli'are vt fig bombard. ber'saglio m target

be'stemmia f swear-word; (maledizione) oath; (sproposito) blasphemy. ~'are vi swear

'bestia f animal; (persona brutale) beast; (persona sciocca) fool; andare in ~a 🔟 blow one's top. ~'ale adj bestial; (espressione, violenza) brutal; 🔟: (freddo, fame) terrible. ~alità f inv bestiality; fig nonsense. ~'ame m livestock

'bettola f fig dive

be'tulla f birch

be'vanda f drink

bevi'tore, -'trice mf drinker

be'vut|a f drink. ~o pp di bere

bi'ada f fodder

bianche'ria f linen. ~ intima underwear

bi'anco adj white; (foglio, pagina ecc) blank • m white; mangiare in ~ not eat rich food; in ~ e nero (film, fotografia) black and white; passare una notte in ~ have a sleepless night

bian'core m whiteness

bianco'spino m hawthorn

biasci'care vt (mangiare) eat noisily; (parlare) mumble

biasi'mare vt blame. bi'asimo m blame

'Bibbia f Bible

bibe'ron m inv [baby's] bottle

bi'bita f [soft] drink

'biblico adj biblical

bibliogra'fia f bibliography

biblio'te|ca f library; (mobile) bookcase. ~'cario, -a mf librarian

bicarbo'nato m bicarbonate

bicchi'ere m glass

bicchie'rino m 🔟 tipple

bici'cletta f bicycle; andare in ~ ride a bicycle

bico'lore adj two-coloured

bidè m inv bidet

bi'dello, -a mf janitor

bido'nata f 🔟 swindle

bi'done m bin; (🔟: truffa) swindle; fare un ~ a qcno 🔟 stand sb up

bien'nale adj biennial

bi'ennio m two-year period

bi'etola f beet

bifo'cale adj bifocal

bi'folco, -a mf fig boor

bifor'c|arsi vr fork. ~azi'one f fork. ~uto adj forked

biga'mia f bigamy. 'bigamo, -a adj bigamous • mf bigamist

bighello'nare vi loaf around. bi-

ghel'lone m loafer

bigiotte'ria f costume jewellery; (negozio) jeweller's

bigliet'taio m booking clerk; (sui treni) ticket-collector. ~e'ria f ticket-office; (Theat) box-office

bigli'et|to m ticket; (lettera breve) note; (cartoncino) card; (di banca) banknote. ~to da visita business card. ~'tone m (🔲: soldi) big one

bignè m inv cream puff

bigo'dino m roller

bi'gotto m bigot

bi'kini m inv bikini

bi'lanci|a f scales pl; (Comm) balance; B~a (Astr) Libra. ~'are vt balance; (Comm) balance sheet; fare il ~o balance the books; fig take stock

'bil|e f bile; fig rage

bili'ardo m billiards sg

'bilico m equilibrium; in ~ in the balance

bi'lingue adj bilingual

bili'one m billion

bilo'cale adj two-room

'bimbo, -a mf child

bimen'sile adj fortnightly

bime'strale adj bimonthly

bi'nario m track; (piattaforma) platform

bi'nocolo m binoculars pl

bio'chimica f biochemistry

biodegra'dabile adj biodegradable

bio'etica f bioethics

bio'fisica f biophysics

biogra'fia f biography. **bio'grafico** adj biographical. **bi'ografo, -a** mf biographer

biolo'gia f biology. **bio'logico** adj biological; (alimento, agricoltura) organic. **bi'ologo, -a** mf biologist

bi'ond|a f blonde. ~o adj blond ●m fair colour; (uomo) fair-haired man

bio'sfera f biosphere

bi'ossido m ~ di carbonio carbon dioxide

bioterro'rismo m bioterrorism

biparti'tismo m two-party system

'birba f, **bir'bante** m rascal, rogue. **bir'bone** adj wicked

biri'chino, -a adj naughty ●mf little devil

bi'rillo m skittle

'birr|a f beer; a tutta ~a fig flat out. ~a chiara lager. ~a scura brown ale. ~e'ria f beer-house; (fabbrica) brewery

bis m inv encore

bi'saccia f haversack

bi'sbetic|a f shrew. ~o adj bad-tempered

bisbigli'are vt/i whisper. **bi'sbiglio** m whisper

'bisca f gambling-house

'biscia f snake

bi'scotto m biscuit

bisessu'ale adj & mf bisexual

bise'stile adj anno ~ leap year

bisetti'nale adj fortnightly

bi'slacco adj peculiar

bis'nonno, -a mf great-grandfather; great-grandmother

biso'gn|are vi ~a agire subito we must act at once; ~a farlo it is necessary to do it; non ~a venire you don't have to come. ~o m need; (povertà) poverty; aver ~o di need. ~oso adj needy; (povero) poor; ~oso di in need of

bi'sonte m bison

bi'stecca f steak

bisticci'are vi quarrel. **bi'sticcio** m quarrel; (gioco di parole) pun

bistrat'tare vt mistreat

bi'torzolo m lump

'bitter m inv (bitter) aperitif

bi'vacco m bivouac
'bivio m crossroads; (di strada) fork
bizan'tino adj Byzantine
'bizza f tantrum; **fare le bizze** (bambini) play up
biz'zarro adj bizarre
biz'zeffe adv **a ~** galore
blan'dire vt soothe; (allettare) flatter. **'blando** adj mild
bla'sone m coat of arms
'blatta f cockroach
blin'da|re vt armour-plate. **~to** adj armoured
blitz m inv blitz
bloc'car|e vt block; (isolare) cut off; (Mil) blockade; (Comm) freeze. **~si** vr (Mech) jam
blocca'sterzo m steering lock
'blocco m block; (Mil) blockade; (dei fitti) restriction; (di carta) pad; (unione) coalition; **in ~** (Comm) in bulk. **~ stradale** road-block
bloc-'notes m inv writing pad
blog'gista mf blogger
blu adj & m blue
blue-'jeans mpl blue-jeans
bluff m inv (carta, fig) bluff
'blusa f blouse
'boa m boa [constrictor]; (sciarpa) [feather] boa • f (Naut) buoy
bo'ato m rumbling
bo'bina f spool; (di film) reel; (Electr) coil
'bocca f mouth; **a ~ aperta** fig dumbfounded; **in ~ al lupo!** [1] break a leg!; **fare la respirazione a ~ a ~** give sb mouth to mouth resuscitation or the kiss of life
boc'caccia f grimace; **far boccacce** make faces
boc'caglio m nozzle
boc'cale m jug; (da birra) tankard
bocca'porto m (Naut) hatch
boc'cata f (di fumo) puff; **prendere una ~ d'aria** take a breath of fresh air
boc'cetta f small bottle
boccheggi'are vi gasp
boc'chino m cigarette holder; (Mus, di pipa) mouthpiece
'boccia f (palla) bowl; **~e** pl (gioco) bowls sg
bocci'a|re vt (agli esami) fail; (respingere) reject; (alle bocce) hit; **essere ~to** fail; (ripetere) repeat a year. **~tura** f failure
bocci'olo m bud
boccon'cino m morsel
boc'cone m mouthful; (piccolo pasto) snack
boc'coni adv face downwards
'boia m executioner
boi'ata f [1] rubbish
boicot'tare vt boycott
bo'lero m bolero
'bolgia f (caos) bedlam
'bolide m meteor; **passare come un ~** shoot past [like a rocket]
Bo'livi|a f Bolivia. **b~ano, -a** agg e mf Bolivian
'bolla f bubble; (pustola) blister
bol'la|re vt stamp; fig brand. **~to** adj fig branded; **carta ~ta** paper with stamp showing payment of duty
bol'lente adj boiling [hot]
bol'let|ta f bill; **essere in ~ta** be hard up. **~tino** m bulletin; (Comm) list
bol'lino m coupon
bol'li|re vt/i boil. **~to** m boiled meat. **~tore** m boiler; (per l'acqua) kettle. **~tura** f boiling
'bollo m stamp
bol'lore m boil; (caldo) intense heat; fig ardour
'bomba f bomb; **a prova di ~** bomb-proof
bombarda'mento m shelling; (con aerei) bombing; fig bombardment. **~ aereo** air raid

bombar'd|are vt shell; (con aerei) bomb; fig bombard. ~**'ere** m bomber

bom'betta f bowler [hat]

'bombola f cylinder. ~ **di gas** gas cylinder

bombo'lone m doughnut

bomboni'era f wedding keep-sake

bo'naccia f (Naut) calm

bonacci'one, -a mf goodnatured person ● adj good-natured

bo'nario adj kindly

bo'nifica f land reclamation. **bonifi'care** vt reclaim

bo'nifico m (Comm) discount; (bancario) [credit] transfer

bontà f goodness; (gentilezza) kindness

'bora f bora (cold north-east wind in the upper Adriatic)

'borchi|a f stud. ~**'ato** adj studded

bor'da|re vt border. ~**'tura** f border

bor'deaux adj inv maroon

bor'dello m brothel; fig bedlam; (disordine) mess

'bordo m border; (estremità) edge; a ~ (Aeron, Naut) on board

bor'gata f hamlet

bor'ghese adj bourgeois; (abito) civilian; **in** ~ in civilian dress; (poliziotto) in plain clothes

borghe'sia f middle classes pl

'borgo m village

'bori|a f conceit. ~**'oso** adj conceited

bor'lotto m [fagiolo] ~ borlotto bean

boro'talco m talcum powder

bor'raccia f flask

'bors|a f bag; (borsetta) handbag; (valori) Stock Exchange. ~**a dell'acqua calda** hot-water bottle. ~**a frigo** cool-box. ~**a della spesa** shopping bag. ~**a di studio** scholarship. ~**ai'olo** m pickpocket. ~**el'lino** m

purse. **bor'sista** mf Fin speculator; (Sch) scholarship holder

bor'se|llo m purse; (borsetto) man's handbag. ~**tta** f handbag. ~**tto** m man's handbag

bo'scaglia f woodlands pl

bosca'iolo m woodman; (guardaboschi) forester

'bosco m wood. **bo'scoso** adj wooded

'Bosnia f Bosnia

'bossolo m cartridge case

bo'tanic|a f botany. ~**o** adj botanical ● m botanist

'botta f blow; (rumore) bang; **fare a botte** come to blows. ~ **e risposta** fig thrust and counter-thrust

'botte f barrel

bot'te|ga f shop; (di artigiano) workshop. ~**gaio, -a** mf shopkeeper. ~**'ghino** m Theatr boxoffice; (del lotto) lottery-shop

bot'tiglia f bottle; **in** ~**a** bottled. ~**e'ria** f wine shop

bot'tino m loot; (Mil) booty

'botto m bang; **di** ~ all of a sudden

bot'tone m button; (Bot) bud

bo'vino adj bovine; **bovini** pl cattle

box m inv (per cavalli) loosebox; (recinto per bambini) play-pen

'boxe f boxing

'bozza f draft; (Typ) proof; (bernoccolo) bump. **boz'zetto** m sketch

'bozzolo m cocoon

brac'care vt hunt

brac'cetto m a ~ **arm in arm**

bracci'a|le m bracelet; (fascia) armband. ~**letto** m bracelet; (di orologio) watch-strap

bracci'ante m day labourer

bracci'ata f (nel nuoto) stroke

'bracci|o m (pl **braccia** f) arm; (di fiume, pl **bracci**) arm. ~**'olo** m (di sedia) arm[rest]; (da nuoto) armband

'bracco m hound

bracconiere | bruciare

bracconi'ere m poacher

'brac|e f embers pl; alla ~e chargrilled. ~i'ere m brazier. ~i'ola f chop

'brado adj allo stato ~ in the wild

'brama f longing. **bra'mare** vt long for. **bramo'sia** f yearning

'branca f branch

'branchia f gill

'branco m (di cani) pack; (pej: di persone) gang

branco'lare vi grope

'branda f camp-bed

bran'dello m scrap; a brandelli in tatters

bran'dire vt brandish

'brano m piece; (di libro) passage

Bra'sile m Brazil. **b~i'ano, -a** agg & mf Brazilian

bra'vata f bragging

'bravo adj good; (abile) clever; (coraggioso) brave; ~! well done!. **bra'vura** f skill

'breccia f breach; sulla ~ fig very successful, at the top

bre'saola f dried, salted beef sliced thinly and eaten cold

bre'tella f shoulder-strap; bretelle pl (di calzoni) braces

'breve adj brief; in ~ briefly; tra ~ shortly

brevet'tare vt patent. **bre'vetto** m patent; (attestato) licence

brevità f shortness

'brezza f breeze

'bricco m jug

bric'cone m blackguard; hum rascal

briciol|a f crumb; fig grain. ~o m fragment

'briga f (fastidio) trouble; (lite) quarrel; attaccar ~ pick a quarrel; prendersi la ~ di fare qcsa go to the trouble of doing sth

brigadi'ere m (dei carabinieri) sergeant

bri'gante m bandit; hum rogue

bri'gare vi intrigue

bri'gata f brigade; (gruppo) group

briga'tista mf (Pol) member of the Red Brigades

'briglia f rein; a ~ sciolta at breakneck speed

bril'lante adj brilliant; (scintillante) sparkling ● m diamond

bril'lare vi shine; (metallo:) glitter; (scintillare) sparkle

'brillo adj tipsy

'brina f hoar-frost

brin'dare vi toast; ~ a qcno drink a toast to sb

'brindisi m inv toast

bri'tannico adj British

'brivido m shiver; (di paura ecc) shudder; (di emozione) thrill

brizzo'lato adj greying

'brocca f jug

broc'cato m brocade

'broccoli mpl broccoli sg

'brodo m broth; (per cucinare) stock. ~ ristretto consommé

'broglio m ~ elettorale gerrymandering

bron'chite f bronchitis

'broncio m sulk; fare il ~ sulk

bronto'lare vi grumble; (tuono ecc:) rumble. ~io m grumbling; (di tuono) rumbling. ~one, -a mf grumbler

'bronzo m bronze

bros'sura f edizione in ~ paperback

bru'care vt (pecora:) graze

bruciacchi'are vt scorch

brucia'pelo adv a ~ point-blank

bruci'a|re vt burn; (scottare) scald; (incendiare) set fire to ● vi burn; (scottare) scald. ~rsi vr burn oneself. ~to adj burnt; fig burnt-out. ~tore m burner. ~tura f burn. **bruci'ore** m burning sensation

'bruco m grub

'brufolo m spot

brugh'iera f heath

bruli'c|are vi swarm

'brullo adj bare

'bruma f mist

'bruno adj brown; (occhi, capelli) dark

brusca'mente adv (di colpo) suddenly

bru'schetta f toasted bread rubbed with garlic and sprinkled with olive oil

'brusco adj sharp; (persona) brusque; (improvviso) sudden

bru'sio m buzzing

bru'tal|e adj brutal. ~ità f inv brutality. ~iz'zare vt brutalize. 'bruto adj & m brute

brut'tezza f ugliness

'brut|to adj ugly; (tempo, tipo, situazione, affare) nasty; (cattivo) bad; ~ta copia rough copy; ~to tiro dirty trick. ~'tura f ugly thing

'buca f hole; (avvallamento) hollow. ~ delle lettere (a casa) letter-box

buca'neve m inv snowdrop

bu'car|e vt make a hole in; (pungere) prick; punch (biglietti) • vi have a puncture. ~si vr prick oneself; (con droga) shoot up

bu'cato m washing

'buccia f peel, skin

bucherel'lare vt riddle

'buco m hole

bu'dello m (pl f budella) bowel

bu'dino m pudding

'bue m (pl buoi) ox; carne di ~ beef

'bufalo m buffalo

bu'fera f storm; (di neve) blizzard

buf'fetto m cuff

'buffo adj funny; (Theat) comic • m funny thing. ~'nata f (scherzo) joke. buf'fone m buffoon; fare il buffone play the fool

bu'gi|a f lie; ~a pietosa white lie. ~'ardo, -a adj lying • mf liar

bugi'gattolo m cubby-hole

'buio adj dark • m darkness; al ~ in the dark; ~ pesto pitch dark

'bulbo m bulb; (dell'occhio) eyeball

Bulga'ria f Bulgaria. 'bulgaro, -a adj & mf Bulgarian

'bullo m bully

bul'lone m bolt

'bunker m inv bunker

buona'fede f good faith

buona'notte int good night

buona'sera int good evening

buon'giorno int good morning; (di pomeriggio) good afternoon

buon'grado: di ~ adv willingly

buongu'staio, -a mf gourmet. buon'gusto m good taste

bu'ono adj good; (momento) right; dar ~ (convalidare) accept; alla buona easy-going; (cena) informal; buona notte/sera good night/evening; buon compleanno/Natale! happy birthday/merry Christmas!; buon senso common sense; di buon'ora early; una buona volta once and for all; buona parte di the best part of; tre ore buone three good hours • m good; (in film) goody; (tagliando) voucher; (titolo) bond; con le buone gently; ~ sconto money-off coupon • mf buono, -a a nulla dead loss

buontem'pone, -a mf happy-go-lucky person

buonu'more m good temper

buonu'scita f retirement bonus; (di dirigente) golden handshake

burat'tino m puppet

'burbero adj surly; (nei modi) rough

bu'rocra|te m bureaucrat. buro'cratico adj bureaucratic. ~'zia f bureaucracy

bur'ra|sca f storm. ~'scoso adj stormy

'burro m butter

bur'rone m ravine

bu'scar|e vt, **~si** vr catch

bus'sare vt knock

'bussola f compass; perdere la ~ lose one's bearings

'busta f envelope; (*astuccio*) case. ~ **paga** pay packet. **~rella** f bribe.

bu'stina f (*di tè*) tea bag; (*per medicine*) sachet

'busto m bust; (*indumento*) girdle

but'tar|e vt throw; **~e giù** (*demolire*) knock down; (*inghiottire*) gulp down; scribble down (*scritto*); Ⅱ put on (*pasta*); (*scoraggiare*) dishearten; **~e via** throw away. **~si** vr throw oneself; (*saltare*) jump

butte'rato adj pock-marked

Cc

caba'ret m inv cabaret

ca'bina f (*Aeron, Naut*) cabin; (*balneare*) beach hut. ~ **elettorale** polling booth. ~ **di pilotaggio** cockpit. ~ **telefonica** telephone box. **cabi'nato** m cabin cruiser

ca'cao m cocoa

'cacca f Ⅱ pooh

'caccia f hunt; (*con fucile*) shooting; (*inseguimento*) chase; (*selvaggina*) game ●m inv (*Aeron*) fighter; (*Naut*) destroyer

cacciabombardi'ere m fighter-bomber

cacciagi'one f game

cacci'ar|e vt hunt; (*mandar via*) chase away; (*scacciare*) drive out; (*ficcare*) shove ●vi go hunting. **~rsi** vr (*nascondersi*) hide; (*andare a finire*) get to; **~rsi nei guai** get into trouble; **alla ~tora** adj (*Culin*) chasseur. **~'tore, ~'trice** mf hunter. **~'tore di frodo**

poacher

caccia'vite m inv screwdriver

ca'chet m inv (*Med*) capsule; (*colorante*) colour rinse; (*stile*) cachet

'cachi m inv (*albero, frutta*) persimmon

'cacio m (*formaggio*) cheese

'cactus m inv cactus

ca'da|vere m corpse. **~'verico** adj fig deathly pale

ca'dente adj falling; (*casa*) crumbling

ca'denza f cadence; (*ritmo*) rhythm; (*Mus*) cadenza

ca'dere vi fall; (*capelli ecc*:) fall out; (*capitombolare*) tumble; (*vestito ecc*:) hang; **far ~** (*di mano*) drop; **~ dal sonno** feel very sleepy; **lasciar ~** drop; **~ dalle nuvole** fig be taken aback

ca'detto m cadet

ca'duta f fall; (*di capelli*) loss; fig downfall

caffè m inv coffee; (*locale*) café. ~ **corretto** espresso coffee with a dash of liquer. ~ **lungo** weak black coffee. ~ **macchiato** coffee with a dash of milk. ~ **ristretto** strong espresso coffee. ~ **solubile** instant coffee. **caffe'ina** f caffeine. **caffè l'latte** m inv white coffee.

> **Caffè** If you ask for a *caffè* in an Italian bar you will be served an *espresso*, a small amount of very strong coffee in a small cup. A *macchiato* is the same, but with the addition of a little frothy milk. *Cappuccino* is drunk in the morning or afternoon, never at the end of a meal. A *corretto* has a dash of spirits in it.

caffetti'era f coffee-pot

cafo'naggine f boorishness

cafo'nata f boorishness

ca'fone, -a mf boor

ca'gare vi 🔲 crap

cagio'nare vt cause

cagio'nevole adj delicate

cagli'ar|e vi, ~**si** vr curdle

'cagna f bitch

ca'gnara f 🔲 din

ca'gnesco adj guardare qcno in ~ scowl at sb

'cala f creek

cala'brone m hornet

cala'maio m inkpot

cala'mari mpl squid sg

cala'mita f magnet

calamità f inv calamity

ca'lar|e vi come down; (vento:) drop; (diminuire) fall; (tramontare) set ●vt (abbassare) lower; (nei lavori a maglia) decrease ●vm (di luna) waning. ~**si** vr lower oneself

'calca f throng

cal'cagno m heel

cal'care[1] m limestone

cal'care[2] vt tread; (premere) press [down]; ~ **la mano** fig exaggerate; ~ **le orme di qcno** fig follow in sb's footsteps

'calce[1] f lime

'calce[2] m in ~ at the foot of the page

calce'struzzo m concrete

cal'cetto m Sport five-a-side [football]

calci'a|re vt kick. ~**tore** m footballer

cal'cina f mortar

calci'naccio m (pezzo di intonaco) flake of plaster

'calcio[1] m kick; (Sport) football; (di arma da fuoco) butt; **dare un** ~ a kick. ~ **d'angolo** corner [kick]

'calcio[2] m (chimica) calcium

'calco m tracing; (arte) cast

calco'la|re vt calculate; (considerare) consider. ~**tore** adj calculating ●m calculator; (macchina elettronica)

computer

'calcolo m calculation; (Med) stone

cal'daia f boiler

caldar'rosta f roast chestnut

'caldo adj warm; (molto caldo) hot ●m heat; **avere** ~ be warm/hot; **fa** ~ it is warm/hot

calen'dario m calendar

'calibro m calibre; (strumento) callipers pl; **di grosso** ~ (persona) top attrib

'calice m goblet; (Relig) chalice

ca'ligine f fog; (industriale) smog

call centre m inv call centre

calligra'fia f handwriting; (cinese) calligraphy

cal'lista mf chiropodist. **'callo** m corn; **fare il callo a** become hardened to. cal'**loso** adj callous

'calma f calm. cal'**mante** adj calming ●m sedative. cal'**mare** vt calm [down]; (lenire) soothe. cal'**marsi** vr calm down; (vento:) drop; (dolore:) die down. **'calmo** adj calm

'calo m (Comm) fall; (di volume) shrinkage; (di peso) loss

ca'lore m heat; (moderato) warmth; **in** ~ (animale) on heat. calo'**roso** adj warm

calo'ria f calorie

ca'lorico adj calorific

calo'rifero m radiator

calorosa'mente adv (cordialmente) warmly

calpe'stare vt trample [down]; fig trample on (diritti, sentimenti); **vietato** ~ **l'erba** keep off the grass

calpe'stio m (passi) footsteps

ca'lunni|a f slander. ~**are** vt slander. ~**oso** adj slanderous

ca'lura f heat

cal'vario m Calvary; fig trial

cal'vizie f baldness. **'calvo** adj bald

'calz|a f (da donna) stocking; (da uomo)

sock. ~a'maglia f tights pl; (per danza) leotard

cal'zante adj fig fitting

cal'za|re vt (indossare) wear; (mettersi) put on ● vi fit

calza'scarpe m inv shoehorn

calza'tura f footwear

calzatu' rificio m shoe factory

cal'zetta f è una mezza ~ fig he's no use

calzet'tone m knee-length woollen sock. cal'zino m sock

calzo'l|aio m shoemaker. ~e'ria f (negozio) shoe shop

calzon'cini mpl shorts. ~ da bagno swimming trunks

cal'zone m folded pizza with tomato and mozzarella or ricotta

cal'zoni mpl trousers, pants Am

camale'onte m chameleon

cambi'ale f bill of exchange

cambia'mento m change. ~ climatico climate change

cambi'ar|e vt/i change; move (casa); (fare cambio di) exchange. ~si vr change. 'cambio m change, (Comm, scambio) exchange; (Mech) gear; dare il ~ a qcno relieve sb; in ~ di in exchange for

'camera f room; (mobili) [bedroom] suite; (Phot) camera; C~ (Comm, Pol) Chamber. ~ ardente funeral parlour. ~ d'aria inner tube. C~ di Commercio Chamber of Commerce. C~ dei Deputati ≈ House of Commons. ~ doppia double room. ~ da letto bedroom. ~ matrimoniale double room. ~ oscura darkroom. ~ singola single room

came'rata[1] f (dormitorio) dormitory; (Mil) barrack room

came'ra|ta[2] mf (amico) mate; (Pol) comrade. ~'tismo m comradeship

cameri'era f maid; (di ristorante) waitress; (in albergo) chamber-maid; (di bordo) stewardess

cameri'ere m manservant; (di ristorante) waiter; (di bordo) steward

came'rino m dressing-room

'camice m overall. cami'cetta f blouse. ca'micia f shirt; uovo in ~ poached egg. camicia da notte nightdress

cami'netto m fireplace

ca'mino m chimney; (focolare) fireplace

'camion m inv truck, lorry Br

camion'cino m van

camio'netta f jeep

camio'nista mf truck driver

cam'mello m camel; (tessuto) camel-hair ● adj inv (colore) camel

cam'meo m cameo

cammi'na|re vi walk; (auto, orologio) go. ~ta f walk; fare una ~ta go for a walk. cam'mino m way; essere in ~ be on the way; mettersi in ~ set out

camo'milla f camomile; (bevanda) camomile tea

ca'morra f local mafia

ca'moscio m chamois; (pelle) suede

cam'pagna f country; (paesaggio) countryside; (Comm, Mil) campaign; in ~ in the country. ~ elettorale election campaign. ~ pubblicitaria marketing campaign. campa'gnolo, -a adj rustic ● m countryman ● f countrywoman

cam'pale adj field attrib; giornata ~ fig strenuous day

cam'pa|na f bell; (di vetro) belljar. ~'nella f (di tenda) curtain ring. ~'nello m door-bell; (cicalino) buzzer

campa'nile m belfry

campani'lismo m parochialism

campani'lista mf person with a parochial outlook

cam'panula f (Bot) campanula

cam'pare vi live; (a stento) get by

cam'pato adj ~ in aria unfounded

campeggi'a|re vi camp; (spiccare)

stand out. ~**tore**, ~**trice** mf camper. **cam'peggio** m camping; (terreno) campsite

cam'pestre adj rural

'camping m inv camping

campio'nario m [set of] samples ●adj samples; **fiera** ~**a** trade fair

campio'nato m championship

campiona'tura f (di merce) range of samples

campi'on|e m champion; (Comm) sample; (esemplare) specimen. ~**essa** f ladies' champion

'campo m field; (accampamento) camp. ~ **da calcio** football pitch. ~ **di concentramento** concentration camp. ~ **da golf** golf course. ~ **da tennis** tennis court. ~ **profughi** refugee camp

campo'santo m cemetery

camuf'far|e vt disguise. ~**si** vr disguise oneself

'Cana|da m Canada. ~**dese** agg & mf Canadian

ca'naglia f scoundrel; (plebaglia) rabble

ca'nal|e m channel; (artificiale) canal. ~**iz'zare** vt channel (acque). ~**izza-zi'one** f channelling; (rete) pipes pl

'canapa f hemp

cana'rino m canary

cancel'la|re vt cross out; (con la gomma) rub out; (annullare) cancel; (Comput) delete. ~**tura** f erasure. ~**zi'one** f cancellation; (Comput) deletion

cancelle'ria f chancellery; (articoli per scrivere) stationery

cancelli'ere m chancellor; (di tribunale) clerk

can'cello m gate

cance'ro|geno m carcinogen ●adj carcinogenic. ~**so** adj cancerous

can'crena f gangrene

'cancro m cancer. C~ (Astr) Cancer

candeg'gi|na f bleach. ~**are** vt

bleach. **can'deggio** m bleaching

can'de|la f candle; (Auto) spark plug. ~**li'ere** m candlestick

candi'da|rsi vr stand as a candidate. ~**to**, -**a** mf candidate. ~**tura** f (Pol) candidacy; (per lavoro) application

'candido adj snow-white; (sincero) candid; (puro) pure

can'dito adj candied

can'dore m whiteness; fig innocence

'cane m dog; (di arma da fuoco) cock; **un tempo da cani** foul weather. ~ **da caccia** hunting dog

ca'nestro m basket

cangi'ante adj iridescent; **seta** ~ shot silk

can'guro m kangaroo

ca'nile m kennel; (di allevamento) kennels pl. ~ **municipale** dog pound

ca'nino adj & m canine

'canna f reed; (da zucchero) cane; (di fucile) barrel; (bastone) stick; (di bicicletta) crossbar; (asta) rod; (🎣: hascisc) joint; **povero in** ~ destitute. ~ **da pesca** fishingrod

can'nella f cinnamon

can'neto m bed of reeds

canni'ba|le m cannibal. ~**lismo** m cannibalism

cannocchi'ale m telescope

canno'nata f cannon shot; **è una** ~ fig it's brilliant

cannon'cino m (dolce) cream horn

can'none m cannon; fig ace

can'nuccia f [drinking] straw; (di pipa) stem

ca'noa f canoe

'canone m canon; (affitto) rent; **equo** ~ fair rents act

ca'noni|co m canon. ~**z'zare** vt canonize. ~**zzazi'one** f canonization

ca'noro adj melodious

ca'notta f (estiva) vest top

canot'taggio m canoeing; (voga) rowing

canotti'era f singlet

canotti'ere m oarsman

ca'notto m [rubber] dinghy

cano'vaccio m (trama) plot; (straccio) duster

can'tante mf singer

can't|are vt/i sing. **~au'tore, ~au'trice** mf singer-songwriter. **~ic'chi'are** vi sing softly; (a bocca chiusa) hum

canti'ere m yard; (Naut) shipyard; (di edificio) construction site. **~ navale** naval dockyard

canti'lena f singsong; (ninna-nanna) lullaby

can'tina f cellar; (osteria) wine shop

'canto[1] m singing; (canzone) song; (Relig) chant; (poesia) poem

'canto[2] m (angolo) corner; (lato) side; **dal ~ mio** for my part; **d'altro ~** on the other hand

canto'nata f prendere una **~** fig be sadly mistaken

can'tone m canton; (angolo) corner

can'tuccio m nook

canzo'na|re vt tease. **~'torio** adj teasing. **~'tura** f teasing

can'zo|ne f song. **~'netta** f 🎵 pop song. **~ni'ere** m songbook

---

Canzone Italians are very proud of their tradition of popular song and it is celebrated at the Festival of Sanremo (Festival della Canzone Italiana). The festival has been held since 1951 and is watched by millions on Italian TV every year. The festival includes a competition for the best new song and the winner is guaranteed chart success.

'caos m chaos. **ca'otico** adj chaotic

C.A.P. m abbr (Codice di Avviamento Postale) post code, zip code Am

ca'pace adj able; (esperto) skilled; (stadio, contenitore) big; **~ di** (disposto a) capable of. **~ità** f ability; (attitudine) skill; (capienza) capacity

capaci'tarsi vr **~ di** (rendersi conto) understand; (accorgersi) realize

ca'panna f hut

capan'nello m fare **~ intorno a** qcno/qcsa gather round sb/sth

capan'none m shed; (Aeron) hangar

ca'parbio adj obstinate

ca'parra f deposit

capa'tina f short visit; **fare una ~ in città/da qcno** pop into town/in on sb

ca'pel|lo m hair; **~li** pl (capigliatura) hair sg. **~'lone** m hippie. **~'luto** adj hairy

capez'zale m bolster; fig bedside

ca'pezzolo m nipple

capi'ente adj capacious. **~za** f capacity

capigli'atura f hair

ca'pire vt understand; **~ male** misunderstand; **si capisce!** naturally!; **sì, ho capito** yes, I see

capi'ta|le adj (Jur) capital; (principale) main • f (città) capital. • m (Comm) capital. **~'lismo** m capitalism. **~'lista** mf capitalist. **~'listico** adj capitalist

capitane'ria f **~ di porto** port authorities pl

capi'tano m captain

capi'tare vi (giungere per caso) come; (accadere) happen

capi'tello m (Archit) capital

capito'la|re vi capitulate. **~zi'one** f capitulation

ca'pitolo m chapter

capi'tombolo m headlong fall; **fare un ~** tumble down

'capo m head; (chi comanda) boss 🔑; (di vestiario) item; (Geog) cape; (in tribù) chief; (parte estrema) top; **a ~** new paragraph; **da ~** over again; **in ~ a**

un mese within a month; giramento di ~ dizziness; mal di ~ headache; ~ d'abbigliamento item of clothing. ~ d'accusa (Jur) charge. ~ di bestiame head of cattle

capo'banda m (Mus) bandmaster; (di delinquenti) ringleader

ca'poccia m (🔲: testa) nut

capocci'one, -a mf 🔲 brainbox

capo'danno m New Year's Day

capofa'miglia m head of the family

capo'fitto m a ~ headlong

capo'giro m giddiness

capola'voro m masterpiece

capo'linea m terminus

capo'lino m fare ~ peep in

capo'luogo m main town

capo'rale m lance-corporal

capo'squadra mf Sport team captain

capo'stipite mf (di famiglia) progenitor

capo'tavola mf head of the table

capo'treno m guard

capouf'ficio mf head clerk

capo'verso m first line

capo'vol|gere vt overturn; fig reverse. ~gersi vr overturn (barca): capsize; fig be reversed. ~to pp di capovolgere ● adj upside-down

'cappa f cloak; (di camino) cowl; (di cucina) hood

cap'pel|la f chapel. ~'lano m chaplain

cap'pello m hat. ~ a cilindro top hat

'cappero m caper

'cappio m noose

cap'pone m capon

cap'potto m [over]coat

cappuc'cino m (frate) Capuchin; (bevanda) white coffee

cap'puccio m hood; (di penna stilografica) cap

'capra f goat. ca'pretto m kid

ca'pricci|o m whim; (bizzarria) freak; fare i capricci have tantrums. ~'oso adj capricious; (bambino) naughty

Capri'corno m (Astr) Capricorn

capri'ola f somersault

capri'olo m roe-deer

'capro m [billy-]goat. ~ espiatorio scapegoat.

ca'prone m [billy] goat

'capsula f capsule; (di proiettile) cap; (di dente) crown

cap'tare vt (Radio, TV) pick up; catch (attenzione)

carabini'ere m carabiniere; carabini'eri pl Italian police

Carabinieri The Carabinieri are a national Italian police force which is part of the army. They deal with issues of public order and serious crimes, but there is a certain amount of overlap with the duties of the Polizia di Stato, which is not part of the army and is controlled by the Interior Ministry. Carabinieri wear a distinctive dark uniform with a red stripe.

ca'raffa f carafe

Ca'raibi mpl (zona) Caribbean sg; (isole) Caribbean Islands; il mar dei ~ the Caribbean [Sea]

cara'mella f sweet

cara'mello m caramel

ca'rato m carat

ca'ratte|re m character; (caratteristica) characteristic; (Typ) type; di buon~re good-natured. ~'ristico, -a adj characteristic; (pittoresco) quaint ● f characteristic. ~riz'zare vt characterize

carbon'cino m charcoal

car'bone m coal

car'bonio m carbon

carbu'rante m fuel

carbura'tore *m* carburettor

car'cassa *f* carcass; *fig* old wreck

carce'ra|rio *adj* prison *attrib.* ~to, -a *mf* prisoner. ~zi'one *f* imprisonment. ~zione preventiva preventive detention

'carcer|e *m* prison; (*punizione*) imprisonment. ~i'ere, -a *mf* gaoler

carci'ofo *m* artichoke

cardi'nale *adj* & *m* cardinal

'cardine *m* hinge

cardio|chi'rurgo *m* heart surgeon. ~lo'gia *f* cardiology. cardi'ologo *m* heart specialist. ~'tonico *m* heart stimulant

'cardo *m* thistle

ca'rena *f* (*Naut*) bottom

ca'ren|te *adj* ~ di lacking in. ~za *f* lack; (*scarsità*) scarcity

ca'rezza *f* caress

cari'a|rsi *vi* decay. ~to *adj* decayed

'carica *f* office; (*Electr, Mil*) charge; *fig* drive. cari'care *vt* load; (*Electr, Mil*) charge; wind up (orologio). ~ *m* (*per proiettile*) magazine

carica'tu|ra *f* caricature. ~'rale *adj* grotesque. ~'rista *mf* caricaturist

'carico *adj* loaded (di with); (*colore*) strong; (orologio) wound [up]; (*batteria*) charged ● *m* load; (*di nave*) cargo; (*il caricare*) loading; a ~ di (*Comm*) to be charged to; (*persona*) dependent on

'carie *f* [tooth] decay

ca'rino *adj* pretty; (*piacevole*) agreeable

ca'risma *m* charisma

carit|à *f* charity; per ~à! (*come rifiuto*) God forbid!. ~a'tevole *adj* charitable

carnagi'one *f* complexion

car'naio *m fig* shambles

car'nale *adj* carnal; cugino ~ first cousin

'carne *f* flesh; (*alimento*) meat; ~ di manzo/maiale/vitello beef/pork/veal

car'nefi|ce *m* executioner. ~'cina *f* slaughter

carne'va|le *m* carnival. ~'lesco *adj* carnival

car'noso *adj* fleshy

'caro, -a *adj* dear; cari saluti kind regards ● *mf* 🔟 darling, dear; i miei cari my nearest and dearest

ca'rogna *f* carcass; *fig* bastard

caro'sello *m* merry-go-round

ca'rota *f* carrot

caro'vana *f* caravan; (*di veicoli*) convoy

caro'vita *m* high cost of living

'carpa *f* carp

carpenti'ere *m* carpenter

car'pire *vt* seize; (*con difficoltà*) extort

car'poni *adv* on all fours

car'rabile *adj* suitable for vehicles; passo ~ ▷CARRAIO

car'raio *adj* passo ~ entrance to driveway, garage etc where parking is forbidden

carreggi'ata *f* roadway; doppia ~ dual carriageway, divided highway *Am*

carrel'lata *f* (*TV*) pan

car'rello *m* trolley; (*di macchina da scrivere*) carriage; (*Aeron*) undercarriage; (*Cinema, TV*) dolly. ~ d'atterraggio (*Aeron*) landing gear

car'retto *m* cart

carri'e|ra *f* career; di gran ~ra at full speed; fare ~ra get on. ~'rismo *m* careerism

carri'ola *f* wheelbarrow

'carro *m* cart. ~ armato tank. ~ attrezzi breakdown vehicle. ~ funebre hearse. ~ merci truck

car'rozza *f* carriage; (*Rail*) car. ~ cuccette sleeping car. ~ ristorante restaurant car

carroz'zella *f* (*per bambini*) pram;

(per disabili) wheelchair

carrozze'ria f bodywork; (officina) bodyshop

carroz'zina f pram; (pieghevole) push-chair, stroller Am

carroz'zone m (di circo) caravan

'**carta** f paper; (da gioco) card; (statuto) charter; (Geog) map. **~ d'argento** ≈ senior citizens' railcard. **~ assorbente** blotting-paper. **~ di credito** credit card. **~ geografica** map. **~ d'identità** identity card. **~ igienica** toilet-paper. **~ di imbarco** boarding card or pass. **~ da lettere** writing-paper. **~ da parati** wallpaper. **~ SIM** SIM card. **~ stagnola** silver paper; (Culin) aluminium foil. **~ straccia** waste paper. **~ stradale** road map. **~ velina** tissue-paper. **~ verde** (Auto) green card. **~ vetrata** sandpaper

cartacar'bone f carbon paper

car'taccia f waste paper

carta'modello m pattern

cartamo'neta f paper money

carta'pesta f papier mâché

carta'straccia f waste paper

cartave'trare vt sand [down]

car'tella f briefcase; (di cartone) folder; (di scolaro) satchel. **~la clinica** medical record. **~'lina** f folder

cartel'lino m (etichetta) label; (dei prezzi) price-tag; (di presenza) time-card; **timbrare il ~** clock in; (all'uscita) clock out

car'tello m sign; (pubblicitario) poster; (stradale) road sign; (di protesta) placard; (Comm) cartel. **~'lone** m poster; (Theat) bill

carti'era f paper-mill

car'tina f map

car'toccio m paper bag; **al ~** (Culin) baked in foil

carto'laio, -a mf stationer. **~le'ria** f stationer's. **~libre'ria** f stationer's and book shop

---

carto'lina f postcard. **~ postale** postcard

carto'mante mf fortune-teller

carton'cino m (materiale) card

car'tone m cardboard; (arte) cartoon. **~ animato** [animated] cartoon

car'tuccia f cartridge

'**casa** f house; (abitazione propria) home; (ditta) firm; **amico di ~** family friend; **andare a ~** go home; **essere di ~** be like one of the family; **fatto in ~** home-made; **padrone di ~** (di pensione ecc) landlord; (proprietario) house owner. **~ di cura** nursing home. **~ popolare** council house. **~ dello studente** hall of residence

ca'sacca f military coat; (giacca) jacket

ca'saccio adv **a ~** at random

casa'ling|a f housewife. **~o** adj domestic; (fatto in casa) home-made; (amante della casa) home-loving; (semplice) homely

ca'scante adj falling; (floscio) flabby

ca'sca|re vi fall [down]. **~ta** f (di acqua) waterfall

ca'schetto m [capelli a] **~ bob**

ca'scina f farm building

'**casco** m crash-helmet; (asciuga-capelli) [hair-]drier; **~ di banane** bunch of bananas

caseggi'ato m apartment block

casei'ficio m dairy

ca'sella f pigeon-hole. **~ postale** post office box; (Comput) mailbox

casel'lante mf (per treni) signalman

casel'lario m **~ giudiziario** record of convictions; **avere il ~ giudiziario vergine** have no criminal record

ca'sello [autostra'dale] m [motorway] toll booth

case'reccio adj home-made

ca'serma f barracks pl; (dei carabinieri) [police] station

casi'nista mf 🔢 muddler. **ca'sino** m 🔢 (bordello) brothel; (fig: confusione) racket; (disordine) mess; un casino di loads of

casinò m inv casino

ca'sistica f (classificazione) case records pl

'caso m chance; (Gram, Med), (fatto, circostanza) case; a ~ at random; ~ mai if need be; far ~ a pay attention to; non far ~ a take no account of; per ~ by chance. ~ [giudiziario] [legal] case

caso'lare m farmhouse

'caspita int good gracious!

'cassa f till; cash; (luogo di pagamento) cash desk; (mobile) chest; (istituto bancario) bank. ~ automatica prelievi cash dispenser, ATM. ~ da morto coffin. ~ toracica ribcage

cassa'forte f safe

cassa'panca f linen chest

casseru'ola f saucepan

cas'setta f case; (per registratore) cassette. ~ delle lettere letterbox. ~ di sicurezza strong-box

cas'set|to m drawer. ~tone m chest of drawers

cassi'ere, -a mf cashier; (di supermercato) checkout assistant; (di banca) teller

'casta f caste

ca'stagn|a f chestnut. casta'gneto m chestnut grove. ~o m chestnut[-tree]

ca'stano adj chestnut

ca'stello m castle; (impalcatura) scaffold

casti'gare vt punish

casti'gato adj (casto) chaste

ca'stigo m punishment

casti'tà f chastity. 'casto adj chaste

ca'storo m beaver

ca'strare vt castrate

casu'al|e adj chance attrib. ~'mente adv by chance

ca'supola f little house

cata'clisma m fig upheaval

cata'comba f catacomb

cata'fascio m andare a ~ a go to rack and ruin

cata'litico adj marmitta catalitica (Auto) catalytic converter

cataliz'za|re vt heighten. ~'tore m (Auto) catalytic converter

catalo'gare vt catalogue. ca'talogo m catalogue

catama'rano m (da diporto) catamaran

cata'pecchia f hovel; 🔳 dump

catapul'tar|e vt eject. ~si vr (precipitarsi) dive

catarifran'gente m reflector

ca'tarro m catarrh

ca'tasta f pile

ca'tasto m land register

ca'tastrofe f catastrophe. cata'strofico adj catastrophic

cate'chismo m catechism

cate'go|ria f category. ~'gorico adj categorical

ca'tena f chain. ~ montuosa mountain range. catene pl da neve tyre-chains. cate'naccio m bolt

cate|'nella f (collana) chain. ~'nina f chain

cate'ratta f cataract

ca'terva f una ~ di heaps of

cati'nell|a f basin; piovere a ~e bucket down

ca'tino m basin

ca'trame m tar

'cattedra f (tavolo di insegnante) desk; (di università) chair

catte'drale f cathedral

catti'veria f wickedness; (azione) wicked action

cattività f captivity

cat'tivo adj bad; (bambino)

naughty

cattoli'cesimo m Catholicism

cat'tolico, -a adj & mf [Roman] Catholic

cat'tura f capture. **~rare** vt capture

cauccìù m rubber

'causa f cause; (Jur) lawsuit; far a ~ a qcno sue sb. **cau'sare** vt cause

'caustico adj caustic

cauta'mente adv cautiously

cau'tela f caution

caute'lar|e vt protect. **~si** vr take precautions

cauteriz'z|are vt cauterize. **cauterizzazi'one** f cauterization

'cauto adj cautious

cauzi'one f security; (per libertà provvisoria) bail

'cava f quarry; fig mine

caval'ca|re vt ride; (stare a cavalcioni) sit astride. **~ta** f ride; (corteo) cavalcade. **~via** m flyover

cavalci'oni : a ~ adv astride

cavali'ere m rider; (titolo) knight; (accompagnatore) escort; (al ballo) partner

caval'le|resco adj chivalrous. **~ria** f chivalry; (Mil) cavalry. **~rizzo, -a** m horseman •f horsewoman

caval'letta f grasshopper

caval'letto m trestle; (di macchina fotografica) tripod; (di pittore) easel

caval'lina f (ginnastica) horse

ca'vallo m horse; (misura di potenza) horsepower; (scacchi) knight; (dei pantaloni) crotch; a ~ on horseback; andare a ~ go horse-riding. **~ a dondolo** rocking-horse

caval'lone m (ondata) roller

caval'luccio ma'rino m sea horse

ca'var|e vt take out; (di dosso) take

off; **~sela** get away with it; se la cava bene he's doing all right

cava'tappi m inv corkscrew

ca'ver|na f cave. **~'noso** adj (voce) deep

'cavia f guinea-pig

cavi'ale m caviar

ca'viglia f ankle

cavil'lare vi quibble. **ca'villo** m quibble

cavità f inv cavity

'cavo adj hollow •m cavity; (di metallo) cable; (Naut) rope

cavo'lata f 🔟 rubbish

cavo'letto m ~ di Bruxelles Brussels sprout

cavolfi'ore m cauliflower

'cavolo m cabbage; ~! 🔟 sugar!

caz'zo int vulg fuck!

caz'zott|o m punch; prendere qcno a ~i beat sb up

cazzu'ola f trowel

c/c abbr (conto corrente) c/a

CD-Rom m inv CD-Rom

ce pers pron (a noi) (to) us •adv there; ~ ne sono molti there are many

'cece m chick-pea

cecità f blindness

ceco, -a adj & mf Czech; la Repubblica Ceca the Czech Republic

'cedere vi (arrendersi) surrender; (concedere) yield; (sprofondare) subside •vt give up; make over (proprietà ecc). **ce'devole** adj (terreno ecc) soft; (fig) yielding. **cedi'mento** m (di terreno) subsidence

'cedola f coupon

'cedro m (albero) cedar; (frutto) citron

'ceffo m (muso) snout; (pej: persona) mug

cef'fone m slap

ce'lar|e vt conceal. **~si** vr hide

cele'bra|re vt celebrate. **~zi'one** f

celebration

'celebr|e *adj* famous. ∼ità *f inv* celebrity

'celere *adj* swift

ce'leste *adj* (*divino*) heavenly ● *agg & m* (*colore*) sky-blue

celi'bato *m* celibacy

'celibe *adj* single ● *m* bachelor

'cella *f* cell

'cellofan *m inv* cellophane; (*Culin*) cling film

'cellula *f* cell. ∼ fotoelettrica electronic eye

cellu'lare *m* (*telefono*) cellular phone ● *adj* [*furgone*] ∼ *m* police van. [telefono] ∼ *m* cellular phone

cellu'lite *f* cellulite

cellu'loide *adj* celluloid

cellu'losa *f* cellulose

'Celt|i *mpl* Celts. ∼ico *adj* Celtic

cemen'tare *vt* cement. ce'mento *m* cement. cemento armato reinforced concrete

'cena *f* dinner; (*leggera*) supper

Cena Cena is the evening meal, traditionally a lighter meal than *pranzo*, although it too may start with a *primo* (often small pasta shapes in broth). A *cena* can also be a dinner party or a dinner at a restaurant, two of the principal ways in which Italians socialize.

ce'nacolo *m* circle

ce'nare *vi* have dinner

'cenci|o *m* rag; (*per spolverare*) duster. ∼oso *adj* in rags

'cenere *f* ash; (*di carbone ecc*) cinders

ce'netta *f* (*cena semplice*) informal dinner

'cenno *m* sign; (*col capo*) nod; (*con la mano*) wave; (*allusione*) hint; (*breve resoconto*) mention

ce'none *m* il ∼ di Capodanno/ Natale special New Year's Eve/Christmas Eve dinner

censi'mento *m* census

cen's|ore *m* censor. ∼ura *f* censorship. ∼u'rare *vt* censor

'cent *m inv* cent

centelli'nare *vt* sip

cente'n|ario, -a *adj* & *mf* centenarian ● *m* centenary. ∼'nale *adj* centennial

cen'tesimo *adj* hundredth ● *m* (*di moneta*) cent; non avere un ∼ be penniless

centi'grado *adj* centigrade. ∼metro *m* centimetre

centi'naio *m* hundred

'cento *adj* & *m* one or a hundred; per ∼ per cent

centome'trista *mf* Sport one hundred metres runner

cento'mila *m* one or a hundred thousand

cen'trale *adj* central ● *f* (*di società ecc*) head office. ∼ atomica atomic power station. ∼ elettrica power station. ∼ nucleare nuclear power station. ∼ telefonica [telephone] exchange

centra'li|na *f* (Teleph) switchboard. ∼'nista *mf* operator

centra'lino *m* (Teleph) exchange; (*di albergo ecc*) switchboard

centra'li|smo *m* centralism. ∼z'zare *vt* centralize

cen'trare *vt* ∼ qcsa hit sth in the centre; (*fissare nel centro*) centre; fig hit on the head (idea)

cen'trifu|ga *f* spin-drier. centrifuga [asciugaverdure] shaker. ∼'gare *vt* centrifuge; (*lavatrice*): spin

'centro *m* centre. ∼ [*città*] city centre. ∼ commerciale mall. ∼ di accoglienza reception centre. ∼ sociale community centre

Centro storico The layout and much of the fabric of most Italian town and city centres derive from medieval or even Roman times, with the result that the *centro storico* is a place of narrow streets. Some (like Lucca) are surrounded by city walls. This makes life difficult for the motorist, and cars have been banned from many city centres.

'**ceppo** *m* (*di albero*) stump; (*da ardere*) log; (*fig: gruppo*) stock

'**cera** *f* wax; (*aspetto*) look. ~ **per il pavimento** floor-polish

ce'**ramica** *f* (*arte*) ceramics; (*materia*) pottery; (*oggetto*) pot

ce'**rato** *adj* (*tela*) waxed

cerbi'**atto** *m* fawn

'**cerca** *f* **andare in ~ di** look for

cercaper'**sone** *m inv* beeper

cer'**care** *vt* look for ● *vi* ~ **di** try to

'**cerchia** *f* circle. ~**are** *vt* circle (*parola*). ~'**ato** *adj* (*occhi*) black-ringed. ~'**etto** *m* (*per capelli*) hairband

cerchi'**o** *m* circle; (*giocattolo*) hoop. ~'**one** *m* alloy wheel

cere'**ale** *m* cereal

cere'**brale** *adj* cerebral

'**cereo** *adj* waxen

ce'**retta** *f* depilatory wax

ceri'**monia** *f* ceremony. ~**ale** *m* ceremonial. ~**oso** *adj* ceremonious

ce'**rino** *m* [wax] match

cerni'**era** *f* hinge; (*di borsa*) clasp. ~ **lampo** zip[-fastener], zipper *Am*

cer'**nita** *f* selection

'**cero** *m* candle

ce'**rone** *m* grease-paint

ce'**rotto** *m* [sticking] plaster

certa'**mente** *adv* certainly

cer'**tezza** *f* certainty

certifi'**care** *vt* certify. ~**to** *m* certificate

'**certo** *adj* certain; (*notizia*) definite; (*indeterminativo*) some; **sono ~ di riuscire** I am certain to succeed; **certi giorni** some days; **un ~ signor Giardini** a Mr Giardini; **una certa Anna** somebody called Anna; **certa gente** *pej* some people; **ho certi dolori!** I'm in such pain!. **certi** *pron* some; (*alcune persone*) some people ● *adv* of course; **sapere per ~** know for certain; **di ~** surely; **~ che sì!** of course!

cer'**vello** *m* brain.

'**cervo** *m* deer

ce'**sareo** *adj* (*Med*) Caesarean

cesel'**lare** *vt* chisel. ~**to** *adj* chiselled. ce'**sello** *m* chisel

ce'**soie** *fpl* shears

ce'**spuglio** *m* bush. ~'**oso** *adj* (*terreno*) bushy

ces'**sare** *vi* stop, cease ● *vt* stop. ~**te il fuoco** ceasefire

cessi'**one** *f* handover

'**cesso** *m* ⊠ (*gabinetto*) bog, john *Am*; (*fig: locale, luogo*) dump

'**cesta** *f* [large] basket. ce'**stello** *m* (*di lavatrice*) drum

cesti'**nare** *vt* throw away. ce'**stino** *m* [small] basket; (*per la carta straccia*) waste-paper basket. '**cesto** *m* basket

'**ceto** *m* [social] class

'**cetra** *f* lyre

cetrio'**lino** *m* gherkin. cetri'**olo** *m* cucumber

cfr *abbr* (*confronta*) cf.

chat'**tare** *vi* (*Comput*) chat

che

● *pron rel* (*persona: soggetto*) who; (*persona: oggetto*) that, who, whom *fml*; (*cosa, animale*) that, which; **questa è la casa ~ ho comprato** this is the house [that] I've bought; **il ~ mi sorprende** which surprises me; **dal**

~ **deduco che...** from which I gather that...; **avere di ~ vivere** have enough to live on; **grazie! – non c'è di ~!** thank you! – don't mention it!; **il giorno ~ ti ho visto** 1 the day I saw you

● adj inter what, which; (esclamativo; con aggettivo) how; (con nome) what a; ~ **macchina prendiamo, la tua o la mia?** which car are we taking, yours or mine?; ~ **bello!** how nice!; ~ **idea!** what an idea!; ~ **bella giornata!** what a lovely day!

● pron inter what; **a ~ pensi?** what are you thinking about?

● conj that; (con comparazioni) than; **credo ~ abbia ragione** I think [that] he is right; **era così commosso ~ non riusciva a parlare** he was so moved [that] he couldn't speak; **aspetto ~ telefoni** I'm waiting for him to phone; **è da un po' ~ non lo vedo** it's been a while since I saw him; **mi piace più Roma ~ Milano** I like Rome better than Milan; ~ **ti piaccia o no** whether you like it or not; ~ **io sappia** as far as I know

checché indef pron whatever

chemioterapia f chemotherapy

cherosene m paraffin

chetichella: alla ~ silently

'**cheto** adj quiet

chi

● rel pron whoever; (coloro che) people who; **ho trovato ~ ti può aiutare** I found somebody who can help you; **c'è ~ dice che...** some people say that...; **senti ~ parla!** listen to who's talking!

● inter pron (soggetto) who; (oggetto, con preposizione) who, whom fml; (possessivo) **di ~** whose; ~ **sei?** who are you?; ~ **hai incontrato?** who did you meet?; **di ~ sono questi libri?** whose books are these?; **con ~ parli?** who are you talking to?; **a ~ lo dici!** tell me about it!

chiacchie|ra f chat; (pettegolezzo) gossip. ~**rare** vi chat; (far pettegolezzi) gossip. ~**rato** adj **essere** ~**rato** (persona:) be the subject of gossip; **far quattro** ~**re** have a chat. ~**rone, -a** adj talkative ● mf chatterer

chia|mare vt call; (far venire) send for; **come ti chiami?** what's your name?; **mi chiamo Roberto** my name is Robert; ~**re alle armi** call up. ~**rsi** vr be called. ~**ta** f call; (Mil) call-up

chiappa f 1 cheek

chiara|mente adv clearly

chia'rezza f clarity; (limpidezza) clearness

chiarifi|care vt clarify. ~**tore** adj clarificatory. ~**zi'one** f clarification

chiari'mento m clarification

chia'rir|e vt make clear; (spiegare) clear up. ~**si** vi become clear

chi'aro adj clear; (luminoso) bright; (colore) light. **chia'rore** m glimmer

chiaroveg'gente adj clear-sighted ● mf clairvoyant

chi'asso m din. ~**'soso** adj rowdy

chi'av|e f key; **chiudere a ~e** lock. ~**e inglese** spanner. ~**i'stello** m latch

chiaz|za f stain. ~**zare** vt stain

chic adj inv chic

chicches'sia pron anybody

'**chicco** m grain; (di caffè) bean; (d'uva) grape

chi'eder|e vt ask; (per avere) ask for; (esigere) demand. ~**si** vr wonder

chi'esa f church

chi'esto pp di **chiedere**

'chiglia f keel

'chilo m kilo

chilo'grammo m kilogram[me]

chilome'traggio m (Auto) mileage

chilo'metrico adj in kilometres

chi'lometro m kilometre

chi'mera f fig illusion

'chimic|a f chemistry. **~o, -a** adj chemical ● mf chemist

'china f (declivio) slope; **inchiostro di ~** Indian ink

chi'nar|e vt lower. **~si** vr stoop

chincaglie'rie fpl knick-knacks

chinesitera'pia f physiotherapy

chi'nino m quinine

'chino adj bent

chi'notto m sparkling soft drink

chi'occia f sitting hen

chi'occiola f snail; (Comput) at sign; **scala a ~** spiral staircase

chi'odo m nail; (idea fissa) obsession. **~ di garofano** clove

chi'oma f head of hair; (fogliame) foliage

chi'osco m kiosk

chi'ostro m cloister

chiro'man|te mf palmist. **~'zia** f palmistry

chirur'gia f surgery. **chi'rurgico** adj surgical. **chi'rurgo** m surgeon

chissà adv who knows; **~ quando arriverà** I wonder when he will arrive

chi'tar|ra f guitar. **~'rista** mf guitarist

chi'uder|e vt close; (con la chiave) lock; turn off (luce, acqua); (per sempre) close down (negozio ecc); (recingere) enclose ● vi shut, close. **~si** vr shut; (tempo:) cloud over; (ferita:) heal up.

chi'unque pron anyone, anybody ● rel pron whoever

chi'usa f enclosure; (di canale) lock; (conclusione) close

chi'u|so pp di **chiudere** ● adj shut; (tempo) overcast; (persona) reserved. **~sura** f closing; (sistema) lock; (allacciatura) fastener. **~sura lampo** zip, zipper Am

---

ci

● pron (personale) us; (riflessivo) ourselves; (reciproco) each other; (a ciò, di ciò ecc) about it; **non ci disturbare** don't disturb us; **aspettateci** wait for us; **ci ha detto tutto** he told us everything; **ce lo manderanno** they'll send it to us; **ci consideriamo...** we consider ourselves...; **ci laviamo le mani** we wash our hands; **ci odiamo** we hate each other; **non ci penso mai** I never think about it; **pensaci!** think about it!

● adv (qui) here; (lì) there; (moto per luogo) through it; **ci siamo** we are here; **ci siete?** are you there? **ci siamo passati tutti** we all went through it; **c'è** there is; **ce ne sono molti** there are many; **ci vuole pazienza** it takes patience; **non ci vedo/sento** I can't see/hear

---

cia'bat|ta f slipper. **~'tare** vi shuffle

ciabat'tino m cobbler

ci'alda f wafer

cial'trone m scoundrel

ciam'bella f (Culin) ring-shaped cake; (salvagente) lifebelt; (gonfiabile) rubber ring

cianci'are vi gossip

cia'notico adj (colorito) puce

ci'ao int 🔁 (all' arrivo) hello!, hi!; (alla partenza) bye-bye!

ciar'la|re vi chat. **~'tano** m charlatan

cias'cuno adj each ● pron everyone,

c

everybody; (*distributivo*) each [one];
per ~ each
ci'bar|e *vt* feed. **~ie** *fpl* provisions
~ si *vt* eat; **~si di** live on
ciber'netico *adj* cybernetic
'cibo *m* food
ci'cala *f* cicada
cica'lino *m* buzzer
cica'tri|ce *f* scar. **~z'zante** *m*
ointment
cicatriz'zarsi *vr* heal [up]. **cicatriz-
zazi'one** *f* healing
'cicca *f* cigarette end; (囗: *sigaretta*)
fag; (囗: *gomma*) [chewing] gum
cic'chetto *m* 囗 (*bicchierino*) nip; (*rimprovero*) telling-off
'ciccia *f* fat, flab
cice'rone *m* guide
cicla'mino *m* cyclamen
ci'cli|smo *m* cycling. **~ta** *mf* cyclist
'ciclo *m* cycle; (*di medicina*) course
ciclomo'tore *m* moped
ci'clone *m* cyclone
ci'cogna *f* stork
ci'coria *f* chicory
ci'eco, -a *adj* blind **•** *m* blind man
• *f* blind woman
ci'elo *m* sky; (*Relig*) heaven; **santo
~!** good heavens!
'cifra *f* figure; (*somma*) sum; (*mono-
gramma*) monogram; (*codice*) code
ci'fra|re *vt* embroider with a mono-
gram; (*codificare*) code. **~to** *adj*
monogrammed; coded
'ciglio *m* (*bordo*) edge; (*pl f* **ciglia**:
delle palpebre) eyelash
'cigno *m* swan
cigo'l|are *vi* squeak. **~io** *m* squeak
'Cile *m* Chile
ci'lecca *f* far ~ miss
ci'leno, -a *adj & mf* Chilean
cili'egi|a *f* cherry. **~o** *m* cherry
[tree]
cilin'drata *f* cubic capacity; **macchina di alta ~** highpowered car

ci'lindro *m* cylinder; (*cappello*)
top hat
'cima *f* top; (*fig*: *persona*) genius; **da
~ a fondo** from top to bottom
ci'melio *m* relic
cimen'tar|e *vt* put to the test. **~si**
vr (*provare*) try one's hand
'cimice *f* bug; (*puntina*) drawing pin,
thumbtack *Am*
cimini'era *f* chimney; (*Naut*) funnel
cimi'tero *m* cemetery
ci'murro *m* distemper
'Cina *f* China
cin cin! *int* cheers!
cincischi'are *vi* fiddle
'cine *m* 囗 cinema
cine'asta *mf* film maker
'cinema *m inv* cinema. **cine'presa** *f*
cine-camera
ci'nese *adj & mf* Chinese
cine'teca *f* film collection
'cingere *vt* (*circondare*) surround
'cinghia *f* strap; (*cintura*) belt
cinghi'ale *m* wild boar; **pelle di ~**
pigskin
cinguet't|are *vi* twitter. **~io** *m*
twittering
'cinico *adj* cynical
ci'niglia *f* (*tessuto*) chenille
ci'nismo *m* cynicism
ci'nofilo *adj* dog-loving
cin'quanta *adj & m* fifty. **cinquan-
'tenne** *adj & mf* fifty-year-old. **cin-
quan'tesimo** *adj* fiftieth. **cinquan-
'tina** *f* una cinquantina di
about fifty
'cinque *adj & m* five
cinquecen'tesco *adj* sixteenth-
century
cinque'cento *adj* five hundred **•** *m*
il C~ the sixteenth century
cinque'mila *adj & m* five thousand
'cinta *f* (*di pantaloni*) belt; **muro di ~**
(*boundary*) wall. **cin'tare** *vt* enclose
'cintola *f* (*di pantaloni*) belt

cin'tura f belt. ∼ **di salvataggio** lifebelt. ∼ **di sicurezza** (Aeron), (Auto) seat-belt

cintu'rino m ∼ **dell'orologio** watch-strap

ciò pron this; that; ∼ **che** what; ∼ **nondimeno** nevertheless

ci'occa f lock

ciocco'la|ta f chocolate; (bevanda) [hot] chocolate. ∼ **tino** m chocolate. ∼ **to** m chocolate. ∼ **to al latte/ fondente** milk/plain chocolate

cioè adv that is

ciondo'lare vi dangle. **ci'ondolo** m pendant

ciono'nostante adv nonetheless

ci'otola f bowl

ci'ottolo m pebble

ci'polla f onion; (bulbo) bulb

ci'presso m cypress

'cipria f [face] powder

'Cipro m Cyprus. **cipri'ota** adj & mf Cypriot

'circa adv & prep about

'circo m circus

circo'la|re adj circular ● f circular; (di metropolitana) circle line ● vi circulate. ∼ **torio** m (Med) circulatory. ∼ **zi'one** f circulation; (traffico) traffic

'circolo m circle; (società) club

circon'ci|dere vt circumcise. ∼ **si'one** f circumcision

circon'dare vt surround. ∼ **io** m (amministrativo) administrative district. ∼ **si di** vr surround oneself with

circonfe'renza f circumference. ∼ **dei fianchi** hip measurement

circonvallazi'one f ring road

circo'scritto adj limited

circoscrizi'one f area. ∼ **elettorale** constituency

circo'spetto adj wary

circospezi'one f con ∼ **warily**

circo'stante adj surrounding

circo'stanza f circumstance; (occa-

sione) occasion

circu'ire vt (ingannare) trick

cir'cuito m circuit

circumnavi'ga|re vt circumnavigate. ∼ **zi'one** f circumnavigation

ci'sterna f cistern; (serbatoio) tank

'cisti f inv cyst

ci'ta|re vt quote; (come esempio) cite; (Jur) summons. ∼ **zi'one** f quotation; (Jur) summons sg

citofo'nare vt buzz. **ci'tofono** m entry phone; (in ufficio, su aereo ecc) intercom

ci'trullo, -a mf ⬜ dimwit

città f inv town; (grande) city

citta'della f citadel

citta|di'nanza f citizenship; (popolazione) citizens pl. ∼ **dino, -a** mf citizen; (abitante di città) city dweller

ciucci'are vt ⬜ suck. **ci'uccio** m ⬜ dummy

ci'uffo m tuft

ci'urma f (Naut) crew

ci'vet|ta f owl; (fig: donna) flirt; [auto] ∼ **ta** unmarked police car. ∼ **tare** vi flirt. ∼ **te'ria** f coquettishness

'civico adj civic

ci'vil|e adj civil. ∼ **iz'zare** vt civilize. ∼ **iz'zato** adj (paese) civilized. ∼ **izza-zi'one** f civilization. ∼ **mente** adv civilly

civiltà f inv civilization; (cortesia) civility

'clacson m inv (car) horn

clacso'nare vi hoot; honk

cla'mo|re m clamour; **fare** ∼ **re** cause a sensation. ∼ **rosa'mente** adv (sbagliare) sensationally. ∼ **roso** adj noisy; (sbaglio) sensational

clan m inv clan; fig clique

clandestinità f secrecy

clande'stino adj secret; **movimento** ∼ underground movement; **passeggero** ∼ stowaway

clari'netto m clarinet

'classe f class. ~ turistica tourist class

classi'cis|mo m classicism. ~ta mf classicist

'classico adj classical; (tipico) classic • m classic

clas'sifi|ca f classification; Sport results pl. ~'care vt classify. ~'carsi vr be placed. ~ca'tore m (cartella) folder. ~cazi'one f classification

clas'sista mf class-conscious person

'clausola f clause

claustro'fo'bia f claustrophobia. ~'fobico adj claustrophobic

clau'sura f (Relig) enclosed order

clavi'cembalo m harpsichord

cla'vicola f collar-bone

cle'men|te adj merciful; (tempo) mild. ~za f mercy

cleri'cale adj clerical. 'clero m clergy

clic m (Comput) click; fare ~ su click on; fare doppio ~ su double-click on

clic'care vi click (su on)

cli'en|te mf client; (di negozio) customer. ~tela f customers pl

'clima m climate. cli'matico adj climatic; stazione climatica health resort

'clinica f clinic. clinico adj clinical • m clinician

clo'na|re vt clone. ~'zione f cloning

'cloro m chlorine

clou m inv i momenti ~ the highlights

coabi'ta|re vi live together. ~zi'one f cohabitation

coagu'la|re vt, ~rsi vr coagulate. ~zi'one f coagulation

coalizi'one f coalition. ~'zarsi vr unite

co'atto adj (Jur) compulsory

coca'ina f cocaine. coca'inomane mf cocaine addict

cocci'nella f ladybird

'coccio m earthenware; (frammento) fragment

cocci'u'taggine f stubbornness. ~'uto adj stubborn

'cocco m coconut palm; ① love; noce di ~ coconut

cocco'drillo m crocodile

cocco'lare vt cuddle

co'cente adj (sole) burning

'cocktail m inv (ricevimento) cocktail party

co'comero m watermelon

co'cuzzolo m top; (di testa, cappello) crown

'coda f tail; (di abito) train; (fila) queue; fare la ~ queue [up], stand in line Am. ~ di cavallo (acconciatura) ponytail.

co'dardo, -a adj cowardly • mf coward

'codice m code. ~ di avviamento postale postal code, zip code Am. ~ a barre bar-code. ~ fiscale tax code. ~ della strada highway code.

codifi'care vt codify

coe'ren|te adj consistent. ~za f consistency

coesi'one f cohesion

coe'taneo, -a adj & mf contemporary

cofa'netto m casket. 'cofano m chest; (Auto) bonnet, hood Am

'cogliere vt pick; (sorprendere) catch; (afferrare) seize; (colpire) hit

co'gnato, -a mf brother-in-law; sister-in-law

cognizi'one f knowledge

co'gnome m surname

'coi = con + i

coinci'denza f coincidence; (di treno ecc) connection

coin'cidere vi coincide

coinqui'lino m flatmate

coin'vol|gere vt involve. ∼**gi**'mento m involvement. ∼**to** adj involved

'**coito** m coitus

col = **con** + **il**

colà adv there

cola|'brodo m inv strainer; ridotto a un ∼**brodo** 🅸 full of holes. ∼**pasta** m inv colander

co'la|re vt strain; (versare lentamente) drip ● vi (gocciolare) drip; (perdere) leak; ∼**re a picco** (Naut) sink. ∼**ta** f (di metallo) casting; [di lava] flow

colazi'one f (del mattino) breakfast; (di mezzogiorno) lunch; **prima** ∼ breakfast; **far** ∼ have breakfast/lunch. ∼ **al sacco** packed lunch

co'lei pron f the one

co'lera m cholera

coleste'rolo m cholesterol

colf f abbr (collaboratrice familiare) home help

'**colica** f colic

co'lino m [tea] strainer

'**colla** f glue; (di farina) paste. ∼ **di pesce** gelatine

collabo'ra|re vi collaborate. ∼**tore**, ∼**trice** mf collaborator. ∼**zi'one** f collaboration

col'lana f necklace; (serie) series

col'lant m inv tights pl

col'lare m collar

col'lasso m collapse

collau'dare vt test. **col'laudo** m test

'**colle** m hill

col'lega mf colleague

collega'mento m connection; (Mil) liaison; Radio link; ∼ **iperte-stuale** hypertext link. **colle'gar|e** vt connect. ∼**si** vr link up

collegi'ale mf boarder ● adj (responsabilità, decisione) collective

col'legio m (convitto) boarding-school. ∼ **elettorale** constituency

'**collera** f anger; **andare in** ∼ get

angry. **col'lerico** adj irascible

col'letta f collection

collet|tività f inv community. ∼**tivo** adj collective; (interesse) general; **biglietto** ∼**tivo** group ticket

col'letto m collar

collezi|o'nare vt collect. ∼**one** f collection. ∼**o'nista** mf collector

colli'mare vi coincide

col'li|na f hill. ∼**noso** adj (terreno) hilly

col'lirio m eyewash

collisi'one f collision

'**collo** m neck; (pacco) package; **a** ∼ **alto** high-necked. ∼ **del piede** instep

colloca'mento m placing; (impiego) employment

collo'ca|re vt place. ∼**rsi** vr take one's place. ∼**zi'one** f placing

colloqui'ale adj (termine) colloquial. **col'loquio** m conversation; (udienza ecc) interview; (esame) oral [exam]

collusi'one f collusion

colluttazi'one f scuffle

col'mare vt fill [to the brim]; bridge (divario); ∼ **qcno di gentilezze** overwhelm sb with kindness. '**colmo** adj full ● m top; fig height; **al colmo della disperazione** in the depths of despair; **questo è il colmo!** (con indignazione) this is the last straw!; (con stupore) I don't believe it!

co'lomb|a f dove. ∼**o** m pigeon

co'loni|a[1] f colony; ∼ **[estiva]** (per bambini) holiday camp. ∼**'ale** adj colonial

co'lonia[2] f **[acqua di]** ∼ **[eau de]** Cologne

co'lonico adj (terreno, casa) farm

coloniz'za|re vt colonize. ∼**tore**, ∼**trice** mf colonizer

co'lon|na f column. ∼ **sonora** sound-track. ∼ **vertebrale** spine.

~'nato m colonnade

colon'nello m colonel

co'lono m tenant farmer

colo'rante m colouring

colo'rare vt colour; colour in (disegno)

co'lore m colour; a colori in colour; di ~ coloured. colo'rito adj coloured; (viso) rosy; (racconto) colourful • m complexion

co'loro pron pl the ones

colos'sale adj colossal. co'losso m colossus

'colpa f fault; (biasimo) blame; (colpevolezza) guilt; (peccato) sin; dare la ~ a blame; essere in ~ be at fault; per ~ di because of. col'pevole adj guilty • mf culprit

col'pire vt hit, strike

'colpo m blow; (di arma da fuoco) shot; (urto) knock; (emozione) shock; (Med, Sport) stroke; (furto) raid; di ~ suddenly; far ~ make a strong impression; far venire un ~ a qcno fig give sb a fright; perdere colpi (motore:) keep missing; a ~ d'occhio at a glance; a ~ sicuro for certain. ~ d'aria chill. ~ di sole sunstroke; colpi di sole (su capelli) highlights. ~ di stato coup [d'état]. ~ di telefono ring; dare un ~ di telefono a qn give sb a ring. ~ di testa [sudden] impulse. ~ di vento gust of wind

col'poso adj omicidio ~ manslaughter

coltel'lata f stab. col'tello m knife

colti'va|re vt cultivate. ~'tore, ~'trice mf farmer. ~zi'one f farming; (di piante) growing

'colto pp di cogliere • adj cultured

'coltre f blanket

col'tura f cultivation

col'lui pron inv m the one

'coma m coma; in ~ in a coma

comanda'mento m

commandment

coman'dante m commander; (Aeron, Naut) captain

coman'dare vt command; (Mech) control • vi be in charge. co'mando m command; (di macchina) control

co'mare f (madrina) godmother

combaci'are vi fit together; (testimonianze:) concur

combat'tente adj fighting • m combatant. ex ~ ex-serviceman

com'bat|tere vt/i fight. ~ti'mento m fight; (Mil) battle; fuori ~timento (pugilato) knocked out. ~'tuto adj (gara) hard fought

combi'na|re vt/i arrange; (mettere insieme) combine; (🆃: fare) do; cosa stai ~ndo? what are you doing? ~rsi vr combine; (mettersi d'accordo) come to an agreement. ~zi'one f combination; (caso) coincidence; per ~zione by chance

com'briccola f gang

combu'sti|bile adj combustible • m fuel. ~'one f combustion

com'butta f gang; in ~ in league

'come

● adv like; (in qualità di) as; (interrogativo, esclamativo) how; questo vestito è ~ il tuo this dress is like yours; ~ stai? how are you?; ~ va? how are things?; ~ mai? how come?; ~ what?; non sa ~ fare he doesn't know what to do; ~ sta bene! how well he looks!; ~ no! that will be right!; ~ tu sai as you know; fa ~ vuoi do as you like; ~ se as if

● conj (non appena) as soon as

co'meta f comet

'comico, -a adj comic • m funny side • mf (attore) comedian • f (a torta in faccia) slapstick sketch

co'mignolo m chimney-pot

cominci'are vt/i begin, start; a ~ da oggi from today.

comi'tato m committee

comi'tiva f party, group

co'mizio m meeting

com'mando m inv commando

com'media f comedy; (opera teatrale) play; fig sham. ~ione f comedy musical. ~ante mf comedian; fig pej phoney. ~'ografo, -a f playwright

commemo'ra|re vt commemorate. ~zi'one f commemoration

commen'sale mf fellow diner

commen't|are vt comment on; (annotare) annotate. ~ario m commentary. ~a'tore, ~a'trice mf commentator. com'mento m comment

commerci'ale adj commercial; (relazioni, trattative) trade; (attività) business. centro ~e shopping centre. ~'lista mf business consultant; (contabile) accountant. ~liz'zare vt market. ~lizzazi'one f marketing

commerci'ante mf trader; (negoziante) shopkeeper. ~ all'ingrosso wholesaler

commerci'are vi ~ in deal in

com'mercio m commerce; (internazionale) trade; (affari) business; in ~ (prodotto) on sale. ~ equo e solidale fair trade. ~ all'ingrosso wholesale trade. ~ al minuto retail trade

com'messo, -a pp di commettere •mf shop assistant. ~ viaggiatore commercial traveller •f (ordine) order

comme'stibile adj edible. commestibili mpl groceries

com'mettere vt commit; make (sbaglio)

commi'ato m leave; prendere ~ da take leave of

commise'rar|e vt commiserate with. ~si vr feel sorry for oneself

commissari'ato m (di polizia) police station

commis's|ario m [police] superin-

tendent; (membro di commissione) commissioner; Sport steward; (Comm) commission agent. ~ario d'esame examiner. ~i'one f (incarico) errand; (comitato ecc) commission; (Comm: di merce) order; ~ioni pl (acquisti) fare ~ioni go shopping. ~ione d'esame board of examiners. C~ione Europea European Commission

commit'tente mf purchaser

com'mo|sso pp di commuovere •adj moved. ~'vente adj moving

commozi'one f emotion. ~ cerebrale concussion

commu'over|e vt touch, move. ~si vr be touched

commu'tare vt change; (Jur) commute

comò m inv chest of drawers

comoda'mente adv comfortably

como'dino m bedside table

comodità f inv comfort; (convenienza) convenience

'comodo adj comfortable; (conveniente) convenient; (spazioso) roomy; (facile) easy; stia ~! don't get up!; far ~ be useful •m comfort; fare il proprio ~ do as one pleases

compae'sano, -a mf fellow countryman

com'pagine f (squadra) team

compa'gnia f company; (gruppo) party; fare ~ a qcno keep sb company; essere di ~ be sociable. ~ aerea airline

com'pagno, -a mf companion; (Comm, Sport, in coppia) partner; (Pol) comrade. ~ di scuola schoolmate

compa'rabile adj comparable

compa'ra|re vt compare. ~'tivo adj e m comparative. ~zi'one f comparison

com'pare m (padrino) godfather; (testimone di matrimonio) witness

compa'rire vi appear; (spiccare) stand out; ~ in giudizio appear in court

com'parso, -a pp di comparire • f appearance; Cinema extra

compartecipazi'one f sharing; (quota) share

comparti'mento m compartment; (amministrativo) department

compas'sato adj calm and collected

compassi'one f compassion; aver ~ne per feel pity for; far ~ne arouse pity. ~**nevole** adj compassionate

com'passo m [pair of] compasses pl

compa'tibil|e adj (conciliabile) compatible; (scusabile) excusable. ~**ità** f compatibility. ~**mente** adv ~**mente con i miei impegni** if my commitments allow

compa'tire vt pity; (scusare) make allowances for

compat'tezza f (di materia) compactness. **com'patto** adj compact; (denso) dense; (solido) solid; fig united

compene'trare vt pervade

compen'sar|e vt compensate; (supplire) make up for. ~**si** vr balance each other out

compen'sato m (legno) plywood

compensazi'one f compensation

com'penso m compensation; (retribuzione) remuneration; in ~ (in cambio) in return; (d'altra parte) on the other hand; (invece) instead

'comper|a f purchase; far ~e do some shopping

compe'rare vt buy

compe'ten|te adj competent. ~**za** f competence; (responsabilità) responsibility

com'petere vi compete; ~ a (compito:) be the responsibility of

competi'tività f competitiveness. ~**tivo** adj (prezzo, carattere) competitive. ~**tore, -trice** mf competitor. ~**zi'one** f competition

compia'cen|te adj obliging. ~**za** f obligingness

compia'cer|e vt/i please. ~**ersi** vr (congratularsi) congratulate. ~**ersi di** (degnarsi) condescend. ~**i'mento** m satisfaction; pej smugness. ~**i'uto** adj satisfied; (aria, sorriso) smug

compi'an|gere vt pity; (per lutto ecc) sympathize with. ~**to** adj lamented • m grief

'compier|e vt (concludere) complete; commit (delitto); ~**e gli anni** have one's birthday. ~**si** vr end; (avverarsi) come true

compi'lare vt compile; fill in (modulo). ~**zi'one** f compilation

compi'mento m portare a ~ qcsa conclude sth

com'pire vt = COMPIERE

compi'tare vt spell

com'pito¹ adj polite

'compito² m task; (Sch) homework

compi'uto adj avere 30 anni ~**i** be over 30

comple'anno m birthday

complemen'tare adj complementary; (secondario) subsidiary

comple'mento m complement; (Mil) draft. ~ **oggetto** direct object

comples|sità f complexity. ~**siva'mente** adv on the whole. ~**sivo** adj comprehensive; (totale) total. **com'plesso** adj complex; (difficile) complicated • m complex; (di cantanti ecc) group; (di circostanze, fattori) combination; in ~**so** on the whole

completa'mente adv completely

comple'tare vt complete

com'pleto adj complete; (pieno) full [up]; essere al ~ (teatro:) be sold out; la famiglia al ~ the whole family • m (vestito) suit; (insieme di cose) set

compli'ca|re vt complicate. ~**rsi** vr become complicated. ~**to** adj complicated. ~**zi'one** f complication; salvo ~**zioni** all being well 'complic|e *mf* accomplice ● *adj* (sguardo) knowing. ~ità *f* complicity

complimen'tar|e *vt* compliment. ~si *vr* ~si con congratulate

compli'menti *mpl* (ossequi) regards; (congratulazioni) congratulations; far ~ stand on ceremony

compli'mento *m* compliment

complot'tare *vi* plot

compo'nente *adj & m* component ● *mf* member

compo'nibile *adj* (cucina) fitted; (mobili) modular

componi'mento *m* composition; (letterario) work

com'por|re *vt* compose; (ordinare) put in order; (Typ) set. ~si *vi* ~si di be made up of

comporta'mento *m* behaviour

comport'tar|e *vt* involve; (consentire) allow. ~si *vr* behave

composi'tore, -'trice *mf* composer; (Typ) compositor. ~zi'one *f* composition

com'posta *f* stewed fruit; (concime) compost

compo'stezza *f* composure

com'posto *pp di* comporre ● *adj* composed; (costituito) comprising; stai ~! sit properly! ● *m* (Chem) compound

com'pra|re *vt* buy. ~'tore, ~'trice *mf* buyer

compra'vendita *f* buying and selling

com'pren|dere *vt* understand; (includere) comprise. ~'sibile *adj* understandable. ~sibil'mente *adv* understandably. ~si'one *f* understanding. ~'sivo *adj* understanding; (che include) inclusive. ~'preso *pp di* comprendere ● *adj* included; tutto compreso (prezzo) all-in

com'pressa *f* compress; (pastiglia) tablet

compressi'one *f* compression. com'presso *pp di* comprimere ● *adj* compressed

com'primere *vt* press; (reprimere) repress

compro'me|sso *pp di* compromettere ● *m* compromise. ~t'tente *adj* compromising. ~ttere *vt* compromise

compropri'età *f* multiple ownership

compro'vare *vt* prove

compu'tare *vt* calculate

com'puter *m inv* computer. ~iz'zare *vt* computerize. ~iz'zato *adj* computerized

computiste'ria *f* book-keeping. 'computo *m* calculation

comu'nale *adj* municipal

co'mune *adj* common; (condiviso) mutual; (ordinario) ordinary ● *m* borough; (amministrativo) commune; fuori del ~ extraordinary. ~'mente *adv* commonly

comuni'ca|re *vt* communicate; pass on (malattia); (Relig) administer Communion to. ~rsi *vr* receive Communion. ~'tiva *f* communicativeness. ~'tivo *adj* communicative. ~to *m* communiqué. ~to stampa press release. ~zi'one *f* communication; (Teleph) [phone] call; avere la ~zione get through; dare la ~zione a qcno put sb through

comuni'one *f* communion; (Relig) [Holy] Communion

comu'nis|mo *m* communism. ~ta *adj & mf* communist

comunità *f inv* community. C~ [Economica] Europea European [Economic] Community

co'munque *conj* however ● *adv* anyhow

con *prep* with; (mezzo) by; ~ facilità easily; ~ mia grande gioia to my great delight; è gentile ~ tutti he is kind to everyone; col treno by train; ~ questo tempo in this weather

co'nato m ~ di vomito retching

'conca f basin; (valle) dell

concate'na|re vt link together. ~zi'one f connection

'concavo adj concave

con'ceder|e vt grant; award (premio); (ammettere) admit. ~si vr allow oneself (pausa)

concentra'mento m concentration

concen'tra|re vt, ~rsi vr concentrate. ~to adj concentrated ● m ~to di pomodoro tomato purée. ~zi'one f concentration

concepi'mento m conception

conce'pire vt conceive (bambino); (capire) understand; (figurarsi) conceive of; devise (piano ecc)

con'cernere vt concern

concer'tar|e vt (Mus) harmonize; (organizzare) arrange. ~si vr agree

concer'tista mf concert performer. con'certo m concert; (composizione) concerto

concessio'nario m agent

concessi'one f concession

con'cesso pp di concedere

con'cetto m concept; (opinione) opinion

concezi'one f conception; (idea) concept

con'chiglia f [sea] shell

'concia f tanning; (di tabacco) curing

conci'a|re vt tan; cure (tabacco). ~re qcno per le feste give sb a good hiding. ~rsi vr (sporcarsi) get dirty; (vestirsi male) dress badly. ~to adj (pelle, cuoio) tanned

concili'abile adj compatible

concili'a|re vt reconcile; settle (contravvenzione); (favorire) induce. ~rsi vr go together; (mettersi d'accordo) become reconciled. ~zi'one f

reconciliation; (Jur) settlement

con'cilio m (Relig) council; (riunione) assembly

conci'mare vt feed (pianta). con-'cime m fertilizer; (chimico) fertilizer

concisi'one f conciseness. con'ciso adj concise

conci'tato adj excited

concitta'dino, -a mf fellow citizen

con'clu|dere vt conclude; (finire con successo) achieve. ~dersi vr come to an end. ~si'one f conclusion; in ~sione (insomma) in short. ~sivo adj conclusive. ~so pp di concludere

concomi'tanza f (di circostanze, fatti) combination

concor'da|nza f agreement. ~re vt agree; (Gram) make agree. ~to m agreement; (Comm, Jur) arrangement

con'cord|e adj in agreement; (unanime) unanimous

concor'ren|te adj concurrent; (rivale) competing ● mf (Comm), Sport competitor; (candidato) candidate. ~za f competition. ~zi'ale adj competitive

con'cor|rere vi (contribuire) concur; (andare insieme) go together; (competere) compete. ~so pp di concorrere ● m competition; fuori ~so not in the official competition. ~so di bellezza beauty contest

concreta'mente adv specifically

concre'|tare vt (concludere) achieve. ~tiz'zare vt put into concrete form (idea, progetto)

con'creto adj concrete; in ~ in concrete terms

concussi'one f extortion

con'danna f sentence; pronunziare una ~ pass a sentence. con-dan'nare vt condemn; (Jur) sentence. condan'nato, -a mf convict

conden'sa|re vt, ~rsi vr condense. ~zi'one f condensation

condi'mento m seasoning; (salsa) dressing. **con'dire** vt flavour; dress (insalata)

condiscen'den|te adj indulgent; pej condescending. **~za** f indulgence; pej condescension

condi'videre vt share

condizio'na|le adj & m conditional ●f (Jur) suspended sentence

condizio'na|re vt condition. **~to** adj conditional. **~tore** m air conditioner

condizi'one f condition; a **~** che on condition that

condogli'anze fpl condolences; fare le **~** a offer condolences to

condomini'ale adj (spese) common. **condo'minio** m joint ownership; (edificio) condominium

condo'nare vt remit. **con'dono** m remission

con'dotta pp di condurre ●adj medico **~** district doctor ●m pipe; (Anat) duct

condu'cente m driver

con'du|rre vt lead; drive (veicoli); (accompagnare) take; conduct (gas, elettricità ecc); (gestire) run. **~rsi** vr behave. **~t'tore**, **~t'trice** mf (TV) presenter; (di veicolo) driver ●m (Electr) conductor. **~t'tura** f duct

confabu'lare vi have a confab

confa'cente adj suitable. **con'farsi** vr confarsi a suit

confederazi'one f confederation

confe'renz|a f (discorso) lecture; (congresso) conference. **~a stampa** news conference. **~i'ere**, **-a** mf lecturer

confe'rire vt (donare) give ●vi confer

con'ferma f confirmation. **confer'mare** vt confirm

confes'sa|re vt, **~rsi** vr confess. **~io'nale** adj & m confessional. **~i'one** f confession. **~ore** m confessor

con'fetto m sugared almond

confet'tura f jam

confezio'na|re vt manufacture; make (abiti); package (merci). **~to** adj (vestiti) off-the-peg; (gelato) wrapped

confezi'one f manufacture; (di abiti) tailoring; (di pacchi) packaging; **confezioni** pl clothes. **~ regalo** gift pack

confic'car|e vt thrust. **~si** vr run into

confi'd|are vi **~are** in trust ●vt confide. **~arsi** vr **~arsi con** confide in. **~ente** adj confident ●mf confidant

confi'denz|a f confidence; (familiarità) familiarity; **prendersi delle ~e** take liberties. **~i'ale** adj confidential; (rapporto, tono) familiar

configu'ra|re vt (Comput) configure. **~zi'one** f configuration

confi'nante adj neighbouring

confi'na|re vi (relegare) confine ●vi **~re con** border on. **~rsi** vr withdraw. **~to** adj confined

con'fin|e m border; (tra terreni) boundary. **~o** m political exile

con'fisca f (di proprietà) forfeiture. **~'scare** vt confiscate

con'flitt|o m conflict. **~u'ale** adj adversarial

conflu'enza f confluence; (di strade) junction

conflu'ire vi (fiumi:) flow together; (strade:) meet

con'fonder|e vt confuse; (turbare) confound; (imbarazzare) embarrass. **~si** vr (mescolarsi) mingle; (turbarsi) become confused; (sbagliarsi) be mistaken

confor'ma|re vt adapt. **~rsi** vr conform. **~zi'one** f conformity (a

with); (del terreno) composition
con'forme adj according. **~mente**
adv accordingly
confor'mi|smo m conformity.
~sta mf conformist. **~tà** f (a norma)
conformity
confor'tante adj comforting
confor't|are vt comfort. **~evole**
adj (comodo) comfortable. **con'forto** m
comfort
confron'tare vt compare
con'fronto m comparison; **in ~ a**
by comparison with; **nei tuoi con-
fronti** towards you; **senza ~** far
and away
confusi|o'nario adj (persona)
muddle-headed. **~'ne** f confusion;
(baccano) racket; (disordine) mess; (imbarazzo) embarrassment. **con'fuso** pp
di **confondere** ● adj confused; (indi-
stinto) indistinct; (imbarazzato) embarrassed
conge'dar|e vt dismiss; (Mil) dis-
charge. **~si** vr take one's leave
con'gedo m leave; **essere in ~** be
on leave. **~ malattia** sick leave. **~
maternità** maternity leave
conge'gnare vt devise; (mettere insieme) assemble. **con'gegno** m device
congela'mento m freezing; (Med)
frost-bite
congela're vt freeze. **~to** adj
(cibo) deep-frozen. **~tore** m freezer
congeni'ale adj congenial
con'genito adj congenital
congestio'na|re vt congest. **~to**
adj (traffico) congested. **conge-
sti'one** f congestion
conget'tura f conjecture
congi'unger|e vt join; combine
(sforzi). **~si** vr join
congiunti'vite f conjunctivitis
congiun'tivo m subjunctive
congi'unto pp di **congiungere** ● adj
joined ● m relative
congiun'tu|ra f joint; (circostanza)

juncture; (situazione) situation. **~'rale**
adj economic
congiunzi'one f conjunction
congi'u|ra f conspiracy. **~'rare** vi
conspire
conglome'rato m conglomerate;
fig conglomeration; (da costruzione)
concrete
congratu'la|rsi vr **~rsi con qcno
per** congratulate sb on. **~zi'oni** fpl
congratulations
con'grega f band
congre'ga|re vt, **~rsi** vr congre-
gate. **~zi'one** f congregation
con'gresso m congress
'congruo adj proper; (giusto) fair
conguagli'are vt balance. **con-
gu'aglio** m balance
coni'are vt coin
'conico adj conical
co'nifera f conifer
co'niglio m rabbit
coniu'gale adj marital; (vita)
married
coniu'ga|re vt conjugate. **~rsi** vr
get married. **~zi'one** f conjugation
'coniuge mf spouse
connessi'one f connection. **con-
'nesso** pp di **connettere**
con'netter|e vt connect ● vi think
rationally. **~rsi** vr go online
conni'vente adj conniving
conno'ta|re vt feature. **~to** m
distinguishing feature; **~ti** pl description
con'nubio m fig union
'cono m cone
cono'scen|te mf acquaintance.
~za f knowledge; (persona) acquaint-
ance; (sensi) consciousness; **perdere
~za** lose consciousness; **riprendere
~za** regain consciousness
co'nosc|ere vt know; (essere a cono-
scenza di) be acquainted with; (fare la
conoscenza di) meet. **~i'tore**, **~i'trice**
mf connoisseur. **~i'uto** pp di **cono-**

scere ● adj well-known

con'quist|a f conquest. conqui-'stare vt conquer; fig win

consa'cra|re vt consecrate; ordain (sacerdote); (dedicare) dedicate. ~rsi vr devote oneself

consangu'ineo, -a mf bloodrelation

consa'pevo|le adj conscious. ~'lezza f consciousness. ~l'mente adv consciously

'conscio adj conscious

consecu'tivo adj consecutive; (seguente) next

con'segna f delivery; (merce) consignment; (custodia) care; (di prigioniero) handover; (Mil: ordine) orders pl; (Mil: punizione) confinement; pagamento alla ~ cash on delivery

conse'gnare vt deliver; (affidare) give in charge; (Mil) confine to barracks

consegu'en|te adj consequent. ~za f consequence; di ~za (perciò) consequently

consegui'mento m achievement

consegu'ire vt achieve ● vi follow

con'senso m consent

consensu'ale adj consensus-based

consen'tire vi consent ● vt allow

con'serva f preserve; (di frutta) jam; (di agrumi) marmalade. ~ di pomodoro tomato sauce

conser'var|e vt preserve; (mantenere) keep. ~si vr keep; ~si in salute keep well

conserva'tore, -'trice mf (Pol) conservative

conserva'torio m conservatory

conservazi'one f preservation; a lunga ~ long-life

conside'ra|re vt consider; (stimare) regard. ~to adj (stimato) esteemed. ~zi'one f consideration; (osservazione, riflessione) remark

conside'revole adj considerable

consigli'abile adj advisable

consigli'ar|e vt advise; (raccomandare) recommend. ~'arsi vr ~arsi con qcno ask sb's advice. ~'ere, -a mf adviser; (membro di consiglio) councillor

con'siglio m advice; (ente) council. ~ d'amministrazione board of directors. C~ dei Ministri Cabinet

consi'sten|te adj substantial; (spesso) thick; (fig: argomento) valid. ~za f consistency

con'sistere vi ~ in consist of

consoci'ata f associate company

conso'lar|e[1] vt console; (rallegrare) cheer. ~si vr console oneself

conso'la|re[2] adj consular. ~to m consulate

consolazi'one f consolation; (gioia) joy

'console m consul

consoli'dar|e vt, ~si vr consolidate

conso'nante f consonant

'consono adj consistent

con'sorte mf consort

con'sorzio m consortium

con'stare vi ~ di consist of; (risultare) appear; a quanto mi consta as far as I know; mi consta che it appears that

consta'tare vt ascertain. ~zi'one f observation

consu'e|to adj & m usual. ~tudi-'nario adj (diritto) common; (persona) set in one's ways. ~'tudine f habit; (usanza) custom

consu'len|te mf consultant. ~za f consultancy

consul'tare vt consult. ~rsi con consult with. ~zi'one f consultation

consul'tivo adj consultative. ~orio m clinic

consu'ma|re vt (usare) consume; wear out (abito, scarpe); consummate (matrimonio); commit (delitto). ~rsi vr consume; (abito, scarpe) wear out; (*struggersi*) pine

consu'mato *adj* (politico) seasoned; (scarpe, tappeto) worn

consuma'tore, -'trice *mf* consumer. ~**zi'one** *f* (bibita) drink; (spuntino) snack

consu'mismo *m* consumerism. ~**ta** *mf* consumerist

con'sumo *m* consumption; (di abito, scarpe) wear; (uso) use; **generi di ~** consumer goods or items. **~ [di carburante]** [fuel] consumption

consun'tivo *m* [bilancio] **~** final statement

conta'balle *mf* 🛈 storyteller

con'tabil|e *adj* book-keeping ● *mf* accountant. ~**ità** *f* accounting; **tenere la ~ità** keep the accounts

contachilo'metri *m inv* mileometer, odometer *Am*

conta'dino, -a *mf* farm-worker; (medievale) peasant

contagi'are *vt* infect. **con'tagio** *m* infection. ~**oso** *adj* infectious

conta'gocce *m inv* dropper

contami'na|re *vt* contaminate. ~**zi'one** *f* contamination

con'tante *m* cash; **pagare in contanti** pay cash

con'tare *vt/i* count; (tenere conto di) take into account; (proporsi) intend

conta'scatti *m inv* (Teleph) time-unit counter

conta'tore *m* meter

contat'tare *vt* contact. **con'tatto** *m* contact

'conte *m* count

conteggi'are *vt* put on the bill ● *vi* calculate. **con'teggio** *m* calculation. **conteggio alla rovescia** countdown

con'te|gno *m* behaviour; (atteggiamento) attitude. ~**'gnoso** *adj* dignified

contem'pla|re *vt* contemplate; (fissare) gaze at. ~**zi'one** *f* contemplation

con'tempo *m* **nel ~** in the meantime

contempo|ranea'mente *adv* at once. ~**raneo, -a** *adj & mf* contemporary

conten'dente *mf* competitor. **con'tendere** *vi* compete; (litigare) quarrel ● *vt* contend

conte'n|ere *vt* contain; (reprimere) repress. ~**ersi** *vr* contain oneself. ~**i'tore** *m* container

conten'tarsi *vr* **~ di** be content with

conten'tezza *f* joy

conten'tino *m* placebo

con'tento *adj* glad; (soddisfatto) contented

conte'nuto *m* contents *pl*; (soggetto) content

contenzi'oso *m* legal department

con'tesa *f* disagreement; Sport contest. **~o** *pp di* contendere ● *adj* contested

con'tessa *f* countess

conte'sta|re *vt* contest; (Jur) notify. ~**tario** *adj* anti-establishment. ~**'tore, ~'trice** *mf* protester. ~**zi'one** *f* (disputa) dispute

con'testo *m* context

con'tiguo *adj* adjacent

continen'tale *adj* continental. **conti'nente** *m* continent

conti'nenza *f* continence

contin'gen|te *m* contingent; (quota) quota. ~**za** *f* contingency

continua'mente *adv* (senza interruzione) continuously; (frequentemente) continually

continu'a|re *vt/i* continue; (riprendere) resume. ~**tivo** *adj* permanent. ~**zi'one** *f* continuation. ~**ità** *f* continuity

con'tinuo *adj* continuous; (molto frequente) continual. **corrente ~a** direct current; **di ~o** continually

'conto *m* calculation; (Comm) account; (di ristorante ecc) bill; (stima) consideration; a conti fatti all things considered; far ~ di (supporre) suppose; (proporsi) intend; far ~ su rely on; in fin dei conti when all is said and done; per ~ di on behalf of; per ~ mio (a mio parere) in my opinion; (da solo) on my own; starsene per ~ proprio be on one's own; rendersi ~ di qcsa realize sth; sul ~ di qcno (voci, informazioni) about sb; tener ~ di qcsa take sth into account; tenere da ~ qcsa look after sth. ~ corrente current account, checking account Am. ~ alla rovescia countdown

con'torcer|e vt twist. ~si vr twist about

contor'nare vt surround

con'torno m contour; (Culin) vegetables pl

contorsi'one f contortion. con'torto pp di contorcere

contrabban|'dare vt smuggle. ~di'ere, -a mf smuggler. contrab'bando m contraband

contrab'basso m double bass

contraccambi'are vt return. contrac'cambio m return

contracce't'tivo m contraceptive. ~zi'one f contraception

contrac'col|po m rebound; (di arma a fuoco) recoil; fig repercussion

con'trada f (rione) district

contrad'detto pp di contraddire

contrad'di|re vt contradict. ~t'torio adj contradictory. ~zi'one f contradiction

contraddi'stin|guere vt differentiate. ~to adj distinct

contra'ente mf contracting party

contra'ereo adj anti-aircraft

contraf'fa|re vt disguise; (imitare) imitate; (falsificare) forge. ~tto adj forged. ~zi'one f disguising; (imitazione) imitation; (falsificazione) forgery

con'tralto m countertenor ● f

contralto

contrap'peso m counterbalance

contrap'por|re vt counter; (confrontare) compare. ~si vr contrast; ~si a be opposed to

contraria'mente adv contrary (a to)

contrari'are vt oppose; (infastidire) annoy. ~arsi vr get annoyed. ~età f inv adversity; (ostacolo) set-back

con'trario adj contrary; (direzione) opposite; (sfavorevole) unfavourable ● m contrary; al ~ on the contrary

con'trarre vt contract

contras'se|gnare vt mark. ~'segno m mark; [in] ~segno (spedizione) cash on delivery

contra'stare vt oppose; (contestare) contest ● vi clash. con'trasto m contrast; (litigio) dispute

contrattac'care vt counterattack. contrat'tacco m counter-attack

contrat'ta|re vt/i negotiate; (mercanteggiare) bargain. ~zi'one f (salariale) bargaining

contrat'tempo m hitch

con'tratt|o pp di contrarre ● m contract. ~o a termine fixed-term contract. ~u'ale adj contractual

contravve'n|ire vi contravene. ~zi'one f contravention; (multa) fine

contrazi'one f contraction; (di prezzi) reduction

contribu'ente mf contributor; (del fisco) taxpayer

contribu'ire vi contribute. contri'buto m contribution

'contro prep against; ~ di me against me ● m i pro e i ~ the pros and cons

contro'battere vt counter

controbilanci'are vt counterbalance

controcor'rente adj nonconformist ● adv upriver; fig upstream

controffen'siva f counteroffensive

controfi'gura f stand-in

controindicazi'one f (Med) contraindication

control'la|re vt check; (verificare) check; (collaudare) test. **~rsi** vr have self-control. **~to** adj controlled

con'trol|lo m control; (verifica) check; (Med) check-up. **~lo delle nascite** birth control. **~lore** m controller; (sui treni ecc) [ticket] inspector. **~lore di volo** air-traffic controller

contro'mano adv in the wrong direction

contromi'sura f countermeasure

contropi'ede m **prendere in ~** catch off guard

controprodu'cente adj self-defeating

con'trordin|e m counter order; **salvo ~i** unless I/you hear to the contrary

contro'senso m contradiction in terms

controspio'naggio m counter-espionage

contro'vento adv against the wind

contro'vers|ia f controversy; (Jur) dispute. **~o** adj controversial

contro'voglia adv unwillingly

contu'macia f default; **in ~** in one's absence

contun'dente adj (corpo, arma) blunt

contusi'one f bruise

convale'scen|te adj convalescent

con'vali|da f validation. **~'dare** vt confirm; validate (atto, biglietto)

con'vegno m meeting; (congresso) congress

conve'nevol|e adj suitable; **~i** pl pleasantries

conveni'en|te adj convenient; (prezzo) attractive; (vantaggioso) ad-

vantageous. **~za** f convenience; (interesse) advantage; (di prezzo) attractiveness

conve'nire vi (riunirsi) gather; (concordare) agree; (ammettere) admit; (essere opportuno) be convenient ● vt agree on; **ci conviene andare** it is better to go; **non mi conviene stancarmi** I'd better not tire myself out

con'vento m (di suore) convent; (di frati) monastery

conve'nuto adj fixed

convenzio'nale adj conventional. **~'one** f convention

conver'gen|te adj converging. **~za** f fig confluence

con'vergere vi converge

conver'sa|re vi converse. **~zi'one** f conversation

conversi'one f conversion

con'verso pp di convergere

conver'tibile f (Auto) convertible

conver'ti|re vt convert. **~rsi** vr be converted. **~to, -a** mf convert

con'vesso adj convex

convin'cente adj convincing

con'vin|cere vt convince. **~to** adj convinced. **~zi'one** f conviction

con'vitto m boarding school

convi'ven|te m common-law husband ● f common-law wife. **~za** f cohabitation. **con'vivere** vi live together

convivi'ale adj convivial

convo'ca|re vt convene. **~zi'one** f convening

convogli'are vt convey; convoy (navi) **con'voglio** m convoy; (ferroviario) train

convulsi'one f convulsion. **con'vulso** adj convulsive; (febbrile) feverish

coope'ra|re vi co-operate. **~'tiva** f co-operative. **~zi'one** f co-operation

coordina'mento m co-ordination

coordi'na|re vt co-ordinate. ∼ta f (Math) coordinate. ∼te bancarie bank (account) details. ∼zi'one f co-ordination

co'perchio m lid; (copertura) cover

co'perta f blanket; (copertura) cover; (Naut) deck

coper'tina f cover; (di libro) dust-jacket

co'perto pp di coprire ● adj covered; (cielo) overcast ● m (a tavola) place; (prezzo del coperto) cover charge; al ∼ under cover

coper'tone m tarpaulin; (gomma) tyre

coper'tura f covering; (Comm, Fin) cover

'copia f copy; bella/brutta ∼ fair/rough copy; ∼ carbone carbon copy. ∼ su carta hardcopy. copi'are vt copy

copi'one m script

copi'oso adj plentiful

'coppa f (calice) goblet; (per gelato ecc) dish; Sport cup. ∼ [di] gelato ice-cream (served in a dish)

cop'petta f bowl; (di gelato) small tub

'coppia f couple; (in carte) pair

co'prente adj (cipria, vernice) covering

copri'capo m headgear

copri'fuoco m curfew

copri'letto m bedspread

copripiu'mino m duvet cover

co'pri|re vt cover; drown (suono); hold (carica). ∼si vr (vestirsi) cover up; fig cover oneself; (cielo) become overcast

coque f alla ∼ (uovo) soft-boiled

co'raggi|o m courage; (sfacciaggine) nerve; ∼o! come on. ∼'oso adj courageous

co'rale adj choral

co'rallo m coral

Co'rano m Koran

co'raz|za f armour; (di animali) shell. ∼'zata f battleship. ∼'zato adj (nave) armour-clad

corbelle'ria f nonsense; (sproposito) blunder

'corda f cord; (Mus, spago) string; (fune) rope; (cavo) cable; essere giù di ∼ be depressed; dare ∼ a qcno encourage sb. corde vocali vocal cords

cordi'al|e adj cordial ● m (bevanda) cordial; ∼i saluti best wishes. ∼ità f cordiality

'cordless m inv cordless phone

cor'doglio m grief; (lutto) mourning

cor'done m cord; (schieramento) cordon

core ogra'fia f choreography. ∼'ografo, -a mf choreographer

cori'andoli mpl confetti sg

cori'andolo m (spezia) coriander

cori'car|e vt put to bed. ∼si vr go to bed

co'rista mf choir member

corna ▷CORNO

cor'nacchia f crow

corna'musa f bagpipes pl

cor'nett|a f (Mus) cornet; (del telefono) receiver. ∼o m (brioche) croissant

cor'ni|ce f frame. ∼ci'one m cornice

'corno m (pl ∼a corna) horn; fare le corna a qcno be unfaithful to sb; fare le corna (per scongiuro) touch wood. cor'nuto adj horned ● m (꞊: marito tradito) cuckold; (insulto) bastard

'coro m chorus; (Relig) choir

co'rolla f corolla

co'rona f crown; (di fiori) wreath; (rosario) rosary. ∼'mento m (di impresa) crowning. coro'nare vt crown; (sogno) fulfil

cor'petto m bodice

'corpo m body; (Mil, diplomatico) corps inv; ∼ a ∼ man to man; andare di ~ move one's bowels. ~ di ballo corps de ballet. ~ insegnante teaching staff. ~ del reato incriminating item

corpo'rale adj corporal

corporati'vismo m corporatism

corpora'tura f build

corporazi'one f corporation

cor'poreo adj bodily

cor'poso adj full-bodied

corpu'lento adj stout

cor'puscolo m corpuscle

corre'dare vt equip

corre'dino m (per neonato) layette

cor'redo m (nuziale) trousseau

cor'reggere vt correct; lace (bevanda)

corre'lare vt correlate

cor'rente adj running; (in vigore) current; (frequente) everyday; (inglese ecc) fluent ● f current; (d'aria) draught; essere al ~ be up to date. ~'mente adv (parlare) fluently

'correre vi run; (affrettarsi) hurry; Sport race; (notizie:) circulate; ~ dietro a run after ● vt run; ~ un pericolo run a risk; lascia ~! don't bother!

corret|ta'mente adv correctly. cor'retto pp di correggere ● adj correct; (caffè) with a drop of alcohol. ~zi'one f correction

cor'rida f bullfight

corri'doio m corridor; (Aeron) aisle

corri'|dore, -'trice mf racer; (a piedi) runner

corri'era f coach, bus

corri'ere m courier; (posta) mail; (spedizioniere) carrier

corri'mano m bannister

corrispet'tivo m amount due

corrispon'den|te adj corresponding ● mf correspondent. ~za f correspondence; scuola/corsi per ~za correspondence course; vendite per ~za mail-order [shopping]. corri-

'spondere vi correspond; (stanza:) communicate; corrispondere a (contraccambiare) return

corri'sposto adj (amore) reciprocated

corrobo'rare vt strengthen; fig corroborate

cor'roder|e vt, ~si vr corrode

cor'rompere vt corrupt; (con denaro) bribe

corrosi'one f corrosion. corro'sivo adj corrosive

cor'roso pp di corrodere

cor'rotto pp di corrompere ● adj corrupt

corrucci'a|rsi vr be vexed. ~to adj upset

corru'gare vt wrinkle; ~ la fronte knit one's brows

corruzi'one f corruption; (con denaro) bribery

'corsa f running; (rapida) dash; Sport race; (di treno ecc) journey; di ~ at a run; fare una ~ run

cor'sia f gangway; (di ospedale) ward; (Auto) lane; (di supermercato) aisle

cor'sivo m italics pl

'corso pp di correre ● m course; (strada) main street; (Comm) circulation; lavori in ~ work in progress; nel ~ di during. ~ d'acqua watercourse

'corte f [court]yard; (Jur, regale) court; fare la ~ a qcno court sb. ~ d'appello court of appeal

cor'teccia f bark

corteggia'mento m courtship

corteggi'a|re vt court. ~tore m admirer

cor'teo m procession

cor'te|se adj courteous. ~sia f courtesy; per ~sia please

cortigi'ano, -a mf courtier ● f courtesan

cor'tile m courtyard

cor'tina f curtain; (schermo) screen

'corto adj short; essere a ∼ di be short of. ∼ **circuito** m short [circuit]

cortome'traggio m Cinema short

cor'vino adj jet-black

'corvo m raven

'cosa f thing; (faccenda) matter; inter, rel what; [che] ∼ what; nessuna ∼ nothing; ogni ∼ everything; per prima ∼ first of all; tante cose so many things; (augurio) all the best

'cosca f clan

'coscia f thigh; (Culin) leg

cosci'en|te adj conscious. ∼**za** f conscience; (consapevolezza) consciousness

co'scri|tto m conscript. ∼**zi'one** f conscription

così adv so; (in questo modo) like this, like that; (perciò) therefore; le cose stanno ∼ that's how things stand; fermo ∼! I hold it; proprio ∼! exactly!; basta ∼! that will do!; ah, è ∼? it's like that, is it?; ∼ ∼ so-so; e ∼ via and so on; per ∼ dire so to speak; più di ∼ any more; una ∼ cara ragazza! such a nice girl!; è stato ∼ generoso da aiutarti he was kind enough to help you ●conj (allora) so ●adj inv (tale) like that; una ragazza ∼ a girl like that

cosicché conj and so

cosid'detto adj so-called

co'smesi f cosmetics

co'smetico adj & m cosmetic

'cosmico adj cosmic

'cosmo m cosmos

cosmopo'lita adj cosmopolitan

co'spargere vt sprinkle; (disseminare) scatter

co'spetto m al ∼ di in the presence of

co'spicuo adj conspicuous; (somma ecc) considerable

cospi'ra|re vi conspire. ∼**tore**, ∼**'trice** mf conspirator. ∼**zi'one** f conspiracy

'costa f coast; (Anat) rib

co'stà adv there

co'stan|te adj & f constant. ∼**za** f constancy

co'stare vi cost; quanto costa? how much is it?

co'stata f chop

costeggi'are vt (per mare) coast; (per terra) skirt

co'stei pers pron ▷COSTUI

costellazi'one f constellation

coster'na|to adj dismayed. ∼**zi'one** f consternation

costi'era f stretch of coast. ∼**o** adj coastal

costi'pa|to adj constipated. ∼**zi'one** f constipation; (raffreddore) bad cold

costitu'ir|e vt constitute; (formare) form; (nominare) appoint. ∼**si** vr (Jur) give oneself up

costituzio'nale adj constitutional. **costituzi'one** f constitution; (fondazione) setting up

'costo m cost; ad ogni ∼ at all costs; a nessun ∼ on no account

'costola f rib; (di libro) spine

co'stoletta f cutlet

co'storo pron ▷COSTUI

co'stoso adj costly

co'stretto pp di costringere

co'strin|gere vt compel; (stringere) constrict. ∼**'tivo** adj coercive

costru'ir|e vt build. ∼**t'tivo** adj constructive. ∼**zi'one** f construction

co'stui, **co'stei**, pl co'storo pron (soggetto) he, she, pl they; (complemento) him, her, pl them

co'stume m (usanza) custom; (condotta) morals pl; (indumento) costume. ∼ **da bagno** swim-suit; (da uomo) swimming trunks

co'tenna f pigskin; (della pancetta) rind

coto'letta f cutlet

co'tone m cotton. ~ **idrofilo** cotton wool, absorbent cotton Am

'cottimo m lavorare a ~ do piece-work

'cotto pp di **cuocere** ● adj done; (fig: infatuato) in love; (fig: sbronzo) drunk; **ben** ~ (carne) well done

'cotton fi'oc® m inv cotton bud

cot'tura f cooking

co'vare vt hatch; sicken for (malattia); harbour (odio) ● vi smoulder

'covo m den

co'vone m sheaf

'cozza f mussel

coz'zare vi ~ **contro** bump into. **'cozzo** m fig clash

C.P. abbr (Casella Postale) PO Box

'crampo m cramp

'cranio m skull

cra'tere m crater

cra'vatta f tie; (a farfalla) bow-tie

cre'anza f politeness; **mala** ~ bad manners

cre'a|re vt create; (causare) cause. ~**tività** f creativity. ~**tivo** adj creative. ~**to** m creation. ~**tore**, ~**trice** m creator. ~**zi'one** f creation

crea'tura f creature; (bambino) baby; **povera** ~! poor thing!

cre'den|te mf believer. ~**za** f belief; (Comm) credit; (mobile) sideboard. ~**zi'ali** fpl credentials

'crede|re vt believe; (pensare) think ● vi ~**e in** believe in; **credo di sì** I think so; **non ti credo** I don't believe you. ~**si** vr think oneself to be. **cre'dibile** adj credible. **credibilità** f credibility

'credi|to m credit; (stima) esteem; **comprare a** ~**to** buy on credit. ~**tore**, ~**trice** m creditor

credulità f credulity

'credu|lo adj credulous. ~**lone**, ~**a** mf simpleton

'crema f cream; (di uova e latte) custard. ~ **idratante** moisturizer. ~ **pasticcera** egg custard. ~ **solare** suntan lotion

cre'ma|re vt cremate. ~**torio** m crematorium. ~**zi'one** f cremation

'crème cara'mel f crème caramel

creme'ria f dairy (also selling ice cream and cakes)

'crepa f crack

cre'paccio m cleft; (di ghiacciaio) crevasse

crepacu'ore m heart-break

crepa'pelle: **a** ~ adv fit to burst; **ridere a** ~ split one's sides with laughter

cre'pare vi crack; (fam: morire) kick the bucket; ~ **dal ridere** laugh fit to burst

crepa'tura f crevice

crêpe f inv pancake

crepi'tare vi crackle

cre'puscolo m twilight

cre'scendo m crescendo

'cresc|ere vi grow; (aumentare) increase ● vt (allevare) bring up; (aumentare) increase. ~**ita** f growth; (aumento) increase. ~**i'uto** pp di **crescere**

cresi'ma f confirmation. ~**mare** vt confirm

'crespo adj frizzy ● m crêpe

'cresta f crest; (cima) peak

'creta f clay

'Creta f Crete

cre'tino, -a adj stupid ● mf idiot

cric m inv jack

cri'ceto m hamster

crimi'na|le adj & mf criminal. ~**ità** f crime. **'crimine** m crime

crimi'noso adj criminal

'crin|e m horsehair. ~**i'era** f mane

'cripta f crypt

crisan'temo m chrysanthemum

'crisi f inv crisis; (Med) fit

cristal'lino m crystalline

cristalliz'zar|e vt, ~**si** vr crystallize; *fig:* (parola, espressione:) become part of the language

cri'stallo *m* crystal

Cristia'nesimo *m* Christianity

cristi'ano, -a *adj* & *mf* Christian

'Cristo *m* Christ; **un povero c~** a poor beggar

cri'terio *m* criterion; (*buon senso*) [common] sense

'criti|ca *f* criticism; (*recensione*) review. **criti'care** *vt* criticize. **~co** *adj* critical ● *m* critic. **~cone, -a** *mf* fault-finder

crivel'lare *vt* riddle (**di** with)

cri'vello *m* sieve

Cro'azia *f* Croatia

croc'cante *adj* crisp ● *m* type of crunchy nut biscuit

croc'chetta *f* croquette

'croce *f* cross; **a occhio e ~** roughly. **C~ Rossa** Red Cross

croce'via *m inv* crossroads *sg*

croci'ata *f* crusade

cro'cicchio *m* crossroads *sg*

croci'era *f* cruise; (*Archit*) crossing

croci'fi|ggere *vt* crucify. **~ssi'one** *f* crucifixion. **~sso** *pp di* **crocifiggere** ● *adj* crucified ● *m* crucifix

crogio'larsi *vr* bask

crogi|u'olo *m* crucible; *fig* melting pot

crol'lare *vi* collapse; (*prezzi:*) slump. **'crollo** *m* collapse; (*dei prezzi*) slump

cro'mato *adj* chromium-plated.

'cromo *m* chrome. **cromo'soma** *m* chromosome

'cronaca *f* chronicle; (*di giornale*) news; (*Radio, TV*) commentary; **fatto di ~** news item. **~ nera** crime news

'cronico *adj* chronic

cro'nista *mf* reporter

crono'logico *adj* chronological

crono'metrare *vt* time

cro'nometro *m* chronometer

'crosta *f* crust; (*di formaggio*) rind; (*di ferita*) scab; (*quadro*) daub

cro'staceo *m* shellfish

cro'stata *f* tart

cro'stino *m* croûton

crucci'arsi *vr* worry. **'cruccio** *m* worry

cruci'ale *adj* crucial

cruci'verba *m inv* crossword [puzzle]

cru'del|e *adj* cruel. **~tà** *f inv* cruelty

'crudo *adj* raw; (*rigido*) harsh

cru'ento *adj* bloody

cru'miro *m* blackleg, scab

'crusca *f* bran

cru'scotto *m* dashboard

'Cuba *f* Cuba

cu'betto *m* **~ di ghiaccio** ice cube

'cubico *adj* cubic

cubi'tal|e *adj* **a caratteri ~i** in enormous letters

'cubo *m* cube

cuc'cagna *f* abundance; (*baldoria*) merry-making; **paese della ~** land of plenty

cuc'cetta *f* (*su un treno*) couchette; (*Naut*) berth

cucchia'ino *m* teaspoon

cucchi'a|io *m* spoon; **al ~io** (*dolce*) creamy. **~i'ata** *f* spoonful

'cuccia *f* dog's bed; **fa la ~!** lie down!

cuccio'lata *f* litter

'cucciolo *m* puppy

cu'cina *f* kitchen; (*il cucinare*) cooking; (*cibo*) food; (*apparecchio*) cooker; **far da ~** cook; **libro di ~** cook[ery] book. **~ a gas** gas cooker

cuci'n|are *vt* cook. **~ino** *m* kitchenette

cu'ci|re *vt* sew; **macchina per ~re** sewing-machine. **~to** *m* sewing. **~tura** *f* seam

cucù *m inv* cuckoo

'cuculo *m* cuckoo

'cuffia f bonnet; (da bagno) bathing-cap; (ricevitore) headphones pl

cu'gino, -a mf cousin

'cui pron rel (persona: con prep) who, whom fml; (cose, animali: con prep) which; (tra articolo e nome) whose; la persona con ~ ho parlato the person [who] I spoke to; la ditta per ~ lavoro the company I work for, the company for which I work; l'amico di ~ (dove) where; (quando) when; that; per ~ (perciò) so; la città in ~ vivo the city I live in, the city where I live; il giorno in ~ l'ho visto the day [that] I saw him

culi'nari|a f cookery. ~o adj culinary

'culla f cradle. cul'lare vt rock

culmi'na|nte adj culminating. ~re vi culminate. 'culmine m peak

'culto m cult; (Relig) religion; (adorazione) worship

cul'tu|ra f culture. ~ra generale general knowledge. ~rale adj cultural

cultu'ris|mo m body-building

cumula'tivo adj cumulative; biglietto ~ group ticket

'cumulo m pile; (mucchio) heap; (nuvola) cumulus

'cuneo m wedge

cu'netta f gutter

cu'ocere vt/i cook; fire (ceramica)

cu'oco, -a mf cook

cu'oio m leather. ~ capelluto scalp

cu'ore m heart; cuori pl (carte) hearts; nel profondo del ~ in one's heart of hearts; di [buon] ~ (persona) kind-hearted; nel ~ della notte in the middle of the night; stare a ~ a qcno be very important to sb

cupi'digia f greed

'cupo adj gloomy; (suono) deep

'cupola f dome

'cura f care; (amministrazione) management; (Med) treatment; a ~ di edited by; in ~ under treatment. ~ dimagrante diet. cu'rante adj medico curante GP, doctor

cu'rar|e vt take care of; (Med) treat; (guarire) cure; edit (testo). ~si vr take care of oneself; (Med) follow a treatment; ~si di (badare a) mind

cu'rato m parish priest

cura'to|re, -'trice mf trustee; (di testo) editor

'curia f curia

curio's|are vi be curious; (mettere il naso) pry (in into); (nei negozi) look around. ~ità f inv curiosity. curi'oso adj curious; (strano) odd

cur'sore m (Comput) cursor

'curva f curve; (stradale) bend. ~ a gomito U-bend. cur'vare vt/i curve; (strada:) bend. cur'varsi vr bend. 'curvo adj curved; (piegato) bent

cusci'netto m pad; (Mech) bearing

cu'scino m cushion; (guanciale) pillow. ~ d'aria air cushion

'cuspide f spire

cu'stod|e m caretaker. ~e giudiziario official receiver. ~ia f care; (Jur) custody; (astuccio) case. custo'dire vt keep; (badare) look after

cu'taneo adj skin attrib

'cute f skin

Dd

da prep from; (con verbo passivo) by; (moto a luogo) to; (moto per luogo) through; (stato in luogo) at; (continuativo) for; (causale) with; (in qualità di) as; (con caratteristica) with; (come) like; (temporale) since, for

da si traduce con **for** quando si tratta di un periodo di tempo e con **since** quando si riferisce al momento in cui qualcosa è cominciato. Nota che in inglese si usa il passato prossimo invece del presente: aspetto da mesi I've been waiting for months; aspetto da lunedì I've been waiting since Monday

···▶ da Roma a Milano from Rome to Milan; staccare un quadro dalla parete take a picture off the wall; i bambini dai 5 ai 10 anni children between 5 and 10; vedere qcsa da vicino/lontano see sth from up close/from a distance; scritto da written by; andare dal panettiere go to the baker's; passo da te più tardi I'll come over to your place later; passiamo da qui let's go this way; un appuntamento dal dentista an appointment at the dentist's; il treno passa da Venezia the train goes through Venice; dall'anno scorso since last year; vivo qui da due anni I've been living here for two years; da domani from tomorrow; piangere dal dolore cry with pain; ho molto da fare I have a lot to do; occhiali da sole sunglasses; qualcosa da mangiare something to eat; un uomo dai capelli scuri a man with dark hair; è un oggetto da poco it's not worth much; l'ho fatto da solo I did it by myself; si è fatto da sé he is a self-made man; non è da lui it's not like him

dac'capo adv again; (dall'inizio) from the beginning

dacché conj since

'dado m dice; (Culin) stock cube; (Techn) nut

daf'fare m work

'dagli = DA + GLI. **'dai** = DA + I

'dai int come on!

'daino m deer; (pelle) buckskin

dal = DA + IL. **'dalla** = DA + LA. **'dalle** = DA + LE. **'dallo** = DA + LO

'dalia f dahlia

dal'tonico adj colour-blind

'dama f lady; (nei balli) partner; (gioco) draughts sg

dami'gella f (di sposa) bridesmaid

damigi'ana f demijohn

dam'meno adv non essere ~ (di qcno) be no less good (than sb)

da'naro m = DENARO

dana'roso adj (fam: ricco) loaded

da'nese adj Danish ● mf Dane ● m (lingua) Danish

Dani'marca f Denmark

dan'na|re vt damn; far ~re qcno drive sb mad. ~to adj damned. ~zi'one f damnation

danneggia'mento m damage. ~'are vt damage; (nuocere) harm

'danno m damage; (a persona) harm. **dan'noso** adj harmful

'danza f dance; (il danzare) dancing. **dan'zare** vi dance

dapper'tutto adv everywhere

dap'poco adj worthless

dap'prima adv at first

'dardo m dart

'dar|e vt give; take (esame); have (festa); ~ qcsa a qcno give sb sth; ~ da mangiare a qcno give sb something to eat; ~ il benvenuto a qcno welcome sb; ~ la buonanotte a qcno say good night to sb; ~ del tu/del lei a qcno address sb as "tu"/"lei"; ~ del cretino a qcno call sb an idiot; ~ qcsa per scontato take sth for granted; **cosa danno alla TV stasera?** what's on TV tonight? ♦ *vi* ~ **nell'occhio** be conspicuous; ~ **alla testa go to one's head**; ~ **su** (finestra, casa:) look on to; ~ **sui o ai nervi a qcno** get on sb's nerves ●*m* (Comm) debit. ~**si** *vr* (scambiarsi) give each other; ~**si da fare** get down to it; **si è dato tanto da fare!** he went to so much trouble!; ~**si a** (cominciare) take up; ~**si al bere** take to drink; ~**si per** (malato) pretend to be; ~**si per vinto** give up; **può** ~**si** maybe

'darsena *f* dock

'data *f* date. ~ **di emissione** date of issue. ~ **di nascita** date of birth. ~ **di scadenza** cut-off date

da'ta|re *vt* date; **a** ~**re da** as from. ~**to** *adj* dated

'dato *adj* given; (dedito) addicted; ~ **che** given that ●*m* datum. ~ **di fatto** well-established fact; **dati** *pl* data. **da'tore** *m* giver. **datore, datrice** *mf* **di lavoro** employer

'dattero *m* date

dattilogra'f|are *vt* type. ~**ia** *f* typing. **datti'lografo, -a** *mf* typist

dat'torno *adv* **togliersi** ~ clear off

da'vanti *adv* before; (dirimpetto) opposite; (di fronte) in front ●*adj* *inv* front ●*m* front; ~ **a** *prep* in front of

da'vanzo *adv* more than enough

dav'vero *adv* really; **per** ~ in earnest; **dici** ~? honestly?

'dazio *m* duty; (ufficio) customs *pl*

d.C. *abbr* (dopo Cristo) AD

'dea *f* goddess

debel'lare *vt* defeat

debili'ta|nte *adj* weakening. ~**re** *vt* weaken. ~**rsi** *vr* become weaker

debita'mente *adv* duly

'debi|to *adj* due; **a tempo** ~**to** in due course ●*m* debt. ~**tore, ~trice** *mf* debtor

'debo|le *adj* weak; (luce) dim; (suono) faint ●*m* weak point; (prefe-

renza) weakness. ~**lezza** *f* weakness

debor'dare *vi* overflow

debosci'ato *adj* debauched

debut'ta|nte *m* (attore) actor making his début ●*f* actress making her début. ~**re** *vi* make one's début. **de'butto** *m* début

deca'den|te *adj* decadent. ~**tismo** *m* decadence. ~**za** *f* decline; (Jur) loss. **deca'dere** *vi* lapse. **decadi'mento** *m* (delle arti) decline

decaffei'nato *adj* decaffeinated ●*m* decaffeinated coffee

decan'tare *vt* (lodare) praise

decapi'ta|re *vt* decapitate; behead (condannato). ~**zi'one** *f* decapitation; beheading

decap'pottabile *adj* convertible

de'ce|dere *vi* (morire) die. ~**duto** *adj* deceased

decele'rare *vt* decelerate

decen'nale *adj* ten-yearly. **de'cennio** *m* decade

de'cen|te *adj* decent. ~**te'mente** *adv* decently. ~**za** *f* decency

decentra'mento *m* decentralization

de'cesso *m* death; **atto di** ~ death certificate

de'cider|e *vt* decide; settle (questione). ~**si** *vr* make up one's mind

deci'frare *vt* decipher; (documenti cifrati) decode

deci'male *adj* decimal

deci'mare *vt* decimate

'decimo *adj* tenth

de'cina *f* (Math) ten; **una** ~ **di** (circa dieci) about ten

decisa'mente *adv* definitely

decisio'nale *adj* decision-making

deci'si|one *f* decision. ~**sivo** *adj* decisive. **de'ciso** *pp* di **decidere** ●*adj* decided

decla'ma|re *vt/i* declaim. ~**torio** *adj* (stile) declamatory

declas'sare *vt* downgrade

decli'na|re vt decline; ~re ogni responsabilità disclaim all responsibility ● vi go down; (tramontare) set. ~zi'one f declension. **de'clino** m decline; in declino on the decline

decodificazi'one f decoding

decol'lare vi take off

décolle'té m inv décolleté

de'collo m take-off

decolo'ra|nte m bleach. ~re vt bleach

decolorazi'one f bleaching

decom'po|rre vt, ~rsi vr decompose. ~sizi'one f decomposition

deconcen'trarsi vr become distracted

deconge'lare vt defrost

decongestio'nare vt relieve congestion in

deco'ra|re vt decorate. ~'tivo adj decorative. ~to adj (ornato) decorated. ~'tore, ~'trice mf decorator. ~zi'one f decoration

de'coro m decorum

decorosa'mente adv decorously. **decoroso** adj dignified

decor'renza f ~ dal... starting from...

de'correre vi pass; a ~ da with effect from. **de'corso** pp di decorrere ● m passing; (Med) course

de'crepito adj decrepit

decre'scente adj decreasing. **de'crescere** vi decrease; (prezzi:) go down; (acque:) subside

decre'tare vt decree. **de'creto** m decree. **decreto legge** decree which has the force of law

'dedalo m maze

'dedica f dedication

dedi'car|e vt dedicate. ~si vr dedicate oneself

'dedi|to adj ~ a given to; (assorto) engrossed in; addicted to (vizi). ~zi'one f dedication

de'dotto pp di dedurre

dedu'cibile adj (tassa) allowable

de'du|rre vt deduce; (sottrarre) deduct. ~t'tivo adj deductive. ~zi'one f deduction

defal'care vt deduct

defe'rire vt (Jur) remit

defezio'nare vi (abbandonare) defect. ~'one f defection

defici'en|te adj (mancante) deficient; (Med) mentally deficient ● mf mental defective ~za f deficiency; (lacuna) gap; (Med) mental deficiency

'defici|t m inv deficit. ~'tario adj (bilancio) deficit attrib

defi'larsi vr (scomparire) slip away

défilé m inv fashion show

defi'ni|re vt define; (risolvere) settle. ~tiva'mente adv for good. ~'tivo adj definitive. ~to adj definite. ~zi'one f definition; (soluzione) settlement

deflazi'one f deflation

deflet'tore m (Auto) quarterlight

deflu'ire vi (liquidi:) flow away; (persone:) stream out

de'flusso m (di marea) ebb

defor'ma|re vt deform (arto); fig distort. ~si vr lose its shape. **de'forme** adj deformed. ~ità f deformity

defor'ma|to adj warped. ~zi'one f (di fatti) distortion

defrau'dare vt defraud

de'funto, -a adj & mf deceased

degene'ra|re vi degenerate. ~zi'one f degeneration. **de'genere** adj degenerate

de'gen|te mf patient. ~za f confinement

'degli = DI + GLI

deglu'tire vt swallow

de'gna|re vt ~ qcno di uno sguardo deign to look at sb

'degno adj worthy; (meritevole) deserving

degrada'mento m degradation

d

degra'da|re vt degrade. ~**rsi** vr lower oneself; (città) fall into disrepair. ~**zi'one** f degradation

de'grado m damage; ~ **ambientale** m environmental damage

degu'sta|re vt taste. ~**zi'one** f tasting

'dei = DI + I. **'del** = DI + IL

dela'|tore, -'trice mf [police] informer. ~**zi'one** f informing

'delega f proxy

dele'ga|re vt delegate. ~**to** m delegate. ~**zi'one** f delegation

dele'terio adj harmful

del'fino m dolphin; (stile di nuoto) butterfly [stroke]

de'libera f bylaw

delibe'ra|re vt/i deliberate; ~ **su**/**in** rule on/in. ~**to** adj deliberate

delicata'mente adv delicately

delica'tezza f delicacy; (fragilità) frailty; (tatto) tact

deli'cato adj delicate

delimi'tare vt delimit

deline'a|re vt outline. ~**rsi** vr be outlined; fig take shape. ~**to** adj defined

delin'quen|te mf delinquent. ~**za** f delinquency

deli'rante adj (Med) delirious; (assurdo) insane

deli'rare vi be delirious. **de'lirio** m delirium; fig frenzy

de'litt|o m crime. ~**u'oso** adj criminal

de'lizia f delight. ~**'are** vt delight. ~**'oso** adj delightful; (cibo) delicious

'della = DI + LA. **'delle** = DI + LE. **'dello** = DI + LO

delocaliz'zare vt relocate

'delta m inv delta

delta'piano m hang-glider; **fare** ~ go hang-gliding

delucidazi'one f clarification

delu'dente adj disappointing

de'lu|dere vt disappoint. ~**si'one** f disappointment. **de'luso** adj disappointed

demar'ca|re vt demarcate. ~**zi'one** f demarcation

de'men|te adj demented. ~**za** f dementia. ~**zi'ale** adj (assurdo) zany

demilitariz'za|re vt demilitarize. ~**zi'one** f demilitarization

demistifi'cazi'one f debunking

demo'cra|tico adj democratic. ~**'zia** f democracy

democristi'ano, -a adj & mf Christian Democrat

demogra'fia f demography. **demo'grafico** adj demographic

demo'li|re vt demolish. ~**zi'one** f demolition

'demone m demon. **de'monio** m demon

demoraliz'zar|e vt demoralize. ~**si** vr become demoralized

de'mordere vi give up

demoti'vato adj demotivated

de'nari mpl (nelle carte) diamonds

de'naro m money

deni'gra|re vt denigrate. ~**'torio** adj denigratory

denomi'na|re vt name. ~**tore** m denominator. ~**zi'one** f denomination; ~**zione di origine controllata** guarantee of a wine's quality

deno'tare vt denote

densità f inv density. **'denso** adj dense

den'ta|le adj dental. ~**rio** adj dental. ~**ta** f bite. ~**tura** f teeth pl

'dente m tooth; (di forchetta) prong; **al** ~ (Culin) slightly firm. ~ **del giudizio** wisdom tooth. ~ **di latte** milk tooth. **denti'era** f false teeth pl

denti'fricio m toothpaste

den'tista mf dentist

'dentro adv in, inside; (in casa) indoors; **da** ~ from within; **qui** ~ in here ● prep in, inside; (di tempo)

within, by ●**m** inside
denu'dar|e vt bare. ~**si** vr strip
de'nunci|a, de'nunzia f denunciation; (alla polizia) report; (dei redditi) [income] tax return. ~'**are** vt denounce; (accusare) report
denutrizi'one f malnutrition
deodo'rante adj & m deodorant
dépendance f inv outbuilding
depe'ri|bile adj perishable. ~'**mento** m wasting away; (di merci) deterioration. ~**re** vi waste away
depi'la|re vt depilate. ~**rsi** vr shave (gambe); pluck (sopracciglia). ~'**torio** m depilatory
deplo'rabile adj deplorable
deplo'r|are vt deplore; (dolersi di) grieve over. ~'**evole** adj deplorable
de'porre vt put down; lay (uova); (togliere da una carica) depose; (testimoniare) testify
depor'ta|re vt deport. ~**to, -a** mf deportee. ~**zi'one** f deportation
deposi'tar|e vt deposit; (lasciare in custodia) leave; (in magazzino) store. ~**io, -a** mf (di segreto) repository. ~**si** vr settle
de'posito m deposit; (luogo) warehouse; (Mil) depot. ~**to bagagli** left-luggage office. ~**zi'one** f deposition; (da una carica) removal
depra'va|re vt deprave. ~**to** adj depraved
depre'ca|bile adj appalling. ~**re** vt deprecate
depre'dare vt plunder
depressi'one f depression. **de'presso** pp di **deprimere** ●adj depressed
deprez'zar|e vt depreciate. ~**si** vr depreciate
depri'mente adj depressing
de'primer|e vt depress. ~**si** vr become depressed
depu'ra|re vt purify. ~'**tore** m purifier

depu'ta|re vt delegate. ~**to, -a** mf Member of Parliament, MP
deraglia'mento m derailment
deragli'are vi go off the lines; far ~ derail
'derby m inv Sport local Derby
deregolamentazi'one f deregulation
dere'litto adj derelict
dere'tano m backside, bottom
de'ri|dere vt deride. ~**si'one** f derision. ~'**sorio** adj derisory
deri'va|re vi ~**re da** (provenire) derive from ● vt derive; (sviare) divert. ~**zi'one** f derivation; (di fiume) diversion
dermato'lo'gia f dermatology. **derma'tologo, -a** mf dermatologist
'deroga f dispensation. **dero'gare** vi **derogare a** depart from
der'rat|a f merchandise. ~**e alimentari** foodstuffs
deru'bare vt rob
descrit'tivo adj descriptive. **de'scritto** pp di **descrivere**
des'crivere vt describe. ~'**vibile** adj describable. ~**zi'one** f description
de'serto adj uninhabited ●m desert
deside'rabile adj desirable
deside'rare vt wish; (volere) want; (intensamente) long for; **desidera?** can I help you?; **lasciare a ~** leave a lot to be desired
desi'de|rio m wish; (brama) desire; (intenso) longing. ~'**roso** adj desirous; (bramoso) longing
desi'gnare vt designate; (fissare) fix
de'sistere vi ~ **da** desist from
'desktop 'publishing m desktop publishing
deso'la|re vt distress. ~**to** adj desolate; (spiacente) sorry. ~**zi'one** f desolation
'despota m despot
de'star|e vt waken; fig awaken. ~**si**

vr waken; *fig* awaken

desti'na|re vt destine; (*nominare*) appoint; (*assegnare*) assign; (*indirizzare*) address. ~**'tario** m addressee. ~**zi'one** f destination; *fig* purpose

de'stino m destiny; (*fato*) fate

destitu'ire vt dismiss. ~**zi'one** f dismissal

'desto *adj liter* awake

'destra f (*parte*) right; (*mano*) right hand; **prendere a** ~ turn right

de'strezza f dexterity, skill

'destro *adj* right; (*abile*) skilful

detei'nato *adj* tannin-free

dete'ne|re vt hold; (*polizia*): detain. ~**uto, -a** mf prisoner. ~**zi'one** f detention

deter'gente *adj* cleaning; (*latte, crema*) cleansing ● m detergent; (*per la pelle*) cleanser

deteriora'mento m deterioration

deterio'rar|e vt deteriorate. ~**si** vr deteriorate

determi'nante *adj* decisive

determi'na|re vt determine. ~**rsi** vr ~**rsi** a resolve to. ~**'tezza** f determination. ~**'tivo** *adj* (*Gram*) definite. ~**to** *adj* (*risoluto*) determined; (*particolare*) specific. ~**zi'one** f determination; (*decisione*) decision

deter'rente *adj* & m deterrent

deter'sivo m detergent. ~ **per i piatti** washing-up liquid

dete'stare vt detest, hate

deto'nare vi detonate

de'tra|rre vt deduct (**da** from). ~**zi'one** f deduction

detri'mento m detriment; **a** ~ **di** to the detriment of

de'trito m debris

'detta f **a** ~ **di** according to

dettagli'ante mf retailer

dettagli'a|re vt detail. ~**ta'mente** *adv* in detail

det'taglio m detail; **al** ~ (*Comm*) retail

det'ta|re vt dictate. ~**to** m, ~**'tura** f dictation

'detto *adj* said; (*chiamato*) called; (*soprannominato*) nicknamed; ~ **fatto** no sooner said than done ● m saying

detur'pare vt disfigure

deva'sta|re vt devastate. ~**to** *adj* devastated

devi'a|re vi deviate ● vt divert. ~**zi'one** f deviation; (*stradale*) diversion

devitaliz'zare vt deaden (*dente*)

devo'lu|to *pp* di **devolvere** ● *adj* devolved. ~**zi'one** f devolution

de'volvere vt devolve

de'vo|to *adj* devout; (*affezionato*) devoted. ~**zi'one** f devotion

---

di *prep* of; (*partitivo*) some; (*scritto da*) by; (*parlare, pensare ecc*) about; (*con causa, mezzo*) with; (*con provenienza*) from; (*in comparazioni*) than; (*con infinito*) to; **la casa di mio padre/dei miei genitori** my father's house/my parents' house; **compra del pane** buy some bread; **hai del pane?** do you have any bread?; **un film di guerra** a war film; **piangere di dolore** cry with pain; **coperto di neve** covered with snow; **sono di Genova** I'm from Genoa; **uscire di casa** leave one's house; **più alto di te** taller than you; **è ora di partire** it's time to go; **crede di aver ragione** he thinks he's right; **dire di si** say yes; **di domenica** on Sundays; **di sera** in the evening; **una pausa di un'ora** an hour's break; **un corso di due mesi** a two-month course

dia'bet|e m diabetes. ~**ico, -a** *adj* & mf diabetic

diabolico | differente

dia'bolico adj diabolical
dia'dema m diadem; (di donna) tiara
di'afano adj diaphanous
dia'framma m diaphragm; (divisione) screen
dia'gnosi f inv diagnosis. ~ti'care vt diagnose
diago'nale adj & f diagonal
dia'gramma m diagram
dia'letto m dialect

Dialetto As Italy was not unified until 1861, standard Italian was slow to become widely used except by the cultural elite. As a result dialects are used by many Italians, with 60% using their dialect regularly. Ranging from Neapolitan and Sicilian to Milanese and Venetian, they vary considerably from each other. Tuscan dialects are the closest to standard Italian.

---

di'alogo m dialogue
dia'mante m diamond
di'ametro m diameter
di'amine int che ~... what on earth...
diaposi'tiva f slide
di'ario m diary
diar'rea f diarrhoea
di'avolo m devil
di'batt|ere vt debate. ~ersi vr struggle. ~ito m debate; (meno formale) discussion
dica'stero m office
di'cembre m December
dice'ria f rumour
dichia'ra|re vt state; (ufficialmente) declare. ~rsi vr si dichiara innocente he says he's innocent. ~zi'one f statement; (documento, di guerra) declaration
dician'nove adj & m nineteen
dicias'sette adj & m seventeen

dici'otto adj & m eighteen
dici'tura f wording
didas'calia f (di film) subtitle; (di illustrazione) caption
di'dattico adj didactic; (televisione) educational
di'dentro adv inside
didi'etro adv behind ● m hum hindquarters pl
di'eci adj & m ten
die'cina = DECINA
'diesel adj & f inv diesel
di'esis m inv sharp
di'eta f diet; essere a ~ be on a diet. **die'tetico** adj diet. **die'tista** mf dietician. **die'tologo, -a** mf dietician
di'etro adv behind ● prep behind; (dopo) after ● adj back; (di zampe) hind ● m back; **le stanze di ~** the back rooms
dietro'front m inv about-turn; fig U-turn
di'fatti adv in fact
di'fen|dere vt defend. ~dersi vr defend oneself. ~'siva f stare sulla ~siva be on the defensive. ~'sivo adj defensive. ~'sore m defender; **avvocato** ~sore defence counsel
di'fes|a f defence; **prendere le ~e di** qcno come to sb's defence. ~o pp di difendere
difet'tare vi be defective; ~are di lack. ~'ivo adj defective
di'fet|to m defect; (morale) fault, flaw; (mancanza) lack; (in tessuto, abito) flaw; **essere in ~to** be at fault; far ~to be lacking. ~'toso adj defective; (abito) flawed
diffa'ma|re vt (con parole) slander; (per iscritto) libel. ~'torio adj slanderous; (per iscritto) libellous; ~zi'one f slander; (scritta) libel
diffe'ren|te adj different. ~za f difference; a ~za di unlike; non fare ~za make no distinction (fra between). ~zi'ale adj & m

differential

differenzi'ar|e vt differentiate. ~**si** vr ~**si da** differ from

diffe'ri|re vt postpone ●vi be different. ~**ta f in** ~**ta** (TV) prerecorded

dif'ficil|e adj difficult; (duro) hard; (improbabile) unlikely ●m difficulty. ~**mente** adv with difficulty

difficoltà f inv difficulty

dif'fida f warning

diffi'd|are vi ~**are di** distrust ●vt warn. ~**ente** adj mistrustful. ~**enza** f mistrust

dif'fond|ere vt spread; diffuse (calore, luce ecc). ~**si** vr spread. **diffusi'one** f diffusion; (di giornale) circulation

dif'fu|so pp di diffondere ●adj common; (malattia) widespread; (luce) diffuse

difi'lato adv straight; (subito) straightaway

'diga f dam; (argine) dike

dige'ribile adj digestible

dige|'rire vt digest; ⊞ stomach. ~**sti'one** f digestion; ~**stivo** adj digestive ●m digestive; (dopo cena) liqueur

digi'tale adj digital; (delle dita) finger attrib ●f (fiore) foxglove

digitaliz'zare vt digitize

digi'tare vt key in

digiu'nare vi fast

digi'uno adj essere ~ have an empty stomach ●m fast; a ~ (bere ecc) on an empty stomach

digni|tà f dignity. ~**tario** m dignitary. ~**toso** adj dignified

digressi'one f digression

digri'gnare vt ~ **i denti** grind one's teeth

dila'gare vi flood; fig spread

dila'niare vt tear to pieces

dilapi'dare vt squander

dila'ta|re vt, ~**rsi** vr dilate; (metallo, gas) expand

dilazio'nabile adj postponable

dilazi|o'nare vt delay. ~**one** f delay

dilegu'ar|e vt disperse. ~**si** vr disappear

di'lemma m dilemma

dilet'tante mf amateur

dilet'tare vt delight

di'letto, -a adj beloved ●m delight ●mf (persona) beloved

dili'gen|te adj diligent; (lavoro) accurate. ~**za** f diligence

dilu'ire vt dilute

dilun'gar|e vt prolong. ~**si** vr ~**si su** dwell on (argomento)

diluvi'are vi pour [down]. **di'luvio** m downpour; fig flood

dima'gran|te adj slimming. ~**i'mento** m weight loss. ~**ire** vi slim

dime'nar|e vt wave; wag (coda). ~**si** vr be agitated

dimensi'one f dimension; (misura) size

dimenti'canza f forgetfulness; (svista) oversight

dimenti'car|e vt, ~**si** vr ~ [di] forget. **dimentico** adj **dimentico di** (che non ricorda) forgetful of

di'messo pp di dimettere ●adj humble; (trasandato) shabby; (voce) low

dimesti'chezza f familiarity

di'metter|e vt dismiss; (da ospedale ecc) discharge. ~**si** vr resign

dimez'zare vt halve

dimin|u'ire vt/i diminish; (in maglia) decrease. ~**tivo** adj & m diminutive. ~**zi'one** f decrease; (riduzione) reduction

dimissi'oni fpl resignation sg; dare le ~ resign

di'mo|ra f residence. ~**rare** vi reside

dimo'strante mf demonstrator

dimo'stra|re vt demonstrate; (provare) prove; (*mostrare*) show. **~rsi** vr prove [to be]. **~tivo** adj demonstrative. **~zi'one** f demonstration; (*Math*) proof

di'namico, -a adj dynamic. **dina-'mismo** m dynamism

dinami'tardo adj attentato **~** bomb attack

dina'mite f dynamite

'dinamo f inv dynamo

di'nanzi adv in front ● prep **~** a in front of

dina'stia f dynasty

dini'ego m denial

dinocco'lato adj lanky

dino'sauro m dinosaur

din'torn|i mpl outskirts; nei **~i** di in the vicinity of. **~o** adv around

'dio m (pl **'dei**) god; D**~** God

di'ocesi f inv diocese

dipa'nare vt wind into a ball; fig unravel

diparti'mento m department

dipen'den|te adj depending ● mf employee. **~za** f dependence; (*edificio*) annexe

di'pendere vi **~** da depend on; (*provenire*) derive from; dipende it depends

di'pinger|e vt paint; (*descrivere*) describe. **~si** vr (*truccarsi*) make up. di-'pinto pp di dipingere ● adj painted ● m painting

di'plo|ma m diploma. **~'marsi** vr graduate

diplo'matico adj diplomatic ● m diplomat; (*pasticcino*) millefeuille (*with alcohol*)

diplo'mato mf person with school-leaving qualification ● adj qualified

diploma'zia f diplomacy

di'porto m imbarcazione da **~** pleasure craft

dira'dar|e vt thin out; make less frequent (*visite*). **~si** vr thin out; (*nebbia:*) clear

dira'ma|re vt issue ● vi, **~rsi** vr branch out; (*diffondersi*) spread. **~zi'one** f (*di strada*) fork

'dire vt say; (*raccontare, riferire*) tell; **~** quello che si pensa speak one's mind; voler **~** mean; volevo ben **~!** I wondered!; **~** di sì/no say yes/ no; si dice che... rumour has it that...; come si dice "casa" in inglese? what's the English for "casa"?; che ne dici di...? how about...?; non c'è che **~** there's no disputing that; e **~** che... to think that...; a dir poco/tanto at least/ most ● vi **~** bene/male di speak highly/ill of; dica pure how can I help you?; dici sul serio? are you serious?

diretta'mente adv directly

diret'tissima f per **~** (*Jur*) omitting normal procedure

diret'tissimo m fast train

diret'tiva f directive

di'retto pp di dirigere ● adj direct. **~** a (*inteso*) meant for. essere **~** a be heading for. in diretta (*trasmissione*) live ● m (*treno*) through train

diret'tore, -'trice mf manager; manageress; (*di scuola*) headmaster; headmistress. **~tore d'orchestra** conductor

direzi'one f direction; (*di società*) management; (*Sch*) headmaster's/ headmistress's office (*primary school*)

diri'gen|te adj ruling ● mf executive; (*Pol*) leader. **~za** f management. **~zi'ale** adj managerial

di'riger|e vt direct; conduct (*orchestra*); run (*impresa*). **~si** vr **~si verso** head for

dirim'petto adv opposite ● prep **~** a facing

di'ritto¹, dritto adj straight; (*destro*) right ● adv straight; andare **~** go straight on ● m right side; (*Tennis*) forehand

di'ritt|o² m right; (*Jur*) law. **~i** pl

d'autore royalties

dirit'tura f straight line; fig honesty. ~ d'arrivo Sport home straight

diroc'cato adj tumbledown

dirom'pente adj fig explosive

dirot'ta|re vt reroute (treno, aereo); (illegalmente) hijack; divert (traffico) •vi alter course. ~'tore, ~'trice mf hijacker

di'rotto adj (pioggia) pouring; (pianto) uncontrollable; piovere a ~ rain heavily

di'rupo m precipice

dis'abile mf disabled person

disabi'tato adj uninhabited

disabitu'arsi vr ~ a get out of the habit of

disac'cordo m disagreement

disadat'tato, -a adj maladjusted •mf misfit

disa'dorno adj unadorned

disa'gevole adj (scomodo) uncomfortable

disagi'ato adj poor; (vita) hard

di'sagio m discomfort; (difficoltà) inconvenience; (imbarazzo) embarrassment; sentirsi a ~ feel uncomfortable; disagi pl (privazioni) hardships

disappro'va|re vt disapprove of. ~zi'one f disapproval

disap'punto m disappointment

disar'mante adj fig disarming

disar'mare vt/i disarm. di'sarmo m disarmament

disa'strato, -a adj devastated

di'sastro m disaster; (🄵: grande confusione) mess; (🄵: persona) disaster area. disa'stroso adj disastrous

disat'ten|to adj inattentive. ~zi'one f inattention; (svista) oversight

disatti'vare vt de-activate

disa'vanzo m deficit

disaven'tura f misadventure

dis'brigo m dispatch

dis'capito m a ~ di to the detriment of

dis'carica f scrap-yard

discen'den|te adj descending •mf descendant. ~za f descent; (discendenti) descendants pl

di'scendere vt/i descend; (dal treno) get off; (da cavallo) dismount; (sbarcare) land. ~ da (trarre origine da) be a descendant of

di'scepolo, -a mf disciple

di'scernere vt discern

di'sce|sa f descent; (pendio) slope; ~a in picchiata (di aereo) nosedive; essere in ~a (strada:) go downhill. ~a libera (in sci) downhill race. disce'sista mf (sciatore) downhill skier. ~o pp di discendere

di'schetto m (Comput) diskette

dischi'udere vt open; (svelare) disclose. ~si vr open up

disci'oglier|e vt, ~si vr dissolve; (fondersi) melt. disci'olto pp di disciogliere

disci'pli|na f discipline. ~'nare adj disciplinary ~'nato adj disciplined

'disco m disc; (Comput) disk; Sport discus; (Mus) record; ernia del ~ slipped disc. ~ fisso (Comput) hard disk. ~ volante flying saucer

discogra'fia f (insieme di incisioni) discography. disco'grafico adj (industria) recording; casa discografica recording company

'discolo mf rascal •adj unruly

discol'par|e vt clear. ~si vr clear oneself

disconnet'tersi vr go offline

disco'noscere vt disown (figlio)

discontinuità f (nel lavoro) irregularity. discon'tinuo adj intermittent; (rendimento) uneven

discor'dan|te adj discordant. ~za f mismatch

discor'dare vi (opinioni:) conflict. dis'corde adj clashing. dis'cordia f discord; (*dissenso*) dissension

dis'cor|rere vi talk (**di** about). ~**sivo** adj colloquial. **dis'corso** pp di **discorrere** ●m speech; (*conversazione*) talk

dis'costo adj distant ● adv far away; stare ~ stand apart

disco'te|ca f disco; (*raccolta*) record library

discre'pante adj contradictory. ~**za** f discrepancy

dis'cre|to adj discreet; (*moderato*) moderate; (*abbastanza buono*) fairly good. ~**zi'one** f discretion; (*giudizio*) judgement; a ~**zione di** at the discretion of

discrimi'nante adj extenuating

discrimi'na|re vt discriminate. ~**'torio** adj (*atteggiamento*) discriminatory. ~**zi'one** f discrimination

discussi'one f discussion; (*alterco*) argument. **dis'cusso** pp di **discutere** ●adj controversial

dis'cutere vt discreet; (*formale*) debate; (*litigare*) argue; ~ **sul prezzo** bargain. **discu'tibile** adj debatable; (*gusto*) questionable

disde'gnare vt disdain. **dis'degno** m disdain

disdi'cevole adj unbecoming

dis'dire vt retract; (*annullare*) cancel

diseduca'tivo adj boorish

dise'gna|re vt draw; (*progettare*) design. ~**tore**, ~**trice** mf designer. **di'segno** m drawing; (*progetto, linea*) design

diser'bante m herbicide ●adj herbicidal

disere'da|re vt disinherit ●mf i ~**ti** the dispossessed

diser'tare vt/i desert; ~**tare la scuola** stay away from school. ~**tore** m deserter. ~**zi'one** f desertion

disfaci'mento m decay

dis'fa|re vt undo; strip (*letto*); (*smantellare*) take down; (*annientare*) defeat; ~**re le valigie** unpack [one's bags]. ~**rsi** vi fall to pieces; (*sciogliersi*) melt; ~**rsi di** (*liberarsi di*) get rid of; ~**rsi in lacrime** dissolve into tears. ~**tta** f defeat. ~**tto** adj fig worn out

disfat'tis|mo m defeatism. ~**ta** adj & mf defeatist

disfunzi'one f disorder

dis'gelo m thaw

dis'grazi|a f misfortune; (*incidente*) accident; (*sfavore*) disgrace. ~**ata'mente** adv unfortunately. ~**ato, -a** adj unfortunate ●mf wretch

disgre'gar|e vt break up. ~**si** vr disintegrate

disgu'ido m ~ **postale** mistake in delivery

disgu'st|are vt disgust. ~**arsi** vr ~**arsi di** be disgusted by. **dis'gusto** m disgust. ~**oso** adj disgusting

disidra'ta|re vt dehydrate. ~**to** adj dehydrated

disil'lu|dere vt disenchant. ~**si'one** f disenchantment. ~**so** adj disillusioned

disimbal'lare vt unpack

disimpa'rare vt forget

disimpe'gnar|e vt release; (*compiere*) fulfil; redeem (*oggetto dato in pegno*). ~**si** vi disengage oneself; (*cavarsela*) manage. **disim'pegno** m (*locale*) vestibule

disincan'tato adj (*disilluso*) disillusioned

disinfe'sta|re vt disinfest. ~**zi'one** f disinfestation

disinfet'tante adj & m disinfectant

disinfet'ta|re vt disinfect. ~**zi'one** f disinfection

disinfor'mato adj uninformed

disini'bito adj uninhibited

disinne'scare vt defuse (*mina*), disin'nesco m (di bomba) bomb disposal

disinse'rire vt disconnect

disinte'gra|re vt, ~rsi vr disintegrate. ~zi'one f disintegration

disinteres'sarsi vr ~ di take no interest in. disinte'resse m indifference; (oggettività) disinterestedness

disintossi'ca|re vt detoxify. ~rsi vr come off alcohol/drugs. ~zi'one f giving up alcohol/drugs

disin'volto adj natural. disinvol'tura f confidence

disles'sia f dyslexia

disli'vello m difference in height; fig inequality

dislo'care vt (Mil) post

dismi'sura f excess; a ~ excessively

disobbedi'ente adj disobedient

disobbe'dire vt disobey

disoccu'pa|to, -a adj unemployed • m/f unemployed person. ~zi'o·ne f unemployment

disonestà f dishonesty. diso'nesto adj dishonest

disono'rare vt dishonour. diso'nore m dishonour

di'sopra adv above • adj upper • m top

disordi'na|re vt disarrange. ~ta'mente adv untidily. ~to adj untidy; (sregolato) immoderate. di'sordine m disorder

disorganiz'za|re vt disorganize. ~to adj disorganized. ~zi'one f disorganization

disorienta'mento m disorientation

disorien'ta|re vt disorientate. ~rsi vr lose one's bearings. ~to adj fig bewildered

di'sotto adv below • adj lower • m bottom

dis'paccio m dispatch

dispa'rato adj disparate

'dispari adj odd. ~tà f inv disparity

dis'parte adv in ~ apart; stare in ~ stand aside

dis'pendi|o m (spreco) waste. ~'oso adj expensive

dis'pen|sa f pantry; (distribuzione) distribution; (mobile) cupboard; (Jur) exemption; (Relig) dispensation; (pubblicazione periodica) number. ~'sare vt distribute; (esentare) exonerate

dispe'ra|re vi despair (di of). ~rsi vr despair. ~ta'mente (piangere) desperately. ~to adj desperate. ~zi'one f despair

dis'per|dere vt, ~dersi vr disperse. ~si'one f dispersion; (di truppe) dispersal. ~'sivo adj disorganized. ~so pp di disperdere • adj scattered; (smarrito) lost • m missing soldier

dis'pet|to m spite; a ~to di in spite of. ~'toso adj spiteful

dispia'c|ere m upset; (rammarico) regret; (dolore) sorrow; (preoccupazione) worry • vi mi dispiace I'm sorry; non mi dispiace I don't dislike it; se non ti dispiace if you don't mind. ~i'uto adj upset; (dolente) sorry

dispo'nibil|e adj available; (gentile) helpful. ~ità f availability; (gentilezza) helpfulness

dis'por|re vt arrange • vi dispose; (stabilire) order; ~re di have at one's disposal. ~si vr line up

disposi'tivo m device

disposizi'one f disposition; (ordine) order; (libera disponibilità) disposal. di'sposto pp di disporre • adj ready; (incline) disposed; essere ben disposto verso be favourably disposed towards

di'spotico adj despotic

dispregia'tivo adj disparaging

disprez'zare vt despise. dis'prezzo m contempt

'disputa f dispute

dispu'tar|e vi dispute; (gareggiare)

compete. ~si vr ~si qcsa contend for sth

dissacra'torio adj debunking

dissangua'mento m loss of blood

dissangu'a|re vt, ~rsi vr bleed. ~rsi vr fig become impoverished. ~to adj bloodless; fig impoverished

dissa'pore m disagreement

dissec'car|e vt, ~si vr dry up

dissemi'nare vt disseminate; (notizie) spread

dis'senso m dissent; (disaccordo) disagreement

dissente'ria f dysentery

dissen'tire vi disagree (da with)

dissertazi'one f dissertation

disser'vizio m poor service

disse'sta|re vt upset; (Comm) damage. ~to adj (strada) uneven. dis'sesto m ruin

disse'tante adj thirst-quenching

disse'ta|re vt ~re qcno quench sb's thirst

dissi'dente adj & mf dissident

dis'sidio m disagreement

dis'simile adj unlike, dissimilar

dissimu'lare vt conceal; (fingere) dissimulate

dissi'pa|re vt dissipate; (sperperare) squander. ~rsi vr (nebbia:) clear; (dubbio:) disappear. ~to adj dissipated. ~zi'one f squandering

dissoci'ar|e vt, ~si vr dissociate

disso'dare vt till

dis'solto pp di dissolvere

disso'luto adj dissolute

dis'solver|e vt, ~si vr dissolve; (disperdere) dispel

disso'nanza f dissonance

dissua'dere vt dissuade. ~si'one f dissuasion. ~'sivo adj dissuasive

distac'car|e vt detach; Sport leave behind. ~si vr be detached. di'stacco m detachment; (separazione)

separation; Sport lead

di'stan|te adj far away; fig: (person) detached ●adv far away. ~za f distance. ~zi'are vt space out; Sport outdistance

di'stare vi be distant; quanto dista? how far is it?

di'sten|dere vt stretch out (parte del corpo); (spiegare) spread; (deporre) lay. ~dersi vr stretch; (sdraiarsi) lie down; (rilassarsi) relax. ~si'one f stretching; (rilassamento) relaxation; (Pol) détente. ~'sivo adj relaxing

di'steso, -a pp di distendere ●f expanse

distil'la|re vt/i distil. ~azi'one f distillation. ~e'ria f distillery

di'stingu|ere vt distinguish. ~si vr distinguish oneself. distin'guibile adj distinguishable

di'stinta f (Comm) list. ~ di pagamento receipt. ~ di versamento paying-in slip

distinta'mente adv individually; (chiaramente) clearly

distin'tivo adj distinctive ●m badge

di'stin|to, -a pp di distinguere ●adj distinct; (signorile) distinguished; ~ti saluti Yours faithfully. ~zi'one f distinction

di'stogliere vt ~ da remove from; (dissuadere) dissuade from. di'stolto pp di distogliere

di'storcere vt twist

distorsi'one f (Med) sprain; (alterazione) distortion

di'stra|rre vt distract; (divertire) amuse. ~rsi vr get distracted; (svagarsi) amuse oneself; non ti distrarre! pay attention!. ~tta'mente adv absently. ~tto pp di distrarre ●adj absent-minded; (disattento) inattentive. ~zi'one f absent-mindedness; (errore) inattention; (svago) amusement di'stretto m district

distribu|'ire vt distribute; (disporre) arrange; deal (carte). ~'tore m distributor; (di benzina) petrol pump; (automatico) slot-machine. ~zi'one f distribution

distri'car|e vt disentangle; ~si fig get out of it

di|stru'ggere vt destroy. ~t'tivo adj destructive; (critica) negative. ~tto pp di distruggere. ~zi'one f destruction

distur'bar|e vt disturb; (sconvolgere) upset. ~si vr trouble oneself. di'sturbo m bother; (indisposizione) trouble; (Med) problem; (Radio, TV) interference; disturbi pl (Radio, TV) static. disturbi di stomaco stomach trouble

disubbidi'en|te adj disobedient. ~za f disobedience

disubbi'dire vi ~ a disobey

disugu|agli'anza f disparity. ~'ale adj unequal; (irregolare) irregular

di'suso m cadere in ~ fall into disuse

di'tale m thimble

di'tata f poke; (impronta) finger-mark

'dito m (pl f dita) finger; (di vino) finger. ~ del piede toe

'ditta f firm

dit'tafono m dictaphone

ditta'tor|e m dictator. ~i'ale adj dictatorial. ditta'tura f dictatorship

dit'tongo m diphthong

di'urno adj daytime; spettacolo ~ matinée

'diva f diva

diva'ga|re vi digress. ~zi'one f digression

divam'pare vi burst into flames; fig spread like wildfire

di'vano m sofa. ~ letto sofa bed

divari'care vt open

di'vario m discrepancy; un ~ di

opinioni a difference of opinion

dive'n|ire vi = DIVENTARE. ~uto pp di divenire

diven'tare vi become; (lentamente) grow; (rapidamente) turn

di'verbio m squabble

diver'gen|te adj divergent. ~za f divergence; ~za di opinioni difference of opinion. di'vergere vi diverge

diversa'mente adv otherwise; (in modo diverso) differently

diversifi'ca|re vt diversify. ~rsi vr differ. ~zi'one f diversification

diversi'one f diversion. ~sità f inv difference. ~'sivo m diversion. di'verso adj different; diversi pl (parecchi) several • pron several [people]

diver'tente adj amusing. diverti'mento m amusement

diver'tir|e vt amuse. ~si vr enjoy oneself

divi'dendo m dividend

di'vider|e vt divide; (condividere) share. ~si vr (separarsi) separate

divi'eto m prohibition; ~ di sosta no parking

divin'colarsi vr wriggle

divinità f inv divinity. di'vino adj divine

di'visa f uniform; (Comm) currency

divisi'one f division

di'vismo m worship; (atteggiamento) superstar mentality

di'vi|so pp di dividere. ~'sore m divisor. ~'sorio adj dividing

'divo, -a mf star

divo'rar|e vt devour. ~si vr ~si da be consumed with

divorzi'a|re vi divorce. ~to, -a mf divorcee. di'vorzio m divorce

divul'ga|re vt divulge; (rendere popolare) popularize. ~rsi vr spread. ~'tivo adj popular. ~zi'one f popularization

dizio'nario m dictionary

dizi'one f diction

do m (Mus) C

> **DOC** Italian wines which are grown in certain specified areas and which conform to certain regulations may be styled DOC (*Denominazione di Origine Controllata*). The classification DOCG (*Denominazione di Origine Controllata e Garantita*) is awarded to DOC wines of particular quality. Wines must conform to the DOC criteria for at least five years before they can be classified as DOCG.

'**doccia** f shower; (grondaia) gutter; **fare la ~** have a shower

do'cen|te adj teaching ● mf teacher; (Univ) lecturer. **~za** f (Univ) lecturer's qualification

'**docile** adj docile

documen'tar|e vt document. **~si** vr gather information (**su** about)

documen'tario adj & m documentary

documen'ta|to adj well-documented; (persona) well-informed. **~zi'one** f documentation

docu'mento m document

dodi'cesimo adj & m twelfth. '**dodici** adj & m twelve

do'gan|a f customs pl; (dazio) duty. **doga'nale** adj customs. **~i'ere** m customs officer

'**doglie** fpl labour pains

'**dogma** m dogma. **dog'matico** adj dogmatic. **~tismo** m dogmatism

'**dolce** adj sweet; (clima) mild; (voce, consonante) soft; (acqua) fresh ● m (portata) dessert; (torta) cake; **non mangio dolci** I don't eat sweet things. **~mente** adv sweetly. **dol'cezza** f sweetness; (di clima) mildness

dolce'vita adj inv (maglione) rollneck

dolci'ario adj confectionery

dolci'astro adj sweetish

dolcifi'cante m sweetener ● adj sweetening

dolci'umi mpl sweets

do'lente adj painful; (spiacente) sorry

do'le|re vi ache, hurt; (dispiacere) regret. **~rsi** vi regret; (protestare) complain; **~rsi di** be sorry for

do'llaro m dollar

'**dolo** m (Jur) malice; (truffa) fraud

Dolo'miti fpl **le ~** the Dolomites

do'lore m pain; (morale) sorrow. **do'loroso** adj painful

do'loso adj malicious

do'manda f question; (richiesta) request; (scritta) application; (Comm) demand; **fare una ~ (a qcno)** ask (sb) a question. **~ di impiego** job application

doman'dar|e vt ask; (esigere) demand; **~e qcsa a qcno** ask sb for sth. **~si** vr wonder

do'mani adv tomorrow; **~ sera** tomorrow evening ● m il **~** the future; **a ~** see you tomorrow

do'mare vt tame; fig control (emozioni). **~tore** m tamer

domat'tina adv tomorrow morning

do'meni|ca f Sunday. **~'cale** adj Sunday attrib

do'mestico, -a adj domestic ● m servant ● f maid

domicili'are adj **arresti domiciliari** (Jur) house arrest

domicili'arsi vr settle

domi'cilio m domicile; (abitazione) home; **recapitiamo a ~** we do home deliveries

domi'na|re vt dominate; (controllare) control ● vi rule over; (prevalere) be dominant. **~rsi** vr control oneself. **~tore**, **~'trice** mf ruler. **~zi'one** f domination

do'minio m control; (Pol) dominion; (ambito) field; di ~ pubblico common knowledge

don m inv (ecclesiastico) Father

do'na|re vt give; donate (sangue, organo); •vi ~re a (giovane esteticamente) suit. ~tore, ~'trice mf donor. ~zi'one f donation

dondo'l|are vt swing; (cullare) rock •vi sway. ~arsi vr swing. ~io m rocking. 'dondolo m gift; cavallo/sedia a dondolo rocking-horse/chair

dongio'vanni m inv Romeo

'donna f woman. ~ di servizio domestic help

don'naccia f pej whore

'dono m gift

'dopo prep after; (a partire da) since •adv afterwards; (più tardi) later; (in seguito) later on; ~ di me after me

dopo'barba m inv aftershave

dopo'cena m inv evening

dopodiché adv after which

dopodo'mani adv the day after tomorrow

dopogu'erra m inv post-war period

dopo'pranzo m inv afternoon

dopo'sci adj & m inv après-ski

doposcu'ola m inv after-school activities pl

dopo-'shampoo m inv conditioner •adj inv conditioning

dopo'sole m inv aftersun cream •adj inv aftersun

dopo'tutto adv after all

doppi'aggio m dubbing

doppia'mente adv doubly

doppi'a|re vt double; Sport lap; Cinema dub. ~'tore, ~'trice mf dubber

'doppio adj & adv double. ~ clic m (Comput) double click. ~ fallo m Tennis double fault. ~ gioco m double-dealing. ~ mento m double chin. ~ senso m double entendre. doppi

vetri mpl double glazing •m double; Tennis doubles pl. ~ misto Tennis mixed doubles

doppi'one m duplicate

doppio'petto adj double-breasted

dop'pista mf doubles player

do'ra|re vt gild; (Culin) brown. ~to adj gilt; (color oro) golden. ~'tura f gilding

dor'mecchi'are vi doze

dormigli'one, -a mf sleepyhead; fig lazy-bones

dor'mi|re vi sleep; (essere addormentato) be asleep; fig be asleep. ~ta f good sleep. ~'tina f nap. ~'torio m dormitory

dormi'veglia m essere in ~ be half asleep

dor'sale adj dorsal •f (di monte) ridge

'dorso m back; (di libro) spine; (di monte) crest; (nel nuoto) backstroke

do'saggio m dosage

do'sare vt dose; fig measure; ~ le parole weigh one's words

dosa'tore m measuring jug

'dose f dose; in buona ~ fig in good measure. ~ eccessiva overdose

dossi'er m inv file

'dosso m (dorso) back; levarsi di ~ gli abiti take off one's clothes

do'ta|re vt endow; (di accessori) equip. ~to adj (persona) gifted; (fornito) equipped. ~zi'one f (attrezzatura) equipment; in ~zione at one's disposal

'dote f dowry; (qualità) gift

'dotto adj learned •m scholar; (Anat) duct

dotto'rato m doctorate. dot'tore, ~'ressa mf doctor

dot'trina f doctrine

'dove adv where; di ~ sei? where do you come from; fin ~? how far?;

per ∼? which way?

do'vere vi (obbligo) have to, must; **devo andare** I have to go, I must go; **devo venire anch'io?** do I have to come too?; **avresti dovuto dirmelo** you should have told me, you ought to have told me; **devo sedermi un attimo** I must sit down for a minute, I need to sit down for a minute; **dev'essere successo qualcosa** something must have happened; **come si deve** properly • vt (essere debitore di, derivare) owe; **essere dovuto a** be due to • m duty; **per ∼** out of duty. **dove'roso** adj only right and proper

do'vunque adv (dappertutto) everywhere; (in qualsiasi luogo) anywhere • conj wherever

do'vuto adj due; (debito) proper

doz'zi|na f dozen. **∼nale** adj cheap

dra'gare vt dredge

'drago m dragon

'dramm|a m drama. **dram'matico** adj dramatic. **∼atiz'zare** vt dramatize. **∼a'turgo** m playwright. **dram'mone** m (film) tear-jerker

drappeggi'are vt drape. **drap'peggio** m drapery

drap'pello m (Mil) squad; (gruppo) band

'drastico adj drastic

dre'nare vt drain

drib'blare vt (in calcio) dribble

'dritta f (mano destra) right hand; (Naut) starboard; (informazione) pointer, tip; **a ∼ e a manca** left, right and centre

'dritto adj = DIRITTO • mf ⓘ crafty so-and-so

driz'zar|e vt straighten; (rizzare) prick up; **∼si** vr straighten [up]; (alzarsi) raise

'dro|ga f drug. **∼'gare** vt drug. **∼'garsi** vr take drugs. **∼'gato, -a** mf drug addict

drogh|e'ria f grocery. **∼i'ere, -a** mf grocer

'dubbi|o adj doubtful; (ambiguo) dubious • m doubt; (sospetto) suspicion; **mettere in ∼** doubt; **essere fuori ∼** be beyond doubt; **essere in ∼** be doubtful. **∼'oso** adj doubtful

dubi'ta|re vi doubt; **∼re di** doubt; (diffidare) mistrust; **dubito che venga** I doubt whether he'll come. **∼'tivo** adj ambiguous

'duca, du'chessa mf duke; duchess

'due adj & m two

due'cento adj & m two hundred

du'ello m duel

due'mila adj & m two thousand

due'pezzi m inv (bikini) bikini

du'etto m duo; (Mus) duet

'duna f dune

'dunque conj therefore; (allora) well [then]

'duo m inv duo; (Mus) duet

du'omo m cathedral

dupli'ca|re vt duplicate. **∼to m** duplicate. **'duplice** adj double; **in ∼plice** in duplicate

dura'mente adv (lavorare) hard; (rimproverare) harshly

du'rante prep during

du'r|are vi last; (cibo:) keep; (resistere) hold out. **∼ata** f duration. **∼a'turo, ∼evole** adj lasting, enduring

du'rezza f hardness; (di carne) toughness; (di voce, padre) harshness

'duro, -a adj hard; (persona, carne) tough; (voce) harsh; (pane) stale • mf tough person

du'rone m hardened skin

'duttile adj (materiale) ductile; (carattere) malleable

DVD m inv DVD

Ee

e, ed *conj* and

'ebano *m* ebony

eb'bene *conj* well [then]

eb'brezza *f* inebriation; (*euforia*) elation; guida in stato di ~za drink-driving. **'ebbro** *adj* inebriated; (*di gioia*) ecstatic

'ebete *adj* stupid

ebollizi'one *f* boiling

e'braico *adj* Hebrew ●*m* (*lingua*) Hebrew. **e'breo, -a** *adj* Jewish ●*mf* Jew

eca'tombe *f* fare un'~ wreak havoc

ecc *abbr* (eccetera) etc

ecce'den|te *adj* (peso, bagaglio) excess. **~za** *f* excess; (*d'avanzo*) surplus; avere qcsa in ~za have an excess of sth; bagagli in ~za excess baggage. **~za di cassa** surplus. **ec'cedere** *vt* exceed ●*vi* go too far; eccedere nel bere drink too much

eccel'len|te *adj* excellent. **~za** *f* excellence; (*titolo*) Excellency; per **~za** par excellence. **ec'cellere** *vi* excel (in at)

ec'centrico, -a *adj* & *mf* eccentric

ecces'siva'mente *adv* excessively. **ec'cessivo** *adj* excessive

ec'cesso *m* excess; andare agli eccessi go to extremes; **all'~** to excess. **~ di velocità** speeding

ec'cetera *adv* et cetera

ec'cetto *prep* except; **~ che** (*a meno che*) unless. **eccettu'are** *vt* except

eccezio'nal|e *adj* exceptional. **~'mente** *adv* exceptionally; (*contrariamente alla regola*) as an exception

eccezi'one *f* exception; (*Jur*) objection; **a ~ di** with the exception of. **eccita'mento** *m* excitement. **ecci-**

'tante *adj* exciting; (*sostanza*) stimulant ●*m* stimulant

ecci'ta|re *vt* excite. **~rsi** *vr* get excited. **~to** *adj* excited

eccitazi'one *f* excitement

ecclesi'astico *adj* ecclesiastical ●*m* priest

'ecco *adv* (*qui*) here; (*là*) there; **~!** exactly!; **~ fatto** there we are; **~ la tua borsa** here is your bag; **~ [li] mio figlio** there is my son; **~mi** here I am; **~ tutto** that is all

ec'come *adv* & *int* and how!

echeggi'are *vi* echo

e'clissi *f inv* eclipse

'eco *f* (*pl m* echi) echo

ecogra'fia *f* scan

ecolo'gia *f* ecology. **eco'logico** *adj* ecological; (*prodotto*) environmentally friendly

e commerci'ale *f* ampersand

econo'mia *f* economy; (*scienza*) economics; fare ~la economize (di on). **eco'nomico** *adj* economic; (*a buon prezzo*) cheap. **~ista** *mf* economist. **~iz'zare** *vt/i* economize; save (tempo, denaro). **e'conomo, -a** *adj* thrifty ●*mf* (*di collegio*) bursar

é'cru *adj inv* raw

ec'zema *m* eczema

ed *conj vedi* e

'edera *f* ivy

e'dicola *f* [newspaper] kiosk

edifi'cabile *adj* (area, terreno) *classified as* suitable for development

edifi'cante *adj* edifying

edifi'care *vt* build

edi'ficio *m* building; *fig* structure

e'dile *adj* building *attrib*

edi'lizi|a *f* building trade. **~o** *adj* building *attrib*

edi'to|re, -'trice *adj* publishing ●*mf* publisher; (*curatore*) editor. **~to'ria** *f* publishing. **~tori'ale** *adj* publishing ●*m* editorial

edizi'one *f* edition; (*di manifestazione*)

performance. ~ **ridotta** abridg[e]ment. ~ **della sera** (*di telegiornale*) evening news

edu'ca|re vt educate; (*allevare*) bring up. ~'**tivo** adj educational. ~**to** adj polite. ~'**tore**, ~'**trice** mf educator. ~**zi'one** f education; (*di bambini*) upbringing; (*buone maniere*) [good] manners pl. ~**zione fisica** physical education

e'felide f freckle

effemi'nato adj effeminate

efferve'scente adj effervescent; (*frizzante*) fizzy; (*aspirina*) soluble

effettiva'mente adv è troppo tardi – ~ it's too late - so it is

effet'tivo adj actual; (*efficace*) effective; (*personale*) permanent; (*Mil*) regular ●m sum effect

ef'fetto m effect; (*impressione*) impression; in ~**i** in fact; ~**i personali** personal belongings. ~**u'are** vt carry out (controllo, sondaggio). ~**u'arsi** vr take place

effi'cace adj effective. ~**ia** f effectiveness

effici'en|te adj efficient. ~**za** f efficiency

ef'fimero adj ephemeral

effusi'one f effusion

E'geo m l'~ the Aegean [Sea]

E'gitto m Egypt. **egizi'ano**, -**a** agg & mf Egyptian

'**egli** pers pron he; ~ **stesso** he himself

ego'centrico, -**a** adj egocentric

ego'is|mo m selfishness. ~**ta** adj selfish ●mf selfish person. ~**tico** adj selfish

e'gregio adj distinguished; **E**~ **Signore** Dear Sir

eiaculazi'one f ejaculation

elabo'ra|re vt elaborate; process (dati). ~**to** adj elaborate. ~**zi'one** f elaboration; (*di dati*) processing. ~**zione [di] testi** word processing

elar'gire vt lavish

elastici'tà f elasticity. ~**z'zato** adj (stoffa) elasticated. **e'lastico** adj elastic; (*tessuto*) stretch; (*orario*, *mente*) flexible; (*persona*) easygoing ●m elastic; (*fascia*) rubber band

ele'fante m elephant

ele'gan|te adj elegant. ~**za** f elegance

e'leggere vt elect. **eleg'gibile** adj eligible

elemen'tare adj elementary; **scuola** ~ primary school

ele'mento m element; **elementi** pl (*fatti*) data; (*rudimenti*) elements

ele'mosina f charity; **chiedere l'**~ beg. **elemosi'nare** vt/i beg

elen'care vt list

e'lenco m list. ~ **abbonati** telephone directory. ~ **telefonico** telephone directory

elet'tivo adj (carica) elective. **e'letto**, -**a** pp di **eleggere** ●adj chosen ●mf elected member

eletto'ra|le adj electoral. ~**to** m electorate

elet'|tore, -'**trice** mf voter

elet'trauto m inv garage for electrical repairs

elettri'cista m electrician

elettri'cità f electricity. **e'lettrico** adj electric. ~**z'zante** adj (notizia, gara) electrifying. ~**z'zare** vt fig electrify. ~**z'zato** adj fig electrified

elettrocardio'gramma m electrocardiogram

e'lettrodo m electrode

elettrodo'mestico m [electrical] household appliance

elet'trone m electron

elet'tronica, -**a** adj electronic ●f electronics

ele'va|re vt raise; (*promuovere*) promote; (*erigere*) erect; (*fig: migliorare*) better; ~ **al quadrato/cubo** square/cube. ~**rsi** vr rise; (*edificio*): stand.

~to adj high. ~zi'one f elevation

elezi'one f election

'elica f (Aeron, Naut) propeller; (del ventilatore) blade

eli'cottero m helicopter

elimi'na|re vt eliminate. ~'toria f Sport preliminary heat. ~zi'one f elimination

é'li|te f inv élite. ~'tista adj élitist

'ella pers pron she

el'metto m helmet

elogi'are vt praise

elo'quen|te adj eloquent; fig telltale. ~za f eloquence

e'lu|dere vt elude; evade (sorveglianza). ~'sivo adj elusive

el'vetico adj Swiss

emaci'ato adj emaciated

'e-mail f e-mail; indirizzo ~ e-mail address. ~ spazzatura junk e-mail

ema'na|re vt give off; pass (legge) ● vi emanate

emanci'pa|re vt emancipate. ~rsi vr become emancipated. ~to adj emancipated. ~zi'one f emancipation

emargi'na|to m marginalized person. ~zi'one f marginalization

em'bargo m embargo

em'ble|ma m emblem. ~'matico adj emblematic

embrio'nale adj embryonic. em'bri|one m embryo

emen|da'mento m amendment. ~'dare vt amend

emer'gen|te adj emergent. ~za f emergency; in caso di ~ in an emergency

e'mergere vi emerge; (sottomarino:) surface; (distinguersi) stand out

e'merso pp di emergere

e'messo pp di emettere

e'mettere vt emit; give out (luce, suono); let out (grido); (mettere in circolazione) issue

emi'crania f migraine

emi'gra|re vi emigrate. ~to, -a mf immigrant. ~zi'one f emigration

emi'nen|te adj eminent. ~za f eminence

e'miro m emir

emis'fero m hemisphere

emis'sario m emissary

emissi'one f emission; (di denaro) issue; (trasmissione) broadcast

emit'tente adj issuing; (trasmittente) broadcasting ● f transmitter

emorra'gia f haemorrhage

emor'roidi fpl piles

emotività f emotional make-up. emo'tivo adj emotional

emozio'na|nte adj exciting; (commovente) moving. ~re vt excite; (commuovere) move. ~rsi vr become excited; (commuoversi) be moved. ~to adj excited; (commosso) moved. emozi'one f emotion; (agitazione) excitement

'empio adj impious; (spietato) pitiless; (malvagio) wicked

em'pirico adj empirical

em'porio m emporium; (negozio) general store

emu'la|re vt emulate. ~zi'one f emulation

emulsi'one f emulsion

en'ciclica f encyclical

enciclope'dia f encyclopaedia

encomi'are vt commend. en'comio m commendation

en'demico adj endemic

endo've|na f intravenous injection. ~'noso adj intravenous; per via ~nosa intravenously

ener'getico adj (risorse, crisi) energy attrib; (alimento) energy-giving

ener'gia f energy. e'nergico adj energetic; (efficace) strong

'enfasi f emphasis

en'fatico adj emphatic. ~z'zare vt emphasize

e'nigma m enigma. enig'matico adj enigmatic. enig'mistica f puzzles pl

E.N.I.T. m abbr (Ente Nazionale Italiano per il Turismo) Italian State Tourist Office

en'nesimo adj (Math) nth; 🄃 umpteenth

e'norm|e adj enormous. ~e'mente adv massively. ~ità f inv enormity; (assurdità) absurdity

eno'teca f wine-tasting shop

'ente m board; (società) company; (filosofia) being

entità f inv entity; (gravità) seriousness; (dimensione) extent

entou'rage m inv entourage

en'trambi adj & pron both

en'tra|re vi go in, enter; ~re in go into; (stare in, trovar posto in) fit into; (arruolarsi) join; ~rci (avere a che fare) have to do with; tu che c'entri? what has it got to do with you? ~ta f entrance; ~te pl (Comm) takings; (reddito) income sg

'entro prep (tempo) within

entro'terra m inv hinterland

entusias'mante adj fascinating

entusias'mar|e vt arouse enthusiasm in. ~si vr be enthusiastic (per about)

entusi'as|mo m enthusiasm. ~ta adj enthusiastic ●mf enthusiast. ~tico adj enthusiastic

enume'ra|re vt enumerate. ~zi'one f enumeration

enunci'a|re vt enunciate. ~zi'one f enunciation

epa'tite f hepatitis

'epico adj epic

epide'mia f epidemic

epi'dermide f epidermis

Epifa'nia f Epiphany

epi'gramma m epigram

epil|es'sia f epilepsy. epi'lettico, -a adj & mf epileptic

e'pilogo m epilogue

epi'sodi|co adj episodic; caso ~co one-off case. ~o m episode

'epoca f age; (periodo) period; a quell'~ in those days; auto d'~ vintage car

ep'pure conj [and] yet

epu'rare vt purge

equa'tore m equator. equatori'ale adj equatorial

equazi'one f equation

e'questre adj equestrian; circo ~ circus

equili'bra|re vt balance. ~to adj well-balanced. equi'librio m balance; (buon senso) common sense; (di bilancia) equilibrium

equili'brismo m fare ~ do a balancing act

e'quino adj horse attrib

equi'nozio m equinox

equipaggia'mento m equipment

equipaggi'are vt equip; (di persone) man

equi'paggio m crew; (Aeron) cabin crew

equipa'rare vt make equal

é'quipe f inv team

equità f equity

equitazi'one f riding

equiva'len|te adj & m equivalent. ~za f equivalence

equiva'lere vi ~ a be equivalent to

equivo'care vi misunderstand

e'quivoco adj equivocal; (sospetto) suspicious ●m misunderstanding

'equo adj fair, just

'era f era

'erba f grass; (aromatica, medicinale) herb. ~ cipollina chives pl. er'baccia f weed. er'baceo adj herbaceous

erbi'cida m weed-killer

erbo'rist|a mf herbalist. ∼e'ria f herbalist's shop

er'boso adj grassy

er'culeo adj (forza) herculean

e'red|e mf heir; heiress. ∼ità f inv inheritance; (Biol) heredity. ∼i'tare vt inherit. ∼itarietà f heredity. ∼i'tario adj hereditary

ere'sia f heresy. e'retico, e'retico, -a adj heretical • mf heretic

e're|tto pp di erigere • adj erect. ∼zi'one f erection; (costruzione) building

er'gastolo m life sentence; (luogo) prison

'erica f heather

e'rigere vt erect; (fig: fondare) found

eri'tema m (cutaneo) inflammation; (solare) sunburn

er'metico adj hermetic; (a tenuta d'aria) airtight

'ernia f hernia

e'rodere vi erode

e'ro|e m hero. ∼ico adj heroic. ∼ismo m heroism

ero'ga|re vt distribute; (fornire) supply. ∼zi'one f supply

ero'ina f heroine; (droga) heroin

erosi'one f erosion

e'rotico adj erotic

er'rante adj wandering. **er'rare** vi wander; (sbagliare) be mistaken

er'rato adj (sbagliato) mistaken

erronea'mente adv mistakenly

er'rore m error; (di stampa) misprint; **essere in** ∼ be wrong

'erta f **stare all'**∼ be on the alert

eru'di|rsi vr get educated. ∼to adj learned

erut'tare vt (vulcano:) erupt • vi (ruttare) belch. **eruzi'one** f eruption; (Med) rash

esage'ra|re vt exaggerate • vi exaggerate; (nel comportamento) go over the top; ∼**re nel mangiare** eat too much. ∼ta'mente adv excessively. ∼to adj exaggerated; (prezzo) exorbitant • m **è un** ∼to he exaggerates. ∼zi'one f exaggeration; **è costato un'**∼zione it cost the earth

esa'lare vt/i exhale

esal'ta|re vt exalt; (entusiasmare) elate. ∼to adj (fanatico) fanatical • m fanatic. ∼zi'one f exaltation; (in discorso) fervour

e'same m examination, exam; **dare un** ∼ take an exam; **prendere in** ∼ examine. ∼ **del sangue** blood test. **esami** pl **di maturità** ≈ A-levels

esami'na|re vt examine. ∼'tore, ∼'trice mf examiner

e'sangue adj bloodless

e'sanime adj lifeless

esaspe'rante adj exasperating

esaspe'ra|re vt exasperate. ∼**rsi** vr get exasperated. ∼zi'one f exasperation

esatta'mente adv exactly. ∼'tezza f exactness; (precisione) precision; (di risultato) accuracy

e'satto pp di esigere • adj exact; (risposta, risultato) correct; (orologio) right; **hai l'ora esatta?** do you have the right time?; **sono le due esatte** it's two o'clock exactly

esat'tore m collector

esau'dire vt grant; fulfil (speranze)

esau'riente adj exhaustive

esau'ri|re vt exhaust. ∼**rsi** vr exhaust oneself; (merci ecc:) run out. ∼to adj exhausted; (merci) sold out; (libro) out of print; **fare il tutto** ∼to (spettacolo:) play to a full house

'esca f bait

escande'scenz|a f outburst; **dare in** ∼**e** lose one's temper

escla'ma|re vi exclaim. ∼'tivo adj exclamatory. ∼zi'one f exclamation

es'clu|dere vt exclude (possibilità,

ipotesi). ∼si'one f exclusion. ∼'siva f exclusive right; in ∼siva exclusive. ∼siva'mente adv exclusively. ∼'sivo adj exclusive. ∼so pp di **escludere** ● adj non è ∼so che ci sia it's not out of the question that he'll be there

escogi'tare vt contrive

escursi'one f excursion; (scorreria) raid; (di temperatura) range

ese'cra|bile adj abominable. ∼re vt abhor

esecu'tivo adj & m executive. ∼tore, ∼trice mf executor; (Mus) performer. ∼zi'one f execution; (Mus) performance

esegu'ire vt carry out; (Jur) execute; (Mus) perform

e'sempio m example; ad o per ∼ for example; dare l'∼ a qcno set sb an example; fare un ∼ give an example

esem'plare m specimen; (di libro) copy

esen'tar|e vt exempt. ∼si vr free oneself. e'sente adj exempt. esente da imposta duty-free. esente da IVA VAT-exempt

esen'tasse adj duty-free

e'sequie fpl funeral rites

eser'cente mf shopkeeper

eserci'ta|re vt exercise; (addestrare) train; (fare uso di) exert; (professione) practise; ∼rsi vr practise. ∼zi'one f exercise; (Mil) drill

e'sercito m army

eser'cizio m exercise; (pratica) practice; (Comm) financial year; (azienda) business; essere fuori ∼ be out of practice

esi'bi|re vt show off; produce (documenti). ∼rsi vr (Theat) perform; fig show off. ∼zi'one f (Theat) performance; (di documenti) production

esibizio'nis|mo m showing off

esi'gen|te adj exacting; (pignolo) fastidious. ∼za f demand; (bisogno) need. e'sigere vt demand; (riscuotere) collect

e'siguo adj meagre

esila'rante adj exhilarating

e'sile adj slender; (voce) thin

esili'a|re vt exile. ∼rsi vr go into exile. ∼to, -a adj exiled ● mf exile. e'silio m exile

e'simer|e vt release. ∼si vr si dà get out of

esi'sten|te adj existing. ∼za f existence.

e'sistere vi exist

esi'tante adj hesitating; (voce) faltering

esi'ta|re vi hesitate. ∼zi'one f hesitation

'esito m result; avere buon ∼ be a success

'esodo m exodus

e'sofago m oesophagus

esone'rare vt exempt. e'sonero m exemption

esorbi'tante adj exorbitant

esorciz'zare vt exorcize

esordi'ente mf person making his/her début. e'sordio m opening; (di attore) début. esor'dire vi début

esor'tare vt (pregare) beg; (incitare) urge

e'sotico adj exotic

espa'drillas fpl espadrilles

es'pan|dere vt expand. ∼dersi vr expand; (diffondersi) extend. ∼si'one f expansion. ∼'sivo adj expansive; (persona) friendly

espatri'are vi leave one's country. es'patrio m expatriation

espedi'ente m expedient; vivere di ∼i live by one's wits

es'pellere vt expel

esperi'enza f experience; parlare per ∼enza speak from experience. ∼'mento m experiment es'perto, -a *adj & mf* expert

espi'a|re *vt* atone for. ~'torio *adj* expiatory

espi'rare *vt/i* breathe out

espli'care *vt* carry on

esplicita'mente *adv* explicitly. es'plicito *adj* explicit

es'plodere *vi* explode ● *vt* fire

esplo'ra|re *vt* explore. ~'tore, ~'trice *mf* explorer; giovane ~'tore boy scout. ~zi'one *f* exploration

explo|si'one *f* explosion. ~'sivo *adj & m* explosive

es'por|re *vt* expose; display (merci); (spiegare) expound; exhibit (quadri ecc). ~si *vr* (compromettersi) compromise oneself; (al sole) expose oneself

espor'ta|re *vt* export. ~'tore, ~'trice *mf* exporter. ~zi'one *f* export

esposizi'one *f* (mostra) exhibition; (in vetrina) display; (spiegazione ecc) exposition; (posizione, fotografia) exposure. es'posto *pp di* esporre ● *adj* exposed; esposto a (rivolto) facing ● *m* (Jur) statement

espressa'mente *adv* expressly; non l'ha detto ~ he didn't put it in so many words

espres|si'one *f* expression. ~'sivo *adj* expressive

es'presso *pp di* esprimere ● *adj* express ● *m* (lettera) express letter; (treno) express train; (caffè) espresso; per ~ (spedire) [by] express [post]

es'primer|e *vt* express. ~si *vr* express oneself

espropri'a|re *vt* dispossess. ~zi'one *f* (Jur) expropriation. es'proprio *m* expropriation

espulsi'one *f* expulsion. es'pulso *pp di* espellere

es'senz|a *f* essence. ~i'ale *adj* essential ● *m* important thing. ~ial'mente *adj* essentially

'essere

● *vi* be; c'è there is; ci sono there are; che ora è? – sono le dieci what time is it? – it's ten o'clock; chi è? – sono io who is it? – it's me; ci siamo! (siamo arrivati) here we are at last!; siamo in due there are two of us; questa camicia è da lavare this shirt is to be washed; non è da te it's not like you; ~ di (provenire da) be from; ~ per (favorevole) be in favour of; se fossi in te,... if I were you,...; sarà if you say so!; come sarebbe a dire? what are you getting at?

● *v aux* have; (in passivi) be; siamo arrivati we have arrived; ci sono stato ieri I was there yesterday; sono nato a Torino I was born in Turin; è riconosciuto come... he is recognized as...; è stato detto che it has been said that

● *m* being. ~ umano human being. ~ vivente living creature

essic'cato *adj* dried

'esso, -a *pers pron* he, she; (cosa, animale) it

est *m* east

'estasi *f* ecstasy; andare in ~ per go into raptures over

e'state *f* summer

e'sten|dere *vt* extend. ~dersi *vr* spread; (allungarsi) stretch. ~si'one *f* extension; (ampiezza) expanse; (Mus) range. ~sivo *adj* extensive

estenu'ante *adj* exhausting

estenu'a|re *vt* wear out; deplete (risorse, casse). ~rsi *vr* wear oneself out

esteri'or|e *adj & m* exterior. ~'mente *adv* externally; (di persone) outwardly esterna'mente adv on the outside

ester'nare vt express, show

e'sterno adj external; per uso ~ for external use only ● m (allievo) day-boy; (Archit) exterior; (in film) location shot

'estero adj foreign ● m foreign countries pl; all'~ abroad

esterre'fatto adj horrified

e'steso pp di estendere ● adj extensive; (diffuso) widespread; per ~ (scrivere) in full

e'stetic|a f aesthetics sg. ~a'mente adv aesthetically. ~o, -a adj aesthetic; (chirurgia, chirurgo) plastic. este'tista f beautician

'estimo m estimate

e'stin|guere vt extinguish. ~guersi vr die out. ~to, -a pp di estinguere ● mf deceased. ~tore m [fire] extinguisher. ~zi'one f extinction; (di incendio) putting out

estir'pa|re vt uproot; extract (dente); fig eradicate (crimine, malattia). ~zi'one f eradication; (di dente) extraction

e'stivo adj summer

e'stor|cere vt extort. ~si'one f extortion. ~to pp di estorcere

estradizi'one f extradition

e'straneo, -a adj extraneous; (straniero) foreign ● mf stranger

estrani'ar|e vt estrange. ~si vr become estranged

e'stra|rre vt extract; (sorteggiare) draw. ~tto pp di estrarre ● m extract; (brano) excerpt; (documento) abstract. ~tto conto statement [of account], bank statement. ~zi'one f extraction; (sorte) draw

estrema'mente adv extremely

estre'mis|mo m extremism. ~ta mf extremist

estremità f inv extremity; (di una corda) end ● fpl (Anat) extremities

e'stremo adj extreme; (ultimo) last; misure estreme drastic measures; l'E~ Oriente the Far East ● m (limite) extreme. estremi pl (di documento) main points; (di reato) essential elements; essere agli estremi be at the end of one's tether

'estro m (disposizione artistica) talent; (ispirazione) inspiration; (capriccio) whim. e'stroso adj talented; (capriccioso) unpredictable

estro'mettere vt expel

estro'verso adj extroverted ● m extrovert

estu'ario m estuary

esube'ran|te adj exuberant. ~za f exuberance

'esule mf exile

esul'tante adj exultant

esul'tare vi rejoice

esu'mare vt exhume

età f inv age; raggiungere la maggiore ~ come of age; un uomo di mezz'~ a middle-aged man

'etere m ether. e'tereo adj ethereal

eterna'mente adv eternally

eternità f eternity; è un'~ che non la vedo I haven't seen her for ages

e'terno adj eternal; (questione, problema) age-old; in ~ 🔲 for ever

eterosessu'ale mf heterosexual

'etica f ethics

eti'chetta¹ f label; price-tag

eti'chetta² f etiquette

etichet'tare vt label

'etico adj ethical

eti'lometro m Breathalyzer®

Eti'opia f Ethiopia

'etnico adj ethnic

e'trusco adj & mf Etruscan

'ettaro m hectare

'etto, ettogrammo m hundred grams, ≈ quarter pound

eucari'stia f Eucharist

eufe'mismo m euphemism
eufo'ria f elation; (Med) euphoria. **eu'forico** adj elated; (Med) euphoric
'euro m inv Fin euro
Euro'city m international Intercity
eurodepu'tato m Euro MP, MEP
Eu'ropa f Europe. **euro'peo, -a** agg & mf European
eutana'sia f euthanasia
evacu'a|re vt evacuate. **~zi'one** f evacuation
e'vadere vt evade; (sbrigare) deal with ●vi **~ da** escape from
evane'scente adj vanishing
evan'gel|ico adj evangelical. **evange'lista** m evangelist
evapo'ra|re vi evaporate. **~zi'one** f evaporation
evasi'one f escape; (fiscale) evasion; fig escapism. **eva'sivo** adj evasive
e'vaso pp di evadere ●m fugitive
eva'sore m **~ fiscale** tax evader
eveni'enza f eventuality
e'vento m event
eventu'al|e adj possible. **~ità** f inv eventuality
evi'den|te adj evident; **è ~te che** it is obvious that. **~te'mente** adv evidently. **~za** f evidence; mettere in **~za** emphasize; mettersi in **~za** make oneself conspicuous
evidenzi'a|re vt highlight. **~'tore** m (penna) highlighter
evi'tare vt avoid; (risparmiare) spare
evo'care vt evoke
evo'lu|to pp di evolvere ●adj evolved; (progredito) progressive; (civiltà, nazione) advanced; **una donna evoluta** a modern woman. **~zi'one** f evolution; (di ginnastica, aereo) circle
e'volver|e vt develop. **~si** vr evolve
ev'viva int hurray; **~ il Papal** long live the Pope!; **gridare ~** cheer
ex+ pref ex+, former

'extra adj inv extra; (qualità) first-class ●m inv extra
extracomuni'tario adj non-EU
extrater'restre mf extra-terrestrial

Extravergine Olive oil which is obtained from the first pressing of the olives is called *extravergine* (extra virgin). It has a distinctive peppery flavour and is often a cloudy greenish colour. A less refined grade, suitable for cooking, is obtained by using chemical methods. This is called simply *olio d'oliva*.

Ff

fa¹ m inv (Mus) F
fa² adv ago; **due mesi ~** two months ago
fabbi'sogno m requirements pl
'fabbrica f factory
fabbri'cabile adj (area, terreno) that can be built on
fabbri'cante m manufacturer
fabbri'ca|re vt build; (produrre) manufacture; (fig: inventare) fabricate. **~to** m building. **~zi'one** f manufacturing; (costruzione) building
'fabbro m blacksmith
fac'cend|a f matter; **~e** pl (lavori domestici) housework sg. **~i'ere** m wheeler-dealer
fac'chino m porter
'facci|a f face; (di foglio) side; **~a a ~a** face to face; **~a tosta** cheek; **voltar ~a** change sides; **di ~a** (palazzo) opposite; **alla ~a di** in spite of. **~'ata** f façade; (di foglio) side; (fig: esteriorità) outward

appearance

fa'ceto *adj* facetious; **tra il serio e il ~** half joking

fa'chiro *m* fakir

'facil|e *adj* easy; *(affabile)* easygoing; **essere ~e alle critiche** be quick to criticize; **essere ~e al riso** laugh a lot; **~e a farsi easy to do; è ~e che piova** it's likely to rain. **~ità** *f* ease; *(disposizione)* aptitude; **avere ~ità di parola** express oneself well

facili'tare *vt* facilitate. **~zi'one** *f* facility; **~zioni** *fpl* special terms

facil'mente *adv* *(con facilità)* easily; *(probabilmente)* probably

faci'lone *adj* slapdash. **~'ria** *f* slapdash attitude

facino'roso *adj* violent

facoltà *f inv* faculty; *(potere)* power. **facolta'tivo** *adj* optional; **fermata facoltativa** request stop

facol'toso *adj* wealthy

'faggio *m* beech

fagi'ano *m* pheasant

fagio'lino *m* French bean

fagi'olo *m* bean; **a ~** *(arrivare, capitare)* at the right time

fagoci'tare *vt* gobble up *(società)*

fa'gotto *m* bundle; *(Mus)* bassoon

'faida *f* feud

fai da te *m* do-it-yourself, DIY

fal'cata *f* stride

'falc|e *f* scythe. **fal'cetto** *m* sickle. **~i'are** *vt* cut; *fig* mow down. **~ia'trice** *f* [lawn-]mower

'falco *m* hawk

fal'cone *m* falcon

'falda *f* stratum; *(di neve)* flake; *(di cappello)* brim; *(pendio)* slope

fale'gname *m* carpenter. **~'ria** *f* carpentry

'falla *f* leak

fal'lace *adj* deceptive

fallimen'tare *adj* disastrous; *(Jur)* bankruptcy. **falli'mento** *m* Fin bank-

ruptcy; *fig* failure

fal'li|re *vi* Fin go bankrupt; *fig* fail **•** *vt* miss *(colpo)*. **~to, -a** *adj* unsuccessful; Fin bankrupt **•** *mf* failure; Fin bankrupt

'fallo *m* fault; *(errore)* mistake; Sport foul; *(imperfezione)* flaw; **senza ~** without fail

falò *m inv* bonfire

fal'sare *vt* alter; *(falsificare)* falsify. **~io, -a** *mf* forger; *(di documenti)* counterfeiter

falsifi'ca|re *vt* fake; *(contraffare)* forge. **~zi'one** *f* *(di documento)* falsification

falsità *f* falseness

'falso *adj* false; *(sbagliato)* wrong; *(opera d'arte ecc)* fake; *(gioielli, oro)* imitation **•** *m* forgery; **giurare il ~** commit perjury

'fama *f* fame; *(reputazione)* reputation

'fame *f* hunger; **aver ~** be hungry; **fare la ~** barely scrape a living. **fa'melico** *adj* ravenous

famige'rato *adj* infamous

fa'miglia *f* family

famili'ar|e *adj* family *attrib*; *(ben noto)* familiar; *(senza cerimonie)* informal **•** *mf* relative, relation. **~ità** *f* familiarity; *(informalità)* informality. **~iz'zarsi** *vr* familiarize oneself

fa'moso *adj* famous

fa'nale *m* lamp; *(Auto)* light. **fanali** *pl* **posteriori** *(Auto)* rear lights

fa'natico, -a *adj* fanatical; **essere ~ di calcio** be a football fanatic **•** *mf* fanatic. **fana'tismo** *m* fanaticism

fanci'ul|la *f* young girl. **~'lezza** *f* childhood. **~lo** *m* young boy

fan'donia *f* lie; **fandonie!** nonsense!

fan'fara *f* fanfare; *(complesso)* brass band

fanfaro'nata *f* brag. **fanfa'rone, -a** *mf* braggart

fan'ghiglia *f* mud. **'fango** *m* mud.

fan'goso adj muddy

fannul'lone, -a mf idler

fantasci'enza f science fiction

fanta'si|a f fantasy; (immaginazione) imagination; (capriccio) fancy; (di tessuto) pattern. ~'oso adj (stilista, ragazzo) imaginative; (resoconto) improbable

fan'tasma m ghost

fantasti'c|are vi day-dream. ~he'ria f day-dream. fan'tastico adj fantastic; (racconto) fantasy

'fante m infantryman; (nelle carte) jack. ~'ria f infantry

fan'tino m jockey

fan'toccio m puppet

fanto'matico adj phantom attrib

fara'butto m trickster

fara'ona f (uccello) guinea-fowl

far'ci|re vt stuff; fill (torta). ~to adj stuffed; (dolce) filled

far'dello m bundle; fig burden

● vt do; make (dolce, letto ecc); (recitare la parte di) play; (trascorrere) spend; ~ una pausa/un sogno have a break/a dream; ~ colpo su impress; ~ paura a frighten; ~ piacere a please; farla finita put an end to it; ~ l'insegnante be a teacher; ~ lo scemo play the idiot; ~ una settimana al mare spend a week at the seaside; 3 più 3 fa 6 3 and 3 makes 6; quanto fa? – fanno 10 000 euros how much is it? – it's 10,000 euros; far ~ qcsa a qcno get sb to do sth; (costringere) make sb do sth; ~ vedere show; fammi parlare let me speak; niente a che ~ con nothing to do with; non c'è niente da ~ (per copiare) there is nothing we/you/etc. can do; fa caldo/buio it's warm/dark; non fa niente it doesn't matter; strada facendo on the way; farcela (riuscire) manage

● vi fai in modo di venire try and come; ~ da act as; ~ per make as if to; ~ presto be quick; non fa per me it's not for me

● m way; sul far del giorno at daybreak.

● farsi vr (diventare) get; farsi avanti come forward; farsi i fatti propri mind one's own business; farsi la barba shave; farsi il ragazzo [I] find a boyfriend; farsi male hurt oneself; farsi strada (aver successo) make one's way in the world

fa'retto m spot[light]

far'falla f butterfly

farfal'lino m (cravatta) bow tie

farfugli'are vt mutter

fa'rina f flour. fari'nacei mpl starchy food sg

fa'ringe f pharynx

fari'noso adj (neve) powdery; (mela) soft; (patata) floury

farma|'ceutico adj pharmaceutical. ~'cia f pharmacy; (negozio) chemist's [shop]. ~cia di turno duty chemist. ~'cista mf chemist.

'farmaco m drug

> **Farmacia** A *farmacia* in Italy sells medicines and health-related products, whereas a *profumeria* sells not only perfume, but also beauty and personal hygiene products. For film and developing services it is necessary to go to a shop specializing in photographic equipment.

'faro m (Auto) headlight; (Aeron) beacon; (costruzione) lighthouse

'farsa f farce

'fascia f band; (zona) area; (ufficiale)

sash; (*benda*) bandage. **~'are** vt bandage; cling to (*fianchi*). **~a'tura** f dressing; (*azione*) bandaging

fa'scicolo m file; (*di rivista*) issue; (*libretto*) booklet

'fascino m fascination

'fascio m bundle; (*di fiori*) bunch

fa'scis|mo m fascism. **~ta** mf fascist

'fase f phase

fa'stidi|o m nuisance; (*scomodo*) inconvenience; dar **~o** a qcno bother sb; **~i** pl (*preoccupazioni*) worries; (*disturbi*) troubles. **~'oso** adj tiresome

'fasto m pomp. **fa'stoso** adj sumptuous

fa'sullo adj bogus

'fata f fairy

fa'tale adj fatal; (*inevitabile*) fated

fatal'ismo m fatalism. **~ista** mf fatalist. **~ità** f inv fate; (*caso sfortunato*) misfortune. **~'mente** adv inevitably

fa'tica f effort; (*lavoro faticoso*) hard work; (*stanchezza*) fatigue; a **~** with great difficulty; è **~** sprecata it's a waste of time; fare **~** a fare qcsa find it difficult to do sth; fare **~** a finire qcsa struggle to finish sth. fa·ti'caccia f pain

fati'ca|re vi toil; **~re a** (*stentare*) find it difficult to do. **~ta** f effort; (*sfacchinata*) grind. fati'coso adj tiring; (*difficile*) difficult

'fato m fate

fat'taccio m hum foul deed

fat'tezze fpl features

fat'tibile adj feasible

'fatto pp di fare ●adj done, made; **~** a mano hand-made ●m fact; (*azione*) action; (*avvenimento*) event; bada ai fatti tuoi mind your own business; di **~** in fact; in quanto al **~** as regards

fat'to|re m (Math, causa) factor; (*di fattoria*) farm manager. **~'ria** f farm; (*casa*) farmhouse

fatto'rino m messenger [boy]

fattucchi'era f witch

fat'tura f (*stile*) cut; (*lavorazione*) workmanship; (Comm) invoice

fattu'ra|re vt invoice; (*adulterare*) adulterate. **~to** m turnover, sales pl. **~zi'one** f invoicing, billing

'fatuo adj fatuous

fau'tore m supporter

'fava f broad bean

fa'vella f speech

fa'villa f spark

'favo|la f fable; (*fiaba*) story; (*oggetto di pettegolezzi*) laughing-stock; (*meraviglia*) dream. **~'loso** adj fabulous

fa'vore m favour; essere a **~** di be in favour of; per **~** please; di **~** (*condizioni, trattamento*) preferential. **~ggia'mento** m (Jur) aiding and abetting. favo'revole adj favourable. **~vol'mente** adv favourably

favo'ri|re vt favour; (*promuovere*) promote; vuol **~re?** (*a cena, pranzo*) will you have some?; (*entrare*) will you come in?. **~to,** -a adj & mf favourite

fax m inv fax. **fa'xare** vt fax

fazi'one f faction

faziosità f bias. **fazi'oso** adj sectarian

fazzolet'tino m **~** [di carta] [paper] tissue

fazzo'letto m handkerchief; (*da testa*) headscarf

feb'braio m February

'febbre f fever; avere la **~** have o run a temperature. **~ da fieno** hay fever. **feb'brile** adj feverish

'feccia f dregs pl

'fecola f potato flour

fecon'da|re vt fertilize. **~tore** m fertilizer. **~zi'one** f fertilization. **~zione artificiale** artificial insemination. fe'condo adj fertile

'fede f faith; (*fiducia*) trust; (*anello*) wedding-ring; in buona/mala **~** in good/bad faith; **prestar ~ a** believe; **tener ~ alla parola** keep one's word. **fe'dele** adj faithful ● mf believer; (seguace) follower. **~l'mente** adv faithfully. **~ltà** f faithfulness

'federa f pillowcase

fede'ra|le adj federal. **~lismo** m federalism. **~zi'one** f federation

fe'dina f **avere la ~ penale sporca/pulita** have a/no criminal record

'fegato m liver; fig guts pl

'felce f fern

fe'lic|e adj happy; (fortunato) lucky. **~ità** f happiness

felici'ta|rsi vr **~rsi con** congratulate. **~zi'oni** fpl congratulations

'felpa f (indumento) sweatshirt

fel'pato adj brushed; (passo) stealthy

'feltro m felt; (cappello) felt hat

'femmin|a f female. **femmi'nile** adj feminine; (abbigliamento) women's; (sesso) female ● m feminine. **~ilità** f femininity. **femmi'nismo** m feminism

'femore m femur

'fend|ere vt split. **~i'tura** f split; (in roccia) crack

feni'cottero m flamingo

fenome'nale adj phenomenal. **fe-'nomeno** m phenomenon

fe'retro m coffin

feri'ale adj weekday; **giorno ~** weekday

'ferie fpl holidays; (di università, tribunale ecc) vacation sg; **andare in ~** go on holiday

feri'mento m wounding

fe'ri|re vt wound; (in incidente) injure; fig hurt. **~rsi** vr injure oneself. **~ta** f wound. **~to** adj wounded ● m wounded person; (Mil) casualty

'ferma f (Mil) period of service

ferma'capelli m inv hairslide

ferma'carte m inv paperweight

fermacra'vatta m inv tiepin

fer'maglio m clasp; (spilla) brooch; (per capelli) hair slide

ferma'mente adv firmly

fer'ma|re vt stop; (fissare) fix; (Jur) detain ● vi stop. **~rsi** vr stop. **~ta** f stop. **~ta dell'autobus** bus-stop. **~ta a richiesta** request stop

fermen'ta|re vi ferment. **~zi'one** f fermentation. **fer'mento** m ferment; (lievito) yeast

fer'mezza f firmness

'fermo adj still; (veicolo) stationary; (stabile) steady; (orologio) not working ● m (Jur) detention; (Mech) catch; **in stato di ~** in custody

fe'roc|e adj ferocious; (bestia) wild; (dolore) unbearable. **~e'mente** adv fiercely. **~ia** f ferocity

fer'raglia f scrap iron

ferra'gosto m 15 August (bank holiday in Italy); (periodo) August holidays pl

ferra'menta fpl ironmongery sg; **negozio di ~** ironmonger's

fer'ra|re vt shoe (cavallo). **~to** adj **~to in** (preparato in) well up in

'ferreo adj iron

'ferro m iron; (attrezzo) tool; (di chirurgo) instrument; **bistecca ai ferri** grilled steak; **di ~** (memoria) excellent; (alibi) cast-iron; **salute di ~** iron constitution. **~ battuto** wrought iron. **~ da calza** knitting needle. **~ di cavallo** horseshoe. **~ da stiro** iron

ferro'vecchio m scrap merchant

ferro'vi|a f railway. **~'ario** adj railway. **~'ere** m railwayman

fer'tile adj fertile. **~ità** f fertility. **~iz'zante** m fertilizer

fer'vente adj blazing; fig fervent

fer'vere vi (preparativi:) be well under way

'fervido adj fervent; **~i auguri** best wishes

fer'vore m fervour

109

fesse'ria | fiera

fesse'ria f nonsense
'fesso pp di fendere ● adj cracked; (🔲: sciocco) foolish ● m 🔲 (idiota) fool; far ~ qcno con sb
fes'sura f crack; (per gettone ecc) slot
'festa f feast; (giorno festivo) holiday; (compleanno) birthday; (ricevimento) party; fig joy; fare ~ a qcno welcome sb; essere in ~ be on holiday; far ~ celebrate. ~l'olo adj festive
festeggia'mento m celebration; (manifestazione) festivity
festeggi'are vt celebrate; (accogliere festosamente) give a hearty welcome to
fe'stino m party
festività fpl festivities. **fe'stivo** adj holiday; (lieto) festive. **festivi** mpl public holidays
fe'stoso adj merry
fe'tente adj evil smelling; fig revolting ● mf 🔲 bastard
fe'ticcio m fetish
'feto m foetus
fe'tore m stench
'fetta f slice; a fette sliced. ~ biscottata slices of crispy toast-like bread
fet'tuccia f tape; (con nome) name tape
feu'dale adj feudal. **'feudo** m feud
FFSS abbr (Ferrovie dello Stato) Italian state railways
fi'aba f fairy-tale. **fia'besco** adj fairy-tale
fi'acca f weariness; (indolenza) laziness; battere la ~a be sluggish
fiac'care vt weaken. ~**rsi** vr weak; (indolente) slack; (stanco) weary; (partita) dull
fi'acco|la f torch. ~**lata** f torchlight procession
fi'ala f phial
fi'amma f flame; (Naut) pennant; in fiamme aflame. andare in fiamme go up in flames. ~ **ossidrica** blowtorch

fiam'ma|nte adj flaming; nuovo ~nte brand new. ~**ta** f blaze
fiammeggi'are vi blaze
fiam'mifero m match
fiam'mingo, -a adj Flemish ● mf Fleming ● m (lingua) Flemish
fiancheggi'are vt border; fig support
fi'anco m side; (di persona) hip; (di animale) flank; (Mil) wing; al mio ~ by my side; ~ a ~ (lavorare) side by side
fi'asco m flask; fig fiasco; fare ~ be a fiasco
fia'tare vi breathe; (parlare) breathe a word
fi'ato m breath; (vigore) stamina; strumenti a ~ wind instruments; senza ~ breathlessly; tutto d'un ~ (bere, leggere) all in one go
'fibbia f buckle
'fibra f fibre; fibre pl (alimentari) roughage. ~ **ottica** optical fibre
ficca'naso mf nosey parker
fic'car|e vt thrust; drive (chiodo ecc); (🔲: mettere) shove. ~**si** vr thrust oneself; (nascondersi) hide; ~**si nei guai** get oneself into trouble
fiche f inv (gettone) chip
'fico m (albero) fig-tree; (frutto) fig. ~ **d'India** prickly pear
'fico, -a 🔲 mf cool sort ● adj cool
fidanza'mento m engagement
fidan'za|rsi vr get engaged. ~**to, -a** mf (ufficiale) fiancé; fiancée
fi'dar|si vr ~**rsi di** trust. ~**to** adj trustworthy
'fido m devoted follower; (Comm) credit
fi'ducia f confidence; degno di ~a trustworthy; persona di ~a reliable person; di ~a (fornitore) usual. ~**oso** adj trusting
fi'ele m bile; fig bitterness
fie'nile m barn. **fi'eno** m hay
fi'era f fair

fie'rezza f (dignità) pride. **fi'ero** adj proud

fi'evole adj faint; (luce) weak

'fifa f 🔲 jitters; aver ~ have the jitters

'figli|a f daughter; ~a unica only child. ~'astra f stepdaughter. ~'astro m stepson. ~o m son; (generico) child. ~o unico only child

---

Figlio di papà With the rapid rise in living standards which took place in Italy after 1945, many more children grew up in affluent families than was previously the case, and *figli unici* (only children) are often the norm. Children, both young and grown-up, are often given considerable financial help by their parents, and are sometimes termed *figli di papà*, implying that they are also spoilt.

---

figli'occi|a f goddaughter. ~o m godson

figli'ol|a f girl. ~'lanza f offspring. ~lo m boy

'figo, -a ⊳ **FICO, -A**

fi'gura f figure; (aspetto esteriore) shape; (illustrazione) illustration; (far bella/brutta) make a good/bad impression; **mi hai fatto fare una brutta ~** you made me look a fool; **che ~!** how embarrassing!. **figu'rac-cia** f bad impression

figu'ra|re vt represent; (simboleggiare) symbolize; (immaginare) imagine ●vi (far figura) cut a dash; (in lista) appear. ~**rsi** vr (immaginarsi) imagine ~**ti!** imagine that!; **posso? - [ma] ~ti!** may I? - of course!. ~'tivo adj figurative

figu'rina f = cigarette card

figu|ri'nista mf dress designer. ~'rino m fashion sketch. ~'rone m **fare un ~rone** make an excellent impression

'fila f line; (di soldati ecc) file; (di oggetti) row; (coda) queue; **di ~** in succession; **fare la ~** queue [up], stand in line Am

fi'lare vt spin; (Naut) pay out ●vi (andarsene) run away; (liquido:) trickle; **filal** 🔲 scram!; ~ **con** (🔲: amoreggiare) go out with

filar'monica f (orchestra) orchestra

fila'strocca f rigmarole; (per bambini) nursery rhyme

fi'la|to adj spun; (ininterrotto) running; (continuato) uninterrupted; **di ~to** (subito) immediately ●m yarn

fil di 'ferro m wire

fi'letto m (bordo) border; (di vite) thread; (Culin) fillet

fili'ale adj filial ●f (Comm) branch

fili'grana f filigree; (su carta) watermark

film m inv film. ~ **giallo** thriller. ~ **a lungo metraggio** feature film

fil'ma|re vt film. ~**to** m short film. **fil'mino** m cine film

'filo m thread; (tessile) yarn; (metallico) wire; (di lama) edge; (venatura) grain; (di perle) string; (d'erba) blade; (di luce) ray; **con un ~ di voce** in a whisper; **fare il ~ a qcno** fancy sb; **perdere il ~** lose the thread. ~ **spinato** barbed wire

'filobus m inv trolleybus

filodiffusi'one f rediffusion

fi'lone m vein; (di pane) long loaf

filoso'fia f philosophy. **fi'losofo, -a** mf philosopher

fil'trare vt filter. **'filtro** m filter

'filza f string

fin ⊳ **FINE, FINO**

fi'nal|e adj final ●m end ●f Sport final. **fina'lista** mf finalist. ~**ità** f inv finality; (scopo) aim. ~'**mente** adv at last; (in ultimo) finally

fi'nanz|a f finance; ~i'**ario** adj financial. ~i'**ere** m financier; (guardia di finanza) customs officer. ~ia'**mento**

m funding

finanzia|re *vt* fund, finance. ∼**tore**, ∼**trice** *mf* backer

finché *conj* until; (*per tutto il tempo che*) as long as

'fine *adj* fine; (*sottile*) thin; (*udito, vista*) keen; (*raffinato*) refined ●*f* end; **alla** ∼ **in the end; alla fin** ∼ **after all; in fin dei conti** when all's said and done; **senza** ∼ endless ●*m* aim. ∼ **settimana** weekend

fi'nestra *f* window. fine'strella *f* di aiuto (*Comput*) help box. fine'strino *m* (*Auto, Rail*) window

fi'nezza *f* fineness; (*sottigliezza*) thinness; (*raffinatezza*) refinement

'finger|e *vt* pretend; feign (*affetto ecc.*). ∼**si** *vr* pretend to be

fini'menti *mpl* finishing touches; (*per cavallo*) harness *sg*

fini'mondo *m* end of the world; *fig* pandemonium

fi'ni|re *vt/i* finish, end; (*smettere*) stop; (*diventare, andare a finire*) end up; ∼**scila!** stop it!. ∼**to** *adj* finished; (*abile*) accomplished. ∼**tura** *f* finish

finlan'dese *adj* Finnish ●*mf* Finn ●*m* (*lingua*) Finnish

Fin'landia *f* Finland

'fino[1] *prep* ∼ **a** till, until; (*spazio*) as far as; ∼ **all'ultimo** to the last; **fin da** (*tempo*) since; (*spazio*) from; **fin qui** as far as here; **fin troppo** too much; ∼ **a ora** how far for much

'fino[2] *adj* fine; (*acuto*) subtle; (*puro*) pure

fi'nocchio *m* fennel; (☐: *omosessuale*) poof

fi'nora *adv* so far, up till now

'finta *f* sham; *Sport* feint; **far** ∼ **di** pretend to; **far** ∼ **di niente** act as if nothing had happened; **per** ∼ (*per scherzo*) for a laugh

'fint|o, -a *pp di* fingere ●*adj* false; (*artificiale*) artificial; **fare il** ∼**o tonto** act dumb

finzi'one *f* pretence

fi'occo *m* bow; (*di neve*) flake; (*nappa*) tassel; **coi fiocchi** *fig* excellent. ∼ **di neve** snowflake

fi'ocina *f* harpoon

fi'oco *adj* weak; (*luce*) dim

fi'onda *f* catapult

fio'raio, -a *mf* florist

fiorda'liso *m* cornflower

fi'ordo *m* fiord

fi'ore *m* flower; (*parte scelta*) cream; **fiori** *pl* (*nelle carte*) clubs; **a fior d'acqua** on the surface of the water; **fior di** (*abbondanza*) a lot of; **ha i nervi a fior di pelle** his nerves are on edge; **a fiori** flowery

fioren'tino *adj* Florentine

fio'retto *m* (*scherma*) foil; (*Relig*) act of mortification

fio'rire *vi* flower; (*albero:*) blossom; *fig* flourish

fio'rista *mf* florist

fiori'tura *f* (*di albero*) blossoming

fi'otto *m* scorrere a fiotti pour out; **piove a fiotti** the rain is pouring down

Fi'renze *f* Florence

'firma *f* signature; (*nome*) name

fir'ma|re *vt* sign. ∼**tario, -a** *mf* signatory. ∼**to** *adj* (*abito, borsa*) designer *attrib*

fisar'monica *f* accordion

fi'scale *adj* fiscal

fischi'are *vi* whistle ●*vt* whistle; (*in segno di disapprovazione*) boo

fischiet'tare *vt* whistle. ∼**io** *m* whistling

fischi'etto *m* whistle. '**fischio** *m* whistle

'fisco *m* treasury; (*tasse*) taxation; **il** ∼ **the taxman**

'fisica *f* physics

'fisico, -a *adj* physical ●*mf* physicist ●*m* physique

'fisima *f* whim

fisio|lo'gia f physiology. ~**logico** adj physiological

fisiono'mia f features, face; (di paesaggio) appearance

fisiotera'pia f physiotherapy. ~**sta** mf physiotherapist

fis'sa|re vt fix, fasten; (guardare fissamente) stare at; arrange (appuntamento, ora). ~**rsi** vr (stabilirsi) settle; (fissare lo sguardo) stare; ~**rsi su** (ostinarsi) set one's mind on; ~**rsi di fare qcsa** become obsessed with doing sth. ~**to** m obsessive. ~**zi'one** f fixation; (ossessione) obsession

'fisso adj fixed; **un lavoro** ~ a regular job; **senza fissa dimora** of no fixed abode

fit'tizio adj fictitious

fitto¹ adj thick; ~ **di full of** ● m depth

fitto² m (affitto) rent; **dare a** ~ let; **prendere a** ~ rent; (noleggiare) hire

fiu'mana f swollen river; fig stream

fi'ume m river; fig stream

fiu'tare vt smell. **fi'uto** m [sense of] smell; fig nose

'flaccido adj flabby

fla'cone m bottle

fla'gello m scourge

fla'grante adj flagrant; **in** ~ in the act

fla'nella f flannel

'flash m inv Journ newsflash

'flauto m flute

'flebile adj feeble

'flemma f calm; (Med) phlegm

fles'sibil|e adj flexible. ~**ità** f flexibility

flessi'one f (del busto in avanti) forward bend

'flesso pp di flettere

flessu'oso adj supple

'flettere vt bend

flir'tare vi flirt

F.lli abbr (fratelli) Bros

'floppy disk m inv floppy disk

'florido adj flourishing

'floscio adj limp; (flaccido) flabby

'flotta f fleet. **flot'tiglia** f flotilla

flu'ente adj fluent

flu'ido m fluid

flu'ire vi flow

fluore'scente adj fluorescent

flu'oro m fluorine

'flusso m flow; (Med) flux; (del mare) flood[-tide]; ~ **e riflusso** ebb and flow

fluttu'ante adj fluctuating

fluttu'a|re vi (prezzi, moneta:) fluctuate. ~**zi'one** f fluctuation

fluvi'ale adj river

fo'bia f phobia

'foca f seal

fo'caccia f (pane) flat bread; (dolce) ≈ raisin bread

fo'cale adj (distanza, punto) focal. **focaliz'zare** vt get into focus (fotografia); focus (attenzione); define (problema)

'foce f mouth

foco'laio m (Med) focus; fig centre

foco'lare m hearth; (caminetto) fireplace; (Techn) furnace

fo'coso adj fiery

foder|a f lining; (di libro) dust-jacket; (di poltrona ecc) loose cover. **fode'rare** vt line; cover (libro). ~**o** m sheath

'foga f impetuosity

foggi|a f fashion; (maniera) manner; (forma) shape. ~**'are** vt mould

'foglia f leaf; (di metallo) foil

fogli'etto m (pezzetto di carta) piece of paper

'foglio m sheet; (pagina) leaf. ~ **elettronico** (Comput) spreadsheet. ~ **rosa** (Auto) provisional licence

'fogna f sewer. ~**'tura** f sewerage

fo'lata f gust

fol'clo|re m folklore. ~**'ristico** adj

folk; (*bizzarro*) weird

folgo'ra|re vi (*splendere*) shine ● vt (*con un fulmine*) strike. ~**zi'one** f (*da fulmine, elettrica*) electrocution; (*idea*) brainwave

'**folgore** f thunderbolt

'**folla** f crowd

'**folle** adj mad; **in ~** (*Auto*) in neutral

folle'mente adv madly

fol'lia f madness; **alla ~** (*amare*) to distraction

'**folto** adj thick

fomen'tare vt stir up

fonda'le m (*Theat*) backcloth

fonda'men|ta fpl foundations. ~**tale** adj fundamental. ~**to** m (*di principio, teoria*) foundation

fon'da|re vt establish; base (*ragionamento, accusa*). ~**to** adj (*ragionamento*) well-founded. ~**zi'one** f establishment; ~**zioni** pl (*di edificio*) foundations

fon'delli mpl **prendere qcno per i ~** 🔲 pull sb's leg

fon'dente adj (*cioccolato*) dark

'**fonder|e** vt/i melt; (*colori:*) blend. ~**si** vr melt; (*Comm*) merge

'**fondi** mpl (*denaro*) funds; (*di caffè*) grounds

'**fondo** adj deep; **è notte fonda** it's the middle of the night ● m bottom; (*fine*) end; (*sfondo*) background; (*indole*) nature; (*somma di denaro*) fund; (*feccia*) dregs pl; **andare a ~** (*nave:*) sink; **da cima a ~** from beginning to end; **in ~** after all; **in ~ in ~** deep down; **fino in ~** right to the end; (*capire*) thoroughly. **~ d'investimento** investment trust

fondo'tinta m foundation cream

fon'duta f ≈ fondue

fo'netica f phonetics. ~**o** adj phonetic

fon'tana f fountain

'**fonte** f spring; *fig* source ● m font

fo'raggio m forage

fo'rar|e vt pierce; punch (*biglietto*) ● vi puncture. ~**si** vr (*gomma, pallone:*) go soft

'**forbici** fpl scissors

forbi'cine fpl (*per le unghie*) nail scissors

'**forca** f fork; (*patibolo*) gallows pl

for'cella f fork; (*per capelli*) hairpin

for'chet|ta f fork. ~**tata** f (*quantità*) forkful

for'cina f hairpin

'**forcipe** m forceps pl

for'cone m pitchfork

fo'resta f forest. **fore'stale** adj forest attrib

foresti'ero, -a adj foreign ● mf foreigner

for'fait m inv fixed price; **dare ~** (*abbandonare*) give up

for'fora f dandruff

forgi|a f forge. ~'**are** vt forge

'**forma** f form; (*sagoma*) shape; (*Culin*) mould; (*da calzolaio*) last; **essere in ~** be in good form; **a ~ di** in the shape of; **forme** pl (*del corpo*) figure sg; (*convenzioni*) appearances

formag'gino m processed cheese. **for'maggio** m cheese

for'male adj formal. ~**ità** f inv formality. ~**iz'zarsi** vr stand on ceremony. ~'**mente** adv formally

for'mare vt form. ~**rsi** vr form; (*svilupparsi*) develop. ~**to** m size; (*di libro*) format; ~**to tessera** (*fotografia*) passportsize

format'tare vt format

formazi'one f formation; *Sport* line-up. ~ **professionale** vocational training

formico'l|are vi (*braccio ecc:*) tingle; ~**are di** be swarming with; **mi ~a la mano** I have pins and needles in my hand. ~**io** m swarming; (*di braccio ecc*) pins and needles pl

formi'dabile adj (*tremendo*) formidable; (*eccezionale*) tremendous

for'mina f mould

for'moso adj shapely

'formula f formula. **formu'lare** vt formulate; (esprimere) express

for'nace f furnace; (per laterizi) kiln

for'naio m baker; (negozio) bakery

for'nello m stove; (di pipa) bowl

for'ni|re vt supply (di with). **~tore** m supplier. **~tura** f supply

'forno m oven; (panetteria) bakery; al **~** roast. **~ a microonde** microwave [oven]

'foro m hole; (romano) forum; (tribunale) [law] court

'forse adv perhaps, maybe; essere in **~** be in doubt

forsen'nato, -a adj mad ●mf madman; madwoman

'forte adj strong; (colore) bright; (suono) loud; (resistente) tough; (spesa) considerable; (dolore) severe; (pioggia) heavy; (a tennis, calcio) good; (Ⅲ: simpatico) great; (taglia) large ●adv strongly; (parlare) loudly; (velocemente) fast; (piovere) heavily ●m (fortezza) fort; (specialità) strong point

for'tezza f fortress; (forza morale) fortitude

fortifi'care vt fortify

for'tino m (Mil) blockhouse

for'tuito adj fortuitous; **incontro ~** chance encounter

for'tuna f fortune; (successo) success; (buona sorte) luck. **atterraggio di ~** forced landing; **aver ~** be lucky; **buona ~!** good luck!; **di ~** makeshift; **per ~** luckily. **fortu'nato** adj lucky, fortunate; (impresa) successful. **~ta'mente** adv fortunately

fo'runcolo m pimple; (grosso) boil

'forza f strength; (potenza) power; (fisica) force; **di ~** by force; **a ~ di** by dint of; **con ~** hard; **~! come on!**; **~ di volontà** will-power; **~ maggiore** circumstances beyond one's control; **la ~ pubblica** the police; **per ~** against one's will; (natu-

ralmente) of course; **farsi ~** bear up; **mare ~ 8 force 8 gale; bella ~!** ⓘ big deal. **le forze armate** the armed forces

for'za|re vt force; (scassare) break open; (sforzare) strain. **~to** adj forced; (sorriso) strained ●m convict

forzi'ere m coffer

for'zuto adj strong

fo'schia f haze

'fosco adj dark

fo'sfato m phosphate

'fosforo m phosphorus

'fossa f pit; (tomba) grave. **~ biologica** cesspool. **fos'sato** m (di fortificazione) moat

fos'setta f dimple

'fossile m fossil

'fosso m ditch; (Mil) trench

'foto f inv ⓘ photo; **fare delle ~** take some photos

foto'camera f camera

foto'cellula f photocell

fotocomposizi'one f filmsetting, photocomposition

foto'copi|a f photocopy. **~'are** vt photocopy. **~a'trice** f photocopier

foto'finish m inv photo finish

fotogra'fare vt photograph. **~'fia** f (arte) photography; (immagine) photograph; **fare ~fie** take photographs. **foto'grafico** adj photographic; **macchina fotografica** camera. **fo'tografo, -a** mf photographer

foto'gramma m frame

fotomo'dello, -a mf [photographer's] model

fotoro'manzo m photo story

fou'lard m inv scarf

fra prep (in mezzo a due) between; (in un insieme) among; (tempo, distanza) in; **detto ~ noi** between you and me; **~ sé e sé** to oneself; **~ l'altro** what's more; **~ breve** soon; **~ quindici giorni** in two weeks' time;

~ **tutti, siamo in venti** there are twenty of us altogether

fracas'sar|e *vt* smash. ~**si** *vr* shatter

fra'casso *m* din; (*di cose che cadono*) crash

'fradicio *adj* (*bagnato*) soaked; (*guasto*) rotten; **ubriaco** ~ blind drunk

'fragile *adj* fragile; *fig* frail. ~**ità** *f* fragility; *fig* frailty

'fragola *f* strawberry

fra'gor|e *m* uproar; (*di cose rotte*) clatter; (*di tuono*) rumble. ~**roso** *adj* uproarious; (*tuono*) rumbling; (*suono*) clanging

fra'grante *adj* fragrant. ~**za** *f* fragrance

frain'tendere *vt* misunderstand. ~**ndersi** *vr* be at cross-purposes. ~**so** *pp di* fraintendere

frammen'tario *adj* fragmentary

'frana *f* landslide. **fra'nare** *vi* slide down

franca'mente *adv* frankly

fran'cese *adj* French ● *mf* Frenchman; Frenchwoman ● *m* (*lingua*) French

fran'chezza *f* frankness

'Francia *f* France

'franco[1] *adj* frank; (*Comm*) free; **farla franca** get away with sth

'franco[2] *m* (*moneta*) franc

franco'bollo *m* stamp

fran'gente *m* (*onda*) breaker; (*scoglio*) reef; (*fig: momento difficile*) crisis; **in quel** ~ given the situation

'frangia *f* fringe

fra'noso *adj* subject to landslides

fran'toio *m* olive-press

frantu'mar|e *vt*, ~**si** *vr* shatter. **fran'tumi** *mpl* splinters; **andare in frantumi** be smashed to pieces

frappé *m inv* milkshake

frap'por|re *vt* interpose. ~**si** *vr* intervene

fra'sario *m* vocabulary; (*libro*)

phrase book

'frase *f* sentence; (*espressione*) phrase. ~ **fatta** cliché

'frassino *m* ash[-tree]

frastagli'a|re *vt* make jagged. ~**to** *adj* jagged

frastor'na|re *vt* daze. ~**to** *adj* dazed

frastu'ono *m* racket

'frate *m* friar; (*monaco*) monk

fratel'la|nza *f* brotherhood. ~**stro** *m* half-brother

fra'tell|i *mpl* (*fratello e sorella*) brother and sister. ~**o** *m* brother

fraterniz'zare *vi* fraternize. **fra'terno** *adj* brotherly

frat'taglie *fpl* (*di pollo ecc*) giblets

frat'tanto *adv* in the meantime

frat'tempo *m* **nel** ~ meanwhile, in the meantime

frat'tur|a *f* fracture. ~**rare** *vt*, ~**rarsi** *vr* break

fraudo'lento *adj* fraudulent

frazi'one *f* fraction; (*borgata*) hamlet

'frecci|a *f* arrow; (*Auto*) indicator. ~**'ata** *f* (*osservazione pungente*) cutting remark

fredda'mente *adv* coldly

fred'dare *vt* cool; (*fig: con sguardo, battuta*) cut down; (*uccidere*) kill

fred'dezza *f* coldness

'freddo *adj & m* cold; **aver** ~ be cold; **fa** ~ it's cold

freddo'loso *adj* sensitive to cold

fred'dura *f* pun

fre'ga|re *vt* rub; (Ⅱ: *truffare*) cheat; (Ⅱ: *rubare*) swipe. ~**rsene** Ⅱ not give a damn; **chi se ne frega!** what the heck!. ~**si** *vr* rub (**occhi**). ~**ta** *f* rub. ~**tura** *f* (Ⅱ: *truffa*) swindle; (*delusione*) letdown

'fregio *m* (*Archit*) frieze; (*ornamento*) decoration

'frem|ere *vi* quiver. ~**ito** *m* quiver

fre'na|re vt brake; fig restrain; hold back (lacrime) ●vi brake. ~rsi vr check oneself. ~ta f fare una ~ta brusca brake sharply

frene'sia f frenzy; (desiderio smodato) craze. fre'netico adj frenzied

'freno m brake; fig check; togliere il ~ release the brake; usare il ~ apply the brake; tenere a ~ restrain. ~ a mano handbrake

frequen'tare vt frequent; attend (scuola ecc); mix with (persone)

fre'quen|te adj frequent; di ~te frequently. ~za f frequency; (assiduità) attendance

fre'schezza f freshness; (di temperatura) coolness

'fresco adj fresh; (temperatura) cool; stai ~! you're for it! ● m coolness; far ~ be cool; mettere/tenere in ~ put/keep in a cool place

'fretta f hurry, haste; aver ~ be in a hurry; far ~ a qcno hurry sb; in ~ e furia in a great hurry. frettolosa'mente adv hurriedly. fretto'loso adj (persona) in a hurry; (lavoro) rushed, hurried

fri'abile adj crumbly

'friggere vt fry; vai a farti ~! get lost! ● vi sizzle

friggi'trice f chip pan

frigidità f frigidity. 'frigido adj frigid

fri'gnare vi whine

'frigo m inv fridge

frigo'bar m inv minibar

frigo'rifero adj refrigerating ● m refrigerator

frit'tata f omelette

frit'tella f fritter; (🄸: macchia d'unto) grease stain

'fritto pp di friggere ● adj fried; essere ~ be done for ● m fried food. ~ misto mixed fried fish/vegetables. frit'tura f fried dish

frivo'lezza f frivolity. 'frivolo adj frivolous

frizio'nare vt rub. frizi'one f friction; (Mech) clutch; (di pelle) rub

friz'zante adj fizzy; (vino) sparkling; (aria) bracing

'frizzo m gibe

fro'dare vt defraud

'frode f fraud. ~ fiscale tax evasion

'frollo adj tender; (selvaggina) high; (persona) spineless; pasta frolla short[crust] pastry

'fronda f [leafy] branch; fig rebellion. fron'doso adj leafy

fron'tale adj frontal; (scontro) head-on

'fronte f forehead; (di edificio) front; di ~ opposite; di ~ a opposite, facing; (a paragone) compared with; far ~ a face ● m (Mil, Pol) front. ~ggi'are vt face

fronti'era f frontier, border

fron'tone m pediment

fron'zolo m frill

'frotta f swarm; (di animali) flock

'frottola f fib; frottole pl nonsense sg

fru'gale adj frugal

fru'gare vi rummage ● vt search

frul'la|re vt (Culin) whisk ● vi (ali:) whirr. ~to m ~to di frutta fruit drink with milk and crushed ice. ~'tore m [electric] mixer. frul'lino m whisk

fru'mento m wheat

frusci'are vi rustle

fru'scio m rustle; (radio, giradischi) background noise; (di acque) murmur

'frusta f whip; (frullino) whisk

fru'sta|re vt whip. ~ta f lash. fru'stino m riding crop

fru'stra|re vt frustrate. ~to adj frustrated. ~zi'one f frustration

'frutt|a f fruit; (portata) dessert. frut'tare vi bear fruit ● vt yield. frut'teto *m* orchard. **~i'vendolo, -a** *mf* greengrocer. **~o** *m* fruit; *Fin* yield; **~i di bosco** fruits of the forest. **~i di mare** seafood *sg.* **~u'oso** *adj* profitable

f.to *abbr* (firmato) signed

fu *adj* (defunto) late; **il ~ signor Rossi** the late Mr Rossi

fuci'la|re *vt* shoot. **~ta** *f* shot

fu'cile *m* rifle

fu'cina *f* forge

'fuga *f* escape; (perdita) leak; (Mus) fugue; **darsi alla ~** escape

fu'gace *adj* fleeting

fug'gevole *adj* short-lived

fuggi'asco, -a *mf* fugitive

fuggi'fuggi *m* stampede

fuggi're *vi* flee; (innamorati:) elope; *fig* fly. **~'tivo, -a** *mf* fugitive

'fulcro *m* fulcrum

ful'gore *m* splendour

fu'liggine *f* soot

fulmi'nar|e *vt* strike by lightning; (con sguardo) look daggers at; (con scarica elettrica) electrocute. **~si** *vr* burn out. **'fulmine** *m* lightning. **ful'mineo** *adj* rapid

'fulvo *adj* tawny

fumai'olo *m* funnel; (di casa) chimney

fumar|e *vt/i* smoke; (in ebollizione) steam. **~'tore, ~'trice** *mf* smoker; **non fumatori** non-smoker, non-smoking

fu'metto *m* comic strip; **fumetti** *pl* comics

'fumo *m* smoke; (vapore) steam; *fig* hot air; **andare in ~** vanish. **fu'moso** *adj* smoky; (discorso) vague

fu'nambolo, -a *mf* tightrope walker

'fune *f* rope; (cavo) cable

'funebre *adj* funeral; (cupo) gloomy

fune'rale *m* funeral

> **Funghi** Wild mushrooms are an Italian passion, and the most prized is the *porcino* (cep), which can be bought fresh or dried. However, many Italians are also avid mushroom-pickers and are expert at differentiating edible mushrooms (funghi commestibili) from poisonous ones. Local authorities often have a department controlling the picking and selling of mushrooms.

'fungo *m* mushroom; (Bot) fungus

funico'lare *f* funicular [railway]

funi'via *f* cableway

funzio'nal|e *adj* functional. **~ità** *f* functionality

funziona'mento *m* functioning

funzio'nare *vi* work, function; **~ da** (fungere da) act as

funzio'nario *m* official

funzi'one *f* function; (carica) office; (Relig) service; **entrare in ~** take up office

fu'oco *m* fire; (fisica, fotografia) focus; **far ~** fire; **dar ~ a** set fire to; **prendere ~** catch fire. **fuochi** *pl* **d'artificio** fireworks

fuorché *prep* except

fu'ori *adv* out; (all'esterno) outside; (all'aperto) outdoors; **andare di ~** (traboccare) spill over; **essere ~ di sé** be beside oneself; **essere in ~** (sporgere) stick out; **far ~** 🄸 do in; **~ luogo** (inopportuno) out of place; **~ mano** out of the way; **~ moda** old-fashioned; **~ pasto** between meals; **~ pericolo** out of danger; **~ questione** out of the question; **~ uso** out of use ●*m* outside

fuori'bordo *m* speedboat (with outboard motor)

fuori'classe *mf inv* champion

fuorigi'oco *m & adv* offside

fuori'legge *mf* outlaw

fuori'serie *adj* custom-made ●*f* (*Auto*) custom-built model

fuori'strada *m* off-road vehicle

fuorvi'are *vt* lead astray ● *vi* go astray

furbe'ria *f* cunning. **fur'bizia** *f* cunning

'furbo *adj* cunning; (*intelligente*) clever; (*astuto*) shrewd; bravo ~! nice one!; fare il ~ try to be clever

fu'rente *adj* furious

fur'fante *m* scoundrel

furgon'cino *m* delivery van. **fur-'gone** *m* van

'furi|a *f* fury; (*fretta*) haste; a ~a di by dint of. **~'bondo**, **~'oso** *adj* furious

fu'rore *m* fury; (*veemenza*) frenzy; far ~ be all the rage. **~ggi'are** *vi* be a great success

furtiva'mente *adv* covertly. **fur-'tivo** *adj* furtive

'furto *m* theft; (*con scasso*) burglary; commettere un ~ steal. ~ d'iden-tità identity theft

'fusa *fpl* fare le ~ purr

fu'scello *m* (*di legno*) twig; (*di paglia*) straw; sei un ~ you're as light as a feather

fu'seaux *mpl* leggings

fu'sibile *m* fuse

fusi'one *f* fusion; (*Comm*) merger

'fuso *pp di* fondere ● *adj* melted ●*m* spindle. ~ **orario** time zone

fusoli'era *f* fuselage

fu'stagno *m* corduroy

fu'stino *m* (*di detersivo*) box

'fusto *m* stem; (*tronco*) trunk; (*reci-piente di metallo*) drum; (*di legno*) barrel

'futile *adj* futile

fu'turo *adj & m* future

Gg

gab'bar|e *vt* cheat. **~si** *vr* ~si di make fun of

'gabbia *f* cage; (*da imballaggio*) crate. ~ **degli imputati** dock. ~ **toracica** rib cage

gabbi'ano *m* [sea]gull

gabi'netto *m* consulting room; (*Pol*) cabinet; (*bagno*) lavatory; (*labora-torio*) laboratory

'gaffe *f inv* blunder

gagli'ardo *adj* vigorous

gai'ezza *f* gaiety. **'gaio** *adj* cheerful

'gala *f* gala

ga'lante *adj* gallant. **~'ria** *f* gal-lantry. **galantu'omo** *m* (*pl* galantuo-mini) gentleman

ga'lassia *f* galaxy

gala'teo *m* [good] manners *pl*; (*trat-tato*) book of etiquette

gale'otto *m* (*rematore*) galley-slave; (*condannato*) convict

ga'lera *f* (*nave*) galley; Ⓘ prison

'galla *f* (*Bot*) gall; a ~ *adv* afloat; ve-nire a ~ surface

galleggi'are *vi* float

galle'ria *f* tunnel; (*d'arte*) gallery; (*Theat*) circle; (*arcata*) arcade. ~ **d'arte** art gallery

'Galles *m* Wales. **gal'lese** *adj* welsh ●*m* Welshman; (*lingua*) Welsh ●*f* Welshwoman

gal'letto *m* cockerel; fare il ~ show off

gal'lina *f* hen

gal'lismo *m* machismo

'gallo *m* cock

gal'lone *m* stripe; (*misura*) gallon

galop'pare *vi* gallop. **ga'loppo** *m* gallop; al galoppo at a gallop

'gamba *f* leg; (*di lettera*) stem; a

quattro gambe on all fours; essere in ~ (*essere forte*) be strong; (*capace*) be smart

gamba'letto *m* pop sock

gambe'retto *m* shrimp. '**gambero** *m* prawn; (*di fiume*) crayfish

'**gambo** *m* stem; (*di pianta*) stalk

'**gamma** *f* (*Mus*) scale; *fig* range

ga'**nascia** *f* jaw; ganasce *pl* del freno brake shoes

'**gancio** *m* hook

'**ganghero** *m* uscire dai gangheri *fig* get into a temper

'**gara** *f* competition; (*di velocità*) race; fare a ~ compete

ga'**rage** *m inv* garage

ga'**ran|te** *mf* guarantor. ~'**tire** *vt* guarantee; (*rendersi garante*) vouch for; (*assicurare*) assure. ~'**zia** *f* guarantee; in ~**zia** under guarantee

gar'**ba|re** *vi* like; non mi garba I don't like it. ~**to** *adj* courteous

'**garbo** *m* courtesy; (*grazia*) grace; con ~ graciously

gareggi'**are** *vi* compete

garga'**nella** *f* a ~ from the bottle

garga'**rismo** *m* gargle; fare i gargarismi gargle

ga'**rofano** *m* carnation

'**garza** *f* gauze

gar'**zone** *m* boy. ~ di stalla stable-boy

gas *m inv* gas; dare ~ (*Auto*) accelerate; a tutto ~ flat out. ~ lacrimogeno tear gas. ~ *pl* di scarico exhaust fumes

gas'**dotto** *m* natural gas pipeline

ga'**solio** *m* diesel oil

ga'**sometro** *m* gasometer

gas'**s|are** *vt* aerate; (*uccidere col gas*) gas. ~**ato** *adj* gassy. ~**oso, -a** *adj* gassy; (*bevanda*) fizzy ●*f* lemonade

'**gastrico** *adj* gastric. ga'**strite** *f* gastritis

gastro|no'**mia** *f* gastronomy. ~'**nomico** *adj* gastronomic. ga'**stro**-

nomo, -a *mf* gourmet

'**gatta** *f* una ~ da pelare a headache

gatta'**buia** *f hum* clink

gat'**tino, -a** *mf* kitten

'**gatto, -a** *mf* cat. ~ delle nevi snowmobile

gat'**toni** *adv* on all fours

gay *adj inv* gay

'**gazza** *f* magpie

gaz'**zarra** *f* racket

gaz'**zella** *f* gazelle; (*Auto*) police car

gaz'**zetta** *f* gazette

gaz'**zosa** *f* clear lemonade

'**geco** *m* gecko

ge'**la|re** *vt/i* freeze. ~**ta** *f* frost

gela'**t|aio, -a** *mf* ice-cream seller; (*negozio*) ice-cream shop. ~**e'ria** *f* ice-cream parlour. ~**i'era** *f* ice-cream maker

gela'**ti|na** *f* gelatine; (*dolce*) jelly. ~**na di frutta** fruit jelly.

ge'**lato** *adj* frozen ●*m* ice-cream

'**gelido** *adj* freezing

'**gelo** *m* (*freddo intenso*) freezing cold; (*brina*) frost; *fig* chill

ge'**lone** *m* chilblain

gelosa'**mente** *adv* jealously

gelo'**sia** *f* jealousy. ge'**loso** *adj* jealous

'**gelso** *m* mulberry[-tree]

gel'**somino** *m* jasmine

gemel'**laggio** *m* twinning

ge'**mello, -a** *adj & mf* twin; (*di polsino*) cuff-link; Gemelli *pl* (*Astr*) Gemini *sg*

'**gem|ere** *vi* groan; (*tubare*) coo. ~**ito** *m* groan

'**gemma** *f* gem; (*Bot*) bud

'**gene** *m* gene

genea|lo'**gia** *f* genealogy

gene'**ral|e**[1] *adj* general; spese ~**i** overheads

gene'**rale**[2] *m* (*Mil*) general

genera|lità *f* (*qualità*) generality, general nature; ~ pl (dati personali) particulars

generaliz'za|re vt generalize. ~zi'one f generalization. general'mente adv generally

gene'ra|re vt give birth to; (causare) breed; (Techn) generate. ~'tore m (Techn) generator. ~zi'one f generation

'genere m kind; (Biol) genus; (Gram) gender; (letterario, artistico) genre; (prodotto) product; il ~ umano mankind; in ~ generally. generi pl alimentari provisions

ge'nerico adj generic; medico generico general practitioner

'genero m son-in-law

generosità f generosity. gene'roso adj generous

'genesi f inv genesis

ge'netico, -a adj genetic ● f genetics

gen'giva f gum

geni'ale adj ingenious; (congeniale) congenial

'genio m genius; andare a ~ to be to one's taste. ~ civile civil engineering. ~ [militare] Engineers

geni'tale adj genital. genitali mpl genitals

geni'tore m parent

gen'naio m January

'Genova f Genoa

gen'taglia f rabble

'gente f people pl

gen'til|e adj kind; G~e Signore (in lettere) Dear Sir. genti'lezza f kindness; per gentilezza (per favore) please. ~'mente adv kindly. ~u'omo (pl ~u'omini) m gentleman

genu'ino adj genuine; (cibo, prodotto) natural

geogra'fia f geography. geo'grafico adj geographical. ge'ografo, -a mf geographer

geolo'gia f geology. geo'logico adj geological. ge'ologo, -a mf geologist

ge'ometra mf surveyor

geome'tria f geometry

ge'ranio m geranium

gerar'chia f hierarchy

ge'rente m manager ● f manageress

'gergo m slang; (di professione ecc) jargon

geria'tria f geriatrics sg

Ger'mania f Germany

'germe m germ; (fig: principio) seed

germogli'are vi sprout. ger'moglio m sprout

gero'glifico m hieroglyph

'gesso m chalk; (Med, scultura) plaster

gestazi'one f gestation

gestico'lare vi gesticulate

gesti'one f management

ge'stir|e vi manage. ~si vr budget one's time and money

'gesto m gesture; (azione pl f gesta) deed

ge'store m manager

Gesù m Jesus. ~ bambino baby Jesus

gesu'ita m Jesuit

get'ta|re vt throw; (scagliare) fling; (emettere) spout; (Techn, fig cast; ~re via throw away. ~rsi vr throw oneself; ~rsi in (fiume:) flow into. ~ta f throw

'getto m throw; (di liquidi, gas) jet; a ~ continuo in a continuous stream; di ~ straight off

getto'nato adj popular. get'tone m token; (per giochi) counter

'ghetto m ghetto

ghiacci'aio m glacier

ghiacci'a|re vt/i freeze. ~to adj frozen; (freddissimo) ice-cold

ghi'acci|o m ice; (Auto) black ice. ~'olo m icicle; (gelato) ice lolly

ghi'aia f gravel

ghi'anda f acorn

ghi'andola f gland

ghigliot'tina f guillotine

ghi'gnare vi sneer

ghi'ot|to adj greedy; (appetitoso) appetizing. **~tone, -a** mf glutton. **~tone'ria** f (qualità) gluttony; (cibo) tasty morsel

ghir'landa f (corona) wreath; (di fiori) garland

'ghiro m dormouse; **dormire come un ~** sleep like a log

'ghisa f cast iron

già adv already; (un tempo) formerly; **~!** indeed!; **~ da ieri** since yesterday

gi'acca f jacket. **~ a vento** windcheater

giacché conj since

giac'cone m jacket

gia'cere vi lie

giaci'mento m deposit. **~ di petrolio** oil deposit

gia'cinto m hyacinth

gi'ada f jade

giaggi'olo m iris

giagu'aro m jaguar

gial'lastro adj yellowish

gi'allo adj & m yellow; [libro] **~** thriller

Giap'pone m Japan. **giappo'nese** adj & mf Japanese

giardi'n|aggio m gardening. **~i'ere, -a** mf gardener **•** f (Auto) estate car; (sottaceti) pickles pl

giar'dino m garden. **~ d'infanzia** kindergarten. **~ pensile** roofgarden. **~ zoologico** zoo

giarretti'era f garter

giavel'lotto m javelin

gi'gan|te adj gigantic **•** m giant. **~'tesco** adj gigantic

gigantogra'fia f blow-up

'giglio m lily

gilè m inv waistcoat

gin m inv gin

gineco|lo'gia f gynaecology. **~lo'gico** adj gynaecological. **gine'cologo, -a** mf gynaecologist

gi'nepro m juniper

gingil'larsi vr fiddle; (perder tempo) potter. **gin'gillo** m plaything; (ninnolo) knick-knack

gin'nasio m ≈ grammar school

gin'nast|a mf gymnast. **~ica** f gymnastics; (esercizi) exercises pl

ginocchi'ata f prendere una **~** bang one's knee

gi'nocchi|o m (pl m ginocchi o f ginocchia) knee; **in ~o** on one's knees; **mettersi in ~o** kneel down; (per supplicare) go down on one's knees. **~oni** adv kneeling

gio'ca|re vt/i play; (giocherellare) toy; (d'azzardo) gamble; (puntare) stake; (ingannare) trick. **~rsi la carriera** throw one's career away. **~'tore, ~'trice** mf player; (d'azzardo) gambler

gio'cattolo m toy

giocherel'l|are vi toy; (nervosamente) fiddle. **~one** adj skittish

gi'oco m (anche: Techn) play; (d'azzardo) gambling; (scherzo) joke; (insieme di pezzi ecc) set; **fare il doppio ~ con** qcno double-cross sb

giocoli'ere m juggler

gio'coso adj playful

gi'oia f joy; (gioiello) jewel; (appellativo) sweetie

gioiell|e'ria f jeweller's [shop]. **~i'ere, -a** mf jeweller; (negozio) jeweller's. **gioi'ello** m jewel; **gioielli** pl jewellery

gioi'oso adj joyous

gio'ire vi **~ per** rejoice at

Gior'dania f Jordan

giorna'laio, -a mf newsagent

gior'nale m [news]paper; (diario) journal. **~ di bordo** logbook. **~ radio** news bulletin

giornali'ero adj daily ●m (per sciare) day pass

giorna'lino m comic

giorna'lis|mo m journalism. ~ta mf journalist

giornal'mente adv daily

gior'nata f day; in ~ today

gi'orno m day; al ~ per day; al ~ d'oggi nowadays; di ~ by day; un ~ sì, un ~ no every other day

gi'ostra f merry-go-round

giova'mento m trarre ~ da derive benefit from

gi'ova|ne adj young; (giovanile) youthful ●m young man ●f young woman. ~nile adj youthful. ~'notto m young man

gio'var|e vi ~e a be useful to; (far bene) be good for. ~si vr ~si di avail oneself of

giovedì m inv Thursday. ~ grasso last Thursday before Lent

gioventù f youth; (i giovani) young people pl

giovi'ale adj jovial

giovi'nezza f youth

gira'dischi m inv record-player

gi'raffa f giraffe; Cinema boom

gira'ndola f (fuoco d'artificio) Catherine wheel; (giocattolo) windmill; (banderuola) weathercock

gi'ra|re vt turn; (andare intorno, visitare) go round; (Comm) endorse; Cinema shoot ●vi turn; (aerei, uccelli): circle; (andare in giro) wander; ~re al largo steer clear. ~rsi vr turn [round]; mi gira la testa I'm dizzy

girar'rosto m spit

gira'sole m sunflower

gi'rata f turn; (Comm) endorsement; (in macchina ecc) ride; fare una ~ (a piedi) go for a walk; (in macchina) go for a ride

gira'volta f spin; fig U-turn

gi'rello m (per bambini) babywalker; (Culin) topside

gi'revole adj revolving

gi'rino m tadpole

'giro m turn; (circolo) circle; (percorso) round; (viaggio) tour; (passeggiata) short walk; (in macchina) drive; (in bicicletta) ride; (circolazione di denaro) circulation; nel ~ di un mese within a month; senza giri di parole without beating about the bush; a ~ di posta by return mail. ~ d'affari (Comm) turnover. giri pl al minuto rpm. ~ turistico sightseeing tour. ~ vita waist measurement

giro'collo m choker; a ~ crewneck

gi'rone m round

gironzo'lare vi wander about

girova'gare vi wander about. gi'rovago m wanderer

'gita f trip; andare in ~ go on a trip. ~ scolastica school trip. gi'tante mf tripper

giù adv down; (sotto) below; (dabbasso) downstairs; in ~ down; a (capofitto) headlong; essere ~ be down; (di salute) be run down; ~ di corda down; ~ di lì, su per ~ more or less; non andare ~ a qcno stick in sb's craw

gi'ub|ba f jacket; (Mil) tunic. ~'botto m bomber jacket

giudi'care vt judge; (ritenere) consider

gi'udice m judge. ~ conciliatore justice of the peace. ~ di gara umpire. ~ di linea linesman

giu'dizi|o m judge[e]ment; (opinione) opinion; (senno) wisdom; (processo) trial; (sentenza) sentence; mettere ~o become wise. ~'oso adj sensible

gi'ugno m June

giu'menta f mare

gi'ungere vi arrive; ~ a (riuscire) succeed in ●vt (unire) join

gi'ungla f jungle

gi'unta f addition; (Mil) junta; per ~ in addition. ~ comunale district council

gi'unto pp di giungere ● m (Mech) joint

giun'tura f joint

giuo'care, giu'oco = GIO-CARE, GIOCO

giura'mento m oath; prestare ~ take the oath

giu'ra|re vt/i swear. ~to, -a adj sworn ● mf juror

giu'ria f jury

giu'ridico adj legal

giurisdizi'one f jurisdiction

giurispru'denza f jurisprudence

giu'rista mf jurist

giustifi'ca|re vt justify. ~zi'one f justification

giu'stizi|a f justice. ~'are vt execute. ~'ere m executioner

gi'usto adj just, fair; (adatto) right; (esatto) exact ● m (uomo retto) just man; (cosa giusta) right ● adv exactly; ~ ora just now

glaci'ale adj glacial

gla'diolo m gladiolus

'glassa f (Culin) icing

gli def art mpl (before vowel and s + consonant, gn, ps, z) the; ▶IL ● pron (a lui) [to] him; (a essa) [to] it; (a loro) [to] them

glice'rina f glycerine

'glicine m wisteria

gli'e|lo, -a pron [to] him/her/them; (forma di cortesia) [to] you; ~ chiedo I'll ask him/her/them/you; gliel'ho prestato I've lent it to him/her/them/you. ~ne (di ciò) [of] it; ~ne ho dato un po' I gave him/her/them/you some

glo'bal|e adj global; fig overall. ~za'zione f globalization. ~'mente adv globally

'globo m globe. ~ oculare eyeball. ~ terrestre globe

'globulo m globule; (Med) corpuscle. ~ bianco white corpuscle. ~ rosso red corpuscle

'glori|a f glory. ~'arsi vr ~arsi di be proud of. ~'oso adj glorious

glos'sario m glossary

glu'cosio m glucose

'gluteo m buttock

'gnorri m fare lo ~ play dumb

'gobb|a f hump. ~o, -a adj hunchbacked ● mf hunchback

'gocci|a f drop; (di sudore) bead; è stata l'ultima ~a it was the last straw. ~o'lare vi drip. ~o'lio m dripping

go'der|e vi (sessualmente) come; ~e di enjoy. ~sela vr have a good time. ~si vr ~si qcsa enjoy sth

godi'mento m enjoyment

goffa'mente adv awkwardly. **'goffo** adj awkward

'gola f throat; (ingordigia) gluttony; (Geog) gorge; (di camino) flue; avere mal di ~ have a sore throat; far ~ a qcno tempt sb

golf m inv jersey; Sport golf

'golfo m gulf

golosi'tà f inv greediness; (cibo) tasty morsel. **go'loso** adj greedy

'golpe m inv coup

gomi'tata f nudge

'gomito m elbow; alzare il ~ raise one's elbow

go'mitolo m ball

'gomma f rubber; (colla, da masticare) gum; (pneumatico) tyre. ~ da masticare chewing gum

gommapi'uma f foam rubber

gom'mista m tyre specialist

gom'mone m [rubber] dinghy

'gondol|a f gondola. ~i'ere m gondolier

gonfa'lone m banner

gonfi'abile adj inflatable

gonfi'ar|e vi swell ● vt blow up; pump up (pneumatico); (esagerare) exaggerate. ~si vr swell; (acque:) rise. **'gonfio** adj swollen; (pneumatico) inflated. **gonfi'ore** m swelling

gongo'la|nte adj overjoyed. ∼re vi be overjoyed

'gonna f skirt. ∼ pantalone culottes pl

goo'glare vt/i google

gorgogli'are vi gurgle

go'rilla m inv gorilla; (guardia del corpo) bodyguard

'gotico adj & m Gothic

gover'nante f housekeeper

gover'na|re vt govern; (dominare) rule; (dirigere) manage; (curare) look after. ∼tore m governor

go'verno m government; (dominio) rule; al ∼ in power

gps m gps

gracchi'are vi caw; fig: (persona:) screech

graci'dare vi croak

'gracile adj delicate

gra'dasso m braggart

gradata'mente adv gradually

gradazi'one f gradation. ∼ alcolica alcohol[ic] content

gra'devole adj agreeable.

gradi'mento m liking; indice di ∼ (Radio, TV) popularity rating; non è di mio ∼ it's not to my liking

gradi'nata f flight of steps; (di stadio) stand; (di teatro) tiers pl

gra'dino m step

gra'di|re vt like; (desiderare) wish. ∼to adj pleasant; (bene accetto) welcome

'grado m degree; (rango) rank; di buon ∼ willingly; essere in ∼ di fare qcsa be in a position to do sth; (essere capace a) be able to do sth

gradu'ale adj gradual

gradu'a|re vt graduate. ∼to adj graded; (provvisto di scala graduata) graduated ● m (Mil) non-commissioned officer. ∼toria f list. ∼zi'one f graduation

'graffa f clip

graf'fetta f staple

graffi'a|re vt scratch. ∼tura f scratch

'graffio m scratch

gra'fia f [hand]writing; (ortografia) spelling

'grafic|a f graphics; ∼a pubblicitaria commercial art. ∼a'mente adv graphically. ∼o adj graphic ● m graph; (persona) graphic designer

gra'migna f weed

gram'matica f grammar

'grammo m gram[me]

gran adj ▷GRANDE

'grana f grain; (formaggio) parmesan; (𝕀: seccatura) trouble; (𝕀: soldi) readies pl

gra'naio m barn

gra'na|ta f (Mil) grenade; (frutto) pomegranate. ∼i'ere m (Mil) grenadier

Gran Bre'tagna f Great Britain

'granchio m crab; (errore) blunder; prendere un ∼ make a blunder

grandango'lare m wide-angle lens

'grande (a volte gran) adj (ampio) large; (grosso) big; (alto) tall; (largo) wide; (fig: senso morale) great; (grandioso) grand; (adulto) grown-up; ho una gran fame I'm very hungry; fa un gran caldo it is very hot; in ∼ on a large scale; in gran parte to a great extent; un gran ballo a grand ball ● m f (persona adulta) grown-up; (persona eminente) great man/woman. ∼ggi'are vi ∼ggiare su tower over; (darsi arie) show off

gran'dezza f greatness; (ampiezza) largeness; (larghezza) width, breadth; (dimensione) size; (fasto) grandeur; (prodigalità) lavishness; a ∼ naturale life-size

grandi'nare vi hail; grandina it's hailing. **'grandine** f hail

grandiosità f grandeur. grandi'oso adj grand

gran'duca m grand duke

gra'nello m grain; (di frutta) pip

gra'nita f crushed ice drink

gra'nito m granite

grano m grain; (frumento) wheat

gran'turco m maize

granulo m granule

grappa f grappa; (morsa) cramp

grappolo m bunch. ~ d'uva bunch of grapes

gras'setto m bold [type]

gras'sezza f fatness

grasso adj fat; (cibo) fatty; (unto) greasy; (terreno) rich; (grossolano) coarse ●m fat; (sostanza) grease. ~'soccio adj plump

grata f grating. gra'tella, gra'ticola f (Culin) grill

grati'fica f bonus. ~zi'one f satisfaction

grati'nare vt cook au gratin. ~to adj au gratin

grati'tudine f gratitude. 'grato adj grateful; (gradito) pleasant

gratta'capo m trouble

grattaci'elo m skyscraper

gratta e 'vinci m inv scratch card

grat'tare vt scratch; (raschiare) scrape; (grattugiare) grate; (☞: rubare) pinch ●vi grate. ~si vr scratch oneself

grat'tugia f grater. ~'are vt grate

gratuita'mente adv free [of charge]. gra'tuito adj free [of charge]; (ingiustificato) gratuitous

gra'vare vt burden ●vi ~ su weigh on

grave adj (pesante) heavy; (serio) serious; (difficile) hard; (voce, suono) low; (fonetica) grave; essere ~ (ammalato) be seriously ill. ~'mente adv seriously

gravi'danza f pregnancy. 'gravido adj pregnant

gravità f seriousness; (Phys) gravity

gra'voso adj onerous

grazia f grace; (favore) favour; (Jur)

pardon; entrare nelle ~e di qcno get into sb's good books. ~'are vt pardon

grazie int thank you!, thanks!; ~ mille! many thanks!

grazi'oso adj charming; (carino) pretty

Grecia f Greece. g~o, -a agg & mf Greek

gregge m flock

greggio adj raw ●m crude oil

grembi'ale, grembi'ule m apron

grembo m lap; (utero) womb; fig bosom

gre'mire vt pack. ~rsi vr become crowded (di with). ~to adj packed

gretto adj stingy; (di vedute ristrette) narrow-minded

grezzo adj = GREGGIO

gri'dare vi shout; (di dolore) scream; (animale:) cry ●vt shout

grido m (pl m gridi o f grida) shout; (di animale) cry; l'ultimo ~ the latest fashion

grigio adj & m grey

griglia f grill; alla ~ grilled

gril'letto m trigger

grillo m cricket; (fig: capriccio) whim

grin'fia f fig clutch

grinta f grit. ~'toso adj determined

grinza f wrinkle; (di stoffa) crease

grip'pare vi (Mech) seize

gris'sino m bread-stick

gronda f eaves pl

gron'daia f gutter

gron'dare vi pour; (essere bagnato fradicio) be dripping

groppa f back

groppo m knot

gros'sezza f size; (spessore) thickness

gros'sista mf wholesaler

grosso adj big, large; (spesso) thick;

(*grossolano*) coarse; (*grave*) serious ● *m* big part; (*massa*) bulk; **farla grossa** do a stupid thing

grosso|lanità *f inv* (*qualità*) coarseness; (*di errore*) grossness; (*azione, parola*) coarse thing. **~'lano** *adj* coarse; (*errore*) gross

grosso'modo *adv* roughly

'grotta *f* cave, grotto

grovi'era *m* Gruyère

gro'viglio *m* tangle; *fig* muddle

gru *f inv* (*uccello, edilizia*) crane

'gruccia *f* (*stampella*) crutch; (*per vestito*) hanger

gru'gni|re *vi* grunt. **~to** *m* grunt

'grugno *m* snout

'grullo *adj* silly

'grumo *m* clot; (*di farina ecc*) lump. **gru'moso** *adj* lumpy

'gruppo *m* group; (*comitiva*) party. **~ sanguigno** blood group

gruvi'era *m* Gruyère

'gruzzolo *m* nest-egg

guada'gnare *vt* earn; gain (*tempo, forza ecc*). **gua'dagno** *m* gain; (*profitto*) profit; (*entrate*) earnings *pl*

gu'ado *m* ford; **passare a ~** ford

gu'aina *f* sheath; (*busto*) girdle

gu'aio *m* trouble; **che ~!** that's just brilliant!; **essere nei guai** be in a fix; **guai a te se lo tocchi!** don't you dare touch it!

gu'ancia *f* cheek. **~'ale** *m* pillow

gu'anto *m* glove. **guantoni** *pl* [da boxe] boxing gloves

guarda'coste *m inv* coastguard

guarda'linee *m inv Sport* linesman

guar'dar|e *vt* look at; (*osservare*) watch; (*badare a*) look after; (*dare su*) look out on ● *vi* look; (*essere orientato verso*) face. **~si** *vr* look at oneself; **~si da** beware of; (*astenersi*) refrain from

guarda'rob|a *m inv* wardrobe; (*di locale pubblico*) cloakroom. **~i'ere, -a**

mf cloakroom attendant

gu'ardia *f* guard; (*poliziotto*) policeman; (*vigilanza*) watch; **essere di ~** be on guard; (*medico:*) be on duty; **fare la ~ a** keep guard over; **mettere in ~ qcno** warn sb. **~ carceraria** prison warder. **~ del corpo** bodyguard. **~ di finanza** ≈ Fraud Squad. **~ forestale** forest ranger. **~ medica** duty doctor

guardi'ano, -a *mf* caretaker. **~ notturno** night watchman

guar'dingo *adj* cautious

guardi'ola *f* gatekeeper's lodge

guarigi'one *f* recovery

gua'rire *vt* cure ● *vi* recover; (*ferita:*) heal [up]

guarnigi'one *f* garrison

guar'ni|re *vt* trim; (*Culin*) garnish. **~zi'one** *f* trimming; (*Culin*) garnish; (*Mech*) gasket

gua'star|e *vt* spoil; (*rovinare*) ruin; break (*meccanismo*). **~si** *vr* spoil; (*andare a male*) go bad; (*tempo:*) change for the worse; (*meccanismo:*) break down. **gu'asto** *adj* broken; (*ascensore, telefono*) out of order; (*auto*) broken down; (*cibo, dente*) bad ● *m* breakdown; (*danno*) damage

guazza'buglio *m* muddle

guaz'zare *vi* wallow

gu'ercio *adj* cross-eyed

gu'err|a *f* war; (*tecnica bellica*) warfare. **~ mondiale** world war. **~eggi'are** *vi* wage war. **guer'resco** *adj* (*di guerra*) war; (*bellicoso*) warlike. **~i'ero** *m* warrior

guer'rigli|a *f* guerrilla warfare. **~'ero, -a** *mf* guerrilla

'gufo *m* owl

gu'glia *f* spire

gu'id|a *f* guide; (*direzione*) guidance; (*comando*) leadership; (*Auto*) driving; (*tappeto*) runner; **~a a destra/sinistra** right-/left-hand drive. **~a telefonica** telephone directory. **~a**

turistica tourist guide. **gui'dare** vt guide; (Auto) drive; steer (nave). ~a'tore, ~a'trice mf driver

guin'zaglio m leash

guiz'zare vi dart; (luce:) flash. **gu'izzo** m dart; (di luce) flash

'guscio m shell

gu'stare vt taste ● vi like. 'gusto m taste; (piacere) liking; mangiare di gusto eat well; prenderci gusto develop a taste for. gu'stoso adj tasty; fig delightful

guttu'rale adj guttural

....

Hh

habitué mf inv regular

ham'burger m inv hamburger

'handicap m inv handicap

handicap'pa|re vt handicap. ~to, -a mf disabled person ●adj disabled

'hascisc m hashish

henné m henna

hi-fi m inv hi-fi

'hippy adj hippy

hockey m hockey. ~ su ghiaccio ice hockey. ~ su prato hockey

hollywoodi'ano adj Hollywood

ho'tel m inv hotel

....

Ii

i def art mpl the; ▷IL

iber'na|re vi hibernate. ~zi'one f hibernation

i'bisco m hibiscus

'ibrido adj & m hybrid

'iceberg m inv iceberg

i'cona f icon

Id'dio m God

i'dea f idea; (opinione) opinion; (ideale) ideal; (indizio) inkling; (piccola quantità) hint; (intenzione) intention; cambiare ~ change one's mind; neanche per ~! not on your life!; chiarirsi le idee get one's ideas straight. ~ fissa obsession

ide'a|le adj & m ideal. ~lista mf idealist. ~liz'zare vt idealize

ide'a|re vt conceive. ~'tore, ~'trice mf originator

'idem adv the same

i'dentico adj identical

identifi'cabile adj identifiable

identifi'ca|re vt identify. ~zi'one f identification

identità f inv identity

ideolo'gia f ideology. **ideo'logico** adj ideological

idi'oma m idiom. **idio'matico** adj idiomatic

idi'ota adj idiotic ●mf idiot. **idio'zia** f (cosa stupida) idiocy

idola'trare vt worship

idoleggi'are vt idolize. **'idolo** m idol

idoneità f suitability; (Mil) fitness; esame di ~ qualifying examination. **i'doneo** adj idoneo a suitable for; (Mil) fit for

i'drante m hydrant

idra'ta|nte adj (crema, gel) moisturizing. ~zi'one f moisturizing

i'draulico adj hydraulic ●m plumber

'idrico adj water attrib

idrocar'buro m hydrocarbon

idroe'lettrico adj hydroelectric

i'drofilo adj ▷COTONE

i'drogeno m hydrogen

i'ella f [!] bad luck; portare ~ be bad luck. **iel'lato** adj [!] jinxed, plagued by bad luck

i'ena f hyena

i'eri adv yesterday; ~ l'altro, l'altro ~ the day before yesterday; ~ pomeriggio yesterday afternoon; il giornale di ~ yesterday's paper

ietta'tore, -'trice f jinx. ~tura f (sfortuna) bad luck

igi'ene f hygiene. ~ico adj hygienic. **igie'nista** mf hygienist

i'gnaro adj unaware

i'gnobile adj base; (non onorevole) dishonourable

igno'ran|te adj ignorant • mf ignoramus. ~za f ignorance

igno'rare vt (non sapere) be unaware of; (trascurare) ignore

i'gnoto adj unknown

'ilare adj merry. ~ità f hilarity

illazi'one f inference

illecita'mente adv illicitly. **il'lecito** adj illicit

ille'gal|e adj illegal. ~ità f illegality. ~'mente adv illegally

illeg'gibile adj illegible; (libro) unreadable

illegittimità f illegitimacy. **ille'gittimo** adj illegitimate

il'leso adj unhurt

illette'rato, -a adj & mf illiterate

illimi'tato adj unlimited

illivi'dire vt bruise • vi (per rabbia) become livid

il'logico adj illogical

il'luder|e vt deceive. ~si vr deceive oneself

illumi'na|re vt light [up]; fig enlighten; ~re a giorno floodlight. ~rsi vr light up. ~zi'one f lighting; fig enlightenment

Illumi'nismo m Enlightenment

illusi'one f illusion; farsi illusioni delude oneself

il'luso, -a pp di illudere • adj deluded • mf day-dreamer.

illu'stra|re vt illustrate. ~tivo adj illustrative. ~tore, ~trice mf illustrator. ~zi'one f illustration

il'lustre adj distinguished

imbacuc'ca|re vt, ~rsi vr wrap up. ~to adj wrapped up

imbal'la|ggio m packing. ~re vt pack; (Auto) race

imbalsa'ma|re vt embalm; stuff (animale). ~to adj embalmed; (animale) stuffed

imbambo'lato adj vacant

imbaraz'zante adj embarrassing

imbaraz'za|re vt embarrass; (ostacolare) encumber. ~to adj embarrassed

imba'razzo m embarrassment; (ostacolo) hindrance; trarre qcno d'~ help sb out of a difficulty. ~ di stomaco indigestion

imbarca'dero m landing-stage

imbar'ca|re vt embark; (①: rimorchiare) score. ~rsi vr embark. ~zi'one f boat. ~zione di salvataggio lifeboat. **im'barco** m embarkation; (banchina) landing-stage

imba'sti|re vt tack; fig sketch. ~tura f tacking, basting

im'battersi vr ~ in run into

imbat'ti|bile adj unbeatable. ~uto adj unbeaten

imbavagli'are vt gag

imbe'cille adj stupid • mf imbecile

imbel'li|re vt embellish

imbestia'li|re vi, **~rsi** vr fly into a rage. **~to** adj enraged

im'bever|e vt imbue (**di** with). **~si** vr absorb

imbe'v|ibile adj undrinkable. **~uto** adj **~uto di** (acqua) soaked in; (nozioni) imbued with

imbian'c|are vt whiten • vi turn white. **~hino** m house painter

imbizzar'rir|e vi, **~si** vr become restless; (arrabbiarsi) get angry

imboc'ca|re vt feed; (entrare) enter; fig prompt. **~'tura** f opening; (ingresso) entrance; (Mus: di strumento) mouthpiece. **~m'bocco** m entrance

imbo'scar|e vt hide. **~si** vr (Mil) shirk military service

imbo'scata f ambush

imbottigli'a|re vt bottle. **~rsi** vr get snarled up in a traffic jam. **~to** adj (vino, acqua) bottled

imbot'ti|re vt stuff; pad (giacca); (Culin) fill. **~rsi** vr **~rsi di** (fig: di pasticche) stuff oneself with. **~ta** f quilt. **~to** adj (spalle) padded; (cuscino) stuffed; (panino) filled. **~'tura** f stuffing; (di giacca) padding; (Culin) filling

imbra'nato adj clumsy

imbrat'tar|e vt mark. **~si** vr dirty oneself

imbroc'car|e vt hit; **~la giusta** hit the nail on the head

imbrogli'|are vt muddle; (raggirare) cheat. **im'broglio** m tangle; (pasticcio) mess; (inganno) trick. **~'one, -a** mf cheat

imbronci'a|re vi, **~rsi** vr sulk. **~to** adj sulky

imbru'nire vi get dark; **all'~** at dusk

imbrut'tire vt make ugly • vi become ugly

imbu'care vt post, mail; (nel biliardo) pot

imbur'rare vt butter

im'buto m funnel

IMC m abbr (indice di massa corporea) BMI

imi'ta|re vt imitate. **~'tore, ~'trice** mf imitator. **~zi'one** f imitation

immaco'lato adj immaculate

immagazzi'nare vt store

immagi'na|re vt imagine; (supporre) suppose; s'immagini! imagine that!. **~rio** adj imaginary. **~zi'one** f imagination. **im'magine** f image

imman'cabil|e adj unfailing. **~'mente** adv without fail

im'mane adj huge; (orribile) terrible

imma'nente adj immanent

immangi'abile adj inedible

immatrico'la|re vt register. **~rsi** vr (studente): matriculate. **~zi'one** f registration; (di studente) matriculation

immaturità f immaturity. **imma'turo** adj unripe; (persona) immature; (precoce) premature

immedesi'ma|rsi vr **~rsi in** identify oneself with. **~zi'one** f identification

immedia|ta'mente adv immediately. **~'tezza** f immediacy. **imme-di'ato** adj immediate

immemo'rabile adj immemorial

immens|a'mente adv enormously. **~ità** f immensity. **im-'menso** adj immense

immensu'rabile adj immeasurable

im'merger|e vt immerse. **~si** vr plunge; (sommergibile) dive; **~si in** immerse oneself with.

immersi'one f immersion; (di sommergibile) dive. **im'merso** pp di **immergere**

immi'gra|nte adj & mf immigrant. **~re** vi immigrate. **~to, -a** mf immigrant. **~zi'one** f immigration

immi'nen|te adj imminent. **~za** f imminence

immischi'ar|e vt involve. ∼**si** vr ∼**si** in meddle in

immis'sario m tributary

immissi'one f insertion

im'mobile adj motionless

im'mobili mpl real estate. ∼**are** vt società ∼**are** building society, savings and loan Am

immobili|tà f immobility. ∼**z'zare** vt immobilize; (Comm) tie up

immo'lare vt sacrifice

immondez'zaio m rubbish tip. **immon'dizia** f filth; (spazzatura) rubbish. **im'mondo** adj filthy

immo'rale adj immoral. ∼**ità** f immorality

immorta'lare vt immortalize. **immor'tale** adj immortal

immoti'vato adj (gesto) unjustified

im'mun|e adj exempt; (Med) immune. ∼**ità** f immunity. ∼**iz'zare** vt immunize. ∼**izzazi'one** f immunization

immunodefici'enza f immunodeficiency

immuso'ni|rsi vr sulk. ∼**to** adj sulky

immu'tabile adj unchangeable. ∼**to** adj unchanging

impacchet'tare vt wrap up

impacci'a|re vt hamper; (disturbare) inconvenience; (imbarazzare) embarrass. ∼**to** adj embarrassed; (goffo) awkward. **im'paccio** m embarrassment; (ostacolo) hindrance; (situazione difficile) awkward situation

im'pacco m compress

impadro'nirsi vr ∼ **di** take possession of; (fig: imparare) master

impa'gabile adj priceless

impagi'na|re vt paginate. ∼**zi'one** f pagination

impagli'are vt stuff (animale)

impa'lato adj fig stiff

impalca'tura f scaffolding; fig structure

impalli'dire vi turn pale; (fig: perdere d'importanza) pale into insignificance

impa'nare vt roll in breadcrumbs

impanta'narsi vr get bogged down

impape'rarsi, impappi'narsi vr falter, stammer

impa'rare vt learn

impareggi'abile adj incomparable

imparen'ta|rsi vr ∼ **con** become related to. ∼**to** adj related

'impari adj unequal; (dispari) odd

impar'tire vt impart

imparzi'al|e adj impartial. ∼**ità** f impartiality

impas'sibile adj impassive

impas'ta|re vt (Culin) knead; blend (colori). **im'pasto** m (Culin) dough; (miscuglio) mixture

im'patto m impact

impau'rir|e vt frighten. ∼**si** vr become frightened

im'pavido adj fearless

impazi'en|te adj impatient; ∼**te di fare** qcsa eager to do sth. ∼**tirsi** vr lose patience. ∼**za** f impatience

impaz'zata f all'∼ full speed

impaz'zire vi go mad; (maionese): separate; far ∼ qcno drive sb mad; ∼ **per** le crazy about; **da** ∼ (mal di testa) blinding

impec'cabile adj impeccable

impedi'mento m hindrance; (ostacolo) obstacle

impe'dire vt ∼ **di** prevent from; (impacciare) hinder; (ostruire) obstruct; ∼ **a qcno di fare** qcsa prevent sb [from] doing sth

impe'gna|re vt (dare in pegno) pawn; (vincolare) bind; (prenotare) reserve; (assorbire) take up. ∼**rsi** vr apply oneself; ∼**rsi a fare** qcsa commit oneself to doing sth. ∼**tiva**

f referral. ∼'tivo *adj* binding; (lavoro) demanding. ∼ato *adj* engaged; (Pol) committed. im'pegno *m* engagement; (Comm) commitment; (zelo) care

impel'lente *adj* pressing

impen'na|rsi *vr* (cavallo:) rear; *fig* bristle. ∼ta *f* sharp rise; (di cavallo) rearing; (di moto) wheelie

impen'sabile *adj* unthinkable. ∼to *adj* unexpected

impensie'rir|e *vt*, ∼si *vr* worry

impe'ra|nte *adj* prevailing. ∼re *vi* reign; (tendenza:) prevail

impera'tivo *adj & m* imperative

impera'tore, -'trice *m* emperor ● *f* empress

impercet'tibile *adj* imperceptible

imperdo'nabile *adj* unforgivable

imper'fe|tto *adj & m* imperfect. ∼zi'one *f* imperfection

imperi'a|le *adj* imperial. ∼'lismo *m* imperialism

imperi'oso *adj* imperious; (impellente) urgent

impe'rizia *f* lack of skill

imperme'abile *adj* waterproof ● *m* raincoat

imperni'ar|e *vt* pivot; (fondare) base. ∼si *vr* ∼si su be based on

im'pero *m* empire; (potere) rule

imperscru'tabile *adj* inscrutable

imperso'nale *adj* impersonal

imperso'nare *vt* personify; (interpretare) act [the part of]

imper'territo *adj* undaunted

imperti'nen|te *adj* impertinent. ∼za *f* impertinence

imperver'sare *vi* rage

im'pervio *adj* inaccessible

'impet|o *m* impetus; (impulso) impulse; (slancio) transport. ∼u'oso *adj* impetuous; (vento) blustering

impet'tito *adj* stiff

impian'tare *vt* install; set up

(azienda)

impi'anto *m* plant; (sistema) system; (operazione) installation. ∼ radio (Auto) car stereo system

impia'strare *vt* plaster; (sporcare) dirty. impi'astro *m* poultice; (persona noiosa) bore; (pasticcione) cack-handed person

impic'car|e *vt* hang. ∼si *vr* hang oneself

impicci'arsi *vr* meddle. im'piccio *m* hindrance; (seccatura) bother. ∼'one, -a *mf* nosey parker

impie'ga|re *vt* employ; (usare) use; spend (tempo, denaro); Fin invest; l'autobus ha ∼to un'ora it took the bus an hour. ∼rsi *vr* get [oneself] a job

impie'gatizio *adj* clerical

impie'gato, -a *mf* employee. ∼ di banca bank clerk. impi'ego *m* employment; (posto) job; Fin investment

impieto'sir|e *vt* move to pity. ∼si *vr* be moved to pity

impie'trito *adj* petrified

impigli'ar|e *vt* entangle. ∼si *vr* get entangled

impi'grir|e *vt* make lazy. ∼si *vr* get lazy

impli'car|e *vt* implicate; (sottintendere) imply. ∼rsi *vr* become involved. ∼zi'one *f* implication

implicita'mente *adv* implicitly. im'plicito *adj* implicit

implo'rar|e *vt* implore. ∼zi'one *f* entreaty

impolve'ra|re *vt* cover with dust. ∼rsi *vr* get covered with dust. ∼to *adj* dusty

imponde'rabile *adj* imponderable; (causa, evento) unpredictable

impo'nen|te *adj* imposing. ∼za *f* impressiveness

impo'nibile *adj* taxable ● *m* taxable income

impopo'lar|e *adj* unpopular. ~ità *f* unpopularity

im'por|re *vt* impose; (*ordinare*) order. ~si *vr* assert oneself; (*aver successo*) be successful; ~si di (*prefiggersi di*) set oneself the task of

impor'tan|te *adj* important ● *m* important thing. ~za *f* importance

impor'ta|re *vt* import; (*comportare*) cause ● *vi* matter; (*essere necessario*) be necessary. non ~ I it doesn't matter!; non me ne ~ nientel I couldn't care less!. ~'tore, -'trice *mf* importer. ~zi'one *f* importation; (*merce importata*) import

im'porto *m* amount

importu'nare *vt* pester. impor'tuno *adj* troublesome; (*inopportuno*) untimely

imposizi'one *f* imposition; (*imposta*) tax

imposses'sarsi *vr* ~ di seize

impos'sibil|e *adj* impossible ● *m* fare l'~e do absolutely all one can. ~ità *f* impossibility

im'posta¹ *f* tax; ~ sul reddito income tax; ~ sul valore aggiunto value added tax

im'posta² *f* (*di finestra*) shutter

impo'sta|re *vt* (*progettare*) plan; (*basare*) base; (*Mus*) pitch; (*imbucare*) post, mail; set out (*domanda, problema*). ~zi'one *f* planning; (*di voce*) pitching

im'posto *pp di* imporre

impo'store, -a *mf* impostor

impo'ten|te *adj* powerless; (*Med*) impotent. ~za *f* powerlessness; (*Med*) impotence

impove'rir|e *vt* impoverish. ●si *vr* become poor

imprati'cabile *adj* impracticable; (*strada*) impassable

imprati'chir|e *vt* train. ~si *vr* ~si in o a get practice in

impre'care *vi* curse

impreci'sabile *adj* indeterminable. ~ato *adj* indeterminate. ~i'one *f* inaccuracy. impre'ciso *adj* inaccurate

impre'gnar|e *vt* impregnate; (*imbevere*) soak; *fig* imbue. ~si *vr* become impregnated with

imprendi'tor|e, -'trice *mf* entrepreneur. ~i'ale *adj* entrepreneurial

imprepa'rato *adj* unprepared

im'presa *f* undertaking; (*gesta*) exploit; (*azienda*) firm

impre'sario *m* impresario; (*appaltatore*) contractor

imprescin'dibile *adj* inescapable

impressio'na|bile *adj* impressionable. ~nte *adj* impressive; (*spaventoso*) frightening

impressio'nare *vt* impress; (*spaventare*) frighten; expose (*foto*). ~o'narsi *vr* be affected; (*spaventarsi*) be frightened. ~o'ne *f* impression; (*sensazione*) sensation; (*impronta*) mark; far ~one a qcno upset sb

impressio'nismo *m* impressionism. ~ta *mf* impressionist

im'presso *pp di* imprimere ● *adj* printed

impre'stare *vt* lend

impreve'dibile *adj* unexpected

imprevi'dente *adj* improvident

impre'visto *adj* unforeseen ● *m* unforeseen event

imprigio|na'mento *m* imprisonment. ~'nare *vt* imprison

im'primere *vt* impress; (*stampare*) print; (*comunicare*) impart

impro'babil|e *adj* unlikely, improbable. ~ità *f* improbability

improdut'tivo *adj* unproductive

im'pronta *f* impression; *fig* mark. ~ digitale fingerprint. ~ ecologica carbon footprint. ~ del piede footprint

impro'perio *m* insult; improperi

pl abuse *sg*

im'proprio *adj* improper

improvvi'sa|re *vt/i* improvise.
~**rsi** *vr* turn oneself into a. ~**ta** *f*
surprise. ~**zi'one** *f* improvisation

improv'viso *adj* sudden; **all'~** unexpectedly

impru'den|te *adj* imprudent. ~**za**
f imprudence

impu'gna|re *vt* grasp; (*Jur*) contest. ~**tura** *f* grip; (*manico*) handle

impulsività *f* impulsiveness. **impul'sivo** *adj* impulsive

im'pulso *m* impulse; **agire d'~** act
on impulse

impune'mente *adv* with impunity. **impu'nito** *adj* unpunished

impun'tura *f* stitching

impurità *f inv* impurity. **im'puro** *adj*
impure

impu'tabile *adj* attributable (a to)

impu'ta|re *vt* attribute; (*accusare*)
charge. ~**to, -a** *mf* accused. ~**zi'one**
f charge

imputri'dire *vi* rot

in *prep* in; (*moto a luogo*) to; (*su*) on;
(*entro*) within; (*mezzo*) by; (*con materiale*) made of; **essere in casa/ufficio**
be at home/at the office; **in mano/**
tasca in one's hand/pocket; **andare**
in Francia/campagna go to France/
the country; **salire in treno** get on
the train; **versa la birra nel bic-**
chiere pour the beer into the glass;
in alto up there; **in giornata** within
the day; **nel 1997 in** 1997; **una**
borsa in pelle a bag made of leather, a leather bag; **in macchina**
(*viaggiare, venire*) by car; **in con-**
tanti [in] cash; **in vacanza** on holiday; **se fossi in te** if I were you;
siamo in sette there are seven of us

inabbor'dabile *adj* unapproachable

i'nabil|e *adj* incapable; (*fisicamente*)
unfit. ~**ità** *f* incapacity

inabi'tabile *adj* uninhabitable

inacces'sibile *adj* inaccessible;
(*persona*) unapproachable

inaccet'tabil|e *adj* unacceptable.
~**ità** *f* unacceptability

inacer'bi|re *vt* embitter; exacerbate (*rapporto*). ~**si** *vr* grow bitter

inaci'di|re *vt* turn sour. ~**si** *vr* go
sour; (*persona*): become bitter

ina'datto *adj* unsuitable

inadegu'ato *adj* inadequate

inadempi'ente *mf* defaulter.
~**'mento** *m* nonfulfilment

ina'la|re *vt* inhale. ~**tore** *m* inhaler.
~**zi'one** *f* inhalation

inalbe'rar|e *vt* hoist. ~**si** *vr* (*cavallo*:) rear [up]; (*adirarsi*) lose one's
temper

inalte'rabile *adj* unchangeable;
(*colore*) fast. ~**to** *adj* unchanged

inami'da|re *vt* starch. ~**to** *adj*
starched

inammis'sibile *adj* inadmissible

inamovi'bile *adj* irremovable

inani'mato *adj* inanimate; (*senza*
vita) lifeless

inappa'ga|bile *adj* unsatisfiable.
~**to** *adj* unfulfilled

inappe'tenza *f* lack of appetite

inappli'cabile *adj* inapplicable

inappun'tabile *adj* faultless

inar'ca|re *vt* arch; raise (*sopracciglia*). ~**si** *vr* (*legno*:) warp; (*ripiano*:)
sag; (*linea*:) curve

inari'dir|e *vt* parch; empty of feelings (*persona*). ~**si** *vr* dry up; (*persona*:) become empty of feelings

inarti'co'lato *adj* inarticulate

inaspettata'mente *adv* unexpectedly. **inaspet'tato** *adj* unexpected

inaspri'mento *m* embitterment;
(*di conflitto*) worsening

ina'sprir|e *vt* embitter. ~**si** *vr* become embittered

inattac'cabile *adj* unassailable; (*ir-*

reprensibile) irreproachable

inatten'dibile *adj* unreliable. **inat-'teso** *adj* unexpected

inattività *f* inactivity. **inat'tivo** *adj* inactive

inattu'abile *adj* impracticable

inau'dito *adj* unheard of

inaugu'rale *adj* inaugural; viaggio ~ maiden voyage

inaugu'ra|re *vt* inaugurate; open (mostra); unveil (statua); christen (lavastoviglie ecc.). **~zi'one** *f* inauguration; *(di mostra)* opening; *(di statua)* unveiling

inavver't|enza *f* inadvertence. **~ita'mente** *adv* inadvertently

incagli'ar|e *vi* ground • *vt* hinder. **~si** *vr* run aground

incalco'labile *adj* incalculable

incal'li|rsi *vr* grow callous; *(abituarsi)* become hardened. **~to** *adj* callous; *(abituato)* hardened

incal'za|nte *adj* (ritmo) driving; (richiesta) urgent. **~re** *vt* pursue; *fig* press

incame'rare *vt* appropriate

incammi'nar|e *vt* get going; *(fig: guidare)* set off. **~si** *vr* set out

incana'lar|e *vt* canalize; *fig* channel. **~si** *vr* converge on

incande'scen|te *adj* incandescent; *(discussione)* burning

incan'ta|re *vt* enchant. **~rsi** *vr* stand spellbound; *(inceppparsi)* jam. **~tore,** **~trice** *m* enchanter • *f* enchantress

incan'tesimo *m* spell

incan'tevole *adj* enchanting

in'canto *m* spell; *fig* delight; *(asta)* auction; come per ~ as if by magic

incanu'tire *vt* turn white. **~to** *adj* white

inca'pace *adj* incapable. **~ità** *f* incapability

incapo'nirsi *vr* be set (a fare un doing)

incap'pare *vi* ~ in run into

incappucci'arsi *vr* wrap up

incapricci'arsi *vr* ~ di take a fancy to

incapsu'lare *vt* seal; crown (dente)

incarce'ra|re *vt* imprison. **~zi'one** *f* imprisonment

incari'ca|re *vt* charge. **~rsi** *vr* take upon oneself; me ne incarico io I will see to it. **~to, -a** *adj* in charge • *mf* representative. **in'carico** *m* charge; per incarico di on behalf of

incar'nare *vt* embody. **~rsi** *vr* become incarnate

incarta'mento *m* documents pl. **incar'tare** *vt* wrap [in paper]

incas'sa|re *vt* pack; *(Mech)* embed; box in (mobile, frigo); *(riscuotere)* cash; take (colpo). **~to** *adj* set; (fiume) deeply embanked. **in'casso** *m* collection; *(introito)* takings pl

incasto'na|re *vt* set. **~tura** *f* setting. **~to** *adj* embedded; (anello) inset (di with)

inca'strar|e *vt* fit in; *(⊡: in situazione)* corner. **~si** *vr* fit. **in'castro** *m* joint; a incastro (pezzi) interlocking

incate'nare *vt* chain

incatra'mare *vt* tar

incatti'vire *vt* turn nasty

in'cauto *adj* imprudent

inca'va|re *vt* hollow out. **~to** *adj* hollow. **~tura** *f* hollow. **in'cavo** *m* hollow; *(scanalatura)* groove

incendi'ar|e *vt* set fire to; *fig* inflame. **~si** *vr* catch fire. **~io, -a** *adj* incendiary; *(discorso)* inflammatory; *fig:* (bellezza) sultry • *mf* arsonist. **in'cendio** *m* fire. incendio doloso arson

incene'ri|re *vt* burn to ashes; *(cremare)* cremate. **~rsi** *vr* be burnt to ashes. **~tore** *m* incinerator

in'censo *m* incense

incensu'rato *adj* blameless; essere ~ *(Jur)* have a clean record

incenti'vare vt motivate. **incen-
'tivo** m incentive

incen'trarsi vr ~ **su** centre on

incep'par|e vt block; fig hamper.
~**si** vr jam

ince'rata f oilcloth

incerot'tato adj with a plaster on

incer'tezza f uncertainty. **in'certo**
adj uncertain ●m uncertainty

inces'sante adj unceasing.
~'**mente** adv incessantly

in'cest|o m incest. ~**u'oso** adj in-
cestuous

in'cetta f buying up; **fare** ~ **di**
stockpile

inchi'esta f investigation

inchi'nar|e vt, ~**si** vr bow. **in'chino**
m bow; (di donna) curtsy

inchio'dare vt nail; nail down (coperchio); ~ **a letto** (malattia:) confine to bed

inchi'ostro m ink

inciam'pare vi stumble; ~ **in** (imbattersi) run into. **inci'ampo** m hindrance

inciden'tale adj incidental

inci'den|te m (episodio) incident; (in-
fortunio) accident. ~**za** f incidence

in'cidere vt cut; (arte) engrave; (registrare) record ●vi ~ **su** (gravare)
weigh upon

in'cinta adj pregnant

incipi'ente adj incipient

incipri'ar|e vt powder. ~**si** vr pow-
der one's face

in'circa adv **all'**~ more or less

incisi'one f incision; (arte) engrav-
ing; (acquaforte) etching; (registrazione)
recording

inci'sivo adj incisive ●m (dente)
incisor

in'ciso m **per** ~ incidentally

incita'mento m incitement. **inci-
'tare** vt incite

inci'vil|e adj uncivilized; (maleducato)
impolite. ~**tà** f barbarism; (maleduca-*

*zione) rudeness

incle'men|te adj harsh

incli'nabile adj reclining

incli'na|bile vt tilt ●vi ~**re a** be in-
clined to. ~**rsi** vr list. ~**to** adj tilted;
(terreno) sloping. ~**zi'one** f slope,
inclination. **in'cline** adj inclined

in'clud|ere vt include; (allegare) en-
close. ~**si'one** f inclusion. ~**sivo** adj
inclusive. ~**so** pp di **includere** ●adj
included; (compreso) inclusive; (allegato) enclosed

incoe'ren|te adj (contraddittorio) in-
consistent. ~**za** f inconsistency

in'cognit|a f unknown quantity.
~**o** adj unknown ●m **in** ~**o**
incognito

incol'lar|e vt stick; (con colla liquida)
glue. ~**si** vr stick to; ~**si a qcno**
stick close to sb

incolle'ri|rsi vr lose one's temper.
~**to** adj enraged

incol'mabile adj (differenza) un-
bridgeable; (vuoto) unfillable

incolon'nare vt line up

inco'lore adj colourless

incol'pare vt blame

in'colto adj uncultivated; (persona)
uneducated

in'colume adj unhurt

incom'ben|te adj impending. ~**za**
f task

in'combere vi ~ **su** hang over; ~
a (spettare) be incumbent on

incominci'are vt/i begin, start

incomo'dar|e vt inconvenience.
~**si** vr trouble. **in'comodo** adj uncomfortable; (inopportuno) inconvenient ●m inconvenience

incompa'rabile adj incomparable

incompe'ten|te adj incompetent.
~**za** f incompetence

incompi'uto adj unfinished

incom'pleto adj incomplete

incompren'si|bile adj incompre-
hensible. ~**one** f lack of under-

standing; (malinteso) misunderstanding. **incom'preso** adj misunderstood

inconce'pibile adj inconceivable

inconclu'dente adj inconclusive; (persona) ineffectual

incondizio|nata'mente adv unconditionally. **~'nato** adj unconditional

inconfes'sabile adj unmentionable

inconfon'dibile adj unmistakable

incongru'ente adj inconsistent

in'congruo adj inadequate

inconsa'pevol|e adj unaware; (inconscio) unconscious. **~'mente** adv unwittingly

'inconscia'mente adv unconsciously. **in'conscio** adj & m (Psych) unconscious

inconsi'sten|te adj insubstantial; (notizia ecc) unfounded. **~za** f (di ragionamento, prove) flimsiness

inconsu'eto adj unusual

incon'sulto adj rash

incontami'nato adj uncontaminated

inconte'nibile adj irrepressible

inconten'tabile adj insatiable; (esigente) hard to please

inconti'nen|te adj incontinent. **~za** f incontinence

incon'trar|e vt meet; encounter, meet with (difficoltà). **~si** vr meet (con qcno sb)

incon'trario: all'**~** adv the other way around; (in modo sbagliato) the wrong way around

incontra'stabile adj incontrovertible. **~to** adj undisputed

in'contro m meeting; Sport match. **~** al vertice summit meeting • prep **~** a towards; andare **~** a qcno go to meet sb; fig meet sb half way

inconveni'ente m drawback

incoraggia|'mento m encouragement. **~'ante** adj encouraging.

~'are vt encourage

incornici'a|re vt frame. **~'tura** f framing

incoro'na|re vt crown. **~zi'one** f coronation

incorpo'rar|e vt incorporate; (mescolare) blend. **~si** vr blend; (territori:) merge

incorreg'gibile adj incorrigible

in'correre vt **~** in incur; **~** nel pericolo di... run the risk of...

incorrut'tibile adj incorruptible

incosci'en|te adj unconscious; (irresponsabile) reckless • mf irresponsible person. **~za** f unconsciousness; recklessness

inco'stan|te adj changeable; (persona) fickle. **~za** f changeableness; (di persona) fickleness

incre'dibile adj unbelievable, incredible

incredulità f incredulity. **in'credulo** adj incredulous

incremen'tare vt increase; (intensificare) step up. **incre'mento** m increase. incremento demografico population growth

incresci'oso adj regrettable

incre'spar|e vt ruffle; wrinkle (tessuto); make frizzy (capelli); **~e** la fronte frown. **~si** vr (acqua:) ripple; (tessuto:) wrinkle; (capelli:) go frizzy

incrimi'na|re vt indict; fig incriminate. **~zi'one** f indictment

incri'na|re vt crack; fig affect (amicizia). **~rsi** vr crack; (amicizia:) be affected. **~'tura** f crack

incroci'a|re vt cross • vi (Aeron, Naut) cruise. **~rsi** vr cross. **~'tore** m cruiser

in'crocio m crossing; (di strade) crossroads sg

incrol'labile adj indestructible

incro'sta|re vt encrust. **~zi'one** f encrustation

incuba|'trice f incubator. **~zi'one**

f incubation

'incubo m nightmare

in'cudine f anvil

incu'rabile adj incurable

incu'rante adj careless

incurio'sir|e vt make curious. **∼si** vr become curious

incursi'one f raid. **∼ aerea** air raid

incurva'mento m bending

incur'va|re vt, **∼rsi** vr bend. **∼tura** f bending

in'cusso pp di incutere

incusto'dito adj unguarded

in'cutere vt arouse

'indaco m indigo

indaffa'rato adj busy

inda'gare vt/i investigate

inda'gine f research; (giudiziaria) investigation. **∼ di mercato** market survey

indebi'tar|e vt, **∼si** vr get into debt

in'debito adj undue

indeboli'mento m weakening

indebo'lir|e vt, **∼si** vr weaken

inde'cen|te adj indecent. **∼za** f indecency; (vergogna) disgrace

indeci'frabile adj indecipherable

indecisi'one f indecision. **inde-'ciso** adj undecided

inde'fesso adj tireless

indefi'ni|bile adj indefinable. **∼to** adj indefinite

indefor'mabile adj crushproof

in'degno adj unworthy

indelica'tezza f indelicacy; (azione) tactless act. **indeli'cato** adj indiscreet; (grossolano) indelicate

in'denn|e adj uninjured; (da malattia) unaffected. **∼ità** f inv allowance; (per danni) compensation. **∼ità di trasferta** travel allowance. **∼iz'zare** vt compensate. **inden'nizzo** m compensation

---

indero'gabile adj binding

indeside'ra|bile adj undesirable. **∼to** adj (figlio, ospite) unwanted

indetermi'na|bile adj indeterminable. **∼'tezza** f vagueness. **∼to** adj indeterminate

'Indi|a f India. **i∼'ano, -a** adj & mf Indian; **in fila i∼ana** in single file

indiavo'lato adj possessed; (vivace) wild

indi'ca|re vt show, indicate; (col dito) point at; (far notare) point out; (consigliare) advise. **∼'tivo** adj indicative ● m (Gram) indicative. **∼'tore** m indicator; (Techn) gauge; (prontuario) directory. **∼zi'one** f indication; (istruzione) direction

'indice m (dito) forefinger; (lancetta) pointer; (di libro, statistica) index; (fig: segno) sign

indietreggi'are vi draw back; (Mil) retreat

indi'etro adv back, behind; **all'∼** backwards; **avanti e ∼** back and forth; **essere ∼** be behind; (mentalmente) be backward; (con pagamenti) be in arrears; (di orologio) be slow; **fare marcia ∼** reverse; **rimandare ∼** send back; **rimanere ∼** be left behind; **torna ∼!** come back!

indi'feso adj undefended; (inerme) helpless

indiffe'ren|te adj indifferent; **mi è ∼te** it is all the same to me. **∼za** f indifference

in'digeno, -a adj indigenous ● mf native

indi'gen|te adj needy. **∼za** f poverty

indigesti'one f indigestion. **indi-'gesto** adj indigestible

indi'gna|re vt make indignant. **∼rsi** vr be indignant. **∼to** adj indignant. **∼zi'one** f indignation

indimenti'cabile adj unforgettable

indipen'den|te adj independent

~te'mente adv independently; ~te-mente dal tempo regardless of the weather, whatever the weather. ~za f independence

in'dire vt announce

indiretta'mente adv indirectly. indi'retto adj indirect

indiriz'zar|e vt address; (mandare) send; (dirigere) direct. ~si vr direct one's steps. indi'rizzo m address; (direzione) direction

indisci'pli|na f lack of discipline. ~'nato adj undisciplined

indi'scre|to adj indiscreet. ~zi'one f indiscretion

indi'scusso adj unquestioned

indiscu'tibil|e adj unquestionable. ~'mente adv unquestionably

indispen'sabile adj essential, indispensable

indispet'tir|e vt irritate. ~si vr get irritated

indi'spo|rre vt antagonize. ~sto pp di indisporre ●adj indisposed. ~sizi'one f indisposition

indisso'lubile adj indissoluble

indistin'guibile adj indiscernible

indistinta'mente adv without exception. indi'stinto adj indistinct

indistrut'tibile adj indestructible

indistur'bato adj undisturbed

in'divia f endive

individu'a|le adj individual. ~'lista mf individualist. ~lità f individuality. ~re vt individualize; (localizzare) locate; (riconoscere) single out

indi'viduo m individual

indivi'sibile adj indivisible. indi-'viso adj undivided

indizi'a|re vt throw suspicion on. ~to, -a adj suspected ●mf suspect. in'dizio m sign; (Jur) circumstantial evidence

'indole f nature

indolenzi'mento m stiffness

indolenzi'rsi vr go stiff.

~to adj stiff

indo'lore adj painless

indo'mani m l'~ the following day

Indo'nesia f Indonesia

indo'rare vt gild

indos'sa|re vt wear; (mettere addosso) put on. ~tore, ~trice mf model

in'dotto pp di indurre

indottri'nare vt indoctrinate

indovi'n|are vt guess; (predire) foretell. ~ato adj successful; (scelta) well-chosen. ~ello m riddle. indo-'vino, -a mf fortune-teller

indubbia'mente adv undoubtedly. in'dubbio adj undoubted

indugi'ar|e vi, ~si vr linger. in'du-gio m delay

indul'gen|te adj indulgent. ~za f indulgence

in'dul|gere vi ~gere a indulge in. ~to pp di indulgere ●m (Jur) pardon

indu'mento m garment; indu-menti pl clothes

induri'mento m hardening

indu'rir|e vt, ~si vr harden

in'durre vt induce

in'dustri|a f industry. ~'ale adj industrial ●mf industrialist

industrializza're vt industrialize. ~to adj industrialized. ~zi'one f industrialization

industri'arsi vr try one's hardest. ~oso adj industrious

induzi'one f induction

inebe'tito adj stunned

inebri'ante adj intoxicating, exciting

i'nedia f starvation

i'nedito adj unpublished

ineffi'cace adj ineffective

ineffici'en|te adj inefficient. ~za f inefficiency

ineguagli'abile adj incomparable

inegu'ale adj unequal;

(superficie) uneven

inelut'tabile *adj* inescapable

ine'rente *adj* ~ a concerning

i'nerme *adj* unarmed; *fig* defenceless

inerpi'carsi *vr* ~ su clamber up; (pianta:) climb up

i'ner|te *adj* inactive; (*Phys*) inert. ~za *f* inactivity; (*Phys*) inertia

inesat'tezza *f* inaccuracy. ine-'satto *adj* inaccurate; (*erroneo*) incorrect; (*non riscosso*) uncollected

inesau'ribile *adj* inexhaustible

inesi'sten|te *adj* non-existent. ~za *f* non-existence

inesperi'enza *f* inexperience. ine-'sperto *adj* inexperienced

inespli'cabile *adj* inexplicable

ine'sploso *adj* unexploded

inesti'mabile *adj* inestimable

inetti'tudine *f* ineptitude. i'netto *adj* inept; inetto a unsuited to

ine'vaso *adj* (*pratiche*) pending; (*corrispondenza*) unanswered

inevi'tabil|e *adj* inevitable. ~'mente *adv* inevitably

i'nezia *f* trifle

infagot'tare *vt* wrap up. ~si *vr* wrap [oneself] up

infal'libile *adj* infallible

infa'mare *vt* defame. ~'torio *adj* defamatory

in'fam|e *adj* infamous; (🔢: *orrendo*) awful, shocking. ~ia *f* infamy

infan'garsi *vr* get muddy

infan'tile *adj* children's; (*ingenuità*) childlike; *pej* childish

in'fanzia *f* childhood; (*bambini*) children *pl*; prima ~ infancy

infar'cire *vt* pepper (*discorso*) (di with)

infari'na|re *vt* flour; ~re di sprinkle with. ~'tura *f fig* smattering

in'farto *m* coronary

infasti'dir|e *vt* irritate. ~si *vr* get irritated

ineluttabile | **infierire**

infati'cabile *adj* untiring

in'fatti *conj* as a matter of fact; (*veramente*) indeed

infatu'a|rsi *vr* become infatuated (di with). ~to *adj* infatuated. ~zi'one *f* infatuation

infe'condo *adj* infertile

infe'del|e *adj* unfaithful. ~tà *f* unfaithfulness; ~ *pl* affairs

infe'lic|e *adj* unhappy; (*inappropriato*) unfortunate; (*cattivo*) bad. ~ità *f* unhappiness

infel'tri|rsi *vr* get matted. ~to *adj* matted

inferi'or|e *adj* (*più basso*) lower; (*qualità*) inferior • *mf* inferior. ~ità *f* inferiority

infer'meria *f* infirmary; (*di nave*) sick-bay

infermi'er|a *f* nurse. ~e *m* [male] nurse

infermità *f* sickness. ~ mentale mental illness. in'fermo, -a *adj* sick • *mf* invalid

infer'nale *adj* infernal; (*spaventoso*) hellish

in'ferno *m* hell; va all'~! go to hell!

infero'cirsi *vr* become fierce

inferri'ata *f* grating

infervo'rar|e *vt* arouse enthusiasm in. ~si *vr* get excited

infe'stare *vt* infest

infet't|are *vt* infect. ~arsi *vr* become infected. ~ivo *adj* infectious. in'fetto *adj* infected. infezi'one *f* infection

infiac'chir|e *vt/i*, ~si *vr* weaken

infiam'mabile *adj* [in]flammable

infiam'ma|re *vt* set on fire; (*Med, fig*) inflame. ~rsi *vr* catch fire; (*Med*) become inflamed. ~zi'one *f* (*Med*) inflammation

in'fido *adj* treacherous

infie'rire *vi* (*imperversare*) rage; ~ su

attack furiously

in'figger|e vt drive. **~si** vr **~si in** penetrate

infil'lar|e vt thread; (mettere) insert; (indossare) put on. **~si** vr slip on (vestito); **~si in** (introdursi in) slip into

infil'tra|rsi vr infiltrate. **~zi'one** f infiltration; (d'acqua) seepage; (Med: iniezione) injection

infil'zare vt pierce; (infilare) string; (conficcare) stick

'infimo adj lowest

in'fine adv finally; (insomma) in short

infinità f infinity; **un'~ di** masses of. **infi'nito** adj infinite; (Gram) infinitive ● m infinite; (Gram) infinitive; (Math) infinity; **all'infinito** endlessly

infinocchi'are vt 🄵 hoodwink

infischi'arsi vr ~ **di** not care about; **me ne infischio** 🄵 I couldn't care less

in'fisso pp di infiggere ● m fixture; (di porta, finestra) frame

infit'tir|e vt/i, **~si** vr thicken

inflazi'one f inflation

infles'sibil|e adj inflexible. **~ità** f inflexibility

inflessi'one f inflection

in'fli|ggere vt inflict. **~tto** pp di infliggere

influ'en|te adj influential. **~za** f influence; (Med) influenza

influen'za|bile adj (mente, opinione) impressionable. **~re** vt influence. **~to** adj (malato) with the flu

influ'ire vi ~ **su** influence

in'flusso m influence

info'carsi vr catch fire; (viso:) go red; (discussione:) become heated

infol'tire vt/i thicken

infon'dato adj unfounded

in'fondere vt instil

infor'care vt fork up; get on (bici); put on (occhiali)

infor'male adj informal

infor'ma|re vt inform. **~rsi** vr inquire (di about).

infor'matic|a f computing, IT. **~o** adj computer attrib

infor'ma|tivo adj informative. infor'mato adj informed; **male informato** ill-informed. **~tore**, **~trice** mf (di polizia) informer. **~zi'one** f information (solo sg); **un'~zione** a piece of information

in'forme adj shapeless

infor'nare vt put into the oven

infortu'narsi vr have an accident.

infor'tu|nio m accident. **~nio sul lavoro** industrial accident

infos'sa|rsi vr sink; (guance, occhi:) become hollow. **~to** adj sunken, hollow

infradici'ar|e vt drench. **~si** vr get drenched; (diventare marcio) rot

infra'dito m pl (scarpe) flip-flops

in'frang|ere vt break; (in mille pezzi) shatter. **~ersi** vr break. **~'gibile** adj unbreakable

in'franto pp di infrangere ● adj shattered; (cuore) broken

infra'rosso adj infra-red

infrastrut'tura f infrastructure

infrazi'one f offence

infredda'tura f cold

infreddo'li|rsi vr feel cold. **~to** adj cold

infruttu'oso adj fruitless

infuo'care vt make red-hot. **~to** adj burning

infu'ori adv **all'~** outwards; **all'~ di** except

infuri'a|re vi rage. **~rsi** vr fly into a rage. **~to** adj blustering

infusi'one f infusion. **in'fuso** pp di infondere ● m infusion

Ing. abbr ingegnere

ingabbi'are vt cage; (fig: mettere in prigione) jail

ingaggi'are vt engage; sign up

(calciatori ecc); begin (lotta, battaglia). in'gaggio m engagement; (di calciatore) signing [up]

ingan'nar|e vt deceive; (essere infedele a) be unfaithful to. ~si vr deceive oneself; se non m'inganno if I am not mistaken

ingan'nevole adj deceptive. in'ganno m deceit; (frode) fraud

ingarbugli'ar|e vt entangle; (confondere) confuse. ~rsi vr get entangled; (confondersi) become confused. ~to adj confused

inge'gnarsi vr do one's best

inge'gnere vt engineer. ingegne-'ria f engineering

in'gegno m brains pl; (genio) genius; (abilità) ingenuity. ~sa'mente adv ingeniously

ingelo'sir|e vt make jealous. ~si vr become jealous

in'gente adj huge

ingenu|a'mente adv naïvely. ~ità f naïvety. in'genuo adj ingenuous; (credulone) naïve

inge'renza f interference

inghiot'tire vt swallow

inges'sar|e vt put in plaster. ~tura f plaster

Inghil'terra f England

inghiot'tire vt swallow

in'ghippo m trick

ingial'li|re vi, ~rsi vr turn yellow. ~to adj yellowed

ingigan'tir|e vt magnify ●vi, ~si vr grow to enormous proportions

inginocchi|a|rsi vr kneel [down]. ~to adj kneeling. ~'toio m prie-dieu

ingiù adv down; all'~ downwards; a testa ~ head downwards

ingi'un|gere vt order. ~zi'one f injunction. ~zione di pagamento final demand

ingi'uri|a f insult; (torto) wrong; (danno) damage. ~'are vt insult; (fare

un torto a) wrong. ~'oso adj insulting

ingiu'stizia f injustice. ingi'usto adj unjust, unfair

in'glese adj English ●m Englishman; (lingua) English ●f Englishwoman

ingoi'are vt swallow

ingol'far|e vt flood (motore). ~si vr fig get involved; (motore:) flood

ingom'bra|nte adj cumbersome. ~re vt clutter up; fig cram (mente)

in'gombro m encumbrance; essere d'~ be in the way

ingor'digia f greed. in'gordo adj greedy

ingor'gar|e vt block. ~si vr be blocked [up]. in'gorgo m blockage; (del traffico) jam

ingoz'zar|e vt gobble up; (nutrire eccessivamente) stuff; fatten (animali)

ingra'naggio m gear; fig mechanism. ~re vt engage ●vi be in gear

ingrandi'mento m enlargement

ingran'di|re vt enlarge; (esagerare) magnify. ~rsi vr become larger; (aumentare) increase

ingras'sar|e vt fatten up; (Mech) grease ●vi, ~si vr put on weight

ingrati'tudine f ingratitude. in'grato adj ungrateful; (sgradevole) thankless

ingredi'ente m ingredient

in'gresso m entrance; (accesso) admittance; (sala) hall; ~ gratuito/libero admission free; vietato l'~ no entry; no admittance

ingros'sar|e vt make big; (gonfiare) swell ●vi, ~si vr grow big; (gonfiare) swell

in'grosso m; all'~ wholesale; (pressappoco) roughly

ingua'ribile adj incurable

'inguine m groin

ingurgi'tare vt gulp down

ini'bi|re vt inhibit; (vietare) forbid

i

~to adj inhibited. ~zi'one f inhibition; (divieto) prohibition

iniet'tar|e vt inject. ~si vr ~si di sangue (occhi:) become bloodshot. iniezi'one f injection

inimi'carsi vr make an enemy of. inimi'cizia f enmity

inimi'tabile adj inimitable

ininter|rotta'mente adv continuously. ~rotto adj continuous

iniquità f iniquity. i'niquo adj iniquitous

inizi'are vt begin; (avviare) open; ~ qcno a qcsa initiate sb in sth ● vi begin

inizia'tiva f initiative; prendere l'~ take the initiative

inizi'a|to, -a adj initiated ● mf initiate; gli ~ti the initiated. ~'tore, ~'trice mf initiator. ~zi'one f initiation

i'nizio m beginning, start; dare ~ a start; avere ~ get under way

innaffi'a|re vt water. ~'toio m watering-can

innal'zar|e vt raise; (erigere) erect. ~si vr rise

innamo'ra|rsi vr fall in love (di with). ~ta f girl-friend. ~to adj in love ● m boy-friend

in'nanzi adv (stato in luogo) in front; (di tempo) ahead; (avanti) forward; (prima) before; d'ora ~ from now on ● prep (prima) before; ~ a in front of. ~'tutto adv first of all; (soprattutto) above all

in'nato adj innate

innatu'rale adj unnatural

inne'gabile adj undeniable

innervo'sir|e vt make nervous. ~si vr get irritated

inne'scare vt prime. in'nesco m primer

inne'stare vt graft; (Mech) engage; (inserire) insert. in'nesto m graft; (Mech) clutch; (Electr) connection

inne'vato adj covered in snow

'inno m hymn. ~ nazionale national anthem

inno'cen|te adj innocent ~te- 'mente adv innocently

in'nocuo adj innocuous

inno'va|re vt make changes in. ~tivo adj innovative. ~'tore adj trail-blazing. ~zi'one f innovation

innume'revole adj innumerable

ino'doro adj odourless

inoffen'sivo adj harmless

inol'trar|e vt forward. ~si vr advance

inol'trato adj late

i'noltre adv besides

inon'da|re vt flood. ~zi'one f flood

inope'roso adj idle

inoppor'tuno adj untimely

inorgo'glir|e vt make proud. ~si vr become proud

inorri'dire vt horrify ● vi be horrified

inosser'vato adj unobserved; (non rispettato) disregarded; passare ~ go unnoticed

inossi'dabile adj stainless

'inox adj inv (acciaio) stainless

inqua'dra|re vt frame; fig put in context (scrittore, problema). ~rsi vr fit into. ~'tura f framing

inqualifi'cabile adj unspeakable

inquie'tar|e vt worry. ~si get worried; (impazientirsi) get cross. inqui'eto adj restless; (preoccupato) worried. inquie'tudine f anxiety

inqui'lino, -a mf tenant

inquina'mento m pollution

inqui'na|re vt pollute. ~to adj polluted

inqui'rente adj (Jur) (magistrato) examining; commissione ~ commission of enquiry

inqui'sire vt/i investigate. ~to adj under investigation. ~'tore, ~'trice *adj* inquiring. ●*mf* inquisitor. ~**zi'one** *f* inquisition

insabbi'are *vt* shelve

insa'lat|a *f* salad. ~**a belga** endive. ~**i'era** *f* salad bowl

insa'lubre *adj* unhealthy

insa'nabile *adj* incurable

insangui'na|re *vt* cover with blood. ~**to** *adj* bloody

insa'po|re *adj* tasteless. ~'**rire** *vt* flavour

insa'puta *f* all'~ di unknown to

insazi'abile *adj* insatiable

insce'nare *vt* stage

inscin'dibile *adj* inseparable

inse'dia|**mento** *m* installation. ~'**are** *vt* install. ~**si** *vr* install oneself

in'segna *f* sign; (*bandiera*) flag; (*decorazione*) decoration; (*emblema*) insignia *pl*; (*stemma*) symbol. ~ **luminosa** neon sign

insegna'mento *m* teaching. **inse-'gnante** *adj* teaching ●*mf* teacher

inse'gnare *vt/i* teach; ~ qcsa a qcno teach sb sth

insegui'mento *m* pursuit

insegu'i|re *vt* pursue. ~'**tore**, ~'**trice** *m* pursuer

insemi'na|re *vt* inseminate. ~**zi'one** *f* insemination. ~**zione artificiale** artificial insemination

insena'tura *f* inlet

insen'sato *adj* senseless; (*folle*) crazy

insen'sibil|e *adj* insensitive; (*braccio ecc*) numb. ~**ità** *f* insensitivity

inseri'mento *m* insertion

inse'rir|e *vt* insert; place (*annuncio*); (*Electr*) connect. ~**si** *vr* ~**si in** get into. **in'serto** *m* file; (*in un film ecc*) insert

inservi'ente *mf* attendant

inserzi'o|ne *f* insertion; (*avviso*) advertisement. ~'**nista** *mf* advertiser

insetti'cida *m* insecticide

in'setto *m* insect

insicu'rezza *f* insecurity. **insi'curo** *adj* insecure

in'sidi|a *f* trick; (*tranello*) snare. ~'**are** *vt/i* lay a trap for. ~'**oso** *adj* insidious

insi'eme *adv* together; (*contemporaneamente*) at the same time ●*prep* ~ **a** [together] with ●*m* whole; (*completo*) outfit; (*Theat*) ensemble; (*Math*) set; **nell'**~ as a whole; **tutto** ~ all together; (*bere*) at one go

in'signe *adj* renowned

insignifi'cante *adj* insignificant

insi'gnire *vt* decorate

insin'dacabile *adj* final

insinu'ante *adj* insinuating

insinu'a|re *vt* insinuate. ~**rsi** *vr* penetrate; ~**rsi in** *fig* creep into

in'sipido *adj* insipid

insi'sten|te *adj* insistent. ~**te-'mente** *adv* repeatedly. ~**za** *f* insistence. **in'sistere** *vi* insist; (*perseverare*) persevere

insoddisfa'cente *adj* unsatisfactory

insoddi'sfa|tto *adj* unsatisfied; (*scontento*) dissatisfied. ~**zi'one** *f* dissatisfaction

insoffe'ren|te *adj* intolerant. ~**za** *f* intolerance

insolazi'one *f* sunstroke

inso'len|te *adj* rude, insolent. ~**za** *f* rudeness, insolence; (*commento*) insolent remark

in'solito *adj* unusual

inso'lubile *adj* insoluble

inso'luto *adj* unsolved; (*non pagato*) unpaid

insol'venza *f* insolvency

in'somma *adv* in short; ~**!** well really!; (*così così*) so so

in'sonn|e *adj* sleepless. ~**ia** *f* insomnia

insonno'lito *adj* sleepy

insonoriz'zato adj soundproofed

insoppor'tabile adj unbearable

insor'genza f onset

in'sorgere vi revolt, rise up; (sorgere) arise; (difficoltà) crop up

insormon'tabile adj (ostacolo, difficoltà) insurmountable

in'sorto pp di **insorgere●** adj rebellious ● m rebel

insospet'tabile adj unsuspected

insospet'tire vt make suspicious ● vi, ~**si** vr become suspicious

insoste'nibile adj untenable; (insopportabile) unbearable

insostitu'ibile adj irreplaceable

inspe'rabile adj una sua vittoria è ~**bile** there is no hope of him winning. ~**to** adj unhoped-for

inspie'gabile adj inexplicable

inspi'rare vt breathe in

in'stabile adj unstable; (tempo) changeable. ~**ità** f instability; (di tempo) changeability

instal'lare vt install. ~**rsi** vr settle in. ~**zi'one** f installation

instau'rare vt found. ~**rsi** vr become established. ~**zi'one** f foundation

instra'dare vt direct

insù adv all'~ upwards

insuc'cesso m failure

insudici'are vt dirty. ~**si** vr get dirty

insuffici'en|te adj insufficient; (inadeguato) inadequate ● m (Sch) fail. ~**za** f insufficiency; (inadeguatezza) inadequacy; (Sch) fail. ~**za cardiaca** heart failure. ~**za di prove** lack of evidence

insu'lare adj insular

insu'lina f insulin

in'sulso adj insipid; (sciocco) silly

insul'tare vt insult. **in'sulto** m insult

insupe'rabile adj insuperable; (eccezionale) incomparable

insussi'stente adj groundless

intac'care vt nick; (corrodere) corrode; draw on (capitale); (danneggiare) damage

intagli'are vt carve. **in'taglio** m carving

intan'gibile adj untouchable

in'tanto adv meanwhile; (per ora) for the moment; (avversativo) but; ~ **che** while

intarsi'a|re vt inlay. ~**to** adj ~**to di** inset with. **in'tarsio** m inlay

inta'sa|re vt clog; block (traffico). ~**rsi** vr get blocked. ~**to** adj blocked

inta'scare vt pocket

in'tatto adj intact

intavo'lare vt start

inte'gra|le adj whole; edizione ~**le** unabridged edition; pane ~**le** wholemeal bread. ~**nte** adj integral. **'integro** adj complete; (retto) upright

inte'gra|re vt integrate; (aggiungere) supplement. ~**rsi** vr integrate. ~**tivo** adj (corso) supplementary. ~**zi'one** f integration

integrità f integrity

intelaia'tura f framework

intel'letto m intellect

intellettu'al|e adj & mf intellectual. ~'**mente** adv intellectually

intelli'gen|te adj intelligent. ~**te'mente** adv intelligently. ~**za** f intelligence

intelli'gibile adj intelligible

intempe'ranza f intemperance

intem'perie fpl bad weather

inten'den|te m superintendent. ~**za** f ~**za di finanza** inland revenue office

in'tender|e vt (comprendere) understand; (udire) hear; (avere intenzione) intend; (significare) mean. ~**sela con** have an understanding with; ~**si** vr (capirsi) understand each other; ~**si di** (essere esperto) have a good knowledge of

intendi'mento *m* understanding; (*intenzione*) intention. ~**tore**, ~**trice** *mf* connoisseur

intene'rir|e *vt* soften; (*commuovere*) touch. ~**si** *vr* be touched

intensifi'car|e *vt*, ~**si** *vr* intensify

intensità *f* intensity. **inten'sivo** *adj* intensive. **in'tenso** *adj* intense

inten'tare *vt* start up; ~ **causa contro qcno** bring o institute proceedings against sb

in'tento *adj* engrossed (**a** in) ● *m* purpose

intenzio|'nale *adj* intentional. **intenzi'one** *f* intention; **senza** ~**ne** unintentionally; **avere** ~**ne di fare qcsa** intend to do sth, have the intention of doing sth.

intenzio'nato *adj* **essere** ~ **a fare qcsa** have the intention of doing sth

intera'gire *vi* interact

intera'mente *adv* completely

intera|t'tivo *adj* interactive. ~**zi'one** *f* interaction

interca'lare[1] *m* stock phrase

interca'lare[2] *vt* insert

intercambi'abile *adj* interchangeable

interca'pedine *f* cavity

inter'ce|dere *vi* intercede. ~**ssi'one** *f* intercession

intercet'ta|re *vt* intercept; tap (telefono). ~**zi'one** *f* interception. ~**zione telefonica** telephone tapping

inter'city *m inv* inter-city

intercontinen'tale *adj* intercontinental

inter'correre *vi* (tempo:) elapse; (esistere) exist

inter'detto *pp di* **interdire** ● *adj* astonished; (proibito) forbidden; **rimanere** ~ be taken aback

inter'di|re *vt* forbid; (Jur) deprive of civil rights. ~**zi'one** *f* prohibition

interessa'mento *m* interest

interes'sante *adj* interesting; **essere in stato** ~ be pregnant

interes'sa|re *vt* interest; (riguardare) concern ● *vi* ~ **a** matter to. ~**rsi** *vr* ~**rsi a** take an interest in. ~**rsi di** take care of. ~**to**, -a *adj* interested party ● *adj* interested; **essere** ~**to** *pej* have an interest

inte'resse *m* interest; **fare qcsa per** ~ do sth out of self-interest

inter'faccia *f* (Comput) interface

interfe'renza *f* interference

interfe'r|ire *vi* interfere

interiezi'one *f* interjection

interi'ora *fpl* entrails

interi'ore *adj* interior

inter'ludio *m* interlude

intermedi'ario, -a *adj* & *mf* intermediary

inter'medio *adj* in-between

inter'mezzo *m* (Mus, Theat) intermezzo

intermit'ten|te *adj* intermittent; (luce) flashing. ~**za** *f* **luce a** ~**za** flashing light

interna'mento *m* internment; (in manicomio) committal

inter'nare *vt* intern; (in manicomio) commit [to a mental institution]

internazio'nale *adj* international

'Internet *f* Internet, internet

in'terno *adj* internal; (Geog) inland; (interiore) inner; (politica) national; **alunno** ~ boarder ● *m* interior; (di condominio) flat; (Teleph) extension; (Cinema) interior shot; **all'**~ inside

in'tero *adj* whole, entire; (intatto) intact; (completo) complete; **per** ~ in full

interpel'lare *vt* consult

inter'por|re *vt* place (ostacolo). ~**si** *vr* come between

interpre'ta|re *vt* interpret; (Mus) perform. ~**zi'one** *f* interpretation;

(*Mus*) performance. in'terprete *mf* interpreter; (*Mus*) performer

inter'ra|re *vt* (*seppellire*) bury; plant (*pianta*). ~**to** *m* basement

interro'ga|re *vt* question; (*Sch*) test; examine (*studenti*). ~**tivo** *adj* interrogative; (*sguardo*) questioning; punto ~**tivo** question mark ●*m* question. ~**torio** *adj & m* questioning. ~**zi'one** *f* question; (*Sch*) oral [test]

inter'rompere *vt* interrupt; (*sospendere*) stop; cut off (*collegamento*). ~**si** *vr* break off

interrut'tore *m* switch

interruzi'one *f* interruption; senza ~ non-stop. ~ **di gravidanza** termination of pregnancy

interse'ca|re *vt*, ~**rsi** *vr* intersect. ~**zi'one** *f* intersection

interur'ban|a *f* long-distance call. ~**o** *adj* inter-city; telefonata ~**a** long-distance call

interval'lare *vt* space out. inter'vallo *m* interval; (*spazio*) space; (*Sch*) break. intervallo pubblicitario commercial break

interve'nire *vi* intervene; (*Med: operare*) operate; ~ **a** take part in. inter'vento *m* intervention; (*presenza*) presence; (*chirurgico*) operation; pronto intervento emergency services

inter'vista *f* interview

intervi'sta|re *vt* interview. ~**tore**, ~**trice** *mf* interviewer

in'tes|a *f* understanding; cenno d'~**a** acknowledgement. ~**o** *pp di* intendere ●*adj* resta ~**o** che...; needless to say,...; ~**il** agreed!; ~**o a** meant to

inte'sta|re *vt* head; write one's name and address at the top of (*lettera*); (*Comm*) register. ~**rsi** *vr* ~**rsi a** fare qcsa take it into one's head to do sth. ~**tario, -a** *mf* holder. ~**zi'one** *f* heading; (*su carta da lettere*)

letterhead

inte'stino *adj* (*lotte*) internal ●*m* intestine

intima'mente *adv* intimately

inti'ma|re *vt* order; ~**re l'alt a** qcno order sb to stop. ~**zi'one** *f* order

intimi'dire *vt* intimidate

intimità *f* cosiness. 'intimo *adj* intimate; (*interno*) innermost; (*amico*) close ●*m* (*amico*) close friend; (*dell'animo*) heart

intimo'ri|re *vt* frighten. ~**rsi** *vr* get frightened. ~**to** *adj* frightened

in'tingere *vt* dip

in'tingolo *m* sauce; (*pietanza*) stew

intiriz'zi|re *vt* numb. ~**rsi** *vr* grow numb. ~**to** *adj* essere ~**to** (*dal freddo*) be perished

intito'lar|e *vt* entitle; (*dedicare*) dedicate. ~**si** *vr* be called

intolle'rabile *adj* intolerable

intona'care *vt* plaster. in'tonaco *m* plaster

into'na|re *vt* start to sing; tune (*strumento*); (*accordare*) match. ~**rsi** *vr* match. ~**to** *adj* (*persona*) able to sing in tune; (*colore*) matching

intonazi'one *f* (*inflessione*) intonation; (*ironica*) tone

inton'tire *vt* daze; (*gas:*) make dizzy ●*vi* be dazed. ~**to** *adj* dazed

intop'pare *vi* ~ **in** run into

in'toppo *m* obstacle

in'torno *adv* around ●*prep* ~ **a** around; (*circa*) about

intorpi'dire *vt* numb. ~**rsi** *vr* become numb. ~**to** *adj* torpid

intossi'ca|re *vt* poison. ~**rsi** *vr* be poisoned. ~**zi'one** *f* poisoning

intral'ci|are *vt* hamper

in'tralcio *m* hitch; essere d'~ be a hindrance (a to)

intrallaz'zare vi intrigue. intral-'lazzo m racket

intramon'tabile adj timeless

intransi'gen|te adj uncompromising. ~za f intransigence

intransi'tivo adj intransitive

intrappo'lato adj rimanere ~ be trapped

intrapren'den|te adj enterprising. ~za f initiative

intra'prendere vt undertake

intrat'tabile adj very difficult

intratte'n|ere vt entertain. ~ersi vr linger. ~i'mento m entertainment

intrave'dere vt catch a glimpse of; (presagire) foresee

intrecci'ar|e vt interweave; plait (capelli, corda). ~si vr intertwine; (aggrovigliarsi) become tangled; ~e le mani clasp one's hands

in'treccio m (trama) plot

intri'cato adj tangled

intri'gante adj scheming; (affascinante) intriguing

intri'ga|re vt entangle; (incuriosire) intrigue ● vi intrigue, scheme. ~rsi vr meddle. in'trigo m plot; intrighi pl intrigues

in'triso adj ~ di soaked in

intri'stirsi vr grow sad

intro'du|rre vt introduce; (inserire) insert; ~rre a (iniziare a) introduce to. ~rsi vr get in (in to). ~t'tivo adj (pagine, discorso) introductory. ~zi'one f introduction

in'troito m income, revenue; (incasso) takings pl

intro'metter|e vt introduce. ~si vr interfere; (interporsi) intervene. in-tromissi'one f intervention

intro'vabile adj that can't be found; (prodotto) unobtainable

intro'verso, -a adj introverted ● mf introvert

intrufo'larsi vr sneak in

in'truglio m concoction

intrusi'one f intrusion. in'truso, -a mf intruder

intu'i|re vt perceive

intui'tivo adj intuitive. in'tuito m intuition. ~zi'one f intuition

inuguagli'anza f inequality

inu'mano adj inhuman

inu'mare vt inter

inumi'dir|e vt dampen; moisten (labbra). ~si vr become damp

i'nutil|e adj useless; (superfluo) unnecessary. ~ità f uselessness

inutiliz'za|bile adj unusable. ~to adj unused

inva'dente adj intrusive

in'vadere vt invade; (affollare) overrun

invali'd|are vt invalidate. ~ità f disability; (Jur) invalidity. in'valido, -a adj invalid; (handicappato) disabled ● mf disabled person

in'vano adv in vain

invari'abile adj invariable

invari'ato adj unchanged

invasi'one f invasion. in'vaso pp di invadere. inva'sore adj invading ● m invader

invecchia'mento m (di vino) maturation

invecchi'are vt/i age

in'vece adv instead; (anzi) but; ~ di instead of

inve'ire vi ~ contro inveigh against

inven'd|ibile adj unsaleable. ~uto adj unsold

inven'tare vt invent

inventari'are vt make an inventory of. inven'tario m inventory

inven'tivo, -a adj inventive ● f inventiveness; (capacità) resourcefulness. ~'tore, ~'trice mf inventor. ~zi'one f invention

inver'nale adj wintry. in'verno m winter

invero'simile adj improbable

inversi'one f inversion; (Mech) reversal. in'verso *adj* inverse; *(opposto)* opposite ● *m* opposite

inverte'brato *adj* & *m* invertebrate

inver'ti|re *vt* reverse; *(capovolgere)* turn upside down.

investi'ga|re *vt* investigate. ∼tore *m* investigator. ∼zi'one *f* investigation

investi'mento *m* investment; *(incidente)* crash

inve'sti|re *vt* invest; *(urtare)* collide with; *(travolgere)* run over; ∼re qcno di invest sb with. ∼tura *f* investiture

invi'a|re *vt* send. ∼to, -a *a mf* envoy; *(di giornale)* correspondent

invidi|a *f* envy. ∼'are *vt* envy. ∼'oso *adj* envious

invigo'rir|e *vt* invigorate. ∼si *vr* become strong

invin'cibile *adj* invincible

in'vio *m* dispatch; *(Comput)* enter

invipe'ri|rsi *vr* get nasty. ∼to *adj* furious

invi'sibil|e *adj* invisible. ∼ità *f* invisibility

invi'tante *adj* *(piatto, profumo)* enticing

invi'ta|re *vt* invite. ∼to, -a *mf* guest. in'vito *m* invitation

invo'ca|re *vt* invoke; *(implorare)* beg. ∼zi'one *f* invocation

invogli'ar|e *vt* tempt; *(indurre)* induce. ∼si *vr* ∼si di take a fancy to

involon'taria'mente *adv* involuntarily. ∼'tario *adj* involuntary

invol'tino *m* *(Culin)* beef olive

in'volto *m* parcel; *(fagotto)* bundle

in'volucro *m* wrapping

invulne'rabile *adj* invulnerable

inzacche'rare *vt* splash with mud

inzup'par|e *vt* soak; *(intingere)* dip. ∼si *vr* get soaked

'io *pers pron* I; chi è? - [sono] io who is it? - [it's] me; l'ho fatto io [stesso] I did it myself ● *m* l'∼ the ego

i'odio *m* iodine

l'onio *m* lo ∼ the Ionian [Sea]

i'osa: a ∼ *adv* in abundance

iperat'tivo *adj* hyperactive

ipermer'cato *m* hypermarket

iper'metrope *adj* long-sighted

ipertensi'one *f* high blood pressure

ip'no|si *f* hypnosis. ∼tico *adj* hypnotic. ∼'tismo *m* hypnotism. ∼tiz-'zare *vt* hypnotize

ipoca'lorico *adj* low-calorie

ipocon'driaco, -a *adj* & *mf* hypochondriac

ipocri'sia *f* hypocrisy. i'pocrita *adj* hypocritical ● *mf* hypocrite

ipo'te|ca *f* mortgage. ∼'care *vt* mortgage

i'potesi *f inv* hypothesis; *(caso, eventualità)* eventuality. ipo'tetico *adj* hypothetical. ipotiz'zare *vt* hypothesize

'ippico, -a *adj* horse *attrib* ● *f* riding

ippo'castano *m* horse-chestnut

ip'podromo *m* racecourse

ippo'potamo *m* hippopotamus

'ira *f* anger. ∼'scibile *adj* irascible

i'rato *adj* irate

'iride *f* *(Anat)* iris; *(arcobaleno)* rainbow

Ir'lan|da *f* Ireland. ∼da del Nord Northern Ireland. i∼'dese *adj* Irish ● *m* Irishman; *(lingua)* Irish ● *f* Irishwoman

iro'nia *f* irony. i'ronico *adj* ironic[al]

irradi'a|re *vt/i* radiate. ∼zi'one *f* radiation

irraggiun'gibile *adj* unattainable

irragio'nevole *adj* unreasonable; *(speranza, timore)* irrational; *(assurdo)* absurd

irrazio'nal|e *adj* irrational. ∼ità *f* irrationality

irre'a|le adj unreal. ∼**listico** adj unrealistic. ∼**liz'zabile** adj unattainable. ∼**ltà** f unreality

irrecupe'rabile adj irrecoverable

irrego'lar|e adj irregular. ∼**ità** f irregularity

irremo'vibile adj fig adamant

irrepa'rabile adj irreparable

irrepe'ribile adj not to be found; **sarò ∼ I** won't be contactable

irrepren'sibile adj irreproachable

irrepri'mibile adj irrepressible

irrequi'eto adj restless

irresi'stibile adj irresistible

irrespon'sabil|e adj irresponsible. ∼**ità** f irresponsibility

irrever'sibile adj irreversible

irricono'scibile adj unrecognizable

irri'ga|re vt irrigate; (fiume:) flow through. ∼**zi'one** f irrigation

irrigidi'mento m stiffening

irrigi'dir|e vt, ∼**si** vr stiffen

irrile'vante adj unimportant

irrimedi'abile adj irreparable

irripe'tibile adj unrepeatable

irri'sorio adj derisive; (differenza, particolare, somma) insignificant

irri'ta|bile adj irritable. ∼**nte** adj aggravating

irri'ta|re vt irritate. ∼**rsi** vr get annoyed. ∼**to** adj irritated; (gola) sore. ∼**zi'one** f irritation

irrobu'stir|e vt fortify. ∼**si** vr get stronger

ir'rompere vi burst (**in** into)

irro'rare vt sprinkle

irru'ente adj impetuous

irruzi'one f **fare ∼ in** burst into

i'scritto, -a pp di **iscrivere** ●adj registered ●mf member; **per ∼ in** writing

i'scriver|e vt register, ∼**si** vr **si a**

register at, enrol at (scuola); join (circolo ecc.) **iscrizi'one** f registration; (epigrafe) inscription

i'sla|mico adj Islamic. ∼**'mismo** m Islam

I'slan|da f Iceland. **i∼'dese** adj Icelandic ●mf Icelander

'isola f island. **le isole britanniche** the British Isles. **∼ pedonale** pedestrian precinct. **∼ spartitraffico** traffic island

iso'lante adj insulating ●m insulator

iso'la|re vt isolate; (Electr, Mech) insulate; (acusticamente) soundproof. ∼**to** adj isolated ●m (di appartamenti) block

ispes'sir|e vt, ∼**si** vr thicken

ispetto'rato m inspectorate. **ispet'tore** m inspector. **ispezio'nare** vt inspect. **ispezi'one** f inspection

'ispido adj bristly

ispi'ra|re vt inspire; suggest (idea, soluzione). ∼**rsi** vr ∼**rsi a** be based on. ∼**to** adj inspired. ∼**zi'one** f inspiration; (idea) idea

Isra'el|e m Israel. **i∼i'ano, -a** agg & mf Israeli

istan'taneo, -a adj instantaneous ●f snapshot

i'stante m instant; **all'∼** instantly

i'stanza f petition

i'sterico adj hysterical. **iste'rismo** m hysteria

isti'ga|re vt instigate; ∼**re qcno al male** incite sb to evil. ∼**zi'one** f instigation

istin'tivo adj instinctive. **i'stinto** m instinct; **d'istinto** instinctively

istitu'ire vt institute; (fondare) found; initiate (manifestazione)

isti'tu|to m institute; (universitario) department; (Sch) secondary school. ∼**to di bellezza** beauty salon. ∼**tore**, ∼**trice** mf (insegnante) tutor;

(*fondatore*) founder
istituzio'nale *adj* institutional. **istituzi'one** *f* institution
'istrice *m* porcupine
istru'i|re *vt* instruct; (*addestrare*) train; (*informare*) inform; (*Jur*) prepare. **∼to** *adj* educated
istrut't|ivo *adj* instructive. **∼ore**, **∼rice** *mf* instructor; **giudice ∼ore** examining magistrate. **∼oria** *f* (*Jur*) investigation. **istruzi'one** *f* education; (*indicazione*) instruction
I'tali|a *f* Italy. **i∼ano, -a** *adj* & *mf* Italian

Italo- Descendants of those who emigrated from Italy are often referred to as *italo-americani*, *italo-brasiliani*, etc. Massive emigration started in the 1870s, mainly from the north of Italy to South America. Buenos Aires and Sao Paulo have the highest concentrations of Italians outside Italy. Subsequently more and more southern Italians emigrated to the United States.

itine'rario *m* route, itinerary
itte'rizia *f* jaundice
'ittico *adj* fishing *attrib*
I.V.A. *f abbr* (*imposta sul valore aggiunto*) VAT

Jj

jack *m inv* jack
jazz *m* jazz. **jaz'zista** *mf* jazz player
jeep *f inv* jeep
'jolly *m inv* (*carta da gioco*) joker
ju'niores *mfpl Sport* juniors

Kk

ka'jal *m inv* kohl
kara'oke *m inv* karaoke
kara'te *m* karate
kg *abbr* (*chilogrammo*) kg
km *abbr* (*chilometro*) km

Ll

l' *def art mf* (*before vowel*) the; ▸ IL
la *def art f* the; ▸ IL ● *pron* (*oggetto, riferito a persona*) her; (*riferito a cosa, animale*) it; (*forma di cortesia*) you ● *m inv* (*Mus*) A
là *adv* there; **di là** (*in quel luogo*) in there; (*da quella parte*) that way; **eccolo là** there he is!; **farsi più in là** (*far largo*) make way; **là dentro** in there; **là fuori** out there; [ma] **va là!** come off it!; **più in là** (*nel tempo*) later on; (*nello spazio*) further on
'labbro *m* (*pl f* (*Anat*) labbra) lip
labi'rinto *m* labyrinth; (*di sentieri ecc*) maze
labora'torio *m* laboratory; (*di negozio, officina ecc*) workshop
labori'oso *adj* industrious; (*faticoso*) laborious
labu'rista *adj* Labour ● *mf* member of the Labour Party
'lacca *f* lacquer; (*per capelli*) hairspray. **lac'care** *vt* lacquer
'laccio *m* noose; (*lazo*) lasso; (*trappola*) snare; (*stringa*) lace
lace'rante *adj* (*grido*) earsplitting
lace'ra|re *vt* tear; lacerate (*carne*).

~**rsi** vr tear. ~**zi'one** f laceration.

'lacero adj torn; (cencioso) ragged

'lacri|ma f tear; (goccia) drop. ~**'mare** vi weep. ~**'mevole** adj tearjerking

lacri'mogeno adj gas ~ tear gas

la'cuna f gap. **lacu'noso** adj (preparazione, resoconto) incomplete

la'custre adj lake attrib

>
>
> **Ladino** Ladin (ladino in Italian) is a direct descendant of the Latin spoken in the valleys in north-eastern Italy. Western Ladin is spoken in Alto Adige alongside German, and Eastern Ladin (also called Friulian) in Friuli-Venezia Giulia. Numbers of speakers are shrinking as gradually German or Italian predominate.

'ladro, -a mf thief; al ~**l** stop thief!; ~**'cinio** m theft. **la'druncolo** m petty thief

'lager m inv concentration camp

laggiù adv down there; (lontano) over there

'lagna f (🔲: persona) moaning Minnie; (film) bore

la'gna|nza f complaint. ~**rsi** vr moan; (protestare) complain (di about)

'lago m lake

la'guna f lagoon

'laico, -a adj lay; (vita) secular ● m layman ● f laywoman

'lama f blade ● m inv llama

lambic'carsi vr ~ il cervello rack one's brains

lam'bire vt lap

lamé m inv lamé

lamen'tar|e vt lament. ~**si** vr moan. ~**si di** complain about

lamen'te|la f complaint. ~**vole** adj mournful; (pietoso) pitiful. **la'mento** m moan

la'metta f ~ [da barba] razor blade

lami'era f sheet metal

'lamina f foil. ~ **d'oro** gold leaf

lami'na|re vt laminate. ~**to** adj laminated ● m laminate; (tessuto) lamé

'lampa|da f lamp. ~ **da abbronzante** sunlamp. ~**da** f pila torch. ~**'dario** m chandelier. ~**'dina** f light bulb

lam'pante adj clear

lampeggi'a|re vi flash. ~**'tore** m (Auto) indicator

lampi'one m street lamp

'lampo m flash of lightning; (luce) flash; **lampi** pl lightning sg. ~ **di genio** stroke of genius. [cerniera] ~ **zip** [fastener]; zipper Am

lam'pone m raspberry

'lana f wool; **di** ~ woollen. ~ **d'acciaio** steel wool. ~ **vergine** new wool. ~ **di vetro** glass wool

lan'cetta f pointer; (di orologio) hand

'lancia f spear; (Naut) launch

lanci'ar|e vt throw; (da un aereo) drop; launch (missile, prodotto); give (grido); ~ **e uno sguardo a** glance at. ~**si** vr fling oneself; (intraprendere) launch out

lanci'nante adj piercing

'lancio m throwing; (da aereo) drop; (di missile, prodotto) launch. ~ **del disco** discus [throwing]. ~ **del giavellotto** javelin [throwing]

'landa f heath

lani'ero adj wool

lani'ficio m woollen mill

lan'terna f lantern; (faro) lighthouse

la'nugine f down

lapi'dare vt stone; fig demolish

lapi'dario adj (conciso) terse

'lapide f tombstone; (commemorativa) memorial tablet

'lapis m inv pencil

'lapsus m inv lapse, error

'**lardo** m lard

larga'mente adv widely

lar'ghezza f breadth; fig liberality. ~ **di vedute** broadmindedness

'**largo** adj wide; (ampio) broad; (abito) loose; (liberale) liberal; (abbondante) generous; **stare alla larga** keep away; ~ **di manica** fig generous; ~ **di spalle/vedute** broad-shouldered/-minded ● m width; **andare al** ~ (Naut) go out to sea; **fare** ~ make room; **farsi** ~ make one's way; **al** ~ **di** off the coast of

'**larice** m larch

la'ringe f larynx. **larin'gite** f laryngitis

'**larva** f larva; (persona emaciata) shadow

la'sagne fpl lasagna sg

lasciapas'sare m inv pass

lasci'ar|e vt leave; (rinunciare) give up; (rimetterci) lose; (smettere di tenere) let go [of]; (concedere) let; ~**e di fare** qcsa (smettere) stop doing sth; **lascia perdere!** forget it!; **lascialo venire** let him come. ~**si** vr (reciproco) leave each other; ~**si andare** let oneself go

'**lascito** m legacy

'**laser** adj & m inv [raggio] ~ laser [beam]

lassa'tivo adj & m laxative

'**lasso** m ~ **di tempo** period of time

lassù adv up there

'**lastra** f slab; (di ghiaccio) sheet; (Phot, di metallo) plate; (radiografia) X-ray [plate]

lastri'ca|re vt pave. ~**to**, '**lastrico** m pavement

la'tente adj latent

late'rale adj side attrib; (Med, Techn ecc) lateral; **via** ~ side street

late'rizi mpl bricks

lati'fondo m large estate

la'tino adj & m Latin

lati'tan|te adj in hiding ● mf fugitive [from justice]

lati'tudine f latitude

'**lato** adj (ampio) broad; **in senso** ~ broadly speaking ● m side; (aspetto) aspect; **a** ~ **di** beside; **dal** ~ **mio** (punto di vista) for my part; **d'altro** ~ fig on the other hand

la'tra|re vi bark. ~**to** m barking

la'trina f latrine

'**latta** f tin, can

lat'taio, -a m milkman ● f milkwoman

lat'tante adj breast-fed ● mf suckling

'**latt|e** m milk. ~**e acido** sour milk. ~**e condensato** condensed milk. ~**e detergente** cleansing milk. ~**e in polvere** powdered milk. ~**e scremato** skimmed milk. ~**eo** adj milky. ~**e'ria** f dairy. ~**i'cini** mpl dairy products. ~**i'era** f milk jug

lat'tina f can

lat'tuga f lettuce

'**laure|a** f degree; **prendere la** ~**a** graduate. ~'**ando**, -**a** mf final-year student

laure'a|rsi vr graduate. ~**to**, -**a** agg & mf graduate

'**lauro** m laurel

'**lauto** adj lavish; ~ **guadagno** handsome profit

'**lava** f lava

la'vabile adj washable

la'vabo m wash-basin

la'vaggio m washing. ~ **automatico** (per auto) carwash. ~ **a secco** dry-cleaning

la'vagna f slate; (Sch) blackboard

la'van|da f wash; (Bot) lavender; **fare una** ~**da gastrica** have one's stomach pumped. ~'**daia** f washer-woman. ~**de'ria** f laundry. ~**deria automatica** launderette

lavan'dino m sink; (① persona) bottomless pit

lavapi'atti mf inv dishwasher

la'var|e *vt* wash; ~**e i piatti** wash up. ~**si** *vr* wash, have a wash; ~**si i denti** brush one's teeth; ~**si le mani** wash one's hands

lava'secco *mf inv* dry-cleaner's

lavasto'viglie *f inv* dishwasher

la'vata *f* wash; **darsi una** ~ have a wash; ~ **di capo** *fig* scolding

lava'tivo, -a *mf* idler

lava'trice *f* washing-machine

lavo'rante *mf* worker

lavo'ra|re *vi* work ● *vt* work; knead (pasta ecc); till (la terra); ~**re a maglia** knit. ~**tivo** *adj* working. ~**to** *adj* (pietra, legno) carved; (cuoio) tooled; (metallo) wrought. ~**tore**, ~**'trice** *mf* worker ● *adj* working. ~**zi'one** *f* manufacture; (di terra) working; (artigianale) workmanship; (del terreno) cultivation. **lavo'rìo** *m* intense activity

la'voro *m* work; (faticoso, sociale) labour; (impiego) job; (Theat) play; **mettersi al** ~ set to work (su on). ~ **a maglia** knitting. ~ **nero** moonlighting. ~ **straordinario** overtime. ~ **a tempo pieno** full-time job. **lavori** *pl* **di casa** housework. **lavori** *pl* **in corso** roadworks. **lavori** *pl* **stradali** roadworks

le *def art fpl* the; ▷**IL** ● *pers pron* (oggetto) them; (a lei) her; (forma di cortesia) you

le'al|e *adj* loyal. ~**'mente** *adv* loyally. ~**tà** *f* loyalty

'lebbra *f* leprosy

'lecca 'lecca *m inv* lollipop

leccapi'edi *mf inv* pej bootlicker

lec'ca|re *vt* lick; *fig* suck up to. ~**rsi** *vr* lick; (fig: agghindarsi) doll oneself up; **da** ~**rsi i baffi** mouth-watering. ~**ta** *f* lick

leccor'nia *f* delicacy

'lecito *adj* lawful; (permesso) permissible

'ledere *vt* damage; (Med) injure

'lega *f* league; (di metalli) alloy; **far** ~

con qcno take up with sb

le'gaccio *m* string; (delle scarpe) shoelace

le'gal|e *adj* legal ● *m* lawyer. ~**ità** *f* legality. ~**iz'zare** *vt* authenticate; (rendere legale) legalize; (connettere) legally

le'game *m* tie; (amoroso) liaison; (connessione) link

lega'mento *m* (Med) ligament

le'gar|e *vt* tie; tie up (persona); tie together (due cose); (unire, rilegare) bind; alloy (metalli); (connettere) connect ● *vi* (far lega) get on well. ~**si** *vr* bind oneself; ~**si a qcno** become attached to sb

le'gato *m* legacy; (Relig) legate

lega'tura *f* tying; (di libro) binding

le'genda *f* legend

'legge *f* law; (parlamentare) act; **a norma di** ~ by law

leg'genda *f* legend; (didascalia) caption. **leggen'dario** *adj* legendary

'leggere *vt/i* read

legge'r|ezza *f* lightness; (frivolezza) frivolity; (incostanza) fickleness. ~**'mente** *adv* slightly

leg'gero *adj* light; (bevanda) weak; (lieve) slight; (frivolo) frivolous; (incostante) fickle

leg'gibile *adj* (scrittura) legible; (stile) readable

leg'gio *m* lectern; (Mus) music stand

legife'rare *vi* legislate

legio'nario *m* legionary. **legi'one** *f* legion

legisla'|tivo *adj* legislative. ~**tore** *m* legislator. ~**tura** *f* legislature. ~**zi'one** *f* legislation

legittimità *f* legitimacy. **le'gittimo** *adj* legitimate; (giusto) proper; **legittima difesa** self-defence

'legna *f* firewood

le'gname *m* timber

'legno *m* wood; **di** ~ wooden. ~ **compensato** plywood. **le'gnoso**

adj woody

le'gume m pod

'lei pers pron (soggetto) she; (oggetto, con prep) her; (forma di cortesia) you; **lo ha fatto ~ stessa** she did it herself

'lembo m edge; (di terra) strip

'lena f vigour

le'nire vt soothe

lenta'mente adv slowly

'lente f lens. **~ a contatto** contact lens. **~ d'ingrandimento** magnifying glass

len'tezza f slowness

len'ticchia f lentil

len'tiggine f freckle

'lento adj slow; (allentato) slack; (abito) loose

'lenza f fishing-line

len'zuolo m (pl f lenzuola) m sheet

le'one m lion; (Astr) Leo

leo'pardo m leopard

'lepre f hare

'lercio adj filthy

'lesbica f lesbian

lesi'nare vt grudge ● vi be stingy

lesio'nare vt damage. **lesi'one** f lesion

'leso pp di ledere ● adj injured

'lessare vt boil

'lessico m vocabulary

'lesso adj boiled ● m boiled meat

'lesto adj quick; (mente) sharp

le'tale adj lethal

le'targi|co adj lethargic. **~o** m lethargy; (di animali) hibernation

le'tizia f joy

'lettera f letter; **alla ~** literally; **maiuscola** capital letter; **~ minuscola** small letter; **lettere** pl (letteratura) literature sg; (Univ) Arts; **dottore in lettere** BA, Bachelor of Arts

lette'rale adj literal

lette'rario adj literary

lette'rato adj well-read

lettera'tura f literature

let'tiga f stretcher

let'tino m cot; (Med) couch

'letto m bed. **~ a castello** bunkbed. **~ a una piazza** single bed. **~ a due piazze** double bed. **~ matrimoniale** double bed

letto'rato m (corso) ≈ tutorial

let'tore, -'trice mf reader; (Univ) language assistant ● m (Comput) disk drive. **~ CD-ROM** CD-Rom drive. **~ MP3** MP3 player

let'tura f reading

leuce'mia f leukaemia

'leva f lever; (Mil) call-up; **far ~ lever. ~ del cambio** gear lever

le'vante m East; (vento) east wind

le'va|re vt (alzare) raise; (togliere) take away; (rimuovere) take off; (estrarre) pull out; **~re di mezzo qcsa** get sth out of the way. **~rsi** vr rise; (da letto) get up; **~rsi di mezzo, ~rsi dai piedi** get out of the way. **~ta** f rising; (di posta) collection

leva'taccia f **fare una ~** get up at the crack of dawn

leva'toio adj **ponte ~** drawbridge

levi'ga|re vt smooth; (con carta vetro) rub down. **~to** adj (superficie) polished

levri'ero m greyhound

lezi'one f lesson; (Univ) lecture; (rimprovero) rebuke

lezi'oso adj (stile, modi) affected

li pers pron mpl them

lì adv there; **fin lì** as far as there; **giù di lì** thereabouts; **lì per lì** there and then

Li'bano m Lebanon

'libbra f (peso) pound

li'beccio m south-west wind

li'bellula f dragon-fly

libe'rale adj liberal; (generoso) generous ● mf liberal

libe'ra|re vt free; release (prigioniero); vacate (stanza); (salvare) rescue. **~rsi** vr (stanza:) become vacant; (Teleph) become free; (da impegno) get out of it; **~rsi** di get rid of. **~'tore**, **~'trice** adj liberating •mf liberator. **~zi'one** f liberation; la L~zione Liberation Day

'liber|o adj free; (strada) clear. **~o docente** qualified university lecturer. **~o professionista** selfemployed person. **~tà** f inv freedom; (di prigioniero) release. **~tà provvisoria** (Jur) bail; **~tà** pl (confidenze) liberties

'liberty m & adj inv Art Nouveau

'Libi|a f Libya. **l~co**, **-a** adj & mf Libyan

'libra|io m bookseller

libre'ria f (negozio) bookshop; (mobile) bookcase; (biblioteca) library

li'bretto m booklet; (Mus) libretto. **~ degli assegni** cheque book. **~ di circolazione** logbook. **~ d'istruzioni** instruction booklet. **~ di risparmio** bankbook. **~ universitario** student record of exam results

'libro m book. **~ giallo** thriller. **~ paga** payroll

lice'ale mf secondary-school student •adj secondary-school attrib

li'cenza f licence; (permesso) permission; (Mil) leave; (Sch) school-leaving certificate; **essere in ~** be on leave

licenzia'mento m dismissal

licenzi'a|re vt dismiss, sack 🗆. **~rsi** vr (da un impiego) resign; (accomiatarsi) take one's leave

li'ceo m secondary school. **~ classico** secondary school emphasizing humanities. **~ scientifico** secondary school emphasizing science

Liceo There are two main types of secondary school in Italy: the licei, which offer an academic syllabus, and the istituti, which have a more vocational syllabus, offering subjects like accountancy, electronics, and catering. Licei may specialize in particular subjects such as science, languages or classical studies.

'lido m beach

li'eto adj glad; (evento) happy; **molto ~!** pleased to meet you!

li'eve adj light; (debole) faint; (trascurabile) slight

lievi'tare vi rise •vt leaven. **li'evito** m yeast. **lievito in polvere** baking powder

'lifting m inv face-lift

'ligio adj **essere ~ al dovere** have a sense of duty

'lilla[1] (colore) lilac

'lillà[2] m (Bot) lilac

'lima f file

limacci'oso adj slimy

li'mare vt file

li'metta f nail-file

limi'ta|re m threshold •vt limit. **~rsi** vr **~rsi a fare qcsa** restrict oneself to doing sth; **~rsi in qcsa** cut down on sth. **~'tivo** adj limiting. **~zi'one** f limitation

'limite m limit; (confine) boundary. **~ di velocità** speed limit

li'mitrofo adj neighbouring

limo'nata f (bibita) lemonade; (succo) lemon juice

li'mone m lemon; (albero) lemon tree

'limpido adj clear; (occhi) limpid

'lince f lynx

linci'are vt lynch

'lindo adj neat; (pulito) clean

'linea f line; (di autobus, aereo) route; (di metro) line; (di abito) cut; (di auto, mobile) design; (fisico) figure; **è caduta la ~** I've been cut off; **in ~** (Comput) on line; **mantenere la ~** keep one's figure; **mettersi in ~** line up; **nave di ~** liner; **volo di ~** scheduled flight. **~ d'arrivo** finishing line. **~ continua** unbroken line

linea'menti mpl features

line'are adj linear; (discorso) to the point; (ragionamento) consistent

line'etta f (tratto lungo) dash; (d'unione) hyphen

lin'gotto m ingot

'lingu|a f (Anat, linguaggio) language. ~'accia f (persona) backbiter. ~'aggio m language. ~'etta f (di scarpa) tongue; (di strumento) reed; (di busta) flap

lingu'ist|a mf linguist. ~ica f linguistics sg. ~ico adj linguistic

'lino m (Bot) flax; (tessuto) linen

li'noleum m linoleum

liofiliz'za|re vt freeze-dry. ~to adj freeze-dried

liposuzi'one f liposuction

lique'far|e vt, ~si vr liquefy; (sciogliersi) melt

liqui'da|re vt liquidate; settle (conto); pay off (debiti); clear (merce); (🄵: uccidere) get rid of. ~zi'one f liquidation; (di conti) settling; (di merce) clearance sale

'liquido adj & m liquid

liqui'rizia f liquorice

li'quore m liqueur; **liquori** pl (bevande alcooliche) liquors

'lira f lira; (Mus) lyre

'lirico, -a adj lyrical; (poesia) lyric; (cantante, musica) opera attrib ● f lyric poetry; (Mus) opera

lisci'are vt smooth; (accarezzare) stroke; (liscio adj smooth; (capelli) straight; (liquore) neat; (acqua minerale) still; **passarla liscia** get away with it

'liso adj worn [out]

'lista f list; (striscia) strip. ~ **di attesa** waiting list; **in ~ di attesa** (Aeron) stand-by. ~ **elettorale** electoral register. ~ **nera** blacklist. ~ **di nozze** wedding list. **li'stare** vt edge; (Comput) list

li'stino m list. ~ **prezzi** price list

Lit. abbr (lire italiane) Italian lire

'lite f quarrel; (baruffa) row; (Jur) lawsuit

liti'gare vi quarrel. **li'tigio** m quarrel. **litigi'oso** adj quarrelsome

lito'rale adj coastal ● m coast

'litro m litre

li'turgico adj liturgical

li'vella f level. ~ **a bolla d'aria** spirit level

livel'lar|e vt level. ~**si** vr level out

li'vello m level; **passaggio a ~** level crossing; **sotto/sul ~ del mare** below/above sea level

'livido adj livid; (per il freddo) blue; (per una botta) black and blue ● m bruise

Li'vorno f Leghorn

'lizza f lists pl; **essere in ~ per qcsa** be in the running for sth

lo def art m (before s + consonant, gn, ps, z) the; ▶IL ● pron (riferito a oggetto) it; (riferito a persona) him; (riferito a cosa) it; **non lo so** I don't know

'lobo m lobe

lo'cal|e adj local ● m (stanza) room; (treno) local train; ~i pl (edifici) premises. ~e **notturno** night-club. ~**ità** f inv locality

localiz'zare vt localize; (trovare) locate

localizza'zione f localization

lo'canda f inn

locan'dina f bill, poster

loca|'tario, -a mf tenant. ~'tore, ~'trice m landlord ● f landlady. ~**zi'one** f tenancy

locomo'tiva f locomotive. ~**zi'one** f locomotion; **mezzi di** ~**zione** means of transport

'loculo m burial niche

lo'custa f locust

locuzi'one f expression

lo'dare vt praise. **'lode** f praise; **laurea con lode** first-class degree

'loden m inv (cappotto) loden coat

'lodola f lark

'loggia f loggia; (massonica) lodge

loggi'one m gallery, the gods

'logica f logic

logica'mente adv (in modo logico) logically; (ovviamente) of course

'logico adj logical

lo'gistica f logistics sg

logo'ra|re vt wear out; (sciupare) waste. **~rsi** vr wear out; (persona:) wear oneself out. **logo'rìo** m wear and tear. **'logoro** adj worn-out

lom'baggine f lumbago

Lombar'dia f Lombardy

lom'bata f loin. **'lombo** m (Anat) loin

lom'brico m earthworm

'Londra f London

lon'gevo adj long-lived

longi'lineo adj tall and slim

longi'tudine f longitude

lontana'mente adv distantly; (vagamente) vaguely; **neanche ~** not for a moment

lonta'nanza f distance; (separazione) separation; **in ~** in the distance

lon'tano adj far; (distante) distant; (nel tempo) far-off, distant; (parente) distant; (vago) vague; (assente) absent; **più ~** further ● adv far [away]; **da ~** from a distance

'lontra f otter

lo'quace adj talkative

'lordo adj dirty; (somma, peso) gross

'loro¹ pron pl (soggetto) they; (oggetto) them; (forma di cortesia) you; **sta a ~** it is up to them

'loro² (il ~ m, la ~ f, i ~ mpl, le ~ fpl) poss adj their; (forma di cortesia) your; **un ~ amico** a friend of theirs; (forma di cortesia) a friend of yours ● poss pron theirs; (forma di cortesia) yours; **i ~** (famiglia) their folk

lo'sanga f lozenge; **a losanghe** diamond-shaped

'losco adj suspicious

'lott|a f fight, struggle; (contrasto) conflict; Sport wrestling. **lot'tare** vi fight, struggle; Sport, fig wrestle. **~a'tore** m wrestler

lotte'ria f lottery

'lotto m [national] lottery; (porzione) lot; (di terreno) plot

lozi'one f lotion

lubrifi'ca|nte adj lubricating ● m lubricant. **~re** vt lubricate

luc'chetto m padlock

lucci'ca|nte adj sparkling. **~re** vi sparkle. **lucci'chio** m sparkle

'luccio m pike

'lucciola f glow-worm

'luce f light; **far ~ su** shed light on; **dare alla ~** give birth to. **~ della luna** moonlight; **luci** pl di posizione sidelights. **~ del sole** sunlight

lu'cen|te adj shining. **~'tezza** f shine

lucer'nario m skylight

lu'certola f lizard

lucida'labbra m inv lip gloss

luci'da|re vt polish. **~'trice** f [floor-]polisher. **'lucido** adj shiny; (pavimento, scarpe) polished; (chiaro) clear; (persona, mente) lucid; (occhi) watery ● m shine. **lucido** [da scarpe] [shoe] polish

lucra'tivo adj lucrative

'luglio m July

'lugubre adj gloomy

'lui pron (soggetto) he; (oggetto, con prep) him; **lo ha fatto ~ stesso** he did it himself

lu'maca f (mollusco) snail; fig slowcoach

'lume m lamp; (luce) light; **a ~ di candela** by candlelight

luminosità f brightness. **lumi'noso** adj luminous; (stanza, cielo ecc) bright

'luna f moon; **chiaro di ~** moonlight. ~ di miele honeymoon

luna park m inv fairground

lu'nario m almanac; sbarcare il ~ make both ends meet

lu'natico a moody

lunedì m inv Monday

lu'netta f half-moon [shape]

lun'gaggine f slowness

lun'ghezza f length. ~ d'onda wavelength

'lungi adv ero [ben] ~ dall'immaginare che... I never dreamt for a moment that...

lungimi'rante adj far-sighted

'lungo adj long; (diluito) weak; (lento) slow; saperla lunga be shrewd ●m length; di gran lunga by far; andare per le lunghe drag on ●prep (durante) throughout; (per la lunghezza di) along

lungofi'ume m riverside

lungo'lago m lakeside

lungo'mare m sea front

lungome'traggio m feature film

lu'notto m rear window

lu'ogo m place; (punto preciso) spot; (passo d'autore) passage; aver ~ take place; dar ~ a give rise to; del ~ (usanze) local. ~ pubblico public place

luogote'nente m (Mil) lieutenant

lu'petto m Cub [Scout]

'lupo m wolf

'luppolo m hop

'lurido adj filthy. luri'dume m filth

lusin'g|are vt flatter. ~arsi vr flatter oneself; (illudersi) fool oneself. ~hi'ero a flattering

lus'sa|re vt, ~rsi vr dislocate. ~zi'one f dislocation

Lussem'burgo m Luxembourg

'lusso m luxury; di ~ luxury attrib

lussu'oso adj luxurious

lus'suria f lust

lu'strare vt polish

'lustro adj shiny ●m sheen; fig prestige; (quinquennio) five-year period

'lutto m mourning; ~o stretto deep mourning. ~u'oso a mournful

Mm

m abbr (metro) m

ma conj but; (eppure) yet; ma! (dubbio) I don't know; (indignazione) really!; ma davvero? really?; ma sì why not!; (certo che sì) of course!

'macabro adj macabre

macché int of course not!

macche'roni mpl macaroni sg

macche'ronico adj (italiano) broken

'macchia[1] f stain; (di diverso colore) spot; (piccola) speck; senza ~ spotless

'macchia[2] f (boscaglia) scrub

macchi'a|re vt, ~rsi vr stain. ~to adj (caffè) with a dash of milk; ~to di (sporco) stained with

'macchina f machine; (motore) engine; (automobile) car. ~ da cucire sewing machine. ~ da presa cine camera. ~ da scrivere typewriter. ~ fotografica (digitale) (digital) camera

macchinal'mente adv mechanically

macchi'nare vt plot

macchi'nario m machinery

macchi'netta f (per i denti) brace

macchi'nista m (Rail) enginedriver; (Naut) engineer; (Theat) stagehand

macchi'noso adj complicated

mace'donia f fruit salad

Mace'donia f Macedonia

macel'laio m butcher. ~re vt slaughter, butcher. macelle'ria f butcher's [shop]. ma'cello m (mattatoio) slaughterhouse; fig shambles sg; andare al macello fig go to the slaughter

mace'rar|e vt macerate; fig distress. ~si vr be consumed

ma'cerie fpl rubble sg; (rottami) debris sg

ma'cigno m boulder

'macina f millstone

macinacaffè m inv coffee mill

macina'pepe m inv pepper mill

maci'na|re vt mill. ~to adj ground ● m (carne) mince. maci'nino m mill; (hum) old banger

maciul'lare vt (stritolare) crush

macrobiotic|a f negozio di ~a health-food shop. ~o adj macrobiotic

macu'lato adj spotted

'madido adj ~ di moist with

Ma'donna f Our Lady

mador'nale adj gross

'madre f mother. ~lingua adj inv inglese ~lingua English native speaker. ~'patria f native land. ~'perla f mother-of-pearl

ma'drina f godmother

maestà f majesty

maestosità f majesty. mae'stoso adj majestic

mae'strale m northwest wind

mae'stranza f workers pl

mae'stria f mastery

ma'estro, -a mf teacher ● m master; (Mus) maestro. ~ di cerimonie master of ceremonies ● adj (principale) chief; (di grande abilità) skilful

'mafi|a f Mafia. ~'oso adj of the Mafia ● m member of the Mafia, Mafioso

Mafia The Mafia developed in Sicily in the nineteenth century, where it continues to wield considerable power in opposition to the authorities. Strictly speaking, the term Mafia applies only to Sicily, and its equivalents in other regions (Camorra in Naples and 'ndrangheta in Calabria) are separate organizations, although often working in collaboration with each other.

ma'gagna f fault

ma'gari adv (forse) maybe ● int I wish! ● conj (per esprimere desiderio) if only; (anche se) even if

magazzini'ere m storesman, warehouseman. magaz'zino m warehouse; (emporio) shop; grande magazzino department store

'maggio m May

maggio'lino m May bug

maggio'rana f marjoram

maggio'ranza f majority

maggio'rare vt increase

maggior'domo m butler

maggi'ore adj (di dimensioni, numero) bigger, larger; (superlativo) biggest, largest; (di età) older; (superlativo) oldest; (di importanza, musica) major; (superlativo) greatest; la maggior parte di most; la maggior parte del tempo most of the time ● pron (di dimensioni) the bigger, the larger; (superlativo) the biggest, the largest; (di età) the older; (superlativo) the oldest; (di importanza) the major; (superlativo) the greatest ● m (Mil) major; (Aeron) squadron leader. maggio'renne adj of age ● mf adult

maggiori'tario adj (sistema) first-past-the-post attrib. ~'mente adv [all] the more; (più di tutto) most

'Magi mpl i re ~ the Magi

ma'gia f magic; (trucco) magic trick. magica'mente adv magically. 'magico adj magic

magi'stero m (*insegnamento*) teaching; (*maestria*) skill; **facoltà di ~ arts** faculty

magi'stra|le adj masterly; **istituto ~e** teachers' training college

magi'stra|to m magistrate. **~'tura** f magistrature. **la ~'tura del Bench**

'magli|a f stitch; (*lavoro ai ferri*) knitting; (*tessuto*) jersey; (*di rete*) mesh; (*di catena*) link; (*indumento*) vest; **fare una ~a** knit. **~a diritta** knit. **~a rosa** (*ciclismo*) ≈ yellow jersey. **~a rovescia** purl. **~e'ria** f knitwear. **~'etta** f **~'etta [a maniche corte]** tee-shirt. **~'ficio** m knitwear factory. **ma'glina** f (*tessuto*) jersey

magli'one m sweater

'magma m magma

ma'gnanimo adj magnanimous

ma'gnate m magnate

ma'gnesi|a f magnesia. **~o** m magnesium

ma'gne|te m magnet. **~tico** adj magnetic. **~tismo** m magnetism

magne'tofono m tape recorder

magnifica'mente adv magnificently. **~cenza** f magnificence; (*generosità*) munificence. **ma'gnifico** adj magnificent; (*generoso*) munificent

ma'gnolia f magnolia

ma'gone m **avere il ~ be down;** **mi è venuto il ~ I've got a lump in my throat**

'magr|a f low water. **ma'grezza** f thinness. **~o** adj thin; (*carne*) lean; (*scarso*) meagre

'mai adv never; (*inter, talvolta*) ever; **caso ~ if anything; caso ~ tornasse in case he comes back; come ~? why?; cosa ~? what on earth?; più che ~ never again; più che ~ more than ever; quando ~? whenever?; quasi ~ hardly ever**

mai'ale m pig; (*carne*) pork

mai'olica f majolica

maio'nese f mayonnaise

'mais m maize

mai'uscol|a f capital [letter]. **~o** adj capital

mal ▷ **MALE**

'mala f la ~ 🗵 the underworld

mala'fede f bad faith

malaf'fare m **gente di ~** shady characters pl

mala'lingua f backbiter

mala'mente adv (*ridotto*) badly

malan'dato adj in bad shape; (*di salute*) in poor health

ma'lanimo m ill will

ma'lanno m misfortune; (*malattia*) illness; **prendersi un ~** catch something

mala'pena: a ~ adv hardly

ma'laria f malaria

mala'ticcio adj sickly

ma'lato, -a adj ill, sick; (*pianta*) diseased ● mf sick person. **~ di mente** mentally ill person. **malat'tia** f disease, illness; **ho preso due giorni di malattia** I had two days off sick. **malattia venerea** venereal disease

malau'gurato adj ill-omened. **ma-lau'gurio** m **bad o ill omen**

mala'vita f underworld

mala'voglia f unwillingness; **di ~** unwillingly

malcapi'tato adj wretched

malce'lato adj ill-concealed

mal'concio adj battered

malcon'tento m discontent

malco'stume m immorality

mal'destro adj awkward; (*inesperto*) inexperienced

maldi'cen|te adj slanderous. **~za** f slander

maldi'sposto adj ill-disposed

'male adv badly; **funzionare ~ not work properly; ~ a qcno (vestito ecc.) not suit sb; ri-**

manerci ~ be hurt; non c'è ~! not bad at all! ● m evil; (dolore) pain; (malattia) illness; (danno) harm. distinguere il bene dal ~ know right from wrong; andare a ~ go off; aver ~ a have a pain in; dove hai ~? where does it hurt?; far ~ a qcno (provocare dolore) hurt sb; (cibo:) be bad for sb; le cipolle mi fanno ~ onions don't agree with me; mi fa ~ la schiena my back is hurting; mal d'auto car-sickness. mal di denti toothache. mal di gola sore throat. mal di mare sea-sickness; avere il mal di mare be sea-sick. mal di pancia stomach ache. mal di testa headache

male'detto adj cursed; (orribile) awful

male'di|re vt curse. ~zi'one f curse; (maledizione) damn!

maledu|'cato adj ill-mannered. ~cazi'one f rudeness

male'fatta f misdeed

ma'lefico adj (azione) evil; (nocivo) harmful

maleodo'rante adj foul-smelling

ma'lessere m indisposition; fig uneasiness

ma'levolo adj malevolent

malfa'mato adj of ill repute

mal'fat|to adj badly done; (malformato) ill-shaped. ~'tore m wrongdoer

mal'fermo adj unsteady; (salute) poor

malfor'ma|to adj misshapen. ~zi'one f malformation

mal'grado prep in spite of ● conj although

ma'lia f spell

mali'gn|are vi malign. ~ità f malice; (Med) malignancy. ma'ligno adj malicious; (perfido) evil; (Med) malignant

malinco'ni|a f melancholy. malin'conico adj melancholy

malincu'ore: a ~ adv reluctantly

malinfor'mato adj misinformed

malintenzio'nato, -a mf miscreant

malin'teso adj mistaken ● m misunderstanding

ma'lizi|a f malice; (astuzia) cunning; (espediente) trick. ~'oso oso adj malicious; (birichino) mischievous

malle'abile adj malleable

malme'nare vt ill-treat

mal'messo adj (vestito male) shabbily dressed; (casa) poorly furnished; (fig: senza soldi) hard up

malnu'tri|to adj undernourished. ~zi'one f malnutrition

'malo adj in ~ modo badly

ma'locchio m evil eye

ma'lora f ruin; della ~ awful; andare in ~ go to ruin

ma'lore m illness; essere colto da ~ be suddenly taken ill

malri'dotto adj (persona) in a sorry state

mal'sano adj unhealthy

'malta f mortar

mal'tempo m bad weather

'malto m malt

maltrat|ta'mento m ill-treatment. ~'tare vt ill-treat

malu'more m bad mood; di ~ in a bad mood

mal'vagi|o adj wicked. ~tà f wickedness

malversazi'one f embezzlement

mal'visto adj unpopular (da with)

malvi'vente m criminal

malvolenti'eri adv unwillingly

malvo'lere vt farsi ~ make oneself unpopular

'mamma f mummy, mum; ~ mia! good gracious!

mam'mella f breast

mam'mifero m mammal

'mammola f violet

m

ma'nata f handful; (colpo) slap

'manca f ▶MANCO

manca'mento m avere un ~ faint

man'can|te adj missing. ~za f lack; (assenza) absence; (insufficienza) shortage; (fallo) fault; (imperfezione) defect; sento la sua ~za I miss her

man'care vi be lacking; (essere assente) be missing; (venir meno) fail; (morire) pass away; ~ di be lacking in; ~ a fail to keep (promessa); mi manca casa I miss home; mi manchi I miss you; mi è mancato il tempo I didn't have [the] time; mi manca un euro I'm one euro short; quanto manca alla partenza? how long before we leave?; è mancata la corrente there was a power failure; sentirsi ~ feel faint; sentirsi il respiro be unable to breathe [properly] • vt miss (bersaglio); è mancato poco che cadesse he nearly fell

'manche f inv heat

man'chevole adj defective

'mancia f tip

manci'ata f handful

man'cino adj left-handed

'manco, -a adj left • f left hand • adv (nemmeno) not even

man'dante mf (di delitto) instigator

manda'rancio m clementine

man'dare vt send; (emettere) give off; utter (suono); ~ a chiamare send for; ~ avanti la casa run the house; ~ giù (ingoiare) swallow

manda'rino m (Bot) mandarin

man'data f consignment; (di serratura) turn; chiudere a doppia ~ double lock

man'dato m (incarico) mandate; (Jur) warrant; (di pagamento) money order. ~ di comparizione [in giudizio] subpoena. ~ di perquisizione search warrant

man'dibola f jaw

mando'lino m mandolin

'mandor|la f almond; a ~la (occhi) almond-shaped. ~lato m nut brittle (type of nougat). ~lo m almond[-tree]

'mandria f herd

maneg'gevole adj easy to handle. maneggi'are vt handle

ma'neggio m handling; (intrigo) plot; (scuola di equitazione) riding school

ma'netta f hand lever; manette pl handcuffs

man'forte m dare ~ a qcno support sb

manga'nello m truncheon

manga'nese m manganese

mange'reccio adj edible

mangia'dischi® m inv type of portable record player

mangia'fumo adj inv candela ~ air-purifier in the form of candle

mangia'nastri m inv cassette player

mangi'a|re vt/i eat; (consumare) eat up; (corrodere) eat away; take (scacchi, carte ecc) • m eating; (cibo) food; (pasto) meal. ~rsi vr ~rsi le parole mumble; ~rsi le unghie bite one's nails

mangi'ata f big meal; farsi una bella ~ di... feast on...

man'gime m fodder

mangiucchi'are vt nibble

'mango m mango

ma'nia f mania. ~ di grandezza delusions of grandeur • mf maniac

'manica f sleeve; (🇬🇧: gruppo) band; a maniche lunghe long-sleeved; essere in maniche di camicia be in shirt sleeves

'Manica f la ~ the [English] Channel

mani'caretto m tasty dish

mani'chetta f hose

mani'chino m dummy

'manico *m* handle; (*Mus*) neck

mani'comio *m* mental home; (☐: *confusione*) tip

mani'cotto *m* muff; (*Mech*) sleeve

mani'cure *f* manicure ●*mf inv* (*persona*) manicurist

mani'e|ra *f* manner; in ~ra che so that. ~'rato *adj* affected; (*stile*) mannered. ~'rismo *m* mannerism

manifat'tura *f* manufacture; (*fabbrica*) factory

manife'stante *mf* demonstrator

manife'sta|re *vt* show; (*esprimere*) express ●*vi* demonstrate. ~rsi *vr* show oneself. ~zi'one *f* show; (*espressione*) expression; (*sintomo*) manifestation; (*dimostrazione pubblica*) demonstration

mani'festo *adj* evident ●*m* poster; (*dichiarazione pubblica*) manifesto

ma'niglia *f* handle; (*sostegno, in autobus ecc*) strap

manipo'la|re *vt* handle; (*massaggiare*) massage; (*alterare*) adulterate; *fig* manipulate. ~'tore, ~'trice *mf* manipulator. ~zi'one *f* handling; (*massaggio*) massage; (*alterazione*) adulteration; *fig* manipulation

mani'scalco *m* smith

man'naia *f* axe; (*da macellaio*) cleaver

man'naro *adj* lupo ~ werewolf

'mano *f* hand; (*strato di vernice ecc*) coat; alla ~ informal; fuori ~ out of the way; man ~ little by little; man ~ che as; sotto ~ to hand

mano'dopera *f* labour

ma'nometro *m* gauge

mano'mettere *vt* tamper with; (*violare*) violate

ma'nopola *f* knob; (*guanto*) mitten; (*su pullman*) handle

mano'scritto *adj* handwritten ●*m* manuscript

mano'vale *m* labourer

mano'vella *f* handle; (*Techn*) crank

ma'no|vra *f* manoeuvre; (*Rail*)

shunting; fare le ~vre (*Auto*) manoeuvre. ~'vrabile *adj fig* easy to manipulate. ~'vrare *vt* operate; *fig* manipulate (*persona*) ●*vi* manoeuvre

manro'vescio *m* slap

man'sarda *f* attic

mansi'one *f* task; (*dovere*) duty

mansu'eto *adj* meek; (*animale*) docile

man'tell|a *f* cape. ~o *m* cloak; (*soprabito, di animale*) coat; (*di neve*) mantle

mante'ner|e *vt* keep; (*in buono stato, sostentare*) maintain. ~si *vr* ~si in forma keep fit. manteni'mento *m* maintenance

'mantice *m* bellows *pl*; (*di automobile*) hood

'manto *m* cloak; (*coltre*) mantle

manto'vana *f* (*di tende*) pelmet

manu'al|e *adj* & *m* manual. ~e d'uso user manual. ~'mente *adv* manually

ma'nubrio *m* handle; (*di bicicletta*) handlebars *pl*; (*per ginnastica*) dumb-bell

manu'fatto *adj* manufactured

manutenzi'one *f* maintenance

'manzo *m* steer; (*carne*) beef

'mappa *f* map

mappa'mondo *m* globe

mar ▷**MARE**

ma'rasma *m fig* decline

mara'to|na *f* marathon. ~'neta *mf* marathon runner

'marca *f* brand; (*Comm*) brand; (*fabbricazione*) make; (*scontrino*) ticket. ~ da bollo revenue stamp

mar'ca|re *vt* mark; *Sport* score. ~ta'mente *adv* markedly. ~to *adj* (*tratto, accento*) strong. ~'tore *m* (*nel calcio*) scorer

mar'chese, -a *m* marquis ●*f* marchioness

marchi'are *vt* brand

'marchio *m* brand; (*caratteristica*) mark. ~ di fabbrica trademark. ~

registrato registered trademark

'marcia f march; (Auto) gear; Sport walk; mettere in ~ put into gear; mettersi in ~ start off; fare ~ indietro reverse; fig back-pedal. ~ funebre funeral march. ~ nuziale wedding march

marciapi'ede m pavement; (di stazione) platform

marci'a|re vi march; (funzionare) go, work. ~'tore, ~'trice mf walker

'marcio adj rotten ● m rotten part; fig corruption. mar'cire vi go bad, rot

'marco m (moneta) mark

'mare m sea; (luogo di mare) seaside; sul ~ (casa) at the seaside; (città) on the sea; in alto ~ on the high seas. ~ Adriatico Adriatic Sea. mar Ionio Ionian Sea. mar Mediterraneo Mediterranean. mar Tirreno Tyrrhenian Sea

ma'rea f tide; una ~ di hundreds of; alta ~ high tide; bassa ~ low tide

mareggi'ata f [sea] storm

mare'moto m tidal wave, seaquake

maresci'allo m marshal; (sottufficiale) warrantofficer

marga'rina f margarine

marghe'rita f marguerite. margherri'tina f daisy

margi'nale adj marginal

'margine m margin; (orlo) brink; (bordo) border. ~ di errore margin of error. ~ di sicurezza safety margin

ma'rina f navy; (costa) seashore; (quadro) seascape. ~ mercantile merchant navy. ~ militare navy

mari'naio m sailor

mari'na|re vt marinate. ~ta f marinade. ~to adj (Culin) marinated

ma'rino adj sea attrib, marine

mario'netta f puppet

ma'rito m husband

ma'rittimo adj maritime

mar'maglia f rabble

marmel'lata f jam; (di agrumi) marmalade

mar'mitta f pot; (Auto) silencer. ~ catalitica catalytic converter

'marmo m marble

mar'mocchio m 🔤 brat

mar'mor|eo adj marble. ~iz'zato adj marbled

mar'motta f marmot

Ma'rocco m Morocco

ma'roso m breaker

mar'rone adj brown ● m brown; (castagna) chestnut; marroni pl canditi marrons glacés

mar'sina f tails pl

mar'supio m (borsa) bumbag

marte'dì m inv Tuesday. ~ grasso Shrove Tuesday

martel'la|re vt hammer ● vi throb. ~ta f hammer blow

martel'letto m (di giudice) gavel

mar'tello m hammer; (di battente) knocker. ~ pneumatico pneumatic drill

marti'netto m (Mech) jack

'martire mf martyr. mar'tirio m martyrdom

'martora f marten

martori'are vt torment

mar'xis|mo m Marxism. ~ta agg & mf Marxist

marza'pane m marzipan

marzi'ale adj martial

marzi'ano, -a mf Martian

'marzo m March

mascal'zone m rascal

ma'scara m inv mascara

mascar'pone m full-fat cream cheese

ma'scella f jaw

'masche|ra f mask; (costume) fancy dress; (Cinema,Theat) usher m, usherette f; (nella commedia dell'arte) stock character. ~a antigas gas mask. ~a di bellezza face pack. ~a ad ossigeno oxygen mask. ~a'mento m masking; (*Mil*) camouflage. masche'rare vt mask. ~arsi vr put on a mask; ~arsi da dress up as. ~ata f masquerade

maschi'accio m tomboy

ma'schi|le adj masculine; (*sesso*) male ● m masculine [gender]. ~lista adj sexist. 'maschio adj male; (*virile*) manly ● m male; (*figlio*) son. masco'lino adj masculine

ma'scotte f inv mascot

maso'chis|mo m masochism. ~ta adj & mf masochist

'**massa** f mass; (*Electr*) earth, ground Am; comunicazioni di ~ mass media

massa'crare vt massacre. mas'sacro m massacre; fig mess

massaggi'a|re vt massage. mas'saggio m massage. ~'tore, ~'trice m masseur ● f masseuse

mas'saia f housewife

masse'rizie fpl household effects

mas'siccio adj massive; (*oro ecc*) solid; (*corporatura*) heavy ● m massif

'**massim|a** f maxim; (*temperatura*) maximum. ~o adj greatest; (*quantità*) maximum, greatest ● il ~o the maximum; al ~o at [the] most, as a maximum

'**masso** m rock

mas'sone m [Free]mason. ~'ria Freemasonry

ma'stello m wooden box for the grape or olive harvest

masteriz'zare vt (*Comput*) burn

masterizza'tore m (*Comput*) burner

masti'care vt chew; (*borbottare*) mumble

'**mastice** m mastic; (*per vetri*) putty

ma'stino m mastiff

masto'dontico adj gigantic

'**mastro** m master; libro ~ ledger

mastur'ba|rsi vr masturbate. ~zi'one f masturbation

ma'tassa f skein

mate'matic|a f mathematics, maths. ~o, -a adj mathematical ● mf mathematician

materas'sino m ~ gonfiabile air bed

mate'rasso m mattress. ~ a molle spring mattress

ma'teria f matter; (*materiale*) material; (*di studio*) subject. ~ prima raw material

materi'a|le adj material; (*grossolano*) coarse ● m material. ~lismo m materialism. ~lista adj materialistic ● mf materialist. ~liz'zarsi vr materialize. ~l'mente adv physically

materni'tà f motherhood; ospedale di ~ maternity hospital

ma'terno adj maternal; lingua materna mother tongue

ma'tita f pencil

ma'trice f matrix; (*origini*) roots pl; (*Comm*) counterfoil

ma'tricola f (*registro*) register; (*Univ*) fresher

ma'trigna f stepmother

matrimoni'ale adj matrimonial; vita ~ married life. matri'monio m marriage; (*cerimonia*) wedding

ma'trona f matron

'**matta** f (*nelle carte*) joker

matta'toio m slaughterhouse

matte'rello m rolling-pin

mat'ti|na f morning; la ~na in the morning. ~'nata f morning; (*Theat*) matinée. ~no m morning

'**matto, -a** adj mad, crazy; (*Med*) insane; (*falso*) false; (*opaco*) matt; ~ da legare barking mad; avere una voglia matta di be dying for ● mf madman; madwoman

mat'tone m brick; (*libro*) bore

matto'nella f tile

mattu'tino adj morning attrib

matu'rare vt ripen. **maturità** f maturity; (Sch) school-leaving certificate. **ma'turo** adj mature; (frutto) ripe

Maturità The Italian secondary school-leaving exam is called the *Esame di Maturità*. Candidates are examined by a committee consisting of external examiners and their own teachers, and the exams may be oral or written, depending on the subject. Candidates are tested on a wide range of subjects, including philosophy and history of art.

mauso'leo m mausoleum

maxi+ pref maxi+

'mazza f club; (martello) hammer; (da baseball, cricket) bat. ~ da golf golfclub. **maz'zata** f blow

maz'zetta f (di banconote) bundle

'mazzo m bunch; (carte da gioco) pack

me pers pron me; me lo ha dato he gave it to me; fai come me do as I do; è più veloce di me he is faster than me o faster than I am

me'andro m meander

M.E.C. m abbr (Mercato Comune Europeo) EEC

mec'canica f mechanics sg

meccanica'mente adv mechanically

mec'canico adj mechanical ●m mechanic. **mecca'nismo** m mechanism

mèche fpl [farsi] fare le ~ have one's hair streaked

me'daglia f medal. ~'one m medallion; (gioiello) locket

me'desimo adj same

'media f average; (Sch) average mark; (Math) mean; essere nella ~a be in the mid-range. ~'ano adj middle ●m (calcio) half-back

medi'ante prep by

medi'a|re vt act as intermediary in. ~'tore, ~'trice mf mediator; (Comm) middleman

medica'mento m medicine

medi'ca|re vt treat; dress (ferita). ~zi'one f medication; (di ferita) dressing

medi'cina f medicine. ~ina legale forensic medicine. ~i'nale adj medicinal ●m medicine

'medico adj medical ●m doctor. ~ generico general practitioner. ~ legale forensic scientist. ~ di turno duty doctor

medie'vale adj medieval

'medio adj average; (punto) middle; (statura) medium ●m (dito) middle finger

medi'ocre adj mediocre; (scadente) poor

medio'evo m Middle Ages pl

medi'ta|re vt meditate; (progettare) plan; (considerare attentamente) think over ●vi meditate. ~zi'one f meditation

mediter'raneo adj Mediterranean; il [mar] M~ the Mediterranean [Sea]

me'dusa f jellyfish

me'gafono m megaphone

mega'lomane mf megalomaniac

me'gera f hag

'meglio adv better; tanto ~, ~ così so much the better ●adj better; (superlativo) best ●mf best ● avere la ~ su have the better of; fare qcsa alla [bell'e] ~ do sth as best one can ●m fare del proprio ~ do one's best; fare qcsa il ~ possibile make an excellent job of sth; al ~ to the best of one's ability

'mela f apple. ~ cotogna quince

mela'grana f pomegranate

mela'nina f melanin

melan'zana f aubergine,

eggplant Am

me'lassa f molasses sg

me'lenso adj (persona, film) dull

mel'lifluo adj (parole) honeyed; (voce) sugary

'melma f slime. **mel'moso** adj slimy

melo m apple[-tree]

melo'di|a f melody. **me'lodico** adj melodic. ~**oso** adj melodious

melo'dram|ma m melodrama. ~**matico** adj melodramatic

melo'grano m pomegranate tree

me'lone m melon

'membro m member; (pl f membra (Anat)) limb

memo'rabile adj memorable

'memore adj mindful; (riconoscente) grateful

me'mori|a f memory; (oggetto ricordo) souvenir. imparare a ~a learn by heart. ~a tampone (Comput) buffer. ~a volatile (Comput) volatile memory; memorie pl (biografiche) memoirs. ~**'ale** m memorial. ~**z'zare** vt memorize; (Comput) save, store

mena'dito : a ~ adv perfectly

me'nare vt lead; (![]: picchiare) hit

mendi'ca|nte mf beggar. ~**re** vt/i beg

me'ningi fpl spremersi le ~ rack one's brains

menin'gite f meningitis

'meno adv less; (superlativo) least; (in operazioni, con temperatura) minus; far qcsa alla ~ peggio do sth as best one can; fare a ~ di qcsa do without sth; non posso fare a ~ di ridere I can't help laughing; ~ male! thank goodness!; sempre ~ less and less; venir ~ (svenire) faint; venir ~ a qcno (coraggio:) fail sb; sono le tre ~ un quarto it's a quarter to three; che tu venga o ~ whether you're coming or not; quanto ~ at least ● adj inv less; (con

nomi plurali) fewer ● m least; (Math) minus sign; il ~ possibile as little as possible; per lo ~ at least ● prep except [for] ● conj a ~ che unless

meno'ma|re vt (incidente:) maim. ~**to** adj disabled

meno'pausa f menopause

'mensa f table; (Mil) mess; (Sch, Univ) refectory

men'sil|e adj monthly ● m (stipendio) [monthly] salary; (rivista) monthly. ~**ità** f inv monthly salary. ~**mente** adv monthly

'mensola f bracket; (scaffale) shelf

'menta f mint. ~ **peperita** peppermint

men'tal|e adj mental. ~**ità** f inv mentality

'mente f mind; a ~ fredda in cold blood; venire in ~ a qcno occur to sb

men'tina f mint

men'tire vi lie

'mento m chin

'mentre conj (temporale) while; (invece) whereas

menu m inv menu. ~ **fisso** set menu. ~ **a tendina** (Comput) pull-down menu

menzio'nare vt mention. **menzi'one** f mention

men'zogna f lie

mera'viglia f wonder; a ~ marvellously; che ~! how wonderful!; con mia grande ~ to much to my amazement; mi fa ~ che... I am surprised that...

meravigli'ar|e vt surprise. ~**si** vr ~**si di** be surprised at

meravigli'oso adj marvellous

mer'can|te m merchant. ~**teggi'are** vi trade; (sul prezzo) bargain. ~**zia** f merchandise, goods pl ● m merchant ship

mer'cato m market; Fin market[-place]. à buon ~ (comprare)

m

cheap[ly]; (articolo) cheap. ~ dei cambi foreign exchange market. ~ coperto covered market. ~ libero free market. ~ nero black market

'**merce** f goods pl

mercé f alla ~ di at the mercy of

merce'nario adj & m mercenary

merce'ria f haberdashery; (negozio) haberdasher's

mercoledì m inv Wednesday. ~ delle Ceneri Ash Wednesday

mer'curio m mercury

me'renda f afternoon snack; far ~ have an afternoon snack

meridi'ana f sundial

meridi'ano adj midday ●m meridian

meridio'nale adj southern ●mf southerner. meridi'one m south

me'rin|ga f meringue. ~'gata f meringue pie

meri'tare vt deserve. meri'tevole adj deserving

'**meri|to** m merit; (valore) worth; in ~to a as to; per ~to di thanks to. ~'torio adj meritorious

mer'letto m lace

'**merlo** m blackbird

mer'luzzo m cod

'**mero** adj mere

meschine'ria f meanness. me'schino adj wretched; (gretto) mean ●m wretch

mesco|la'mento m mixing. ~'lanza f mixture

mesco'la|re vt mix; shuffle (carte); (confondere) mix up; blend (tè, tabacco ecc). ~rsi vr mix; (immischiarsi) meddle. ~ta f (a carte) shuffle; (Culin) stir

'**mese** m month

me'setto m un ~ about a month

'**messa**[1] f Mass

'**messa**[2] f (il mettere) putting. ~ in moto (Auto) starting. ~ in piega (di capelli) set. ~ a punto adjustment.

~ in scena production. ~ a terra earthing, grounding Am

messag'gero m messenger. mes'saggio m message

'**messe** f harvest

Mes'sia m Messiah

messi'cano, -a adj & mf Mexican

'**Messico** m Mexico

messin'scena f staging; fig act

'**messo** pp di **mettere** ●m messenger

mesti'ere m trade; (lavoro) job; essere del ~ be an expert

'**mesto** adj sad

'**mestola** f (di cuoco) ladle

mestru'a|le adj menstrual. ~zi'one f menstruation. ~zi'oni pl period

'**meta** f destination; fig aim

metà f inv half; (centro) middle; a ~ strada half-way; fare a ~ con qcno go halves with sb

metabo'lismo m metabolism

meta'done m methadone

me'tafora f metaphor. meta'forico adj metaphorical

me'talli|co adj metallic. ~z'zato adj (grigio) metallic

me'tallo m metal. ~ur'gia f metallurgy

metalmec'canico adj engineering ●m engineering worker

me'tano m methane. ~'dotto m methane pipeline

meta'nolo m methanol

me'teora f meteor. meteo'rite m meteorite

meteoro|lo'gia f meteorology. ~'logico adj meteorological

me'ticcio, -a mf half-caste

meti'co'loso adj meticulous

me'tod|ico adj methodical. 'metodo m method. ~olo'gia f methodology

me'traggio m length (in metres)

'metrico, -a adj metric; (in poesia) metrical •f metrics sg

'metro m metre; (nastro) tape measure •f inv (🔲: metropolitana) tube Br, subway

me'tronomo m metronome

metro'notte mf inv night security guard

me'tropoli f inv metropolis. **~'tana** f subway, underground Br. **~'tano** adj metropolitan

'metter|e vt put; (indossare) put on; (🔲: installare) put in; **~e al mondo** bring into the world; **~e da parte** set aside; **~e fiducia** inspire trust; **~e qcsa in chiaro** make sth clear; **~e in mostra** display; **~e a posto** tidy up; **~e in vendita** put up for sale; **~e su** set up (casa, azienda); **ci ho messo un'ora** it took me an hour; **mettiamo che...** let's suppose that... **~si** vr (indossare) put on; (diventare) turn out; **~si** a start to; **~si con qcno** (🔲: formare una coppia) start to go out with sb; **~si a letto** go to bed; **~si a sedere** sit down; **~si in viaggio** set out

'mezza f è la **~** it's half past twelve; **sono le quattro e ~** it's half past four

mezza'luna f half moon; (simbolo islamico) crescent; (coltello) two-handled chopping knife

mezza'manica f a **~** (maglia) short-sleeved

mez'zano adj middle

mezza'notte f midnight

mezz'asta a **~** adv at half mast

'mezzo adj half; di mezza età middle-aged; **~ bicchiere** half a glass; **una mezza idea** a vague idea; **sono le quattro e ~** it's half past four. **mezz'ora** f half an hour. **mezza pensione** f half board. **mezza stagione** f una giacca di mezza stagione a spring/autumn jacket •adv (a metà) half •m (metà) half; (centro)

middle; (per raggiungere un fine) means sg; **uno e ~** one and a half; **tre anni e ~** three and a half years; **in ~ a** in the middle of; **il giusto ~** the happy medium; **levare di ~** clear away; **per ~ di** by means of; a **~ posta** by mail; **via di ~** fig halfway house; (soluzione) middle way. **mezzi** pl (denaro) means pl. **mezzi pubblici** public transport. **mezzi di trasporto** [means of] transport

mezzo'busto a **~** adj (foto, ritratto) half-length

mezzo'fondo m middle-distance running

mezzogi'orno m midday; (sud) South. **il M~** Southern Italy. **~ in punto** high noon

mi[1] pers pron me; (refl) myself; **mi ha dato un libro** he gave me a book; **mi lavo le mani** I wash my hands; **eccomi here I am**

mi[2] m (Mus) E

'mica[1] f mica

'mica[2] adv 🔲 (per caso) by any chance; **hai ~ visto Paolo?** have you seen Paul, by any chance?; **non è ~ bello** it is not at all nice; **male not bad**

'miccia f fuse

midici'ale adj deadly

'micio m pussy-cat

'microbo m microbe

micro'cosmo m microcosm

micro'fiche f inv microfiche

micro'film m inv microfilm

mi'crofono m microphone

microorga'nismo m microorganism

microproces'sore m microprocessor

micro'scopi|o m microscope

micro'solco m (disco) long-playing record

mi'dollo m (pl f midolla, Anat) marrow; **fino al ~** through and through. ~ spinale spinal cord

mi'ele m honey

'mie, mi'ei ▷ MIO

mi'et|ere vt reap. ~i'trice f (Mech) harvester. ~i'tura f harvest

migli'aio m (pl f migliaia) thousand. a migliaia in thousands

'miglio m (Bot) millet; (misura: pl f miglia) mile

migliora'mento m improvement

miglio'rare vt/i improve

migli'ore adj better; (superlativo) the best ● mf il/la ~ the best

'mignolo m little finger; (del piede) little toe

mi'gra|re vi migrate. ~zi'one f migration

'mila ▷ MILLE

Mi'lano f Milan

miliar'dario, -a m millionaire; (plurimiliardario) billionaire ● f million-airess; billionairess. **mili'ardo** m billion

mili'are adj pietra f ~ milestone

milio'nario, -a m millionaire ● f millionairess

mili'one m million

milio'nesimo adj millionth

mili'tante adj & mf militant

mili'tare vi ~ in be a member of (partito ecc) ● adj military ● m soldier; fare il ~ do one's military service. ~ di leva national serviceman

mi'lite m soldier. **mil'izia** f militia

'mille adj & m (pl mila) a o one thousand; due/tre mila two/three thousand; ~ grazie! thanks a lot!

mille'foglie m inv (Culin) vanilla slice

mil'lennio m millennium

millepi'edi m inv centipede

mil'lesimo adj & m thousandth

milli'grammo m milligram

milli'metro m millimetre

mi'mare vt mimic (persona)

● vi mime

mi'metico adj camouflage attrib

mimetiz'zar|e vt camouflage. ~si vr camouflage oneself

'mim|ica f mime. ~ico adj mimic. ~o m mime

mi'mosa f mimosa

'mina f mine; (di matita) lead

mi'naccia f threat

minacci'|are vt threaten. ~'oso adj threatening

mi'nare vt mine; fig undermine

mina'tor|e m miner. ~io adj threatening

mine'ra|le adj & m mineral. ~rio adj mining attrib

mi'nestra f soup. mine'strone m vegetable soup; (🇮🇹: insieme confuso) hotchpotch

mini+ pref mini+

minia'tura f miniature. miniaturiz'zato adj miniaturized

mini'era f mine

mini'golf m miniature golf

mini'gonna f miniskirt

minima'mente adv minimally

mini'market m inv minimarket

minimiz'zare vt minimize

'minimo adj least, slightest; (il più basso) lowest; (salario, quantità ecc) minimum ● m minimum

mini'stero m ministry; (governo) government

mi'nistro m minister. M~ del Tesoro Finance Minister

mino'ranza f minority attrib

Minoranza linguistica Minoranze linguistiche (linguistic minorities) are protected by the Italian constitution. As well as dialects of Italian, and the related languages Sardinian and Ladin, other languages spoken.

They include German in Alto Adige; French in Valdaosta; Greek, Albanian, and Serbo-Croat in the rural south; Slovenian in the north-east and Catalan in Alghero.

mino'rato, -a adj disabled ● mf disabled person

mi'nore adj (gruppo, numero) smaller; (superlativo) smallest; (distanza) shorter; (superlativo) shortest; (prezzo) lower; (superlativo) lowest; (di età) younger; (superlativo) youngest; (di importanza) minor; (superlativo) least important ● mf younger; (superlativo) youngest; (Jur) minor; **i minori di 14 anni** children under 14. mino'renne adj under age ● mf minor

minori'tario adj minority attrib

minu'etto m minuet

mi'nuscolo, -a adj tiny ● f small letter

mi'nuta f rough copy

mi'nuto[1] adj minute; (persona) delicate; (ricerca) detailed; (pioggia, neve) fine; **al ~** (Comm) retail

mi'nuto[2] m (di tempo) minute; **spaccare il ~** be dead on time

mi'nuzia f trifle. ~'oso adj detailed; (persona) meticulous

'mio (il mio m, la mia f, i miei mpl, le mie fpl) adj poss my; **questa macchina è mia** this car is mine; **~ padre** my father; **un ~ amico** a friend of mine ● poss pron mine; **i miei** (genitori ecc) my folks

'miope adj short-sighted. mio'pia f short-sightedness

'mira f aim; (bersaglio) target; **prendere la ~** take aim

mi'racolo m miracle. ~sa'mente adv miraculously. miraco'loso adj miraculous

mi'raggio m mirage

mi'rar|e vi [take] aim. ~si vr (guardarsi) look at oneself

mi'riade f myriad

mi'rino m sight; (Phot) view-finder

mir'tillo m blueberry

mi'santropo, -a mf misanthropist

mi'scela f mixture; (di caffè, tabacco ecc) blend. ~'tore m (di acqua) mixer tap

miscel'lanea f miscellany

'mischia f scuffle; (nel rugby) scrum

mischi'ar|e vt mix; (carte da gioco). ~si vr mix; (immischiarsi) interfere

misco'noscere vt not appreciate

mi'scuglio m mixture

mise'rabile adj wretched

misera'mente adv (finire) miserably; (vivere) in abject poverty

mi'seria f poverty; (infelicità) misery; **guadagnare una ~** earn a pittance; **porca ~!** hell!

miseri'cordi|a f mercy. ~'oso adj merciful

'misero adj (miserabile) wretched; (povero) poor; (scarso) paltry

mi'sfatto m misdeed

mi'sogino m misogynist

mis'saggio m vision mixer

'missile m missile

missio'nario, -a mf missionary. missi'one f mission

misteri'oso adj mysterious. mi'stero m mystery

'mistica f mysticism. ~'cismo m mysticism. ~co adj mystic[al] ● m mystic

mistifi'ca|re vt distort (verità). ~zi'one f (della verità) distortion

'misto adj mixed; **scuola mista** mixed or co-educational school ● m mixture; **~ lana/cotone** wool/cotton mix

mi'sura f measure; (dimensione) measurement; (taglia) size; (limite) limit; **su ~** (abiti) made to measure; (mobile) custom-made; **a ~** (andare, calzare) perfectly. **~ di sicurezza** safety measure. misu'rare vt measure; try on (indumenti); (limitare) limit. **misu'rarsi** vr misurarsi con (gareggiare) compete with. **misu'rato** adj measured. misu'rino m measuring spoon

'**mite** adj mild; (prezzo) moderate

'**mitico** adj mythical

miti'gar|e vt mitigate. ~**si** vr calm down; (clima) become mild

'**mito** m myth. ~**lo'gia** f mythology. ~'**logico** adj mythological

'**mitra** f (Relig) mitre ● m inv (Mil) machine-gun

mitragli'a|re vt machine-gun; ~**re di domande** fire questions at. ~'**trice** f machine-gun

mit'tente mf sender

mo' m a ~ **di** by way of (esempio, consolazione)

'**mobbing** m harassment

'**mobile**[1] adj mobile; (voluble) fickle; (che si può muovere) movable; **beni mobili** personal estate; **squadra** ~ flying squad

'**mobile**[2] m piece of furniture; **mobili** pl furniture sg. **mo'bilia** f furniture. ~**li'ficio** m furniture factory

mo'bilio m furniture

mobilità f mobility

mobili'ta|re vt mobilize. ~**zi'one** f mobilization

mocas'sino m moccasin

'**moccolo** m candle-end; (moccio) snot

'**moda** f fashion; **di** ~ in fashion; **alla** ~ (musica, vestiti) up-to-date; **fuori** ~ unfashionable

modalità f inv formality; ~ **d'uso** instruction

mo'della f model. **model'lare** vt model

model'li|no m model. ~**sta** mf designer

mo'dello m model; (stampo) mould; (di carta) pattern; (modulo) form

'**modem** m inv modem

mode'ra|re vt moderate; (diminuire) reduce. ~**rsi** vr control oneself. ~**ta'mente** adv moderately ~**to** adj moderate. ~'**tore**, ~'**trice** mf (in tavola rotonda) moderator. ~**zi'one** f moderation

modern|a'mente adv (in modo moderno) in a modern style. ~**iz'zare** vt modernize. **mo'derno** adj modern

mo'dest|ia f modesty. ~**o** adj modest

'**modico** adj reasonable

mo'difica f modification

modifi'ca|re vt modify. ~**zi'one** f modification

mo'dista f milliner

'**modo** m way; (garbo) manners pl; (occasione) chance; (Gram) mood; **ad ogni** ~ anyhow; **di** ~ **che** so that; **fare in** ~ **di** try to; **in che** ~ (inter) how; **in qualche** ~ somehow; **in questo** ~ like this; ~ **di dire** idiom; **per** ~ **di dire** so to speak

modu'la|re vt modulate. ~**zi'one** f modulation. ~**zione di frequenza** frequency modulation

'**modulo** m form; (lunare, di comando) module. ~ **continuo** continuous paper

'**mogano** m mahogany

'**mogio** adj dejected

'**moglie** f wife

'**mola** f millstone; (Mech) grindstone

mo'lare m molar

'**mole** f mass; (dimensione) size

mo'lecola f molecule

mole'stare vt bother; (più forte) molest. **mo'lestia** f nuisance. **mo'lesto** adj bothersome

'**molla** f spring; **molle** pl tongs

mol'lare vt let go; (🔲: lasciare) leave; (🔲: give (ceffone); (Naut) cast off ● vi cease; **mollala**! 🔲 stop that!

'**molle** adj soft; (bagnato) wet

mol'letta f (per capelli) hair-grip; (per bucato) clothes-peg; **mollette** pl

173

(*per ghiaccio ecc*) tongs

mol'lezza f softness; ~e pl fig luxury

mol'lica f crumb

'**molo** m pier; (*banchina*) dock

mol'teplic|e adj manifold; (*numeroso*) numerous. ~**ità** f multiplicity

multipli'ca|re vt, ~**rsi** vr multiply. ~**tore** m multiplier. ~**trice** f calculating machine. ~**zi'one** f multiplication

molti'tudine f multitude

'**molto**

● adj a lot of; (*con negazione e interrogazione*) much, a lot of; (*con nomi plurali*) many, a lot of; non ~ tempo not much time, not a lot of time

● adv very; (*con verbi*) a lot; (*con avverbi*) much; ~ **stupido** very stupid; **mangiare** ~ eat a lot; ~ **più veloce** much faster; **non mangiare** ~ not eat much

● pron a lot; (*molto tempo*) a lot of time; (*con negazione e interrogazione*) much, a lot; (*plurale*) many; **non ne ho** ~ I don't have much; **non ne ho molti** I don't have many, I don't have a lot; **non ci metterò** ~ I won't be long; **fra non** ~ before long; **molti** (*persone*) a lot of people; **eravamo in molti** there were a lot of us

---

momentanea'mente adv momentarily; **è** ~ **assente** he's not here at the moment. **momen'taneo** adj momentary

mo'mento m moment; a **momenti** (*a volte*) sometimes; (*fra un momento*) in a moment; **dal** ~ **che** since; **per il** ~ for the time being; **da un** ~ **all'altro** (*cambiare idea ecc*) from one moment to the next; (*aspettare qcno ecc*) at any moment

'**monac|a** f nun. ~**o** m monk

'**Monaco** m Monaco ● f (*di Baviera*) Munich

mo'narc|a m monarch. **monar'chia** f monarchy

mona'stero m (*di monaci*) monastery; (*di monache*) convent. **mo'nastico** adj monastic

monche'rino m stump

'**monco, -a** adj maimed; (*fig: troncato*) truncated; ~ **di un braccio** one-armed

mon'dano adj worldly; **vita mondana** social life

mondi'ale adj world attrib; **di fama** ~ world-famous

'**mondo** m world; **il bel** ~ fashionable society; **un** ~ (*molto*) a lot

mondovisi'one f in ~ transmitted worldwide

mo'nello, -a m urchin

mo'neta f coin; (*denaro*) money; (*denaro spicciolo*) [small] change. ~ **estera** foreign currency. ~ **legale** legal tender. ~ **unica** single currency. **mone'tario** adj monetary

mongolfi'era f hot air balloon

mo'nile m jewel

'**monito** m warning

moni'tore m monitor

monoco'lore adj (*Pol*) one-party

mono'dose adj inv individually packaged

monogra'fia f monograph

mono'gramma m monogram

mono'kini m inv monokini

mono'lingue adj monolingual

monolo'cale m studio apartment

mo'nologo m monologue

mono'pattino m [child's] scooter

mono'poli|o m monopoly. ~**o** di Stato state monopoly. ~**z'zare** vt monopolize

mono'sci m inv monoski

monosil'labico adj monosyllabic. **mono'sillabo** m monosyllable

monoto'nia f monotony. **mo'no-**

m

tono adj monotonous

mono'uso adj disposable

monsi'gnore m monsignor

mon'sone m monsoon

monta'carichi m inv hoist

mon'taggio m (Mech) assembly; Cinema editing; catena di ~ production line

mon'tagna f (mountain; (zona) mountains pl. montagne pl russe big dipper. ~'gnoso adj mountainous. ~'naro, -a mf highlander. ~no adj mountain attrib

mon'tante m (di finestra, porta) upright

mon'tare vt/i mount; get on (veicolo); (aumentare) rise; (Mech) assemble; frame (quadro); (Culin) whip; edit (film); (a cavallo) ride; fig blow up; ~rsi la testa get big-headed. ~to, -a mf poser. ~tura f (Mech) assembling; (di occhiali) frame; (di gioiello) mounting; fig exaggeration

'monte m mountain; a ~ up-stream; andare a ~ be ruined; mandare a ~ qcsa ruin sth. ~ di pietà pawnshop

Monte'negro m Montenegro

monte'premi m inv jackpot

mon'tone m ram; carne di ~ mutton

montu'oso adj mountainous

monumen'tale adj monumental. monu'mento m monument

mo'quette f fitted carpet

'mora f (del gelso) mulberry; (del rovo) blackberry

mo'rale adj moral ●f morals pl; (di storia) moral ●m morale. mora'lista mf moralist. ~ità f morality; (condotta) morals pl. ~iz'zare vt/i moralize. ~'mente adv morally

morbi'dezza f softness

'morbido adj soft

mor'billo m measles sg

'morbo m disease. ~sità f (qualità)

morbidity

mor'boso adj morbid

mor'dente adj biting. 'mordere vt bite; (corrodere) bite into. mordic-chi'are vt gnaw

mor'fina f morphine. morfi'nomane mf morphine addict

mori'bondo adj dying; (istituzione) moribund

morige'rato adj moderate

mo'rire vi die; fig die out; fa un freddo da ~ it's freezing cold, it's perishing; ~ di noia be bored to death

mor'mone mf Mormon

mormo'r|are vt/i murmur; (brontolare) mutter. ~io m murmuring; (lamentela) grumbling

'moro adj dark ●m Moor

mo'roso adj in arrears

'morsa f vice; fig grip

'morse adj alfabeto ~ Morse code

mor'setto m clamp

morsi'care vt bite. 'morso m bite; (di cibo, briglia) bit; i morsi della fame hunger pangs

morta'della f mortadella (type of salted pork)

mor'taio m mortar

mor'tal|e adj mortal; (simile a morte) deadly; di una noia ~e deadly. ~ità f mortality. ~'mente adv (ferito) fatally; (offeso) mortally

morta'retto m firecracker

'morte f death

mortifi'ca|re vt mortify. ~rsi vr be mortified. ~to adj mortified. ~zi'one f mortification

'morto, -a pp di morire ●adj dead; ~ di freddo frozen to death; stanco ~ dead tired ●m dead man ●f dead woman

mor'torio m funeral

mo'saico m mosaic

'mosca f fly. ~ cieca blindman's buff

'Mosca f Moscow

mo'scato adj muscat; noce moscata nutmeg ● m muscatel

mosce'rino m midge

mo'schea f mosque

moschi'cida adj fly attrib

'moscio adj limp; avere l'erre moscia not be able to say one's r's properly

mo'scone m bluebottle; (barca) pedalo

'moss|a f movement; (passo) move. ~o pp di **muovere** ● adj (mare) rough; (capelli) wavy; (fotografia) blurred

mo'starda f mustard

'mostra f show; (d'arte) exhibition; far ~ di pretend; in ~ on show; mettersi in ~ make oneself conspicuous

mo'stra|re vt show; (indicare) point out; (spiegare) explain. ~rsi vr show oneself; (apparire) appear

'mostro m monster; (fig: persona) genius; ~ sacro fig sacred cow

mostru|osa'mente adv tremendously. ~'oso adj monstrous; (incredibile) enormous

mo'tel m inv motel

moti'va|re vt cause; (Jur) justify. ~to adj (persona) motivated. ~zi'one f motivation; (giustificazione) justification

mo'tivo m reason; (movente) motive; (in musica, letteratura) theme; (disegno) motif

'moto m motion; (esercizio) exercise; (gesto) movement; (sommossa) rising ● f inv (motocicletta) motor bike; mettere in ~ start (motore)

moto'carro m three-wheeler

motoci'cl|etta f motor cycle. ~ismo m motorcycling. ~ista mf motor-cyclist

moto'cros|s m motocross. ~'sista mf scrambler

moto'lancia f motor launch

moto'nave f motor vessel

mo'tore adj motor ● m motor, engine. ~ di ricerca (Comput) search engine. moto'retta f motor scooter. moto'rino m moped. motorino d'avviamento starter

motoriz'za|to adj (Mil) motorized. ~zi'one f (ufficio) vehicle licensing office

moto'scafo m motorboat

motove'detta f patrol vessel

'motto m motto; (facezia) witticism; (massima) saying

mouse m inv (Comput) mouse

mo'vente m motive

movimen'ta|re vt enliven. ~to adj lively. movi'mento m movement; essere sempre in movimento be always on the go

mozi'one f motion

mozzafi'ato adj inv nail-biting

moz'zare vt cut off; dock (coda); ~ il fiato a qcno take sb's breath away

mozza'rella f mozzarella (mild, white cheese)

mozzi'cone m (di sigaretta) stub

'mozzo m (Mech) hub; (Naut) ship's boy ● adj (coda) truncated; (testa) severed

'mucca f cow. morbo della ~ pazza mad cow disease

'mucchio m heap, pile; un ~ di fig lots of

'muco m mucus

'muffa f mould; fare la ~ go mouldy. muf'fire vi go mouldy

muf'fole fpl mittens

mug'gi|re vi (mucca): moo, low; (toro:) bellow

mu'ghetto m lily of the valley

mugo'lare vi whine; (persona:) moan. mugo'lio m whining

mulatti'era f mule track

mu'latto, -a mf mulatto

muli'nello m (d'acqua) whirl-pool;

(di vento) eddy; (giocattolo) windmill

mu'lino m mill. ~ **a vento** windmill

'**mulo** m mule

'**multa** f fine. mul'tare vt fine

multico'lore adj multicoloured

multi'lingue adj multilingual

multi'media mpl multimedia

multimedi'ale adj multimedia attrib

multimiliar'dario, -a m f multimillionaire

multinazio'nale f multinational

'**multiplo** adj & m multiple

multiproprietà f inv time-share

multi'uso adj (utensile) all-purpose

'**mummia** f mummy

'**mungere** vt milk

munici'pal|e adj municipal. ~**ità** f inv town council. **muni'cipio** m town hall

mu'nifico adj munificent

mu'nire vt fortify; ~ **di** (provvedere) supply with

munizi'oni fpl ammunition sg

'**munto** pp di mungere

mu'over|e vt move; (suscitare) arouse. ~**si** vr move

mura fpl (cinta di città) walls

mu'raglia f wall

mu'rale adj mural; (pittura) wall attrib

mur'ar|e vt wall up. ~**tore** m bricklayer; (con pietre) mason; (operaio edile) builder. ~**tura** f (di pietra) masonry, stonework; (di mattoni) brickwork

mu'rena f moray eel

'**muro** m wall; (di nebbia) bank; **a** ~ (armadio) built-in. ~ **portante** load-bearing wall. ~ **del suono** sound barrier

'**muschio** m (Bot) moss

musco'lar|e adj muscular. ~**tura** f muscles pl. '**muscolo** m muscle

mu'seo m museum

museu'ola f muzzle

'**musi|ca** f music. ~**cal** m inv musical. ~**cale** adj musical. ~**cista** m f musician.

'**muso** m muzzle; (pej: di persona) mug; (di aeroplano) nose; **fare il** ~ sulk. **mu'sone, -a** m f sulker

'**mussola** f muslin

musul'mano, -a m f Moslem

'**muta** f (cambio) change; (di penne) moult; (di cani) pack; (per immersione subacquea) wetsuit

muta'mento m change

mu'tan|de fpl pants; (da donna) knickers. ~**doni** mpl (da uomo) long johns; (da donna) bloomers

mu'tare vt change

mu'tevole adj changeable

muti'lar|e vt mutilate. ~**to, -a** m f disabled person. ~**to di guerra** disabled ex-serviceman

mu'tismo m dumbness; fig obstinate silence

'**muto** adj dumb; (silenzioso) silent; (fonetica) mute

mutu|a f [cassa f ~] sickness benefit fund. ~**ato, -a** m f ≈ NHS patient

'**mutuo**[1] adj mutual

'**mutuo**[2] m loan; (per la casa) mortgage; **fare un** ~ take out a mortgage. ~ **ipotecario** mortgage

Nn

n° abbr (numero) No

nacchera f castanet

'**nafta** f naphtha; (per motori) diesel oil

'**naia** f cobra; (X: servizio militare) national service

'**nailon** m nylon

'**nano, -a** adj & m f dwarf

napole'tano, -a *adj & mf* Neapolitan

'Napoli *f* Naples

'nappa *f* tassel; (*pelle*) soft leather

nar'ciso *m* narcissus

nar'cotico *adj & m* narcotic

na'rice *f* nostril

nar'ra|re *vt* tell. ~**tivo, -a** *adj* narrative ● *f* fiction. ~**tore, ~'trice** *mf* narrator. ~**zi'one** *f* narration; (*racconto*) story

na'sale *adj* nasal

'nasc|ere *vi* (*venire al mondo*) be born; (*germogliare*) sprout; (*sorgere*) rise; ~**ere da** *fig* arise from. ~**ita** *f* birth. ~**i'turo** *m* unborn child

na'scond|ere *vt* hide. ~**si** *vr* hide

nascon'di|glio *m* hiding-place. ~**no** *m* hide-and-seek. **na'scosto** *pp di* **nascondere** ● *adj* hidden; **di na'scosto** secretly

na'sello *m* (*pesce*) hake

'naso *m* nose

'nastro *m* ribbon; (*di registratore ecc*) tape. ~ **adesivo** adhesive tape. ~ **isolante** insulating tape. ~ **trasportatore** conveyor belt

na'tale *adj* (*paese*) of one's birth. **N~e** *m* Christmas; ~**i** *pl* parentage. ~**ità** *f* [number of] births. **nata'lizio** *adj* (*del Natale*) Christmas *attrib*; (*di nascita*) of one's birth

na'tante *adj* floating ● *m* craft

'natica *f* buttock

na'tio *adj* native

Nativi'tà *f* Nativity. **na'tivo, -a** *agg & mf* native

'nato *pp di* **nascere** ● *adj* born; **uno scrittore** ~ a born writer; **nata Rossi** née Rossi

NATO *f* Nato, NATO

na'tura *f* nature; **pagare in** ~ pay in kind. ~ **morta** still life

natu'ra|le *adj* natural; **al** ~**le** (*alimento*) plain, natural; ~**le!** naturally, of course. ~**lezza** *f* naturalness. ~**liz'zare** *vt* naturalize. ~**l'mente** *adv*

naturally

natu'rista *mf* naturalist

naufra'gare *vi* be wrecked; (*persona*) be shipwrecked. **nau'fragio** *m* shipwreck; *fig* wreck. **'naufrago, -a** *mf* survivor

'nause|a *f* nausea; **avere la** ~**a** feel sick. ~**ante** *adj* nauseating. ~**are** *vt* nauseate

'nautic|a *f* navigation. ~**o** *adj* nautical

na'vale *adj* naval

na'vata *f* nave; (*laterale*) aisle

'nave *f* ship. ~ **cisterna** tanker. ~ **da guerra** warship. ~ **spaziale** spaceship

na'vetta *f* shuttle

navicella *f* ~ **spaziale** nose cone

navi'gabile *adj* navigable

navi'ga|re *vi* sail; ~**re in Internet** surf the Net. ~**tore, ~'trice** *mf* navigator. ~**zi'one** *f* navigation

na'viglio *m* fleet; (*canale*) canal

nazio'na|le *adj* national ● *f Sport* national team. ~**lismo** *m* nationalism. ~**lista** *mf* nationalist ~**lità** *f inv* nationality.

nazionaliz'zare *vt* nationalize. **nazi'one** *f* nation

na'zista *adj & mf* Nazi

N.B. *abbr* (nota bene) N.B.

---

ne

Spesso non si traduce: **Ne ho cinque** I've got five (of them)

● *pers pron* (*di lui*) about him; (*di lei*) about her; (*di loro*) about them; (*di ciò*) of it; (*da ciò*) from that; (*di un insieme*) of it; (*di un gruppo*) of them

····▸ **non ne conosco nessuno** I don't know any of them; **ne ho**

I have some; **non ne ho più** I don't have any left

● *adv* from there; **ne vengo ora** I've just come from there; **me ne vado** I'm off

né *conj* né... né... nor...; **non ne ho il tempo né la voglia** I don't have either the time or the inclination; **né tu né io vogliamo andare** neither you nor I want to go; **né l'uno né l'altro** neither [of them/us]

ne'anche *adv* (*neppure*) not even; (*senza neppure*) without even ● *conj* (*e neppure*) neither... nor; **non parlo inglese, e lui** ~ I don't speak English, neither does he **o** and he **o** not either

'nebbia *f* mist; (*in città, su strada*) fog. ~'**oso** *adj* misty; foggy

necessaria'mente *adv* necessarily. **neces'sario** *adj* necessary

necessità *f inv* necessity; (*bisogno*) need

necessi'tare *vi* ~ **di** need; (*essere necessario*) be necessary

necro'logio *m* obituary

ne'fando *adj* wicked

ne'fasto *adj* ill-omened

ne'ga|re *vt* deny; (*rifiutare*) refuse; **essere** ~**to** per qcsa be no good at sth. ~'**tivo, -a** *adj* negative ● *f* negative. ~**zi'one** *f* negation; (*diniego*) denial; (*Gram*) negative

ne'gletto *adj* neglected

'negli = IN + GLI

negli'gen|te *adj* negligent. ~**za** *f* negligence

negozi'abile *adj* negotiable

negozi'ante *mf* dealer; (*bottegaio*) shopkeeper

negozi'a|re *vt* negotiate ● *vi* ~**re** in trade in. ~**ti** *mpl* negotiations

ne'gozio *m* shop

'negro, -a *adj* black ● *mf* black; (*scrittore*) ghost writer

'nei = IN + I. **nel** = IN + IL.
'nella = IN + LA. **'nelle** = IN + LE.
'nello = IN + LO

'nembo *m* nimbus

ne'mico, -a *adj* hostile ● *mf* enemy

nem'meno *conj* not even

'nenia *f* dirge; (*per bambini*) lullaby; (*piagnucolio*) wail

'neo+ *pref* neo+

neofa'scismo *m* neofascism

neo'litico *adj* Neolithic

'neon *m* neon

neo'nato, -a *adj* newborn ● *mf* newborn baby

neozelan'dese *adj* New Zealand ● *mf* New Zealander

nep'pure *conj* not even

'nerb|o *m* (*forza*) strength; *fig* backbone. ~**o'ruto** *adj* brawny

ne'retto *m* (*Typ*) bold [type]

'nero *adj* black; ((🄻): *arrabbiato*) fuming ● *m* black; **mettere** ~ **su bianco** put in writing

nerva'tura *f* nerves *pl*; (*Bot*) veining; (*di libro*) band

'nervo *m* nerve; (*Bot*) vein; **avere i nervi** be bad-tempered; **dare ai nervi a qcno** get on sb's nerves. ~'**vismo** *m* nerviness

ner'voso *adj* nervous; (*irritabile*) bad-tempered; **avere il** ~ be irritable; **esaurimento** ~ nervous breakdown

'nespol|a *f* medlar. ~**o** *m* medlar[-tree]

'nesso *m* link

nes'suno *adj* no, not... any; (*qualche*) any; **non ho nessun problema** I don't have any problems, I have no problems; **non lo trovo da nessuna parte** I can't find it anywhere; **in nessun modo** on no account ● *pron* nobody, no one, not... anybody, not... anyone; (*qualcuno*) anybody, anyone; **hai delle domande? – nessuna** do you have any questions? –

none; ~ di voi none of you; ~ dei due *(di voi due)* neither of you; non ho visto ~ dei tuoi amici I haven't seen any of your friends; c'è ~? is anybody there?

net'tare *vt* clean

net'tezza *f* cleanliness. ~ urbana cleansing department

'netto *adj* clean; *(chiaro)* clear; *(Comm)* net; di ~ just like that

nettur'bino *m* dustman

neu'trale *adj* & *m* neutral. ~ità *f* neutrality. ~iz'zare *vt* neutralize. **'neutro** *adj* neutral; *(Gram)* neuter ● *m* *(Gram)* neuter

neu'trone *m* neutron

'neve *f* snow

nevi'care *vi* snow; ~ca it is snowing. ~cata *f* snowfall. ne'vischio *m* sleet. ne'voso *adj* snowy

nevral'gia *f* neuralgia

ne'vro|si *f inv* neurosis. ~tico *adj* neurotic

'nibbio *m* kite

'nicchia *f* niche

nicchi'are *vi* shilly-shally

'nichel *m* nickel

nichi'lista *adj* & *mf* nihilist

nico'tina *f* nicotine

nidi'ata *f* brood. 'nido *m* nest; *(giardino d'infanzia)* crèche

ni'ente *pron* nothing, not... anything; *(qualcosa)* anything; non ho fatto ~ di male I didn't do anything wrong; non ho fatto ~ di male I didn't do anything wrong; grazie! – di ~! thank you! – don't mention it!; non serve a ~ it's no use; vuoi ~? do you want anything?; da ~ *(poco importante)* minor; *(di poco valore)* worthless ● *adj inv* [Ⓣ] non ho ~ fame I'm not the slightest bit hungry ● *adv* non fa ~ *(non importa)* it doesn't matter; per ~ at all; *(litigare)* over nothing; ~ affatto! no way! ● *m* un bel ~ absolutely nothing

nientedi'meno, niente'meno *adv* ~ che no less than ● *int* fancy that!

'ninfa *f* nymph

nin'fea *f* water-lily

'ninnolo *m* plaything; *(fronzolo)* knick-knack

ni'pote *m* *(di zii)* nephew; *(di nonni)* grandson, grandchild ● *f* *(di zii)* niece; *(di nonni)* granddaughter, grandchild

'nitido *adj* neat; *(chiaro)* clear

ni'trato *m* nitrate

ni'tri|re *vi* neigh. ~to *m* *(di cavallo)* neigh

no *adv* no; *(con congiunzione)* not; dire di no say no; credo di no I don't think so; perché no? why not?; io no not me; fa freddo, no? it's cold, isn't it?

'nobil|e *adj* noble ● *m* noble, nobleman ● *f* noble, noblewoman. ~i'are *adj* noble. ~tà *f* nobility

'nocca *f* knuckle

nocci'ol|a *f* hazelnut. ~o *m* *(albero)* hazel

'nocciolo *m* stone; *fig* heart

'noce *f* walnut ● *m* *(albero, legno)* walnut. ~ moscata nutmeg. ~'pesca *f* nectarine

no'civo *adj* harmful

'nodo *m* knot; *fig* lump; *(Comput)* node; fare il ~ della cravatta do up one's tie. no'doso *adj* knotty

'noi *pers pron* *(soggetto)* we; *(oggetto, con prep)* us; chi è? – siamo ~ who is it? – it's us

'noia *f* boredom; *(fastidio)* bother; *(persona)* bore; dar ~ annoy

noi'altri *pers pron* we

noi'oso *adj* boring; *(fastidioso)* tiresome

noleggi'are *vt* hire; *(dare a noleggio)* hire out; charter *(nave, aereo)*. no'leggio *m* hire; *(di nave, aereo)* charter. 'nolo *m* hire; *(Naut)* freight; a nolo for hire

n

'**nomade** adj nomadic • mf nomad

'**nome** m name; (Gram) noun; a ~ di in the name of; di ~ by name. ~ di famiglia surname. ~ da ragazza maiden name. no'mea f reputation

nomencla'tura f nomenclature

no'mignolo m nickname

'**nomina** f appointment. nomi'nale adj nominal; (Gram) noun attrib

nomi'nare vt name; (menzionare) mention; (eleggere) appoint. ~'tivo adj nominative; (Comm) registered • m nominative; (nome) name

non adv not; ~ ti amo I do not love you; ~ c'è di che not at all

Per formare il negativo dei verbi regolari si usa l'ausiliare do: Non mi piace I don' like it

nonché conj (tanto meno) let alone (e anche) as well as

noncu'ran|te adj nonchalant; (negligente) indifferent. ~za f nonchalance; (negligenza) indifference

nondi'meno conj nevertheless

'**nonna** f grandmother

'**nonno** m grandfather; **nonni** pl grandparents

non'nulla m inv trifle

'**nono** adj & m ninth

nono'stante prep in spite of • conj although

nonvio'lento adj nonviolent

nord m north; del ~ northern

nord-'est m northeast; a ~ northeasterly

'**nordico** adj northern

nordocciden'tale adj northwestern

nordorien'tale adj northeastern

nord-'ovest m northwest; a ~ northwesterly

'**norma** f rule; (istruzione) instruction; a ~ di legge according to law; è buona ~ it's advisable

nor'mal|e adj normal. ~ità f normality. ~iz'zare vt normalize. ~'mente adv normally

norve'gese adj & mf Norwegian. Nor'vegia f Norway

'**nossignore** adv no way

nostal'gia f (di casa, patria) homesickness; (del passato) nostalgia; aver ~ be homesick; aver ~ di qcno miss sb. no'stalgico, -a adj nostalgic • mf reactionary

no'strano adj local; (fatto in casa) home-made

'**nostro** (il nostro m, la nostra f, i nostri mpl, le nostre fpl) poss adj our; quella macchina è nostra that car is ours; ~ padre our father; un ~ amico a friend of ours • poss pron ours

'**nota** f (segno) sign; (comunicazione, commento, musica) note; (conto) bill; (lista) list; degno di ~ noteworthy; prendere ~ take note. note pl caratteristiche distinguishing marks

no'tabile adj & m notable

no'taio m notary

no'ta|re vt (segnare) mark; (annotare) note down; (osservare) notice; far ~re qcsa point sth out. ~zi'one f marking; (annotazione) notation

'**notes** m inv notepad

no'tevole adj (degno di nota) remarkable; (grande) considerable

no'tifica f notification. notifi'care vt notify; (Comm) advise. ~zi'one f notification

no'tizi|a f una ~a a piece of news; (informazione) a piece of information; le ~e the news sg. ~'ario m news sg

'**noto** adj [well-]known; rendere ~ (far sapere) announce

notori'età f fame; raggiungere la ~ become famous. no'torio adj well-known; pej notorious

not'tambulo m night-bird

not'tata f night; far ~ stay up all night

'notte f night; di ~ at night; ~ **bianca** sleepless night. **~'tempo** adv at night

not'turno adj nocturnal; (servizio ecc) night

no'vanta adj & m ninety

novan't|enne adj & mf ninety-year-old. **~esimo** adj ninetieth. **~ina** f about ninety. **'nove** adj & m nine. nove'cento adj & m nine hundred. il Novecento the twentieth century

no'vella f short story

novel'lino, -a adj inexperienced ● mf novice, beginner. no'vello adj new

no'vembre m November

novità f inv novelty; (notizie) news sg; l'ultima ~ (moda) the latest fashion

novizi'ato m (Relig) novitiate; (tirocinio) apprenticeship

nozi'one f notion; nozioni pl rudiments

'nozze fpl marriage sg; (cerimonia) wedding sg. ~ d'argento silver wedding [anniversary]. ~ d'oro golden wedding [anniversary]

'nub|e f cloud. **~e tossica** toxic cloud. **~i'fragio** m cloudburst

'nubile adj unmarried ● f unmarried woman

'nuca f nape

nucle'are adj nuclear

'nucleo m nucleus; (unità) unit

nu'di|sta mf nudist. **~tà** f inv nudity

'nudo adj naked; (spoglio) bare; a occhio ~ to the naked eye

'nugolo m large number

'nulla pron = NIENTE

nulla'osta m inv permit

nullità f inv (persona) nonentity

'nullo adj (Jur) null and void

nume'ra|bile adj countable. **~le** adj & m numeral

nume'ra|re vt number. **~zi'one** f

numbering. nu'merico adj numerical

'numero m number; (romano, arabo) numeral; (di scarpe ecc) size; dare i numeri be off one's head. ~ cardinale cardinal [number]. ~ decimale decimal. ~ ordinale ordinal [number]. ~ di telefono phone number. ~ verde Freephone®. nume'roso adj numerous

'nunzio m nuncio

nu'ocere vi ~ a harm

nu'ora f daughter-in-law

nuo'ta|re vi swim; fig wallow. nu'oto m swimming. **~'tore, ~'trice** mf swimmer

nu'ov|a f (notizia) news sg. **~a'mente** adv again. **~o** adj new; di ~o again; rimettere a ~o give a new lease of life to

nutri'ente adj nourishing. **~'mento** m nourishment

nu'tri|re vt nourish; harbour (sentimenti). **~rsi** eat; **~rsi di** fig live on. **~'tivo** adj nourishing. **~zi'one** f nutrition

'nuvola f cloud. nuvo'loso adj cloudy

nuzi'ale adj nuptial; (vestito, anello ecc) wedding attrib

Oo

o conj or; ~ l'uno ~ l'altro one or the other, either

O abbr (ovest) W

'oasi f inv oasis

obbedi'ente ecc = UBBIDIENTE ecc

obbli'ga|re vt force, oblige; **~rsi** vr **~rsi a** undertake to. **~to** adj obliged. **~'torio** adj compulsory. **~zi'one** f obligation; (Comm) bond. **'obbligo** m obligation; (dovere) duty;

avere obblighi verso be under an obligation to; d'obbligo obligatory

obbligatoria'mente adv fare qcsa ~ be obliged to do sth

ob'bro|brio m disgrace. ~brioso adj disgraceful

obe'lisco m obelisk

obe'rare vt overburden

obesità f obesity. o'beso adj obese

obiet'tare vt/i object; ~ su object to

obiettivi'tà f objectivity. obiet'tivo adj objective ●m objective; (scopo) object

obie|t'tore m objector. ~ttore di coscienza conscientious objector. ~zi'one f objection

obi'torio m mortuary

o'blio m oblivion

o'bliquo adj oblique; fig underhand

oblite'rare vt obliterate

oblò m inv porthole

'oboe m oboe

obso'leto adj obsolete

'oca f (pl oche) goose

occasio'nal|e adj occasional. ~'mente** adv occasionally

occasi'one f occasion; (buon affare) bargain; (motivo) cause; (opportunità) chance; d'~ secondhand

occhi'aia f eye socket; occhiaie pl shadows under the eyes

occhi'ali mpl glasses, spectacles. ~ da sole sunglasses. ~ da vista glasses, spectacles

occhi'ata f look; dare un'~ a have a look at

occhieggi'are vt ogle ●vi peep

occhi'ello m buttonhole; (asola) eyelet

'occhio m eye; ~! watch out!; a quatt'occhi in private; tenere d'~ qcno keep an eye on sb; ~ [e croce] roughly; chiudere un'~ turn a blind eye; dare nell'~ attract attention; pagare o spendere un ~

pay an arm and a leg. ~ nero (pesto) black eye. ~ di pernice (callo) corn. ~'lino m fare l'~lino a qcno wink at sb

occiden'tale adj western ●mf westerner. occi'dente m west

oc'clu|dere vt obstruct. ~si'one f occlusion

occor'ren|te adj necessary ●m the necessary. ~za f need; all'~za if need be

oc'correre vi be necessary

occulta'mento m ~ di prove concealment of evidence

occul't|are vt hide. ~ismo m occult. oc'culto adj hidden; (magico) occult

occu'pante mf occupier. (abusivo) squatter

occu'pa|re vt occupy; spend (tempo); take up (spazio); (dar lavoro a) employ. ~rsi vr occupy oneself; (trovare lavoro) find a job; (badare) look after. ~to adj engaged; (persona) busy; (posto) taken. ~zi'one f occupation

o'ceano m ocean. ~ Atlantico Atlantic [Ocean]. ~ Pacifico Pacific [Ocean]

'ocra f ochre

ocu'lare adj ocular; (testimone, bagno) eye attrib

ocula'tezza f care. ocu'lato adj (scelta) wise

ocu'lista mf optician; (per malattie) ophthalmologist

od conj or

'ode f ode

odi'are vt hate

odi'erno adj of today; (attuale) present

'odi|o m hatred; avere in ~o hate. ~'oso adj hateful

odo'ra|re vt smell; (profumare) perfume ●vi ~re di smell of. ~to m sense of smell. o'dore m smell; (pro-

fumo) scent; **c'è odore di...** there's a smell of...; **sentire odore di** smell; **odori** pl (Culin) herbs. **odo'roso** adj fragrant

of'fender|e vt offend; (*ferire*) injure. **∼si** vr take offence

offen'siv|a f (Mil) offensive. **∼o** adj offensive

offe'rente mf offerer; (*in aste*) bidder

of'fert|a f offer; (*donazione*) donation; (Comm) supply; (*nelle aste*) bid; **in ∼a speciale** on special offer. **∼o** pp di **offrire**

of'fes|a f offence. **∼o** pp di **offendere** ● adj offended

offi'ciare vt officiate

offi'cina f workshop; **∼** [**meccanica**] garage

of'frir|e vt offer. **∼si** vr offer oneself; (*occasione:*) present itself; **∼si di fare qcsa** offer to do sth

offu'scar|e vt darken; *fig* dull (*memoria, bellezza*); blur (*vista*). **∼si** vr darken; *fig:* (*memoria, bellezza*) fade away; (*vista:*) become blurred

of'talmico adj ophthalmic

oggettività f objectivity. **ogget'tivo** adj objective

og'getto m object; (*argomento*) subject; **oggetti** pl **smarriti** lost property, lost and found Am

'oggi adv & m today; (*al giorno d'oggi*) nowadays; **da ∼ in poi** from today on; **∼ a otto** a week today; **dall'∼ al domani** overnight; **al giorno d'∼** nowadays. **∼gi'orno** adv nowadays

'ogni adj inv every; (*qualsiasi*) any; **∼ tre giorni** every three days; **ad ∼ costo** at any cost; **ad ∼ modo** anyway; **∼ cosa** everything; **∼ tanto** now and then; **∼ volta che** whenever

o'gnuno pron everyone, everybody; **∼ di voi** each of you

'ola f inv Mexican wave

O'lan|da f Holland. **o∼'dese** adj

Dutch ● m Dutchman; (*lingua*) Dutch ● f Dutchwoman

ole'andro m oleander

ole'at|o adj oiled; **carta ∼a** greaseproof paper

oleo'dotto m oil pipeline. **ole'oso** adj oily

ol'fatto m sense of smell

oli'are vt oil

oli'era f cruet

olim'piadi fpl Olympic Games. **o'limpico** adj Olympic. **olim'pionico** adj (*primato, squadra*) Olympic

'olio m oil; **sott'∼** in oil; **colori a ∼** oils; **quadro a ∼** oil painting. **∼ di mais** corn oil. **∼ d'oliva** olive oil. **∼ di semi** vegetable oil. **∼ solare** suntan oil

o'liv|a f olive. **oli'vastro** adj olive. **oli'veto** m olive grove. **∼o** m olive tree

'olmo m elm

oltraggi'are vt offend. **ol'traggio** m offence

ol'tranza f **ad ∼** to the bitter end

'oltre adv (*di luogo*) further; (*di tempo*) longer ● prep (*di luogo*) over; (*di tempo*) later than; (*più di*) more than; (*in aggiunta*) besides; **∼ a** (*eccetto*) except, apart from; **per ∼ due settimane** for more than two weeks. **∼'mare** adv overseas. **∼'modo** adv extremely

oltrepas'sare vt go beyond; (*eccedere*) exceed

o'maggio m homage; (*dono*) gift; **in ∼** con free with; **omaggi** pl (*saluti*) respects

ombeli'cale adj umbilical. **ombe'lico** m navel

'ombr|a f (*zona*) shade; (*immagine oscura*) shadow; **all'∼a** in the shade. **∼eggi'are** vt shade

om'brello m umbrella. **ombrel'lone** m beach umbrella

om'bretto m eye-shadow

om'broso adj shady

ome**'lette** f inv omelette

ome**'lia** f (Relig) sermon

omeopa**'tia** f homoeopathy. omeo**'patico** adj homoeopathic ●m homoeopath

omertà f conspiracy of silence

o**'messo** pp di omettere

o**'mettere** vt omit

OMG m abbr (organismo modificato geneticamente) GMO

omi**'cid|a** adj murderous ●mf murderer. ~io m murder. ~io colposo manslaughter

omissi**'one** f omission

omogeneiz**'zato** adj homogenized. omo**'geneo** adj homogeneous

omolo**'gare** vt approve

o**'monimo, -a** mf namesake ●m (parola) homonym

omosessu**'al|e** adj & mf homosexual. ~ità f homosexuality

On. abbr (onorevole) MP

'oncia f ounce

'onda f wave; andare in ~ Radio go on the air. onde pl corte short wave. onde pl lunghe long wave. onde pl medie medium wave. on**'data** f wave

ondeggi**'are** vi wave; (barca:) roll

ondula**|'torio** adj undulating. ~zi**'one** f undulation; (di capelli) wave

'oner|e m burden. ~**'oso** adj onerous

onestà f honesty; (rettitudine) integrity. o**'nesto** adj honest; (giusto) just

'onice f onyx

onnipo**'tente** adj omnipotent

onnipre**'sente** adj ubiquitous; Rel omnipresent

ono**'mastico** m name-day

ono**ra'bile** adj honourable. ~re vt (fare onore a) be a credit to; honour (promessa). ~rio adj honorary ●m fee. ~rsi vr ~rsi di be proud of

o**'nore** m honour; in ~ di (festa, ri-

cevimento) in honour of; fare ~ a do justice to (pranzo); farsi ~ in excel in

ono**'revole** adj honourable. ●mf Member of Parliament

onorifi**'cenza** f honour; (decorazione) decoration. ono**'rifico** adj honorary

O.N.U. f abbr (Organizzazione delle Nazioni Unite) UN

o**'paco, -a** adj opaque; (colori ecc) dull; (fotografia, rossetto) matt

o**'pale** f opal

'opera f (lavoro) work; (azione) deed; (Mus) opera; (teatro) opera house; (ente) institution; mettere in ~ put into effect; mettersi all'~ get to work; opere pl pubbliche public works. ~ d'arte work of art. ~ lirica opera

ope**'raio, -a** adj working ●mf worker; ~ specializzato skilled worker

ope**'ra|re** vt (Med) operate on; farsi ~re have an operation ●vi operate; (agire) work. ~**'tivo**, ~**'torio** adj operating attrib. ~**'tore, -'trice** mf operator; (TV) cameraman. ~**'tore** turistico tour operator. ~zi**'one** f operation; (Comm) transaction

ope**'retta** f operetta

ope**'roso** adj industrious

opini**'one** f opinion. ~ pubblica public opinion, vox pop

'oppio m opium

oppo**'nente** adj opposing ●mf opponent

op**'por|re** vt oppose; (obiettare) object; ~re resistenza offer resistance. ~**si** vr ~**si** a oppose

opportu**'ni|smo** m expediency. ~**sta** mf opportunist. ~tà f inv opportunity; (l'essere opportuno) timeliness. oppor**'tuno** adj opportune; (adeguato) appropriate; il momento opportuno the right moment

opposi**|'tore** m opposer. ~zi**'one** f

opposition; d'∼**zione** (giornale, partito) opposition

op'posto pp di opporre ● adj opposite; (opinioni) opposing ● m opposite; all'∼ on the contrary

oppres|si'one f oppression. ∼'sivo adj oppressive. op'presso pp di **opprimere** adj oppressed. ∼'sore m oppressor

oppri'me|nte adj oppressive. op'primere vt oppress; (gravare) weigh down

op'pure conj otherwise, or [else]; lunedì ∼ martedì Monday or Tuesday

op'tare vi ∼ per opt for

opu'lento adj opulent

o'puscolo m booklet; (pubblicitario) brochure

opzio'nale adj optional. opzi'one f option

'ora[1] f time; (unità) hour; di buon'∼ early; che ∼ è?, che ore sono? what time is it?; mezz'∼ half an hour; a ore (lavorare, pagare) by the hour; 50 km all'∼ 50 km an hour; a un'∼ di macchina one hour by car. ∼ d'arrivo arrival time. l'∼ esatta (Teleph) speaking clock. ∼ legale daylight saving time. ∼ di punta, ore pl di punta peak time; (per il traffico) rush hour

'ora[2] adv now; (tra poco) presently; ∼ come ∼ at the moment; d'∼ in poi from now on; per ∼ for the time being, for now; è ∼ di finirla! that's enough now! ● conj (dunque) now [then]; ∼ che ci penso,... now that I come to think about it,...

'orafo m goldsmith

o'rale adj & m oral; per via ∼ by mouth

ora'mai adv = ORMAI

o'rario adj (tariffa) hourly; (segnale) time attrib; (velocità) per hour ● m time; (tabella dell'orario) timetable, schedule Am; essere in ∼ to be on time; in senso ∼ clockwise. ∼ di chiusura closing time. ∼ flessibile flexitime. ∼ di sportello banking hours. ∼ d'ufficio business hours. ∼ di visita (Med) consulting hours

o'rata f gilthead

ora'tore, -'trice mf speaker

ora'torio, -a adj oratorical ● m (Mus) oratorio ● f oratory. orazi'one f (Relig) prayer

'orbita f orbit; (Anat) [eye-]socket

or'chestra f orchestra; (parte del teatro) pit

orche'stra|le adj orchestral ● mf member of an/the orchestra. ∼re vt orchestrate

orchi'dea f orchid

'orco m ogre

'orda f horde

or'digno m device; (arnese) tool. ∼ esplosivo explosive device

ordi'nale adj & m ordinal

ordina'mento m order; (leggi) rules pl.

ordi'nanza f bylaw; d'∼ (soldato) on duty

ordi'nare vt (sistemare) arrange; (comandare) order; (prescrivere) prescribe; (Relig) ordain

ordi'nario adj ordinary; (grossolano) common; (professore) with tenure; di ordinaria amministrazione routine ● m ordinary; (Univ) professor

ordi'nato adj (in ordine) tidy

ordinazi'one f order; fare un'∼ place an order

'ordine m order; (di avvocati, medici) association; mettere in ∼ put in order; di prim'∼ first-class; di terz'∼e (film, albergo) third- rate; di ∼ pratico/economico of a practical/economic nature; fino a nuovo ∼ until further notice; parola d'∼ password. ∼ del giorno agenda. ordini sacri pl Holy Orders

or'dire vt (tramare) plot

orec'chino m ear-ring

o'recchi|o m (pl f orecchie) ear; avere ~o have a good ear; mi è giunto all'~o che... I've heard that...; ~'oni pl (Med) mumps sg

o'refice m jeweller. ~'ria f (arte) goldsmith's art; (negozio) goldsmith's [shop]

'orfano, -a adj orphan. ● mf orphan. ~'trofio m orphanage

orga'netto m barrel-organ; (a bocca) mouth-organ; (fisarmonica) accordion

or'ganico adj organic ● m personnel

orga'nismo m organism; (corpo umano) body

orga'nista mf organist

organiz'za|re vt organize. ~rsi vr get organized. ~'tore, ~'trice mf organizer. ~zi'one f organization

'organo m organ

or'gasmo m orgasm

'orgia f orgy

or'gogli|o m pride. ~'oso adj proud

orien'tale adj eastern; (cinese ecc) oriental

orienta'mento m orientation; perdere l'~ lose one's bearings; senso dell'~ sense of direction

orien'ta|re vt orientate. ~rsi vr find one's bearings; (tendere) steer

ori'ente m east. l'Estremo O~ the Far East. il Medio O~ the Middle East

o'rigano m oregano

origi'na|le adj original; (eccentrico) odd ● m original. ~lità f originality. ~re vt/i originate. ~rio adj (nativo) native

o'rigine f origin; in ~ originally; aver ~ da originate from; dare ~ a give rise to

o'rina f urine. ori'nale m chamberpot. ori'nare vi urinate

ori'undo adj native

orizzon'tale adj horizontal

orizzon'tare vt = ORIENTARE. oriz'zonte m horizon

or'la|re vt hem. ~'tura f hem. 'orlo m edge; (di vestito ecc) hem

'orma f track; (di piede) footprint; (impronta) mark

or'mai adv by now; (passato) by then; (quasi) almost

ormeggi'are vt moor

ormo'nale adj hormonal. or'mone m hormone

ornamen'tale adj ornamental. orna'mento m ornament

or'na|re vt decorate. ~rsi vr deck oneself; (di festa) deck. ~to adj (stile) ornate

ornitolo'gia f ornithology

'oro m gold; d'~ gold; fig golden

orologi'aio, -a mf clockmaker, watchmaker

oro'logio m watch; (da tavolo, muro ecc) clock. ~ a pendolo grandfather clock. ~ da polso wrist-watch. ~ a sveglia alarm clock

o'roscopo m horoscope

or'rendo adj awful, dreadful

or'ribile adj horrible

orripi'lante adj horrifying

or'rore m horror; avere qcsa in ~ hate sth

orsacchi'otto m teddy bear

'orso m bear; (persona scontrosa) hermit. ~ bianco polar bear

or'taggio m vegetable

or'tensia f hydrangea

or'tica f nettle

orticol'tura f horticulture. 'orto m vegetable plot

orto'dosso adj orthodox

ortogo'nale adj perpendicular

orto|gra'fia f spelling. ~'grafico adj spelling attrib

orto'lano m market gardener; (ne-gozio) greengrocer's

orto|pe'dia f orthopaedics sg. ~'pedico adj orthopaedic ●m orthopaedist

orzai'olo m sty

or'zata f barley-water

o'sare vt/i dare; (avere audacia) be daring

oscenità f inv obscenity. o'sceno adj obscene

oscil'la|re vi swing; (prezzi ecc:) fluctuate; Tech oscillate; (fig: essere indeciso) vacillate. ~zi'one f swinging; (di prezzi) fluctuation; Tech oscillation

oscura'mento m darkening; (di vista, mente) dimming; (totale) black-out

oscu'r|are vt darken; fig obscure. ~arsi vr get dark. ~ità f darkness. o'scuro adj dark; (triste) gloomy; (incomprensibile) obscure

ospe'dal|e m hospital. ~i'ero adj hospital attrib

ospi'ta|le adj hospitable. ~lità f hospitality. ~re vt give hospitality to. 'ospite m (chi ospita) host; (chi viene ospitato) guest ●f hostess; guest

o'spizio m [old people's] home

ossa'tura f bone structure; (di romanzo) structure, framework. 'osseo adj bone attrib

ossequi'|are vt pay one's respects to. os'sequio m homage; ossequi pl respects. ~'oso adj obsequious

osser'van|te adj (cattolico) practising. ~za f observance

osser'va|re vt observe; (notare) notice; keep (ordine, silenzio). ~tore, ~trice mf observer. ~'torio m (Astr) observatory; (Mil) observation post. ~zi'one f observation; (rimprovero) reproach

ossessio'na|nte adj haunting; (persona) nagging. ~re vt obsess; (infastidire) nag. ossessi'one f obses-

sion. osses'sivo adj obsessive. os-'sesso adj obsessed

os'sia conj that is

ossi'dabile adj liable to tarnish

ossi'dar|e vt, ~si vr oxidize

'ossido m oxide. ~ di carbonio carbon monoxide

os'sidrico adj fiamma ossidrica blowlamp

ossige'nar|e vt oxygenate; (decolorare) bleach; fig put back on its feet (azienda). ~si vr ~si i capelli dye one's hair blonde. os'sigeno m oxygen

'osso m ((Anat): pl f ossa) bone; (di frutto) stone

osso'buco m marrowbone

os'suto adj bony

osta'co|lare vt hinder, obstruct. o'stacolo m obstacle; Sport hurdle

o'staggio m hostage; prendere in ~ take hostage

o'stello m ~ della gioventù youth hostel

osten'ta|re vt show off; ~re indifferenza pretend to be indifferent. ~zi'one f ostentation

oste'ria f inn

o'stetrico, -a adj obstetric ●mf obstetrician

'ostia f host; (cialda) wafer

'ostico adj tough

o'stil|e adj hostile. ~ità f inv hostility

osti'na|rsi vr persist (a in). ~to adj obstinate. ~zi'one f obstinacy

'ostrica f oyster

ostru'ire vt obstruct. ~zi'one f obstruction

otorinolaringoi'atra mf ear, nose and throat specialist

ottago'nale adj octagonal. ot'tagono m octagon

ot'tan|ta adj & m eighty. ~'tenne

adj & mf eighty-year-old. ~'tesimo adj eightieth. ~'tina f about eighty

ot'tav|a f octave. ~o adj eighth

otte'nere vt obtain; (più comune) get; (conseguire) achieve

'ottico, -a adj optic[al] • mf optician • f (scienza) optics sg; (di lenti ecc) optics pl

otti'ma|le adj optimum. ~'mente adv very well

otti'mis|mo m optimism. ~ta mf optimist. ~tico adj optimistic

'ottimo adj very good • m optimum

'otto adj & m eight

ot'tobre m October

otto'cento adj & m eight hundred; l'O~ the nineteenth century

ot'tone m brass

ottu'ra|re vt block; fill (dente). ~rsi vr clog. ~'tore m (Phot) shutter. ~zi'one f stopping; (di dente) filling

ot'tuso pp di ottundere • adj obtuse

o'vaia f ovary

o'vale adj & m oval

o'vatta f cotton wool

ovazi'one f ovation

over'dose f inv overdose

'ovest m west

o'vi|le m sheep-fold. ~no adj sheep attrib

ovo'via f two-seater cable car

ovulazi'one f ovulation

o'vunque adv = DOVUNQUE

ov'vero conj or; (cioè) that is

ovvia'mente adv obviously

ovvi'are vi ~ a qcsa counter sth. 'ovvio adj obvious

ozi'are vi laze around. 'ozio m idleness. ozi'oso adj idle; (questione) pointless

o'zono m ozone; buco nell'~ hole in the ozone layer

Pp

pa'ca|re vt quieten. ~to adj quiet

pac'chetto m packet; (postale) parcel, package; (di sigarette) pack, packet. ~ software software package

'pacchia f 🔢 bed of roses

pacchi'ano adj garish

'pacco m parcel; (involto) bundle. ~ regalo gift-wrapped package

paccot'tiglia f junk, rubbish

'pace f peace; darsi ~ forget it; fare ~ con qcno make it up with sb; lasciare in ~ qcno leave sb in peace

pachi'stano, -a mf & adj Pakistani

pacifi'ca|re vt reconcile; (mettere pace) pacify. ~zi'one f reconciliation

pa'cifico adj pacific; (calmo) peaceful; il P~ the Pacific

paci'fis|mo m pacifism. ~ta mf pacifist

pa'dano adj pianura padana Po Valley

pa'del|la f frying-pan; (per malati) bedpan

padigli'one m pavilion

'padr|e m father; ~i pl (antenati) forefathers. ~'drino m godfather. ~e'nostro m il ~enostro the Lord's Prayer. ~e'terno m God Almighty

padro'nanza f mastery. ~ di sé self-control

pa'drone, -a mf master; mistress; (datore di lavoro) boss; (proprietario) owner. ~ggi'are vt master

pae'sag|gio m scenery; (pittura) landscape. ~'gista mf landscape architect

pae'sano, -a adj country • mf villager

pa'ese m (*nazione*) country; (*territorio*) land; (*villaggio*) village; il Bel P~ Italy; va' a quel ~! get lost!; Paesi pl Bassi Netherlands

paf'futo adj plump

'paga f pay, wages pl

pa'gabile adj payable

pa'gaia f paddle

paga'mento m payment; a ~ (*parcheggio*) which you have to pay to use. ~ anticipato (Comm) advance payment. ~ alla consegna cash on delivery, COD

pa'gano, -a adj & mf pagan

pa'gare vt/i pay; ~ da bere a qcno buy sb a drink

pa'gella f [school] report

'pagina f page. Pagine pl Gialle® Yellow Pages. ~ web (Comput) web page

'paglia f straw

pagliac'cetto m (*per bambini*) rompers pl

pagliac'ciata f farce

pagli'accio m clown

pagli'aio m haystack

paglie'riccio m straw mattress

pagli'etta f (*cappello*) boater; (*per pentole*) steel wool

pagli'uzza f wisp of straw; (*di metallo*) particle

pa'gnotta f [round] loaf

pail'lette f inv sequin

'paio m (pl **paia**) pair; un ~ (*circa due*) a couple; un ~ di (*scarpe, forbici*) a pair of

'Pakistan m Pakistan

'pala f shovel; (*di remo, elica*) blade; (*di ruota*) paddle

pala'fitta f pile-dwelling

pala'sport m inv indoor sports arena

pa'late fpl a ~ (*fare soldi*) hand over fist

pa'lato m palate

palaz'zetto m ~ dello sport indoor sports arena

palaz'zina f villa

pa'lazzo m palace; (*edificio*) building. ~ delle esposizioni exhibition centre. ~ di giustizia law courts pl, courthouse. ~ dello sport indoor sports arena

'palco m (*pedana*) platform; (Theat) box. ~['scenico] m stage

pale'sar|e vt disclose. ~si vr reveal oneself. **pa'lese** adj evident

Pale'sti|na f Palestine. ~'nese mf Palestinian

pa'lestra f gymnasium, gym; (*ginnastica*) gymnastics pl

pa'letta f spade; (*per focolare*) shovel. ~ [della spazzatura] dustpan

pa'letto m peg

'palio m (*premio*) prize. il P~ horse-race held at Siena

paliz'zata f fence

'palla f ball; (*proiettile*) bullet; (🎱: *bugia*) porkie; che palle! 🎱 this is a pain in the arse!. ~ di neve snowball. ~ al piede fig millstone round one's neck

pallaca'nestro f basketball

palla'mano f handball

pallanu'oto f water polo

palla'volo f volley-ball

palleggi'are vi (*calcio*) practise ball control; Tennis knock up

pallia'tivo m palliative

'pallido adj pale

pal'lina f (*di vetro*) marble

pal'lino m avere il ~ del calcio be crazy about football

pallon'cino m balloon; (*lanterna*) Chinese lantern; (🎈: *etilometro*) Breathalyzer®

pal'lone m ball; (*calcio*) football; (*aerostato*) balloon

pal'lore m pallor

pal'loso adj 🅇 boring

pal'lottola f pellet; (proiettile) bullet

'palm|a f (Bot) palm. ~o m (Anat) palm; (misura) hand's-breadth; restare con un ~o di naso feel disappointed

pal'mare m palmtop

'palo m pole; (di sostegno) stake; (in calcio) goalpost; fare il ~ (ladro:) keep a lookout. ~ della luce lamppost

palom'baro m diver

pal'pare vt feel

'palpebra f eyelid

palpi'ta|re vi throb; (fremere) quiver. ~zi'one f palpitation. 'palpito m throb; (del cuore) beat

pa'lude f marsh, swamp

palu'doso adj marshy

pa'lustre adj marshy; (piante, uccelli) marsh attrib

'pampino m vine leaf

'panca f bench; (in chiesa) pew

pancar'ré f sliced bread

pan'cetta f (Culin) bacon; (di una certa età) paunch

pan'chetto m [foot]stool

pan'china f garden seat; (in calcio) bench

'pancia f belly; mal di ~ stomachache; metter su ~ develop a paunch; a ~ in giù lying face down

panci'olle: stare in ~ lounge about

panci'one m (persona) pot belly

panci'otto m waistcoat

pande'monio m pandemonium

pan'doro m sponge cake eaten at Christmas

'pane m bread; (pagnotta) loaf; (di burro) block. ~ a cassetta sliced bread. pan grattato breadcrumbs pl. ~ di segale rye bread. ~ di Spagna sponge cake. ~ tostato toast

panett'e'ria f bakery; (negozio) baker's [shop]. ~i'ere, -a rf baker

panet'tone m kind of Christmas cake

'panfilo m yacht

pan'forte m nougat-like delicacy from Siena

'panico m panic; lasciarsi prendere dal ~ panic

pani'ere m basket; (cesta) hamper

pani'ficio m bakery; (negozio) baker's [shop]

pa'nino m [bread] roll. ~ imbottito filled roll. ~ al prosciutto ham roll. ~'teca f sandwich bar

'panna f cream. ~ da cucina [single] cream. ~ montata whipped cream

'panne f (Mech) in ~ broken down; restare in ~ break down

pan'nello m panel. ~ solare solar panel

'panno m cloth; panni pl (abiti) clothes

pan'nocchia f (di granoturco) cob

panno'lino m (per bambini) nappy; (da donna) sanitary towel

pano'rama m panorama; fig overview. ~ico adj panoramic

pantacol'lant mpl leggings

pantalon'cini mpl ~ [corti] shorts

panta'loni mpl trousers, pants Am

pan'tano m bog

pan'tera f panther; (auto della polizia) high-speed police car

pan'tofo|la f slipper

pan'zana f fib

pao'nazzo adj purple

'papa m Pope

papà m inv dad[dy]

pa'pale adj papal

papa'lina f skull-cap

papa'razzo m paparazzo

pa'pato m papacy

pa'pavero m poppy

'paper|a f (errore) slip of the tongue. ~o m gosling

papil'lon m inv bow tie

pa'piro m papyrus

'**pappa** f (per bambini) pap

pappa'gallo m parrot

pappa'molle mf wimp

'**para** f suole fpl di ~ crêpe soles

pa'rabola f parable; (curva) parabola. ~ satellitare satellite dish

para'bolico adj parabolic

para'brezza m inv windscreen, windshield Am

paracadu'tar|e vt parachute. ~si vr parachute

paraca'du|te m inv parachute. ~'tista** mf parachutist

para'carro m roadside post

paradi'siaco adj heavenly

para'diso m paradise. ~ terrestre Eden, earthly paradise

parados'sale adj paradoxical. pa-ra'dosso m paradox

para'fango m mudguard

paraf'fina f paraffin

parafra'sare vt paraphrase

para'fulmine m lightning-conductor

pa'raggi mpl neighbourhood sg

parago'na|bile adj comparable (a to). ~re vt compare. para'gone m comparison; a paragone di in comparison with

pa'ragrafo m paragraph

pa'ra|lisi f inv paralysis. ~'litico, -a adj & mf paralytic. ~liz'zare vt paralyse

paral'lel|a f parallel line. ~a'mente adv in parallel. ~o agg & m parallel; ~e pl parallel bars. ~o'gramma m parallelogram

para'lume m lampshade

para'medico m paramedic

pa'rametro m parameter

para'noia f paranoia

para'occhi mpl blinkers. parao'recchie mpl earmuffs

Paraolim'piadi fpl Paralympic Games

para'petto m parapet

para'piglia m turmoil

para'plegico, -a adj & mf paraplegic

pa'rar|e vt (addobbare) adorn; (riparare) shield; save (tiro, pallone); ward off, parry (schiaffo, pugno) ● vi (mirare) lead up to. ~si vr (abbigliarsi) dress up; (da pioggia, pugni) protect oneself; ~si dinanzi a qcno appear in front of sb

para'sole m inv parasol

paras'sita adj parasitic ● m parasite

parasta'tale adj government-controlled

pa'rata f parade; (in calcio) save; (in scherma, pugilato) parry

para'urti m inv (Auto) bumper, fender Am

para'vento m screen

par'cella f bill

parcheggi'a|re vt park. par'cheggio m parking; (posteggio) carpark, parking lot Am. ~'tore, ~'trice mf parking attendant. ~'tore abusivo person extorting money for guarding cars

par'chimetro m parking-meter

'**parco**[1] adj sparing; (moderato) moderate

'**parco**[2] m park. ~ a tema theme park. ~ di divertimenti fun fair. ~ giochi playground. ~ naturale wildlife park. ~ nazionale national park. ~ regionale [regional] wildlife park

pa'recchi adj a good many ● pron several

pa'recchio adj quite a lot of ● pron quite a lot ● adv rather; (parecchio tempo) quite a time

pareggi'are vt level; (eguagliare) equal; (Comm) balance ● vi draw

pa'reggio m (Comm) balance; Sport draw

paren'tado m relatives pl; (vincolo di sangue) relationship

pa'rente mf relative. ~ stretto

close relation

paren'tela f relatives pl; (vincolo di sangue) relationship

pa'rentesi f inv parenthesis; (segno grafico) bracket; (fig: pausa) break. ~ pl graffe curly brackets. ~ quadre square brackets. ~ tonde round brackets

pa'reo m sarong

pa'rere[1] m opinion; a mio ~ in my opinion

pa'rere[2] vi seem; (pensare) think; che te ne pare? what do you think of it?; pare di sì it seems so

pa'rete f wall; (in alpinismo) face. ~ divisoria partition wall

'pari adj inv equal; (numero) even; andare di ~ passo keep pace; arrivare a ~ draw; ~ ~ (copiare, ripetere) word for word ● m/f inv equal; ragazza alla ~ au pair [girl] ● m (titolo nobiliare) peer

Pa'rigi f Paris

pa'riglia f pair

pari|tà f equality; Tennis deuce. ~'tario adj parity attrib

parlamen'tare adj parliamentary ● m/f Member of Parliament ● vi discuss. **parla'mento** m Parliament. il Parlamento europeo the European Parliament

par'la|re vt/i speak, talk; (confessare) talk; ~ bene/male di qcno speak well/ill of somebody; non parliamone più let's forget about it; non se ne parla nemmeno! don't even mention it!. ~to adj (lingua) spoken. ~'torio m parlour; (in prigione) visiting room

parlot'tare vi mutter. **parlot'tio** m muttering

parmigi'ano m Parmesan

paro'dia f parody

pa'rola f word; (facoltà) speech; parole pl (di canzone) words, lyrics; parole la ~ a address; dare a qcno la propria ~ give sb one's

word; **in parole povere** crudely speaking. **parole** pl incrociate crossword [puzzle] sg. ~ **d'ordine** password. **paro'laccia** f swear-word

par'quet m inv (pavimento) parquet flooring

par'rocchi|a f parish. ~'ale adj parish attrib. ~'ano, -a m/f parishioner. **'parroco** m parish priest

par'rucca f wig

parrucchi'ere, -a m/f hairdresser

parruc'chino m toupée, hairpiece

parsi'monia f thrift

'parso pp di parere

'parte f part; (lato) side; (partito) party; (porzione) share; a ~ apart from; in ~ in part; la maggior ~ di the majority of; d'altra ~ on the other hand; da ~ aside; (in disparte) to one side; farsi da ~ stand aside; da ~ di from; (per conto di) on behalf of; è gentile da ~ tua it is kind of you; fare una brutta ~ a qcno behave badly towards sb; da che ~ è...? whereabouts is...?; da una ~..., dall'altra... on the one hand..., on the other hand...; dall'altra ~ on the other side of; da nessuna ~ nowhere; da tutte le parti (essere) everywhere; da questa ~ (in questa direzione) this way; da un anno a questa ~ for about a year now; essere dalla ~ di qcno be on sb's side; essere ~ in causa be involved; prendere ~ a take part in. ~ civile plaintiff

parteci'pante m/f participant

parteci'pa|re vi ~re a participate in, take part in; (condividere) share in. ~zi'one f participation; (annuncio) announcement; Fin shareholding; (presenza) presence. **par'tecipe** adj participating

parteggi'are vi ~ per side with

par'tenza f departure; Sport start; in ~ per leaving for

parti'cella f particle

parti'cipio m participle

partico'lar|e adj particular; (privato) private ●m detail, particular; fin nei minimi ~i down to the smallest detail. ~eggi'ato adj detailed. ~ità f inv particularity; (dettaglio) detail

partigi'ano, -a adj & mf partisan

par'tire vi leave; (aver inizio) start; a ~ da [beginning] from

par'tita f game; (incontro) match; (Comm) lot; (contabilità) entry. ~ a calcio football match. ~ a carte game of cards

par'tito m party; (scelta) choice; (occasione di matrimonio) match

'parto m childbirth; un ~ facile an easy birth o labour; dolori pl del ~ labour pains. ~ cesareo Caesarean section. ~'rire vt give birth to

par'venza f appearance

parzi'al|e adj partial. ~ità f partiality. ~mente adv (non completamente) partially; ~mente scremato semi-skimmed

pasco'lare vt graze. **'pascolo** m pasture

'Pasqua f Easter. **pa'squale** adj Easter attrib

'passa: e ~ adv (e oltre) plus

pas'sabile adj passable

pas'saggio m passage; (traversata) crossing; Sport pass; (su veicolo) lift; essere di ~ be passing through. ~ a livello level crossing, grade crossing Am. ~ pedonale pedestrian crossing

pas'sante mf passer-by ●m (di cintura) loop ● adj Tennis passing

passa'porto m passport

pas'sa|re vi pass; (attraversare) pass through; (far visita) call; (andare) go; (essere approvato) be passed; ~re alla storia go down in history; mi è ~to di mente it slipped my mind; ~re per un genio/idiota be taken for a genius/an idiot ●vt (far scorrere) pass over; (sopportare) go through; (al tele-

fono) put through; (Culin) strain; ~re di moda go out of fashion; le passo il signor Rossi I'll put you through to Mr Rossi; ~rsela bene be well off; come la passi? how are you doing?. ~ta f (di vernice) coat; (spolverata) dusting; (occhiata) look

passa'tempo m pastime

pas'sato adj past; l'anno ~ last year; sono le tre passate it's past o after three o'clock ●m past; (Culin) purée; (Gram) past tense. ~ prossimo (Gram) present perfect. ~ remoto (Gram) [simple] past. ~ di verdure cream of vegetable soup

passaver'dure m inv food mill

passeg'gero, -a adj passing ●mf passenger

passeggi'a|re vi walk, stroll. ~ta f walk, stroll; (luogo) public walk; (in bicicletta) ride; fare una ~ta go for a walk

passeg'gino m pushchair, stroller Am

pas'seggio m walk; (luogo) promenade; andare a ~ go for a walk; scarpe da ~ walking shoes

passe-partout m inv master-key

passe'rella f gangway; (Aeron) boarding bridge; (per sfilate) catwalk

'passero m sparrow. **passe'rotto** m (passero) sparrow

pas'sibile adj ~ di liable to

passio'nale adj passionate. **pas'sione** f passion

pas'sivo adj passive ●m passive; (Comm) liabilities pl; in ~ (bilancio) loss-making

pass magnetico m inv swipe card

'passo m step; (orma) footprint; (andatura) pace; (brano) passage; (valico) pass; a due passi da qui a stone's throw away; a ~ d'uomo at walking pace; fare due passi go for a stroll; di pari ~ fig hand in hand. ~ carrabile, ~ carraio driveway

'past|a f (impasto per pane ecc) dough; (per dolci, pasticcino) pastry; (pasta-sciutta) pasta; (massa molle) paste; fig nature. ~a frolla shortcrust pastry. pa'stella f batter

> **Pasta** A popular myth says that Marco Polo brought pasta back from China. Italians like to make their own pasta for special occasions (pasta fatta in casa), usually with eggs and sometimes with various fillings. Traditional pasta varies enormously from region to region, and sometimes the same name can be used for different types.

pastasci'utta f pasta
pa'stello m pastel
pa'sticca f pastille; ([I]: pastiglia) pill
pasticc|e'ria f cake shop, patisserie; (pasticcini) pastries pl; (arte) confectionery
pasticci'are vi make a mess • vt make a mess of
pasticci'ere, -a mf confectioner
pastic'cino m little cake
pa'sticci|o m (Culin) pie; (lavoro disordinato) mess. ~one, -a mf bungler • adj bungling
pasti'ficio m pasta factory
pa'stiglia f (Med) pill, tablet; (di menta) sweet. ~ dei freni brake pad
'pasto m meal
pasto'rale adj pastoral. pa'store m shepherd; (Relig) pastor. pastore tedesco German shepherd
pastoriz'za|re vt pasteurize. ~zi'one f pasteurization
pa'stoso adj doughy; fig mellow
pa'stura f pasture; (per pesci) bait
pa'tacca f (macchia) stain; (fig: oggetto senza valore) piece of junk
pa'tata f potato. patate pl fritte chips Br, French fries. pata'tine fpl [potato] crisps, chips Am

pata'trac m inv (crollo) crash
pâté m inv pâté
pa'tella f limpet
pa'tema m anxiety
pa'tente f licence. ~ di guida driving licence
pater'na|le f scolding. ~lista m paternalist
paternità f paternity. pa'terno adj paternal; (affetto ecc) fatherly
pa'tetico adj pathetic. 'pathos m pathos
pa'tibolo m gallows sg
'patina f patina; (sulla lingua) coating
pa'ti|re vt/i suffer. ~to, -a adj suffering • mf fanatic. ~to della musica music lover
patolo'gia f pathology. pato'logico adj pathological
'patria f native land
patri'arca m patriarch
pa'trigno m stepfather
patrimoni'ale adj property attrib. patri'monio m estate
patri'o|ta mf patriot
pa'trizio, -a adj & mf patrician
patro|ci'nare vt support. ~'cinio m support
patro'nato m patronage. pa'trono m (Relig) patron saint; (Jur) counsel
'patta¹ f (di tasca) flap
'patta² f (pareggio) draw
patteggi|a'mento m bargaining. ~'are** vt/i negotiate
patti'naggio m skating. ~ su ghiaccio ice skating. ~ a rotelle roller skating
patti'na|re vi skate; (auto:) skid. ~'tore, ~'trice mf skater. 'pattino m skate; (Aeron) skid. pattino da ghiaccio iceskate. pattino a rotelle roller skate; pattini mpl in linea roller blades®.
'patto m deal; (Pol) pact; a ~ che on condition that

pat'tuglia f patrol. ~ stradale patrol car; highway patrol

pattu'ire vt negotiate

pattumi'era f dustbin, trashcan Am

pa'ura f fear; (spavento) fright; aver ~ be afraid; mettere ~ a frighten. pau'roso adj (che fa paura) frightening; (che ha paura) fearful; (🆒: enorme) awesome

'pausa f pause; (nel lavoro) break; fare una ~ pause; (nel lavoro) have a break

pavimen'ta|re vt pave (strada). ~zi'one f (operazione) paving. pavi'mento m floor

pa'vone m peacock

pazien'tare vi be patient

pazi'ente adj & mf patient. ~'mente adv patiently. pazi'enza f patience

'pazza f madwoman. ~'mente adv madly

paz'z|esco adj foolish; (esagerato) crazy. ~ia f madness; (azione) [act of] folly. 'pazzo adj mad; fig crazy • m madman; essere pazzo di/per be crazy about; darsi alla pazza gioia live it up. paz'zoide adj whacky

'pecca f fault; senza ~ flawless. peccami'noso adj sinful

pec'ca|re vi sin; ~re di be guilty of (ingratitudine). ~to m sin; ~to che... it's a pity that...; [che] ~to! [what a] pity!. ~'tore, ~'trice mf sinner

'pece f pitch

'peco|ra f sheep. ~ra nera black sheep. ~'raio m shepherd. ~'rella f cielo a ~relle sky full of fluffy white clouds. ~'rino m (formaggio) sheep's milk cheese

peculi'ar|e adj ~ di peculiar to. ~ità f inv peculiarity

pe'daggio m toll

pedago'gia f pedagogy. peda'gogico adj pedagogical

peda'lare vi pedal. pe'dale m pedal. pedalò m inv pedalo

pe'dana f footrest; Sport springboard

pe'dante adj pedantic. ~'ria f pedantry. pedan'tesco adj pedantic

pe'data f (in calcio) kick; (impronta) footprint

pede'rasta m pederast

pe'destre adj pedestrian

pedi'atra mf paediatrician. pedia-'tria f paediatrics sg

pedi'cure mf inv chiropodist, podiatrist Am • m pedicure

pedi'gree m inv pedigree

pe'dina f (nella dama) piece; fig pawn. ~'mento m shadowing. pedi'nare vt shadow

pe'dofilo, -a mf paedophile

pedo'nale adj pedestrian. pe'done, -a mf pedestrian

peeling m inv exfoliation treatment

'peggio adv worse; ~ per te! too bad!; la persona ~ vestita the worst dressed person • adj worse; niente di ~ nothing worse • m il ~ è che... the worst of it is that...; pensare al ~ think the worst • f alla ~ at worst; avere la ~ get the worst of it; alla meno ~ as best I can

peggiora'mento m worsening

peggio'ra|re vt make worse, worsen • vi get worse. ~'tivo adj pejorative

peggi'ore adj worse; (superlativo) worst • m il/la ~ the worst

'pegno m pledge; (nei giochi di società) forfeit; fig token

pelan'drone m slob

pe'la|re vt (spennare) pluck; (spellare) skin; (sbucciare) peel; (🆒: spillare denaro) fleece. ~rsi vr 🆒 lose one's hair. ~to adj bald. ~ti mpl (pomodori) peeled tomatoes

pel'lame m skins pl

'**pelle** f skin; (cuoio) leather; (buccia) peel; avere la ~ d'oca have goose-flesh

pellegri'naggio m pilgrimage. pelle'grino, -a mf pilgrim

pelle'rossa m Red Indian

pellette'ria f leather goods pl

pelli'cano m pelican

pellicce'ria f furrier's [shop]. pel-'licc'ia f fur; (indumento) fur coat. ~i'aio, -a mf furrier

pel'licola f film. ~ [trasparente] cling film

'pelo m hair; (di animale) coat; (di lana) pile; per un ~ by the skin of one's teeth. pe'loso adj hairy

'peltro m pewter

pe'luche m: giocattolo di ~ soft toy

pe'luria f down

'pelvico adj pelvic

'pena f (punizione) punishment; (sofferenza) pain; (dispiacere) sorrow; (disturbo) trouble; a mala ~ hardly; mi fa ~ I pity him; vale la ~ andare it is worth [while] going. ~ di morte death sentence

pe'nalle adj criminal; diritto m ~ e criminal law. ~ità f inv penalty

penaliz'zare vt penalize. ~zi'one f (penalità) penalty

pe'nare vi suffer; (faticare) find it difficult

pen'daglio m pendant

pen'dant m inv fare ~ [con] match

pen'denǀte adj hanging; (Comm) outstanding ● m (ciondolo) pendant; ~ti pl drop earrings. ~za f slope; (Comm) outstanding account

'pendere vi hang; (superficie:) slope; (essere inclinato) lean

pen'dio m slope; in ~ sloping

pendo'lare adj pendulum ● mf commuter; ~ino m (treno) special, first class only, fast train

'pendolo m pendulum

'pene m penis

pene'trante adj penetrating; (freddo) biting

pene'traǀre vt/i penetrate; (trafiggere) pierce ● vt (odore:) get into ● vi (entrare furtivamente) steal in. ~zi'one f penetration

penicil'lina f penicillin

pe'nisola f peninsula

peni'tenǀte adj & m penitent. ~za f penitence; (in gioco) forfeit. ~zi'ario m penitentiary

'penna f pen; (di uccello) feather. ~ a feltro felt-tip[ped pen]. ~ a sfera ball-point [pen]

pen'nacchio m plume

penna'rello m felt-tip[ped pen]

pennel'laǀre vt paint. ~ta f brushstroke. pen'nello m brush; a pennello (alla perfezione) perfectly

pen'nino m nib

pen'none m flagpole

pen'nuto adj feathered

pe'noso adj (🔢: pessimo) painful

pen'saǀre vt/i think; penso di sì think so; ~re a think of; remember to (chiudere il gas ecc); ci penso io I'll take care of it; ~re di fare qcsa think of doing sth; ~re fra sé e sé think to oneself ● vt think. ~ta f idea

pensi'eǀro m thought; (mente) mind; (preoccupazione) worry; stare in ~ro per be anxious about. ~'roso adj pensive

'pensiǀle adj hanging; giardino ~le roof-garden ● m (mobile) wall unit. ~'lina f bus shelter

pensio'nante mf boarder; (ospite pagante) lodger

pensio'nato, -a mf pensioner ● m (per anziani) [old folks'] home; (per studenti) hostel. pensi'one f pension; (albergo) boarding-house; (vitto e alloggio) board and lodging; andare in pensione retire; **mezza pensione** half board. **pensione completa** full board

pen'soso adj pensive

pen'tagono m pentagon

Pente'coste f Whitsun

penti|rsi vr ∼**rsi di** repent of; (rammaricarsi) regret. ∼**tismo** m turning informant. ∼**to** m Mafioso turned informant

'pentola f saucepan; (contenuto) potful. ∼ **a pressione** pressure cooker

pe'nultimo adj penultimate

pe'nuria f shortage

penzo'l|are vi dangle. ∼**oni** adv dangling

pe'pa|re vt pepper. ∼**to** adj peppery

'pepe m pepper; **grano di** ∼ peppercorn. ∼ **in grani** whole peppercorns. ∼ **macinato** ground pepper

pepero'n|ata f peppers cooked in olive oil with onion, tomato and garlic. ∼**'cino** m chilli pepper. **pepe'rone** m pepper. **peperone verde** green pepper

pe'pita f nugget

per prep for; (attraverso) through; (stato in luogo) in, on; (distributivo) per; (mezzo, entro) by; (causa) with; (in qualità di) as; ∼ **strada** in the street; ∼ **la fine del mese** by the end of the month; **in fila** ∼ **due** in double file; **l'ho sentito** ∼ **telefono** I spoke to him on the phone; ∼ **iscritto** in writing; ∼ **caso** by chance; **ho aspettato** ∼ **ore** I've been waiting for hours; ∼ **tempo** in time; ∼ **sempre** forever; ∼ **scherzo** as a joke; **gridare** ∼ **il dolore** scream with pain; **vendere** ∼ **10 milioni** sell for 10 million; **uno** ∼ **volta** one at a time; **uno** ∼ **uno** one by one; **venti** ∼ **cento** twenty per cent; ∼ **fare qcsa** [in order to] do sth; **stare** ∼ be about to

'pera f pear; **farsi una** ∼ (🔲: di eroina) shoot up

per'cento adv per cent. **percentu'ale** f percentage

perce'pibile adj perceivable; (somma) payable

perce'pi|re vt perceive; (riscuotere) cash

perce|t'tibile adj perceptible. ∼**zi'one** f perception

perché conj (in interrogazioni) why; (per il fatto che) because; (affinché) so that; ∼ **non vieni?** why don't you come?; **dimmi** ∼ tell me why; ∼ **no/sì** because!; **la ragione** ∼ **l'ho fatto** the reason [that] I did it, the reason why I did it; **è troppo difficile** ∼ **lo possa capire** it's too difficult for me to understand ∼**m** inv reason [why]; **senza un** ∼ without any reason

perciò conj so

per'correre vt cover (distanza); (viaggiare) travel. **per'corso** pp di percorrere ∼**m** (distanza) distance; (viaggio) journey

per'cossa f blow. ∼**o** pp di percuotere. **percu'otere** vt strike

percussi'o|ne f percussion; **strumenti** pl a ∼**ne** percussion instruments. ∼**nista** mf percussionist

per'dente mf loser

'perde|re vt lose; (sprecare) waste; (non prendere) miss; fig: ruin; (vizio): ∼**e tempo** waste time ∼**vi** lose; (recipiente): leak; **lascia** ∼**el** forget it!. ∼**si** vr get lost; (reciproco) lose touch

perdigi'orno mf inv idler

'perdita f loss; (spreco) waste; (falla) leak; **a** ∼ **d'occhio** as far as the eye can see. ∼ **di tempo** waste of time. **perdi'tempo** m time-waster

perdo'nare vt forgive; (scusare) excuse. **per'dono** m forgiveness; (Jur) pardon

perdu'rare vi last; (perseverare) persist

perduta'mente adv hopelessly. **per'duto** pp di perdere ∼**adj** lost; (rovinato) ruined pe'renne adj everlasting; (Bot) perennial. ~'mente adv perpetually

peren'torio adj peremptory

per'fetto adj perfect • m (Gram) perfect [tense]

perfezio'nar|e vt perfect; (migliorare) improve. ~si vr improve oneself; (specializzarsi) specialize

perfezi'o|ne f perfection; alla ~ne to perfection. ~'nista mf perfectionist

per'fidia f wickedness; (atto) wicked act. 'perfido adj treacherous; (malvagio) perverse

per'fino adv even

perfo'ra|re vt pierce; punch (schede); (Mech) drill. ~'tore, ~'trice mf punch-card operator • m perforator. ~zi'one f perforation; (di schede) punching

per'formance f inv performance

perga'mena f parchment

perico'lante adj precarious; (azienda) shaky

pe'rico|lo m danger; (rischio) risk; mettere in ~lo endanger. ~'loso adj dangerous

perife'ria f periphery; (di città) outskirts pl; fig fringes pl

peri'feric|a f peripheral; (strada) ring road. ~o adj (quartiere) outlying

pe'rifrasi f inv circumlocution

pe'rimetro m perimeter

peri'odico m periodical • adj periodical; (vento, mal di testa) (Math) recurring. pe'riodo m period; (Gram) sentence. periodo di prova trial period

peri'pezie fpl misadventures

pe'rire vi perish

pe'ri|to, -a adj skilled • mf expert

perito'nite f peritonitis

pe'rizia f skill; (valutazione) survey

'perla f pearl. per'lina f bead

perlo'meno adv at least

perlu'stra|re vt patrol. ~zi'one f patrol; andare in ~zione go on patrol

perma'loso adj touchy

perma'ne|nte adj permanent • f perm; farsi [fare] la ~nte have a perm. ~nza f permanence; (soggiorno) stay; in ~nza permanently. ~re vi remain

perme'are vt permeate

per'messo pp di permettere • m permission; (autorizzazione) permit; (Mil) leave; [è] ~? (posso entrare?) may I come in?; (posso passare?) excuse me. ~ di lavoro work permit

per'mettere vt allow, permit; potersi ~ qcsa (finanziariamente) afford sth; come si permette? how dare you?

permutazi'one f exchange; (Math) permutation

per'nic|e f partridge. ~i'oso adj pernicious

'perno m pivot

pernot'tare vi stay overnight

'pero m pear-tree

però conj but; (tuttavia) however

pero'rare vt plead

perpendico'lare adj & f perpendicular

perpe'trare vt perpetrate

perpetu'are vt perpetuate. per'petuo adj perpetual

perplessità f inv perplexity; (dubbio) doubt. per'plesso adj perplexed

perqui'si|re vt search. ~zi'one f search. ~zione domiciliare search of the premises

persecu'tore, -'trice mf persecutor. ~zi'one f persecution

persegu'ire vt pursue

persegui'tare vt persecute

perseve'ra|nza f perseverance. ~re vi persevere

persi'ano, -a adj Persian • f (di finestra) shutter. 'persico adj Persian

per'sino adv = PERFINO

persi'sten|te *adj* persistent. ~**za** *f* persistence. **per'sistere** *vi* persist

'perso *pp di* perdere ●*adj* lost; **a tempo** ~ in one's spare time

per'sona *f* person; (*un tale*) somebody; **di** ~, **in** ~ in person, personally; **per** ~ per person, a head; **per interposta** ~ through an intermediary; **persone** *pl* people

perso'naggio *m* personality; (*Theat*) character

perso'nal|e *adj* personal ●*m* staff. ~**e di terra** ground crew. ~**ità** *f inv* personality. ~**iz'zare** *vt* customize (*auto ecc*); personalize (*penna ecc*)

personifi'ca|re *vt* personify. ~**zi'one** *f* personification

perspi'cace *adj* shrewd

persua|'dere *vt* convince; impress (*critici*). ~**dere qcno a fare qcsa** persuade sb to do sth. ~**si'one** *f* persuasion. ~**'sivo** *adj* persuasive. **persu'aso** *pp di* persuadere

per'tanto *conj* therefore

'pertica *f* pole

perti'nente *adj* relevant

per'tosse *f* whooping cough

pertur'ba|re *vt* perturb. ~**rsi** *vr* be perturbed. ~**zi'one** *f* disturbance. ~**zione atmosferica** atmospheric disturbance

per'va|dere *vt* pervade. ~**so** *pp di* pervadere

perve'nire *vi* reach; **far** ~ **qcsa a qcno** send sth to sb

pervers|i'one *f* perversion. ~**ità** *f inv* perversity. **per'verso** *adj* perverse

perver'ti|re *vt* pervert. ~**to** *adj* perverted ●*m* pervert

per'vinca *m* (*colore*) blue with a touch of purple

p.es. *abbr* (per esempio) e.g.

'pesa *f* weighing; (*bilancia*) weighing machine; (*per veicoli*) weighbridge

pe'sante *adj* heavy; (*stomaco*) overfull ●*adv* (*vestirsi*) warmly. ~**'mente** *adv* (cadere) heavily. **pesan'tezza** *f* heaviness

pe'sar|e *vt/i* weigh; ~**e su** *fig* lie heavy on; ~**e le parole** weigh one's words. ~**si** *vr* weigh oneself

'pesca¹ *f* (*frutto*) peach

'pesca² *f* fishing; **andare a** ~ go fishing. ~ **subacquea** underwater fishing. **pe'scare** *vt* fish for; (*prendere*) catch; (*fig: trovare*) fish out. ~**'tore** *m* fisherman

'pesce *m* fish. ~ **d'aprile!** April Fool!!. ~ **grosso** *fig* big fish. ~ **piccolo** *fig* small fry. ~ **rosso** goldfish. ~ **spada** swordfish. **Pesci** *pl* (*Astr*) Pisces

pesce'cane *m* shark

pesche'reccio *m* fishing boat

pesc|he'ria *f* fishmonger's [shop]. ~**hi'era** *f* fish-pond. ~**i'vendolo** *m* fishmonger

'pesco *m* peach-tree

'peso *m* weight; **essere di** ~ **per qcno** be a burden to sb; **di poco** ~ (*senza importanza*) not very important

pessi'mis|mo *m* pessimism. ~**ta** *mf* pessimist ●*adj* pessimistic. **'pessimo** *adj* very bad

pe'staggio *m* beating-up. **pe'stare** *vt* tread on; (*schiacciare*) crush; (*picchiare*) beat; crush (aglio, prezzemolo)

'peste *f* plague; (*persona*) pest

pe'stello *m* pestle

pesti'cida *m* pesticide

pesti'len|za *f* pestilence; (*fetore*) stench. ~**zi'ale** *adj* noxious

'pesto *adj* ground; **occhio** ~ black eye ●*m* basil and garlic sauce

'petalo *m* petal

pe'tardo *m* banger

petizi'one *f* petition; **fare una** ~ draw up a petition

petro|li'era *f* [oil] tanker. ~**'lifero** *adj* oil-bearing. ~**'trolio** *m* oil

pettego|'lare *vi* gossip. ~**'lezzo** *m* piece of gossip; **far** ~**lezzi** gossip

pet'tegolo, -a *adj* gossipy ●*mf*

P

gossip

petti'na|re vt comb. **~rsi** vr comb one's hair. **~'tura** f combing; (acconciatura) hair-style. **'pettine** m comb

'petting m petting

petti'nino m (fermaglio) comb

petti'rosso m robin

'petto m chest; (seno) breast; a doppio ~ double-breasted

petto'rale m (in gare sportive) number. **~rina** f (di salopette) bib. **~'ruto** adj (donna) full-breasted; (uomo) broad-chested

petu'lante adj impertinent

'pezza f cloth; (toppa) patch; (rotolo di tessuto) roll

pez'zente mf tramp; (avaro) miser

'pezzo m piece; (parte) part; un ~ (di tempo) some time; (di spazio) a long way; al ~ (costare) each; fare a pezzi tear to shreds. ~ grosso bigwig

pia'cente adj attractive

pia'ce|re ● m pleasure; (favore) favour; a ~re as much as one likes; per ~re! please!; ~re [di conoscerla]! pleased to meet you!; con ~re with pleasure

● vi la Scozia mi piace I like Scotland; mi piacciono i dolci I like sweets; ti piace? do you like it?; faccio come mi pare e piace I do as I please; lo spettacolo è piaciuto the show was a success.

Nota che il soggetto in italiano corrisponde al complemento oggetto in inglese, mentre il complemento indiretto in italiano corrisponde al soggetto in inglese: **Non mi piace** I don't like it

pia'vole adj pleasant

piaci'mento m a ~ as much as you like

pia'dina f unleavened bread

pi'aga f sore; scourge; (persona noiosa) pain; (fig: ricordo doloroso) wound

piagni'steo m whining

piagnuco'lare vi whimper

pi'alla f plane. **pial'lare** vt plane

pi'ana f plane. **pianeggi'ante** adj level

piane'rottolo m landing

pia'neta m planet

pi'angere vi cry; (disperatamente) weep ● vt (lamentare) lament; (per un lutto) mourn

pianifi'ca|re vt plan. **~zi'one** f planning

pia'nista mf (Mus) pianist

pi'ano adj flat; (a livello) flush; (regolare) smooth; (facile) easy ● adv slowly; (con cautela) gently; andarci ~ go carefully ● m plain; (di edificio) floor; (livello) plane; (progetto) plan; (Mus) piano; **di primo ~** first-rate; **primo ~** (Phot) close-up; **in primo ~** in the foreground. **~ regolatore** town plan. **~ di studi** syllabus

piano'forte m piano. **~ a coda** grand piano

piano'terra m inv ground floor

pi'anta f plant; (del piede) sole; (disegno) plan; **di sana ~** (totalmente) entirely; **in ~ stabile** permanently. **~ stradale** road map. **~gi'one** f plantation

pian'tar|e vt plant; (conficcare) drive; (🄼: abbandonare) dump; **piantala!** (🄼: stop it!. **~si** vr plant oneself; (🄼: lasciarsi) leave each other

pianter'reno m ground floor

pi'anto pp di piangere ● m crying; (disperato) weeping; (lacrime) tears pl

pian|to'nare vt guard. **~'tone** m guard

pia'nura f plain

p'iastra f plate; (*lastra*) slab; (*Culin*) griddle. ~ **elettronica** circuit board. ~ **madre** (*Comput*) motherboard

pia'strella f tile

pia'strina f (*Mil*) identity disc; (*Med*) platelet; (*Comput*) chip

piatta'forma f platform. ~ **di lancio** launch pad

piat'tino m saucer

pi'atto adj flat ● m plate; (*da portata, vivanda*) dish; (*portata*) course; (*parte piatta*) flat; (*di giradischi*) turntable; **piatti** pl (*Mus*) cymbals; **lavare i piatti** do the washing-up. ~ **fondo** soup plate. ~ **piano** (*ordinary*) plate

pi'azza f square; (*Comm*) market; **letto a una ~** single bed; **letto a due piazze** double bed; **far ~ pulita** make a clean sweep. ~**forte** m stronghold. **piaz'zale** m large square. ~**mento** m (*in classifica*) placing

piaz'za|re vt place. ~**rsi** vr Sport be placed; ~**rsi secondo** come second. ~**to** adj (*cavallo*) placed; **ben ~to** (*robusto*) well built

piaz'zista m salesman

piaz'zuola f ~ **di sosta** pull-in

pic'cante adj hot; (*pungente*) sharp; (*salace*) spicy

pic'carsi vr (*risentirsi*) take offence; ~ **di** (*vantarsi di*) claim to

'picche fpl (*in carte*) spades

picchet'tare vt stake; (*scioperanti:*) picket. **pic'chetto** m picket

picchi'a|re vt beat, hit ● vi (*bussare*) knock; (*Aeron*) nosedive; ~**re in testa** (*motore:*) knock. ~**ta** f beating; (*Aeron*) nosedive; **scendere in ~ta** nosedive

picchiet'tare vt tap; (*punteggiare*) spot

'picchio m woodpecker

pic'cino adj tiny; (*gretto*) mean; (*di poca importanza*) petty ● m little one, child

picci'one m pigeon

'picco m peak; **a ~** vertically; **colare a ~** sink

'piccolo, -a adj small, little; (*di età*) young; (*di statura*) short; (*gretto*) petty ● mf child; **da ~** as a child

pic'cone m pickaxe. ~**zza** f ice axe

pic'nic m inv picnic

pi'docchio m louse

piè m inv **a ~ di pagina** at the foot of the page; **saltare a ~ pari** skip

pi'ede m foot; **a piedi** on foot; **andare a piedi** walk; **a piedi nudi** barefoot; **a piedi libero** free; **in piedi** standing; **alzarsi in piedi** stand up; **ai piedi di** (*montagna*) at the foot of; **prendere ~** fig gain ground; (*moda:*) catch on; **mettere in piedi** (*allestire*) set up

piedi'stallo m pedestal

pi'ega f (*piegatura*) fold; (*di gonna*) pleat; (*di pantaloni*) crease; (*grinza*) wrinkle; (*andamento*) turn; **non fare una ~** (*ragionamento:*) be flawless

pie'ga|re vt fold; (*flettere*) bend ● vi bend. ~**rsi** vr bend. ~**rsi a** fig yield to. ~**tura** f folding

pieghet'tare vt pleat. ~**to** adj pleated. **pie'ghevole** adj pliable; (*tavolo*) folding ● m leaflet

piemon'tese adj Piedmontese

pi'ena f (*di fiume*) flood; (*folla*) crowd. ~**o** adj full; (*massiccio*) solid; **in ~a estate** in the middle of summer; **a ~i voti** (*diplomarsi*) ≈ with A-grades, with first class honours ● m (*colmo*) height; (*carico*) full load; **in ~o** (*completamente*) fully; **fare il ~o** (*di benzina*) fill up

pie'none m **c'era il ~** the place was packed

'piercing m inv body piercing

pietà f pity; (*misericordia*) mercy; **senza ~** (*persona*) pitiless; (*spietatamente*) pitilessly; **avere ~ di qcno** take pity on sb; **far ~** (*far pena*) be pitiful

pie'tanza f dish

pie'toso adj pitiful, merciful; (pessimo) terrible

pi'etr|a f stone. ~a dura semi-precious stone. ~a preziosa precious stone. ~a dello scandalo cause of the scandal. pie'trame m stones pl. ~ifi'care vt petrify. pie'trina f flint. pie'troso adj stony

pigi'ama m pyjamas pl

'pigia 'pigia m inv crowd, crush. pigi'are vt press

pigi'one f rent; dare a ~ let, rent out; prendere a ~ rent

pigli'are vt (🔲: afferrare) catch. 'piglio m air

pig'mento m pigment

'pigna f cone

pi'gnolo adj pedantic

pigo'lare vi chirp. pigo'lio m chirping

pi'grizia f laziness. 'pigro adj lazy; (intelletto) slow

'pila f pile; (Electr) battery; (🔲: lampadina tascabile) torch; (vasca) basin; a pile battery powered

pi'lastro m pillar

'pillola f pill; prendere la ~ be on the pill

pi'lone m pylon; (di ponte) pier

pi'lota mf pilot • m (Auto) driver. pilo'tare vt pilot; drive (auto)

pinaco'teca f art gallery

pi'neta f pine-wood

ping-'pong m table tennis, ping-pong 🔲

'pingue adj fat. ~'edine f fatness

pingu'ino m penguin; (gelato) choc ice on a stick

'pinna f fin; (per nuotare) flipper

'pino m pine[-tree]; ~ marittimo cluster pine. pi'nolo m pine kernel

'pinta f pint

'pinza f pliers pl; (Med) forceps pl

pin'za|re vt (con pinzatrice) staple. ~'trice f stapler

pin'zette fpl tweezers pl

pinzi'monio m sauce for crudités

'pio adj pious; (benefico) charitable

pi'oggia f rain; (fig: di pietre, insulti) hail, shower; sotto la ~ in the rain. ~ acida acid rain

pi'olo m (di scala) rung

piom'ba|re vi fall heavily; ~re su fall upon • vt fill (dente). ~'tura f (di dente) filling. piom'bino m (sigillo) [lead] seal; (da pesca) sinker; (in gonne) weight

pi'ombo m lead; (sigillo) [lead] seal; a ~ plumb; senza ~ (benzina) lead-free

pioni'ere, -a mf pioneer

pi'oppo m poplar

pio'vano adj acqua piovana rainwater

pi'ov|ere vi rain; ~e it's raining; ~iggi'nare vi drizzle. pio'voso adj rainy

'pipa f pipe

pipì f fare [la] ~ pee

pipi'strello m bat

pi'ramide f pyramid

pi'ranha m inv piranha

pi'ra|ta m pirate. ~ della strada road-hog • adj inv pirate. ~e'ria f piracy

pi'rofil|a f (tegame) oven-proof dish. ~o adj heat-resistant

pi'romane mf pyromaniac

pi'roscafo m steamer. ~ di linea liner

pi'scina f swimming pool. ~ coperta indoor swimming pool. ~ scoperta outdoor swimming pool

pi'sello m pea; (🔲: pene) willie

piso'lino m nap; fare un ~ have a nap

'pista f track; (Aeron) runway; (orma) footprint; (sci) slope, piste. ~ d'atterraggio airstrip. ~ da ballo dance floor. ~ ciclabile cycle track

pi'stacchio m pistachio

pi'stola f pistol; (*per spruzzare*) spray-gun. ∼ a spruzzo paint spray

pi'stone m piston

pi'tone m python

pit'to|re, -'trice mf painter. ∼'resco adj picturesque. **pit'torico** adj pictorial

pit'tu|ra f painting. ∼'rare vt paint

---

più

● adv more; (*superlativo*) most

Il comparativo e il superlativo di aggettivi di una sillaba o che terminano in -y si formano con i suffissi -er e -est: più breve shorter il più giovane the youngest

∼ importante more important; il ∼ importante the most important; ∼ caro more expensive; il ∼ caro the most expensive; di ∼ more; una coperta in ∼ an extra blanket; non ho ∼ soldi I don't have any more money; non vive ∼ a Milano he doesn't live in Milan any longer; ∼ o meno more or less; il ∼ lentamente possibile as slowly as possible; per di ∼ what's more; mai ∼! I never again!; ∼ di more than; sempre ∼ more and more; (*Math*) plus

● adj more; (*superlativo*) most; ∼ tempo more time; la classe con ∼ alunni the class with most pupils; ∼ volte several times

● m most; (*Math*) plus sign; il ∼ è fatto the worst is over; parlare del ∼ e del meno make small talk; i ∼ the majority

---

piucche'fetto m pluperfect

pi'uma f feather. piu'maggio m plumage. piu'mino m (*di cigni*) down; (*copriletto*) eiderdown; (*per cipria*) powder-puff; (*per spolverare*) feather duster; (*giacca*) down jacket. piu-'mone® m duvet

piut'tosto adv rather; (*invece*) instead

pi'vello m 🔢 greenhorn

'pizza f pizza; *Cinema* reel.

pizza'iola f slices of beef in tomato sauce, oregano and anchovies

pizze'ria f pizza restaurant

pizzi'c|are vt pinch; (*pungere*) sting; (*di sapore*) taste sharp; (🔢: *sorprendere*) catch; (*Mus*) pluck ● vi scratch; (*cibo:*) be spicy **'pizzico** m, ∼**otto** m pinch

'pizzo m lace; (*di montagna*) peak

pla'car|e vt placate; assuage (*fame, dolore*). ∼**si** vr calm down

'placca f plate; (*commemorativa, dentale*) plaque; (*Med*) patch

plac'ca|re vt plate. ∼**to adj** ∼**to d'argento** silver-plated. ∼**to d'oro** gold-plated. ∼**tura** f plating

pla'centa f placenta

'placido adj placid

plagi'are vt plagiarize; plagiarize (*persona*). **'plagio** m plagiarism

plaid m inv tartan rug

pla'nare vi glide

'plancia f (*Naut*) bridge; (*passerella*) gangplank

pla'smare vt mould

'plastic|a f (*arte*) plastic art; (*Med*) plastic surgery; (*materia*) plastic. ∼**o** adj plastic ● m plastic model

'platano m plane[-tree]

pla'tea f stalls pl; (*pubblico*) audience

'platino m platinum

plau'sibil|e adj plausible. ∼**ità** f plausibility

ple'baglia f pej mob

pleni'lunio m full moon

'plettro m plectrum

pleu'rite f pleurisy

'plico m packet; in ∼ a parte under separate cover

p

plissé adj inv plissé; (gonna) accordeon-pleated

plo'tone m platoon; (di ciclisti) group. ~ d'esecuzione firing-squad

'plumbeo adj leaden

plu'ral|e adj & m plural; al ~e in the plural. ~ità f majority

pluridiscipli'nare adj multidisciplinary

plurien'nale adj ~ esperienza many years' experience

pluripar'titico adj (Pol) multi-party

plu'tonio m plutonium

pluvi'ale adj rain attrib

pneu'matico adj pneumatic ● m tyre

pneu'monia f pneumonia

po' ▷ POCO

po'chette f inv clutch bag

po'chino m un ~ a little bit

'poco
● adj little; (tempo) short; (con nomi plurali) few
● adv (con verbi) not much; (con avverbi) not very; parla ~ he doesn't speak much; lo conosco ~ I don't know him very well

poco + aggettivo spesso si traduce con un aggettivo specifico: ~ probabile unlikely, ~ profondo shallow

● pron little; (poco tempo) a short time; (plurale) few
● m little; un po' a little [bit]; un po' di a little, some; a ~ a little by little; fra ~ soon; per ~ (a poco prezzo) cheap; (quasi) nearly; ~ fa a little while ago; sono arrivato da ~ I have just arrived; un bel po' quite a lot

po'dere m farm

pode'roso adj powerful

'podio m dais; (Mus) podium

po'dis|mo m walking. ~ta mf walker

po'e|ma m poem. ~sia f poetry; (componimento) poem. ~ta m poet. ~tessa f poetess. ~tico adj poetic

poggiapi'edi m inv footrest

poggi'a|re vt lean; (posare) place ● vi ~re su be based on. ~testa m inv head-rest

poggi'olo m balcony

'poi adv (dopo) then; (più tardi) later [on]; (finalmente) finally. d'ora in ~ from now on; questa ~! well!

poiché conj since

pois m inv a ~ a polka-dot

'poker m poker

po'lacco, -a adj Polish ● mf Pole ● m (lingua) Polish

po'lar|e adj polar. ~iz'zare vt polarize

'polca f polka

po'lemic|a f controversy. ~camente adv controversially. ~co adj controversial. ~z'zare vi engage in controversy

po'lenta f cornmeal porridge

poli'clinico m general hospital

poli'estere m polyester

polio[mie'lite] f polio[myelitis]

'polipo m polyp

poli'sti'rolo m polystyrene

poli'tecnico m polytechnic

po'litic|a f politics sg; (linea di condotta) policy; fare ~a be in politics. ~iz'zare vt politicize. ~o, -a adj political ● mf politician

poliva'lente adj catch-all

poli'zi|a f police. ~a giudiziaria f Criminal Investigation Department. ~a stradale traffic police. ~'esco adj police attrib; (romanzo, film) detective attrib. ~'otto m policeman

'polizza f policy

pol'la|io m chicken run; (🔒: *luogo chiassoso*) mad house. ~**me** m poultry. ~**strello** m spring chicken. ~**stro** m cockerel

'pollice m thumb; (*unità di misura*) inch

'polline m pollen; **allergia al** ~ hay fever

polli'vendolo, -a mf poulterer

'pollo m chicken; (🔒: *sempliciotto*) simpleton

polmo'nare adj pulmonary. pol'**mone** m lung. ~**nite** f pneumonia

'polo m pole; Sport polo; (*maglietta*) polo top. ~ **nord** North Pole. ~ **sud** South Pole

Po'lonia f Poland

'polpa f pulp

pol'paccio m calf

polpa'strello m fingertip

pol'pet|ta f meatball. ~**tone** m meat loaf

'polpo m octopus

pol'sino m cuff

'polso m pulse; (Anat) wrist; fig authority; **avere** ~ be strict

pol'tiglia f mush

pol'trire vi lie around

pol'tron|a f armchair; (Theat) seat in the stalls. ~**e** adj lazy

'polve|re f dust; (*sostanza polverizzata*) powder; **in** ~**re** powdered; **sapone in** ~**re** soap powder. ~**rina** f (*medicina*) powder. ~**riz'zare** vt pulverize; (*nebulizzare*) atomize. ~**rone** m cloud of dust. ~**roso** adj dusty

po'mata f ointment, cream

po'mello m knob; (*guancia*) cheek

pomeridi'ano adj afternoon attrib; **alle tre pomeridiane** at three in the afternoon. **pome'riggio** m afternoon

'pomice f pumice

'pomo m (*oggetto*) knob. ~ **d'Adamo** Adam's apple

pomo'doro m tomato

'pompa f pump; (*sfarzo*) pomp. **pompe** pl **funebri** (*funzione*) funeral. **pom'pare** vt pump; (*gonfiare d'aria*) pump up; (*fig: esagerare*) exaggerate; **pompare fuori** pump out

pom'pelmo m grapefruit

pompi'ere m fireman; **i pompieri** the fire brigade

pom'poso adj pompous

ponde'rare vt ponder

po'nente m west

'ponte m bridge; (Naut) deck; (*impalcatura*) scaffolding; **fare il** ~ make a long weekend of it

pon'tefice m pontiff

pontifi'ca|re vi pontificate. ~**to** m pontificate

ponti'ficio adj papal

pon'tile m jetty

popò f inv 🔒 pooh

popo'lano adj of the people

popo'la|re adj popular; (*comune*) common • vt populate. ~**rsi** vr get crowded. ~**rità** f popularity. ~**zi'one** f population. **'popolo** m people. **popo'loso** adj populous

'poppa f (Naut) stern; (*mammella*) breast; **a** ~ astern

pop'pa|re vt suck. ~**ta** f (*pasto*) feed. ~**toio** m [feeding-]bottle

popu'lista mf populist

por'cata f load of rubbish; **porcate** pl (🔒: *cibo*) junk food

porcel'lana f porcelain

porcel'lino m piglet. ~ **d'India** guinea-pig

porche'ria f dirt; (*cosa orrenda*) piece of filth; (*robaccia*) rubbish

por'ci|le m pigsty. ~**no** adj pig attrib • m (*fungo*) edible mushroom. **'porco** m pig; (*carne*) pork

'porgere vt give; (*offrire*) offer; **porgo distinti saluti** (*in lettera*) I remain, yours sincerely

porno'gra'fia f pornography. ~'**grafico** adj pornographic '**poro** m pore. po'**roso** adj porous

'**porpora** f purple

'**por|re** vt (collocare) place; (supporre) suppose; ask (domanda); present (candidatura); poniamo il caso che... let us suppose that...; ~re fine o termine a put an end to. ~si vr put oneself; ~si a sedere sit down; ~si in cammino set out

'**porro** m (Bot) leek; (verruca) wart

'**porta** f door; Sport goal; (di città) gate; (Comput) port. ~ a ~ door-to-door; mettere alla ~ show sb the door. ~ di servizio tradesmen's entrance

portaba'gagli m inv porter; (di treno ecc) luggage rack; (Auto) boot, trunk Am; (sul tetto di un'auto) roof rack

portabot'tiglie m inv bottle rack, wine rack

porta'cenere m inv ashtray

portachi'avi m inv keyring

porta'cipria m inv compact

portadocu'menti m inv document wallet

porta'erei f inv aircraft carrier

portafi'nestra f French window

porta'foglio m wallet; (per documenti) portfolio; (ministero) ministry

portafor'tuna m inv lucky charm ● adj inv lucky

portagi'oie m inv jewellery box

por'tale m door

portama'tite m inv pencil case

porta'mento m carriage; (condotta) behaviour

porta'mina m inv propelling pencil

portamo'nete m inv purse

portaom'brelli m inv umbrella stand

porta'pacchi m inv roof rack; (su bicicletta) luggage rack

porta'penne m inv pencil case

por'ta|re vt (verso chi parla) bring; (lontano da chi parla) take; (sorreggere) (Math) carry; (condurre) lead; (indossare) wear; (avere) bear. ~rsi vr (trasferirsi) move; (comportarsi) behave; ~rsi bene/male gli anni look young/old for one's age

portari'viste m inv magazine rack

porta'sci m inv ski rack

portasiga'rette m inv cigarette-case

por'tata f (di pranzo) course; (Auto) carrying capacity; (di arma) range; (fig: abilità) capability; a ~ta di mano within reach. por'tatile agg & m portable. ~to adj (indumento) worn; (dotato) gifted; essere ~to per qcsa have a gift for sth; essere ~to a (tendere a) be inclined to. ~tore, ~'trice mf bearer; al ~tore to the bearer. ~tore di handicap disabled person

portatovagli'olo m napkin ring

portau'ovo m inv egg-cup

porta'voce m inv spokesman ● f inv spokeswoman

por'tento m marvel; (persona dotata) prodigy

'**portico** m portico

porti'er|a f door; (tendaggio) door curtain. ~e m porter, doorman; Sport goalkeeper. ~e di notte night porter

porti'n|aio, -a mf caretaker. ~e'ria f concierge's room; (di ospedale) porter's lodge

'**porto** pp di porgere ● m harbour; (complesso) port; (vino) port [wine]; (spesa di trasporto) carriage; andare in ~ succeed. ~ d'armi gun licence

Porto'gallo m Portugal. p~hese adj & mf Portuguese

por'tone m main door

portu'ale m docker

porzi'one f portion

'**posa** f flaying; (riposo) rest; (Phot) exposure; (atteggiamento) pose; mettersi in ~ pose

po'sa|re vt put; (giù) put [down] ● vi (poggiare) rest; (per un ritratto) pose.

~**rsi** *vr* alight; (*sostare*) rest; (*Aeron*) land. ~**ta** *f* piece of cutlery; ~**te** *pl* cutlery *sg*. ~**to** *adj* sedate

po'scritto *m* postscript

posi'tivo *adj* positive

posizio'nare *vt* position

posizi'one *f* position; farsi una ~ get ahead

posolo'gia *f* dosage

po'spo|rre *vt* place after; (*posticipare*) postpone. ~**sto** *pp di* posporre

posse'd|ere *vt* possess, own. ~**i'mento** *m* possession

posses'sivo *adj* possessive. possesso *m* ownership; (*bene*) possession. ~**sore** *m* owner

pos'sibil|e *adj* possible; il più presto ~e as soon as possible ●*m* fare [tutto] il ~e do one's best. ~**ità** *f inv* possibility; (*occasione*) chance ●*fpl* (*mezzi*) means

possi'dente *mf* land-owner

'posta *f* post, mail; (*ufficio postale*) post office; (*al gioco*) stake; spese di ~ postage; per ~ by post, by mail; a bella ~ on purpose; Poste e Telecomunicazioni *pl* [Italian] Post Office. ~ elettronica e-mail. ~ prioritaria ≈ first-class mail. ~ vocale voice-mail

posta'giro *m* postal giro

po'stale *adj* postal

postazi'one *f* position

postda'tare *vt* postdate (assegno)

posteggi'a|re *vt/i* park. ~'tore, ~'trice *mf* parking attendant. po'steggio *m* car-park, parking lot *Am*; (*di taxi*) taxi-rank

'posteri *mpl* descendants. ~'ore *adj* rear; (*nel tempo*) later ~tà *f* posterity

po'sticcio *adj* artificial; (*baffi, barba*) false ●*m* hair-piece

postici'pare *vt* postpone

po'stilla *f* note; (*Jur*) rider

po'stino *m* postman, mailman *Am*

'posto *pp di* porre ●*m* place; (*spazio*)

room; (*impiego*) job; (*Mil*) post; (*sedile*) seat; a/fuori ~ in/out of place; prendere ~ take up room; sul ~ on-site; essere a ~ (*casa, libri*) be tidy; fare ~ a make room for; al ~ di (*invece di*) in place of, instead of. ~ di blocco checkpoint. ~ di guida driving seat. ~ di lavoro workstation. posti *pl* in piedi standing room. ~ di polizia police station

post-'partum *adj* post-natal

'postumo *adj* posthumous ●*m* after-effect

po'tabile *adj* drinkable; acqua ~ drinking water

po'tare *vt* prune

po'tassio *m* potassium

po'ten|te *adj* powerful; (*efficace*) potent. ~**za** *f* power; (*efficacia*) potency. ~**zi'ale** *adj* & *n* potential

po'tere *m* power; al ~ in power ●*vi* can, be able to; posso entrare? may I come in?; posso fare qualche cosa? can I do something?; che tu possa essere felice! may you be happy!; non ne posso più (*sono stanco*) I can't go on; (*sono stufo*) I can't take any more; può darsi perhaps; può darsi che sia vero perhaps it's true; potrebbe aver ragione he could be right, he might be right; avresti potuto telefonare you could have phoned, you might have phoned; spero di poter venire I hope to be able to come

potestà *f inv* power

'pover|o, -a *adj* poor; (*semplice*) plain ●*m* poor man ●*f* poor woman; i ~i the poor. ~tà *f* poverty

'pozza *f* pool. poz'zanghera *f* puddle

'pozzo *m* well; (*minerario*) pit. ~ petrolifero oil-well

PP.TT. *abbr* (Poste e Telegrafi) [Italian] Post Office

prali'nato *adj* (mandorla, gelato)

praline-coated

pram'matica *f* essere di ∼ be customary

pran'zare *vi* dine; *(a mezzogiorno)* lunch. **'pranzo** *m* dinner; *(a mezzogiorno)* lunch. **pranzo di nozze** wedding breakfast

Pranzo *Pranzo* is traditonally the day's main meal and school timetables and hours of business are geared to a break between one and four o'clock. It starts with a *primo* (usually pasta), followed by a *secondo* (main course). Gradually Italians, especially city-dwellers, are adopting a more northern European timetable and making less of *pranzo*.

'prassi *f* standard procedure

prate'ria *f* grassland

'prati|ca *f* practice; *(esperienza)* experience; *(documentazione)* file; **avere** ∼**ca di qcsa** be familiar with sth; **far** ∼**ca** gain experience. ∼**'cabile** *adj* practicable; *(strada)* passable. ∼**ca'mente** *adv* practically. ∼**'cante** *mf* apprentice; *(Relig)* [regular] church-goer

prati'ca|re *vt* practise; *(frequentare)* associate with; *(fare)* make

praticità *f* practicality. **'pratico** *adj* practical; *(esperto)* experienced; **essere pratico di qcsa** know about sth

'prato *m* meadow; *(di giardino)* lawn

pre'ambolo *m* preamble

preannunci'are *vt* give advance notice of

preavvi'sare *vt* forewarn. **preav-'viso** *m* warning

pre'cario *adj* precarious

precauzi'one *f* precaution; *(cautela)* care

prece'den|te *adj* previous ● *m* precedent. ∼**te'mente** *adv* previously.

∼**za** *f* precedence; *(di veicoli)* right of way; **dare la** ∼**za** give way. **pre'cedere** *vt* precede

pre'cetto *m* precept

precipi'ta|re *vt* ∼**re le cose** precipitate events ● *vi* fall headlong; *(situazione, eventi)* come to a head. ∼**rsi** *vr* *(gettarsi)* throw oneself; *(affrettarsi)* rush; ∼**rsi a fare qcsa** rush to do sth. ∼**zi'one** *f* *(fretta)* haste; *(atmosferica)* precipitation. **precipi-'toso** *adj* hasty; *(avventato)* reckless; *(caduta)* headlong

preci'pizio *m* precipice; **a** ∼ headlong

precisa'mente *adv* precisely

preci'sa|re *vt* specify; *(spiegare)* clarify. ∼**zi'one** *f* clarification

precisi'one *f* precision. **pre'ciso** *adj* precise; *(ore)* sharp; *(identico)* identical

pre'clu|dere *vt* preclude. ∼**so** *pp di* precludere

pre'coc|e *adj* precocious; *(prematuro)* premature

precon'cetto *adj* preconceived ● *m* prejudice

pre'corr|ere *vt* ∼**ere i tempi** be ahead of one's time

precur'sore *m* precursor

'preda *f* prey; *(bottino)* booty; **essere in** ∼ **al panico** be panic-stricken; **in** ∼ **alle fiamme** engulfed in flames. **pre'dare** *vt* plunder. ∼**'tore** *m* predator

predeces'sore *mf* predecessor

pre'del|la *f* platform. ∼**'lino** *m* step

predesti'na|re *vt* predestine. ∼**to** *adj* *(Relig)* predestined, preordained

predetermi'nato *adj* predetermined, preordained

pre'detto *pp di* predire

'predica *f* sermon; *fig* lecture

predi'care *vt* preach

predi'le|tto, -a *pp di* prediligere ● *adj* favourite ● *mf* pet. ∼**zi'one** *f* predilection. **predi'ligere** vt prefer

pre'dire vt foretell

predi'spo|rre vt arrange. ~**rsi** vr ~**rsi a** prepare oneself for. ~**si-zi'one** f predisposition; (al disegno ecc) bent (a for). ~**sto** pp di **predisporre**

predizi'one f prediction

predomi'na|nte adj predominant. ~**re** vi predominate. **predo'minio** m predominance

pre'done m robber

prefabbri'cato adj prefabricated • m prefabricated building

prefazi'one f preface

prefe'renz|a f preference; **di** ~**a** preferably. ~**i'ale** adj preferential; **corsia** ~**iale** bus and taxi lane

prefe'ribil|e adj preferable. ~'**mente** adv preferably

prefe'ri|re vt prefer. ~**to, -a** agg & mf favourite

pre'fet|to m prefect. ~'**tura** f prefecture

pre'figgersi vr be determined

pre'fisso pp di **prefiggere** • m pre-fix; (Teleph) (dialling) code

pre'gare vt/i pray; (supplicare) beg; **farsi** ~ need persuading

pre'gevole adj valuable

preghi'era f prayer; (richiesta) request

pregi'ato adj esteemed; (prezioso) valuable. '**pregio** m esteem; (valore) value; (di persona) good point; **di pregio** valuable

pregiudi'ca|re vt prejudice; (dan-neggiare) harm. ~**to** adj prejudiced • m (Jur) previous offender

pregiu'dizio m prejudice; (danno) detriment

'**prego** int (non c'è di che) don't men-tion it!; (per favore) please; ~? I beg your pardon?

pregu'stare vt look forward to

pre'lato m prelate

prela'vaggio m prewash

preleva'mento m withdrawal. **prele'vare** vt withdraw (denaro); col-lect (merci); (Med) take. **preli'evo** m (di soldi) withdrawal. **prelievo di san-gue** blood sample

prelimi'nare adj preliminary • m **preliminari** pl preliminaries

pre'ludio m prelude

prema'man m inv maternity dress • adj maternity attrib

prema'turo, -a adj premature • mf premature baby

premedi'ta|re vt premeditate. ~**zi'one** f premeditation

'**premere** vt press; (Comput) hit (tasto) • vi ~ **a** (importare) matter to; **mi preme sapere** I need to know; ~ **su** press on; push (pulsante)

pre'messa f introduction

pre'me|sso pp di **premettere**. ~**sso che** bearing in mind that. ~**ttere** vt put forward; (mettere prima) put before.

premi'a|re vt give a prize to; (ricom-pensare) reward. ~**zi'one** f prize giving

premi'nente adj pre-eminent

'**premio** m prize; (ricompensa) re-ward; (Comm) premium. ~ **di conso-lazione** booby prize

premoni'|tore adj (sogno, segno) premonitory. ~**zi'one** f premonition

premu'ni|re vt fortify. ~**si** vr take protective measures; ~**si di** provide oneself with; ~**si contro** protect oneself against

pre'mu|ra f (fretta) hurry; (cura) care. ~**roso** adj thoughtful

prena'tale adj antenatal

'**prender|e** vt take; (afferrare) seize; catch (treno, malattia, ladro, pesce); have (cibo, bevanda); (far pagare) charge; (assumere) take on; (ottenere) get; (occupare) take up; ~**e informa-zioni** make inquiries; ~**e a calci/**

pugni kick/punch; **quanto prende?** what do you charge?; **~e una persona per un'altra** mistake a person for someone else ● *vi* (*voltare*) turn; (*attechire*) take root; (*rapprendersi*) set; **~e a destra/sinistra** turn right/left; **~e a fare qcsa** start doing sth. **~si** *vr* **~si a pugni** come to blows; **~si cura di** take care of (*ammalato*)

prendi'sole *m inv* sundress

preno'ta|re *vt* book, reserve. **~to** *adj* booked, reserved **~zi'one** *f* booking, reservation

preoccu'pante *adj* alarming

preoccu'pa|re *vt* worry. **~rsi** *vr* **~rsi** worry (di about); **~rsi di fare qcsa** take the trouble to do sth. **~to** *adj* (*ansioso*) worried. **~zi'one** *f* worry; (*apprensione*) concern

prepa'gato *adj* prepaid

prepa'ra|re *vt* prepare. **~rsi** *vr* get ready. **~tivi** *mpl* preparations. **~to** *m* (*prodotto*) preparation. **~torio** *adj* preparatory. **~zi'one** *f* preparation

prepensiona'mento *m* early retirement

prepode'ran|te *adj* predominant. **~za** *f* prevalence

pre'porre *vt* place before

preposizi'one *f* preposition

pre'posto *pp di* **preporre** ● *adj* **~ a** (*addetto a*) in charge of

prepo'ten|te *adj* overbearing ● *mf* bully

preroga'tiva *f* prerogative

'presa *f* taking; (*conquista*) capture; (*stretta*) hold; (*di cemento ecc*) setting; (*Electr*) socket; (*pizzico*) pinch; **essere alle prese con** be struggling with; **~ rapida** (*cemento, colla*) quick-setting; **fare ~ su qcno** influence sb. **~ d'aria** air vent. **~ multipla** adaptor

pre'sagio *m* omen. **presa'gire** *vt* foretell

'presbite *adj* long-sighted

presbi'terio *m* presbytery

pre'scelto *adj* selected

pre'scindere *vi* **~ da** leave aside; **a ~ da** apart from

presco'lare *adj* **in età ~** pre-school

pre'scritto *pp di* **prescrivere**

pre'scri|vere *vt* prescribe. **~zi'one** *f* prescription; (*norma*) rule

preselezi'one *f* **chiamare qcno in ~** call sb via the operator

presen'ta|re *vt* present; (*far conoscere*) introduce; show (*documento*); (*inoltrare*) submit. **~rsi** *vr* present oneself; (*farsi conoscere*) introduce oneself; (*alla ufficio*) attend; (*alla polizia ecc*) report; (*come candidato*) stand, run; (*occasione:*) occur; **~rsi bene/male** (*persona:*) make a good/bad impression; (*situazione:*) look good/bad. **~tore, ~trice** *mf* presenter; (*di notizie*) announcer. **~zi'one** *f* presentation; (*per conoscersi*) introduction

pre'sente *adj* present; (*attuale*) current; (*questo*) this; **aver ~** remember ● *m* present; **i presenti** those present ● *f* **allegato alla ~** (*in lettera*) enclosed

presenti'mento *m* foreboding

pre'senza *f* presence; (*aspetto*) appearance; **in ~ di, alla ~ di** in the presence of; **di bella ~** personable. **~ di spirito** presence of mind

presenzi'are *vi* **~ a** attend

pre'sepe *m*, **pre'sepio** *m* crib

> **Presepe** The *presepe* (also
> called *presepio*) is a traditional nativity scene made
> with ceramic or wooden figures.
> Most homes have small ones and
> large-scale models are assembled
> in churches during Advent. *Presepi*
> from Naples, sometimes made of
> porcelain, are particularly prized.

preser'va|re vt preserve; (proteggere) protect (da from). ∼'tivo m condom. ∼zi'one f preservation

'preside m headmaster; (Univ) dean ●f headmistress; (Univ) dean

presi'den|te m chairman; (Pol) president ●f chairwoman; (Pol) president. ∼ del consiglio [dei ministri] Prime Minister. ∼ della repubblica President of the Republic. ∼za f presidency; (di assemblea) chairmanship

presidi'are vt garrison. **pre'sidio** m garrison

presi'edere vt preside over

'preso pp di **prendere**

'pressa f (Mech) press

pres'sante adj urgent

pressap'poco adv about

pres'sare vt press

pressi'one f pressure. ∼ del sangue blood pressure

'presso prep near; (a casa di) with; (negli indirizzi) care of, c/o; (lavorare) for ●pressi mpl: **nei pressi di...** in the neighbourhood o vicinity of...

pressoché adv almost

pressuriz'za|re vt pressurize. ∼to adj pressurized

prestabi'li|re vt arrange in advance. ∼to adj agreed

prestam'pato adj printed ●m (modulo) form

pre'stante adj good-looking

pre'star|e vt lend; ∼e attenzione pay attention; ∼e aiuto lend a hand; **farsi** ∼e borrow (da from). ∼si vr (frase:) lend itself; (persona:) offer

prestazi'one f performance; **prestazioni** pl (servizi) services

prestigia'tore, -'trice mf conjurer

pre'stigi|o m prestige; **gioco di** ∼o conjuring trick. ∼'oso m pres-

tigious

'prestito m loan; **dare in** ∼ lend; **prendere in** ∼ borrow

'presto adv soon; (di buon'ora) early; (in fretta) quickly; **a** ∼ see you soon; **al più** ∼ as soon as possible; ∼ **o tardi** sooner or later

pre'sumere vt presume; (credere) think

presu'mibile adj è ∼ **che...** presumably,...

pre'sunto adj (colpevole) presumed

presun'tu'oso adj presumptuous. ∼zi'one f presumption

presup'po|rre vt suppose; (richiedere) presuppose. ∼sizi'one f presupposition. ∼sto m essential requirement

'prete m priest

preten'dente mf pretender ●m (corteggiatore) suitor

pre'ten|dere vt (sostenere) claim; (esigere) demand ●vi ∼dere a claim to; ∼dere di (esigere) demand to. ∼si'one f pretension. ∼zi'oso adj pretentious

pre'tes|a f pretension; (esigenza) claim; **senza** ∼e unpretentious. ∼o pp di **pretendere**

pre'testo m pretext

pre'tore m magistrate

pre'tura f magistrate's court

preva'le|nte adj prevalent. ∼nte'mente adv primarily. ∼nza f prevalence. ∼re vi prevail

pre'valso pp di **prevalere**

preve'dere vt foresee; forecast (tempo); (legge ecc:) provide for

preve'nire vt precede; (evitare) prevent; (avvertire) forewarn

preven'ti'vare vt estimate; (aspettarsi) budget for. ∼'tivo adj preventive ●m (Comm) estimate

preve'n|uto adj forewarned; (mal

disposto) prejudiced. **~zi'one** *f* prevention; (*preconcetto*) prejudice

previ'den|te *adj* provident. **~za** *f* foresight. **~za sociale** social security, welfare *Am.* **~zi'ale** *adj* provident

'previo *adj* **~ pagamento** on payment

previsi'one *f* forecast; **in ~ di** in anticipation of

pre'visto *pp di* prevedere **●** *adj* foreseen **●** **più/meno/prima del ~** more/less/earlier than expected

prezi'oso *adj* precious

prez'zemolo *m* parsley

'prezzo *m* price. **~ di fabbrica** factory price. **~ all'ingrosso** wholesale price. [a] **metà ~** half price

prigi'on|e *f* prison; (*pena*) imprisonment. **prigio'nia** *f* imprisonment. **~i'ero, -a** *adj* imprisoned **●** *mf* prisoner

'prima *adv* before; (*più presto*) earlier; (*in primo luogo*) first; **~, finiamo questo** let's finish this first; **~ o poi** sooner or later; **quanto ~** as soon as possible **●** *prep* **~ di** before; **~ d'ora** before now **●** *conj* **~ che** before **●** *f* first class; (*Theat*) first night; (*Auto*) first [gear]

pri'mario *adj* primary; (*principale*) principal

pri'mat|e *m* primate. **~o** *m* supremacy; *Sport* record

prima've|ra *f* spring. **~rile** *adj* spring *attrib*

primeggi'are *vi* excel

primi'tivo *adj* primitive; (*originario*) original

pri'mizie *fpl* early produce *sg*

'primo *adj* first; (*fondamentale*) principal; (*precedente di due*) former; (*iniziale*) early; (*migliore*) best **●** *m* first; **primi** *pl* (*i primi giorni*) the beginning; **in un ~ tempo** at first. **prima copia** master copy

Primo In Italy, lunch invariably includes a *primo*, or first course, before the main course. The most common *primi* are pasta (traditional in the Centre and South) and risotto (traditional in the North), but a *primo* may also consist of soup (often containing small pasta shapes) or *gnocchi* (potato dumplings).

primordi'ale *adj* primordial

'primula *f* primrose

princi'pale *adj* main **●** *m* head, boss 🗓

princi'pato *m* principality. **'principe** *m* prince. **~'pessa** *f* princess

princi'piante *mf* beginner

prin'cipio *m* beginning; (*concetto*) principle; (*causa*) cause; **per ~** on principle

pri'ore *m* prior

priori'tà *f inv* priority. **~'tario** *adj* having priority

'prisma *m* prism

pri'va|re *vt* deprive. **~rsi** *vr* deprive oneself

privatizzazi'one *f* privatization. **pri'vato, -a** *adj* private **●** *mf* private citizen

privazi'one *f* deprivation

privile'gi|are *vt* privilege; (*considerare più importante*) favour. **privi'legio** *m* privilege

'privo *adj* **~ di** devoid of; (*mancante*) lacking in

pro *prep* for **●** *m* advantage; **a che ~?** what's the point?

pro'babil|e *adj* probable. **~ità** *f inv* probability. **~'mente** *adv* probably

pro'ble|ma *m* problem. **~'matico** *adj* problematic

pro'boscide *f* trunk

procacci'ar|e *vt*, **~si** *vr* obtain

pro'cace *adj* (*ragazza*) provocative

pro'ced|ere *vi* proceed; (*iniziare*)

start; **~ere contro** (*Jur*) start legal proceedings against. **~i'mento** *m* process; (*Jur*) proceedings *pl*. **proce'dura** *f* procedure

proces'sare *vt* (*Jur*) try

processi'one *f* procession

pro'cesso *m* process; (*Jur*) trial

proces'sore *m* processor

processu'ale *adj* trial

pro'cinto *m* essere in **~** di be about to

pro'clama *m* proclamation

procla'ma|re *vt* proclaim. **~zi'one** *f* proclamation

procreazi'one *f* procreation

pro'cura *f* power of attorney; per **~** by proxy

procu'ra|re *vt/i* procure; (*causare*) cause; (*cercare*) try. **~'tore** *m* attorney. P**~'tore** Generale Attorney General. **~'tore legale** lawyer. **~'tore della repubblica** public prosecutor

'prode *adj* brave. **pro'dezza** *f* bravery

prodi'gar|e *vt* lavish. **~si** *vr* do one's best

pro'digi|o *m* prodigy. **~'oso** *adj* prodigious

pro'dotto *pp di* **produrre** ●*m* product. **prodotti agricoli** farm produce *sg*. **~ derivato** by-product. **~ interno lordo** gross domestic product. **~ nazionale lordo** gross national product

pro'du|rre *vt* produce. **~rsi** *vr* (*attore:*) play; (*accadere*) happen. **~ttività** *f* productivity. **~t'tivo** *adj* productive. **~t'tore**, **~t'trice** *mf* producer. **~zi'one** *f* production

Prof. *abbr* (*Professore*) Prof.

profa'na|re *vt* desecrate

profe'rire *vt* utter

Prof.essa *abbr* (*Professoressa*) Prof.

profes'sare *vt* profess; practise (*professione*)

professio'nale *adj* professional

professi'o|ne *f* profession; **libera ~ne** profession. **~'nismo** *m* professionalism. **~'nista** *mf* professional

profes'sor|e, **-'essa** *mf* (*Sch*) teacher; (*Univ*) lecturer; (*titolare di cattedra*) professor

pro'feta *m* prophet

pro'ficuo *adj* profitable

profi'lar|e *vt* outline; (*ornare*) border; (*Aeron*) streamline. **~si** *vr* stand out

profi'lattico *adj* prophylactic ●*m* condom

pro'filo *m* profile; (*breve studio*) outline; **di ~** in profile

profit'tare *vi* **~ di** (*avvantaggiarsi*) profit by; (*approfittare*) take advantage of. **pro'fitto** *m* profit; (*vantaggio*) advantage

profond|a'mente *adv* deeply, profoundly. **~ità** *f inv* depth

pro'fondo *adj* deep; *fig* profound; (*cultura*) great

'profugo, **-a** *mf* refugee

profu'mar|e *vt* perfume. **~si** *vr* put on perfume

profu'mato *adj* (*fiore*) fragrant; (*fazzoletto ecc*) scented

profume'ria *f* perfumery. **pro'fumo** *m* perfume, scent

profusi'one *f* profusion; **a ~** in profusion. **pro'fuso** *pp di* **profondere** ●*adj* profuse

proget'tare *vt* plan. **~'tista** *mf* designer. **pro'getto** *m* plan; (*di lavoro importante*) project. **progetto di legge** bill

prog'nosi *f inv* prognosis; **in ~ riservata** on the danger list

pro'gramma *m* programme; (*Comput*) program. **~ scolastico** syllabus

program'ma|re *vt* programme; (*Comput*) program. **~'tore**, **~'trice** *mf* [*computer*] programmer. **~zi'one** *f* programming

progre'dire *vi* [make] progress

progres|si'one *f* progression.

∼'sivo adj progressive. pro'gresso m progress

proi'bi|re vt forbid. ∼'tivo adj prohibitive. ∼to adj forbidden. ∼zi'one f prohibition

proie|t'tare vt project; show (film). ∼t'tore m projector; (Auto) headlight

proi'ettile m bullet

proiezi'one f projection

'prole f offspring. prole'tario agg e m proletarian

prolife'rare vi proliferate. pro'lifico adj prolific

pro'lisso adj verbose, prolix

'prologo m prologue

pro'lunga f (Electr) extension

prolun'gar|e vt prolong; (allungare) lengthen; extend (contratto, scadenza). ∼si vr continue; ∼si su (dilungarsi) dwell upon

prome'moria m memo; (per se stessi) reminder, note; (formale) memorandum

pro'me|ssa f promise. ∼sso pp di promettere. ∼ttere vt/i promise

promet'tente adj promising

promi'nente adj prominent

promiscuità f promiscuity. pro'miscuo adj promiscuous

promon'torio m promontory

pro'mo|sso pp di promuovere e adj (Sch) who has gone up a class; (Univ) who has passed an exam. ∼'tore, ∼'trice mf promoter

promozio'nale adj promotional. promozi'one f promotion

promul'gare vt promulgate

promu'overe vt promote; (Sch) move up a class

proni'pote m (di bisnonno) great-grandson; (di prozio) great-nephew e f (di bisnonno) great-granddaughter; (di prozio) great-niece

pro'nome m pronoun

pronosti'care vt forecast. pro'nostico m forecast

pron'tezza f readiness; (rapidità) quickness

'pronto adj ready; (rapido) quick; ∼! (Teleph) hello!; tenersi ∼ be ready (per fqc); pronti, via! (in gare) ready! steady! go!. ∼ soccorso first aid; (in ospedale) accident and emergency

prontu'ario m handbook

pro'nuncia f pronunciation

pronunci'a|re vt pronounce; (dire) utter; deliver (discorso). ∼rsi vr (su un argomento) give one's opinion. ∼to adj pronounced; (prominente) prominent

pro'nunzia ecc = PRONUNCIA ecc

propa'ganda f propaganda

propa'ga|re vt propagate. ∼rsi vr spread. ∼zi'one f propagation

prope'deutico adj introductory

pro'pen|dere vi ∼dere per be in favour of. ∼so pp di propendere e adj essere ∼so a fare qcsa be inclined to do sth

propi'nare vt administer

pro'pizio adj favourable

proponi'mento m resolution

pro'por|re vt propose; (suggerire) suggest. ∼si vr set oneself (obiettivo, meta); ∼si di intend to

proporzio'na|le adj proportional. ∼re vt proportion. proporzi'one f proportion

pro'posito m purpose; a ∼ by the way; a ∼ di with regard to; di ∼ (apposta) on purpose

proposizi'one f clause; (frase) sentence

pro'post|a f proposal. ∼o pp di proporre

proprietà f inv property; (diritto) ownership; (correttezza) propriety. ∼ immobiliare m property. ∼ privata private property. proprie'taria f owner; (di casa affittata) landlady. proprie'tario m owner; (di casa affittata) landlord

'proprio adj one's [own]; (caratteristico) typical; (appropriato) proper ●adv just; (veramente) really; non ~ not really, not exactly; (affatto) not... at all ●pron one's own ●m one's [own]; lavorare in ~ be one's own boss; mettersi in ~ set up on one's own

propul|si'one f propulsion. ~'sore m propeller

'proroga f extension

proro'ga|bile adj extendable. ~re vt extend

pro'rompere vi burst out

'prosa f prose. **pro'saico** adj prosaic

pro'scio|gliere vt release; (Jur) acquit. ~lto pp di prosciogliere

prosciu'gar|e vt dry up; (bonificare) reclaim. ~si vr dry up

prosci'utto m ham. ~ cotto cooked ham. ~ crudo Parma ham

pro'scri|tto, -a pp di proscrivere ●mf exile

prosecuzi'one f continuation

prosegui'mento m continuation; buon ~! (viaggio) have a good journey!; (festa) enjoy the rest of the party!

prosegu'ire vt continue ●vi go on, continue

prospe'r|are vi prosper. ~ità f prosperity. **'prospero** adj prosperous; (favorevole) favourable. ~oso adj flourishing; (ragazza) buxom

prospet'tar|e vt show. ~si vr seem

prospet'tiva f perspective; (panorama) view; fig prospect. **pro'spetto** m (vista) view; (facciata) façade; (tabella) table

prospici'ente adj facing

prossima'mente adv soon

prossimità f proximity

'prossimo, -a adj near; (seguente) next; (molto vicino) close; l'anno ~ next year ●m neighbour

prosti'tu|ta f prostitute. ~zi'one f

prostitution

protago'nista mf protagonist

pro'teggere vt protect; (favorire) favour

prote'ina f protein

pro'tender|e vt stretch out. ~si vr (in avanti) lean out. **pro'teso** pp di protendere

pro'te|sta f protest; (dichiarazione) protestation. ~'stante adj & mf Protestant. ~'stare vt/i protest

prote|t'tivo adj protective. ~tto pp di proteggere. ~t'tore, ~t'trice mf protector; (sostenitore) patron ●m (di prostituta) pimp. ~zi'one f protection

protocol'lare adj (visita) protocol ●vt register

proto'collo m protocol; (registro) register; carta ~ official stamped paper

proto'tipo m prototype

pro'tra|rre vt protract; (differire) postpone. ~rsi vr go on, continue. ~tto pp di protrarre

protube'ran|te adj protuberant. ~za f protuberance

'prova f test; (dimostrazione) proof; (tentativo) try; (di abito) fitting; Sport heat; (Theat) rehearsal; (bozza) proof; in ~ (assumere) for a trial period; mettere alla ~ put to the test. ~ generale dress rehearsal

pro'var|e vt test; (dimostrare) prove; (tentare) try; try on (abiti ecc); (sentire) feel; (Theat) rehearse. ~si vr try

proveni'enza f origin. **prove'nire** vi provenire da come from

pro'vento m proceeds pl

prove'nuto pp di provenire

pro'verbio m proverb

pro'vetta f test-tube; bambino in ~ test-tube baby

pro'vetto adj skilled

'provider m inv ISP, Internet Service Provider

pro'vinci|a f province; (strada) B road, secondary road. ~'ale adj provincial; strada ~ale B road

pro'vino m specimen; Cinema screen test

provo'ca|nte adj provocative. ~re vt provoke; (causare) cause. ~'tore, ~'trice mf trouble-maker. ~'torio adj provocative. ~zi'one f provocation

provve'd|ere vi ~ere a provide for. ~i'mento m measure; (previdenza) precaution

provvi'denz|a f providence. ~i'ale adj providential

provvigi'one f commission

provvi'sorio adj provisional

prov'vista f supply

pro'zio, -a m great-uncle ● f great-aunt

'prua f prow

pru'den|te adj prudent. ~za f prudence; per ~za as a precaution

'prudere vi itch

prugn|a f plum. ~a secca prune. ~o m plum[-tree]

pru'rito m itch

pseu'donimo m pseudonym

psica'na|lisi f psychoanalysis. ~'lista mf psychoanalyst. ~liz'zare vt psychoanalyse

'psiche f psyche

psichi'a|tra mf psychiatrist. ~'tria f psychiatry. ~trico adj psychiatric

'psichico adj mental

psico|lo'gia f psychology. ~'logico adj psychological. psi'cologo, -a mf psychologist

psico'patico, -a mf psychopath

PT abbr (Posta e Telecomunicazioni) PO

pubbli'ca|re vt publish. ~zi'one f publication. ~zioni pl (di matrimonio) banns

pubbli'cista mf Journ correspondent

pubbli'cità f inv publicity; (annuncio) advertisement, advert; fare ~ a qcsa advertise sth; piccola ~ small advertisements. pubbli'citario adj advertising

'pubblico adj public; scuola pubblica state school ● m public; (spettatori) audience; grande ~ general public. Pubblica Sicurezza Police. ~ ufficiale civil servant

'pube m pubis

puber'tà f puberty

pu'dico adj modest

pue'rile adj children's; pej childish

pugi'lato m boxing. 'pugile m boxer

pugna'la|re vt stab. ~ta f stab. pu'gnale m dagger

'pugno m fist; (colpo) punch; (manciata) fistful; (numero limitato) handful; dare un ~ a punch

'pulce f flea; (microfono) bug

pul'cino m chick; (nel calcio) junior

pu'ledra f filly

pu'ledro m colt

pu'li|re vt clean. ~re a secco dry-clean. ~to adj clean. ~'tura f cleaning. ~'zia f (il pulire) cleaning; (l'essere pulito) cleanliness; ~zie pl housework; fare le ~zie do the cleaning

'pullman m inv bus, coach; (urbano) bus

pul'mino m minibus

'pulpito m pulpit

pul'sante m button; (Electr) [push-]button. ~ di accensione on/off switch

pul'sa|re vi pulsate. ~zi'one f pulsation

pul'viscolo m dust

'puma m inv puma

pun'gente adj prickly; (insetto) stinging; (odore ecc) sharp

'pungere vt prick; (insetto:) sting

pungigli'one m sting

pu'ni|re vt punish. ~'tivo adj punitive. ~zi'one f punishment; Sport free kick

'**punta** f point; (estremità) tip; (di monte) peak; (un po') pinch; Sport forward; **doppie punte** (di capelli) split ends

pun'tare vt point; (spingere con forza) push; (scommettere) bet; (⬚: appuntare) fasten ● vi ~ **su** fig rely on; ~ **verso** (dirigersi) head for; ~ **a** aspire to

punta'**spilli** m inv pincushion

pun'tat|a f (di una storia) instalment; (televisiva) episode; (al gioco) stake, bet; (breve visita) flying visit; **a ~e** serialized, in instalments

punteggia'tura f punctuation

pun'teggio m score

puntel'lare vt prop. pun'tello m prop

pun'tigli|o m spite; (ostinazione) obstinacy. ~oso adj punctilious, pernickety pej

pun'tin|a f (da disegno) drawing pin, thumb tack Am; (di giradischi) stylus. ~o m dot; (a ~o) perfectly; (cotto) to a T

'**punto** m point; (Med, in cucito), stitch; (in punteggiatura) full stop; in che ~? where, exactly?; **due punti** colon; **in** ~ sharp; **mettere a** ~ put right; fig fine tune; tune up (motore); **essere sul** ~ **di fare qcsa** be about to do sth, be on the point of doing sth. ~ **esclamativo** exclamation mark. ~ **interrogativo** question mark. ~ **nero** blackhead. ~ **di riferimento** landmark; (per la qualità) benchmark. ~ **di vendita** point of sale. ~ **e virgola** semicolon. ~ **di vista** point of view

puntu'al|e adj punctual. ~ità f punctuality. ~mente adv punctually

pun'tura f (di insetto) sting; (di ago ecc) prick; (Med) puncture; (iniezione) injection; (fitta) stabbing pain

punzecchi'are vt prick; fig tease

'**pupa** f doll. pu'pazzo m puppet.

pupazzo di neve snowman

pup'illa f (Anat) pupil

pu'pillo, -a mf (di professore) favourite

purché conj provided

'**pure** adv too, also; (concessivo) fate ~! please do! ● conj (tuttavia) yet; (anche se) even if; **pur di** just to

purè m inv purée. ~ **di patate** creamed potatoes

pu'rezza f purity

'**purga** f purge. pur'gante m laxative. pur'gare vt purge

purga'torio m purgatory

purifi'care vt purify

puri'tano, -a adj & mf Puritan

'**puro** adj pure; (vino ecc) undiluted; **per** ~ **caso** purely by chance

puro'sangue adj & m thoroughbred

pur'troppo adv unfortunately

pus m pus. '**pustola** f pimple

puti'ferio m uproar

putre'far|e vi, ~si vr putrefy

'**putrido** adj putrid

'**puzza** f = PUZZO

puz'zare vi stink; ~ **di bruciato** fig smell fishy

'**puzzo** m stink, bad smell. ~la f polecat. ~'lente adj stinking

p.zza abbr (piazza) Sq.

Qq

qua adv here; **da un anno in** ~ for the last year; **da quando in** ~? since when?; **di** ~ **this way**; **di** ~ **di** on this side of; ~ **dentro** in here; **sotto** ~ **under here**; ~ **vicino** near here; ~ **e là** here and there

qua'**derno** m exercise book; (per

appunti) notebook

quadrango'lare *adj* (*forma*) quadrangular. **qua'drangolo** *m* quadrangle

qua'drante *m* quadrant; (*di orologio*) dial

qua'dra|re *vt* square; (*contabilità*) balance ●*vi* fit in. ~**to** *adj* square; (*equilibrato*) level-headed ●*m* square; (*pugilato*) ring; al ~**to** squared

quadret'tato *adj* squared; (*carta*) graph *attrib.* **qua'dretto** *m* square; (*piccolo quadro*) small picture; a quadretti (*tessuto*) check

quadrien'nale *adj* (*che dura quattro anni*) four-year

quadri'foglio *m* four-leaf clover

quadri'latero *m* quadrilateral

quadri'mestre *m* four-month period

'quadro *m* picture, painting; (*quadrato*) square; (*fig: scena*) sight; (*tabella*) table; (*Theat*) scene; (*Comm*) executive quadri *pl* (*carte*) diamonds; a quadri (*tessuto, giacca, motivo*) check. quadri *pl* direttivi senior management

quaggiù *adv* down here

'quaglia *f* quail

'qualche *adj* (*alcuni*) a few, some; (*un certo*) some; (*in interrogazioni*) any; ho ~ problema I have a few problems, I have some problems; ~ tempo fa some time ago; hai ~ libro italiano? have you any Italian books?; posso pren-dere ~ libro? can I take some books?; in ~ modo somehow; in ~ posto somewhere; ~ volta sometimes; ~ cosa = QUALCOSA

qual'cosa *pron* something; (*in interrogazioni*) anything; ~'altro something else; vuoi ~'altro? would you like anything else?; ~a di strano something strange; vuoi ~a da mangiare? would you like something to eat?

qual'cuno *pron* someone, somebody; (*in interrogazioni*) anyone, anybody; (*alcuni*) some; (*in interrogazioni*) any; c'è ~? is anybody in?; qualcun altro someone else, somebody else; c'è qualcun altro che aspetta? is anybody else waiting?; ho letto ~ dei suoi libri I've read some of his books; conosci ~ dei suoi amici? do you know any of his friends?

'quale *adj* which; (*indeterminato*) what; (*come*) as, like; ~ macchina è la tua? which car is yours?; ~ motivo avrà di parlare così? what reason would he have to speak like that?; ~ onore! what an honour!; città quali Venezia towns like Venice; ~ che sia la tua opinione whatever you may think ●*pron inter* which [one]; ~ preferisci? which [one] do you prefer? ●*pron rel* il/la ~ (*persona*) who; (*animale, cosa*) that, which; (*oggetto: con prep*) whom; (*animale, cosa*) which; ho incontrato tua madre, la ~ mi ha detto... I met your mother, who told me...; l'ufficio nel ~ lavoro the office in which I work; l'uomo con il ~ parlavo the man to whom I was speaking ●*adv* (*come*) as

qua'lifica *f* qualification; (*titolo*) title

qualifi'ca|re *vt* qualify; (*definire*) define. ~**rsi** *vr* be placed. ~**'tivo** *adj* qualifying. ~**to** *adj* (*operaio*) semi-skilled. ~**zi'one** *f* qualification

qualità *f inv* quality; (*specie*) kind; in ~ di in one's capacity as. **qualita'tivo** *adj* qualitative

qua'lora *conj* in case

qual'siasi, qua'lunque *adj* any; (*non importa quale*) whatever; (*ordinario*) ordinary; dammi una penna ~ give me any pen [whatsoever]; farei ~ cosa I would do anything; ~ cosa io faccia whatever I do; ~ persona anyone; in ~ caso in any case; in ~ modo in any way; ~ any one, whichever; l'uomo qua-lunque the man in the street

qualunqu'ismo m lack of political views

'quando conj & adv when; da ~ ti ho visto since I saw you; da ~ esci con lui? how long have you been going out with him?; da ~ in qua? since when?; ~..., ~... sometimes..., sometimes...

quantifi'care vt quantify

quantità f inv quantity; una ~ di (gran numero) a great deal of. **quanti'tativo** m amount ● adj quantitative

'quanto

● adj inter how much; (con nomi plurali) how many; (in esclamazione) what a lot of; ~ tempo? how long?; quanti anni hai? how old are you?

● adj rel as much... as; (con nomi plurali) as many... as; prendi ~ denaro ti serve take as much money as you need; prendi quanti libri vuoi take as many books as you like

● pron inter how much; (quanto tempo) how long; (plurale) how many; quanti ne abbiamo oggi? what date is it today?, what's the date today?

● pron rel as much as; (quanto tempo) as long as; (plurale) as many as; prendine ~/quanti ne vuoi take as much/as many as you like; stai ~ vuoi stay as long as you like; questo è ~ that's it

● adv inter how much; (quanto tempo) how long; ~ sei alto? how tall are you?; ~ hai aspettato? how long did you wait for?; ~ costa? how much is it?; ~ mi dispiace! I'm so sorry!; ~ è bello! how nice!

● adv rel as much as; lavoro ~ posso I work as much as I can; è tanto intelligente ~ bello

he's as intelligent as he's good-looking; in ~ (in qualità di) as; (poiché) since; in ~ a me as far as I'm concerned; per ~ however; per ~ ne sappia as far as I know; per ~ mi riguarda as far as I'm concerned; ~ a as for; ~ prima (al più presto) as soon as possible

quan'tunque conj although

qua'ranta adj & m forty

quaran'tena f quarantine

quaran'tenn|e adj forty-year-old. ~io m period of forty years

quaran't|esimo adj fortieth. ~ina f una ~ina about forty

qua'resima f Lent

quar'tetto m quartet

quarti'ere m district; (Mil) quarters pl. ~ generale headquarters

'quarto adj fourth ● m fourth; (quarta parte) quarter; le sette e un ~ a quarter past seven. quarti pl di finale quarterfinals. ~ d'ora quarter of an hour. quar'tultimo, -a mf fourth from the end

'quarzo m quartz

'quasi adv almost, nearly; ~ mai hardly ever ● conj (come se) as if; ~ ~ sto a casa I'm tempted to stay home

quassù adv up here

'quatto adj crouching; (silenzioso) silent

quat'tordici adj & m fourteen

quat'trini mpl money sg

'quattro adj & m four; dirne ~ a qcno give sb a piece of one's mind; farsi in ~ (per qcno/per fare qcsa) go to a lot of trouble for sb/to do sth); in ~ e quatt'otto in a flash. ~ per ~ m inv (Auto) four-wheel drive [vehicle]

quat'trocchi: a ~ adv in private

quattro'cento adj & m four hundred; il Q~cento the

fifteenth century

quattro'mila adj & m four thousand

'quell|o adj that (pl those); quell'albero that tree; quegli alberi those trees; quel cane that dog; quei cani those dogs ● pron that [one] (pl those [ones]); ~o li that one over there; ~o che the one that; (ciò che) what; quelli che the ones that, those that; ~o a destra the one on the right

'quercia f oak

que'rela f [legal] action

quere'lare vt bring an action against

que'sito m question

questio'nario m questionnaire

quest'ione f question; (faccenda) matter; (litigio) quarrel; in ~ in doubt; è fuori ~ it's out of the question

'quest|o adj this (pl these) ● pron this [one] (pl these [ones]); ~o qui, ~o qua this one here; ~o è quello che ha detto that's what he said; per ~o for that reason. que-st'oggi today

que'store m chief of police

que'stura f police headquarters

qui adv here; da ~ in poi from now on; fin ~ (di tempo) up till now, until now; ~ dentro in here; ~ sotto under here; ~ vicino near here ● m ~ pro quo misunderstanding

quie'scienza f trattamento di ~ retirement package

quie'tanza f receipt

quie'tar|e vt calm. ~si vr quieten down

qui'et|e f quiet; disturbo della ~e pubblica breach of the peace. ~o adj quiet

'quindi adv then ● conj therefore

'quindi|ci adj & m fifteen. ~'cina f una ~cina una about fifteen; una ~cina di giorni two weeks pl

quinquen'nale adj (che dura cinque anni) five-year. quin'quennio m [period of] five years

quin'tale m a hundred kilograms

'quinte fpl (Theat) wings

quin'tetto m quintet

'quinto adj fifth

quin'tuplo adj quintuple

'quota f quota; (rata) instalment; (altitudine) height; (Aeron) altitude, height; (ippica) odds pl; perdere ~ lose altitude; prendere ~ gain altitude. ~ di iscrizione entry fee

quo'ta|re vt (Comm) quote. ~to adj quoted; essere ~to in Borsa be quoted on the Stock Exchange. ~zi'one f quotation

quotidi'ana'mente adv daily. ~'ano adj daily; (ordinario) everyday ● m daily [paper]

quozi'ente m quotient. ~ d'intelligenza intelligence quotient, IQ

Rr

ra'barbaro m rhubarb

'rabbia f rage; (ira) anger; (Med) rabies sg; che ~! what a nuisance!; mi fa ~ it makes me angry

rab'bino m rabbi

rabbiosa'mente adv furiously. rabbi'oso adj hot-tempered; (Med) rabid; (violento) violent

rabbo'nir|e vt pacify. ~si vr calm down

rabbrivi'dire vi shudder; (di freddo) shiver

rabbui'arsi vr become dark

raccapez'zar|e vt put together. ~si vr see one's way ahead

raccapricci'ante adj horrifying

raccatta'palle m inv ball boy ● f inv ball girl

raccat'tare vt pick up

rac'chetta f racket. ~ da ping pong table-tennis bat. ~ da sci ski pole. ~ da tennis tennis racket

racchi'udere vt contain

rac'cogli|ere vt pick; (da terra) pick up; (mietere) harvest; (collezionare) collect; (radunare) gather; win (voti ecc); (dare asilo a) take in. ~ersi vr gather; (concentrarsi) collect one's thoughts. ~'mento m concentration. ~'tore, ~'trice f collector ● m (cartella) ring-binder

rac'colto, -a pp di **raccogliere** ● adj (rannicchiato) hunched; (intimo) cosy; (concentrato) engrossed ● m (mietitura) harvest ● f collection; (di scritti) compilation; (del grano ecc) harvesting; (adunata) gathering

raccoman'dabile adj recommendable; poco ~ (persona) shady

raccoman'da|re vt recommend; (affidare) entrust. ~rsi vr (implorare) beg. ~ta f registered letter; ~ta con ricevuta di ritorno recorded delivery. ~espresso f next-day delivery of recorded items. ~zi'one f recommendation

raccon'tare vt tell. **rac'conto** m story

raccorci'are vt shorten

raccor'dare vt join. **rac'cordo** m connection; (stradale) feeder. **rac-cordo anulare** ring road. **raccordo ferroviario** siding

ra'chitico adj rickety; (poco sviluppato) stunted

racimo'lare vt scrape together

'racket m inv racket

'radar m inv radar

raddol'cir|e vt sweeten; fig soften. ~si vr become milder; (carattere:) mellow

raddoppi'are vt double. **rad'dop-pio** m doubling

raddriz'zare vt straighten

'rader|e vt shave; graze (muro); ~e al suolo raze. ~si vr shave

radi'are vt strike off; ~ dall'albo strike off

radia'tore m radiator. ~zi'one f radiation

'radica f briar

radi'cale adj radical ● m (Gram) root; (Pol) radical

ra'dicchio m chicory

ra'dice f root

'radio f inv radio; via ~ by radio. ~ a transistor transistor radio ● m (Chem) radium.

radioama'tore, -'trice mf [radio] ham

radioascolta'tore, -'trice mf listener

radioat'tività f radioactivity. ~'tivo adj radioactive

radio'cro|naca f radio commentary; fare la ~naca di commentate on. ~'nista mf radio reporter

radiodiffusi'one f broadcasting

radio'fonico adj radio attrib

radiogra'fare vt X-ray. ~'fia f X-ray [photograph]; (radiologia) radiography; fare una ~fia (paziente:) have an X-ray; (dottore:) take an X-ray

radio'lina f transistor

radi'ologo, -a mf radiologist

radi'oso adj radiant

radio'sveglia f radio alarm

radio'taxi m inv radio taxi

radiote'lefono m radiotelephone; (privato) cordless [phone]

radiotelevi'sivo adj broadcasting attrib

'rado adj sparse; (non frequente) rare; di ~ seldom

radu'nar|e vt, ~si vr gather [together]. **ra'duno** m meeting; Sport rally

ra'dura f clearing

r

'rafano m horseradish

raf'fermo adj stale

'raffica f gust; (di armi da fuoco) burst; (di domande) barrage

raffigu'ra|re vt represent. ~zi'one f representation

raffi'na|re vt refine. ~ta'mente adv elegantly. ~to adj refined. raffine'ria f refinery

rafforza|'mento m reinforcement; (di muscolatura) strengthening. ~re vt reinforce. ~'tivo m (Gram) intensifier

raffredda'mento m (processo) cooling

raffred'd|are vt cool. ~arsi vr get cold; (prendere un raffreddore) catch a cold. ~ore m cold. ~ore da fieno hay fever

raf'fronto m comparison

'rafia f raffia

Rag. abbr ragioniere

ra'gaz|za f girl; (fidanzata) girlfriend. ~za alla pari au pair [girl]. ~'zata f prank. ~zo m boy; (fidanzato) boyfriend

ragge'lar|e vt fig freeze. ~si vr fig turn to ice

raggi'ante adj radiant; ~ di successo flushed with success

raggi'era f a ~ with a pattern like spokes radiating from a centre

'raggio m ray; (Math) radius; (di ruota) spoke; ~ d'azione range. ~ laser laser beam

raggi'rare vt trick. rag'giro m trick

raggi'un|gere vt reach; (conseguire) achieve. ~gibile adj (luogo) within reach

raggomito'lar|e vt wind. ~si vr curl up

raggranel'lare vt scrape together

raggrin'zir|e vt, ~si vr wrinkle

raggrup|pa'mento m (gruppo) group; (azione) grouping. ~'pare vt group together

ragguagli'are vt compare; (informare) inform. raggu'aglio m comparison; (informazione) information

ragguar'devole adj considerable

'ragia f resin; acqua ~ turpentine

ragiona'mento m reasoning; (discussione) discussion. ragio'nare vi reason; (discutere) discuss

ragi'one f reason; (ciò che è giusto) right; a ~ o a torto rightly or wrongly; aver ~ be right; perdere la ~ go out of one's mind

ragione'ria f accountancy

ragio'nevol|e adj reasonable. ~'mente adv reasonably

ragioni'ere, -a mf accountant

ragli'are vi bray

ragna'tela f cobweb. 'ragno m spider

ragù m inv meat sauce

RAI f abbr (Radio Audizioni Italiane) Italian public broadcasting company

ralle'gra|re vt gladden. ~rsi vr rejoice; ~rsi con qcno congratulate sb. ~'menti mpl congratulations

rallenta'mento m slowing down

rallen'ta|re vt/i slow down; (allentare) slacken. ~rsi vr slow down. ~'tore m speed bump; al ~tore in slow motion

raman'zina f reprimand

ra'marro m type of lizard

ra'mato adj copper[-coloured]

'rame m copper

ramifi'ca|re vi, ~rsi vr branch out; (strada:) branch. ~zi'one f ramification

rammari'carsi vr ~ di regret; (lamentarsi) complain (di about). ram'marico m regret

rammen'dare vt darn. ram'mendo m darning

rammen'tar|e vt remember; ~e qcsa a qcno (richiamare alla memoria) remind sb of sth. ~si vr remember

rammol'li|re vt soften. ~rsi vr go

soft. ∼to, -a *mf* wimp

'**ramo** *m* branch. ∼'scello *m* twig

'**rampa** *f* (*di scale*) flight. ∼ d'accesso slip road. ∼ di lancio launch[ing] pad

ram'pante *adj* giovane ∼ yuppie

rampi'cante *adj* climbing ●*m* (*Bot*) creeper

ram'pollo *m* hum brat; (*discendente*) descendant

ram'pone *m* harpoon; (*per scarpe*) crampon

'**rana** *f* frog; (*nel nuoto*) breaststroke; uomo ∼ frogman

ran'core *m* resentment

ran'dagio *adj* stray

'**rango** *m* rank

rannicchi'arsi *vr* huddle up

rannuvo'larsi *vr* cloud over

ra'nocchio *m* frog

ranto'lare *vi* wheeze. '**rantolo** *m* wheeze; (*di moribondo*) deathrattle

'**rapa** *f* turnip

ra'pace *adj* rapacious; (*uccello*) predatory

ra'pare *vt* crop

'**rapida** *f* rapids *pl*. ∼'mente *adv* rapidly

rapidità *f* speed

'**rapido** *adj* swift ●*m* (*treno*) express [train]

rapi'mento *m* kidnapping

ra'pina *f* robbery; ∼ a mano armata armed robbery. ∼ in banca bank robbery. **rapi'nare** *vt* rob. ∼'tore *m* robber

ra'pi|re *vt* abduct; (*a scopo di riscatto*) kidnap; (*estasiare*) ravish. ∼'tore, ∼'trice *mf* kidnapper

rappacifi'ca|re *vt* pacify. ∼**rsi** *vr* be reconciled. ∼**zi'one** *f* reconciliation

rappor'tare *vt* reproduce (*disegno*); (*confrontare*) compare

rap'porto *m* report; (*connessione*) re-

lation; (*legame*) relationship; (*Math, Techn*) ratio; **rapporti** *pl* relationship; essere in buoni rapporti be on good terms. ∼ di lancio launch-[ing] pad ∼ di amicizia friendship. ∼ di lavoro working relationship. **rapporti** *pl* sessuali sexual intercourse

rap'prendersi *vr* set; (*latte:*) curdle

rappre'saglia *f* reprisal

rappresen'tan|te *mf* representative. ∼**te di commercio** sales representative. ∼**za** *f* delegation; (*Comm*) agency; **spese** *pl* **di** ∼**za** entertainment expenses; **di** ∼**za** (*appartamento ecc*) company

rappresen'ta|re *vt* represent; (*Theat*) perform. ∼**tivo** *adj* representative. ∼**zi'one** *f* representation; (*spettacolo*) performance

rap'preso *pp* **di rapprendersi**

rapso'dia *f* rhapsody

'**raptus** *m inv* fit of madness

rara'mente *adv* rarely, seldom

rare'fa|re *vt*, ∼**rsi** *vr* rarefy. ∼**tto** *adj* rarefied

rarità *f inv* rarity. '**raro** *adj* rare

ra'sa|re *vt* shave; trim (*siepe ecc*). ∼**rsi** *vr* shave

raschi'are *vt* scrape; (*togliere*) scrape off

rasen'tare *vt* go close to. **ra'sente** *prep* very close to

'**raso** *pp* **di radere** ●*adj* smooth; (*colmo*) full to the brim; (*barba*) close-cropped; ∼ **terra** close to the ground; **un cucchiaio** ∼ a level spoonful ●*m* satin

ra'soio *m* razor

ras'segna *f* review; (*mostra*) exhibition; (*musicale, cinematografica*) festival; passare in ∼ review; (*Mil*) inspect

rasse'gna|re *vt* present. ∼**rsi** *vr* resign oneself. ∼**to** *adj* (*persona, aria, tono*) resigned. ∼**zi'one** *f* resignation

rassere'nar|e *vt* clear; *fig* cheer up.

~**si** vr become clear; fig cheer up

rasset'tare vt tidy up; (ripa-rare) mend

rassicu'ra|nte adj reassuring. ~re vt reassure. ~zi'one f reassurance

rasso'dare vt harden; fig strengthen

rassomigli'a|nza f resemblance. ~re vi ~re a resemble

rastrella'mento m (di fieno) raking; (perlustrazione) combing. **rastrel'lare** vt rake; (perlustrare) comb

rastrelli'era f rack; (per biciclette) bicycle rack; (scolapiatti) [plate] rack. **ra'strello** m rake

'**rata** f instalment; **pagare a rate** pay by instalments. **rate'ale** adj by instalments; **pagamento rateale** payment by instalments

rate'are, **rateiz'zare** vt divide into instalments

ra'tifica f (Jur) ratification

ratifi'care vt (Jur) ratify

'**ratto** m abduction; (roditore) rat

rattop'pare vt patch. **rat'toppo** m patch

rattrap'pir|e vt make stiff. ~**si** vr become stiff

rattri'star|e vt sadden. ~**si** vr become sad

rau'cedine f hoarseness. '**rauco** adj hoarse

rava'nello m radish

ravi'oli mpl ravioli

ravve'dersi vr mend one's ways

ravvicina'mento m reconciliation; (Pol) rapprochement

ravvici'nar|e vt bring closer; (riconciliare) reconcile. ~**si** vr be reconciled

ravvi'sare vt recognize

ravvi'var|e vt revive; fig brighten up. ~**si** vr revive

'**rayon** m rayon

razio'cinio m rational thought; (buon senso) common sense

razio'nal|e adj rational. ~**ità** f (ra-ziocinio) rationality; (di ambiente) functional nature. ~**iz'zare** vt rationalize (programmi, metodi, spazio). ~'**mente** adv rationally

razio'nare vt ration. **razi'one** f ration

'**razza** f race; (di cani ecc) breed; (genere) kind; **che ~ di idiota!** ⚠ what an idiot!

raz'zia f raid

razzi'ale adj racial

raz'zis|mo m racism. ~**ta** adj & mf racist

'**razzo** m rocket. **~ da segnalazione** flare

razzo'lare vi (polli:) scratch about

re m inv king; (Mus) D

rea'gire vi react

re'ale adj real; (di re) royal

rea'lis|mo m realism. ~**ta** mf realist; (fautore del re) royalist

realistica'mente adv realistically. **rea'listico** adj realistic

'**reality tv** f reality tv

realiz'zabile adj feasible

realiz'zar|e vt (attuare) carry out, realize; (Comm) make; score (gol, canestro); (rendersi conto di) realize. ~**si** vr come true; (nel lavoro ecc) fulfil oneself. ~**zi'one** f realization; (di sogno, persona) fulfilment. ~**zione scenica** production

real'mente adv really

realtà f inv reality. **~ virtuale** virtual reality

re'ato m crime

reat'tivo adj reactive

reat'tore m reactor; (Aeron) jet [aircraft]

reazio'nario, -a adj & mf reactionary

reazi'one f reaction. **~ a catena** chain reaction

'**rebus** m inv rebus; (enigma) puzzle

recapi'tare vt deliver. **re'capito** m address; (consegna) delivery. **recapito a domicilio** home delivery. **recapito telefonico** contact telephone number

re'car|e vt bear; (produrre) cause. **~si** vr go

re'cedere vi recede; fig give up

recensi'one f review

recen's|ire vt review. **~ore** m reviewer

re'cente adj recent; **di ~** recently. **~mente** adv recently

recessi'one f recession

re'cesso m recess

re'cidere vt cut off

reci'divo, -a adj (Med) recurrent ● mf repeat offender

recin'tare vt close off. **re'cinto** m enclosure; (per animali) pen; (per bambini) play-pen. **~zi'one** f (muro) wall; (rete) wire fence; (cancellata) railings pl

recipi'ente m container

re'ciproco adj reciprocal

re'ciso pp di recidere

'recita f performance. **reci'tare** vt recite; (Theat) act; play (ruolo). **~zi'one** f recitation; (Theat) acting

recla'mare vi protest ● vt claim

ré'clame f inv advertising; (avviso pubblicitario) advertisement

re'clamo m complaint; **ufficio reclami** complaints department

recli'na|bile adj reclining; **sedile ~bile** reclining seat. **~re** vt tilt (sedile); lean (capo)

reclusi'one f imprisonment. **re'cluso, -a** adj secluded ● mf prisoner

'recluta f recruit

reclu|ta'mento m recruitment. **~'tare** vt recruit

'record m inv record ● adj inv (cifra) record attrib

recrimi'na|re vi recriminate

recupe'rare vt recover. **re'cupero** m recovery; **corso di recupero** additional classes; **minuti di recupero** Sport injury time

redargu'ire vt rebuke

re'datto pp di redigere

redat'tore, -'trice mf editor; (di testo) writer

redazi'one f (ufficio) editorial office; (di testi) editing

reddi'tizio adj profitable

'reddito m income. **~ imponibile** taxable income

re'den|to pp di redimere. **~'tore** m redeemer. **~zi'one** f redemption

re'digere vt write; draw up (documento)

re'dimer|e vt redeem. **~si** vr redeem oneself

'redini fpl reins

'reduce adj **~ da** back from ● mf survivor

refe'rendum m inv referendum

refe'renza f reference

refet'torio m refectory

refrat'tario adj refractory; **essere ~ a** have no aptitude for

refrige'ra|re vt refrigerate. **~zi'o-ne** f refrigeration

refur'tiva f stolen goods pl

rega'lare vt give

re'galo m present, gift

re'gata f regatta

reg'gen|te m regent. **~za** f regency

'regger|e vt (sorreggere) bear; (tenere in mano) hold; (dirigere) run; (governare) govern; (Gram) take ● vi (resistere) hold out; (durare) last; fig stand. **~si** vr stand

'reggia f royal palace

reggi'calze m inv suspender belt

reggi'mento m regiment

reggi'petto, reggi'seno m bra

re'gia f Cinema direction; (Theat) production

re'gime m regime; (dieta) diet;

(Mech) speed

re'gina f queen

'regio adj royal

regio'na|le adj regional. ~**lismo** m (parola) regionalism

regi'one f region

re'gista mf (Cinema) director; (Theat, TV) producer

regi'stra|re vt register; (Comm) enter; (incidere su nastro) tape, record; (su disco) record. ~**tore** m recorder; (magnetofono) tape-recorder. ~**tore di cassa** cash register. ~**zi'one** f (di registrazione); (Comm) entry; (di programma) recording

re'gistro m register; (ufficio) registry. ~ **di cassa** ledger

re'gnare vi reign

'regno m kingdom; (sovranità) reign. R~ **Unito** United Kingdom

'regola f rule; essere in ~ be in order; (persona): have one's papers in order. **rego'labile** adj (meccanismo) adjustable. ~**'mento** m regulation; (Comm) settlement

rego'lar|e adj regular ● vt regulate; (ridurre, moderare) limit; (sistemare) settle. ~**si** vr (agire) act; (moderarsi) control oneself. ~**ità** f regularity. ~**iz'zare** vt settle (debt)

rego'la|ta f darsi una ~**ta** pull oneself together. ~**tore**, ~**'trice** adj **piano** ~**tore** urban development plan

'regolo m ruler

regres'sivo adj regressive. **re'gresso** m decline

reinseri'mento m (di persona) reintegration

reinse'rirsi vr (in ambiente) reintegrate

reinte'grare vt restore

relativa'mente adv relatively; ~ **a** as regards. **rela'tivo** adj relative

rela'tore, ~**'trice** mf (in una conferenza) speaker

re'lax m relaxation

relazi'one f relation[ship]; (rapporto amoroso) [love] affair; (resoconto) report; **pubbliche relazioni** pl public relations

rele'gare vt relegate

religi'o|ne f religion. ~**so, -a** adj religious ● m monk ● f nun

re'liqui|a f relic. ~**'ario** m reliquary

re'litto m wreck

re'ma|re vi row. ~**tore**, ~**'trice** mf rower

remini'scenza f reminiscence

remissi'one f remission; (sottomissione) submissiveness. **remis'sivo** adj submissive

'remo m oar

'remora f senza remore without hesitation

re'moto adj remote

remune'ra|re vt remunerate. ~**zi'one** f remuneration

'render|e vt (restituire) return; (esprimere) render; (fruttare) yield; (far diventare) make. ~**si** vr become; ~**si conto di qcsa** realize sth; ~**si utile** make oneself useful

rendi'conto m report

rendi'mento m rendering; (produzione) yield

'rendita f income; (dello Stato) revenue

'rene m kidney. ~ **artificiale** kidney machine

'reni fpl (schiena) back

reni'tente adj essere ~ **a** (consigli di qcno) be unwilling to accept

'renna f reindeer (pl inv); (pelle) buckskin

'reo, -a adj guilty ● mf offender

re'parto m department; (Mil) unit

repel'lente adj repulsive

repen'taglio m **mettere a** ~ risk

repen'tino adj sudden

reper'ibile adj available; **non è** ~

(*perduto*) it's not to be found

repe'rire vt trace (*fondi*)

re'perto m ~ archeologico find

reper'torio m repertory; (*elenco*) index; **immagini** pl di ~ archive footage

'replica f reply; (*obiezione*) objection; (*copia*) replica; (*Theat*) repeat performance. **repli'care** vt reply; (*Theat*) repeat

repor'tage m inv report

repres|si'one f repression. ~**si'vo** adj repressive. **re'presso** pp di reprimere. **re'primere** vt repress

re'pubbli|ca f republic. ~**'cano, -a** adj & mf republican

repu'tare vt consider

reputazi'one f reputation

requi'sito m requirement

requi'sitoria f (*arringa*) closing speech

'resa f surrender; (*Comm*) rendering. ~ **dei conti** rendering of accounts

'residence m inv residential hotel

resi'den|te adj & mf resident. ~**za** f residence; (*soggiorno*) stay. ~**zi'ale** adj residential; **zona** ~**ziale** residential district

re'siduo adj residual ●m remainder

'resina f resin

resi'sten|te adj resistant; ~**te all'acqua** water-resistant. ~**za** f resistance; (*fisica*) stamina; (*Electr*) resistor; **la R~za** the Resistance

re'sistere vi ~ [a] resist; (*a colpi, scosse*) stand up to; ~ **alla pioggia/al vento** be rain-/wind-resistant

'reso pp di rendere

reso'conto m report

re'spin|gere vt repel; (*rifiutare*) reject; (*bocciare*) fail. ~**to** pp di respingere

respi'ra|re vt/i breathe. ~**'tore** m respirator. ~**tore [a tubo]** snorkel; ~**'torio** adj respiratory. ~**zi'one** f breathing; (*Med*) respiration. ~**zione**

bocca a bocca mouth-to-mouth resuscitation, kiss of life. **re'spiro** m breath; (*il respirare*) breathing; fig respite

respon'sabile adj responsible (di for); (*Jur*) liable ●mf person responsible. ~**e della produzione** production manager. ~**ità** f inv responsibility; (*Jur*) liability. ~**iz'zare** vt give responsibility to

re'sponso m response

'ressa f crowd

re'stante adj remaining ●m remainder

re'stare vi = RIMANERE

restau'ra|re vt restore. ~**'tore, ~'trice** mf restorer. ~**zi'one** f restoration. **re'stauro** m (*riparazione*) repair

re'stio adj restive; ~ **a** a reluctant to

resti'tu|'ire vt return; (*reintegrare*) restore. ~**zi'one** f return; (*Jur*) restitution

'resto m remainder; (*saldo*) balance; (*denaro*) change; **resti** pl (*avanzi*) remains; **del** ~ besides

re'string|ere vt contract; take in (*vestiti*); (*limitare*) restrict; shrink (*stoffa*). ~**si** vr contract; (*farsi più vicini*) close up; (*stoffa:*) shrink. **re'stringi'mento** m (*di tessuto*) shrinkage

restri'ttivo adj restrictive. ~**zi'one** f restriction

resurrezi'one f resurrection

resusci'tare vt/i revive

re'tata f round-up

'rete f net; (*sistema*) network; (*televisiva*) channel; (*in calcio*) goal; fig trap; (*per la spesa*) string bag. ~ **locale** (*Comput*) local [area] network. ~ **stradale** road network. ~ **televisiva** television channel

reti'cen|te adj reticent. ~**za** f reticence

retico'lato m grid; (*rete metallica*) wire netting. **re'ticolo** m network

re'torico, -a adj rhetorical; **domanda retorica** rhetorical question

● f rhetoric

retribu'ire vt remunerate. ~zi'one f remuneration

'**retro** adv behind; vedi ~ see over ● m inv back. ~ **di copertina** outside back cover

retroat'tivo adj retroactive

retro'ce|dere vi retreat ● vt (Mil) demote; Sport relegate. ~ssi'one f Sport relegation

retroda'tare vt backdate

re'trogrado adj retrograde; fig old-fashioned; (Pol) reactionary

retrogu'ardia f (Mil) rearguard

retro'marcia f reverse [gear]

retro'scena m inv (Theat) backstage; fig background details pl

retrospet'tivo adj retrospective

retro'stante adj il palazzo ~ the building behind

retrovi'sore m rear-view mirror

'**retta**[1] f (Math) straight line; (di collegio, pensionato) fee

'**retta**[2] f dar ~ a qcno take sb's advice

rettango'lare adj rectangular. ret'tangolo m rectangle

ret'tifi|ca f rectification. ~'care vt rectify

'**rettile** m reptile

retti'lineo adj rectilinear; (retto) upright ● m Sport back straight

'**retto** pp di reggere ● adj straight; fig upright; (giusto) correct; **angolo** ~ right angle

ret'tore m (Relig) rector; (Univ) principal, vice-chancellor

reu'matico adj rheumatic

reuma'tismi mpl rheumatism

reve'rendo adj reverend

rever'sibile adj reversible

revisio'nare vt revise; (Comm) audit; (Auto) overhaul. **revisi'one** f revision; (Comm) audit; (Auto) overhaul. **revi'sore** m (di conti) auditor; (di bozze) proof-reader; (di traduzioni) revisor

re'vival m inv revival

'**revoca** f repeal. **revo'care** vt repeal

riabili'ta|re vt rehabilitate. ~zi'one f rehabilitation

riabitu'ar|e vt reaccustom. ~**si** vr reaccustom oneself

riac'cender|e vt rekindle (fuoco). ~**si** vr (luce:) come back on

riacqui'stare vt buy back; regain (libertà, prestigio); recover (vista, udito)

riagganci'are vt replace (ricevitore); ~ **la cornetta** hang up ● vi hang up

riallac'ciare vt refasten; reconnect (corrente); renew (amicizia)

rial'zare vt raise ● vi rise. ri'alzo m rise

riani'mar|e vt (Med) resuscitate; (ridare forza a) revive; (ridare coraggio a) cheer up. ~**si** vr regain consciousness; (riprendere forza) revive; (riprendere coraggio) cheer up

riaper'tura f reopening

ria'prir|e vt, ~**si** vr reopen

rias'sumere vt summarize

riassun'tivo adj summarizing. rias'sunto pp di riassumere ● m summary

ria'ver|e vt get back; regain (salute, vista). ~**si** vr recover

riavvicina'mento m reconciliation

riavvici'nar|e vt reconcile (paesi, persone). ~**si** vr (riconciliarsi) be reconciled, make it up

riba'dire vt (confermare) reaffirm

ri'balta f flap; (Theat) footlights pl; fig limelight

ribal'tar|e vt/i, ~**si** vr tip over; (Naut) capsize

ribas'sare vt lower ● vi fall. ri'basso m fall; (sconto) discount

ri'battere vt (a macchina) retype; (controbattere) deny ● vi answer back

ribel'l|arsi vr rebel. ri'belle adj

rebellious ● *mf* rebel. ~'**ione** *f* rebellion

ri'bes *m inv* (*rosso*) redcurrant; (*nero*) blackcurrant

ribol'lire *vi* ferment; *fig* seethe

ri'brezzo *m* disgust; far ~ a disgust

rica'dere *vi* fall back; (*nel peccato ecc*) lapse; (*pendere*) hang [down]; ~ su (*riversarsi*) fall on. **rica'duta** *f* relapse

rical'care *vt* trace

rica'mare *vt* embroider. ~**to** *adj* embroidered

ri'cambi *mpl* spare parts

ricambi'are *vt* return; reciprocate (*sentimento*); ~ qcsa a qcno repay sb for sth. **ri'cambio** *m* replacement; (*Biol*) metabolism; pezzo di ricambio spare [part]

ri'camo *m* embroidery

ricapito'la|re *vt* sum up. ~**zi'one** *f* summary, recap Ⓘ

ri'carica *f* (*di sveglia*) rewinding; (*Teleph*) top-up card

ricari'care *vt* reload (*macchina fotografica, fucile, camion*); recharge (*batteria*); (*Comput*) reboot

ricat'ta|re *vt* blackmail. ~**tore**, ~**trice** *mf* blackmailer. **ri'catto** *m* blackmail

rica'va|re *vt* get; (*ottenere*) obtain; (*dedurre*) draw. ~**to** *m* proceeds *pl*. **ri'cavo** *m* proceeds *pl*

'ricca *f* rich woman. ~'**mente** *adv* lavishly

ric'chezza *f* wealth; *fig* richness

'riccio *adj* curly ● *m* curl; (*animale*) hedgehog. ~ di mare sea-urchin. ~**lo** *m* curl. ~'**luto** *adj* curly. **ric'ciuto** *adj* (*barba*) curly

'ricco *adj* rich ● *m* rich man

ri'cerca *f* search; (*indagine*) investigation; (*scientifica*) research; (*Sch*) project

ricer'ca|re *vt* search for; (*fare ricer-*

che su) research. ~**ta** *f* wanted woman. ~'**tezza** *f* refinement. ~**to** *adj* sought-after; (*raffinato*) refined; (*affettato*) affected ● *m* (*dalla polizia*) wanted man

ricetrasmit'tente *f* transceiver

ri'cetta *f* prescription; (*Culin*) recipe

ricet'tacolo *m* receptacle

ricet'tario *m* (*di cucina*) recipe book

ricetta|'tore, -'trice *mf* fence, receiver of stolen goods. ~**zi'one** *f* receiving [stolen goods]

rice'vente *adj* (*apparecchio, stazione*) receiving ● *mf* receiver

ri'cev|ere *vt* receive; (*dare il benvenuto*) welcome; (*di albergo*) accommodate. ~**i'mento** *m* receiving; (*accoglienza*) welcome; (*trattenimento*) reception

ricevi'tor|e *m* receiver. ~'**la** *f* ~**ia del lotto** agency authorized to sell lottery tickets

rice'vuta *f* receipt

ricezi'one *f* (*Radio, TV*) reception

richia'mare *vt* (*al telefono*) call back; (*far tornare*) recall; (*rimproverare*) rebuke; (*attirare*) draw; ~ **alla mente** call to mind. **richi'amo** *m* recall; (*attrazione*) call

richi'edere *vt* ask for; (*di nuovo*) ask again for; ~ a qcno di fare qcsa ask o request sb to do sth. **richi'esta** *f* request; (*Comm*) demand

ri'chiuder|e *vt* close again. ~**si** *vr* (*ferita*) heal

rici'claggio *m* recycling

rici'clare *vt* recycle (*carta, vetro*); launder (*denaro sporco*)

'ricino *m* olio di ~ castor oil

ricognizi'one *f* reconnaissance

ri'colmo *adj* full

ricominci'are *vt/i* start again

ricompa'rire *vi* reappear

ricom'pen|sa *f* reward. ~'**sare** *vt* reward

ricom'por|re *vt* (*riscrivere*) rewrite;

(*ricostruire*) reform; (*Typ*) reset. ∼si *vr* regain one's composure

riconcili'a|re *vt* reconcile. ∼rsi *vr* be reconciled. ∼zi'one *f* reconciliation

ricono'scen|te *adj* grateful. ∼za *f* gratitude

rico'nosc|ere *vt* recognize; (*ammettere*) acknowledge. ∼i'mento *m* recognition; (*ammissione*) acknowledgement; (*per la polizia*) identification. ∼i'uto *adj* recognized

riconside'rare *vt* rethink

rico'prire *vt* re-cover; (*rivestire*) coat; (*di insulti*) shower (di with); hold (*carica*)

ricor'dar|e *vt* remember; (*richiamare alla memoria*) recall; (*far ricordare*) remind; (*rassomigliare*) look like. ∼si ∼si [di] remember. ri'cordo *m* memory; (*oggetto*) memento; (*di viaggio*) souvenir; ricordi *pl* (*memorie*) memoirs

ricor'ren|te *adj* recurrent. ∼za *f* recurrence; (*anniversario*) anniversary

ri'correre *vi* recur; (*accadere*) occur; (*data*) fall; ∼ a have recourse to; (*rivolgersi a*) turn to. ri'corso *pp di* ricorrere ● *m* recourse; (*Jur*) appeal

ricostitu'ente *m* tonic

ricostitu'ire *vt* re-establish

ricostru'|ire *vt* reconstruct. ∼zi'one *f* reconstruction

ricove'rare *vt* give shelter to; ∼re in ospedale admit to hospital, hospitalize. ∼to, -a *mf* hospital patient. ri'covero *m* shelter; (*ospizio*) home

ricre'a|re *vt* re-create; (*ristorare*) restore. ∼rsi *vr* amuse oneself. ∼tivo *adj* recreational. ∼zi'one *f* recreation; (*Sch*) break

ri'credersi *vr* change one's mind

ricupe'rare *vt* recover; rehabilitate (*tossicodipendente*); ∼ il tempo perduto make up for lost time. ri'cupero *m* recovery; (*di tossicodipendente*) rehabilitation; (*salvataggio*) res-

cue; [minuti *mpl* di] ricupero injury time

ri'curvo *adj* bent

ri'dare *vt* give back, return

ri'dente *adj* (*piacevole*) pleasant

'ridere *vi* laugh; ∼ di (*deridere*) laugh at

ri'detto *pp di* ridire

ridicoliz'zare *vt* ridicule. ri'dicolo *adj* ridiculous

ridimensio'nare *vt* reshape; *fig* see in the right perspective

ri'dire *vt* repeat; (*criticare*) find fault with

ridon'dante *adj* redundant

ri'dotto *pp di* ridurre ● *m* (*Theat*) foyer ● *adj* reduced

ri'du|rre *vt* reduce. ∼rsi *vr* diminish. ∼rsi a be reduced to. ∼t'tivo *adj* reductive. ∼zi'one *f* reduction; (*per cinema, teatro*) adaptation

rieducazi'one *f* (*di malato*) rehabilitation

riem'pi|re *vt* fill [up]; fill in (*moduli ecc*). ∼rsi *vr* fill [up]. ∼'tivo *adj* filling ● *m* filler

rien'tranza *f* recess

rien'trare *vi* go/come back in; (*tornare*) return; (*piegare indentro*) recede; ∼ in (*far parte*) fall within. ri'entro *m* return; (*di astronave*) re-entry

riepilo'gare *vt* recapitulate. rie'pilogo *m* roundup

riesami'nare *vt* reappraise

riesu'mare *vt* exhume

rievo'ca|re *vt* commemorate. ∼zi'one *f* commemoration

rifaci'mento *m* remake

ri'fa|re *vt* do again; (*creare*) make again; (*riparare*) repair; (*imitare*) imitate; make (*letto*). ∼rsi *vr* (*rimettersi*) recover; (*vendicarsi*) get even; ∼rsi una vita/carriera make a new life/career for oneself; ∼rsi di make up for. ∼tto *pp di* rifare

riferi'mento *m* reference

rife'rir|e vt report; ~e a attribute to • vi make a report. ~si vr ~si a refer to

rifi'lare vt (tagliare a filo) trim; (🔲: affibbiare) saddle

rifi'ni|re vt finish off. ~tura f finish

rifiu'tare vt refuse. rifi'uto m refusal; rifiuti pl (immondizie) rubbish sg. rifiuti pl urbani urban waste sg

riflessi'one f reflection; (osservazione) remark. rifles'sivo adj thoughtful; (Gram) reflexive

ri'flesso pp di riflettere • m (luce) reflection; (Med) reflex; per ~ indirectly

ri'fletter|e vt reflect • vi think. ~si vr be reflected

riflet'tore m reflector; (proiettore) searchlight

ri'flusso m ebb

rifocil'lar|e vt restore. ~si vr liter, hum take some refreshment

ri'fondere vt refund

ri'forma f reform; (Relig) reformation; (Mil) medical exemption

rifor'ma|re vt re-form; (migliorare) reform; (Mil) declare unfit for military service. ~to adj (chiesa) Reformed. ~'tore, ~'trice mf reformer. ~'torio m reformatory. rifor'mista adj reformist

riforni'mento m supply; (scorta) stock; (di combustibile) refuelling; stazione f di ~ petrol station

rifor'nir|e vt ~ di provide with. ~si vr restock, stock up (di with)

ri'fra|ngere vt refract. ~tto pp di rifrangere. ~zi'one f refraction

rifug'gire vi ~ da fig shun

rifugi'a|rsi vr take refuge. ~to, -a mf refugee. ~to economico economic refugee

ri'fugio m shelter; (nascondiglio) hideaway

'riga f line; (fila) row; (striscia) stripe; (scriminatura) parting; (regolo) rule; a

righe (stoffa) striped; (quaderno) ruled; mettersi in ~ line up

ri'gagnolo m rivulet

ri'gare vt rule (foglio) • vi ~ dritto behave well

rigatti'ere m junk dealer

rigene'rare vt regenerate

riget'tare vt throw back; (respingere) reject; (vomitare) throw up. ri'getto m rejection

ri'ghello m ruler

rigid|a'mente adv rigidly. ~ità f rigidity; (di clima) severity; (severità) strictness. 'rigido adj rigid; (freddo) severe; (severo) strict

rigi'rar|e vt turn again; (ripercorrere) go round; fig twist (argomentazione) • vi walk about. ~si vr turn round; (nel letto) turn over. ri'giro m (imbroglio) trick

'rigo m line; (Mus) staff

ri'goglio m bloom. ~'oso adj luxuriant

ri'gonfio adj swollen

ri'gore m rigours pl; a ~ strictly speaking; calcio di ~ penalty [kick]; area di ~ penalty area; essere di ~ be compulsory

rigo'roso adj (severo) strict; (scrupoloso) rigorous

riguada'gnare vt regain (quota, velocità)

riguar'dar|e vt look at again; (considerare) regard; (concernere) concern; per quanto riguarda with regard to. ~si vr take care of oneself. ri'guardo m care; (considerazione) consideration; nei riguardi di towards; riguardo a with regard to

ri'gurgito m regurgitation

rilanci'are vt throw back (palla); (di nuovo) throw again; increase (offerta); revive (moda); relaunch (prodotto) • vi (a carte) raise the stakes

rilasci'ar|e vt (concedere) grant; (liberare) release; issue (documento). ~si vr relax. ri'lascio m release; (di documento) issue

rilassa'mento m relaxation

rilas'sa|re vt, **~rsi** vr relax. **~to** adj (ambiente) relaxed

rile'ga|re vt bind (libro). **~to** adj bound. **~tura** f binding

ri'leggere vt reread

ri'lento: a **~** adv slowly

rileva'mento m survey; (Comm) buyout

rile'vante adj considerable

rile'va|re vt (trarre) get; (mettere in evidenza) point out; (notare) notice; (topografia) survey; (Comm) take over; (Mil) relieve. **~zi'one** f (statistica) survey

rili'evo m relief; (Geog) elevation; (topografia) survey; (importanza) importance; (osservazione) remark; mettere in **~** qcsa point sth out

rilut'tan|te adj reluctant. **~za** f reluctance

'rima f rhyme

riman'dare vt (posporre) postpone; (mandare indietro) send back; (mandare di nuovo) send again; (far ridare un esame) make resit an examination. ri'mando m return; (in un libro) cross-reference

rima'nen|te adj remaining **●** m remainder. **~za** f remainder

rima'ne|re vi stay, remain; (essere d'avanzo) be left; (venirsi a trovare) be; (restare stupito) be astonished; (restare d'accordo) agree

rimar'chevole adj remarkable

ri'mare vt/i rhyme

rimargi'nar|e vt, **~si** vr heal

ri'masto pp di rimanere

rimbal'zare vi rebound; (proiettile) ricochet; far **~** bounce. rim'balzo m rebound; (di proiettile) ricochet

rimbam'bi|re vi be in one's dotage **●** vt stun. **~to** adj in one's dotage

rimboc'care vt turn up; roll up (maniche); tuck in (coperte)

rimbom'bare vi resound

rimbor'sare vt reimburse, repay. rim'borso m reimbursement, repayment. rimborso spese reimbursement of expenses

rimedi'are vi **~** a remedy; make up for (errore); (procurare) scrape up. ri'medio m remedy

rimesco'lare vt mix [up]; shuffle (carte); (rivangare) rake up

ri'messa f (locale per veicoli) garage; (per aerei) hangar; (per autobus) depot; (di denaro) remittance; (di merci) consignment

ri'messo pp di rimettere

ri'metter|e vt put back; (restituire) return; (affidare) entrust; (perdonare) remit; (rimandare) put off; (vomitare) bring up. **~si** vr (ristabilirsi) recover; (tempo) clear up; **~si** a start again

'rimmel® m inv mascara

rimoder'nare vt modernize

rimon'tare vt (risalire) go up; (Mech) reassemble **●** vi remount; **~** a (risalire) go back to

rimorchi'a|re vt tow; Ⓣ pick up (ragazza). **~'tore** m tug[boat]. ri'morchio m tow; (veicolo) trailer

ri'morso m remorse

rimo'stranza f complaint

rimozi'one f removal; (da un incarico) dismissal. **~** forzata illegally parked vehicles removed at owner's expense

rim'pasto m (Pol) reshuffle

rimpatri'are vt/i repatriate. rim'patrio m repatriation

rimpian|gere vt regret. **~to** pp di rimpiangere **●** m regret

rimpiaz'zare vt replace

rimpiccio'lire vi become smaller

rimpin'za|re vt **~e** di stuff with. **~si** vr stuff oneself

rimprove'rare vt reproach; **~** qcsa a qcno reproach sb for sth.

rim'provero m reproach

rimune'ra|re vt remunerate. ~**tivo** adj remunerative. ~**zi'one** f remuneration

ri'muovere vt remove

ri'nascere vi be reborn

rinascimen'tale adj Renaissance. Rinasci'mento m Renaissance

ri'nascita f rebirth

rincal'zare vt (sostenere) support; (rimboccare) tuck in. rin'calzo m support; rincalzi pl (Mil) reserves

rincantucci'arsi vr hide oneself away in a corner

rinca'rare vt increase the price of ● vi become more expensive. rin'caro m price increase

rinca'sare vi return home

rinchi'uder|e vt shut up. ~si vr shut oneself up

rin'correre vt run after

rin'cors|a f run-up. ~o pp di rincorrere

rin'crescere vi mi rincresce di non... I'm sorry o I regret that I can't...; se non ti ~e if you don't mind. ~i'mento m regret. ~i'uto pp di rincrescere

rincreti'nire vi be stupid

rincu'lare vi (arma:) recoil; (cavallo:) shy. rin'culo m recoil

rincuo'rar|e vt encourage. ~si vr take heart

rinfacci'are vt ~ qcsa a qcno throw sth in sb's face

rinfor'zar|e vt strengthen; (rendere più saldo) reinforce. ~si vr become stronger. rin'forzo m reinforcement; fig support

rinfran'care vt reassure

rinfre'scante adj cooling

rinfre'scar|e vt cool; (rinnovare) freshen up ● vi get cooler. ~si vr freshen [oneself] up. rin'fresco m light refreshment; (ricevimento) party

rin'fusa f alla ~ at random

ringhi'era f railing; (di scala) banisters pl

ringiova'nire vt rejuvenate (pelle, persona); (vestito:) make look younger ● vi become young again; (sembrare) look young again

ringrazi|a'mento m thanks pl. ~'are vt thank

rinne'ga|re vt disown. ~to, -a mf renegade

rinnova'mento m renewal; (di edifici) renovation

rinno'var|e vt renew; renovate (edifici). ~si vr be renewed; (ripetersi) recur, happen again. rin'novo m renewal

rinoce'ronte m rhinoceros

rino'mato adj renowned

rinsal'dare vt consolidate

rinsa'vire vi come to one's senses

rinsec'chi|re vi shrivel up. ~to adj shrivelled up

rinta'narsi vr hide oneself away; (animale:) retreat into its den

rintoc'care vi (campana:) toll; (orologio:) strike. rin'tocco m toll; (di orologio) stroke

rinton'ti|re vt stun. ~to adj dazed

rintracci'are vt trace

rintro'nare vt stun ● vi boom

ri'nuncia f renunciation

rinunci|a|re vi ~re a renounce, give up. ~'tario adj defeatist

ri'nunzia, rinunzi'are = RINUNCIA, RINUNCIARE

rinveni'mento m (di reperti) discovery; (di refurtiva) recovery. rinve'nire vt find ● vi (riprendere i sensi) come round; (ridiventare fresco) revive

rinvi'are vt put off; (mandare indietro) return; (in libro) refer; ~ a giudizio indict

rin'vio m Sport goal kick; (in libro) cross-reference; (di appuntamento) postponement; (di merce) return

rio'nale adj local. ri'one m district

riordi'nare vt tidy [up]; (*ordinare di nuovo*) reorder; (*riorganizzare*) reorganize

riorganiz'zare vt reorganize

ripa'gare vt repay

ripa'ra|re vt protect; (*aggiustare*) repair; (*porre rimedio*) remedy ●vi ~re a make up for. ~rsi vr take shelter. ~to adj (*luogo*) sheltered. ~zi'one f repair; fig reparation. ri'paro m shelter; (*rimedio*) remedy

ripar'ti|re vt (*dividere*) divide ●vi leave again. ~zi'one f division

ripas'sa|re vt recross; (*rivedere*) revise ●vi pass again. ri'passo m (*di lezione*) revision

ripensa'mento m second thoughts pl

ripen'sare vi change one's mind; ~ a think of; ripensaci! think again!

riper'correre vt go back over

riper'cosso pp di ripercuotere

ripercu'oter|e vt strike again. ~si vr (*suono*) reverberate; ~si su (*avere conseguenze*) impact on. ripercussi'one f repercussion

ripe'scare vt fish out (*oggetti*)

ripe'tente mf student repeating a year

ri'pet|ere vt repeat. ~ersi vr (*evento*) recur. ~izi'one f repetition; (*di lezione*) revision; (*lezione privata*) private lesson. ~uta'mente adv repeatedly

ri'piano m (*di scaffale*) shelf; (*terreno pianeggiante*) terrace

ri'picc|a f fare qcsa per ~a do sth out of spite. ~o m spite

'ripido adj steep

ripie'ga|re vt refold; (*abbassare*) lower ●vi (*indietreggiare*) retreat. ~si vr bend; (*sedile*) fold. ripi'ego m expedient; (*via d'uscita*) way out

ripi'eno adj full; (*Culin*) stuffed ●m filling; (*Culin*) stuffing

ri'porre vt put back; (*mettere da parte*) put away; (*collocare*) place; repeat (*domanda*)

ripor'tar|e vt (*restituire*) bring/take back; (*riferire*) report; (*subire*) suffer; (*Math*) carry; win (*vittoria*); transfer (*disegno*). ~si vr go back; (*riferirsi*) refer

ripo'sante adj (*colore*) restful, soothing

ripo'sa|re vi rest ●vt put back. ~rsi vr rest. ~to adj (*mente*) fresh. ri'poso m rest; andare a riposo retire; riposo! (*Mil*) at ease!; giorno di riposo day off

ripo'stiglio m cupboard

ri'posto pp di riporre

ri'prender|e vt take again; (*prendere indietro*) take back; (*riconquistare*) recapture; (*ricuperare*) recover; (*ricominciare*) resume; (*rimproverare*) reprimand; take in (*cucitura*); *Cinema* shoot. ~si vr recover; (*correggersi*) correct oneself

ri'presa f resumption; (*ricupero*) recovery; (*Theat*) revival; *Cinema* shot; (*Auto*) acceleration; (*Mus*) repeat. ~ aerea bird's-eye view

ripresen'tar|e vt resubmit (*domanda, certificato*). ~si vr go/come back again; (*come candidato*) run again; (*occasione*) arise again

ri'preso pp di riprendere

ripri'stinare vt restore

ripro'dotto pp di riprodurre

ripro'du|rre vt, ~rsi vr reproduce. ~t'tivo adj reproductive. ~zi'one f reproduction

ripro'mettersi vr intend

ri'prova f confirmation

ripudi'are vt repudiate

ripu'gnan|te adj repugnant. ~za f disgust. ripu'gnare vi ripugnare a disgust

ripu'li|re vt clean [up]; fig polish

ripuls|i'one f repulsion. ~'ivo adj repulsive

ri'quadro m square; (*pannello*) panel

ri'sacca f undertow

risa'lire vt go back up ●vi ~ a (nel tempo) go back to; (essere datato a) date back to, go back to

risal'tare vi stand out. **ri'salto** m prominence; (rilievo) relief

risa'nare vt heal; (bonificare) reclaim

risa'puto adj well-known

risarci'mento m compensation. **risar'cire** vt indemnify

ri'sata f laugh

riscalda'mento m heating. ~ autonomo central heating (for one flat)

riscal'dar|e vt heat; warm (persona). ~si vr warm up

riscat'tar|e vt ransom. ~si vr redeem oneself. **ri'scatto** m ransom; (morale) redemption

rischiara're vt light up; brighten (colore). ~si vr light up; (cielo:) clear up

rischi|'are vt risk ●vi run the risk. **'rischio** m risk. ~'oso adj risky

risciac'quare vt rinse

riscon'trare vt (confrontare) compare; (verificare) check; (rilevare) find. **ri'scontro** m comparison; check; (Comm: risposta) reply

ri'scossa f revolt; (riconquista) recovery

riscossi'one f collection

ri'scosso pp di **riscuotere**

riscu'oter|e vt shake; (percepire) draw; (ottenere) gain; cash (assegno). ~si vr rouse oneself

risen'ti|re vt hear again; (provare) feel ●vi ~re di feel the effect of. ~rsi vr (offendersi) take offence. ~to adj resentful

ri'serbo m reserve; mantenere il ~ remain tight-lipped

ri'serva f reserve; (di caccia, pesca) preserve; Sport substitute, reserve. ~ di caccia game reserve. ~ naturale wildlife reserve

riser'va|re vt reserve; (prenotare)

book; (per occasione) keep. ~rsi vr (ripromettersi) plan for oneself (cambiamento). ~'tezza f reserve. ~to adj reserved

ri'siedere vi ~ a live in/at

'riso[1] m (cereale) rice

'riso[2] pp di **ridere** ●m (pl f risa) laughter; (singolo) laugh. ~'lino m giggle

ri'solto pp di **risolvere**

risolu'tezza f determination. **riso'luto** adj resolute, determined. ~zi'one f resolution

ri'solver|e vt resolve; (Math) solve. ~si vr (decidersi) decide; ~si in turn into

riso'na|nza f resonance; aver ~nza arouse great interest. ~re vi resound; (rimbombare) echo

ri'sorgere vi rise again

risorgi'mento m revival; (storico) Risorgimento

ri'sorsa f resource; (espediente) resort

ri'sorto pp di **risorgere**

ri'sotto m risotto

ri'sparmi mpl (soldi) savings

risparmi'a|re vt save; (salvare) spare. ~'tore, ~'trice mf saver ri'sparmio m saving

rispecchi'are vt reflect

rispet'tabil|e adj respectable. ~ità f respectability

rispet'tare vt respect; farsi ~ command respect

rispet'tivo adj respective

ri'spetto m respect; ~ a as regards; (in confronto a) compared to

rispet'tosa'mente adv respectfully. ~'oso adj respectful

risplen'dente adj shining. **ri'splendere** vi shine

rispon'den|te adj ~te a in keeping with. ~za f correspondence

ri'spondere vi answer; (rimbeccare) answer back; (obbedire) respond; ~ a reply to; ~ **di** (rendersi responsabile) answer for

ri'spost|a f answer, reply; (reazione) response. ~**o** pp di **rispondere**

'rissa f brawl. **ris'soso** adj pugnacious

ristabi'lir|e vt re-establish. ~**si** vr (in salute) recover

rista'gnare vi stagnate; (sangue:) coagulate. **ri'stagno** m stagnation

ri'stampa f reprint; (azione) reprinting. **ristam'pare** vt reprint

risto'rante m restaurant

risto'ra|re vt refresh. ~**rsi** vr liter take some refreshment; (riposarsi) take a rest. ~**tore**, ~**trice** mf (proprietario di ristorante) restaurateur; (fornitore) caterer ● adj refreshing. **ri'storo** m refreshment; (sollievo) relief

ristret'tezza f narrowness; (povertà) poverty

ri'stretto pp di **restringere** ● adj narrow; (condensato) condensed; (limitato) restricted; **di idee ristrette** narrow-minded

ristruttu'rare vt restructure (ditta); refurbish (casa)

risucchi'are vt suck in. **ri'succhio** m whirlpool; (di corrente) undertow

risul'ta|re vi result; (riuscire) turn out. ~**to** m result

risuo'nare vi echo; (Phys) resonate

risurrezi'one f resurrection

risusci'tare vt resuscitate; fig revive ● vi return to life

risve'gli|are vt reawaken (interesse). ~**si** vr wake up; (natura:) awake; (desiderio:) be aroused. **ri'sveglio** m waking up; (dell'interesse) revival; (del desiderio) arousal

ri'svolto m lapel; (di pantaloni) turn-up, cuff Am; (di manica) cuff; (di tasca) flap; (di libro) inside flap

ritagli'are vt cut out. **ri'taglio** m cutting; (di stoffa) scrap

ritar'da|re vi be late; (orologio:) be

slow ● vt delay; slow down (progresso); (differire) postpone. ~**'tario**, -a mf late-comer

ri'tardo m delay; **essere in ~** be late; (volo:) be delayed

ri'tegno m reserve

rite'n|ere vt retain; deduct (somma); (credere) believe. ~**uta** f deduction

riti'ra|re vt throw back (palla); (prelevare) withdraw; (riscuotere) draw; collect (pacco). ~**rsi** vr withdraw; (stoffa:) shrink; (da attività) retire; (marea:) recede. ~**ta** f retreat; (WC) toilet. **ri'tiro** m withdrawal; (Relig) retreat; (da attività) retirement. ritiro bagagli baggage reclaim

'ritmo m rhythm

'rito m rite; **di ~** customary

ritoc'care vt touch up

ritor'nare vi return; (andare venire indietro) go/come back; (ricorrere) recur; (ridiventare) become again

ritor'nello m refrain

ri'torno m return

ritorsi'one f retaliation

ri'trarre vt withdraw; (distogliere) turn away; (rappresentare) portray

ritrat'ta|re vt deal with again; retract (dichiarazione). ~**zi'one** f withdrawal, retraction

ritrat'tista mf portrait painter. **ri'tratto** pp di **ritrarre** ● m portrait

ritro'sia f shyness. **ri'troso** adj backward; (timido) shy; **a ritroso** backwards; **ritroso a** a reluctant to

ritro'va|re vt find [again]; regain (salute). ~**rsi** vr meet; (di nuovo) meet again; (capitare) find oneself; (raccapezzarsi) see one's way. ~**to** m discovery. **ri'trovo** m meeting-place; (notturno) night-club

'ritto adj upright; (diritto) straight

ritu'ale adj ● m ritual

riunifi'ca|re vt reunify. ~**rsi** vr be reunited. ~**zi'one** f reunification

riuni'one f meeting; (fra amici) reunion

riu'nir|e vt (unire) join together; (radunare) gather. **~si** vr be re-united; (adunarsi) meet

riusc'i|re vi (aver successo) succeed; (in matematica ecc) be good (**in** at); (aver esito) turn out; **le è riuscito simpatico** she found him likeable. **~ta** f result; (successo) success

'riva f shore; (di fiume) bank

ri'val|e mf rival. **~ità** f inv rivalry

rivalutazi'one f revaluation

rive'dere vt see again; revise (lezione); (verificare) check

rive'la|re vt reveal. **~rsi** vr (dimostrarsi) turn out. **~'tore** adj revealing ● m (Techn) detector. **~zi'one** f revelation

ri'vendere vt resell

ri'vendi|care vt claim. **~zi'one** f claim

ri'vendi|ta f (negozio) shop. **~tore,** **~trice** mf retailer. **~tore autorizzato** authorized dealer

ri'verbero m reverberation; (bagliore) glare

rive'renza f reverence; (inchino) curtsy; (di uomo) bow

rive'rire vt respect; (ossequiare) pay one's respects to

river'sar|e vt pour. **~si** vr (fiume:) flow

rivesti'mento m covering

rive'sti|re vt (rifornire di abiti) clothe; (ricoprire) cover; (internamente) line; hold (carica). **~rsi** vr get dressed again; (per una festa) dress up

rivi'era f coast; **la ~ ligure** the Italian Riviera

ri'vincita f Sport return match; (vendetta) revenge

rivis'suto pp di rivivere

ri'vista f review; (pubblicazione) magazine; (Theat) revue; **passare in ~** review

ri'vivere vi come to life again; (riprendere le forze) revive ● vt relive

ri'volger|e vt turn; (indirizzare) address; **~e da** (distogliere) turn away from. **~si** vr turn round; **~si a** (indirizzarsi) turn to

ri'volta f revolt

rivol'tante adj disgusting

rivol'tar|e vt turn [over]; (mettendo l'interno verso l'esterno) turn inside out; (sconvolgere) upset. **~si** vr (ribellarsi) revolt

rivol'tella f revolver

ri'volto pp di rivolgere

rivoluzio'nar|e vt revolutionize. **~io, -a** adj & mf revolutionary. **rivoluzi'one** f revolution; (fig: disordine) chaos

riz'zar|e vt raise; (innalzare) erect; prick up (orecchie). **~si** vr stand up; (capelli:) stand on end; (orecchie:) prick up

'roaming m inv (Teleph) **~ [internazionale]** roaming

'roba f stuff; (personale) belongings pl, stuff; (faccenda) thing; (⊠: droga) drugs pl. **~ da mangiare** things to eat

ro'baccia f rubbish

ro'bot m inv robot. **~ da cucina** food processor

robu'stezza f sturdiness, robustness; (forza) strength. **ro'busto** adj sturdy, robust; (forte) strong

'rocca f fortress. **~'forte** f stronghold

roc'chetto m reel

'roccia f rock

ro'da|ggio m running in. **~re** vt run in

'roder|e vt gnaw; (corrodere) corrode. **~si** vr **~si da** be consumed with. **rodi'tore** m rodent

rodo'dendro m rhododendron

ro'gnone m (Culin) kidney

'rogo m (supplizio) stake; (per

cadaveri) pyre

'**Roma** f Rome

Roma'nia f Romania

ro'manico *adj* Romanesque

ro'mano, -a *adj & mf* Roman

romanti'cismo *m* romanticism.
ro'mantico *adj* romantic

ro'man|za f romance. ~'zato *adj*
romanticized. ~'zesco *adj* fictional;
(stravagante) wild, unrealistic. ~zi'ere
m novelist

ro'manzo *adj* Romance ●*m* novel.
~ giallo thriller

'**rombo** *m* rumble; *(Math)* rhombus;
(pesce) turbot

'**romper|e** *vt* break; break off (rela-
zione); non ~e [le scatole]! (🔟:
seccare) don't be a pain [in the
neck]!. ~si *vr* break; ~si una
gamba break one's leg

rompi'capo *m* nuisance; *(indovinello)*
puzzle

rompi'collo *m* daredevil; a ~ at
breakneck speed

rompighi'accio *m* ice-breaker

rompi'scatole *mf inv* 🔟 pain

'**ronda** f rounds *pl*

ron'della f *(Mech)* washer

'**rondine** f swallow

ron'done *m* swift

ron'fare *vi* snore

ron'zino *m* jade

ron'zio *m* buzz

'**rosa** f rose. ~ dei venti wind rose
●*adj & m* pink. ro'saio *m* rose-bush

ro'sario *m* rosary

ro'sato *adj* rosy ●*m (vino)* rosé

'**roseo** *adj* pink

ro'seto *m* rose garden

rosma'rino *m* rosemary

'**roso** *pp di* rodere

roso'lare *vt* brown

roso'lia f German measles

ro'sone *m* rosette; *(apertura)* rose-
window

'**rospo** *m* toad

ros'setto *m (per labbra)* lipstick

'**rosso** *adj & m* red; passare con il ~
jump a red light. ~ d'uovo [egg]
yolk. ros'sore *m* redness; *(della
pelle)* flush

rosticce'ria f *shop selling cooked meat
and other prepared food*

ro'tabile *adj* strada ~ carriageway

ro'taia f rail; *(solco)* rut

ro'tar|e *vt/i* rotate. ~zi'one f ro-
tation

rote'are *vt/i* roll

ro'tella f small wheel; *(di mobile)*
castor

roto'lar|e *vt/i* roll. ~si *vr* roll
[about]. 'rotolo *m* roll; andare a rotoli go to rack and ruin

rotondità f *inv* roundness; ~ *pl (curve
femminili)* curves. ro'tondo, -a *adj*
round ●f *(spiazzo)* terrace

ro'tore *m* rotor

'**rotta**¹ f *(Naut)*, *(Aeron)* course; far ~
per make course for; fuori ~ off
course

'**rotta**² f a ~ di collo at breakneck
speed; essere in ~ con be on bad
terms with

rot'tame *m* scrap; *fig* wreck

'**rotto** *pp di* rompere ●*adj* broken;
(stracciato) torn

rot'tura f break

rotula f kneecap

rou'lette f *inv* roulette

rou'lotte f *inv* caravan, trailer *Am*

rou'tine f *inv* routine; di ~ *(operazioni, controlli)* routine

ro'vente *adj* scorching

'**rovere** *m (legno)* oak

rovesci'ar|e *vt* knock over; *(sottoso-
pra)* turn upside down; *(rivoltare)* turn
inside out; spill *(liquido)*; overthrow
(governo); reverse *(situazione)*. ~si
vr (capovolgersi) overturn; *(riversarsi)*
pour. ro'vescio *adj (contrario)* reverse;
alla rovescia *(capovolto)* upside down;

(con l'interno all'esterno) inside out ● m reverse; (nella maglia) purl; (di pioggia) downpour; Tennis backhand

ro'vina f ruin; (crollo) collapse

rovi'na|re vt ruin; (guastare) spoil ● vi crash. ~rsi vr be ruined. ~to adj (oggetto) ruined. rovi'noso adj ruinous

rovi'stare vt ransack

'rovo m bramble

'rozzo adj rough

R.R. abbr (ricevuta di ritorno) return receipt for registered mail

'ruba f andare a ~ sell like hot cakes

ru'bare vt steal

rubi'netto m tap, faucet Am

ru'bino m ruby

ru'brica f column; (in programma televisivo) TV report; (quaderno con indice) address book. ~ telefonica telephone and address book

'rude adj rough

'rudere m ruin

rudimen'tale adj rudimentary. rudi'menti mpl rudiments

ruffi'an|a f procuress. ~o m pimp; (adulatore) bootlicker

'ruga f wrinkle

'ruggine f rust; fare la ~ go rusty

rug'gi|re vi roar. ~to m roar

rugi'ada f dew

ru'goso adj wrinkled

rul'lare vi roll; (Aeron) taxi

rul'lino m film

rul'lio m rolling; (Aeron) taxiing

rum m inv rum

ru'meno, -a adj & mf Romanian

ru'mor|e m noise; fig rumour. ~eggi'are vi rumble. rumo'roso adj noisy; (sonoro) loud

ru'olo m role; (Theat) role; di ~ on the staff

ru'ota f wheel; andare a ~ libera free-wheel. ~ di scorta spare wheel

'rupe f cliff

ru'rale adj rural

ru'scello m stream

'ruspa f bulldozer

rus'sare vi snore

'Russ|ia f Russia. r~o, -a adj & mf Russian; (lingua) Russian

'rustico adj rural; (carattere) rough

rut'tare vi belch. 'rutto m belch

'ruvido adj coarse

ruzzo'l|are vi tumble down. ~one m tumble; cadere ruzzoloni tumble down

Ss

'sabato m Saturday

'sabb|ia f sand. ~e pl mobili quicksand. ~oso a sandy

sabo'ta|ggio m sabotage. ~re vt sabotage. ~tore, ~trice mf saboteur

'sacca f bag. ~ da viaggio travelling-bag

sacca'rina f saccharin

sac'cente adj pretentious ● mf know-all

saccheggi'a|re vt sack; hum raid (frigo)

sac'chetto m bag

'sacco m sack; (Anat) sac; mettere nel ~ fig swindle; (mottissimo) a lot; un ~ di (gran quantità) lots of. ~ a pelo sleeping-bag

sacer'do|te m priest

sacra'mento m sacrament

sacrifi'ca|re vt sacrifice. ~rsi vr sacrifice oneself. ~to adj (non valorizzato) wasted. sacri'ficio m sacrifice

sa'crilego adj sacrilegious

'sacro adj sacred ● m (Anat) sacrum

r
s

sacro'santo adj sacrosanct

'sadico, -a adj sadistic • mf sadist. **sa'dismo** m sadism

sa'etta f arrow

sa'fari m inv safari

'saga f saga

sa'gace adj shrewd

sag'gezza f wisdom

saggi'are vt test

'saggio¹ m (scritto) essay; (prova) proof; (di metallo) assay; (campione) sample; (esempio) example

'saggio² adj wise

sag'gistica f non-fiction

Sagit'tario m (Astr) Sagittarius

'sagoma f shape; (profilo) outline. **sago'mato** adj shaped

'sagra f festival

sagre|'stano m sacristan. **∼'stia** f sacristy

'sala f hall; (stanza) room; (salotto) living room. **∼ d'attesa** waiting room. **∼ da ballo** ballroom. **∼ d'imbarco** departure lounge. **∼ macchine** engine room. **∼ operatoria** operating theatre. **∼ parto** delivery room. **∼ da pranzo** dining room

sa'lame m salami

sala'moia f brine

sa'lare vt salt

sa'lario m wages pl

sa'lasso m essere un ∼ fig cost a fortune

sala'tini mpl savouries (eaten with aperitifs)

sa'lato adj salty; (costoso) dear

sal'ciccia f = SALSICCIA

sal'dar|e vt weld; set (osso); pay off (debito); settle (conto); **∼e a stagno** solder. **∼si** vr (Med: osso:) knit

salda'trice f welder; (a stagno) soldering iron

salda'tura f weld; (azione) welding; (di osso) knitting

'saldo adj firm; (resistente) strong • m

settlement; (svendita) sale; (Comm) balance

'sale m salt. **∼ fine** table salt. **∼ grosso** cooking salt. **sali** pl e **tabacchi** tobacconist's shop

'salice m willow. **∼ piangente** weeping willow

sali'ente adj outstanding; **i punti salienti di un discorso** the main points of a speech

sali'era f salt-cellar

sa'lina f salt-works sg

sa'li|re vi go/come up; (levarsi) rise; (su treno ecc) get on; (in macchina) get in • vt go/come up (scale). **∼ta** f climb; (aumento) rise; **in ∼ta** uphill

sa'liva f saliva

'salma f corpse

'salmo m psalm

sal'mone m & adj inv salmon

sa'lone m hall; (salotto) living room; (di parrucchiere) salon. **∼ di bellezza** beauty parlour

salo'pette f inv dungarees pl

salot'tino m boudoir

sa'lotto m drawing room; (soggiorno) sitting room; (mobili) [three-piece] suite

sal'pare vt/i sail; **∼ l'ancora** weigh anchor

'salsa f sauce

sal'sedine f saltiness

sal'siccia f sausage

sal'ta|re vi jump; (venir via) come off; (balzare) leap; (esplodere) blow up; **∼r fuori** spring from nowhere; (oggetto cercato:) turn up; **∼to fuori che...** it emerged that...; **∼re fuori con...** come out with...; **∼re in mente** spring to mind • vt jump [over]; skip (pasti, lezioni); (Culin) sauté. **∼to** adj (Culin) sautéed

saltel'lare vi hop; (di gioia) skip

saltim'banco m acrobat

'salto m jump; (balzo) leap; (dislivello) drop; (omissione, lacuna) gap; **fare un**

~ **da** drop in on. ~ **in alto** high jump. ~ **con l'asta** pole-vault. ~ **in lungo** long jump. ~ **pagina** (*Comput*) page down

saltuaria'mente *adv* occasionally. **saltu'ario** *adj* desultory; **lavoro saltuario** casual work

sa'lubre *adj* healthy

salume'ria *f* delicatessen. **sa'lumi** *mpl* cold cuts

salu'tare *vt* greet; (*congedandosi*) say goodbye to; (*portare i saluti a*) give one's regards to; (*Mil*) salute ● *adj* healthy

sa'lute *f* health; ~**!** (*dopo uno starnuto*) bless you!; (*a un brindisi*) your health!

sa'luto *m* greeting; (*di addio*) goodbye; (*Mil*) salute; **saluti** *pl* (*ossequi*) regards

'salva *f* salvo; **sparare a salve** fire blanks

salvada'naio *m* money box

salva'gente *m* lifebelt; (*a giubbotto*) life-jacket; (*ciambella*) rubber ring; (*spartitraffico*) traffic island

salvaguar'dare *vt* safeguard. **sal-vagu'ardia** *f* safeguard

sal'var|e *vt* save; (*proteggere*) protect. ~**si** *vr* save oneself

salva'slip *m inv* panty-liner

salva|'taggio *m* rescue; (*Naut*) salvage; (*Comput*) saving; **battello di** ~**taggio** lifeboat

sal'vezza *f* safety; (*Relig*) salvation

'salvia *f* sage

salvi'etta *f* serviette

'salvo *adj* safe ● *prep* except [for] ● *conj* ~ **che** (*a meno che*) unless; (*eccetto che*) except that

samari'tano, -a *adj & mf* Samaritan

sam'buco *m* elder

san *m* S~ **Francesco** Saint Francis

sa'nare *vt* heal

sana'torio *m* sanatorium

san'cire *vt* sanction

'sandalo *m* sandal

'sangu|e *m* blood; **al** ~ (*carne*) rare; **farsi cattivo** ~**e per** worry about. ~**e freddo** composure; **a** ~**e freddo** in cold blood. ~**igno** *adj* blood

sangui'naccio *m* (*Culin*) black pudding

sangui'nante *adj* bleeding

sangui'nar|e *vi* bleed. ~**io** *adj* bloodthirsty

sangui'noso *adj* bloody

sangui'suga *f* leech

sanità *f* soundness; (*salute*) health. ~ **mentale** mental health

sani'tario *adj* sanitary; **Servizio S~** Health Service

'sano *adj* sound; (*salutare*) healthy; ~ **di mente** sane; ~ **come un pesce** as fit as a fiddle

San Sil'vestro *m* New Year's Eve

santifi'care *vt* sanctify

'santo *adj* holy; (*con nome proprio*) saint ● *m* saint. **san'tone** *m* guru. **santu'ario** *m* sanctuary

sanzi'one *f* sanction

sa'pere *vt* know; (*essere capace di*) be able to; (*venire a sapere*) hear; **saperla lunga** know a thing or two ● *vi* ~ **di** know about; (*aver sapore di*) taste of; (*aver odore di*) smell of; **saperci fare** have the know-how ● *m* knowledge

sapi'en|te *adj* wise; (*esperto*) expert ● *m* (*uomo colto*) sage. ~**za** *f* wisdom

sa'pone *m* soap. ~ **da bucato** washing soap. **sapo'netta** *f* bar of soap

sa'pore *m* taste. **saporita'mente** *adv* soundly. **sapo'rito** *adj* tasty

sapu'tello, -a *adj & m* 🅇 know-all, know-it-all *Am*

saraci'nesca *f* roller shutter

sar'cas|mo *m* sarcasm. ~**tico** *adj* sarcastic

Sar'degna *f* Sardinia

sar'dina f sardine

'sardo, -a adj & mf Sardinian

 Sardo Sardo is Sardinia's traditional language. It is considered to be an independent language because of its many differences from Italian and its long independent history. Sardinian preserves many features derived from Latin which were lost in Italian, e.g. the k-sound in words like *chelu* (Italian *cielo*).

sar'donico adj sardonic

'sarto, -a m tailor ● f dressmaker. ~ria f tailor's; dressmaker's; (arte) couture

'sasso m stone; (ciottolo) pebble

sassofo'nista mf saxophonist. sas'sofono m saxophone

sas'soso adj stony

sa'tellite adj inv & nm satellite

sati'nato adj glossy

'satira f satire. sa'tirico adj satirical

satu'ra|re vt saturate. ~zi'one f saturation. 'saturo adj saturated; (pieno) full

'sauna f sauna

savoi'ardo m (biscotto) sponge finger

sazi'ar|e vt satiate. ~si vr ~si di fig grow tired of

sazi'età f mangiare a ~ eat one's fill. 'sazio adj satiated

sbaciucchi'ar|e vt smother with kisses. ~si vr kiss and cuddle

sbada'ta|ggine f carelessness; è stata una ~ggine it was careless. ~'mente adv carelessly. sba'dato adj careless

sbadigli'are vi yawn. sba'diglio m yawn

sba'fa|re vt sponge

'sbafo m sponging; a ~ without paying

sbagli'ar|e vi make a mistake; (aver torto) be wrong ● vt make a mistake in; ~e strada go the wrong way; ~e numero get the number wrong; (Teleph) dial a wrong number. ~si vr make a mistake. 'sbaglio m mistake; per sbaglio by mistake

sbal'l|are vt unpack; ⊞ screw up (conti) ● vi ⊞ go crazy. ~ato adj (squilibrato) unbalanced

sbal'lottare vt toss about

sbalor'di|re vt stun ● vi be stunned. ~'tivo adj amazing. ~to adj stunned

sbal'zare vt throw; (da una carica) dismiss ● vi bounce; (saltare) leap. 'sbalzo m bounce; (sussulto) jolt; (di temperatura) sudden change; a sbalzi in spurts; a sbalzo (lavoro a rilievo) embossed

sban'care vt bankrupt; ~ il banco break the bank

sbanda'mento m (Auto) skid; (Naut) list; fig going off the rails

sban'da|re vi (Auto) skid; (Naut) list. ~rsi vr (disperdersi) disperse. ~ta f skid; (Naut) list. ~to, -a adj mixed-up ● mf mixed-up person

sbandie'rare vt wave; fig display

sbarac'care vt/i clear up

sbaragli'are vt rout. sba'raglio m rout; mettere allo sbaraglio rout

sbaraz'zar|e vt clear. ~si vr ~si di get rid of

sbaraz'zino, -a adj mischievous ● mf scamp

sbar'bar|e vt, ~si vr shave

sbar'care vt/i disembark; ~ il lunario make ends meet. 'sbarco m landing; (di merci) unloading

'sbarra f bar; (di passaggio a livello) barrier. ~'mento m barricade. sbar'rare vt bar; (ostruire) block; cross (assegno); (spalancare) open wide

sbatacchi'are vt/i ⊠ bang

'sbatter|e vt bang; slam, bang (porta); (urtare) knock; (Culin) beat;

flap (ali); shake (tappeto) ● *vi* bang; (porta:) slam, bang. ~**si** *vr* ⊠ rush around; ~**sene** di qcsa not give a damn about sth. **sbat'tuto** *adj* tossed; (*Culin*) beaten; *fig* run down

sba'va|re *vi* dribble; (colore:) smear. ~**tura** *f* smear; **senza** ~**ture** *fig* faultless

sbelli'carsi *vr* ~ **dalle risa** split one's sides [with laughter]

'**sberla** *f* slap

sbia'di|re *vt/i*, ~**rsi** *vr* fade. ~**to** *adj* faded; *fig* colourless

sbian'car|e *vt/i*, ~**si** *vr* whiten

sbi'eco *adj* slanting; **di** ~ **on the** slant; (guardare) sidelong; guardare qcno **di** ~ look askance at sb; tagliare **di** ~ cut on the bias

sbigot'ti|re *vt* dismay ● *vi*, ~**rsi** *vr* be dismayed. ~**to** *adj* dismayed

sbilanci'ar|e *vt* unbalance ● *vi* (*perdere l'equilibrio*) overbalance. ~**si** *vr* lose one's balance

sbizzar'rirsi *vr* satisfy one's whims

sbloc'care *vt* unblock; (*Mech*) release; decontrol (prezzi)

sboc'care *vi* ~ **in** (fiume:) flow into; (strada:) lead to; (folla:) pour into

sboc'cato *adj* foul-mouthed

sbocci'are *vi* blossom

'**sbocco** *m* flowing; (*foce*) mouth; (*Comm*) outlet

sbolo'gnare *vt* 🔲 get rid of

'**sbornia** *f* **prendere una** ~ get drunk

sbor'sare *vt* pay out

sbot'tare *vi* burst out

sbotto'nar|e *vt* unbutton. ~**si** *vr* (🔲: *confidarsi*) open up; ~**si la camicia** unbutton one's shirt

sbra'carsi *vr* put on something more comfortable; ~ **dalle risate** 🔲 kill oneself laughing

sbracci'a|rsi *vr* wave one's arms. ~**to** *adj* bare-armed; (abito)

sleeveless

sbrai'tare *vi* bawl

sbra'nare *vt* tear to pieces

sbricio'lar|e *vt*, ~**si** *vr* crumble

sbri'ga|re *vt* expedite; (*occuparsi di*) attend to. ~**rsi** *vr* be quick. ~'**tivo** *adj* quick

sbrindel'lare *vt* tear to shreds. ~**to** *adj* in rags

sbrodo'l|are *vt* stain

'**sbronza** *f* **prendersi una** ~**a** get tight. **sbron'zarsi** *vr* get tight. ~**o** *adj* (*ubriaco*) tight

sbruffo'nata *f* boast. **sbruf'fone, -a** *mf* boaster

sbu'care *vi* come out

sbucci'ar|e *vt* peel; shell (piselli). ~**si** *vr* graze oneself

sbuf'fare *vi* snort; (*per impazienza*) fume. '**sbuffo** *m* puff

'**scabbia** *f* scabies *sg*

sca'broso *adj* rough; *fig* difficult; (scena) indecent

scacci'are *vt* chase away

'**scacc|o** *m* check; ~**hi** *pl* (*gioco*) chess; (*pezzi*) chessmen; **dare** ~**o matto** a checkmate; **a** ~**hi** (tessuto) checked. ~**hi'era** *f* chess-board

sca'dente *adj* shoddy

sca'de|nza *f* expiry; (*Comm*) maturity; (*di progetto*) deadline; **a breve**/ **lunga** ~**nza** short-/long-term. ~**re** *vi* expire; (valore:) decline; (debito:) be due. **sca'duto** *adj* out-of-date

sca'fandro *m* diving suit; (*di astronauta*) spacesuit

scaf'fale *m* shelf; (libreria) bookshelf

sca'fista *m* motor-boat operator; (*pej*) refugee smuggler (using motorboat)

'**scafo** *m* hull

scagion'are *vt* exonerate

'**scaglia** *f* scale; (*di sapone*) flake; (*scheggia*) chip

scagli'ar|e *vt* fling. ~**si** *vr* fling oneself; ~**si contro** *fig* rail against

s ⟩

scaglio'na|re vt space out. ~one m group; a ~oni in groups. ~one di reddito tax bracket

'scala f staircase; (*portatile*) ladder; (*Mus, misura, fig*) scale; **scale** pl stairs. ~ **mobile** escalat-or; (*dei salari*) cost of living index

scalla|re vt climb; layer (capelli); (*detrarre*) deduct. ~**ta** f climb; (*dell'Everest ecc*) ascent; **fare delle** ~**te** go climbing. ~**tore**, ~**trice** mf climber

scalca'gnato adj down at heel

scalci'are vi kick

scalci'nato adj shabby

scalda'bagno m water heater

scalda'muscoli m inv leg-warmer

scal'dar|e vt heat. ~**si** vr warm up; (*eccitarsi*) get excited

scal'fi|re vt scratch. ~**t'tura** f scratch

scali'nata f flight of steps. **sca'lino** m step; (*di scala a pioli*) rung

scalma'narsi vr get worked up

'scalo m slipway; (*Aeron, Naut*) port of call; **fare** ~ **a** call at; (*Aeron*) land at

sca'lo|gna f bad luck. ~'**gnato** adj unlucky

scalop'pina f escalope

scal'pello m chisel

'scalpo m scalp

scal'pore m noise; **far** ~ fig cause a sensation

scal'trezza f shrewdness. **'scaltro** adj shrewd

scal'zare vt bare the roots of (albero); fig undermine; (*da una carica*) oust

'scalzo adj & adv barefoot

scambi'are vt exchange; ~**are** qcno per qualcun altro mistake sb for somebody else. ~'**evole** adj reciprocal

'scambio m exchange; (*Comm*) trade; **libero** ~ free trade

scamosci'ato adj suede

scampa'gnata f trip to the country

scampa'nato adj (gonna) flared

scampanel'lata f [loud] ring

scam'pare vt save; (*evitare*) escape. **'scampo** m escape

'scampolo m remnant

scanala'tura f groove

scandagli'are vt sound

scanda'listico adj sensational

scandaliz'zare vt scandalize. ~**iz'zarsi** vr be scandalized

'scanda|lo m scandal. ~'**loso** adj (*somma*) ecc scandalous; (*fortuna*) outrageous

Scandi'navia f Scandinavia. **scan'di'navo, -a** adj & mf Scandi-navian

scan'dire vt scan (verso); pronounce clearly (parole)

scan'nare vt slaughter

'scanner m inv scanner

scanneriz'zare vt (*Comput*) scan

scan'sar|e vt shift; (*evitare*) avoid. ~**si** vr get out of the way

scansi'one f (*Comput*) scanning

'scanso m a ~ **di** in order to avoid; a ~ **di equivoci** to avoid any misunderstanding

scanti'nato m basement

scanto'nare vi turn the corner; (*svignarsela*) sneak off

scanzo'nato adj easy-going

scapacci'one m smack

scape'strato adj dissolute

'scapito m loss

'scapola f shoulder-blade

'scapolo m bachelor

scappa'mento m (*Auto*) exhaust

scap'pa|re vi escape; (*andarsene*) dash [off]; (*sfuggire*) slip; **mi** ~ **da ridere!** I want to burst out laughing. ~**ta** f short visit. ~'**tella** f escapade; (*infedeltà*) fling. ~'**toia** f way out

scappel'lotto m cuff

scarabocchi'are vt scribble

scara'bocchio m scribble

scara'faggio m cockroach

scara'muccia f skirmish

scaraven'tare vt hurl

scardi'nare vt unhinge

'scarica f discharge; (di arma di fuoco) volley; fig shower

scari'ca|re vt discharge; unload (arma, merci); (Comput) download; fig unburden. **~rsi** vr (fiume:) flow; (orologio, batteria:) run down; fig unwind. **~'tore** m loader; (di porto) docker. **'scarico** adj unloaded; (vuoto) empty; (orologio) run-down; (batteria) flat; fig untroubled ● m unloading; (di rifiuti) dumping; (di acqua) draining; (di sostanze inquinanti) discharge; (luogo) [rubbish] dump; (Auto) exhaust; (idraulico) drain; (tubo) waste pipe

scarlat'tina f scarlet fever

scar'latto adj scarlet

'scarno adj thin; (stile) bare

sca'ro|gna f bad luck. **~'gnato** adj [T] unlucky

'scarpa f shoe. scarpe pl da ginnastica trainers, gym shoes

scar'pata f slope; (burrone) escarpment

scarpi'nare vi hike

scar'pone m boot. scarponi pl da sci ski boot. scarponi pl da trekking walking boots

scarroz'zare vt/i drive around

scarseggi'are vi be scarce; **~ di** (mancare) be short of

scar'sezza f scarcity, shortage. scarsità f shortage. **'scarso** adj scarce; (manchevole) short

scarta'mento m (Rail) gauge. **~ ridotto** narrow gauge

scar'tare vt discard; unwrap (pacco); (respingere) reject ● vi (deviare) swerve. **'scarto** m scrap; (in carte) discard; (deviazione) swerve; (distacco) gap

scas'sa|re vt break. **~to** adj [T] clapped out

scassi'nare vt force open

scassina'tore, -'trice mf burglar. **'scasso** m (furto) house-breaking

scate'na|re vt fig stir up. **~rsi** vr break out; fig (temporale:) break; ([T]:) inflammarsi) get excited. **~to** adj crazy

'scatola f box; (di latta) can, tin Br; in **~** (cibo) canned, tinned Br

scat'tare vi go off; (balzare) spring up; (adirarsi) lose one's temper; take (foto). **'scatto** m (balzo) spring; (d'ira) outburst; (di telefono) unit; (dispositivo) release; a scatti jerkily; di scatto suddenly

scatu'rire vi spring

scaval'care vt jump over (muretto); climb over (muro); (fig superare) overtake

sca'vare vt dig (buca); dig up (tesoro); excavate (città sepolta). **'scavo** m excavation

'scegliere vt choose, select

scelle'rato adj wicked

'scel|ta f choice; (di articoli) range; ...a **~a** (in menu) choice of...; prendine uno a **~a** take your choice o pick; di prima **~a** top-grade, choice. **~o** pp di **scegliere** ● adj select; (merce ecc) choice

sce'mare vt/i diminish

sce'menza f silliness; (azione) silly thing to do/say. **'scemo** adj silly

'scempio m havoc; (fig: di paesaggio) ruination; fare **~ di** play havoc with

'scena f scene; (palcoscenico) stage; entrare in **~** go/come on; fig enter the scene; fare **~** put on an act; fare una **~** make a scene; andare in **~** (Theat) be staged, be put on. sce'nario m scenery

sce'nata f row, scene

'scendere vi go/come down; (da treno, autobus) get off; (da macchina) get out; (strada:) slope; (notte, prezzi:)

fall ●vt go/come down (scale)
sceneggi'a|re vt dramatize. ～to m television serial. ～tura f screenplay

'scenico adj scenic

scervel'la|rsi vr rack one's brains. ～to adj brainless

'sceso pp di scendere

scetti'cismo m scepticism. 'scettico, -a adj sceptical ●mf sceptic

'scheda f card. ～ elettorale ballotpaper. ～ di espansione (Comput) expansion card. ～ telefonica phonecard. sche'dare vt file. sche'dario m file; (mobile) filing cabinet

sche'dina f ≈ pools coupon; giocare la ～ do the pools

scheggi'a|re f fragment; (di legno) splinter. ～arsi vr chip; (legno:) splinter

'scheletro m skeleton

'schema m diagram; (abbozzo) outline. sche'matico adj schematic

'scherma f fencing

scher'mirsi vr protect oneself

'schermo m screen; grande ～ big screen

scher'nire vt mock. 'scherno m mockery

scher'zare vi joke; (giocare) play

'scherzo m joke; (trucco) trick; (effetto) play; (Mus) scherzo; fare uno ～ a qcno play a joke on sb. scher'zoso adj playful

schiaccia'noci m inv nutcrackers pl

schiacci'ante adj damning

schiacci'are vt crush; Sport smash; press (pulsante); crack (noce)

schiaffeggi'are vt slap. schi'affo m slap; dare uno schiaffo a slap

schiamaz'zare vi make a racket; (galline:) cackle

schian'tar|e vt break. ～si vr crash ●vi schianto dalla fatica I'm wiped out. 'schianto m crash; ⬆ knockout; (divertente) scream

schia'rir|e vt clear; (sbiadire) fade

●vi, ～si vr brighten up; ～si la gola clear one's throat

schiavitù f slavery. schi'avo, -a mf slave

schi'ena f back; mal di ～ backache. schie'nale m (di sedia) back

schi'er|a f (Mil) rank; (moltitudine) crowd. ～a'mento m lining up

schie'rar|e vt draw up. ～si vr draw up; ～si con (parteggiare) side with

schiet'tezza f frankness. schi'etto adj frank; (puro) pure

schi'fezza f una ～ rubbish. schifil'toso adj fussy. 'schifo m disgust; mi fa schifo it makes me sick. schi'foso adj disgusting; (di cattiva qualità) rubbishy

schioc'care vt crack; snap (dita). schi'occo m (di frusta) crack; (di bacio) smack; (di dita, lingua) click

schi'uder|e vt, ～si vr open

schi'u|ma f foam; (di sapone) lather; (feccia) scum. ～ma da barba shaving foam. ～mare vt skim ●vi foam

schi'uso pp di schiudere

schi'vare vt avoid. 'schivo adj bashful

schizo'frenico adj schizophrenic

schiz'zare vt squirt; (inzaccherare) splash; (abbozzare) sketch ●vi spurt; ～ via scurry away

schizzi'noso adj squeamish

'schizzo m squirt; (di fango) splash; (abbozzo) sketch

sci m inv ski; (sport) skiing. ～ d'acqua water-skiing

'scia f wake; (di fumo ecc) trail

sci'abola f sabre

scia'callo m jackal; fig profiteer

sciac'quar|e vt rinse. ～si vr rinse oneself. sci'acquo m mouthwash

scia'gura f disaster. ～rato adj unfortunate; (scellerato) wicked

scialac'quare vt squander

scia'lare vi squander

sci'albo adj pale; fig dull

sci'alle m shawl

scia'luppa f dinghy. ∼ di salvataggio lifeboat

sci'ame m swarm

sci'ampo m shampoo

scian'cato adj lame

sci'are vi ski

sci'arpa f scarf

sci'atica f (Med) sciatica

scia'tore, -'trice mf skier

sci'atto adj slovenly; (stile) careless. **sciat'tone, -a** mf slovenly person

scienti'fico adj scientific

sci'enz|a f science; (sapere) knowledge. ∼i'ato, -a mf scientist

'scimmi|a f monkey. ∼ott'are vt ape

scimpanzé m inv chimpanzee, chimp

scimu'nito adj idiotic

'scinder|e vt, ∼si vr split

scin'tilla f spark. **scintil'lante** adj sparkling. **scintil'lare** vi sparkle

scioc'ca|nte adj shocking. ∼re vt shock

scioc'chezza f foolishness; (assurdità) nonsense. **sci'occo** adj foolish

sci'oglier|e vt untie; (liberare) release; (liquefare) melt; dissolve (contratto, qcsa nell'acqua); loosen up (muscoli). ∼si vr release oneself; (liquefarsi) melt; (contratto:) be dissolved; (pastiglia:) dissolve

sciogli'lingua m inv tongue-twister

scio'lina f wax

sciol'tezza f agility; (disinvoltura) ease

sci'olto pp di sciogliere ● adj loose; (agile) agile; (disinvolto) easy; versi sciolti blank verse sg

sciope'ra|nte mf striker. ∼re vi go on strike, strike. **sci'opero** m strike. sciopero a singhiozzo on-off strike

sciori'nare vt fig show off

sci'pito adj insipid

scip'pa|re vt 🄵 snatch. ∼'tore, ∼'trice mf bag snatcher. **'scippo** m bag-snatching

sci'rocco m sirocco

scirop'pato adj (frutta) in syrup. **sci'roppo** m syrup

'scisma m schism

scissi'one f division

'scisso pp di scindere

sciu'par|e vt spoil; (sperperare) waste. ∼si vr get spoiled; (deperire) wear oneself out. **sciu'pio** m waste

scivo'l|are vi slide; (involontariamente) slip. **'scivolo** m slide; (Techn) chute. ∼oso adj slippery

scoc'care vt shoot ● vi (scintilla:) shoot out; (ora:) strike

scocci'a|re vt (dare noia a) bother. ∼rsi vr be bothered. ∼to adj 🄵 narked. ∼'tore, ∼'trice mf bore. ∼'tura f nuisance

sco'della f bowl

scodinzo'lare vi wag its tail

sco'glie|ra f cliff; (a fior d'acqua) reef. **'scoglio** m rock; (fig: ostacolo) stumbling block

scoi'attolo m squirrel

scola'|pasta m inv colander. ∼pi'atti m inv dish drainer

sco'lara f schoolgirl

sco'lare vt drain; strain (pasta, verdura) ● vi drip

sco'la|ro m schoolboy. ∼'resca f pupils pl. ∼'stico adj school attrib

scol'la|re vt cut away the neck of (abito); (staccare) unstick. ∼to adj low-necked. ∼'tura f neckline

'scolo m drainage

scolo'ri|re vt, ∼rsi vr fade. ∼to adj faded

scol'pire vt carve; (imprimere) engrave

scombi'nare vt upset

scombusso'lare vt muddle up

scom'mess|a f bet. ∼o pp di

s.

scommettere, **scom'mettere** vt bet

scomo'dar|e vt, ~si vr trouble. scomodità f discomfort. 'scomodo adj uncomfortable

scompa'rire vi disappear; (morire) pass on. **scom'parsa** f disappearance; (morte) passing, death. **scom'parso**, **-a** pp di **scomparire** ●mf departed

scomparti'mento m compartment. **scom'parto** f compartment

scom'penso m imbalance

scompigli'are vt disarrange. **scom'piglio** m confusion

scom'po|rre vt take to pieces; (fig: turbare) upset. ~rsi vr get flustered. ~sto pp di **scomporre** ●adj (sguaiato) unseemly; (disordinato) untidy

sco'muni|ca f excommunication. ~'care vt excommunicate

sconcer'ta|re vt disconcert; (rendere perplesso) bewilder. ~to adj disconcerted; bewildered

scon'cezza f obscenity. 'sconcio adj dirty ●m è uno sconcio che... it's a disgrace that...

sconclusio'nato adj incoherent

scon'dito adj unseasoned; (insalata) with no dressing

sconfes'sare vt disown

scon'figgere vt defeat

sconfi'na|re vi cross the border; (in proprietà privata) trespass. ~to adj unlimited

scon'fitt|a f defeat. ~o pp di **sconfiggere**

scon'forto m dejection

sconge'lare vt thaw out (cibo), defrost

scongiu'rare vt beseech; (evitare) avert. ~'uro m fare gli scongiuri touch wood, knock on wood Am

scon'nesso pp di **sconnettere** ●adj fig incoherent. **scon'nettere** vt disconnect

sconosci'uto, **-a** adj unknown

●mf stranger

sconquas'sare vt smash; (sconvolgere) upset

conside'rato adj inconsiderate

sconsigli'a|bile adj not advisable. ~re vt advise against

sconso'lato adj disconsolate

scon'ta|re vt discount; (dedurre) deduct; (pagare) pay off; serve (pena). ~to adj discount; (ovvio) expected; ~to del 10% with 10% discount

scon'tento adj displeased ●m discontent

'sconto m discount; fare uno ~ give a discount

scon'trarsi vr clash; (urtare) collide

scon'trino m ticket; (di cassa) receipt

'scontro m clash; (urto) collision

scon'troso adj unsociable

conveni'ente adj unprofitable; (scorretto) unseemly

sconvol'gente adj mind-blowing

sconvol'ge|re vt upset; (mettere in disordine) disarrange. ~gi'mento m upheaval. ~to pp di **sconvolgere** ●adj distraught

'scopa f broom. **sco'pare** vt sweep

scoperchi'are vt take the lid off (pentola); take the roof off (casa)

sco'pert|a f discovery. ~o pp di **scoprire** ●adj uncovered; (senza riparo) exposed; (conto) overdrawn; (spoglio) bare

'scopo m aim; allo ~ di in order to

scoppi'are vi burst; fig break out. **scoppiet'tare** vi crackle. **'scoppio** m burst; (di guerra) outbreak; (esplosione) explosion

sco'prire vt discover; (togliere la copertura a) uncover

scoraggi'a|re vt discourage. ~rsi vr lose heart

scor'butico adj peevish

scorcia'toia f short cut

'scorcio m (di epoca) end; (di cielo)

249 | scordare | scrollare

patch; (in arte) foreshortening; di ~
(vedere) from an angle. ~ panoramico panoramic view

scor'da|re vt, ~rsi vr forget. ~to
adj (Mus) out of tune

'scorgere vt make out; (notare)
notice

'scoria f waste; (di metallo, carbone)
slag; scorie pl radioattive radioactive waste

scor'nato adj fig hangdog. 'scorno
m humiliation

scorpi'one m scorpion; (Astr) S ~
Scorpio

scorraz'zare vi run about

'scorrere vt (dare un'occhiata) glance
through ● vi run; (scivolare) slide;
(fluire) flow; (Comput) scroll. scor'revole adj porta scorrevole slid-
ing door

scorre'ria f raid

scorret'tezza f (mancanza di educazione) bad manners pl. scor'retto adj
incorrect; (sconveniente) improper

scorri'banda f raid; fig excursion

'scors|a f glance. ~o pp di scorrere
● adj last

scor'soio adj nodo ~ noose

'scor|ta f escort; (provvista) supply.
~tare vt escort

scor'te|se adj discourteous. ~'sia f
discourtesy

scorti'ca|re vt skin. ~'tura f graze

'scorto pp di scorgere

'scorza f peel; (crosta) crust; (corteccia) bark

sco'sceso adj steep

'scoss|a f shake; (Electr; fig) shock;
prendere la ~ get an electric
shock. ~ elettrica electric shock. ~
sismica earth tremor

'scosso pp di scuotere ● adj shaken;
(sconvolto) upset

sco'stante adj off-putting

sco'sta|re vt push away. ~rsi vr
stand aside

scostu'mato adj dissolute; (maleducato) ill-mannered

scot'tante adj dangerous

scot'ta|re vt scald ● vi burn; (be-
vanda:) be too hot; (sole, pentola:)
be very hot. ~rsi vr burn oneself; (al
sole) get sunburnt; fig get one's
fingers burnt. ~tura f burn; (da liquido) scald; ~tura solare sunburn;
fig painful experience

'scotto adj overcooked

sco'vare vt (scoprire) discover

'Scozia f Scotland. ~zese adj
Scottish ●mf Scot

scredi'tare vt discredit

scre'mare vt skim

screpo'la|re vt, ~rsi vr crack. ~to
adj (labbra) chapped. ~tura f crack

screzi'ato adj speckled

'screzio m disagreement

scribac|chi'are vt scribble.
~'chino, -a mf scribbler; (impiegato)
penpusher

scric|chio'l|are vi creak. ~io m
creaking

'scricciolo m wren

'scrigno m casket

scrimina'tura f parting

'scrit|ta f writing; (su muro) graffiti.
~to pp di scrivere ● adj written ●m
writing; (lettera) letter. ~'toio m
writing-desk. ~'tore, ~'trice mf
writer. ~'tura f writing; (Relig)
scripture

scrittu'rare vt engage

scriva'nia f desk

'scrivere vt write; (descrivere) write
about; ~ a macchina type

scroc'ca|re vt ~are a sponge off.
'scrocco m (da) a scrocco 🅸 without
paying. ~one, -a mf sponger

'scrofa f sow

scrol'lar|e vt shake; ~e le spalle
shrug one's shoulders. ~si vr shake
oneself; ~si qcsa di dosso shake
sth off

s

scrosci'are vi roar; (pioggia:) pelt down. 'scroscio m roar; (di pioggia) pelting

scro'star|e vt scrape. ~si vr peel off

'scrupo|lo m scruple; (diligenza) care; senza scrupoli unscrupulous, without scruples. ~loso adj scrupulous

scru'ta|re vt scan; (indagare) search. ~tore m (alle elezioni) returning officer

scruti'nare vt scrutinize. scru'tinio m (di voti alle elezioni) poll; (Sch) assessment of progress

scu'deria f stable

scu'detto m Sport championship shield

'scudo m shield

sculacci'|are vt spank. ~ata f spanking. ~one m spanking

sculet'tare vi wiggle one's hips

scul'tore, -'trice m sculptor ●f sculptress. ~tura f sculpture

scu'ola f school. ~ elementare primary school. ~ guida driving school. ~ materna day nursery. ~ media [inferiore] secondary school (10-13). ~ media [superiore] secondary school (13-18)

scu'oter|e vt shake. ~si vr (destarsi) rouse oneself; ~si di dosso shake off

'scure f axe

scu'reggia|re vi 🔢 fart. scureggi'are vi 🔢 fart

scu'rire vt/i darken

'scuro adj dark ●m darkness; (imposta) shutter

'scusa f excuse; (giustificazione) apology; chiedere ~ apologize; chiedo ~! I'm sorry!

scu'sar|e vt excuse. ~si vr ~si apologize (di for); [mi] scusi! excuse me!; (chiedendo perdono) [I'm] sorry!

sdebi'tarsi vr repay a kindness

sde'gna|re vt despise. ~rsi vr get angry. ~to adj indignant. 'sdegno m disdain. sde'gnoso adj disdainful

sdolci'nato adj sentimental

sdoppi'are vt halve

sdrai'arsi vr lie down. 'sdraio m [sedia a] sdraio deckchair

sdrammatiz'zare vi provide some comic relief

sdruccio'levole adj slippery

<hr>

se

● conj if; (interrogativo) whether, if; se mai (caso mai) if need be; se mai telefonasse,... should he call,..., if he calls,...; se no otherwise, or else; se non altro at least, if nothing else; se pure (sebbene) even though; (anche se) even if; non so se sia vero I don't know whether it's true, I don't know if it's true; come se as if; se lo avessi saputo prima! if only I had known before!; e se andassimo fuori a cena? how about going out for dinner?

● m inv if

<hr>

sé pers pron oneself; (lui) himself; (lei) herself; (esso, essa) itself; (loro) themselves; l'ha fatto da sé he did it himself; ha preso i soldi con sé he took the money with him; si sono tenuti le notizie per sé they kept the news to themselves

seb'bene conj although

'secca f shallows pl; in ~ (nave) aground

sec'cante adj annoying

sec'ca|re vt dry; (importunare) annoy ●vi dry up. ~rsi vr dry up; (irritarsi) get annoyed; (annoiarsi) get bored. ~tore, ~trice mf nuisance. ~tura f bother

secchi'ello m pail

'secchio m bucket. ~ della spazzatura rubbish bin, trash can Am

'secco, -a adj dry; (dissecato) dried; (magro) thin; (brusco) curt; (preciso) sharp ● m (siccità) drought; lavare a ~ dry-clean

secessi'one f secession

seco'lare adj age-old; (laico) secular.

'secolo m century; (epoca) age

se'cond|a f (Rail, Sch) second class; (Auto) second [gear]. **~o** adj second ● m second; (secondo piatto) main course ● prep according to; **~o me** in my opinion

secrezi'one f secretion

'sedano m celery

seda'tivo adj & m sedative

'sede f seat; (centro) centre; (Relig) see; (Comm) head office. ~ **sociale** registered office

seden'tario adj sedentary

se'der|e vi sit. **~si** vr sit down ● m (deretano) bottom

'sedia f chair. ~ **a dondolo** rocking chair. ~ **a rotelle** wheelchair

sedi'cente adj self-styled

'sedici adj & m sixteen

se'dile m seat

sedizi'o|ne f sedition. **~so** adj seditious

se'dotto pp di sedurre

sedu'cente adj seductive

se'durre vt seduce

se'duta f session; (di posa) sitting. ~ **stante** adv here and now

seduzi'one f seduction

'sega f saw

'segala f rye

se'gare vt saw

'seggio m seat. ~ **elettorale** polling station

seg'gio|la f chair. **~lino** m seat; (da bambino) child's seat. **~lone** m (per bambini) high chair

seggio'via f chair lift

seghe'ria f sawmill

se'ghetto m hacksaw

seg'mento m segment

segna'lar|e vt signal; (annunciare) announce; (indicare) point out. **~si** vr distinguish oneself

se'gna|le m signal; (stradale) sign. ~**le acustico** beep. ~**le orario** time signal. **~lética** f signals pl. **~letica stradale** road signs pl

se'gnar|e vt mark; (prendere nota) note; (indicare) indicate; Sport score. **~si** vr cross oneself. **'segno** m sign; (traccia, limite) mark; (bersaglio) target; **far segno** (col capo) nod; (con la mano) beckon. **segno zodiacale** birth sign

segre'ga|re vt segregate. **~zi'one** f segregation

segretari'ato m secretariat

segre'tario, -a mf secretary. ~ **comunale** town clerk

segrete'ria f (administrative) office; (segretariato) secretariat. ~ **telefonica** answering machine

segre'tezza f secrecy

se'greto adj & m secret; **in ~** in secret

segu'ace mf follower

segu'ente adj following, next

se'gugio m bloodhound

segu'ire vt/i follow; (continuare) continue

segui'tare vt/i continue

'seguito m retinue; (sequela) series; (continuazione) continuation; **di ~** in succession; **in ~** later on; **in ~ a** following; **owing to**; **fare ~ a** follow up

'sei adj & m six. **sei'cento** adj & m six hundred; **il Seicento** the seventeenth century. **sei'mila** adj & m six thousand

sel'ciato m paving

selet'tivo adj selective. **selezio'nare** vt select. **selezi'one** f selection

'sella f saddle. **sel'lare** vt saddle

seltz m soda water

'selva f forest

selvag'gina f game

sel'vaggio, -a adj wild; (primitivo) savage • mf savage

sel'vatico adj wild

se'maforo m traffic lights pl

se'mantica f semantics sg

sem'brare vi seem; (assomigliare) look like; **che te ne sembra?** what do you think?; **mi sembra che...** I think...

'seme m seed; (di mela) pip; (di carte) suit; (sperma) semen

se'mestre m half-year

semi'cerchio m semicircle

semifi'nale f semifinal

semi'freddo m ice cream and sponge dessert

'semina f sowing

semi'nare vt sow; 🔟 shake off (inseguitori)

semi'nario m seminar; (Relig) seminary

seminter'rato m basement

se'mitico adj Semitic

sem'mai conj in case • adv è lui, ~, che... if anyone, it's him who...

'semola f bran. **semo'lino** m semolina

'semplice adj simple; **in parole semplici** in plain words. **~'cemente** adv simply. **~'cità** f simplicity. **~fi'care** vt simplify

'sempre adv always; (ancora) still; **per ~** for ever

sempre'verde adj & m evergreen

'senape f mustard

se'nato m senate. **sena'tore** m senator

se'nile adj senile. **~ità** f senility

'senno m sense

'seno m breast; (Math) sine

sen'sato adj sensible

sensazio'nale adj sensational. **~'one** f sensation

sen'sibile adj sensitive; (percepibile) perceptible; (notevole) considerable. **~ità** f sensitivity. **~iz'zare** vt make more aware (a of)

sensi'tivo, -a adj sensory • mf sensitive person; (medium) medium

'senso m sense; (significato) meaning; (direzione) direction; **non ha ~** it doesn't make sense; **perdere i sensi** lose consciousness. **~ dell'umorismo** sense of humour. **~ unico** (strada) one-way; **~ vietato** no entry

sensu'ale adj sensual. **~ità** f sensuality

sen'tenza f sentence; (massima) saying. **~i'are** vi pass judgment

senti'ero m path

sentimen'tale adj sentimental. **senti'mento** m feeling

senti'nella f sentry

sen'tire vt feel; (udire) hear; (ascoltare) listen to; (gustare) taste; (odorare) smell • vi feel; (udire) hear; **~re caldo/freddo** feel hot/cold. **~rsi** vr feel; (udire) hear; **~rsi di fare qcsa** feel like doing sth; **~rsi bene** feel well; **~rsi poco bene** feel unwell. **~to** adj sincere

sen'tore m inkling

'senza prep without; **~ correre** without running; **senz'altro** certainly; **~ ombrello** without an umbrella

senza'tetto m inv i **~ the** homeless

sepa'rare vt separate. **~rsi** vr separate; (amici:) part; **~rsi da** be separated from. **~ta'mente** adv separately. **~zi'one** f separation

se'polcro m sepulchre. **~to** pp of seppellire. **~tura** f burial

seppel'lire vt bury

'seppia f cuttle fish; **nero di ~** sepia

sep'pure *conj* even if

se'quenza *f* sequence

seque'strare *vt* (*rapire*) kidnap; (*Jur*) impound; (*confiscare*) confiscate. **se'questro** *m* impounding; (*di persona*) kidnap[ping]

'sera *f* evening; **di ~** in the evening. **se'rale** *adj* evening. **se'rata** *f* evening; (*ricevimento*) party

ser'bare *vt* keep; harbour (*odio*); cherish (*speranza*)

serba'toio *m* tank. ~ **d'acqua** water tank; (*per una città*) reservoir

'Serbia *f* Serbia

'serbo, -a *adj & mf* Serbian ● *m* (*lingua*) Serbian

sere'nata *f* serenade

serenità *f* serenity. **se'reno** *adj* serene; (*cielo*) clear

ser'gente *m* sergeant

seria'mente *adv* seriously

'serie *f inv* series; (*complesso*) set; *Sport* division; **fuori ~** custom-built; **produzione in ~** mass production; **di ~ B** second-rate

serietà *f* seriousness. **'serio** *adj* serious; (*degno di fiducia*) reliable; **sul serio** seriously; (*davvero*) really

ser'mone *m* sermon

'serpe *f liter* viper. **~ggi'are** *vi* meander; (*diffondersi*) spread

ser'pente *m* snake

'serra *f* greenhouse; **effetto ~** greenhouse effect

ser'randa *f* shutter

ser'ra|re *vt* shut; (*stringere*) tighten; (*incalzare*) press on. **~'tura** *f* lock

'server *m inv* (*Comput*) server

ser'vir|e *vt* serve; (*al ristorante*) wait on ● *vi* serve; (*essere utile*) be of use; **non serve** it's no good. **~si** *vr* (*di cibo*) help oneself; **~si da** buy from; **~si di** use

servitù *f* servitude; (*personale di servizio*) servants *pl*

ser'vizio *m* service; (*da caffè ecc*) set;

(*di cronaca, sportivo*) report; **servizi** *pl* bathroom; **essere di ~** be on duty; **fare ~** (*autobus ecc*:) run; **fuori ~** (bus) not in service; (*ascensore*) out of order; **~ compreso** service charge included. **~ in camera** room service. **~ civile** civilian duties done instead of national service. **~ militare** military service. **~ pubblico** utility company. **~ al tavolo** waiter service

'servo, -a *mf* servant

servo'sterzo *m* power steering

ses'san|ta *adj & m* sixty. **~'tina** *f* **una ~tina** about sixty

sessi'one *f* session

'sesso *m* sex

sessu'al|e *adj* sexual. **~ità** *f* sexuality

'sesto[1] *adj* sixth

'sesto[2] *m* (*ordine*) order

'seta *f* silk

setacci'are *vt* sieve. **se'taccio** *m* sieve

'sete *f* thirst; **avere ~** be thirsty

'setta *f* sect

set'tan|ta *adj & m* seventy. **~'tina** *f* **una ~tina** about seventy

'sette *adj & m* seven. **~'cento** *agg & m* seven hundred; **il S~cento** the eighteenth century

set'tembre *m* September

settentri|o'nale *adj* northern ● *mf* northerner. **~'one** *m* north

setti'ma|na *f* week. **~'nale** *agg & m* weekly

'settimo *adj* seventh

set'tore *m* sector

severità *f* severity. **se'vero** *adj* severe; (*rigoroso*) strict

se'vizi|a *f* torture; **se'vizie** *pl* tortures *sg*. **~'are** *vt* torture

sezio'nare *vt* divide; (*Med*) dissect. **sezi'one** *f* section; (*reparto*) department; (*Med*) dissection

sfaccen'dato *adj* idle

sfacchi'na|re *vi* toil. **~ta** *f*

drudgery

sfaccia|taggine f insolence. ∼**ato** adj cheeky, fresh Am

sfa'celo m ruin; **in** ∼ in ruins

sfal'darsi vr flake off

sfa'mar|e vt feed. ∼**si** vr satisfy one's hunger

sfar'zoso adj sumptuous

sfa'sato adj 🔲 confused; (motore) which needs tuning

sfasci'a|re vt unbandage; (fracassare) smash. ∼**rsi** vr fall to pieces. ∼**to** adj beat-up

sfa'tare vt explode

sfati'cato adj lazy

sfavil'lare vi sparkle

sfavo'revole adj unfavourable

sfavo'rire vt disadvantage

sfer|a f sphere. ∼**ico** adj spherical

sfer'rare vt unshoe (cavallo); (scagliare) land

sfer'zare vt whip

sfian'carsi vr wear oneself out

sfi'bra|re vt exhaust. ∼**to** adj exhausted

sfida f challenge. **sfi'dare** vt challenge

sfi'ducia f mistrust. ∼**'ato** adj discouraged

sfigu'rare vt disfigure ● vi (far cattiva figura) look out of place

sfilacci'ar|e vt, ∼**si** vr fray

sfi'la|re vt unthread; (togliere di dosso) take off ● vi (truppe:) march past; (in parata) parade. ∼**rsi** vr come unthreaded; (collant:) ladder; take off (pantaloni). ∼**ta** f parade; (sfilza) series. ∼**ta di moda** fashion show

'sfilza f (di errori) string

'sfinge f sphinx

sfi'nito adj worn out

sfio'rare vt skim; touch on (argomento)

sfio'rire vi wither; (bellezza:) fade

'sfitto adj vacant

'sfizio m whim, fancy; **togliersi uno** ∼ satisfy a whim

sfo'cato adj out of focus

sfoci'are vi ∼ **in** flow into

sfode'ra|re vt draw (pistola, spada). ∼**to** adj unlined

sfo'gar|e vt vent. ∼**si** vr give vent to one's feelings

sfoggi'are vt/i show off. **'sfoggio** m show, display; **fare sfoggio di** show off

'sfoglia f sheet of pastry; **pasta** ∼ puff pastry

sfogli'are vt leaf through

'sfogo m outlet; fig outburst; (Med) rash; **dare** ∼ **a** give vent to

sfolgo'rare vi blaze

sfol'lare vt clear ● vi (Mil) be evacuated

sfol'tire vt thin [out]

sfon'dare vt break down ● vi (aver successo) make a name for oneself

'sfondo m background

sfor'ma|re vt pull out of shape (tasche). ∼**rsi** vr lose its shape; (persona:) lose one's figure. ∼**to** m (Culin) flan

sfor'nito adj ∼ **di** (negozio) out of

sfor'tuna f bad luck. ∼**ta'mente** adv unfortunately. **sfortu'nato** adj unlucky

sfor'zar|e vt force. ∼**si** vr try hard. **'sforzo** m effort; (tensione) strain

'sfottere vt 🔲 tease

sfracel'larsi vr smash

sfrat'tare vt evict. **'sfratto** m eviction

sfrecci'are vi flash past

sfregi'a|re vt slash. ∼**to** adj scarred

'sfregio m slash

sfre'na|rsi vr run wild. ∼**to** adj wild

sfron'tato adj shameless

sfrutta'mento m exploitation.

sfrut'tare vt exploit

sfug'gente adj elusive; (mento) receding

sfug'gire vi escape; ~re a escape [from]; mi sfugge it escapes me; mi è sfuggito di mano I lost hold of it ● vt avoid. ~ta f di ~ta in passing

sfu'mare vi (svanire) vanish; (colore:) shade off ● vt soften (colore). ~'tura f shade

sfuri'ata f outburst [of anger]

sga'bello m stool

sgabuz'zino m cupboard

sgambet'tare vi kick one's legs; (camminare) trot. sgam'betto m fare lo sgambetto a qcno trip sb up

sganasci'arsi vr ~ dalle risa roar with laughter

sganci'ar|e vt unhook; (Rail) uncouple; drop (bombe); 🔲 cough up (denaro). ~si vr become unhooked; fig get away

sanghe'rato adj ramshackle

sgar'bato adj rude. 'sgarbo m discourtesy

sgargi'ante adj garish

sgar'rare vi be wrong; (da regola) stray from the straight and narrow. 'sgarro m mistake, slip

sgattaio'lare vi sneak away; ~ via decamp

sghignaz'zare vi laugh scornfully, sneer

sgoccio'lare vi drip

sgo'larsi vr shout oneself hoarse

sgomb[e]'rare vt clear [out]. 'sgombro adj clear ● m (trasloco) removal; (pesce) mackerel

sgomen'tar|e vt dismay. ~si vr be dismayed. sgo'mento m dismay

sgomi'nare vt defeat

sgom'mata f screech of tyres

sgonfi'ar|e vt deflate. ~si vr go down. 'sgonfio adj flat

'sgorbio m scrawl; (fig: vista sgradevole) sight

sgor'gare vi gush [out] ● vt flush out, unblock (lavandino)

sgoz'zare vt ~ qcno cut sb's throat

sgra'd|evole adj disagreeable. ~ito adj unwelcome

sgrammati'cato adj ungrammatical

sgra'nare vt shell (piselli); open wide (occhi)

sgran'chir|e vt, ~si vr stretch

sgranocchi'are vt munch

sgras'sare vt remove the grease from

sgrazi'ato adj ungainly

sgreto'lar|e vt, ~si vr crumble

sgri'da|re vt scold. ~ta f scolding

sgros'sare vt rough-hew (marmo); fig polish

sgual'ato adj coarse

sgual'cire vt crumple

sgu'ardo m look; (breve) glance

sguaz'zare vi splash; (nel fango) wallow

sguinzagli'are vt unleash

sgusci'are vt shell ● vi (sfuggire) slip away; ~ fuori slip out

shake'rare vt shake

---

si

● *pers pron* (*riflessivo*) oneself; (*lui*) himself; (*lei*) herself; (*esso, essa*) itself; (*loro*) themselves; (*reciproco*) each other; (*tra più di due*) one another; (*impersonale*) you, one; lavarsi wash [oneself]; si è lavata she washed [herself]; lavarsi le mani wash one's hands; si è lavata le mani she washed her hands; si è mangiato un pollo intero he ate an entire chicken by himself; incontrarsi meet each other; la gente si aiuta a vicenda people help one another; non

si sa mai you never know, one never knows *fml*; queste cose si dimenticano facilmente these things are easily forgotten
● *m* (*chiave, nota*) B

sì *adv* yes
'sia¹ *f* ~ ESSERE
'sia² *conj* ~...~... (*entrambi*) both...and...; (*o l'uno o l'altro*) either...or...; (*che*) ~ che non venga whether he comes or not; scegli ~ questo ~ quello choose either this one or that one; voglio ~ questo che quello I want both this one and that one
sia'mese *adj* Siamese
sibi'lare *vi* hiss
si'cario *m* hired killer
sicché *conj* (*perciò*) so [that]; (*allora*) then
sicci'tà *f* drought
sic'come *conj* as
Si'cilia *f* Sicily. s~ano, -a *adj* & *mf* Sicilian
si'cura *f* safety catch; (*di portiera*) child-proof lock. ~mente *adv* definitely
sicu'rezza *f* certainty; (*salvezza*) safety; uscita di ~ emergency exit. ~ delle frontiere homeland security
si'curo *adj* safe; (*certo*) sure; (*saldo*) steady; (*Comm*) sound ● *adv* certainly ● *m* safety; al ~ safe; andare sul ~ play [it] safe; di ~, definitely; di ~, sarà arrivato he must have arrived
siderur'gia *f* iron and steel industry
'sidro *m* cider
si'epe *f* hedge
si'ero *m* serum
sieroposi'tivo *adj* HIV positive
si'esta *f* afternoon nap
si'fone *m* siphon
Sig. *abbr* (*signore*) Mr

Sig.a *abbr* (*signora*) Mrs, Ms
siga'retta *f* cigarette
'sigaro *m* cigar
Sigg. *abbr* (*signori*) Messrs
sigil'lare *vt* seal. si'gillo *m* seal
'sigla *f* initials *pl.* ~ musicale signature tune. si'glare *vt* initial
Sig.na *abbr* (*signorina*) Miss, Ms
signifi'care *vt* mean. ~'tivo *adj* significant. ~to *m* meaning
si'gnora *f* lady; (*davanti a nome proprio*) Mrs; (*non sposata*) Miss; (*in lettere ufficiali*) Dear Madam; il signor Venè e ~ Mr and Mrs Venè
si'gnore *m* gentleman; (*Relig*) lord; (*davanti a nome proprio*) Mr; (*in lettere ufficiali*) Dear Sir. signo'rile *adj* gentlemanly; (*di lusso*) luxury
signo'rina *f* young lady; (*seguito da nome proprio*) Miss
silenzia'tore *m* silencer
si'lenzio *m* silence. ~'oso *adj* silent
silhou'ette *f* silhouette
si'licio *m* piastrina di ~ silicon chip
sili'cone *m* silicone
'sillaba *f* syllable
silu'rare *vt* torpedo. si'luro *m* torpedo
simboleggi'are *vt* symbolize
sim'bolico *adj* symbolic[al]
'simbolo *m* symbol
similarità *f inv* similarity
'simile *adj* similar; (*tale*) such; ~e a like ● *m* (*il prossimo*) fellow man. ~'mente *adv* similarly. ~'pelle *f* Leatherette®
simme'tria *f* symmetry. sim'metrico *adj* symmetric[al]
simpa'tia *f* liking; (*compenetrazione*) sympathy; prendere qcno in ~ take a liking to sb. sim'patico *adj* nice. ~iz'zante *mf* well-wisher. ~iz'zare *vt* ~izzare con take a liking to sb; ~izzare per qcsa/qcno lean towards sth/sb

sim'posio m symposium

simu'la|re vt simulate; feign (amicizia, interesse). **~zi'one** f simulation

simul'taneo adj simultaneous

sina'goga f synagogue

since'rità f sincerity. **sin'cero** adj sincere

'sincope f syncopation; (Med) fainting fit

sincron'ia f synchronization

sincroniz'zare vt synchronize

sinda'ca|le adj [trade] union, [labor] union Am. **~lista** mf trade unionist, labor union member Am. **~re** vt inspect. **~to** m [trade] union, [labor] union Am; (associazione) syndicate

'sindaco m mayor

'sindrome f syndrome

sinfo'nia f symphony. **sin'fonico** adj symphonic

singhi|oz'zare vi (di pianto) sob. **~'ozzo** m hiccup; (di pianto) sob

singo'lar|e adj singular ● m singular. **~'mente** adv individually; (stranamente) peculiarly

'singolo adj single ● m individual; Tennis singles pl

si'nistra f left; a **~** on the left; girare a **~** turn to the left; tenere la guida a **~** (auto) with left-hand drive

sini'strato adj injured

si'nistr|o, -a adj left[-hand]; (avverso) sinister ● m accident ● f left [hand]; (Pol) left [wing]

'sino prep = FINO

si'nonimo adj synonymous ● m synonym

sin'tassi f syntax

'sintesi f inv synthesis; (riassunto) summary

sin'teti|co adj synthetic; (conciso) summary. **~z'zare** vt summarize

sintetiz'zatore m synthesizer

sinto'matico adj symptomatic

'sintomo m symptom

sinto'nia f tuning; in **~** on the same wavelength

si'pario m curtain

si'rena f siren

'Siri|a f Syria. **s~ano, -a** adj & mf Syrian

si'ringa f syringe

'sismico adj seismic

si'stema m system. **~a operativo** (Comput) operating system

siste'ma|re vt (mettere) put; tidy up (casa, camera); (risolvere) sort out; (procurare lavoro a) fix up with a job; (trovare alloggio a) find accommodation for; (sposare) marry off; (🆒: punire) sort out. **~rsi** vr settle down; (trovare un lavoro) find a job; (trovare alloggio) find accommodation; (sposarsi) marry. **~tico** adj systematic. **~zi'one** f arrangement; (di questione) settlement; (lavoro) job; (alloggio) accommodation; (matrimonio) marriage

'sito m site. **~ web** web site

situ'are vt place

situazi'one f situation

ski-'lift m inv ski tow

slacci'are vt unfasten

slanci'a|rsi vr hurl oneself. **~to** adj slender. **'slancio** m impetus; (impulso) impulse

sla'vato adj fair

'slavo adj Slav[onic]

sle'al|e adj disloyal. **~tà** f disloyalty

sle'gare vt untie

'slitta f sledge, sleigh. **~'mento** m (di macchina) skid; (fig: di riunione) postponement

slit'ta|re vi (Auto) skid; (riunione:) be put off. **~ta** f skid

slit'tino m toboggan

'slogan m inv slogan

slo'ga|re vt dislocate. **~rsi** vr **~rsi una caviglia** sprain one's ankle. **~'tura** f dislocation

sloggi'are vi move out

Slo'vacchia f Slovakia

Slo'venia f Slovenia

smacchi'a|re vt clean. ~'**tore** m stain remover

'**smacco** m humiliating defeat

smagli'ante adj dazzling

smagli'a|rsi vr (calza): run. ~'**tura** f run

smalizi'ato adj cunning

smal'ta|re vt enamel; glaze (ceramica); varnish (unghie). ~**to** adj enamelled

smalti'mento m disposal; (di merce) selling off. ~ **rifiuti** waste disposal; (di grassi) burning off

smal'tire vt burn off; (merce) sell off; fig get through (corrispondenza); ~ **la sbornia** sober up

'**smalto** m enamel; (di ceramica) glaze; (per le unghie) nail varnish

smantella'mento m dismantling. ~**lare** vt dismantle

smarri'mento m loss; (psicologico) bewilderment

smar'ri|re vt lose; (temporaneamente) mislay. ~**rsi** vr get lost; (turbarsi) be bewildered

smasche'rar|e vt unmask. ~**si** vr (tradirsi) give oneself away

smemo'rato, -a adj forgetful • mf scatterbrain

smen'ti|re vt deny. ~**ta** f denial

sme'raldo m & adj emerald

smerci'are vt sell off

smerigli'ato adj emery; vetro ~ frosted glass. **sme'riglio** m emery

'**smesso** pp di smettere • adj (abiti) cast-off

'**smett|ere** vt stop; stop wearing (abiti); ~**ila!** stop it!

smidol'lato adj spineless

sminu'ir|e vt diminish. ~**si** vr fig belittle oneself

sminuz'zare vt crumble; (fig: analizzare) analyse in detail

smista'mento m clearing; (postale) sorting. **smi'stare** vt sort; (Mil) post

smisu'rato adj boundless; (esorbitante) excessive

smobili'ta|re vt demobilize. ~**zi'one** f demobilization

smo'dato adj immoderate

smog m smog

'**smoking** m inv dinner jacket, tuxedo Am

smon'tar|e vt take to pieces; (scoraggiare) dishearten • vi (da veicolo) get off; (da cavallo) dismount; (dal servizio) go off duty. ~**si** vr lose heart

'**smorfi|a** f grimace; (moina) simper; **fare** ~ **e** make faces. ~'**oso** adj affected

'**smorto** adj pale; (colore) dull

smor'zare vt dim (luce); tone down (colori); deaden (suoni); quench (sete)

'**smosso** pp di smuovere

smotta'mento m landslide

sms m inv (short message service) text message

'**smunto** adj emaciated

smu'over|e vt shift; (commuovere) move. ~**si** vr move; (commuoversi) be moved

smus'sar|e vt round off; (fig: attenuare) tone down. ~**si** vr go blunt

snatu'rato adj inhuman

snel'lir|e vt slim down. ~**si** vr slim [down]. '**snello** adj slim

sner'va|re vt enervate. ~**rsi** vr get exhausted

sni'dare vt drive out

snif'fare vt snort

snob'bare vt snub. **sno'bismo** m snobbery

snoccio'lare vt stone; fig blurt out

sno'da|re vt (scogliere) loosen. ~**rsi** vr come untied; (strada): wind. ~**to** adj (persona) double-jointed; (dita) flexible

so'ave adj gentle

sobbal'zare vi jerk; (*trasalire*) start. **sob'balzo** m jerk; (*trasalimento*) start

sobbar'carsi vr ~ a undertake

sob'borgo m suburb

sobil'la|re vt stir up

'sobrio adj sober

soc'chiu|dere vt half-close. ~**so** pp di socchiudere ● adj (occhi) half-closed; (porta) ajar

soc'cor|rere vt assist. ~**so** pp di soccorrere ● m assistance; soccorsi pl rescuers; (dopo disastro) relief workers. ~**so stradale** breakdown service

socialdemo'cra|tico, -a adj Social Democratic ● mf Social Democrat. ~'**zia** f Social Democracy

soci'ale adj social

socia'li|smo m Socialism. ~**sta** agg & mf Socialist. ~'**zzare** vi socialize

società f inv society; (Comm) company. ~ **per azioni** plc. ~ **a responsabilità limitata** limited liability company

soci'evole adj sociable

'socio, -a mf member; (Comm) partner

sociolo'gia f sociology. **socio'logico** adj sociological

'soda f soda

soddisfa'cente adj satisfactory

soddi'sfa|re vt/i satisfy; meet (richiesta); make amends for (offesa). ~**tto** pp di soddisfare ● adj satisfied. ~**zi'one** f satisfaction

'sodo adj hard; fig firm; (uovo) hard-boiled ● adv hard; **dormire** ~ sleep soundly

sofà m inv sofa

soffe'ren|te adj ill

soffer'marsi vr pause; ~ **su** dwell on

sof'ferto pp di soffrire

soffi'a|re vt blow; reveal (segreto); (rubare) pinch 🔢 ● vi blow. ~**ta** f fig 🔲 tip-off

'soffice adj soft

'soffio m puff; (Med) murmur

sof'fitt|a f attic. ~**o** m ceiling

soffo'ca|mento m suffocation

soffo'ca|nte adj suffocating. ~**re** vt/i suffocate; (con cibo) choke; fig stifle

sof'friggere vt fry lightly

sof'frire vt/i suffer; (sopportare) bear; ~ **di** suffer from

sof'fritto pp di soffriggere

sof'fuso adj (luce) soft

sofisti'ca|re vt (adulterare) adulterate ● vi (sottilizzare) quibble. ~**to** adj sophisticated

sog'get|tivo adj subjective

sog'getto m subject ● adj subject; **essere** ~ **a** be subject to

soggezi'one f subjection; (rispetto) awe

sogghi'gnare vi sneer

soggio'gare vt subdue

soggior'nare vi stay. **soggi'orno** m stay; (stanza) living room

soggi'ungere vt add

'soglia f threshold

'sogliola f sole

so'gna|re vt/i dream; ~**re a occhi aperti** daydream. ~'**tore, -'trice** mf dreamer. '**sogno** m dream; **fare un sogno** have a dream; **neanche per sogno!** not at all!

'soia f soya

sol m (Mus) G

so'laio m attic

sola'mente adv only

so'lar|e adj (energia, raggi) solar; (crema) sun attrib. ~**ium** m inv solarium

sol'care vt plough. '**solco** m furrow; (di ruota) track; (di nave) wake; (di disco) groove

sol'dato m soldier

'soldo m non ha un ~ he hasn't got a penny; **senza un** ~ penniless;

soldi *pl* (denaro) money *sg*

'**sole** *m* sun; (*luce del sole*) sun[light]; al ~ in the sun; prendere il ~ sunbathe

soleggi'ato *adj* sunny

so'lenn|e *adj* solemn. ~ità *f* solemnity

so'lere *vi* be in the habit of; come si suol dire as they say

sol'fato *m* sulphate

soli'da|le *adj* in agreement. ~rietà *f* solidarity

solidifi'car|e *vt/i*, ~si *vr* solidify

solidità *f* solidity; (*di colori*) fastness. '**solido** *adj* solid; (*robusto*) sturdy; (*colore*) fast ●*m* solid

so'lista *adj* solo ●*mf* soloist

solita'mente *adv* usually

soli'tario *adj* solitary; (*isolato*) lonely ●*m* (*brillante*) solitaire; (*gioco di carte*) patience, solitaire

'**solito** *adj* usual; essere ~ fare qcsa be in the habit of doing sth ●*m* usual; di ~ usually

soli'tudine *f* solitude

solleci'ta|re *vt* speed up; urge (*persona*). ~zi'one *f* (*richiesta*) request; (*preghiera*) entreaty

sol'lecito *adj* prompt ●*m* reminder. ~'tudine *f* promptness; (*interessamento*) concern

solle'one *m* noonday sun; (*periodo*) dog days of summer

solleti'care *vt* tickle

solleva'mento *m* ~ pesi weightlifting

solle'var|e *vt* lift; (*elevare*) raise; (*confortare*) comfort. ~si *vr* rise; (*riaversi*) recover

solli'evo *m* relief

'**solo**, **-a** *adj* alone; (*isolato*) lonely; (*unico*) only; (*Mus*) solo; da ~ by myself/yourself/himself etc ●*m* if un ~, la sola the only one ●*m* (*Mus*) solo ●*adv* only

sol'stizio *m* solstice

sol'tanto *adv* only

so'lubile *adj* soluble; (*caffè*) instant

soluzi'one *f* solution; (*Comm*) payment

sol'vente *adj* & *m* solvent; ~ per unghie nail polish remover

so'maro *m* ass; (*Sch*) dunce

so'matico *adj* somatic

somigli'an|te *adj* similar. ~za *f* resemblance

somigli'ar|e *vi* ~e a resemble. ~si *vr* be alike

'**somma** *f* sum; (*Math*) addition

som'mare *vt* add; (*totalizzare*) add up

som'mario *adj* & *m* summary

som'mato *adj* tutto ~ all things considered

sommeli'er *m inv* wine waiter

som'mer|gere *vt* submerge. ~'gibile *m* submarine. ~so *pp di* sommergere

som'messo *adj* soft

sommini'stra|re *vt* administer. ~zi'one *f* administration

sommità *f inv* summit

'**sommo** *adj* highest; *fig* supreme ●*m* summit

som'mossa *f* rising

sommozza'tore *m* frogman

so'naglio *m* bell

so'nata *f* sonata; *fig* 🔲 beating

'**sonda** *f* (*Mech*) drill; (*Med, spaziale*). son'daggio *m* drilling; (*Med, spaziale*) probe; (*indagine*) survey. sondaggio d'opinioni opinion poll. son'dare *vt* sound; (*investigare*) probe

sonnambu'lismo *m* sleepwalking. son'nambulo, -a *mf* sleepwalker

sonnecchi'are *vi* doze

son'nifero *m* sleeping-pill

'**sonno** *m* sleep; aver ~ be sleepy. ~'lenza *f* sleepiness

so'noro *adj* resonant; (*rumoroso*) loud; (*onde, scheda*) sound *attrib*

sontu'oso adj sumptuous

sopo'rifero adj soporific

sop'palco m platform

soppe'rire vi ~ a qcsa provide for sth

soppe'sare vt weigh up

soppor'ta|re vt support; (tollerare) stand; bear (dolore)

soppressi'one f removal; (di legge) abolition; (di diritti, pubblicazione) suppression; (annullamento) cancellation. **sop'presso** pp di **sopprimere**

sop'primere vt get rid of; abolish (legge); suppress (diritti, pubblicazione); (annullare) cancel

'sopra adv on top; (più in alto) higher [up]; (al piano superiore) upstairs; (in testo) above; **mettilo lì** ~ put it up there; **di** ~ upstairs; **pensarci** ~ think about it; **vedi** ~ see above ● prep ~ [a] on; (senza contatto, oltre) over; (riguardo a) about; **è** ~ **al tavolo, è** ~ **il tavolo** it's on the table; **il quadro è appeso** ~ **al camino** the picture is hanging over the fireplace; **il ponte passa** ~ **all'autostrada** the bridge crosses over the motorway; **è caduto** ~ **il tetto** it fell on the roof; **l'uno** ~ **l'altro** one above the other; (senza contatto) one above the other; **abita** ~ **di me** he lives upstairs from me; **i bambini** ~ **i dieci anni** children over ten; **20°** ~ **lo zero** 20° above zero; ~ **il livello del mare** above sea level; **rifletti** ~ **quello che è successo** think about what happened ● m il [di] ~ the top

so'prabito m overcoat

soprac'ciglio m (pl f **sopracciglia**) eyebrow

sopracco'per|ta f bedspread; (di libro) [dust-]jacket. ~**tina** f book jacket

soprad'detto adj above-mentioned

sopraele'vata f elevated railway

sopraf'fa|re vt overwhelm. ~**tto** pp di **sopraffare**. ~**zi'one** f abuse of power

sopraf'fino adj excellent; (gusto, udito) highly refined

sopraggi'ungere vi (persona:) turn up; (accadere) happen

soprallu'ogo m inspection

sopram'mobile m ornament

soprannatu'rale adj & m supernatural

sopran'nome m nickname

so'prano mf soprano

soprappensi'ero adv lost in thought

sopras'salto m di ~ with a start

soprasse'dere vi ~ a postpone

soprat'tutto adv above all

sopravvalu'tare vt overvalue

soprav've'nire vi turn up; (accadere:) happen. ~**'vento** m fig upper hand

sopravvi|s'suto pp di **sopravvivere**. ~**'venza** f survival. **soprav'vivere** vi survive; **sopravvivere a** outlive (persona)

soprinten'den|te mf supervisor; (di museo ecc) keeper. ~**za** f supervision; (ente) board

so'pruso m abuse of power

soq'quadro m mettere a ~ turn upside down

sor'betto m sorbet

'sordido adj sordid; (avaro) stingy

sor'dina f mute; in ~ on the quiet

sordità f deafness. **'sordo, -a** adj deaf; (rumore, dolore) dull ● mf deaf person. **sordo'muto, -a** adj deaf-and-dumb

so'rel|la f sister. ~**'lastra** f step-sister

sor'gente f spring; (fonte) source

'sorgere vi rise; fig arise

sormon'tare vt surmount

sorni'one adj sly

sorpas'sa|re vt surpass; (eccedere) exceed; overtake (veicolo). ~to adj old-fashioned. sor'passo m overtaking

sorpren'dente adj surprising; (straordinario) remarkable

sor'prendere vt surprise; (cogliere in flagrante) catch

sor'pres|a f surprise; di ~a by surprise. ~o pp di sorprendere

sor're|ggere vt support; (tenere) hold up. ~ggersi vr support oneself. ~tto pp di sorreggere

sor'ri|dere vi smile. ~so pp di sorridere ●m smile

sorseg'giare vt sip. 'sorso m sip; (piccola quantità) drop

'sorta f sort; di ~ whatever; ogni ~ di all sorts of

'sorte f fate; (caso imprevisto) chance; tirare a ~ draw lots. sor'teggio m draw

sorti'legio m witchcraft

sor'ti|re vi come out. ~ta f (Mil) sortie; (battuta) witticism

'sorto pp di sorgere

sorvegli'an|te mf keeper; (controllore) overseer. ~za f watch; (Mil ecc) surveillance

sorvegli'are vt watch over; (controllare) oversee; (polizia:) keep under surveillance

sorvo'lare vt fly over; fig skip

'sosia m inv double

so'spen|dere vt hang; (interrompere) stop; (privare di una carica) suspend. ~si'one f suspension

so'speso pp di sospendere ●adj (impiegato, alunno) suspended; ~ a hanging from; ~ a un filo fig hanging by a thread ●m in ~ pending; (emozionato) in suspense

sospet'ta|re vt suspect. so'spetto adj suspicious; persona sospetta suspicious person ●m suspicion; (persona) suspect. ~toso adj suspicious

so'spin|gere vt drive. ~to pp di sospingere

sospi'rare vi sigh ●vt long for. so-'spiro m sigh

'sosta f stop; (pausa) pause; senza ~ non-stop; "divieto di ~" "no parking"

sostan'tivo m noun

so'stan|za f substance; ~e pl (patrimonio) property sg. ~i'oso adj substantial; (cibo) nourishing

so'stare vi stop; (fare una pausa) pause

so'stegno m support

soste'ner|e vt support; (sopportare) bear; (resistere) withstand; (affermare) maintain; (nutrire) sustain; sit (esame); ~e le spese meet the costs. ~si vr support oneself

sosteni'tore, -'trice mf supporter

sostenta'mento m maintenance

soste'nuto adj (stile) formal; (prezzi, velocità) high

sostitu'ir|e vt substitute (a for), replace (con with). ~si vr ~si a replace

sostitu'to, -ta mf replacement, stand-in ●m (surrogato) substitute. ~zi'one f substitution

sot'tana f petticoat; (di prete) cassock

sotter'raneo adj underground ●m cellar

sotter'rare vt bury

sottigli'ezza f slimness; fig subtlety

sot'til|e adj thin; (udito, odorato) keen; (osservazione, distinzione) subtle. ~iz'zare vi split hairs

sottin'ten|dere vt imply. ~so pp di sottintendere ~i'one f allusion; senza ~i openly ●adj implied

'sotto adv below; (più in basso) lower [down]; (al di sotto) underneath; (al piano di sotto) downstairs; è li ~ it's underneath; ~ ~ deep down; (di na-scosto) on the quiet; di ~ down-stairs; mettersi ~ fig get down to it; mettere ~ [a] under; (al di sotto di) under[neath]; abita ~ di me he lives downstairs from me; i bambini ~ i dieci anni children under ten; 20° ~ zero 20° below zero; ~ il li-vello del mare below sea level; ~ la pioggia in the rain; ~ calmante under sedation; ~ condizione che... on condition that...; ~ giuramento under oath; ~ sorveglianza under surveillance; ~ Natale/gli esami around Christmas/exam time; al di ~ di under; andare ~ i 50 all'ora do less than 50km an hour • m il [di] ~ the bottom

sotto'banco adv under the counter

sottobicchi'ere m coaster

sotto'bosco m undergrowth

sotto'braccio adv arm in arm

sotto'fondo m background

sottoline'are vt underline; fig stress

sot'tolio adv in oil

sotto'mano adv within reach

sottoma'rino, -a adj & m submarine

sotto'messo pp di sottomettere

sotto'metter|e vt submit; subdue (popolo). ~si vr submit. sottomis-si'one f submission

sottopas'saggio m underpass; (pedonale) subway

sotto'por|re vt submit; (costringere) subject. ~si vr submit oneself; ~si a undergo. sotto'posto pp di sot-toporre

sotto'scala m cupboard under the stairs

sotto'scritto pp di sottoscrivere • m undersigned

sotto'scri|vere vt sign; (approvare) sanction, subscribe to. ~zi'one f (petizione) petition; (approvazione) sanc-tion; (raccolta di denaro) appeal

sotto'sopra adv upside down

sotto'stante adj la strada ~ the road below

sottosu'olo m subsoil

sottosvilup'pato adj under-developed

sotto'terra adv underground

sotto'titolo m subtitle

sottovalu'tare vt underestimate

sotto'veste f slip

sotto'voce adv in a low voice

sottovu'oto adj vacuum-packed

sot'tra|rre vt remove; embezzle (fondi) (Math) subtract. ~rsi vr ~rsi a escape from; avoid (re-sponsabilità). ~tto pp di sottrarre. ~zi'one f removal; (di fondi) em-bezzlement; (Math) subtraction

sottuffici'ale m non-commissioned officer; (Naut) petty officer

sou'brette f inv showgirl

so'vietico, -a adj & mf Soviet

sovraccari'care vt overload. so-vrac'carico adj overloaded (di with) • m overload

sovrannatu'rale adj & m = SO-PRANNATURALE

so'vrano, -a adj sovereign; fig su-preme • mf sovereign

sovrap'por|re vt superimpose. ~si vr overlap

sovra'stare vt dominate; fig: (peri-colo:) hang over

sovrinten'den|te, ~za = SO-PRINTENDENTE, SOPRINTENDENZA

sovru'mano adj superhuman

sovvenzi'one f subsidy

sovver'sivo adj subversive

'sozzo adj filthy

S.p.A. abbr (società per azioni) plc

spac'ca|re vt split; chop (legna). ~rsi vr split. ~'tura f split

spacci'a|re vt deal in, push (droga); ~re qcsa per qcsa pass sth off as sth. ~**rsi** vr ~**rsi per** pass oneself off as. ~**tore**, ~**trice** mf (di droga) pusher; (di denaro falso) distributor of forged bank notes. '**spaccio** m (di droga) dealing; (negozio) shop

'**spacco** m split

spac'cone, -a mf boaster

'**spada** f sword. ~c'cino m swordsman

spae'sato adj disorientated

spa'ghetti mpl spaghetti sg

spa'ghetto m (🄸: spavento) fright

'**Spagna** f Spain

spa'gnolo, -a a adj Spanish ●mf Spaniard ●m (lingua) Spanish

'**spago** m string; dare ~ a qcno encourage sb

spai'ato adj odd

spalan'ca|re vt, ~**rsi** vr open wide. ~**to** adj wide open

spa'lare vt shovel

'**spall|a** f shoulder; (di comico) straight man; (di schiena) back; alle ~**e** pl (schiena) back; alle ~**e di** qcno (ridere) behind sb's back. ~**eggia're** vt back up

spal'letta f parapet

spalli'era f back; (di letto) headboard; (ginnastica) wall bars pl

spal'lina f strap; (imbottitura) shoulder pad

spal'mare vt spread

'**spander|e** vt spread; (versare) spill. ~**si** vr spread

spappo'lare vt crush

spa'ra|re vt/i shoot; ~**rle grosse** talk big. ~**toria** f shooting

sparecchi'are vt clear

spa'reggio m (Comm) deficit; Sport play-off

'**sparg|ere** vt scatter; (diffondere) spread; shed (lacrime, sangue). ~**ersi** vr spread. ~**i'mento** m scattering; ~**imento di sangue** bloodshed

spa'ri|re vi disappear; ~**sci!** get lost!. ~**zi'one** f disappearance

spar'lare vi ~ **di** run down

'**sparo** m shot

sparpagli'ar|e vt, ~**si** vr scatter

'**sparso** pp di spargere ●adj scattered; (sciolto) loose

spar'tire vt share out; (separare) separate

sparti'traffico m inv traffic island; (di autostrada) central reservation, median strip Am

spartizi'one f division

spa'ruto adj gaunt; (gruppo) small; (peli, capelli) sparse

sparvi'ero m sparrow-hawk

'**spasimo** m spasm

spa'smodico adj spasmodic

spas'sar|si vr amuse oneself; ~**sela** have a good time

spassio'nato adj dispassionate

'**spasso** m fun; essere uno ~ be hilarious; andare a ~ go for a walk. spas'soso adj hilarious

'**spatola** f spatula

spau'racchio m scarecrow; fig bugbear. spau'rire vt frighten

spa'valdo adj defiant

spaventa'passeri m inv scarecrow

spaven'tar|e vt frighten. ~**si** vr be frightened. spa'vento m fright. spa'ven'toso adj frightening; (🄸: enorme) incredible

spazi'ale adj spatial; (cosmico) space attrib

spazi'are vt space out ●vi range

spazien'tirsi vr lose patience

'**spazi|o** m space. ~**'oso** adj spacious

spaz'z|are vt sweep; ~**are via** sweep away; (🄸: mangiare) devour. ~**a'tura** f rubbish. ~**ino** m road sweeper; (netturbino) dustman

'**spazzo|la** f brush; (di tergicristallo) blade. ~**'lare** vt brush. ~**'lino** m small brush. ~**lino da denti** toothbrush. ~**'lone** m scrubbing brush

specchi'ar|si vr look at oneself in the mirror; (*riflettersi*) be mirrored; ~ in qcno model oneself on sb

specchi'etto m ~ retrovisore driving mirror

'specchio m mirror

speci'a|le adj special ●m (TV) special [programme]. ~'lista mf specialist. ~lità f inv specialty

specializ'za|re vt, ~rsi vr specialize. ~to adj skilled

special'mente adv especially

'specie f inv species; (*tipo*) kind; fare ~ a surprise

specifi'care vt specify. **spe'cifico** adj specific

specu'lare[1] vi speculate; ~ su (*indagare*) speculate on; (*Fin*) speculate in

specu'lare[2] adj mirror attrib

specula|'tore, -'trice mf speculator. ~zi'one f speculation

spe'di|re vt send. ~to pp di spedire ●adj quick; (*parlata*) fluent. ~zi'one f dispatch; (*Comm*) consignment; (*scientifica*) expedition

'spegner|e vt put out; turn off (gas, luce); switch off (motore); slake (sete). ~si vr go out; (*morire*) pass away

spelacchi'ato adj (*tappeto*) threadbare; (*cane*) mangy

spe'lar|e vt skin (*coniglio*). ~si vr (*cane*) moult

speleolo'gia f potholing

spel'lar|e vt skin; fig fleece. ~si vr peel off

spe'lonca f cave; fig hole

spendacci'one, -a mf spendthrift

'spendere vt spend; ~ fiato waste one's breath

spen'nare vt pluck; 🔲 fleece (*cliente*)

spennel'lare vt brush

spensie|ra'tezza f lightheartedness. ~'rato adj carefree

'spento pp di spegnere ●adj off; (*gas*) out; (*smorto*) dull

spe'ranza f hope; pieno di ~ hopeful; senza ~ hopeless

spe'rare vt hope for; (*aspettarsi*) expect ●vi ~ in trust in; spero di sì I hope so

'sper|dersi vr get lost. ~'duto adj lost; (*isolato*) secluded

spergi'uro, -a mf perjurer ●m perjury

sperimen'ta|le adj experimental. ~re vt experiment with; test (*resistenza, capacità, teoria*). ~zi'one f experimentation

'sperma m sperm

spe'rone m spur

sperpe'rare vt squander. **'sperpero** m waste

'spes|a f expense; (*acquisto*) purchase; andare a far ~e go shopping; fare la ~a do the shopping; fare le ~e di pay for. ~e pl bancarie bank charges. ~e a carico del destinatario carriage forward. spe'sato adj all-expenses-paid. ~o pp di spendere

'spesso[1] adj thick

'spesso[2] adv often

spes'sore m thickness; (*fig: consistenza*) substance

spet'tabile f (*Comm*) abbr (**Spett.**) S~ ditta Rossi Messrs Rossi

spettaco'lare adj spectacular. spet'tacolo m spectacle; (*rappresentazione*) show. ~'loso adj spectacular

spet'tare vi ~ a be up to; (*diritto:*) be due to

spetta|'tore, -'trice mf spectator; spettatori pl audience sg

spettego'lare vi gossip

spet'trale adj ghostly. **'spettro** m ghost; (*Phys*) spectrum

'spezie fpl spices

spez'zar|e vt, ~si vr break

spezza'tino m stew

spez'zato *m* coordinated jacket and trousers

spezzet'tare *vt* break into small pieces

'spia *f* spy; (*della polizia*) informer; (*di porta*) peep-hole; **fare la ∼** sneak. **∼[luminosa] ∼** dell'olio oil [warning] light

spiacci'care *vt* squash

spia'ce|nte *adj* sorry. **∼vole** *adj* unpleasant

spi'aggia *f* beach

spia'nare *vt* level; (*rendere liscio*) smooth; roll out (*pasta*); raze to the ground (*edificio*)

spian'tato *adj fig* penniless

spi'are *vt* spy on; wait for (*occasione ecc*)

spiat'tellare *vt* blurt out; shove (*oggetto*)

spi'azzo *m* (*radura*) clearing

spic'ca|re *vt* **∼re un salto** jump; **∼re il volo** take flight **●** *vi* stand out. **∼to** *adj* marked

'spicchio *m* (*di agrumi*) segment; (*di aglio*) clove

spicci'a|rsi *vr* hurry up. **∼tivo** *adj* speedy

'spicciolo *adj* (*comune*) banal; (*denaro, 5 euro*) in change. **spiccioli** *pl* change *sg*

'spicco *m* relief; **fare ∼** stand out

'spider *f inv* open-top sports car

spie'dino *m* kebab. **spi'edo** *m* spit; **allo spiedo** on a spit, spit-roasted

spie'ga|re *vt* explain; open out (*cartina*); unfurl (*vele*). **∼rsi** *vr* explain oneself; (*vele, bandiere*): unfurl. **∼zi'one** *f* explanation

spiegaz'zato *adj* crumpled

spie'tato *adj* ruthless

spiffe'rare *vt* blurt out **●** *vi* (*vento:*) whistle. **'spiffero** *m* draught

'spiga *f* spike; (*Bot*) ear

spigli'ato *adj* self-possessed

'spigolo *m* edge; (*angolo*) corner

'spilla *f* brooch. **∼ da balia** safety pin. **∼ di sicurezza** safety pin

spil'lare *vt* tap

'spillo *m* pin. **∼ di sicurezza** safety pin; (*in arma*) safety catch

spi'lorcio *adj* stingy

'spina *f* thorn; (*di pesce*) bone; (*Electr*) plug. **∼ dorsale** spine

spi'naci *mpl* spinach

spi'nale *adj* spinal

spi'nato *adj* (*filo*) barbed; (*pianta*) thorny

spi'nello *m* ⚄ joint

'spinger|e *vt* push; *fig* drive. **∼si** *vr* (*andare*) proceed

spi'noso *adj* thorny

'spint|a *f* push; (*violenta*) thrust; *fig* spur. **∼o** *pp di* **spingere**

spio'naggio *m* espionage

spio'vente *adj* sloping

spi'overe *vi liter* stop raining; (*ricadere*) fall; (*scorrere*) flow down

'spira *f* coil

spi'raglio *m* small opening; (*soffio d'aria*) breath of air; (*raggio di luce*) gleam of light

spi'rale *adj* spiral **●** *f* spiral; (*negli orologi*) hairspring; (*anticoncezionale*) coil

spi'rare *vi* (*soffiare*) blow; (*morire*) pass away

spirit'a|to *adj* possessed; (*espressione*) wild. **'spirito** *m* spirit; (*arguzia*) wit; (*intelletto*) mind; **fare dello spirito** be witty; **sotto spirito** in brandy. **∼o'saggine** *f* witticism. **spi'ritoso** *adj* witty

spiritu'ale *adj* spiritual

'splend|ere *vi* shine. **∼dido** *adj* splendid. **∼'dore** *m* splendour

'spoglia *f* (*di animale*) skin; **spoglie** *pl* (*salma*) mortal remains; (*bottino*) spoils

spogli'a|re *vt* strip; (*svestire*) undress; (*fare lo spoglio di*) go through. **∼rello** *m* strip-tease. **∼rsi** *vr* strip, undress. **∼toio** *m* dressing room; *Sport* changing room; (*guardaroba*) cloakroom, checkroom *Am.* 'spoglio *adj* undressed; (albero, muro) bare ● *m* (scrutinio) perusal

'spola *f* shuttle; fare la ~ shuttle

spol'pare *vt* flesh; *fig* fleece

spolve'rare *vt* dust; 🔲 devour (cibo)

'sponda *f* shore; (di fiume) bank; (bordo) edge

sponsoriz'zare *vt* sponsor

spon'taneo *adj* spontaneous

spopo'lar|e *vt* depopulate ● *vi* (avere successo) draw the crowds. ~si *vr* become depopulated

sporadica'mente *adv* sporadically. spo'radico *adj* sporadic

spor'c|are *vt* dirty; (macchiare) soil. ~arsi *vr* get dirty. ~izia *f* dirt. 'sporco *adj* dirty; avere la coscienza sporca have a guilty conscience ● *m* dirt

spor'gen|te *adj* jutting. ~za *f* projection

'sporger|e *vt* stretch out; ~e querela contro take legal action against ● *vi* jut out. ~si *vr* lean out

sport *m inv* sport

'sporta *f* shopping basket

spor'tello *m* door; (di banca ecc) window. ~ automatico cash dispenser

spor'tivo, -a *adj* sports attrib; (persona) sporty ● *m* sportsman ● *f* sportswoman

'sporto *pp di* sporgere

'sposa *f* bride. ~'lizio *m* wedding

spo'sa|re *vt* marry; *fig* espouse. ~rsi *vr* get married; (vino:) go (con with). ~to *adj* married. 'sposo *m* bridegroom; sposi *pl* [novelli] newlyweds

spossa'tezza *f* exhaustion. spos'sato *adj* exhausted, worn out

spo'sta|re *vt* move; (differire) postpone; (cambiare) change. ~rsi *vr* move. ~to, -a *adj* ill-adjusted ● *mf*

(disadattato) misfit

'spranga *f* bar. spran'gare *vt* bar

'sprazzo *m* (di colore) splash; (di luce) flash; *fig* glimmer

spre'care *vt* waste. 'spreco *m* waste

spre'g|evole *adj* despicable. ~ia'tivo *adj* pejorative. 'spregio *m* contempt

spregiudi'cato *adj* unscrupulous

'spremer|e *vt* squeeze. ~si *vr* ~si le meningi rack one's brains

spremia'grumi *m* lemon squeezer

spre'muta *f* juice. ~ d'arancia fresh orange [juice]

sprez'zante *adj* contemptuous

sprigio'nar|e *vt* emit. ~si *vr* burst out

spriz'zare *vt/i* spurt; be bursting with (salute, gioia)

sprofon'dar|e *vi* sink; (crollare) collapse. ~si *vr* ~si in sink into; *fig* be engrossed in

'sprone *m* spur; (sartoria) yoke

sproporzio'nato *adj* disproportionate. ~'one *f* disproportion

spropo'sitato *adj* full of blunders; (enorme) huge. spro'posito *m* blunder; (eccesso) excessive amount

sprovve'duto *adj* unprepared; ~ di lacking in

sprov'visto *adj* ~ di out of; lacking in (fantasia, pazienza); alla sprovvista unexpectedly

spruz'za|re *vt* sprinkle; (vaporizzare) spray; (inzaccherare) spatter. ~'tore *m* spray; 'spruzzo *m* spray; (di fango) splash

spudo|ra'tezza *f* shamelessness. ~'rato *adj* shameless

'spugna *f* sponge; (tessuto) towelling. spu'gnoso *adj* spongy

'spuma *f* foam; (schiuma) froth; (Culin) mousse. spu'mante *m* sparkling wine. spumeg'giare *vi* foam

spun'ta|re *vt* break the point of;

trim (capelli); ~**rla** *fig* win ● *vi*
(pianta:) sprout; (capelli:) begin to
grow; (*sorgere*) rise; (*apparire*) appear.
~**rsi** *vr* get blunt. ~**ta** *f* trim

spun'tino *m* snack

'**spunto** *m* cue; *fig* starting point;
dare ~ a give rise to

spur'gar|e *vt* purge. ~**si** *vr* (*Med*)
expectorate

spu'tare *vt/i* spit; ~ sentenze pass
judgment. '**sputo** *m* spit

'**squadra** *f* team, squad; (*di polizia
ecc*) squad; (*di disegno*) square. **squa-
'drare** *vt* square; (*guardare*) look up
and down

squa'dr|iglia *f*, ~**one** *m* squadron

squagli'ar|e *vt*, ~**si** *vr* melt; ~**sela**
(Ⅰ:) *svignarsela*) steal out

squa'lifi|ca *f* disqualification.
~'**care** *vt* disqualify

'**squallido** *adj* squalid. **squal'lore** *m*
squalor

'**squalo** *m* shark

'**squama** *f* scale; (*di pelle*) flake

squa'mar|e *vt* scale. ~**arsi** *vr*
(pelle:) flake off. ~'**moso** *adj* scaly;
(pelle) flaky

squarcia'gola: a ~ *adv* at the top
of one's voice

squarci'are *vt* rip. '**squarcio** *m* rip;
(*di ferita, in nave*) gash; (*di cielo*) patch

squattri'nato *adj* penniless

squili'bra|re *vt* unbalance. ~**to**, -**a**
adj unbalanced ● *mf* lunatic. **squi'li-
brio** *m* imbalance

squil'lan|te *adj* shrill. ~**re** *vi* (cam-
pana:) peal; (tromba:) blare; (tele-
fono:) ring. '**squillo** *m* blare; (*Teleph*)
ring ● *f* (*ragazza*) call girl

squi'sito *adj* exquisite

sradi'care *vt* uproot; eradicate
(vizio, male)

sragio'nare *vi* rave

srego'lato *adj* inordinate; (*dissoluto*)
dissolute

s.r.l. *abbr* (società a responsabilità li-

mitata) Ltd

sroto'lare *vt* uncoil

SS *abbr* (strada statale) national road

'**stabile** *adj* stable; (*permanente*) lasting; (saldo) steady; **compagnia** ~
(*Theat*) repertory company ● *m* (*edificio*) building

stabili'mento *m* factory; (*industriale*) plant; (*edificio*) establishment.
~ **balneare** lido

stabi'li|re *vt* establish; (*decidere*) de-
cide. ~**rsi** *vr* settle. ~**tà** *f* stability

stabiliz'za|re *vt* stabilize. ~**rsi** *vr*
stabilize. ~'**tore** *m* stabilizer

stac'car|e *vt* detach; pronounce
clearly (parole); (*separare*) separate;
turn off (corrente) ● *vi* (Ⅰ: *finire di lavorare*) knock off. ~**si** *vr* come off;
~**si da** break away from (partito, famiglia)

staccio'nata *f* fence

'**stacco** *m* gap

'**stadio** *m* stadium

'**staffa** *f* stirrup

staf'fetta *f* dispatch rider

stagio'nale *adj* seasonal

stagio'na|re *vt* season (legno);
mature (formaggio). ~**to** *adj* (legno)
seasoned; (formaggio) matured

stagi'one *f* season; **alta/bassa** ~
high/low season

stagli'arsi *vr* stand out

sta'gnan|te *adj* stagnant. ~**re** *vt*
(saldare) solder; (chiudere ermeticamente)
seal ● *vi* stagnate. '**stagno** *adj* water-
tight ● *m* pond; (metallo) tin

sta'gnola *f* tinfoil

'**stall|a** *f* stable; (*per buoi*) cowshed.
~'**iere** *m* groom

stal'lone *m* stallion

sta'mani, stamat'tina *adv* this
morning

stam'becco *m* ibex

stam'berga *f* hovel

'**stampa** *f* (*Typ*) printing; (giornali,
giornalisti) press; (riproduzione) print

stam'pa|nte f printer. ∼**nte laser** laser printer. ∼**re** vt print. ∼**tello** m block letters pl

stam'pella f crutch

'**stampo** m mould; **di vecchio** ∼ (persona) of the old school

sta'nare vt drive out

stan'car|e vt tire; (annoiare) bore. ∼**si** vr get tired

stan'chezza f tiredness. '**stanco** adj tired; **stanco di fed up with. stanco morto** dead tired, exhausted

'standard adj & m inv standard. ∼**iz'zare** vt standardize

'**stan|ga** f bar; (persona) beanpole. ∼'**gata** f fig blow; (ﬁg): **nel calcio) big kick. **stan'ghetta** f (di occhiali) leg

sta'notte adv tonight; (la notte scorsa) last night

'**stante** prep on account of; **a se** ∼ separate

stan'tio adj stale

stan'tuffo m piston

'**stanza** f room; (metrica) stanza

stanzi'are vt allocate

stap'pare vt uncork

'**stare**

● vi (rimanere) stay; (abitare) live; (con gerundio) be; **sto solo cinque minuti** I'll stay only five minutes; **sto in piazza Peyron** I live in Peyron Square; **sta dormendo** he's sleeping; ∼ **a** (attenersi) keep to; (spettare) be up to; ∼ **bene** (economicamente) be well off; (di salute) be well; (addirsi) suit; ∼ **dietro a** (seguire) follow; (sorvegliare) keep an eye on; (corteggiare) run after; ∼ **in piedi** stand; ∼ **per** be about to; **come stai/sta?** how are you?; **lasciar** ∼ leave alone; **starci** (essere contenuto) be in; (essere d'accordo) agree; **il 3 nel 12 ci sta 4 volte** 3 into 12

goes 4; **non sa** ∼ **agli scherzi** he can't take a joke; ∼ **sulle proprie** keep oneself to oneself.

● **starsene** vr (rimanere) stay

starnu'tire vi sneeze. **star'nuto** m sneeze

sta'sera adv this evening, tonight

sta'tale adj state attrib ● mf state employee ● f main road

'**statico** adj static

sta'tista m statesman

sta'tistic|a f statistics sg. ∼**o** adj statistical

'**stato** pp di essere, stare ● m state; (posizione sociale) position; (Jur) status. ∼ **d'animo** frame of mind. ∼ **civile** marital status. S∼ **Maggiore** (Mil) General Staff. **Stati** pl **Uniti** [**d'America**] United States [of America]

'**statua** f statue

statuni'tense adj United States attrib, US attrib ● mf citizen of the United States, US citizen

sta'tura f height; **di alta** ∼ tall; **di bassa** ∼ short

sta'tuto m statute

stazio'nario adj stationary

stazi'one f station; (città) resort. ∼ **balneare** seaside resort. ∼ **ferroviaria** train station. ∼ **di servizio** service station. ∼ **termale** spa

'**stecca** f stick; (di ombrello) rib; (da biliardo) cue; (Med) splint; (di sigarette) carton; (di reggiseno) stiffener

stec'cato m fence

stec'chito adj skinny; (rigido) stiff; (morto) stone cold dead

'**stella** f star; **salire alle stelle** (prezzi) rise sky-high. ∼ **alpina** edelweiss. ∼ **cadente** shooting star. ∼ **filante** streamer. ∼ **di mare** starfish

stel'lare adj stellar

'**stelo** m stem; **lampada** f **a** ∼

standard lamp

'**stemma** m coat of arms

stempi'ato adj bald at the temples

sten'dardo m standard

'**stender|e** vt spread out; (*appendere*) hang out; (*distendere*) stretch [out]; (*scrivere*) write down. ~**si** vr stretch out

stendibianche'ria f inv, **stendi'toio** m clothes horse

stenodatti|logra'fia f shorthand typing

stenogra'f|are vt take down in shorthand. ~**ia** f shorthand

sten'ta|re vi ~**re** a find it hard to. ~**to** adj laboured. '**stento** m effort; a stento with difficulty; stenti pl hardships, privations

'**sterco** m dung

stereo['fonico] adj stereo[phonic]

stereoti'pato adj stereotyped; (*sorriso*) insincere. **stere'otipo** m stereotype

'**steril|e** adj sterile; (*terreno*) barren. ~**ità** f sterility. ~**iz'zare** vt sterilize. ~**izzazi'one** f sterilization

ster'lina f pound; lira ~ [pound] sterling

stermi'nare vt exterminate

stermi'nato adj immense

ster'minio m extermination

ste'roide m steroid

ster'zare vi steer. '**sterzo** m steering

'**steso** pp di stendere

'**stesso** adj same; io ~ myself; tu ~ yourself; me ~ myself; se ~ himself; in quel momento ~ at that very moment; dalla stessa regina by the Queen herself; coi miei stessi occhi with my own eyes ● pron lo ~ the same one; (*la stessa cosa*) the same; fa lo ~ it's all the same; ci vado lo ~ I'll go just the same

ste'sura f drawing up; (*documento*) draft

stick m colla a ~ glue stick; deodorante a ~ stick deodorant

'**stigma** m stigma. ~**te** fpl stigmata

sti'lare vt draw up

'**stil|e** m style. sti'lista mf stylist. ~**iz'zato** adj stylized

stil'lare vi ooze

stilo'grafic|a f fountain pen. ~**o** adj penna ~**a** fountain pen

'**stima** f esteem; (*valutazione*) estimate. **sti'mare** vt esteem; (*valutare*) estimate; (*ritenere*) consider

stimo'la|nte adj stimulating ● m stimulant. ~**re** vt stimulate; (*incitare*) incite

'**stimolo** m stimulus; (*fitta*) pang

'**stinco** m shin

'**stinger|e** vt/i fade. ~**si** vr fade. '**stinto** pp di stingere

sti'par|e vt cram. ~**si** vr crowd together

stipendi'ato adj salaried ● m salaried worker. **sti'pendio** m salary

'**stipite** m doorpost

stipu'la|re vt stipulate. ~**zi'one** f stipulation; (*accordo*) agreement

stira'mento m sprain

sti'ra|re vt iron; (*distendere*) stretch. ~**rsi** vr (*distendersi*) stretch; pull (muscolo). ~**tura** f ironing. '**stiro** m ferro da stiro iron

'**stirpe** f stock

stiti'chezza f constipation. '**stitico** adj constipated

'**stiva** f (*Naut*) hold

sti'vale m boot. stivali pl di gomma Wellington boots

'**stizza** f anger

stiz'zir|e vt irritate. ~**rsi** vr become irritated. ~**to** adj irritated. **stiz'zoso** adj peevish

stocca'fisso m stockfish

stoc'cata f stab; (*battuta pungente*) gibe

'stoffa *f* material; *fig* stuff

'stola *f* stole

'stolto *adj* foolish

stoma'chevole *adj* revolting

'stomaco *m* stomach; mal di ~ stomach-ache

sto'na|re *vt/i* sing/play out of tune ●*vi* (*non intonarsi*) clash. ~to *adj* out of tune; (*discordante*) clashing; (*confuso*) bewildered. ~tura *f* false note; (*discordanza*) clash

'stoppia *f* stubble

stop'pino *m* wick

stop'poso *adj* tough

'storcer|e *vt*, ~si *vr* twist

stor'di|re *vt* stun; (*intontire*) daze. ~rsi *vr* dull one's senses. ~to *adj* stunned; (*intontito*) dazed; (*sventato*) heedless

'storia *f* history; (*racconto, bugia*) story; (*pretesto*) excuse; fare [delle] storie make a fuss

'storico, -a *adj* historical; (*di importanza storica*) historic ●*mf* historian

stori'one *m* sturgeon

'stormo *m* flock

'storno *m* starling

storpi'a|re *vt* cripple; mangle (*parole*). ~tura *f* deformation. 'storpio, -a *adj* crippled ●*mf* cripple

'stort|a *f* (*distorsione*) sprain; prendere una ~a alla caviglia sprain one's ankle. ~o *pp di* storcere ●*adj* crooked; (*ritorto*) twisted; (*gambe*) bandy; *fig* wrong

sto'viglie *fpl* crockery *sg*

'strabico *adj* cross-eyed

strabili'ante *adj* astonishing

stra'bismo *m* squint

straboc'care *vi* overflow

stra'carico *adj* overloaded

stracci'a|re *vt* tear; (⚫: *vincere*) thrash. ~ato *adj* torn; (*persona*) in rags; (*prezzi*) slashed; a un prezzo ~ato dirt cheap. 'straccio *adj* torn ●*m* rag; (*strofinaccio*) cloth. ~one

m tramp

stra'cotto *adj* overdone; (⚫: *innamorato*) head over heels ●*m* stew

'strada *f* road; (*di città*) street; essere fuori ~ be on the wrong track; fare ~ lead the way; farsi ~ make one's way. ~ maestra main road. ~ a senso unico one-way street. ~ senza uscita blind alley. stra'dale *adj* road *attrib*

strafalci'one *m* blunder

stra'fare *vi* overdo things

stra'foro: di ~ *adv* on the sly

strafot'ten|te *adj* arrogant. ~za *f* arrogance

'strage *f* slaughter

'stralcio *m* (*parte*) extract

stralu'na|re *vt* ~re gli occhi open one's eyes wide. ~to *adj* (*occhi*) staring; (*persona*) distraught

stramaz'zare *vi* fall heavily

stram'be'ria *f* oddity. 'strambo *adj* strange

stampa'lato *adj* odd

stra'nezza *f* strangeness

strango'lare *vt* strangle

strani'ero, -a *adj* foreign ●*mf* foreigner

'strano *adj* strange

straordi|naria'mente *adv* extraordinarily. ~nario *adj* extraordinary; (*notevole*) remarkable; (*edizione*) special; lavoro ~nario overtime; treno ~nario special train

strapaz'zar|e *vt* ill-treat; scramble (*uova*). ~si *vr* tire oneself out. stra'pazzo *m* strain; da strapazzo *fig* worthless

strapi'eno *adj* overflowing

strapi'ombo *m* projection; a ~ sheer

strap'par|e *vt* tear; (*per distruggere*) tear up; pull out (*dente, capelli*); (*sradicare*) pull up; (*estorcere*) wring. ~si *vr* get torn; (*allontanarsi*) tear oneself away. 'strappo *m* tear; (*strattone*) jerk; (🔲: *passaggio*) lift; fare uno strappo alla regola make an exception to the rule. ~ **muscolare** muscle strain

strapun'tino m folding seat

strari'pare vi flood

strasci'c|are vt trail; shuffle (piedi); drawl (parole). **'strascico** m train; *fig* after-effect

strass m inv rhinestone

strata'gemma m stratagem

strate'gia f strategy. **stra'tegico** adj strategic

'strato m layer; (di vernice ecc) coat; (roccioso, sociale) stratum. ~'sfera f stratosphere. ~'sferico adj stratospheric

stravac'carsi vr 🔲 slouch

strava'gan|te adj extravagant; (eccentrico) eccentric. ~za f extravagance; (eccentricità) eccentricity

stra'vecchio adj ancient

strave'dere vt ~ per worship

stravizi'are vi indulge oneself. **stra'vizio** m excess

stra'volg|ere vt twist; (turbare) upset. ~i'mento m twisting. **stra'volto** adj distraught; (🔲: stanco) done in

strazi'a|nte adj heartrending; (dolore) agonizing. ~re vt grate on (orecchie); break (cuore). **'strazio** m agony; che strazio! it's awful!

'strega f witch. **stre'gare** vt bewitch. **stre'gone** m wizard

'stregua f alla ~ di like

stre'ma|re vt exhaust. ~to adj exhausted

'strenuo adj strenuous

strepi'ta|re vi make a din. **'strepito** m noise. ~'toso adj noisy; *fig* resounding

stres'sa|nte adj (lavoro, situazione) stressful. ~to adj stressed [out]

stretta f grasp; (dolore) pang; essere alle strette be in dire straits.

~ **di mano** handshake

stret'tezza f narrowness; **stret'tezze** pl (difficoltà finanziarie) financial difficulties

'stret|to pp di stringere ● adj narrow; (serrato) striped; (vicino) close; (dialetto) broad; (rigoroso) strict; lo ~to necessario the bare minimum ● m (Geog) strait. ~'toia f bottleneck; (🔲: difficoltà) tight spot

stri'a|to adj striped. ~'tura f streak

stri'dente adj strident

'stridere vi squeak; *fig* clash. **stri'dore** m screech

'stridulo adj shrill

strigli'a|re vt groom. ~ta f grooming; *fig* dressing down

stril'l|are vt i scream. **'strillo** m scream

strimin'zito adj skimpy; (magro) skinny

strimpel'lare vt strum

'strin|ga f lace; (Comput) string. ~'gato adj *fig* terse

'stringer|e vt press; (serrare) squeeze; (tenere stretto) hold tight; take in (abito); (comprimere) be tight; (restringere) tighten; ~e la mano a shake hands with ● vi (premere) press. ~si vr (accostarsi) draw close (a to); (avvicinarsi) squeeze up

'striscia f strip; (riga) stripe. **strisce** pl [pedonali] zebra crossing sg

strisci'ar|e vi crawl; (sfiorare) graze ● vt drag (piedi); ~si vr ~si a rub against. **'striscio** m graze; (Med) smear; colpire di striscio graze

strisci'one m banner

strito'lare vt grind

striz'zare vt squeeze; (torcere) wring [out]; ~ l'occhio wink

'strofa f strophe

strofi'naccio m cloth; (per spolverare) duster

strofi'nare vt rub

strombaz'zare vt boast about ● vi hoot

strombaz'zata f hoot

stron'care vt cut off; (reprimere) crush; (criticare) tear to shreds

stropicci'are vt rub; crumple (vestito)

stroz'zare vt strangle. **~'tura** f strangling; (di strada) narrowing

strozzi'naggio m loan-sharking

stroz'zino m pej usurer; (truffatore) shark

strug'gente adj all-consuming

strumen'tale adj instrumental

strumentaliz'zare vt make use of

stru'mento m instrument; (arnese) tool. **~** a corda string instrument. **~** musicale musical instrument

strusci'are vt rub

'strutto m lard

strut'tura f structure. **struttu'rale** adj structural

struttu'rare vt structure

strutturazi'one f structuring

'struzzo m ostrich

stuc'ca|re vt stucco

stuc'chevole adj nauseating

'stucco m stucco

stu'den|te, -'tessa mf student; (di scuola) schoolboy; schoolgirl. **~'tesco** adj student; (di scolaro) school attrib

studi'ar|e vt study. **~si** vr **~si di** try to

'studi|o m studying; (stanza, ricerca) study; (di artista, TV ecc) studio; (di professionista) office. **~'oso, -a** adj studious ● mf scholar

'stufa f stove. **~** elettrica electric fire

stu'fa|re vt (Culin) stew; (dare fastidio) bore. **~rsi** vr get bored. **~to** m stew

'stufo adj bored; **essere ~ di** be fed up with

stu'oia f mat

stupefa'cente adj amazing ● m drug

stu'pendo adj stupendous

stupi'd|aggine f (azione) stupid thing; (cosa da poco) nothing. **~ata** f stupid thing. **~ità** f stupidity. **'stupido** adj stupid

stu'pir|e vt astonish ● vi, **~si** vr be astonished. **stu'pore** m amazement

stu'pra|re vt rape. **~'tore** m rapist. **'stupro** m rape

sturalavan'dini m inv plunger

stu'rare vt uncork; unblock (lavandino)

stuzzi'care vt prod [at]; pick (denti); poke (fuoco); (molestare) tease; whet (appetito)

stuzzi'chino m (Culin) appetizer

su prep on; (senza contatto) over; (riguardo a) about; (circa, intorno a) about; around; le chiavi sono sul tavolo the keys are on the table; il quadro è appeso sul camino the picture is hanging over the fireplace; un libro sull'antico Egitto a book on o about Ancient Egypt; costa sul 25 euro it costs about 25 euros; decidere sul momento decide at the time; su commissione on commission; su due piedi on the spot; uno su dieci one out of ten ● adv (sopra) up; (al piano di sopra) upstairs; (addosso) on; ho su il cappotto I've got my coat on; in su (guardare) up; dalla vita in su from the waist up; su! come on!

su'bacqueo adj underwater

subaffit'tare vt sublet. **subaf'fitto** m sublet

subal'terno adj & m subordinate

sub'buglio m turmoil

sub'conscio adj & m subconscious

'subdolo adj devious

suben'trare vi (circostanze:) come up; **~** a take the place of

su'bire vt undergo; (patire) suffer

subis'sare vt fig ~ di overwhelm with

'subito adv at once; ~ dopo straight after

su'blime adj sublime

subodo'rare vt suspect

subordi'nato, -a adj & mf subordinate

subur'bano adj suburban

suc'ceder|e vi (accadere) happen; ~e a succeed; (venire dopo) follow; ~e al trono succeed to the throne. ~si vr happen one after the other

successi'one f succession; in ~ in succession

succes|siva'mente adv subsequently. ~'sivo adj successive

suc'ces|so pp di succedere ● m success; (esito) outcome; (disco ecc) hit

succes'sore m successor

succhi'are vt suck [up]

suc'cinto adj (conciso) concise; (abito) scanty

'succo m juice; fig essence; ~ di frutta fruit juice. **suc'coso** adj juicy

succu'lento adj succulent

succur'sale f branch [office]

sud m south; del ~ southern

su'da|re vi (faticare) sweat blood; ~re freddo be in a cold sweat. ~ta f sweat. ~'ticcio adj sweaty. ~to adj sweaty

sud'detto adj above-mentioned

'suddito, -a mf subject

suddi'vi|dere vt subdivide. ~si'one f subdivision

su'd-est m southeast

'sudici|o adj filthy. ~'ume m filth

su'dore m sweat; fig sweat

su'd-ovest m southwest

suffici'en|te adj sufficient; (presuntuoso) conceited ● m bare essentials pl; (Sch) pass mark. ~za f sufficiency; (presunzione) conceit; (Sch) pass; a ~za enough

suf'fisso m suffix

suf'fragio m vote. ~ universale universal suffrage

suggeri'mento m suggestion

sugge'ri|re vt suggest; (Theat) prompt. ~'tore, ~'trice mf (Theat) prompter

suggestiona'bile adj suggestible

suggestio'na|re vt influence suggestio'ne f influence

sugge'stivo adj suggestive; (musica ecc) evocative

'sughero m cork

'sugli = su + gli

'sugo m (di frutta) juice; (di carne) gravy; (salsa) sauce; (sostanza) substance

'sui = su + i

sui'cid|a adj suicidal ● mf suicide. **suici'darsi** vr commit suicide. ~io m suicide

su'ino adj carne suina pork ● m swine

sul = su + il. **'sullo** = su + lo. **'sulla** = su + la. **'sulle** = su + le

sul'ta|na f sultana. ~'nina adj uva ~nina sultana. ~no m sultan

'sunto m summary

'suo, -a poss adj il ~, i suoi his; (di cosa, animale) its; (forma di cortesia) your; la sua, le sue her; (di cosa, animale) its; (forma di cortesia) your; questa macchina è sua this car is his/ hers; ~ padre his/her/your father; un ~ amico a friend of his/hers/ yours ● poss pron il ~, i suoi his; (di cosa, animale) its; (forma di cortesia) yours; la sua, le sue hers; (di cosa animale) its; (forma di cortesia) yours; i suoi his/her folk

su'ocera f mother-in-law

su'ocero m father-in-law

su'ola f sole

su'olo m ground; (terreno) soil

suo'na|re vt/i (Mus) play; ring (campanello); sound (allarme, clacson);

(orologio:) strike. ~'tore, ~'trice mf player. suone'ria f alarm; (di cellulare) ringtone. su'ono m sound

su'ora f nun; Suor Maria Sister Maria

superal'colico m spirit ● adj bevande pl superalcoliche spirits

supera'mento m (di timidezza) overcoming; (di esame) success (di in)

supe'rare vt surpass; (eccedere) exceed; (vincere) overcome; overtake (veicolo); pass (esame)

su'perbo adj haughty; (magnifico) superb

superdo'tato adj highly gifted

superfici'al|e adj superficial ● mf superficial person. ~ità f superficiality. super'ficie f surface; (area) area

su'perfluo adj superfluous

superi'or|e adj superior; (di grado) senior; (più elevato) higher; (sovrastante) upper; (al di sopra) above ● mf superior. ~ità f superiority

superla'tivo adj & m superlative

supermer'cato m supermarket

super'sonico adj supersonic

su'perstite adj surviving ● mf survivor

superstizi'o|ne f superstition. ~so adj superstitious

super'strada f toll-free motorway

supervi|si'one f supervision. ~'sore m supervisor

su'pino adj supine

suppel'lettili fpl furnishings

suppergiù adv about

supplemen'tare adj supplementary

supple'mento m supplement; ~ rapido express train supplement

sup'plen|te adj temporary ● mf (Sch) supply teacher. ~za f temporary post

'suppli|ca f plea; (domanda) petition. ~'care vt beg

sup'plire vt replace ● vi ~ a (com-

pensare) make up for

sup'plizio m torture

sup'porre vt suppose

sup'porto m support

supposizi'one f supposition

sup'posta f suppository

sup'posto pp di supporre

supre'ma|zia f supremacy. su'premo adj supreme

sur'fare vi ~ in Internet surf the Net

surge'la|re vt deep-freeze. ~ti mpl frozen food sg. ~to adj frozen

surrea'lis|mo m surrealism. ~ta mf surrealist

surriscal'dare vt overheat

surro'gato m substitute

suscet'tibil|e adj touchy. ~ità f touchiness

susci'tare vt stir up; arouse (ammirazione ecc)

su'sin|a f plum. ~o m plumtree

su'spense f suspense

sussegu'|ente adj subsequent. ~'irsi vr follow one after the other

sussidi'ar|e vt subsidize. ~io adj subsidiary. sus'sidio m subsidy; (aiuto) aid. sussidio di disoccupazione unemployment benefit

sus'siego m haughtiness

sussi'stenza f subsistence. sus'sistere vi subsist; (essere valido) hold good

sussul'tare vi start. sus'sulto m start

sussur'rare vt whisper. sus'surro m whisper

sva'gar|e vt amuse. ~si vr amuse oneself. ~'svago m relaxation; (divertimento) amusement

svali'gia|re vt rob; burgle (casa)

svalu'ta|re vt devalue; fig underestimate. ~rsi vr lose value. ~zi'one f devaluation

svam'pito adj absent-minded

sva'nire vi vanish

svantaggi'ato adj at a disadvantage; (bambino, paese) disadvantaged. **svan'taggio** m disadvantage; **essere in svantaggio** Sport be losing; **~oso** adj disadvantageous

svapo'rare vi evaporate

svari'ato adj varied

sva'sato adj flared

'svastica f swastika

sve'dese adj & m (lingua) Swedish •mf Swede

'sveglia f (orologio) alarm [clock]; **~!** get up!; **mettere la ~** set the alarm [clock]

svegli'are vt wake up; fig awaken. **~si** vr wake up. **'sveglio** adj awake; (di mente) quick-witted

sve'lare vt reveal

svel'tezza f speed; fig quick-wittedness

svel'tire vt quicken. **~si** vr (persona:) liven up. **'svelto** adj quick; (slanciato) svelte; **alla svelta** quickly

'svendere vt undersell. **~ita** f [clearance] sale

sve'nire vi faint

sven'tare vt foil. **~to** adj thoughtless •mf thoughtless person

'sventola f slap

svento'lare vt/i wave

sven'trare vt disembowel; fig demolish (edificio)

sven'tura f misfortune. **sventu'rato** adj unfortunate

sve'nuto pp di svenire

svergo'gnato adj shameless

sver'nare vi winter

sve'stire vt undress

'Svezia f Sweden

svez'zare vt wean

svi'are vt divert; (corrompere) lead astray. **~si** vr fig go astray

svico'lare vi turn down a side
street; (dalla questione ecc) evade the issue; (da una persona) dodge out of the way

svi'gnarsela vr slip away

svi'lire vt debase

svilup'par|e vt, **~si** vr develop. **svi'luppo** m development; **paese in via di sviluppo** developing country

svinco'lar|e vt release; clear (merce). **~si** vr free oneself. **'svincolo** m clearance; (di autostrada) exit

svisce'rar|e vt gut; fig dissect. **~to** adj passionate; (ossequioso) obsequious

'svista f oversight

svi'tare vt unscrew. **~to** adj (🔲: matto) cracked, nutty

'Svizzer|a f Switzerland. **s~o, -a** adj & mf Swiss

Svizzera Italian is one of the four national languages of Switzerland, but is spoken widely only in the canton of Ticino in the south of the country, and to a lesser extent in Grisons. Around half a million people in Switzerland have Italian as their first language. Their language rights are protected by the Swiss constitution.

svogli'a|tezza f half-hearted-ness. **~'ato** adj lazy

svolaz'za|nte adj (capelli) windswept. **~re** vi flutter

'svolger|e vt unwind; unwrap (pacco); (risolvere) solve; (portare a termine) carry out; (sviluppare) develop. **~si** vr (accadere) take place. **svolgi'mento** m course; (sviluppo) development

'svolta f turning; fig turning-point. **svol'tare** vi turn

'svolto pp di svolgere

svuo'tare vt empty [out]

Tt

---

tabac'c|aio, -a *mf* tobacconist. ~he'ria *f* tobacconist's. ta'bacco *m* tobacco

> **Tabaccheria** By law, cigarettes and other tobacco products can be sold only in *tabaccherie*, which must be licensed by the State. They can be recognized by a sign with a large T. As well as tobacco, *tabaccherie* have a monopoly on postage stamps, lottery tickets, and other items controlled by the State.

ta'bel|la *f* table; (*lista*) list. ~la dei prezzi price list. ~lina *f* (*Math*) multiplication table. ~lone *m* wall chart. ~lone del canestro backboard

taber'nacolo *m* tabernacle

tabù *adj & m inv* taboo

tabu'lato *m* [data] printout

'tacca *f* notch; di mezza ~ (*attore, giornalista*) second-rate

tac'cagno *adj* 🄵 stingy

tac'cheggio *m* shoplifting

tac'chetto *m Sport* stud

tac'chino *m* turkey

tacci'are *vt* ~ qcno di qcsa accuse sb of sth

'tacco *m* heel; alzare i tacchi take to one's heels; scarpe senza ~ flat shoes. tacchi *pl* a spillo stiletto heels

taccu'ino *m* notebook

ta'cere *vi* be silent ●*vt* say nothing about; mettere a ~ qcsa (*scandalo*) hush sth up

ta'chimetro *m* speedometer

'tacito *adj* silent; (*inespresso*) tacit.

taci'turno *adj* taciturn

ta'fano *m* horsefly

taffe'ruglio *m* scuffle

'taglia *f* (*riscatto*) ransom; (*ricompensa*) reward; (*statura*) height; (*misura*) size. ~ unica one size

taglia'carte *m inv* paperknife

taglia'erba *m inv* lawn-mower

tagliafu'oco *adj inv* porta ~ fire door; striscia ~ fire break

tagli'ando *m* coupon; fare il ~ ≈ put one's car in for its MOT

tagli'ar|e *vt* cut; (*attraversare*) cut across; (*interrompere*) cut off; (*togliere*) cut out; carve (*carne*); mow (*erba*); farsi ~e i capelli have a haircut ●*vi* cut. ~**si** *vr* cut oneself; ~si i capelli have a haircut

taglia'telle *fpl* tagliatelle *sg*, thin, flat strips of egg pasta

taglieggi'are *vt* extort money from

tagli'e|nte *adj* sharp ●*m* cutting edge. ~**re** *m* chopping board

'taglio *m* cut; (*il tagliare*) cutting; (*di stoffa*) length; (*parte tagliente*) edge. ~ cesareo Caesarean section

tagli'ola *f* trap

tagliuz'zare *vt* cut

tail'leur *m inv* (*lady's*) suit

'talco *m* talcum powder

'tale *adj* such a; (*con nomi plurali*) such; c'è un ~ disordine there is such a mess; non accetto tali scuse I won't accept such excuses; il rumore era ~ che non si sentiva nulla there was so much noise you couldn't hear yourself think; ~ il giorno su such and such a day; quel tal signore that gentleman; ~ quale just like ●*pron* un ~ someone; quel ~ that man; il tal dei tali such and such a person

ta'lento *m* talent

tali'smano *m* talisman

tallo'nare *vt* be hot on the heels of

tallon'cino m coupon

tal'lone m heel

tal'mente adv so

ta'lora adv = TALVOLTA

'talpa f mole

tal'volta adv sometimes

tamburel'lare vi (con le dita) drum; (pioggia:) beat, drum. **tambu'rello** m tambourine. **tambu'rino** m drummer. **tam'buro** m drum

tampona'mento m (Auto) collision; (di ferita) dressing; (di falla) plugging. ~ a catena pile-up. **tampo'nare** vt (urtare) crash into; (otturare) plug. **tam'pone** m swab; (per timbri) pad; (per mestruazioni) tampon; (Comput) (per treni) buffer

'tana f den

'tanfo m stench

'tanga m inv tanga

tan'gen|te adj tangent ● f tangent; (somma) bribe. ~'topoli f widespread corruption in Italy in the early 90s. ~zi'ale f orbital road

tan'gibile adj tangible

'tango m tango

tan'tino: un ~ adv a little [bit]

'tanto adj [so] much; (con nomi plurali) [so] many, [such] a lot of; ~ tempo [such] a long time; non ho tanta pazienza he doesn't have much patience; ~ tempo quanto ti serve as much time as you need; non è ~ intelligente quanto suo padre he's not as intelligent as his father; tanti amici quanti parenti as many friends as relatives ● pron much; (plurale) many; (tanto tempo) a long time; è un uomo come tanti he's just an ordinary man; tanti (molte persone) many people; non ci vuole così ~ it doesn't take that long; ~ quanto as much as; tanti quanti as many as ● conj (comunque) anyway, in any case ● adv (così) so; (con verbi) so much; ~ debole so weak; è ~ ingenuo da crederle he's naive enough to be-

lieve her; di ~ in ~ every now and then; ~ l'uno come l'altro both; ~ quanto as much as; tre volte ~ three times as much; una volta ~ once in a while; tant'è non much so; ~ per cambiare for a change

'tappa f stop; (parte di viaggio) stage

tappa'buchi m inv stopgap

tap'par|e vt plug; cork (bottiglia); ~e la bocca a qcno [f] shut sb up. ~si vr ~si gli occhi cover one's eyes; ~si il naso hold one's nose

tappa'rella f [f] roller blind

tappe'tino m mat; (Comput) mouse mat

tap'peto m carpet; (piccolo) rug; mandare qcno al ~ knock sb down

tappez'z|are vt paper (pareti); (rivestire) cover. ~e'ria f tapestry; (di carta) wallpaper; (arte) upholstery. ~i'ere m upholsterer; (imbianchino) decorator

'tappo m plug; (di sughero) cork; (di metallo, per penna) top; ([f]: persona piccola) dwarf. ~ di sughero cork

'tara f (difetto) flaw; (ereditaria) hereditary defect; (peso) tare

ta'rantola f tarantula

ta'ra|re vt calibrate (strumento). ~to adj (Comm) discounted; (Techn) calibrated; (Med) with a hereditary defect; [f] crazy

tarchi'ato adj stocky

tar'dare vi be late ● vt delay

'tard|i adv late; al più ~i at the latest; più ~i later [on]; sul ~i late in the day; far ~i (essere in ritardo) be late; (con gli amici) stay up late; a più ~i see you later. **tar'divo** adj late; (bambino) retarded. ~o adj slow; (tempo) late

'targ|a f plate; (Auto) numberplate. ~a di circolazione numberplate. **tar'gato** adj un'auto targata... a car with the registration number.... ~'hetta f (su porta) nameplate; (sulla *valigia)* name tag

ta'rif|fa *f* tariff. **~'fario** *m* price list

'tarlo *m* woodworm

'tarma *f* moth

ta'rocco *m* tarot; **ta'rocchi** *pl* tarot

tartagli'are *vi* stutter

'tartaro *adj & m* tartar

tarta'ruga *f* tortoise; *(di mare)* turtle; *(per pettine ecc)* tortoiseshell

tartas'sare *vt* harass

tar'tina *f* canapé

tar'tufo *m* truffle

'tasca *f* pocket; *(in borsa)* compartment; **da ~** pocket *attrib*. **~ da pasticciere** icing bag

ta'scabile *adj* pocket *attrib* ●*m* paperback

tasca'pane *m inv* haversack

ta'schino *m* breast pocket

'tassa *f* tax; *(d'iscrizione ecc)* fee; *(doganale)* duty. **~ di circolazione** road tax. **~ d'iscrizione** registration fee

tas'sametro *m* taximeter

tas'sare *vt* tax

tassa'tiva'mente *adv* without question

tassazi'one *f* taxation

tas'sello *m* wedge; *(di stoffa)* gusset

'tassi *m inv* taxi. **tas'sista** *mf* taxi driver

'tasso[1] *m* yew; *(animale)* badger

'tasso[2] *m* rate. **~ di cambio** exchange rate. **~ di interesse** interest rate

ta'stare *vt* feel; *(sondare)* sound; **~ il terreno** *fig* test the water

tasti'e|ra *f* keyboard. **~'rista** *mf* keyboarder

'tasto *m* key; *(tatto)* touch. **~ delicato** *fig* touchy subject. **~ funzione** *(Comput)* function key. **~ tabulatore** tab key

'tattica *f* tactics *pl*

'tattico *adj* tactical

'tatto *m* (*senso*) touch; *(accortezza)*

tact; **aver ~** be tactful

tatu'a|ggio *m* tattoo. **~re** *vt* tattoo

'tavola *f* table; *(illustrazione)* plate; *(asse)* plank. **~ calda** snackbar

tavo'lato *m* boarding; *(pavimento)* wood floor

tavo'letta *f* bar; *(medicinale)* tablet; **andare a ~** *(Auto)* drive flat out

tavo'lino *m* small table

'tavolo *m* table. **~ operatorio** *(Med)* operating table

tavo'lozza *f* palette

'tazza *f* cup; *(del water)* bowl. **~ da caffè/tè** coffee-cup/teacup

taz'zina *f* **~ da caffè** espresso coffee cup

T.C.I. *abbr* (Touring Club Italiano) Italian Touring Club

te *pers pron* you; **te l'ho dato** I gave it to you

tè *m inv* tea

TEAM *f abbr* (Tessera Europea di Assicurazione Malattia) EHIC

tea'trale *adj* theatrical

te'atro *m* theatre. **~ all'aperto** open-air theatre. **~ di posa** *Cinema* set. **~ tenda** marquee *for theatre performances*

'tecnico, -a *adj* technical ●*mf* technician **~** technique

tecno|lo'gia *f* technology. **~'logico** *adj* technological

te'desco, -a *adj & mf* German

tedi'oso *adj* tedious

te'game *m* saucepan

'teglia *f* baking tin

'tegola *f* tile; *fig* blow

tei'era *f* teapot

tek *m* teak

'tela *f* cloth; *(per quadri, vele)* canvas; *(Theat)* curtain. **~ cerata** oilcloth. **~ di lino** linen

te'laio *m* (*di bicicletta, finestra*) frame; *(Auto)* chassis; *(per tessere)* loom

tele'camera f television camera

teleco|man'dato adj remote-controlled, remote control attrib. **∼'mando** m remote control

Telecom Italia f Italian State telephone company

telecomunicazi'oni fpl telecommunications

tele'cro|naca f [television] commentary. **∼naca diretta** live [television] coverage. **∼nista** mf television commentator

tele'ferica f cableway

telefo'na|re vt/i [tele]phone, ring. **∼ta** f call. **∼ta interurbana** long-distance call

telefonica'mente adv by [tele-]phone

tele'fo|nico adj [tele]phone attrib. **∼'nino** m mobile [phone]. **∼nista** mf operator

te'lefono m [tele]phone. **∼ senza filo** cordless [phone]. **∼ interno** internal telephone. **∼ satellitare** satphone. **∼ a schede** cardphone

telegior'nale m television news sg

tele'grafico adj telegraphic; (risposta) monosyllabic; **sii telegrafico** keep it brief

tele'gramma m telegram

telela'voro m teleworking

tele'matica f data communications, telematics

teleno'vela f soap opera

teleobiet'tivo m telephoto lens

telepa'tia f telepathy

telero'manzo m television serial

tele'scopio m telescope

teleselezi'one f subscriber trunk dialling, STD; **chiamare in ∼** dial direct

telespetta'tore, -'trice mf viewer

tele'text® m Teletext®

televisi'one f television; **guardare la ∼** watch television

televi'sivo adj television attrib; operatore **∼** television cameraman; apparecchio **∼** television set

televi'sore m television [set]

'tema m theme; (Sch) essay. **te'matica** f main theme

teme'rario adj reckless

te'mere vt be afraid of, fear ● vi be afraid, fear

temperama'tite m inv pencil-sharpener

tempera'mento m temperament

tempe'ra|re vt temper; sharpen (matita). **∼to** adj temperate. **∼'tura** f temperature. **∼tura ambiente** room temperature

tempe'rino m penknife

tem'pe|sta f storm. **∼sta di neve** snowstorm. **∼sta di sabbia** sandstorm

tempe|stiva'mente adv quickly. **∼'stivo** adj timely. **∼'stoso** adj stormy

'tempia f (Anat) temple

'tempio m (Relig) temple

tem'pismo m timing

'tempo m time; (atmosferico) weather; (Mus) tempo; (Gram) tense; (di film) part; (di partita) half; **a suo ∼** in due course; **∼ fa** some time ago; **un ∼** once; **ha fatto il suo ∼** it's superannuated. **∼ supplementare** Sport extra time, overtime Am. **∼'rale** adj temporal ● m [thunder] storm. **∼ranea'mente** adv temporarily. **∼'raneo** adj temporary. **∼reggi'are** vi play for time

tem'prare vt temper

te'nac|e adj tenacious. **∼ia** f tenacity

te'naglia f pincers pl

'tenda f curtain; (per campeggio) tent; (tendone) awning. **∼ a ossigeno** oxygen tent

ten'denz|a f tendency. **∼ial'mente** adv by nature

'**tendere** vt (allargare) stretch [out]; (tirare) tighten; (porgere) hold out; fig lay (trappola) ● vi ~ a aim at; (essere portato a) tend to

'**tendine** m tendon

ten'do|ne m awning; (di circo) tent. ~poli f inv tent city

tene'broso adj gloomy

te'nente m lieutenant

tenera'mente adv tenderly

te'ner|e vt hold; (mantenere) keep; (gestire) run; (prendere) take; (seguire) follow; (considerare) consider ● vi hold; ~ci a, ~e a be keen on; ~e per support (squadra). ~si vr hold on (a to); (in una condizione) keep oneself; (seguire) stick to; ~si indietro stand back

tene'rezza f tenderness. '**tenero** adj tender

'**tenia** f tapeworm

'**tennis** m tennis. ~ da tavolo table tennis. **ten'nista** mf tennis player

te'nore m standard; (Mus) tenor; ~ di legge by law. ~ di vita standard of living

tensi'one f tension; (Electr) voltage; alta ~ high voltage

ten'tacolo m tentacle

ten'ta|re vt attempt; (sperimentare) try; (indurre in tentazione) tempt. ~'tivo m attempt. ~zi'one f temptation

tenten'nare vi waver

'**tenue** adj fine; (debole) weak; (esiguo) small; (leggero) slight

te'nuta f (capacità) capacity; (Sport: resistenza) stamina; (possedimento) estate; (divisa) uniform; (abbigliamento) clothes pl; a ~ d'aria airtight. ~ di strada road holding

teolo'gia f theology. **teo'logico** adj theological. **te'ologo** m theologian

teo'rema m theorem

teo'ria f theory

teorica'mente adv theoretically.

te'orico adj theoretical

te'pore m warmth

'**teppa** f mob. **tep'pismo** m hooliganism. **tep'pista** m hooligan

tera'peutico adj therapeutic. **tera'pia** f therapy

tergicri'stallo m windscreen wiper, windshield wiper Am

tergilu'notto m rear windscreen wiper

tergiver'sare vi hesitate

'**tergo** m a ~ behind

ter'male adj thermal; **stazione** ~ spa. '**terme** fpl thermal baths

'**termico** adj thermal

termi'na|le adj & m terminal; **malato** ~le terminally ill person. ~re vt/i finish, end. '**termine** m (limite) limit; (fine) end; (condizione, espressione) term

terminolo'gia f terminology

'**termite** f termite

termoco'perta f electric blanket

ter'mometro m thermometer

'**termos** m inv thermos®

termosi'fone m radiator; (sistema) central heating

ter'mostato m thermostat

'**terra** f earth; (regione) land; (terreno) ground; (argilla) clay; (cosmetico) dark face powder (for impression of tan); a ~ (sulla costa) ashore; (installazioni) onshore; per ~ on the ground; sotto ~ underground. ~'cotta f terracotta; vasellame di ~cotta earthenware. ~'pi'eno m embankment

ter'razz|a f, ~o m balcony

terremo'tato, -a adj (zona) affected by an earthquake ● mf earthquake victim. **terre'moto** m earthquake

ter'reno adj earthly ● m ground; (suolo) soil; (proprietà terriera) land; **perdere/guadagnare** ~ lose/gain ground. ~ di gioco playing field

ter'restre adj terrestrial; esercito ~ land forces pl

ter'ribil|e adj terrible. ~'mente adv terribly

ter'riccio m potting compost

terrifi'cante adj terrifying

territori'ale adj territorial. terri'torio m territory

ter'rore m terror

terro'ris|mo m terrorism. ~ta mf terrorist

terroriz'zare vt terrorize

'terso adj clear

ter'zetto m trio

terzi'ario adj tertiary

'terzo adj third; di terz'ordine (locale, servizio) third-rate; la terza età the third age ● m third; terzi pl (Jur) third party sg. ter'zultimo, -a agg & mf third from last

'tesa f brim

'teschio m skull

'tesi f inv thesis

'teso pp di tendere ● adj taut; fig tense

tesor|e'ria f treasury. ~i'ere m treasurer

te'soro m treasure; (tesoreria) treasury

'tessera f card; (abbonamento all'autobus) season ticket

'tessere vt weave; hatch (complotto)

tesse'rino m travel card

'tessile adj textile. tessili mpl textiles; (operai) textile workers

tessi'l|tore, -'trice mf weaver

tes'suto m fabric; (Anat) tissue

'testa f head; (cervello) brain; essere in ~ a be ahead of; in ~ Sport in the lead; ~ o croce? heads or tails?

'testa-'coda m inv fare un ~ spin right round

testa'mento m will; T~ (Relig) Testament

testar'daggine f stubbornness. te'stardo adj stubborn

te'stata f head; (intestazione) heading; (colpo) butt

'teste mf witness

te'sticolo m testicle

testi'mon|e mf witness. ~e oculare eye witness

testi'monial mf inv celebrity promoting brand of cosmetics

testimoni'anza f testimony. ~'are vt testify to ● vi give evidence

'testo m text; far ~ be an authority

te'stone, -a mf blockhead

testu'ale adj textual

'tetano m tetanus

'tetro adj gloomy

tetta'rella f teat

'tetto m roof. ~ apribile sunshine roof. tet'toia f roofing. tet'tuccio m tettuccio apribile sun-roof

'Tevere m Tiber

ti pers pron you; (riflessivo) yourself; ti ha dato un libro he gave you a book; lavati le mani wash your hands; eccoti here you are!; sbrigati! hurry up!

ti'ara f tiara

ticchet't|are vi tick. ~io m ticking

'ticchio m tic; (ghiribizzo) whim

'ticket m inv (per farmaco, esame) amount paid by National Health patients

tiepida'mente adv half-heartedly. ti'epido adj lukewarm

ti'fare vi ~ per shout for. 'tifo m (Med) typhus; fare il tifo per fig be a fan of

tifoi'dea f typhoid

ti'fone m typhoon

ti'foso, -a mf fan

'tiglio m lime

ti'grato adj gatto ~ tabby [cat]

'tigre f tiger

'tilde mf tilde

tim'ballo m (Culin) pie

tim'brare vt stamp; ~ il cartellino clock in/out

'timbro m stamp; (di voce) tone

timida'mente adv timidly, shyly. timi'dezza f timidity, shyness. 'timido adj timid, shy

'timo m thyme

ti'mon|e m rudder. ~i'ere m helmsman

ti'more m fear; (soggezione) awe

'timpano m eardrum; (Mus) kettledrum

ti'nello m dining-room

'tinger|e vt dye; (macchiare) stain. ~si vi (viso, cielo): be tinged (di with); ~si i capelli have one's hair dyed; (da solo) dye one's hair

'tino m, **ti'nozza** f tub

'tint|a f dye; (colore) colour; in ~a unita plain. ~a'rella f 🔲 suntan

tintin'nare vi tinkle

'tinto pp di tingere. ~'ria f (negozio) cleaner's. tin'tura f dyeing; (colorante) dye.

'tipico adj typical

'tipo m type; (individuo) guy

tipogra'fia f printery; (arte) typography. tipo'grafico adj typographic[al]. ti'pografo m printer

tip tap m tap dancing

ti'raggio m draught

tiramisù m inv dessert made of coffee-soaked sponge, eggs, Marsala, cream and cocoa powder

tiran'nia f tyranny. ti'ranno, -a adj tyrannical ● mf tyrant

ti'rar|e vt pull; (gettare) throw; kick (palla); (sparare) fire; (tracciare) draw; (stampare) print ● vi pull; (vento:) blow; (abito:) be tight; (sparare) fire; ~e avanti get by; ~e su (crescere) bring up; (da terra) pick up. ~si vr ~si indietro fig back out

tiras'segno m target shooting; (alla fiera) rifle range

ti'rata f tug; in una ~ in one go

tira'tore m shot. ~ scelto marksman

tira'tura f printing; (di giornali) circulation; (di libri) [print] run

'tirchio adj mean

tiri'tera f spiel

'tiro m (traino) draught; (lancio) throw; (sparo) shot; (scherzo) trick. ~ con l'arco archery. ~ alla fune tug-of-war. ~ a segno rifle-range

tiro'cinio m apprenticeship

ti'roide f thyroid

Tir'reno m il [mar] ~ the Tyrrhenian Sea

ti'sana f herb[al] tea

tito'lare adj regular ● mf principal; (proprietario) owner; (calcio) regular player

'titolo m title; (accademico) qualification; (Comm) security; a ~ di as; a ~ di favore as a favour. titoli pl di studio qualifications

titu'ba|nte adj hesitant. ~nza f hesitation. ~re vi hesitate

tivù f inv 🔲 TV, telly

'tizio m fellow

tiz'zone m brand

toc'cante adj touching

toc'ca|re vt touch; touch on (argomento); (tastare) feel; (riguardare) concern ● vi ~ a (capitare) happen to; mi tocca aspettare I'll have to wait; tocca a te it's your turn; (pagare da bere) it's your round

tocca'sana m inv cure-all

'tocco m touch; (di pennello, orologio) stroke; (di pane ecc) chunk ● adj 🔲 crazy, touched

'toga f toga; (accademica, di magistrato) gown

'toglier|e vt take off (coperta); take away (bambino da scuola, sete); (Math); take out, remove (dente); ~e qcsa di mano a qcno take sth away from sb; ~e qcno dai guai get sb out of trouble; ciò non toglie che... nevertheless... ∼si *vr* take off (abito); ∼si la vita take one's [own] life

toilette *f inv*, **to'letta** *f* toilet; (*mobile*) dressing table

tolle'ra|nte *adj* tolerant. ∼nza *f* tolerance. ∼re *vt* tolerate

'tolto *pp di* togliere

to'maia *f* upper

'tomba *f* grave, tomb

tom'bino *m* manhole cover

'tombola *f* bingo; (*caduta*) tumble

'tomo *m* tome

'tonaca *f* habit

tonalità *f inv* (*Mus*) tonality

'tondo *adj* round ● *m* circle

'tonico *adj* & *m* tonic

tonifi'care *vt* brace

tonnel'la|ggio *m* tonnage. ∼ta *f* ton

'tonno *m* tuna [fish]

'tono *m* tone

ton'sil|la *f* tonsil. ∼'lite *f* tonsillitis

'tonto *adj* ① thick

top *m inv* (*indumento*) sun-top

to'pazio *m* topaz

'topless *m inv* in ∼ topless

'topo *m* mouse. ∼ di biblioteca *fig* bookworm

to'ponimo *m* place name

'toppa *f* patch; (*serratura*) keyhole

to'race *m* chest

'torba *f* peat

'torbido *adj* cloudy; *fig* troubled

'torcer|e *vt* twist; wring [out] (*biancheria*). ∼si *vr* twist

'torchio *m* press

'torcia *f* torch

torci'collo *m* stiff neck

'tordo *m* thrush

to'rero *m* bullfighter

To'rino *f* Turin

tor'menta *f* snowstorm

tormen'tare *vt* torment.

tor'mento *m* torment

torna'conto *m* benefit

tor'nado *m* tornado

tor'nante *m* hairpin bend

tor'nare *vi* return, go/come back; (*ridiventare*) become again; (*conto:*) add up; ∼ a sorridere become happy again

tor'neo *m* tournament

'tornio *m* lathe

'torno *m* togliersi di ∼ get out of the way

'toro *m* bull; (*Astr*) T∼Taurus

tor'pedin|e *f* torpedo

tor'pore *m* torpor

'torre *f* tower; (*scacchi*) castle. ∼ di controllo control tower

torrefazi'one *f* roasting

tor'ren|te *m* torrent, mountain stream; (*fig: di lacrime*) flood. ∼zi'ale *adj* torrential

tor'retta *f* turret

'torrido *adj* torrid

torri'one *m* keep

tor'rone *m* nougat

'torso *m* torso; (*di mela, pera*) core; a ∼ nudo bare-chested

'torsolo *m* core

'torta *f* cake; (*crostata*) tart

tortel'lini *mpl* tortellini, small packets of pasta stuffed with pork, ham, Parmesan and nutmeg

torti'era *f* baking tin

tor'tino *m* pie

'torto *pp di* torcere ● *adj* twisted ● *m* wrong; (*colpa*) fault; aver ∼ be wrong; a ∼ wrongly

'tortora *f* turtle-dove

tortu'oso *adj* winding; (*ambiguo*) tortuous

tor'tu|ra *f* torture. ∼'rare *vt* torture

'torvo *adj* grim

to'sare *vt* shear

tosa'tura *f* shearing

To'scana *f* Tuscany

'tosse f cough

'tossico adj toxic ●m poison. tossi'comane mf drug addict

tos'sire vi cough

tosta'pane m inv toaster

to'stare vt toast (pane); roast (caffè)

'tosto adv (subito) soon ●adj 🄵 cool

tot adj inv una cifra ~ such and such a figure ●m un ~ so much

to'tal|e adj & m total. ~ità f entirety; la ~ità dei presenti all those present

totali'tario adj totalitarian

totaliz'zare vt total; score (punti)

total'mente adv totally

'totano m squid

toto'calcio m ≈ [football] pools pl

tournée f inv tour

to'vaglia f tablecloth. ~etta f ~etta [all'americana] place mat. ~olo m napkin

'tozzo adj squat

tra = FRA

trabal'la|nte adj staggering; (sedia) rickety. ~re vi stagger; (veicolo:) jolt

tra'biccolo m 🄵 contraption; (auto) jalopy

traboc'care vi overflow

traboc'chetto m trap

tracan'nare vt gulp down

'tracci|a f track; (orma) footstep; (striscia) trail; (residuo) trace; fig sign. ~'are vt trace; sketch out (schema); draw (linea). ~'ato m (schema) layout

tra'chea f windpipe

tra'colla f shoulder-strap; borsa a ~ shoulder-bag

tra'collo m collapse

tradi'mento m betrayal

tra'di|re vt betray; be unfaithful to (moglie, marito). ~tore, ~trice mf traitor

tradizio'nale adj traditional.

~'lista mf traditionalist. ~l'mente adv traditionally. tradizi'one f tradition

tra'dotto pp di tradurre

tra'du|rre vt translate. ~t'tore, ~t'trice mf translator. ~ttore elettronico electronic phrasebook. ~zi'one f translation

tra'ente mf (Comm) drawer

trafe'lato adj breathless

traffi'ca|nte mf dealer. ~nte di droga [drug] pusher. ~re vi (affaccendarsi) busy oneself; ~ttore in pej traffic in. 'traffico m traffic; (Comm) trade

tra'figgere vt stab; (straziare) pierce

tra'fila f fig rigmarole

trafo'rare vt bore, drill. tra'foro m boring; (galleria) tunnel

trafu'gare vt steal

tra'gedia f tragedy

traghet'tare vt ferry. tra'ghetto m ferrying; (nave) ferry

tragica'mente adv tragically. 'tragico adj tragic

tra'gitto m journey; (per mare) crossing

tragu'ardo m finishing post; (meta) goal

traiet'toria f trajectory

trai'nare vt drag; (rimorchiare) tow

tralasci'are vt interrupt; (omettere) leave out

'tralcio m (Bot) shoot

tra'liccio m trellis

tram m inv tram, streetcar Am

'trama f weft; (di film ecc) plot

traman'dare vt hand down

tra'mare vt weave; (macchinare) plot

tram'busto m turmoil

trame'stio m bustle

tramez'zino m sandwich

tra'mezzo m partition

'tramite prep through ●m link; fare da ~ act as go-between

tramon'tana f north wind

tramon'tare vi set; (declinare) decline. tra'monto m sunset; (declino) decline

tramor'tire vt stun ● vi faint

trampo'lino m springboard; (per lo sci) ski-jump

'**trampolo** m stilt

tramu'tare vt transform

'**trancia** f shears pl; (fetta) slice

tra'nello m trap

trangugi'are vt gulp down

'**tranne** prep except

tranquilla'mente adv peacefully

tranquil'lante m tranquillizer

tranquilli'tà f calm; (di spirito) tranquility. ~z'zare vt reassure. tran'quillo adj quiet; (pacifico) peaceful; (coscienza) easy

transat'lantico adj transatlantic ● m ocean liner

tran'satto pp di transigere. ~zi'one f (Comm) transaction

tran'senna f (barriera) barrier

trans'genico adj genetically modified, transgenic

tran'sigere vi reach an agreement; (cedere) yield

transi'tabile adj passable. ~re vi pass

transi'tivo adj transitive

'**transito** m transit; diritto di ~to right of way; "divieto di ~to" no thoroughfare". ~'torio adj transitory. ~zi'one f transition

tranvi'ere m tram driver

'**trapano** m drill

trapas'sare vt go [right] through ● vi (morire) pass away

tra'passo m passage

tra'pezio m trapeze; (Math) trapezium

trapian'tare vt transplant. ~'anto m transplant

'**trappola** f trap

tra'punta f quilt

'**trarre** vt draw; (ricavare) obtain; ~ in inganno deceive

trasa'lire vi start

trasan'dato adj shabby

trasbor'dare vt transfer; (Naut) tran[s]ship ● vi change. tra'sbordo m trans[s]hipment

tra'scendere vt transcend ● vi (eccedere) go too far

trasci'nare vt drag; (entusiasmo:) carry away. ~si vr drag oneself

tra'scorrere vt spend ● vi pass

tra'scritto pp di trascrivere. ~vere vt transcribe. ~zi'one f transcription

trascu'rabile adj negligible. ~re vt neglect; (non tenere conto di) disregard. ~'tezza f negligence. ~to adj negligent; (curato male) neglected; (nel vestire) slovenly

traseco'lato adj amazed

trasferi'mento m transfer; (trasloco) move

trasfe'ri|re vt transfer. ~rsi vr move

tra'sferta f transfer; (indennità) subsistence allowance; Sport away match; giocare in ~ play away

trasfigu'rare vt transfigure

trasfor'ma|re vt transform; (in rugby) convert. ~'tore m transformer. ~zi'one f transformation; (in rugby) conversion

trasfor'mista mf quick-change artist

trasfusi'one f transfusion

trasgre'dire vt disobey; (Jur) infringe

trasgredi'trice f transgressor

trasgres|si'one f infringement. ~'sore m transgressor

tra'slato adj metaphorical

traslo'car|e vt move ● vi, ~si vr move house. tra'sloco m removal

tra'smesso pp di trasmettere

tra'smett|ere vt pass on; (Radio, TV) broadcast; (Med, Techn) transmit. ~i'tore m transmitter

trasmis'si|bile adj transmissible. ~one f transmission; (Radio, TV) programme

trasmit'tente m transmitter •f broadcasting station

traso'gna|re vi day-dream

traspa'ren|te adj transparent. ~za f transparency; in ~za against the light. traspa'rire vi show [through]

traspi'ra|re vi perspire; fig transpire. ~zi'one f perspiration

tra'sporre vt transpose

traspor'tare vt transport; lasciarsi ~ da get carried away by. tra'sporto m transport; (passione) passion

trastul'lar|e vt amuse. ~si vr amuse oneself

trasu'dare vt ooze •vi sweat

trasver'sale adj transverse

trasvo'la|re vt fly over •vi ~re su fig skim over. ~ta f crossing [by air]

'tratta f illegal trade; (Comm) draft

trat'tabile adj or near offer

tratta'mento m treatment. ~ di riguardo special treatment

trat'ta|re vt treat; (commerciare in) deal in; (negoziare) negotiate •vi ~re di deal with. ~rsi vr di che si tratta? what is it about?; si tratta di... it's about.... ~'tive fpl negotiations. ~to m treaty; (opera scritta) treatise

tratteggi'are vt outline; (descrivere) sketch

tratte'ner|e vt (far restare) keep; hold (respiro, in questura); hold back (lacrime, riso); (frenare) restrain; (da paga) withhold; sono stato trattenuto (ritardato) I got held up. ~si vr restrain oneself; (fermarsi) stay; ~si su (indugiare) dwell on. tratteni-'mento m entertainment; (ricevimento) party

tratte'nuta f deduction

trat'tino m dash; (in parole composte) hyphen

'tratto pp di trarre •m (di spazio, tempo) stretch; (di penna) stroke; (linea) line; (brano) passage; tratti pl features; a tratti at intervals; ad un ~ suddenly

trat'tore m tractor

tratto'ria f restaurant

'trauma m trauma. trau'matico adj traumatic

tra'vaglio m labour; (angoscia) anguish

trava'sare vt decant

'trave f beam

tra'versa f crossbar; è una ~ di Via Roma it's off Via Roma

traver'sa|re vt cross. ~ta f crossing

traver'sie fpl misfortunes

traver'sina f (Rail) sleeper

tra'vers|o adj crosswise •adv di ~o crossways; andare di ~o (cibo): go down the wrong way; camminare di ~o not walk in a straight line. ~one m (in calcio) cross

travesti'mento m disguise

trave'sti|re vt disguise. ~rsi vr disguise oneself. ~to adj disguised •m transvestite

travi'are vt lead astray

travi'sare vt distort

tra'vol|gere vt sweep away; (sopraffare) overwhelm. ~to pp di travolgere

trazi'one f traction. ~ anteriore/posteriore front-/rear-wheel drive

tre adj & m three

trebbi'a|re vt thresh

'treccia f plait, braid

tre'cento adj & m three hundred; il T~ the fourteenth century

tredi'cesima f Christmas bonus of one month's pay

'tredici *adj* & *m* thirteen

'tregua *f* truce; *fig* respite

tre'mare *vi* tremble; (*di freddo*) shiver

tremenda'mente *adv* terribly. tre'mendo *adj* terrible; ho una fame tremenda I'm very hungry

tremen'tina *f* turpentine

tre'mila *adj* & *m* three thousand

'tremito *m* tremble

tremo'lare *vi* shake; (*luce:*) flicker. tre'more *m* trembling

tre'nino *m* miniature railway

'treno *m* train

'tren|ta *adj* & *m* thirty; ~ta e lode top marks. ~tatré giri *m inv* LP. ~'tenne *adj* & *mf* thirty-year-old. ~'tesimo *adj* & *m* thirtieth. ~'tina *f* una ~tina di about thirty

trepi'dare *vi* be anxious. 'trepido *adj* anxious

treppi'ede *m* tripod

'tresca *f* intrigue; (*amorosa*) affair

tri'angolo *m* triangle

tri'bale *adj* tribal

tribo'la|re *vi* suffer; (*fare fatica*) go through trials and tribulations. ~zi'one *f* tribulation

tribù *f inv* tribe

tri'buna *f* tribune; (*per uditori*) gallery; *Sport* stand. ~ coperta stand

tribu'nale *m* court

tribu'tare *vt* bestow

tribu'tario *adj* tax *attrib.* tri'buto *m* tribute; (*tassa*) tax

tri'checo *m* walrus

tri'ciclo *m* tricycle

trico'lore *adj* three-coloured ● *m* (*bandiera*) tricolour

tri'dente *m* trident

trien'nale *adj* (*ogni tre anni*) three-yearly; (*lungo tre anni*) three-year. tri'ennio *m* three-year period

tri'foglio *m* clover

trifo'lato *adj* sliced and cooked with olive oil, parsley and garlic

'triglia *f* mullet

trigonome'tria *f* trigonometry

tri'mestre *m* quarter; (*Sch*) term

'trina *f* lace

trin'cea *f* trench

trincia'pollo *m inv* poultry shears *pl*

trinci'are *vt* cut up

Trinità *f* Trinity

'trio *m* trio

trion'fa|le *adj* triumphal. ~nte *adj* triumphant. ~re *vi* triumph; ~re su triumph over. tri'onfo *m* triumph

tripli'care *vt* triple. 'triplice *adj* triple; in triplice [copia] in triplicate. 'triplo *adj* treble ● *m* il triplo (di) three times as much (as)

'trippa *f* tripe; (🔲: *pancia*) belly

'trist|e *adj* sad; (*luogo*) gloomy. tri'stezza *f* sadness. ~o *adj* wicked; (*meschino*) miserable

trita'carne *m inv* mincer

tri'ta|re *vt* mince. 'trito *adj* trito e ritrito well-worn, trite

'trittico *m* triptych

tritu'rare *vt* chop finely

triumvi'rato *m* triumvirate

tri'vella *f* drill. trivel'lare *vt* drill

trivi'ale *adj* vulgar

tro'feo *m* trophy

'trogolo *m* (*per maiali*) trough

'troia *f* sow; (🔲 *donna*) whore

'tromba *f* trumpet; (*Auto*) horn; (*delle scale*) well. ~ d'aria whirlwind

trom'b|etta *m* toy trumpet. ~one *m* trombone

trom'bosi *f* thrombosis

tron'care *vt* sever; truncate (*parola*)

'tronco *adj* truncated; licenziare in ~ fire on the spot ● *m* trunk; (*di strada*) section. tron'cone *m* stump

troneggi'are *vi* ~ su tower over

'trono *m* throne

tropi'cale adj tropical. **'tropico** m tropic

'troppo adj too much; (con nomi plurali) too many ● pron too much; (plurale) too many; (troppo tempo) too long; **troppi** (troppa gente) too many people ● adv too; (con verbi) too much; ∼ **stanco** too tired; **ho mangiato** ∼ I ate too much; **hai fame? - non** ∼ are you hungry? - not very

'trota f trout

trot'tare vi trot. **trotterel'lare** vi trot along; (bimbo:) toddle

'trotto m trot; **andare al** ∼ trot

'trottola f [spinning] top; (movimento) spin

troupe f inv ∼ **televisiva** camera crew

tro'va|re vt find; (scoprire) find out; (incontrare) meet; (ritenere) think; andare a ∼re go and see. ∼**rsi** vr find oneself; (luogo:) be; (sentirsi) feel. ∼**ta** f bright idea. ∼**ta pubblicitaria** advertising gimmick

truc'ca|re vt make up; (falsificare) fix 🗵. ∼**rsi** vr make up

'trucco m (cosmetico) make-up; (imbroglio) trick

'truce adj fierce; (delitto) appalling

truci'dare vt slay

'truciolo m shaving

trucu'lento adj truculent

'truffa f fraud. **truf'fare** vt swindle. ∼**tore,** ∼**trice** mf swindler

'truppa f troops pl; (gruppo) group

tu pers pron you; **sei tu?** is that you?; **l'hai fatto tu?** did you do it yourself?; **a tu per tu** in private; **darsi del tu** use the familiar tu

'tuba f tuba; (cappello) top hat

tuba'tura f piping

tubazi'oni fpl piping sg, pipes

tuberco'losi f tuberculosis

tu'betto m tube

tu'bino m (vestito) shift

'tubo m pipe; (Anat) canal; non ho

capito un ∼ 🔟 I understood zilch. ∼ **di scappamento** exhaust [pipe]

tuf'fa|re vt plunge. ∼**rsi** vr dive. ∼**tore,** ∼**trice** mf diver

'tuffo m dive; (bagno) dip; **ho avuto un** ∼ **al cuore** my heart missed a beat. ∼ **di testa** dive

'tufo m tufa

tu'gurio m hovel

tuli'pano m tulip

'tulle m tulle

tume'fa|tto adj swollen. ∼**zi'one** f swelling. **'tumido** adj swollen

tu'more m tumour

tumulazi'one f burial

tu'mul|to m turmoil; (sommossa) riot. ∼**u'oso** adj uproarious

'tunica f tunic

Tuni'sia f Tunisia

'tunnel m inv tunnel

'tuo (il ∼ m, la tua f, i ∼i mpl, le tue fpl) poss adj your; **è tua questa macchina?** is this car yours?; **un** ∼ **amico** a friend of yours; ∼ **padre** your father ● poss pron yours; **i tuoi** your folks

tuo'nare vi thunder. **tu'ono** m thunder

tu'orlo m yolk

tu'racciolo m stopper; (di sughero) cork

tu'rar|e vt stop; cork (bottiglia). ∼**si** vr become blocked; ∼**si il naso** hold one's nose

turba'mento m disturbance; (sconvolgimento) upsetting. ∼ **della quiete pubblica** breach of the peace

tur'bante m turban

tur'ba|re vt upset. ∼**rsi** vr get upset. ∼**to** adj upset

tur'bina f turbine

turbi'nare vi whirl. **'turbine** m whirl. **turbine di vento** whirlwind

turbo'lenza f turbulence

turboreat'tore m turbo-jet

t

tur'chese adj & mf turquoise

Tur'chia f Turkey

tur'chino adj & m deep blue

'turco, -a adj Turkish; •mf Turk •m (lingua) Turkish; fig double Dutch; fumare come un ~ smoke like a chimney

tu'rismo m tourism. ~ culturale heritage tourism. ~ta mf tourist. ~tico adj tourist attrib

'turno m turn; a ~ in turn; di ~ on duty; fare a ~ take turns. ~ di notte night shift

'turple adj base

'tuta f overalls pl; Sport tracksuit. ~ da lavoro overalls pl. ~ mimetica camouflage. ~ spaziale spacesuit. ~ subacquea wetsuit

tu'tela f (Jur) guardianship; (protezione) protection. tute'lare vt protect

tu'tina f sleepsuit; (da danza) leotard

tu'tore, -'trice mf guardian

'tutta f mettercela ~ per fare qcsa go flat out for sth

tutta'via conj nevertheless

'tutto adj whole; (con nomi plurali) all; (ogni) every; tutta la classe the whole class, all the class; tutti gli alunni all the pupils; a tutta velocità at full speed; ho aspettato ~ il giorno I waited all day [long]; in ~ il mondo all over the world; noi tutti all of us; era tutta contenta she was delighted; tutti e due both; tutti e tre all three •pron all; (tutta la gente) everybody; (tutte le cose) everything; (qualunque cosa) anything; l'ho mangiato ~ I ate it all; le ho lavate tutte I washed them all; raccontami ~ tell me everything; lo sanno tutti everybody knows; è capace di anything; ~ compreso all in; del ~ quite; in ~ altogether •adv completely; tutt'a un tratto all at once; tutt'altro not at all; tutt'altro che anything but •m whole. ~'fare a inv & nmf [impiegato] ~ general handyman; donna

~ general maid

tut'tora adv still

tutù m inv tutu, ballet dress

tv f inv TV

Uu

ubbidi'en|te adj obedient. ~za f obedience. ubbi'dire vi ~ (a) obey

ubi'cato adj located. ~zi'one f location

ubria'car|e vt get drunk. ~si vr get drunk; ~si di fig become intoxicated with

ubria'chezza f drunkenness; in stato di ~ inebriated

ubri'aco, -a adj drunk •mf drunk

ubria'cone m drunkard

uccelli'era f aviary. uc'cello m bird; (ⓧ: pene) cock

uc'cider|e vt kill. ~si vr kill oneself

ucci|si'one f killing. uc'ciso pp di uccidere. ~'sore m killer

u'dente adj i non udenti the hearing-impaired

u'dibile adj audible

udi'enza f audience; (colloquio) interview; (Jur) hearing

u'di|re vt hear. ~'tivo adj auditory. ~to m hearing. ~'tore, ~'trice mf listener; (Sch) unregistered student (allowed to attend lectures). ~'torio m audience

uffici'al|e adj official •m officer; (funzionario) official; pubblico ~e public official. ~iz'zare vt make official

uf'ficio m office; (dovere) duty. ~ di collocamento employment office. ~ informazioni information office. ~ del personale personnel department. ~sa'mente adv unofficially

uffici'oso *adj* unofficial

'ufo[1] *m inv* ufo

'ufo[2]: **a** ~ *adv* without paying

uggi'oso *adj* boring

uguagli'a|nza *f* equality. ~**re** *vt* make equal; (*essere uguale*) equal; (*livellare*) level. ~**rsi** *vr* ~**rsi a** compare oneself to

ugu'al|e *adj* equal; (*lo stesso*) the same; (*simile*) like. ~**mente** *adv* equally; (*malgrado tutto*) all the same

'ulcera *f* ulcer

uli'veto *m* olive grove

ulteri'or|e *adj* further. ~**mente** *adv* further

ultima'mente *adv* lately

ulti'ma|re *vt* complete. ~**tum** *m inv* ultimatum

ulti'missime *fpl* stop press *sg*

'ultimo *adj* last; (*notizie ecc*) latest; (*più lontano*) farthest; *fig* ultimate ● *m* last; **fino all'**~ to the last; **per** ~ at the end; **l'**~ **piano** the top floor

ultrà *mf inv Sport* fanatical supporter

ultramo'derno *adj* ultramodern

ultra'rapido *adj* extra-fast

ultrasen'sibile *adj* ultrasensitive

ultra's|onico *adj* ultrasonic. ~**u'ono** *m* ultrasound

ultravio'letto *adj* ultraviolet

ulu'la|re *vi* howl. ~**to** *m* howling

umana'mente *adv* (*trattare*) humanely; ~ **impossibile** not humanly possible

uma'nesimo *m* humanism

umanità *f* humanity. **umani'tario** *adj* humanitarian. **u'mano** *adj* human; (*benevolo*) humane

umidifica'tore *m* humidifier

umidità *f* dampness; (*di clima*) humidity. **'umido** *adj* damp; (*clima*) humid; (*mani, occhi*) moist ● *m* dampness; **in umido** (*Culin*) stewed

'umile *adj* humble

umili'a|nte *adj* humiliating. ~**re** *vt* humiliate. ~**rsi** *vr* humble oneself.

~**zi'one** *f* humiliation. **umil'mente** *adv* humbly. **umiltà** *f* humility

u'more *m* humour; (*stato d'animo*) mood; **di cattivo/buon** ~ in a bad/good mood

umo'ris|mo *m* humour. ~**ta** *mf* humorist. ~**tico** *adj* humorous

---

un *in def art*

> Un/una si traduce con *one* quando si tratta di un numero

a;

····▶ (*davanti a vocale o h muta*)

an; ▷**UNO**

---

una *indef art f* a; ▷**UN**

u'nanim|e *adj* unanimous. ~**e'mente** *adv* unanimously. ~**ità** *f* unanimity; **all'**~**ità** unanimously

unci'nato *adj* hooked; (*parentesi*) angle

un'cino *m* hook

'undici *adj & m* eleven

'unger|e *vt* grease; (*sporcare*) get greasy; (*Relig*) anoint; (*blandire*) flatter. ~**si** *vr* (*con olio solare*) oil oneself; ~**si le mani** get one's hands greasy

unghe'rese *adj & mf* Hungarian. **Unghe'ria** *f* Hungary

'ungh|ia *f* nail; (*di animale*) claw. ~**ata** *f* (*graffio*) scratch

ungu'ento *m* ointment

unica'mente *adv* only. **'unico** *adj* only; (*singolo*) single; (*incomparabile*) unique

unifi'ca|re *vt* unify. ~**zi'one** *f* unification

unifor'ma|re *vt* level. ~**rsi** *vr* conform (**a** to)

uni'form|e *adj & f* uniform. ~**ità** *f* uniformity

unilate'rale *adj* unilateral

uni'one *f* union; (*armonia*) unity. **U**~ **Europea** European Union. **U**~ **Mo-**

netaria Europea European Monetary Union. ~ **sindacale** trade union

u'ni|re vt unite; (collegare) join; blend (colori ecc). ~**rsi** vr unite; (collegarsi) join

'unisex adj inv unisex

unità f inv unity; (Math, Mil) unit; (Comput) drive. ~**rio** adj unitary

u'nito adj united; (tinta) plain

univer'sal|e adj universal. ~**mente** adv universally

università f inv university. ~**rio, -a** adj university attrib ● mf (insegnante) university lecturer; (studente) undergraduate

---

Università Italy's first university was founded in Bologna in 1088, and they are still run on traditional lines. Oral exams are the norm. Students study for a number of exams, which can be taken in a flexible order. For this reason Italian students often combine study with a job. The drop-out rate is high.

---

uni'verso m universe

uno, -a indef art (before s + consonant, gn, ps, z) a
● pron one; a ~ a ~ one by one; l'~ e l'altro both [of them]; né l'~ né l'altro neither [of them]; ~ di noi one of us; ~ fa quello che può you do what you can
● adj a, one
● m (numerale) one; (un tale) some man;
● f some woman

'unt|o pp di **ungere** ● adj greasy ● m grease. ~**u'oso** adj greasy. unzi'one f **l'Estrema Unzione** Extreme Unction

u'omo m (pl **uomini**) man. ~ **d'affari** business man. ~ **di fiducia** right-hand man. ~ **di Stato** statesman

u'ovo m (pl f **uova**) egg. ~ **in camicia** poached egg. ~ **alla coque** boiled egg. ~ **di Pasqua** Easter egg. ~ **sodo** hard-boiled egg. ~ **strapazzato** scrambled egg

ura'gano m hurricane

u'ranio m uranium

urba'n|esimo m urbanization. ~**ista** mf town planner. ~**istica** f town planning. ~**istico** adj urban. urbanizzazi'one f urbanization. ur'bano adj urban; (cortese) urbane

ur'gen|te adj urgent. ~**te'mente** adv urgently. ~**za** f urgency; **in caso d'~za** in an emergency; **d'~za** (misura, chiamata) emergency

'urgere vi be urgent

u'rina f urine. uri'nare vi urinate

ur'lare vi yell; (cane, vento) howl. **'urlo** m (pl m **urli**, f **urla**) shout; (di cane, vento) howling

'urna f urn; (elettorale) ballot box; **andare alle urne** go to the polls

urrà int hurrah!

ur'tar|e vt knock against; (scontrarsi) bump into; fig irritate. ~**si** vr collide; fig clash

'urto m knock; (scontro) crash; (contrasto) conflict; fig clash; **d'~** (misure, terapia) shock

usa e getta adj inv (rasoio, siringa) disposable

u'sanza f custom; (moda) fashion

u'sa|re vt use; (impiegare) employ; (esercitare) exercise; ~**re** fare qcsa be in the habit of doing sth ● vi (essere di moda) be fashionable; **non si usa più** it's out of fashion; it's not used any more. ~**to** adj used; (non nuovo) second-hand

u'scente adj (presidente) outgoing

usci'ere m usher. **'uscio** m door

u'sci|re vi come out; (andare fuori) go out; (sfuggire) get out; (essere sorteggiato) come up; (giornale) come out; ~**re da** (Comput) exit from, quit; ~**re di strada** leave the road. ~**ta** f exit, way out; (spesa) outlay; (di autostrada) junction; (*battuta*) witty remark; essere in libera ∼ta be off duty. ∼ta di servizio back door. ∼ta di sicurezza emergency exit

usi'gnolo *m* nightingale

'uso *m* use; (*abitudine*) custom; (*usanza*) usage; fuori ∼ out of use; per ∼ esterno for external use only

U.S.S.L. *f abbr* (Unità Socio-Sanitaria Locale) local health centre

ustio'narsi *vr* burn oneself ●*adj* burnt. usti'one *f* burn

usu'ale *adj* usual

usufru'ire *vi* ∼ di take advantage of

u'sura *f* usury

usur'pare *vt* usurp

u'tensile *m* tool; (*Culin*) utensil; cassetta degli utensili tool box

u'tente *mf* user. ∼ finale end user

u'tenza *f* use; (*utenti*) users pl. ∼ finale end users

ute'rino *adj* uterine. 'utero *m* womb

'util|e *adj* useful ●*m* (*Comm*) profit. ∼ità *f* usefulness; (*Comput*) utility. ∼i'taria *f* (*Auto*) small car. ∼i'tario *adj* utilitarian

utiliz'za|re *vt* utilize. ∼zi'one *f* utilization. uti'lizzo *m* use

uto'pistico *adj* Utopian

'uva *f* grapes pl; chicco d'∼ grape. ∼ passa raisins pl. ∼ sultanina currants pl

---

V v

---

va'cante *adj* vacant

va'canza *f* holiday; (*posto vacante*) vacancy. essere in ∼ be on holiday

'vacca *f* cow. ∼ da latte dairy cow

vacci'nare *vt* vaccinate. ∼nazi'one *f* vaccination. vac'cino *m*

vaccine

vacil'la|nte *adj* tottering; (*oggetto*) wobbly; (*luce*) flickering; *fig* wavering. ∼re *vi* totter; (*oggetto*): wobble; (*luce*): flicker; *fig* waver

'vacuo *adj* (*vano*) vain; *fig* empty ●*m* vacuum

vagabon'dare *vi* wander. vaga'bondo, -a *adj* (*cane*) stray; gente vagabonda tramps pl ●*mf* tramp

va'gare *vi* wander

vagheggi'are *vt* long for

va'gina *f* vagina. ∼'nale *adj* vaginal

va'gi|re *vi* whimper

'vaglia *m inv* money order. ∼ bancario bank draft. ∼ postale postal order

vagli'are *vt* sift; *fig* weigh

'vago *adj* vague

vagon'cino *m* (*di funivia*) car

va'gone *m* (*per passeggeri*) carriage; (*per merci*) wagon. ∼ letto sleeper. ∼ ristorante restaurant car

vai'olo *m* smallpox

va'langa *f* avalanche

va'lente *adj* skilful

va'ler|e *vi* be worth; (*contare*) count; (*regola*): apply (per to); (*essere valido*) be valid; far ∼e i propri diritti assert one's rights; farsi ∼e assert oneself; non vale! that's not fair! ●*vt* ∼re qcsa a qcno (*procurare*) earn sb sth; ∼ne la pena be worth it; vale la pena di vederlo it's worth seeing; ∼si di avail oneself of

valeri'ana *f* valerian

va'levole *adj* valid

vali'care *vt* cross. 'valico *m* pass

validità *f* validity; con ∼ illimitata valid indefinitely

'valido *adj* valid; (*efficace*) efficient; (*contributo*) valuable

valige'ria *f* (*fabbrica*) leather factory; (*negozio*) leather goods shop

va'ligia f suitcase; fare le valigie pack one's bags. ~ diplomatica diplomatic bag

val'lata f valley. 'valle f valley; a valle downstream

val'lett|a f (TV) assistant. ~o m valet; (TV) assistant

val'lone m (valle) deep valley

va'lor|e m value; (merito) merit; (coraggio) valour; ~i pl (Comm) securities; di ~e (oggetto) valuable; oggetti pl di ~e valuables; senza ~e worthless. ~iz'zare vt (mettere in valore) use to advantage; (aumentare di valore) increase the value of; (migliorare l'aspetto di) enhance

valo'roso adj courageous

'valso pp di valere

va'luta f currency. ~ estera foreign currency

valu'ta|re vt value; weigh up (situazione); (stabilire) (mercato, norme) currency. ~rio adj (mercato, norme) currency. ~zi'one f valuation

'valva f valve. **'valvola** f valve; (Electr) fuse

vam'pata f blaze; (di calore) blast; (al viso) flush

vam'piro m vampire

vana'mente adv in vain

van'da|lico adj atto ~lico act of vandalism. ~'lismo m vandalism. 'vandalo m vandal

vaneggi'are vi rave

'vanga f spade. van'gare vt dig

van'gelo m Gospel; (🔲: verità) gospel [truth]

vanifi'care vt nullify

va'nigli|a f vanilla. ~'ato adj (zucchero) vanilla attrib

vanità f vanity. vani'toso adj vain

'vano adj vain ● m (stanza) room; (spazio vuoto) hollow

van'taggio m advantage; Sport lead; Tennis advantage; trarre ~o da qcsa derive benefit from sth. ~'oso adj advantageous

van't|are vt praise; (possedere) boast. ~arsi vr boast. ~e'ria f boasting. 'vanto m boast

vanvera f a ~ at random; parlare a ~ talk nonsense

va'por|e m steam; (di benzina, cascata) vapour; a ~e steam attrib; al ~e (Culin) steamed. ~e acqueo steam, water vapour; battello a ~e steamboat. vapo'retto m ferry. ~i'era f steam engine

vaporiz'za|re vt vaporize. ~'tore m spray

vapo'roso adj (vestito) filmy; capelli vaporosi big hair sg

va'rare vt launch

var'care vt cross. 'varco m passage; aspettare al varco lie in wait

vari'abil|e adj variable ● f variable. ~ità f variability

vari'a|nte m variant. ~re vt/i vary; ~re di umore change one's mood. ~zi'one f variation

va'rice f varicose vein

vari'cella f chickenpox

vari'coso adj varicose

varie'gato adj variegated

varietà f inv variety ● m inv variety show

'vario adj varied; (al pl, parecchi) various; vari pl (molti) several; varie ed eventuali any other business

vario'pinto adj multicoloured

'varo m launch

va'saio m potter

'vasca f tub; (piscina) pool; (lunghezza) length. ~ da bagno bath

va'scello m vessel

va'schetta f tub

vase'lina f Vaseline®

vasel'lame m china. ~ d'oro/ d'argento gold/silver plate

'vaso m pot; (da fiori) vase; (Anat) vessel; (per cibi) jar. ~ da notte chamber pot

vas'soio m tray

vastità f vastness. 'vasto adj vast; di vaste vedute broad-minded

Vati'cano m Vatican

ve pers pron you; ve l'ho dato I gave it to you

vecchia f old woman. vecchi'aia f old age. 'vecchio adj old ●mf old man; i vecchi old people

've**ce** f in ~ di in place of; fare le veci di qcno take sb's place

ve'**dente** adj i non vedenti the visually handicapped

ve'**der|e** vt/i see; far ~e show; farsi ~e show one's face; non vedo l'ora di... I can't wait to...; ~si vr see oneself; (reciproco) see each other

ve'**detta** f lookout; (Naut) patrol vessel

'**vedovo, -a** m widower ●f widow

ve'**duta** f view

vee'**mente** adj vehement

vege'**ta|le** adj & m vegetable. ~li'ano adj & mf vegan. ~re vi vegetate. ~ri'ano, -a adj & mf vegetarian. ~zi'one f vegetation

'**vegeto** adj ▷VIVO

veg'**gente** mf clairvoyant

'**veglia** f watch; fare la ~ keep watch. ~ funebre vigil

vegli'**are** vi be awake; ~su are su watch over. ~one m ~one di Capodanno New Year's Eve celebration

ve'**icolo** m vehicle

'**vela** f sail; (Sport) sailing; far ~ set sail

ve'**la|re** vt veil; (fig: nascondere) hide. ~rsi vr (vista): mist over; (voce:) go husky. ~ta'mente adv indirectly. ~to adj veiled; (occhi) misty; (collant) sheer

'**velcro**® m velcro®

veleggi'**are** vi sail

ve'**leno** m poison. vele'noso adj poisonous

veli'**ero** m sailing ship

ve'**lina** f (carta) ~ tissue paper;

(copia) carbon copy

ve'**lista** m yachtsman ●f yachtswoman

ve'**livolo** m aircraft

vellei'**tario** adj unrealistic

'**vello** m fleece

vellu'**tato** adj velvety. vel'luto m velvet. velluto a coste corduroy

'**velo** m veil; (di zucchero, cipria) dusting; (tessuto) voile

ve'**loc|e** adj fast. ~e'mente adv quickly. velo'cista mf (Sport) sprinter. ~ità f inv speed; (Auto: marcia) gear. ~iz'zare vt speed up

ve'**lodromo** m cycle track

'**vena** f vein; essere in ~ di be in the mood for

ve'**nale** adj venal; (persona) mercenary, venal

ve'**nato** adj grainy

vena'**torio** adj hunting attrib

vena'**tura** f (di legno) grain; (di foglia, marmo) vein

ven'**demmia** f grape harvest. ~are vt harvest

'**vender|e** vt sell. ~si vr sell oneself; "vendesi" "for sale"

ven'**detta** f revenge

vendi'**care** vt avenge. ~rsi vr get one's revenge. ~tivo adj vindictive

'**vendita** f sale; in ~ta on sale. ~ta all'asta sale by auction. ~ta al dettaglio retailing. ~ta all'ingrosso wholesaling. ~ta al minuto retailing. ~tore, ~trice mf seller. ~tore ambulante hawker, pedlar

vene'**ra|bile**, ~**ndo** adj venerable

vene'**rare** vt revere

vener'**dì** m inv Friday. V~ Santo Good Friday

'**Venere** f Venus. ve'nereo adj venereal

Ve'**nezi|a** f Venice. v~'ano, -a agg & mf Venetian ●f (persiana) Venetian blind; (Culin) sweet bun

veni'**ale** adj venial

v

ve'nire vi come; (riuscire) turn out; (costare) cost; (in passivi) be; ~ a sapere learn; ~ in mente occur; ~ meno (svenire) faint; ~ meno a un contratto go back on a contract; ~ via come away; (staccarsi) come off; **vieni a prendermi** come and pick me up

ven'taglio m fan

ven'tata f gust [of wind]; fig breath

ven'tenne adj & mf twenty-year-old. **~simo**, **~simo** adj & m twentieth. **'venti** adj & m twenty

venti'lare vt air. **~'tore** m fan. **~zi'one** f ventilation

ven'tina f una ~ (circa venti) about twenty

ventiquat'trore f inv (valigia) overnight case

'vento m wind; **farsi ~** fan oneself

ven'tosa f sucker

ven'toso adj windy

'ventre m stomach. **ven'triloquo** m ventriloquist

ven'tura f fortune

ven'turo adj next

ve'nuta f coming

vera'mente adv really

ve'randa f veranda

ver'bal|e adj verbal ● m (di riunione) minutes pl. **~'mente** adv verbally

'verbo m verb. **~ ausiliare** auxiliary [verb]

'verde adj green ● m green; (vegetazione) greenery; (semaforo) green light. **~ oliva** olive green. **~'rame** m verdigris

ver'detto m verdict

ver'dura f vegetables pl; una ~ a vegetable

'verga f rod

vergi'n|ale adj virginal. **'vergine** f virgin; (Astr) V~ Virgo ● adj virgin; (cassetta) blank. **~ità** f virginity

ver'gogna f shame; (timidezza) shyness

vergo'gn|arsi vr feel ashamed; (essere timido) feel shy. **~oso** adj ashamed; (timido) shy; (disonorevole) shameful

ve'rifica f check. **verifi'cabile** adj verifiable

verifi'car|e vt check. **~si** vr come true

ve'rismo m realism

verit|à f truth. **~i'ero** adj truthful

'verme m worm. **~ solitario** tapeworm

ver'miglio adj & m vermilion

'vermut m inv vermouth

ver'nacolo m vernacular

ver'nic|e f (trasparente) varnish; (pelle) patent leather; fig veneer; **"vernice fresca"** "wet paint". **~i'are** vt paint; (con vernice trasparente) varnish. **~ia'tura** f painting; (strato) paintwork; fig veneer

'vero adj true; (autentico) real; (perfetto) perfect; **è ~?** is that so?; **sei stanca, ~?** you're tired, aren't you ● m truth; (realtà) life

verosimigli'anza f probability. **vero'simile** adj probable

ver'ruca f wart; (sotto la pianta del piede) verruca

versa'mento m payment; (in banca) deposit

ver'sante m slope

ver'sa|re vt pour; (spargere) shed; (rovesciare) spill; pay (denaro). **~rsi** vr spill; (sfociare) flow

ver'satil|e adj versatile. **~ità** f versatility

ver'setto m verse

versi'one f version; (traduzione) translation; **"~ integrale"** "unabridged version"

'verso [1] m (verse); (grido) cry; (gesto) gesture; (senso) direction; (modo) manner; **non c'è ~ di** there is no way of

'verso [2] prep towards; (nei pressi di)

round about; ~ **dove?** which way?

'vertebra f vertebra

'vertere vi ~ **su** focus on

verti'cal|e adj vertical; (in parole crociate) down ● m vertical ● f handstand. ~**'mente** adv vertically

'vertice m summit; (Math) vertex; **conferenza al** ~ summit conference

ver'tigine f dizziness; (Med) vertigo. **vertigini** pl giddy spells

vertigi|nosa'mente adv dizzily. ~**'noso** adj dizzy; (velocità) breakneck; (prezzi) sky-high; (scollatura) plunging

ve'scica f bladder; (sulla pelle) blister

'vescovo m bishop

'vespa f wasp

vespasi'ano m urinal

'vespro m vespers pl

ves'sillo m standard

ve'staglia f dressing gown

'vest|e f dress; (rivestimento) covering; **in** ~**e di** in the capacity of. ~**i'ario** m clothing

ve'stibolo m hall

ve'stigio m (pl m **vestigi**, pl f **vestigia**) trace

ve'sti|re vt dress. ~**rsi** vr get dressed. ~**ti** pl clothes. ~**to** adj dressed ● m (da uomo) suit; (da donna) dress

vete'rano, -a adj & mf veteran

veteri'naria f veterinary science

veteri'nario adj veterinary ● m veterinary surgeon

'veto m inv veto

ve'tra|io m glazier. ~**ta** f big window; (in chiesa) stained-glass window; (porta) glass door. ~**to** adj glazed. **vetre'ria** f glass works

ve'tri|na f [shop-]window; (mobile) display cabinet. ~**nista** mf window dresser

vetri'olo m vitriol

'vetro m glass; (di finestra, porta) pane. ~**resina** f fibreglass

'vetta f peak

vet'tore m vector

vetto'vaglie fpl provisions

vet'tura f coach; (ferroviaria) carriage; (Auto) car. **vettu'rino** m coachman

vezzeggi'a|re vt fondle. ~**tivo** m pet name. **'vezzo** m habit; (attrattiva) charm; **vezzi** pl (moine) affectation sg. **vez'zoso** adj charming; pej affected

vi pers pron you; (riflessivo) yourselves; (reciproco) each other; (tra più persone) one another; **vi ho dato un libro** I gave you a book; **lavatevi le mani** wash your hands; **eccovi!** here you are! ● adv = **ci**

'via¹ f street, road; fig way; (Anat) tract; **in** ~ **di** in the course of; **per** ~ **di** on account of; ~ ~ **che** as; **per** ~ **aerea** by airmail

'via² adv away; (fuori) out; **andar** ~ go away; **e così** ~ and so on; **e** ~ **dicendo** and whatnot ● int ~! go away!; Sport go!; (andiamo) come on! ● m starting signal

viabilità f road conditions pl; (rete) road network; (norme) road and traffic laws pl

via'card f inv motorway card

viaggi'a|re vi travel. ~**tore, -trice** mf traveller

vi'aggio m journey; (breve) trip; **buon** ~! safe journey!, have a good trip!; **fare un** ~ go on a journey. ~ **di nozze** honeymoon

vi'ale m avenue; (privato) drive

vi'bra|nte adj vibrant. ~**re** vi vibrate; (fremere) quiver. ~**zi'one** f vibration

vi'cario m vicar

'vice+ m deputy. ~**diret'tore** m assistant manager

vi'cenda f event; **a** ~ (fra due) each other; (a turno) in turn[s]

vice'versa adv vice versa

vici'na|nza f nearness; (paraggi) neighbourhood. ~**to** m neighbourhood; (vicini) neighbours pl

vi'cino, -a adj near; (accanto) next ●adv near, close. ~ a prep near [to] ●mf neighbour. ~ di casa nextdoor neighbour

'vicolo m alley

'video m video. ~'camera f camcorder. ~cas'setta f video cassette

videoci'tofono m video entry phone

video'clip m inv video clip

videogi'oco m video game

videoregistra'tore m videorecorder

video'teca f video library

video'tel® m ≈ Videotex®

videote'lefono m videophone

videotermi'nale m visual display unit, VDU

vidi'mare vt authenticate

vie'ta|re vt forbid; sosta ~ta no parking; ~to fumare no smoking

vi'gente adj in force. 'vigere vi be in force

vigi'lante adj vigilant. ~nza f vigilance. ~re vt keep an eye on ●vi keep watch

'vigile adj watchful ●m ~ [urbano] policeman. ~ del fuoco fireman

vi'gilia f eve

vigliacche'ria f cowardice. vigli'acco, -a adj cowardly ●mf coward

'vigna f, **vi'gneto** m vineyard

vi'gnetta f cartoon

vi'gore m vigour; entrare in ~ come into force. vigo'roso adj vigorous

'vile adj cowardly; (abietto) vile

'villa f villa

vil'laggio m village. ~ turistico holiday village

vil'lano adj rude ●m boor; (contadino) peasant

villeggia'|nte mf holiday-maker. ~re vi spend one's holidays. ~'tura

f holiday[s] [pl]

vil'l|etta f small detached house. ~ino m detached house

viltà f cowardice

'vimine m wicker

'vinc|ere vt win; (sconfiggere) beat; (superare) overcome. ~ita f win; (somma vinta) winnings pl. ~i'tore, ~i'trice mf winner

vinco'la|nte adj binding. ~re vt bind; (Comm) tie up. 'vincolo m bond

vi'nicolo adj wine attrib

vinil'pelle® f Leatherette®

'vino m wine. ~ spumante sparkling wine. ~ da taglio blending wine. ~ da tavola table wine

'vinto pp di vincere

vi'ola f (Bot) violet; (Mus) viola. viola adj & m inv purple

vio'la|re vt violate. ~zi'one f violation. ~zione di domicilio breaking and entering

violen'tare vt rape

vio'len|to adj violent. ~za f violence. ~za carnale rape

vio'letta f violet

vio'letto adj & m (colore) violet

violi'nista mf violinist. vio'lino m violin. violon'cello m cello

'vipera f viper

vi'raggio m (Phot) toning; (Aeron, Naut) turn. ~re vi turn

'virgol|a f comma. ~ette fpl inverted commas

vi'ril|e adj virile; (da uomo) manly. ~ità f virility; manliness

virtù f inv virtue; in ~ di (legge) under. virtu'ale adj virtual. virtu'oso adj virtuous ●m virtuoso

viru'lento adj virulent

'virus m inv virus

visa'gista mf beautician

visce'rale adj visceral; (odio) deepseated; (reazione) gut '**viscere** *m* internal organ ●*fpl* guts

'**vischi|o** *m* mistletoe. ~'**oso** *adj* viscous; (*appiccicoso*) sticky

vi'**scont|e** *m* viscount. ~'**essa** *f* viscountess

vi'**scoso** *adj* viscous

vi'**sibile** *adj* visible

visi'**bilio** *m* profusion; andare in ~ go into ecstasies

visibilità *f* visibility

visi'**era** *f* (*di elmo*) visor; (*di berretto*) peak

visio'**nare** *vt* examine; *Cinema* screen. visi'**one** *f* vision; prima visione *Cinema* first showing

'**visit|a** *f* visit; (*breve*) call; (*Med*) examination. ~**a di controllo** (*Med*) checkup. visi'**tare** *vt* visit; (*brevemente*) call on; (*Med*) examine; ~**a'tore**, ~**a'trice** *mf* visitor

vi'**sivo** *adj* visual

'**viso** *m* face

vi'**sone** *m* mink

'**vispo** *adj* lively

vis'**suto** *pp di* vivere ●*adj* experienced

'**vist|a** *f* sight; (*veduta*) view; a ~**a d'occhio** (*crescere*) visibly; (*estendersi*) as far as the eye can see; in ~**a di** in view of; ~**o che** since ●*m* visa. vi'**stoso** *adj* showy; (*notevole*) considerable

visu'**al|e** *adj* visual. ~**izza'tore** *m* (*Comput*) display, VDU. ~**izzazi'one** *f* (*Comput*) display

'**vita** *f* life; (*durata della vita*) lifetime; (*Anat*) waist; a ~ **for** life; essere in ~ be alive

vi'**tal|e** *adj* vital. ~**ità** *f* vitality

vita'**lizio** *adj* life *attrib* ●*m* [life] annuity

vita'**min|a** *f* vitamin. ~**iz'zato** *adj* vitamin-enriched

'**vite** *f* (*Mech*) screw; (*Bot*) vine

vi'**tello** *m* calf; (*Culin*) veal; (*pelle*) calfskin

vi'**ticcio** *m* tendril

viticol'**t|ore** *m* wine grower. ~**ura** *f* wine growing

'**vitreo** *adj* vitreous; (*sguardo*) glassy

'**vittima** *f* victim

'**vitto** *m* food; (*pasti*) board. ~ **e alloggio** board and lodging

vit'**toria** *f* victory

vittori'**oso** *adj* victorious

vi'**uzza** *f* narrow lane

'**viva** *int* hurrah!; ~ **la Regina!** long live the Queen!

vi'**vac|e** *adj* vivacious; (*mente*) lively; (*colore*) bright. ~**ità** *f* vivacity; (*di mente*) liveliness; (*di colore*) brightness. ~**iz'zare** *vt* liven up

vi'**vaio** *m* nursery; (*per pesci*) pond; *fig* breeding ground

viva'**mente** *adv* (*ringraziare*) warmly

vi'**vanda** *f* food; (*piatto*) dish

vi'**vente** *adj* living ●*mpl* i viventi the living

'**vivere** *vi* live; ~ **di** live on ●*vt* (*passare*) go through ●*m* life

'**viveri** *mpl* provisions

'**vivido** *adj* vivid

vivisezi'**one** *f* vivisection

'**vivo** *adj* alive; (*vivente*) living; (*vivace*) lively; (*colore*) bright; ~ **e vegeto** alive and kicking; farsi ~ keep in touch; (*arrivare*) turn up ●*m* dal ~ (*trasmissione*) live; (*disegnare*) from life; i vivi the living

vizi'**are** *vt* spoil (*bambino ecc*); (*guastare*) vitiate. ~**'ato** *adj* spoilt; (*aria*) stale. '**vizio** *m* vice; (*cattiva abitudine*) bad habit; (*difetto*) flaw. ~**'oso** *adj* dissolute; (*difettoso*) faulty; circolo ~**oso** vicious circle

vocabo'**lario** *m* dictionary; (*lessico*) vocabulary. vo'**cabolo** *m* word

vo'**cale** *adj* vocal ●*f* vowel. vo'**calico** *adj* (*corde*) vocal; (*suono*) vowel *attrib*

v

vocazi'one f vocation

'voce f voice; (diceria) rumour; (di bilancio, dizionario) entry

voci'are vi (spettegolare) gossip ● m buzz of conversation

vocife'rare vi shout

'voga f rowing; (lena) enthusiasm; (moda) vogue; essere in ~a be in fashion. **vo'gare** vi row. **~a'tore** m oarsman; (attrezzo) rowing machine

'voglia f desire; (volontà) will; (della pelle) birthmark; aver ~a di fare qcsa feel like doing sth

'voi pers pron you; **siete ~?** is that you?; **l'avete fatto ~?** did you do it yourself?. **~a'ltri** pers pron you

vo'lano m shuttlecock; (Mech) flywheel

vo'lante adj flying; (foglio) loose ● m steering-wheel

volan'tino m leaflet

vo'la|re vi fly. **~ta** f Sport final sprint; **di ~ta** in a rush

vo'latile adj (liquido) volatile ● m bird

volée f inv Tennis volley

vo'lente adj ~ o nolente whether you like it or not

volenti'eri adv willingly; **~!** with pleasure!

vo'lere vt want; (chiedere di) ask for; (aver bisogno di) need; **vuole che lo faccia io** he wants me to do it; **fai come vuoi** do as you like; **se tuo padre vuole**, **ti porto al cinema** if your father agrees, I'll take you to the cinema; **vorrei un caffè** I'd like a coffee; **la vuoi smettere?** will you stop that!; **senza ~** without meaning to; **voler bene/male** a qcno love/have something against sb; **voler dire** mean; **ci vuole il latte** we need milk; **ci vuole tempo/pazienza** it takes time/patience; **volerne** a have a grudge against; **vuoi ... vuoi...** either... or... ● m will; **vo'leri** pl wishes

vol'gar|e adj vulgar; (popolare) common. **~ità** f inv vulgarity. **~iz'zare** vt popularize. **~'mente** adv (grossolanamente) vulgarly, coarsely; (comunemente) commonly

'volger|e vt/i turn. **~si** vr turn [round]; **~si a** (dedicarsi) take up

voli'era f aviary

voli'tivo adj strong-minded

'volo m flight; al ~ (fare qcsa) quickly; (prendere qcsa) in mid-air; **alzarsi in ~** (uccello:) take off; **in ~** airborne. **~ di linea** scheduled flight. **~ nazionale** domestic flight. **~ a vela** gliding.

volontà f inv will; (desiderio) wish; **a ~** (mangiare) as much as you like. **volonta'mente** adv voluntarily. **volon'tario** adj voluntary ● m volunteer

volonte'roso adj willing

'volpe f fox

volt m inv volt

'volta f time; (turno) turn; (curva) bend; (Archit) vault; **4 volte 4** 4 times 4; **a volte** sometimes; **c'era una ~...** once upon a time, there was...; **una ~** once; **due volte** twice; **tre/quattro volte** three/four times; **una ~ per tutte** once and for all; **uno per ~** one at a time; **uno alla ~** one at a time; **alla ~ di** in the direction of

volta'faccia m inv volte-face

vol'taggio m voltage

vol'ta|re vt/i turn; (rigirare) turn round; (rivoltare) turn over. **~rsi** vr turn [round]

volta'stomaco m nausea

volteggi'are vi circle; (ginnastica) vault

'volto pp di volgere ● m face; **mi ha mostrato il suo vero ~** he revealed his true colours

vo'lubile adj fickle

vo'lum|e m volume. **~i'noso** adj voluminous

voluta'mente adv deliberately
voluttu'osità f voluptuousness. ~'oso adj voluptuous
vomi'tare vt vomit, be sick. 'vomito m vomit
'vongola f clam
vo'race adj voracious
vo'ragine f abyss
'vortice m whirl; (gorgo) whirlpool; (di vento) whirlwind
'vostro (il ~ m, la vostra f, i vostri mpl, le vostre fpl) poss adj your; è vostra questa macchina? is this car yours?; un ~ amico a friend of yours; ~ padre your father ●poss pron yours; i vostri your folks
vo'ta|nte mf voter. ~re vi vote. ~zi'one f voting; (Sch) marks pl. 'voto m vote; (Sch) mark; (Relig) vow
vs. abbr (Comm) (vostro) yours
vul'canico adj volcanic. vul'cano m volcano
vulne'rabil|e adj vulnerable. ~ità f vulnerability
vuo'tare vt, **vuo'tarsi** vr empty
vu'oto adj empty; (non occupato) vacant; ~ di (sprovvisto) devoid of ●m empty space; (Phys) vacuum; fig void; assegno a ~ dud cheque; sotto ~ (prodotto) vacuum-packed; ~ a perdere no deposit. ~ d'aria air pocket

Ww

W abbr (viva) long live
'wafer m inv (biscotto) wafer
walkie-'talkie m inv walkie-talkie
watt m inv watt
WC m WC
'Web m inv Web

'webmaster m webmaster
'western adj inv cowboy attrib ●m Cinema western

X, x adj raggi pl X X-rays; il giorno X D-day
xenofo'bia f xenophobia. xe'nofobo, -a adj xenophobic ●mf xenophobe
xi'lofono m xylophone

yacht m inv yacht
yen m inv Fin yen
'yoga m yoga; (praticante) yogi
'yogurt m inv yoghurt. ~i'era f yoghurt-maker

Zz

zaba[gl]i'one m zabaglione (dessert made from eggs, wine or marsala and sugar)
zaf'fata f whiff; (di fumo) cloud
zaffe'rano m saffron
zaf'firo m sapphire
'zaino m rucksack
'zampa f leg; a quattro zampe (animale) four-legged; (carponi) on

v
w
x
y
z

all fours

zampil'la|nte adj spurting. ~re vi spurt. zam'pillo m spurt

zam'pogna f bagpipe

zam'pone fpl stuffed pig's trotter with lentils

'zanna f fang; (di elefante) tusk

zan'zar|a f mosquito. ~i'era f (velo) mosquito net; (su finestra) insect screen

'zappa f hoe. zap'pare vt hoe

'zattera f raft

zatte'roni mpl (scarpe) wedge shoes

za'vorra f ballast; fig dead wood

'zazzera f mop of hair

'zebra f zebra; zebre pl (passaggio pedonale) zebra crossing

'zecca[1] f mint; nuovo di ~ brand-new

'zecca[2] f (parassita) tick

zec'chino m sequin; oro ~ pure gold

ze'lante adj zealous. 'zelo m zeal

'zenit m zenith

'zenzero m ginger

'zeppa f wedge

'zeppo adj packed full; pieno ~ di crammed o packed with

zer'bino m doormat

'zero m zero, nought; (in calcio) nil; Tennis love; due a ~ (in partite) two nil

'zeta f zed, zee Am

'zia f aunt

zibel'lino m sable

'zigomo m cheek-bone

zig'zag m inv zigzag; andare a ~ zigzag

zim'bello m decoy; (oggetto di scherno) laughing-stock

'zinco m zinc

'zingaro, -a mf gypsy

'zio m uncle

zi'tel|la f spinster; pej old maid. ~lona f pej old maid

zit'tire vi fall silent ● vt silence. 'zitto adj silent; sta' zitto! keep quiet!

ziz'zania f (discordia) discord

'zoccolo m clog; (di cavallo) hoof; (di terra) clump; (di parete) skirting board, baseboard Am; (di colonna) base

zodia'cale adj of the zodiac. zo'diaco m zodiac

'zolfo m sulphur

'zolla f clod; (di zucchero) lump

zol'letta f sugar lump

'zombi mf inv fig zombi

'zona f zone; (area) area. ~ di depressione area of low pressure. ~ disco area for parking discs only. ~ pedonale pedestrian precinct. ~ verde green belt

'zonzo adv andare a ~ stroll about

zoo m inv zoo

zoolo'gia f zoology. zoo'logico adj zoological. zo'ologo, -a mf zoologist

zoo sa'fari m inv safari park

zoppi'ca|nte adj limping; fig shaky. ~re vi limp; (essere debole) be shaky. 'zoppo, -a adj lame ● mf cripple

zoti'cone m boor

'zucca f marrow; (🗎: testa) head; (🗎: persona) thickie

zucche'r|are vt sugar. ~i'era f sugar bowl. ~i'ficio m sugar refinery. zucche'rino adj sugary ● m sugar lump

'zucchero m sugar. ~ di canna cane sugar. ~ vanigliato vanilla sugar. ~ a velo icing sugar. zucche'roso adj honeyed

zuc'chin|a f, ~o m courgette, zucchini Am

'zuffa f scuffle

zufo'lare vt/i whistle

zu'mare vi zoom

'zuppa f soup. ~ inglese trifle

zup'petta f fare ~ [con] dunk

zuppi'era f soup tureen

'zuppo adj soaked

Phrasefinder/Frasi utili

Key phrases — Frasi chiave

yes, please	sì, grazie
no, thank you	no, grazie
sorry!	scusa
excuse me	mi scusi
you're welcome	prego
I'm sorry, I don't understand	scusi, non capisco

Meeting people — Incontri

hello/goodbye	ciao/arrivederci
how do you do?	come sta?
how are you?	come stai?
nice to meet you	piacere

1

Asking questions	Fare domande
do you speak English/Italian?	parli inglese/italiano?
what's your name?	come ti chiami?
where are you from?	di dove sei?
where is...?	dov'è...?
can I have...?	posso avere... ?
would you like...?	vuoi...?
do you mind if...?	le dispiace se...?

About you	Presentarsi
my name is...	mi chiamo...
I'm English/Italian/American	sono inglese/italiano/-a/americano/-a
I don't speak Italian/English very well	non parlo molto bene l'italiano/l'inglese
I'm here on holiday	sono qui in vacanza
I live near York/Pisa	abito vicino a York/Pisa

Emergencies	Emergenze
can you help me, please?	mi può aiutare, per favore?
I'm lost	mi sono perso/-a
I'm ill	sto male
call an ambulance	chiami un'ambulanza
watch out!	attenzione!

Reading signs	Segnali e cartelli
no entry	vietato l'ingresso
no smoking	vietato fumare
fire exit	uscita di sicurezza
for sale	in vendita/vendesi
push	spingere
pull	tirare
press	premere

Going Places/In viaggio

By rail and underground	In treno e sul metrò
where can I buy a ticket?	dove si fanno i biglietti?
what time is the next train to Milan/New York?	a che ora è il prossimo treno per Milano/New York?
do I have to change?	devo cambiare?
can I take my bike on the train?	posso portare la bicicletta sul treno?
which platform for the train to Bath/Florence?	da quale binario parte il treno per Bath/Firenze?
a single/return, (*Amer*) round trip to Baltimore/Turin, please	un biglietto di sola andata/di andata e ritorno per Baltimora/Torino, per favore
I'd like an all-day ticket	vorrei un biglietto giornaliero
I'd like to reserve a seat	vorrei prenotare un posto
is there a student/senior citizen discount?	c'è uno sconto per studenti/anziani?
is this the train for Rome/Manchester?	è questo il treno per Roma/Manchester?
what time does the train arrive in Naples/London?	a che ora arriva il treno a Napoli/Londra?
have I missed the train?	ho perso il treno?
which line do I need to take for the Colosseum/London Eye?	che linea si prende per il Colosseo/London Eye?

YOU WILL HEAR:	SENTIRAI:
il treno è in arrivo sul binario 2	the train is arriving at platform 2
c'è un treno per Roma alle 10	there's a train to Rome at 10 o'clock
il treno è in ritardo/orario	the train is delayed/on time
la prossima fermata è ...	the next stop is...
il suo biglietto non è valido	your ticket isn't valid

MORE USEFUL WORDS:	ALTRE PAROLE UTILI:
underground station, (*Amer*) subway station	stazione di metropolitana
timetable	orario
connection	coincidenza
express train	treno espresso
local train	treno locale
high-speed train	treno ad alta velocità

DID YOU KNOW...? — LO SAPEVI...?

In an Italian train station, before you get on the train you must validate your ticket, i.e. have it stamped in the special yellow machine on the platform to make it valid for your journey. You risk a fine if you forget to do this.

Dall'aeroporto di Heathrow è possibile raggiungere il centro di Londra in meno di venti minuti grazie all'Heathrow Express..

At the airport All'aeroporto

when's the next flight to Paris/Rome?	quand'è il prossimo volo per Parigi/Roma?
what time do I have to check in?	a che ora si fa il check-in?
where do I check in?	dov'è il check-in?
I'd like to confirm my flight	vorrei confermare il mio volo
I'd like a window seat/an aisle seat	vorrei un posto accanto al finestrino/di corridoio
I want to change/cancel my reservation	vorrei cambiare/annullare la mia prenotazione
can I carry this in my hand luggage, (*Amer*) carry-on luggage?	posso portare questo nel bagaglio a mano?
my luggage hasn't arrived	il mio bagaglio non è arrivato

YOU WILL HEAR:	SENTIRAI:
il volo BA7057 è in ritardo/cancellato	flight BA7057 is delayed/cancelled
presentarsi all'uscita 29	please go to gate 29
la sua carta d'imbarco, per favore	your boarding card, please

MORE USEFUL WORDS:	ALTRE PAROLE UTILI:
arrivals	arrivi
departures	partenze
baggage claim	ritiro bagagli

Asking how to get there — Chiedere e dare indicazioni

how do I get to the airport?	come si arriva all'aeroporto?
how long will it take to get there?	quanto ci vuole per arrivarci?
how far is it from here?	quanto dista da qui?
which bus do I take for the cathedral?	quale autobus devo prendere per andare al duomo?
where does this bus go?	dove va questo autobus?
does this bus/train go to...?	questo autobus/treno va a...?
where should I get off?	può dirmi dove devo scendere?
how much is it to the town centre?	quant'è la tariffa per il centro?
what time is the last bus?	che ora è l'ultimo autobus?
where's the nearest underground station, (Amer) subway station?	dov'è la metropolitana più vicina?
is this the turning for...?	si svolta qui per...?
can you call me a taxi?	può chiamarmi un taxi, per favore?

YOU WILL HEAR: — SENTIRAI:

prenda la prima a destra	take the first turning on the right
dopo il semaforo/la chiesa svolti a sinistra	turn left at the traffic lights/just past the church

Disabled travellers — Viaggiatori disabili

I'm disabled	sono disabile
is there wheelchair access?	c'è l'accesso per sedia a rotelle?
are guide dogs permitted?	sono ammessi i cani guida per non vedenti?

On the road   Sulla strada

where's the nearest petrol station, (*Amer*) gas station?	dov'è la stazione di servizio più vicina?
what's the best way to get there?	qual è la strada migliore per arrivarci?
I've got a puncture, (*Amer*) flat tire	ho bucato
I'd like to hire, (*Amer*) rent a bike/car	vorrei noleggiare una bicicletta/una macchina
where can I park around here?	c'è un parcheggio qui vicino?
there's been an accident	c'è stato un incidente
my car's broken down	ho la macchina in panne
the car won't start	la macchina non parte
where's the nearest garage?	dov'è l'officina più vicina?
pump number six, please	pompa numero sei, grazie
fill it up, please	il pieno, per favore
can I wash my car here?	c'è l'autolavaggio?
can I park here?	posso parcheggiare qui?
there's a problem with the brakes/lights	i freni/fari hanno qualcosa che non va
the clutch/gearstick isn't working	la frizione/leva del cambio non funziona
take the third exit off the roundabout, (*Amer*) traffic circle	alla rotatoria prenda la terza uscita
turn right at the next junction	al prossimo incrocio svolti a destra
slow down	rallenta
I can't drink – I'm driving	non posso bere, devo guidare
can I buy a road map here?	vendete cartine stradali?

YOU WILL HEAR:	SENTIRAI:
favorisca la patente	can I see your driving licence?
deve compilare la denuncia di sinistro	you need to fill out an accident report
questa strada è a senso unico	this road is one-way
qui non si può parcheggiare	you can't park here

MORE USEFUL WORDS:	ALTRE PAROLE UTILI:
diesel	gasolio
unleaded	senza piombo/verde
motorway, (*Amer*) expressway	autostrada
toll	pedaggio
satnav, (*Amer*) GPS	navigatore satellitare
speed camera	autovelox
roundabout	rotatoria
crossroads	crocevia
dual carriageway, (*Amer*) divided highway	strada a due carreggiate
exit	uscita
traffic lights	semaforo
driver	conducente

DID YOU KNOW...?	LO SAPEVI...?
In Italy, all drivers are required to wear a reflective vest and to use a reflective triangle warning sign if they need to stop at the roadside.	Il pedaggio per circolare e sostare in auto nel centro di Londra, nei giorni lavorativi, si può pagare presso le stazioni di servizio o le edicole.

COMMON ITALIAN ROAD SIGNS

Alt polizia	Stop for police check
Consentito ai soli mezzi autorizzati	Authorized vehicles only
Passo carrabile	No blocking of passageway
Lavori in corso	Roadworks ahead
Zona pedonale	Pedestrian zone
Rallentare	Slow down
Zona rimozione	Tow-away zone
ZTL (Zona traffico limitato)	Traffic restricted area
Postazione fissa di misuratore della velocità	Speed cameras ahead
Passaggio a livello	Train crossing

SEGNALI STRADALI COMUNI NEI PAESI ANGLOFONI

Cattle	Animali domestici vaganti
Contraflow	Doppio senso di circolazione
Ford	Guado
Get in lane	Immettersi in corsia
Give way	Dare precedenza
Keep clear	Lasciare libero il passaggio
No overtaking, (Amer) Do not pass	Divieto di sorpasso
Pedestrians crossing	Attraversamento pedonale
Red route – no stopping	Divieto di sosta e fermata
Reduce speed now	Rallentare
Stop	Stop

Keeping in touch/Comunicazioni

On the phone | Al telefono

where can I buy a phone card?	dove si comprano le schede telefoniche?
may I use your phone?	posso usare il telefono?
do you have a mobile, (Amer) cell phone?	hai il cellulare?
what is your phone number?	qual è il tuo numero di telefono?
what is the area code for Venice/ Sheffield?	qual è il prefisso di Venezia/ Sheffield?
I want to make a phone call	vorrei fare una telefonata
I'd like to reverse the charges, (Amer) call collect	vorrei fare una telefonata a carico del destinatario
the line's engaged/busy	è occupato
there's no answer	non risponde nessuno
hello, this is Natalie	pronto, sono Natalie
is Riccardo there, please?	c'è Riccardo, per favore?
who's calling?	chi parla?
sorry, wrong number	ha sbagliato numero
just a moment, please	un attimo, prego
would you like to hold?	vuole attendere in linea?
it's a business/personal call	è una chiamata di lavoro/personale
I'll put you through to him/her	le passo la comunicazione
s/he cannot come to the phone at the moment	in questo momento non può venire al telefono
please tell him/her I called	gli/le dica che ho chiamato
I'd like to leave a message for him/her	vorrei lasciare un messaggio

I'll try again later	riproverò più tardi
please tell him/her that Maria called	gli/le dica che ha chiamato Maria
can he/she ring me back?	mi può richiamare?
my home number is...	il mio numero è...
my business number is...	il mio numero al lavoro è...
my fax number is...	il mio numero di fax è...
we were cut off	è caduta la linea
I'll call you later	ti chiamo più tardi
I need to top up my phone	mi serve una ricarica per il cellulare
the battery's run out	ho la batteria scarica
I'm running low on credit	sto esaurendo il credito
send me a text	mandami un sms/messaggino
there's no signal here	non c'è campo
you're breaking up	la linea è molto disturbata
could you speak a little louder?	puoi parlare più forte?

YOU WILL HEAR:	SENTIRAI:
pronto?	hello
chiamami sul cellulare	call me on my mobile, (*Amer*) cell phone
vuole lasciare un messaggio?	would you like to leave a message?

MORE USEFUL WORDS:	ALTRE PAROLE UTILI:
text message	SMS/messaggino
top-up card	ricarica
phone box, (*Amer*) phone booth	cabina telefonica
dial	comporre il numero
directory enquiries	elenco abbonati

Writing Corrispondenza

what's your address?	qual è il tuo indirizzo?
where is the nearest post office?	dov'è l'ufficio postale più vicino?
could I have a stamp for the UK/ Italy, please?	mi dà un francobollo per la Gran Bretagna/l'Italia, per favore?
I'd like to send a parcel	vorrei spedire un pacco
where is the nearest postbox, (*Amer*) mailbox?	dov'è la buca delle lettere più vicina?
dear Isabella/Fred	cara Isabella/caro Fred
dear Sir or Madam	gentili Signori
yours sincerely	distinti saluti
yours faithfully	cordialmente
best wishes	cari saluti

YOU WILL HEAR: SENTIRAI:

vuole spedirla per posta prioritaria?	would you like to send it first class?
c'è qualcosa di valore?	is it valuable?

MORE USEFUL WORDS: ALTRE PAROLE UTILI:

letter	lettera
postcode, (*Amer*) ZIP code	codice di avviamento postale/CAP
airmail	posta aerea
postcard	cartolina
fragile	fragile
urgent	urgente
registered post, (*Amer*) mail	raccomandata

On line | Internet

are you on the Internet?	siete su Internet?
what's your e-mail address?	qual è il tuo indirizzo email?
I'll e-mail it to you on Tuesday	te lo mando per email martedì
I looked it up on the Internet	l'ho cercato su Internet
the information is on their website	le informazioni si trovano sul sito web
my e-mail address is anna dot rossi at rapido dot com	il mio indirizzo email è: anna punto rossi chiocciola rapido punto com
can I check my e-mail here?	posso controllare l'email qui?
I have broadband/dial-up	ho la linea veloce/connessione dial-up
do you have wireless internet access?	avete accesso internet wireless?
I'll send you the file as an attachment	ti mando il file in allegato

YOU WILL SEE: | VEDRAI:

ricerca	search
fare doppio click sull'icona	double-click on the icon
apri l'applicazione	open (up) the application
scarica il file	download file

MORE USEFUL WORDS: | ALTRE PAROLE UTILI:

subject (*of an email*)	oggetto
password	password
social networking site	sito di social network
search engine	motore di ricerca
mouse	mouse
keyboard	tastiera

Meeting up Appuntamenti

what shall we do this evening?	cosa facciamo stasera?
do you want to go out tonight?	ti va di uscire stasera?
where shall we meet?	dove ci diamo appuntamento?
I'll see you outside the café at 6 o'clock	ci vediamo davanti al bar alle 6
see you later	a più tardi
I can't today, I'm busy	oggi non posso, sono impegnato
I'm sorry, I've got something planned	mi dispiace, ho già altri programmi
let's meet for a coffee in town	troviamoci al centro per un caffè
would you like to see a show/film, (*Amer*) movie?	ti va di andare a teatro/al cinema?
what about next week instead?	che ne dici se facciamo la prossima settimana?
shall we go for something to eat?	andiamo a mangiare qualcosa?

YOU WILL HEAR:	SENTIRAI:
piacere	nice to meet you
posso offrirti qualcosa da bere?	can I buy you a drink?

MORE USEFUL WORDS:	ALTRE PAROLE UTILI:
bar	bar
bar (*serving counter in a bar/pub*)	banco
meal	pasto
snack	spuntino
date	appuntamento
cigarette	sigaretta

Food and Drink/Mangiare e bere

Booking a table / Prenotare un ristorante

can you recommend a good restaurant?	può consigliarmi un buon ristorante?
I'd like to reserve a table for four	vorrei prenotare un tavolo per quattro
a reservation for tomorrow evening at eight o'clock	una prenotazione per domani sera alle otto
I booked a table for two	ho prenotato un tavolo per due

Ordering / Per Ordinare

could we see the menu/wine list, please?	possiamo avere il menù/la carta dei vini, per favore?
do you have a vegetarian menu?	avete un menù vegetariano?
could we have some more bread?	possiamo avere dell'altro pane?
could I have the bill, (Amer) check?	il conto, per favore
what would you recommend?	che cosa consiglia?
I'd like a black/white coffee	vorrei un caffè/un caffè macchiato

YOU WILL HEAR: / IL CAMERIERE CHIEDE …

Volete ordinare?	Are you ready to order?
Prendete un antipasto?	Would you like a starter?
Che cosa prendete come secondo?	What will you have for the main course?
Posso consigliare …	I can recommend …
Altro?	Anything else?
Buon appetito!	Enjoy your meal!
Il servizio non è compreso.	Service is not included.

The menu Il menu

starters	antipasti	antipasti	starters
melon	melone	antipasto di mare	seafood starter
omelette	frittata	antipasto di terra	assorted hams etc
soup	zuppa	prosciutto crudo	cured ham
salad	insalata	zuppa	soup

fish	pesce	pesce	fish
cod	merluzzo	acciughe	anchovies
hake	nasello	calamari	squid
halibut	ippoglosso	cozze	mussels
herring	aringa	dentice	sea bream
monk fish	squadro	frutti di mare	seafood
mussels	cozze	gamberetti	shrimp
oysters	ostriche	gamberi	prawns
plaice	platessa	merluzzo	cod
prawns	gamberi	nasello	hake
red mullet	triglie	ostriche	oysters
salmon	salmone	pesce spada	swordfish
seafood	frutti di mare	platessa	plaice
sea bass	spigola	rombo	turbot
shrimp	gamberetti	salmone	salmon
sole	sogliola	sogliola	sole
squid	calamari	spigola	sea bass
trout	trota	tonno	tuna
tuna	tonno	triglie	red mullet
turbot	rombo	trota	trout

meat	carne	carne	meat
beef	manzo	agnello	lamb
chicken	pollo	anatra	duck

duck	anatra		bistecca	steak
goose	oca		cinghiale	wild boar
hare	lepre		coniglio	rabbit
lamb	agnello		fegato	liver
liver	fegato		lepre	hare
pork	maiale		maiale	pork
rabbit	coniglio		manzo	beef
steak	bistecca		oca	goose
veal	vitello		pollo	chicken
wild boar	cinghiale		vitello	veal

vegetables	**verdure**		**verdure**	**vegetables**
artichokes	carciofi		asparagi	asparagus
asparagus	asparagi		carciofi	artichokes
aubergines	melanzane		carote	carrots
beans	fagioli		cavolfiore	cauliflower
cabbage	cavolo		cavolo	cabbage
carrots	carote		cipolle	onions
cauliflower	cavolfiore		fagioli	beans
celery	sedano		fagiolini	green beans
courgettes	zucchini		funghi	mushrooms
green beans	fagiolini		insalata	salad
mushrooms	funghi		melanzane	aubergines
onions	cipolle		patate	potatoes
peas	piselli		peperoni	peppers
peppers	peperoni		piselli	peas
potatoes	patate		sedano	celery
salad	insalata		zucchini	courgettes

the way it's cooked	**cottura**		**cottura**	**the way it's cooked**
boiled	lesso		al forno	cooked in the oven
fried	fritto		al pomodoro	in tomato sauce
grilled	alla griglia			

griddled	alla piastra	al ragù	in a meat sauce
puree	purè	al sangue	rare
roast	arrosto	alla griglia	grilled
stewed	in umido	arrosto	roast
rare	al sangue	ben cotta	well done
medium	cotta al punto giusto	cotta al punto giusto	medium
well done	ben cotta	fritto	fried
		in umido	stewed
		lesso	boiled

desserts	**dolci**	**dolci**	**desserts**
cream	panna	crostata	tart
fruit	frutta	frutta	fruit
ice cream	gelato	gelato	ice cream
pie	torta	panna	cream
tart	crostata	torta	pie

sundries	**contorni, salse, ecc.**	**contorni, salse, ecc.**	**sundries**
bread	pane	aceto	vinegar
butter	burro	burro	butter
cheese	formaggio	condimento	seasoning
herbs	erbe	erbe	herbs
mayonnaise	maionese	formaggio	cheese
mustard	senape	maionese	mayonnaise
olive oil	olio d'oliva	olio d'oliva	olive oil
pepper	pepe	pane	bread
rice	riso	pepe	pepper
salt	sale	riso	rice
sauce	salsa	sale	salt
seasoning	condimento	salsa	sauce
vinegar	aceto	senape	mustard

drinks	bevande		bevande	drinks
beer	birra		acqua minerale	mineral water
bottle	bottiglia		bibite analcoliche	soft drinks
carbonated	gassato		birra	beer
coffee	caffè		bottiglia	bottle
decaffeinated coffee	decaffeinato		caffè	coffee
espresso	espresso		decaffeinato	decaffeinated coffee
half-bottle	mezza bottiglia		espresso	espresso
liqueur	liquore		gassato	carbonated
mineral water	acqua minerale		liquore	liqueur
red wine	vino rosso		mezza bottiglia	half-bottle
soft drinks	bibite analcoliche		naturale	still
sparkling wine	spumante		spumante	sparkling wine
still	naturale		vino	wine
table wine	vino da tavola		vino bianco	white wine
white wine	vino bianco		vino da tavola	table wine
wine	vino		vino rosso	red wine

Places to stay/Dove alloggiare

Camping	In campeggio
can we pitch our tent here?	possiamo montare la tenda qui?
can we park our caravan here?	possiamo parcheggiare la roulotte qui?
what are the facilities like?	che attrezzature ci sono?
how much is it per night?	quant'è a notte?
where do we park the car?	dov'è il parcheggio?
we're looking for a campsite	stiamo cercando un campeggio
this is a list of local campsites	questo è l'elenco dei campeggi della zona
we go on a camping holiday every year	andiamo in campeggio tutti gli anni

At the hotel	In albergo
I'd like a double/single room with bath	vorrei una camera doppia/singola con bagno
we have a reservation in the name of Morris	abbiamo prenotato a nome Morris
we'll be staying three nights, from Friday to Sunday	ci fermiamo tre notti, da venerdì a domenica
how much does the room cost?	quant'è la camera?
I'd like to see the room, please	vorrei vedere la camera, per favore
what time is breakfast?	a che ora è la colazione?
can I leave this in your safe?	posso lasciare questo nella cassaforte?
bed and breakfast	camera e prima colazione
we'd like to stay another night	vorremmo fermarci un'altra notte
please call me at 7:30	mi chiami alle 7:30, per favore
are there any messages for me?	ci sono messaggi per me?

★ ★ ★

Hostels · Ostelli

could you tell me where the youth hostel is?	mi sa dire dov'è l'ostello della gioventù?
what time does the hostel close?	a che ora chiude l'ostello?
I'm staying in a hostel	alloggio in un ostello
the hostel we're staying in is great value	l'ostello in cui alloggiamo è molto conveniente
I know a really good hostel in Dublin	conosco un ottimo ostello a Dublino
I'd like to go backpacking in Australia	mi piacerebbe girare l'Australia con zaino e sacco a pelo

Rooms to let · In affitto

I'm looking for a room with a reasonable rent	vorrei affittare una camera a prezzo modico
I'd like to rent an apartment for a few weeks	vorrei affittare un appartamento per qualche settimana
where do I find out about rooms to let?	dove posso informarmi su camere in affitto?
what's the weekly rent?	quant'è l'affitto alla settimana?
I'm staying with friends at the moment	al momento alloggio presso amici
I rent an apartment on the outskirts of town	affitto un appartamento in periferia
the room's fine—I'll take it	la camera mi piace, la prendo
the deposit is one month's rent in advance	la caparra è di un mese d'affitto

Shopping and money/Spese e soldi

At the bank   In banca

I'd like to change some money	vorrei cambiare dei soldi
I want to change some euros into pounds	vorrei cambiare degli euro in sterline
do you take Eurocheques?	accettate Eurochèque?
what's the exchange rate today?	quant'è il tasso di cambio oggi?
I prefer traveller's cheques, (Amer) traveler's checks to cash	preferisco i traveller's cheque al contante
I'd like to transfer some money from my account	vorrei fare un bonifico
I'll get some money from the cash machine	prenderò dei soldi dal bancomat®
I'm with another bank	ho il conto in un'altra banca

Finding the right shop   Il negozio giusto

where's the main shopping district?	dov'è la zona commerciale principale?
where's a good place to buy sunglasses/shoes?	qual è il posto migliore per comprare occhiali da sole/scarpe?
where can I buy batteries/postcards?	dove posso comprare pile/cartoline?
where's the nearest chemist/bookshop?	dov'è la farmacia/libreria più vicina?
is there a good food shop around here?	c'è un buon negozio di generi alimentari qui vicino?
what time do the shops open/close?	a che ora aprono/chiudono i negozi?
where can I hire a car?	dove posso noleggiare una macchina?
where did you get those?	dove le/li hai comprate/-i?
I'm looking for presents for my family	sto cercando dei regali per la mia famiglia
we'll do all our shopping on Saturday	faremo la spesa sabato
I love shopping	adoro fare spese

....

Are you being served? Nei negozi

how much does that cost?	quanto costa quello?
can I try it on?	posso provarlo?
can you keep it for me?	me lo mette da parte?
could you wrap it for me, please?	me lo incarta, per favore?
can I pay by credit card/cheque, (Amer) check?	posso pagare con la carta di credito/un assegno?
do you have this in another colour, (Amer) color?	c'è in altri colori?
could I have a bag, please?	mi dà un sacchetto, per favore?
I'm just looking	sto solo dando un'occhiata
I'll think about it	ci devo pensare
I'd like a receipt, please	mi dà lo scontrino, per favore?
I need a bigger/smaller size	mi serve la taglia più grande/piccola
I take a size 10/a medium	porto la 42/la media
it doesn't suit me	non mi sta bene
I'm sorry, I don't have any change/anything smaller	mi dispiace, non ho spiccioli/biglietti più piccoli
that's all, thank you	nient'altro, grazie

Changing things Cambiare un acquisto

can I have a refund?	rimborsate i soldi?
can you mend it for me?	può ripararlo?
can I speak to the manager?	posso parlare con il direttore?
it doesn't work	non funziona
I'd like to change it, please	vorrei cambiarlo, per favore
I bought this here yesterday	l'ho comprato qui ieri

23

Currency Convertor		Convertitore di valute	
€/$	£/$	£/$	€/$
0.25		0.25	
0.50		0.50	
0.75		0.75	
1		1	
1.5		1.5	
2		2	
3		3	
5		5	
10		10	
20		20	
30		30	
40		40	
50		50	
100		100	
200		200	
1000		1000	

Sport and leisure/Sport e tempo libero

Keeping fit	Tenersi in forma
where can we play tennis/badminton?	dove si può giocare a tennis/badminton?
I'm looking for a swimming pool/golf course	sto cercando una piscina/un campo da golf
is there a hotel gym?	c'è una palestra in albergo?
are there any yoga/pilates classes here?	ci sono corsi di yoga/pilates?
I would like to go cycling/riding	mi piacerebbe andare in bici/a cavallo
I love swimming/football	mi piace nuotare/il calcio
where can I get tickets for the match, (Amer) game on Saturday?	dove si comprano i biglietti per la partita di sabato?

Going out	Uscire
what's on at the theatre/cinema?	cosa danno a teatro/al cinema?
how much are the tickets?	quanto costano i biglietti?
what time does the concert/performance start?	a che ora inizia il concerto/lo spettacolo?
I'd like to book tickets for tonight	vorrei prenotare dei biglietti per stasera
we'd like to go to a club	vorremmo andare in qualche locale

Good timing/L'Ora giusta

Telling the time — Dire l'ora

could you tell me the time?	mi dica che ore sono?
what time is it?	che ora è?
it's 2 o'clock	sono le due
at about 8 o'clock	verso le otto
at 9 o'clock tomorrow	domani mattina alle nove
from 10 o'clock onwards	dalle dieci in poi
at 8 a.m./p.m.	alle otto di mattina/di sera
at 5 o'clock in the morning/afternoon	alle cinque del mattino/di sera
it's five past/quarter past/half past one	è l'una e cinque/e un quarto/e mezza
it's twenty-five to/quarter to/five to one	è l'una meno venticinque/meno un quarto/meno cinque
a quarter /three quarters of an hour	un quarto/tre quarti d'ora

Days and dates — Giorni, mesi e date

Sunday, Monday, Tuesday, Wednesday, Thursday, Friday, Saturday	domenica, lunedì, martedì, mercoledì, giovedì, venerdì, sabato
January, February, March, April, May, June, July, August, September, October, November, December	gennaio, febbraio, marzo, aprile, maggio, giugno, luglio, agosto, settembre, ottobre, novembre, dicembre
what's the date?	quanti ne abbiamo oggi?
it's the second of June	è il due giugno
we meet up every Monday	ci incontriamo ogni lunedì
she comes on Tuesdays	viene di martedì
we're going away in August	saremo via ad agosto
it was the first of April	era il primo aprile
on November 8th	l'otto novembre

Public holidays and special days	Festività
Bank holiday	festa civile
Bank holiday Monday	festa civile che cade di lunedì
long weekend	ponte
New Year's Day (Jan 1)	Capodanno (1 gennaio)
Epiphany (Jan 6)	Epifania (la Befana: 6 gennaio)
St Valentine's Day (Feb 14)	San Valentino (14 febbraio)
Shrove Tuesday/Pancake Day	martedì grasso
Ash Wednesday	mercoledì delle Ceneri
St Joseph's Day (Mar 19)	San Giuseppe (19 marzo)
Mother's Day	Festa della mamma
Palm Sunday	domenica delle Palme
Maundy Thursday	giovedì grasso
Good Friday	venerdì santo
Easter Day	Pasqua
Easter Monday	lunedì dell'Angelo (pasquetta)
Anniversary of the liberation of Italy in 1945	anniversario della Liberazione (25 aprile)
May Day (May 1)	Festa del lavoro (1 maggio)
Father's Day	Festa del papà
Independence Day (Jul 4)	anniversario dell'Indipendenza (4 luglio)
Assumption (Aug 15)	Assunzione (ferragosto: 15 agosto)
Halloween (Oct 31)	vigilia d'Ognissanti
All Saints' Day (Nov 1)	Ognissanti (1 novembre)
Thanksgiving	giorno del Ringraziamento
Christmas Eve (Dec 24)	vigilia di Natale (24 dicembre)
Christmas Day (Dec 25)	Natale (25 dicembre)
Boxing Day (Dec 26)	Santo Stefano (26 dicembre)
New Year's Eve (Dec 31)	San Silvestro (31 dicembre)

Health and Beauty/Salute e bellezza

At the doctor's	Dal medico

can I see a doctor?	potrei vedere un medico?
I don't feel well	non mi sento bene
it hurts here	mi fa male qui
I have a migraine/stomachache	ho l'emicrania/il mal di stomaco
are there any side effects?	ci sono effetti collaterali?
I have a sore ankle/wrist/knee	mi fa male la caviglia/il polso/il ginocchio

YOU WILL HEAR:	SENTIRAI:

deve prendere un appuntamento	you need to make an appointment
si accomodi	please take a seat
ha la Tessera Europea di Assicurazione Malattia (TEAM)?	do you have a European Health Insurance Card (EHIC)?
ha l'assistenza medica?	do you have Health Insurance?
devo misurarle la pressione	I need to take your blood pressure

MORE USEFUL WORDS:	ALTRE PAROLE UTILI:

nurse	infermiere/a
antibiotics	antibiotici
medicine	medicina
infection	infezione
treatment	cura
rest	riposo

At the pharmacy In farmacia

can I have some painkillers?	mi dà un antidolorifico/analgesico?
I have asthma/hay fever/eczema	soffro d'asma/di rinite allergica/d'eczema
I've been stung by a wasp/bee	mi ha punto una vespa/un'ape
I've got a cold/cough/the flu	ho il raffreddore/la tosse/l'influenza
I need something for diarrhoea/stomachache	vorrei qualcosa per la diarrea/il mal di stomaco
I'm pregnant	sono incinta

YOU WILL HEAR: SENTIRAI

ha già preso questo farmaco?	have you taken this medicine before?
le sue medicine sono pronte tra dieci minuti	your prescription will be ready in ten minutes
da assumere durante i pasti/tre volte al giorno?	take at mealtimes/three times a day?
è allergico/-a a qualcosa?	are you allergic to anything?
sta prendendo qualche altro farmaco?	are you taking any other medication?

MORE USEFUL WORDS: ALTRE PAROLE UTILI:

plasters, (Amer) Band-Aid™	cerotti
insect repellent	insettifugo
contraception	anticoncezionali
sun cream	solare
aftersun	doposole
dosage	dosi

At the hairdresser's/ beauty salon
Dal parrucchiere/ dall'estetista

I'd like a cut and blow dry	taglio e asciugatura spazzola e phon
just a trim please	solo una spuntatina, per favore
a grade 3 back and sides	9 mm sia sui lati che dietro
I'd like my hair washed first please	mi faccia lo shampoo prima, per favore
can I have a manicure/pedicure/ facial?	fate la manicure/pedicure/pulizia del viso?
how much is a head/back massage?	quant'è il massaggio alla testa/ schiena?
can I see a price list?	potrei vedere il listino prezzi?
do you offer reflexology/ aromatherapy treatments?	fate riflessologia/aromaterapia?

YOU WILL HEAR:	SENTIRAI:
vuole l'asciugatura a spazzola e phon?	would you like your hair blow-dried?
da che lato porta la riga?	where is your parting?
le faccio un taglio scalato?	would you like your hair layered?

MORE USEFUL WORDS:	ALTRE PAROLE UTILI:
dry/greasy/fine/flyaway/frizzy hair	capelli secchi/grassi/sottili/ sfibrati/crespi
highlights	colpi di sole
extensions	allungamento capelli/extensions
sunbed	lettino solare
leg/arm/bikini wax	ceretta gambe/braccia/inguine

At the dentist's Dal dentista

I have toothache	ho mal di denti
I'd like an emergency appointment	vorrei un appuntamento d'urgenza
I have cracked a tooth	mi si è spezzato un dente
my gums are bleeding	mi sanguinano le gengive

YOU WILL HEAR: SENTIRAI:

apra bene la bocca	open your mouth
bisogna fare un'otturazione	you need a filling
devo farle una radiografia	we need to take an X-ray
sciacqui bene	please rinse

MORE USEFUL WORDS: ALTRE PAROLE UTILI:

anaesthetic	anestesia
root canal treatment	devitalizzazione del dente
injection	iniezione
floss	filo interdentale

Weights & measures/ Pesi e misure

Length/Lunghezza

inches/pollici	0.39	3.9	7.8	11.7	15.6	19.7	39
cm/centimetri	1	10	20	30	40	50	100

Distance/Distanze

miles/miglia	0.62	6.2	12.4	18.6	24.9	31	62
km/chilometri	1	10	20	30	40	50	100

Weight/Pesi

pounds/libbre	2.2	22	44	66	88	110	220
kg/chilogrammi	1	10	20	30	40	50	100

Capacity/Capacità

gallons/galloni	0.22	2.2	4.4	6.6	8.8	11	22
litres/litri	1	10	20	30	40	50	100

Temperature/Temperatura

°C	0	5	10	15	20	25	30	37	38	40
°F	32	41	50	59	68	77	86	98.4	100	104

Clothing and shoe sizes/Taglie e numeri di scarpe

Women's clothing sizes/Abbigliamento femminile

UK	8	10	12	14	16	18
US	6	8	10	12	14	16
Continent	36	38	40	42	44	46

Men's clothing sizes/Abbigliamento maschile

UK/US	36	38	40	42	44	46
Continent	46	48	50	52	54	56

Men's and women's shoes/Scarpe da uomo e da donna

UK women	4	5	6	7	7.5	8			
UK men			6	7	8	9	10	11	
US	6.5	7.5	8.5	9.5	10.5	11.5	12.5	13.5	14.5
Continent	37	38	39	40	41	42	43	44	45

Aa

a /ə/, accentato /eɪ/ *indef art*; davanti a una vocale **an**
  ⋯➤ un *m*, una *f*; *(before s + consonant, gn, ps and z)* uno; *(before feminine noun starting with a vowel)* un'; **a tiger is a feline** la tigre è un felino; **a knife and fork** un coltello e una forchetta; **a Mr Smith is looking for you** un certo signor Smith ti sta cercando
  ⋯➤ *(each)* a; **£2 a kilo/a head** due sterline al chilo/a testa

> when *a* refers to professions, it is not translated: **I am a lawyer** sono avvocato

A /eɪ/ *n (Mus)* la *m inv*

aback /ə'bæk/ *adv* **be taken** ∼ essere preso in contropiede

abandon /ə'bændən/ *vt* abbandonare; *(give up)* rinunciare a ● *n* abbandono *m*. ∼**ed** *adj* abbandonato

abashed /ə'bæʃt/ *adj* imbarazzato

abate /ə'beɪt/ *vi* calmarsi

abattoir /'æbətwɑ:(r)/ *n* mattatoio *m*

abbey /'æbɪ/ *n* abbazia *f*

abbreviat|e /ə'bri:vɪeɪt/ *vt* abbreviare. ∼**ion** *n* abbreviazione *f*

abdicat|e /'æbdɪkeɪt/ *vi* abdicare ● *vt* rinunciare a. ∼**ion** *n* abdicazione *f*

abdom|en /'æbdəmən/ *n* addome *m*. ∼**inal** *adj* addominale

abduct /əb'dʌkt/ *vt* rapire. ∼**ion** *n* rapimento *m*

abhor /əb'hɔ:(r)/ *vt (pt/pp abhorred)* aborrire. ∼**rence** *n* orrore *m*

abid|e /ə'baɪd/ *vt (pt/pp abided) (tolerate)* sopportare ● **abide by** *vi* rispettare. ∼**ing** *adj* perpetuo

ability /ə'bɪlətɪ/ *n* capacità *f inv*

abject /'æbdʒekt/ *adj (poverty)* degradante; *(apology)* umile; *(coward)* abietto

ablaze /ə'bleɪz/ *adj* in fiamme; **be** ∼ **with light** risplendere di luci

able /'eɪbl/ *adj* capace, abile; **be** ∼ **to do sth** poter fare qcsa; **were you** ∼ **to...?** sei riuscito a...? ∼**-bodied** *adj* robusto; *(Mil)* abile

ably /'eɪblɪ/ *adv* abilmente

abnormal /æb'nɔ:ml/ *adj* anormale. ∼**ity** *n* anormalità *f inv*. ∼**ly** *adv* in modo anormale

aboard /ə'bɔ:d/ *adv & prep* a bordo

abolish /ə'bɒlɪʃ/ *vt* abolire. ∼**ition** *n* abolizione *f*

abominable /ə'bɒmɪnəbl/ *adj* abominevole

abort /ə'bɔ:t/ *vt* fare abortire; *fig* annullare. ∼**ion** *n* aborto *m*; **have an** ∼**ion** abortire. ∼**ive** *adj (attempt)* infruttuoso

abound /ə'baʊnd/ *vi* abbondare; ∼ **in** abbondare di

about /ə'baʊt/ *adv (here and there)* [di] qua e [di] là; *(approximately)* circa; **be** ∼ *(illness, tourists)*: essere in giro; **be up and** ∼ essere alzato; **leave sth lying** ∼ lasciare in giro qcsa ● *prep (concerning)* su; *(in the region of)* intorno a; *(here and there in)* per; **what is the book/the film** ∼? di cosa parla il libro/il film?; **he wants to see you – what** ∼? ti vuole vedere – a che proposito?; **talk** ∼ parlare/sapere di; **I know nothing** ∼ **it** non ne so niente; ∼ **5**

o'clock intorno alle 5; travel ~ the world viaggiare per il mondo; be ~ to do sth stare per fare qcsa; how ~ going to the cinema? e se andassimo al cinema?

about: ~-'face n, ~-'turn n dietro front m inv

above /ə'bʌv/ adv & prep sopra; ~ all soprattutto

above: ~-'board adj onesto. ~-'mentioned adj suddetto

abrasive /ə'breɪsɪv/ adj abrasivo; (remark) caustico ● n abrasivo m

abreast /ə'brest/ adv fianco a fianco; come ~ of allinearsi con; keep ~ of tenersi al corrente di

abroad /ə'brɔːd/ adv all'estero

abrupt /ə'brʌpt/ adj brusco

abscess /'æbsɪs/ n ascesso m

abscond /əb'skɒnd/ vi fuggire

absence /'æbsəns/ n assenza f; (lack) mancanza f

absent¹ /'æbsənt/ adj assente

absent² /æb'sent/ vt ~ oneself essere assente

absentee /æbsən'tiː/ n assente mf

absent-minded /æbsənt maɪndɪd/ adj distratto

absolute /'æbsəluːt/ adj assoluto; an ~ idiot un perfetto idiota. ~ly adv assolutamente; ([]: indicating agreement) esattamente

absolve /əb'zɒlv/ vt assolvere

absorb /əb'sɔːb/ vt assorbire; ~ed in assorto in. ~ent adj assorbente

absorption /əb'sɔːpʃn/ n assorbimento m; (in activity) concentrazione f

abstain /əb'steɪn/ vi astenersi (from da)

abstemious /əb'stiːmɪəs/ adj moderato

abstention /əb'stenʃn/ n (Pol) astensione f

abstract /'æbstrækt/ adj astratto ● n astratto m; (summary) estratto m

absurd /əb'sɜːd/ adj assurdo. ~ity n

assurdità f inv

abundan|ce /ə'bʌndəns/ n abbondanza f. ~t adj abbondante

abuse¹ /ə'bjuːz/ vt (misuse) abusare di; (insult) insultare; (ill-treat) maltrattare

abus|e² /ə'bjuːs/ n abuso m; (verbal) insulti mpl; (ill-treatment) maltrattamento m. ~ive adj offensivo

abysmal /ə'bɪzml/ adj [] pessimo; (ignorance) abissale

abyss /ə'bɪs/ n abisso m

academic /ækə'demɪk/ adj teorico; (qualifications, system) scolastico; be ~ (person): avere predisposizione allo studio ● n docente mf universitario, -a

academy /ə'kædəmɪ/ n accademia f; (of music) conservatorio m

accelerat|e /ək'seləreɪt/ vt/i accelerare. ~ion n accelerazione f. ~or n (Auto) acceleratore m

accent /'æksənt/ n accento m

accept /ək'sept/ vt accettare. ~able adj accettabile. ~ance n accettazione f

access /'ækses/ n accesso m. ~ible adj accessibile

accession /ək'seʃn/ n (to throne) ascesa f al trono

accessory /ək'sesərɪ/ n accessorio m; (Jur) complice mf

accident /'æksɪdənt/ n incidente m; (chance) caso m; by ~ per caso; (unintentionally) senza volere; I'm sorry, it was an ~ mi dispiace, non l'ho fatto apposta. ~al adj (meeting) casuale; (death) incidentale; (unintentional) involontario. ~ally adv per caso; (unintentionally) inavvertitamente

acclaim /ə'kleɪm/ n acclamazione f ● vt acclamare (as come)

accolade /'ækəleɪd/ n riconoscimento m

accommodat|e /ə'kɒmədeɪt/ vt ospitare; (oblige) favorire. ~ing adj accomodante. ~ion n (place to stay) sistemazione f

accompan|iment /ə'kʌmpənɪmənt/ n accompagnamento m. **~ist** n (Mus) accompagnatore, -trice f

accompany /ə'kʌmpəni/ vt (pt/pp -ied) accompagnare

accomplice /ə'kʌmplɪs/ n complice f

accomplish /ə'kʌmplɪʃ/ vt (achieve) concludere; realizzare (aim). **~ed** adj dotato; (fact) compiuto. **~ment** n realizzazione f; (achievement) risultato m; (talent) talento m

accord /ə'kɔːd/ n (treaty) accordo m; with one **~** tutti d'accordo; of his own **~** di sua spontanea volontà. **~ance** n in **~ance** with in conformità di o a

according /ə'kɔːdɪŋ/ adv **~** to secondo. **~ly** adv di conseguenza

accordion /ə'kɔːdɪən/ n fisarmonica f

accost /ə'kɒst/ vt abbordare

account /ə'kaʊnt/ n conto m; (report) descrizione f; (of eye-witness) resoconto m; **~s** pl (Comm) conti mpl; on **~** of a causa di; on no **~** per nessun motivo; on this **~** per questo motivo; on my **~** per causa mia; of no **~** di nessuna importanza; take into **~** tener conto di ● **account for** vt (explain) spiegare; (person:) render conto di; (constitute) costituire. **~ability** n responsabilità f inv. **~able** adj responsabile (for di)

accountant /ə'kaʊntənt/ n (bookkeeper) contabile mf; (consultant) commercialista mf

accumulat|e /ə'kjuːmjʊleɪt/ vt accumulare ● vi accumularsi. **~ion** n accumulazione f

accura|cy /'ækjʊrəsɪ/ n precisione f. **~te** adj preciso. **~tely** adv con precisione

accusation /ækjʊ'zeɪʃn/ n accusa f

accuse /ə'kjuːz/ vt accusare; **~ sb** of doing sth accusare qcno di fare

qcsa. **~d** n the **~d** l'accusato m, l'accusata f

accustom /ə'kʌstəm/ vt abituare (to a); grow or get **~ed** to abituarsi a. **~ed** adj abituato

ace /eɪs/ n (Cards) asso m; (tennis) ace m inv

ache /eɪk/ n dolore m ● vi dolere, far male; **~** all over essere tutto indolenzito

achieve /ə'tʃiːv/ vt ottenere (success); realizzare (goal, ambition). **~ment** n (feat) successo m

acid /'æsɪd/ adj acido ● n acido m. **~ity** n acidità f. **~ 'rain** n pioggia f acida

acknowledge /ək'nɒlɪdʒ/ vt riconoscere; rispondere a (greeting); far cenno di aver notato (sb's presence); **~** receipt of accusare ricevuta di. **~ment** n riconoscimento m; send an **~ment** of a letter confermare il ricevimento di una lettera

acne /'æknɪ/ n acne f

acorn /'eɪkɔːn/ n ghianda f

acoustic /ə'kuːstɪk/ adj acustico. **~s** npl acustica fsg

acquaint /ə'kweɪnt/ vt **~ sb** with metter qcno al corrente di; be **~ed** with conoscere (person); essere a conoscenza di (fact). **~ance** n (person) conoscente mf; make sb's **~ance** fare la conoscenza di qcno

acquiesce /ækwɪ'es/ vi acconsentire (to, in a). **~nce** n acquiescenza f

acquire /ə'kwaɪə(r)/ vt acquisire

acquisit|ion /ækwɪ'zɪʃn/ n acquisizione f. **~ive** adj avido

acquit /ə'kwɪt/ vt (pt/pp acquitted) assolvere; **~ oneself well** cavarsela bene. **~tal** n assoluzione f

acre /'eɪkə(r)/ n acro m (= 4 047 m²)

acrid /'ækrɪd/ adj acre

acrimon|ious /ækrɪ'məʊnɪəs/ adj aspro. **~y** n asprezza f

acrobat /'ækrəbæt/ n acrobata mf. **~ic** adj acrobatico

across /əˈkrɒs/ adv dall'altra parte; (wide) in larghezza; (not lengthwise) attraverso; (in crossword) orizzontale; come ~ sth imbattersi in qcsa; go ~ attraversare ● prep (crosswise) di traverso su; (on the other side of) dall'altra parte di

act /ækt/ n atto m; (in variety show) numero m; put on an ~ ① fare scena ● vi agire; (behave) comportarsi; (Theat) recitare; (pretend) fingere; ~ as fare da ● vt recitare (role). ~ing adj (deputy) provvisorio ● n (Theat) recitazione f; (profession) teatro m. ~ing profession n professione f dell'attore

action /ˈækʃn/ n azione f; (Mil) combattimento m; (Jur) azione f legale; out of ~ (machine:) fuori uso; take ~ agire. ~ replay n replay m inv

active /ˈæktɪv/ adj attivo. ~ely adv attivamente. ~ity n attività f inv

act|or /ˈæktə(r)/ n attore m. ~ress n attrice f

actual /ˈæktʃʊəl/ adj (real) reale. ~ly adv in realtà

acute /əˈkjuːt/ adj acuto; (shortage, hardship) estremo

ad /æd/ n ① pubblicità f inv

AD abbr (Anno Domini) d.C.

adapt /əˈdæpt/ vt adattare (play) ● vi adattarsi. ~ability n adattabilità f. ~able adj adattabile

adaptation /ædæpˈteɪʃn/ n (Theat) adattamento m

adapter, adaptor /əˈdæptə(r)/ n adattatore m; (two-way) presa f multipla

add /æd/ vt aggiungere; (Math) addizionare ● vi addizionare; ~ to (fig: increase) aggravare. □ ~ up vt addizionare (figures) ● vi addizionare; ~ up to ammontare a; it doesn't ~ up fig non quadra

adder /ˈædə(r)/ n vipera f

addict /ˈædɪkt/ n tossicodipendente

mf; fig fanatico, -a mf

addict|ed /əˈdɪktɪd/ adj assuefatto (to a); ~ed to drugs tossicodipendente; he's ~ed to television è videodipendente. ~ion n dipendenza f; (to drugs) tossicodipendenza f. ~ive adj be ~ive dare assuefazione

addition /əˈdɪʃn/ n (Math) addizione f; (thing added) aggiunta f; in ~ in aggiunta. ~al adj supplementare. ~ally adv in più

additive /ˈædɪtɪv/ n additivo m

address /əˈdres/ n indirizzo m; (speech) discorso m; form of ~ formula f di cortesia ● vt indirizzare; (speak to) rivolgersi a (person); tenere un discorso a (meeting). ~ee n destinatario, -a mf

adept /ˈædept/ adj & n esperto, -a mf (at in)

adequate /ˈædɪkwət/ adj adeguato. ~ly adv adeguatamente

adhere /ədˈhɪə(r)/ vi aderire; ~ to attenersi a (principles, rules)

adhesive /ədˈhiːsɪv/ adj adesivo ● n adesivo m

adjacent /əˈdʒeɪsənt/ adj adiacente

adjective /ˈædʒɪktɪv/ n aggettivo m

adjourn /əˈdʒɜːn/ vt/i aggiornare (until a). ~ment n aggiornamento m

adjust /əˈdʒʌst/ vt modificare; regolare (focus, sound etc) ● vi adattarsi. ~able adj regolabile. ~ment n adattamento m; (Techn) regolamento m

administer /ədˈmɪnɪstə(r)/ vt amministrare; somministrare (medicine)

administrat|ion /ədmɪnɪˈstreɪʃn/ n amministrazione f; (Pol) governo m. ~or n amministratore, -trice mf

admirable /ˈædmərəbl/ adj ammirevole

admiral /ˈædmərəl/ n ammiraglio m

admiration /ædməˈreɪʃn/ n ammirazione f

admire /ədˈmaɪə(r)/ vt ammirare.

~r n ammiratore, -trice mf

admission /ədˈmɪʃn/ n ammissione f; (to hospital) ricovero m; (entry) ingresso m

admit /ədˈmɪt/ vt (pt/pp **admitted**) (let in) far entrare; (to hospital) ricoverare; (acknowledge) ammettere ● vi **~ to** sth ammettere qcsa. **~tance** n ammissione f; 'no **~tance**' 'vietato l'ingresso'. **~tedly** adv bisogna riconoscerlo

admonish /ədˈmɒnɪʃ/ vt ammonire

ado /əˈduː/ n without more ~ senza ulteriori indugi

adolescen|ce /ædəˈlesns/ n adolescenza f. **~t** adj & n adolescente mf

adopt /əˈdɒpt/ vt adottare; (Pol) scegliere (candidate). **~ion** n adozione f. **~ive** adj adottivo

ador|able /əˈdɔːrəbl/ adj adorabile. **~ation** n adorazione f

adore /əˈdɔː(r)/ vt adorare

adrenalin /əˈdrenəlɪn/ n adrenalina f

Adriatic /eɪdrɪˈætɪk/ adj & n the ~ [Sea] il mare Adriatico, l'Adriatico m

adrift /əˈdrɪft/ adj alla deriva; be ~ andare alla deriva; come ~ staccarsi

adult /ˈædʌlt/ n adulto, -a mf

adultery /əˈdʌltəri/ n adulterio m

advance /ədˈvɑːns/ n avanzamento m; (Mil) avanzata f; (payment) anticipo m; in ~ in anticipo ● vi avanzare; (make progress) fare progressi ● vt avanzare (theory); promuovere (cause); anticipare (money). **~ booking** n prenotazione f [in anticipo]. **~d** adj avanzato. **~ment** n promozione f

advantage /ədˈvɑːntɪdʒ/ n vantaggio m; take ~ of approfittare di. **~ous** adj vantaggioso

advent /ˈædvent/ n avvento m

adventur|e /ədˈventʃə(r)/ n avventura f. **~ous** adj avventuroso

adverb /ˈædvɜːb/ n avverbio m

adversary /ˈædvəsəri/ n avversario, -a f

advers|e /ˈædvɜːs/ adj avverso. **~ity** n avversità f

advert /ˈædvɜːt/ n ① = advertisement

advertise /ˈædvətaɪz/ vt reclamizzare; mettere un annuncio per (job, flat) ● vi fare pubblicità; (for job, flat) mettere un annuncio

advertisement /ədˈvɜːtɪsmənt/ n pubblicità f inv; (in paper) inserzione f, annuncio m

advertis|er /ˈædvətaɪzə(r)/ n (in newspaper) inserzionista mf. **~ing** n pubblicità f ● attrib pubblicitario

advice /ədˈvaɪs/ n consigli mpl; piece of ~ consiglio m

advisable /ədˈvaɪzəbl/ adj consigliabile

advis|e /ədˈvaɪz/ vt consigliare; (inform) avvisare; **~e sb to do** sth consigliare a qcno di fare qcsa; **~e sb against** sth sconsigliare qcsa a qcno. **~er** n consulente mf. **~ory** adj consultivo

advocate¹ /ˈædvəkət/ n (supporter) fautore, -trice mf

advocate² /ˈædvəkeɪt/ vt propugnare

aerial /ˈeərɪəl/ adj aereo ● n antenna f

aerobics /eəˈrəʊbɪks/ n aerobica fsg

aero|drome /ˈeərədrəʊm/ n aerodromo m. **~plane** n aeroplano m

aerosol /ˈeərəsɒl/ n bomboletta f spray

aesthetic /iːsˈθetɪk/ adj estetico

afar /əˈfɑː(r)/ adv from ~ da lontano

affable /ˈæfəbl/ adj affabile

affair /əˈfeə(r)/ n affare m; (scandal) caso m; (sexual) relazione f

affect /əˈfekt/ vt influire su; (emotionally) colpire; (concern) riguardare.

~**ation** n affettazione f. ~**ed** adj affettato

affection /əˈfekʃn/ n affetto m. ~**ate** adj affettuoso

affirm /əˈfɜːm/ vt affermare; (Jur) dichiarare solennemente

affirmative /əˈfɜːmətɪv/ adj affermativo ●n in the ~ affermativamente

afflict /əˈflɪkt/ vt affliggere. ~**ion** n afflizione f

affluen|ce /ˈæfluəns/ n agiatezza f. ~**t** adj agiato

afford /əˈfɔːd/ vt be able to ~ sth potersi permettere qcsa. ~**able** adj abbordabile

affront /əˈfrʌnt/ n affronto m

afield /əˈfiːld/ adv further ~ più lontano

afloat /əˈfləʊt/ adj a galla

afraid /əˈfreɪd/ adj be ~ aver paura; I'm ~ not purtroppo no; I'm ~ so temo di sì; I'm ~ I can't help you mi dispiace, ma non posso esserle d'aiuto

afresh /əˈfreʃ/ adv da capo

Africa /ˈæfrɪkə/ n Africa f. ~**n** adj & n africano, -a f

after /ˈɑːftə(r)/ adv dopo; the day ~ il giorno dopo; be ~ cercare ●prep dopo; ~ all dopotutto; the day ~ tomorrow dopodomani ●conj dopo che

after: ~**-effect** n conseguenza f. ~**math** /-mɑːθ/ n conseguenze fpl; the ~math of war il dopoguerra; in the ~math of the period successivo a. ~**noon** n pomeriggio m; good ~noon! buon giorno!. ~**shave** n [lozione f.] dopobarba m inv. ~**thought** n added as an ~thought aggiunto in un secondo momento; ~**wards** adv in seguito

again /əˈgen/ adv di nuovo; [then] ~ (besides) inoltre; (on the other hand) d'altra parte; ~ and ~ continuamente

against /əˈgenst/ prep contro

age /eɪdʒ/ n età f inv; (era) era f; ~s 🗓 secoli; what ~ are you? quanti anni hai?; be under ~ non avere l'età richiesta; he's two years of ~ ha due anni ●vt/i (pres p ageing) invecchiare

aged[1] /eɪdʒd/ adj ~ two di due anni

aged[2] /ˈeɪdʒɪd/ adj anziano ●n the ~ pl gli anziani

agency /ˈeɪdʒənsi/ n agenzia f; have the ~ for essere un concessionario di

agenda /əˈdʒendə/ n ordine m del giorno; on the ~ all'ordine del giorno; fig in programma

agent /ˈeɪdʒənt/ n agente mf

aggravat|e /ˈægrəveɪt/ vt aggravare; (annoy) esasperare. ~**ion** n aggravamento m; (annoyance) esasperazione f

aggress|ion /əˈgreʃn/ n aggressione f. ~**ive** adj aggressivo. ~**iveness** n aggressività f. ~**or** n aggressore m

aghast /əˈgɑːst/ adj inorridito

agil|e /ˈædʒaɪl/ adj agile. ~**ity** n agilità f

agitat|e /ˈædʒɪteɪt/ vt mettere in agitazione; (shake) agitare ●vi fig ~e for creare delle agitazioni per. ~**ed** adj agitato. ~**ion** n agitazione f. ~**or** n agitatore, -trice mf

ago /əˈgəʊ/ adv fa; a long time/a month ~ molto tempo/un mese fa

agoniz|e /ˈægənaɪz/ vi angosciarsi (over per). ~**ing** adj angosciante

agony /ˈægəni/ n agonia f; (mental) angoscia f; be in ~ avere dei dolori atroci

agree /əˈgriː/ vt accordarsi su; ~ to do sth accettare di fare qcsa; ~ that essere d'accordo [sul fatto] che ●vi essere d'accordo; (figures:) concordare; (*reach agreement*) mettersi d'accordo; (*get on*) andare d'accordo; (*consent*) acconsentire (to a); it doesn't ~ with me mi fa male; ~ with sth (*approve of*) approvare qcsa

agreeable /əˈgriːəbl/ adj gradevole; (*willing*) d'accordo

agreed /əˈgriːd/ adj convenuto

agreement /əˈgriːmənt/ n accordo m; in ~ d'accordo

agricultur|al /ægrɪˈkʌltʃərəl/ adj agricolo. ~e n agricoltura f

aground /əˈgraʊnd/ adv run ~ (ship:) arenarsi

ahead /əˈhed/ adv avanti; be ~ of essere davanti a; fig essere avanti rispetto a; draw ~ passare davanti (of a); get ~ (*in life*) riuscire; go ~! fai pure!; look ~ pensare all'avvenire; plan ~ fare progetti per l'avvenire

aid /eɪd/ n aiuto m; in ~ of a favore di ● vt aiutare

Aids /eɪdz/ n AIDS m

aim /eɪm/ n mira f; fig scopo m; take ~ prendere la mira ● vt puntare (gun) (at contro) ● vi mirare; ~ to do sth aspirare a fare qcsa. ~less adj, ~lessly adv senza scopo

air /eə(r)/ n aria f; be on the ~ (*programme:*) essere in onda; put on ~s darsi delle arie; by ~ in aereo; (*airmail*) per via aerea ● vt arieggiare; fig far conoscere (views)

air: ~-conditioned adj con aria condizionata. ~-conditioning n aria f condizionata. ~craft n aereo m. ~craft carrier n portaerei f inv. ~field n campo m d'aviazione. ~ force n aviazione f. ~ freshener n deodorante m per l'ambiente. ~gun n fucile m pneumatico. ~ hostess n hostess f inv. ~ in compagnia f aerea. ~mail n posta f aerea. ~plane n Am aereo m. ~port n aeroporto m. ~tight adj ermetico. ~-traffic controller n controllore m

di volo

airy /ˈeəri/ adj (-ier, -iest) arieggiato; (*manner*) noncurante

aisle /aɪl/ n corridoio m; (*in supermarket*) corsia f; (*in church*) navata f

ajar /əˈdʒɑː(r)/ adj socchiuso

alarm /əˈlɑːm/ n allarme m; set the ~ (*of alarm clock*) mettere la sveglia ● vt allarmare. ~ clock n sveglia f

Albania /ælˈbeɪnɪə/ n Albania f

album /ˈælbəm/ n album m inv

alcohol /ˈælkəhɒl/ n alcol m. ~ic adj alcolico ● n alcolizzato, -a mf. ~ism n alcolismo m

alcove /ˈælkəʊv/ n alcova f

alert /əˈlɜːt/ adj sveglio; (*watchful*) vigile ● n segnale m d'allarme; be on the ~ stare allerta ● vt allertare

algebra /ˈældʒɪbrə/ n algebra f

Algeria /ælˈdʒɪərɪə/ n Algeria f. ~n adj & n algerino, -a mf

alias /ˈeɪlɪəs/ n pseudonimo m ● adv alias

alibi /ˈælɪbaɪ/ n alibi m inv

alien /ˈeɪlɪən/ adj straniero; fig estraneo ● n straniero, -a mf; (*from space*) alieno, -a mf

alienat|e /ˈeɪlɪəneɪt/ vt alienare. ~ion n alienazione f

alight[1] /əˈlaɪt/ vi scendere; (bird:) posarsi

alight[2] adj be ~ essere in fiamme; set ~ dar fuoco a

align /əˈlaɪn/ vt allineare. ~ment n allineamento m; out of ~ment non allineato

alike /əˈlaɪk/ adj simile; be ~ rassomigliarsi ● adv in modo simile; look ~ rassomigliarsi; summer and winter ~ sia d'estate che d'inverno

alimony /ˈælɪmənɪ/ n alimenti mpl

alive /əˈlaɪv/ adj vivo; ~ with brulicante di; ~ to sensibile a; ~ and kicking vivo e vegeto

alkali /ˈælkəlaɪ/ n alcali m

all /ɔːl/.

● adj tutto; ~ the children, ~ children tutti i bambini; ~ day tutto il giorno; he refused to help ha rifiutato qualsiasi aiuto; for ~ that (nevertheless) ciononostante; in ~ sincerity in tutta sincerità; be ~ for essere favorevole a

● pron tutto; ~ of you/them tutti voi/loro; ~ of it tutto; ~ of the town tutta la città; in ~ tutto; ~ in ~ tutto sommato; most of ~ più di ogni altra cosa; once and for ~ una volta per tutte

● adv completamente; ~ but quasi; ~ at once (at the same time) tutto in una volta; ~ at once, ~ of a sudden all'improvviso; ~ too soon troppo presto; ~ the same (nevertheless) ciononostante; ~ the better meglio ancora; she's not ~ that good an actress non è poi così brava come attrice; ~ in tutto; 🄣 esausto; thirty-three ~ (in sport) trenta/tre pari; ~ over (finished) tutto finito; (everywhere) dappertutto; it's ~ right (I don't mind) non fa niente; I'm ~ right (not hurt) non ho niente; ~ right! va bene!

allay /əˈleɪ/ vt placare (suspicions, anger)

allegation /ælɪˈɡeɪʃn/ n accusa f

allege /əˈledʒ/ vt dichiarare. ~d adj presunto. ~dly adv a quanto si dice

allegiance /əˈliːdʒəns/ n fedeltà f

allerg|ic /əˈlɜːdʒɪk/ adj allergico. ~y n allergia f

alleviate /əˈliːvɪeɪt/ vt alleviare

alley /ˈælɪ/ n vicolo m; (for bowling) corsia f

alliance /əˈlaɪəns/ n alleanza f

alligator /ˈælɪɡeɪtə(r)/ n alligatore m

allocat|e /ˈæləkeɪt/ vt assegnare; distribuire (resources). ~ion n assegnazione f; (of resources) distribuzione f

allot /əˈlɒt/ vt (pt/pp allotted) distribuire. ~ment n distribuzione f; (share) parte f; (land) piccolo lotto m di terreno

allow /əˈlaʊ/ vt permettere; (grant) accordare; (reckon on) contare; (agree) ammettere; ~ for tener conto di; ~ sb to do sth permettere a qcno di fare qcsa; you are not ~ed to... è vietato...

allowance /əˈlaʊəns/ n sussidio m; (Am: pocket money) paghetta f; (for petrol etc) indennità f inv; (of luggage, duty free) limite m; make ~s for essere indulgente verso (sb); tener conto di (sth)

alloy /ˈælɔɪ/ n lega f

allusion /əˈluːʒn/ n allusione f

ally[1] /ˈælaɪ/ n alleato, -a mf

ally[2] /əˈlaɪ/ vt (pt/pp -ied) alleare; ~ oneself with allearsi con

almighty /ɔːlˈmaɪtɪ/ adj (🄘: big) mega inv ● the A~ l'Onnipotente m

almond /ˈɑːmənd/ n mandorla f; (tree) mandorlo m

almost /ˈɔːlməʊst/ adv quasi

alone /əˈləʊn/ adj solo; leave me ~! lasciami in pace!; let ~ (not to mention) figurarsi e oltre a

along /əˈlɒŋ/ prep lungo ● adv ~ with assieme a; all ~ tutto il tempo; come ~! (hurry up) vieni qui!; I'll be ~ in a minute arrivo tra un attimo; move ~ spostarsi; move ~! circolare!

along|side adv lungo bordo ● prep lungo; work ~ sb lavorare fianco a fianco con qcno

aloof /əˈluːf/ adj distante

aloud /əˈlaʊd/ adv ad alta voce

alphabet /ˈælfəbet/ n alfabeto m. ~ical adj alfabetico

Alps /ælps/ npl Alpi fpl

already /ɔːlˈredɪ/ adv già

Alsatian /ælˈseɪʃn/ n (dog) pastore m tedesco

also /ˈɔːlsəʊ/ adv anche; ∼, I need...' [e] inoltre, ho bisogno di...

altar /ˈɔːltə(r)/ n altare m

alter /ˈɔːltə(r)/ vt cambiare; aggiustare (clothes) ● vi cambiare. ∼ation n modifica f

alternate[1] /ˈɔːltənert/ vi alternarsi ● vt alternare

alternate[2] /ɔːlˈtɜːnət/ adj alterno; on ∼ days a giorni alterni

alternative /ɔːlˈtɜːnətɪv/ adj alternativo ● n alternativa f. ∼ly adv alternativamente

although /ɔːlˈðəʊ/ conj benché, sebbene

altitude /ˈæltɪtjuːd/ n altitudine f

altogether /ɔːltəˈɡeðə(r)/ adv (in all) in tutto; (completely) completamente; I'm not ∼ sure non sono del tutto sicuro

aluminium /æljʊˈmɪnɪəm/ n, Ám **aluminum** /əˈluːmɪnəm/ n alluminio m

always /ˈɔːlweɪz/ adv sempre

am /æm/ ▷ BE

a.m. abbr (ante meridiem) del mattino

amalgamate /əˈmælɡəmeɪt/ vt fondere ● vi fondersi

amass /əˈmæs/ vt accumulare

amateur /ˈæmətə(r)/ n non professionista mf; pej dilettante mf ● attrib dilettante; ∼ dramatics filodrammatica f. ∼ish adj dilettantesco

amaze /əˈmeɪz/ vt stupire. ∼d adj stupito. ∼ment n stupore m

amazing /əˈmeɪzɪŋ/ adj incredibile

ambassador /æmˈbæsədə(r)/ n ambasciatore, -trice mf

ambigu|ity /æmbɪˈɡjuːətɪ/ n ambiguità f inv. ∼ous adj ambiguo

ambiti|on /æmˈbɪʃn/ n ambizione

f; (aim) aspirazione f. ∼ous adj ambizioso

ambivalent /æmˈbɪvələnt/ adj ambivalente

amble /ˈæmbl/ vi camminare senza fretta

ambulance /ˈæmbjʊləns/ n ambulanza f

ambush /ˈæmbʊʃ/ n imboscata f ● vt tendere un'imboscata a

amend /əˈmend/ vt modificare. ∼ment n modifica f. ∼s npl make ∼s fare ammenda (for di, per)

amenities /əˈmiːnətɪz/ npl comodità fpl

America /əˈmerɪkə/ n America f. ∼n adj & n americano, -a mf

amiable /ˈeɪmɪəbl/ adj amabile

amicable /ˈæmɪkəbl/ adj amichevole

ammonia /əˈməʊnɪə/ n ammoniaca f

ammunition /æmjʊˈnɪʃn/ n munizioni fpl

amnesty /ˈæmnəstɪ/ n amnistia f

among[st] /əˈmʌŋ[st]/ prep tra, fra

amount /əˈmaʊnt/ n quantità f inv; (sum of money) importo m ● vi ∼ to ammontare a; fig equivalere a

amphibi|an /æmˈfɪbɪən/ n anfibio m. ∼ous adj anfibio

amphitheatre /ˈæmfɪ-/ n anfiteatro m

ampl|e /ˈæmpl/ adj (large) grande; (proportions) ampio; (enough)

a

largamente sufficiente

amplif|ier /ˈæmplɪfaɪə(r)/ n amplificatore m. ~y vt (pt/pp -ied) amplificare (sound)

amputate /ˈæmpjʊteɪt/ vt amputare. ~ion n amputazione f

amuse /əˈmjuːz/ vt divertire. ~ment n divertimento m. ~ment arcade n sala f giochi

amusing /əˈmjuːzɪŋ/ adj divertente

an /ən/, accentato /æn/ ▷A

anaem|ia /əˈniːmɪə/ n anemia f. ~ic adj anemico

anaesthetic /ænəsˈθetɪk/ n anestesia f

anaesthet|ist /əˈniːsθətɪst/ n anestesista f

analogy /əˈnælədʒɪ/ n analogia f

analyse /ˈænəlaɪz/ vt analizzare

analysis /əˈnæləsɪs/ n analisi f inv

analyst /ˈænəlɪst/ n analista mf

analytical /ænəˈlɪtɪkl/ adj analitico

anarch|ist /ˈænəkɪst/ n anarchico, -a mf. ~y n anarchia f

anatom|ical /ænəˈtɒmɪkl/ adj anatomico. ~ically adv anatomicamente. ~y n anatomia f

ancestor /ˈænsestə(r)/ n antenato, -a mf. ~ry n antenati mpl

anchor /ˈæŋkə(r)/ n ancora f • vi gettar l'ancora • vt ancorare

anchovy /ˈæntʃəvɪ/ n acciuga f

ancient /ˈeɪnʃənt/ adj antico; ⊤ vecchio

ancillary /ænˈsɪlərɪ/ adj ausiliario

and /ənd/, accentato /ænd/ conj e; two ~ two due più due; six hundred ~ two seicentodue; more ~ more sempre più; nice ~ warm bello caldo; try ~ come cerca di venire; go ~ get vai a prendere

anecdote /ˈænɪkdəʊt/ n aneddoto m

anew /əˈnjuː/ adv di nuovo

angel /ˈeɪndʒl/ n angelo m. ~ic adj angelico

anger /ˈæŋɡə(r)/ n rabbia f • vt far arrabbiare

angle¹ /ˈæŋɡl/ n angolo m; fig angolazione f; at an ~ storto

angle² vi pescare con la lenza; ~ for fig cercare di ottenere. ~r n pescatore, -trice mf

Anglican /ˈæŋɡlɪkən/ adj & n anglicano, -a mf

angr|y /ˈæŋɡrɪ/ adj (-ier, -iest) arrabbiato; get ~y arrabbiarsi; ~y with or at sb arrabbiato con qcno; ~y at or about sth arrabbiato per qcsa. ~ily adv rabbiosamente

anguish /ˈæŋɡwɪʃ/ n angoscia f

animal /ˈænɪml/ adj & n animale m

animate¹ /ˈænɪmət/ adj animato

animat|e² /ˈænɪmeɪt/ vt animare. ~ed adj animato; (person) vivace. ~ion n animazione f

animosity /ænɪˈmɒsətɪ/ n animosità f inv

ankle /ˈæŋkl/ n caviglia f

annihilat|e /əˈnaɪəleɪt/ vt annientare. ~ion n annientamento m

anniversary /ænɪˈvɜːsərɪ/ n anniversario m

announce /əˈnaʊns/ vt annunciare. ~ment n annuncio m. ~r n annunciatore, -trice mf

annoy /əˈnɔɪ/ vt dare fastidio a; get ~ed essere infastidito. ~ance n seccatura f; (anger) irritazione f. ~ing adj fastidioso

annual /ˈænjʊəl/ adj annuale; (income) annuo • n (Bot) pianta f annua; (children's book) almanacco m

annul /əˈnʌl/ vt (pt/pp annulled) annullare

anonymous /əˈnɒnɪməs/ adj anonimo

anorak /ˈænəræk/ n giacca f a vento

another /əˈnʌðə(r)/ adj & pron; ~ [one] un altro, un'altra; in ~ way diversamente; one ~ l'un l'altro

answer /ˈɑːnsə(r)/ n risposta f; (solution) soluzione f ● vt rispondere a (person, question, letter); esaudire (prayer); ~ the door aprire la porta; ~ the telephone rispondere al telefono ● vi rispondere; ~ back ribattere; ~ for rispondere di. ~able adj responsabile; be ~able to sb rispondere a qcno. ~ing machine n (Teleph) segreteria f telefonica

ant /ænt/ n formica f

antagonis|m /ænˈtægənɪzm/ n antagonismo m. ~tic adj antagonistico

antagonize /ænˈtægənaɪz/ vt provocare l'ostilità di

Antarctic /ænˈtɑːktɪk/ n Antartico m ● adj antartico

antenatal /æntɪˈneɪtl/ adj prenatale

antenna /ænˈtenə/ n antenna f

anthem /ˈænθəm/ n inno m

anthology /ænˈθɒlədʒɪ/ n antologia f

anthropology /ænθrəˈpɒlədʒɪ/ n antropologia f

anti-aircraft /æntɪ-/ adj antiaereo

antibiotic /æntɪbaɪˈɒtɪk/ n antibiotico m

anticipat|e /ænˈtɪsɪpeɪt/ vt prevedere; (forestall) anticipare. ~ion /-ˈpeɪʃn/ n anticipo m; (excitement) attesa f

anti'climax n delusione f

anti'clockwise adj & adv in senso antiorario

antidote /ˈæntɪdəʊt/ n antidoto m

'antifreeze n antigelo m

antiquated /ˈæntɪkweɪtɪd/ adj antiquato

antique /ænˈtiːk/ adj antico ● n antichità f inv. ~ dealer n antiquario, -a mf

antiquity /ænˈtɪkwətɪ/ n antichità f

anti'septic adj & n antisettico m

anti'social adj (behaviour) antisociale; (person) asociale

antlers /ˈæntləz/ npl corna fpl

anus /ˈeɪnəs/ n ano m

anxiety /æŋˈzaɪətɪ/ n ansia f

anxious /ˈæŋkʃəs/ adj ansioso. ~ly adv con ansia

any /ˈenɪ/

● adj (no matter which) qualsiasi, qualunque; ~ colour/number you like qualsiasi colore/numero ti piaccia; we don't have ~ wine/biscuits non abbiamo vino/biscotti; for ~ reason per qualsiasi ragione

any is often not translated: have we ~ wine/biscuits? abbiamo del vino/dei biscotti?

● pron (some) ne; (no matter which) uno qualsiasi; I don't want ~ [of it] non ne voglio [nessuno]; there aren't ~ non ce ne sono; have we ~? ne abbiamo?; have you read ~ of her books? hai letto qualcuno dei suoi libri?

● adv I can't go ~ quicker non posso andare più in fretta; is it ~ better? va un po' meglio?; would you like ~ more? ne vuoi ancora?; I can't eat ~ more non posso mangiare più niente

'anybody pron chiunque; (after negative) nessuno; I haven't seen ~ non ho visto nessuno

'anyhow adv ad ogni modo, comunque; (badly) non importa come

'anyone pron = anybody

'anything pron qualche cosa, qualcosa; (no matter which) qualsiasi cosa; (after negative) niente; take/buy ~ you like prendi/compra quello che vuoi; I don't remember ~ non mi ricordo niente; he's ~ but stupid è tutto, ma non stupido; I'll do ~ but that farò qualsiasi cosa, tranne quello

anyway /ˈenɪweɪ/ adv ad ogni modo, comunque

anywhere /ˈenɪweə(r)/ adv dovunque; (after negative) da nessuna parte; put it ~ mettilo dove vuoi; I can't find it ~ non lo trovo da nessuna parte; ~ else da qualch'altra parte; (after negative) da nessun'altra parte; I don't want to go ~ else non voglio andare da nessun'altra parte

apart /əˈpɑːt/ adv lontano; live ~ vivere separati; 100 miles ~ lontani 100 miglia; ~ from a parte; you can't tell them ~ non si possono distinguere; joking ~ scherzi a parte

apartment /əˈpɑːtmənt/ n (Am: flat) appartamento m; in my ~ a casa mia

apathy /ˈæpəθɪ/ n apatia f

ape /eɪp/ n scimmia f ● vt scimmiottare

aperitif /əˈperətɪːf/ n aperitivo m

aperture /ˈæpətʃə(r)/ n apertura f

apex /ˈeɪpeks/ n vertice m

apologetic /əˌpɒləˈdʒetɪk/ adj (air, remark) di scusa; be ~ essere spiacente

apologize /əˈpɒlədʒaɪz/ vi scusarsi (for per)

apology /əˈpɒlədʒɪ/ n scusa f; fig an ~ for a dinner una sottospecie di cena

apostle /əˈpɒsl/ n apostolo m

apostrophe /əˈpɒstrəfɪ/ n apostrofo m

appal /əˈpɔːl/ vt (pt/pp appalled) sconvolgere. ~ling adj sconvolgente

apparatus /æpəˈreɪtəs/ n apparato m

apparent /əˈpærənt/ adj evidente; (seeming) apparente. ~ly adv apparentemente

apparition /æpəˈrɪʃn/ n apparizione f

appeal /əˈpiːl/ n appello m; (attraction) attrattiva f ● vi fare appello; ~

to (be attractive to) attrarre. ~ing adj attraente

appear /əˈpɪə(r)/ vi apparire; (seem) sembrare; (publication:) uscire; (Theat) esibirsi. ~ance n apparizione f; (look) aspetto m; to all ~ances a giudicare dalle apparenze; keep up ~ances salvare le apparenze

appease /əˈpiːz/ vt placare

appendicitis /əˌpendɪˈsaɪtɪs/ n appendicite f

appendix /əˈpendɪks/ n (pl -ices /-ɪsiːz/) (of book) appendice f; (pl -es) (Anat) appendice f

appetite /ˈæpɪtaɪt/ n appetito m

applau|d /əˈplɔːd/ vt/i applaudire. ~se n applauso m

apple /ˈæpl/ n mela f. ~-tree n melo m

appliance /əˈplaɪəns/ n attrezzo m; [electrical] ~ elettrodomestico m

applicable /ˈæplɪkəbl/ adj be ~ to essere valido per; not ~ (on form) non applicabile

applicant /ˈæplɪkənt/ n candidato, -a mf

application /æplɪˈkeɪʃn/ n applicazione f; (request) domanda f; (for job) candidatura f. ~ form n modulo m di domanda

applied /əˈplaɪd/ adj applicato

apply /əˈplaɪ/ vt (pt/pp -ied) applicare; ~ oneself applicarsi ● vi applicarsi; (law:) essere applicabile; ~ to (ask) rivolgersi a; ~ for fare domanda per (job etc)

appoint /əˈpɔɪnt/ vt nominare; fissare (time). ~ment n appuntamento m; (to job) nomina f; (job) posto m

appraisal /əˈpreɪz(ə)l/ n valutazione f

appreciable /əˈpriːʃəbl/ adj sensibile

appreciat|e /əˈpriːʃɪeɪt/ vt apprezzare; (understand) comprendere ● vi (increase in value) aumentare di valore.

~ion n (gratitude) riconoscenza f; (enjoyment) apprezzamento m; (understanding) comprensione f; (in value) aumento m. ~ive adj riconoscente

apprehens|ion /æprɪˈhenʃn/ n arresto m; (fear) apprensione f. ~ive adj apprensivo

apprentice /əˈprentɪs/ n apprendista mf. ~ship n apprendistato m

approach /əˈprəʊtʃ/ n avvicinamento m; (to problem) approccio m; (access) accesso m; make ~es to fare degli approcci con ● vi avvicinarsi ● vt avvicinarsi a; (with request) rivolgersi a; affrontare (problem). ~able adj accessibile

appropriate¹ /əˈprəʊprɪət/ adj appropriato

appropriate² /əˈprəʊprɪeɪt/ vt appropriarsi di

approval /əˈpruːvl/ n approvazione f; on ~ in prova

approv|e /əˈpruːv/ vt approvare ● vi ~e of approvare (sth); avere una buona opinione di (sb). ~ing adj (smile, nod) d'approvazione

approximate /əˈprɒksɪmət/ adj approssimativo. ~ly adv approssimativamente

approximation /əprɒksɪˈmeɪʃn/ n approssimazione f

apricot /ˈeɪprɪkɒt/ n albicocca f

April /ˈeɪprəl/ n aprile m; ~ Fool's Day il primo d'aprile

apron /ˈeɪprən/ n grembiule m

apt /æpt/ adj appropriato; be ~ to do sth avere tendenza a fare qcsa

aptitude /ˈæptɪtjuːd/ n disposizione f. ~ test n test m inv attitudinale

aquarium /əˈkweərɪəm/ n acquario m

Aquarius /əˈkweərɪəs/ n (Astr) Acquario m

aquatic /əˈkwætɪk/ adj acquatico

Arab /ˈærəb/ adj & n arabo, -a mf. ~ian adj arabo

Arabic /ˈærəbɪk/ adj arabo; ~ numerals numeri mpl arabici ● n arabo m

arable /ˈærəbl/ adj coltivabile

arbitrary /ˈɑːbɪtrərɪ/ adj arbitrario

arbitrat|e /ˈɑːbɪtreɪt/ vi arbitrare. ~ion n arbitraggio m

arc /ɑːk/ n arco m

arcade /ɑːˈkeɪd/ n portico m; (shops) galleria f

arch /ɑːtʃ/ n arco m; (of foot) dorso m del piede

archaeological /ɑːkɪəˈlɒdʒɪkl/ adj archeologico

archaeolog|ist /ɑːkɪˈɒlədʒɪst/ n archeologo, -a mf. ~y n archeologia f

archaic /ɑːˈkeɪɪk/ adj arcaico

arch'bishop /ɑːtʃˈ-/ n arcivescovo m

architect /ˈɑːkɪtekt/ n architetto m. ~ural adj architettonico

architecture /ˈɑːkɪtektʃə(r)/ n architettura f

archives /ˈɑːkaɪvz/ npl archivi mpl

archway /ˈɑːtʃweɪ/ n arco m

Arctic /ˈɑːktɪk/ adj artico ● n the ~ l'Artico

ardent /ˈɑːdənt/ adj ardente

arduous /ˈɑːdjʊəs/ adj arduo

are /ɑː(r)/ ▷ BE

area /ˈeərɪə/ n area f; (region) zona f; (fig: field) campo m. ~ code n prefisso m [telefonico]

arena /əˈriːnə/ n arena f

Argentina /ɑːdʒənˈtiːnə/ n Argentina f

Argentinian /-ˈtɪnɪən/ adj & n argentino, -a mf

argue /ˈɑːgjuː/ vi litigare (about su); (debate) dibattere; don't ~! non discutere! ● vt (debate) dibattere; (reason) ~ that sostenere che

argument /ˈɑːgjumənt/ n argomento m; (reasoning) ragionamento m; have an ~ litigare. ~ative adj polemico

arid /ˈærɪd/ adj arido

Aries /ˈeəriːz/ n (Astr) Ariete m

arise /əˈraɪz/ vi (pt arose, pp arisen) (opportunity, need, problem:) presentarsi; (result) derivare

aristocracy /ærɪˈstɒkrəsɪ/ n aristocrazia f

aristocrat /ˈærɪstəkræt/ n aristocratico, -a mf. ~ic adj aristocratico

arithmetic /əˈrɪθmətɪk/ n aritmetica f

arm /ɑːm/ n braccio m; (of chair) bracciolo m; ~s pl (weapons) armi fpl; ~ in ~ a braccetto; up in ~s 🖪 furioso (about per) •vt armare

'armchair n poltrona f

armed /ɑːmd/ adj armato; ~ forces forze fpl armate; ~ robbery rapina f a mano armata

armour /ˈɑːmə(r)/ n armatura f. ~ed adj (vehicle) blindato

'armpit n ascella f

army /ˈɑːmɪ/ n esercito m; join the ~ arruolarsi

aroma /əˈrəʊmə/ n aroma f. ~tic adj aromatico

arose /əˈrəʊz/ ▷ ARISE

around /əˈraʊnd/ adv intorno; all ~ tutt'intorno; I'm not from ~ here non sono di qui; he's not ~ non c'è •prep intorno a; in giro per (room, shops, world)

arouse /əˈraʊz/ vt svegliare; (sexually) eccitare

arrange /əˈreɪndʒ/ vt sistemare (furniture, books); organizzare (meeting); fissare (date, time); ~ to do sth combinare di fare qcsa. ~ment n (of furniture) sistemazione f; (Mus) arrangiamento m; (agreement) accordo; (of flowers) composizione f; make ~ments prendere disposizioni

arrears /əˈrɪəz/ npl arretrati mpl; be in ~ essere in arretrato; paid in ~ pagato a lavoro eseguito

arrest /əˈrest/ n arresto m; under ~ in stato d'arresto •vt arrestare

arrival /əˈraɪvl/ n arrivo m; new ~s pl nuovi arrivati mpl

arrive /əˈraɪv/ vi arrivare; ~ at fig raggiungere

arrogan|ce /ˈærəgəns/ n arroganza f. ~t adj arrogante

arrow /ˈærəʊ/ n freccia f

arse /ɑːs/ n 🖪 culo m

arsenic /ˈɑːsənɪk/ n arsenico m

arson /ˈɑːsn/ n incendio m doloso. ~ist n incendiario, -a mf

art /ɑːt/ n arte f; ~s and crafts pl artigianato m; the A~s pl l'arte f; A~s degree (Univ) laurea f in Lettere

artery /ˈɑːtərɪ/ n arteria f

'art gallery n galleria f d'arte

arthritis /ɑːˈθraɪtɪs/ n artrite f

artichoke /ˈɑːtɪtʃəʊk/ n carciofo m

article /ˈɑːtɪkl/ n articolo m; ~ of clothing capo m d'abbigliamento

articulate¹ /ɑːˈtɪkjʊlət/ adj (speech) chiaro; be ~ esprimersi bene

articulate² /ɑːˈtɪkjʊleɪt/ vt scandire (words). ~d lorry n autotreno m

artificial /ɑːtɪˈfɪʃl/ adj artificiale. ~ly adv artificialmente; (smile) artificiosamente

artillery /ɑːˈtɪlərɪ/ n artiglieria f

artist /ˈɑːtɪst/ n artista mf

as /æz/ conj come; (since) siccome; (while) mentre; as he grew older diventando vecchio; as you get to know her conoscendola meglio; young as she is per quanto sia giovane •prep come; as a friend come amico; as a child da bambino; as a foreigner in quanto straniero; disguised as travestito da •adv as well (also) anche; as soon as I get home [non] appena arrivo a casa; as you like quanto te; as quick as you can più veloce che puoi; as far as (distance) fino a; as far as I'm concerned per quanto mi riguarda; as long as finché; (provided that) purché

asbestos /æz'bestɒs/ n amianto m

ascend /ə'send/ vi salire ● vt salire a (throne)

Ascension /ə'senʃn/ n (Relig) Ascensione f

ascent /ə'sent/ n ascesa f

ascertain /æsə'teɪn/ vt accertare

ash¹ /æʃ/ n (tree) frassino m

ash² n cenere f

ashamed /ə'ʃeɪmd/ adj be/feel ~ vergognarsi

ashore /ə'ʃɔː(r)/ adv a terra; go ~ sbarcare

ash: ~tray n portacenere m. **A~ 'Wednesday** n mercoledì m inv delle Ceneri

Asia /'eɪʒə/ n Asia f. **~n** adj & n asiatico, -a m. **~tic** adj asiatico

aside /ə'saɪd/ adv take sb ~ prendere qcno a parte; put sth ~ mettere qcsa da parte; **~ from you** Am a parte te

ask /ɑːsk/ vt fare (question); (invite) invitare; ~ sb sth domandare or chiedere qcsa a qcno; ~ sb to do sth domandare o chiedere a qcno di fare qcsa ● vi ~ about sth informarsi su qcsa; ~ after chiedere [notizie] di; ~ for chiedere (sth); chiedere di (sb); ~ for trouble 🔢 andare in cerca di guai. □ ~ in vt ~ sb in invitare qcno ad entrare. □ ~ out vt ~ sb out chiedere a qcno di uscire

askew /ə'skjuː/ adj & adv di traverso

asleep /ə'sliːp/ adj be ~ dormire; fall ~ addormentarsi

asparagus /ə'spærəgəs/ n asparagi mpl

aspect /'æspekt/ n aspetto m

asphalt /'æsfælt/ n asfalto m

aspire /ə'spaɪə(r)/ vi ~ to aspirare a

ass /æs/ n asino m

assassin /ə'sæsɪn/ n assassino, -a mf. **~ate** vt assassinare. **~ation** n as-

sassinio m

assault /ə'sɔːlt/ n (Mil) assalto m; (Jur) aggressione f ● vt aggredire

assemble /ə'sembl/ vi radunarsi ● vt radunare; (Techn) montare

assembly /ə'semblɪ/ n assemblea f; (Sch) assemblea f giornaliera di alunni e professori di una scuola; (Techn) montaggio m. ~ **line** n catena f di montaggio

assent /ə'sent/ n assenso m ● vi acconsentire

assert /ə'sɜːt/ vt asserire; far valere (one's rights); ~ **oneself** farsi valere. **~ion** n asserzione f. **~ive** adj be ~ive farsi valere

assess /ə'ses/ vt valutare; (for tax purposes) stabilire l'imponibile di. **~ment** n valutazione f; (of tax) accertamento m

asset /'æset/ n (advantage) vantaggio m; (person) elemento m prezioso. **~s** pl beni mpl; (on balance sheet) attivo msg

assign /ə'saɪn/ vt assegnare. **~ment** n (task) incarico m

assimilate /ə'sɪmɪleɪt/ vt assimilare; integrare (person)

assist /ə'sɪst/ vt/i assistere; ~ **sb to do sth** assistere qcno nel fare qcsa. **~ance** n assistenza f. **~ant** adj **~ant manager** vicedirettore, -trice mf ● n assistente mf; (in shop) commesso, -a mf

associate¹ /ə'səʊʃɪeɪt/ vt associare (with a); be **~ed with sth** (involved in) essere coinvolto in qcsa ● vi ~e **with** frequentare. **~ion** n associazione f. **A~ion 'Football** n [gioco m del] calcio m

associate² /ə'səʊʃɪət/ adj associato ● n collega m/; (member) socio, -a mf

assort|ed /ə'sɔːtɪd/ adj assortito. **~ment** n assortimento m

assum|e /ə'sjuːm/ vt presumere; assumere (control); **~e office** entrare in carica; **~ing that you're right,....**

assumption /əˈsʌmpʃn/ n supposizione f; **on the ~ that** partendo dal presupposto che; **the A~** (Relig) l'Assunzione f

assurance /əˈʃʊərəns/ n assicurazione f; (confidence) sicurezza f

assure /əˈʃʊə(r)/ vt assicurare. **~d** adj sicuro

asterisk /ˈæstərɪsk/ n asterisco m

asthma /ˈæsmə/ n asma f. **~tic** adj asmatico

astonish /əˈstɒnɪʃ/ vt stupire. **~ing** adj stupefacente. **~ment** n stupore m

astound /əˈstaʊnd/ vt stupire

astray /əˈstreɪ/ adv **go ~** smarrirsi; (morally) uscire dalla retta via; **lead ~** traviare

astronaut /ˈæstrənɔːt/ n astronauta mf

astronom|er /əˈstrɒnəmə(r)/ n astronomo, -a mf. **~ical** adj astronomico. **~y** n astronomia f

astute /əˈstjuːt/ adj astuto

asylum /əˈsaɪləm/ n [political] **~** asilo m politico; [lunatic] **~** manicomio m

at /æt/, accentato /æt/ prep a; **at the station/the market** alla stazione/al mercato; **at the office/the bank** in ufficio/banca; **at the beginning** all'inizio; **at John's** da John; **at the hairdresser's** dal parrucchiere; **at home** a casa; **at work** al lavoro; **at school** a scuola; **at a party/wedding** a una festa/un matrimonio; **at 1 o'clock** all'una; **at 50 km an hour** a 50 all'ora; **at Christmas/Easter** a Natale/Pasqua; **at times** talvolta; **two at a time** due alla volta; **good at languages** bravo nelle lingue; **at sb's request** su richiesta di qcno; **are you at all worried?** sei preoccupato?

ate /et/ ▷EAT

atheist /ˈeɪθɪɪst/ n ateo, -a mf

athlet|e /ˈæθliːt/ n atleta mf. **~ic** adj atletico. **~ics** n atletica fsg

Atlantic /ətˈlæntɪk/ adj & n **the ~** [Ocean] l'[Oceano m] Atlantico m

atlas /ˈætləs/ n atlante m

atmospher|e /ˈætməsfɪə(r)/ n atmosfera f. **~ic** adj atmosferico

atom /ˈætəm/ n atomo m. **~ bomb** n bomba f atomica

atomic /əˈtɒmɪk/ adj atomico

atrocious /əˈtrəʊʃəs/ adj atroce; (meal, weather) abominevole

atrocity /əˈtrɒsəti/ n atrocità f inv

attach /əˈtætʃ/ vt attaccare; attribuire (importance); **be ~ed to** fig essere attaccato a

attachment /əˈtætʃmənt/ n (affection) attaccamento m; (accessory) accessorio m; (to email) allegato m

attack /əˈtæk/ n attacco m; (physical) aggressione f • vt attaccare; (physically) aggredire. **~er** n assalitore, -trice m; (critic) detrattore, -trice mf

attain /əˈteɪn/ vt realizzare (ambition); raggiungere (success, age, goal)

attempt /əˈtempt/ n tentativo m • vt tentare

attend /əˈtend/ vt essere presente a; (go regularly to) frequentare; (doctor:) avere in cura • vi essere presente; (pay attention) prestare attenzione. □ **~ to** vt occuparsi di; (in shop) servire. **~ance** n presenza f. **~ant** n guardiano, -a mf

attention /əˈtenʃn/ n attenzione f; **~!** (Mil) attenti!; **pay ~** prestare attenzione; **need ~** aver bisogno di attenzioni; (skin, hair, plant:) dover essere curato; (car, tyres:) dover essere riparato; **for the ~ of** all'attenzione di

attentive /əˈtentɪv/ adj (pupil, audience) attento

attic /ˈætɪk/ n soffitta f

attitude /ˈætɪtjuːd/ n atteggiamento m

attorney /əˈtɜːnɪ/ n (Am: lawyer) avvocato m; power of ~ delega f

attract /əˈtrækt/ vt attirare. ~ion n attrazione f; (feature) attrattiva f. ~ive adj (person) attraente; (proposal, price) allettante

attribute¹ /ˈætrɪbjuːt/ n attributo m

attribute² /əˈtrɪbjuːt/ vt attribuire

aubergine /ˈəʊbəʒiːn/ n melanzana f

auction /ˈɔːkʃn/ n asta f • vt vendere all'asta. ~eer n banditore m

audaci|ous /ɔːˈdeɪʃəs/ adj sfacciato; (daring) audace. ~ty n sfacciataggine f; (daring) audacia f

audible /ˈɔːdəbl/ adj udibile

audience /ˈɔːdɪəns/ n (Theat) pubblico m; (TV) telespettatori mpl; (Radio) ascoltatori mpl; (meeting) udienza f

audit /ˈɔːdɪt/ n verifica f del bilancio • vt verificare

audition /ɔːˈdɪʃn/ n audizione f • vi fare un'audizione

auditor /ˈɔːdɪtə(r)/ n revisore m di conti

auditorium /ɔːdɪˈtɔːrɪəm/ n sala f

augment /ɔːgˈment/ vt aumentare

augur /ˈɔːgə(r)/ vi ~ well/ill essere di buon/cattivo augurio

August /ˈɔːgəst/ n agosto m

aunt /ɑːnt/ n zia f

au pair /əʊˈpeə(r)/ n ~ [girl] ragazza f alla pari

aura /ˈɔːrə/ n aura f

auster|e /ɒˈstɪə(r)/ adj austero. ~ity n austerità f

Australia /ɒˈstreɪlɪə/ n Australia f. ~n adj & n australiano, -a mf

Austria /ˈɒstrɪə/ n Austria f. ~n adj & n austriaco, -a mf

authentic /ɔːˈθentɪk/ adj autentico. ~ate vt autenticare. ~ity n autenticità f

author /ˈɔːθə(r)/ n autore m

authoritative /ɔːˈθɒrɪtətɪv/ adj autorevole; (manner) autoritario

authority /ɔːˈθɒrətɪ/ n autorità f; (permission) autorizzazione f; be in ~ over avere autorità su

authorization /ɔːθəraɪˈzeɪʃn/ n autorizzazione f

authorize /ˈɔːθəraɪz/ vt autorizzare

autobi|ography /ɔːtə-/ n autobiografia f

autograph /ˈɔːtə-/ n autografo m

automate /ˈɔːtəmeɪt/ vt automatizzare

automatic /ɔːtəˈmætɪk/ adj automatico • n (car) macchina f col cambio automatico; (washing machine) lavatrice f automatica. ~ally adv automaticamente

automation /ɔːtəˈmeɪʃn/ n automazione f

automobile /ˈɔːtəməbiːl/ n automobile f

autonom|ous /ɔːˈtɒnəməs/ adj autonomo. ~y n autonomia f

autopsy /ˈɔːtpsɪ/ n autopsia f

autumn /ˈɔːtəm/ n autunno m. ~al adj autunnale

auxiliary /ɔːgˈzɪlɪərɪ/ adj ausiliario • n ausiliare m

avail /əˈveɪl/ n to no ~ invano • vi ~ oneself of approfittare di

available /əˈveɪləbl/ adj disponibile; (book, record etc) in vendita

avalanche /ˈævəlɑːnʃ/ n valanga f

avarice /ˈævərɪs/ n avidità f

avenue /ˈævənjuː/ n viale m; fig strada f

average /ˈævərɪdʒ/ adj medio; (mediocre) mediocre • n media f; on ~ in media • vt (sales, attendance) etc: raggiungere una media di. □ ~ **out at** vt risultare in media

avers|e /əˈvɜːs/ adj not be ~e to sth non essere contrario a qcsa. ~ion n avversione f (to per)

avert /əˈvɜːt/ vt evitare (crisis); di-

a

stogliere (eyes)

aviation /eɪvɪˈeɪʃn/ n aviazione f

b

avid /ˈævɪd/ adj avido (for di); (reader) appassionato

avocado /ævəˈkɑːdəʊ/ n avocado m

avoid /əˈvɔɪd/ vt evitare. ~able adj evitabile

await /əˈweɪt/ vt attendere

awake /əˈweɪk/ adj sveglio; wide ~ completamente sveglio ● vi (pt awoke, pp awoken) svegliarsi

awaken /əˈweɪkn/ vt svegliare. ~ing n risveglio m

award /əˈwɔːd/ n premio m; (medal) riconoscimento m; (of prize) assegnazione f ● vt assegnare; (hand over) consegnare

aware /əˈweə(r)/ adj be ~ of (sense) percepire; (know) essere conscio di; become ~ of accorgersi di; (learn) venire a sapere di; be ~ that rendersi conto che. ~ness n percezione f; (knowledge) consapevolezza f

awash /əˈwɒʃ/ adj inondato (with di)

away /əˈweɪ/ adv via; go/stay ~ andare/stare via; he's ~ from his desk/the office non è alla sua scrivania/in ufficio; far ~ lontano; four kilometres ~ a quattro chilometri; play ~ (Sport) giocare fuori casa. ~ game n partita f fuori casa

awe /ɔː/ n soggezione f

awful /ˈɔːfl/ adj terribile. ~ly adv terribilmente; (pretty) estremamente

awkward /ˈɔːkwəd/ adj (movement) goffo; (moment, situation) imbarazzante; (time) scomodo. ~ly adv (move) goffamente; (say) con imbarazzo

awning /ˈɔːnɪŋ/ n tendone m

awoke(n) /əˈwəʊk (ən)/ ▷AWAKE

axe /æks/ n scure f ● vt (pres p axing) fare dei tagli a (budget); sopprimere (jobs); annullare (project)

axis /ˈæksɪs/ n (pl axes /-siːz/) asse m

axle /ˈæksl/ n (Techn) asse m

Bb

BA n abbr Bachelor of Arts

babble /ˈbæbl/ vi farfugliare; (stream:) gorgogliare

baby /ˈbeɪbɪ/ n bambino, -a mf; (🔲: darling) tesoro m

baby: ~ **carriage** n Am carrozzina f. ~**ish** adj bambinesco. ~**-sit** vi fare da baby-sitter. ~**-sitter** n baby-sitter mf

bachelor /ˈbætʃələ(r)/ n scapolo m; B~ of Arts/Science laureato, -a mf in lettere/in scienze

back /bæk/ n schiena f; (of horse, hand) dorso m; (of chair) schienale m; (of house, cheque, page) retro m; (in football) difesa f; at the ~ in fondo; in the ~ (Auto) dietro; ~ to front (sweater) il davanti di dietro; at the ~ of beyond in un posto sperduto ● adj posteriore; (taxes, payments) arretrato ● adv indietro; (returned) di ritorno; turn/move ~ tornare/spostarsi indietro; put it ~ here; there rimettilo qui/là; be ~ at home di ritorno a casa; I'll be ~ in five minutes torno fra cinque minuti; I'm just ~ sono appena tornato; when do you want the book ~? quando rivuoi il libro?; pay ~ ripagare (sb); restituire (money); ~ in power di nuovo al potere ● vt (support) sostenere; (with money) finanziare; puntare su (horse); (cover the back of) rivestire il retro di ● vi (Auto) fare retromarcia. □ ~ **down** vi battere in ritirata. □ ~ **in** vi (Auto) entrare in retromarcia; (person:) entrare camminando all'indietro. □ ~ **out** vi (Auto) uscire in retromarcia; (person:) uscire camminando all'indietro; *fig* tirarsi indietro (of da). □~ **up** *vt* sostenere; confermare (person's alibi); (*Comput*) fare una copia di salvataggio di; **be ~ed up** (traffic): essere congestionato ● *vi* (*Auto*) fare retromarcia

back: ~**ache** *n* mal *m* di schiena. ~**bone** *n* spina *f* dorsale. ~**date** *vt* retrodatare (cheque). ~ '**door** *n* porta *f* di servizio

backer /'bækə(r)/ *n* sostenitore, -trice *mf*; (*with money*) finanziatore, -trice *mf*

back: ~ '**fire** *vi* (*Auto*) avere un ritorno di fiamma; (fig: plan) fallire. ~**ground** *n* sfondo *m*; (*environment*) ambiente *m*. ~**hand** *n* (*tennis*) rovescio *m*

backing /'bækɪŋ/ *n* (*support*) supporto *m*; (*material*) riserva *f*; (*Mus*) accompagnamento *m*; ~ **group** gruppo *m* d'accompagnamento

back: ~**lash** *n* *fig* reazione *f* opposta. ~**log** *n* ~**log of work** lavoro *m* arretrato. ~**side** *n* 🅃 fondoschiena *m inv.* ~**slash** *n* (*Typ*) barra *f* retroversa. ~**stage** *adj* & *adv* dietro le quinte. ~**stroke** *n* dorso *m*. ~**up** *n* rinforzi *mpl*; (*Comput*) riserva *f*

backward /'bækwəd/ *adj* (step) indietro; (child) lento nell'apprendimento; (country) arretrato ● *adv* ~**s** (*also Am*) ~) indietro; (fall, walk) all'indietro; ~**s and forwards** avanti e indietro

back: ~**water** *n* *fig* luogo *m* allo scarto. ~ '**yard** *n* cortile *m*

bacon /'beɪkn/ *n* ≈ pancetta *f*

bacteria /bæk'tɪərɪə/ *npl* batteri *mpl*

bad /bæd/ *adj* (worse, worst) cattivo; (weather, habit, news, accident) brutto; (apple etc) marcio; **the light is ~** non c'è una buona luce; **use ~ language** dire delle parolacce; **feel ~** sentirsi male; (*feel guilty*) sentirsi in colpa; **have a ~ back** avere dei problemi alla schiena; **smoking is ~ for you** fumare fa male; **go ~** an-

dare a male; **that's just too ~!** pazienzal; **not ~** niente male

bade /bæd/ *see* ▷**BID**

badge /bædʒ/ *n* distintivo *m*

badger /'bædʒə(r)/ *n* tasso *m* ● *vt* tormentare

badly /'bædlɪ/ *adv* male; (hurt) gravemente; ~ **off** povero; ~ **behaved** maleducato; **need** ~ aver estremamente bisogno di

bad-'mannered *adj* maleducato

badminton /'bædmɪntən/ *n* badminton *m*

bad-'tempered *adj* irascibile

baffle /'bæfl/ *vt* confondere

bag /bæg/ *n* borsa *f*; (*of paper*) sacchetto *m*; **old** ~ 🅇 megera *f*; ~**s under the eyes** occhiaie *fpl*; ~**s of** 🅃 un sacco di

baggage /'bægɪdʒ/ *n* bagagli *mpl*

baggy /'bægɪ/ *adj* (clothes) ampio

'**bagpipes** *npl* cornamusa *fsg*

bail /beɪl/ *n* cauzione *f*; **on** ~ su cauzione ● **bail out** *vt* (*Naut*) aggottare; ~ **sb out** (*Jur*) pagare la cauzione per qcno ● *vi* (*Aeron*) paracadutarsi

bait /beɪt/ *n* esca *f* ● *vt* innescare; (*fig: torment*) tormentare

bake /beɪk/ *vt* cuocere al forno; (make) fare ● *vi* cuocersi al forno

baker /'beɪkə(r)/ *n* fornaio, -a *mf*, panettiere, -a *mf*; ~'**s** [**shop**] panetteria *f*. ~**y** *n* panificio *m*, forno *m*

balance /'bæləns/ *n* equilibrio *m*; (*Comm*) bilancio *m*; (*outstanding sum*) saldo *m*; [**bank**] ~ saldo *m*; **be or hang in the** ~ *fig* essere in sospeso ● *vt* bilanciare; equilibrare (budget); (*Comm*) fare il bilancio di (books) ● *vi* bilanciarsi; (*Comm*) essere in pareggio. ~**d** *adj* equilibrato. ~ **sheet** *n* bilancio *m* [d'esercizio]

balcony /'bælkənɪ/ *n* balcone *m*

bald /bɔːld/ *adj* (person) calvo; (tyre) liscio; (statement) nudo e crudo; **go**

~ perdere i capelli

bale /beɪl/ n balla f

ball[1] /bɔːl/ n palla f; (football) pallone m; (of yarn) gomitolo m; on the ~ 🔟 sveglio

ball[2] n (dance) ballo m

ballad /'bæləd/ n ballata f

ballast /'bæləst/ n zavorra f

ball-'bearing n cuscinetto m a sfera

ballerina /bælə'riːna/ n ballerina f [classica]

ballet /'bæleɪ/ n balletto m; (art form) danza f; ~ **dancer** n ballerino, -a mf [classico, -a]

balloon /bə'luːn/ n pallone m; (Aeron) mongolfiera f

ballot /'bælət/ n votazione f. ~-**box** n urna f. ~-**paper** n scheda f di votazione

ball: ~-**point** ['pen] n penna f a sfera. ~-**room** n sala f da ballo

Baltic /'bɔːltɪk/ adj & n the ~ [Sea] il [mar] Baltico

bamboo /bæm'buː/ n bambù m inv

ban /bæn/ n proibizione f. vt (pt/pp banned) proibire; ~ **from** espellere da (club); she was ~ned from driving le hanno ritirato la patente

banal /bə'nɑːl/ adj banale. ~**ity** /-'nælətɪ/ n banalità f inv

banana /bə'nɑːnə/ n banana f

band /bænd/ n banda f; (stripe) nastro m; (Mus: pop group) complesso m; (Mus: brass ~) banda f; (Mil) fanfara f ● **band together** vi riunirsi

bandage /'bændɪdʒ/ n benda f ● vt fasciare (limb)

b. & b. abbr bed and breakfast

bandit /'bændɪt/ n bandito m

band: ~-**stand** n palco m coperto [dell'orchestra]. ~-**wagon** n **jump on the** ~-**wagon** fig seguire la corrente

bandy[1] /'bændɪ/ vt (pt/pp -ied)

scambiarsi (words). □ ~ **about** vt far circolare

bandy[2] adj (-ier, -iest) be ~ avere le gambe storte

bang /bæŋ/ n (noise) fragore m; (of gun, firework) scoppio m; (blow) colpo m ● adv ~ **in the middle of** 🔟 proprio nel mezzo di; **go** ~ (gun) sparare; (balloon:) esplodere ● int bum! ● vt battere (fist); battere su (table); sbattere (door, head) ● vi scoppiare; (door:) sbattere

banger /'bæŋə(r)/ n (firework) petardo m; (🔟: sausage) salsiccia f; **old** ~ (🔟: car) macinino m

bangle /'bæŋgl/ n braccialetto m

banish /'bænɪʃ/ vt bandire

banisters /'bænɪstəz/ npl ringhiera fsg

bank[1] /bæŋk/ n (of river) sponda f; (slope) scarpata f ● vi (Aeron) inclinarsi in virata

bank[2] n banca f ● vt depositare in banca ● vi ~ **with** avere un conto [bancario] presso. □ ~ **on** vt contare su

'bank card n carta f assegno

banker /'bæŋkə(r)/ n banchiere m

bank: ~ **holiday** n giorno m festivo. ~**ing** n bancario m. ~**note** n banconota f

bankrupt /'bæŋkrʌpt/ adj fallito; **go** ~ fallire ● n persona f che ha fatto fallimento. ● vt far fallire. ~**cy** n bancarotta f

banner /'bænə(r)/ n stendardo m; (of demonstrators) striscione m

banquet /'bæŋkwɪt/ n banchetto m

banter /'bæntə(r)/ n battute fpl di spirito

baptism /'bæptɪzm/ n battesimo m

Baptist /'bæptɪst/ adj & n battista mf

baptize /bæp'taɪz/ vt battezzare

bar /bɑː(r)/ n sbarra f; (Jur) ordine m degli avvocati; (of chocolate) tavoletta f; (café) bar m inv; (counter) banco m; (Mus) battuta f; (fig: obstacle) ostacolo m; ~ of soap/gold saponetta f/lingotto m; behind ~s 🔒 dietro le sbarre ● vt (pt/pp barred) sbarrare (way); sprangare (door); escludere (person) ● prep tranne; ~ none in assoluto

barbarian /bɑːˈbeərɪən/ n barbaro, -a mf

barbar|ic /bɑːˈbærɪk/ adj barbarico. ~ity n barbarie f inv. ~ous adj barbaro

barbecue /ˈbɑːbɪkjuː/ n barbecue m inv; (party) grigliata f, barbecue m inv ● vt arrostire sul barbecue

barber /ˈbɑːbə(r)/ n barbiere m

bare /beə(r)/ adj nudo; (tree, room) spoglio; (floor) senza moquette ● vt scoprire; mostrare (teeth)

bare: ~back adv senza sella. ~faced adj sfacciato. ~foot adv scalzo. ~headed adj a capo scoperto

barely /ˈbeəlɪ/ adv appena

bargain /ˈbɑːgɪn/ n (agreement) patto m; (good buy) affare m; into the ~ per di più ● vi contrattare; (haggle) trattare. ▢ ~ for vt (expect) aspettarsi

barge /bɑːdʒ/ n barcone m ● barge in vi 🔒 (to room) piombare dentro; (into conversation) interrompere bruscamente. ~ into vt piombare dentro a (room); venire addosso a (person)

baritone /ˈbærɪtəʊn/ n baritono m

bark[1] /bɑːk/ n (of tree) corteccia f

bark[2] n abbaiamento m ● vi abbaiare

barley /ˈbɑːlɪ/ n orzo m

bar: ~maid n barista f. ~man n barista m

barmy /ˈbɑːmɪ/ adj 🔒 strampalato

barn /bɑːn/ n granaio m

barometer /bəˈrɒmɪtə(r)/ n barometro m

baron /ˈbærn/ n barone m. ~ess n

baronessa f

baroque /bəˈrɒk/ adj & n barocco m

barracks /ˈbærəks/ npl caserma fsg

barrage /ˈbærɑːʒ/ n (Mil) sbarramento m; (fig: of criticism) sfilza f

barrel /ˈbærl/ n barile m, botte f; (of gun) canna f. ~-organ n organetto m [a cilindro]

barren /ˈbærən/ adj sterile; (landscape) brullo

barricade /ˈbærɪkeɪd/ n barricata f ● vt barricare

barrier /ˈbærɪə(r)/ n barriera f; (Rail) cancello m; fig ostacolo m

barrister /ˈbærɪstə(r)/ n avvocato m

barter /ˈbɑːtə(r)/ vi barattare (for con)

base /beɪs/ n base f ● adj vile ● vt basare; be ~d on basarsi su

base: ~ball n baseball m. ~ment n seminterrato m

bash /bæʃ/ n colpo m [violento] ● vt colpire [violentemente]; (dent) ammaccare; ~ed in ammaccato

bashful /ˈbæʃfl/ adj timido

basic /ˈbeɪsɪk/ adj di base; (condition, requirement) basilare; (living conditions) povero; my Italian is pretty ~ il mio italiano è abbastanza rudimentale; the ~s (of language, science) i rudimenti; (essentials) l'essenziale m. ~ally adv fondamentalmente

basil /ˈbæzɪl/ n basilico m

basin /ˈbeɪsn/ n bacinella f; (washhand ~) lavabo m; (for food) recipiente m; (Geog) bacino m

basis /ˈbeɪsɪs/ n (pl -ses /-siːz/) base f

bask /bɑːsk/ vi crogiolarsi

basket /ˈbɑːskɪt/ n cestino m. ~ball n pallacanestro f

bass /beɪs/ adj basso; ~ voice voce f di basso ● n basso m

bastard /'bɑːstəd/ n (illegitimate child) bastardo, -a mf; ✗ figlio m di puttana

bat[1] /bæt/ n mazza f; (for table tennis) racchetta f; off one's own ~ 🔢 tutto da solo • vt (pt/pp batted) battere; she didn't ~ an eyelid fig non ha battuto ciglio

bat[2] n (Zool) pipistrello m

batch /bætʃ/ n gruppo m; (of goods) partita f; (of bread) infornata f

bated /'beɪtɪd/ adj with ~ breath col fiato sospeso

bath /bɑːθ/ n (pl ~s /bɑːðz/) bagno m; (tub) vasca f da bagno; ~s pl piscina f; have a ~ fare un bagno • vt fare il bagno a

bathe /beɪð/ n bagno m • vi fare il bagno • vt lavare (wound). ~r n bagnante mf

bathing /'beɪðɪŋ/ n bagni mpl. ~-cap n cuffia f. ~-costume n costume m da bagno

bathroom n bagno m

battalion /bə'tæliən/ n battaglione m

batter /'bætə(r)/ n (Culin) pastella f; ~ed adj (car) malandato; (wife, baby) maltrattato

battery /'bætərɪ/ n batteria f; (of torch, radio) pila f

battle /'bætl/ n battaglia f; fig lotta f • vi fig lottare

battle: ~field n campo m di battaglia. ~ship n corazzata f

bawl /bɔːl/ vt/i urlare

bay[1] /beɪ/ n (Geog) baia f

bay[2] n keep at ~ tenere a bada

bay[3] n (Bot) alloro m. ~-leaf n foglia f d'alloro

bayonet /'beɪənɪt/ n baionetta f

bay 'window n bay window f inv (grande finestra sporgente)

bazaar /bə'zɑː(r)/ n bazar m inv

BC abbr (before Christ) a.C.

be /biː/
• vi (pres am, are, is, are; pt was, were; pp been) essere; he is a teacher è insegnante, fa l'insegnante; what do you want to be? cosa vuoi fare?; be quiet! sta' zitto!; I am cold/hot ho freddo/caldo; it's cold/hot, isn't it? fa freddo/caldo, vero?; how are you? come stai?; I am well sto bene; there is c'è; there are ci sono; I have been to Venice sono stato a Venezia; has the postman been? è passato il postino?; you're coming too, aren't you? vieni anche tu, no?; it's yours, is it? è tuo, vero?; was John there? – yes, he was c'era John? – sì; John wasn't there – yes he was! John non c'era – sì che c'era!; three and three are six tre più tre fanno sei; he is five ha cinque anni; that will be £10, please fanno 10 sterline, per favore; how much is it? quanto costa?; that's £5 you owe me mi devi 5 sterline

• v aux I am coming/reading sto venendo/leggendo; I am staying (not leaving) resto; I am being lazy sono pigro; I was thinking of you stavo pensando a te; you are not to tell him non devi dirgielo; you are to do that immediately devi farlo subito

• passive essere; I have been robbed sono stato derubato

beach /biːtʃ/ n spiaggia f. ~wear n abbigliamento m da spiaggia

bead /biːd/ n perlina f

beak /biːk/ n becco m

beaker /'biːkə(r)/ n coppa f

beam /biːm/ n trave f; (of light) raggio m • vi irradiare; (person:) essere raggiante. ~ing adj raggiante

bean /biːn/ n fagiolo m; (of coffee) chicco m

bear[1] /beə(r)/ n orso m

bear[2] v (pt bore, pp borne) • vt (endure) sopportare; mettere al mondo (child); (carry) portare; ∼ in mind tenere presente • vi ∼ left/right andare a sinistra o a destra. □ ∼ with vt aver pazienza con. **∼able** adj sopportabile

beard /bɪəd/ n barba f. **∼ed** adj barbuto

bearer /ˈbeərə(r)/ n portatore, -trice mf; (of passport) titolare mf

bearing /ˈbeərɪŋ/ n portamento m; (Techn) cuscinetto m [a sfera]; have a ∼ on avere attinenza con; get one's ∼s orientarsi

beast /biːst/ n bestia f; (ⅈ: person) animale m

beat /biːt/ n battito m; (rhythm) battuta f; (of policeman) giro m d'ispezione • v (pt beat, pp beaten) • vt battere; picchiare (person); ∼ it! ⅈ darsela a gambel; it ∼s me why... ⅈ non capisco proprio perché... beat up vt picchiare

beating /ˈbiːtɪŋ/ n bastonata f; get a ∼ing (with fists) essere preso a pugni; (team, player:) prendere una batosta

beautician /bjuːˈtɪʃn/ n estetista mf

beauti|ful /ˈbjuːtɪfl/ adj bello. **∼fully** adv splendidamente

beauty /ˈbjuːtɪ/ n bellezza f. ∼ parlour n istituto m di bellezza. ∼ spot n neo m; (place) luogo m pittoresco

beaver /ˈbiːvə(r)/ n castoro m

became /bɪˈkeɪm/ ▷**BECOME**

because /bɪˈkɒz/ conj perché; ∼ you didn't tell me, I... poiché non me lo hai detto,... • adv ∼ of a causa di

beckon /ˈbekn/ vt/i ∼ [to] chiamare con un cenno

becom|e /bɪˈkʌm/ v (pt became, pp

become • vt diventare • vi diventare; what has ∼e of her? che ne è di lei? **∼ing** adj (clothes) bello

bed /bed/ n letto m; (of sea, lake) fondo m; (layer) strato m; (of flowers) aiuola f; in ∼ a letto; go to ∼ andare a letto; ∼ and breakfast pensione f familiare in cui the prezzo della camera comprende la prima colazione. **∼clothes** npl lenzuola fpl e coperte fpl. **∼ding** n biancheria f per il letto, materasso e guanciali

bed: **∼room** n camera f da letto. **∼sitter** n = camera f ammobiliata fornita di cucina. **∼spread** n copriletto m. **∼time** n l'ora f di andare a letto

bee /biː/ n ape f

beech /biːtʃ/ n faggio m

beef /biːf/ n manzo m. **∼burger** n hamburger m inv

bee: **∼hive** n alveare m. **∼line** n make a ∼line for ⅈ precipitarsi verso

been /biːn/ ▷**BE**

beer /bɪə(r)/ n birra f

beetle /ˈbiːtl/ n scarafaggio m

beetroot /ˈbiːtruːt/ n barbabietola f

before /bɪˈfɔː(r)/ prep prima di; the day ∼ yesterday ieri l'altro; ∼ long fra poco • adv prima; never ∼ have I seen... non ho mai visto prima...; ∼ that prima; ∼ going prima di andare • conj (time) prima che; ∼ you go prima che tu vada. **∼hand** adv in anticipo

befriend /bɪˈfrend/ vt trattare da amico

beg /beg/ v (pt/pp begged) • vi mendicare • vt pregare; chiedere (favour, forgiveness)

began /bɪˈgæn/ ▷**BEGIN**

beggar /ˈbegə(r)/ n mendicante mf; poor ∼! povero cristo!

begin /bɪˈgɪn/ vt/i (pt began, pp begun, pres p beginning) cominciare. **∼ner** n principiante mf. **∼ning**

n principio m

begrudge /brɪˈɡrʌdʒ/ vt (envy) essere invidioso di; dare malvolentieri (money)

begun /brɪˈɡʌn/ ▷BEGIN

behalf /brɪˈhɑːf/ n on ~ of a nome di; on my ~ a nome mio

behave /brɪˈheɪv/ vi comportarsi; ~ [oneself] comportarsi bene

behaviour /brɪˈheɪvjə(r)/ n comportamento m; (of prisoner, soldier) condotta f

behead /brɪˈhed/ vt decapitare

behind /brɪˈhaɪnd/ prep dietro; be ~ sth fig stare dietro qcsa ● adv dietro, indietro; (late) in ritardo; a long way ~ molto indietro ● n □ didietro m.
~hand adv indietro

beige /beɪʒ/ adj & n beige m inv

being /ˈbiːɪŋ/ n essere m; come into ~ nascere

belated /brɪˈleɪtɪd/ adj tardivo

belch /beltʃ/ vi ruttare ● vt ~ [out] eruttare (smoke)

belfry /ˈbelfrɪ/ n campanile m

Belgian /ˈbeldʒən/ adj & n belga mf

Belgium /ˈbeldʒəm/ n Belgio m

belief /brɪˈliːf/ n fede f; (opinion) convinzione f

believe /brɪˈliːv/ vt/i credere. ~r n (Relig) credente mf; be a great ~r in credere fermamente in

belittle /brɪˈlɪtl/ vt sminuire (person, achievements)

bell /bel/ n campana f; (on door) campanello m

belligerent /brɪˈlɪdʒərənt/ adj belligerante; (aggressive) bellicoso

bellow /ˈbeləʊ/ vi gridare a squarciagola; (animal:) muggire

bellows /ˈbeləʊz/ npl (for fire) soffietto msg

belly /ˈbelɪ/ n pancia f

belong /brɪˈlɒŋ/ vi appartenere (to a); (be member) essere socio (to di). ~ings npl cose fpl

beloved /brɪˈlʌvɪd/ adj & n amato, -a mf

below /brɪˈləʊ/ prep sotto; (with numbers) al di sotto di ● adv sotto, di sotto; (Naut) sotto coperta; see ~ guardare qui di seguito

belt /belt/ n cintura f; (area) zona f; (Techn) cinghia f ● v (pt/pp belted) ● vt ~ along (□: rush) filare velocemente ● vt (□: hit) picchiare

bench /bentʃ/ n panchina f; (work~) piano m da lavoro; the B~ (Jur) la magistratura

bend /bend/ n curva f; (of river) ansa f ● v (pt/pp bent) ● vt piegare ● vi piegarsi; (road:) curvare; ~ [down] chinarsi. ~ over ● vi inchinarsi

beneath /brɪˈniːθ/ prep sotto, al di sotto di; he thinks it's ~ him fig pensa che sia sotto al suo livello ● adv giù

beneficial /benɪˈfɪʃl/ adj benefico

beneficiary /benɪˈfɪʃərɪ/ n beneficiario, -a mf

benefit /ˈbenɪfɪt/ n vantaggio m; (allowance) indennità f inv ● v (pt/pp -fited, pres p -fiting) ● vt giovare a ● vi trarre vantaggio (from da)

benign /brɪˈnaɪn/ adj benevolo; (Med) benigno

bent /bent/ ▷BEND ● adj (person) ricurvo; (distorted) curvato; (□: dishonest) corrotto; be ~ on doing sth essere ben deciso a fare qcsa ● n predisposizione f

bereave|d /brɪˈviːvd/ n the ~d pl i familiari del defunto. ~ment n lutto m

beret /ˈbereɪ/ n berretto m

berry /ˈberɪ/ n bacca f

berserk /bəˈsɜːk/ adj go ~ diventare una belva

berth /bɜːθ/ n (in bed) cuccetta f; (anchorage) ormeggio m ● vi ormeggiare

beside /brɪˈsaɪd/ prep accanto a; ~ oneself fuori di sé

besides /brɪˈsaɪdz/ prep oltre a

● adv inoltre

besiege /bɪˈsiːdʒ/ vt assediare

best /best/ adj migliore; the ~ part of a year la maggior parte dell'anno; ~ before (Comm) preferibilmente prima di ● n the ~ il meglio; (person) il/la migliore; at ~ tutt'al più; all the ~! tanti auguri; do one's ~ fare del proprio meglio; to the ~ of my knowledge per quel che ne so; make the ~ of it cogliere il lato buono della cosa ● adv meglio, nel modo migliore; as ~ I could meglio che potevo. ~ 'man n testimone m

bestow /bɪˈstəʊ/ vt conferire (on a)

best'seller n bestseller m inv

bet /bet/ n scommessa f ● vt/i (pt/pp bet or betted) scommettere

betray /bɪˈtreɪ/ vt tradire. ~al n tradimento m

better /ˈbetə(r)/ adj migliore, meglio; get ~ migliorare; (after illness) rimettersi ● adv meglio; ~ off meglio; (wealthier) più ricco; all the ~ tanto meglio; the sooner the ~ prima è, meglio è; I've thought ~ of it ci ho ripensato; you'd ~ stay faresti meglio a restare; I'd ~ not è meglio che non lo faccia ● vt migliorare; ~ oneself migliorare le proprie condizioni

between /bɪˈtwiːn/ prep fra; tra; ~ you and me detto fra di noi; ~ us (together) tra me e te ● adv [in] ~ in mezzo; (time) frattempo

beverage /ˈbevərɪdʒ/ n bevanda f

beware /bɪˈweə(r)/ vi guardarsi (of da); ~ of the dog! attenti al cane!

bewilder /bɪˈwɪldə(r)/ vt disorientare; ~ed perplesso. ~ment n perplessità f

beyond /bɪˈjɒnd/ prep oltre; ~ reach irraggiungibile; ~ doubt senza alcun dubbio; ~ me fig ⓘ non riesco proprio a capire ● adv più in là

bias /ˈbaɪəs/ n (preference) preferenza f; pej pregiudizio m ● vt (pt/pp biased) (influence) influenzare. ~ed adj parziale

bib /bɪb/ n bavaglino m

Bible /ˈbaɪbl/ n Bibbia f

biblical /ˈbɪblɪkl/ adj biblico

biceps /ˈbaɪseps/ n bicipite m

bicker /ˈbɪkə(r)/ vi litigare

bicycle /ˈbaɪsɪkl/ n bicicletta f ● vi andare in bicicletta

bid¹ /bɪd/ n offerta f; (attempt) tentativo m ● vt/i (pt/pp bid, pres p bidding) offrire; (in cards) dichiarare

bid² vt (pt bade or bid, pp bidden or bid, pres p bidding) liter (command) comandare; ~ sb welcome dare il benvenuto a qcno

bidder /ˈbɪdə(r)/ n offerente mf

bide /baɪd/ vt ~ one's time aspettare il momento buono

bifocals /baɪˈfəʊklz/ npl occhiali mpl bifocali

big /bɪg/ adj (bigger, biggest) grande; (brother, sister) più grande; (ⓘ: generous) generoso ● adv talk ~ ⓘ sparare grosse

bigam|ist /ˈbɪgəmɪst/ n bigamo, -a mf. ~y n bigamia f

big-'headed adj ⓘ gasato

bigot /ˈbɪgət/ n fanatico, -a mf. ~ed adj di mentalità ristretta

bike /baɪk/ n ⓘ bici f inv

bikini /bɪˈkiːnɪ/ n bikini m inv

bile /baɪl/ n bile f

bilingual /baɪˈlɪŋgwəl/ adj bilingue

bill¹ /bɪl/ n fattura f; (in restaurant etc) conto m; (poster) manifesto m; (Pol) progetto m di legge; (Am: note) biglietto m di banca ● vt fatturare

bill² n (beak) becco m

'billfold n Am portafoglio m

billiards /ˈbɪljədz/ n biliardo m

billion /ˈbɪljən/ n (thousand million) miliardo m; (old-fashioned Br: million million) mille miliardi mpl

bin /bɪn/ n bidone m

bind /baɪnd/ vt (pt/pp bound) legare (to a); (bandage) fasciare; (Jur) obbligare. **~ing** adj (promise, contract) vincolante ● n (of book) rilegatura f; (on ski) attacco m [di sicurezza]

binge /bɪndʒ/ n 🔢 have a ~ fare baldoria; (eat a lot) abbuffarsi ● vi abbuffarsi (on di)

binoculars /bɪˈnɒkjʊləz/ npl [pair of] ~ binocolo msg

biograph|er /baɪˈɒɡrəfə(r)/ n biografo, -a mf. **~y** n biografia f

biological /baɪəˈlɒdʒɪkl/ adj biologico

biolog|ist /baɪˈɒlədʒɪst/ n biologo, -a mf. **~y** n biologia f

birch /bɜːtʃ/ n (tree) betulla f

bird /bɜːd/ n uccello m; (🔢: girl) ragazza f

Biro® /ˈbaɪrəʊ/ n biro® f inv

birth /bɜːθ/ n nascita f

birth: ~ **certificate** n certificato m di nascita. **~-control** n controllo m delle nascite. **~day** n compleanno m. **~mark** n voglia f. **~-rate** n natalità f

biscuit /ˈbɪskɪt/ n biscotto m

bisect /baɪˈsekt/ vt dividere in due [parti]

bishop /ˈbɪʃəp/ n vescovo m; (in chess) alfiere m

bit¹ /bɪt/ n pezzo m; (smaller) pezzetto m; (for horse) morso m; (Comput) bit m inv; a ~ of un pezzo di (cheese, paper); un po' di (time, rain, silence); ~ **by** ~ poco a poco; **do one's** ~ fare la propria parte

bit² ▷ BITE

bitch /bɪtʃ/ n cagna f; 🔳 stronza f. **~y** adj velenoso

bit|e /baɪt/ n morso m; (insect ~) puntura f; (mouthful) boccone m ● vt (pt bit, pp bitten) mordere; (insect:) pungere; **~e one's nails** mangiarsi le unghie ● vi (dog:) mordere; (insect:) pungere. **~ing** adj (wind, criticism) pun-

gente; (remark) mordace

bitter /ˈbɪtə(r)/ adj amaro ● n Br birra f amara. **~ly** adv amaramente; **it's ~ly cold** c'è un freddo pungente. **~ness** n amarezza f

bizarre /bɪˈzɑ:(r)/ adj bizzarro

black /blæk/ adj nero; **be ~ and blue** essere pieno di lividi ● n nero, -a mf ● vt boicottare (goods). □ ~ **out** vt cancellare ● vi (lose consciousness) perdere coscienza

black: **~berry** n mora f. **~bird** n merlo m. **~board** n (Sch) lavagna f. **~currant** n ribes m inv nero; **~ 'eye** n occhio m nero. **~ 'ice** n ghiaccio m (sulla strada). **~leg** n Br crumiro m. **~list** vt mettere sulla lista nera. **~mail** n ricatto m ● vt ricattare. **~mailer** n ricattatore, -trice mf. **~out** n blackout m inv; **have a ~out** (Med) perdere coscienza. **~smith** n fabbro m

bladder /ˈblædə(r)/ n (Anat) vescica f

blade /bleɪd/ n lama f; (of grass) filo m

blame /bleɪm/ n colpa f ● vt dare la colpa a; ~ **sb for doing sth** dare la colpa a qcno per aver fatto qcsa; **no one is to ~** non è colpa di nessuno. **~less** adj innocente

bland /blænd/ adj (food) insipido; (person) insulso

blank /blæŋk/ adj bianco; (look) vuoto ● n spazio m vuoto; (cartridge) a salve. **~ 'cheque** n assegno m in bianco

blanket /ˈblæŋkɪt/ n coperta f

blare /bleə(r)/ vi suonare a tutto volume. □ ~ **out** vt far risuonare ● vi (music, radio:) strillare

blaspheme /blæsˈfi:m/ vi bestemmiare

blasphem|ous /ˈblæsfəməs/ adj blasfemo. **~y** n bestemmia f

blast /blɑ:st/ n (gust) raffica f; (sound) scoppio m ● vt (with explosive)

far saltare ● *int* ⊠ maledizione!. **~ed**
adj ⊠ maledetto

blast-off *n* (*of missile*) lancio *m*

blatant /'bleɪtənt/ *adj* sfacciato

blaze /bleɪz/ *n* incendio *m*; a ~ of
colour un'esplosione *f* di colori ● *vi*
ardere

blazer /'bleɪzə(r)/ *n* blazer *m inv*

bleach /bliːtʃ/ *n* decolorante *m*; (*for
cleaning*) candeggina *f* ● *vt* sbiancare;
ossigenare (*hair*)

bleak /bliːk/ *adj* desolato; (*fig*: pro-
spects, future) tetro

bleat /bliːt/ *vi* belare ● *n* belato *m*

bleed /bliːd/ *v* (*pt/pp* bled) ● *vi* san-
guinare ● *vt* spurgare (brakes, radiator)

bleep /bliːp/ *n* bip *m* ● *vi* suonare
● *vt* chiamare (*col cercapersone*) (doctor). **~er** *n* cercapersone *m inv*

blemish /'blemɪʃ/ *n* macchia *f*

blend /blend/ *n* (*of tea, coffee, whisky*)
miscela *f*; (*of colours*) insieme *m* ● *vt*
mescolare ● *vi* (*colours, sounds*) fondersi (with con). **~er** *n* (Culin) frullatore *m*

bless /bles/ *vt* benedire. **~ed** *adj also*
⊠ benedetto. **~ing** *n* benedizione *f*

blew /bluː/ ▷**BLOW²**

blight /blaɪt/ *n* (*a Bot*) ruggine *f* ● *vt*
far avvizzire (plants)

blind¹ /blaɪnd/ *adj* cieco; the ~ *npl* i
ciechi *mpl*. ~ **man/woman** cieco/
cieca ● *vt* accecare

blind² *n* (roller) ~ avvolgibile *m*;
[Venetian] ~ veneziana *f*

blind: ~ **alley** *n* vicolo *m* cieco.
~fold *adj* be ~fold avere gli occhi
bendati ● *n* benda *f* ● *vt* bendare gli
occhi a. **~ly** *adv* ciecamente. **~ness**
n cecità *f*

blink /blɪŋk/ *vi* sbattere le palpebre;
(light:) tremolare

blinkers /'blɪŋkəz/ *npl* paraocchi *mpl*

bliss /blɪs/ *n* (Rel) beatitudine *f*; (happiness) felicità *f*. **~ful** *adj* beato;

(happy) meraviglioso

blister /'blɪstə(r)/ *n* (Med) vescica *f*;
(in paint) bolla *f* ● *vi* (paint:) formare
una bolla/delle bolle

blizzard /'blɪzəd/ *n* tormenta *f*

bloated /'bləʊtɪd/ *adj* gonfio

blob /blɒb/ *n* goccia *f*

bloc /blɒk/ *n* (Pol) blocco *m*

block /blɒk/ *n* blocco *m*; (building)
isolato *m*; (building ~) cubo *m* (per giochi
di costruzione); ~ **of flats** palazzo *m*
● *vt* bloccare. □ ~ **up** *vt* bloccare

blockade /blɒ'keɪd/ *n* blocco *m* ● *vt*
bloccare

blockage /'blɒkɪdʒ/ *n* ostruzione *f*

block: **~head** *n* ⊞ testone, -a *mf*.
~ **letters** *npl* stampatello *m*

bloke /bləʊk/ *n* ⊞ tizio *m*

blonde /blɒnd/ *adj* biondo ● *n* bi-
onda *f*

blood /blʌd/ *n* sangue *m*

blood: ~ **bath** *n* bagno *m* di sangue. ~ **group** *n* gruppo *m* sanguigno. **~hound** *n* segugio *m*. ~ **pressure** *n* pressione *f* del sangue.
~shed *n* spargimento *m* di sangue.
~shot *adj* iniettato di sangue.
~stream *n* sangue *m*. **~thirsty** *adj*
assetato di sangue

bloody /'blʌdɪ/ *adj* (-ier, -iest) in-
sanguinato; ⊠ maledetto ● *adv* ⊠
easy/difficult facile/difficile da
matti. **~-minded** *adj* scorbutico

bloom /bluːm/ *n* fiore *m*; in ~
(flower:) sbocciato; (tree:) in fiore
● *vi* fiorire; *fig* essere in forma sma-
gliante

blossom /'blɒsəm/ *n* fiori *mpl*
(d'albero); (single one) fiore *m* ● *vi*
sbocciare

blot /blɒt/ *n* also fig macchia *f*. ● blot
out *vt* (*pt/pp* blotted) *fig* cancellare

blotch /blɒtʃ/ *n* macchia *f*. **~y** *adj*
chiazzato

'blotting-paper *n* carta *f* assorbente

blouse /blaʊz/ n camicetta f

blow[1] /bləʊ/ n colpo m

blow[2] v (pt blew, pp blown) • vi (wind:) soffiare; (fuse:) saltare • vt (⚠: squander) sperperare; ~ one's nose soffiarsi il naso. □ ~ **away** vt far volar via (papers) • vi (papers:) volare via. □ ~ **down** vt abbattere • vi abbattersi al suolo. □ ~ **out** vt (extinguish) spegnere. □ ~ **over** vi (storm:) passare; (fuss, trouble:) dissiparsi. □ ~ **up** vt (inflate) gonfiare; (enlarge) ingrandire (photograph); (by explosion) far esplodere • vi esplodere

blow: ~**-dry** vt asciugare col fon. ~**lamp** n fiamma f ossidrica

blowtorch n fiamma f ossidrica

blue /bluː/ adj (pale) celeste; (navy) blu inv; (royal) azzurro; ~ **with** cold livido per il freddo • n blu m inv; have the ~s essere giù [di tono]; out of the ~ inaspettatamente

blue: ~**bell** n giacinto m di bosco. ~**berry** n mirtillo m. ~**bottle** n moscone m. ~ **film** n film m inv a luci rosse. ~**print** n fig riferimento m

bluff /blʌf/ n bluff m inv • vi bluffare

blunder /ˈblʌndə(r)/ n gaffe f inv • vi fare una/delle gaffe

blunt /blʌnt/ adj spuntato; (person) reciso. ~**ly** adv schiettamente

blur /blɜː(r)/ n it's all a ~ fig è tutto un insieme confuso • vt (pt/pp blurred) rendere confuso. ~**red** adj (vision, photo) sfocato

blurb /blɜːb/ n soffietto m editoriale

blurt /blɜːt/ vt ~ **out** spifferare

blush /blʌʃ/ n rossore m • vi arrossire

BMI n abbr (body mass index) IMC m

boar /bɔː(r)/ n cinghiale m

board /bɔːd/ n tavola f; (for notices) tabellone m; (committee) assemblea f; (of directors) consiglio m; full ~ Br pensione f completa; half ~ Br mezza pensione f; ~ and lodging vitto e alloggio m; go by the ~ 🅛

andare a monte • vt (Naut, Aeron) salire a bordo di • vi (passengers:) salire a bordo. □ ~ **up** vt sbarrare con delle assi. □ ~ **with** vi stare a pensione da.

boarder /ˈbɔːdə(r)/ n pensionante mf; (Sch) convittore, -trice mf

board: ~**ing-house** n pensione f. ~**ing-school** n collegio m

boast /bəʊst/ vi vantarsi (about di). ~**ful** adj vanaglorioso

boat /bəʊt/ n barca f; (ship) nave f

bob /bɒb/ n (hairstyle) caschetto m • vi (pt/pp bobbed) (also ~ **up and down**) andare su e giù

bob-sleigh n bob m inv

bode /bəʊd/ vi ~ **well/ill** essere di buono/cattivo augurio

bodily /ˈbɒdɪlɪ/ adj fisico • adv (forcibly) fisicamente

body /ˈbɒdɪ/ n corpo m; (organization) ente m; (amount: of poems etc) quantità f. ~**guard** n guardia f del corpo. ~**part** n pezzo m del corpo. ~**work** n (Auto) carrozzeria f

bog /bɒg/ n palude f • vt (pt/pp bogged) get ~**ged down** impantanarsi

boggle /ˈbɒgl/ vi the mind ~s non posso neanche immaginarlo

bogus /ˈbəʊgəs/ adj falso

boil[1] /bɔɪl/ n (Med) foruncolo m

boil[2] n bring/come to the ~ portare/arrivare ad ebollizione • vt [far] bollire • vi bollire; (fig: with anger) ribollire; the water o kettle's ~**ing** l'acqua bolle. **boil down to** vt fig ridursi a. □ ~ **over** vi straboccare (bollendo). □ ~ **up** vt far bollire

boiler /ˈbɔɪlə(r)/ n caldaia f. ~**suit** n tuta f

boisterous /ˈbɔɪstərəs/ adj chiassoso

bold /bəʊld/ adj audace • n (Typ) neretto m. ~**ness** n audacia f

bolster /ˈbəʊlstə(r)/ n cuscino m (lungo e rotondo) • vt ~ **[up]** sostenere

bolt /bəʊlt/ n (for door) catenaccio m; (for fixing) bullone m ● vt fissare (con i bulloni) (to a); chiudere col chiavistello (door); ingurgitare (food) ● vi svignarsela; (horse:) scappar via ● adv ∼ upright diritto come un fuso

bomb /bɒm/ n bomba f ● vt bombardare

bombard /bɒm'bɑːd/ vt also fig bombardare

bomb|er /'bɒmə(r)/ n (Aeron) bombardiere m; (person) dinamitardo m. ∼er jacket giubbotto m, bomber m inv. ∼shell n (fig: news) bomba f

bond /bɒnd/ n fig legame m, (Comm) obbligazione f ● vt (glue:) attaccare

bondage /'bɒndɪdʒ/ n schiavitù f

bone /bəʊn/ n osso m; (of fish) spina f ● vt disossare (meat); togliere le spine da (fish). ∼-'dry adj secco

bonfire /'bɒn-/ n falò m inv. ∼ night festa celebrata la notte del 5 novembre con fuochi d'artificio e falò

bonnet /'bɒnɪt/ n cuffia f; (of car) cofano m

bonus /'bəʊnəs/ n (individual) gratifica f; (production ∼) premio m; (life insurance) dividendo m. ∼ fig qualcosa in più

bony /'bəʊnɪ/ adj (-ier, -iest) ossuto; (fish) pieno di spine

boo /buː/ interj (to surprise or frighten) bu! ● vt/i fischiare

boob /buːb/ n [] (mistake) gaffe f inv; (breast) tetta f ● vi [] fare una gaffe

book /bʊk/ n libro m; (of tickets) blocchetto m; keep the ∼s (Comm) tenere la contabilità; be in sb's bad/ good ∼s essere nel libro nero/nelle grazie di qcno ● vt (reserve) prenotare; (for offence) multare ● vi (reserve) prenotare

book: ∼case n libreria f. ∼ing-office n biglietteria f. ∼keeping n contabilità f. ∼let n opuscolo m. ∼maker n allibratore m. ∼mark n segnalibro m. ∼seller n libraio, -a mf.

∼shop n libreria f. ∼worm n topo m di biblioteca

boom /buːm/ n (Comm) boom m inv; (upturn) impennata f; (of thunder, gun) rimbombo m ● vi (fig prosperare; (of thunder, gun:) rimbombare; fig prosperare

boost /buːst/ n spinta f ● vt stimolare (sales); sollevare (morale); far crescere (hopes). ∼er n (Med) dose f supplementare

boot /buːt/ n stivale m; (up to ankle) stivaletto m; (football) scarpetta f; (climbing) scarpone m; (Auto) portabagagli m inv ● vt (Comput) inizializzare

booth /buːð/ n (telephone, voting) cabina f; (at market) bancarella f

booze /buːz/ [] n alcolici mpl. ∼-up n bella bevuta f

border /'bɔːdə(r)/ n bordo m; (frontier) frontiera f; (in garden) bordura f ● vi ∼ on confinare con; fig essere ai confini di (madness). ∼line n linea f di demarcazione; ∼line case caso m dubbio

bore[1] /bɔː(r)/ ▷ BEAR[2]

bore[2] vt (Techn) forare

bor|e[3] n (of gun) calibro m; (person) seccatore, -trice m f; (thing) seccatura f ● vt annoiare. ∼edom n noia f. be ∼ed (to tears or to death) annoiarsi (da morire). ∼ing adj noioso

born /bɔːn/ pp be ∼ nascere; I was ∼ in 1966 sono nato nel 1966 ● adj nato; a ∼ liar/actor un bugiardo/ attore nato

borne /bɔːn/ ▷ BEAR[2]

borough /'bʌrə/ n municipalità f inv

borrow /'bɒrəʊ/ vt prendere a prestito (from da); can I ∼ your pen? mi presti la tua penna?

boss /bɒs/ n direttore, -trice mf ● vt (also ∼ about) comandare a bacchetta. ∼y adj autoritario

botanical /bə'tænɪkl/ adj botanico

botan|ist /'bɒtənɪst/ n botanico, -a mf. ∼y n botanica f

both /bəʊθ/ adj & pron tutti e due,

entrambi ● *adv* ~ men and women entrambi uomini e donne; ~ [of] the children tutti e due i bambini; they are ~ dead sono morti entrambi; ~ of them tutti e due

bother /'bɒðə(r)/ *n* preoccupazione *f*; (*minor trouble*) fastidio *m*; it's no ~ non c'è problema ● *int* 🇬🇧 che seccatura! ● *vt* (*annoy*) dare fastidio a; (*disturb*) disturbare ● *vi* preoccuparsi (about di); don't ~ lascia perdere

bottle /'bɒtl/ *n* bottiglia *f*; (*baby's*) biberon *m inv* ● *vt* imbottigliare. □ ~ up *vt fig* reprimere

bottle: ~-neck *n fig* ingorgo *m*. ~-opener *n* apribottiglie *m inv*

bottom /'bɒtm/ *adj* ultimo; the ~ shelf l'ultimo scaffale in basso ● *n* (of *container*) fondo *m*; (of *river*) fondale *m*; (of *hill*) piedi *mpl*; (*buttocks*) sedere *m*; at the ~ of the page in fondo alla pagina; get to the ~ of *fig* vedere cosa c'è sotto. ~less *adj* senza fondo

bough /baʊ/ *n* ramoscello *m*

bought /bɔːt/ ▷BUY

boulder /'bəʊldə(r)/ *n* masso *m*

bounce /baʊns/ *vi* rimbalzare; (🇬🇧: *cheque*) essere respinto ● *vt* far rimbalzare (ball)

bound¹ /baʊnd/ *n* balzo *m* ● *vi* balzare

bound² ▷BIND ● *adj* ~ for (ship) diretto a; be ~ to do (*likely*) dovere fare per forza; (*obliged*) essere costretto a fare

boundary /'baʊndərɪ/ *n* limite *m*

bouquet /bʊ'keɪ/ *n* mazzo *m* di fiori; (of *wine*) bouquet *m*

bout /baʊt/ *n* (*Med*) attacco *m*; (*Sport*) incontro *m*

bow¹ /bəʊ/ *n* (*weapon*) arco *m*; (*Mus*) archetto *m*; (*knot*) nodo *m*

bow² /baʊ/ *n* inchino *m*; (of *ship*) prua *f* ● *vt* piegare (head)

bow³ /baʊ/ *n* (*Naut*) prua *f*

bowl¹ /bəʊl/ *n* (for soup, cereal) scodella *f*; (of *pipe*) fornello *m*

bowl² *n* (ball) boccia *f* ● *vt* lanciare ● *vi* (*Cricket*) servire; (in *bowls*) lanciare. □ ~ over *vt* buttar giù; (fig: *leave speechless*) lasciar senza parole

bowler¹ /'bəʊlə(r)/ *n* (*Cricket*) lanciatore *m*; (Bowls) giocatore *m* di bocce

bowler² *n* ~ [hat] bombetta *f*

bowling /'bəʊlɪŋ/ *n* gioco *m* delle bocce. ~-alley *n* pista *f* da bowling

bow-'tie /bəʊ-/ *n* cravatta *f* a farfalla

box¹ /bɒks/ *n* scatola *f*; (*Theat*) palco *m*

box² *vi* (*Sport*) fare il pugile ● *vt* ~ sb's ears dare uno scappaccione a qcno

boxer /'bɒksə(r)/ *n* pugile *m*. ~ing *n* pugilato *m*. B~ing Day *n* [giorno *m* di] Santo Stefano *m*

box: ~-office *n* (*Theat*) botteghino *m*. ~-room *n Br* sgabuzzino *m*

boy /bɔɪ/ *n* ragazzo *m*; (*younger*) bambino *m*

'boy band *n* boy band *f inv*

boycott /'bɔɪkɒt/ *n* boicottaggio *m* ● *vt* boicottare

boy: ~friend *n* ragazzo *m*. ~ish *adj* da ragazzino

bra /brɑː/ *n* reggiseno *m*

brace /breɪs/ *n* sostegno *m*; (*dental*) apparecchio *m*; ~s *npl* bretelle *fpl* ● *vt* ~ oneself *fig* farsi forza (for per affrontare)

bracelet /'breɪslɪt/ *n* braccialetto *m*

bracken /'brækn/ *n* felce *f*

bracket /'brækɪt/ *n* mensola *f*; (*group*) categoria *f*; (*Typ*) parentesi *f inv* ● *vt* mettere fra parentesi

brag /bræg/ *vi* (*pt/pp* bragged) vantarsi (about di)

braid /breɪd/ *n* (*edging*) passamano *m*

brain /breɪn/ *n* cervello *m*; ~s *pl fig* testa *fsg*

brain: ~child *n* invenzione *f* personale. ~wash *vt* fare il lavaggio del cervello a. ~wave *n* lampo *m* di genio

brainy /'breɪnɪ/ adj (-ier, -iest) intelligente

brake /breɪk/ n freno m ● vi frenare. **~-light** n stop m inv

bramble /'bræmbl/ n rovo m; (fruit) mora f

bran /bræn/ n crusca f

branch /brɑːntʃ/ n also fig ramo m; (Comm) succursale f ● vi (road): biforcarsi. □ ~ **off** vi biforcarsi. □ ~ **out** vi ~ **out into** allargare le proprie attività nel ramo di

brand /brænd/ n marca f; (on animal) marchio m ● vt marcare (animal); fig tacciare (as di)

brandish /'brændɪʃ/ vt brandire

brandy /'brændɪ/ n brandy m inv

brash /bræʃ/ adj sfrontato

brass /brɑːs/ n ottone m; the ~ (Mus) gli ottoni mpl; **top** ~ 🔲 pezzi mpl grossi. ~ **band** n banda f (di soli ottoni)

brassiere /'bræzɪə(r)/ n fml, Am reggipetto m

brat /bræt/ n pej marmocchio, -a mf

bravado /brə'vɑːdəʊ/ n bravata f

brave /breɪv/ adj coraggioso ● vt affrontare. ~**ry** n coraggio m

brawl /brɔːl/ n rissa f ● vi azzuffarsi

brazen /'breɪzn/ adj sfrontato

Brazil /brə'zɪl/ n Brasile m. ~**ian** adj & n brasiliano, -a mf. ~ **nut** n noce f del Brasile

breach /briːtʃ/ n (of law) violazione f; (gap) breccia f; (fig: in party) frattura f. ~ **of contract** inadempienza f di contratto; ~ **of the peace** violazione f della quiete pubblica ● vt recedere (contract)

bread /bred/ n pane m; a slice of ~ and butter una fetta di pane imburrato

breadcrumbs npl briciole fpl; (Culin) pangrattato m

breadth /bredθ/ n larghezza f

'bread-winner n quello, -a mf che porta i soldi a casa

break /breɪk/ n rottura f; (interval) intervallo m; (interruption) interruzione f; (🔲: chance) opportunità f inv ● v (pt broke, pp broken) ● vt rompere; (interrupt) interrompere; ~ **one's arm** rompersi un braccio ● vi rompersi; (day:) spuntare; (storm:) scoppiare; (news:) diffondersi; (boy's voice:) cambiare. □ ~ **away** vi scappare; fig chiudere (from con). □ ~ **down** vi (machine, car:) guastarsi; (emotionally) cedere (psicologicamente) ● vt sfondare (door); ripartire (figures). □ ~ **into** vt introdursi (con la forza) in; forzare (car). □ ~ **off** vt rompere (engagement) ● vi (part of whole:) rompersi. □ ~ **out** vi (fight, war:) scoppiare. □ ~ **up** vt far cessare (fight); disperdere (crowd) ● vi (crowd:) disperdersi; (couple:) separarsi; (Sch) iniziare le vacanze

'break|able /'breɪkəbl/ adj fragile. ~**age** n rottura f. ~**down** n (of car, machine) guasto m; (Med) esaurimento m nervoso; (of figures) analisi f inv. ~**er** n (wave) frangente m

breakfast /'brekfəst/ n [prima] colazione f

break: ~**through** n scoperta f. ~**water** n frangiflutti m inv

breast /brest/ n seno m. ~**-feed** vt allattare [al seno]. ~**-stroke** n nuoto m a rana

breath /breθ/ n respiro m. ~**less** adj senza fiato. ~**-taking** adj mozzafiato. ~ **test** n prova [etilica] f del palloncino

breathalyse /'breθəlaɪz/ vt sottoporre alla prova [etilica] del palloncino. ~**r®** n Br alcoltest m inv

breathe /briːð/ vt/i respirare. □ ~ **in** vi inspirare ● vt respirare (scent, air). □ ~ **out** vt/i espirare

breath|er /'briːðə(r)/ n pausa f. ~**ing** n respirazione f

bred /bred/ ▷**BREED**

breed /briːd/ n razza f ● v (pt/pp

bred) ● vt allevare; (give rise to) generare ● vi riprodursi. ~er n allevatore, -trice mf. ~ing n allevamento m; fig educazione f

breez|e /briːz/ n brezza f. ~y adj ventoso

brew /bruː/ n infuso m ● vt mettere in infusione (tea); produrre (beer) ● vi fig (trouble:) essere nell'aria. ~er n birraio m. ~ery n fabbrica f di birra

bribe /braɪb/ n (money) bustarella f; (large sum of money) tangente f ● vt corrompere. ~ry n corruzione f

brick /brɪk/ n mattone m. '~layer n muratore m ● brick up vt murare

bridal /'braɪdl/ adj nuziale

bride /braɪd/ n sposa f. ~groom n sposo m. ~smaid n damigella f d'onore

bridge[1] /brɪdʒ/ n ponte m; (of nose) dorso m; (of spectacles) ponticello m ● vt fig colmare (gap)

bridge[2] n (Cards) bridge m

bridle /'braɪdl/ n briglia f

brief[1] /briːf/ adj breve

brief[2] n istruzioni fpl; (Jur: case) causa f ● vt dare istruzioni a; (Jur) affidare la causa a. ~case n cartella f

briefs /briːfs/ npl slip m inv

brigad|e /brɪ'geɪd/ n brigata f. ~ier n generale m di brigata

bright /braɪt/ adj (metal, idea) brillante; (day, room, future) luminoso; (clever) intelligente; ~ red rosso m acceso

bright|en /braɪtn/ v ~en up [up] ● vt ravvivare; rallegrare (person) ● vi (weather:) schiarirsi; (face:) illuminarsi; (person:) rallegrarsi. ~ly adv (shine) intensamente; (smile) allegramente. ~ness n luminosità f; (intelligence) intelligenza f

brilliance /'brɪljəns/ n luminosità f; (of person) genialità f

brilliant /'brɪljənt/ adj (very good) eccezionale; (very intelligent) brillante; (sunshine) splendente

brim /brɪm/ n bordo m; (of hat) tesa f ● brim over vi (pt/pp brimmed) traboccare

brine /braɪn/ n salamoia f

bring /brɪŋ/ vt (pt/pp brought) portare (person, object). □ ~ about vt causare. □ ~ along vt portare [con sé]. □ ~ back vt restituire (sth borrowed); reintrodurre (hanging); fare ritornare in mente (memories). □ ~ down vt portare giù; fare cadere (government); fare abbassare (price). □ ~ off vt ~ sth off riuscire a fare qcsa. □ ~ on vt (cause) provocare. □ ~ out vt (emphasize) mettere in evidenza; pubblicare (book). □ ~ round vt portare; (persuade) convincere; far rinvenire (unconscious person). □ ~ up vt (vomit) rimettere; allevare (children); tirare fuori (question, subject)

brink /brɪŋk/ n orlo m

brisk /brɪsk/ adj svelto; (person) sbrigativo; (trade, business) redditizio; (walk) a passo spedito

bristl|e /'brɪsl/ n setola f ● vi ~ling with pieno di. ~ly adj (chin) ispido

Brit|ain /'brɪtn/ n Gran Bretagna f. ~ish adj britannico; (ambassador) della Gran Bretagna ● npl the ~ish il popolo britannico. ~on n cittadino, -a britannico, -a mf

brittle /'brɪtl/ adj fragile

broach /brəʊtʃ/ vt toccare (subject)

broad /brɔːd/ adj ampio; (hint) chiaro; (accent) marcato. two metres ~ largo due metri; in ~ daylight in pieno giorno. ~ band n banda f larga. ~ beans npl fave fpl

'broadcast n trasmissione f ● vt/i (pt/pp -cast) trasmettere. ~er n giornalista m radiotelevisivo, -a. ~ing n diffusione f radiotelevisiva; be in ~ing lavorare per la televisione/radio

broaden /'brɔːdn/ vt allargare ● vi allargarsi

broadly /'brɔːdlɪ/ adv largamente; ~ [speaking] generalmente

broad'minded adj di larghe vedute

broccoli /'brɒkəlɪ/ n inv broccoli mpl

brochure /'brəʊʃə(r)/ n opuscolo m; (travel ~) dépliant m inv

broke /brəʊk/ ⊳**BREAK** ● adj 🔢 al verde

broken /'brəʊkn/ ⊳**BREAK** ● adj rotto; (fig: marriage) fallito. ~ English inglese m stentato. ~-hearted adj affranto

broker /'brəʊkə(r)/ n broker m inv

brolly /'brɒlɪ/ n 🔢 ombrello m

bronchitis /brɒŋ'kaɪtɪs/ n bronchite f

bronze /brɒnz/ n bronzo m ● attrib di bronzo

brooch /brəʊtʃ/ n spilla f

brood /bruːd/ n covata f; (hum: children) prole f ● vi fig rimuginare

brook /brʊk/ n ruscello m

broom /bruːm/ n scopa f. ~stick n manico m di scopa

broth /brɒθ/ n brodo m

brothel /'brɒθl/ n bordello m

brother /'brʌðə(r)/ n fratello m

brother: ~-in-law n (pl ~s-in-law) cognato m. ~ly adj fraterno

brought /brɔːt/ ⊳**BRING**

brow /braʊ/ n fronte f; (of hill) cima f

'browbeat vt (pt -beat, pp -beaten) intimidire

brown /braʊn/ adj marrone; castano (hair) ● n marrone m ● vt rosolare (meat) ● vi (meat:) rosolarsi. ~ 'paper n carta f da pacchi

browse /braʊz/ vi (read) leggicchiare; (in shop) curiosare

bruise /bruːz/ n livido m; (on fruit) ammaccatura f ● vt ammaccare (fruit); ~ one's arm farsi un livido sul braccio. ~d adj contuso

brunette /bruːˈnet/ n bruna f

brunt /brʌnt/ n bear the ~ of sth subire maggiormente qcsa

brush /brʌʃ/ n spazzola f; (with long handle) spazzolone m; (for paint) pennello m; (bushes) boscaglia f; (fig: conflict) breve scontro m ● vt spazzolare (hair); lavarsi (teeth); scopare (stairs, floor). □ ~ **against** vt sfiorare. □ ~ **aside** vt fig ignorare. □ ~ **off** vt spazzolare; (with hands) togliere; ignorare (criticism). □ ~ **up** vt/i fig ~ up [on] rinfrescare

brusque /brʊsk/ adj brusco

Brussels /'brʌslz/ n Bruxelles f. ~ sprouts npl cavoletti mpl di Bruxelles

brutal /'bruːtl/ adj brutale. ~ity n brutalità f

brute /bruːt/ n bruto m. ~ force n forza f bruta

BSc n abbr Bachelor of Science

BSE n abbr (bovine spongiform encephalitis) encefalite f bovina spongiforme

bubble /'bʌbl/ n bolla f; (in drink) bollicina f

buck¹ /bʌk/ n maschio m del cervo; (rabbit) maschio m del coniglio ● vi (horse:) saltare a quattro zampe. □ ~ **up** vi 🔢 tirarsi su; (hurry) sbrigarsi

buck² n Am 🔢 dollaro m

buck³ n pass the ~ scaricare la responsabilità

bucket /'bʌkɪt/ n secchio m

buckle /'bʌkl/ n fibbia f ● vt allacciare ● vi (shelf:) piegarsi; (wheel:) storcersi

bud /bʌd/ n bocciolo m

Buddhis|m /'bʊdɪzm/ n buddismo m. ~t adj & n buddista mf

buddy /'bʌdɪ/ n 🔢 amico, -a mf

budge /bʌdʒ/ vt spostare ● vi spostarsi

budgerigar /'bʌdʒərɪgɑː(r)/ n cocorita f

budget /'bʌdʒɪt/ n bilancio m; (allotted to specific activity) budget m inv ● vi (pt/pp budgeted) prevedere le spese; ~ for sth includere qcsa nelle spese previste

buffalo /'bʌfələʊ/ n (inv or pl -es) bufalo m

buffer /'bʌfə(r)/ n (Rail) respingente m; old ~ 🔟 vecchio bacucco m; ~ zone n zona f cuscinetto

buffet¹ /'bʊfeɪ/ n buffet m inv

buffet² /'bʌfɪt/ vt (pt/pp buffeted) sferzare

bug /bʌg/ n (insect) insetto m; (Comput) bug m inv; (🔟: device) cimice f ● vt (pt/pp bugged) 🔟 installare delle microspie in (room); mettere sotto controllo (telephone); (🔟: annoy) scocciare

buggy /'bʌgɪ/ n [baby] ~ passeggino m

bugle /'bju:gl/ n tromba f

build /bɪld/ n (of person) corporatura f ● vt/i (pt/pp built) costruire. □ ~ **on** vt aggiungere (extra storey); sviluppare (previous work). □ ~ **up** vt ~ up one's strength rimettersi in forza ● vi (pressure, traffic:) aumentare; (excitement, tension:) crescere

builder /'bɪldə(r)/ n (company) costruttore m; (worker) muratore m

building /'bɪldɪŋ/ n edificio m; ~ site n cantiere m [di costruzione]. ~ society n istituto m di credito immobiliare

'build-up n (of gas etc) accumulo m; fig battage m inv pubblicitario

built /bɪlt/ ▷ **BUILD**. ~-**in** adj (unit) a muro; (fig: feature) incorporato. ~-**up area** n (Auto) centro m abitato

bulb /bʌlb/ n bulbo m; (Electr) lampadina f

Bulgaria /bʌl'geərɪə/ n Bulgaria f

bulg|e /bʌldʒ/ n rigonfiamento m ● vi esser gonfio (with di); (stomach, wall:) sporgere; (eyes, with surprise:) uscire dalle orbite. ~**ing** adj gonfio; (eyes) sporgente

bulk /bʌlk/ n volume m; (greater part) grosso m; **in** ~ in grande quantità; (loose) sfuso. ~**y** adj voluminoso

bull /bʊl/ n toro m

'bulldog n bulldog m inv

'bulldozer /'bʊldəʊzə(r)/ n bulldozer m inv

bullet /'bʊlɪt/ n pallottola f

bulletin /'bʊlɪtɪn/ n bollettino m. ~ **board** n (Comput) bacheca f elettronica

'bullet-proof adj antiproiettile inv; (vehicle) blindato

'bullfight n corrida f. ~**er** n torero m

bull: ~**ring** n arena f. ~**'s-eye** n centro m del bersaglio; **score a** ~**'s-eye** fare centro

bully /'bʊlɪ/ n prepotente mf ● vt fare il/la prepotente con. ~**ing** n prepotenze fpl

bum¹ /bʌm/ n 🔳 sedere m

bum² n Am 🔟 vagabondo, -a mf ● **bum around** vi 🔟 vagabondare

bumble-bee /'bʌmbl-/ n calabrone m

bump /bʌmp/ n botta f; (swelling) bozzo m, gonfiore m; (in road) protuberanza f ● vt sbattere. □ ~ **into** vt sbattere contro; (meet) imbattersi in. □ ~ **off** vt 🔟 far fuori

bumper /'bʌmpə(r)/ n (Auto) paraurti m inv ● adj abbondante

bun /bʌn/ n focaccina f (dolce); (hair) chignon m inv

bunch /bʌntʃ/ n (of flowers, keys) mazzo m; (of bananas) casco m; (of people) gruppo m; ~ **of grapes** grappolo m d'uva

bundle /'bʌndl/ n fascio m; (of money) mazzetta f; **a** ~ **of nerves** un fascio di nervi 🔟 ● vt ~ [**up**] affastellare

bungalow /'bʌŋgələʊ/ n bungalow m inv

bungle /'bʌŋgl/ vt fare un

pasticcio di

bunk /bʌŋk/ n cuccetta f. ~-beds npl letti mpl a castello

bunny /bʌnɪ/ n [I] coniglietto m

buoy /bɔɪ/ n boa f

burden /bɜːdn/ n carico m • vt caricare. ~some adj gravoso

bureau /bjʊərəʊ/ n (pl -x /-əʊz/ or ~s) (desk) scrivania f; (office) ufficio m

bureaucracy /bjʊəˈrɒkrəsɪ/ n burocrazia f

bureaucrat /bjʊərəkræt/ n burocrate mf. ~ic adj burocratico

burger /ˈbɜːgə(r)/ n hamburger m inv

burglar /ˈbɜːglə(r)/ n svaligiatore, -trice mf. ~ alarm n antifurto m inv

burgle /ˈbɜːgl/ vt svaligiare

burial /ˈberɪəl/ n sepoltura f. ~ ground cimitero m

burly /ˈbɜːlɪ/ adj (-ier, -iest) corpulento

burn /bɜːn/ n bruciatura f • v (pt/pp burnt or burned) • vt bruciare • vi bruciare. □ ~ down vt/i bruciare. □ ~ out vi fig esaurirsi. ~er n (on stove) bruciatore m (Comput) masterizzatore m

burnt /bɜːnt/ ▷BURN

burp /bɜːp/ n [I] rutto m • vi [I] ruttare

burrow /ˈbʌrəʊ/ n tana f • vt scavare (hole)

bursar /ˈbɜːsə(r)/ n economo, -a mf. ~y n borsa f di studio

burst /bɜːst/ n (of gunfire, energy, laughter) scoppio m; (of speed) scatto m • v (pt/pp burst) • vt far scoppiare • vi scoppiare; ~ into tears scoppiare in lacrime; she ~ into the room ha fatto irruzione nella stanza. □ ~ out vi ~ out laughing/crying scoppiare a ridere/piangere

bury /ˈberɪ/ vt (pt/pp -ied) seppellire; (hide) nascondere

bus /bʌs/ n autobus m inv, pullman m

inv; (long distance) pullman m inv, corriera f

bush /bʊʃ/ n cespuglio m; (land) boscaglia f. ~y adj (-ier, -iest) folto

business /ˈbɪznɪs/ n affare m; (Comm) affari mpl; (establishment) attività f di commercio; on ~ per affari; he has no ~ to non ha alcun diritto di; mind one's own ~ farsi gli affari propri; that's none of your ~ non sono affari tuoi. ~like adj efficiente. ~man n uomo m d'affari. ~woman n donna f d'affari

busker /ˈbʌskə(r)/ n suonatore, -trice mf ambulante

'bus station n stazione f degli autobus

'bus-stop n fermata f d'autobus

bust¹ /bʌst/ n busto m; (chest) petto m

bust² adj [I] rotto; go ~ fallire • v (pt/pp busted or bust) [I] • vt far scoppiare • vi scoppiare

'bust-up n [I] lite f

busy /ˈbɪzɪ/ adj (-ier, -iest) occupato; (day, time) intenso; (street) affollato; (with traffic) pieno di traffico; be ~ doing essere occupato a fare • vt ~ oneself darsi da fare

'busybody n ficcanaso mf inv

but /bʌt/, atono /bət/ conj ma • prep eccetto, tranne; nobody ~ you nessuno tranne te; ~ for (without) se non fosse stato per; the last ~ one il penultimo; the next ~ one il secondo • adv (only) soltanto; there were ~ two ce n'erano soltanto due

butcher /ˈbʊtʃə(r)/ n macellaio m; ~'s [shop] macelleria f • vt macellare; fig massacrare

butler /ˈbʌtlə(r)/ n maggiordomo m

butt /bʌt/ n (of gun) calcio m; (of cigarette) mozzicone m; (for water) barile m; (fig: target) bersaglio m • vt dare una testata a; (goat:) dare una cornata a. □ ~ in vi interrompere

butter /ˈbʌtə(r)/ n burro m • vt imburrare. □ ~ **up** vt 🔤 arruffianarsi

butter: ~**cup** n ranuncolo m. ~**fingers** nsg 🔤 be a ~**fingers** avere le mani di pasta frolla. ~**fly** n farfalla f

button /ˈbʌtn/ n bottone m • ~ [**up**] abbottonare • vi abbottonarsi. ~**hole** n occhiello m, asola f

buy /baɪ/ n good/bad ~ buon/cattivo acquisto m • vt (pt/pp bought) comprare; ~ sb a drink pagare da bere a qcno; I'll ~ this one (drink) questo, lo offro io. ~**er** n compratore, -trice mf

buzz /bʌz/ n ronzio m; give sb a ~ 🔤 (on phone) dare un colpo di telefono a qcno; (excite) mettere in fermento qcno • vi ronzare • vt ~ sb chiamare qcno col cicalino. □ ~ **off** vi 🔤 levarsi di torno

buzzer /ˈbʌzə(r)/ n cicalino m

---

by /baɪ/
● prep (near, next to) vicino a; (at the latest) per; by Mozart di Mozart; he was run over by a bus è stato investito da un autobus; by oneself da solo; by the sea al mare; by sea via mare; by car/bus in macchina/autobus; by day/night di giorno/notte; by the hour/metre a ore/metri; six metres by four sei metri per quattro; he won by six metres ha vinto di sei metri; I missed the train by a minute ho perso il treno per un minuto; I'll be home by six sarò a casa per le sei; by this time next week a quest'ora tra una settimana; he rushed by me mi è passato accanto di corsa
● adv she'll be here by and by sarà qui fra poco; by and large in complesso

---

bye[-bye] /baɪ[ˈbaɪ]/ int 🔤 ciao

by: ~-**election** n elezione f straordinaria indetta per coprire una carica rimasta vacante in Parlamento. ~**law** n legge f locale. ~**pass** n circonvallazione f; (Med) by-pass m inv • vt evitare. ~-**product** n sottoprodotto m. ~**stander** n spettatore, -trice mf

---

Cc

cab /kæb/ n taxi m inv; (of lorry, train) cabina f

cabaret /ˈkæbəreɪ/ n cabaret m inv

cabbage /ˈkæbɪdʒ/ n cavolo m

cabin /ˈkæbɪn/ n (of plane, ship) cabina f; (hut) capanna f

cabinet /ˈkæbɪnɪt/ n armadietto m; [display] ~ vetrina f; C~ (Pol) consiglio m dei ministri. ~-**maker** n ebanista m

cable /ˈkeɪbl/ n cavo m. ~ **railway** n funicolare f. ~ **television** n televisione f via cavo

cackle /ˈkækl/ vi ridacchiare

cactus /ˈkæktəs/ n (pl -ti /-taɪ/ or -tuses) cactus m inv

caddie /ˈkædɪ/ n portabastoni m inv

caddy /ˈkædɪ/ n [tea-]~ barattolo m del tè

cadet /kəˈdet/ n cadetto m

cadge /kædʒ/ vt/i 🔤 scroccare

café /ˈkæfeɪ/ n caffè m inv

cafeteria /kæfəˈtɪərɪə/ n tavola f calda

caffeine /ˈkæfiːn/ n caffeina f

cage /keɪdʒ/ n gabbia f

cake /keɪk/ n torta f, (small) pasticcino m. ~**d** adj incrostato (with di)

calamity /kəˈlæmətɪ/ n calamità f inv

calcium /ˈkælsɪəm/ n calcio m

calculat|e /'kælkjʊleɪt/ vt calcolare. **~ing** adj fig calcolatore. **~ion** n calcolo m. **~or** n calcolatrice f

calendar /'kælɪndə(r)/ n calendario m

calf¹ /kɑːf/ n (pl calves) vitello m

calf² n (pl calves) (Anat) polpaccio m

calibre /'kælɪbə(r)/ n calibro m

call /kɔːl/ n grido m; (Teleph) telefonata f; (visit) visita f; **be on ~** (doctor): essere di guardia ● vt chiamare; indire (strike); **be ~ed** chiamarsi ● vi chiamare; **~ [in** or **round]** passare. □ **~ back** vt/i richiamare. □ **~ for** vt (ask for) chiedere; (require) richiedere; (fetch) passare a prendere. □ **~ off** vt richiamare (dog); disdire (meeting); revocare (strike). □ **~ on** vt chiamare; (appeal to) fare un appello a; (visit) visitare. □ **~ out** vt chiamare ad alta voce (names) ● vi chiamare ad alta voce. □ **~ together** vt riunire. □ **~ up** vt (Mil) chiamare alle armi; (Teleph) chiamare

call: **~box** n cabina f telefonica. **~ centre** n call centre m inv. **~er** n visitatore, -trice mf; (Teleph) persona f che telefona. **~ing** n vocazione f

callous /'kæləs/ adj insensibile

calm /kɑːm/ adj calmo ● n calma f. □ **~ down** vt calmare ● vi calmarsi. **~ly** adv con calma

calorie /'kælərɪ/ n caloria f

calves /kɑːvz/ npl see calf1 &2

camcorder /'kæmkɔːdə(r)/ n videocamera f

came /keɪm/ ▷COME

camel /'kæml/ n cammello m

camera /'kæmərə/ n macchina f fotografica; (TV) telecamera f. **~man** n operatore m [televisivo], cameraman m inv

camouflage /'kæməflɑːʒ/ n mimetizzazione f ● vt mimetizzare

camp /kæmp/ n campeggio f; (Mil) campo m ● vi campeggiare; (Mil) accamparsi

campaign /kæm'peɪn/ n campagna f ● vi fare una campagna

camp: **~-bed** n letto m da campo. **~er** n campeggiatore, -trice mf; (Auto) camper m inv. **~ing** n campeggio m. **~site** n campeggio m

campus /'kæmpəs/ n (pl -puses) (Univ) città f universitaria, campus m inv

can¹ /kæn/ n (for petrol) latta f; (tin) scatola f; **~ of beer** lattina f di birra ● vt mettere in scatola

---

can² /kæn/, atono /kən/ v aux (pres can; pt could) (be able to) potere; (know how to) sapere; **I cannot** or **can't** go non posso andare; **he could not** or **couldn't** go non poteva andare; **she can't swim** non sa nuotare; **I ~ smell something burning** sento odor di bruciato

---

Canad|a /'kænədə/ n Canada m. **~ian** adj & n canadese mf

canal /kə'næl/ n canale m

Canaries /kə'neərɪz/ npl Canarie fpl

canary /kə'neərɪ/ n canarino m

cancel /'kænsl/ v (pt/pp cancelled) ● vt disdire (meeting, newspaper); revocare (contract, order); annullare (reservation, appointment, stamp). **~lation** /-'leɪʃn/ n (of meeting, contract) revoca f; (in hotel, restaurant, for flight) cancellazione f

cancer /'kænsə(r)/ n cancro m; **C~** (Astr) Cancro m. **~ous** adj canceroso

candid /'kændɪd/ adj franco

candidate /'kændɪdət/ n candidato, -a mf

candle /'kændl/ n candela f. **~stick** n portacandele m inv

candour /'kændə(r)/ n franchezza f

candy /'kændɪ/ n Am caramella f; **a [piece of] ~** una caramella. **~floss** n zucchero m filato

cane /keɪn/ n (stick) bastone m; (Sch)

bacchetta f ● vt prendere a bacchet-
tate (pupil)

canister /'kænɪstə(r)/ n barattolo m
(di metallo)

cannabis /'kænəbɪs/ n cannabis f

cannibal /'kænɪbl/ n cannibale mf.
~ism n cannibalismo m

cannon /'kænən/ n inv cannone m.
~-ball n palla f di cannone

cannot /'kænɒt/ ▷CAN²

canoe /kə'nu:/ n canoa f ● vi andare
in canoa

'can-opener n apriscatole m inv

canopy /'kænəpɪ/ n baldacchino f;
(of parachute) calotta f

cantankerous /kæn'tæŋkərəs/ adj
stizzoso

canteen /kæn'ti:n/ n mensa f; ~
of cutlery servizio m di posate

canter /'kæntə(r)/ vi andare a piccolo galoppo

canvas /'kænvəs/ n tela f; (painting)
dipinto m su tela

canvass /'kænvəs/ vi (Pol) fare propaganda elettorale. ~ing n sollecita-
zione f di voti

canyon /'kænjən/ n canyon m inv

cap /kæp/ n berretto m; (nurse's) cuffia f; (top, lid) tappo m ● vt (pt/pp
capped) (fig: do better than) superare

capability /keɪpə'bɪlətɪ/ n capacità f

capabl|e /'keɪpəbl/ adj capace; (skil-
ful) abile; **be ~ of doing** sth essere
capace di fare qcsa. ~y adv con
abilità

capacity /kə'pæsətɪ/ n capacità f;
(function) qualità f; **in my ~ as** in
qualità di

cape¹ /keɪp/ n (cloak) cappa f

cape² n (Geog) capo m

capital /'kæpɪtl/ n (town) capitale f;
(money) capitale m; (letter) lettera f
maiuscola. ~ **city** n capitale f

capital|ism /'kæpɪtəlɪzm/ n capita-
lismo m. ~ist adj & n capitalista mf.

~ize /'kaɪz/ vi ~ize on fig trarre vantaggio
da. ~ 'letter n lettera f maiuscola.
~ 'punishment n pena f capitale

Capitol Situato su Capitol
Hill, nella città di Washing-
ton, il Campidoglio (the Capitol) è la sede del Congresso (Congress) degli Stati Uniti d'America e
per estensione indica il Congresso
stesso.

capitulat|e /kə'pɪtjʊleɪt/ vi capito-
lare. ~ion n capitolazione f

Capricorn /'kæprɪkɔ:n/ n (Astr) Ca-
pricorno m

capsize /kæp'saɪz/ vi capovolgersi
● vt capovolgere

capsule /'kæpsjʊl/ n capsula f

captain /'kæptɪn/ n capitano m ● vt
comandare (team)

caption /'kæpʃn/ n intestazione f;
(of illustration) didascalia f

captivate /'kæptɪveɪt/ vt incantare

captiv|e /'kæptɪv/ adj prigioniero;
hold/take ~e tenere/fare prigioniero m prigioniero, -a mf. ~ity n
prigionia f; (animals) cattività f

capture /'kæptʃə(r)/ n cattura f ● vt
catturare; attirare (attention)

car /kɑ:(r)/ n macchina f; **by ~** in
macchina

carafe /kə'ræf/ n caraffa f

caramel /'kærəmel/ n (sweet) caramella f al mou; (Culin) caramello m

caravan /'kærəvæn/ n roulotte f inv;
(horse-drawn) carovana f

carbohydrate /kɑ:bə'haɪdreɪt/ n
carboidrato m

carbon /'kɑ:bən/ n carbonio m. ~
di'oxide n anidride f carbonica. ~
'footprint n impronta f ecologica

carburettor /kɑ:bjʊ'retə(r)/ n car-
buratore m

carcass /'kɑ:kəs/ n carcassa f

card /kɑ:d/ n (for birthday, Christmas
etc) biglietto m di auguri; (playing ~)

carta f [da gioco]; (membership ~) tessera f; (business ~) biglietto m da visita; (credit ~) carta f di credito; (Comput) scheda f

'**cardboard** n cartone m. ~ '**box** n scatola f di cartone; (large) scatolone m

cardigan /'kɑːdɪgən/ n cardigan m inv

cardinal /'kɑːdɪnl/ adj cardinale; ~ **number** numero m cardinale ● n (Relig) cardinale m

care /keə(r)/ n cura f; (caution) attenzione f; (worry) preoccupazione f; ~ **of** (on letter abbr c/o) presso; **take** ~ (be cautious) fare attenzione; **bye, take** ~ ciao, stammi bene; **take** ~ **of** occuparsi di; **be taken into** ~ essere preso in custodia da un ente assistenziale ● vi ~ **about** interessarsi di; ~ **for** (feel affection for) volere bene a; (look after) aver cura di; **I don't** ~ **for chocolate** non mi piace il cioccolato; **I don't** ~ non me ne importa; **who** ~**s?** chi se ne frega?

career /kə'rɪə(r)/ n carriera f; (profession) professione f ● vi andare a tutta velocità

care: ~**free** adj spensierato. ~**ful** adj attento; (driver) prudente. ~**fully** adv con attenzione. ~**less** adj irresponsabile; (in work) trascurato; (work) fatto con poca cura; (driver) distratto. ~**lessly** adv negligentemente. ~**lessness** n trascuratezza f. ~**r** n persona f che accudisce a un anziano o a un malato

caress /kə'res/ n carezza f ● vt accarezzare

'**caretaker** n custode mf; (in school) bidello m

'**car ferry** n traghetto m (per il trasporto di auto)

cargo /'kɑːgəʊ/ n (pl -es) carico m

Caribbean /kærɪ'biːən/ n the ~ (sea) il Mar dei Caraibi ● adj caraibico

caricature /'kærɪkətjʊə(r)/ n caricatura f

carnage /'kɑːnɪdʒ/ n carneficina f

carnation /kɑː'neɪʃn/ n garofano m

carnival /'kɑːnɪvl/ n carnevale m

carol /'kærəl/ ~ [Christmas] ~ canzone f natalizia

carp[1] /kɑːp/ n inv carpa f

carp[2] vi ~ **at** trovare da ridire su

'**car park** n parcheggio m

carpent|er /'kɑːpɪntə(r)/ n falegname m. ~**ry** n falegnameria f

carpet /'kɑːpɪt/ n tappeto m; (wall-to-wall) moquette f inv ● vt mettere la moquette in (room)

carriage /'kærɪdʒ/ n carrozza f; (of goods) trasporto m; (cost) spese fpl di trasporto; (bearing) portamento m; ~**way** n strada f carrozzabile; north-bound ~**way** carreggiata f nord

carrier /'kærɪə(r)/ n (company) impresa f di trasporti; (Aeron) compagnia f di trasporto aereo; (of disease) portatore m. ~ **bag** n borsa f [per la spesa]

carrot /'kærət/ n carota f

carry /'kærɪ/ v (pt/pp -ied) ● vt portare; (transport) trasportare; **get carried away** ⧫ lasciarsi prender la mano ● vi (sound) trasmettersi. □ ~ **off** vt portare via; vincere (prize). □ ~ **on** vi continuare; (fam: make scene) fare delle storie; ~ **on with** sth continuare qcsa; ~ **on with** sb ⧫ intendersela con qcno ● vt mantenere (business). □ ~ **out** vt portare fuori; eseguire (instructions, task); mettere in atto (threat); effettuare (experiment, survey)

'**carry-cot** n porte-enfant m inv

cart /kɑːt/ n carretto m ● vt (⧫: carry) portare

carton /'kɑːtn/ n scatola f di cartone; (for drink) cartone m; (of cream, yoghurt) vasetto m; (of cigarettes) stecca f

cartoon /kɑːˈtuːn/ n vignetta f; (strip) vignette fpl; (film) cartone m animato; (in art) bozzetto m. ∼ist n vignettista mf; (for films) disegnatore, -trice mf di cartoni animati

cartridge /ˈkɑːtrɪdʒ/ n cartuccia f; (for film) bobina f; (of record player) testina f

carve /kɑːv/ vt scolpire; tagliare (meat)

case[1] /keɪs/ n caso m; in any ∼ in ogni caso; in that ∼ in questo caso; just in ∼ per sicurezza; in ∼ he comes nel caso in cui venisse

case[2] n (container) scatola f; (crate) cassa f; (for spectacles) astuccio m; (suitcase) valigia f; (for display) vetrina f

cash /kæʃ/ n denaro m contante; (I: money) contanti mpl; **pay** [in] ∼ pagare in contanti; ∼ **on delivery** pagamento alla consegna ∼ vt incassare (cheque). ∼ **desk** n cassa f

cashier /kæˈʃɪə(r)/ n cassiere, -a mf

casino /kəˈsiːnəʊ/ n casinò m inv

casket /ˈkɑːskɪt/ n scrigno m; (Am: coffin) bara f

casserole /ˈkæsərəʊl/ n casseruola f; (stew) stufato m

cassette /kəˈset/ n cassetta f. ∼ **recorder** n registratore m (a cassette)

cast /kɑːst/ n (mould) forma f; (Theat) cast m inv; (plaster) (Med) ingessatura f ∼ vt (pt/pp cast) dare (vote); fondere (metal); (throw) gettare; ∼ **an actor** as dare ad un attore il ruolo di; ∼ **a glance at** lanciare uno sguardo a. □ ∼ **off** vi (Naut) sganciare gli ormeggi ∼ vt (in knitting) diminuire. □ ∼ **on** vt (in knitting) avviare

castaway /ˈkɑːstəweɪ/ n naufrago, -a mf

caster /ˈkɑːstə(r)/ n (wheel) rotella f. ∼ **sugar** n zucchero m raffinato

cast iron n ghisa f

cast-iron adj di ghisa; fig solido

castle /ˈkɑːsl/ n castello m;

(in chess) torre f

'cast-offs npl abiti mpl smessi

castrat|**e** /kæˈstreɪt/ vt castrare. ∼**ion** n castrazione f

casual /ˈkæʒʊəl/ adj (chance) casuale; (remark) senza importanza; (glance) di sfuggita; (attitude, approach) disinvolto; (chat) informale; (clothes) casual inv; (work) saltuario; ∼ **wear** abbigliamento m casual. ∼**ly** adv (dress) casual; (meet) casualmente

casualty /ˈkæʒʊəltɪ/ n (injured person) ferito m; (killed) vittima f. ∼ [**department**] n pronto soccorso m

cat /kæt/ n gatto m; pej arpia f

catalogue /ˈkætəlɒg/ n catalogo m ∼ vt catalogare

catalyst /ˈkætəlɪst/ n (Chem) & fig catalizzatore m

catapult /ˈkætəpʌlt/ n catapulta f; (child's) fionda f ∼ vt fig catapultare

catarrh /kəˈtɑː(r)/ n catarro m

catastroph|**e** /kəˈtæstrəfɪ/ n catastrofe f. ∼**ic** adj catastrofico

catch /kætʃ/ n (of fish) pesca f; (fastener) fermaglio m; (on door) fermo m; (on window) gancio m; (I: snag) tranello m ∼ v (pt/pp caught) ∼ vt acchiappare (ball); (grab) afferrare; prendere (illness, fugitive, train); ∼ **a cold** prendersi un raffreddore; ∼ **sight of** scorgere; **I caught him stealing** l'ho sorpreso mentre rubava; ∼ **one's finger in the door** chiudersi il dito nella porta; ∼ **sb's eye or attention** attirare l'attenzione di qcno ∼ vi (fire:) prendere; (get stuck) impigliarsi. □ ∼ **on** vi (I: understand) afferrare; (become popular) diventare popolare. □ ∼ **up** vt raggiungere ∼ vi recuperare; (runner:) riguadagnare terreno; ∼ **up with** raggiungere (sb); mettersi in pari con (work)

catching /ˈkætʃɪŋ/ adj contagioso

catchphrase n tormentone m

catchy /ˈkætʃɪ/ adj (-ier, -iest)

orecchiabile

categor|ical /kætɪˈgɒrɪkl/ adj categorico. ~y n categoria f

cater /ˈkeɪtə(r)/ vi ~ for provvedere a (needs); fig venire incontro alle esigenze di. ~ing n (trade) ristorazione f. (food) rinfresco m

caterpillar /ˈkætəpɪlə(r)/ n bruco m

cathedral /kəˈθiːdrl/ n cattedrale f

Catholic /ˈkæθəlɪk/ adj & n cattolico, -a mf. ~ism n cattolicesimo m

cat's eyes n catarifrangente msg (inserito nell'asfalto)

cattle /ˈkætl/ npl bestiame msg

catwalk /ˈkætwɔːk/ n passerella f

caught /kɔːt/ ▷CATCH

cauliflower /ˈkɒlɪ-/ n cavolfiore m

cause /kɔːz/ n causa f ● vt causare; ~ sb to do sth far fare qcsa a qcno

caution /ˈkɔːʃn/ n cautela f; (warning) ammonizione f ● vt mettere in guardia; (Jur) ammonire

cautious /ˈkɔːʃəs/ adj cauto

cavalry /ˈkævəlrɪ/ n cavalleria f

cave /keɪv/ n caverna f ● cave in vi (roof:) crollare; (fig: give in) capitolare

cavern /ˈkævən/ n caverna f

caviare /ˈkævɪɑː(r)/ n caviale m

cavity /ˈkævɪtɪ/ n cavità f inv; (in tooth) carie f inv

CD n CD m inv. ~ player n lettore m [di] compact

CD-Rom /siːdiːˈrɒm/ n CD-Rom m inv. ~ drive n lettore m [di] CD-Rom

cease /siːs/ n without ~ incessantemente ● vt/i cessare. ~-fire n cessate il fuoco m inv. ~less adj incessante

cedar /ˈsiːdə(r)/ n cedro f

ceiling /ˈsiːlɪŋ/ n soffitto m; fig tetto m [massimo]

celebrat|e /ˈselɪbreɪt/ vt festeggiare (birthday, victory) ● vi far festa. ~ed adj celebre (for per). ~ion n celebrazione f

celebrity /sɪˈlebrətɪ/ n celebrità f inv

celery /ˈselərɪ/ n sedano m

cell /sel/ n cella f; (Biol) cellula f

cellar /ˈselə(r)/ n scantinato m; (for wine) cantina f

cello /ˈtʃeləʊ/ n violoncello m

Cellophane® /ˈseləfeɪn/ n cellofan m inv

cellphone /ˈselfəʊn/ n cellulare m

cellular phone /seljʊləˈfəʊn/ n [telefono] cellulare m

celluloid /ˈseljʊlɔɪd/ n celluloide f

Celsius /ˈselsɪəs/ adj Celsius

cement /sɪˈment/ n cemento m; (adhesive) mastice m ● vt cementare; fig consolidare

cemetery /ˈsemətrɪ/ n cimitero m

censor /ˈsensə(r)/ n censore m ● vt censurare. ~ship n censura f

censure /ˈsenʃə(r)/ vt biasimare

census /ˈsensəs/ n censimento m

cent /sent/ n (of dollar) centesimo m; (of euro) cent m inv, centesimo m

centenary /senˈtiːnərɪ/ n, Am centennial /senˈtenɪəl/ n centenario m

center /ˈsentə(r)/ n Am = centre

centi|grade /ˈsentɪ-/ adj centigrado. ~metre n centimetro m. ~pede n centopiedi m inv

central /ˈsentrəl/ adj centrale. ~ heating n riscaldamento m autonomo. ~ize vt centralizzare. ~ly adv al centro; ~ly heated con riscaldamento autonomo. ~ reservation n (Auto) banchina f spartitraffico

centre /ˈsentə(r)/ n centro m ● v (pt/pp centred) ● vt centrare ● vi ~ on fig incentrarsi su. ~-forward n centravanti m inv

century /ˈsentʃərɪ/ n secolo m

cereal /ˈsɪərɪəl/ n cereale m

ceremon|ial /serɪˈməʊnɪəl/ adj da cerimonia ● n cerimoniale m. ~ious adj cerimonioso

ceremony /ˈserɪmənɪ/ n

cerimonia f

certain /'sɜːtn/ adj certo; for ~ di sicuro; **make ~** accertarsi ; he is ~ to win è certo di vincere; it's not ~ whether he'll come non è sicuro che venga. **~ly** adv certamente; **~ly not!** no di certo! **~ty** n certezza f; it's a ~ty è una cosa certa

certificate /sə'tɪfɪkət/ n certificato m

certify /'sɜːtɪfaɪ/ vt (pt/pp -ied) certificare; (declare insane) dichiarare malato di mente

chafe /tʃeɪf/ vt irritare

chain /tʃeɪn/ n catena f ● vt incatenare (prisoner); attaccare con la catena (dog) (to a). □ ~ **up** vt legare alla catena (dog)

chain: ~ **re'action** n reazione f a catena. **~-smoker** n fumatore, -trice mf accanito, -a. ~ **store** n negozio m appartenente a una catena

chair /tʃeə(r)/ n sedia f; (Univ) cattedra f ● vt presiedere. **~-lift** n seggiovia f. **~man** n presidente m

chalet /'ʃæleɪ/ n chalet m inv; (in holiday camp) bungalow m inv

chalk /tʃɔːk/ n gesso m. **~y** adj gessoso

challeng|e /'tʃælɪndʒ/ n sfida f; (Mil) intimazione f ● vt sfidare; (Mil) intimare il chi va là a; fig mettere in dubbio (statement). **~er** n sfidante mf. **~ing** adj (job) impegnativo

chamber /'tʃeɪmbə(r)/ n C~ of Commerce camera f di commercio

chambermaid n cameriera f [d'albergo]

champagne /ʃæm'peɪn/ n champagne m inv

champion /'tʃæmpɪən/ n (Sport) campione m; (of cause) difensore, difenditrice mf ● vt (defend) difendere; (fight for) lottare per. **~ship** n (Sport) campionato m

chance /tʃɑːns/ n caso m; (possibility) possibilità f inv; (opportunity) occasione f; by ~ per caso; take a ~ provarci; give sb a second ~ dare un'altra possibilità a qcno ● attrib fortuito ● vt I'll ~ it I corro il rischio

chancellor /'tʃɑːnsələ(r)/ n cancelliere m; (Univ) rettore m; C~ of the Exchequer ≈ ministro m del tesoro

chandelier /ʃændə'lɪə(r)/ n lampadario m

change /tʃeɪndʒ/ n cambiamento m; (money) resto m; (small coins) spiccioli mpl; **for a ~** tanto per cambiare; **a ~ of clothes** un cambio di vestiti; the ~ [of life] la menopausa ● vt cambiare; (substitute) scambiare (for con); ~ **one's clothes** cambiarsi [i vestiti]; ~ **trains** cambiare treno ● vi cambiare; (~ clothes) cambiarsi; **all ~!** I stazione terminale!

changeable /'tʃeɪndʒəbl/ adj mutevole; (weather) variabile

'changing-room n camerino m; (for sports) spogliatoio m

channel /'tʃænl/ n canale m; the [English] C~ la Manica; the C~ Islands le Isole del Canale ● vt (pt/pp channelled) ~ **one's energies** into sth convogliare le proprie energie in qcsa

chant /tʃɑːnt/ n cantilena f; (of demonstrators) slogan m inv di protesta ● vt cantare; (demonstrators:) gridare

chaos /'keɪɒs/ n caos m. **~tic** adj caotico

chap /tʃæp/ n I tipo m

chapel /'tʃæpl/ n cappella f

chaperon /'ʃæpərəʊn/ n chaperon f inv ● vt fare da chaperon a (sb)

chapter /'tʃæptə(r)/ n capitolo m

char¹ /tʃɑː(r)/ n I donna f delle pulizie

char² vt (pt/pp charred) (burn) carbonizzare

character /'kærɪktə(r)/ n carattere m; (in novel, play) personaggio m; **quite a** ~ I un tipo particolare

characteristic /kærɪktə'rɪstɪk/ adj

caratteristico • n caratteristica f.
~ally adv tipicamente

characterize /ˈkærɪktəraɪz/ vt caratterizzare

charade /ʃəˈrɑːd/ n farsa f

charcoal /ˈtʃɑː-/ n carbonella f

charge /tʃɑːdʒ/ n (cost) prezzo m; (Electr, Mil) carica f; (Jur) accusa f; free of ~ gratuito; be in ~ essere responsabile (of di); take ~ assumersi la responsabilità; take ~ of occuparsi di • vt far pagare (fee); far pagare a (person); (Electr, Mil) caricare; (Jur) accusare (with di); ~ sb for sth far pagare qcsa a qcno; ~ it to my account lo addebiti sul mio conto • vi (attack) caricare

charitable /ˈtʃærɪtəbl/ adj caritatevole; (kind) indulgente

charity /ˈtʃærətɪ/ n carità f; (organization) associazione f di beneficenza; concert given for ~ concerto m di beneficenza; live on ~ vivere di elemosina

charm /tʃɑːm/ n fascino m; (object) ciondolo m • vt affascinare. ~ing adj affascinante

chart /tʃɑːt/ n carta f nautica; (table) tabella f

charter /ˈtʃɑːtə(r)/ n ~ [flight] [volo m] charter m inv • vt noleggiare. ~ed accountant n commercialista mf

chase /tʃeɪs/ n inseguimento m • vt inseguire. chase away or off vt cacciare via

chassis /ˈʃæsɪ/ n (pl chassis /-sɪz/) telaio m

chastity /ˈtʃæstətɪ/ n castità f

chat /tʃæt/ n chiacchierata f; have a ~ with fare quattro chiacchiere con • vi (pt/pp chatted) chiacchierare; (Comput) chattare. ~ show n talk show m inv

chatter /ˈtʃætə(r)/ n chiacchiere fpl • vi chiacchierare; (teeth:) battere. ~box n 🇬🇧 chiacchierone, -a mf

chauffeur /ˈʃəʊfə(r)/ n autista mf

chauvin|ism /ˈʃəʊvɪnɪzm/ n sciovinismo m. ~ist n sciovinista mf. male ~ist n 🇬🇧 maschilista m

cheap /tʃiːp/ adj a buon mercato; (rate) economico; (vulgar) grossolano; (of poor quality) scadente ~ a buon mercato. ~ly adv a buon mercato

cheat /tʃiːt/ n imbroglione, -a mf; (at cards) baro m • vt imbrogliare; ~ sb out of sth sottrarre qcsa a qcno con l'inganno • vi imbrogliare; (at cards) barare. □ ~ on vt 🇬🇧 tradire (wife)

check¹ /tʃek/ adj (pattern) a quadri • n disegno m a quadri

check² n verifica f; (of tickets) controllo m; (in chess) scacco m; (Am: bill) conto m; (Am: cheque) assegno m; (Am: tick) segnetto m; keep a ~ on controllare; keep in ~ tenere sotto controllo • vt verificare; controllare (tickets); (restrain) contenere; (stop) bloccare • vi controllare; ~ on sth controllare qcsa. □ ~ in vi registrarsi all'arrivo (in albergo); check in f il check-in • vt registrare l'arrivo (in albergo). □ ~ out vi (of hotel) saldare il conto • vt (🇬🇧: investigate) controllare. □ ~ up vi accertarsi; ~ up on prendere informazioni su

check: ~-in n (in airport: place) banco m accettazione, check-in m inv; ~mate int scacco matto!; ~-out n (in supermarket) cassa f. ~-up n (Med) visita f di controllo, check-up m

cheek /tʃiːk/ n guancia f; (impudence) sfacciataggine f. ~y adj sfacciato

cheep /tʃiːp/ vi pigolare

cheer /tʃɪə(r)/ n evviva m inv; three ~s tre urrà; ~s! salute!; (goodbye) arrivederci!; (thanks) grazie! • vt/i acclamare. □ ~ up vt tirare su [di morale] • vi tirarsi su [di morale]; ~ up! su con la vita!. ~ful adj allegro. ~fulness n allegria f. ~ing n acclamazione f

cheerio /tʃɪərɪˈəʊ/ int 🇬🇧 arrivederci

'**cheerless** adj triste, tetro

cheese /tʃiːz/ n formaggio m. ~**cake** n dolce m al formaggio

chef /ʃef/ n cuoco, -a mf, chef mf inv

chemical /ˈkemɪkl/ adj chimico ● n prodotto m chimico

chemist /ˈkemɪst/ n (pharmacist) farmacista mf; (scientist) chimico, -a mf; ~'s [shop] farmacia f. ~ry n chimica f

cheque /tʃek/ n assegno m. ~-**book** n libretto m degli assegni. ~ **card** n carta f assegni

cherish /ˈtʃerɪʃ/ vt curare teneramente; (love) avere caro; nutrire (hope)

cherry /ˈtʃerɪ/ n ciliegia f; (tree) ciliegio m

chess /tʃes/ n scacchi mpl

chessboard n scacchiera f

chest /tʃest/ n petto m; (box) cassapanca f

chestnut /ˈtʃesnʌt/ n castagna f; (tree) castagno m

chest of 'drawers n cassettone m

chew /tʃuː/ vt masticare. ~**inggum** n gomma f da masticare

chic /ʃiːk/ adj chic inv

chick /tʃɪk/ n pulcino m; (🔲: girl) ragazza f

chicken /ˈtʃɪkn/ n pollo m ● adj attrib (soup) di pollo ● **chicken out** vi 🔲 he ~ed out gli è venuta fifa. ~**pox** n varicella f

chicory /ˈtʃɪkərɪ/ n cicoria f

chief /tʃiːf/ adj principale ● n capo m. ~**ly** adv principalmente

chilblain /ˈtʃɪlbleɪn/ n gelone m

child /tʃaɪld/ n (pl ~ren) bambino, -a mf; (son/daughter) figlio, -a mf

child: ~**birth** n parto m. ~**hood** n infanzia f. ~**ish** adj infantile. ~**less** adj senza figli. ~**like** adj ingenuo

Chile /ˈtʃɪlɪ/ n Cile m. ~**an** adj & n cileno, -a mf

chill /tʃɪl/ n freddo m; (illness) infreddatura f ● vt raffreddare

chilli /ˈtʃɪlɪ/ n (pl -es) ~ [pepper] peperoncino m

chilly /ˈtʃɪlɪ/ adj freddo

chime /tʃaɪm/ vi suonare

chimney /ˈtʃɪmnɪ/ n camino m. ~-**pot** n comignolo m. ~-**sweep** n spazzacamino m

chimpanzee /tʃɪmpænˈziː/ n scimpanzé m inv

chin /tʃɪn/ n mento m

china /ˈtʃaɪnə/ n porcellana f

China n Cina f. ~**ese** adj & n cinese mf; (language) cinese m; **the** ~**ese** pl i cinesi

chink¹ /tʃɪŋk/ n (slit) fessura f

chink² /tʃɪŋk/ n (noise) tintinnio m

chip /tʃɪp/ n (fragment) scheggia f; (in china, paintwork) scheggiatura f; (Comput) chip m inv; (in gambling) fiche f inv; ~s pl Br (Culin) patatine fpl fritte; Am (Culin) patatine fpl ● vt (pt/pp chipped) (damage) scheggiare. □ ~ **in** vi 🔲 intromettersi; (with money) contribuire. ~**ped** adj (damaged) scheggiato

chiropod|ist /kɪˈrɒpədɪst/ n podiatra mf inv. ~**y** n podiatria f

chirp /tʃɜːp/ vi cinguettare; (cricket:) fare cri cri. ~**y** adj 🔲 pimpante

chisel /ˈtʃɪzl/ n scalpello m

chival|rous /ˈʃɪvlrəs/ adj cavalleresco. ~**ry** n cavalleria f

chives /tʃaɪvz/ npl erba f cipollina

chlorine /ˈklɔːriːn/ n cloro m

chock-a-block /tʃɒkəˈblɒk/, **chock-full** /tʃɒkˈfʊl/ adj pieno zeppo

chocolate /ˈtʃɒkələt/ n cioccolato m; (drink) cioccolata f; **a** ~ un cioccolatino

choice /tʃɔɪs/ n scelta f ● adj scelto

choir /ˈkwaɪə(r)/ n coro m. ~**boy** n corista m

choke /tʃəʊk/ n (Auto) aria f ● vt/i soffocare

cholera /'kɒlərə/ n colera m
cholesterol /kə'lestərɒl/ n colesterolo m
choose /tʃu:z/ vt/i (pt chose, pp chosen) scegliere; as you ~ come vuoi

chop /tʃɒp/ n (blow) colpo m (d'ascia); (Culin) costata f ● vt (pt/pp chopped) tagliare. □ ~ **down** vt abbattere (tree). □ ~ **off** vt spaccare
chop|per /'tʃɒpə(r)/ n accetta f; 🔲 elicottero m. ~**py** adj increspato
chord /kɔ:d/ n (Mus) corda f
chore /tʃɔ:(r)/ n corvé f inv; [household] ~s faccende fpl domestiche
chorus /'kɔ:rəs/ n coro m; (of song) ritornello m
chose, chosen /tʃəuz/, /'tʃəuzn/ ▷CHOOSE

Christ /kraɪst/ n Cristo m
christen /'krɪsn/ vt battezzare. ~**ing** n battesimo m
Christian /'krɪstʃən/ adj & n cristiano, -a mf. ~**ity** n cristianesimo m. ~ **name** n nome m di battesimo
Christmas /'krɪsməs/ n Natale m ● attrib di Natale. '~ **card** n biglietto m d'auguri di Natale. ~ **Day** n il giorno di Natale. ~ **Eve** n la vigilia di Natale. '~ **present** n regalo m di Natale. '~ **pudding** dolce m natalizio a base di frutta candita e liquore. '~ **tree** n albero m di Natale
chrome /krəum/ n, **chromium** /'krəumɪəm/ n cromo m
chromosome /'krəuməsəum/ n cromosoma m
chronic /'krɒnɪk/ adj cronico
chronicle /'krɒnɪkl/ n cronaca f
chronological /krɒnə'lɒdʒɪkl/ adj cronologico. ~**ly** adv (ordered) in ordine cronologico
chubby /'tʃʌbɪ/ adj (-ier, -iest) paffuto
chuck /tʃʌk/ vt 🔲 buttare. □ ~ **out**

vt 🔲 buttare via (object); buttare fuori (person)
chuckle /'tʃʌkl/ vi ridacchiare
chug /tʃʌg/ vi (pt/pp chugged) the train ~ged out of the station il treno è uscito dalla stazione sbuffando
chum /tʃʌm/ n amico, -a mf. ~**my** adj 🔲 be ~**my with** essere amico di
chunk /tʃʌŋk/ n grosso pezzo m
church /tʃɜ:tʃ/ n chiesa f. ~**yard** n cimitero m
churn /tʃɜ:n/ vt churn out sfornare
chute /ʃu:t/ n scivolo m; (for rubbish) canale m di scarico
cider /'saɪdə(r)/ n sidro m
cigar /sɪ'gɑ:(r)/ n sigaro m
cigarette /sɪgə'ret/ n sigaretta f
cine-camera /'sɪnɪ-/ n cinepresa f
cinema /'sɪnɪmə/ n cinema m inv
cinnamon /'sɪnəmən/ n cannella f
circle /'sɜ:kl/ n cerchio m; (Theat) galleria f; **in a** ~ in cerchio ● vt girare intorno a; cerchiare (mistake) ● vi descrivere dei cerchi
circuit /'sɜ:kɪt/ n giro m; (lap) giro m; (Electr) ~ **board** n circuito m stampato. ~**ous** adj ~**ous route** percorso m lungo e indiretto
circular /'sɜ:kjulə(r)/ adj circolare ● n circolare f
circulat|e /'sɜ:kjuleɪt/ vt far circolare ● vi circolare. ~**ion** n circolazione f; (of newspaper) tiratura f
circumcis|e /'sɜ:kəmsaɪz/ vt circoncidere. ~**ion** n circoncisione f
circumference /ʃə'kʌmfərəns/ n conferenza f
circumstance /'sɜ:kəmstəns/ n circostanza f; ~**s** pl (financial) condizioni fpl finanziarie
circus /'sɜ:kəs/ n circo m
cistern /'sɪstən/ n (tank) cisterna f; (of WC) serbatoio m
cite /saɪt/ vt citare
citizen /'sɪtɪzn/ n cittadino, -a mf;

(of town) abitante mf. ~ship n cittadinanza f

citrus /'sɪtrəs/ n ~ [fruit] agrume m

city /'sɪtɪ/ n città f inv; the C~ la City (di Londra)

> **City** La City è quella parte del centro di Londra dove un tempo si trovava l'antica città. Oggi è il centro finanziario della capitale britannica dove numerose banche e istituti finanziari hanno la propria sede centrale; molto spesso the City indica infatti le istituzioni finanziarie oltre che la zona della città.

civic /'sɪvɪk/ adj civico

civil /'sɪvl/ adj civile

civilian /sɪ'vɪljən/ adj civile; in ~ clothes in borghese ● n civile mf

civilization /sɪvɪlaɪ'zeɪʃn/ n civiltà f inv. ~e vt civilizzare

civil: ~ **'servant** n impiegato, -a mf statale. C~ **'Service** n pubblica amministrazione f

clad /klæd/ adj vestito (in di)

claim /kleɪm/ n richiesta f; (right) diritto m; (assertion) dichiarazione f; lay ~ to sth rivendicare qcsa ● vt richiedere; reclamare (lost property); rivendicare (ownership); ~ that so sostenere che. ~ant n richiedente mf

clairvoyant /kleə'vɔɪənt/ n chiaroveggente mf

clam /klæm/ n (Culin) vongola f ● clam up vi (pt/pp clammed) zittirsi

clamber /'klæmbə(r)/ vi arrampicarsi

clammy /'klæmɪ/ adj (-ier, -iest) appiccicaticcio

clamour /'klæmə(r)/ n (protest) rimostranza f ● vi ~ for chiedere a gran voce

clamp /klæmp/ n morsa f ● vt ammorsare; (Auto) mettere i ceppi bloccaruote a. ◻~ **down** vi 🔢 essere duro; ~ **down on** reprimere

clan /klæn/ n clan m inv

clang /klæŋ/ n suono m metallico. ~**er** n 🔢 gaffe f inv

clap /klæp/ n give sb a ~ applaudire qcno; ~ of thunder tuono m ● vt/i (pt/pp clapped) applaudire; ~ one's hands applaudire. ~**ping** n applausi mpl

clari|fication /klærɪfɪ'keɪʃn/ n chiarimento m. ~**fy** vt/i (pt/pp -ied) chiarire

clarinet /klærɪ'net/ n clarinetto m

clarity /'klærətɪ/ n chiarezza f

clash /klæʃ/ n scontro m; (noise) fragore m ● vi scontrarsi; (colours:) stonare; (events:) coincidere

clasp /klɑːsp/ n chiusura f ● vt agganciare; (hold) stringere

class /klɑːs/ n classe f; (lesson) corso m ● vt classificare

classic /'klæsɪk/ adj classico ● n classico m; ~s pl (Univ) lettere fpl classiche. ~**al** adj classico

classi|fication /klæsɪfɪ'keɪʃn/ n classificazione f. ~**fy** vt (pt/pp -ied) classificare

classroom n aula f

classy /'klɑːsɪ/ adj (-ier, -iest) 🔢 d'alta classe

clatter /'klætə(r)/ n fracasso m ● vi far fracasso

clause /klɔːz/ n clausola f; (Gram) proposizione f

claustrophob|ia /klɔːstrə'fəʊbɪə/ n claustrofobia f

claw /klɔː/ n artiglio m; (of crab, lobster & (Techn)) tenaglia f ● vt (cat:) graffiare

clay /kleɪ/ n argilla f

clean /kliːn/ adj pulito, lindo ● adv completamente ● vt pulire (shoes, windows); ~ one's teeth lavarsi i denti; have a coat ~ed portare un cappotto in lavanderia. **clean up** vt pulire ● vi far pulizia

cleaner /'kli:nə(r)/ n uomo m/donna f delle pulizie; (substance) detersivo m; [dry] ~'s lavanderia f, tintoria f

cleanliness /'klenlɪnɪs/ n pulizia f

cleanse /klenz/ vt pulire. ~r n detergente m

cleansing cream /'klenz-/ n latte m detergente

clear /klɪə(r)/ adj chiaro; (conscience) pulito; (road) libero; (profit, majority) netto; (sky) sereno; (water) limpido; (glass) trasparente; **make sth** ~ mettere qcsa in chiaro; **have I made myself** ~? mi sono fatto capire?; **five** ~ **days** cinque giorni buoni ● adv **stand** ~ **of** allontanarsi da; **keep** ~ **of** tenersi alla larga da ● vt sgombrare (room, street); sparecchiare (table); (acquit) scagionare; (authorize) autorizzare; scavalcare senza toccare (fence, wall); guadagnare (sum of money); passare (Customs); ~ **one's throat** schiarirsi la gola ● vi (face, sky:) rasserenarsi; (fog:) dissiparsi. □ ~ **away** vt metter via. □ ~ **off** □ filar via. □ ~ **out** vt sgombrare ● vi □ filar via. □ ~ **up** vt (tidy) mettere a posto; chiarire (mystery) ● vi (weather:) schiarirsi

clearance /'klɪərəns/ n (space) spazio m libero; (authorization) autorizzazione f; (Customs) sdoganamento m. ~ **sale** n liquidazione f

clear|ing /'klɪərɪŋ/ n radura f. ~ly adv chiaramente. ~**way** n (Auto) strada f con divieto di sosta

cleavage /'kli:vɪdʒ/ n (woman's) décolleté m inv

clench /klentʃ/ vt serrare

clergy /'klɜ:dʒɪ/ npl clero m. ~**man** n ecclesiastico m

cleric /'klerɪk/ n ecclesiastico m. ~**al** adj impiegatizio; (Relig) clericale

clerk /klɑ:k/, Am /klɜ:k/ n impie-

gato, -a mf; (Am: shop assistant) commesso, -a mf

clever /'klevə(r)/ adj intelligente; (skilful) abile

cliché /'kli:ʃeɪ/ n cliché m inv

click /klɪk/ vi scattare; (Comput) cliccare ● n (Comput) click m. **click on** vt (Comput) cliccare su

client /'klaɪənt/ n cliente mf

cliff /klɪf/ n scogliera f

climat|e /'klaɪmət/ n clima f. ~**e change** n cambiamento m climatico. ~**ic** adj climatico

climax /'klaɪmæks/ n punto m culminante

climb /klaɪm/ n salita f ● vt scalare (mountain); arrampicarsi su (ladder, tree) ● vi arrampicarsi; (rise) salire; (road:) salire. □ ~ **down** vi scendere; (from ladder, tree) scendere; fig tornare sui propri passi

climber /'klaɪmə(r)/ n alpinista mf; (plant) rampicante m

clinch /klɪntʃ/ vt □ concludere (deal) ● n (in boxing) clinch m inv

cling /klɪŋ/ vi (pt/pp clung) aggrapparsi; (stick) aderire. ~ **film** n pellicola f trasparente

clinic /'klɪnɪk/ n ambulatorio m. ~**al** adj clinico

clink /klɪŋk/ n tintinnio m; (□: prison) galera f ● vi tintinnare

clip¹ /klɪp/ n fermaglio m; (jewellery) spilla f ● vt (pt/pp clipped) attaccare

clip² /klɪp/ n (extract) taglio m ● vt obliterare (ticket). ~**board** n fermabloc m inv. ~**pers** npl (for hair) rasoio m; (for hedge) tosasiepi m inv; (for nails) tronchesina f. ~**ping** n (from newspaper) ritaglio m

cloak /kləʊk/ n mantello m. ~**room** n guardaroba m inv; (toilet) bagno m

clock /klɒk/ n orologio m; (□: speedometer) tachimetro m. □ ~ **in** vi attaccare. □ ~ **out** vi staccare

clock: ~**wise** adj & adv in senso orario. ~**work** n meccanismo m

clog /klɒg/ n zoccolo m • vt (pt/pp clogged) ∼ [up] intasare (drain); inceppare (mechanism) • vi (drain): intasarsi

cloister /ˈklɔɪstə(r)/ n chiostro m

clone /kləʊn/ n clone m

close[1] /kləʊs/ adj vicino; (friend) intimo; (weather) afoso; have a ∼ shave 🔢 scamparla bella; be ∼ to sb essere unito a qcno • adv vicino; ∼ by vicino; ∼ on five o'clock quasi le cinque

close[2] /kləʊz/ n fine f • vt chiudere • vi chiudersi; (shop:) chiudere. □ ∼ down vt chiudere • vi (TV station:) interrompere la trasmissione; (factory:) chiudere

closely /ˈkləʊslɪ/ adv da vicino; (watch, listen) attentamente

closet /ˈklɒzɪt/ n Am armadio m

close-up /ˈkləʊs-/ n primo piano m

closure /ˈkləʊʒə(r)/ n chiusura f

clot /klɒt/ n grumo m; (🔢: idiot) tonto, -a mf • vi (pt/pp clotted) (blood:) coagularsi

cloth /klɒθ/ n (fabric) tessuto m; (duster etc) straccio m

clothe /kləʊð/ vt vestire

clothes /kləʊðz/ npl vestiti mpl, abiti mpl. ∼-brush n spazzola f per abiti. ∼-line n corda f stendibiancheria

clothing /ˈkləʊðɪŋ/ n abbigliamento m

cloud /klaʊd/ n nuvola f • cloud over vi rannuvolarsi. ∼burst n acquazzone m

cloudy /ˈklaʊdɪ/ adj (-ier, -iest) nuvoloso; (liquid) torbido

clout /klaʊt/ n 🔢 colpo m; (influence) impatto m (with su) • vt 🔢 colpire

clove /kləʊv/ n chiodo m di garofano; ∼ of garlic spicchio m d'aglio

clover /ˈkləʊvə(r)/ n trifoglio m

clown /klaʊn/ n pagliaccio m • vi ∼ [about] fare il pagliaccio

club /klʌb/ n club m inv; (weapon)

clava f; (Sport) mazza f; ∼s pl (Cards) fiori mpl • v (pt/pp clubbed) • vt bastonare. □ ∼ together vi unirsi

cluck /klʌk/ vi chiocciare

clue /kluː/ n indizio m; (in crossword) definizione f; I haven't a ∼ 🔢 non ne ho idea

clump /klʌmp/ n gruppo m

clumsiness /ˈklʌmzɪnɪs/ n goffaggine f

clumsy /ˈklʌmzɪ/ adj (-ier, -iest) maldestro; (tool) scomodo; (remark) senza tatto

clung /klʌŋ/ ▷ CLING

cluster /ˈklʌstə(r)/ n gruppo m • vi raggrupparsi (round intorno a)

clutch /klʌtʃ/ n stretta f; (Auto) frizione f; be in sb's ∼es essere in balia di qcno • vt stringere; (grab) afferrare • vi ∼ at afferrare

clutter /ˈklʌtə(r)/ n caos m • vt ∼ [up] ingombrare

coach /kəʊtʃ/ n pullman m inv; (Rail) vagone m; (horse-drawn) carrozza f; (Sport) allenatore, -trice mf • vt fare esercitare; (Sport) allenare

coal /kəʊl/ n carbone m

coalition /kəʊəˈlɪʃn/ n coalizione f

coarse /kɔːs/ adj grossolano; (joke) spinto

coast /kəʊst/ n costa f • vi (free-wheel) scendere a ruota libera • ∼al adj costiero. ∼er n (mat) sottobicchiere m inv

coast: ∼guard n guardia f costiera. ∼line n litorale m

coat /kəʊt/ n cappotto m; (of animal) manto m; (of paint) mano f; ∼ of arms stemma f • vt coprire; (with paint) ricoprire. ∼-hanger n gruccia f. ∼-hook n gancio m [appendiabiti]

coating /ˈkəʊtɪŋ/ n rivestimento m; (of paint) stato m

coax /kəʊks/ vt convincere con le moine

cobweb /ˈkɒb-/ n ragnatela f

cocaine /kə'keɪn/ n cocaina f

cock /kɒk/ n gallo m; (any male bird) maschio m • vt sollevare (il grilletto di (gun); ∼ **its ears** (animal): drizzare le orecchie

cockerel /'kɒkərəl/ n galletto m

cock-'eyed adj 🔢 storto; (absurd) assurdo

cockney /'kɒknɪ/ n (dialect) dialetto m londinese; (person) abitante mf dell'est di Londra

cock: ∼pit n (Aeron) cabina f. **∼roach** /-rəʊtʃ/ n scarafaggio m. **∼tail** n cocktail m inv. **∼up** n 🔲 **make a ∼up** fare un casino (of con)

cocky /'kɒkɪ/ adj (-ier, -iest) 🔢 presuntuoso

cocoa /'kəʊkəʊ/ n cacao m

coconut /'kəʊkənʌt/ n noce f di cocco

cocoon /kə'ku:n/ n bozzolo m

cod /kɒd/ n inv merluzzo m

COD abbr (cash on delivery) pagamento m alla consegna

code /kəʊd/ n codice m. **∼d** adj codificato

coedu'cational /kəʊ-/ adj misto

coerc|e /kəʊ'ɜːs/ vt costringere. **∼ion** n coercizione f

coffee /'kɒfɪ/ n caffè m inv

coffeepot n caffettiera f

coffin /'kɒfɪn/ n bara f

cog /kɒg/ n (Techn) dente m (di ruota)

coherent /kəʊ'hɪərənt/ adj coerente; (when speaking) logico

coil /kɔɪl/ n rotolo m; (Electr) bobina f; ∼**s** pl spire fpl • vt ∼ [**up**] avvolgere

coin /kɔɪn/ n moneta f • vt coniare (word)

coincide /kəʊɪn'saɪd/ vi coincidere

coinciden|ce /kəʊ'ɪnsɪdəns/ n coincidenza f. ∼**tal** adj casuale. ∼**tally** adv casualmente

coke /kəʊk/ n [carbone m] coke m

Coke® n Coca[-cola]® f

cold /kəʊld/ adj freddo; **I'm ∼** ho freddo • n freddo m; (Med) raffreddore m

cold-'blooded adj spietato

coleslaw /'kəʊlslɔ:/ n insalata f di cavolo crudo, cipolle e carote in maionese

collaborat|e /kə'læbəreɪt/ vi collaborare; ∼**e on sth** collaborare in qcsa. ∼**ion** n collaborazione f; (with enemy) collaborazionismo m. ∼**or** n collaboratore, -trice mf; (with enemy) collaborazionista f

collaps|e /kə'læps/ n crollo m • vi (person): svenire; (roof, building): crollare. ∼**ible** adj pieghevole

collar /'kɒlə(r)/ n colletto m; (for animal) collare m. ∼**bone** n clavicola f

colleague /'kɒli:g/ n collega mf

collect /kə'lekt/ vt andare a prendere (person); ritirare (parcel, tickets); riscuotere (taxes); raccogliere (rubbish); (as hobby) collezionare • vi riunirsi • adv call ∼ Am telefonare a carico del destinatario. ∼**ed** adj controllato

collection /kə'lekʃn/ n collezione f; (in church) questua f; (of rubbish) raccolta f; (of post) levata f

collector /kə'lektə(r)/ n (of stamps etc) collezionista m

college /'kɒlɪdʒ/ n istituto m parauniversitario; C∼ **of**... Scuola f di...

collide /kə'laɪd/ vi scontrarsi

collision /kə'lɪʒn/ n scontro m

colloquial /kə'ləʊkwɪəl/ adj colloquiale. ∼**ism** n espressione f colloquiale

colon /'kəʊlən/ n due punti mpl; (Anat) colon m inv

colonel /'kɜ:nl/ n colonnello m

colonial /kə'ləʊnɪəl/ adj coloniale

colon|ize /'kɒlənaɪz/ vt colonizzare. ∼**y** n colonia f

colossal /kə'lɒsl/ adj colossale

colour /'kʌlə(r)/ n colore m; (com-

plexion) colorito *m*; ~s *pl* (*flag*) bandiera *fsg*; off ~ 🔲 giù di tono ● *vt* colorare; ~ [in] colorare *vt* (*with blush*) arrossire

colour: ~**-blind** *adj* daltonico. ~**ed** *adj* colorato; (*person*) di colore ● *n* (*person*) persona *f* di colore. ~**ful** *adj* pieno di colore. ~**less** *adj* incolore

column /ˈkɒləm/ *n* colonna *f*. ~**ist** *n* giornalista *mf* che cura una rubrica

coma /ˈkəʊmə/ *n* coma *m* inv

comb /kəʊm/ *n* pettine *m*; (*for wearing*) pettinino *m* ● *vt* pettinare; (*fig: search*) setacciare; ~ **one's hair** pettinarsi i capelli

combat /ˈkɒmbæt/ *n* combattimento *m* ● *vt* (*pt/pp* combated) combattere

combination /kɒmbɪˈneɪʃn/ *n* combinazione *f*

combine¹ /kəmˈbaɪn/ *vt* unire; ~ **a job with being a mother** conciliare il lavoro con il ruolo di madre ● *vi* (*chemical elements*) combinarsi

combine² /ˈkɒmbaɪn/ *n* (*Comm*) associazione *f*. ~ **harvester** *n* mietitrebbia *f*

combustion /kəmˈbʌstʃn/ *n* combustione *f*

come /kʌm/ *vi* (*pt* came, *pp* come) venire; **where do you ~ from?** da dove vieni?; ~ **to** (*reach*) arrivare a; **that ~s to £10** fanno 10 sterline; ~ **into money** ricevere dei soldi; ~ **true/open** verificarsi/aprirsi; ~ **first** arrivare primo; *fig* venire prima di tutto; ~ **in two sizes** esistere in due misure; **the years to ~** gli anni a venire; **how ~?** 🔲 come mai? **come about** *vi* succedere. □ ~ **across** *vi* ~ **across as being** 🔲 dare l'impressione di essere ● *vt* (*find*) imbattersi in. □ ~ **along** *vi* venire; (*job, opportunity:*) presentarsi; (*progress*) andare bene. □ ~ **apart** *vi* smontarsi; (*break*) rompersi. □ ~ **away** *vi* venir via; (*button, fastener:*) staccarsi. □ ~ **back** *vi* ritornare. □ ~ **by**

vi passare ● *vt* (*obtain*) avere. □ ~ **down** *vi* scendere; ~ **down to** (*reach*) arrivare a. **come in** *vi* entrare; (*in race*) arrivare; (*tide:*) salire. □ ~ **in for** *vi* ~ **in for criticism** essere criticato. □ ~ **off** *vi* staccarsi; (*take place*) esserci; (*succeed*) riuscire. □ ~ **on** *vi* (*make progress*) migliorare; ~ **on!** (*hurry*) dai!; (*indicating disbelief*) ma va là!. □ ~ **out** *vi* venir fuori; (*book, sun:*) uscire; (*stain:*) andar via. □ ~ **over** *vi* venire. □ ~ **round** *vi* venire; (*after fainting*) riaversi; (*change one's mind*) farsi convincere. □ ~ **to** *vi* (*after fainting*) riaversi. □ ~ **up** *vi* salire; (*sun:*) sorgere; (*plant:*) crescere; **something came up** (*I was prevented*) ho avuto un imprevisto. □ ~ **up with** *vt* tirar fuori

'come-back *n* ritorno *m*

comedian /kəˈmiːdɪən/ *n* comico *m*

comedy /ˈkɒmədɪ/ *n* commedia *f*

comet /ˈkɒmɪt/ *n* cometa *f*

comfort /ˈkʌmfət/ *n* benessere *m*; (*consolation*) conforto *m* ● *vt* confortare

comfortabl|e /ˈkʌmfətəbl/ *adj* comodo; **be ~e** (*person:*) stare comodo; (*fig: in situation*) essere a proprio agio; (*financially*) star bene. ~**y** *adv* comodamente

'comfort station *n* Am bagno *m* pubblico

comic /ˈkɒmɪk/ *adj* comico ● *n* comico, -a *mf*; (*periodical*) fumetto *m*. ~**al** *adj* comico. ~ **strip** *n* striscia *f* di fumetti

coming /ˈkʌmɪŋ/ *n* venuta *f*; ~**s and goings** viavai *m*

comma /ˈkɒmə/ *n* virgola *f*

command /kəˈmɑːnd/ *n* comando *m*; (*order*) ordine *m*; (*mastery*) padronanza *f* ● *vt* ordinare; comandare (*army*)

commandeer /kɒmənˈdɪə(r)/ *vt* requisire

command|er /kəˈmɑːndə(r)/ *n* comandante *m*. ~**ing** *adj* (*view*) impo-

nente; (lead) dominante. **~ing** officer n comandante m. **~ment** n
comandamento m

commemorat|e /kə'memərert/ vt
commemorare. **~ion** n commemo-
razione f. **~ive** adj commemorativo

commence /kə'mens/ vt/i cominciare. **~ment** n inizio m

commend /kə'mend/ vt compli-
mentarsi con (on per); (recommend)
raccomandare (to a). **~able** adj lodevole

comment /'kɒment/ n commento
m •vi fare commenti (on su)

commentary /'kɒməntrɪ/ n commento m; [running] **~** (on radio, (TV)
cronaca f diretta

commentat|e /'kɒməntert/ vt **~**e
on (TV, Radio) fare la cronaca di. **~or**
n cronista mf

commerce /'kɒmɜːs/ n commercio m

commercial /kə'mɜːʃl/ adj commerciale •n (TV) pubblicità f inv.
~ize vt commercializzare

commiserate /kə'mɪzəreɪt/ vi
esprimere il proprio rincrescimento
(with a)

commission /kə'mɪʃn/ n commissione f; receive one's **~** (Mil) essere
promosso ufficiale; out of **~** fuori
uso vt commissionare

commissionaire /kəmɪʃə'neə(r)/
n portiere m

commit /kə'mɪt/ vt (pt/pp committed) commettere; (to prison, hospital)
affidare (to a); impegnare (funds);
~ oneself impegnarsi. **~ment** n
impegno m; (involvement) compromis-
sione f. **~ted** adj impegnato

committee /kə'mɪtɪ/ n comitato m

commodity /kə'mɒdətɪ/ n prodotto m

common /'kɒmən/ adj comune;
(vulgar) volgare •n prato m pubblico;
have in **~** avere in comune; House
of C**~**s Camera f dei Comuni. **~er** n

persona f non nobile

common: **~ law** n diritto m con-
suetudinario. **~ly** adv comunemente.
C**~** 'Market n Mercato m Comune.
~place adj banale. **~room** n sala f
dei professori/degli studenti. **~**
'sense n buon senso m

commotion /kə'məʊʃn/ n confusione f

communicate /kə'mjuːnɪkeɪt/ vt/i
comunicare

communication /kəmjuːnɪ'-
keɪʃn/ n comunicazione f; (of disease)
trasmissione f; be in **~** with sb essere in contatto con qcno; **~s** pl
(technology) telecomunicazioni fpl. **~**
cord n fermata f d'emergenza

communicative /kə'mjuːnɪkətɪv/
adj comunicativo

Communion /kə'mjuːnɪən/ n
[Holy] **~** comunione f

Communis|m /'kɒmjʊnɪzm/ n co-
munismo m. **~t** adj & n comunista mf

community /kə'mjuːnətɪ/ n comunità f. **~ centre** n centro m sociale

commute /kə'mjuːt/ vi fare il pendolare •vt (Jur) commutare. **~r** n
pendolare mf

compact[1] /kəm'pækt/ adj
compatto

compact[2] /'kɒmpækt/ n portacipria *m inv*. ~ disc *n* compact disc *m inv*

companion /kəm'pænjən/ *n* compagno, -a *mf*. ~**ship** *n* compagnia *f*

company /'kʌmpəni/ *n* compagnia *f*; (*guests*) ospiti *mpl*. ~ car *n* macchina *f* della ditta

comparable /'kɒmpərəbl/ *adj* paragonabile

comparative /kəm'pærətɪv/ *adj* comparativo; (*relative*) relativo • *n* (*Gram*) comparativo *m*. ~**ly** *adv* relativamente

compare /kəm'peə(r)/ *vt* paragonare (with/to a) • *vi* essere paragonato

comparison /kəm'pærɪsn/ *n* paragone *m*

compartment /kəm'pɑːtmənt/ *n* compartimento *m*; (*Rail*) scompartimento *m*

compass /'kʌmpəs/ *n* bussola *f*. ~**es** *npl*, pair of ~**es** compasso *msg*

compassion /kəm'pæʃn/ *n* compassione *f*. ~**ate** *adj* compassionevole

compatible /kəm'pætəbl/ *adj* compatibile

compel /kəm'pel/ *vt* (*pt/pp* compelled) costringere. ~**ling** *adj* (*reason*) inconfutabile

compensate /'kɒmpənseɪt/ *vt* risarcire • *vi* ~ for *fig* compensare di. ~**ion** *n* risarcimento *m*; (*fig: comfort*) consolazione *f*

compère /'kɒmpeə(r)/ *n* presentatore, -trice *mf*

compete /kəm'piːt/ *vi* competere; (*take part*) gareggiare

competen|ce /'kɒmpɪtəns/ *n* competenza *f*. ~**t** *adj* competente

competition /kɒmpə'tɪʃn/ *n* concorrenza *f*; (*contest*) gara *f*

competitive /kəm'petɪtɪv/ *adj* competitivo; ~ prices prezzi *mpl* concorrenziali

competitor /kəm'petɪtə(r)/ *n*

concorrente *mf*

complacen|cy /kəm'pleɪsnsi/ *n* compiacimento *m*. ~**t** *adj* compiaciuto

complain /kəm'pleɪn/ *vi* lamentarsi (about di); (*formally*) reclamare; ~ of (*Med*) accusare. ~**t** *n* lamentela *f*; (*formal*) reclamo *m*; (*Med*) disturbo *m*

complement¹ /'kɒmplɪmənt/ *n* complemento *m*

complement² /'kɒmplɪment/ *vt* complementare; ~ each other complementarsi a vicenda. ~**ary** *adj* complementare

complete /kəm'pliːt/ *adj* completo; (*utter*) finito • *vt* completare; compilare (form). ~**ly** *adv* completamente

completion /kəm'pliːʃn/ *n* fine *f*

complex /'kɒmpleks/ *adj* complesso • *n* complesso *m*

complexion /kəm'plekʃn/ *n* carnagione *f*

complexity /kəm'pleksəti/ *n* complessità *f inv*

complicat|e /'kɒmplɪkeɪt/ *vt* complicare. ~**ed** *adj* complicato. ~**ion** *n* complicazione *f*

compliment /'kɒmplɪmənt/ *n* complimento *m*; ~**s** *pl* omaggi *mpl* • *vt* complimentare. ~**ary** *adj* complimentoso; (*given free*) in omaggio

comply /kəm'plaɪ/ *vi* (*pt/pp* -ied) ~ with conformarsi a

component /kəm'pəʊnənt/ *adj* & *n* ~ [part] componente *m*

compose /kəm'pəʊz/ *vt* comporre; ~ oneself ricomporsi; be ~d of essere composto da. ~**d** *adj* (calm) composto. ~**r** *n* compositore, -trice *mf*

composition /kɒmpə'zɪʃn/ *n* composizione *f*; (*essay*) tema *m*

compost /'kɒmpɒst/ *n* composta *f*

composure /kəm'pəʊʒə(r)/ *n* calma *f*

compound /'kɒmpaʊnd/ *adj* composto. ~ fracture *n* frattura *f* esposta. ~ 'interest n interesse m composto ● n (Chem) composto m; (Gram) parola f composta; (enclosure) recinto m

comprehen|d /kɒmprɪ'hend/ vt comprendere. ~**sible** adj comprensibile. ~**sion** n comprensione f

comprehensive /kɒmprɪ'hensɪv/ adj & n comprensivo; ~ [**school**] scuola f media in cui gli allievi hanno capacità d'apprendimento diverse. ~ **insurance** n (Auto) polizza f casco

compress[1] /'kɒmpres/ n compressa f

compress[2] /kəm'pres/ vt comprimere; ~**ed air** aria f compressa

comprise /kəm'praɪz/ vt comprendere; (form) costituire

compromise /'kɒmprəmaɪz/ n compromesso m ● vt compromettere ● vi fare un compromesso

compuls|ion /kəm'pʌlʃn/ n desiderio m irresistibile. ~**ive** adj (Psych) patologico. ~**ive** eating voglia f ossessiva di mangiare. ~**ory** adj obbligatorio

compute /kəm'pjuːt/ vt calcolare

comput|er /kəm'pjuːtə(r)/ n computer m inv. ~**erize** vt computerizzare. ~**ing** n informatica f

comrade /'kɒmreɪd/ n camerata m; (Pol) compagno, -a mf. ~**ship** n cameratismo m

con[1] /kɒn/ ▷**PRO**

con[2] n 🔟 fregatura f ● vt (pt/pp conned) 🔟 fregare

concave /'kɒnkeɪv/ adj concavo

conceal /kən'siːl/ vt nascondere

concede /kən'siːd/ vt (admit) ammettere; (give up) rinunciare a; lasciar fare (goal)

conceit /kən'siːt/ n presunzione f. ~**ed** adj presuntuoso

conceivable /kən'siːvəbl/ adj concepibile

conceive /kən'siːv/ vt (Biol) concepire ● vi aver figli. ▫ ~ **of** vt fig

concepire

concentrat|e /'kɒnsəntreɪt/ vt concentrare ● vi concentrarsi. ~**ion** n concentrazione f. ~**ion camp** n campo m di concentramento

concept /'kɒnsept/ n concetto m. ~**ion** n concezione f; (idea) idea f

concern /kən'sɜːn/ n preoccupazione f; (Comm) attività f inv ● vt (be about, affect) riguardare; (worry) preoccupare; be ~**ed about** essere preoccupato per; ~ **oneself** with preoccuparsi di; as far as I am ~**ed** per quanto mi riguarda. ~**ing** prep riguardo a

concert /'kɒnsət/ n concerto m. ~**ed** adj collettivo

concertina /kɒnsə'tiːnə/ n piccola fisarmonica f

concerto /kən'tʃeətəʊ/ n certo m

concession /kən'seʃn/ n concessione f; (reduction) sconto m. ~**ary** adj (reduced) scontato

concise /kən'saɪs/ adj conciso

conclu|de /kən'kluːd/ vt concludere ● vi concludersi. ~**ding** adj finale

conclusion /kən'kluːʒn/ n conclusione f; in ~ per concludere

conclusive /kən'kluːsɪv/ adj definitivo. ~**ly** adv in modo definitivo

concoct /kən'kɒkt/ vt confezionare; fig inventare. ~**ion** n mistura f; (drink) intruglio m

concrete /'kɒnkriːt/ adj concreto ● n calcestruzzo m

concussion /kən'kʌʃn/ n commozione f cerebrale

condemn /kən'dem/ vt condannare; dichiarare inagibile (building). ~**ation** n condanna f

condensation /kɒndenˈseɪʃn/ n condensazione f

condense /kən'dens/ vt condensare; (Phys) condensare ● vi condensarsi. ~**d milk** n latte m condensato

condescend /kɒndɪ'send/ vi degnarsi. ~ing adj condiscendente

condition /kən'dɪʃn/ n condizione f; on ~ that a condizione che • vt (Psych) condizionare. ~al adj (acceptance) condizionato; (Gram) condizionale • n (Gram) condizionale m. ~er n balsamo m; (for fabrics) ammorbidente m

condolences /kən'dəʊlənsɪz/ npl condoglianze fpl

condom /'kɒndəm/ n preservativo m

condo[minium] /'kɒndə ('mɪnɪəm)/ n Am condominio m

condone /kən'dəʊn/ vt passare sopra a

conduct¹ /'kɒndʌkt/ n condotta f

conduct² /kən'dʌkt/ vt condurre; dirigere (orchestra). ~or n direttore m d'orchestra; (of bus) bigliettaio m; (Phys) conduttore m. ~ress n bigliettaia f

cone /kəʊn/ n cono m; (Bot) pigna f; (Auto) birillo m • **cone off** vt be ~d off (Auto) essere chiuso da birilli

confederation /kənfedə'reɪʃn/ n confederazione f

conference /'kɒnfərəns/ n conferenza f

confess /kən'fes/ vt confessare • vi confessare; (Relig) confessarsi. ~ion n confessione f. ~ional n confessionale m. ~or n confessore m

confetti /kən'fetɪ/ n coriandoli mpl

confide /kən'faɪd/ vt confidare. □ ~ in vt ~ in sb fidarsi di qcno

confidence /'kɒnfɪdəns/ n (trust) fiducia f; (self-assurance) sicurezza f di sé; (secret) confidenza f; in ~ in confidenza. ~ trick n truffa f

confident /'kɒnfɪdənt/ adj fiducioso; (self-assured) sicuro di sé. ~ly adv con aria fiduciosa

confidential /kɒnfɪ'denʃl/ adj confidenziale

configur|ation /kənfɪgə'reɪʃn/ n configurazione f. ~e vt configurare

confine /kən'faɪn/ vt rinchiudere; (limit) limitare; be ~d to bed essere confinato a letto. ~d adj (space) limitato. ~ment n detenzione f; (Med) parto m

confirm /kən'fɜːm/ vt confermare; (Relig) cresimare. ~ation n conferma f; (Relig) cresima f. ~ed adj incallito; ~ed bachelor scapolo m impenitente

confiscat|e /'kɒnfɪskeɪt/ vt confiscare. ~ion n confisca f

conflict¹ /'kɒnflɪkt/ n conflitto m

conflict² /kən'flɪkt/ vi essere in contraddizione. ~ing adj contraddittorio

conform /kən'fɔːm/ vi (person:) conformarsi; (thing:) essere conforme (to a). ~ist n conformista mf

confounded /kən'faʊndɪd/ adj 🔢 maledetto

confront /kən'frʌnt/ vt affrontare; the problems ~ing us i problemi che dobbiamo affrontare. ~ation n confronto m

confus|e /kən'fjuːz/ vt confondere. ~ing adj che confonde. ~ion n confusione f

congeal /kən'dʒiːl/ vi (blood:) coagularsi

congest|ed /kən'dʒestɪd/ adj congestionato. ~ion n congestione f

congratulat|e /kən'grætjʊleɪt/ vt congratularsi con (on per). ~ions npl radunarsi

congregat|e /'kɒŋgrɪgeɪt/ vi radunarsi. ~ion n (Relig) assemblea f

congress /'kɒŋgres/ n congresso m. ~man n Am (Pol) membro m del congresso

conifer /'kɒnɪfə(r)/ n conifera f

conjugat|e /'kɒndʒʊgeɪt/ vt coniugare. ~ion n coniugazione f

conjunction /kən'dʒʌŋkʃn/ n congiunzione f; in ~ with insieme a

conjur|e /'kʌndʒə(r)/ vi ~ing

tricks *npl* giochi *mpl* di prestigio. ~or
n prestigiatore, -trice *mf*. □ ~ up *vt*
evocare (image); tirar fuori dal nulla
(meal)

conk /kɒŋk/ *vi* ~ out 𝕀 truffatore *m*
guastarsi; (person:) crollare

'con-man *n* 𝕀 truffatore *m*

connect /kəˈnekt/ *vt* collegare;
~ed with avere legami con; (be related to) essere imparentato con; be
well ~ed aver conoscenze influenti
● *vi* essere collegato (with a); (train:)
fare coincidenza

connection /kəˈnekʃn/ *n* (between
ideas) nesso *m*; (in travel) coincidenza
f; (Electr) collegamento *m*; in ~ with
con riferimento a. ~s *pl* (people) conoscenze *fpl*

connoisseur /kɒnəˈsɜː(r)/ *n* inten-
ditore, -trice *mf*

conquer /ˈkɒŋkə(r)/ *vt* conquistare;
fig superare (fear). ~or *n* conquista-
tore *m*

conquest /ˈkɒŋkwest/ *n* conquista *f*

conscience /ˈkɒnʃəns/ *n* coscienza *f*

conscientious /kɒnʃɪˈenʃəs/ *adj*
coscienzioso. ~ ob'jector *n* obiet-
tore *m* di coscienza

conscious /ˈkɒnʃəs/ *adj* conscio;
(decision) meditato; [fully] ~ co-
sciente; be/become ~ of sth rendersi conto di qcsa. ~ly *adv* consapevolmente. ~ness *n*
consapevolezza *f*; (Med) conoscenza *f*

conscript[1] /ˈkɒnskrɪpt/ *n* co-
scritto *m*

conscript[2] /kənˈskrɪpt/ *vt* (Mil)
chiamare alle armi. ~ion *n* coscri-
zione *f*, leva *f*

consecrat|e /ˈkɒnsɪkreɪt/ *vt* consa-
crare. ~ion *n* consacrazione *f*

consecutive /kənˈsekjʊtɪv/ *adj*
consecutivo

consensus /kənˈsensəs/ *n* consenso *m*

consent /kənˈsent/ *n* consenso *m*
● *vi* acconsentire

consequen|ce /ˈkɒnsɪkwəns/ *n*
conseguenza *f*; (importance) importanza *f*. ~t *adj* conseguente. ~tly
adv di conseguenza

conservation /kɒnsəˈveɪʃn/ *n*
conservazione *f*. ~ist *n* fautore,
-trice *mf* della tutela ambientale

conservative /kənˈsɜːvətɪv/ *adj*
conservativo; (estimate) ottimistico.
C~ (Pol) *adj* conservatore ● *n* conservatore, -trice *mf*

conservatory /kənˈsɜːvətrɪ/ *n*
spazio *m* chiuso da vetrate adiacente
alla casa

conserve /kənˈsɜːv/ *vt* conservare

consider /kənˈsɪdə(r)/ *vt* considerare; ~ doing sth considerare la
possibilità di fare qcsa. ~able *adj*
considerevole. ~ably *adv* considere-
volmente

consider|ate /kənˈsɪdərət/ *adj*
pieno di riguardo. ~ately *adv* con riguardo. ~ation *n* considerazione *f*;
(thoughtfulness) attenzione *f*; (respect)
riguardo *m*; (payment) compenso *m*;
take sth into ~ation prendere qcsa
in considerazione. ~ing *prep* consi-
derando

consign /kənˈsaɪn/ *vt* affidare.
~ment *n* consegna *f*

consist /kənˈsɪst/ *vi* ~ of consi-
stere di

consisten|cy /kənˈsɪstənsɪ/ *n* coe-
renza *f*; (density) consistenza *f*. ~t *adj*
coerente; (loyalty) costante. ~tly
adv coerentemente; (late, loyal) costantemente

consolation /kɒnsəˈleɪʃn/ *n* consolazione *f*. ~ prize *n* premio *m* di
consolazione

console /kənˈsəʊl/ *vt* consolare

consolidate /kənˈsɒlɪdeɪt/ *vt* consolidare

consonant /ˈkɒnsənənt/ *n* consonante *f*

conspicuous /kən'spɪkjʊəs/ adj facilmente distinguibile

conspiracy /kən'spɪrəsɪ/ n cospirazione f

conspire /kən'spaɪə(r)/ vi cospirare

constable /'kʌnstəbl/ n agente m [di polizia]

constant /'kɒnstənt/ adj costante. ~ly adv costantemente

constellation /kɒnstə'leɪʃn/ n costellazione f

consternation /kɒnstə'neɪʃn/ n costernazione f

constipat|ed /'kɒnstɪpeɪtɪd/ adj stitico. ~ion n stitichezza f

constituency /kən'stɪtjʊənsɪ/ n area f elettorale di un deputato nel Regno Unito

constituent /kən'stɪtjʊənt/ n costituente m; (Pol) elettore, -trice mf

constitut|e /'kɒnstɪtjuːt/ vt costituire. ~ion n costituzione f. ~ional adj costituzionale

construct /kən'strʌkt/ vt costruire. ~ion n costruzione f; under ~ion in costruzione. ~ive adj costruttivo

consul /'kɒnsl/ n console m. ~ar adj consolare. ~ate n consolato m

consult /kən'sʌlt/ vt consultare. ~ant n consulente mf; (Med) specialista mf. ~ation n consultazione f; (Med) consulto m

consume /kən'sjuːm/ vt consumare. ~r n consumatore, -trice mf. ~r goods npl beni mpl di consumo. ~r organization organizzazione f per la tutela dei consumatori

consummate /'kɒnsəmeɪt/ vt consumare

consumption /kən'sʌmpʃn/ n consumo m

contact /'kɒntækt/ n contatto m; (person) conoscenza f ● vt mettersi in contatto con. ~ lenses npl lenti fpl a contatto

contagious /kən'teɪdʒəs/ adj contagioso

contain /kən'teɪn/ vt contenere; ~ oneself controllarsi. ~er n recipiente m; (for transport) container m inv

contaminat|e /kən'tæmɪneɪt/ vt contaminare. ~ion n contaminazione f

contemplat|e /'kɒntəmpleɪt/ vt contemplare; (consider) considerare; ~e doing sth considerare di fare qcsa. ~ion n contemplazione f

contemporary /kən'tempərərɪ/ adj & n contemporaneo, -a mf

contempt /kən'tempt/ n disprezzo m; beneath ~ più che vergognoso; ~ of court oltraggio m alla Corte. ~ible adj spregevole. ~uous adj sprezzante

contend /kən'tend/ vi ~ with occuparsi di ● vt (assert) sostenere. ~er n concorrente mf

content[1] /'kɒntent/ n contenuto m

content[2] /kən'tent/ adj soddisfatto ● vt ~ oneself accontentarsi (with di). ~ed adj soddisfatto. ~edly adv con aria soddisfatta

contentment /kən'tentmənt/ n soddisfazione f

contents /'kɒntents/ npl contenuto m

contest[1] /'kɒntest/ n gara f

contest[2] /kən'test/ vt contestare (statement); impugnare (will); (Pol) (candidates:) contendersi; (one candidate:) aspirare a. ~ant n concorrente mf

context /'kɒntekst/ n contesto m

continent /'kɒntɪnənt/ n continente m; the C~ l'Europa f continentale

continental /kɒntɪ'nentl/ adj continentale. ~ breakfast n prima colazione f a base di pane, burro, marmellata, croissant, ecc. ~ quilt n piumone m

contingency /kən'tɪndʒənsɪ/ n eventualità f inv

continual /kən'tɪnjʊəl/ adj

continuo

continuation /kəntɪnjʊˈeɪʃn/ n continuazione f

continue /kənˈtɪnjuː/ vt continuare; ∼ doing or to do sth continuare a fare qcsa; to be ∼d continua • vi continuare. ∼d adj continuo

continuity /kɒntɪˈnjuːətɪ/ n continuità f

continuous /kənˈtɪnjʊəs/ adj continuo

contort /kənˈtɔːt/ vt contorcere. ∼ion n contorsione f. ∼ionist n contorsionista mf

contour /ˈkɒntʊə(r)/ n contorno m; (line) curva f di livello

contraband /ˈkɒntrəbænd/ n contrabbando m

contracep|tion /kɒntrəˈsepʃn/ n contraccezione f. ∼tive n contraccettivo m

contract¹ /ˈkɒntrækt/ n contratto m

contract² /kənˈtrækt/ vi (get smaller) contrarsi • vt contrarre (illness). ∼ion n contrazione f. ∼or n imprenditore, -trice mf

contradict /kɒntrəˈdɪkt/ vt contraddire. ∼ion n contraddizione f. ∼ory adj contraddittorio

contraption /kənˈtræpʃn/ n 🛈 aggeggio m

contrary¹ /ˈkɒntrərɪ/ adj contrario • adv ∼ to contrariamente a • n contrario m; on the ∼ al contrario

contrary² /kənˈtreərɪ/ adj disobbediente

contrast¹ /ˈkɒntrɑːst/ n contrasto m

contrast² /kənˈtrɑːst/ vt confrontare • vi contrastare. ∼ing adj contrastante

contraven|e /kɒntrəˈviːn/ vt trasgredire. ∼tion n trasgressione f

contribut|e /kənˈtrɪbjuːt/ vt/i contribuire. ∼ion n contribuzione f; (what is contributed) contributo m. ∼or

n contributore, -trice mf

contrive /kənˈtraɪv/ vt escogitare; ∼ to do sth riuscire a fare qcsa

control /kənˈtrəʊl/ n controllo m; ∼s pl (of car, plane) comandi mpl; get out of ∼ sfuggire al controllo • vt (pt/pp controlled) controllare; ∼ oneself controllarsi

controvers|ial /kɒntrəˈvɜːʃl/ adj controverso. ∼y n controversia f

convalesce /kɒnvəˈles/ vi essere in convalescenza

convector /kənˈvektə(r)/ n ∼ [heater] convettore m

convene /kənˈviːn/ vt convocare • vi riunirsi

convenience /kənˈviːnɪəns/ n convenienza f; [public] ∼ gabinetti mpl pubblici; with all modern ∼s con tutti i comfort

convenient /kənˈviːnɪənt/ adj comodo; be ∼ for sb andar bene per qcno; if it is ∼ [for you] se ti va bene. ∼ly adv comodamente; ∼ly located in una posizione comoda

convent /ˈkɒnvənt/ n convento m

convention /kənˈvenʃn/ n convenzione f; (assembly) convegno m. ∼al adj convenzionale

converge /kənˈvɜːdʒ/ vi convergere

conversation /kɒnvəˈseɪʃn/ n conversazione f. ∼al adj di conversazione. ∼alist n conversatore, -trice mf

converse¹ /kənˈvɜːs/ vi conversare

converse² /ˈkɒnvɜːs/ n inverso m. ∼ly adv viceversa

conversion /kənˈvɜːʃn/ n conversione f

convert¹ /ˈkɒnvɜːt/ n convertito, -a mf

convert² /kənˈvɜːt/ vt convertire (into in); sconsacrare (church). ∼ible adj convertibile • n (Auto) macchina f decappottabile

convex /ˈkɒnveks/ adj convesso

convey /kən'veɪ/ vt portare; tra-smettere (idea, message). ∼**or belt** n nastro m trasportatore

convict[1] /'kɒnvɪkt/ n condannato, -a mf

convict[2] /kən'vɪkt/ vt giudicare colpevole. ∼**ion** n condanna f; (belief) convinzione f; **previous** ∼**ion** precedente m penale

convince /kən'vɪns/ vt convincere. ∼**ing** adj convincente

convoluted /'kɒnvəluːtɪd/ adj contorto

convoy /'kɒnvɔɪ/ n convoglio m

convulse /kən'vʌls/ vt sconvolgere; **be** ∼**ed with laughter** contorcersi dalle risa. ∼**ion** n convulsione f

coo /kuː/ vi tubare

cook /kʊk/ n cuoco, -a mf ● vt cucinare; **is it** ∼**ed?** è cotto?; ∼ **the books** 🄴 truccare i libri contabili ● vi (food) cuocere; (person) cucinare. ∼**book** n libro m di cucina

cooker /'kʊkə(r)/ n cucina f; (apple) mela f da cuocere. ∼**y** n cucina f. ∼**y book** n libro m di cucina

cookie /'kʊkɪ/ n Am biscotto m

cool /kuːl/ adj fresco; (calm) calmo; (unfriendly) freddo ● n fresco m ● vt rinfrescare ● vi rinfrescarsi. ∼**box** n borsa f termica. ∼**ness** n freddezza f

coop /kuːp/ n stia f ● vt ∼ **up** rinchiudere

co-operat|e /kəʊ'ɒpəreɪt/ vi cooperare. ∼**ion** n cooperazione f

co-operative /kəʊ'ɒpərətɪv/ adj cooperativo ● n cooperativa f

co-opt /kəʊ'ɒpt/ vt eleggere

co-ordinat|e /kəʊ'ɔːdɪneɪt/ vt coordinare. ∼**ion** n coordinazione f

cop /kɒp/ n 🄴 poliziotto m

cope /kəʊp/ vi 🄴 farcela; **can she** ∼ **by herself?** ce la fa da sola?; ∼ **with** farcela con

copious /'kəʊpɪəs/ adj abbondante

copper[1] /'kɒpə(r)/ n rame m; ∼**s** pl

monete fpl da uno o due pence ● attrib di rame

copper[2] n 🄴 poliziotto m

copy /'kɒpɪ/ n copia f ● vt (pt/pp -ied) copiare

copyright n diritti mpl d'autore

coral /'kɒrəl/ n corallo m

cord /kɔːd/ n corda f; (thinner) cordoncino m; (fabric) velluto m a coste; ∼**s** pl pantaloni mpl di velluto a coste

cordial /'kɔːdɪəl/ adj cordiale ● n analcolico m

cordon /'kɔːdn/ n cordone m (di persone) ● **cordon off** vt mettere un cordone (di persone) intorno a

core /kɔː(r)/ n (of apple, pear) torsolo m; (fig: of organization) cuore m; (of problem, theory) nocciolo m

cork /kɔːk/ n sughero m; (for bottle) turacciolo m. ∼**screw** n cavatappi m inv

corn[1] /kɔːn/ n grano m; (Am: maize) granturco m

corn[2] n (Med) callo m

corned beef /kɔːnd'biːf/ n manzo m sotto sale

corner /'kɔːnə(r)/ n angolo m; (football) calcio m d'angolo, corner m inv ● vt fig bloccare; (Comm) accaparrarsi (market)

cornet /'kɔːnɪt/ n (Mus) cornetta f; (for ice-cream) cono m

corn: ∼**flour** n, Am ∼**starch** n farina f di granturco

corny /'kɔːnɪ/ adj (-ier, -iest) (🄴: joke, film) scontato; (person) banale; (sentimental) sdolcinato

coronary /'kɒrənərɪ/ adj coronario ● n ∼ **[thrombosis]** trombosi f coronarica

coronation /kɒrə'neɪʃn/ n incoronazione f

coroner /'kɒrənə(r)/ n coroner m inv (nel diritto britannico, ufficiale incaricato delle indagini su morti sospette)

corporal[1] /'kɔːpərəl/ n (Mil)

caporale *m*

corporal[2] */adj* corporale; ~ punishment punizione *f* corporale

corporate /'kɔ:pərət/ *adj* (decision,
policy, image) aziendale; ~ life la
vita in un'azienda

corporation /kɔ:pə'reɪʃn/ *n* ente
m; (*of town*) consiglio *m* comunale

corps /kɔ:(r)/ *n* (*pl* **corps** /kɔ:z/)
corpo *m*

corpse /kɔ:ps/ *n* cadavere *m*

corpulent /'kɔ:pjʊlənt/ *adj* corpulento

correct /kə'rekt/ *adj* corretto; be ~
(person:) aver ragione; ~! esatto!
● *vt* correggere. ~ion *n* correzione *f*.
~ly *adv* correttamente

correspond /kɒrɪ'spɒnd/ *vi* corrispondere (to a); (two things:) corrispondere; (*write*) scriversi. ~ence *n*
corrispondenza *f*. ~ent *n* corrispondente *mf*. ~ing *adj* corrispondente.
~ingly *adv* in modo corrispondente

corridor /'kɒrɪdɔ:(r)/ *n* corridoio *m*

corro|de /kə'rəʊd/ *vt* corrodere ● *vi*
corrodersi. ~sion *n* corrosione *f*

corrugated /'kɒrəgeɪtɪd/ *adj* ondulato. ~ iron *n* lamiera *f* ondulata

corrupt /kə'rʌpt/ *adj* corrotto ● *vt*
corrompere. ~ion *n* corruzione *f*

corset /'kɔ:sɪt/ *n* & -s *pl* busto *m*

Corsica /'kɔ:sɪkə/ *n* Corsica *f*. ~n
adj & *n* corso, -a *mf*

cosmetic /kɒz'metɪk/ *adj* cosmetico
● *n* ~s *pl* cosmetici *mpl*

cosmic /'kɒzmɪk/ *adj* cosmico

cosmopolitan /kɒzmə'pɒlɪtən/ *adj*
cosmopolita

cosmos /'kɒzmɒs/ *n* cosmo *m*

cosset /'kɒsɪt/ *vt* coccolare

cost /kɒst/ *n* costo *m*; ~s *pl* (*Jur*)
spese *fpl* processuali; at all ~s a
tutti i costi; I learnt to my ~ ho
imparato a mie spese ● *vt* (*pt/pp*
cost) costare; it ~ me £20 mi è co-
stato 20 sterline ● *vt* (*pt/pp* costed)

~ [out] stabilire il prezzo di

costly /'kɒstlɪ/ *adj* (-ier, -iest)
costoso

costume /'kɒstjuːm/ *n* costume *m*.
~ jewellery *n* bigiotteria *f*

cosy /'kəʊzɪ/ *adj* (-ier, -iest) (pub,
chat) intimo; it's nice and ~ in
here si sta bene qui

cot /kɒt/ *n* lettino *m*; (*Am*: camp-bed)
branda *f*

cottage /'kɒtɪdʒ/ *n* casetta *f*. ~
'cheese *n* fiocchi *mpl* di latte

cotton /'kɒtn/ *n* cotone *m* ● *attrib* di
cotone ● **cotton on** *vi* 🔲 capire

cotton 'wool *n* cotone *m* idrofilo

couch /kaʊtʃ/ *n* divano *m*. ~ potato *n* pantofolaio, -a *mf*

cough /kɒf/ *n* tosse *f* ● *vi* tossire.
□ ~ **up** *vt/i* sputare; (🔲: pay)
sborsare

'cough mixture *n* sciroppo *m* per
la tosse

could /kʊd/, *atono* /kəd/ *v aux*
(*see also* **can**[2]) ~ I have a glass of
water? potrei avere un bicchier
d'acqua?; I ~n't do it even if I
wanted to non potrei farlo nemmeno se lo volessi; I ~n't care
less non potrebbe importarmene
di meno; he ~n't have done it
without help non avrebbe potuto
farlo senza aiuto; you ~ have
phoned avresti potuto telefonare

council /'kaʊnsl/ *n* consiglio *m*. ~
house *n* casa *f* popolare

councillor /'kaʊnsələ(r)/ *n* consigliere, -a *mf*

counsel /'kaʊnsl/ *n* consigli *mpl*;
(*Jur*) avvocato *m* ● *vt* (*pt/pp* coun-
selled) consigliare a (person). ~lor
n consigliere, -a *mf*

count[1] /kaʊnt/ *n* (*nobleman*) conte *m*

count[2] /kaʊnt/ *n* conto *m*; keep ~
tenere il conto ● *vt/i* contare. □ ~ **on** *vt*

contare su

countdown /'kaʊntdaʊn/ n conto m alla rovescia

counter¹ /'kaʊntə(r)/ n banco m; (in games) gettone m

counter² adv ~ to contro, in contrasto a; go ~ to sth andare contro qcsa ● vt/i opporre (measure, effect); parare (blow)

counter'act vt neutralizzare

counter-attack n contrattacco m

counterfeit /-fɪt/ adj contraffatto ● n contraffazione f ● vt contraffare

counterfoil n matrice f

counter-pro'ductive adj controproduttivo

countess /'kaʊntɪs/ n contessa f

countless /'kaʊntlɪs/ adj innumerevole

country /'kʌntrɪ/ n nazione f, paese m; (native land) patria f; (countryside) campagna f; in the ~ in campagna; go to the ~ andare in campagna; (Pol) indire le elezioni politiche. ~man n uomo m di campagna; (fellow ~man) compatriota m. ~side n campagna f

county /'kaʊntɪ/ n contea f (unità amministrativa britannica)

coup /ku:/ n (Pol) colpo m di stato

couple /'kʌpl/ n coppia f; a ~ of un paio di

coupon /'ku:pɒn/ n tagliando m; (for discount) buono m sconto

courage /'kʌrɪdʒ/ n coraggio m. ~ous adj coraggioso

courgette /kʊə'ʒet/ n zucchino m

courier /'kʊrɪə(r)/ n corriere m; (for tourists) guida f

course /kɔːs/ n (Sch) corso m; (Naut) rotta f; (Culin) portata f; (for golf) campo m; ~ of treatment (Med) serie f inv di cure; of ~ naturalmente; in the ~ of durante; in due ~ a tempo debito

court /kɔːt/ n tribunale m; (Sport)

campo m; take sb to ~ citare qcno in giudizio ● vt fare la corte a (woman); sfidare (danger); ~ing couples coppiette fpl

courteous /'kɜːtɪəs/ adj cortese

courtesy /'kɜːtəsɪ/ n cortesia f

court: ~ 'martial n (pl ~s martial) corte f marziale. ~-martial vt (pt ~-martialled) portare davanti alla corte marziale; ~yard n cortile m

cousin /'kʌzn/ n cugino, -a mf

cove /kəʊv/ n insenatura f

cover /'kʌvə(r)/ n copertura f; (of cushion, to protect sth) fodera f; (of book, magazine) copertina f; take ~ mettersi al riparo; under separate ~ a parte ● vt coprire; foderare (cushion); (Journ) fare un servizio su. □ ~ up vt coprire; fig soffocare (scandal)

coverage /'kʌvərɪdʒ/ n (Journ) it got a lot of ~ i media gli hanno dedicato molto spazio

cover: ~ charge n coperto m. ~ing n copertura f; (for floor) rivestimento m; ~ing letter lettera f d'accompagnamento

covet /'kʌvɪt/ vt bramare

cow /kaʊ/ n vacca f, mucca f

coward /'kaʊəd/ n vigliacco, -a mf. ~ice n vigliaccheria f. ~ly adj da vigliacco

cowboy n cowboy m inv; 🔲 buffone m

cower /'kaʊə(r)/ vi acquattarsi

coy /kɔɪ/ adj falsamente timido; (flirtatiously) civettuolo; be ~ about sth essere evasivo su qcsa

crab /kræb/ n granchio m

crack /kræk/ n (in wall) crepa f; (in china, glass, bone) incrinatura f; (noise) scoppio m; (🔲: joke) battuta f; have a ~ (try) fare un tentativo ● adj (🔲: best) di prim'ordine ● vt incrinare (china, glass); schiacciare (nut); decifrare (code); 🔲 risolvere (problem); ~ a joke 🔲 fare una battuta ● vi (china, glass:) incrinarsi; (whip:) schioccare. □~ **down** vi 🔲 prendere seri provvedimenti. □~ **down on** vt 🔲 prendere seri provvedimenti contro

cracker /'krækə(r)/ n (biscuit) cracker m inv; (firework) petardo m; [Christmas] ~ tubo m di cartone colorato contenente una sorpresa

crackle /'krækl/ vi crepitare

cradle /'kreɪdl/ n culla f

craft[1] /krɑːft/ n inv (boat) imbarcazione f

craft[2] n mestiere m; (technique) arte f. ~sman n artigiano m

crafty /'krɑːftɪ/ adj (-ier, -iest) astuto

cram /kræm/ v (pt/pp crammed) • vt stipare (into in) • vi (for exams) sgobbare

cramp /kræmp/ n crampo m. ~ed adj (room) stretto; (handwriting) appiccicato

cranberry /'krænbərɪ/ n (Culin) mirtillo m rosso

crane /kreɪn/ n (at docks, bird) gru f inv • vt ~ one's neck allungare il collo

crank[1] /kræŋk/ n tipo, -a mf strampalato, -a

crank[2] n (Techn) manovella f. ~shaft n albero m a gomiti

cranky /'kræŋkɪ/ adj strampalato; (Am: irritable) irritabile

cranny /'krænɪ/ n fessura f

crash /kræʃ/ n (noise) fragore m; (Aeron, Auto) incidente m; (Comm) crollo m • vi schiantarsi (into contro); (plane:) precipitare • vt schiantare (car)

crash: ~ **course** n corso m intensivo. ~-**helmet** n casco m

crate /kreɪt/ n (for packing) cassa f

crater /'kreɪtə(r)/ n cratere m

crav|e /kreɪv/ vt morire dalla voglia di. ~**ing** n voglia f smodata

crawl /krɔːl/ n (swimming) stile m libero; do the ~ nuotare a stile libero; at a ~ a passo di lumaca • vi andare carponi; ~ **with** brulicare di. ~**er lane** n (Auto) corsia f riservata al traffico lento

crayon /'kreɪən/ n pastello m a cera; (pencil) matita f colorata

craze /kreɪz/ n mania f

crazy /'kreɪzɪ/ adj (-ier, -iest) matto; be ~ **about** andar matto per

creak /kriːk/ n scricchiolio m • vi scricchiolare

cream /kriːm/ n crema f; (fresh) panna f • adj (colour) [bianco] panna inv • vt (Culin) sbattere. ~ '**cheese** n formaggio m cremoso. ~**y** adj cremoso

crease /kriːs/ n piega f • vt stropicciare • vi stropicciarsi. ~-**resistant** adj che non si stropiccia

creat|e /kriː'eɪt/ vt creare. ~**ion** n creazione f. ~**ive** adj creativo. ~**or** n creatore, -trice mf

creature /'kriːtʃə(r)/ n creatura f

crèche /kreʃ/ n asilo m nido

credibility /kredə'bɪlətɪ/ n credibilità f

credible /'kredəbl/ adj credibile

credit /'kredɪt/ n credito m; (honour) merito m; take the ~ for prendersi il merito di • vt (pt/pp credited) accreditare; ~ **sb with** sth (Comm) accreditare qcsa a qcno; fig attribuire qcsa a qcno. ~**able** adj lodevole

credit: ~ **card** n carta f di credito. ~**or** n creditore, -trice mf

creed /kriːd/ n credo m

creek /kriːk/ n insenatura f; (Am: stream) torrente m

creep /kriːp/ vi (pt/pp crept) muoversi furtivamente • n 🔲 tipo m viscido. ~**er** n pianta f rampicante. ~**y** adj che fa venire i brividi

cremat|e /krɪ'meɪt/ vt cremare. ~**ion** n cremazione f

crematorium /kremə'tɔːrɪəm/ n

crematorio m

crept /krept/ ▷**CREEP**

crescent /'kresənt/ n mezzaluna f

crest /krest/ n cresta f; (coat of arms) cimiero m

Crete /kri:t/ n Creta f

crevice /'krevɪs/ n crepa f

crew /kru:/ n equipaggio m; (gang) équipe f inv. ~ cut n capelli mpl a spazzola. ~ neck n girocollo m

crib[1] /krɪb/ n (for baby) culla f

crib[2] vt/i (pt/pp cribbed) ~ copiare

crick /krɪk/ n ~ in the neck torcicollo m

cricket[1] /'krɪkɪt/ n (insect) grillo m

cricket[2] n cricket m. ~er n giocatore m di cricket

crime /kraɪm/ n crimine m; (criminality) criminalità f

criminal /'krɪmɪnl/ adj criminale; (law, court) penale ● n criminale mf

crimson /'krɪmzn/ adj cremisi inv

cringe /krɪndʒ/ vi (cower) acquattarsi; (at bad joke etc) fare una smorfia

crinkle /'krɪŋkl/ vt spiegazzare ● vi spiegazzarsi

cripple /'krɪpl/ n storpio, -a mf ● vt storpiare; fig danneggiare. ~d adj (person) storpio; (ship) danneggiato

crisis /'kraɪsɪs/ n (pl -ses /-siːz/) crisi f inv

crisp /krɪsp/ adj croccante; (air) frizzante; (style) incisivo. ~bread n crostini mpl di pane. ~s npl patatine fpl

criterion /kraɪ'tɪərɪən/ n (pl -ria /-rɪə/) criterio m

critic /'krɪtɪk/ n critico, -a mf. ~al adj critico. ~ally adv in modo critico; ~ally ill gravemente malato

criticism /'krɪtɪsɪzm/ n critica f; he doesn't like ~ non ama le critiche

criticize /'krɪtɪsaɪz/ vt criticare

croak /krəʊk/ vi gracchiare; (frog:) gracidare

Croatia /krəʊ'eɪʃə/ n Croazia f

crochet /'krəʊʃeɪ/ n lavoro m all'uncinetto ● vt fare all'uncinetto. ~-hook n uncinetto m

crockery /'krɒkərɪ/ n terrecotte fpl

crocodile /'krɒkədaɪl/ n coccodrillo m. ~ tears lacrime fpl di coccodrillo

crocus /'krəʊkəs/ n (pl -es) croco m

crook /krʊk/ n (🖪: criminal) truffatore, -trice mf

crooked /'krʊkɪd/ adj storto; (limb) storpiato; (🖪: dishonest) disonesto

crop /krɒp/ n raccolto m; fig quantità f inv ● v (pt/pp cropped) ● vt coltivare. □ ~ up vi 🖪 presentarsi

croquet /'krəʊkeɪ/ n croquet m

croquette /krəʊ'ket/ n crocchetta f

cross /krɒs/ adj (annoyed) arrabbiato; talk at ~ purposes fraintendersi ● n croce f; (Bot, Zool) incrocio m ● vt sbarrare (cheque); incrociare (road, animals); ~ oneself farsi il segno della croce; ~ one's arms incrociare le braccia; ~ one's legs accavallare le gambe; keep one's fingers ~ed for sb tenere le dita incrociate per qcno; it ~ed my mind mi è venuto in mente ● vi (go across) attraversare; (lines:) incrociarsi. □ ~ out vt depennare

cross: ~bar n (of goal) traversa f; (on bicycle) canna f. ~ex'amine vt sottoporre a controinterrogatorio. ~-'eyed adj strabico. ~fire n fuoco m incrociato. ~ing n (for pedestrians) passaggio m pedonale; (sea journey) traversata f. ~-'reference n rimando m. ~roads n incrocio m. ~-'section n sezione f; (of community) campione m. ~word n ~word [puzzle] parole fpl crociate

crouch /kraʊtʃ/ vi accovacciarsi

crow /krəʊ/ n corvo m; as the ~ flies in linea diretta ● vi cantare. ~bar n piede m di porco

crowd /kraʊd/ n folla f ● vt affollare ● vi affollarsi. ~ed adj affollato

crown /kraʊn/ n corona f ● vt incoronare; incapsulare (tooth)

crucial /ˈkruːʃl/ *adj* cruciale

crucifix /ˈkruːsɪfɪks/ *n* crocifisso *m*

crucif|ixion /kruːsɪˈfɪkʃn/ *n* crocifissione *f*. **~y** *vt* (*pt/pp* -**ied**) crocifiggere

crude /kruːd/ *adj* (oil) greggio; (language) crudo; (person) rozzo

cruel /ˈkruːəl/ *adj* (crueller, cruellest) crudele (to verso). **~ly** *adv* con crudeltà. **~ty** *n* crudeltà *f*

cruis|e /kruːz/ *n* crociera *f* ● *vi* fare una crociera; (car:) andare a velocità di crociera. **~er** *n* (Mil) incrociatore *m*; (motor boat) motoscafo *m*. **~ing speed** *n* velocità *f inv* di crociera

crumb /krʌm/ *n* briciola *f*

crumb|le /ˈkrʌmbl/ *vt* sbriciolare ● *vi* sbriciolarsi; (building, society:) sgretolarsi. **~ly** *adj* friabile

crumple /ˈkrʌmpl/ *vt* spiegazzare ● *vi* spiegazzarsi

crunch /krʌntʃ/ *n* 🔟 when it comes to the ~ quando si viene al dunque ● *vt* sgranocchiare ● *vi* (snow:) scricchiolare

crusade /kruːˈseɪd/ *n* crociata *f*. **~r** *n* crociato *m*

crush /krʌʃ/ *n* (crowd) calca *f*; have a ~ on sb essersi preso una cotta per qcno ● *vt* schiacciare; sgualcire (clothes)

crust /krʌst/ *n* crosta *f*

crutch /krʌtʃ/ *n* gruccia *f*; (Anat) inforcatura *f*

crux /krʌks/ *n* *fig* punto *m* cruciale

cry /kraɪ/ *n* grido *m*; have a ~ farsi un pianto; a far ~ from *fig* tutta un'altra cosa rispetto a ● *vi* (*pt/pp* cried) (weep) piangere; (call) gridare

crypt /krɪpt/ *n* cripta *f*. **~ic** *adj* criptico

crystal /ˈkrɪstl/ *n* cristallo *m*; (glassware) cristalli *mpl*. **~lize** *vi* (become clear) concretizzarsi

cub /kʌb/ *n* (animal) cucciolo *m*; C~

[Scout] lupetto *m*

Cuba /ˈkjuːbə/ *n* Cuba *f*

cubby-hole /ˈkʌbɪ-/ *n* (compartment) scomparto *m*; (room) ripostiglio *m*

cub|e /kjuːb/ *n* cubo *m*. **~ic** *adj* cubico

cubicle /ˈkjuːbɪkl/ *n* cabina *f*

cuckoo /ˈkʊkuː/ *n* cuculo *m*. ~ **clock** *n* orologio *m* a cucù

cucumber /ˈkjuːkʌmbə(r)/ *n* cetriolo *m*

cuddl|e /ˈkʌdl/ *vt* coccolare ● *vi* ~**e up to** starsene accoccolato insieme a ● *n* have a ~**e** (child:) farsi coccolare; (lovers:) abbracciarsi. **~y** *adj* tenerone; (wanting cuddles) coccolone. **~y** 'toy *n* pupazzo *m* di peluche

cue[1] /kjuː/ *n* segnale *m*; (Theat) battuta *f* d'entrata

cue[2] *n* (in billiards) stecca *f*. ~ **ball** *n* pallino *m*

cuff /kʌf/ *n* polsino *m*; (Am: turn-up) orlo *m*; (blow) scapaccione *m*; **off the** ~ improvvisando ● *vt* dare una pacca a. **~link** *n* gemello *m*

cul-de-sac /ˈkʌldəsæk/ *n* vicolo *m* cieco

culinary /ˈkʌlɪnərɪ/ *adj* culinario

cull /kʌl/ *vt* scegliere (flowers); (kill) selezionare e uccidere

culminat|e /ˈkʌlmɪneɪt/ *vi* culminare. **~ion** *n* culmine *m*

culprit /ˈkʌlprɪt/ *n* colpevole *mf*

cult /kʌlt/ *n* culto *m*

cultivate /ˈkʌltɪveɪt/ *vt* coltivare; *fig* coltivarsi (person)

cultural /ˈkʌltʃərəl/ *adj* culturale

culture /ˈkʌltʃə(r)/ *n* cultura *f*. **~d** *adj* colto

cumbersome /ˈkʌmbəsəm/ *adj* ingombrante

cunning /ˈkʌnɪŋ/ *adj* astuto ● *n* astuzia *f*

cup /kʌp/ *n* tazza *f*; (prize, of bra) coppa *f*

cupboard /ˈkʌbəd/ *n* armadio *m*.

curator /kjʊəˈreɪtə(r)/ n direttore, -trice mf (di museo)

curb /kɜːb/ vt tenere a freno

curdle /ˈkɜːdl/ vi coagularsi

cure /kjʊə(r)/ n cura f ● vt curare; (salt) mettere sotto sale; (smoke) affumicare

curfew /ˈkɜːfjuː/ n coprifuoco m

curiosity /kjʊərɪˈɒsəti/ n curiosità f

curious /ˈkjʊərɪəs/ adj curioso. ~ly adv (strangely) curiosamente

curl /kɜːl/ n ricciolo m ● vt arricciare ● vi arricciarsi. □ ~ **up** vi raggomitolarsi

curler /ˈkɜːlə(r)/ n bigodino m

curly /ˈkɜːli/ adj (-ier, -iest) riccio

currant /ˈkʌrənt/ n (dried) uvetta f

currency /ˈkʌrənsi/ n valuta f; (of word) ricorrenza f; foreign ~ valuta f estera

current /ˈkʌrənt/ adj corrente ● n corrente f. ~ **affairs** or **events** npl attualità fsg. ~ly adv attualmente

curriculum /kəˈrɪkjʊləm/ n programma m di studi. ~ **vitae** n curriculum vitae m inv

curry /ˈkʌri/ n curry m inv; (meal) piatto m cucinato nel curry ● vt (pt/pp -ied) ~ **favour** with sb cercare d'ingraziarsi qcno

curse /kɜːs/ n maledizione f; (oath) imprecazione f ● vt maledire ● vi imprecare

cursory /ˈkɜːsəri/ adj sbrigativo

curt /kɜːt/ adj brusco

curtain /ˈkɜːtn/ n tenda f; (Theat) sipario m

curtsy /ˈkɜːtsi/ n inchino m ● vi (pt/pp -ied) fare l'inchino

curve /kɜːv/ n curva f ● vi curvare; ~ **to the right/left** curvare a destra/sinistra. ~d adj curvo

cushion /ˈkʊʃn/ n cuscino m ● vt attutire; (protect) proteggere

cushy /ˈkʊʃi/ adj (-ier, -iest) 🄵

facile

custard /ˈkʌstəd/ n (liquid) crema f pasticciera

custody /ˈkʌstədi/ n (of child) custodia f; (imprisonment) detenzione f preventiva

custom /ˈkʌstəm/ n usanza f; (Jur) consuetudine f; (Comm) clientela f. ~ary adj (habitual) abituale; it's ~ary to... è consuetudine.... ~er n cliente mf

customs /ˈkʌstəmz/ npl dogana f. ~ **officer** n doganiere m

cut /kʌt/ n (with knife etc, of clothes) taglio m; (reduction) riduzione f; (in public spending) taglio m ● vt/i (pt/pp cut, pres p cutting) tagliare; (reduce) ridurre; ~ **one's finger** tagliarsi il dito; ~ sb's **hair** tagliare i capelli a qcno ● vi (with cards) alzare. □ ~ **back** vt tagliare (hair); potare (hedge); (reduce) ridurre. □ ~ **down** vt abbattere (tree); (reduce) ridurre. □ ~ **off** vt tagliar via; (disconnect) interrompere; fig isolare; I **was** ~ **off** (Teleph) la linea è caduta. □ ~ **out** vt ritagliare; (delete) eliminare; **be** ~ **out for** 🄵 essere tagliato per; ~ **it out!** 🄵 dacci un taglio!. □ ~ **up** vt (slice) tagliare a pezzi

cute /kjuːt/ adj 🄵 (in appearance) carino; (clever) acuto

cutlery /ˈkʌtləri/ n posate fpl

cutlet /ˈkʌtlɪt/ n cotoletta f

'cut-price adj a prezzo ridotto; (shop) che fa prezzi ridotti

'cut-throat adj spietato

cutting /ˈkʌtɪŋ/ adj (remark) tagliente ● n (from newspaper) ritaglio m; (of plant) talea f

CV n abbr curriculum vitae

cycl|e /ˈsaɪkl/ n ciclo m; (bicycle) bicicletta f, bici f inv 🄵 ● vi andare in bicicletta. ~**ing** n ciclismo m. ~**ist** n ciclista mf

cylind|er /ˈsɪlɪndə(r)/ n cilindro m. ~**rical** adj cilindrico

cynic /'sɪnɪk/ n cinico, -a mf. ~al adj cinico. ~ism n cinismo m

Cyprus /'saɪprəs/ n Cipro m

Czech /tʃek/ adj ceco; ~ Republic Repubblica f Ceca ● n ceco, -a mf

....

Dd

....

dab /dæb/ n colpetto m; a ~ of un pochino di ● vt (pt/pp dabbed) toccare leggermente (eyes). □ ~ on vt mettere un po' di (paint etc)

daddy-'long-legs n zanzarone m [dei boschi]; (Am: spider) ragno m

daffodil /'dæfədɪl/ n giunchiglia f

daft /dɑ:ft/ adj sciocco

dagger /'dægə(r)/ n stiletto m

dahlia /'deɪlɪə/ n dalia f

Dáil Éireann Dáil Éireann è la camera bassa del Parlamento della Repubblica d'Irlanda. È composto di 166 deputati (o TD) in rappresentanza di 41 collegi elettorali. I deputati sono infatti eletti col sistema proporzionale e la Costituzione ne prevede uno per ogni 20.000-30.000 cittadini.

daily /'deɪlɪ/ adj giornaliero ● adv giornalmente ● n (newspaper) quotidiano m; (🗵: cleaner) donna f delle pulizie

dainty /'deɪntɪ/ adj (-ier, -iest) grazioso; (movement) delicato

dairy /'deərɪ/ n caseificio m; (shop) latteria f. ~ cow n mucca f da latte. ~ products npl latticini mpl

daisy /'deɪzɪ/ n margheritina f; (larger) margherita f

dam /dæm/ n diga f ● vt (pt/pp

dammed) costruire una diga su

damag|e /'dæmɪdʒ/ n danno m (to a); ~es pl (Jur) risarcimento msg ● vt danneggiare; fig nuocere a. ~ing adj dannoso

dame /deɪm/ n liter dama f; Am 🗵 donna f

damn /dæm/ adj 🗵 maledetto ● adv (lucky, late) maledettamente ● n I don't give a ~ 🗵 non me ne frega un accidente ● vt dannare. ~ation n dannazione f ● int 🗵 accidenti!

damp /dæmp/ adj umido ● n umidità f ● vt inumidire

dance /dɑ:ns/ n ballo m ● vt/i ballare. ~hall n sala f da ballo. ~ music n musica f da ballo

dancer /'dɑ:nsə(r)/ n ballerino, -a m

dandelion /'dændɪlaɪən/ n dente m di leone

dandruff /'dændrʌf/ n forfora f

Dane /deɪn/ n danese mf; Great ~ danese m

danger /'deɪndʒə(r)/ n pericolo m; in/out of ~ in/fuori pericolo. ~ous adj pericoloso. ~ously adv pericolosamente; ~ously ill in pericolo di vita

dangle /'dæŋgl/ vi penzolare ● vt far penzolare

Danish /'deɪnɪʃ/ adj & n danese m. ~ 'pastry n dolce m a base di pasta sfoglia contenente pasta di mandorle, mele ecc

dare /deə(r)/ vt/i osare; (challenge) sfidare (to a); ~ [to] do sth osare fare qcsa; I ~ say! molto probabilmente! ● n sfida f. ~devil n spericolato, -a mf

daring /'deərɪŋ/ adj audace ● n audacia f

dark /dɑ:k/ adj buio; ~ blue/brown blu/marrone scuro; it's getting ~ sta cominciando a fare buio; ~ horse fig (in race, contest) vincitore m imprevisto; (not much known about) misterioso m; keep sth ~ fig tenere qcsa nascosto ● n after ~ col buio;

in the ~ al buio; keep sb in the ~ *fig* tenere qcno all'oscuro

dark|en /'dɑːkn/ *vt* oscurare ● *vi* oscurarsi. ~**ness** *n* buio *m*

'dark-room *n* camera *f* oscura

darling /'dɑːlɪŋ/ *adj* adorabile; my ~ Joan carissima Joan ● *n* tesoro *m*

darn /dɑːn/ *vt* rammendare. ~**ing-needle** *n* ago *m* da rammendo

dart /dɑːt/ *n* dardo *m*; (*in sewing*) pince *f inv*; ~**s** *sg* (*game*) freccette *fpl* ● *vi* lanciarsi

dartboard /'dɑːtbɔːd/ *n* bersaglio *m* [per freccette]

dash /dæʃ/ *n* (*Typ*) trattino *m*; (*in Morse*) linea *f*; a ~ of milk un goccio di latte; make a ~ for lanciarsi verso ● *vi* I must ~ devo scappare ● *vt* far svanire (hopes). □ ~ **off** *vi* scappar via ● *vt* (*write quickly*) buttare giù. □ ~ **out** *vi* uscire di corsa

'dashboard *n* cruscotto *m*

data /'deɪtə/ *npl & sg* dati *mpl*. ~**base** *n* base [di] dati *f*, database *m inv*. ~**comms** *n* telematica *f*. ~**processing** *n* elaborazione *f* [di] dati

date[1] /deɪt/ *n* (*fruit*) dattero *m*

date[2] *n* data *f*; (*meeting*) appuntamento *m*; to ~ fino ad oggi; out of ~ (*not fashionable*) fuori moda; (*expired*) scaduto; (*information*) non aggiornato; make a ~ with sb dare un appuntamento a qcno; be up to ~ essere aggiornato ● *vt/i* datare; (*go out with*) uscire con. □ ~ **back to** *vi* risalire a

dated /'deɪtɪd/ *adj* fuori moda; (*language*) antiquato

daub /dɔːb/ *vt* imbrattare (walls)

daughter /'dɔːtə(r)/ *n* figlia *f*. ~**-in-law** [*pl* ~s-] *n* nuora *f*

dawdle /'dɔːdl/ *vi* bighellonare; (*over work*) cincischiare

dawn /dɔːn/ *n* alba *f*; at ~ all'alba ● *vi* albeggiare; it ~ed on me *fig* mi è apparso chiaro

day /deɪ/ *n* giorno *m*; (*whole day*) gior-

nata *f*; (*period*) epoca *f*; these ~s oggigiorno; in those ~s a quei tempi; it's had its ~ [1] ha fatto il suo tempo

day: ~**break** *n* at ~break allo spuntar del giorno. ~**dream** *n* sogno *m* ad occhi aperti ● *vi* sognare ad occhi aperti. ~**light** *n* luce *f* del giorno. ~**time** *n* giorno *m*; in the ~time di giorno

daze /deɪz/ *n* in a ~ stordito; *fig* sbalordito. ~**d** *adj* stordito; *fig* sbalordito

dazzle /'dæzl/ *vt* abbagliare

dead /ded/ *adj* morto; (*numb*) intorpidito; ~ **body** morto *m*; ~ **centre** pieno centro *m* ● *adv* ~ **tired** stanco morto; ~ **slow/easy** lentissimo/ facilissimo; **you're** ~ **right** hai perfettamente ragione; **stop** ~ fermarsi di colpo; **be** ~ **on time** essere in perfetto orario ● *n* the ~ *pl* i morti; in the ~ of night nel cuore della notte

deaden /'dedn/ *vt* attutire (sound); calmare (pain)

dead: ~ **end** *n* vicolo *m* cieco. ~**line** *n* scadenza *f*. ~**lock** *n* reach ~**lock** *fig* giungere a un punto morto

deadly /'dedlɪ/ *adj* (**-ier**, **-iest**) mortale; ([1]: *dreary*) barboso; ~ **sins** peccati *mpl* capitali

deaf /def/ *adj* sordo; ~ **and dumb** sordomuto. ~**aid** *n* apparecchio *m* acustico

deaf|en /'defn/ *vt* assordare; (*permanently*) render sordo. ~**ening** *adj* assordante. ~**ness** *n* sordità *f*

deal /diːl/ *n* (*agreement*) patto *m*; (*in business*) accordo *m*; **whose** ~? (*in cards*) a chi tocca dare le carte?; a **good** or **great** ~ molto; **get a raw** ~ [1] ricevere un trattamento ingiusto ● *vt* (*pt/pp* **dealt** /delt/) (*in cards*) dare; ~ **a blow** dare un colpo a qcno. □ ~ **in** *vt* trattare in. □ ~ **out** *vt* (*hand out*) distribuire. □ ~ **with** *vt* (handle) occuparsi di; trattare con (company); (be about) trattare di; that's been ~t with è stato risolto

dealler /'di:lə(r)/ n commerciante mf; (in drugs) spacciatore, -trice mf. ~ings npl have ~ings with avere a che fare con

dean /di:n/ n decano m; (Univ) ≈ preside mf di facoltà

dear /dɪə(r)/ adj caro; (in letter) Caro; (formal) Gentile ● n caro, -a mf ● int oh ~! Dio mio!. ~ly adv (love) profondamente; (pay) profumatamente

death /deθ/ n morte f. ~ **certificate** n certificato m di morte. ~ **duty** n tassa f di successione

death trap n trappola f mortale

debatable /dɪ'beɪtəbl/ adj discutibile

debate /dɪ'beɪt/ n dibattito m ● vt discutere; (in formal debate) dibattere ● vi ~ whether to... considerare se...

debauchery /dɪ'bɔ:tʃərɪ/ n dissolutezza f

debit /'debɪt/ n debito m ● vt (pt/pp debited) (Comm) addebitare (sum)

debris /'debri:/ n macerie fpl

debt /det/ n debito m; be in ~ avere dei debiti. ~**or** n debitore, -trice mf

decade /'dekeɪd/ n decennio m

decaden|ce /'dekədəns/ n decadenza f. ~t adj decadente

decay /dɪ'keɪ/ n (also fig) decadenza f; (rot) decomposizione f; (of tooth) carie f inv ● vi decomporsi; (rot) decomporsi; (tooth:) cariarsi

deceased /dɪ'si:st/ adj defunto ● n the ~d il defunto, la defunta

deceit /dɪ'si:t/ n inganno m. ~**ful** adj falso

deceive /dɪ'si:v/ vt ingannare

December /dɪ'sembə(r)/ n dicembre m

decency /'di:sənsɪ/ n decenza f

decent /'di:sənt/ adj decente; (respectable) rispettabile; very ~ of you molto gentile da parte tua. ~ly adv decentemente; (kindly) gentilmente

decept|ion /dɪ'sepʃn/ n inganno m. ~**ive** adj ingannevole. ~**ively** adv ingannevolmente; it looks ~**ively** easy sembra facile, ma non lo è

decibel /'desɪbel/ n decibel m inv

decide /dɪ'saɪd/ vt decidere ● vi decidere (on di)

decided /dɪ'saɪdɪd/ adj risoluto. ~**ly** adv risolutamente; (without doubt) senza dubbio

decimal /'desɪml/ adj decimale ● n numero m decimale. ~ '**point** n virgola f

decipher /dɪ'saɪfə(r)/ vt decifrare

decision /dɪ'sɪʒn/ n decisione f

decisive /dɪ'saɪsɪv/ adj decisivo

deck¹ /dek/ vt abbigliare

deck² n (Naut) ponte m; on ~ in coperta; top ~ (of bus) piano m di sopra; ~ of cards mazzo m. ~**chair** n [sedia f a] sdraio f inv

declaration /deklə'reɪʃn/ n dichiarazione f

declare /dɪ'kleə(r)/ vt dichiarare; anything to ~? niente da dichiarare?

decline /dɪ'klaɪn/ n declino m ● vt also (Gram) declinare ● vi (decrease) diminuire; (health:) deperire; (say no) rifiutare

decode /di:'kəʊd/ vt decifrare; (Comput) decodificare

decompose /di:kəm'pəʊz/ vi decomporsi

décor /'deɪkɔ:(r)/ n decorazione f; (including furniture) arredamento m

decorat|e /'dekəreɪt/ vt decorare; (paint) pitturare; (wallpaper) tappezzare. ~**ion** n decorazione f. ~**ive** adj decorativo. ~**or** n painter and ~**or** imbianchino m

decoy¹ /'di:kɔɪ/ n esca f

decoy² /dɪˈkɔɪ/ vt adescare

decrease¹ /ˈdiːkriːs/ n diminuzione f

decrease² /dɪˈkriːs/ vt/i diminuire

decree /dɪˈkriː/ n decreto m • vt (pt/pp decreed) decretare

decrepit /dɪˈkrepɪt/ adj decrepito

dedicat|e /ˈdedɪkeɪt/ vt dedicare. ~ed adj (person) scrupoloso. ~ion n dedizione f; (in book) dedica f

deduce /dɪˈdjuːs/ vt dedurre (from da)

deduct /dɪˈdʌkt/ vt dedurre

deduction /dɪˈdʌkʃn/ n deduzione f

deed /diːd/ n azione f; (Jur) atto m di proprietà

deem /diːm/ vt ritenere

deep /diːp/ adj profondo; go off the ~ end 🄵 arrabbiarsi

deepen /ˈdiːpn/ vt approfondire; scavare più profondamente (trench) • vi approfondirsi; (fig: mystery:) infittirsi

deep-'freeze n congelatore m

deeply /ˈdiːplɪ/ adv profondamente

deer /dɪə(r)/ n inv cervo m

deface /dɪˈfeɪs/ vt sfigurare (picture); deturpare (monument)

default /dɪˈfɔːlt/ n (non-payment) morosità f; (failure to appear) contumacia f; win by ~ (Sport) vincere per abbandono dell'avversario; in ~ of per mancanza di • adj ~ drive (Comput) lettore m di default • vi (not pay) venir meno a un pagamento

defeat /dɪˈfiːt/ n sconfitta f • vt sconfiggere; (frustrate) vanificare (attempts); that ~s the object questo fa fallire l'obiettivo

defect¹ /dɪˈfekt/ vi (Pol) fare defezione

defect² /ˈdiːfekt/ n difetto m. ~ive adj difettoso

defence /dɪˈfens/ n difesa f. ~less adj indifeso

defend /dɪˈfend/ vt difendere; (justify) giustificare. ~ant n (Jur) imputato, -a mf

defensive /dɪˈfensɪv/ adj difensivo • n difensiva f; on the ~ sulla difensiva

defer /dɪˈfɜː(r)/ v (pt/pp deferred) • vt (postpone) rinviare • vi ~ to sb rimettersi a qcno

deferen|ce /ˈdefərəns/ n deferenza f. ~tial adj deferente

defian|ce /dɪˈfaɪəns/ n sfida f; in ~ce of sfidando. ~t adj (person) ribelle; (gesture, attitude) di sfida. ~tly adv con aria di sfida

deficit /ˈdefɪsɪt/ n deficit m inv

define /dɪˈfaɪn/ vt definire

definite /ˈdefɪnɪt/ adj definito; (certain) definitivo; (improvement, difference) netto; he was ~ about it è stato chiaro in proposito. ~ly adv sicuramente

definition /defɪˈnɪʃn/ n definizione f

definitive /dɪˈfɪnɪtɪv/ adj definitivo

deflat|e /dɪˈfleɪt/ vt sgonfiare. ~ion n (Comm) deflazione f

deflect /dɪˈflekt/ vt deflettere

deform|ed /dɪˈfɔːmd/ adj deforme. ~ity n deformità f inv

defrost /diːˈfrɒst/ vt sbrinare (fridge); scongelare (food)

deft /deft/ adj abile

defuse /diːˈfjuːz/ vt disinnescare; calmare (situation)

defy /dɪˈfaɪ/ vt (pt/pp -ied) (challenge) sfidare; resistere a (attempt); (not obey) disobbedire a

degenerate¹ /dɪˈdʒenəreɪt/ vi degenerare; ~ into fig degenerare in

degenerate² /dɪˈdʒenərət/ adj degenerato

degree /dɪˈgriː/ n grado m; (Univ)

laurea f; 20 ~s 20 gradi; not to the same ~ non allo stesso livello

deign /deɪn/ vi ~ to do sth degnarsi di fare qcsa

deity /ˈdiːɪtɪ/ n divinità f inv

dejected /dɪˈdʒektɪd/ adj demoralizzato

delay /dɪˈleɪ/ n ritardo m; without ~ senza indugio ● vt ritardare; be ~ed (person): essere trattenuto; (train, aircraft): essere in ritardo ● vi indugiare

delegate[1] /ˈdelɪgət/ n delegato, -a mf

delegat|**e**[2] /ˈdelɪgeɪt/ vt delegare. ~**ion** n delegazione f

delet|**e** /dɪˈliːt/ vt cancellare. ~**ion** n cancellatura f

deliberate[1] /dɪˈlɪbərət/ adj deliberato; (slow) posato. ~**ly** adv deliberatamente; (slowly) in modo posato

deliberat|**e**[2] /dɪˈlɪbəreɪt/ vt/i deliberare. ~**ion** n deliberazione f

delicacy /ˈdelɪkəsɪ/ n delicatezza f; (food) prelibatezza f

delicate /ˈdelɪkət/ adj delicato

delicatessen /delɪkəˈtesn/ n negozio m di specialità gastronomiche

delicious /dɪˈlɪʃəs/ adj delizioso

delight /dɪˈlaɪt/ n piacere m ● vt deliziare ● vi ~ in dilettarsi con. ~**ed** adj lieto. ~**ful** adj delizioso

deli|**rious** /dɪˈlɪrɪəs/ adj be ~**rious** delirare; (fig: very happy) essere pazzo di gioia. ~**rium** n delirio m

deliver /dɪˈlɪvə(r)/ vt consegnare; recapitare (post, newspaper); tenere (speech); dare (message); tirare (blow); (set free) liberare; ~ a baby far nascere un bambino. ~**ance** n liberazione f. ~**y** n consegna f; (of post) distribuzione f; (Med) parto m; cash on ~**y** pagamento m alla consegna

delude /dɪˈluːd/ vt ingannare; ~ oneself illudersi

deluge /ˈdeljuːdʒ/ n diluvio m ● vt

(fig: with requests etc) inondare

delusion /dɪˈluːʒn/ n illusione f

de luxe /dəˈlʌks/ adj di lusso

delve /delv/ vi ~ into (into pocket etc) frugare in; (into notes, the past) fare ricerche in

demand /dɪˈmɑːnd/ n richiesta f; (Comm) domanda f; in ~ richiesto; on ~ a richiesta ● vt esigere (of/ from sb). ~**ing** adj esigente

demented /dɪˈmentɪd/ adj demente

demister /diːˈmɪstə(r)/ n (Auto) sbrinatore m

demo /ˈdeməʊ/ n (pl ~s) 🔲 manifestazione f; ~ **disk** (Comput) demodisk m inv

democracy /dɪˈmɒkrəsɪ/ n democrazia f

democrat /ˈdeməkræt/ n democratico, -a mf. ~**ic** adj democratico

demo|**lish** /dɪˈmɒlɪʃ/ vt demolire. ~**lition** n demolizione f

demon /ˈdiːmən/ n demonio m

demonstrat|**e** /ˈdemənstreɪt/ vt dimostrare; fare una dimostrazione sull'uso di (appliance) ● vi (Pol) manifestare. ~**ion** n dimostrazione f; (Pol) manifestazione f

demonstrator /ˈdemənstreɪtə(r)/ n (Pol) manifestante mf; (for product) dimostratore, -trice mf

demoralize /dɪˈmɒrəlaɪz/ vt demoralizzare

demote /dɪˈməʊt/ vt retrocedere di grado; (Mil) degradare

demure /dɪˈmjʊə(r)/ adj schivo

den /den/ n tana f; (room) rifugio m

denial /dɪˈnaɪəl/ n smentita f

denim /ˈdenɪm/ n [tessuto m] jeans m; ~s pl [blue]jeans mpl

Denmark /ˈdenmɑːk/ n Danimarca f

denounce /dɪˈnaʊns/ vt denunciare

dens|**e** /dens/ adj denso; (crowd, forest) fitto; (stupid) ottuso. ~**ely** adv (populated) densamente; ~ely wooded fittamente ricoperto di alberi. ~ity n densità f inv; (of forest) fittezza f

dent /dent/ n ammaccatura f • vt ammaccare; ~ed adj ammaccato

dental /'dentl/ adj dei denti; (treatment) dentistico; (hygiene) dentale. ~ surgeon n odontoiatria mf, medico m dentista

dentist /'dentɪst/ n dentista mf. ~ry n odontoiatria f

dentures /'dentʃəz/ npl dentiera fsg

deny /dɪ'naɪ/ vt (pt/pp -ied) negare; (officially) smentire; ~ sb sth negare qcsa a qcno

deodorant /diː'əʊdərənt/ n deodorante m

depart /dɪ'pɑːt/ vi (plane, train:) partire; (liter: person) andare via; (deviate) allontanarsi (from da)

department /dɪ'pɑːtmənt/ n reparto m; (Pol) ministero m; (of company) sezione f; (Univ) dipartimento m. ~ store n grande magazzino m

departure /dɪ'pɑːtʃə(r)/ n partenza f; (from rule) allontanamento f; new ~ svolta f

depend /dɪ'pend/ vi dipendere (on da); (rely) contare (on su); it all ~s dipende; ~ing on what he says a seconda di quello che dice. ~able adj fidato. ~ant n persona f a carico. ~ence n dipendenza f. ~ent adj dipendente (on da)

depict /dɪ'pɪkt/ vt (in writing) dipingere; (with picture) rappresentare

deplete /dɪ'pliːt/ vt ridurre; totally ~d completamente esaurito

deplor|able /dɪ'plɔːrəbl/ adj deplorevole. ~e vt deplorare

deploy /dɪ'plɔɪ/ vt (Mil) spiegare • vi schierarsi

deport /dɪ'pɔːt/ vt deportare. ~ation n deportazione f

depose /dɪ'pəʊz/ vt deporre

deposit /dɪ'pɒzɪt/ n deposito m;

(against damage) cauzione f; (first instalment) acconto m • vt (pt/pp deposited) depositare. ~ account n libretto m di risparmio; (without instant access) conto m vincolato

depot /'depəʊ/ n deposito m; Am (Rail) stazione f ferroviaria

depress /dɪ'pres/ vt deprimere; (press down) premere. ~ed adj depresso; ~ed area zona f depressa. ~ing adj deprimente. ~ion n depressione f

deprivation /deprɪ'veɪʃn/ n privazione f

deprive /dɪ'praɪv/ vt ~ sb of sth privare qcno di qcsa. ~d adj (area, childhood) disagiato

depth /depθ/ n profondità f inv; in ~ (study, analyse) in modo approfondito; in the ~s of winter in pieno inverno; be out of one's ~ (in water) non toccare il fondo; fig sentirsi in alto mare

deputize /'depjotaɪz/ vi ~ for fare le veci di

deputy /'depjoti/ n vice mf; (temporary) sostituto, -a mf • attrib ~ leader ≈ vicesegretario, -a mf; ~ chairman vicepresidente mf

derail /dɪ'reɪl/ vt be ~ed (train:) essere deragliato. ~ment n deragliamento m

derelict /'derəlɪkt/ adj abbandonato

deri|de /dɪ'raɪd/ vt deridere. ~sion n derisione f

derisory /dɪ'raɪsərɪ/ adj (laughter) derisorio; (offer) irrisorio

derivation /derɪ'veɪʃn/ n derivazione f

derivative /dɪ'rɪvətɪv/ adj derivato • n derivato m

derive /dɪ'raɪv/ vt (obtain) derivare; be ~d from (word:) derivare da

derogatory /dɪ'rɒgətrɪ/ adj (comments) peggiorativo

descend /dɪ'send/ vi scendere • vt scendere da; be ~ed from discendere da. **~ant** n discendente mf

descent /dɪ'sent/ n discesa f; (lineage) origine f

describe /dɪ'skraɪb/ vt descrivere

descrip|tion /dɪ'skrɪpʃn/ n descrizione f; they had no help of any **~tion** non hanno avuto proprio nessun aiuto. **~tive** adj descrittivo; (vivid) vivido

desecrat|e /'desɪkreɪt/ vt profanare. **~ion** n profanazione f

desert[1] /'dezət/ n deserto m ● adj deserto. **~ island** isola f deserta

desert[2] /dɪ'zɜːt/ vt abbandonare ● vi disertare. **~ed** adj deserto. **~er** n (Mil) disertore m. **~ion** n (Mil) diserzione f; (of family) abbandono m

deserts /dɪ'zɜːts/ npl get one's just **~** ottenere ciò che si merita

deserv|e /dɪ'zɜːv/ vt meritare. **~ing** adj meritevole; **~ing cause** opera f meritoria

design /dɪ'zaɪn/ n progettazione f; (fashion ~, appearance) design m inv; (pattern) modello m; (aim) proposito m ● vt progettare; design (clothes, furniture, model); **be ~ed for** essere fatto per

designat|e /'dezɪgneɪt/ vt designare. **~ion** n designazione f

designer /dɪ'zaɪnə(r)/ n progettista mf; (of clothes) stilista mf; (Theat: of set) scenografo, -a mf

desirable /dɪ'zaɪərəbl/ adj desiderabile

desire /dɪ'zaɪə(r)/ n desiderio m ● vt desiderare

desk /desk/ n scrivania f; (in school) banco m; (in hotel) reception f inv; (cash ~) cassa f. **~top publishing** n desktop publishing m, editoria f da tavolo

desolat|e /'desələt/ adj desolato. **~ion** n desolazione f

despair /dɪ'speə(r)/ n disperazione f; **in ~** disperato; (say) per disperazione ● vi **I ~ of that boy** quel ra-

gazzo mi fa disperare

desperat|e /'despərət/ adj disperato; **be ~e** (criminal): essere un disperato; **be ~e for** sth morire dalla voglia di. **~ely** adv disperatamente; he said **~ely** ha detto, disperato. **~ion** n disperazione f; **in ~ion** per disperazione

despicable /dɪ'spɪkəbl/ adj disprezzevole

despise /dɪ'spaɪz/ vt disprezzare

despite /dɪ'spaɪt/ prep malgrado

despondent /dɪ'spɒndənt/ adj abbattuto

despot /'despɒt/ n despota m

dessert /dɪ'zɜːt/ n dolce m. **~ spoon** n cucchiaio m da dolce

destination /destɪ'neɪʃn/ n destinazione f

destiny /'destɪnɪ/ n destino m

destitute /'destɪtjuːt/ adj bisognoso

destroy /dɪ'strɔɪ/ vt distruggere. **~er** n (Naut) cacciatorpediniere m

destruc|tion /dɪ'strʌkʃn/ n distruzione f. **~tive** adj distruttivo; (fig: criticism) negativo

detach /dɪ'tætʃ/ vt staccare. **~able** adj separabile. **~ed** adj fig distaccato; **~ed house** villetta f

detachment /dɪ'tætʃmənt/ n distacco m; (Mil) distaccamento m

detail /'diːteɪl/ n particolare m, dettaglio m; **in ~** particolareggiatamente ● vt esporre con tutti i particolari; (Mil) assegnare. **~ed** adj particolareggiato, dettagliato

detain /dɪ'teɪn/ vt (police): trattenere; (delay) far ritardare. **~ee** n detenuto, -a mf

detect /dɪ'tekt/ vt individuare; (perceive) percepire. **~ion** n scoperta f

detective /dɪ'tektɪv/ n investigatore, -trice mf. **~ story** n racconto m poliziesco

detector /dɪ'tektə(r)/ n (for metal) metal detector m inv

d

detention /dɪˈtenʃn/ n detenzione f; (Sch) punizione f

deter /dɪˈtɜː(r)/ vt (pt/pp deterred) impedire; ~ sb from doing sth impedire a qcno di fare qcsa

detergent /dɪˈtɜːdʒənt/ n detersivo m

deteriorat|e /dɪˈtɪərɪəreɪt/ vi deteriorarsi. ~ion n deterioramento m

determination /dɪtɜːmɪˈneɪʃn/ n determinazione f

determine /dɪˈtɜːmɪn/ vt (ascertain) determinare; ~ to (resolve) decidere di. ~d adj deciso

deterrent /dɪˈterənt/ n deterrente m

detest /dɪˈtest/ vt detestare. ~able adj detestabile

detonat|e /ˈdetəneɪt/ vt far detonare • vi detonare. ~or n detonatore m

detour /ˈdiːtʊə(r)/ n deviazione f

detract /dɪˈtrækt/ vi ~ from sminuire (merit); rovinare (pleasure, beauty)

detriment /ˈdetrɪmənt/ n to the ~ of a danno di. ~al adj dannoso

de'value vt svalutare (currency)

devastat|e /ˈdevəsteɪt/ vt devastare. ~ed adj ⚠ sconvolto. ~ing adj devastante; (news) sconvolgente. ~ion n devastazione f

develop /dɪˈveləp/ vt sviluppare; contrarre (illness); (add to value of) valorizzare (area) • vi svilupparsi; ~ into divenire. ~er n [property] ~er imprenditore, -trice mf edile

development /dɪˈveləpmənt/ n sviluppo m; (of vaccine etc) messa f a punto

deviant /ˈdiːvɪənt/ adj deviato

deviat|e /ˈdiːvɪeɪt/ vi deviare. ~ion n deviazione f

device /dɪˈvaɪs/ n dispositivo m

devil /ˈdevl/ n diavolo m

devious /ˈdiːvɪəs/ adj (person) subdolo; (route) tortuoso

devise /dɪˈvaɪz/ vt escogitare

devoid /dɪˈvɔɪd/ adj ~ of privo di

devolution /diːvəˈluːʃn/ n (of power) decentramento m

devot|e /dɪˈvəʊt/ vt dedicare. ~ed adj (daughter etc) affezionato; be ~ed to sth consacrarsi a qcsa. ~ee /devəˈtiː/ n appassionato, -a mf

devotion /dɪˈvəʊʃn/ n dedizione f; ~s pl (Relig) devozione fsg

devour /dɪˈvaʊə(r)/ vt divorare

devout /dɪˈvaʊt/ adj devoto

dew /djuː/ n rugiada f

dexterity /dekˈsterətɪ/ n destrezza f

diabet|es /daɪəˈbiːtiːz/ n diabete m. ~ic adj diabetico • n diabetico, -a mf

diabolical /daɪəˈbɒlɪkl/ adj diabolico

diagnose /ˈdaɪəgnəʊz/ vt diagnosticare

diagnosis /daɪəgˈnəʊsɪs/ n (pl -oses /-siːz/) diagnosi f inv

diagonal /daɪˈægənl/ adj diagonale • n diagonale f

diagram /ˈdaɪəgræm/ n diagramma m

dial /ˈdaɪəl/ n (of clock, machine) quadrante m; (Teleph) disco m combinatore • v (pt/pp dialled) • vi (Teleph) fare il numero; ~ direct chiamare in teleselezione • vt fare (number)

dialect /ˈdaɪəlekt/ n dialetto m

dialling: ~ **code** n prefisso m. ~ **tone** n segnale m di linea libera

dialogue /ˈdaɪəlɒg/ n dialogo m

'dial tone n Am (Teleph) segnale m di linea libera

diameter /daɪˈæmɪtə(r)/ n diametro m

diamond /ˈdaɪəmənd/ n diamante m, brillante m; (shape) losanga f; ~s pl (in cards) quadri mpl

diaper /ˈdaɪəpə(r)/ n Am pannolino m

diaphragm /'daɪəfræm/ n diaframma m

diarrhoea /daɪə'rɪːə/ n diarrea f

diary /'daɪərɪ/ n (for appointments) agenda f; (for writing in) diario m

dice /daɪs/ n inv dadi mpl ● vt (Culin) tagliare a dadini

dictate /dɪk'teɪt/ vt/i dettare. ~ion n dettato m

dictator /dɪk'teɪtə(r)/ n dittatore m. ~ial adj dittatoriale. ~ship n dittatura f

dictionary /'dɪkʃənrɪ/ n dizionario m

did /dɪd/ ▷**DO**

didn't /'dɪdnt/ = did not

die /daɪ/ vi (pres p dying) morire (of di); **be dying to do sth** ● morire dalla voglia di fare qcsa. □ ~ **down** vi calmarsi; (fire, flames:) spegnersi. □ ~ **out** vi estinguersi; (custom:) morire

diesel /'diːzl/ n diesel m

diet /'daɪət/ n regime m alimentare; (restricted) dieta f; **be on a** ~ essere a dieta ● vi essere a dieta

differ /'dɪfə(r)/ vi differire; (disagree) non essere d'accordo

difference /'dɪfrəns/ n differenza f; (disagreement) divergenza f

different /'dɪfrənt/ adj diverso, differente; (various) diversi; **be** ~ **from** essere diverso da

differently /'dɪfrəntlɪ/ adv in modo diverso; ~ **from** diversamente da

difficult /'dɪfɪkəlt/ adj difficile. ~**y** n difficoltà f inv

diffuse[1] /dɪ'fjuːs/ adj diffuso; (wordy) prolisso

diffuse[2] /dɪ'fjuːz/ vt (Phys) diffondere

dig /dɪg/ n (poke) spinta f; (remark) frecciata f; (Archaeol) scavo m; ~**s** pl Ⓘ camera fsg ammobiliata ● vt/i (pt/pp dug, pres p digging) scavare

(hole); vangare (garden); (thrust) conficcare; ~ **sb in the ribs** dare una gomitata a qcno. □ ~ **out** vt fig tirar fuori. □ ~ **up** vt scavare (garden, street, object); sradicare (plant); (fig: find) scovare

digest[1] /'daɪdʒest/ n compendio m

digest[2] /daɪ'dʒest/ vt digerire. ~**ible** adj digeribile. ~**ion** n digestione f

digger /'dɪgə(r)/ n (Techn) scavatrice f

digit /'dɪdʒɪt/ n cifra f; (finger) dito m

digital /'dɪdʒɪtl/ adj digitale; ~ **camera** fotocamera f digitale. ~ **clock** orologio m digitale

digitize /'dɪdʒɪtaɪz/ vt digitalizzare

dignified /'dɪgnɪfaɪd/ adj dignitoso

dignitary /'dɪgnɪtərɪ/ n dignitario m

dignity /'dɪgnɪtɪ/ n dignità f

digress /daɪ'gres/ vi divagare. ~**ion** n digressione f

dike /daɪk/ n diga f

dilapidated /dɪ'læpɪdeɪtɪd/ adj cadente

dilate /daɪ'leɪt/ vi dilatarsi

dilemma /dɪ'lemə/ n dilemma m

dilute /daɪ'luːt/ vt diluire

dim /dɪm/ adj (dimmer, dimmest) debole (light); (dark) scuro; (prospect, chance) scarso; (indistinct) impreciso; (Ⓘ: stupid) tonto ● vt/i (pt/pp dimmed) affievolire. ~**ly** adv (see, remember) indistintamente; (shine) debolmente

dime /daɪm/ n Am moneta f da dieci centesimi

dimension /daɪ'menʃn/ n dimensione f

diminish /dɪ'mɪnɪʃ/ vt/i diminuire

dimple /'dɪmpl/ n fossetta f

din /dɪn/ n baccano m

dine /daɪn/ vi pranzare. ~**r** n (Am: restaurant) tavola f calda; **the last** ~**r in the restaurant** l'ultimo cliente nel ristorante

dinghy /'dɪŋgɪ/ n dinghy m; (inflatable) canotto m pneumatico

dingy /'dɪndʒɪ/ adj (-ier, -iest) squallido e tetro

dinner /'dɪnə(r)/ n cena f; (at midday) pranzo m. ~-jacket n smoking m inv

dinosaur /'daɪnəsɔː(r)/ n dinosauro m

dint /dɪnt/ n by ~ of a forza di

dip /dɪp/ n (in ground) inclinazione f; (Culin) salsina f; to go for a ~ andare a fare una nuotata ● v (pt/pp dipped) ● vt (in liquid) immergere; abbassare (head, headlights) ● vi (land:) formare un avvallamento. □ ~ into vt scorrere (book)

diphthong /'dɪfθɒŋ/ n dittongo m

diploma /dɪ'pləʊmə/ n diploma m

diplomacy /dɪ'pləʊməsɪ/ n diplomazia f

diplomat /'dɪpləmæt/ n diplomatico, -a mf. ~ic adj diplomatico. ~ically adv con diplomazia

'dip-stick n (Auto) astina f dell'olio

dire /daɪə(r)/ adj (situation, consequences) terribile

direct /dɪ'rekt/ adj diretto ● adv direttamente ● vt (aim) rivolgere (attention, criticism); (control) dirigere; fare la regia di (film, play); ~ sb (show the way) indicare la strada a qcno; ~ sb to do sth ordinare a qcno di fare qcsa. ~ 'current n corrente m continua

direction /dɪ'rekʃn/ n direzione f; (of play, film) regia f; ~s pl indicazioni fpl

directly /dɪ'rektlɪ/ adv direttamente; (at once) immediatamente ● conj [non] appena

director /dɪ'rektə(r)/ n (Comm) direttore, -trice mf; (of play, film) regista mf

directory /dɪ'rektərɪ/ n elenco m; (Teleph) elenco m [telefonico]; (of streets) stradario m

dirt /dɜːt/ n sporco m; ~ cheap 🆃 a [un] prezzo stracciato

dirty /'dɜːtɪ/ adj (-ier, -iest) sporco; ~ trick brutto scherzo m; ~ word parolaccia f ● vt (pt/pp -ied) sporcare

disa'bility /dɪs-/ n infermità f inv. ~abled adj invalido

disad'van|tage n svantaggio m; at a ~tage in una posizione di svantaggio. ~taged adj svantaggiato. ~tageous adj svantaggioso

disa'gree vi non essere d'accordo; ~ with (food:) far male a

disa'greeable adj sgradevole

disa'greement n disaccordo m; (quarrel) dissidio m

disap'pear vi scomparire. ~ance n scomparsa f

disap'point vt deludere; I'm ~ed sono deluso. ~ing adj deludente. ~ment n delusione f

disap'proval n disapprovazione f

disap'prove vi disapprovare; ~ of sb/sth disapprovare qcno/qcsa

dis'arm vt disarmare ● vi (Mil) disarmarsi. ~ament n disarmo m. ~ing adj (frankness etc) disarmante

disar'ray n in ~ in disordine

disast|er /dɪ'zɑːstə(r)/ n disastro m. ~rous adj disastroso

disband vt sciogliere; smobilitare (troops) ● vi sciogliersi; (regiment:) essere smobilitato

disbe'lief n incredulità f; in ~ con incredulità

disc /dɪsk/ n disco m; (CD) compact disc m inv

discard /dɪ'skɑːd/ vt scartare; (throw away) eliminare; scaricare (boyfriend)

discern /dɪ'sɜːn/ vt discernere. ~ible adj discernibile. ~ing adj perspicace

'discharge[1] n (Electr) scarica f; (dismissal) licenziamento m; (Mil) congedo m; (Med: of blood) emissione f; (of cargo) scarico m

dis'charge² vt scaricare (battery, cargo); (dismiss) licenziare; (Mil) congedare; (Jur) assolvere (accused); dimettere (patient) ● vi (Electr) scaricarsi

disciple /dɪˈsaɪpl/ n discepolo m

disciplinary /ˈdɪsɪplɪnərɪ/ adj disciplinare

discipline /ˈdɪsɪplɪn/ n disciplina f ● vt disciplinare; (punish) punire

'disc jockey n disc jockey m inv

dis'claim vt disconoscere. **~er** n rifiuto m

dis'clos|e vt svelare. **~ure** n rivelazione f

disco /ˈdɪskəʊ/ n discoteca f

dis'colour vt scolorire ● vi scolorirsi

dis'comfort n scomodità f; fig disagio m

disconcert /dɪskənˈsɜːt/ vt sconcertare

discon'nect vt disconnettere

disconsolate /dɪsˈkɒnsələt/ adj sconsolato

discon'tent n scontentezza f. **~ed** adj scontento

discon'tinue vt cessare, smettere; (Comm) sospendere la produzione di; **~d line** fine f serie

'discord n discordia f; (Mus) dissonanza f. **~ant** adj **~ant note** nota f discordante

'discount¹ n sconto m

dis'count² vt (not believe) non credere a; (leave out of consideration) non tener conto di

dis'courage vt scoraggiare; (dissuade) dissuadere

dis'courteous adj scortese

dis'cover /dɪsˈkʌvə(r)/ vt scoprire. **~y** n scoperta f

dis'credit n discredito m ● vt (pt/pp discredited) screditare

discreet /dɪsˈkriːt/ adj discreto

discrepancy /dɪsˈkrepənsɪ/ n discrepanza f

discretion /dɪsˈkreʃn/ n discrezione f

discriminat|e /dɪsˈkrɪmɪneɪt/ vi discriminare (against contro); **~e** between distinguere tra. **~ing** adj esigente. **~ion** n discriminazione f; (quality) discernimento m

discus /ˈdɪskəs/ n disco m

discuss /dɪsˈkʌs/ vt discutere; (examine critically) esaminare. **~ion** n discussione f

disdain /dɪsˈdeɪn/ n sdegno f ● vt sdegnare. **~ful** adj sdegnoso

disease /dɪˈziːz/ n malattia f. **~d** adj malato

disem'bark vi sbarcare

disen'tangle vt districare

dis'figure vt deformare

dis'grace n vergogna f; **I am in ~** sono caduto in disgrazia; **it's a ~** è una vergogna ● vt disonorare. **~ful** adj vergognoso

disgruntled /dɪsˈɡrʌntld/ adj malcontento

disguise /dɪsˈɡaɪz/ n travestimento m; **in ~** travestito ● vt contraffare (voice); dissimulare (emotions); **~d as** travestito da

disgust /dɪsˈɡʌst/ n disgusto m; **in ~** con aria disgustata ● vt disgustare. **~ing** adj disgustoso

dish /dɪʃ/ n piatto m; **do the ~es** lavare i piatti ● **dish out** vt (serve) servire; (distribute) distribuire. ▫ **~ up** vt servire

'dishcloth n strofinaccio m

dis'honest adj disonesto. **~y** n disonestà f

dis'honour n disonore m ● vt disonorare (family); non onorare (cheque). **~able** adj disonorevole. **~ably** adv in modo disonorevole

'dishwasher n lavapiatti f inv

disil'lusion vt disilludere. **~ment** n disillusione f

disin'fect vt disinfettare. **~ant** n

disinfettante *m*
dis'integrate *vi* disintegrarsi
dis'interested *adj* disinteressato
dis'jointed *adj* sconnesso
disk /dɪsk/ *n* (Comput) disco *m*; (disk-ette) dischetto *m*
dis'like *n* avversione *f*; your likes and ~s i tuoi gusti ● *vt* l ~ him/it non mi piace; I don't ~ him/it non mi dispiace
dislocate /'dɪsləkeɪt/ *vt* slogare; ~ one's shoulder slogarsi una spalla
dis'lodge *vt* sloggiare
dis'loyal *adj* sleale. ~ty *n* slealtà *f*
dismal /'dɪzməl/ *adj* (person) abbacchiato; (news, weather) deprimente; (performance) mediocre
dismantle /dɪs'mæntl/ *vt* smontare (tent, machine); *fig* smantellare
dis'may *n* sgomento *m*. ~ed *adj* sgomento
dis'miss *vt* licenziare (employee); (reject) scartare (idea, suggestion). ~al *n* licenziamento *m*
dis'mount *vt* smontare
diso'bedien|ce *n* disubbidienza *f*. ~t *adj* disubbidiente
diso'bey *vt* disubbidire a (rule) ● *vi* disubbidire
dis'order *n* disordine *m*; (Med) disturbo *m*. ~ly *adj* disordinato; (crowd) turbolento; ~ly conduct turbamento *m* della quiete pubblica
dis'organized *adj* disorganizzato
diso'rientate *vt* disorientare
dis'own *vt* disconoscere
disparaging /dɪ'spærɪdʒɪŋ/ *adj* sprezzante
dispatch /dɪ'spætʃ/ *n* (Comm) spedizione *f*; (Mil, report) dispaccio *m*; with ~ con prontezza ● *vt* spedire; (kill) spedire al creatore
dispel /dɪ'spel/ *vt* (pt/pp dispelled) dissipare
dispensable /dɪ'spensəbl/ *adj* dispensabile

dispense /dɪ'spens/ *vt* distribuire; ~ with fare a meno di; dispensing chemist farmacista *mf*; (shop) farmacia *f*. ~r *n* (device) distributore *m*
dispers|al /dɪ'spɜːsl/ *n* disperzione *f*. ~e *vt* disperdere ● *vi* disperdersi
dispirited /dɪ'spɪrɪtɪd/ *adj* scoraggiato
display /dɪ'spleɪ/ *n* mostra *f*; (Comm) esposizione *f*; (of feelings) manifestazione *f*; *pej* ostentazione *f*; (Comput) display *m inv* ● *vt* mostrare; esporre (goods); manifestare (feeling); (Comput) visualizzare
dis'please *vt* non piacere a; be ~d with essere scontento di
dis'pleasure *n* malcontento *m*
disposable /dɪ'spəʊzəbl/ *adj* (throwaway) usa e getta; (income) disponibile
disposal /dɪ'spəʊzl/ *n* (getting rid of) eliminazione *f*; be at sb's ~ essere a disposizione di qcno
dispro'portionate /dɪsprə'pɔːʃə-nət/ *adj* sproporzionato
dis'prove *vt* confutare
dispute /dɪ'spjuːt/ *n* disputa *f*; (industrial) contestazione *f* ● *vt* contestare (statement)
disqualifi'cation *n* squalifica *f*; (from driving) ritiro *m* della patente
dis'qualify *vt* (pt/pp -ied) escludere; (Sport) squalificare; ~ sb from driving ritirare la patente a qcno
disre'gard *n* mancanza *f* di considerazione ● *vt* ignorare
dis'reputable *adj* malfamato
disre'spect *n* mancanza *f* di rispetto. ~ful *adj* irrispettoso
disrupt /dɪs'rʌpt/ *vt* creare scompiglio in; sconvolgere (plans). ~ion *n* scompiglio *m*; (of plans) sconvolgimento *m*. ~ive *adj* (person, behaviour) indisciplinato
dissatis'faction *n* malcontento *m*
dis'satisfied *adj* scontento

dissect /dɪˈsekt/ vt sezionare. ~ion
n dissezione f

dissent /dɪˈsent/ n dissenso m ● vi
dissentire

dissertation /dɪsəˈteɪʃn/ n tesi
f inv

dissident /ˈdɪsɪdənt/ n dissidente mf

dis'similar adj dissimile (to da)

dissolute /ˈdɪsəluːt/ adj dissoluto

dissolve /dɪˈzɒlv/ vt dissolvere ● vi
dissolversi

dissuade /dɪˈsweɪd/ vt dissuadere

distance /ˈdɪstəns/ n distanza f; it's
a short ~ from here to the station la stazione non è lontana da
qui; in the ~ in lontananza; from a
~ da lontano

distant /ˈdɪstənt/ adj distante; (relative) lontano

dis'taste n avversione f. ~ful adj
spiacevole

distil /dɪˈstɪl/ vt (pt/pp distilled) di-
stillare. ~lation n distillazione f.
~lery n distilleria f

distinct /dɪˈstɪŋkt/ adj chiaro; (different) distinto. ~ion n distinzione f;
(Sch) massimo m dei voti. ~ive adj
caratteristica. ~ly adv chiaramente

distinguish /dɪˈstɪŋgwɪʃ/ vt/i distinguere; ~ oneself distinguersi.
~ed adj rinomato; (appearance) distinto; (career) brillante

distort /dɪˈstɔːt/ vt distorcere. ~ion
n distorsione f

distract /dɪˈstrækt/ vt distrarre.
~ed adj assente; (☐: worried) preoccupato. ~ing adj che distoglie. ~ion
n distrazione f; (despair) disperazione
f; drive sb to ~ portare qcno alla
disperazione

distraught /dɪˈstrɔːt/ adj sconvolto

distress /dɪˈstres/ n angoscia f;
(pain) sofferenza f; (danger) difficoltà f
● vt sconvolgere; (sadden) affliggere.
~ing adj penoso; (shocking) sconvolgente. ~ signal n segnale m di ri-

chiesta di soccorso

distribut|e /dɪˈstrɪbjuːt/ vt distri-
buire. ~ion n distribuzione f. ~or n
distributore m

district /ˈdɪstrɪkt/ n regione f;
(Admin) distretto m. ~ nurse n infermiere, -a mf che fa visite a domicilio

dis'trust n sfiducia f ● vt non fidarsi
di. ~ful adj diffidente

disturb /dɪˈstɜːb/ vt disturbare;
(emotionally) turbare; spostare
(papers). ~ance n disturbo m;
~ances (pl: rioting etc) disordini mpl.
~ed adj turbato; [mentally] ~ed
malato di mente. ~ing adj inquietante

dis'used adj non utilizzato

ditch /dɪtʃ/ n fosso m ● vt (☐: abandon) abbandonare (plan, car); piantare (lover)

dither /ˈdɪðə(r)/ vi titubare

divan /dɪˈvæn/ n divano m

dive /daɪv/ n tuffo m; (Aeron) picchiata f; (☐: place) bettola f ● vi tuffarsi; (when in water) immergersi;
(Aeron) scendere in picchiata; (☐:
rush) precipitarsi

diver /ˈdaɪvə(r)/ n (from board) tuffa-
tore, -trice mf; (scuba) sommozzatore,
-trice mf; (deep sea) palombaro m

diver|ge /daɪˈvɜːdʒ/ vi divergere.
~gent adj divergente

diverse /daɪˈvɜːs/ adj vario

diversify /daɪˈvɜːsɪfaɪ/ vt/i (pt/pp
-ied) diversificare

diversion /daɪˈvɜːʃn/ n deviazione
f; (distraction) diversivo m

diversity /daɪˈvɜːsətɪ/ n varietà f

divert /daɪˈvɜːt/ vt deviare (traffic);
distogliere (attention)

divide /dɪˈvaɪd/ vt dividere (by per);
six ~d by two sei diviso due ● vi dividersi

dividend /ˈdɪvɪdend/ n dividendo
m; pay ~s fig ripagare

divine /dɪˈvaɪn/ adj divino

d

diving /'daɪvɪŋ/ n (from board) tuffi mpl; (scuba) immersione f. ~-**board** n trampolino m. ~-**mask** n maschera f [subacquea]. ~-**suit** n muta f; (deep sea) scafandro m

division /dɪ'vɪʒn/ n divisione f; (in sports league) serie f

divorce /dɪ'vɔːs/ n divorzio m ●vt divorziare da. ~**d** adj divorziato; **get** ~**d** divorziare

divorcee /dɪvɔː'siː/ n divorziato, -a mf

divulge /daɪ'vʌldʒ/ vt rendere pubblico

DIY n abbr do-it-yourself

dizziness /'dɪzɪnɪs/ n giramenti mpl di testa

dizzy /'dɪzɪ/ adj (-ier, -iest) vertiginoso; **I feel** ~ mi gira la testa

---

do¹ /duː/

3 sing pres tense **does**; past tense **did**; past participle **done**

● vt fare; (🄵: cheat) fregare; **be done** (Culin) essere cotto; **well done** bravo; (Culin) ben cotto; **do the flowers** sistemare i fiori; **do the washing up** lavare i piatti; **do one's hair** farsi i capelli

● vi (be suitable) andare; (be enough) bastare; **this will do** questo va bene; **that will do!** basta così!; **do well/badly** cavarsela bene/male; **how is he doing?** come sta?

● v aux (used to form questions and negatives; often not translated) **do you speak Italian?** parli italiano?; **you don't like him, do you?** non ti piace, vero?; (expressing astonishment) **don't** dirmi che ti piace!; (emphatic) **invece** sì; **no, I don't** no; **I don't smoke** non fumo; **don't**

you/doesn't he? vero?; **so do I** anch'io; **do come in, John** entra, John; **how do you do?** piacere. □~ **away with** vt abolire (rule). □~ **for** vt done for (🄵: kill) uccidere; farsi male a (back); **done in** (🄵) esausto. □~ **up** vt (fasten) abbottonare; (renovate) rimettere a nuovo; (wrap) avvolgere. □~ **with** vt **I could do with a spanner** mi ci vorrebbe una chiave inglese. □~ **without** vt fare a meno di

do² /duː/ n (pl **dos** or **do's**) (🄵) festa f

docile /'dəʊsaɪl/ adj docile

dock¹ /dɒk/ n (Jur) banco m degli imputati

dock² n (Naut) bacino m ●vi entrare in porto; (spaceship): congiungersi. ~**er** n portuale m. ~**s** npl porto m. ~**yard** n cantiere m navale

doctor /'dɒktə(r)/ n dottore m, dottoressa f ●vt alterare (drink); castrare (cat). ~**ate** n dottorato m

doctrine /'dɒktrɪn/ n dottrina f

document /'dɒkjʊmənt/ n documento m. ~**ary** adj documentario ●n documentario m

dodge /dɒdʒ/ n (🄵) trucco m ●vt schivare (blow); evitare (person) ●vi scansarsi; ~ **out of the way** scansarsi

dodgems /'dɒdʒəmz/ npl autoscontro msg

dodgy /'dɒdʒɪ/ adj (-ier, -iest) (🄵: dubious) sospetto

doe /dəʊ/ n femmina f (di daino, renna, lepre); (rabbit) coniglia f

does /dʌz/ ▷**DO**

doesn't /'dʌznt/ = does not

dog /dɒg/ n cane m ●vt (pt/pp dogged) (illness, bad luck): perseguitare

dogged /'dɒgɪd/ adj ostinato

'**dog house** n **in the** ~ (🄵) in disgrazia

dogma /ˈdɒɡmə/ n dogma m. ~**tic** adj dogmatico

do-it-yourself /duːɪtjəˈself/ n fai da te m, bricolage m. ~ **shop** n negozio m di bricolage

dole /dəʊl/ n sussidio m di disoccupazione; be on the ~ essere disoccupato ● **dole out** vt distribuire

doleful /ˈdəʊlfl/ adj triste

doll /dɒl/ n bambola f. ~ oneself up vt 🖽 mettersi in ghingheri

dollar /ˈdɒlə(r)/ n dollaro m

dollop /ˈdɒləp/ n 🖽 cucchiaiata f

dolphin /ˈdɒlfɪn/ n delfino m

dome /dəʊm/ n cupola f

domestic /dəˈmestɪk/ adj domestico; (Pol) interno; (Comm) nazionale

domesticated /dəˈmestɪkeɪtɪd/ adj (animal) addomesticato

domestic flight n volo m nazionale

dominant /ˈdɒmɪnənt/ adj dominante

dominat|e /ˈdɒmɪnent/ vt/i dominare. ~**ion** n dominio m

domineering /dɒmɪˈnɪərɪŋ/ adj autoritario

dominion /dəˈmɪnjən/ n Br (Pol) dominion m inv

donat|e /dəʊˈneɪt/ vt donare. ~**ion** n donazione f

done /dʌn/ ▷ **DO**

donkey /ˈdɒŋkɪ/ n asino m; ~'s years 🖽 secoli mpl. ~**-work** n sgobbata f

donor /ˈdəʊnə(r)/ n donatore, -trice mf

doodle /ˈduːdl/ vi scarabocchiare

doom /duːm/ n fato m; (ruin) rovina f ● vt be ~ed [to failure] essere destinato al fallimento; ~ed (ship) destinato ad affondare

door /dɔː(r)/ n porta f; (of car) portiera f; out of ~s all'aperto

door: ~**mat** n zerbino m. ~**step** n gradino m della porta. ~**way** n vano

m della porta

dope /dəʊp/ n (drug) droga f leggera; (information) indiscrezioni fpl; (idiot) idiota m ● vt drogare; (Sport) dopare

dormant /ˈdɔːmənt/ adj latente; (volcano) inattivo

dormitory /ˈdɔːmɪtərɪ/ n dormitorio m

dormouse /ˈdɔː-/ n ghiro m

dosage /ˈdəʊsɪdʒ/ n dosaggio m

dose /dəʊs/ n dose f

dot /dɒt/ n punto m; at 8 o'clock on the ~ alle 8 in punto

dot-com /dɒtˈkɒm/ n azienda f legata a Internet

dote /dəʊt/ vi ~ on stravedere per

dotty /ˈdɒtɪ/ adj (-ier, -iest) 🖽 tocco; (idea) folle

double /ˈdʌbl/ adj doppio ●adv cost ~ costare il doppio; see ~ vedere doppio; ~ the amount la quantità doppia ●n doppio m; (person) sosia m inv; ~s pl (Tennis) doppio m; at the ~ di corsa ● vt raddoppiare; (fold) piegare in due ● vi raddoppiare. □ ~ **back** vi (go back) tornare sui propri passi. □ ~ **up** vi (bend) piegarsi in due (with per); (share) dividere una stanza

double: ~**-bass** n contrabbasso m. ~ '**bed** n letto m matrimoniale. ~ '**chin** n doppio mento m. ~-'**click** vt/i cliccare due volte, fare doppio clic (on su). ~-'**cross** vt ingannare. ~-'**decker** n autobus m inv a due piani. ~ '**Dutch** n 🖽 ostrogoto m. ~ '**glazing** n doppiovetro m

doubly /ˈdʌblɪ/ adv doppiamente

doubt /daʊt/ n dubbio m ● vt dubitare di. ~**ful** adj dubbio; (having doubts) in dubbio. ~**fully** adv con aria dubbiosa. ~**less** adv indubbiamente

dough /dəʊ/ n pasta f; (for bread) impasto m; (🖽 money) quattrini mpl. ~**nut** n bombolone m, krapfen m inv

dove /dʌv/ n colomba f. ~**tail** n

(Techn) incastro m a coda di rondine
down[1] /daʊn/ n (feathers) piumino m

down[2] adv giù; go/come ~ scendere; ~ there laggiù; sales are ~ le vendite sono diminuite; £50 ~ 50 sterline d'acconto; ~ 10% ridotto del 10%; ~ with...! abbasso...! ● prep walk ~ the road camminare per strada; ~ the stairs giù per le scale; fall ~ the stairs cadere giù dalle scale; get that ~ you! 🔢 butta giù!; be ~ the pub 🔢 essere al pub ● vt bere tutto d'un fiato (drink)

down: ~-and-out n spiantato, -a mf. ~cast adj abbattuto. ~fall n caduta f; (of person) rovina f. ~-hearted adj scoraggiato. ~hill adv in discesa; go ~ 🔢 essere in declino. ~load vt scaricare. ~payment n deposito m. ~pour n acquazzone m. ~right adj (absolute) totale; (lie) bell'e buono; (idiot) perfetto ● adv (completely) completamente. ~stairs adv al piano di sotto ● adj del piano di sotto. ~stream adv a valle. ~to-earth adj (person) con i piedi per terra. ~town adv Am in centro. ~ward[s] adj verso il basso; (slope) in discesa ● adv verso il basso

> **Downing Street** È una via del centro di Londra, nel quartiere di Westminster. Al numero 10 si trova la residenza ufficiale del Primo Ministro britannico e al numero 11 quella del Chancellor of the Exchequer (il Cancelliere dello Scacchiere, equivalente del Ministro delle Finanze e del Tesoro). Le espressioni Downing Street e Number 10 sono spesso usate dalla stampa per indicare il Primo Ministro.

dowry /'daʊrɪ/ n dote f

doze /daʊz/ n sonnellino m ● vi sonnecchiare. □ ~ off vi assopirsi

dozen /'dʌzn/ n dozzina f; ~s of books libri a dozzine

Dr abbr doctor

drab /dræb/ adj spento

draft[1] /drɑːft/ n abbozzo m; (Comm) cambiale f; Am (Mil) leva f ● vt abbozzare; Am (Mil) arruolare

draft[2] n Am = draught

drag /dræg/ n 🔢 scocciatura f; in ~ 🔢 (man) travestito da donna ● vt (pt/pp dragged) trascinare; dragare (river). □ ~ on vi (time, meeting:) trascinarsi

dragon /'drægən/ n drago m. ~-fly n libellula f

drain /dreɪn/ n tubo m di scarico; (grid) tombino m; the ~s pl le fognature; be a ~ on sb's finances prosciugare le finanze di qcno ● vt drenare (land, wound); scolare (liquid, vegetables); svuotare (tank, glass, person) ● vi ~ [away] andar via

drama /'drɑːmə/ n arte f drammatica; (play) opera f teatrale; (event) dramma m

dramatic /drə'mætɪk/ adj drammatico

dramat|ist /'dræmətɪst/ n drammaturgo, -a mf. ~ize vt adattare per il teatro; fig drammatizzare

drank /dræŋk/ ▷ DRINK

drape /dreɪp/ n Am tenda f ● vt appoggiare (over su)

drastic /'dræstɪk/ adj drastico. ~ally adv drasticamente

draught /drɑːft/ n corrente f; ~s sg (game) [gioco m della] dama fsg

draught beer n birra f alla spina

draughty /'drɑːftɪ/ adj pieno di correnti d'aria; it's ~ c'è corrente

draw /drɔː/ n (attraction) attrazione f; (Sport) pareggio m; (in lottery) sorteggio m ● v (pt drew, pp drawn) ● vt tirare; (attract) attirare; disegnare (picture); tracciare (line); ritirare (money); ~ lots tirare a sorte ● vi (tea:) essere in infusione; (*Sport*) pareggiare; ~ **near** avvicinarsi. □ ~ **back** *vt* tirare indietro; ritirare (hand); tirare (curtains) ● *vi* (recoil) tirarsi indietro. □ ~ **in** *vt* ritirare (claws etc) ● *vi* (train:) arrivare; (days:) accorciarsi. □ ~ **out** *vt* (pull out) tirar fuori; ritirare (money) ● *vi* (train:) partire; (days:) allungarsi. □ ~ **up** *vt* redigere (document); accostare (chair); ~ **oneself** to one's full height farsi grande ● *vi* (stop) fermarsi

draw: ~**back** *n* inconveniente *m*. ~**bridge** *n* ponte *m* levatoio

drawer /drɔː(r)/ *n* cassetto *m*

drawing /'drɔːɪŋ/ *n* disegno *m*

drawing: ~ **pin** *n* puntina *f*. ~ **room** *n* salotto *m*

drawl /drɔːl/ *n* pronuncia *f* strascicata

drawn /drɔːn/ ▷ DRAW

dread /dred/ *n* terrore *m* ● *vt* aver il terrore di

dreadful /'dredfʊl/ *adj* terribile. ~ly *adv* terribilmente

dream /driːm/ *n* sogno *m* ● *attrib* di sogno ● *vt/i* (*pt/pp* dreamt /dremt/ *or* dreamed) sognare (about/of di)

dreary /'drɪərɪ/ *adj* (-ier, -iest) tetro; (boring) monotono

dredge /dredʒ/ *vt/i* dragare

dregs /dregz/ *npl* feccia *fsg*

drench /drentʃ/ *vt* get ~ed inzupparsi; ~ed zuppo

dress /dres/ *n* (woman's) vestito *m*; (clothing) abbigliamento *m* ● *vt* vestire; (decorate) adornare; (Culin) condire; (Med) fasciare; ~ **oneself**, get ~ed vestirsi ● *vi* vestirsi. □ ~ **up** *vi* mettersi elegante; (in disguise) travestirsi (as da)

dress circle *n* (*Theat*) prima galleria *f*

dressing /'dresɪŋ/ *n* (*Culin*) condimento *m*; (Med) fasciatura *f*

dressing: ~-**gown** *n* vestaglia *f*.

~-**room** *n* (in gym) spogliatoio *m*; (*Theat*) camerino *m*. ~-**table** *n* toilette *f inv*

dress: ~**maker** *n* sarta *f*. ~ **rehearsal** *n* prova *f* generale

drew /druː/ ▷ DRAW

dribble /'drɪbl/ *vi* gocciolare; (baby:) sbavare; (*Sport*) dribblare

dried /draɪd/ *adj* (food) essiccato

drier /'draɪə(r)/ *n* asciugabiancheria *m inv*

drift /drɪft/ *n* movimento *m* lento; (of snow) cumulo *m*; (meaning) senso *m* ● *vi* (off course) andare alla deriva; (snow:) accumularsi; (fig: person:) procedere senza meta. □ ~ **apart** *vi* (people:) allontanarsi l'uno dall'altro

drill /drɪl/ *n* trapano *m*; (Mil) esercitazione *f* ● *vt* trapanare; (Mil) fare esercitare ● *vi* (Mil) esercitarsi; ~ for oil trivellare in cerca di petrolio

drink /drɪŋk/ *n* bevanda *f*; (alcoholic) bicchierino *m*; have a ~ bere qualcosa; a ~ of water un po' d'acqua ● *vt/i* (*pt* drank, *pp* drunk) bere. □ ~ **up** *vt* finire ● *vi* finire il bicchiere

drink|able /'drɪŋkəbl/ *adj* potabile. ~**er** *n* bevitore, -trice *mf*

'drinking-water *n* acqua *f* potabile

drip /drɪp/ *n* gocciolamento *m*; (drop) goccia *f*; (Med) flebo *f inv*; (□: person) mollaccione, -a *mf* ● *vi* (*pt/pp* dripped) gocciolare. ~-**'dry** *adj* che non si stira. ~**ping** *n* (*from meat*) grasso *m* d'arrosto ● *adj* ~**ping** [wet] fradicio

drive /draɪv/ *n* (in car) giro *m*; (entrance) viale *m*; (energy) grinta *f*; (Psych) pulsione *f*; (organized effort) operazione *f*; (Techn) motore *m*; (Comput) lettore *m* ● *v* (*pt* drove, *pp* driven) ● *vt* portare (person by car); guidare (car); (*Sport*: hit) mandare; (Techn) far funzionare; ~ **sb mad** far diventare matto qcno ● *vi* guidare. □ ~ **at** *vt* what are you driving at? dove vuoi arrivare? **drive away** *vt* portare via in macchina; (chase) cacciare ● vi andare via in macchina. □ ~ **in** vt piantare (nail) ● vi arrivare [in macchina]. □ ~ **off** vt portare via in macchina; (chase) cacciare ● vi andare via in macchina. □ ~ **on** vi proseguire (in macchina). □ ~ **up** vi arrivare (in macchina)

drivel /ˈdrɪvl/ n 🔳 sciocchezze fpl

driver /ˈdraɪvə(r)/ n guidatore, -trice mf; (of train) conducente mf

driving /ˈdraɪvɪŋ/ adj (rain) violento; (force) motore ● n guida f

driving: ~ **licence** n patente f di guida. ~ **test** n esame m di guida

drizzle /ˈdrɪzl/ n pioggerella f ● vi piovigginare

drone /drəʊn/ n (bee) fuco m; (sound) ronzio m

droop /druːp/ vi abbassarsi; (flowers:) afflosciarsi

drop /drɒp/ n (of liquid) goccia f; (fall) caduta f; (in price, temperature) calo m ● v (pt/pp **dropped**) ● vt far cadere; sganciare (bomb); (omit) omettere; (give up) abbandonare ● vi cadere; (price, temperature, wind:) calare; (ground:) essere in pendenza. □ ~ **in** vi passare. □ ~ **off** vt depositare (person) ● vi cadere; (fall asleep) assopirsi. □ ~ **out** vi cadere; (of race, society) ritirarsi; ~ **out of school** lasciare la scuola

'drop-out n persona f contro il sistema sociale

drought /draʊt/ n siccità f

drove /drəʊv/ ▷**DRIVE**

drown /draʊn/ vi annegare ● vt annegare; coprire (noise); **he was ~ed** è annegato

drowsy /ˈdraʊzɪ/ adj sonnolento

drudgery /ˈdrʌdʒərɪ/ n lavoro m pesante e noioso

drug /drʌg/ n droga f; (Med) farmaco m; **take** ~ **s** drogarsi ● vt (pt/pp **drugged**) drogare

drug: ~ **addict** n tossicomane, -a

mf. ~ **dealer** n spacciatore, -trice mf [di droga]. **~gist** n Am farmacista mf. **~store** n Am negozio m di generi vari, inclusi medicinali, (che funge anche da bar; dispensing) farmacia f

drum /drʌm/ n tamburo m; (for oil) bidone m; ~ **s** (pl: in pop-group) batteria f ● v (pt/pp **drummed**) ● vi suonare il tamburo; (in pop-group) suonare la batteria ● vt ~ **sth into sb** ripetere qcsa a qcno cento volte. **~mer** n percussionista mf; (in pop-group) batterista mf. **~stick** n bacchetta f; (of chicken, turkey) coscia f

drunk /drʌŋk/ ▷**DRINK** ● adj ubriaco; **get** ~ ubriacarsi ● n ubriaco, -a mf

drunk|ard /ˈdrʌŋkəd/ n ubriacone, -a mf. **~en** adj ubriaco; **~en driving** guida f in stato di ebbrezza

dry /draɪ/ adj (**drier, driest**) asciutto; (climate, country) secco ● vt/i (pt/pp **dried**) asciugare; ~ **one's eyes** asciugarsi le lacrime. □ ~ **up** vi seccarsi; (fig: source:) prosciugarsi; (🔳: be quiet) stare zitto; (do dishes) asciugare i piatti

dry: ~-**'clean** vt pulire a secco. ~-**'cleaner's** n (shop) tintoria f. **~ness** n secchezza f

DTD n abbr (digital type definition) DTD f

dual /ˈdjuːəl/ adj doppio

dual 'carriageway n strada f a due carreggiate

dub /dʌb/ vt (pt/pp **dubbed**) doppiare (film); (name) soprannominare

dubious /ˈdjuːbɪəs/ adj dubbio; **be** ~ **about** avere dei dubbi riguardo

duchess /ˈdʌtʃɪs/ n duchessa f

duck /dʌk/ n anatra f ● vt (in water) immergere; ~ **one's head** abbassare la testa ● vi abbassarsi. **~ling** n anatroccolo m

duct /dʌkt/ n condotto m; (Anat) dotto m

dud /dʌd/ 🔳 adj (Mil) disattivato; (coin) falso; (cheque) a vuoto ● n

(*banknote*) banconota *f* falsa

due /dju:/ *adj* dovuto; be ~ (train:)
essere previsto; **the baby is** ~ **next
week** il bambino dovrebbe nascere
la settimana prossima; ~ **to** (*owing
to*) a causa di; **be** ~ **to** (*causally*) essere dovuto a; **I'm** ~ **to... to...** dovrei...;
in ~ **course** a tempo debito ● *adv*
~ **north** direttamente a nord

duel /'dju:əl/ *n* duello *m*

dues /dju:z/ *npl* quota *f* [di
iscrizione]

duet /dju:'et/ *n* duetto *m*

dug /dʌg/ ▷ **DIG**

duke /dju:k/ *n* duca *m*

dull /dʌl/ *adj* (*overcast, not bright*) cupo;
(*not shiny*) opaco; (*sound*) soffocato;
(*boring*) monotono; (*stupid*) ottuso ● *vt*
intorpidire (mind); attenuare (pain)

dumb /dʌm/ *adj* muto; ([T]: *stupid*)
ottuso. **~founded** *adj* sbigottito.
□ ~ **down** vt semplificare il livello di

dummy /'dʌmɪ/ *n* (*tailor's*) mani-
chino *m*; (*for baby*) succhiotto *m*;
(*model*) riproduzione *f*

dump /dʌmp/ *n* (*for refuse*) scarico
m; ([T]: *town*) mortorio *m*; **be down in
the** ~**s** [T] essere depresso ● *vt* scaricare; ([T]: *put down*) lasciare; ([T]: *get rid
of*) liberarsi di

dumpling /'dʌmplɪŋ/ *n* gnocco *m*

dunce /dʌns/ *n* zuccone, -a *mf*

dung /dʌŋ/ *n* sterco *m*

dungarees /dʌŋgə'ri:z/ *npl* tuta *fsg*

dungeon /'dʌndʒən/ *n* prigione *f*
sotterranea

duplicate¹ /'dju:plɪkət/ *adj* doppio
● *n* duplicato *m*; (*document*) copia *f*; **in**
~ in duplicato

duplicat|e² /'dju:plɪkeɪt/ *vt* fare un
duplicato di; (*research:*) essere una
ripetizione di (work)

durable /'djʊərəbl/ *adj* resistente;
durevole (basis, institution)

duration /djʊə'reɪʃn/ *n* durata *f*

duress /djʊə'res/ *n* costrizione *f*;
under ~ sotto minaccia

during /'djʊərɪŋ/ *prep* durante

dusk /dʌsk/ *n* crepuscolo *m*

dust /dʌst/ *n* polvere *f* ● *vt* spolverare; (*sprinkle*) cospargere (cake)
(with di) ● *vi* spolverare

dust: ~**bin** *n* pattumiera *f*. ~**er** *n*
strofinaccio *m*. ~**jacket** *n* sopraccoperta *f*. ~**man** *n* spazzino *m*. ~**pan**
n paletta *f* per la spazzatura

dusty /'dʌstɪ/ *adj* (-ier, -iest) polveroso

Dutch /dʌtʃ/ *adj* olandese; **go** ~ 🇮🇹
fare alla romana ● *n* (*language*) olandese *m*; **the** ~ *pl* gli olandesi. ~**man**
n olandese *m*

duty /'dju:tɪ/ *n* dovere *m*; (task) compito *m*; (tax) dogana *f*; **be on** ~ essere di servizio. ~**-free** *adj* esente da
dogana

duvet /'du:veɪ/ *n* piumone *m*

DVD *n* DVD *m inv*

dwarf /dwɔ:f/ *n* (*pl* -s *or* dwarves)
nano, -a *mf* ● *vt* rimpicciolire

dwell /dwel/ *vi* (*pt/pp* dwelt) *liter* di-
morare. □ ~ **on** *vt fg* soffermarsi su.
~**ing** *n* abitazione *f*

dwindle /'dwɪndl/ *vi* diminuire

dye /daɪ/ *n* tintura *f* ● *vt* (*pres p* dyeing) tingere

dying /'daɪɪŋ/ ▷ **DIE²**

dynamic /daɪ'næmɪk/ *adj* dinamico

dynamite /'daɪnəmaɪt/ *n* di-
namite *f*

dynamo /'daɪnəməʊ/ *n* dinamo *f inv*

dynasty /'dɪnəstɪ/ *n* dinastia *f*

**d
e**

- -

Ee

- -

each /i:tʃ/ *adj* ogni ● *pron* ognuno;
£1 ~ una sterlina ciascuno; **they
love/hate** ~ **other** si amano/
odiano; **we lend** ~ **other money** ci
prestiamo i soldi

eager /'iːgə(r)/ adj ansioso (to do di fare); (pupil) avido di sapere. ~ly adv (wait) ansiosamente; (offer) premurosamente. ~ness n premura f

eagle /'iːgl/ n aquila f

ear¹ /ɪə(r)/ n (of corn) spiga f

ear² n orecchio m. ~ache n mal m d'orecchi. ~drum n timpano m

earl /ɜːl/ n conte m

early /'ɜːlɪ/ adj (-ier, -iest) (before expected time) anticipato; (spring) pre-maturo; (reply) pronto; (works, writings) primo; be here ~! sii puntuale!; you're ~ sei in anticipo!; ~ morning walk passeggiata f mat-tutina; in the ~ morning la mattina presto; in the ~ spring all'inizio della primavera; ~ retirement n pensionamento m ● adv presto; (ahead of time) in anticipo; in the morn-ing la mattina presto

earn /ɜːn/ vt guadagnare; (deserve) meritare

earnest /'ɜːnɪst/ adj serio ● n in ~ sul serio. ~ly adv con aria seria

earnings /'ɜːnɪŋz/ npl guadagni mpl; (salary) stipendio m

ear: ~phones npl cuffia fsg. ~ring n orecchino m. ~shot n within ~shot a portata d'orecchio; he is out of ~shot non può sentire

earth /ɜːθ/ n terra f; where/what on ~? dove/che diavolo? ● vt (Electr) mettere a terra

'**earthquake** n terremoto m

earwig /'ɪəwɪg/ n forbicina f

ease /iːz/ n at ~ a proprio agio; at ~! (Mil) riposo!; ill at ~ a disagio; with ~ con facilità ● vt calmare (pain); alleviare (tension, shortage); (slow down) rallentare; (loosen) allen-tare ● vi (pain, situation, wind:) calmarsi

easel /'iːzl/ n cavalletto m

easily /'iːzɪlɪ/ adv con facilità; ~ the best certamente il meglio

east /iːst/ n est m; to the ~ of a est

di ● adj dell'est ● adv verso est

Easter /'iːstə(r)/ n Pasqua f. ~ egg n uovo m di Pasqua

east|erly /'iːstəlɪ/ adj da levante. ~ern adj orientale. ~ward[s] /-wəd[z]/ adv verso est

easy /'iːzɪ/ adj (-ier, -iest) facile; take it or things ~ prendersela con calma; take it ~! (don't get excited) calma!; go ~ with andarci piano con

easy: ~ chair n poltrona f. ~'going adj conciliante; too ~going troppo accomodante

eat /iːt/ vt/i (pt ate, pp eaten) man-giare. □ ~ into vt intaccare. □ ~ up vt mangiare tutto (food); fig inghiot-tire (profits)

eaves /iːvz/ npl cornicione msg. ~drop vi (pt/pp ~dropped) ori-gliare; ~drop on ascoltare di na-scosto

ebb /eb/ n (tide) riflusso m; at a low ~ fig a terra ● vi rifluire; fig declinare

ebony /'ebənɪ/ n ebano m

eccentric /ɪk'sentrɪk/ adj & n ec-centrico, -a mf

echo /'ekəʊ/ n (pl -es) eco f or m ● v (pt/pp echoed, pres p echoing) ● vt echeggiare; ripetere (words) ● vi ri-suonare (with di)

eclipse /ɪ'klɪps/ n (Astr) eclissi f inv ● vt fig eclissare

ecolog|ical /iːkə'lɒdʒɪkl/ adj ecolo-gico. ~y n ecologia f

e-commerce /'iːkɒmɜːs/ n e-commerce m inv, commercio m elettronico

economic /iːkə'nɒmɪk/ adj economi-co; ~ refugee rifugiato, -a mf economico, -a. ~al adj economico. ~ally adv economicamente; (thriftily) in economia. ~s n economia f

economist /ɪ'kɒnəmɪst/ n econo-mista mf

economize /ɪ'kɒnəmaɪz/ vi econo-mizzare (on su)

economy /ɪ'kɒnəmi/ n economia f

ecstasy /'ekstəsi/ n estasi f inv; (drug) ecstasy f

eczema /'eksɪmə/ n eczema m

edge /edʒ/ n bordo m; (of knife) filo m; (of road) ciglio m; on ~ con i nervi tesi; **have the ~ on** 🎗 avere un vantaggio su ● vt bordare. □ ~ **forward** vi avanzare lentamente

edgeways /'edʒweɪz/ adv di fianco; **I couldn't get a word in** ~ non ho potuto infilare neanche mezza parola nel discorso

edgy /'edʒi/ adj nervoso

edible /'edɪbl/ adj commestibile; **this pizza's not** ~ questa pizza è immangiabile

---

Edinburgh Festival La più importante manifestazione culturale britannica, fondata nel 1947 e tenuta annualmente nella capitale scozzese, in agosto. Il festival offre spettacoli di musica, teatro, danza, ecc. e attira ogni anno moltissimi visitatori. Un settore sempre molto interessante è quello del cosiddetto *Fringe*, ossia gli eventi fuori dal programma ufficiale.   *i*

---

edit /'edɪt/ vt (pt/pp edited) far la revisione di (text); curare l'edizione di (anthology, dictionary); dirigere (newspaper); montare (film); editare (tape); ~**ed by** (book) a cura di

edition /ɪ'dɪʃn/ n edizione f

editor /'edɪtə(r)/ n (of anthology, dictionary) curatore, -trice mf; (of newspaper) redattore, -trice mf; (of film) responsabile mf del montaggio

editorial /edɪ'tɔːrɪəl/ adj redazionale m n (Journ) editoriale m

educate /'edjukeɪt/ vt istruire; educare (mind); **be ~d at** Eton essere educato a Eton. ~**d** adj istruito

education /edju'keɪʃn/ n istru-

zione f; (culture) cultura f, educazione f. ~**al** adj istruttivo; (visit) educativo; (publishing) didattico

eel /iːl/ n anguilla f

eerie /'ɪərɪ/ adj (-ier, -iest) inquietante

effect /ɪ'fekt/ n effetto m; **in** ~ in effetti; **take** ~ (law:) entrare in vigore; (medicine:) fare effetto ● vt effettuare

effective /ɪ'fektɪv/ adj efficace; (striking) che colpisce; (actual) di fatto; ~ **from** in vigore a partire da. ~**ly** adv efficacemente; (actually) di fatto. ~**ness** n efficacia f

effeminate /ɪ'femɪnət/ adj effeminato

efficiency /ɪ'fɪʃənsɪ/ n efficienza f; (of machine) rendimento m

efficient /ɪ'fɪʃənt/ adj efficiente. ~**ly** adv efficientemente

effort /'efət/ n sforzo m; **make an** ~ sforzarsi. ~**less** adj facile. ~**lessly** adv con facilità

e.g. abbr (exempli gratia) per es.

egg[1] /eg/ vt ~ **on** 🎗 incitare

egg[2] n uovo m. ~-**cup** n portauovo m inv. ~**head** n 🎗 intellettuale mf. ~**shell** n guscio m d'uovo. ~**timer** n clessidra f per misurare il tempo di cottura delle uova

ego /'iːgəʊ/ n ego m. ~**centric** adj egocentrico. ~**ism** n egoismo m. ~**ist** n egoista mf. ~**tism** n egotismo m. ~**tist** n egotista mf

Egypt /'iːdʒɪpt/ n Egitto m. ~**ian** adj & n egiziano, -a mf

EHIC n abbr (European Health Insurance Card) TEAM f

eiderdown /'aɪdə-/ n (quilt) piumino m

eight /eɪt/ adj otto ● n otto m. ~**teen** adj diciotto. ~**teenth** adj diciottesimo

eighth /eɪtθ/ adj ottavo ● n ottavo m

eightieth /'eɪtɪəθ/ adj ottantesimo

eighty /'eɪtɪ/ adj ottanta

either /'aɪðə(r)/ adj & pron ▶ [of

them) l'uno o l'altro; I don't like ~
[of them] non mi piace né l'uno né
l'altro; on ~ side da tutte e due le
parti ● adv I don't ~ nemmeno io; I
don't like John or his brother ~
non mi piace John e nemmeno suo
fratello ● conj ~ John or his brother
will be there ci saranno o John o
suo fratello; I don't like ~ John or
his brother non mi piacciono né
John né suo fratello; ~ you go to
bed or else... o vai a letto o altrimenti ...

eject /ɪ'dʒekt/ vt eiettare (pilot);
espellere (tape, drunk)

eke /iːk/ vt ~ out far bastare; (increase) arrotondare; ~ out a living
arrangiarsi

elaborate[1] /ɪ'læbərət/ adj ela-
borato

elaborate[2] /ɪ'læbəreɪt/ vi entrare
nei particolari (on di)

elapse /ɪ'læps/ vi trascorrere

elastic /ɪ'læstɪk/ adj elastico ● n elastico m. ~ 'band n elastico m

elated /ɪ'leɪtɪd/ adj esultante

elbow /'elbəʊ/ n gomito m

elder[1] /'eldə(r)/ n (tree) sambuco m

elder[2] adj maggiore ● n the ~ il/la
maggiore. ~erly adj anziano. ~est
adj maggiore ● n the ~est il/la
maggiore

elect /ɪ'lekt/ adj the president ~ il
futuro presidente ● vt eleggere; ~ to
do sth decidere di fare qcsa. ~ion n
elezione f

elector /ɪ'lektə(r)/ n elettore, -trice
mf. ~al adj elettorale; ~al roll liste
fpl elettorali. ~ate n elettorato m

electric /ɪ'lektrɪk/ adj elettrico

electrical /ɪ'lektrɪkl/ adj elettrico;
~ engineering elettrotecnica f

electric 'blanket n termoco-
perta f

electrician /ɪlek'trɪʃn/ n elettrici-
sta m

electricity /ɪlek'trɪsətɪ/ n

elettricità f

electrify /ɪ'lektrɪfaɪ/ vt (pt/pp -ied)
elettrificare; fig elettrizzare. ~ing adj
fig elettrizzante

electrocute /ɪ'lektrəkjuːt/ vt ful-
minare; (execute) giustiziare sulla
sedia elettrica

electrode /ɪ'lektrəʊd/ n elettrodo m

electron /ɪ'lektrɒn/ n elettrone m

electronic /ɪlek'trɒnɪk/ adj elettronico. ~ mail n posta f elettronica.
~s n elettronica f

elegance /'elɪgəns/ n eleganza f

elegant /'elɪgənt/ adj elegante

element /'elɪmənt/ n elemento m.
~ary adj elementare

elephant /'elɪfənt/ n elefante m

elevat|e /'elɪveɪt/ vt elevare. ~ion n
elevazione f; (height) altitudine f;
(angle) alzo m

elevator /'elɪveɪtə(r)/ n Am ascensore m

eleven /ɪ'levn/ adj undici ● n undici
m. ~th adj undicesimo; at the ~th
hour 🄸 all'ultimo momento

elf /elf/ n (pl elves) elfo m

eligible /'elɪdʒəbl/ adj eleggibile; ~
for aver diritto a

eliminate /ɪ'lɪmɪneɪt/ vt eliminare

élite /eɪ'liːt/ n fior fiore m

ellip|se /ɪ'lɪps/ n ellisse f. ~tical adj
ellittico

elm /elm/ n olmo m

elope /ɪ'ləʊp/ vi fuggire [per
sposarsi]

eloquen|ce /'eləkwəns/ n elo-
quenza f. ~t adj eloquente. ~tly adv
con eloquenza

else /els/ adv altro; who ~? e chi
altro?; he did of course, who ~?
l'ha fatto lui e chi, se no?; nothing
~ nient'altro; or ~ altrimenti;
someone ~ qualcun altro; somewhere ~ da qualche altra parte;
anyone ~ chiunque altro; (as ques-

tion) nessun'altro?; **anything** ~ qualunque altra cosa; (*as question*) altro?. ~**where** *adv* altrove

elude /ɪ'luːd/ *vt* eludere; (*avoid*) evitare; **the name** ~**s me** il nome mi sfugge

elusive /ɪ'luːsɪv/ *adj* elusivo

emaciated /ɪ'meɪsɪeɪtɪd/ *adj* emaciato

e-mail /'iːmeɪl/ *n* posta *f* elettronica ● *vt* spedire via posta elettronica. ~ **address** *n* indirizzo *m* e-mail

embankment /ɪm'bæŋkmənt/ *n* argine *m*; (*Rail*) massicciata *f*

embargo /em'bɑːɡəʊ/ *n* (*pl* -**es**) embargo *m*

embark /ɪm'bɑːk/ *vi* imbarcarsi; ~ **on** intraprendere. ~**ation** *n* imbarco *m*

embarrass /em'bærəs/ *vt* imbarazzare. ~**ed** *adj* imbarazzato. ~**ing** *adj* imbarazzante. ~**ment** *n* imbarazzo *m*

embassy /'embəsɪ/ *n* ambasciata *f*

embedded /ɪm'bedɪd/ *adj* (*in concrete*) cementato; (*traditions, feelings*) radicato

embellish /ɪm'belɪʃ/ *vt* abbellire

embers /'embəz/ *npl* braci *fpl*

embezzle /ɪm'bezl/ *vt* appropriarsi indebitamente di. ~**ment** *n* appropriazione *f* indebita

emblem /'embləm/ *n* emblema *m*

embrace /ɪm'breɪs/ *vt* abbracciare ● *vt* abbracciare ● *vi* abbracciarsi

embroider /ɪm'brɔɪdə(r)/ *vt* ricamare (*design*); *fig* abbellire. ~**y** *n* ricamo *m*

embryo /'embrɪəʊ/ *n* embrione *m*

emerald /'emərəld/ *n* smeraldo *m*

emer|ge /ɪ'mɜːdʒ/ *vi* emergere; (*come into being: nation*) nascere; (*sun, flowers*) spuntare fuori. ~**gence** *n* emergere *m*; (*of new country*) nascita *f*

emergency /ɪ'mɜːdʒənsɪ/ *n* emergenza *f*; **in an** ~ in caso di emergenza. ~ **exit** *n* uscita *f* di sicurezza

emigrant /'emɪɡrənt/ *n* emigrante *m f*

emigrat|e /'emɪɡreɪt/ *vi* emigrare. ~**ion** *n* emigrazione *f*

eminent /'emɪnənt/ *adj* eminente. ~**ly** *adv* eminentemente

emission /ɪ'mɪʃn/ *n* emissione *f*; (*of fumes*) esalazione *f*

emit /ɪ'mɪt/ *vt* (*pt/pp* **emitted**) emettere; esalare (*fumes*)

emotion /ɪ'məʊʃn/ *n* emozione *f*. ~**al** *adj* denso di emozione; (*person, reaction*) emotivo; **become** ~**al** avere una reazione emotiva

emotive /ɪ'məʊtɪv/ *adj* emotivo

emperor /'empərə(r)/ *n* imperatore *m*

emphasis /'emfəsɪs/ *n* enfasi *f*; **put the** ~ **on** sth accentuare qcsa

emphasize /'emfəsaɪz/ *vt* accentuare (*word, syllable*); sottolineare (*need*)

emphatic /ɪm'fætɪk/ *adj* categorico

empire /'empaɪə(r)/ *n* impero *m*

empirical /em'pɪrɪkl/ *adj* empirico

employ /ɪm'plɔɪ/ *vt* impiegare; *fig* usare (*tact*). ~**ee** *n* impiegato, -a *mf*. ~**er** *n* datore *m* di lavoro. ~**ment** *n* occupazione *f*; (*work*) lavoro *m*. ~**ment agency** *n* ufficio *m* di collocamento

empower /ɪm'paʊə(r)/ *vt* autorizzare; (*enable*) mettere in grado

empress /'emprɪs/ *n* imperatrice *f*

empty /'emptɪ/ *adj* vuoto; (*promise, threat*) vano ● *v* (*pt/pp* -**ied**) ● *vt* vuotare (*container*) ● *vi* vuotarsi

emulate /'emjʊleɪt/ *vt* emulare

emulsion /ɪ'mʌlʃn/ *n* emulsione *f*

enable /ɪ'neɪbl/ *vt* ~ **sb to** mettere in grado qcno in grado di

enact /ɪ'nækt/ *vt* (*Theat*) rappresentare; decretare (*law*)

enamel /ɪ'næml/ *n* smalto *m* ● *vt* (*pt/pp* **enamelled**) smaltare

enchant /ɪn'tʃɑ:nt/ vt incantare.
~**ing** adj incantevole. ~**ment** n incanto m

encircle /ɪn'sɜ:kl/ vt circondare

enclave /'enkleɪv/ n enclave f inv; fig territorio m

enclos|e /ɪn'kləʊz/ vt circondare (land); (in letter) allegare (with a). ~**ed** adj (space) chiuso; (in letter) allegato. ~**ure** n (at zoo) recinto m; (in letter) allegato m

encore /'ɒŋkɔ:(r)/ n & int bis m inv

encounter /ɪn'kaʊntə(r)/ n incontro m; (battle) scontro m • vt incontrare

encourag|e /ɪn'kʌrɪdʒ/ vt incoraggiare; promuovere (the arts, independence). ~**ement** n incoraggiamento m; (of the arts) promozione f. ~**ing** adj incoraggiante; (smile) di incoraggiamento

encroach /ɪn'krəʊtʃ/ vi ~ **on** invadere (land, privacy); abusare di (time); interferire con (rights)

encyclop[a]ed|ia /ɪnsaɪklə'pi:dɪə/ n enciclopedia f. ~**ic** adj enciclopedico

end /end/ n fine f; (of box, table, piece of string) estremità f; (of town, room) parte f; (purpose) fine m; **in the** ~ alla fine; **at the** ~ **of May** alla fine di maggio; **at the** ~ **of the street/garden** in fondo alla strada/al giardino; **on** ~ (upright) in piedi; **for days on** ~ per giorni e giorni; **for six days on** ~ per sei giorni di fila; **put an** ~ **to** sth mettere fine a qcsa; **make** ~**s meet** ⊞ sbarcare il lunario; **no** ~ **of** ⊞ un sacco di • vt/i finire. □ ~ **up** vi finire; ~ **up doing** sth finire col fare qcsa

endanger /ɪn'deɪndʒə(r)/ vt rischiare (one's life); mettere a repentaglio (sb else, success of sth)

endear|ing /ɪn'dɪərɪŋ/ adj accattivante. ~**ment** n term of ~**ment** vezzeggiativo m

endeavour /ɪn'devə(r)/ n tentativo m • vi sforzarsi (to do)

ending /'endɪŋ/ n fine f; (Gram) desinenza f

endless /'endlɪs/ adj interminabile; (patience) infinito. ~**ly** adv continuamente; (patient) infinitamente

endorse /ɪn'dɔ:s/ vt girare (cheque); (sports personality:) fare pubblicità a (product); approvare (plan). ~**ment** n (of cheque) girata f; (of plan) conferma f; (on driving licence) registrazione f su patente di un'infrazione

endur|e /ɪn'djʊə(r)/ vt sopportare • vi durare. ~**ing** adj duraturo

enemy /'enəmɪ/ n nemico, -a mf • attrib nemico

energetic /enə'dʒetɪk/ adj energico

energy /'enədʒɪ/ n energia f

enforce /ɪn'fɔ:s/ vt far rispettare (law). ~**d** adj forzato

engage /ɪn'geɪdʒ/ vt assumere (staff); (Theat) ingaggiare; (Auto) ingranare (gear) • vi (Techn) ingranare; ~ **in** impegnarsi in. ~**d** adj (in use, busy) occupato; (person) impegnato; (to be married) fidanzato; **get** ~**d** fidanzarsi (to con). ~**d tone** (Teleph) segnale m di occupato. ~**ment** n fidanzamento m; (appointment) appuntamento m; (Mil) combattimento m; ~**ment ring** anello m di fidanzamento

engine /'endʒɪn/ n motore m; (Rail) locomotrice f. ~**-driver** n macchinista m

engineer /endʒɪ'nɪə(r)/ n ingegnere m; (service, installation) tecnico m; (Naut, Am (Rail) macchinista m • vt fig architettare. ~**ing** n ingegneria f

England /'ɪŋglənd/ n Inghilterra f

English /'ɪŋglɪʃ/ adj inglese; **the** ~ **Channel** la Manica • n (language) inglese m; **the** ~ pl gli inglesi. ~**man** n inglese m. ~**woman** n inglese f

engrav|e /ɪn'greɪv/ vt incidere.

~ing n incisione f

engulf /ɪn'gʌlf/ vt (fire, waves:) inghiottire

enhance /ɪn'hɑːns/ vt accrescere (beauty, reputation); migliorare (performance)

enigma /ɪ'nɪgmə/ n enigma m. ~tic adj enigmatico

enjoy /ɪn'dʒɔɪ/ vt godere di (good health); ~ oneself divertirsi; I ~ cooking/painting mi piace cucinare/dipingere; ~ your meal buon appetito. ~able adj piacevole. ~ment n piacere m

enlarge /ɪn'lɑːdʒ/ vt ingrandire ● vi ~ upon dilungarsi su. ~ment n ingrandimento m

enlighten /ɪn'laɪtn/ vt illuminare. ~ed adj progressista. ~ment n The E~ment l'Illuminismo m

enlist /ɪn'lɪst/ vt (Mil) reclutare; ~ sb's help farsi aiutare da qcno ● vi (Mil) arruolarsi

enliven /ɪn'laɪvn/ vt animare

enormity /ɪ'nɔːmətɪ/ n enormità f

enormous /ɪ'nɔːməs/ adj enorme. ~ly adv estremamente; (grateful) infinitamente

enough /ɪ'nʌf/ adj & n abbastanza; I didn't bring ~ clothes non ho portato abbastanza vestiti; have you had ~? (to eat/drink) hai mangiato/bevuto abbastanza?; I've had ~! ⃞ ne ho abbastanza!; is that ~? basta?; that's ~! basta così!; £50 isn't ~ 50 sterline non sono sufficienti ● adv abbastanza; you're not working fast ~ non lavori abbastanza in fretta; funnily ~ stranamente

enquir|e /ɪn'kwaɪə(r)/ vi domandare; ~e about chiedere informazioni su. ~y n domanda f; (investigation) inchiesta f

enrage /ɪn'reɪdʒ/ vt fare arrabbiare

enrol /ɪn'rəʊl/ vi (pt/pp -rolled) (for exam, in club) iscriversi (for, in a).

~ment n iscrizione f

ensue /ɪn'sjuː/ vi seguire; the ~ing discussion la discussione che ne è seguita

ensure /ɪn'ʃʊə(r)/ vt assicurare; ~ that (person): assicurarsi che; (measure:) garantire che

entail /ɪn'teɪl/ vt comportare; what does it ~? in che cosa consiste?

entangle /ɪn'tæŋgl/ vt get ~d in rimanere impigliato in; fig rimanere coinvolto in

enter /'entə(r)/ vt entrare in; iscrivere (horse, runner in race); cominciare (university); partecipare a (competition); (Comput) immettere (data); (write down) scrivere ● vi entrare; (Theat) entrare in scena; (register as competitor) iscriversi; (take part) partecipare (in a)

enterpris|e /'entəpraɪz/ n impresa f; (quality) iniziativa f. ~ing adj intraprendente

entertain /entə'teɪn/ vt intrattenere; (invite) ricevere; nutrire (ideas, hopes); prendere in considerazione (possibility) ● vi intrattenersi; (have guests) ricevere. ~er n artista mf. ~ing adj (person) di gradevole compagnia; (evening, film, play) divertente. ~ment n (amusement) intrattenimento m

enthral /ɪn'θrɔːl/ vt (pt/pp enthralled) be ~led essere affascinato (by da)

enthusias|m /ɪn'θjuːzɪæzm/ n entusiasmo m. ~t n entusiasta mf. ~tic adj entusiastico

entice /ɪn'taɪs/ vt attirare. ~ment n (incentive) incentivo m

entire /ɪn'taɪə(r)/ adj intero. ~ly adv del tutto; I'm not ~ly satisfied non sono completamente soddisfatto. ~ty n /ɪn'taɪərətɪ/ in its ~ty nell'insieme

entitlement /ɪn'taɪtlmənt/ n diritto m

entity /'entətɪ/ n entità f

entrance¹ /'entrəns/ n entrata f; (*Theat*) entrata f in scena; (*right to enter*) ammissione f; '~ 'no ~' 'ingresso vietato'. ~ **examination** n esame m di ammissione. ~ **fee** n how much is the ~ **fee?** quanto costa il biglietto di ingresso?

entrance² /m'trɑːns/ vt estasiare

entrant /'entrənt/ n concorrente mf

entreat /m'triːt/ vt supplicare

entrenched /m'trentʃt/ adj (ideas, views) radicato

entrust /m'trʌst/ vt ~ sb with sth, ~ **sth to sb** affidare qcsa a qcno

entry /'entri/ n entrata f; (*way in*) entrata f; (*in directory etc*) voce f; (*in appointment diary*) appuntamento m; 'no ~ 'ingresso vietato'; (*Auto*) accesso vietato. ~ **form** n modulo m di ammissione. ~ **visa** n visto m di ingresso

enumerate /r'njuːməreɪt/ vt enumerare

envelop /m'veləp/ vt (pt/pp enveloped) avviluppare

envelope /'envələʊp/ n busta f

enviable /'enviəbl/ adj invidiabile

envious /'enviəs/ adj invidioso. ~**ly** adv con invidia

environment /m'vaɪrənmənt/ n ambiente m

environmental /mvaɪrən'mentl/ adj ambientale. ~**ist** n ambientalista mf. ~**ly** adv ~**ly friendly** che rispetta l'ambiente

envisage /m'vɪzɪdʒ/ vt prevedere

envoy /'envɔɪ/ n inviato, -a m

envy /'envi/ n invidia f • vt (pt/pp -ied) ~ **sb sth** invidiare qcno per qcsa

enzyme /'enzaɪm/ n enzima m

epic /'epɪk/ adj epico • n epopea f

epidemic /epr'demɪk/ n epidemia f

epilep|sy /'epɪlepsi/ n epilessia f. ~**tic** adj n epilettico, -a mf

epilogue /'epɪlɒg/ n epilogo m

episode /'epɪsəʊd/ n episodio m

epitaph /'epɪtɑːf/ n epitaffio m

epitom|e /r'pɪtəmi/ n epitome f. ~**ize** vt essere il classico esempio di

epoch /'iːpɒk/ n epoca f

equal /'iːkwl/ adj (parts, amounts) uguale; of ~ **height** della stessa altezza; **be ~ to the task** essere all'altezza del compito • n pari m inv • vt (pt/pp **equalled**) (*be same in quantity as*) essere pari a; (*rival*) uguagliare; **5 plus 5 ~s 10** 5 più 5 [è] uguale a 10. ~**ity** n uguaglianza f

equalize /'iːkwəlaɪz/ vi (*Sport*) pareggiare. ~**r** n (*Sport*) pareggio m

equally /'iːkwəlɪ/ adv (divide) in parti uguali; ~, **intelligent** della stessa intelligenza; ~,... allo stesso tempo...

equator /r'kweɪtə(r)/ n equatore m

equilibrium /iːkwr'lɪbrɪəm/ n equilibrio m

equinox /'iːkwɪnɒks/ n equinozio m

equip /r'kwɪp/ vt (pt/pp **equipped**) equipaggiare; attrezzare (kitchen, office). ~**ment** n attrezzatura f

equivalent /r'kwɪvələnt/ adj equivalente; **be ~ to** equivalere a • n equivalente m

equivocal /r'kwɪvəkl/ adj equivoco

era /'ɪərə/ n età f; (*geological*) era f

eradicate /r'rædɪkeɪt/ vt eradicare

erase /r'reɪz/ vt cancellare. ~**r** n gomma f [da cancellare]; (*for blackboard*) cancellino m

erect /r'rekt/ adj eretto • vt erigere. ~**ion** n erezione f

ero|de /r'rəʊd/ vt (water:) erodere; (acid:) corrodere. ~**sion** n erosione f; (*by acid*) corrosione f

erotic /r'rɒtɪk/ adj erotico

err /ɜː(r)/ vi errare; (sin) peccare

errand /'erənd/ n commissione f

erratic /r'rætɪk/ adj irregolare; (person, moods) imprevedibile; (exchange rate) incostante

erroneous /ɪˈrəʊnɪəs/ adj erroneo

error /ˈerə(r)/ n errore m; in ~ per errore

erudit|e /ˈeruːdaɪt/ adj erudito. ~ion n erudizione f

erupt /ɪˈrʌpt/ vi eruttare; (spots:) spuntare; (fig: in anger) dare in escandescenze. ~ion n eruzione f; fig scoppio m

escalat|e /ˈeskəleɪt/ vi intensificarsi ● vt intensificare. ~ion n escalation f inv. ~or n scala f mobile

escapade /eskəpeɪd/ n scappatella f

escape /ɪˈskeɪp/ n fuga f; (from prison) evasione f; have a narrow ~ cavarsela per un pelo ● vi (prisoner:) evadere (from da); sfuggire (from sb alla sorveglianza di qcno); (animal:) scappare; (gas:) fuoriuscire ● vt ~ notice passare inosservato; the name ~s me mi sfugge il nome

escapism /ɪˈskeɪpɪzm/ n evasione f [dalla realtà]

escort¹ /ˈeskɔːt/ n accompagnatore, -trice mf; (Mil etc) scorta f

escort² /ɪˈskɔːt/ vt accompagnare; (Mil etc) scortare

Eskimo /ˈeskɪməʊ/ n esquimese mf

especial /ɪˈspeʃl/ adj speciale. ~ly adv specialmente; (kind) particolarmente

espionage /ˈespɪənɑːʒ/ n spionaggio m

essay /ˈeseɪ/ n saggio m; (Sch) tema f

essence /ˈesns/ n essenza f; in ~ in sostanza

essential /ɪˈsenʃl/ adj essenziale ● npl the ~s l'essenziale m. ~ly adv essenzialmente

establish /ɪˈstæblɪʃ/ vt stabilire (contact, lead); fondare (firm); (prove) accertare; ~ oneself as affermarsi come. ~ment n (firm) azienda f; the E~ment l'ordine m costituito

estate /ɪˈsteɪt/ n tenuta f; (possessions) patrimonio m; (housing) quar-

tiere m residenziale. ~ agent n agente m immobiliare. ~ car n giardiniera f

esteem /ɪˈstiːm/ n stima f ● vt stimare; (consider) giudicare

estimate¹ /ˈestɪmət/ n valutazione f; (Comm) preventivo m; at a rough ~ a occhio e croce

estimat|e² /ˈestɪmeɪt/ vt stimare. ~ion n (esteem) stima f; in my ~ion (judgement) a mio giudizio

estuary /ˈestjʊərɪ/ n estuario m

etc /etˈsetərə/ abbr (et cetera) ecc

etching /ˈetʃɪŋ/ n acquaforte f

eternal /ɪˈtɜːnl/ adj eterno

eternity /ɪˈtɜːnətɪ/ n eternità f

ethic /ˈeθɪk/ n etica f. ~al adj etico. ~s n etica f

ethnic /ˈeθnɪk/ adj etnico

etiquette /ˈetɪket/ n etichetta f

EU n abbr (European Union) UE f

euphemis|m /ˈjuːfəmɪzm/ n eufemismo m. ~tic adj eufemistico

euphoria /juːˈfɔːrɪə/ n euforia f

euro /ˈjʊərəʊ/ n euro m inv

Euro- /ˈjʊərəʊ-/ pref ~cheque n eurochèque m inv. ~dollar n eurodollaro m

Europe /ˈjʊərəp/ n Europa f

European /jʊərəˈpɪən/ adj europeo; ~ Union Unione f Europea ● n europeo, -a mf

Euro-sceptic /ˈjʊərəʊˈskeptɪk/ adj euroscettico ● n euroscettico, -a mf

evacuat|e /ɪˈvækjʊeɪt/ vt evacuare (building, area). ~ion n evacuazione f

evade /ɪˈveɪd/ vt evadere (taxes); evitare (the enemy, authorities); ~ the issue evitare l'argomento

evaluat|e /ɪˈvæljʊeɪt/ vt valutare. ~ion /-ˈeɪʃn/ n valutazione f

evangelical /iːvænˈdʒelɪkl/ adj evangelico. ~list n evangelista m

evaporat|e /ɪˈvæpəreɪt/ vi evaporare; fig svanire. ~ion n evaporazione f

evasion /ɪˈveɪʒn/ n evasione f

evasive /ɪˈveɪsɪv/ adj evasivo

eve /iːv/ n liter vigilia f

even /ˈiːvn/ adj (level) piatto; (same, equal) uguale; (regular) regolare; (number) pari; get ~ with vendicarsi di; now we're ~ adesso siamo pari • adv anche, ancora; ~ if anche se; ~ so con tutto ciò; not ~ nemmeno; ~ bigger/hotter ancora più grande/caldo • vt ~ the score (Sport) pareggiare. ~ out vi livellarsi. ~ up vt livellare

evening /ˈiːvnɪŋ/ n sera f; (whole evening) serata f; this ~ stasera; in the ~ la sera. ~ class n corso m serale. ~ dress n abito m scuro; (woman's) abito m da sera

event /ɪˈvent/ n avvenimento m; (function) manifestazione f; (Sport) gara f; in the ~ of nell'eventualità di; in the ~ alla fine. ~ful adj movimentato

eventual /ɪˈventjʊəl/ adj the ~ winner was... alla fine il vincitore è stato.... ~ity n eventualità f. ~ly adv alla fine; ~ly! finalmente!

ever /ˈevə(r)/ adv mai; I haven't ~... non ho mai...; for ~ per sempre; hardly ~ quasi mai; ~ since da quando; (since that time) da allora; ~ so Ⓘ veramente

'evergreen n sempreverde m

ever'lasting adj eterno

every /ˈevrɪ/ adj ogni; ~ one ciascuno; ~ other day un giorno sì un giorno no

every: ~body pron tutti pl. ~day adj quotidiano, di ogni giorno. ~one pron tutti pl; ~thing pron tutto; ~where adv dappertutto; (wherever) dovunque

evict /ɪˈvɪkt/ vt sfrattare. ~ion n sfratto m

eviden|ce /ˈevɪdəns/ n evidenza f; (Jur) testimonianza f; give ~ce te-

stimoniare. ~t adj evidente. ~tly adv evidentemente

evil /ˈiːvl/ adj cattivo • n male m

evocative /ɪˈvɒkətɪv/ adj evocativo; be ~ of evocare

evoke /ɪˈvəʊk/ vt evocare

evolution /iːvəˈluːʃn/ n evoluzione f

evolve /ɪˈvɒlv/ vt evolvere • vi evolversi

ewe /juː/ n pecora f

exact /ɪgˈzækt/ adj esatto • vt esigere. ~ing adj esigente. ~itude n esattezza f. ~ly adv esattamente; not ~ly non proprio. ~ness n precisione f

exaggerat|e /ɪgˈzædʒəreɪt/ vt/i esagerare. ~ion n esagerazione f

exam /ɪgˈzæm/ n esame m

examination /ɪgzæmɪˈneɪʃn/ n esame m; (of patient) visita f

examine /ɪgˈzæmɪn/ vt esaminare; visitare (patient). ~r n (Sch) esaminatore, -trice mf

example /ɪgˈzɑːmpl/ n esempio m; for ~ per esempio; make an ~ of sb punire qcno per dare un esempio; be an ~ to sb dare il buon esempio a qcno

exasperat|e /ɪgˈzæspəreɪt/ vt esasperare. ~ion n esasperazione f

excavat|e /ˈekskəveɪt/ vt scavare; (Archaeol) fare gli scavi di. ~ion n scavo m

exceed /ɪkˈsiːd/ vt eccedere. ~ingly adv estremamente

excel /ɪkˈsel/ v (pt/pp excelled) • vi eccellere • vt ~ oneself superare se stessi

excellen|ce /ˈeksələns/ n eccellenza f. E~cy n (title) Eccellenza f. ~t adj eccellente

except /ɪkˈsept/ prep eccetto, tranne; ~ for eccetto, tranne; ~ that... eccetto che... • vt eccettuare. ~ing prep eccetto, tranne

exception /ɪk'sepʃn/ n eccezione f; take ~ to fare obiezioni a. ~al adj eccezionale. ~ally adv eccezionalmente

excerpt /'eksɜːpt/ n estratto m

excess /ɪk'ses/ n eccesso m; in ~ of oltre. ~ baggage n bagaglio m in eccedenza. ~ fare n supplemento m

excessive /ɪk'sesɪv/ adj eccessivo. ~ly adv eccessivamente

exchange /ɪks'tʃeɪndʒ/ n scambio m; (Teleph) centrale f; (Comm) cambio m; in ~ in cambio (for di) ● vt scambiare (for con); cambiare (money). ~ rate n tasso m di cambio

excise¹ /'eksaɪz/ n dazio m; ~ duty dazio m

excise² /ek'saɪz/ vt recidere

excitable /ɪk'saɪtəbl/ adj eccitabile

excit|e /ɪk'saɪt/ vt eccitare. ~ed adj eccitato; get ~ed eccitarsi. ~edly adv tutto eccitato. ~ement n eccitazione f. ~ing adj eccitante; (story, film) appassionante; (holiday) entusiasmante

exclaim /ɪk'skleɪm/ vt/i esclamare

exclamation /ekskləˈmeɪʃn/ n esclamazione f. ~ mark n, Am ~ point n punto m esclamativo

exclude /ɪk'skluːd/ vt escludere. ~ding prep escluso. ~sion n esclusione f

exclusive /ɪk'skluːsɪv/ adj (rights, club) esclusivo; (interview) in esclusiva; ~ of... ...escluso. ~ly adv esclusivamente

excruciating /ɪk'skruːʃieɪtɪŋ/ adj atroce (pain); (🄵: very bad) spaventoso

excursion /ɪk'skɜːʃn/ n escursione f

excusable /ɪk'skjuːzəbl/ adj perdonabile

excuse¹ /ɪk'skjuːs/ n scusa f

excuse² /ɪk'skjuːz/ vt scusare; ~ from esonerare da; ~ me! (to get attention) scusi!; (to get past) permesso!,

scusi!; (indignant) come ha detto?

ex-di'rectory adj be ~ non figurare sull'elenco telefonico

execute /'eksɪkjuːt/ vt eseguire; (put to death) giustiziare; attuare (plan)

execution /eksɪ'kjuːʃn/ n esecuzione f; (of plan) attuazione f. ~er n boia m

executive /ɪg'zekjʊtɪv/ adj esecutivo ● n dirigente mf; (Pol) esecutivo m

executor /ɪg'zekjʊtə(r)/ n (Jur) esecutore, -trice mf

exempt /ɪg'zempt/ adj esente ● vt esentare (from da). ~ion n esenzione f

exercise /'eksəsaɪz/ n esercizio m; (Mil) esercitazione f; physical ~s ginnastica f; take ~ fare del moto ● vt esercitare (muscles, horse); portare a spasso (dog); mettere in pratica (skills) ● vi esercitarsi. ~ book n quaderno m

exert /ɪg'zɜːt/ vt esercitare; ~ oneself sforzarsi. ~ion n sforzo m

exhale /eks'heɪl/ vt/i esalare

exhaust /ɪg'zɔːst/ n (Auto) scappamento m; (pipe) tubo m di scappamento; ~ fumes fumi mpl di scarico m ● vt esaurire. ~ed adj esausto. ~ing adj estenuante; (climate, person) sfibrante. ~ion n esaurimento m. ~ive adj fig esauriente

exhibit /ɪg'zɪbɪt/ n oggetto m esposto; (Jur) reperto m ● vt esporre; fig dimostrare

exhibition /eksɪ'bɪʃn/ n mostra f; (of strength, skill) dimostrazione f. ~ist n esibizionista mf

exhibitor /ɪg'zɪbɪtə(r)/ n espositore, -trice mf

exhort /ɪg'zɔːt/ vt esortare

exile /'eksaɪl/ n esilio m; (person) esule mf ● vt esiliare

exist /ɪg'zɪst/ vi esistere. ~ence n esistenza f; in ~ esistente; be in

~ence esistere. ~ing adj attuale

exit /'eksɪt/ n uscita f; (Theat) uscita f di scena ● vi (Theat) uscire di scena; (Comput) uscire

exorbitant /ɪgˈzɔːbɪtənt/ adj esorbitante

exotic /ɪgˈzɒtɪk/ adj esotico

expand /ɪkˈspænd/ vt espandere ● vi espandersi; (Comm) svilupparsi; (metal:) dilatarsi; ~ **on** (fig: explain better) approfondire

expanse /ɪkˈspæns/ n estensione f. ~**ion** n espansione f; (Comm) sviluppo m; (of metal) dilatazione f. ~**ive** adj espansivo

expatriate /eksˈpætrɪət/ n espatriato, -a mf

expect /ɪkˈspekt/ vt aspettare (letter, baby); (suppose) pensare; (demand) esigere; I ~ so penso di sì; be ~**ing** essere in stato interessante

expectan|cy /ɪkˈspektənsɪ/ n aspettativa f. ~**t** adj in attesa; ~**t mother** donna f incinta. ~**tly** adv con impazienza

expectation /ekspekˈteɪʃn/ n aspettativa f, speranza f

expedient /ɪkˈspiːdɪənt/ adj conveniente ● n espediente m

expedition /ekspɪˈdɪʃn/ n spedizione f. ~**ary** adj (Mil) di spedizione

expel /ɪkˈspel/ vt (pt/pp expelled) espellere

expend /ɪkˈspend/ vt consumare. ~**able** adj sacrificabile

expenditure /ɪkˈspendɪtʃə(r)/ n spesa f

expense /ɪkˈspens/ n spesa f; business ~**s** pl spese fpl; at my ~ a mie spese; at the ~ of fig a spese di

expensive /ɪkˈspensɪv/ adj caro, costoso. ~**ly** adv costosamente

experience /ɪkˈspɪərɪəns/ n esperienza f ● vt provare (sensation); avere (problem). ~**d** adj esperto

experiment /ɪkˈsperɪmənt/ n esperimento m ● vi sperimentare. ~**al**

adj sperimentale

expert /'ekspɜːt/ adj & n esperto, -a mf. ~**ly** adv abilmente

expertise /ekspɜːˈtiːz/ n competenza f

expire /ɪkˈspaɪə(r)/ vi scadere

expiry /ɪkˈspaɪərɪ/ n scadenza f. ~ **date** n data f di scadenza

explain /ɪkˈspleɪn/ vt spiegare

explana|tion /ekspləˈneɪʃn/ n spiegazione f. ~**tory** adj esplicativo

explicit /ɪkˈsplɪsɪt/ adj esplicito. ~**ly** adv esplicitamente

explode /ɪkˈspləʊd/ vi esplodere ● vt fare esplodere

exploit[1] /'eksplɔɪt/ n impresa f

exploit[2] /ɪkˈsplɔɪt/ vt sfruttare. ~**ation** n sfruttamento m

explora|tion /ekspləˈreɪʃn/ n esplorazione f. ~**tory** adj esplorativo

explore /ɪkˈsplɔː(r)/ vt esplorare; fig studiare (implications). ~**r** n esploratore, -trice mf

explos|ion /ɪkˈspləʊʒn/ n esplosione f. ~**ive** adj & n esplosivo m

export /'ekspɔːt/ n esportazione f ● vt /-ˈspɔːt/ esportare. ~**er** n esportatore, -trice mf

expose /ɪkˈspəʊz/ vt esporre; (reveal) svelare; smascherare (traitor etc). ~**ure** n esposizione f; (Med) esposizione f prolungata al freddo/caldo; (of crimes) smascheramento m; 24 ~**ures** (Phot) 24 pose

express /ɪkˈspres/ adj espresso ● adv (send) per espresso ● n (train) espresso m ● vt esprimere; ~ **oneself** esprimersi. ~**ion** n espressione f. ~**ive** adj espressivo. ~**ly** adv espressamente

expulsion /ɪkˈspʌlʃn/ n espulsione f

exquisite /ekˈskwɪzɪt/ adj squisito

extend /ɪkˈstend/ vt prolungare (visit, road); prorogare (visa, contract); ampliare (building, knowledge; (*stretch out*) allungare; tendere (hand) ●*vi* (garden, knowledge:) estendersi

extension /ɪkˈstenʃn/ *n* prolungamento *m*; (*of visa, contract*) proroga *f*; (*of treaty*) ampliamento *m*; (*part of building*) annesso *m*; (*length of cable*) prolunga *f*; (*Teleph*) interno *m*; ~ 226 interno 226

extensive /ɪkˈstensɪv/ *adj* ampio, vasto. ~**ly** *adv* ampiamente

extent /ɪkˈstent/ *n* (*scope*) portata *f*; **to a certain** ~ fino a un certo punto; **to such an** ~ **that...** fino a punto che...

exterior /ɪkˈstɪərɪə(r)/ *adj* & *n* esterno *m*

exterminat|e /ɪkˈstɜːmɪneɪt/ *vt* sterminare. ~**ion** *n* sterminio *m*

external /ɪkˈstɜːnl/ *adj* esterno; **for** ~ **use only** (*Med*) per uso esterno. ~**ly** *adv* esternamente

extinct /ɪkˈstɪŋkt/ *adj* estinto. ~**ion** *n* estinzione *f*

extinguish /ɪkˈstɪŋgwɪʃ/ *vt* estinguere. ~**er** *n* estintore *m*

extort /ɪkˈstɔːt/ *vt* estorcere. ~**ion** *n* estorsione *f*

extortionate /ɪkˈstɔːʃənət/ *adj* esorbitante

extra /ˈekstrə/ *adj* in più; (train) straordinario; **an** ~ **£10** 10 sterline extra, 10 sterline in più ●*adv* in più; (*especially*) più; **pay** ~ pagare in più, pagare extra ●*n* (*Theat*) comparsa *f*; ~**s** *pl* extra *mpl*

extract[1] /ˈekstrækt/ *n* estratto *m*

extract[2] /ɪkˈstrækt/ *vt* estrarre (tooth, oil); strappare (secret); ricavare (truth). ~**or** [**fan**] *n* aspiratore *m*

extradit|e /ˈekstrədaɪt/ *vt* (*Jur*) estradare. ~**ion** *n* estradizione *f*

extraordinar|y /ɪkˈstrɔːdɪnərɪ/ *adj* straordinario. ~**ily** *adv* straordinariamente

extravagan|ce /ɪkˈstrævəgəns/ *n* (*with money*) prodigalità *f*; (*of behaviour*) stravaganza *f*. ~**t** *adj* spendaccione; (*bizarre*) stravagante; (claim) esagerato

extrem|e /ɪkˈstriːm/ *adj* estremo ●*n* estremo *m*; **in the** ~ al massimo. ~**ely** *adv* estremamente. ~**ist** *n* estremista *m*

extricate /ˈekstrɪkeɪt/ *vt* districare

extrovert /ˈekstrəvɜːt/ *n* estroverso, -a *mf*

exuberant /ɪgˈzjuːbərənt/ *adj* esuberante

exude /ɪgˈzjuːd/ *vt also fig* trasudare

exult /ɪgˈzʌlt/ *vi* esultare

eye /aɪ/ *n* occhio *m*; (*of needle*) cruna *f*; **keep an** ~ **on** tener d'occhio; **see** ~ **to** ~ aver le stesse idee ●*vt* (*pt/pp* eyed, *pres p* ey[e]ing) guardare

eye: ~**ball** *n* bulbo *m* oculare. ~**brow** *n* sopracciglio *m* (*pl* sopracciglia *f*). ~**lash** *n* ciglio *m* (*pl* ciglia *f*). ~**lid** *n* palpebra *f*. ~**opener** *n* rivelazione *f*. ~**shadow** *n* ombretto *m*. ~**sight** *n* vista *f*. ~**sore** *n* Ⓘ pugno *m* nell'occhio. ~**witness** *n* testimone *mf* oculare

Ff

fable /ˈfeɪbl/ *n* favola *f*.

fabric /ˈfæbrɪk/ *n* also *fig* tessuto *m*

fabulous /ˈfæbjʊləs/ *adj* Ⓘ favoloso

façade /fəˈsɑːd/ *n* (of building, person) facciata *f*

face /feɪs/ *n* faccia *f*, viso *m*; (grimace) smorfia *f*; (surface) faccia *f*; (of clock) quadrante *m*; **pull** ~**s** far boccacce; **in the** ~ **of** di fronte a; **on the** ~ **of it** in apparenza ●*vt* essere di fronta a; (*confront*) affrontare; ~

north (house:) dare a nord; ~ the fact that arrendersi al fatto che. □ ~ **up to** vt accettare (facts); affrontare (person)

face: ~**-flannel** n ≈ guanto m di spugna. ~**less** adj anonimo. ~**-lift** n plastica f facciale

facetious /fə'siːʃəs/ adj spiritoso. ~ remarks spiritosaggini mpl

facial /'feɪʃl/ adj facciale ● n trattamento m di bellezza al viso

facile /'fæsaɪl/ adj semplicistico

facilitate /fə'sɪlɪteɪt/ vt rendere possibile; (make easier) facilitare

facility /fə'sɪlətɪ/ n facilità f; ~**ies** pl (of area, in hotel etc) attrezzature fpl

fact /fækt/ n fatto m; in ~ infatti

faction /'fækʃn/ n fazione f

factor /'fæktə(r)/ n fattore m

factory /'fæktərɪ/ n fabbrica f

factual /'fæktʃuəl/ adj be ~ attenersi ai fatti. ~**ly** adv (inaccurate) dal punto di vista dei fatti

faculty /'fækəltɪ/ n facoltà f inv

fad /fæd/ n capriccio m

fade /feɪd/ vi sbiadire; (sound, light:) affievolirsi; (flower:) appassire. □ ~ **in** vt cominciare in dissolvenza (picture). □ ~ **out** vt finire in dissolvenza (picture)

fag /fæg/ n (chore) fatica f; (fam: cigarette) sigaretta f; (Am 🖾 : homosexual) frocio m. ~ **end** n 🖾 cicca f

Fahrenheit /'færənhaɪt/ adj Fahrenheit

fail /feɪl/ n without ~ senz'altro ● vi (attempt:) fallire; (eyesight, memory:) indebolirsi; (engine, machine:) guastarsi; (marriage:) andare a rotoli; (in exam) essere respinto; ~ **to do** sth non fare qcsa; I tried but I ~**ed** ho provato ma non ci sono riuscito ● vt non superare (exam); bocciare (candidate); (disappoint) deludere; words ~ me mi mancano le parole

failing /'feɪlɪŋ/ n difetto m ● prep ~ that altrimenti

failure /'feɪljə(r)/ n fallimento m; (mechanical) guasto m; (person) incapace m f

faint /feɪnt/ adj leggero; (memory) vago; feel ~ sentirsi mancare ● n svenimento m ● vi svenire

faint: ~**-hearted** adj timido. ~**ly** adv (slightly) leggermente

fair¹ /feə(r)/ n fiera f

fair² adj (hair, person) biondo; (skin) chiaro; (weather) bello; (just) giusto; (quite good) discreto; (Sch) abbastanza bene; a ~ **amount** abbastanza ● adv play ~ fare un gioco pulito. ~**ly** adv con giustizia; (rather) discretamente, abbastanza. ~**ness** n giustizia f. ~ **play** n fair play m inv. ~ **trade** n commercio m equo e solidale

fairy /'feərɪ/ n fata f; ~ **story**, ~**-tale** n fiaba f

faith /feɪθ/ n fede f; (trust) fiducia f; in good/bad ~ in buona/mala fede

faithful /'feɪθfl/ adj fedele. ~**ly** adv fedelmente; yours ~**ly** distinti saluti. ~**ness** n fedeltà f

fake /feɪk/ adj falso ● n falsificazione f; (person) impostore m ● vt falsificare; (pretend) fingere

falcon /'fɔːlkən/ n falcone m

fall /fɔːl/ n caduta f; (in prices) ribasso m; (Am: autumn) autunno m; have a ~ fare una caduta ● vi (pt fell, pp fallen) cadere; (night:) scendere; ~ **in love** innamorarsi. □ ~ **about** vi (with laughter) morire dal ridere. ~ **back on** vt ritornare su. □ ~ **for** vt 🖾 innamorarsi di (person); cascarci (sth, trick). □ ~ **down** vi cadere; (building:) crollare. □ ~ **in** vi caderci dentro; (collapse) crollare; (Mil) mettersi in riga; ~ **in with** concordare con (plan). □ ~ **off** vi cadere; (diminish) diminuire. □ ~ **out** vi (quarrel) litigare; his hair is ~**ing out** perde i capelli. □ ~ **over** vi cadere. □ ~ **through** vi (plan:) andare a monte

fallacy /'fæləsɪ/ n errore m

fallible /ˈfæləbl/ adj fallibile

'fall-out n pioggia f radioattiva

false /fɔːls/ adj falso; ~ **bottom** doppio fondo m; ~ **start** (Sport) falsa partenza f. ~**hood** n menzogna f. ~**ness** n falsità f

false 'teeth npl dentiera f

falsify /ˈfɔːlsɪfaɪ/ vt (pt/pp -ied) falsificare

falter /ˈfɔːltə(r)/ vi vacillare; (making speech) esitare

fame /feɪm/ n fama f

familiar /fəˈmɪljə(r)/ adj familiare; be ~ with (know) conoscere. ~**ity** n familiarità f. ~**ize** vt familiarizzare; ~**ize** oneself with familiarizzarsi con

family /ˈfæmɪlɪ/ n famiglia f

family: ~ **'planning** n pianificazione f familiare. ~ **tree** n albero m genealogico

famine /ˈfæmɪn/ n carestia f

famished /ˈfæmɪʃt/ adj be ~ ▣ avere una fame da lupo

famous /ˈfeɪməs/ adj famoso

fan[1] /fæn/ n ventilatore m; (handheld) ventaglio m ●vt (pt/pp fanned) far vento a; ~ oneself sventagliarsi; fig ~ the flames soffiare sul fuoco. ▫ ~ **out** vi spiegarsi a ventaglio

fan[2] n (admirer) ammiratore, -trice mf; (Sport) tifoso m; (of Verdi etc) appassionato, -a mf

fanatic /fəˈnætɪk/ n fanatico, -a mf. ~**al** adj fanatico. ~**ism** n fanatismo m

'fan belt n cinghia f per ventilatore

fanciful /ˈfænsɪfl/ adj fantasioso

fancy /ˈfænsɪ/ n fantasia f; I've taken a real ~ to him mi è molto simpatico; as the ~ takes you come ti pare ●adj [a] fantasia ●vt (pt/pp -ied) (believe) credere; (▣: want) aver voglia di; he fancies you ▣ gli piaci; ~ that! ma guarda un po'! ~ **'dress** n costume m (per maschera)

fanfare /ˈfænfeə(r)/ n fanfara f

fang /fæŋ/ n zanna f; (of snake) dente m

fantas|ize /ˈfæntəsaɪz/ vi fantasticare. ~**tic** adj fantastico. ~**y** n fantasia f

far /fɑː(r)/ adv lontano; (much) molto; by ~ di gran lunga; ~ **away** lontano; as ~ as the church fino alla chiesa; how ~ is it from here? quanto dista da qui?; as ~ as I know per quanto io sappia f (end, side) altro; the F~ East l'Estremo Oriente m

farc|e /fɑːs/ n farsa f. ~**ical** adj ridicolo

fare /feə(r)/ n tariffa f; (food) vitto m. ~-**dodger** n passeggero, -a mf senza biglietto

farewell /feəˈwel/ int liter addio! ●n addio m

far-ˈfetched adj improbabile

farm /fɑːm/ n fattoria f ●vi fare l'agricoltore ●vt coltivare (land). ~**er** n agricoltore m

farm: ~**house** n casa f colonica. ~**ing** n agricoltura f. ~**yard** n aia f

far: ~-**ˈreaching** adj di larga portata. ~-**ˈsighted** adj fig prudente; (Am: long-sighted) presbite

farther /ˈfɑːðə(r)/ adv più lontano ●adj at the ~ end all'altra estremità di

fascinat|e /ˈfæsɪneɪt/ vt affascinare. ~**ing** adj affascinante. ~**ion** n fascino m

fascis|m /ˈfæʃɪzm/ n fascismo m. ~**t** n fascista mf ●adj fascista

fashion /ˈfæʃn/ n moda f; (manner) maniera f ●vt modellare. ~**able** adj di moda; be ~**able** essere alla moda. ~**ably** adv alla moda

fast[1] /fɑːst/ adj veloce; (colour) indelebile; be ~ (clock) andare avanti ●adv velocemente; (firmly) saldamente; ~**er!** più in fretta!; be ~ asleep dormire profondamente

fast² n digiuno m ● vi digiunare

fasten /'fɑːsn/ vt allacciare; chiudere (window); (stop flapping) mettere un fermo a ● vi allacciarsi. ∼er n, ∼ing n chiusura f

fat /fæt/ adj (fatter, fattest) (person, cheque) grasso ● n grasso m

fatal /'feɪtl/ adj mortale; (error) fatale. ∼ism n fatalismo m. ∼ist n fatalista mf. ∼ity n morte f. ∼ly adv mortalmente

fate /feɪt/ n destino m. ∼ful adj fatidico

father /'fɑːðə(r)/ n padre m; F∼ Christmas Babbo m Natale ● vt generare (child)

father: ∼hood n paternità f. ∼-in-law n (pl ∼s-in-law) suocero m. ∼ly adj paterno

fathom /'fæðəm/ n (Naut) braccio m ● vt ∼ [out] comprendere

fatigue /fə'tiːg/ n fatica f

fatten /'fætn/ vt ingrassare (animal). ∼ing adj cream is ∼ing la panna fa ingrassare

fatty /'fæti/ adj grasso ● n [] ciccione, -a mf

fatuous /'fætjʊəs/ adj fatuo

faucet /'fɔːsɪt/ n Am rubinetto m

fault /fɔːlt/ n difetto m; (Geol) faglia f; (Tennis) fallo m; be at ∼ avere torto; find ∼ with trovare da ridire su; it's your ∼ è colpa tua ● vt criticare. ∼less adj impeccabile

faulty /'fɔːlti/ adj difettoso

favour /'feɪvə(r)/ n favore m; be in ∼ of sth essere a favore di qcsa; do sb a ∼ fare un piacere a qcno ● vt (prefer) preferire. ∼able adj favorevole

favourit|e /'feɪv(ə)rɪt/ adj preferito ● n preferito, -a mf; (Sport) favorito, -a mf. ∼ism n favoritismo m

fawn /fɔːn/ adj fulvo ● n (animal) cerbiatto m

fax /fæks/ n (document, machine) fax m inv; by ∼ per fax ● vt faxare. ∼ ma-

chine n fax m inv. ∼-modem n modem-fax m inv, fax-modem m inv

fear /fɪə(r)/ n paura f; no ∼! [] vai tranquillo! ● vt temere ● vi ∼ for sth temere per qcsa

fear|ful /'fɪəfl/ adj pauroso; (awful) terribile. ∼less adj impavido. ∼some adj spaventoso

feas|ibility /fiːzɪ'bɪlɪtɪ/ n praticabilità f. ∼ible adj fattibile; (possible) probabile

feast /fiːst/ n festa f; (banquet) banchetto m ● vi banchettare; ∼ on godersi

feat /fiːt/ n impresa f

feather /'feðə(r)/ n piuma f

feature /'fiːtʃə(r)/ n (quality) caratteristica f; (Journ) articolo m; ∼s (pl: of face) lineamenti mpl ● vt (film): (avere come protagonista a ● vi (on a list etc) comparire. ∼ film n lungometraggio m

February /'febrʊərɪ/ n febbraio m

fed /fed/ ▷FEED ● adj be ∼ up [] essere stufo (with di)

federal /'fed(ə)rəl/ adj federale

federation /fedə'reɪʃn/ n federazione f

fee /fiː/ n tariffa f; (lawyer's, doctor's) onorario m; (for membership, school) quota f

feeble /'fiːbl/ adj debole; (excuse) fiacco

feed /fiːd/ n mangiare m; (for baby) pappa f ● v (pt/pp fed) ● vt dar da mangiare a (animal); (support) nutrire; ∼ sth into sth inserire qcsa in qcsa ● vi mangiare

'feedback n controreazione f; (of information) reazione f, feedback m

feel /fiːl/ v (pt/pp felt) ● vt sentire; (experience) provare; (think) pensare; (touch: searching) tastare; (touch: for texture) toccare ● vi ∼ soft/hard essere duro/morbido al tatto; ∼ hungry aver fame/caldo; ∼ ill sentirsi male; I don't ∼ like it non ne ho

voglia; **how do you ~ about it?**
(*opinion*) che te ne pare?; **it doesn't
~ right** non mi sembra giusto. **~er**
n (*of animal*) antenna f; **put out ~ers**
fig tastare il terreno. **~ing** n sentimento m; (*awareness*) sensazione f

feet /fiːt/ ▷ **FOOT**

feign /feɪn/ vt simulare

fell[1] /fel/ vt (*knock down*) abbattere

fell[2] ▷ **FALL**

fellow /ˈfeləʊ/ n (*of society*) socio m;
(🔲: *man*) tipo m

fellow 'countryman n compatriota m

felony /ˈfeləni/ n delitto m

felt[1] /felt/ ▷ **FEEL**

felt[2] n feltro m. **~[-tipped] 'pen**
/[-tɪpt]/ n pennarello m

female /ˈfiːmeɪl/ adj femminile; **the
~ antelope** l'antilope femmina ● n
femmina f

femin|ine /ˈfemɪnɪn/ adj femminile
● n (*Gram*) femminile m. **~inity** n
femminilità f. **~ist** adj & n femminista m f

fenc|e /fens/ n recinto m; (🔲: *person*)
ricettatore m f. **□ ~ in** (*Sport*) tirar di
scherma. **□ ~ in** chiudere in un
recinto. **~er** n schermidore m. **~ing**
n steccato m; (*Sport*) scherma f

fend /fend/ vi **~ for oneself** badare
a se stesso. **~ off** vt parare; difen-
dersi da (*criticisms*)

fender /ˈfendə(r)/ n parafuoco m inv;
(*Am: on car*) parafango m

fennel /ˈfenl/ n finocchio m

ferment[1] /ˈfɜːment/ n fermento m

ferment[2] /fəˈment/ vi fermentare
● vt far fermentare. **~ation** n fer-
mentazione f

fern /fɜːn/ n felce f

fero|cious /fəˈrəʊʃəs/ adj feroce.
~ity n ferocia f

ferret /ˈferɪt/ n furetto m ● **ferret
out** vt scovare

ferry /ˈferɪ/ n traghetto m ● vt
traghettare

fertil|e /ˈfɜːtaɪl/ adj fertile. **~ity** n
fertilità f

fertilize /ˈfɜːtɪlaɪz/ vt fertilizzare
(land, ovum). **~r** n fertilizzante m

fervent /ˈfɜːvənt/ adj fervente

fervour /ˈfɜːvə(r)/ n fervore m

fester /ˈfestə(r)/ vi suppurare

festival /ˈfestɪvl/ n (*Mus, Theat*) festival m; (*Relig*) festa f

festive /ˈfestɪv/ adj festivo; **~e
season** periodo m delle feste natali-
zie. **~ities** vt andare/venire a prendere; (*be sold for*) raggiungere [il
prezzo di]

fetch /fetʃ/ vt andare/venire a prendere; (*be sold for*) raggiungere [il
prezzo di]

fetching /ˈfetʃɪŋ/ adj attraente

fête /feɪt/ n festa f ● vt festeggiare

fetish /ˈfetɪʃ/ n feticcio m

fetter /ˈfetə(r)/ vt incatenare

feud /fjuːd/ n faida f

feudal /ˈfjuːdl/ adj feudale

fever /ˈfiːvə(r)/ n febbre f. **~ish** adj
febbricitante; *fig* febbrile

few /fjuː/ adj pochi; **every ~ days**
ogni due o tre giorni; **a ~ people**
alcuni; **~er reservations** meno pre-
notazioni; **the ~est number** il numero più basso ● pron pochi; **~ of
us** pochi di noi; **a ~** alcuni; **quite a
~** parecchi; **~er than last year**
meno dell'anno scorso

fiancé /frˈɒnseɪ/ n fidanzato m. **~e** n
fidanzata f

fiasco /frˈæskəʊ/ n fiasco m

fib /fɪb/ n storia f; **tell a ~** raccontare una storia

fibre /ˈfaɪbə(r)/ n fibra f. **~glass** n
fibra f di vetro

fickle /ˈfɪkl/ adj incostante

fiction /ˈfɪkʃn/ n [works of] ~ nar-
rativa f; (*fabrication*) finzione f. **~al** adj
immaginario

fictitious /fɪkˈtɪʃəs/ adj fittizio

fiddle /ˈfɪdl/ n 🎵 violino m; (cheating) imbroglio m • vi gingillarsi (with con) • vt 🎵 truccare (accounts)

fidget /ˈfɪdʒɪt/ vi agitarsi. ~y adj agitato

field /fiːld/ n campo m

field: ~-glasses npl binocolo msg. F~ 'Marshal n feldmaresciallo m. ~work n ricerche fpl sul terreno

fiend /fiːnd/ n demonio m

fierce /fɪəs/ adj feroce. ~ness n ferocia f

fiery /ˈfaɪərɪ/ adj (-ier, -iest) focoso

fifteen /fɪfˈtiːn/ adj & n quindici m. ~th adj quindicesimo

fifth /fɪfθ/ adj quinto

fiftieth /ˈfɪftɪɪθ/ adj cinquantesimo

fifty /ˈfɪftɪ/ adj cinquanta

fig /fɪɡ/ n fico m

fight /faɪt/ n lotta f; (brawl) zuffa f; (argument) litigio m; (boxing) incontro m • v (pt/pp fought) • vt also fig combattere • vi combattere; (brawl) azzuffarsi; (argue) litigare. ~er n combattente mf; (Aeron) caccia m inv. ~ing n combattimento m

figment /ˈfɪɡmənt/ n it's a ~ of your imagination questo è tutta una tua invenzione

figurative /ˈfɪɡjʊrətɪv/ adj (sense) figurato; (art) figurativo

figure /ˈfɪɡə(r)/ n (digit) cifra f; (carving, sculpture, illustration, form) figura f; (body shape) linea f; ~ of speech modo m di dire • vi (appear) figurare • vt (Am: think) pensare. □ ~ out vt dedurre; capire (person)

figurehead n figura f simbolica

file¹ /faɪl/ n scheda f; (set of documents) incartamento m; (folder) cartellina f; (Comput) file m inv • vt archiviare (documents)

file² n (line) fila f; in single ~ in fila

file³ n (Techn) lima f • vt limare

filing cabinet /ˈfaɪlɪŋkæbɪnət/ n schedario m, classificatore m

fill /fɪl/ n eat one's ~ mangiare a sazietà • vt riempire; otturare (tooth) • vi riempirsi. □ ~ in vt compilare (form). □ ~ out vt compilare (form). □ ~ up vi (room, tank:) riempirsi; (Auto) far il pieno • vt riempire

fillet /ˈfɪlɪt/ n filetto m • vt (pt/pp filleted) disossare

filling /ˈfɪlɪŋ/ n (Culin) ripieno m; (of tooth) piombatura f. ~ station n stazione f di rifornimento

film /fɪlm/ n (Cinema) film m inv; (Phot) pellicola f; [cling] ~ pellicola f per alimenti • vt/i filmare. ~ star n star f inv, divo, -a mf

filter /ˈfɪltə(r)/ n filtro m • vt filtrare. □ ~ through vi trapelare. ~-tip n filtro m; (cigarette) sigaretta f col filtro

filth /fɪlθ/ n sudiciume m. ~y adj (-ier, -iest) sudicio; (word) sconcio

fin /fɪn/ n pinna f

final /ˈfaɪnl/ adj finale; (conclusive) decisivo • n (Sport) finale f; ~s pl (Univ) esami mpl finali

finale /fɪˈnɑːlɪ/ n finale m

final|ist /ˈfaɪnəlɪst/ n finalista mf. ~ity n finalità f

final|ize /ˈfaɪnəlaɪz/ vt mettere a punto (text); definire (agreement). ~ly adv (at last) finalmente; (at the end) alla fine; (to conclude) per finire

finance /ˈfaɪnæns/ n finanza f • vt finanziare

financial /faɪˈnænʃl/ adj finanziario

find /faɪnd/ n scoperta f • vt (pt/pp found) trovare; (establish) scoprire; ~ sb guilty (Jur) dichiarare qcno colpevole. □ ~ out vt scoprire • vi (enquire) informarsi

findings /ˈfaɪndɪŋz/ npl conclusioni fpl

fine¹ /faɪn/ n (penalty) multa f • vt multare

fine² /faɪn/ adj bello; (slender) fine; ~ (in health) sta bene. ~ arts npl belle arti fpl. • adv bene; that's cutting it

~ non ci lascia molto tempo ● int
[va] bene. **~ly** adv (cut) finemente

finger /'fɪŋgə(r)/ n dito m (pl dita f)
● vt tastare

finger: **~nail** n unghia f. **~print** n
impronta f digitale. **~tip** n punta f
del dito; **have sth at one's ~tips**
sapere qcsa a menadito; (close at
hand) avere qcsa a portata di mano

finish /'fɪnɪʃ/ n fine f; (finishing line)
traguardo m; (of product) finitura f;
have a good ~ (runner:) avere un
buon finale ● vt finire; (complete; tirare (gun); (🔲: dismiss) buttar fuori
● vi sparare (at a)

finite /'faɪnaɪt/ adj limitato

Finland /'fɪnlənd/ n Finlandia f

Finn /fɪn/ n finlandese mf. **~ish** adj
finlandese ● n (language) finnico m

fiord /fjɔːd/ n fiordo m

fir /fɜː(r)/ n abete m

fire /'faɪə(r)/ n fuoco m; (forest, house)
incendio m; **be on ~** bruciare; **catch
~** prendere fuoco; **set ~ to** dar
fuoco a; **under ~** sotto il fuoco ● vt
cuocere (pottery); sparare (shot); tirare (gun); (🔲: dismiss) buttar fuori
● vi sparare (at a)

fire: **~ alarm** n allarme m antincen-
dio. **~arm** n arma f da fuoco. **~
brigade** n vigili mpl del fuoco.
~-engine n autopompa f.
~-escape n uscita f di sicurezza. **~
extinguisher** n estintore m. **~man**
n pompiere m, vigile m del fuoco.
~place n caminetto m. **~side** n by
or at the **~side** accanto al fuoco.
~wood n legna f (da ardere). **~work**
n fuoco m d'artificio

firm[1] /fɜːm/ n ditta f, azienda f

firm[2] adj fermo; (soil) compatto;
(stable, properly fixed) solido; (resolute)
risoluto. **~ly** adv (hold) stretto; (say)
con fermezza

first /fɜːst/ adj & n primo, -a mf; at ~
all'inizio; **who's ~?** chi è il primo?;
from the ~ [fin] dall'inizio ● adv (arrive, leave) per primo; (beforehand)

prima; (in listing) prima di tutto, in-
nanzitutto

first: **~ aid** n pronto soccorso m.
~-aid kit n cassetta f di pronto
soccorso. **~-class** adj di prim'ordine;
(Rail:) di prima classe ● adv (travel) in
prima classe. **~ floor** n primo piano
m; (Am: ground floor) pianterreno m.
~ly adv in primo luogo. **~ name** n
nome m di battesimo. **~-rate** adj
ottimo

fish /fɪʃ/ n pesce m ● vt/i pescare.
▢ **~ out** vt tirar fuori

fish: **~erman** n pescatore m. **~
'finger** n bastoncino m di pesce

fishing /'fɪʃɪŋ/ n pesca f. **~ boat** n
peschereccio m. **~-rod** n canna f
da pesca

fish: **~monger** /-mʌŋgə(r)/ n pesci-
vendolo m. **~y** adj (🔲: suspicious) sospetto

fission /'fɪʃn/ n (Phys) fissione f

fist /fɪst/ n pugno m

fit[1] /fɪt/ n (attack) attacco m; (of rage)
accesso m; (of generosity) slancio m

fit[2] adj (fitter, fittest) (suitable)
adatto; (healthy) in buona salute;
(Sport) in forma; **be ~ to do sth** essere in grado di fare qcsa; **~ to eat**
buono da mangiare; **keep ~** tenersi
in forma

fit[3] n (of clothes) taglio m; **it's a good
~** (coat) etc: ti/le sta bene ● v (pt/pp
fitted) ● vi (be the right size) andare
bene; **it won't ~** (no room) non ci
sta ● vt (fix) applicare (to a); (install)
installare; **it doesn't ~ me** (coat
etc:) non mi va bene; ~ **with** fornire
di. ▢ **~ in** vi (person:) adattarsi; **it
won't ~ in** (no room) non ci sta ● vt
(in schedule, vehicle) trovare un
buco per

fit|ful /'fɪtfl/ adj irregolare. **~fully**
adv (sleep) a sprazzi. **~ments** npl (in
house) impianti mpl fissi. **~ness** n
(suitability) capacità f. [physical]
~ness forma f, fitness m

fitting /ˈfɪtɪŋ/ adj appropriato ● n (of clothes) prova f; (Techn) montaggio m; ~s pl accessori mpl. ~ room n camerino m

five /faɪv/ adj & n cinque m. ~r n 🔲 biglietto m da cinque sterline

fix /fɪks/ n (🔲: drugs) pera f; **be in a ~** 🔲 essere nei guai ● vt fissare; (repair) aggiustare; preparare (meal). □ ~ **up** vt fissare (meeting)

fixed /fɪkst/ adj fisso

fixture /ˈfɪkstʃə(r)/ n (Sport) incontro m; ~s and fittings impianti mpl fissi

fizz /fɪz/ vi frizzare

fizzle /ˈfɪzl/ vi ~ **out** finire in nulla

fizzy /ˈfɪzɪ/ adj gassoso. ~ **drink** n bibita f gassata

flabbergasted /ˈflæbəgɑːstɪd/ adj **be** ~ rimanere a bocca aperta

flabby /ˈflæbɪ/ adj floscio

flag[1] /flæg/ n bandiera f ● **flag down** vt (pt/pp flagged) far segno di fermarsi a (taxi)

flag[2] vi (pt/pp flagged) cedere

'flag-pole n asta f della bandiera

flagrant /ˈfleɪgrənt/ adj flagrante

flair /fleə(r)/ n (skill) talento m; (style) stile m

flake /fleɪk/ n fiocco m ● vi ~ **[off]** cadere in fiocchi

flaky /ˈfleɪkɪ/ adj a scaglie. ~ **pastry** n pasta f sfoglia

flamboyant /flæmˈbɔɪənt/ adj (personality) brillante; (tie) sgargiante

flame /fleɪm/ n fiamma f

flammable /ˈflæməbl/ adj infiammabile

flan /flæn/ n (fruit) ~ crostata f

flank /flæŋk/ n fianco m ● vt fiancheggiare

flannel /ˈflæn(ə)l/ n flanella f; (for washing) ≈ guanto m di spugna; ~s (trousers) pantaloni mpl di flanella

flap /flæp/ n (of pocket, envelope) risvolto m; (of table) ribalta f; **in a ~** 🔲 in grande agitazione ● v (pt/pp flapped) ● vi sbattere; 🔲 agitarsi ● vt ~ **its wings** battere le ali

flare /fleə(r)/ n (device) razzo m ● **flare up** vi (rash:) venire fuori; (fire:) fare una fiammata; (person, situation:) esplodere. ~**d** adj (garment) svasato

flash /flæʃ/ n lampo m; **in a** 🔲 in un attimo ● vi lampeggiare; ~ **past** passare come un bolide ● vt lanciare (smile); ~ **one's head-lights** lampeggiare; ~ **a torch at** puntare una torcia su

flash: ~**back** n scena f retrospettiva. ~**light** n (Photo) flash m inv (Am: torch) torcia f [elettrica]. ~**y** adj vistoso

flask /flɑːsk/ n fiasco m; (vacuum ~) termos m inv

flat /flæt/ adj (flatter, flattest) piatto; (refusal) reciso; (beer) sgasato; (battery) scarico; (tyre) a terra; **A** ~ (Mus) la bemolle ● n appartamento m; (Mus) bemolle m; (puncture) gomma f a terra

flat: ~**ly** adv (refuse) categoricamente. ~ **rate** n tariffa f unica

flatten /ˈflætn/ vt appiattire

flatter /ˈflætə(r)/ vt adulare. ~**ing** adj (comments) lusinghiero; (colour, dress) che fa sembrare più bello. ~**y** n adulazione f

flaunt /flɔːnt/ vt ostentare

flavour /ˈfleɪvə(r)/ n sapore m ● vt condire; **chocolate** ~**ed** al sapore di cioccolato. ~**ing** n condimento m

flaw /flɔː/ n difetto m. ~**less** adj perfetto

flea /fliː/ n pulce m. ~ **market** n mercato m delle pulci

fleck /flek/ n macchiolina f

fled /fled/ ▷FLEE

flee /fliː/ vt/i (pt/pp fled) fuggire (from da)

fleec|e /fliːs/ n pelliccia f ● vt 🔲

spennare. **~y** adj (lining) felpato

fleet /fliːt/ n flotta f; (of cars) parco m

fleeting /ˈfliːtɪŋ/ adj catch a ~ glance of sth intravedere qcsa; for a ~ moment per un attimo

flesh /fleʃ/ n carne f; in the ~ in persona. **~y** adj carnoso

flew /fluː/ ▷FLY²

flex¹ /fleks/ vt flettere (muscle)

flex² n (Electr) filo m

flexibility /fleksɪˈbɪlətɪ/ n flessibilità f. **~le** adj flessibile

flexitime /ˈfleksɪ-/ n orario m flessibile

flick /flɪk/ vt dare un buffetto a; ~ sth off sth togliere qcsa da qcsa con un colpetto. ~ **through** vt sfogliare

flicker /ˈflɪkə(r)/ vi tremolare

flight¹ /flaɪt/ n (fleeing) fuga f; take ~ darsi alla fuga

flight² n (flying) volo m; ~ of stairs rampa f

flight recorder n registratore m di volo

flimsy /ˈflɪmzɪ/ adj (-ier, -iest) (material) leggero; (shelves) poco robusto; (excuse) debole

flinch /flɪntʃ/ vi (wince) sussultare; (draw back) ritirarsi; ~ **from** a task fig sottrarsi a un compito

fling /flɪŋ/ n have a ~ 🔟: affair) aver un'avventura ●vt (pt/pp flung) gettare

flint /flɪnt/ n pietra f focaia; (for lighter) pietrina f

flip /flɪp/ v (pt/pp flipped) ●vt dare un colpetto a; buttare in aria (coin) ●vi 🔟 uscire dai gangheri; (go mad) impazzire. ~ **through** vt sfogliare

flippant /ˈflɪpənt/ adj irriverente

flipper /ˈflɪpə(r)/ n pinna f

flirt /flɜːt/ n civetta f ●vi flirtare

flit /flɪt/ vi (pt/pp flitted) volteggiare

float /fləʊt/ n galleggiante m; (in pro-cession) carro m; (money) riserva f di cassa ●vi galleggiare; (Fin) fluttuare

flock /flɒk/ n gregge m; (of birds) stormo m ●vi affollarsi

flog /flɒg/ vt (pt/pp flogged) bastonare; (🔟: sell) vendere

flood /flʌd/ n alluvione f; (of river) straripamento m; (fig: of replies, letters, tears) diluvio m; be in ~ (river): essere straripato ●vt allagare ●vi (river): straripare

floodlight n riflettore m ●vt (pt/pp floodlit) illuminare con riflettori

floor /flɔː(r)/ n pavimento m; (storey) piano m; (for dancing) pista f ●vt (baf-fle) confondere; (knock down) stendere (person)

floor polish n cera f per il pavimento

flop /flɒp/ n 🔟 (failure) tonfo m; (Theat) fiasco m ●vi (pt/pp flopped) (🔟: fail) far fiasco. ~ **down** vi accasciarsi

floppy /ˈflɒpɪ/ adj floscio. ~ **disk** n floppy disk m inv. ~ [disk] **drive** n lettore di floppy m

floral /ˈflɔːrəl/ adj floreale

florid /ˈflɒrɪd/ adj (complexion) florido; (style) troppo ricercato

florist /ˈflɒrɪst/ n fioraio, -a mf

flounder¹ /ˈflaʊndə(r)/ vi dibattersi; (speaker): impappinarsi

flounder² n (fish) passera f di mare

flour /ˈflaʊə(r)/ n farina f

flourish /ˈflʌrɪʃ/ n gesto m drammatico; (scroll) ghirigoro m ●vi prosperare ●vt brandire

flout /flaʊt/ vt fregarsene di (rules)

flow /fləʊ/ n flusso m ●vi scorrere; (hang loosely) ricadere

flower /ˈflaʊə(r)/ n fiore m ●vi fiorire

flower: ~**bed** n aiuola f. ~**y** adj fiorito

flown /fləʊn/ ▷FLY²

flu /fluː/ n influenza f

fluctuat|e /ˈflʌktjʊeɪt/ vi fluttuare. ~**ion** n fluttuazione f

fluent /ˈfluːənt/ adj spedito; speak ~ Italian parlare correntemente l'italiano. ~**ly** adv speditamente

fluff /flʌf/ n peluria f. ~**y** adj (-ier, -iest) vaporoso; (toy) di peluche

fluid /ˈfluːɪd/ adj fluido • n fluido m

flung /flʌŋ/ ▷**FLING**

fluorescent /flʊəˈresnt/ adj fluorescente

flush /flʌʃ/ n (blush) [vampata f di] rossore m • vi arrossire • vt lavare con un getto d'acqua; ~ **the toilet** tirare l'acqua • adj a livello (with di); (⫶: affluent) a soldi

flute /fluːt/ n flauto m

flutter /ˈflʌtə(r)/ n battito m • vi svolazzare

flux /flʌks/ n **in a state of** ~ **in uno** stato di flusso

fly[1] /flaɪ/ n (pl **flies**) mosca f

fly[2] v (pt **flew**, pp **flown**) • vi volare; (go by plane) andare in aereo; (flag:) sventolare; (rush) precipitarsi; ~ **open** spalancarsi • vt pilotare (plane); trasportare [in aereo] (troops, supplies); volare con (Alitalia etc)

fly[3] n & **flies** pl (on trousers) patta f

flying /ˈflaɪɪŋ/: ~ **'buttress** n arco m rampante. ~ **'colours: with** ~ **colours** a pieni voti. ~ **'saucer** n disco m volante. ~ **'start** n **get off to a** ~ **start** fare un'ottima partenza. ~ **'visit** n visita f lampo

fly: ~ **leaf** n risguardo m. ~**over** n cavalcavia m inv

foal /fəʊl/ n puledro m

foam /fəʊm/ n schiuma f; (synthetic) gommapiuma® f • vi spumare; ~ **at the mouth** da la bava alla bocca. ~ **'rubber** n gommapiuma® f

fob /fɒb/ vt (pt/pp **fobbed**) ~ **sth off** affibbiare qcsa (on sb a qcno); ~ **sb off** liquidare qcno

focal /ˈfəʊkl/ adj focale

focus /ˈfəʊkəs/ n fuoco m; **in** ~ a fuoco; **out of** ~ sfocato • v (pt/pp **focused** or **focussed**) • vt fig concentrare (on su) • vi (Phot:) ~ **on** mettere a fuoco; fig concentrarsi (on su)

fodder /ˈfɒdə(r)/ n foraggio m

foe /fəʊ/ n nemico, -a mf

foetus /ˈfiːtəs/ n (pl -**tuses**) feto m

fog /fɒg/ n nebbia f

foggy /ˈfɒgɪ/ adj (foggier, foggiest) nebbioso; **it's** ~ c'è nebbia

'fog-horn n sirena f da nebbia

foil[1] /fɔɪl/ n lamina f di metallo

foil[2] vt (thwart) frustrare

foil[3] n (sword) fioretto m

foist /fɔɪst/ vt appioppare (on sb a qcno)

fold[1] /fəʊld/ n (for sheep) ovile m

fold[2] n piega f • vt piegare; ~ **one's arms** incrociare le braccia • vi piegarsi; (fail) crollare. □ ~ **up** vt ripiegare (chair) • vi essere pieghevole; (business:) collassare

fold|er /ˈfəʊldə(r)/ n cartella f. ~**ing** adj pieghevole

folk /fəʊk/ npl gente f; **my** ~**s** (family) i miei; **hello there** ~**s** ciao a tutti

folklore n folclore m

follow /ˈfɒləʊ/ vt/i seguire; **it doesn't** ~ non è necessariamente così; ~ **suit** fig fare lo stesso; **as** ~**s** come segue. □ ~ **up** vt seguire a (letter)

follow|er /ˈfɒləʊə(r)/ n seguace mf. ~**ing** adj seguente • n seguito m; (supporters) seguaci mpl • prep in seguito a

folly /ˈfɒlɪ/ n follia f

fond /fɒnd/ adj affezionato; (hope) vivo; **be** ~ **of** essere appassionato di (music); **I'm** ~ **of...** (food, person) mi piace moltissimo...

fondle /ˈfɒndl/ vt coccolare

fondness /ˈfɒndnɪs/ n affetto m; (for things) amore m

font /fɒnt/ n fonte f battesimale; (Typ) carattere m di stampa

food /fuːd/ n cibo m; (for animals, groceries) mangiare m; let's buy some ~ compriamo qualcosa da mangiare

food processor n tritatutto m inv elettrico

fool[1] /fuːl/ n sciocco, -a mf; she's no ~ non è una stupida; make a ~ of oneself rendersi ridicolo ●vt prendere in giro ●vi ~ around giocare; (husband, wife:) avere l'amante

fool[2] n (Culin) crema f

'fool|hardy adj temerario. ~ish adj stolto. ~ishly adv scioccamente. ~ishness n sciocchezza f. ~proof adj facilissimo

foot /fʊt/ n (pl feet) piede m; (of animal) zampa f; (measure) piede m (= 30,48 cm); on ~ a piedi; on one's feet in piedi; put one's ~ in it fare una gaffe

foot: ~-and-'mouth disease n afta f epizootica. ~**ball** n calcio m; (ball) pallone m. ~**baller** n giocatore m di calcio. ~**bridge** n passerella f. ~**hills** npl colline fpl pedemontane. ~**hold** n punto m d'appoggio. ~**ing** n lose one's ~ing perdere l'appiglio; on an equal ~ing in condizioni di parità. ~**man** n valletto m. ~**note** n nota f a piè di pagina. ~**path** n sentiero m. ~**print** n orma f. ~**step** n passo m; follow in sb's ~steps fig seguire l'esempio di qcno. ~**wear** n calzature fpl

---

for /fə(r)/, accentato /fɔː(r)/

● prep per; ~ this reason per questa ragione; I have lived here ~ ten years vivo qui da dieci anni; ~ supper per cena; ~ all this nonostante questo; what ~? a che scopo?; send ~ a doctor chiamare un dottore; fight ~ a cause lottare per una causa; go ~ a walk

andare a fare una passeggiata; there's no need ~ you to go non c'è bisogno che tu vada; it's not ~ me to say non sta a me dirlo; now you're ~ it ora sei nei pasticci

● conj poiché, perché

forage /ˈfɒrɪdʒ/ n foraggio m ●vi ~ for cercare

forbade /fəˈbæd/ ▷FORBID

forbear|ance /fɔːˈbeərəns/ n pazienza f. ~**ing** adj tollerante

forbid /fəˈbɪd/ vt (pt forbade, pp forbidden) proibire. ~**ding** adj (prospect) che spaventa; (stern) severo

force /fɔːs/ n forza f; in ~ in vigore; (in large numbers) in massa; come into ~ entrare in vigore; the [armed] ~s pl le forze armate ●vt forzare; ~ sth on sb (decision) imporre qcsa a qcno; (drink) costringere qcno a fare qcsa

forced /fɔːst/ adj forzato

force-'feed vt (pt/pp -fed) nutrire a forza. ~**ful** adj energico

forceps /ˈfɔːseps/ npl forcipe m

forcible /ˈfɔːsɪbl/ adj forzato

ford /fɔːd/ n guado m ●vt guadare

fore /fɔː(r)/ n to the ~ in vista; come to the ~ salire alla ribalta

fore: ~arm n avambraccio m. ~**boding** /-ˈbəʊdɪŋ/ n presentimento m. ~**cast** n previsione f ●vt (pt/pp -cast) prevedere. ~**court** n cortile m anteriore. ~**finger** n [dito m] indice m. ~**front** n be in the ~front essere all'avanguardia. ~**gone** adj be a ~gone conclusion essere una cosa scontata. ~**ground** n primo piano m. ~**head** /ˈfɔːhed/, /ˈfɒrɪd/ n fronte f

foreign /ˈfɒrən/ adj straniero; (trade) estero; (not belonging) estraneo; he is ~ è uno straniero. ~ **currency** n valuta f estera. ~**er** n straniero, -a mf. ~ **language** n lingua f straniera

fore: ~man n caporeparto m.
~most adj principale • adv first and
~most in primo luogo

'forerunner n precursore m

fore'see vt (pt -saw, pp -seen) prevedere. **~able** adj in the ~able future in futuro per quanto si possa prevedere

'foresight n previdenza f

forest /'forıst/ n foresta f. **~er** n guardia f forestale

fore'stall vt prevenire

forestry /'forıstrı/ n silvicoltura f

'foretaste n pregustazione f

fore'tell vt (pt/pp -told) predire

forever /fə'revə(r)/ adv per sempre;
he's ~ complaining si lamenta
sempre

fore'warn vt avvertire

foreword /'fɔːwɜːd/ n prefazione f

forfeit /'fɔːfıt/ n (in game) pegno m;
(Jur) penalità f • vt perdere

forgave /fə'geɪv/ ▷ FORGIVE

forge¹ vt (pt -saw) **~ ahead** (runner:)
lasciarsi indietro gli altri; fig farsi
strada

forge² n fucina f • vt fucinare; (counterfeit) contraffare. **~r** n contraffattore m. **~ry** n contraffazione f

forget /fə'get/ vt/i (pt -got, pp
-gotten, pres p -getting) dimenticare; dimenticarsi di (language,
skill). **~ful** adj smemorato. **~fulness**
n smemoratezza f. **~me-not** n nonti-scordar-dimé m inv. **~table** adj
(day, film) da dimenticare

forgive /fə'gɪv/ vt (pt -gave, pp
-given) ~ **sb for sth** perdonare
qcno per qcsa. **~ness** n perdono m

forgo /fɔː'gəʊ/ vt (pt -went, pp
-gone) rinunciare a

forgot(ten) /fə'gɒt(n)/ ▷ FORGET

fork /fɔːk/ n forchetta f; (for digging)
forca f; (in road) bivio m • vi (road:)
biforcarsi; ~ **right** prendere a de-

stra. □ ~ **out** vt [T] sborsare

fork-lift 'truck n elevatore m

forlorn /fə'lɔːn/ adj (look) perduto;
(place) derelitto; ~ **hope** speranza
f vana

form /fɔːm/ n forma f; (document)
modulo m; (Sch) classe f • vt formare;
formulare (opinion) • vi formarsi

formal /'fɔːml/ adj formale. **~ity** n
formalità f inv. **~ly** adv in modo formale; (officially) ufficialmente

format /'fɔːmæt/ n formato m • vt
formattare (disk, page)

formation /fɔː'meɪʃn/ n formazione f

former /'fɔːmə(r)/ adj precedente;
(PM, colleague) ex; the ~, the latter il primo, l'ultimo. **~ly** adv precedentemente; (in olden times) in
altri tempi

formidable /'fɔːmɪdəbl/ adj formidabile

formula /'fɔːmjʊlə/ n (pl -ae /-liː/ or
-s) formula f

formulate /'fɔːmjʊleɪt/ vt formulare

forsake /fə'seɪk/ vt (pt -sook /-sʊk/,
pp -saken) abbandonare

fort /fɔːt/ n (Mil) forte m

forth /fɔːθ/ adv back and ~ avanti e
indietro; **and so** ~ e così via

forth: ~coming adj prossimo; (communicative) communicativo; no response was ~ non arrivava nessuna
risposta. **~right** adj schietto.
~with adv immediatamente

fortieth /'fɔːtɪɪθ/ adj quarantesimo

fortnight /'fɔːt-/ Br n quindicina f.
~ly adj bimensile • adv ogni due settimane

fortress /'fɔːtrıs/ n fortezza f

fortunate /'fɔːtʃənət/ adj fortunato;
that's ~! meno male!. **~ly** adv fortunatamente

fortune /'fɔːtʃuːn/ n fortuna f.
~-teller n indovino, -a mf

forty /ˈfɔːtɪ/ adj & n quaranta m

forum /ˈfɔːrəm/ n foro m

forward /ˈfɔːwəd/ adv avanti; (towards the front) in avanti ● adj in avanti; (presumptuous) sfacciato ● n (Sport) attaccante m ● vt inoltrare (letter); spedire (goods). **~s** adv avanti

fossil /ˈfɒsl/ n fossile m. **~ized** adj fossile; (ideas) fossilizzato

foster /ˈfɒstə(r)/ vt allevare (child). **~-child** n figlio, -a m/f in affidamento. **~-mother** n madre f affidataria

fought /fɔːt/ ▷FIGHT

foul /faʊl/ adj (smell, taste) cattivo; (air) viziato; (language) osceno; (mood, weather) orrendo; **~ play** (Jur) delitto m ● n (Sport) fallo m ● vt inquinare (water); (object) commettere un fallo contro; (nets, rope:) impigliarsi in. **~-smelling** adj puzzo

found¹ /faʊnd/ ▷FIND

found² vt fondare

foundation /faʊnˈdeɪʃn/ n (basis) fondamento m; (charitable) fondazione f; **~s** pl (of building) fondamenta fpl; lay the **~-stone** porre la prima pietra

founder¹ /ˈfaʊndə(r)/ n fondatore, -trice mf

founder² vi (ship:) affondare

fountain /ˈfaʊntɪn/ n fontana f. **~-pen** n penna f stilografica

four /fɔː(r)/ adj & n quattro m

four: ~some /ˈfɔːsəm/ n quartetto m. **~'teen** adj & n quattordici m. **~'teenth** adj & n quattordicesimo

fourth /fɔːθ/ adj quarto

fowl /faʊl/ n pollame m

fox /fɒks/ n volpe f ● vt (puzzle) ingannare

foyer /ˈfɔɪeɪ/ n (Theat) ridotto m; (in hotel) salone m d'ingresso

fraction /ˈfrækʃn/ n frazione f

fracture /ˈfræktʃə(r)/ n frattura f ● vt fratturare ● vi fratturarsi

fragile /ˈfrædʒaɪl/ adj fragile

fragment /ˈfrægmənt/ n frammento m. **~ary** adj frammentario

fragran|ce /ˈfreɪgrəns/ n fragranza f. **~t** adj fragrante

frail /freɪl/ adj gracile

frame /freɪm/ n (of picture, door, window) cornice f; (of spectacles) montatura f; (Anat) ossatura f; (structure, of bike) telaio m; **~ of mind** stato m d'animo ● vt incorniciare (picture); fig formulare; (ⅹ: incriminate) montare. **~work** n struttura f

France /frɑːns/ n Francia f

frank¹ /fræŋk/ vt affrancare (letter)

frank² adj franco. **~ly** adv francamente

frantic /ˈfræntɪk/ adj frenetico; be **~ with worry** essere agitatissimo. **~ally** adv freneticamente

fraternal /frəˈtɜːnl/ adj fraterno

fraud /frɔːd/ n frode f; (person) impostore m. **~ulent** adj fraudolento

fraught /frɔːt/ adj **~ with** pieno di

fray¹ /freɪ/ n mischia f

fray² vi sfilacciarsi

freak /friːk/ n fenomeno m; (person) scherzo m di natura; (ⅹ: weird person) tipo m strambo ● adj anormale. **~ish** adj strambo

freckle /ˈfrekl/ n lentiggine f. **~d** adj lentigginoso

free /friː/ adj (freer, freest) libero; (ticket, copy) gratuito; (lavish) generoso; **~ of charge** gratuito; **set ~** liberare ● vt (pt/pp freed) liberare

free: ~dom n libertà f. **~hold** n proprietà f (fondiaria) assoluta. **~ kick** n calcio m di punizione. **~lance** adj & adv indipendente. **~ly** adv liberamente; (generously) generosamente; **I ~ly admit that...** devo ammettere che.... **f~mason** n massone m. **~-range** adj **~-range egg** uovo m di gallina ruspante. **~style** n stile m libero. **~way** n Am autostrada f

freeze /friːz/ vt (pt froze, pp frozen) gelare; bloccare (wages) •vi (water:) gelare; it's ~ing si gela; my hands are ~ing ho le mani congelate

freezer /ˈfriːzə(r)/ n freezer m inv, congelatore m. ~ing adj gelido •n below ~ing sotto zero

freight /freɪt/ n carico m. ~er n nave f da carico. ~ train n Am treno m merci

French /frentʃ/ adj francese •n (language) francese m; the ~ pl i francesi mpl

French: ~ 'fries npl patate fpl fritte. ~man n francese m. ~ 'window n porta-finestra f. ~woman n francese f

frenzied /ˈfrenzɪd/ adj frenetico

frenzy /ˈfrenzɪ/ n frenesia f

frequency /ˈfriːkwənsɪ/ n frequenza f

frequent¹ /ˈfriːkwənt/ adj frequente. ~ly adv frequentemente

frequent² /frɪˈkwent/ vt frequentare

fresh /freʃ/ adj fresco; (new) nuovo; (Am: cheeky) sfacciato. ~ly adv di recente

freshen /ˈfreʃn/ vi (wind:) rinfrescare. □ ~ up vt dare una rinfrescata a •vi rinfrescarsi

freshness /ˈfreʃnɪs/ n freschezza f

fret /fret/ vi (pt/pp fretted) inquietarsi. ~ful adj irritabile

friction /ˈfrɪkʃn/ n frizione f

Friday /ˈfraɪdeɪ/ n venerdì m inv

fridge /frɪdʒ/ n frigo m

fried /fraɪd/ ▷FRY •adj fritto; ~ egg uovo m fritto

friend /frend/ n amico, a mf. ~ly adj (-ier, -iest) (relations, meeting, match) amichevole; (neighbourhood, smile) piacevole; (software) di facile uso; be ~ly with essere amico di. ~ship n amicizia f

frieze /friːz/ n fregio m

fright /fraɪt/ n paura f; take ~ spaventarsi

frighten /ˈfraɪtn/ vt spaventare. ~ed adj spaventato; be ~ed aver paura (of di). ~ing adj spaventoso

frightful /ˈfraɪtfl/ adj terribile

frigid /ˈfrɪdʒɪd/ adj frigido. ~ity n freddezza f; (Psych) frigidità f

frill /frɪl/ n volant m inv. ~y adj (dress) con tanti volant

fringe /frɪndʒ/ n frangia f; (of hair) frangetta f; (fig: edge) margine m. ~ benefits npl benefici mpl supplementari

fritter /ˈfrɪtə(r)/ n frittella f •fritter away vt sprecare

frivol|ity /frɪˈvɒlɪtɪ/ n frivolezza f. ~ous adj frivolo

fro /frəʊ/ ▷TO

frock /frɒk/ n abito m

frog /frɒg/ n rana f. ~man n uomo m rana

frolic /ˈfrɒlɪk/ vi (pt/pp frolicked) (lambs:) sgambettare; (people:) folleggiare

from /frɒm/ prep da; ~ Monday da lunedì; ~ that day da quel giorno; he's ~ London è di Londra; this is a letter ~ my brother questa è una lettera di mio fratello; documents ~ the 16th century documenti del XVI secolo; made ~ fatto con; she felt ill ~ fatigue si sentiva male dalla stanchezza; ~ now on d'ora in poi

front /frʌnt/ n parte f anteriore; (fig: organization etc) facciata f; (of garment) davanti m; (sea~) lungomare m; (Mil, Pol, Meteorol) fronte m; in ~ of davanti a; in or at the ~ davanti; to the ~ avanti •adj davanti; (page, row, wheel) anteriore

frontal /ˈfrʌntl/ adj frontale

front 'door n porta f d'entrata

frontier /ˈfrʌntɪə(r)/ n frontiera f

frost /frɒst/ n gelo m; (hoar~) brina f

~**bite** *n* congelamento *m.* ~**bitten** *adj* congelato

frost|ed /ˈfrɒstɪd/ *adj* ~**ed glass** vetro *m* smerigliato. ~**ily** *adv* gelidamente. ~**ing** *n* Am (Culin) glassa *f.* ~**y** *adj* also *fig* gelido

froth /frɒθ/ *n* schiuma *f* ● *vi* far schiuma. ~**y** *adj* schiumoso

frown /fraʊn/ *n* cipiglio *m* ● *vi* aggrottare le sopracciglia. □ ~ **on** *vt* disapprovare

froze /frəʊz/ ▷FREEZE

frozen /ˈfrəʊzn/ ▷FREEZE ● *adj* (corpse, hand) congelato; (wastes) gelido; (Culin) surgelato; **I'm** ~ sono gelato. ~ **food** *n* surgelati *mpl*

frugal /ˈfruːgl/ *adj* frugale

fruit /fruːt/ *n* frutto *m;* (collectively) frutta *f;* **eat more** ~ mangia più frutta. ~ **cake** *n* dolce *m* con frutta candita

fruition /fruːˈɪʃn/ *n* **come to** ~ dare dei frutti

fruit: ~**less** *adj* infruttuoso. ~ **'salad** *n* macedonia *f* [di frutta]

frustrat|e /frʌˈstreɪt/ *vt* frustrare; rovinare (plans). ~**ing** *adj* frustrante. ~**ion** *n* frustrazione *f*

fry[1] *vt/i* (*pt/pp* fried) friggere

fry[2] /fraɪ/ *n inv* **small** ~ *fig* pesce *m* piccolo

frying pan *n* padella *f*

fudge /fʌdʒ/ *n* caramella *f* a base di zucchero, burro e latte

fuel /ˈfjuːəl/ *n* carburante *m;* *fig* nutrimento *m* ● *vt fig* alimentare

fugitive /ˈfjuːdʒɪtɪv/ *n* fuggiasco, -a *mf*

fulfil /fʊlˈfɪl/ *vt* (*pt/pp* -filled) soddisfare (conditions, need); realizzare (dream, desire); ~ **oneself** realizzarsi. ~**ling** *adj* soddisfacente. ~**ment** *n* **sense of** ~**ment** senso *m* di appagamento

full /fʊl/ *adj* pieno (of di); (detailed) esauriente; (bus, hotel) completo;

(skirt) ampio; **at** ~ **speed** a tutta velocità; **in** ~ **swing** in pieno fervore ● *n* **in** ~ per intero

full: ~ '**moon** *n* luna *f* piena. ~**-scale** *adj* (model) in scala reale; (alert) di massima gravità. ~ '**stop** *n* punto *m.* ~**-time** *adj* & *adv* a tempo pieno

fully /ˈfʊli/ *adv* completamente; (in detail) dettagliatamente; ~ **booked** (hotel, restaurant) tutto prenotato

fumble /ˈfʌmbl/ *vi* ~ **in** rovistare in; ~ **with** armeggiare con; ~ **for one's keys** rovistare alla ricerca delle chiavi

fume /fjuːm/ *vi* (be angry) essere furioso

fumes /fjuːmz/ *npl* fumi *mpl;* (from car) gas *mpl* di scarico

fumigate /ˈfjuːmɪgeɪt/ *vt* suffumicare

fun /fʌn/ *n* divertimento *m;* **for** ~ per ridere; **make** ~ **of** prendere in giro; **have** ~ divertirsi

function /ˈfʌŋkʃn/ *n* funzione *f;* (event) cerimonia *f* ● *vi* funzionare; ~ **as** (serve as) funzionare da. ~**al** *adj* funzionale

fund /fʌnd/ *n* fondo *m; fig* pozzo *m;* ~**s** *pl* fondi *mpl* ● *vt* finanziare

fundamental /fʌndəˈmentl/ *adj* fondamentale

funeral /ˈfjuːnərəl/ *n* funerale *m*

funeral directors *n* impresa *f* di pompe funebri

'**funfair** *n* luna park *m inv*

fungus /ˈfʌŋgəs/ *n* (*pl* -gi /-gaɪ/) fungo *m*

funnel /ˈfʌnl/ *n* imbuto *m;* (on ship) ciminiera *f*

funnily /ˈfʌnɪli/ *adv* comicamente; (oddly) stranamente; ~ **enough** strano a dirsi

funny /ˈfʌni/ *adj* (-ier, -iest) buffo; (odd) strano. ~ **business** *n* affare *m* losco

f

fur /fɜː(r)/ n pelo m; (for clothing) pelliccia f; (in kettle) deposito m. ~ 'coat n pelliccia f

furious /ˈfjʊərɪəs/ adj furioso

furnace /ˈfɜːnɪs/ n fornace f

furnish /ˈfɜːnɪʃ/ vt ammobiliare (flat); fornire (supplies). ~ed adj ~ed room stanza f ammobiliata. ~ings npl mobili mpl

furniture /ˈfɜːnɪtʃə(r)/ n mobili mpl

furrow /ˈfʌrəʊ/ n solco m

furry /ˈfɜːrɪ/ adj (animal) peloso; (toy) di peluche

further /ˈfɜːðə(r)/ adj (additional) ulteriore; at the ~ end all'altra estremità; until ~ notice fino a nuovo avviso ● adv più lontano; ~,... inoltre,...; ~ off più lontano ● vt promuovere

further'more adv per di più

furthest /ˈfɜːðɪst/ adj più lontano ● adv più lontano

furtive /ˈfɜːtɪv/ adj furtivo

fury /ˈfjʊərɪ/ n furore m

fuse¹ /fjuːz/ n (of bomb) detonatore m; (cord) miccia f

fuse² n (Electr) fusibile m ● vt fondere; (Electr) far saltare ● vi fondersi; (Electr) saltare; the lights have ~d sono saltate le luci. ~-box n scatola f dei fusibili

fuselage /ˈfjuːzəlɑːʒ/ n (Aeron) fusoliera f

fusion /ˈfjuːʒn/ n fusione f

fuss /fʌs/ n storie fpl; make a ~ fare storie; make a ~ of colmare di attenzioni ● vi fare storie

fussy /ˈfʌsɪ/ adj (-ier, -iest) (person) difficile da accontentare; (clothes etc) pieno di fronzoli

futile /ˈfjuːtaɪl/ adj inutile. ~ity n futilità f

future /ˈfjuːtʃə(r)/ adj & n futuro; in ~ in futuro. ~ perfect futuro m anteriore

futuristic /fjuːtʃəˈrɪstɪk/ adj futuristico

fuzz /fʌz/ n the ~ (🔲: police) la pula

fuzzy /ˈfʌzɪ/ adj (-ier, -iest) (hair) crespo; (photo) sfuocato

Gg

gab /gæb/ n 🔢 have the gift of the ~ avere la parlantina

gabble /ˈgæbl/ vi parlare troppo in fretta

gad /gæd/ vi (pt/pp gadded) ~ about andarsene in giro

gadget /ˈgædʒɪt/ n aggeggio m

Gaelic /ˈgeɪlɪk/ adj & n gaelico m

gaffe /gæf/ n gaffe f inv

gag /gæg/ n bavaglio m; (joke) battuta f ● vt (pt/pp gagged) imbavagliare

gaily /ˈgeɪlɪ/ adv allegramente

gain /geɪn/ n guadagno m; (increase) aumento m ● vt acquisire; ~ weight aumentare di peso; ~ access accedere ● vi (clock:) andare avanti. ~ful adj ~ful employment lavoro m remunerativo

gait /geɪt/ n andatura f

gala /ˈgɑːlə/ n gala f; swimming ~ manifestazione f di nuoto ● attrib di gala

galaxy /ˈgæləksɪ/ n galassia f

gale /geɪl/ n bufera f

gall /gɔːl/ n (impudence) impudenza f

gallant /ˈgælənt/ adj coraggioso; (chivalrous) galante. ~ry n coraggio m

'gall-bladder n cistifellea f

gallery /ˈgælərɪ/ n galleria f

galley /ˈgælɪ/ n (ship's kitchen) cambusa f; ~ [proof] bozza f in colonna

gallivant /'gælɪvænt/ vi andare in giro

gallon /'gælən/ n gallone m (= 4,5 l; Am = 3,7 l)

gallop /'gæləp/ n galoppo m • vi galoppare

gallows /'gæləʊz/ n forca f

galore /gə'lɔ:(r)/ adv a bizzeffe

galvanize /'gælvənaɪz/ vt (Techn) galvanizzare; fig stimolare (into a)

gambl|e /'gæmbl/ n rischio m; (risk) azzardo m • vi giocare; (on Stock Exchange) speculare; ~e on (rely) contare su. ~er n giocatore, -trice mf [d'azzardo]. ~ing n gioco m [d'azzardo]

game /geɪm/ n gioco m; (match) partita f; (animals, birds) selvaggina f; ~s (Sch) ≈ ginnastica f (brave) coraggioso; are you ~? ti va?; be ~ for essere pronto per. ~keeper n guardacaccia m inv

gammon /'gæmən/ n coscia f di maiale

gamut /'gæmət/ n fig gamma f

gander /'gændə(r)/ n oca f maschio

gang /gæŋ/ n banda f; (of workmen) squadra f • gang up vi far comunella (on contro)

gangling /'gæŋglɪŋ/ adj spilungone

gangmaster /'gæŋmɑ:stə(r)/ n caporale m (di manodopera abusiva)

gangrene /'gæŋgri:n/ n cancrena f

gangster /'gæŋstə(r)/ n gangster m inv

gangway /'gæŋweɪ/ n passaggio m; (Aeron, Naut) passerella f

gaol /dʒeɪl/ n carcere m • vt incarcerare. ~er n carceriere m

gap /gæp/ n spazio m; (in ages, between teeth) scarto m; (in memory) vuoto m; (in story) punto m oscuro

gap|e /geɪp/ vi stare a bocca aperta; (be wide open) spalancarsi; ~e at guardare a bocca aperta. ~ing adj aperto

gap year In Gran Bretagna il gap year è l'anno di intervallo che gli studenti si prendono tra la fine della scuola secondaria e l'università. Molti studenti utilizzano questo periodo sabbatico per intraprendere attività completamente diverse da ciò che hanno studiato o che studieranno e alcuni lo utilizzano per lavorare e mettere da parte qualche risparmio. Altri, infine, ne approfittano per viaggiare all'estero e conoscere il mondo.

garage /'gærɑ:ʒ/ n garage m inv; (for repairs) meccanico m; (for petrol) stazione f di servizio

garbage /'gɑ:bɪdʒ/ n immondizia f; (nonsense) idiozie fpl. ~ can n Am bidone m dell'immondizia

garden /'gɑ:dn/ n giardino m; [public] ~s pl giardini mpl pubblici • vi fare giardinaggio. ~ centre n negozio m di piante e articoli da giardinaggio. ~er n giardiniere, -a mf. ~ing n giardinaggio m

gargle /'gɑ:gl/ n gargarismo m • vi fare gargarismi

gargoyle /'gɑ:gɔɪl/ n gargouille f inv

garish /'geərɪʃ/ adj sgargiante

garland /'gɑ:lənd/ n ghirlanda f

garlic /'gɑ:lɪk/ n aglio m. ~ bread n pane m condito con aglio

garment /'gɑ:mənt/ n indumento m

garnish /'gɑ:nɪʃ/ n guarnizione f • vt guarnire

garrison /'gærɪsn/ n guarnigione f

garter /'gɑ:tə(r)/ n giarrettiera f; (for socks) reggicalze m inv da uomo

gas /gæs/ n gas m inv; (Am ɪ: petrol) benzina f • v (pt/pp gassed) • vt asfissiare • vi ɪ blaterare. ~ cooker n cucina f a gas. ~ 'fire n stufa f a gas

gash /gæʃ/ n taglio m • vt tagliare

gasket /'gæskɪt/ n (Techn) guarnizione f

gas: ∼ **mask** n maschera f antigas.
∼-**meter** n contatore m del gas

gasoline /'gæsəli:n/ n Am benzina f

gasp /gɑ:sp/ vi avere il fiato mozzato

'**gas station** n Am distributore m di
benzina

gastric /'gæstrɪk/ adj gastrico. ∼
flu n influenza f gastro-intestinale.
∼ '**ulcer** n ulcera f gastrica

gate /geɪt/ n cancello m; (at airport)
uscita f

gate: ∼**crash** vt entrare senza invito
a. ∼**crasher** n intruso, -a mf. ∼**way**
n ingresso m

gather /'gæðə(r)/ vt raccogliere;
(conclude) dedurre; (in sewing) arricciare; ∼ **speed** acquistare velocità;
∼ **together** radunare (people, belongings); (obtain gradually) acquistare
● vi (people:) radunarsi. ∼**ing** n family ∼**ing** ritrovo m di famiglia

gaudy /'gɔ:dɪ/ adj (-ier, -iest) pacchiano

gauge /geɪdʒ/ n calibro m; (Rail)
scartamento m; (device) indicatore m
● vt misurare; fig stimare

gaunt /gɔ:nt/ adj (thin) smunto

gauze /gɔ:z/ n garza f

gave /geɪv/ ▷GIVE

gawky /'gɔ:kɪ/ adj (-ier, -iest)
sgraziato

gawp /gɔ:p/ vi ∼ [at] 🆅 guardare
con aria da ebete

gay /geɪ/ adj gaio; (homosexual) omosessuale; (bar, club) gay

gaze /geɪz/ n sguardo m fisso ● vi
guardare; ∼ **at** fissare

GB abbr (Great Britain) GB

gear /gɪə(r)/ n equipaggiamento m;
(Techn) ingranaggio m; (Auto) marcia f;
in ∼ con la marcia innestata;
change ∼ cambiare marcia ● vt fina-
lizzare (to a)

gearbox n (Auto) scatola f del
cambio

geese /gi:s/ ▷GOOSE

gel /dʒel/ n gel m inv

gelatine /'dʒelətɪn/ n gelatina f

gelignite /'dʒelɪgnaɪt/ n gelatina
esplosiva f

gem /dʒem/ n gemma f

Gemini /'dʒemɪnaɪ/ n (Astr) Gemelli mpl

gender /'dʒendə(r)/ n (Gram)
genere m

gene /dʒi:n/ n gene m

genealogy /dʒi:nɪ'ælədʒɪ/ n ge-
nealogia f

general /'dʒenrəl/ adj generale ● n
generale m; in ∼ in generale. ∼
e'lection n elezioni fpl politiche

generaliz|ation /dʒenrəlar'zeɪʃn/
n generalizzazione f. ∼**e** vi genera-
lizzare

generally /'dʒenrəlɪ/ adv generalmente

general prac'titioner n medico
m generico

generate /'dʒenəreɪt/ vt generare

generation /dʒenə'reɪʃn/ n generazione f

generator /'dʒenəreɪtə(r)/ n gene-
ratore m

generosity /dʒenə'rɒsɪtɪ/ n generosità f

generous /'dʒenərəs/ adj generoso.
∼**ly** adv generosamente

genetic /dʒɪ'netɪk/ adj genetico. ∼
engineering n ingegneria f genetica.
∼**s** n genetica f

Geneva /dʒɪ'ni:və/ n Ginevra f

genial /'dʒi:nɪəl/ adj gioviale

genitals /'dʒenɪtlz/ npl genitali mpl

genitive /'dʒenɪtɪv/ adj & n ∼
[case] genitivo m

genius /'dʒi:nɪəs/ n (pl -uses)
genio m

genocide /'dʒenəsaɪd/ n geno-
cidio m

genre /'ʒæŋ.rə/ n genere m [let-
terario]

gent /dʒent/ n 🆅 signore m; the ∼**s**

sg il bagno per uomini

genteel /dʒen'ti:l/ *adj* raffinato

gentle /'dʒentl/ *adj* delicato; (breeze, tap, slope) leggero

gentleman /'dʒentlmən/ *n* signore *m*; (well-mannered) gentiluomo *m*

gent|leness /'dʒentlnɪs/ *n* delicatezza *f*. ~ly *adv* delicatamente

genuine /'dʒenjʊɪn/ *adj* genuino. ~ly *adv* (sorry) sinceramente

geograph|ical /dʒɪə'græfɪkl/ *adj* geografico. ~y *n* geografia *f*

geological /dʒɪə'lɒdʒɪkl/ *adj* geologico

geolog|ist /dʒɪ'ɒlədʒɪst/ *n* geologo, -a *mf*. ~y *n* geologia *f*

geranium /dʒə'reɪnɪəm/ *n* geranio *m*

geriatric /dʒerɪ'ætrɪk/ *adj* geriatrico; ~ ward *n* reparto *m* geriatria. ~s *n* geriatria *f*

germ /dʒɜːm/ *n* germe *m*; ~s *pl* microbi *mpl*

German /'dʒɜːmən/ *n* & *adj* tedesco, -a *mf*; (language) tedesco *m*

Germanic /dʒə'mænɪk/ *adj* germanico

German 'measles *n* rosolia *f*

Germany /'dʒɜːmənɪ/ *n* Germania *f*

germinate /'dʒɜːmɪneɪt/ *vi* germogliare

gesticulate /dʒe'stɪkjʊleɪt/ *vi* gesticolare

gesture /'dʒestʃə(r)/ *n* gesto *m*

---

get /get/ *verb*

past tense/past participle **got**, past participle *Am* **gotten**, pres participle **getting**)

● *vt* (receive) ricevere; (obtain) ottenere; trovare (job); (buy, catch, fetch) prendere; (transport, deliver to airport etc) portare; (reach on

---

telephone) trovare; (**Ⅰ**: understand) comprendere; preparare (meal); ~ sb to do sth far fare qcsa a qcno

● *vi* (become) ~ tired/bored/angry stancarsi/annoiarsi/arrabbiarsi; I'm ~ting hungry mi sta venendo fame; ~ dressed/married vestirsi/sposarsi; ~ sth ready preparare qcsa; ~ nowhere non concludere nulla; this is ~ting us nowhere questo non ci è di nessun aiuto; ~ to (reach) arrivare a. □ ~ at *vi* (criticize) criticare; I see what you're ~ting at ho capito cosa vuoi dire; what are you ~ting at? dove vuoi andare a parare?. □ ~ away *vi* (leave) andarsene; (escape) scappare. □ ~ back *vi* tornare ● *vt* (recover) riavere; ~ one's own back rifarsi. □ ~ by *vi* passare; (manage) cavarsela. □ ~ down *vi* scendere; ~ down to work mettersi al lavoro ● *vt* (depress) buttare giù. □ ~ in *vi* entrare ● *vt* mettere dentro (washing); far venire (plumber). □ ~ off *vi* scendere; (from work) andarsene; (Jur) essere assolto; ~ off the bus/one's bike scendere dal pullman/dalla bici ● *vt* (remove) togliere. □ ~ on *vi* salire; (be on good terms) andare d'accordo; (make progress) andare avanti; (in life) riuscire; ~ on the bus/one's bike salire sul pullman/sulla bici; how are you ~ting on? come va?. □ ~ out *vi* uscire; (of car) scendere; ~ out! fuori!; ~ out of (avoid doing) evitare ● *vt* togliere (cork, stain). □ ~ over *vi* andare di là ● *vt fig* riprendersi da (illness). □ ~ round *vt* aggirare (rule); rigirare (person) ● *vi* I never ~ round to it non mi sono mai deciso a farlo. □ ~ through *vi* (on telephone) prendere la linea. □~ **up** vi alzarsi; (climb) salire; ~ **up a hill** salire su una collina

geyser /'giːzə(r)/ n scaldabagno m; (Geol) geyser m inv

ghastly /'gɑːstlɪ/ adj (-ier, -iest) terribile; feel ~ sentirsi da cani

gherkin /'gɜːkɪn/ n cetriolino m

ghetto /'getəʊ/ n ghetto m

ghost /ɡəʊst/ n fantasma m. ~**ly** adj spettrale

giant /'dʒaɪənt/ n gigante m ●adj gigante

gibberish /'dʒɪbərɪʃ/ n stupidaggini fpl

gibe /dʒaɪb/ n malignità f

giblets /'dʒɪblɪts/ npl frattaglie fpl

giddiness /'ɡɪdɪnɪs/ n vertigini fpl

giddy /'ɡɪdɪ/ adj (-ier, -iest) vertiginoso; feel ~ avere le vertigini

gift /ɡɪft/ n dono m; (to charity) donazione f. ~**ed** adj dotato. ~**-wrap** vt impacchettare in carta da regalo

gig /ɡɪg/ n (Mus) ① concerto m

gigantic /dʒaɪˈɡæntɪk/ adj gigantesco

giggle /'ɡɪgl/ n risatina f ●vi ridacchiare

gild /ɡɪld/ vt dorare

gills /ɡɪlz/ npl branchia fsg

gilt /ɡɪlt/ adj dorato ●n doratura f. ~**-edged stock** n investimento m sicuro

gimmick /'ɡɪmɪk/ n trovata f

gin /dʒɪn/ n gin m inv

ginger /'dʒɪndʒə(r)/ adj rosso fuoco inv; (cat) rosso ●n zenzero m. ~ **ale** n, ~ **beer** n bibita f allo zenzero. ~**bread** n panpepato m

gipsy /'dʒɪpsɪ/ n = gypsy

giraffe /dʒɪˈrɑːf/ n giraffa f

girder /'ɡɜːdə(r)/ n (Techn) trave f

girl /ɡɜːl/ n ragazza f; (female child) femmina f. ~**band** n girl band f inv. ~**friend** n amica f; (of boy) ragazza f

~**ish** adj da ragazza

giro /'dʒaɪərəʊ/ n bancogiro m; (cheque) sussidio m di disoccupazione

girth /ɡɜːθ/ n circonferenza f

gist /dʒɪst/ n **the** ~ la sostanza

give /ɡɪv/ n elasticità f ●v (pt gave, pp given) vt dare; (as present) regalare (to a); fare (lecture, present, shriek); donare (blood); ~ **birth** partorire ●vi (to charity) fare delle donazioni; (yield) cedere. ~ **away** vt dar via; (betray) tradire; (distribute) assegnare; ~ **away the bride** portare la sposa all'altare. □~ **back** vt restituire. □~ **in** vt consegnare ●vi (yield) arrendersi. □~ **off** vt emanare. □~ **over** vi overi piantala!. □~ **up** vt rinunciare a; ~ **oneself up** arrendersi ●vi rinunciare. □~ **way** vi cedere; (Auto) dare la precedenza; (collapse) crollare

given /'ɡɪvn/ ▷**GIVE** ●adj ~ **name** nome m di battesimo

glacier /'ɡlæsɪə(r)/ n ghiacciaio m

glad /ɡlæd/ adj contento (of di). ~**den** vt rallegrare

gladly /'ɡlædlɪ/ adv volentieri

glamour /'ɡlæmə(r)/ n fascino m

glance /ɡlɑːns/ n sguardo m ●vi ~ **at** dare un'occhiata a. □~ **up** vi alzare gli occhi

gland /ɡlænd/ n glandola f

glare /ɡleə(r)/ n bagliore m; (look) occhiataccia f ●vi ~ **at** dare un'occhiataccia a

glaring /'ɡleərɪŋ/ adj sfolgorante; (mistake) madornale

glass /ɡlɑːs/ n vetro m; (for drinking) bicchiere m; ~**es** (pl: spectacles) occhiali mpl. ~**y** adj vitreo

glaze /ɡleɪz/ n smalto m ●vt mettere i vetri a (door, window); smaltare (pottery); (Culin) spennellare. ~**d** adj (eyes) vitreo

gleam /gliːm/ n luccichio m • vi luccicare

glean /gliːn/ vt racimolare (information)

glee /gliː/ n gioia f. ~**ful** adj gioioso

glib /glɪb/ adj pej insincero

glid|e /glaɪd/ vi scorrere; (through the
air) planare. ~**er** n aliante m

glimmer /ˈglɪmə(r)/ n barlume m
• vi emettere un barlume

glimpse /glɪmps/ n catch a ~ of
intravedere • vt intravedere

glint /glɪnt/ n luccichio • vi luccicare

glisten /ˈglɪsn/ vi luccicare

glitter /ˈglɪtə(r)/ vi brillare

gloat /gləʊt/ vi gongolare (over su)

global /ˈgləʊbl/ adj mondiale.
~**ization** n globalizzazione f

globe /gləʊb/ n globo m; (map) map-
pamondo m

gloom /gluːm/ n oscurità f; (sadness)
tristezza f. ~**ily** adv (sadly) con
aria cupa

gloomy /ˈgluːmɪ/ adj (-ier,
-iest) cupo

glorif|y /ˈglɔːrɪfaɪ/ vt (pt/pp -ied)
glorificare; a ~**ied** waitress niente
più che una cameriera

glorious /ˈglɔːrɪəs/ adj splendido;
(deed, hero) glorioso

glory /ˈglɔːrɪ/ n gloria f; (splendour)
splendore m; (cause for pride) vanto m
• vi (pt/pp -ied) n ~ in vantarsi di

gloss /glɒs/ n lucentezza f. ~ **paint**
n vernice f lucida • **gloss over** vt sor-
volare su

glossary /ˈglɒsərɪ/ n glossario m

glossy /ˈglɒsɪ/ adj (-ier, -iest) lucido;
~ [**magazine**] rivista f femminile

glove /glʌv/ n guanto m. ~ **compartment** n (Auto) cruscotto m

glow /gləʊ/ n (in cheeks) rossore m; (of
candle) luce f soffusa • vi risplendere;
(candle:) brillare; (person:) avvampare.
~**ing** adj ardente; (account) entusiastico.

~**worm** n lucciola f

glucose /ˈgluːkəʊs/ n glucosio m

glue /gluː/ n colla f • vt (pres p glu-
ing) incollare

glum /glʌm/ adj (glummer, glum-
mest) tetro

glutton /ˈglʌtən/ n ghiottone, -a mf.
~**ous** adj ghiotto. ~**y** n ghiotto-
neria f

gnarled /nɑːld/ adj nodoso

gnash /næʃ/ vt ~ one's teeth digrignare i denti

gnaw /nɔː/ vt rosicchiare

go¹ /gəʊ/ n (pl goes) energia f; (attempt) tentativo m; on the go in movimento; at one go in una sola
volta; it's your go tocca a te; make
a go of it riuscire

---

go² /gəʊ/

---

3 sing pres tense **goes**, past tense
went, past participle **gone**

• vi andare; (leave) andar via; (vanish) sparire; (become) diventare;
(be sold) vendersi; go and see
andare a vedere; go swim-
ming/shopping andare a
nuotare/fare spese; where's
the time gone? come ha fatto
il tempo a volare così?; it's all
gone è finito; be going to do
stare per fare; I'm not going to
non ne ho nessuna intenzione;
to go (🍴 hamburgers etc) da
asporto; a coffee to go un
caffè da portar via. □ ~ **about**
vi andare in giro. □ ~ **away** vi
andarsene. □ ~ **back** vi ritornare. □ ~ **by** vi passare. □ ~
down vi scendere; (sun:) tramontare; (ship:) affondare;
(swelling:) diminuire. □ ~ **for** vt
andare a prendere; andare a
cercare (doctor); (choose) optare
per; (🍴 attack) aggredire; he's

not the kind I go for non è il genere che mi attira. □~ **in** vi entrare. □~ **in for** vt partecipare a (competition); darsi a (tennis). □~ **off** vi andarsene; (alarm:) scattare; (gun, bomb:) esplodere; (food, milk:) andare a male; go off well riuscire. □~ **on** vi andare avanti; what's going on? cosa succede? go on at vt 1 scocciare. □~ **out** vi uscire; (light, fire:) spegnersi. □~ **over** vi andare ● vt (check) controllare. □~ **round** vi andare in giro; (visit) andare; (turn) girare; is there enough to go round? ce n'è abbastanza per tutti? **go through** vi (bill, proposal:) passare ● vt (suffer) subire; (check) controllare; (read) leggere. □~ **under** vi passare sotto; (ship, swimmer:) andare sott'acqua; (fail) fallire. □~ **up** vi salire; (Theat: curtain:) aprirsi. □~ **with** vt accompagnare. □~ **without** vt fare a meno di (supper, sleep) ● vi fare senza

goad /gəʊd/ vt spingere (into a); (taunt) spronare

'**go-ahead** adj (person, company) intraprendente ● n okay m

goal /gəʊl/ n porta f; (point scored) gol m inv; (in life) obiettivo m; score a ~ segnare. ~**ie** 1, ~**keeper** n portiere m. ~**post** n palo m

goat /gəʊt/ n capra f

gobble /'gɒbl/ vt ~ [down, up] tranguiare

God, god /gɒd/ n Dio m, dio m

god: ~**child** n figlioccio m, -a mf. ~**daughter** n figlioccia f. ~**dess** /'gɒdes/ n dea f. ~**father** n padrino m. ~**forsaken** /'gɒdfəseɪkən/ adj dimenticato da Dio. ~**mother** n madrina f. ~**send** n manna f. ~**son** n figlioccio m

going /'gəʊɪŋ/ adj (price, rate) corrente; ~ concern azienda f florida

● n it's hard ~ è una faticaccia; while the ~ is good finché si può. ~**s-'on** npl avvenimenti mpl

gold /gəʊld/ n oro m ● adj d'oro

golden /'gəʊldn/ adj dorato. ~ 'handshake n buonuscita f (al termine di un rapporto di lavoro). ~ **mean** n giusto mezzo m. ~ '**wedding** n nozze fpl d'oro

gold: ~**fish** n inv pesce m rosso. ~**mine** n miniera f d'oro. ~**plated** adj placcato d'oro. ~**smith** n orefice m

golf /gɒlf/ n golf m

golf: ~**club** n circolo m di golf; (implement) mazza f da golf. ~**course** n campo m di golf. ~**er** n giocatore, -trice mf di golf

gondola /'gɒndələ/ n gondola f. ~**lier** n gondoliere m

gone /gɒn/ ▷**GO**

gong /gɒŋ/ n gong m inv

good /gʊd/ adj (better, best) buono; (child, footballer, singer) bravo; (holiday, film) bello; ~ at bravo in; a ~ deal of anger molta rabbia; as ~ as (almost) quasi; ~ morning, ~ afternoon buon giorno; ~ evening buona sera; ~ **night** buonanotte; have a ~ time divertirsi ● n good; for ~ per sempre; do ~ far del bene; do sb a ~ turn far del bene; it's no ~ è inutile; be up to no ~ combinare qualcosa

goodbye /gʊd'baɪ/ int arrivederci

good: ~**for-nothing** n buono, -a mf a nulla. G~ '**Friday** n Venerdì m Santo

good-'looking adj bello

goodness /'gʊdnɪs/ n bontà f; my ~! santo cielo!; thank ~! grazie al cielo!

goods /gʊdz/ npl prodotti mpl. ~ **train** n treno m merci

good'will n buona volontà f; (Comm) avviamento m

goody /'gʊdɪ/ n (🔲: person) buono m. ~-**goody** n santarellino, -a mf

gooey /'guːɪ/ adj 🔲 appiccicaticcio; fig sdolcinato

google /'guːgl/ vt/i googlare

goose /guːs/: ~-**flesh** n, ~-**pimples** npl pelle fsg d'oca

gooseberry /'gʊzbərɪ/ n uva f spina

gore[1] /gɔː(r)/ n sangue m

gore[2] vt incornare

gorge /gɔːdʒ/ n (Geog) gola f ● vt ~ oneself ingozzarsi

gorgeous /'gɔːdʒəs/ adj stupendo

gorilla /gə'rɪlə/ n gorilla m inv

gorse /gɔːs/ n ginestrone m

gory /'gɔːrɪ/ adj (-ier, -iest) cruento

gosh /gɒʃ/ int 🔲 caspita

gospel /'gɒspl/ n vangelo m. ~ **truth** n sacrosanta verità f

gossip /'gɒsɪp/ n pettegolezzi mpl; (person) pettegolo, -a mf ● vi pettegolare. ~**y** adj pettegolo

got /gɒt/ ▷ GET; **have** ~ avere; **have** ~ **to do** sth dover fare qcsa

gotten /'gɒtn/ Am see GET

gouge /gaʊdʒ/ vt ~ **out** cavare

gourmet /'gʊəmeɪ/ n buongustaio, -a mf

govern /'gʌv(ə)n/ vt/i governare; (determine) determinare

government /'gʌvnmənt/ n governo m. ~**al** adj governativo

governor /'gʌvənə(r)/ n governatore m; (of school) membro m del consiglio di istituto; (of prison) direttore, -trice mf; (🔲: boss) capo m

gown /gaʊn/ n vestito m; (Jur, Univ) toga f

GP n abbr general practitioner

GPS abbr (Global Positioning System) GPS m

grab /græb/ vt (pt/pp grabbed) ~ [hold of] afferrare

grace /greɪs/ n grazia f; (before meal) benedicite m inv; **with good** ~ volentieri; **three days'** ~ tre giorni di proroga. ~**ful** adj aggraziato. ~**fully** adv con grazia

gracious /'greɪʃəs/ adj cortese; (elegant) lussuoso

grade /greɪd/ n livello m; (Comm) qualità f; (Sch) voto m; (Am Sch: class) classe f; Am = **gradient** ● vt (Comm) classificare; (Sch) dare il voto a. ~ **crossing** n Am passaggio m a livello

gradient /'greɪdɪənt/ n pendenza f

gradual /'grædʒʊəl/ adj graduale. ~**ly** adv gradualmente

graduate[1] /'grædʒʊət/ n laureato, -a mf

graduate[2] /'grædʒʊeɪt/ vi (Univ) laurearsi

graduation /grædʒʊ'eɪʃn/ n laurea f

graffiti /grə'fiːtɪ/ npl graffiti mpl

graft /grɑːft/ n (Bot, Med) innesto m; (Med: organ) trapianto m; (🔲: hard work) duro lavoro m; (🔲: corruption) corruzione f ● vt innestare; trapiantare (organ)

grain /greɪn/ n (of sand, salt) granello m; (of rice) chicco m; (cereals) cereali mpl; (in wood) venatura f; **it goes against the** ~ fig è contro la mia/sua natura

gram /græm/ n grammo m

grammar /'græmə(r)/ n grammatica f. ~ **school** n ≈ liceo m

grammatical /grə'mætɪkl/ adj grammaticale

grand /grænd/ adj grandioso; (🔲: excellent) eccellente

'**grandchild** n nipote mf

'**granddaughter** n nipote f

grandeur /'grændʒə(r)/ n grandiosità f

'**grandfather** n nonno m. ~ **clock** n pendolo m (che poggia a terra)

grandiose /'grændɪəʊs/ adj

grandioso

grand: ~**mother** n nonna f. ~**parents** npl nonni mpl. ~**pi'ano** n pianoforte m a coda. ~**son** n nipote m. ~**stand** n tribuna f

granite /'grænɪt/ n granito m

granny /'grænɪ/ n 🔲 nonna f

grant /grɑːnt/ n (money) sussidio m; (Univ) borsa f di studio ● vt accordare; (admit) ammettere; **take sth for** ~**ed** dare per scontato qcsa

granule /'grænjuːl/ n granello m

grape /greɪp/ n acino m; ~**s** pl uva fsg

grapefruit /'greɪpfruːt/ n inv pompelmo m

graph /grɑːf/ n grafico m

graphic /'græfɪk/ adj grafico; (vivid) vivido. ~**s** n grafica f

grapple /'græpl/ vi ~ **with** also fig essere alle prese con

grasp /grɑːsp/ n stretta f; (understanding) comprensione f ● vt afferrare. ~**ing** adj avido

grass /grɑːs/ n erba f; **at the** ~ **roots** alla base. ~**hopper** n cavalletta f. ~**land** n prateria f

grassy /'grɑːsɪ/ adj erboso

grate[1] /greɪt/ n grata f

grate[2] (Culin) grattugiare ● vi stridere

grateful /'greɪtfl/ adj grato. ~**ly** adv con gratitudine

grater /'greɪtə(r)/ n (Culin) grattugia f

gratif|y /'grætɪfaɪ/ vt (pt/pp -ied) appagare. ~**ied** adj appagato. ~**ying** adj appagante

grating /'greɪtɪŋ/ n grata f

gratitude /'grætɪtjuːd/ n gratitudine f

gratuitous /grə'tjuːɪtəs/ adj gratuito

gratuity /grə'tjuːɪtɪ/ n gratifica f

grave[1] /greɪv/ adj grave

grave[2] n tomba f

gravel /'grævl/ n ghiaia f

grave: ~**stone** n lapide f. ~**yard** n cimitero m

gravitate /'grævɪteɪt/ vi gravitare

gravity /'grævɪtɪ/ n gravità f

gravy /'greɪvɪ/ n sugo m della carne

gray /greɪ/ adj Am = grey

graze[1] /greɪz/ vi (animal:) pascolare

graze[2] n escoriazione f ● vt (touch lightly) sfiorare; (scrape) escoriare; sbucciarsi (knee)

grease /griːs/ n grasso m ● vt ungere. ~**proof** '**paper** n carta f oleata

greasy /'griːsɪ/ adj (-ier, -iest) untuoso; (hair, skin) grasso

great /greɪt/ adj grande; (🔲: marvellous) eccezionale

great: **G~** '**Britain** n Gran Bretagna f. ~'**grandfather** n bisnonno m. ~'**grandmother** n bisnonna f

great|ly /'greɪtlɪ/ adv enormemente. ~**ness** n grandezza f

Greece /griːs/ n Grecia f

greed /griːd/ n avidità f; (for food) ingordigia f

greedy /'griːdɪ/ adj (-ier, -iest) avido; (for food) ingordo

Greek /griːk/ adj & n greco, -a mf; (language) greco m

green /griːn/ adj verde; (fig: inexperienced) immaturo ● n verde m; ~**s** pl verdura f; **the G~s** pl (Pol) i verdi. ~ **belt** n zona f verde intorno a una città. ~ **card** n (Auto) carta f verde

---

Green Card Negli Stati Uniti è un documento ufficiale che concede a qualsiasi persona priva della cittadinanza americana il permesso di risiedere e lavorare indefinitamente negli Stati Uniti. Nel Regno Unito, invece, è un documento che i conducenti o proprietari di autoveicoli devono richiedere alla propria compagnia di assicurazione per convalidare la polizza in occasione di viaggi all'estero.

greenery /'gri:nərɪ/ n verde m

green: ~**grocer** n fruttivendolo, -a mf. ~**house** n serra f. ~**house effect** n effetto m serra. ~ **light** n 1 verde m

greet /gri:t/ vt salutare; (welcome) accogliere. ~**ing** n saluto m; (welcome) accoglienza f. ~**ings card** n biglietto m d'auguri

gregarious /grɪ'geərɪəs/ adj gregario; (person) socievole

grenade /grɪ'neɪd/ n granata f

grew /gru:/ ▷GROW

grey /greɪ/ adj grigio; (hair) bianco ● n grigio m. ~**hound** n levriero m

grid /grɪd/ n griglia f; (on map) reticolato m; (Electr) rete f

grief /gri:f/ n dolore m; come to ~ (plans) naufragare

grievance /'gri:vəns/ n lamentela f

grieve /gri:v/ vt addolorare ● vi essere addolorato

grill /grɪl/ n graticola f; (for grilling) griglia f; **mixed** ~ grigliata f mista ● vt/i cuocere alla griglia; (interrogate) sottoporre al terzo grado

grille /grɪl/ n grata f

grim /grɪm/ adj (grimmer, grimmest) arcigno; (determination) accanito

grimace /grɪ'meɪs/ n smorfia f ● vi fare una smorfia

grime /graɪm/ n sudiciume m

grimy /'graɪmɪ/ adj (-ier, -iest) sudicio

grin /grɪn/ n sorriso m ● vi (pt/pp grinned) fare un gran sorriso

grind /graɪnd/ n (1: hard work) sfacchinata f ● vt (pt/pp ground) macinare; affilare (knife); (Am: mince) tritare; ~ **one's teeth** digrignare

i denti

grip /grɪp/ n presa f; fig controllo m; (bag) borsone m; **get a** ~ **on oneself** controllarsi ● vt (pt/pp gripped) afferrare; (tyres:) far presa su; tenere avvinto (attention)

grisly /'grɪzlɪ/ adj (-ier, -iest) raccapricciante

gristle /'grɪsl/ n cartilagine f

grit /grɪt/ n graniglia f; (for roads) sabbia f; (courage) coraggio m ● vt (pt/pp gritted) spargere sabbia su (road); ~ **one's teeth** serrare i denti

groan /grəʊn/ n gemito m ● vi gemere

grocer /'grəʊsə(r)/ n droghiere, -a mf; ~**'s** [shop] drogheria f. ~**ies** npl generi mpl alimentari

groggy /'grɒgɪ/ adj (-ier, -iest) stordito; (unsteady) barcollante

groin /grɔɪn/ n (Anat) inguine m

groom /gru:m/ n sposo m; (for horse) stalliere m ● vt strigliare (horse); fig preparare; **well-**~**ed** ben curato

groove /gru:v/ n scanalatura f

grope /grəʊp/ vi brancolare; ~ **for** cercare a tastoni

gross /grəʊs/ adj obeso; (coarse) volgare; (glaring) grossolano; (salary, weight) lordo ● inv grossa f. ~**ly** adv (very) enormemente

grotesque /grəʊ'tesk/ adj grottesco

ground¹ /graʊnd/ ▷GRIND

ground² n terra f; (Sport) terreno m; (reason) ragione f; ~**s** pl (park) giardini mpl; (of coffee) fondi mpl ● vi (ship:) arenarsi ● vt bloccare a terra (aircraft); Am (Electr) mettere a terra

ground: ~ **floor** n pianterreno m. ~**ing** n base f. ~**less** adj infondato. ~**sheet** n telone m impermeabile. ~**work** n lavoro m di preparazione

group /gru:p/ n gruppo m ● vt raggruppare ● vi raggrupparsi

grouse¹ /graʊs/ n inv gallo m

cedrone

grouse² vi 🗌 brontolare

grovel /'grɒvl/ vi (pt/pp grovelled) strisciare. ~**ling** adj leccapiedi inv

grow /grəʊ/ v (pt grew, pp grown) ● vi crescere; (become) diventare; (un-employment, fear:) aumentare; (town:) ingrandirsi ● vt coltivare; ~ one's hair farsi crescere i capelli. □ ~ **up** vi crescere; (town:) svilupparsi

growl /graʊl/ n grugnito m ● vi ringhiare

grown /grəʊn/ ▷GROW ● adj adulto. ~-**up** adj & n adulto, -a mf

growth /grəʊθ/ n crescita f; (increase) aumento m; (Med) tumore m

grub /grʌb/ n larva f; (🗌: food) mangiare m

grubby /'grʌbɪ/ adj (-ier, -iest) sporco

grudge /grʌdʒ/ n rancore m; bear sb a ~e portare rancore a qcno ● vt dare a malincuore. ~**ing** adj reluttante. ~**ingly** adv a malincuore

gruelling /'gruːəlɪŋ/ adj estenuante

gruesome /'gruːsəm/ adj macabro

gruff /grʌf/ adj burbero

grumble /'grʌmbl/ vi brontolare (at over)

grumpy /'grʌmpɪ/ adj (-ier, -iest) scorbutico

grunt /grʌnt/ n grugnito m ● vi fare un grugnito

guarant|ee /gærən'tiː/ n garanzia f ● vt garantire. ~**or** n garante mf

guard /gɑːd/ n guardia f; (security) guardiano m; (on train) capotreno m; (Techn) schermo m protettivo; be on ~ essere di guardia ● vt sorvegliare; (protect) proteggere. □ ~ **against** vt guardarsi da. ~**dog** n cane m da guardia

guarded /'gɑːdɪd/ adj guardingo

guardian /'gɑːdɪən/ n (of minor) tutore, -trice mf

guerrilla /gə'rɪlə/ n guerrigliero, -a mf. ~ **warfare** n guerriglia f

guess /ges/ n supposizione f ● vt indovinare ● vi indovinare; (Am: suppose) supporre. ~**work** n supposizione f

guest /gest/ n ospite mf; (in hotel) cliente mf. ~-**house** n pensione f

guffaw /gʌ'fɔː/ n sghignazzata f ● vi sghignazzare

guidance /'gaɪdəns/ n guida f; (advice) consigli mpl

guide /gaɪd/ n guida f; [Girl] G~ giovane esploratrice f ● vt guidare. ~**book** n guida f turistica

guide: ~-**dog** n cane m per ciechi. ~-**lines** npl direttive fpl

guild /gɪld/ n corporazione f

guile /gaɪl/ n astuzia f

guillotine /'gɪlətiːn/ n ghigliottina f; (for paper) taglierina f

guilt /gɪlt/ n colpa f. ~**ily** adv con aria colpevole

guilty /'gɪltɪ/ adj (-ier, -iest) colpevole; have a ~ conscience avere la coscienza sporca

guinea-pig /'gɪnɪ-/ n porcellino m d'India; (fig: used for experiments) cavia f

guitar /gɪ'tɑː(r)/ n chitarra f. ~**ist** n chitarrista m

gulf /gʌlf/ n (Geog) golfo m; fig abisso m

gull /gʌl/ n gabbiano m

gullet /'gʌlɪt/ n esofago m; (throat) gola f

gullible /'gʌlɪbl/ adj credulone

gully /'gʌlɪ/ n burrone m; (drain) canale m di scolo

gulp /gʌlp/ n azione f di deglutire; (of food) boccone m; (of liquid) sorso m ● vi deglutire. □ ~ **down** vt trangugiare (food); scolarsi (liquid)

gum¹ /gʌm/ n (Anat) gengiva f

gum² n gomma f; (chewing gum) gomma f da masticare, chewing gum m inv ● vt (pt/pp gummed) ingommare (**to a**)

gun /gʌn/ n pistola f; (rifle) fucile m; (cannon) cannone m ● **gun down** vt (pt/pp **gunned**) freddare

gun: ~**fire** n spari mpl; (of cannon) colpi mpl [di cannone]. ~**man** uomo m armato

gun: ~**powder** n polvere f da sparo. ~**shot** n colpo m [di pistola]

gurgle /ˈgɜːgl/ vi gorgogliare; (baby:) fare degli urletti

gush /gʌʃ/ vi sgorgare; (enthuse) parlare con troppo entusiasmo (over di). □ ~ **out** vi sgorgare. ~**ing** adj eccessivamente entusiastico

gust /gʌst/ n (of wind) raffica f

gusto /ˈgʌstəʊ/ n **with** ~ con trasporto

gusty /ˈgʌsti/ adj ventoso

gut /gʌt/ n intestino m; ~**s** pl pancia f; (🄵: courage) fegato m ● vt (pt/pp **gutted**) (Culin) svuotare delle interiora; ~**ted by fire** sventrato da un incendio

gutter /ˈgʌtə(r)/ n canale m di scolo; (on roof) grondaia f; fig bassifondi mpl

guttural /ˈgʌtərəl/ adj gutturale

guy /gaɪ/ n 🄵 tipo m, tizio m

guzzle /ˈgʌzl/ vt ingozzarsi con (food); **he's ~d the lot** si è sbafato tutto

gym /dʒɪm/ n 🄵 palestra f; (gymnastics) ginnastica f

gymnasium /dʒɪmˈneɪzɪəm/ n palestra f

gymnast /ˈdʒɪmnæst/ n ginnasta mf. ~**ics** n ginnastica f

gymslip /n (Sch) ≈ grembiule m (da bambina)

gynaecolog|ist /gaɪnɪˈkɒlədʒɪst/ n ginecologo, -a mf. ~**y** n ginecologia f

gypsy /ˈdʒɪpsi/ n zingaro, -a mf

gyrate /dʒaɪˈreɪt/ vi roteare

Hh

haberdashery /hæbəˈdæʃərɪ/ n merceria f; Am negozio m d'abbigliamento da uomo

habit /ˈhæbɪt/ n abitudine f; (Relig: costume) tonaca f; **be in the** ~ **of doing sth** avere l'abitudine di fare qcsa

habitable /ˈhæbɪtəbl/ adj abitabile

habitat /ˈhæbɪtæt/ n habitat m inv

habitation /hæbɪˈteɪʃn/ n **unfit for human** ~ inagibile

habitual /həˈbɪtjʊəl/ adj abituale; (smoker, liar) inveterato. ~**ly** adv regolarmente

hack[1] /hæk/ n (writer) scribacchino, -a mf

hack[2] vt tagliare; ~ **to pieces** tagliare a pezzi

hackneyed /ˈhæknɪd/ adj trito [e ritrito]

had /hæd/ ▷HAVE

haddock /ˈhædək/ n inv eglefino m

haemorrhage /ˈhemərɪdʒ/ n emorragia f

haemorrhoids /ˈhemərɔɪdz/ npl emorroidi fpl

hag /hæg/ n **old** ~ vecchia befana f

haggard /ˈhægəd/ adj sfatto

hail[1] /heɪl/ vt salutare; far segno a (taxi) ● vi ~ **from** provenire da

hail[2] n grandine f ● vi grandinare. ~**stone** n chicco m di grandine. ~**storm** n grandinata f

hair /heə(r)/ n capelli mpl; (on body, of animal) pelo m

hair: ~**brush** n spazzola f per capelli. ~**cut** n taglio m di capelli; **have a** ~**cut** farsi tagliare i capelli. ~**do** n 🄵 pettinatura f. ~**dresser** n parrucchiere, -a mf. ~**dryer** n fon m *inv*; (with hood) casco m [asciugaca-pelli]. ~**grip** n molletta f. ~**pin** n forcina f. ~**pin 'bend** n tornante m, curva f a gomito. ~**raising** adj terrificante. ~**style** n acconciatura f

hairy /ˈheərɪ/ adj (-ier, -iest) peloso; (🗊: *frightening*) spaventoso

half /hɑːf/ n (pl **halves**) metà f inv; **cut in** ~ tagliare a metà; **one and a** ~ uno e mezzo; ~ **a dozen** mezza dozzina; ~ **an hour** mezz'ora ● adj mezzo; [at] ~ **price** [a] metà prezzo ● adv a metà; ~ **past two** le due e mezza

half: ~**'hearted** adj esitante. ~**'mast** n at ~ **mast** a mezz'asta. ~**'term** n vacanza f di metà trimestre. ~**'time** n (Sport) intervallo m. ~**'way** adj the ~**way mark/stage** il livello intermedio ● adv a metà strada; **get** ~**way** fig arrivare a metà

hall /hɔːl/ n (entrance) ingresso m; (room) sala f; (mansion) residenza f di campagna; ~ **of residence** (Univ) casa f dello studente

'hallmark n marchio m di garanzia; fig marchio m

hallo /hə'ləʊ/ int ciao!; (on telephone) pronto!; **say** ~ to salutare

Hallowe'en /hæləʊ'iːn/ n vigilia f d'Ognissanti e notte delle streghe, celebrata soprattutto dai bambini

hallucination /həluːsɪ'neɪʃn/ n allucinazione f

halo /ˈheɪləʊ/ n (pl -es) aureola f; (Astr) alone m

halt /hɔːlt/ n alt m inv; **come to a** ~ fermarsi; (traffic:) bloccarsi ● vi fermarsi; ~**! alt!** ● vt fermare. ~**ing** adj esitante

halve /hɑːv/ vt dividere a metà; (reduce) dimezzare

ham /hæm/ n prosciutto m; (Theat) attore, -trice mf da strapazzo

hamburger /ˈhæmbɜːɡə(r)/ n hamburger m inv

hammer /ˈhæmə(r)/ n martello m ● vt martellare ● vi ~ **at/on** picchiare a

hammock /ˈhæmək/ n amaca f

hamper¹ /ˈhæmpə(r)/ n cesto m; [gift] ~ cestino m

hamper² vt ostacolare

hamster /ˈhæmstə(r)/ n criceto m

hand /hænd/ n mano f; (of clock) lancetta f; (writing) scrittura f; (worker) manovale m; **at** ~, **to** ~ a portata di mano; **on the one** ~ da un lato; **on the other** ~ d'altra parte; **out of** ~ (uncontrollable; (summarily) su due piedi; **give sb a** ~ dare una mano a qcno ● vt porgere. □ ~ **down** vt tramandare. □ ~ **in** vt consegnare. □ ~ **out** vt distribuire. □ ~ **over** vt passare; (to police) consegnare

hand: ~**bag** n borsa f (da signora). ~**brake** n freno m a mano. ~**cuffs** npl manette fpl. ~**ful** n manciata f; **be** [quite] a ~**ful** 🗊 essere difficile da tenere a freno

handicap /ˈhændɪkæp/ n handicap m inv. ~**ped** adj **mentally/physically** ~**ped** mentalmente/fisicamente handicappato

handi|craft /ˈhændɪkrɑːft/ n artigianato m. ~**work** n opera f

handkerchief /ˈhæŋkətʃɪf/ n (pl ~s & -**chieves**) fazzoletto m

handle /ˈhændl/ n manico m; (of door) maniglia f; **fly off the** ~ 🗊 perdere le staffe ● vt maneggiare; occuparsi di (problem, customer); prendere (difficult person); trattare (subject). ~**bars** npl manubrio m

hand: ~**out** n (at lecture) foglio m informativo; (🗊: money) elemosina f. ~**shake** n stretta f di mano

handsome /ˈhænsəm/ adj bello; (fig: generous) generoso

handwriting n calligrafia f

handy /ˈhændɪ/ adj (-ier, -iest) utile; (person) abile; **have/keep** ~ avere/ tenere a portata di mano. ~**man** n tuttofare m inv

hang /hæŋ/ vt (pt/pp **hung**) appendere (picture); (pt/pp **hanged**) impiccare (criminal); ~ **oneself** impiccarsi ● vi (pt/pp **hung**) pendere; (hair): scendere ● n **get the** ~ **of it** 🔳 afferrare. □ ~ **about** vi gironzolare. □ ~ **on** vi tenersi stretto; (🔳: wait) aspettare; (Teleph) restare in linea. □ ~ **on to** vt tenersi stretto a; (keep) tenere. □ ~ **out** vi spuntare; **where does he usually** ~ **out?** 🔳 dove bazzica di solito? ● vt stendere (washing). □ ~ **up** vt appendere; (Teleph) riattaccare ● vi essere appeso; (Teleph) riattaccare

hangar /ˈhæŋə(r)/ n (Aeron) hangar m inv

hanger /ˈhæŋə(r)/ n gruccia f. ~**-on** n leccapiedi mf

hang: ~**glider** n deltaplano m. ~**over** n 🔳 postumi mpl da sbornia. ~**up** n 🔳 complesso m

hanky /ˈhæŋkɪ/ n 🔳 fazzoletto m

haphazard /hæpˈhæzəd/ adj a casaccio

happen /ˈhæpn/ vi capitare, succedere; **as it** ~**s** per caso; **I** ~**ed to meet him** mi è capitato di incontrarlo; **what has** ~**ed to him?** cosa gli è capitato?; (become of) che fine ha fatto? ~**ing** n avvenimento m

happi|ly /ˈhæpɪlɪ/ adv felicemente; (fortunately) fortunatamente. ~**ness** n felicità f

happy /ˈhæpɪ/ adj (-ier, -iest) contento, felice. ~**go-lucky** adj spensierato

harass /ˈhærəs/ vt perseguitare. ~**ed** adj stressato. ~**ment** n persecuzione f; sexual ~**ment** molestie fpl sessuali

harbour /ˈhɑːbə(r)/ n porto m ● vt dare asilo a; nutrire (grudge)

hard /hɑːd/ adj duro; (question, problem) difficile; ~ **of hearing** duro d'orecchi; **be** ~ **on sb** (person) essere duro con qcno ● adv (work) duramente; (pull, hit, rain,

snow) forte; ~ **hit by unemployment** duramente colpito dalla disoccupazione; **take sth** ~ non accettare qcsa; **think** ~! pensaci bene!; **try** ~ mettercela tutta; **try** ~**er** metterci più impegno; ~ **done by** 🔳 trattato ingiustamente

hard: **hard-boiled** adj (egg) sodo. ~ **disk** n hard disk m inv, disco m rigido

harden /ˈhɑːdn/ vi indurirsi

hard: ~**headed** adj (businessman) dal sangue freddo. ~**line** adj duro

hard|ly /ˈhɑːdlɪ/ adv appena; ~**ly ever** quasi mai. ~**ness** n durezza f. ~**ship** n avversità f inv

hard: ~ **'shoulder** n (Auto) corsia f d'emergenza. ~**ware** n ferramenta fpl; (Comput) hardware m inv. ~**working** adj **be** ~**working** essere un gran lavoratore

hardy /ˈhɑːdɪ/ adj (-ier, -iest) dal fisico resistente; (plant) che sopporta il gelo

hare /heə(r)/ n lepre f. ~**brained** adj 🔳 (scheme) da scervellati

hark /hɑːk/ vi ~ **back to** fig ritornare su

harm /hɑːm/ n male m; (damage) danni mpl; **out of** ~**'s way** in un posto sicuro; **it won't do any** ~ non farà certo male a; vt far male a; (damage) danneggiare. ~**ful** adj dannoso. ~**less** adj innocuo

harmonica /hɑːˈmɒnɪkə/ n armonica f [a bocca]

harmonious /hɑːˈməʊnɪəs/ adj armonioso. ~**ly** adv in armonia

harness /ˈhɑːnɪs/ n finimenti mpl; (of parachute) imbracatura f ● vt bardare (horse); sfruttare (resources)

harp /hɑːp/ n arpa f ● **harp on** vi 🔳 insistere (about su). ~**ist** n arpista mf

harpoon /hɑːˈpuːn/ n arpione m

harpsichord /ˈhɑːpsɪkɔːd/ n clavicembalo m

harrowing /ˈhærəʊɪŋ/ adj straziante

harsh /hɑːʃ/ adj duro; (light) abbagliante. ~**ness** n durezza f

harvest /ˈhɑːvɪst/ n raccolta f; (of grapes) vendemmia f; (crop) raccolto m ● vt raccogliere

has /hæz/ ▷ HAVE

hassle /ˈhæsl/ 🔲 n rottura f ● vt rompere le scatole a

haste /heɪst/ n fretta f

hast|y /ˈheɪstɪ/ adj (-ier, -iest) frettoloso; (decision) affrettato. ~**ily** adv frettolosamente

hat /hæt/ n cappello m

hatch[1] /hætʃ/ n (for food) sportello m passavivande; (Naut) boccaporto m

hatch[2] vi ~[out] rompere il guscio; (egg:) schiudersi ● vt covare; tramare (plot)

ˈhatchback n tre/cinque porte m inv; (door) porta f del bagagliaio

hatchet /ˈhætʃɪt/ n ascia f

hate /heɪt/ n odio m ● vt odiare. ~**ful** adj odioso

hatred /ˈheɪtrɪd/ n odio m

haught|y /ˈhɔːtɪ/ adj (-ier, -iest) altezzoso. ~**ily** adv altezzosamente

haul /hɔːl/ n (fish) pescata f; (loot) bottino m; (pull) tirata f ● vt tirare; trasportare (goods) ● vi ~ on tirare. ~**age** n trasporto m. ~**ier** n autotrasportatore m

haunt /hɔːnt/ n ritrovo m ● vt frequentare; (linger in the mind) perseguitare; this house is ~ed questa casa è abitata dai fantasmi

have /hæv/

● vt (3 sg pres tense has; pt/pp had) avere; fare (breakfast, bath, walk etc); ~ a drink bere qualcosa; ~ lunch/dinner pranzare/cenare; ~ a rest riposarsi; I had my hair cut mi sono tagliata i capelli; we had the house painted abbiamo fatto tinteggiare la casa; I had it made l'ho fatto fare; ~ to do sth dover fare qcsa; ~ him telephone me tomorrow digli di telefonarmi domani; he has or he's got two houses ha due case; you've got the money, ~n't you? hai i soldi, no?

● v aux avere; (with verbs of motion & some others) essere; I ~ seen him l'ho visto; he has never been there non ci è mai stato. □ ~ on vt (be wearing) portare; (dupe) prendere in giro; I've got something on tonight ho un impegno stasera. □ ~ out vt ~ it out with sb chiarire le cose con qcno

● npl the ~s and the ~-nots i ricchi e i poveri

haven /ˈheɪvn/ n fig rifugio m

haversack /ˈhævə-/ n zaino m

havoc /ˈhævək/ n strage f; play ~ with fig scombussolare

hawk /hɔːk/ n falco m

hay /heɪ/ n fieno m. ~ fever n raffreddore m da fieno. ~**stack** n pagliaio m

ˈhaywire adj 🔲 go ~ dare i numeri; (plans:) andare all'aria

hazard /ˈhæzəd/ n (risk) rischio m ● vt rischiare; ~ a guess azzardare un'ipotesi. ~**ous** adj rischioso. ~ [warning] lights npl (Auto) luci fpl d'emergenza

haze /heɪz/ n foschia f

hazel /ˈheɪz(ə)l/ n nocciolo m; (colour) [color m] nocciola m. ~**-nut** n nocciola f

hazy /ˈheɪzɪ/ adj (-ier, -iest) nebbioso; (fig: person) confuso; (memories) vago

he /hiː/ pron lui; he's tired è stanco; I'm going but he's not io vengo, ma lui no

head /hed/ n testa f; (of firm) capo

427 **heady | hedge**

m; (of primary school) direttore, -trice mf; (of secondary school) preside mf; (on beer) schiuma f; be off one's ~ essere fuori di testa; have a good ~ for business avere il senso degli affari; have a good ~ for heights non soffrire di vertigini; **10 pounds a ~ 10** sterline a testa; **20** ~ of cattle 20 capi di bestiame; ~ **first** a capofitto; ~ **over** heels in love innamorato pazzo; ~s or tails? testa o croce? ● vt essere a capo di; essere in testa a (list); colpire di testa (ball) ● vi ~ **for** dirigersi verso.

head: ~**ache** n mal m di testa. ~**er** /'hedə(r)/ n rinvio m di testa; (dive) tuffo m di testa. ~**ing** n (in list etc) titolo m. ~**lamp** n (Auto) fanale m. ~**land** n promontorio m. ~**line** n titolo m. ~**long** adj & adv a capofitto. ~'**master** n (of primary school) direttore m; (of secondary school) preside m. ~'**mistress** n (of primary school) direttrice f; (of secondary school) preside f. ~-**on** adj (collision) frontale ● adv frontalmente. ~**phones** npl cuffie fpl. ~**quarters** npl sede fsg; (Mil) quartier m generale msg. ~**strong** adj testardo

heady /'hedi/ adj che dà alla testa

heal /hi:l/ vt/i guarire

health /helθ/ n salute f

health|y /'helθi/ adj (-ier, -iest) sano. ~**ily** adv in modo sano

heap /hi:p/ n mucchio m; ~**s pl** 🗐 un sacco di ● vt ~ [up] ammucchiare; ~**ed teaspoon** un cucchiaino abbondante

hear /hiə(r)/ vt/i (pt/pp heard) sentire; ~, ~**!** bravo! ~ **from** vi aver notizie di; □ ~ **of** vi sentir parlare di; he would not ~ **of it** non ne ha voluto sentir parlare

hearing /'hiəriŋ/ n udito m; (Jur) udienza f. ~-**aid** n apparecchio m acustico

'**hearsay** n **from** ~ per sentito dire

hearse /hɜ:s/ n carro m funebre

heart /hɑ:t/ n cuore m; ~**s pl** (in cards) cuori mpl; **by** ~ a memoria

heart: ~**ache** n pena f. ~ **attack** n infarto m. ~-**break** n afflizione f. ~-**breaking** adj straziante. ~-**burn** n mal m di stomaco. ~**felt** adj di cuore

hearth /hɑ:θ/ n focolare m

heart|ily /'hɑ:tili/ adv di cuore; (eat) con appetito; **be** ~**ily sick of** sth non poterne più di qcsa. ~**less** adj spietato. ~-**searching** n esame m di coscienza. ~-**to**-~ n conversazione f a cuore aperto ● adj a cuore aperto. ~**y** adj caloroso; (meal) copioso; (person) gioviale

heat /hi:t/ n calore m; (Sport) prova f eliminatoria ● vt scaldare ● vi scaldarsi. ~**ed** adj (swimming pool) riscaldato; (discussion) animato. ~**er** n (for room) stufa f; (for water) boiler m inv; (Auto) riscaldamento m

heath /hi:θ/ n brughiera f

heathen /'hi:ðn/ adj & n pagano, -a mf

heather /'heðə(r)/ n erica f

heating /'hi:tiŋ/ n riscaldamento m

heat: ~-**stroke** n colpo m di sole. ~ **wave** n ondata f di calore

heave /hi:v/ vt/i tirare; (lift) tirare su; (🗐: throw) gettare; emettere (sigh) ● vi tirare

heaven /'hev(ə)n/ n paradiso m; ~ **help you** Dio ti scampi se...; **H~s!** santo cielo! ~**ly** adj celeste; 🗐 delizioso

heav|y /'hevi/ adj (-ier, -iest) pesante; (traffic) intenso; (rain, cold) forte; **be a** ~**y smoker/drinker** essere un gran fumatore/bevitore. ~**ily** adv pesantemente; (smoke, drink etc) molto. ~**yweight** n peso m massimo

Hebrew /'hi:bru:/ adj ebreo

heckle /'hekl/ vt interrompere di continuo. ~**r** n disturbatore, -trice mf

hectic /'hektik/ adj frenetico

hedge /hedʒ/ n siepe f ● vi fig essere

evasivo. ~hog n riccio m

heed /hiːd/ n pay ~ to prestare ascolto a ● v t prestare ascolto a. ~less adj noncurante

heel¹ /hiːl/ n tallone m; (of shoe) tacco m; take to one's ~s 🄳 darsela a gambe

heel² vi ~ over (Naut) inclinarsi

hefty /ˈheftɪ/ adj (-ier, -iest) massiccio

heifer /ˈhefə(r)/ n giovenca f

height /haɪt/ n altezza f; (of plane) altitudine f; (of season, fame) culmine m. ~en v t fig accrescere

heir /eə(r)/ n erede mf. ~ess n ereditiera f. ~loom n cimelio m di famiglia

held /held/ ▷HOLD²

helicopter /ˈhelɪkɒptə(r)/ n elicottero m

hell /hel/ n inferno m; go to ~! 🄳 va' al diavolo! ● int porca miseria!

hello /həˈləʊ/ int & n = hallo

helm /helm/ n timone m; at the ~ fig al timone

helmet /ˈhelmɪt/ n casco m

help /help/ n aiuto m; (employee) aiuto m domestico; that's no ~ non è d'aiuto ● v t aiutare; ~ oneself to sth servirsi di qcsa; ~ yourself (at table) serviti pure; I could not ~ laughing non ho potuto trattenermi dal ridere; it cannot be ~ed non c'è niente da fare; I can't ~ it non ci posso far niente ● vi aiutare

help|er /ˈhelpə(r)/ n aiutante mf. ~ful adj (person) di aiuto; (advice) utile. ~ing n porzione f. ~less adj (unable to manage) incapace; (powerless) impotente

hem /hem/ n orlo m ● v t (pt/pp hemmed) orlare. □ ~ in v t intrappolare

hemisphere /ˈhemɪ-/ n emisfero m

hen /hen/ n gallina f; (any female bird) femmina f

hence /hens/ adv (for this reason) quindi. ~forth adv d'ora innanzi

henpecked adj tiranneggiato dalla moglie

her /hɜː(r)/ poss adj il suo m, la sua f, i suoi mpl, le sue fpl; ~ mother/father sua madre/suo padre ● pers pron (direct object) la; (indirect object) le; (after prep) lei; I know ~ la conosco; give ~ the money dalle i soldi; give it to ~ daglielo; I came with ~ sono venuto con lei; it's ~ è lei; I've seen ~ l'ho vista; I've seen ~, but not him ho visto lei, ma non lui

herb /hɜːb/ n erba f

herbal /hɜːb(ə)l/ adj alle erbe; ~ tea tisana f

herd /hɜːd/ n gregge m ● v t (tend) sorvegliare; (drive) far muovere; fig ammassare

here /hɪə(r)/ adv qui, qua; in ~ qui dentro; come/bring ~ vieni/porta qui; ~ is..., ~ are... ecco...; ~ you are! ecco qua!. ~'after adv in futuro. ~by adv con la presente

hered|itary /həˈredɪtərɪ/ adj ereditario. ~y n eredità f

here|sy /ˈherəsɪ/ n eresia f. ~tic n eretico, -a mf

here'with adv (Comm) con la presente

heritage /ˈherɪtɪdʒ/ n eredità f. ~ 'tourism n turismo m culturale

hernia /ˈhɜːnɪə/ n ernia f

hero /ˈhɪərəʊ/ n (pl -es) eroe m

heroic /hɪˈrəʊɪk/ adj eroico

heroin /ˈherəʊɪn/ n eroina f (drug)

hero|ine /ˈherəʊɪn/ n eroina f. ~ism n eroismo m

heron /ˈherən/ n airone m

herring /ˈherɪŋ/ n aringa f

hers /hɜːz/ poss pron il suo m, la sua f, i suoi mpl, le sue fpl; a friend of ~ un suo amico; friends of ~ dei suoi amici; that is ~ quello è suo; (as opposed to mine) quello è il suo her'self *pers pron (reflexive)* si; (*emphatic*) lei stessa; (*after prep*) sé, se stessa; **she poured** ~ **a drink** si è versata da bere; **she told me so** ~ me lo ha detto lei stessa; **she's proud of** ~ è fiera di sé; **by** ~ da sola

hesitant /'hezɪtənt/ *adj* esitante. ~ly *adv* con esitazione

hesitate /'hezɪteɪt/ *vi* esitare. ~ion *n* esitazione *f*

hetero'sexual /hetərəʊ-/ *adj* eterosessuale

hexagon /'heksəgən/ *n* esagono *m*. ~al *adj* esagonale

hey /heɪ/ *int* ehi

heyday /'heɪ-/ *n* tempi *mpl* d'oro

hi /haɪ/ *int* ciao!

hibernat|e /'haɪbəneɪt/ *vi* andare in letargo. ~ion *n* letargo *m*

hiccup /'hɪkʌp/ *n* singhiozzo *m*; (⬚: *hitch*) intoppo *m* ● *vi* fare un singhiozzo

hide¹ /haɪd/ *n* (*leather*) pelle *f* (*di animale*)

hide² *vt* (*pt* hid, *pp* hidden) nascondere ● *vi* nascondersi. ~-**and-'seek** *n* play ~-**and-seek** giocare a nascondino

hideous /'hɪdɪəs/ *adj* orribile

'hide-out *n* nascondiglio *m*

hiding¹ /'haɪdɪŋ/ *n* (⬚: *beating*) bastonata *f*; (*defeat*) batosta *f*

hiding² *n* **go into** ~ sparire dalla circolazione

hierarchy /'haɪərɑːkɪ/ *n* gerarchia *f*

hieroglyphics /haɪərə'glɪfɪks/ *npl* geroglifici *mpl*

hi-fi /'haɪfaɪ/ *n* stereo *m*, hi-fi *m inv* ● *adj* ⬚ ad alta fedeltà

high /haɪ/ *adj alto*; (*meat*) che comincia ad andare a male; (*wind*) forte; (*on drugs*) fatto; **it's** ~ **time we did something about it** è ora di fare qualcosa in proposito ● *adv* in alto; ~ **and low** in lungo e in largo

● *n* massimo *m*; (*temperature*) massima *f*; **be on a** ~ ⬚ essere fatto

high: ~**er education** *n* formazione *f* universitaria. ~**-handed** *adj* dispotico. ~ **heels** *npl* tacchi *mpl* alti

highlight /'haɪlaɪt/ *n fig* momento *m* clou; ~**s** *pl* (*in hair*) mèche *fpl* ● *vt* (*emphasize*) evidenziare. ~**er** *n* (*marker*) evidenziatore *m*

highly /'haɪlɪ/ *adv* molto; **speak** ~ *di* lodare; **think** ~ *of* avere un'alta opinione di. ~**-strung** *adj* nervoso

high: ~**-rise** *adj* (*building*) molto alto ● *n* edificio *m* molto alto. ~**school** *n* ≈ scuola *f* superiore. ~**street** *n* strada *f* principale. ~**way code** *n* codice *m* stradale

High School Negli Stati Uniti indica la scuola superiore, generalmente compresa tra i 14 e i 18 anni. In Gran Bretagna il termine è usato solo nella denominazione di alcune scuole.

hijack /'haɪdʒæk/ *vt* dirottare ● *n* dirottamento *m*. ~**er** *n* dirottatore, -trice *mf*

hike /haɪk/ *n* escursione *f* a piedi ● *vi* fare un'escursione a piedi. ~**r** *n* escursionista *mf*

hilarious /hɪ'leərɪəs/ *adj* esilarante

hill /hɪl/ *n* collina *f*; (*mound*) collinetta *f*; (*slope*) altura *f*

hill: ~**side** *n* pendio *m*. ~**y** *adj* collinoso

hilt /hɪlt/ *n* impugnatura *f*; **to the** ~ (*support*) fino in fondo; (*mortgaged*) fino al collo

him /hɪm/ *pers pron* (*direct object*) lo; (*indirect object*) gli; (*with prep*) lui; **I know** ~ lo conosco; **give** ~ **the money** dagli i soldi; **give it to** ~ daglielo; **I spoke to** ~ gli ho parlato; **it's** ~ è lui; **she loves** ~ lo ama; **she loves** ~, **not you** ama lui, non te. ~'**self** *pers pron* (*reflexive*) si;

(emphatic) lui stesso; (after prep) sé, se stesso; he poured ∼ a drink si è versato da bere; he told me so ∼self me lo ha detto lui stesso; he's proud of ∼self è fiero di sé; by ∼self da solo

hind|er /'hɪndə(r)/ vt intralciare. ∼rance n intralcio m

hindsight /'haɪnd-/ n with ∼ con il senno del poi

Hindu /'hɪnduː/ n indù mf inv ● adj indù. ∼ism n induismo m

hinge /hɪndʒ/ n cardine m ● vi ∼ on fig dipendere da

hint /hɪnt/ n (clue) accenno m; (advice) suggerimento m; (indirect suggestion) allusione f; (trace) tocco m ● vt ∼ that... far capire che... ● vi ∼ at alludere a

hip /hɪp/ n fianco m

hippie /'hɪpi/ n hippy mf inv

hippopotamus /hɪpə'pɒtəməs/ n (pl -muses or -mi /-maɪ/) ippopotamo m

hire /'haɪə(r)/ vt affittare; assumere (person); ∼ [out] affittare ● n noleggio m; 'for ∼' 'affittasi'; ∼ car n macchina f a noleggio. ∼ purchase n acquisto m rateale

his /hɪz/ poss adj il suo m, la sua f, i suoi mpl, le sue fpl; ∼ mother/father sua madre/suo padre ● poss pron il suo m, la sua f, i suoi mpl, le sue fpl; a friend of ∼ un suo amico; friends of ∼ dei suoi amici; that is ∼ questo è suo; (as opposed to mine) questo è il suo

hiss /hɪs/ n sibilo m; (of disapproval) fischio m ● vt fischiare ● vi sibilare; (in disapproval) fischiare

historian /hɪ'stɔːrɪən/ n storico, -a mf

history /'hɪstərɪ/ n storia f; make ∼ passare alla storia

hit /hɪt/ n (blow) colpo m; (🔢: success) successo m; score a direct ∼ (missile:) colpire in pieno ● vt/i (pt/pp hit,

pres p hitting) colpire; ∼ one's head on the table battere la testa contro il tavolo; the car ∼ the wall la macchina ha sbattuto contro il muro; ∼ the roof 🔢 perdere le staffe. □ ∼ off vt fig trovare

hitch /hɪtʃ/ n intoppo m; technical ∼ problema m tecnico ● vt attaccare; ∼ a lift chiedere un passaggio. □ ∼ up vt tirarsi su (trousers). ∼hike vi fare l'autostop. ∼hiker n autostoppista mf

hither /'hɪðə(r)/ adv ∼ and thither di qua e di là. ∼'to adv finora

hit-or-'miss adj on a very ∼ basis all'improvvisata

hive /haɪv/ n alveare m; ∼ of industry fucina f di lavoro ● hive off vt (Comm) separare

hoard /hɔːd/ n provvista f; (of money) gruzzolo m ● vt accumulare

hoarding /'hɔːdɪŋ/ n palizzata f; (with advertisements) tabellone m per manifesti pubblicitari

hoarse /hɔːs/ adj rauco. ∼ly adv con voce rauca. ∼ness n raucedine f

hoax /həʊks/ n scherzo m; (false alarm) falso allarme m. ∼er n burlone, -a mf

hob /hɒb/ n piano m di cottura

hobble /'hɒbl/ vi zoppicare

hobby /'hɒbɪ/ n hobby m inv. ∼-horse n fig fissazione f

hockey /'hɒkɪ/ n hockey m

hoe /həʊ/ n zappa f

hog /hɒg/ n maiale m ● vt (pt/pp hogged) 🔢 monopolizzare

hoist /hɔɪst/ n montacarichi m inv; (🔢: push) spinta f in su ● vt sollevare; innalzare (flag); levare (anchor)

hold[1] /həʊld/ n (Aeron, Naut) stiva f

hold[2] n presa f; (fig: influence) ascendente m; get ∼ of trovare; procurarsi (information) ● vt (pt/pp held) ● vt tenere; (container:) contenere; essere titolare di (licence, passport);

trattenere (breath, suspect); mantenere vivo (interest); (civil servant etc:) occupare (position); (retain) mantenere; ~ sb's hand tenere qcno per mano; ~ one's tongue tenere la bocca chiusa; ~ sb responsible considerare qcno responsabile; ~ that (believe) ritenere che ● vi tenere; (weather, luck:) durare; (offer:) essere valido; (Teleph) restare in linea; I don't ~ with the idea that... 🔲 non sono d'accordo sul fatto che... □ ~ back vt rallentare ● vi esitare. □ ~ down vt tenere a bada (sb). □ ~ on vi (wait) attendere; (Teleph) restare in linea. □ ~ on to vt aggrapparsi a; (keep) tenersi. □ ~ out vt porgere (hand); fig offrire (possibility) ● vi (resist) resistere. □ ~ up vt tenere su; (delay) rallentare; (rob) assalire; ~ one's head up fig tenere la testa alta

'hold: ~all n borsone m. ~er n titolare mf; (of record) detentore, -trice mf; (container) astuccio m. ~up n ritardo m; (attack) rapina f a mano armata

hole /həʊl/ n buco m

holiday /'hɒlɪdeɪ/ n vacanza f; (public) giorno m festivo; (day off) giorno m di ferie; go on ~ andare in vacanza ● vi andare in vacanza. ~-maker n villeggiante mf

holiness /'həʊlɪnɪs/ n santità f; Your H~ Sua Santità

Holland /'hɒlənd/ n Olanda f

hollow /'hɒləʊ/ adj cavo; (promise) a vuoto; (voice) assente; (cheeks) infossato ● n cavità f inv; (in ground) affossamento m

holly /'hɒlɪ/ n agrifoglio m

holocaust /'hɒləkɔːst/ n olocausto m

holster /'həʊlstə(r)/ n fondina f

holy /'həʊlɪ/ adj (-ier, -est) santo; (water) benedetto. H~ Ghost or Spirit n Spirito m Santo. H~ Scriptures npl sacre scritture fpl. H~ Week n settimana f santa

homage /'hɒmɪdʒ/ n omaggio m; pay ~ to rendere omaggio a

home /həʊm/ n casa f; (for children) istituto m; (for old people) casa f di riposo; (native land) patria f ● adv at ~ a casa; (football) in casa; feel at ~ sentirsi a casa propria; come/go ~ venire/andare a casa; drive a nail ~ piantare un chiodo a fondo ● adj domestico; (movie, video) casalingo; (team) ospitante; (Pol) nazionale

home: ~ad'dress n indirizzo m di casa. ~land n patria f; ~land se'curity n sicurezza f delle frontiere. ~less adj senza tetto

homely /'həʊmlɪ/ adj (-ier, -iest) semplice; (atmosphere) familiare; (Am: ugly) bruttino

home: ~-'made adj fatto in casa. H~ Office n Br ministero m degli interni. ~sick adj be ~sick avere nostalgia (for di). ~ 'town n città f inv natia. ~work n (Sch) compiti mpl

homicide /'hɒmɪsaɪd/ n (crime) omicidio m

homoeopath|ic /həʊmɪə'pæθɪk/ adj omeopatico. ~y n omeopatia f

homogeneous /hɒmə'dʒiːnɪəs/ adj omogeneo

homo'sexual adj & n omosessuale mf

honest /'ɒnɪst/ adj onesto; (frank) sincero. ~ly adv onestamente; (frankly) sinceramente; ~ly! ma insommal. ~y n onestà f; (frankness) sincerità f

honey /'hʌnɪ/ n miele m; (🔲: darling) tesoro m

honey: ~comb n favo m. ~moon n luna f di miele. ~suckle n caprifoglio m

honorary /'ɒnərərɪ/ adj onorario

honour /'ɒnə(r)/ n onore m ● vt onorare. ~able adj onorevole. ~ably adv con onore. ~s degree n ≈ diploma m di laurea

hood /hʊd/ n cappuccio m; (of pram)

tettuccio m; (over cooker) cappa f; Am (Auto) cofano m

hoodlum /'hu:dləm/ n teppista m

'hoodwink vt 🔲 infinocchiare

hoof /hu:f/ n (pl ~s or hooves) zoccolo m

hook /hʊk/ n gancio m; (for fishing) amo m; off the ~ (Teleph) staccato; fig fuori pericolo ● vt agganciare ● vi agganciarsi

hook|ed /hʊkt/ adj (nose) adunco ~ed on (🔲: drugs) dedito a; be ~ed on skiing essere un fanatico dello sci. ~er n Am 🔲 battona f

hookey /'hʊki/ n play ~ Am 🔲 marinare la scuola

hooligan /'hu:lɪgən/ n teppista mf. ~ism n teppismo m

hoop /hu:p/ n cerchio m

hooray /hʊ'reɪ/ int & n = hurrah

hoot /hu:t/ n colpo m di clacson; (of siren) ululato m; (of owl) grido m ● vi (owl:) gridare; (car:) clacsonare; (siren:) ululare; (jeer) fischiare. ~er n (of factory) sirena f; (Auto) clacson m inv

hoover® /'hu:və(r)/ n aspirapolvere m inv ● vt passare l'aspirapolvere su (carpet); passare l'aspirapolvere in (room)

hop /hɒp/ n saltello m ● vi (pt/pp hopped) saltellare; ~ it! 🔲 tela!. □ ~ in vi 🔲 saltar su

hope /həʊp/ n speranza f ● vi sperare (for in); I ~ so/not spero di sì/ no ● vt ~ that sperare che

hope|ful /'həʊpfl/ adj pieno di speranza; (promising) promettente; be ~ful that avere buone speranze che. ~fully adv con speranza; (it is hoped) se tutto va bene. ~less adj senza speranze; (useless) impossibile; (incompetent) incapace. ~lessly adv disperatamente; (inefficient, lost) completamente. ~lessness n disperazione f

horde /hɔ:d/ n orda f

horizon /hə'raɪzn/ n orizzonte m

horizontal /hɒrɪ'zɒntl/ adj orizzontale

hormone /'hɔ:məʊn/ n ormone m

horn /hɔ:n/ n corno m; (Auto) clacson m inv

horoscope /'hɒrəskəʊp/ n oroscopo m

horrible /'hɒrɪbl/ adj orribile. ~y adv spaventosamente

horrid /'hɒrɪd/ adj orrendo

horrific /hə'rɪfɪk/ adj raccapricciante; (accident, prices, story) terrificante

horrify /'hɒrɪfaɪ/ vt (pt/pp -ied) far inorridire; I was horrified ero sconvolto. ~ing adj terrificante

horror /'hɒrə(r)/ n orrore m. ~ film n film m dell'orrore

horse /hɔ:s/ n cavallo m

horse: ~back n on ~back a cavallo. ~power n cavallo m [vapore]. ~-racing n corse fpl di cavalli. ~shoe n ferro m di cavallo

horti'cultural /hɔ:tɪ-/ adj di orticoltura

'horticulture n orticoltura f

hose /həʊz/ n (pipe) manichetta f ● hose down vt lavare con la manichetta

hospice /'hɒspɪs/ n (for the terminally ill) ospedale m per i malati in fase terminale

hospitabl|e /hɒ'spɪtəbl/ adj ospitale. ~y adv con ospitalità

hospital /'hɒspɪtl/ n ospedale m

hospitality /hɒspɪ'tælətɪ/ n ospitalità f

host¹ /həʊst/ n a ~ of una moltitudine di

host² n ospite m

host³ n (Relig) ostia f

hostage /'hɒstɪdʒ/ n ostaggio m; hold sb ~ tenere qcno in ostaggio

hostel /'hɒstl/ n ostello m

hostess /'həʊstɪs/ n padrona f di

casa; (Aeron) hostess f inv

hostile /'hɒstaɪl/ adj ostile

hostilit|y /hɒ'stɪlətɪ/ n ostilità f; **~ies** pl ostilità fpl

hot /hɒt/ adj (hotter, hottest) caldo; (spicy) piccante; **I am** or **feel ~** ho caldo; **it is ~** fa caldo

'hotbed n fig focolaio m

hotchpotch /'hɒtʃpɒtʃ/ n miscuglio m

'hot-dog n hot dog m inv

hotel /həʊ'tel/ n albergo m. **~ier** n albergatore, -trice mf

hot: **~house** n serra f. **~plate** n piastra f riscaldante. **~-'water bottle** n borsa f dell'acqua calda

hound /haʊnd/ n cane m da caccia ● vt fig perseguire

hour /'aʊə(r)/ n ora f. **~ly** adj ad ogni ora; (pay, rate) a ora ● adv ogni ora

house /haʊs/: **~boat** n casa f galleggiante. **~breaking** n furto m con scasso. **~hold** n casa f, famiglia f. **~holder** n capo m di famiglia. **~keeper** n governante f di casa. **~keeping** n governo m della casa; (money) soldi mpl per le spese di casa. **~plant** n pianta f da appartamento. **~trained** adj che non sporca in casa. **~warming party** n festa f di inaugurazione della nuova casa. **~wife** n casalinga f. **~work** n lavoro m domestico

house¹ /haʊs/ n casa f; (Pol) camera f; (Theat) sala f; **at my ~** a casa mia, da me

house² /haʊz/ vt alloggiare (person)

housing /'haʊzɪŋ/ n alloggio m. **~ estate** n zona f residenziale

hovel /'hɒvl/ n tugurio m

hover /'hɒvə(r)/ vi librarsi; (linger) indugiare. **~craft** n hovercraft m inv

how /haʊ/ adv come; **~ are you?** come stai?; **~ about a coffee/ going on holiday?** che ne diresti di un caffè/di andare in vacanza?; **~**

do you do? molto lieto!; **~ old are you?** quanti anni hai?; **~ long** quanto tempo; **~ many** quanti; **~ much** quanto; **~ often** ogni quanto; **and ~!** eccome!; **~ odd!** che strano!

how'ever adv (nevertheless) comunque; **~ small** per quanto piccolo

howl /haʊl/ n ululato m ● vi ululare; (cry, with laughter) singhiozzare. **~er** n 🔢 strafalcione m

HP n abbr hire purchase; n abbr (horse power) C.V.

hub /hʌb/ n mozzo m; fig centro m

'hub-cap n coprimozzo m

huddle /'hʌdl/ vi **~ together** rannicchiarsi

hue¹ /hjuː/ n colore m

hue² n **~ and cry** clamore m

huff /hʌf/ n **be in/go into a ~** fare il broncio

hug /hʌɡ/ n abbraccio m ● vt (pt/pp hugged) abbracciare; (keep close to) tenersi vicino a

huge /hjuːdʒ/ adj enorme

hull /hʌl/ n (Naut) scafo m

hullo /hə'ləʊ/ int = hallo

hum /hʌm/ n ronzio m ● v (pt/pp hummed) ● vt canticchiare ● vi (motor:) ronzare; fig fervere (of activity); **~ and haw** esitare

human /'hjuːmən/ adj umano ●n essere m umano. **~ 'being** n essere m umano

humane /hjuː'meɪn/ adj umano

humanitarian /hjuːmænɪ-'teərɪən/ adj & n umanitario, -a mf

humanit|y /hjuː'mænətɪ/ n umanità f; **~ies** pl (Univ) dottrine fpl umanistiche

humbl|e /'hʌmbl/ adj umile ● vt umiliare

'humdrum adj noioso

humid /'hjuːmɪd/ adj umido. **~ifier** n umidificatore m. **~ity** /-'mɪdətɪ/ n umidità f

humiliat|e /hju:'mɪlɪeɪt/ vt umiliare. **~ion** n umiliazione f

humility /hju:'mɪlɪtɪ/ n umiltà f

humorous /'hju:mərəs/ adj umoristico. **~ly** adv con spirito

humour /'hju:mə(r)/ n umorismo m; (mood) umore m; have a sense of ~ avere il senso dell'umorismo • vt compiacere

hump /hʌmp/ n protuberanza f; (of camel, hunchback) gobba f

hunch /hʌntʃ/ n (idea) intuizione f

'hunch|back n gobbo, -a mf. **~ed** adj ~ed up incurvato

hundred /'hʌndrəd/ adj one/a ~ cento • n cento m; **~s** of centinaia di. **~th** adj centesimo • n centesimo m. **~weight** n cinquanta chili m

hung /hʌŋ/ ▷HANG

Hungarian /hʌŋ'geərɪən/ n & adj ungherese mf; (language) ungherese m

Hungary /'hʌŋgərɪ/ n Ungheria f

hunger /'hʌŋgə(r)/ n fame f. **~-strike** n sciopero m della fame m

hungr|y /'hʌŋgrɪ/ adj (-ier, -iest) affamato; be **~y** aver fame. **~ily** adv con appetito

hunk /hʌŋk/ n [grosso] pezzo m

hunt /hʌnt/ n caccia f • vt andare a caccia di (animal); dare la caccia a (criminal) • vi andare a caccia; ~ for cercare. **~er** n cacciatore m. **~ing** n caccia f

hurl /hɜ:l/ vt scagliare

hurrah /hʊ'rɑ:/, **hurray** /hʊ'reɪ/ int urrà! • n urrà m

hurricane /'hʌrɪkən/ n uragano m

hurried /'hʌrɪd/ adj affrettato; (job) fatto in fretta. **~ly** adv in fretta

hurry /'hʌrɪ/ n fretta f; be in a ~ aver fretta • vi (pt/pp -ied) affrettarsi. □~ **up** vi sbrigarsi • vt fare sbrigare (person); accelerare (things)

hurt /hɜ:t/ v (pt/pp hurt) • vt far male a; (offend) ferire • vi far male; my leg **~s** mi fa male la gamba.

~ful adj fig offensivo

hurtle /hɜ:tl/ vi ~ along andare a tutta velocità

husband /'hʌzbənd/ n marito m

hush /hʌʃ/ n silenzio m • **hush up** vt mettere a tacere. **~ed** adj (voice) sommesso. **~-'hush** adj 🔢 segretissimo

husky /'hʌskɪ/ adj (-ier, -iest) (voice) rauco

hustle /'hʌsl/ vt affrettare • n attività f incessante; ~ and bustle trambusto m

hut /hʌt/ n capanna f

hybrid /'haɪbrɪd/ adj ibrido • n ibrido m

hydrant /'haɪdrənt/ n [fire] ~ idrante m

hydraulic /haɪ'drɔ:lɪk/ adj idraulico

hydroe'lectric /haɪdrəʊ-/ adj idroelettrico

hydrofoil /'haɪdrə-/ n aliscafo m

hydrogen /'haɪdrədʒən/ n idrogeno m

hyena /haɪ'i:nə/ n iena f

hygien|e /'haɪdʒi:n/ n igiene f. **~ic** adj igienico

hymn /hɪm/ n inno m. **~-book** n libro m dei canti

hypermarket /'haɪpəmɑ:kɪt/ n ipermercato m

hyphen /'haɪfn/ n lineetta f. **~ate** vt unire con lineetta

hypno|sis /hɪp'nəʊsɪs/ n ipnosi f. **~tic** adj ipnotico

hypno|tism /'hɪpnətɪzm/ n ipnotismo m. **~tist** n ipnotizzatore, -trice mf. **~tize** vt ipnotizzare

hypochondriac /haɪpə'kɒndrɪæk/ adj ipocondriaco • n ipocondriaco, -a mf

hypocrisy /hɪ'pɒkrəsɪ/ n ipocrisia f

hypocrit|e /'hɪpəkrɪt/ n ipocrita mf. **~ical** adj ipocrita

hypodermic /haɪpə'dɜ:mɪk/ adj & n ~ [syringe] siringa f ipodermica

hypothe|sis /haɪˈpɒθəsɪs/ *n* ipotesi *f inv.* ~**tical** *adj* ipotetico. ~**tically** *adv* in teoria; (speak) per ipotesi

hyster|ia /hɪˈstɪərɪə/ *n* isterismo *m.* ~**ical** *adj* isterico. ~**ically** *adv* istericamente; ~**ically funny** da morir dal ridere. ~**ics** *npl* attacco *m* isterico

. . . .

I i

. . . .

I /aɪ/ *pron* io; **I'm tired** sono stanco; **he's going, but I'm not** lui va, ma io no

ice /aɪs/ *n* ghiaccio *m* ● *vt* glassare (cake). □ ~ **over/up** vi ghiacciarsi

ice: ~**-axe** *n* piccozza *f* per il ghiaccio. ~**berg** /-bɜːg/ *n* iceberg *m inv.* ~**box** *n Am* frigorifero *m.* ~**-cream** *n* gelato *m.* ~**-cube** *n* cubetto *m* di ghiaccio

Iceland /ˈaɪslənd/ *n* Islanda *f.* ~**er** *n* islandese *mf*; ~**ic** /-ˈlændɪk/ *adj* & *n* islandese *m*

ice: ~**-lolly** *n* ghiacciolo *m.* ~ **rink** *n* pista *f* di pattinaggio. ~ **skater** pattinatore, -trice *mf* sul ghiaccio. ~ **skating** pattinaggio *m* su ghiaccio

icicle /ˈaɪsɪkl/ *n* ghiacciolo *m*

icing /ˈaɪsɪŋ/ *n* glassa *f.* ~ **sugar** *n* zucchero *m* a velo

icon /ˈaɪkɒn/ *n* icona *f*

ic|y /ˈaɪsɪ/ *adj* (-ier, -iest) ghiacciato; *fig* gelido. ~**ily** *adv* gelidamente

idea /aɪˈdɪə/ *n* idea *f*; **I've no** ~**!** non ne ho idea!

ideal /aɪˈdɪəl/ *adj* ideale ● *n* ideale *m.* ~**ism** *n* idealismo *m.* ~**ist** *n* idealista *mf.* ~**istic** *adj* idealistico. ~**ize** *vt* idealizzare. ~**ly** *adv* idealmente

identical /aɪˈdentɪkl/ *adj* identico

identi|fication /aɪdentɪfɪˈkeɪʃn/ *n* identificazione *f*; (proof of identity) documento *m* di riconoscimento. ~**fy** *vt* (pt/pp -ied) identificare

identity /aɪˈdentɪtɪ/ *n* identità *f inv.* ~ **card** *n* carta *f* d'identità. ~ **theft** *n* furto *m* d'identità

ideolog|ical /aɪdɪəˈlɒdʒɪkl/ *adj* ideologico. ~**y** *n* ideologia *f*

idiom /ˈɪdɪəm/ *n* idioma *f.* ~**atic** *adj* idiomatico

idiot /ˈɪdɪət/ *n* idiota *mf.* ~**ic** *adj* idiota

idl|e /ˈaɪd(ə)l/ *adj* (lazy) pigro, ozioso; (empty) vano; (machine) fermo ● *vi* oziare; (engine) girare a vuoto. ~**eness** *n* ozio *m.* ~**y** *adv* oziosamente

idol /ˈaɪdl/ *n* idolo *m.* ~**ize** *vt* idolatrare

idyllic /ɪˈdɪlɪk/ *adj* idillico

i.e. *abbr* (id est) cioè

if /ɪf/ *conj* se; **as if** come se

ignite /ɪgˈnaɪt/ *vt* dar fuoco a ● *vi* prender fuoco

ignition /ɪgˈnɪʃn/ *n* (Auto) accensione *f.* ~ **key** *n* chiave *f* d'accensione

ignoramus /ɪgnəˈreɪməs/ *n* ignorante *mf*

ignoran|ce /ˈɪgnərəns/ *n* ignoranza *f.* ~**t** *adj* (lacking knowledge) ignaro; (rude) ignorante

ignore /ɪgˈnɔː(r)/ *vt* ignorare

ill /ɪl/ *adj* ammalato; **feel** ~ **at ease** sentirsi a disagio ● *adv* male ● *n* male *m.* ~**-advised** *adj* avventato. ~**-bred** *adj* maleducato

illegal /ɪˈliːgl/ *adj* illegale

illegible /ɪˈledʒɪbl/ *adj* illeggibile

illegitima|cy /ɪlɪˈdʒɪtɪməsɪ/ *n* illegittimità *f.* ~**te** *adj* illegittimo

illitera|cy /ɪˈlɪtərəsɪ/ *n* analfabetismo *m.* ~**te** *adj* & *n* analfabeta *mf*

illness /ˈɪlnɪs/ *n* malattia *f*

illogical /ɪˈlɒdʒɪkl/ *adj* illogico

illuminat|e /ɪˈluːmɪneɪt/ vt illuminare. **~ing** adj chiarificatore. **~ion** n illuminazione f

illusion /ɪˈluːʒn/ n illusione f; **be under the ~ that** avere l'illusione che

illustrat|e /ˈɪləstreɪt/ vt illustrare. **~ion** n illustrazione f. **~or** n illustratore, -trice mf

illustrious /ɪˈlʌstrɪəs/ adj illustre

ill 'will n malanimo m

image /ˈɪmɪdʒ/ n immagine f; (exact likeness) ritratto m

imagin|able /ɪˈmædʒɪnəbl/ adj immaginabile. **~ary** adj immaginario

imaginat|ion /ɪmædʒɪˈneɪʃn/ n immaginazione f, fantasia f; **it's your ~ion** è solo una tua idea. **~ive** adj fantasioso. **~ively** adv con fantasia or immaginazione

imagine /ɪˈmædʒɪn/ vt immaginare; (wrongly) inventare

im'balance n squilibrio m

imbecile /ˈɪmbəsiːl/ n imbecille mf

imitat|e /ˈɪmɪteɪt/ vt imitare. **~ion** n imitazione f. **~or** n imitatore, -trice mf

immaculate /ɪˈmækjʊlət/ adj immacolato. **~ly** adv immacolatamente

imma'ture adj immaturo

immediate /ɪˈmiːdɪət/ adj immediato; (relative) stretto; **in the ~ vicinity** nelle immediate vicinanze. **~ly** adv immediatamente; **~ly next to** subito accanto a ● conj [non] appena

immense /ɪˈmens/ adj immenso

immers|e /ɪˈmɜːs/ vt immergere; **be ~ed in** fig essere immerso in. **~ion** n immersione f. **~ion heater** n scaldabagno m elettrico

immigrant /ˈɪmɪgrənt/ n immigrante mf

imminent /ˈɪmɪnənt/ adj imminente

immobil|e /ɪˈməʊbaɪl/ adj immo-

bile. **~ize** vt immobilizzare

immoderate /ɪˈmɒdərət/ adj smodato

immoral /ɪˈmɒrəl/ adj immorale. **~ity** n immoralità f

immortal /ɪˈmɔːtl/ adj immortale. **~ity** n immortalità f. **~ize** vt immortalare

immune /ɪˈmjuːn/ adj immune (to/from da). **~ system** n sistema m immunitario

immunity /ɪˈmjuːnəti/ n immunità f

immuniz|e /ˈɪmjʊnaɪz/ vt immunizzare

imp /ɪmp/ n diavoletto m

impact /ˈɪmpækt/ n impatto m

impair /ɪmˈpeə(r)/ vt danneggiare

impale /ɪmˈpeɪl/ vt impalare

impart /ɪmˈpɑːt/ vt impartire

im'partial adj imparziale. **~ality** n imparzialità f

im'passable adj impraticabile

im'passive adj impassibile

im'patien|ce n impazienza f. **~t** adj impaziente. **~tly** adv impazientemente

impeccabl|e /ɪmˈpekəbl/ adj impeccabile. **~y** adv in modo impeccabile

impede /ɪmˈpiːd/ vt impedire

impediment /ɪmˈpedɪmənt/ n impedimento m; (in speech) difetto m

impending /ɪmˈpendɪŋ/ adj imminente

impenetrable /ɪmˈpenɪtrəbl/ adj impenetrabile

imperative /ɪmˈperətɪv/ adj imperativo ● n (Gram) imperativo m

imper'ceptible adj impercettibile

im'perfect adj imperfetto; (faulty) difettoso ● n (Gram) imperfetto m. **~ion** n imperfezione f

imperial /ɪmˈpɪərɪəl/ adj imperiale. **~ism** n imperialismo m. **~ist** n imperialista mf

im'personal *adj* impersonale

impersonat|e /ɪm'pɜːsəneɪt/ *vt* impersonare. **~or** *n* imitatore, -trice *mf*

impertinen|ce /ɪm'pɜːtɪnəns/ *n* impertinenza *f*. **~t** *adj* impertinente

impervious /ɪm'pɜːvɪəs/ *adj* **~ to** *fig* indifferente a

impetuous /ɪm'petjʊəs/ *adj* impetuoso. **~ly** *adv* impetuosamente

impetus /'ɪmpɪtəs/ *n* impeto *m*

implacable /ɪm'plækəbl/ *adj* implacabile

im'plant[1] *vt* trapiantare; *fig* inculcare

'implant[2] *n* trapianto *m*

implement[1] /'ɪmplɪmənt/ *n* attrezzo *m*

implement[2] /'ɪmplɪment/ *vt* mettere in atto. **~ation** /-'eɪʃn/ *n* attuazione *f*

implicat|e /'ɪmplɪkeɪt/ *vt* implicare. **~ion** *n* implicazione *f*; **by ~ion** implicitamente

implicit /ɪm'plɪsɪt/ *adj* implicito; (*absolute*) assoluto

implore /ɪm'plɔː(r)/ *vt* implorare

imply /ɪm'plaɪ/ *vt* (*pt/pp* -ied) implicare; **what are you ~ing?** che cosa vorresti insinuare?

impo'lite *adj* sgarbato

import[1] /'ɪmpɔːt/ *n* (*Comm*) importazione *f*

import[2] /ɪm'pɔːt/ *vt* importare

importan|ce /ɪm'pɔːtəns/ *n* importanza *f*. **~t** *adj* importante

importer /ɪm'pɔːtə(r)/ *n* importatore, -trice *mf*

impos|e /ɪm'pəʊz/ *vt* imporre (**on** a) ● *vi* imporsi; **~e on** abusare di. **~ing** *adj* imponente. **~ition** *n* imposizione *f*

impossi'bility *n* impossibilità *f*

im'possibl|e *adj* impossibile

impostor /ɪm'pɒstə(r)/ *n* impostore, -trice *mf*

impoten|ce /'ɪmpətəns/ *n* impotenza *f*. **~t** *adj* impotente

impound /ɪm'paʊnd/ *vt* confiscare

impoverished /ɪm'pɒvərɪʃt/ *adj* impoverito

im'practical *adj* non pratico

impregnable /ɪm'pregnəbl/ *adj* imprendibile

impregnate /'ɪmpregneɪt/ *vt* impregnare (**with** di); (*Biol*) fecondare

im'press *vt* imprimere; *fig* colpire (*positivamente*); **~ sth on sb** fare capire qcsa a qcno

impression /ɪm'preʃn/ *n* impressione *f*; (*imitation*) imitazione *f*. **~able** *adj* (child, mind) influenzabile. **~ism** *n* impressionismo *m*. **~ist** *n* imitatore, -trice *mf*; (*artist*) impressionista *mf*

impressive /ɪm'presɪv/ *adj* imponente

'imprint[1] *n* impressione *f*

im'print[2] *vt* imprimere; **~ed on my mind** impresso nella mia memoria

im'prison *vt* incarcerare. **~ment** *n* reclusione *f*

im'probable *adj* improbabile

impromptu /ɪm'prɒmptjuː/ *adj* improvvisato

im'proper *adj* (use) improprio; (behaviour) scorretto. **~ly** *adv* scorrettamente

improve /ɪm'pruːv/ *vt/i* migliorare. **improve on** *vt* perfezionare. **~ment** *n* miglioramento *m*

improvis|e /'ɪmprəvaɪz/ *vt/i* improvvisare

impuden|ce /'ɪmpjʊdəns/ *n* sfrontatezza *f*. **~t** *adj* sfrontato

impuls|e /'ɪmpʌls/ *n* impulso *m*; **on [an] ~e** impulsivamente. **~ive** *adj* impulsivo

im'pur|e *adj* impuro. **~ity** *n* impurità *f inv*; **~ities** *pl* impurità *fpl*

in /ɪn/ *prep* in; (with names of towns) a;

in the garden in giardino; in the street in *or* per strada; in bed/hospital a letto/all'ospedale; in the world nel mondo; in the rain sotto la pioggia; in the sun al sole; in this heat con questo caldo; in summer/winter in estate/inverno; in 1995 nel 1995; in the evening la sera; he's arriving in two hours time arriva fra due ore; deaf in one ear sordo da un orecchio; in the army nell'esercito; in English/Italian in inglese/italiano; in ink/pencil a penna/matita; in red (dressed, circled) di rosso; the man in the raincoat l'uomo con l'impermeabile; in a soft/loud voice a voce bassa/alta; one in ten people una persona su dieci; in doing this, he... nel far questo,...; in himself in sé; in that in quanto ● adv (at home) a casa; (indoors) dentro; he's not in yet non è ancora arrivato; in there/here li/qui dentro; ten in all dieci in tutto; day in, day out giorno dopo giorno; have it in for sb ⚀ avercela con qcno; send him in fallo entrare; come in entrare; bring in the washing portare dentro i panni ● adj (⚀: in fashion) di moda ● n the ins and outs i dettagli

ina'bility n incapacità f

inac'cessible adj inaccessibile

in'accuracy n inesattezza f. **~te** adj inesatto

in'active adj inattivo. **~'tivity** n inattività f

in'adequate adj inadeguato. **~ly** adv inadeguatamente

inadvertently /ɪnəd'vɜːtntlɪ/ adv inavvertitamente

inad'visable adj sconsigliabile

inane /ɪ'neɪn/ adj stupido

in'animate adj esanime

inap'propriate adj inadatto

inar'ticulate adj inarticolato

inat'tentive adj disattento

in'audible adj impercettibile

inaugurate /ɪ'nɔːɡjʊreɪt/ vt inaugurare. **~ion** n inaugurazione f

inborn /'ɪnbɔːn/ adj innato

inbred /ɪn'bred/ adj congenito

incalculable /ɪn'kælkjʊləbl/ adj incalcolabile

in'capable adj incapace

incapacitate /ɪnkə'pæsɪteɪt/ vt rendere incapace

incarnate /ɪn'kɑːnət/ adj the devil **~e** il diavolo in carne e ossa

incendiary /ɪn'sendɪərɪ/ adj incendiario

incense[1] /'ɪnsens/ n incenso m

incense[2] /ɪn'sens/ vt esasperare

incentive /ɪn'sentɪv/ n incentivo m

incessant /ɪn'sesənt/ adj incessante

incest /'ɪnsest/ n incesto m

inch /ɪntʃ/ n pollice m (= 2.54 cm) ● vi **~** forward avanzare gradatamente

inciden|ce /'ɪnsɪdəns/ n incidenza f. **~t** n incidente m

incidental /ɪnsɪ'dentl/ adj incidentale; **~** expenses spese fpl accessorie. **~ly** adv incidentalmente; (by the way) a proposito

incinerate /ɪn'sɪnəreɪt/ vt incenerire. **~or** n inceneritore m

incision /ɪn'sɪʒn/ n incisione f

incite /ɪn'saɪt/ vt incitare. **~ment** n incitamento m

inclination /ɪnklɪ'neɪʃn/ n inclinazione f

incline[1] /ɪn'klaɪn/ vt inclinare; be **~d** to do sth essere propenso a fare qcsa

incline[2] /'ɪnklaɪn/ n pendio m

include /ɪn'kluːd/ vt includere. **~ding** prep incluso. **~sion** n inclusione f

inclusive /ɪn'kluːsɪv/ adj incluso; **~** of comprendente; be **~** of comprendere ● adv incluso

incognito /ɪnkɒg'niːtəʊ/ adv incognito

inco'herent adj incoerente; (be-

cause drunk etc) incomprensibile

income /'ɪnkʌm/ n reddito m. ~ **tax** n imposta f sul reddito

'incoming adj in arrivo. ~ **tide** n marea f montante

in'comparable adj incomparabile

incom'patible adj incompatibile

in'competen|ce n incompetenza f. ~**t** adj incompetente

incom'plete adj incompleto

incompre'hensible adj incomprensibile

incon'ceivable adj inconcepibile

incon'clusive adj inconcludente

incongruous /ɪn'kɒŋgruəs/ adj contrastante

incon'siderate adj trascurabile

incon'sistency n incoerenza f

incon'sistent adj incoerente; be ~ with non essere coerente con. ~**ly** adv in modo incoerente

incon'spicuous adj non appariscente. ~**ly** adv modestamente

incon'venien|ce n scomodità f; *(drawback)* inconveniente m; put sb to ~**ce** dare disturbo a qcno. ~**t** adj scomodo; *(time, place)* inopportuno. ~**tly** adv in modo inopportuno

incorporate /ɪn'kɔːpəreɪt/ vt incorporare; *(contain)* comprendere

incor'rect adj incorretto. ~**ly** adv scorrettamente

increase[1] /'ɪŋkriːs/ n aumento m; on the ~ in aumento

increas|e[2] /ɪn'kriːs/ vt/i aumentare. ~**ing** adj *(impatience etc)* crescente; *(numbers)* in aumento. ~**ingly** adv sempre più

in'credible adj incredibile

incredulous /ɪn'kredjʊləs/ adj incredulo

incriminate /ɪn'krɪmɪneɪt/ vt *(Jur)* incriminare

incubat|e /'ɪŋkjʊbeɪt/ vt incubare. ~**ion** n incubazione f. ~**ion period** n *(Med)* periodo m di incubazione.

~**or** n *(for baby)* incubatrice f

incur /ɪn'kɜː(r)/ vt *(pt/pp* incurred*)* incorrere; contrarre *(debts)*

in'curable adj incurabile

indebted /ɪn'detɪd/ adj obbligato (to verso)

in'decent adj indecente

inde'cision n indecisione f

inde'cisive adj indeciso. ~**ness** n indecisione f

indeed /ɪn'diːd/ adv *(in fact)* difatti; yes ~! sì, certamente!; ~ I am/do veramente!; very much ~ moltissimo; thank you very much ~ grazie infinite; ~? davvero?

inde'finable adj indefinibile

in'definite adj indefinito. ~**ly** adv indefinitamente; *(postpone)* a tempo indeterminato

indelible /ɪn'delɪbl/ adj indelebile

indemnity /ɪn'demnɪtɪ/ n indennità f pl

indent[1] /'ɪndent/ n *(Typ)* rientranza f dal margine

indent[2] /ɪn'dent/ vt *(Typ)* fare rientrare dal margine. ~**ation** n *(notch)* intaccatura f

inde'penden|ce n indipendenza f. ~**t** adj indipendente. ~**tly** adv indipendentemente

indescribable /ɪndɪ'skraɪbəbl/ adj indescrivibile

indestructible /ɪndɪ'strʌktəbl/ adj indistruttibile

indeterminate /ɪndɪ'tɜːmɪnət/ adj indeterminato

index /'ɪndeks/ n indice m

index: ~ **finger** n dito m indice. ~**-linked** adj *(pension)* legato al costo della vita

India /'ɪndɪə/ n India f. ~**n** adj indiano; *(American)* indiano [d'America] ● n indiano, -a *mf*; *(American)* indiano, -a *mf* [d'America]

indicat|e /'ɪndɪkeɪt/ vt indicare; *(register)* segnare ● vi *(Auto)* mettere la freccia. ~**ion** n indicazione f

indicative /ɪnˈdɪkətɪv/ adj be ~ of essere indicativo di ●n (Gram) indicativo m

indicator /ˈɪndɪkeɪtə(r)/ n (Auto) freccia f

indict /ɪnˈdaɪt/ vt accusare. ~**ment** n accusa f

in'differen|ce n indifferenza f. ~**t** adj indifferente; (not good) mediocre

indi'gestible adj indigesto. ~**ion** n indigestione f

indigna|nt /ɪnˈdɪɡnənt/ adj indignato. ~**ntly** adv con indignazione. ~**tion** n indignazione f

indi'rect adj indiretto. ~**ly** adv indirettamente

indis'creet adj indiscreto

indis'cretion n indiscrezione f

indiscriminate /ɪndɪˈskrɪmɪnət/ adj indiscriminato. ~**ly** adv senza distinzione

indi'spensable adj indispensabile

indisposed /ɪndɪˈspəʊzd/ adj indisposto

indis'putable adj indiscutibile, indisputabile

indistinguishable /ɪndɪˈstɪŋɡwɪʃəbl/ adj indistinguibile

individual /ɪndɪˈvɪdʒʊəl/ adj individuale ●n individuo m. ~**ity** n individualità f

indoctrinate /ɪnˈdɒktrɪneɪt/ vt indottrinare

indomitable /ɪnˈdɒmɪtəbl/ adj indomito

indoor /ˈɪndɔː(r)/ adj interno; (shoes) per casa; (plant) da appartamento; (swimming pool etc) coperto. ~**s** adv dentro

induce /ɪnˈdjuːs/ vt indurre (to a); (produce) causare. ~**ment** n (incentive) incentivo m

indulge /ɪnˈdʌldʒ/ vt soddisfare; viziare (child) ●vi ~ in concedersi. ~**nce** n lusso m; (leniency) indulgenza

f. ~**nt** adj indulgente

industrial /ɪnˈdʌstrɪəl/ adj industriale; take ~ action scioperare. ~**ist** n industriale mf. ~**ized** adj industrializzato

industr|ious /ɪnˈdʌstrɪəs/ adj industrioso. ~**y** n industria f; (zeal) operosità f

inebriated /ɪˈniːbrɪeɪtɪd/ adj ebbro

in'edible adj immangiabile

inef'fective adj inefficace

ineffectual /ɪnɪˈfektʃʊəl/ adj inutile; (person) inconcludente

inef'ficien|cy n inefficienza f. ~**t** adj inefficiente

in'eligible adj inadatto

inept /ɪˈnept/ adj inetto

ine'quality n ineguaglianza f

inert /ɪˈnɜːt/ adj inerte. ~**ia** n inerzia f

inescapable /ɪnɪˈskeɪpəbl/ adj inevitabile

inevitabl|e /ɪnˈevɪtəbl/ adj inevitabile. ~**y** adv inevitabilmente

ine'xact adj inesatto

inex'cusable adj imperdonabile

inex'pensive adj poco costoso

inex'perience n inesperienza f. ~**d** adj inesperto

inexplicable /ɪnɪkˈsplɪkəbl/ adj inesplicabile

in'fallible adj infallibile

infam|ous /ˈɪnfəməs/ adj infame; (person) famigerato. ~**y** n infamia f

infan|cy /ˈɪnfənsɪ/ n infanzia f; in its ~**cy** fig agli inizi. ~**t** n bambino, -a mf piccolo, -a. ~**tile** adj infantile

infantry /ˈɪnfəntrɪ/ n fanteria f

infatuat|ed /ɪnˈfætʃʊeɪtɪd/ adj infatuato (with di). ~**ion** n infatuazione f

infect /ɪnˈfekt/ vt infettare; become ~**ed** (wound:) infettarsi. ~**ion** adj infettivo

infer /ɪnˈfɜː(r)/ vt (pt/pp inferred) dedurre (from da); (imply) implicare.

~**ence** n deduzione f

inferior /ɪnˈfɪərɪə(r)/ adj inferiore; (goods) scadente; (in rank) subalterno ●n inferiore mf; (in rank) subalterno, -a mf

inferiority /ɪnfɪərɪˈɒrətɪ/ n inferiorità f. ~ **complex** n complesso m di inferiorità

in'fertile adj sterile. ~**tility** n sterilità f

infest /ɪnˈfest/ vt be ~ed with essere infestato di

infi'delity n infedeltà f

infiltrate /ˈɪnfɪltreɪt/ vt infiltrare; (Pol) infiltrarsi in

infinite /ˈɪnfɪnət/ adj infinito

infinitive /ɪnˈfɪnɪtɪv/ n (Gram) infinito m

infinity /ɪnˈfɪnətɪ/ n infinità f

infirm /ɪnˈfɜːm/ adj debole. ~**ary** n infermeria f. ~**ity** n debolezza f

inflame /ɪnˈfleɪm/ vt infiammare. ~**d** adj infiammato; become ~**d** infiammarsi

in'flammable adj infiammabile

inflammation /ɪnfləˈmeɪʃn/ n infiammazione f

inflat|e /ɪnˈfleɪt/ vt gonfiare. ~**ion** n inflazione f. ~**ionary** adj inflazionario

in'flexible adj inflessibile

inflict /ɪnˈflɪkt/ vt infliggere (on a)

influen|ce /ˈɪnflʊəns/ n influenza f ●vt influenzare. ~**tial** adj influente

influenza /ɪnflʊˈenzə/ n influenza f

influx /ˈɪnflʌks/ n affluenza f

inform /ɪnˈfɔːm/ vt informare; keep sb ~ed tenere qcno al corrente ●vi ~ against denunciare

in'for|mal adj informale; (agreement) ufficioso. ~**mality** n informalità f inv. ~**mally** adv in modo informale. ~**mality** n informalità f inv

informat|ion /ɪnfəˈmeɪʃn/ n informazioni fpl; a piece of ~ un'informazione. ~**ion highway** n autostrada f telematica. ~**ion**

technology n informatica f. ~**ive** adj informativo; (film, book) istruttivo

informer /ɪnˈfɔːmə(r)/ n informatore, -trice mf; (Pol) delatore, -trice mf

infra-'red /ɪnfrə-/ adj infrarosso

infringe /ɪnˈfrɪndʒ/ vt ~ on usurpare. ~**ment** n violazione f

infuriat|e /ɪnˈfjʊərɪeɪt/ vt infuriare. ~**ing** adj esasperante

ingenious /ɪnˈdʒiːnɪəs/ adj ingegnoso

ingenuity /ɪndʒɪˈnjuːətɪ/ n ingegnosità f

ingot /ˈɪŋgət/ n lingotto m

ingrained /ɪnˈgreɪnd/ adj (in person) radicato; (dirt) incrostato

ingratiate /ɪnˈgreɪʃɪeɪt/ vt ~ oneself with sb ingraziarsi qcno

in'gratitude n ingratitudine f

ingredient /ɪnˈgriːdɪənt/ n ingrediente m

ingrowing /ˈɪngrəʊɪŋ/ adj (nail) incarnito

inhabit /ɪnˈhæbɪt/ vt abitare. ~**ant** n abitante mf

inhale /ɪnˈheɪl/ vt aspirare; (Med) inalare ●vi inspirare; (when smoking) aspirare. ~**r** n (device) inalatore m

inherent /ɪnˈhɪərənt/ adj inerente

inherit /ɪnˈherɪt/ vt ereditare. ~**ance** n eredità f inv

inhibit /ɪnˈhɪbɪt/ vt inibire. ~**ed** adj inibito. ~**ion** n inibizione f

inho'spitable adj inospitale

initial /ɪˈnɪʃl/ adj iniziale ●n iniziale f ●vt (pt/pp **initialled**) siglare. ~**ly** adv all'inizio

initiat|e /ɪˈnɪʃɪeɪt/ vt iniziare. ~**ion** n iniziazione f

initiative /ɪˈnɪʃətɪv/ n iniziativa f

inject /ɪnˈdʒekt/ vt iniettare. ~**ion** n iniezione f

injur|e /ˈɪndʒə(r)/ vt ferire; (wrong) nuocere. ~**y** n ferita f; (wrong) torto m in'justice n ingiustizia f; do sb an ~ giudicare qcno in modo sbagliato

ink /ɪŋk/ n inchiostro m

inland /'ɪnlənd/ adj interno ● adv all'interno. I~ Revenue n fisco m

in-laws /'ɪnlɔːz/ npl 🔢 parenti mpl acquisiti

inlay /'ɪnleɪ/ n intarsio m

inlet /'ɪnlet/ n insenatura f; (Techn) entrata f

inmate /'ɪnmeɪt/ n (of hospital) degente mf; (of prison) carcerato, -a mf

inn /ɪn/ n locanda f

innate /ɪ'neɪt/ adj innato

inner /'ɪnə(r)/ adj interno. ~most adj il più profondo. ~ tube camera f d'aria

innocen|ce /'ɪnəsəns/ n innocenza f. ~t adj innocente

innocuous /ɪ'nɒkjʊəs/ adj innocuo

innovat|e /'ɪnəveɪt/ vi innovare. ~ion n innovazione f. ~ive adj innovativo. ~or n innovatore, -trice mf

innuendo /ɪnjʊ'endəʊ/ n (pl -es) insinuazione f

innumerable /ɪ'njuːmərəbl/ adj innumerevole

inoculat|e /ɪ'nɒkjʊleɪt/ vt vaccinare. ~ion n vaccinazione f

inof'fensive adj inoffensivo

in'opportune adj inopportuno

input /'ɪnput/ n input m inv, ingresso m

inquest /'ɪnkwest/ n inchiesta f

inquir|e /ɪn'kwaɪə(r)/ vi informarsi (about su); ~e into far indagini su ● vt domandare. ~y n domanda f; (investigation) inchiesta f

inquisitive /ɪn'kwɪzətɪv/ adj curioso

in'sane adj pazzo; fig insensato

in'sanity n pazzia f

insatiable /ɪn'seɪʃəbl/ adj insaziabile

inscri|be /ɪn'skraɪb/ vt iscrivere. ~ption n iscrizione f

inscrutable /ɪn'skruːtəbl/ adj impenetrabile

insect /'ɪnsekt/ n insetto m. ~icide n insetticida m

inse'cur|e adj malsicuro; (fig: person) insicuro. ~ity n mancanza f di sicurezza

in'sensitive adj insensibile

in'separable adj inseparabile

insert¹ /'ɪnsɜːt/ n inserto m

insert² /ɪn'sɜːt/ vt inserire. ~ion n inserzione f

inside /ɪn'saɪd/ n interno m. ~s npl 🔢 pancia f ● attrib (Auto) ~ lane n corsia f interna ● adv dentro; ~ out a rovescio; (thoroughly) a fondo ● prep dentro; (of time) entro

insight /'ɪnsaɪt/ n intuito m (into per); an ~ into un quadro di

insig'nificant adj insignificante

insin'cere adj poco sincero. ~ity n mancanza f di sincerità

insinuat|e /ɪn'sɪnjʊeɪt/ vt insinuare. ~ion n insinuazione f

insipid /ɪn'sɪpɪd/ adj insipido

insist /ɪn'sɪst/ vi insistere (on per) ● vt ~ that insistere che. ~ence n insistenza f. ~ent adj insistente

insolen|ce /'ɪnsələns/ n insolenza f. ~t adj insolente

in'soluble adj insolubile

insomnia /ɪn'sɒmnɪə/ n insonnia f

inspect /ɪn'spekt/ vt ispezionare; controllare (ticket). ~ion n ispezione f; (of ticket) controllo m. ~or n ispettore, -trice mf; (of tickets) controllore m

inspiration /ɪnspə'reɪʃn/ n ispirazione f

inspire /ɪn'spaɪə(r)/ vt ispirare

insta'bility n instabilità f

install /ɪn'stɔːl/ vt installare. ~ation n installazione f

instalment /ɪn'stɔːlmənt/ n (Comm) rata f; (of serial) puntata f; (of publication) fascicolo m

instance /'ɪnstəns/ n (case) caso m; (example) esempio m; **in the first ~** in primo luogo; **for ~** per esempio

instant /'ɪnstənt/ adj immediato; (Culin) espresso ● n istante m. **~aneous** adj istantaneo

instead /ɪn'sted/ adv invece; **~ of doing** anziché fare; **~ of me** al mio posto; **~ of going** invece di andare

instigat|e /'ɪnstɪgeɪt/ vt istigare. **~ion** n istigazione f; **at his ~ion** dietro suo suggerimento. **~or** n istigatore, -trice mf

instinct /'ɪnstɪŋkt/ n istinto m. **~ive** adj istintivo

institut|e /'ɪnstɪtjuːt/ n istituto m ● vt istituire (scheme); intentare (search); intentare (legal action). **~ion** n istituzione f; (home for elderly) istituto m per anziani; (for mentally ill) istituto m per malati di mente

instruct /ɪn'strʌkt/ vt istruire; (order) ordinare. **~ion** n istruzione f; **~s** (orders) ordini mpl. **~ive** adj istruttivo. **~or** n istruttore, -trice mf

instrument /'ɪnstrəmənt/ n strumento m. **~al** adj strumentale; **be ~al in** contribuire a. **~alist** n strumentista mf

insu'bordi|nate adj insubordinato. **~nation** n insubordinazione f

in'sufferable adj insopportabile

insuf'ficient adj insufficiente

insular /'ɪnsjʊlə(r)/ adj fig gretto

insulat|e /'ɪnsjʊleɪt/ vt isolare. **~ing tape** n nastro m isolante. **~ion** n isolamento m

insulin /'ɪnsjʊlɪn/ n insulina f

insult[1] /'ɪnsʌlt/ n insulto m

insult[2] /ɪn'sʌlt/ vt insultare

insur|ance /ɪn'ʃʊərəns/ n assicurazione f. **~e** vt assicurare

intact /ɪn'tækt/ adj intatto

integral /'ɪntɪɡrəl/ adj integrale

integrat|e /'ɪntɪɡreɪt/ vt integrare ● vi integrarsi. **~ion** n integrazione f

integrity /ɪn'teɡrətɪ/ n integrità f

intellect /'ɪntəlekt/ n intelletto m. **~ual** adj & n intellettuale m

intelligen|ce /ɪn'telɪdʒəns/ n intelligenza f; (Mil) informazioni fpl. **~t** adj intelligente

intelligible /ɪn'telɪdʒəbl/ adj intelligibile

intend /ɪn'tend/ vt destinare; (have in mind) aver intenzione di; **be ~ed for** essere destinato a. **~ed** adj (effect) voluto ● n my **~ed** 🄸 il mio/la mia fidanzato, -a

intense /ɪn'tens/ adj intenso; (person) dai sentimenti intensi. **~ly** adv intensamente; (very) estremamente

intensity /ɪn'tensətɪ/ n intensità f

intensive /ɪn'tensɪv/ adj intensivo. **~ care** (for people in coma) rianimazione f; **~ care [unit]** terapia f intensiva

intent /ɪn'tent/ adj intento; **~ on** (absorbed in) preso da; **be ~ on doing** sth essere intento a fare qcsa ● n intenzione f; **to all ~s and purposes** a tutti gli effetti. **~ly** adv attentamente

intention /ɪn'tenʃn/ n intenzione f. **~al** adj intenzionale. **~ally** adv intenzionalmente

inter'action n cooperazione f. **~ve** adj interattivo

intercept /ɪntə'sept/ vt intercettare

'interchange n scambio m; (Auto) raccordo m [autostradale]

inter'changeable adj interscambiabile

'intercourse n (sexual) rapporti mpl [sessuali]

interest /'ɪntrəst/ n interesse m; **have an ~ in** (Comm) essere cointeressato in; **be of ~** essere interessante; **~ rate** n tasso m di interesse ● vt interessare. **~ed** adj interessato. **~ing** adj interessante

interface /'ɪntəfeɪs/ n interfaccia f ● vt interfacciare ● vi interfacciarsi

interfere /ɪntəˈfɪə(r)/ vi interferire; ~ **with** interferire con. ~**nce** n interferenza f

interior /ɪnˈtɪərɪə(r)/ adj interiore ● n interno m. ~ **designer** n arredatore, -trice f

interlude /ˈɪntəluːd/ n intervallo m

intermediary /ɪntəˈmiːdɪərɪ/ n intermediario, -a mf

interminable /ɪnˈtɜːmɪnəbl/ adj interminabile

intermittent /ɪntəˈmɪtənt/ adj intermittente

intern /ɪnˈtɜːn/ vt internare

internal /ɪnˈtɜːnl/ adj interno. I~ 'Revenue (Am) n fisco m. ~**ly** adv internamente; (deal with) all'interno

inter'national adj internazionale ● n (game) incontro m internazionale; (player) competitore, -trice mf in gare internazionali. ~**ly** adv internazionalmente

Internet /ˈɪntənet/ n Internet m

interpret /ɪnˈtɜːprɪt/ vt interpretare ● vi fare l'interprete. ~**ation** n interpretazione f. ~**er** n interprete mf

interrogate /ɪnˈterəgeɪt/ vt interrogare. ~**ion** n interrogazione f; (by police) interrogatorio m

interrogative /ɪntəˈrɒgətɪv/ adj & n ~ [pronoun] interrogativo m

interrupt /ɪntəˈrʌpt/ vt/i interrompere. ~**ion** n interruzione f

intersect /ɪntəˈsekt/ vi intersecarsi ● vt intersecare. ~**ion** n intersezione f; (of street) incrocio m

inter'twine vi attorcigliarsi

interval /ˈɪntəvl/ n intervallo m; bright ~s pl schiarite fpl

intervene /ɪntəˈviːn/ vi intervenire. ~**tion** n intervento m

interview /ˈɪntəvjuː/ n (Journ) intervista f; (for job) colloquio m [di lavoro] ● vt intervistare. ~**er** n intervistatore, -trice mf

intestine /ɪnˈtestɪn/ n intestino m.

~**al** adj intestinale

intimacy /ˈɪntɪməsɪ/ n intimità f

intimate[1] /ˈɪntɪmət/ adj intimo. ~**ly** adv intimamente

intimate[2] /ˈɪntɪmeɪt/ vt far capire; (imply) suggerire

intimidate /ɪnˈtɪmɪdeɪt/ vt intimidire. ~**ion** n intimidazione f

into /ˈɪntə/, di fronte a una vocale /ˈɪntʊ/ prep dentro, in; go ~ the house andare dentro [casa] o in casa; be ~ (fam: like) essere appassionato di; I'm not ~ that questo non mi piace; 7 ~ 21 goes 3 il 7 nel 21 ci sta 3 volte; translate ~ French tradurre in francese; get ~ trouble mettersi nei guai

in'tolerable adj intollerabile

in'toleran|ce n intolleranza f. ~**t** adj intollerante

intoxicat|ed /ɪnˈtɒksɪkeɪtɪd/ adj inebriato. ~**ion** n ebbrezza f

in'transitive adj intransitivo

intravenous /ɪntrəˈviːnəs/ adj endovenoso. ~**ly** adv per via endovenosa

intrepid /ɪnˈtrepɪd/ adj intrepido

intricate /ˈɪntrɪkət/ adj complesso

intrigu|e /ɪnˈtriːg/ n intrigo m ● vt intrigare ● vi tramare. ~**ing** adj intrigante

intrinsic /ɪnˈtrɪnsɪk/ adj intrinseco

introduce /ɪntrəˈdjuːs/ vt presentare; (bring in, insert) introdurre

introduct|ion /ɪntrəˈdʌkʃn/ n (to person) presentazione f; (to book) prefazione f. ~**ory** adj introduttivo

introvert /ˈɪntrəvɜːt/ n introverso, -a mf

intru|de /ɪnˈtruːd/ vi intromettersi. ~**der** n intruso, -a mf. ~**sion** n intrusione f

intuit|ion /ɪntjuˈɪʃn/ n intuito m. ~**ive** adj intuitivo

inundate /ˈɪnəndeɪt/ vt (flood)

inondare (with di)

invade /ɪnˈveɪd/ vt invadere. ∼r n invasore m

invalid[1] /ˈɪnvəlɪd/ n invalido, -a mf

invalid[2] /ɪnˈvælɪd/ adj non valido. ∼ate vt invalidare

in'valuable adj prezioso; (priceless) inestimabile

in'variabl|e adj invariabile. ∼y adv invariabilmente

invasion /ɪnˈveɪʒn/ n invasione f

invent /ɪnˈvent/ vt inventare. ∼ion n invenzione f. ∼ive adj inventivo. ∼or n inventore, -trice mf

inventory /ˈɪnvəntrɪ/ n inventario m

invest /ɪnˈvest/ vt investire ● vi fare investimenti; ∼ in (fig: buy) comprarsi

investigat|e /ɪnˈvestɪɡeɪt/ vt investigare. ∼ion n investigazione f

invest|ment /ɪnˈvestmənt/ n investimento m. ∼or n investitore, -trice mf

inveterate /ɪnˈvetərət/ adj inveterato

invidious /ɪnˈvɪdɪəs/ adj ingiusto; (position) antipatico

invincible /ɪnˈvɪnsəbl/ adj invincibile

in'visible adj invisibile

invitation /ɪnvɪˈteɪʃn/ n invito m

invit|e /ɪnˈvaɪt/ vt invitare; (attract) attirare. ∼ing adj invitante

invoice /ˈɪnvɔɪs/ n fattura f ● vt ∼ sb emettere una fattura a qcno

in'voluntar|y adj involontario

involve /ɪnˈvɒlv/ vt comportare; (affect, include) coinvolgere; (entail) implicare; get ∼d with sb legarsi a qcno; (romantically) legarsi sentimentalmente a qcno. ∼d adj complesso. ∼ment n coinvolgimento m

inward /ˈɪnwəd/ adj interno; (thoughts etc) interiore; ∼ investment (Comm) investimento m stra-

niero. ∼ly adv interiormente. ∼[s] adv verso l'interno

iodine /ˈaɪədiːn/ n iodio m

iota /aɪˈəʊtə/ n briciolo m

IOU n abbr (I owe you) pagherò m inv

IQ n abbr (intelligence quotient) Q.I.

Iran /ɪˈrɑːn/ n Iran m. ∼ian adj & n iraniano, -a mf

Iraq /ɪˈrɑːk/ n Iraq m. ∼i adj & n iracheno, -a mf

irate /aɪˈreɪt/ adj adirato

Ireland /ˈaɪələnd/ n Irlanda f

iris /ˈaɪrɪs/ n (Anat) iride f; (Bot) iris f inv

Irish /ˈaɪrɪʃ/ adj irlandese ● n the ∼ pl gli irlandesi mpl. ∼man n irlandese m. ∼woman n irlandese f

iron /ˈaɪən/ adj di ferro. I∼ Curtain n cortina f di ferro ● n ferro m; (appliance) ferro m [da stiro] ● vt/i stirare. □ ∼ out vt eliminare stirando; fig appianare

'**ironmonger** /-ˌmʌŋɡə(r)/ n ∼'s [shop] negozio m di ferramenta

irony /ˈaɪrənɪ/ n ironia f

irrational /ɪˈræʃənl/ adj irrazionale

irrefutable /ɪrɪˈfjuːtəbl/ adj irrefutabile

irregular /ɪˈreɡjʊlə(r)/ adj irregolare. ∼ity n irregolarità f inv

irrelevant /ɪˈreləvənt/ adj non pertinente

irreparabl|e /ɪˈrepərəbl/ adj irreparabile. ∼y adv irreparabilmente

irreplaceable /ɪrɪˈpleɪsəbl/ adj insostituibile

irresistible /ɪrɪˈzɪstəbl/ adj irresistibile

irrespective /ɪrɪˈspektɪv/ adj ∼ of senza riguardo per

irresponsible /ɪrɪˈspɒnsɪbl/ adj irresponsabile

irreverent /ɪˈrevərənt/ adj irreverente

irrevocabl|e /ɪˈrevəkəbl/ adj irrevocabile. ∼y adv irrevocabilmente

irrigat|e /'ɪrɪgeɪt/ vt irrigare. **~ion** n irrigazione f

irritable /'ɪrɪtəbl/ adj irritabile

irrita|te /'ɪrɪteɪt/ vt irritare. **~ing** adj irritante. **~ion** n irritazione f

is /ɪz/ ▷BE

Islam /'ɪzlɑːm/ n Islam m. **~ic** adj islamico

island /'aɪlənd/ n isola f; (in road) isola f spartitraffico. **~er** n isolano, -a mf

isolat|e /'aɪsəleɪt/ vt isolare. **~ed** adj isolato. **~ion** n isolamento m

Israel /'ɪzreɪl/ n Israele m. **~i** adj & n israeliano, -a mf

issue /'ɪʃuː/ n (outcome) risultato m; (of magazine) numero m; (of stamps etc) emissione f; (offspring) figli mpl; (matter, question) questione f; **at** ~ in questione; **take** ~ **with sb** prendere posizione contro qcno ● vt distribuire (supplies); rilasciare (passport); emettere (stamps, order); pubblicare (book); **be** ~**d with** sth ricevere qcsa ● vi ~ **from** uscire da

it /ɪt/ pron (direct object) lo m, la f; (indirect object) gli m, le f; **it's broken** è rotto/rotta; **will it be enough?** basterà?; **it's hot** fa caldo; **it's raining** piove; **it's me** sono io; **who is it?** chi è?; **it's two o'clock** sono le due; **I doubt it** ne dubito; **take it with you** prendilo con te; **give it a wipe** dagli una pulita

Italian /ɪ'tæljən/ adj & n italiano, -a mf; (language) italiano m

Italy /'ɪtəlɪ/ n Italia f

itch /ɪtʃ/ n prurito m ● vi avere prurito, prudere; **be** ~**ing to** 𝕀 avere una voglia matta di. **~y** adj che prude; **my foot is** ~**y** ho prurito al piede

item /'aɪtəm/ n articolo m; (on agenda, programme) punto m; (on invoice) voce f; ~ [of news] notizia f. **~ize** vt dettagliare (bill)

itinerary /aɪ'tɪnərərɪ/ n itinerario m

itself /ɪt'self/ pron (reflexive) si; (emphatic) essa stessa; **the baby looked at** ~ **in the mirror** il bambino si è guardato nello specchio; **by** ~ da solo; **the machine in** ~ **is simple** la macchina di per sé è semplice

ITV n abbr (Independent Television) stazione f televisiva privata britannica

ivory /'aɪvərɪ/ n avorio m

ivy /'aɪvɪ/ n edera f

> **The Ivy League** Il gruppo delle più antiche e rinomate università statunitensi, situate nel nordest del paese: Harvard, Yale, Columbia University, Cornell University, Dartmouth College, Brown University, Princeton University e la University of Pennsylvania. L'espressione deriva dall'edera che cresce sugli antichi edifici universitari.

Jj

jab /dʒæb/ n colpo m secco; (𝕀: injection) puntura f ● vt (pt/pp jabbed) punzecchiare

jack /dʒæk/ n (Auto) cric m inv; (in cards) fante m, jack m inv ● **jack up** vt (Auto) sollevare [con il cric]

jackdaw /'dʒækdɔː/ n taccola f

jacket /'dʒækɪt/ n giacca f; (of book) sopraccoperta f. ~ **po'tato** n patata f cotta al forno con la buccia

jackpot /'dʒækpɒt/ n premio m (di una lotteria); **win the** ~ vincere alla lotteria; **hit the** ~ fig fare un colpo grosso

jade /dʒeɪd/ n giada f ● attrib di giada

jagged /'dʒægɪd/ adj dentellato

jail /dʒeɪl/ = gaol

jam¹ /dʒæm/ n marmellata f

jam² n (Auto) ingorgo m; (🔲: difficulty) guaio m ● v t /pt/pp jammed/ ● vt (cram) pigiare; disturbare (broadcast); inceppare (mechanism, drawer etc); be ~med (roads): essere congestionato ● vi (mechanism): incepparsi; (window, drawer): incastrarsi

Jamaica /dʒə'meɪkə/ n Giamaica f. ~n adj & n giamaicano, -a mf

jangle /'dʒæŋgl/ vt far squillare ● vi squillare

janitor /'dʒænɪtə(r)/ n (caretaker) custode m; (in school) bidello, -a mf

January /'dʒænjʊərɪ/ n gennaio m

Japan /dʒə'pæn/ n Giappone m. ~ese /-'niːz/ adj & n giapponese mf; (language) giapponese m

jar¹ /dʒɑː(r)/ n (glass) barattolo m

jar² vi /pt/pp jarred/ (sound): stridere

jargon /'dʒɑːgən/ n gergo m

jaundice /'dʒɔːndɪs/ n itterizia f. ~d adj /dʒɑː/ fig inacidito

jaunt /dʒɔːnt/ n gita f

jaunty /'dʒɔːntɪ/ adj (-ier, -iest) sbarazzino

jaw /dʒɔː/ n mascella f; (bone) mandibola f

jay-walker /'dʒeɪwɔːkə(r)/ n pedone m distratto

jazz /dʒæz/ n jazz m ● jazz up vt ravvivare. ~y adj vistoso

jealous /'dʒeləs/ adj geloso. ~y n gelosia f

jeans /dʒiːnz/ npl [blue] jeans mpl

jeep /dʒiːp/ n jeep f inv

jeer /dʒɪə(r)/ n scherno m ● vi schernire; ~ at prendersi gioco di ● vt (boo) fischiare

jelly /'dʒelɪ/ n gelatina f. ~fish n medusa f

jeopar|dize /'dʒepədaɪz/ vt mettere in pericolo. ~dy n in ~dy in pericolo

jerk /dʒɜːk/ n scatto m, scossa f ● vt scattare ● vi sobbalzare; (limb,

muscle:) muoversi a scatti. ~ily adv a scatti. ~y adj traballante

jersey /'dʒɜːzɪ/ n maglia f; (Sport) maglietta f; (fabric) jersey m

jest /dʒest/ n scherzo m; in ~ per scherzo ● vi scherzare

Jesus /'dʒiːzəs/ n Gesù m

jet¹ /dʒet/ n (stone) giaietto m

jet² n (of water) getto m; (nozzle) becco m; (plane) aviogetto m, jet m inv

jet: ~'black adj nero ebano. ~lag n scombussolamento m da fuso orario. ~pro'pelled adj a reazione

jettison /'dʒetɪsn/ vt gettare a mare; fig abbandonare

jetty /'dʒetɪ/ n molo m

Jew /dʒuː/ n ebreo m

jewel /'dʒuːəl/ n gioiello m. ~ler n gioielliere m; ~ler's [shop] gioielleria f. ~lery n gioielli mpl

jiffy /'dʒɪfɪ/ n 🔲 in a ~ un batter d'occhio

jigsaw /'dʒɪgsɔː/ n ~ [puzzle] puzzle m inv

jilt /dʒɪlt/ vt piantare

jingle /'dʒɪŋgl/ n (rhyme) canzoncina f pubblicitaria ● vi tintinnare

job /dʒɒb/ n lavoro m; this is going to be quite a ~ 🔲 [questa] non sarà un'impresa facile; it's a good ~ that... meno male che.... ~centre n ufficio m statale di collocamento. ~less adj senza lavoro

jockey /'dʒɒkɪ/ n fantino m

jocular /'dʒɒkjʊlə(r)/ adj scherzoso

jog /dʒɒg/ n colpetto m; at a ~ in un balzo; (Sport) go for a ~ andare a fare jogging ● v t /pt/pp jogged/ ● vt (hit) urtare; ~ sb's memory farlo ritornare in mente a qcno ● vi (Sport) fare jogging. ~ging n jogging m

join /dʒɔɪn/ n giuntura f ● vt raggiungere, unire; raggiungere (person); (become member of) iscriversi a; entrare in (firm) ● vi (roads:) congiungersi. □~ **in** vi partecipare. □~ **up** vi (Mil) arruolarsi ●vt unire

joiner /'dʒɔɪnə(r)/ n falegname m

joint /dʒɔɪnt/ adj comune ● n articolazione f; (in wood, brickwork) giuntura f; (Culin) arrosto m; (Ⅲ: bar) bettola f; (Ⅸ:drug) spinello m. **~ly** adv unitamente

joist /dʒɔɪst/ n travetto m

jok|e /dʒəʊk/ n (trick) scherzo m; (funny story) barzelletta f ● vi scherzare. **~er** n burlone, -a mf; (in cards) jolly m inv. **~ing** n ~**ing apart** scherzi a parte. **~ingly** adv per scherzo

jolly /'dʒɒlɪ/ adj (-ier, -iest) allegro ● adv Ⅲ molto

jolt /dʒəʊlt/ n scossa f, sobbalzo m ● vt far sobbalzare ● vi sobbalzare

jostle /'dʒɒsl/ vt spingere

jot /dʒɒt/ n nulla f ● **jot down** vt (pt/pp jotted) annotare. **~ter** n taccuino m

journal /'dʒɜːnl/ n giornale m; (diary) diario m. **~ese** n gergo m giornalistico. **~ism** n giornalismo m. **~ist** n giornalista mf

journey /'dʒɜːnɪ/ n viaggio m

jovial /'dʒəʊvɪəl/ adj gioviale

joy /dʒɔɪ/ n gioia f. **~ful** adj gioioso. **~ride** n Ⅲ giro m con una macchina rubata. **~stick** n (Comput) joystick m inv

jubil|ant /'dʒuːbɪlənt/ adj giubilante. **~ation** n giubilo m

jubilee /'dʒuːbɪliː/ n giubileo m

judge /dʒʌdʒ/ n giudice m ● vt giudicare; (estimate) valutare; (consider) ritenere ● vi giudicare (by da). **~ment** n giudizio m; (Jur) sentenza f

judic|ial /dʒuːˈdɪʃl/ adj giudiziario. **~iary** n magistratura f. **~ious** adj giudizioso

judo /'dʒuːdəʊ/ n judo m

jug /dʒʌg/ n brocca f; (small) bricco m

juggernaut /'dʒʌgənɔːt/ n Ⅲ grosso autotreno m

juggle /'dʒʌgl/ vi fare giochi di destrezza. **~r** n giocoliere, -a mf

juice /dʒuːs/ n succo m

juicy /'dʒuːsɪ/ adj (-ier, -iest) succoso; (Ⅲ: story) piccante

juke-box /'dʒuːk-/ n juke-box m inv

July /dʒʊ'laɪ/ n luglio m

jumble /'dʒʌmbl/ n accozzaglia f ● vt ~ **[up]** mischiare. ~ **sale** n vendita f di beneficenza

jumbo /'dʒʌmbəʊ/ n ~ **[jet]** jumbo jet m inv

jump /dʒʌmp/ n salto m; (in prices) balzo m; (in horse racing) ostacolo m ● vi saltare; (with fright) sussultare; (prices:) salire rapidamente; ~ **to conclusions** saltare alle conclusioni ● vt saltare; ~ **the gun** fig precipitarsi; ~ **the queue** non rispettare la fila. □~ **at** vt fig accettare con entusiasmo (offer). □~ **up** vi rizzarsi in piedi

jumper /'dʒʌmpə(r)/ n (sweater) golf m inv

jumpy /'dʒʌmpɪ/ adj nervoso

junction /'dʒʌŋkʃn/ n (of roads) incrocio m; (of motorway) uscita f; (Rail) nodo m ferroviario

June /dʒuːn/ n giugno m

jungle /'dʒʌŋgl/ n giungla f

junior /'dʒuːnɪə(r)/ adj giovane; (in rank) subalterno; (Sport) junior inv ● n **the** ~ **s** (Sch) i più giovani. ~ **school** n scuola f elementare

junk /dʒʌŋk/ n cianfrusaglie fpl. ~ **food** n Ⅲ cibo m poco sano, porcherie fpl. ~ **mail** posta f spazzatura

junkie /'dʒʌŋkɪ/ n Ⅸ tossico, -a mf

'junk-shop n negozio m di rigattiere

jurisdiction /dʒʊərɪs'dɪkʃn/ n giurisdizione f

juror /'dʒʊərə(r)/ n giurato, -a mf

jury /'dʒʊərɪ/ n giuria f

just /dʒʌst/ adj giusto ● adv (barely)

appena; (simply) solo; (exactly) esattamente; ~ **as tall** altrettanto alto; ~ **as I was leaving** proprio quando stavo andando via; **I've ~ seen her** l'ho appena vista; **it's ~ as well** meno male; ~ **at that moment** proprio in quel momento; ~ **listen!** ascolta!; **I'm ~ going** sto andando proprio ora

justice /'dʒʌstɪs/ n giustizia f; **do ~ to** rendere giustizia a; **J~ of the Peace** giudice m conciliatore

justifiabl|e /'dʒʌstɪfaɪəbl/ adj giustificabile

justi|fication /dʒʌstɪfɪ'keɪʃn/ n giustificazione f. **~fy** vt (pt/pp -ied) giustificare

jut /dʒʌt/ vi (pt/pp jutted) ~ **out** sporgere

juvenile /'dʒu:vənaɪl/ adj giovanile; (childish) infantile; (for the young) per i giovani ●n giovane mf. ~ **delinquency** n delinquenza f giovanile

Kk

kangaroo /kæŋgə'ru:/ n canguro m

karate /kə'rɑ:tɪ/ n karate m

keel /ki:l/ n chiglia f ● **keel over** vi capovolgersi

keen /ki:n/ adj (intense) acuto; (interest) vivo; (eager) entusiastico; (competition) feroce; (wind, wild) tagliente; ~ **on** entusiasta di; **she's ~ on him** le piace molto; **be ~ to do** sth avere voglia di fare qcsa. ~**ness** n entusiasmo m

keep /ki:p/ n (maintenance) mantenimento m; (of castle) maschio m; **for ~s** per sempre ● vt (pt/pp kept) ●vt tenere; (not throw away) conservare; (detain) trattenere; mantenere (family,

promise); avere (shop); allevare (animals); rispettare (law, rules); ~ **sth hot** tenere qcsa in caldo; ~ **sb from doing sth** impedire a qcno di fare qcsa; ~ **sb waiting** far aspettare qcno; ~ **sth to oneself** tenere qcsa per sé; ~ **sth from sb** tenere nascosto qcsa a qcno ●vi (remain) rimanere; (food:) conservarsi; ~ **calm** rimanere calmo; ~ **left/right** tenere la destra/la sinistra; ~ [on] **doing sth** continuare a fare qcsa. □ ~ **back** vt trattenere (person); ~ **sth back from sb** tenere nascosto qcsa a qcno ●vi tenersi indietro. □ ~ **in with** vt mantenersi in buoni rapporti con. □ ~ **on** vi 🔢 assillare (at sb qcno). □ ~ **up** vi stare al passo ●vt (continue) continuare

kennel /'kenl/ n canile m; ~**s** pl (boarding) canile m; (breeding) allevamento m di cani

Kenya /'kenjə/ n Kenia m. ~**n** adj & n keniota mf

kept /kept/ ▷KEEP

kerb /kɜ:b/ n bordo m del marciapiede

kerosene /'kerəsi:n/ n Am cherosene m

ketchup /'ketʃʌp/ n ketchup m

kettle /'ket(ə)l/ n bollitore m; **put the ~ on** mettere l'acqua a bollire

key /ki:/ n also (Mus) chiave f; (of piano, typewriter) tasto m ●vt ~ **[in]** digitare (character); **could you ~ this?** puoi battere questo?

key: ~**board** n (Comput, Mus) tastiera f. ~**hole** n buco m della serratura. ~**ring** n portachiavi m inv

khaki /'kɑ:kɪ/ adj cachi inv ●n cachi m

kick /kɪk/ n calcio m; (🔢: thrill) piacere m; **for ~s** 🔢 per spasso ●vt dar calci a; ~ **the bucket** 🔢 crepare ●vi (animal:) scalciare; (person:) dare calci. □ ~ **off** vi (Sport) dare il calcio d'inizio; 🔢 iniziare. □ ~ **up** vt ~ **up**

a row fare una scenata

'kick-off n (Sport) calcio m d'inizio

kid /kɪd/ n capretto m; (⊤: child) ragazzino, -a mf ● v (pt/pp **kidded**) ● vt ⊤ prendere in giro ● vi ⊤ scherzare

kidnap /'kɪdnæp/ vt (pt/pp -napped) rapire, sequestrare. ~**per** n sequestrare, -trice mf, rapitore, -trice mf. ~**ping** n rapimento m, sequestro m [di persona]

kidney /'kɪdnɪ/ n rene m; (Culin) rognone m. ~ **machine** n rene m artificiale

kill /kɪl/ vt uccidere; fig metter fine a; ammazzare (time). ~**er** n assassino, -a mf. ~**ing** n uccisione f; (murder) omicidio m; **make a ~ing** fig fare un colpo grosso

kiln /kɪln/ n fornace f

kilo /'kiːlə/: ~**byte** n kilobyte m inv. ~**gram** n chilogrammo m. ~**metre** n chilometro m. ~**watt** n chilowatt m inv

kilt /kɪlt/ n kilt m inv (gonnellino degli scozzesi)

kin /kɪn/ n congiunti mpl; **next of ~** parente m stretto; parenti mpl stretti

kind¹ /kaɪnd/ n genere m, specie f; (brand, type) tipo m; ~ **of** fam alquanto; **two of a ~** due della stessa specie

kind² adj gentile, buono; ~ **to animals** amante degli animali; ~ **regards** cordiali saluti

kindergarten /'kɪndəgɑːtn/ n asilo m infantile

kindle /'kɪndl/ vt accendere

kind|ly /'kaɪndlɪ/ adj (-ier, -iest) benevolo ● adv gentilmente; (if you please) per favore. ~**ness** n gentilezza f

king /kɪŋ/ n re m inv. ~**dom** n regno m

king: ~**fisher** n martin m inv pescatore. ~**-sized** adj (cigarette) kingsize inv, lungo; (bed) matrimoniale

grande

kink /kɪŋk/ n nodo m. ~**y** adj ⊤ bizzarro

kiosk /'kiːɒsk/ n chiosco m; (Teleph) cabina f telefonica

kipper /'kɪpə(r)/ n aringa f affumicata

kiss /kɪs/ n bacio m; ~ **of life** respirazione f bocca a bocca ● vt baciare ● vi baciarsi

kit /kɪt/ n equipaggiamento m, kit m inv; (tools) attrezzi mpl; (construction ~) pezzi mpl da montare, kit m inv ● **kit out** vt (pt/pp **kitted**) equipaggiare. ~**bag** n sacco m a spalla

kitchen /'kɪtʃɪn/ n cucina f ● attrib di cucina. ~**ette** n cucinino m

kitchen towel n Scottex® m inv

kite /kaɪt/ n aquilone m

kitten /'kɪtn/ n gattino m

knack /næk/ n tecnica f; **have the ~ for doing sth** avere la capacità di fare qcsa

knead /niːd/ vt impastare

knee /niː/ n ginocchio m. ~**cap** n rotula f

kneel /niːl/ vi (pt/pp **knelt**) ~ [**down**] inginocchiarsi; **be ~ing** essere inginocchiato

knelt /nelt/ ▷KNEEL

knew /njuː/ ▷KNOW

knickers /'nɪkəz/ npl mutandine fpl

knife /naɪf/ n (pl **knives**) coltello m ● vt ⊤ accoltellare

knight /naɪt/ n cavaliere m; (in chess) cavallo m ● vt nominare cavaliere

knit /nɪt/ vt/i (pt/pp **knitted**) lavorare a maglia; ~ **one, purl one** un diritto, un rovescio. ~**ting** n lavorare m a maglia; (work) lavoro m a maglia. ~**ting-needle** n ferro m da calza. ~**wear** n maglieria f

knives /naɪvz/ ▷KNIFE

knob /nɒb/ n pomello m; (of stick) pomo m; (of butter) noce f. ~**bly** adj nodoso; (bony) spigoloso

knock /nɒk/ n colpo m; there was a ~ at the door hanno bussato alla porta ● vt bussare a (door); (🔲: criticize) denigrare; ~ a hole in sth fare un buco in qcsa; ~ one's head battere la testa con (on contro) ● vi (at door) bussare. □ ~ **about** vt malmenare ● vi 🔲 girovagare. □ ~ **down** vt far cadere; (with fist) stendere con un pugno; (in car) investire; (demolish) abbattere; (reduce) ribassare (price). □ ~ **off** vt (🔲: steal) fregare; (🔲: complete quickly) fare alla bell'e meglio ● vi (🔲: cease work) staccare. □ ~ **out** vt eliminare; (make unconscious) mettere K.O.; (🔲: anaesthetize) addormentare. □ ~ **over** vt rovesciare; (in car) investire

knock: ~**er** n battente m. ~**-kneed** /-'ni:d/ adj con gambe storte. ~**-out** n (in boxing) knock-out m inv

knot /nɒt/ n nodo m ● vt (pt/pp knotted) annodare

know /nəʊ/ v (pt knew, pp known) ● vt sapere; conoscere (person, place); (recognize) riconoscere; get to ~ sb conoscere qcno; ~ how to swim sapere nuotare ● vi sapere; did you ~ about this? lo sapevi? ● n in the ~ 🔲 al corrente

know: ~**-all** n 🔲 sapientone; ~ a mf. ~**-how** n abilità f. ~**ingly** adv (intentionally) consapevolmente; (smile etc) con un'aria d'intesa

knowledge /'nɒlɪdʒ/ n conoscenza f. ~**able** adj ben informato

known /nəʊn/ ▷ **KNOW** ● adj noto

knuckle /'nʌkl/ n nocca f ● **knuckle down** vi darci sotto (to con). □ ~ **under** vi sottomettersi

Koran /kə'rɑːn/ n Corano m

Korea /kə'rɪə/ n Corea f. ~**n** adj & n coreano, -a mf

kosher /'kəʊʃə(r)/ adj kasher inv

kudos /'kju:dɒs/ n 🔲 gloria f

L

lab /læb/ n laboratorio m

label /'leɪbl/ n etichetta f ● vt (pt/pp labelled) mettere un'etichetta a; fig etichettare (person)

laboratory /ləˈbɒrətrɪ/ n laboratorio m

laborious /ləˈbɔːrɪəs/ adj laborioso

labour /'leɪbə(r)/ n lavoro m; (workers) manodopera f; (Med) doglie fpl; be in ~ avere le doglie; L~ (Pol) partito m laburista ● attrib (Pol) laburista ● vi lavorare ● vt ~ **the point** fig ribadire il concetto. ~**er** n manovale m

lace /leɪs/ n pizzo m; (of shoe) laccio m ● attrib di pizzo ● vt allacciare (shoes); correggere (drink)

lacerate /'læsəreɪt/ vt lacerare

lack /læk/ n mancanza f ● vt mancare di; I ~ the time mi manca il tempo ● vi be ~ing mancare; be ~ing in sth mancare di qcsa

lad /læd/ n ragazzo m

ladder /'lædə(r)/ n scala f; (in tights) sfilatura f

laden /'leɪdn/ adj carico (with di)

ladle /'leɪdl/ n mestolo m ● vt ~ [out] versare (col mestolo)

lady /'leɪdɪ/ n signora f; (title) Lady; ladies [room] bagno m per donne

lady: ~**bird** n, Am ~**bug** n coccinella f. ~**like** adj signorile

lag[1] /læg/ vi (pt/pp lagged) ~ behind restare indietro

lag[2] vt (pt/pp lagged) isolare (pipes)

lager /'lɑːgə(r)/ n birra f chiara

lagoon /lə'gu:n/ n laguna f

laid /leɪd/ ▷ **LAY**[3]

lain /leɪn/ ▷ **LIE**[2]

lair /leə(r)/ n tana f

k
l

lake /leɪk/ n lago m

lamb /læm/ n agnello m

lame /leɪm/ adj zoppo; fig (argument) zoppicante; (excuse) traballante

lament /lə'ment/ n lamento m • vt lamentare • vi lamentarsi

lamentable /'læməntəbl/ adj deplorevole

lamp /læmp/ n lampada f; (in street) lampione m. ~**post** n lampione m. ~**shade** n paralume m

lance /lɑːns/ n fiocina f • vt (Med) incidere. ~'**corporal** n appuntato m

land /lænd/ n terreno m; (country) paese m; (as opposed to sea) terra f; **plot of** ~ pezzo m di terreno • vt (Naut) sbarcare; (fam: obtain) assicurarsi; **be** ~**ed with sth** ⬛ ritrovarsi fra capo e collo qcsa • vi (Aeron) atterrare; (fall) cadere. □ ~ **up** vi ⬛ finire

landing /'lændɪŋ/ n (Naut) sbarco m; (Aeron) atterraggio m; (top of stairs) pianerottolo m. ~**stage** n pontile m da sbarco. ~ **strip** n pista f d'atterraggio di fortuna

land: ~**lady** n proprietaria f; (of flat) padrona f di casa. ~**lord** n proprietario m; (of flat) padrone m di casa. ~**mark** n punto m di riferimento; fig pietra f miliare. ~**scape** /-skeɪp/ n paesaggio m. ~**slide** n frana f; (Pol) valanga f di voti

lane /leɪn/ n sentiero m; (Auto, Sport) corsia f

language /'læŋgwɪdʒ/ n lingua f; (speech, style) linguaggio m. ~ **laboratory** n laboratorio m linguistico

lank /læŋk/ adj (hair) diritto

lanky /'læŋkɪ/ adj (-ier, -iest) allampanato

lantern /'læntən/ n lanterna f

lap[1] /læp/ n grembo m

lap[2] n (of journey) tappa f; (Sport) giro m • v (pt/pp lapped) • vi (water:) ~ **against** lambire • vt (Sport) doppiare

lap[3] vt (pt/pp lapped) ~ **up** bere avidamente; bersi completamente (lies); credere ciecamente a (praise)

lapel /lə'pel/ n bavero m

lapse /læps/ n sbaglio m; (moral) sbandamento m [morale]; (of time) intervallo m • vi (expire) scadere; (morally) scivolare; ~ **into** cadere in

laptop /'læptɒp/ n ~ [**computer**] computer m inv portabile, laptop m inv

lard /lɑːd/ n strutto m

larder /'lɑːdə(r)/ n dispensa f

large /lɑːdʒ/ adj grande; (number, amount) grande, grosso; **by and** ~ in complesso; **at** ~ in libertà; (in general) ampiamente. ~**ly** adv ampiamente; ~**ly because of** in gran parte a causa di

lark[1] /lɑːk/ n (bird) allodola f

lark[2] n (joke) burla f • **lark about** vi giocherellare

larva /'lɑːvə/ n (pl -**vae** /-viː/) larva f

laser /'leɪzə(r)/ n laser m inv. ~ **printer** n stampante f laser

lash /læʃ/ n frustata f; (eyelash) ciglio m • vt (whip) frustare; (tie) legare fermamente. □ ~ **out** vi attaccare; (spend) sperperare (on in)

lashings /'læʃɪŋz/ npl ~ **of** ⬛ una marea di

lass /læs/ n ragazzina f

lasso /lə'suː/ n lazo m

last /lɑːst/ adj (final) ultimo; (recent) scorso; ~ **year** l'anno scorso; ~ **night** ieri sera; **at** ~ alla fine; **at** ~! finalmente!; **that's the** ~ **straw** ⬛ questa è l'ultima goccia • n ultimo, -a m; **the** ~ **but one** il penultimo • adv per ultimo; (last time) l'ultima volta • vi durare. ~**ing** adj durevole. ~**ly** adv infine

late /leɪt/ adj (delayed) in ritardo; (at a late hour) tardo; (deceased) defunto; **it's** ~ (at night) è tardi; **in** ~ **November** alla fine di Novembre • adv tardi; **stay up** ~ stare alzati fino a tardi;

~**comer** n ritardatario, -a mf; (to political party etc) nuovo, -a arrivato, -a mf. ~**ly** adv recentemente. ~**ness** n ora f tarda; (delay) ritardo m

latent /'leɪtnt/ adj latente

later /'leɪtə(r)/ adj (train) che parte più tardi; (edition) più recente ● adv più tardi; ~ **on** più tardi, dopo

lateral /'lætərəl/ adj laterale

latest /'leɪtɪst/ adj ultimo; (most recent) più recente; **the** ~ [**news**] le ultime notizie **at six o'clock at the** ~ alle sei al più tardi

lathe /leɪð/ n tornio m

lather /'lɑːðə(r)/ n schiuma f ● vt insaponare ● vi far schiuma

Latin /'lætɪn/ adj latino ● n latino m. ~ **A'merica** n America f Latina. ~ **A'merican** adj & n latino-americano, -a mf

latitude /'lætɪtjuːd/ n (Geog) latitudine f; fig libertà f d'azione

latter /'lætə(r)/ adj ultimo ● n **the** ~ quest'ultimo. ~**ly** adv ultimamente

Latvia /'lætvɪə/ n Lettonia f. ~**n** adj & n lettone mf

laugh /lɑːf/ n risata f ● vi ridere (at/ about di); ~ **at sb** (mock) prendere in giro qcno. ~**able** adj ridicolo. ~**ing-stock** n zimbello m

laughter /'lɑːftə(r)/ n risata f

launch[1] /lɔːntʃ/ n (boat) varo m

launch[2] n lancio m; (of ship) varo m ● vt lanciare (rocket, product); varare (ship); sferrare (attack)

launder /'lɔːndə(r)/ vt lavare e stirare; ~ **money** fig riciclare denaro sporco. ~**ette** n lavanderia f automatica

laundry /'lɔːndrɪ/ n lavanderia f; (clothes) bucato m

lava /'lɑːvə/ n lava f

lavatory /'lævətrɪ/ n gabinetto m

lavish /'lævɪʃ/ adj copioso; (wasteful) prodigo; **on a** ~ **scale** su vasta scala

● vt ~ **sth on sb** ricoprire qcno di qcsa. ~**ly** adv copiosamente

law /lɔː/ n legge f; **study** ~ studiare giurisprudenza, studiare legge; ~ **and order** ordine m pubblico

lawcourt n tribunale m

lawn /lɔːn/ n prato m [all'inglese]. ~**-mower** n tosaerbe m inv

'**law suit** n causa f

lawyer /'lɔːjə(r)/ n avvocato m

lax /læks/ adj negligente; (morals etc) lassista

laxative /'læksətɪv/ n lassativo m

lay[1] /leɪ/ adj laico; fig profano

lay[2] ▸**LIE**[2]

lay[3] vt (pt/pp laid) porre, mettere; apparecchiare (table); ~ **a** (hen:) fare le uova. □ ~ **down** vt posare; stabilire (rules, conditions). □ ~ **off** vt licenziare (workers) ● vi (□: stop) ~ off! smettila! **lay out** vt (display, set forth) esporre; (plan) pianificare (garden); (spend) sborsare; (Typ) impaginare

lay: ~**about** n fannullone, -a mf. ~**-by** n corsia f di sosta

layer /'leɪə(r)/ n strato m

lay: ~**man** n profano m. ~**out** n disposizione f; (Typ) impaginazione f, layout m inv

laze /leɪz/ vi ~ [**about**] oziare

laziness /'leɪzɪnɪs/ n pigrizia f

lazy /'leɪzɪ/ adj (-ier, -iest) pigro. ~**bones** n poltrone, -a mf

lead[1] /led/ n piombo m; (of pencil) mina f

lead[2] /liːd/ n guida f; (leash) giunzaglio m; (flex) filo m; (clue) indizio m; (Theat) parte f principale; (distance ahead) distanza f (over su); **in the** ~ in testa ● v (pt/pp led) vt condurre; dirigere (expedition, party etc); (induce) indurre; ~ **the way** mettersi in testa ● vi (be in front) condurre; (in race, competition) essere in testa; (at cards) giocare (per primo). □ ~ **away** vt portar via. □ ~ **to** vt portare a.

□ ~ **up to** vt preludere; what's this ~ing **up to?** dove porta questo?

leader /'liːdə(r)/ n capo m (of orchestra) primo violino m; (in newspaper) articolo m di fondo. ~**ship** n direzione f, leadership f inv; **show** ~**ship** mostrare capacità di comando

leading /'liːdɪŋ/ adj principale; ~ **lady/man** attrice f/attore m principale; ~ **question** domanda f tendenziosa

leaf /liːf/ n (pl **leaves**) foglia f; (of table) asse f ● **leaf through** vt sfogliare. ~**let** n dépliant m inv; (advertising) dépliant m inv pubblicitario; (political) manifestino m

league /liːg/ n lega f; (Sport) campionato m; **be in** ~ **with** essere in combutta con

leak /liːk/ n (hole) fessura f; (Naut) falla f; (of gas & fig) fuga f ● vi colare; (ship:) fare acqua; (liquid, gas:) fuoriuscire ● vt ~ **sth to sb** fig far trapelare qcsa a qcno. ~**y** adj che perde; (Naut) che fa acqua

lean[1] /liːn/ adj magro

lean[2] v (pt/pp **leaned** or **leant** /lent/) ● vt appoggiare (**against**/**on** contro/su) ● vi appoggiarsi (**against**/**on** contro/su); (not be straight) pendere; **be** ~**ing against** essere appoggiato contro; ~ **on sb** (depend on) appoggiarsi a qcno; (𝕀: exert pressure on) stare alle calcagne di qcno. □ ~ **back** vi piegarsi indietro. □ ~ **forward** vi piegarsi in avanti. □ ~ **out** vi sporgersi. □ ~ **over** vi piegarsi

leaning /'liːnɪŋ/ adj pendente; **the L~ Tower of Pisa** la torre di Pisa, la torre pendente ● n tendenza f

leap /liːp/ n salto m ● vi (pt/pp **leapt** /lept/ or **leaped**) saltare; **he leapt at** it 𝕀 l'ha preso al volo. ~**frog** n cavallina f. ~ **year** n anno m bisestile

learn /lɜːn/ v (pt/pp **learnt** or **learned**) ● vt imparare; ~ **to swim** imparare a nuotare; **I have** ~**ed that...** (heard) sono venuto a sapere

che... ● vi imparare

learn|ed /'lɜːnɪd/ adj colto. ~**er** n also (Auto) principiante mf. ~**ing** n cultura f. ~**ing curve** n curva f d'apprendimento

lease /liːs/ n contratto m d'affitto; (rental) affitto m ● vt affittare

leash /liːʃ/ n guinzaglio m

least /liːst/ adj più piccolo m; (amount) minore; **you've got** ~ **luggage** hai meno bagagli di tutti ● n **the** ~ **il meno; at** ~ **almeno; not in the** ~ niente affatto ● adv meno; **the** ~ **expensive wine** il vino meno caro

leather /'leðə(r)/ n pelle f; (of soles) cuoio m ● attrib di pelle/cuoio. ~**y** adj (meat, skin) duro

leave /liːv/ n (holiday) congedo m; (Mil) licenza f; **on** ~ **in** congedo/licenza ● v (pt/pp **left**) ● vt lasciare; uscire da (house, office); (forget) dimenticare; **there is nothing left** non è rimasto niente ● vi andare via; (train, bus:) partire. □ ~ **behind** vt lasciare; (forget) dimenticare. □ ~ **out** vt omettere; (not put away) lasciare fuori

leaves /liːvz/ ▷ **LEAF**

Leban|on /'lebənən/ n Libano m. ~**ese** /-'niːz/ adj & n libanese mf

lecture /'lektʃə(r)/ n conferenza f; (Univ) lezione f; (reproof) ramanzina f ● vi fare una conferenza (**on su**); (Univ) insegnare (**on qcsa**) ● vt ~ **sb** rimproverare qcno. ~**r** n conferenziere, -a mf; (Univ) docente mf universitario, -a

led /led/ ▷ **LEAD**[2]

ledge /ledʒ/ n cornice f; (of window) davanzale m

leek /liːk/ n porro m

leer /lɪə(r)/ n sguardo m libidinoso ● vi ~ [**at**] guardare in modo libidinoso

left[1] /left/ ▷ **LEAVE**

left[2] adj sinistro ● adv a sinistra ● n also (Pol) sinistra f; **on the** ~

a sinistra;
left: ~-'**handed** adj mancino.
~-'**luggage office** n deposito m bagagli. ~**overs** npl rimasugli mpl.
~-'**wing** adj (Pol) di sinistra

leg /leg/ n gamba f; (of animal) zampa f; (of journey) tappa f; (Culin: of chicken) coscia f; (: of lamb) cosciotto m

legacy /'legəsɪ/ n lascito m

legal /'liːgl/ adj legale; take ~ action intentare un'azione legale. ~**ly** adv legalmente

legality /lɪ'gælətɪ/ n legalità f

legalize /'liːgəlaɪz/ vt legalizzare

legend /'ledʒənd/ n leggenda f.
~**ary** adj leggendario

legib|le /'ledʒəbl/ adj leggibile. ~**ly**
adv in modo leggibile

legislat|e /'ledʒɪsleɪt/ vi legiferare.
~**ion** n legislazione f

legitima|te /lɪ'dʒɪtɪmət/ adj legittimo; (excuse) valido

leisure /'leʒə(r)/ n tempo m libero;
at your ~ con comodo. ~**ly** adj
senza fretta

lemon /'lemən/ n limone m. ~**ade** n
limonata f

lend /lend/ vt (pt/pp lent) prestare;
~ a hand fig dare una mano. ~**ing**
library n biblioteca f per il prestito

length /leŋθ/ n lunghezza f; (piece)
pezzo m; (of wallpaper) parte f; (of play)
durata f; at ~ a lungo; (at last)
alla fine

length|en /'leŋθən/ vt allungare ●vi
allungarsi. ~**ways** adv per lungo

lengthy /'leŋθɪ/ adj (-ier,
-iest) lungo

lens /lenz/ n lente f; (Phot) obiettivo
m; (of eye) cristallino m

lent /lent/ ▷LEND

Lent n Quaresima f

Leo /'liːəʊ/ n (Astr) Leone m

leopard /'lepəd/ n leopardo m

leotard /'liːətɑːd/ n body m inv

lesbian /'lezbɪən/ adj lesbico ●n lesbica f

less /les/ adj meno di; ~ **and** ~
sempre meno ●adv & prep meno ●n
meno m

lessen /'lesn/ vt/i diminuire

lesson /'lesn/ n lezione f

lest /lest/ conj liter per timore che

let /let/ vt (pt/pp let, pres p letting)
lasciare, permettere; (rent) affittare;
~ **alone** (not to mention) tanto meno;
'**to** ~' 'affittasi'; ~ **us** go andiamo;
~ **sb** do sth lasciare fare qcsa a
qcno, permettere a qcno di fare
qcsa; ~ **me know** fammi sapere;
just ~ him try! che ci provi solamente!; ~ **oneself** in for sth 🔢 impelagarsi in qcsa. □ ~ **down** vt sciogliersi (hair); abbassare (blinds);
(lengthen) allungare; (disappoint) deludere; don't ~ **me down** conto su di
te. □ ~ **in** vt far entrare. □ ~ **off** vt
far partire; (not punish) perdonare; ~
sb off doing sth abbonare qcsa a
qcno. □ ~ **out** vt far uscire; (make
larger) allargare; emettere (scream,
groan). □ ~ **through** vt far passare.
□ ~ **up** vi 🔢 diminuire

'**let-down** n delusione f

lethal /'liːθl/ adj letale

letharg|ic /lɪ'θɑːdʒɪk/ adj apatico.
~**y** n apatia f

letter /'letə(r)/ n lettera f. ~-**box** n
buca f per le lettere. ~-**head** n carta
f intestata. ~**ing** n caratteri mpl

lettuce /'letɪs/ n lattuga f

'**let-up** n 🔢 pausa f

leukaemia /luː'kiːmɪə/ n leucemia f

level /'levl/ adj piano; (in height, competition) allo stesso livello; (spoonful)
raso; draw ~ **with sb** affiancare
qcno ●n livello m; on the ~ 🔢 giusto ●vt (pt/pp levelled) livellare; (aim)
puntare (at su)

level 'crossing n passaggio m a
livello

lever /'liːvə(r)/ n leva f ● **lever up** vt sollevare (con una leva). ~**age** n azione f di una leva; fig influenza f

levy /'levɪ/ vt (pt/pp levied) imporre (tax)

lewd /ljuːd/ adj osceno

liabil|ity /laɪə'bɪlətɪ/ n responsabilità f; (🄵 burden) peso m; ~**ies** pl debiti mpl

liable /'laɪəbl/ adj responsabile (for di); be ~ to (rain, break etc) rischiare di; (tend to) tendere a

liaise /lɪ'eɪz/ vi essere in contatto

liaison /lɪ'eɪzɒn/ n contatti mpl; (Mil) collegamento m; (affair) relazione f

liar /'laɪə(r)/ n bugiardo, -a mf

libel /'laɪbl/ n diffamazione f ● vt (pt/pp libelled) diffamare. ~**lous** adj diffamatorio

liberal /'lɪb(ə)rəl/ adj (tolerant) di larghe vedute; (generous) generoso. L~ adj (Pol) liberale ● n liberale mf

liberat|e /'lɪbəreɪt/ vt liberare. ~**ed** adj (woman) emancipata. ~**ion** n liberazione f; (of women) emancipazione f. ~**or** n liberatore, -trice mf

liberty /'lɪbətɪ/ n libertà f; take the ~ of doing sth prendersi la libertà di fare qcsa; at ~ to do sth essere libero di fare qcsa

Libra /'liːbrə/ n (Astr) Bilancia f

librarian /laɪ'breərɪən/ n bibliotecario, -a mf

library /'laɪbrərɪ/ n biblioteca f

Libya /'lɪbɪə/ n Libia f. ~**n** adj & n libico, -a mf

lice /laɪs/ ▷**LOUSE**

licence /'laɪsns/ n licenza f; (for TV) canone m televisivo; (for driving) patente f; (freedom) sregolatezza f. ~**plate** n targa f

license /'laɪsns/ vt autorizzare; be ~**d** (car:) avere il bollo; (restaurant:) essere autorizzato alla vendita di alcolici

lick /lɪk/ n leccata f; a ~ of paint

una passata leggera di pittura ● vt leccare; (🄵 defeat) battere; leccarsi (lips)

lid /lɪd/ n coperchio m; (of eye) palpebra f

lie[1] /laɪ/ n bugia f; tell a ~ mentire ● vi (pt/pp lied, pres p lying) mentire

lie[2] vi (pt lay, pp lain, pres p lying) (person:) sdraiarsi; (object:) stare; (remain) rimanere; leave sth lying about or around lasciare qcsa in giro. ▫ ~ **down** vi sdraiarsi

lie-in n 🄵 have a ~ restare a letto fino a tardi

lieutenant /lef'tenənt/ n tenente m

life /laɪf/ n (pl lives) vita f

life: ~**belt** n salvagente m. ~**boat** n lancia f di salvataggio; (on ship) scialuppa f di salvataggio. ~**buoy** n salvagente m. ~**coach** n life coach m/f inv. ~**guard** n bagnino m. ~**jacket** n giubbotto m di salvataggio. ~**less** adj inanimato. ~**like** adj realistico. ~**long** adj di tutta la vita. ~**size[d]** adj in grandezza naturale. ~**time** n vita f; the chance of a ~**time** un'occasione unica

lift /lɪft/ n ascensore m; (Auto) passaggio m ● vt sollevare; revocare (restrictions); (🄵 steal) rubare ● vi (fog:) alzarsi. ▫ ~ **up** vt sollevare

lift-off n decollo m (di razzo)

light[1] /laɪt/ adj (not dark) luminoso; ~ **green** verde chiaro ● n luce f; (lamp) lampada f; in the ~ of fig alla luce di; have you got a ~? ha da accendere?; come to ~ essere rivelato ● vt (pt/pp lit or lighted) accendere; (illuminate) illuminare. ▫ ~ **up** vi (face:) illuminarsi

light[2] adj (not heavy) leggero ● adv travel ~ viaggiare con poco bagaglio

light-bulb n lampadina f

lighten[1] /'laɪtn/ vt illuminare

lighten[2] vt alleggerire (load)

lighter /'laɪtə(r)/ n accendino m

light: ~-**hearted** adj spensierato.
~**house** n faro m. ~**ly** adv leggermente; (accuse) con leggerezza;
(without concern) senza dare importanza alla cosa; **get off** ~**ly** cavarsela a buon mercato

lightning /'laɪtnɪŋ/ n lampo m, fulmine m. ~-**conductor** n parafulmine m

lightweight adj leggero ● n (in boxing) peso m leggero

like¹ /laɪk/ adj simile ● prep come; ~
this/that così; what's he ~?
com'è? ● conj (fam): as) come; (Am: as if) come se

like² vt piacere, gradire; I would ~
would ~ vorrei, gradirei; I ~ him
mi piace; I ~ this car mi piace questa macchina; I ~ dancing mi piace
ballare; I ~ that! [fam] questa mi è
piaciuta! ● n ~s and dislikes pl
gusti mpl

like|able /'laɪkəbl/ adj simpatico.
~**lihood** n probabilità f. ~**ly** adj
(-ier, -iest) probabile ● adv probabilmente; **not** ~**ly!** [fam] neanche per
sogno!

liken /'laɪkn/ vt paragonare (to a)

like|ness /'laɪknɪs/ n somiglianza f.
~**wise** adv lo stesso

liking /'laɪkɪŋ/ n gusto m; **is it to
your** ~? è di suo gusto?; **take a** ~
to sb prendere qcno in simpatia

lilac /'laɪlək/ n lillà m ● adj color lillà

lily /'lɪlɪ/ n giglio m. ~ **of the valley**
n mughetto m

limb /lɪm/ n arto m

lime¹ /laɪm/ n (fruit) cedro m; (tree)
tiglio m

lime² n calce f. ~**light** n be in the
~**light** essere molto in vista.
~**stone** n calcare m

limit /'lɪmɪt/ n limite m; **that's the**
~**!** [fam] questo è troppo! ● vt limitare
(to a). ~**ation** n limite m. ~**ed** adj ristretto; ~**ed company** società f

anonima

limousine /'lɪməziːn/ n limousine
f inv

limp¹ /lɪmp/ n andatura f zoppicante; **have a** ~ zoppicare ● vi zoppicare

limp² vt floscio

line¹ /laɪn/ n linea f; (length of rope,
cord) filo m; (of writing) riga f; (of poem)
verso m; (row) fila f; (wrinkle) ruga f; (of
business) settore m; (Am: queue) coda f;
in ~ **with** in conformità con ● vt segnare; (fiancheggiare (street). ⏍ ~
up vi allinearsi ● vt allineare

line² vt foderare (garment)

lined¹ /laɪnd/ adj (face) rugoso;
(paper) a righe

lined² (garment) foderato

linen /'lɪnɪn/ n lino m; (articles) biancheria f ● attrib di lino

liner /'laɪnə(r)/ n nave f di linea

linger /'lɪŋgə(r)/ vi indugiare

lingerie /'læ̃ʒ.əriː/ n biancheria f
intima (da donna)

linguist /'lɪŋgwɪst/ n linguista mf

linguistic /lɪŋ'gwɪstɪk/ adj linguistico. ~**s** n linguistica fsg

lining /'laɪnɪŋ/ n (of garment) fodera
f; (of brakes) guarnizione f

link /lɪŋk/ n (of chain) anello m; fig legame m ● vt collegare. ⏍ ~ **up** vi
unirsi (with a); (TV) collegarsi

lino /'laɪnəʊ/ n, **linoleum** /lɪ'nəʊlɪəm/ n linoleum m

lint /lɪnt/ n garza f

lion /'laɪən/ n leone m. ~**ess** n leonessa f

lip /lɪp/ n labbro m (pl labbra f);
(edge) bordo m

lip: ~-**read** vi leggere le labbra;
~-**service** n pay ~-**service** to approvare soltanto a parole. ~**salve** n
burro m [di] cacao. ~**stick** n rossetto m

liqueur /lɪ'kjʊə(r)/ n liquore m

liquid /'lɪkwɪd/ n liquido m ● adj

liquido

liquidat|e /'lɪkwɪdeɪt/ vt liquidare. ~ion n liquidazione f; (Comm) **go into** ~ion andare in liquidazione

liquidize /'lɪkwɪdaɪz/ vt rendere liquido. ~r n (Culin) frullatore m

liquor /'lɪkə(r)/ n bevanda f alcoolica

liquorice /'lɪkərɪs/ n liquirizia f

liquor store n Am negozio m di alcolici

lisp /lɪsp/ n pronuncia f con la lisca ●vi parlare con la lisca

list¹ /lɪst/ n lista f ●vt elencare

list² vi (ship): inclinarsi

listen /'lɪsn/ vi ascoltare; ~ **to** ascoltare. ~er n ascoltatore, -trice mf

listless /'lɪstlɪs/ adj svogliato

lit /lɪt/ ▷ LIGHT

literacy /'lɪtərəsɪ/ n alfabetizzazione f

literal /'lɪtərəl/ adj letterale. ~ly adv letteralmente

literary /'lɪtərərɪ/ adj letterario

literate /'lɪtərət/ adj be ~ saper leggere e scrivere

literature /'lɪtrətʃə(r)/ n letteratura f

Lithuania /lɪθjʊ'eɪnɪə/ n Lituania f. ~n adj & n lituano, -a mf

litre /'liːtə(r)/ n litro m

litter /'lɪtə(r)/ n immondizie fpl; (Zool) figliata f ●vt be ~ed with essere ingombrato di. ~bin n bidone m della spazzatura

little /'lɪtl/ adj piccolo; (not much) poco ●adv & n poco m; a ~ un po'; a ~ water un po' d'acqua; a ~ better un po' meglio; ~ by ~ a poco a poco

live¹ /laɪv/ adj vivo; (ammunition) carico; ~ broadcast trasmissione f in diretta; be ~ (Electr) essere sotto tensione; ~ **wire** n fig persona f dinamica ●adv (broadcast) in diretta

live² /lɪv/ vi vivere; (reside) abitare; ~ **with** convivere con. □ ~ **down** vt far dimenticare. □ ~ **off** vt vivere alle spalle di. □ ~ **on** vt vivere di ●vi sopravvivere. □ ~ **up** vt ~ it up far la bella vita. □ ~ **up to** vt essere all'altezza di

liveli|hood /'laɪvlɪhʊd/ n mezzi mpl di sostentamento. ~ness n vivacità f

lively /'laɪvlɪ/ adj (-ier, -iest) vivace

liver /'lɪvə(r)/ n fegato m

lives /laɪvz/ ▷ LIFE

livestock /'laɪv-/ n bestiame m

livid /'lɪvɪd/ adj 🔢 livido

living /'lɪvɪŋ/ adj vivo ●n **earn** one's ~ guadagnarsi da vivere; **the** ~ pl i vivi. ~-**room** n soggiorno m

lizard /'lɪzəd/ n lucertola f

load /ləʊd/ n carico m; ~s of 🔢 un sacco di ●vt caricare. ~ed adj carico; (🔢: rich) ricchissimo

loaf¹ /ləʊf/ n (pl loaves) pagnotta f

loaf² vi oziare

loan /ləʊn/ n prestito m; on ~ in prestito ●vt prestare

loath|e /ləʊð/ vt detestare. ~ing n disgusto m. ~some adj disgustoso

lobby /'lɒbɪ/ n atrio m; (Pol) gruppo m di pressione, lobby m inv

lobster /'lɒbstə(r)/ n aragosta f

local /'ləʊkl/ adj locale; **I'm not** ~ non sono del posto ●n abitante mf del luogo; (🔢: public house) pub m locale. ~ **au'thority** n autorità f locale. ~ **call** n (Teleph) telefonata f urbana. ~ **government** n autorità f inv locale

locality /ləʊ'kælətɪ/ n zona f

local|ization /ləʊklaɪ'zeɪʃn/ n localizzazione f. ~ized adj localizzato

locally /'ləʊkəlɪ/ adv localmente; (live, work) nei paraggi

locat|e /ləʊ'keɪt/ vt situare; trovare (person); **be** ~ed essere situato. ~ion n posizione f; filmed on ~ion girato in esterni

lock¹ /lɒk/ n (hair) ciocca f

lock² n (on door) serratura f; (on canal) chiusa f • vt chiudere a chiave; bloccare (wheels) • vi chiudersi. □ ~ **in** vt chiudere dentro. □ ~ **out** vt chiudere fuori. □ ~ **up** vt (in prison) mettere dentro • vi chiudere

locker /ˈlɒkə(r)/ n armadietto m

locket /ˈlɒkɪt/ n medaglione m

lock: ~**-out** n serrata f. ~**smith** n fabbro m

locomotive /ləʊkəˈməʊtɪv/ n locomotiva f

lodge /lɒdʒ/ n (porter's) portineria f; (masonic) loggia f • vt presentare (claim, complaint); (with bank, solicitor) depositare; be ~d essersi conficcato • vi essere a pensione (with da); (become fixed) conficcarsi. ~**r** n inquilino, -a mf

lodgings /ˈlɒdʒɪŋz/ npl camere fpl in affitto

loft /lɒft/ n soffitta f

lofty /ˈlɒftɪ/ adj (-ier, -iest) alto; (haughty) altezzoso

log /lɒg/ n ceppo m; (Auto) libretto m di circolazione; (Naut) giornale m di bordo • vt (pt logged) registrare. □ ~ **on to** vt (Comput) connettersi a

logarithm /ˈlɒgərɪðm/ n logaritmo m

log-book n (Naut) giornale m di bordo; (Auto) libretto m di circolazione

loggerheads /ˈlɒgə-/ npl be at ~ 🆸 essere in totale disaccordo

logic /ˈlɒdʒɪk/ n logica f. ~**al** adj logico. ~**ally** adv logicamente

logistics /ləˈdʒɪstɪks/ npl logistica f

logo /ˈləʊgəʊ/ n logo m inv

loin /lɔɪn/ n (Culin) lombata f

loiter /ˈlɔɪtə(r)/ vi gironzolare

lollipop /ˈlɒlɪpɒp/ n lecca-lecca m inv. ~**y** n lecca-lecca m; (🆸: money)

quattrini mpl

London /ˈlʌndən/ n Londra f • attrib londinese, di Londra. ~**er** n londinese mf

lone /ləʊn/ adj solitario. ~**liness** n solitudine f

lonely /ˈləʊnlɪ/ adj (-ier, -iest) solitario; (person) solo

lone|r /ˈləʊnə(r)/ n persona f solitaria. ~**some** adj solo

long¹ /lɒŋ/ adj lungo; a ~ **time** molto tempo; a ~ **way** distante; in the ~ **run** a lungo andare; (in the end) alla fin fine • adv a lungo, lungamente; how ~ **is?** quanto è lungo?; (in time) quanto dura?; **all day** ~ tutto il giorno; **not** ~ **ago** non molto tempo fa; **before** ~ fra breve; **he's no** ~**er here** non è più qui; **as or so** ~ **as** finché; (provided that) purché; **so** ~! 🆸 ciao!; **will you be** ~? [ti] ci vuole molto?

long² vi ~ **for** desiderare ardentemente

long-'distance adj a grande distanza; (Sport) di fondo; (call) interurbano

longing /ˈlɒŋɪŋ/ adj desideroso • n brama f. ~**ly** adv con desiderio

longitude /ˈlɒŋgɪtjuːd/ n (Geog) longitudine f

long: ~**jump** n salto m in lungo. ~**-range** adj (Aeron, Mil) a lunga portata; (forecast) a lungo termine. ~**-sighted** adj presbite. ~**-term** adj a lunga scadenza. ~**-winded** /-ˈwɪndɪd/ adj prolisso

loo /luː/ n 🆸 gabinetto m

look /lʊk/ n occhiata f; (appearance) aspetto m; [**good**] ~**s** pl bellezza f; **have a** ~ **at** dare un'occhiata a • vi guardare; (seem) sembrare; ~ **here!** mi ascolti bene!; ~ **at** guardare; ~ **for** cercare; ~ **like** (resemble) assomigliare a. □ ~ **after** vt badare a. □ ~ **down** vi guardare in basso; ~ **down on sb** fig guardare dall'alto in basso qcno. □ ~ **forward to** vt essere impaziente di. □ ~ **in on** vt passare da. □ ~ **into** vt (examine) esaminare. □ ~ **on to** vt (room): dare su. □ ~ **out** vi guardare fuori; (take care) fare attenzione; ~ out for cercare; ~ out! look out! □ ~ **round** vi girarsi; (in shop, town etc) dare un'occhiata. □ ~ **through** vt dare un'occhiata a (script, notes). □ ~ **up** vi guardare in alto; ~ up to sb fig rispettare qcno ●vt cercare [nel dizionario] (word); (visit) andare a trovare

'look-out n guardia f; (prospect) prospettiva f; **be on the** ~ **for** tenere gli occhi aperti per

loom /luːm/ vi apparire; fig profilarsi

loony /'luːnɪ/ adj & n 🆇 matto, -a mf. ~ **bin** n manicomio m

loop /luːp/ n cappio m; (on garment) passante m. ~**hole** n (in the law) scappatoia f

loose /luːs/ adj libero; (knot) allentato; (page) staccato; (clothes) largo; (morals) dissoluto; (inexact) vago; **be at a** ~ **end** non sapere cosa fare; **come** ~ (knot): sciogliersi; **set** ~ liberare. ~ **change** n spiccioli mpl. ~**ly** adv scorrevolmente; (defined) vagamente

loosen /'luːsn/ vt sciogliere

loot /luːt/ n bottino m ●vt/i depredare. ~**er** n predatore, -trice mf. ~**ing** n saccheggio m

lop /lɒp/ ~ **off** vt (pt/pp lopped) potare

lop'sided adj sbilenco

lord /lɔːd/ n signore m; (title) Lord m; **House of L~s** Camera f dei Lords; **the L~'s Prayer** il Padrenostro; **good L~!** Dio mio!

lorry /'lɒrɪ/ n camion m inv; ~ **driver** camionista mf

lose /luːz/ v (pt/pp lost) ●vt perdere ●vi perdere; (clock): essere indietro; **get lost** perdersi; **get lost!** 🆇 va a quel paese! ~**r** n perdente mf

loss /lɒs/ n perdita f; (Comm) ~**es** perdite fpl; **be at a** ~ essere perplesso; **be at a** ~ **for words** non trovare le parole

lost /lɒst/ ▷LOSE ●adj perduto. ~ **'property office** n ufficio m oggetti smarriti

lot [1] /lɒt/ (at auction) lotto m; **draw** ~**s** tirare a sorte

lot [2] n **the** ~ il tutto; **a** ~ **of,** ~**s of** molto/i; **the** ~ **of you** tutti voi; **it has changed a** ~ è cambiato molto

lotion /'ləʊʃn/ n lozione f

lottery /'lɒtərɪ/ n lotteria f. ~ **ticket** n biglietto m della lotteria

loud /laʊd/ adj sonoro, alto; (colours) sgargiante ●adv forte; **out** ~ ad alta voce. ~ **'hailer** n megafono m. ~**ly** adv forte. ~ **'speaker** n altoparlante m

lounge /laʊndʒ/ n salotto m; (in hotel) salone m ●vi poltrire. ~ **suit** n vestito m da uomo, completo m da uomo

louse /laʊs/ n (pl lice) pidocchio m

lousy /'laʊzɪ/ adj (-ier, -iest) 🆇 schifoso

lout /laʊt/ n zoticone m. ~**ish** adj rozzo

lovable /'lʌvəbl/ adj adorabile

love /lʌv/ n amore m; (Tennis) zero m; **in** ~ innamorato (with di) ●vt amare (person, country); **I** ~ **watching tennis** mi piace molto guardare il tennis. ~**affair** n relazione f [sentimentale]. ~ **letter** n lettera f d'amore

lovely /'lʌvlɪ/ adj (-ier, -iest) bello; (in looks) bello, attraente; (in character) piacevole; (meal) delizioso; **have a** ~ **time** divertirsi molto

lover /'lʌvə(r)/ n amante mf

loving /'lʌvɪŋ/ adj affettuoso

low /ləʊ/ adj basso; (depressed) giù inv ●adv basso; **feel** ~ sentirsi giù ●n minimo m; (Meteorol) depressione f;

at an all-time ~ (prices etc) al livello minimo

lower /'ləʊə(r)/ adj & adv ▷**LOW** vt abbassare; ~ oneself abbassarsi

loyal /'lɔɪəl/ adj leale. ~ty n lealtà f; ~ card carta f fedeltà

lozenge /'lɒzɪndʒ/ n losanga f; (tablet) pastiglia f

LP n abbr long-playing record

Ltd abbr (Limited) s.r.l.

lubricat|e /'lu:brɪkeɪt/ vt lubrificare. ~ion n lubrificazione f

lucid /'lu:sɪd/ adj (explanation) chiaro; (sane) lucido. ~ity n lucidità f; (of explanation) chiarezza f

luck /lʌk/ n fortuna f; bad ~ sfortuna f; good ~! buona fortuna! ~ily adv fortunatamente

lucky /'lʌkɪ/ adj (-ier, -iest) fortunato; be ~ essere fortunato; (thing:) portare fortuna. ~ 'charm n portafortuna m inv

lucrative /'lu:krətɪv/ adj lucrativo

ludicrous /'lu:dɪkrəs/ adj ridicolo. ~ly adv (expensive, complex) eccessivamente

lug /lʌg/ vt (pt/pp **lugged**) 🄸 trascinare

luggage /'lʌgɪdʒ/ n bagaglio m; ~-rack n portabagagli m inv. ~ trolley n carrello m portabagagli. ~-van n bagagliaio m

lukewarm /'lu:k-/ adj tiepido; fig poco entusiasta

lull /lʌl/ n pausa f ●vt ~ to sleep cullare

lullaby /'lʌləbaɪ/ n ninna nanna f

lumber /'lʌmbə(r)/ n cianfrusaglie fpl; (Am: timber) legname m ●vt 🄸 ~ sb with sth affibbiare qcsa a qcno. ~ jack n tagliaboschi m inv

luminous /'lu:mɪnəs/ adj luminoso

lump[1] /lʌmp/ n (of sugar) zolletta f; (swelling) gonfiore m; (in breast) nodulo m; (in sauce) grumo m ●vt ~

together ammucchiare

lump[2] vt ~ it 🄸 you'll just have to ~ it ci che ti piaccia o no è così

lump sum n somma f globale

lumpy /'lʌmpɪ/ adj (-ier, -iest) grumoso

lunacy /'lu:nəsɪ/ n follia f

lunar /'lu:nə(r)/ adj lunare

lunatic /'lu:nətɪk/ n pazzo, -a mf

lunch /lʌntʃ/ n pranzo m ●vi pranzare

luncheon /'lʌntʃn/ n (formal) pranzo m. ~ meat n carne f in scatola. ~ voucher n buono m pasto

lung /lʌŋ/ n polmone m. ~ cancer n cancro m al polmone

lunge /lʌndʒ/ vi lanciarsi (at su)

lurch[1] /lɜːtʃ/ n leave in the ~ 🄸 lasciare nei guai

lurch[2] vi barcollare

lure /lʊə(r)/ n esca f; fig lusinga f ●vt adescare

lurid /'lʊərɪd/ adj (gaudy) sgargiante; (sensational) sensazionalistico

lurk /lɜːk/ vi appostarsi

luscious /'lʌʃəs/ adj saporito; fig sexy inv

lush /lʌʃ/ adj lussureggiante

lust /lʌst/ n lussuria f ●vi ~ after desiderare [fortemente]. ~ful adj lussurioso

lute /lu:t/ n liuto m

luxuriant /lʌg'ʒʊərɪənt/ adj lussureggiante

luxurious /lʌg'ʒʊərɪəs/ adj lussuoso

luxury /'lʌkʃərɪ/ n lusso m ●attrib di lusso

lying /'laɪɪŋ/ ▷**LIE**[1] & [2] ●n mentire

lynch /lɪntʃ/ vt linciare

lyric /'lɪrɪk/ adj lirico. ~al adj lirico; (🄸: enthusiastic) entusiasta. ~s npl parole fpl

Mm

mac /mæk/ n 🇬🇧 impermeabile m

macaroni /mækəˈrəʊnɪ/ n maccheroni mpl

mace[1] /meɪs/ n (staff) mazza f

mace[2] n (spice) macis m o f

machine /məˈʃiːn/ n macchina f • vt (sew) cucire a macchina; (Techn) lavorare a macchina. **~-gun** n mitragliatrice f

machinery /məˈʃiːnərɪ/ n macchinario m

mackerel /ˈmæk(ə)l/ n inv sgombro m

mackintosh /ˈmækɪntɒʃ/ n impermeabile m

mad /mæd/ adj (madder, maddest) pazzo, matto; (🇬🇧: angry) furioso (at con); like **~** 🇬🇧 come un pazzo; be **~** about sb/sth (🇬🇧: keen on) andare matto per qcno/qcsa

madam /ˈmædəm/ n signora f

mad cow disease n morbo m della mucca pazza

madden /ˈmædən/ vt (make angry) far diventare matto

made /meɪd/ ▷ **MAKE**; **~ to measure** [fatto] su misura

mad|ly /ˈmædlɪ/ adv (🇬🇧) follemente; **~ly in love** innamorato pazzo. **~man** n pazzo m. **~ness** n pazzia f

madonna /məˈdɒnə/ n madonna f

magazine /mægəˈziːn/ n rivista f; (Mil, Phot) magazzino m

maggot /ˈmægət/ n verme m

magic /ˈmædʒɪk/ n magia f; (tricks) giochi mpl di prestigio • adj magico; (trick) di prestigio. **~al** adj magico

magician /məˈdʒɪʃ(ə)n/ n mago, -a mf; (entertainer) prestigiatore, -trice m

magistrate /ˈmædʒɪstreɪt/ n magistrato m

magnet /ˈmægnɪt/ n magnete m, calamita f. **~ic** adj magnetico. **~ism** n magnetismo m

magnification /mægnɪfɪˈkeɪʃn/ n ingrandimento m

magnificen|ce /mægˈnɪfɪsəns/ n magnificenza f. **~t** adj magnifico

magnify /ˈmægnɪfaɪ/ vt (pt/pp -ied) ingrandire; (exaggerate) ingigantire. **~ing glass** n lente f d'ingrandimento

magnitude /ˈmægnɪtjuːd/ n grandezza f; (importance) importanza f

magpie /ˈmægpaɪ/ n gazza f

mahogany /məˈhɒgənɪ/ n mogano m • attrib di mogano

maid /meɪd/ n cameriera f; old **~** pej zitella f

maiden /ˈmeɪdn/ n (liter) fanciulla f • adj (speech, voyage) inaugurale. **~ aunt** n zia f zitella. **~ name** n nome m da ragazza

mail /meɪl/ n posta f • vt impostare. **~-bag** n sacco m postale. **~box** n Am cassetta f delle lettere; (e-mail) casella f di posta elettronica. **~ing list** n elenco m d'indirizzi per un mailing. **~man** n Am postino m. **~-order** n vendita f per corrispondenza. **~-order firm** n ditta f di vendita per corrispondenza. **~shot** n mailing m inv

maim /meɪm/ vt menomare

main[1] /meɪn/ n (water, gas, electricity) conduttura f principale

main[2] /meɪn/ adj principale; **the ~ thing is to...** la cosa essenziale è di... • n in **the ~** in complesso

main: **~land** /-lænd/ n continente m. **~ly** adv principalmente. **~ street** n via f principale

maintain /meɪnˈteɪn/ vt mantenere; (keep in repair) curare la manutenzione di; (claim) sostenere

maintenance /ˈmeɪntənəns/ n mantenimento m; (care) manutenzione f; (allowance) alimenti mpl

maisonette /meɪzə'net/ n appartamento m a due piani

majestic /mə'dʒestɪk/ adj maestoso

majesty /'mædʒəstɪ/ n maestà f; His/Her M~ Sua Maestà

major /'meɪdʒə(r)/ adj maggiore; ~ road strada f con diritto di precedenza •n (Mil, Mus) maggiore m •vi Am ~ in specializzarsi in

Majorca /mə'jɔːkə/ n Maiorca f

majority /mə'dʒɒrətɪ/ n maggioranza f; be in the ~ avere la maggioranza

make /meɪk/ n (brand) marca f •v (pt/pp made) •vt fare; (earn) guadagnare; rendere (happy, clear); prendere (decision); ~ sb laugh far ridere qcno; ~ sb do sth far fare qcsa a qcno; ~ it (to party, top of hill etc) farcela; what time do you ~ it? che ore fai? •v as if to fare per; □ ~ do vi arrangiarsi. □ ~ for vi dirigersi verso. □ ~ off vi fuggire. □ ~ out vt (distinguish) distinguere; (write out) rilasciare (cheque); compilare (list); (claim) far credere. □ ~ over vt cedere. □ ~ up vt (constitute) comporre; (complete) completare; (invent) inventare; (apply cosmetics to) truccare; fare (parcel); ~ up one's mind decidersi; ~ it up (after quarrel) riconciliarsi •vi (after quarrel) fare la pace; ~ up for compensare; ~ up for lost time recuperare il tempo perso

'make-believe n finzione f

maker /'meɪkə(r)/ n fabbricante mf; M~ Creatore m

make: ~ **shift** adj di fortuna •n espediente m. ~-**up** n trucco m; (character) natura f

making /'meɪkɪŋ/ n have the ~s of aver la stoffa di

maladjust|ed /mælə'dʒʌstɪd/ adj disadattato

malaria /mə'leərɪə/ n malaria f

Malaysia /mə'leɪzɪə/ n Malesia f

male /meɪl/ adj maschile •n maschio m. ~ **nurse** n infermiere m

malfunction /mæl'fʌŋkʃn/ n funzionamento m imperfetto •vi funzionare male

malice /'mælɪs/ n malignità f; bear sb ~ voler del male a qcno

malicious /mə'lɪʃəs/ adj maligno

mallet /'mælɪt/ n martello m di legno

malnu'trition /mæl-/ n malnutrizione f

mal'practice n negligenza f

malt /mɔːlt/ n malto m

Malta /'mɔːltə/ n Malta f. ~**ese** adj & n maltese m

mammal /'mæml/ n mammifero m

mammoth /'mæməθ/ adj mastodontico •n mammut m inv

man /mæn/ n (pl **men**) uomo m; (chess, draughts) pedina f •vt (pt/pp **manned**) equipaggiare; essere di servizio a (counter, telephones)

manage /'mænɪdʒ/ vt dirigere; gestire (shop, affairs); (cope with) farcela; ~ to do sth riuscire a fare qcsa •vi riuscire; (cope) farcela (on con). ~**able** adj (hair) docile; (size) maneggevole. ~**ment** n gestione f; the ~**ment** la direzione

manager /'mænɪdʒə(r)/ n direttore m; (of shop, bar) gestore m; (Sport) manager m inv. ~**ess** n direttrice f. ~**ial** adj staff personale m direttivo

mandat|e /'mændeɪt/ n mandato m. ~**ory** adj obbligatorio

mane /meɪn/ n criniera f

mangle /'mæŋgl/ vt (damage) maciullare

man: ~**handle** vt malmenare. ~**hole** n botola f. ~**hood** n età f adulta; (quality) virilità f. ~**hour** n ora f lavorativa. ~**hunt** n caccia f all'uomo

man|ia /'meɪnɪə/ n mania f. ~**iac** n maniaco, -a mf

manicure /'mænɪkjʊə(r)/ n manicure f ● vt fare la manicure a

manifest /'mænɪfest/ adj manifesto ● vt ~ itself manifestarsi. ~ly adv palesemente

manifesto /mænɪ'festəʊ/ n manifesto m

manipulat|e /mə'nɪpjʊleɪt/ vt manipolare. ~ion n manipolazione f

man'kind n genere m umano

manly /'mænlɪ/ adj virile

'man-made adj artificiale. ~ fibre n fibra f sintetica

manner /'mænə(r)/ n maniera f; in this ~ in questo modo; have no ~s avere dei pessimi modi; good/bad ~s buone/cattive maniere fpl. ~ism n affettazione f

manor /'mænə(r)/ n maniero m

'manpower n manodopera f

mansion /'mænʃn/ n palazzo m

'manslaughter n omicidio m colposo

mantelpiece /'mæntl-/ n mensola f di caminetto

manual /'mænjʊəl/ adj manuale ● n manuale m

manufacture /mænjʊ'fæktʃə(r)/ vt fabbricare ● n manifattura f. ~r n fabbricante m

manure /mə'njʊə(r)/ n concime m

manuscript /'mænjʊskrɪpt/ n manoscritto m

many /'menɪ/ adj & pron molti; there are as ~ boys as girls ci sono tanti ragazzi quante ragazze; as ~ as 500 ben 500; as ~ as that così tanti; as ~ altrettanti; very ~, a good/great ~ moltissimi; ~ a time molte volte

map /mæp/ n carta f geografica; (of town) mappa f ● map out vt (pt/pp mapped) fig programmare

mar /mɑː(r)/ vt (pt/pp marred) rovinare

marathon /'mærəθən/ n maratona f

marble /'mɑːbl/ n marmo m; (for game) pallina f ● attrib di marmo

march n marcia f; (protest) dimostrazione f ● vi marciare ● vt far marciare; ~ sb off scortare qcno fuori

March /mɑːtʃ/ n marzo m

mare /meə(r)/ n giumenta f

margarine /mɑːdʒə'riːn/ n margarina f

margin /'mɑːdʒɪn/ n margine m. ~al adj marginale. ~ally adv marginalmente

marijuana /mærʊ'wɑːnə/ n marijuana f

marina /mə'riːnə/ n porticciolo m

marine /mə'riːn/ adj marino ● n (sailor) soldato m di fanteria marina

marionette /mærɪə'net/ n marionetta f

mark[1] /mɑːk/ n (currency) marco m

mark[2] n (stain) macchia f; (sign, indication) segno m; (Sch) voto m ● vt segnare; (stain) macchiare; (Sch) correggere; (Sport) marcare; ~ time (Mil) segnare il passo; fig non far progressi; ~ my words ricordati quello che dico. □~ out vt delimitare; fig designare

marked /mɑːkt/ adj marcato. ~ly adv notevolmente

marker /'mɑːkə(r)/ n (for highlighting) evidenziatore m; (Sport) marcatore m; (of exam) esaminatore, -trice mf

market /'mɑːkɪt/ n mercato m ● vt vendere al mercato; (launch) commercializzare; on the ~ sul mercato. ~ing n marketing m. ~ re'search n ricerca f di mercato

marksman /'mɑːksmən/ n tiratore m scelto

marmalade /'mɑːməleɪd/ n marmellata f d'arance

maroon /mə'ruːn/ adj marrone rossastro

marquee /mɑː'kiː/ n tendone m

marriage /'mærɪdʒ/ n

matrimonio *m*

married /'mærɪd/ *adj* sposato; (life) coniugale

marrow /'mærəʊ/ *n* (Anat) midollo *m*; (vegetable) zucca *f*

marr|y /'mærɪ/ *vt* (pt/pp **married**) sposare; **get ~ied** sposarsi ● *vi* sposarsi

marsh /mɑːʃ/ *n* palude *f*

marshal /'mɑːʃl/ *n* (steward) cerimoniere *m* ● *vt* (pt/pp **marshalled**) fig organizzare (arguments)

marshy /'mɑːʃɪ/ *adj* paludoso

martial /'mɑːʃl/ *adj* marziale

martyr /'mɑːtə(r)/ *n* martire *mf* ● *vt* martoriare. **~dom** *n* martirio *m*. **~ed** *adj* ﹇ da martire

marvel /'mɑːvl/ *n* meraviglia *f* ● *vi* (pt/pp **marvelled**) meravigliarsi (at di). **~lous** *adj* meraviglioso

Marxis|m /'mɑːksɪzm/ *n* marxismo *m*. **~t** *adj* & *n* marxista *mf*

marzipan /'mɑːzɪpæn/ *n* marzapane *m*

mascara /mæ'skɑːrə/ *n* mascara *m inv*

mascot /'mæskət/ *n* mascotte *f inv*

masculin|e /'mæskjʊlɪn/ *adj* maschile ● *n* (Gram) maschile *m*. **~ity** *n* mascolinità *f*

mash /mæʃ/ *vt* impastare. **~ed potatoes** *npl* purè *m inv* di patate

mask /mɑːsk/ *n* maschera *f* ● *vt* mascherare

masochis|m /'mæsəkɪzm/ *n* masochismo *m*. **~t** *n* masochista *mf*

mason /'meɪsn/ *n* muratore *m*

Mason *n* massone *m*. **~ic** *adj* massonico

masonry /'meɪsnrɪ/ *n* massoneria *f*

masquerade /mæskə'reɪd/ *n* fig mascherata *f* ● *vi* **~ as** (pose) farsi passare per

mass¹ /mæs/ *n* (Relig) messa *f*

mass² *n* massa *f*; **~es of** ﹇ un sacco di ● *vi* ammassarsi

massacre /'mæsəkə(r)/ *n* massacro *m* ● *vt* massacrare

massage /'mæsɑːʒ/ *n* massaggio *m* ● *vt* massaggiare; fig manipolare (statistics)

masseu|r /mæ'sɜː(r)/ *n* massaggiatore *m*. **~se** *n* massaggiatrice *f*

massive /'mæsɪv/ *adj* enorme

mass: **~ media** *npl* mezzi *mpl* di comunicazione di massa, mass media *mpl*. **~-pro'duce** *vt* produrre in serie

mast /mɑːst/ *n* (Naut) albero *m*; (for radio) antenna *f*

master /'mɑːstə(r)/ *n* maestro *m*, padrone *m*; (teacher) professore *m*; (of ship) capitano *m*; M**~** (boy) signorino *m*

master: **~-key** *n* passe-partout *m inv*. **~-mind** *n* cervello *m* ● *vt* ideare e dirigere. **~-piece** *n* capolavoro *m*. **~-stroke** *n* colpo *m* da maestro. **~y** *n* (of subject) padronanza *f*

masturbat|e /'mæstəbeɪt/ *vi* masturbarsi. **~ion** *n* masturbazione *f*

mat /mæt/ *n* stuoia *f*; (on table) sottopiatto *m*

match¹ /mætʃ/ *n* (Sport) partita *f*; (equal) uguale *mf*; (marriage) matrimonio *m*; (person to marry) partito *m*; **be a good ~** (colours): intonarsi bene; **be no ~ for** non essere dello stesso livello di ● *vt* (equal) uguagliare; (be like) andare bene con ● *vi* intonarsi

match² *n* fiammifero *m*. **~box** *n* scatola *f* di fiammiferi

matching /'mætʃɪŋ/ *adj* intonato

mate¹ /meɪt/ *n* compagno, -a *mf*; (assistant) aiuto *m*; (Naut) secondo *m*; (﹇: friend) amico, -a *mf* ● *vi* accoppiarsi ● *vt* accoppiare

mate² *n* (in chess) scacco *m* matto

material /mə'tɪərɪəl/ *n* materiale *m*; (fabric) stoffa *f*; **raw ~s** materie *fpl* prime ● *adj* materiale

maternal /mə'tɜːnl/ *adj* materno

maternity /mə'tɜːnətɪ/ *n* maternità *f*. **~ clothes** *npl* abiti *mpl* premaman

~ **ward** n maternità f inv

mathematic|al /mæθə'mætɪkl/ adj matematico. ~**ian** n matematico, -a mf

mathematics /mæθ'mætɪks/ n matematica fsg

maths /mæθs/ n 🅱 matematica fsg

matinée /'mætɪneɪ/ n (Theat) matinée m

matriculat|e /mə'trɪkjuleɪt/ vi immatricolarsi. ~**ion** n immatricolazione f

matrix /'meɪtrɪks/ n (pl **matrices** /-siːz/) n matrice f

matted /'mætɪd/ adj ~ hair capelli mpl tutti appiccicati tra loro

matter /'mætə(r)/ n (affair) faccenda f; (question) questione f; (pus) pus m; (phys: substance) materia f; as a ~ of fact a dire la verità; what is the ~? che cosa c'è? ●vi importare; ~ to sb essere importante per qcno; it doesn't ~ non importa. ~**-of-fact** adj pratico

mattress /'mætrɪs/ n materasso m

matur|e /mə'tʃʊə(r)/ adj maturo; (Comm) in scadenza ●vi maturare ●vt far maturare. ~**ity** n maturità f; (Fin) maturazione f

maul /mɔːl/ vt malmenare

mauve /məʊv/ adj malva

maxim /'mæksɪm/ n massima f

maximum /'mæksɪməm/ adj massimo; ten minutes ~ dieci minuti al massimo ●n (pl **-ima**) massimo m

may /meɪ/ v aux (solo al presente) potere; ~ I come in? posso entrare?; if I ~ say so se mi posso permettere; ~ you be very happy siate felici; I ~ as well stay potrei anche rimanere; it ~ be true potrebbe esser vero; she ~ be old, but... sarà anche vecchia, ma...

May /meɪ/ n maggio m

maybe /'meɪbiː/ adv forse, può darsi

'**May Day** n il primo maggio

mayonnaise /meɪə'neɪz/ n maionese f

mayor /'meə(r)/ n sindaco m. ~**ess** n sindaco m; (wife of mayor) moglie f del sindaco

maze /meɪz/ n labirinto m

me /miː/ pron (object) mi; (with preposition) me; she called me mi ha chiamato; she called me, not you ha chiamato me, non te; give me the money dammi i soldi; give it to me dammelo; he gave it to me me lo ha dato; it's ~ sono io

meadow /'medəʊ/ n prato m

meagre /'miːgə(r)/ adj scarso

meal¹ /miːl/ n pasto m

meal² n (grain) farina f

mean¹ /miːn/ adj avaro; (unkind) meschino

mean² adj medio n (average) media f; Greenwich ~ **time** ora f media di Greenwich

mean³ vt (pt/pp **meant**) voler dire; (signify) significare; (intend) intendere; I ~ it lo dico seriamente; ~ **well** avere buone intenzioni; be meant for (present:) essere destinato a; (remark:) essere riferito a

meander /mɪ'ændə(r)/ vi vagare

meaning /'miːnɪŋ/ n significato m. ~**ful** adj significativo. ~**less** adj senza senso

means /miːnz/ n mezzo m; ~ of transport mezzo m di trasporto; by ~ of per mezzo di; by all ~! certamente!; by no ~ niente affatto ●npl (resources) mezzi mpl

meant /ment/ ▷**MEAN³**

'**meantime** n in the ~ nel frattempo ●adv intanto

'**meanwhile** adv intanto

measles /'miːzlz/ n morbillo m

measly /'miːzlɪ/ adj 🅱 misero

measure /'meʒə(r)/ n misura f ●vt/i misurare. ¤ ~ **up to** vt fig essere all'altezza di. ~**d** adj misurato.

~ment n misura f.

meat /miːt/ n carne f. ~ **ball** n (Culin) polpetta f di carne. ~ **loaf** n polpettone m

mechan|ic /mɪˈkænɪk/ n meccanico m. ~**ical** adj meccanico; ~**ical engineering** ingegneria f meccanica. ~**ically** adv meccanicamente. ~**ics** n meccanica f •npl meccanismo msg

mechan|ism /ˈmekənɪzm/ n meccanismo m. ~**ize** vt meccanizzare

medal /ˈmedl/ n medaglia f

medallist /ˈmedəlɪst/ n vincitore, -trice mf di una medaglia

meddle /ˈmedl/ vi immischiarsi (in di); (tinker) armeggiare (with con)

media /ˈmiːdɪə/ ▶**MEDIUM** •npl the ~ i mass media

mediat|e /ˈmiːdɪeɪt/ vi fare da mediatore. ~**ion** n mediazione f. ~**or** n mediatore, -trice mf

medical /ˈmedɪkl/ adj medico •n visita f medica. ~ **insurance** n assicurazione f sanitaria. ~ **student** n studente, -essa mf di medicina

medicat|ed /ˈmedɪkeɪtɪd/ adj medicato. ~**ion** n (drugs) medicinali mpl

medicinal /mɪˈdɪsɪnl/ adj medicinale

medicine /ˈmedsən/ n medicina f

medieval /medɪˈiːvl/ adj medievale

mediocr|e /miːdɪˈəʊkə(r)/ adj mediocre. ~**ity** n mediocrità f

meditat|e /ˈmedɪteɪt/ vi meditare (on su). ~**ion** n meditazione f

Mediterranean /medɪtəˈreɪnɪən/ n the ~ [Sea] il [mare m] Mediterraneo m •adj mediterraneo

medium /ˈmiːdɪəm/ adj medio; (Culin) di media cottura •n (pl media) mezzo m; (pl -s) (person) medium mf inv

medium-sized adj di taglia media

medley /ˈmedlɪ/ n miscuglio m; (Mus) miscellanea f

meek /miːk/ adj mite, mansueto.

~**ly** adv docilmente

meet /miːt/ v (pt/pp met) •vt incontrare; (at station, airport) andare incontro a; (for first time) fare la conoscenza di; (pay) pagare (bill); (satisfy) soddisfare (requirements) •vi incontrarsi; (committee:) riunirsi; ~ **with** incontrare (problem); incontrarsi con (person) •n raduno m [sportivo]

meeting /ˈmiːtɪŋ/ n riunione f, meeting m inv; (large) assemblea f; (by chance) incontro m

megabyte /ˈmegəbaɪt/ n megabyte m

megaphone /ˈmegəfəʊn/ n megafono m

melancholy /ˈmelənkəlɪ/ adj malinconico •n malinconia f

mellow /ˈmeləʊ/ adj (wine) generoso; (sound, colour) caldo; (person) dolce •vi (person:) addolcirsi

melodrama /ˈmelə-/ n melodramma m. ~**tic** adj melodrammatico

melody /ˈmelədɪ/ n melodia f

melon /ˈmelən/ n melone m

melt /melt/ vt sciogliere •vi sciogliersi. □ ~ **down** vt fondere. ~**ing-pot** n fig crogiuolo m

member /ˈmembə(r)/ n membro m; ~ **countries** paesi mpl membri; M~ **of Parliament** deputato, -a mf; M~ **of the European Parliament** eurodeputato, -a mf. ~**ship** n iscrizione f; (members) soci mpl

membrane /ˈmembreɪn/ n membrana f

memo /ˈmeməʊ/ n promemoria m inv

memorable /ˈmemərəbl/ adj memorabile

memorandum /meməˈrændəm/ n promemoria m inv

memorial /mɪˈmɔːrɪəl/ n monumento m. ~ **service** n funzione f commemorativa

memorize /ˈmeməraɪz/ vt

m

memorizzare

memory /'meməri/ n also (Comput) memoria f; (thing remembered) ricordo m; from ~ a memoria; in ~ of in ricordo di

men /men/ ▷MAN

menac|e /'menəs/ n minaccia f; (nuisance) piaga f ● vt minacciare. ~ing adj minaccioso

mend /mend/ vt riparare; (darn) rammendare ● n on the ~ in via di guarigione

'menfolk n uomini mpl

menial /'mi:nɪəl/ adj umile

meningitis /menɪn'dʒaɪtɪs/ n meningite f

menopause /'menə-/ n menopausa f

menstruat|e /'menstrʊeɪt/ vi mestruare. ~ion n mestruazione f

mental /'mentl/ adj mentale; (**[]**: mad) pazzo. ~ a'rithmetic n calcolo m mentale. ~ 'illness n malattia f mentale

mental|ity /men'tæləti/ n mentalità f inv. ~ly adv mentalmente; ~ly ill malato di mente

mention /'menʃn/ n menzione f ● vt menzionare; don't ~ it non c'è di che

menu /'menju:/ n menu m inv

MEP n abbr Member of the European Parliament

mercenary /'mɜːsɪnəri/ adj mercenario ● n mercenario m

merchandise /'mɜːtʃəndaɪz/ n merce f

merchant /'mɜːtʃənt/ n commerciante mf. ~ bank n banca f d'affari. ~ 'navy n marina f mercantile

merci|ful /'mɜːsɪfl/ adj misericordioso. ~fully adv **[]** grazie a Dio. ~less adj spietato

mercury /'mɜːkjʊri/ n mercurio m

mercy /'mɜːsi/ n misericordia f; be at sb's ~ essere alla mercé di qcno,

essere in balìa di qcno

mere /mɪə(r)/ adj solo. ~ly adv solamente

merge /mɜːdʒ/ vi fondersi

merger /'mɜːdʒə(r)/ n fusione f

meringue /mə'ræŋ/ n meringa f

merit /'merɪt/ n merito m; (advantage) qualità f ● vt meritare

mermaid /'mɜːmeɪd/ n sirena f

merri|ly /'merɪli/ adv allegramente. ~ment n baldoria f

merry /'meri/ adj (-ier, -iest) allegro; ~ Christmas! Buon Natale!

merry: ~-**go-round** n giostra f. ~-**making** n festa f

mesh /meʃ/ n maglia f

mesmerize /'mezməraɪz/ vt ipnotizzare. ~d adj fig ipnotizzato

mess /mes/ n disordine m, casino m **[]**; (trouble) guaio m; (something spilt) sporco m; (Mil) mensa f; make a ~ of (botch) fare un pasticcio di ● mess about vi perder tempo; ~ about with armeggiare con ● vt prendere in giro (person). □ ~ up vt mettere in disordine, incasinare **[]**; (botch) mandare all'aria

message /'mesɪdʒ/ n messaggio m

messenger /'mesɪndʒə(r)/ n messaggero m

Messiah /mɪ'saɪə/ n Messia m

Messrs /'mesəz/ npl (on letter) ~ Smith Spett. ditta Smith

messy /'mesi/ adj (-ier, -iest) disordinato; (in dress) sciatto

met /met/ ▷MEET

metal /'metl/ n metallo m ● adj di metallo. ~lic adj metallico

metaphor /'metəfə(r)/ n metafora f. ~ical adj metaforico

meteor /'mi:tɪə(r)/ n meteora f. ~ic adj fig fulmineo

meteorological /mi:tɪərə'lɒdʒɪkl/ adj meteorologico

meteo|rologist /mi:tɪə'rɒlədʒɪst/ n meteorologo, -a mf. ~rology n meteorologia *f*

meter¹ /'mi:tə(r)/ *n* contatore *m*

meter² *n* Am = **metre**

method /'meθəd/ *n* metodo *m*

methodical /mɪ'θɒdɪkl/ *adj* metodico. **~ly** *adv* metodicamente

methylated /'meθɪleɪtɪd/ *adj* **~ spirit[s]** alcol *m* denaturato

meticulous /mɪ'tɪkjʊləs/ *adj* meticoloso. **~ly** *adv* meticolosamente

metre /'mi:tə(r)/ *n* metro *m*

metric /'metrɪk/ *adj* metrico

metropolis /mɪ'trɒpəlɪs/ *n* metropoli *f inv*

mew /mju:/ *n* miao *m* ●*vi* miagolare

Mexican /'meksɪkən/ *adj & n* messicano, -a *mf*. **'Mexico** *n* Messico *m*

miaow /mɪ'aʊ/ *n* miao *m* ●*vi* miagolare

mice /maɪs/ ▷**MOUSE**

mickey /'mɪkɪ/ *n* **take the ~ out of** prendere in giro

micro /'maɪkrəʊ/: **~chip** *n* microchip *m*. **~computer** *n* microcomputer *m*. **~film** *n* microfilm *m*. **~phone** *n* microfono *m*. **~processor** *n* microprocessore *m*. **~scope** *n* microscopio *m*. **~scopic** *adj* microscopico. **~wave** *n* microonda *f*; (oven) forno *m* a microonde

microbe /'maɪkrəʊb/ *n* microbo *m*

mid /mɪd/ *adj* **~ May** metà maggio; **in ~ air** a mezz'aria

midday /mɪd'deɪ/ *n* mezzogiorno *m*

middle /'mɪdl/ *adj* di centro; the M**~ Ages** il medioevo; the **M~ class[es]** la classe media; the **M~ East** il Medio Oriente ●*n* mezzo *m*; **in the ~ of** (room, floor etc) in mezzo a; **in the ~ of the night** nel pieno della notte, a notte piena

middle: **~-aged** *adj* di mezza età. **~-class** *adj* borghese. **~ man** *n* (Comm) intermediario *m*

middling /'mɪdlɪŋ/ *adj* discreto

midge /mɪdʒ/ *n* moscerino *m*

midget /'mɪdʒɪt/ *n* nano, -a *mf*

Midlands /'mɪdləndz/ *npl* the **~** l'Inghilterra *fsg* centrale

'midnight *n* mezzanotte *f*

midriff /'mɪdrɪf/ *n* diaframma *m*

midst /mɪdst/ *n* **in the ~ of** in mezzo a; **in our ~** fra di noi, in mezzo a noi

mid: **~summer** *n* mezza estate *f*. **~way** *adv* a metà strada. **~wife** *n* ostetrica *f*. **~'winter** *n* pieno inverno *m*

might¹ /maɪt/ *v aux* **I ~** potrei; **will you come? – I ~** vieni? – può darsi; **it ~ be true** potrebbe essere vero; **I ~ as well stay** potrei anche restare; **you ~ have drowned** avresti potuto affogare; **you ~ have said so!** avresti potuto dirlo!

might² *n* potere *m*

mighty /'maɪtɪ/ *adj* (-ier, -iest) potente ●*adv* **॥** molto

migraine /'mi:greɪn/ *n* emicrania *f*

migrant /'maɪgrənt/ *adj & n* migratore ●*n* (bird) migratore, -trice *mf*; (person: for work) emigrante *mf*

migrat|e /maɪ'greɪt/ *vi* migrare. **~ion** *n* migrazione *f*

Milan /mɪ'læn/ *n* Milano *f*

mild /maɪld/ *adj* (weather) mite; (person) dolce; (flavour) delicato; (illness) leggero

mildew /'mɪldju:/ *n* muffa *f*

mild|ly /'maɪldlɪ/ *adv* moderatamente; (say) dolcemente; **to put it ~ly** a dir poco, senza esagerazione. **~ness** *n* (of person, words) dolcezza *f*; (of weather) mitezza *f*

mile /maɪl/ *n* miglio *m* (= 1,6 km); **~s nicer** **॥** molto più bello

mile|age /-ɪdʒ/ *n* chilometraggio *m*. **~stone** *n* pietra *f* miliare

militant /'mɪlɪtənt/ *adj & n* militante *mf*

military /'mɪlɪtrɪ/ *adj* militare. **~ service** *n* servizio *m* militare

m

militia /mɪˈlɪʃə/ n milizia f

milk /mɪlk/ n latte m • vt mungere

milk: ~**man** n lattaio m. ~ **shake** n frappé m inv

milky /ˈmɪlkɪ/ adj (-ier, -iest) latteo; (tea etc) con molto latte. M~ **Way** n (Astr) Via f Lattea

mill /mɪl/ n mulino m; (factory) fabbrica f; (for coffee etc) macinino m • vt macinare (grain). **mill about**, **mill around** vi brulicare

millennium /mɪˈlenɪəm/ n millennio m

miller /ˈmɪlə(r)/ n mugnaio m

million /ˈmɪljən/ n milione m; a ~ **pounds** un milione di sterline. ~**aire** n miliardario, -a mf

millstone n fig peso m

mime /maɪm/ n mimo m • vt mimare

mimic /ˈmɪmɪk/ n imitatore, -trice mf • vt (pt/pp **mimicked**) imitare. ~**ry** n mimetismo m

mince /mɪns/ n carne f tritata • vt (Culin) tritare; **not** ~ **one's words** parlare senza mezzi termini

mince 'pie n pasticcino m a base di frutta secca

mincer /ˈmɪnsə(r)/ n tritacarne m inv

mind /maɪnd/ n mente f; (sanity) ragione f; **to my** ~ a mio parere; **give sb a piece of one's** ~ dire chiaro e tondo a qcno quello che si pensa; **make up one's** ~ decidersi; **have sth in** ~ avere qcsa in mente; **bear sth in** ~ tenere presente qcsa; **have something on one's** ~ essere preoccupato; **have a good** ~ **to** avere una gran voglia di; **I have changed my** ~ ho cambiato idea; **in two** ~**s** indeciso; **are you out of your** ~? sei diventato matto? • vt (look after) occuparsi di; **I don't** ~ **the noise** il rumore non mi dà fastidio; **I don't** ~ **what we do** non mi importa quello che facciamo; ~ **the**

step! attenzione al gradino! • vi **I don't** ~ non mi importa; **never** ~! non importa!; **do you** ~ **if...?** ti dispiace se...? **mind out** vi ~ **out!** [fai] attenzione!

mind|ful adj ~**ful of** attento a. ~**less** adj noncurante

mine[1] /maɪn/ poss pron il mio m, la mia f, i miei mpl, le mie fpl; **a friend of** ~ un mio amico; **friends of** ~ dei miei amici; **that is** ~ questo è mio; (as opposed to yours) questo è il mio

mine[2] n miniera f; (explosive) mina f • vt estrarre; (Mil) minare. ~ **detector** n rivelatore m di mine. ~**field** n campo m minato

mineral /ˈmɪnərəl/ n minerale m • adj minerale. ~ **water** n acqua f minerale

mingle /ˈmɪŋgl/ vi ~ **with** mescolarsi a

mini /ˈmɪnɪ/ n (skirt) mini f

miniature /ˈmɪnɪtʃə(r)/ adj in miniatura • n miniatura f

mini|bus /ˈmɪnɪ-/ n minibus m, pulmino m. ~**cab** n taxi m inv

minim|al /ˈmɪnɪməl/ adj minimo. ~**ize** vt minimizzare. ~**um** n (pl -**ima**) minimo m • adj minimo; **ten minutes** ~**um** minimo dieci minuti

mining /ˈmaɪnɪŋ/ n estrazione f • adj estrattivo

miniskirt /ˈmɪnɪ-/ n minigonna f

minist|er /ˈmɪnɪstə(r)/ n ministro m; (Relig) pastore m. ~**erial** adj ministeriale

ministry /ˈmɪnɪstrɪ/ n (Pol) ministero m; **the** ~ (Relig) il ministero sacerdotale

mink /mɪŋk/ n visone m

minor /ˈmaɪnə(r)/ adj minore • n minorenne mf

minority /maɪˈnɒrətɪ/ n minoranza f; (age) minore età f

mint[1] /mɪnt/ n Ⓣ patrimonio m • adj **in** ~ **condition** in condizione perfetta

mint² n (herb) menta f

minus /ˈmaɪnəs/ prep meno; ([[.]] without) senza ●n ~ [sign] meno m

minute¹ /ˈmɪnɪt/ n minuto m; in a ~ (shortly) in un minuto; ~s pl (of meeting) verbale msg

minute² /maɪˈnjuːt/ adj minuto; (precise) minuzioso

mirac|le /ˈmɪrəkl/ n miracolo m. ~ulous adj miracoloso

mirage /ˈmɪrɑːʒ/ n miraggio m

mirror /ˈmɪrə(r)/ n specchio m ●vt rispecchiare

mirth /mɜːθ/ n ilarità f

misappre'hension n malinteso m; be under a ~ avere frainteso

misbe'have vi comportarsi male

mis'calcu|late vt/i calcolare male. ~lation n calcolo m sbagliato

'miscarriage n aborto m spontaneo; ~ of justice errore m giudiziario. mis'carry vi abortire

miscellaneous /mɪsəˈleɪnɪəs/ adj assortito

mischief /ˈmɪstʃɪf/ n malefatta f; (harm) danno m

mischievous /ˈmɪstʃɪvəs/ adj (naughty) birichino; (malicious) dannoso

miscon'ception n concetto m erroneo

mis'conduct n cattiva condotta f

misde'meanour n reato m

miser /ˈmaɪzə(r)/ n avaro m

miserab|le /ˈmɪzrəbl/ adj (unhappy) infelice; (wretched) miserabile; (fig: weather) deprimente. ~ly adv (live, fail) miseramente; (say) tristemente

miserly /ˈmaɪzəli/ adj avaro; (amount) ridicolo

misery /ˈmɪzəri/ n miseria f; ([[.]] person) piagnone, -a mf

mis'fire vi (gun:) far cilecca; (plan etc:) non riuscire

'misfit n disadattato, -a mf

mis'fortune n sfortuna f

mis'guided adj fuorviato

mishap /ˈmɪshæp/ n disavventura f

misin'terpret vt fraintendere

mis'judge vt giudicar male; (estimate wrongly) valutare male

mis'lay vt (pt/pp -laid) smarrire

mis'lead vt (pt/pp -led) fuorviare. ~ing adj fuorviante

mis'manage vt amministrare male. ~ment n cattiva amministrazione f

'misprint n errore m di stampa

miss /mɪs/ n colpo m mancato ●vt (fail to hit or find) mancare; perdere (train, bus, class); (feel the loss of) sentire la mancanza di; I ~ed that part (failed to notice) mi è sfuggita quella parte ●vi but he ~ed (failed to hit) ma l'ha mancato. □ ~ out saltare, omettere

Miss n (pl -es) signorina f

misshapen /mɪsˈʃeɪpən/ adj malformato

missile /ˈmɪsaɪl/ n missile m

missing /ˈmɪsɪŋ/ adj mancante; (person) scomparso; (Mil) disperso; be ~ essere introvabile

mission /ˈmɪʃn/ n missione f

missionary /ˈmɪʃənri/ n missionario, -a mf

mist /mɪst/ n (fog) foschia f ●mist up vi appannarsi, annebbiarsi

mistake /mɪˈsteɪk/ n sbaglio m; by ~ per sbaglio ●vt (pt mistook, pp mistaken) sbagliare (road, house); fraintendere (meaning, words); ~ for prendere per

mistaken /mɪˈsteɪkən/ adj sbagliato; be ~ sbagliarsi; ~ identity errore m di persona. ~ly adv erroneamente

mistletoe /ˈmɪsltəʊ/ n vischio m

mistress /ˈmɪstrɪs/ n padrona f; (teacher) maestra f; (lover) amante f

mis'trust n sfiducia f ●vt non aver fiducia in

misty /ˈmɪstɪ/ adj (-ier, -iest) nebbioso

misunder'stand vt (pt/pp -stood) fraintendere. ~ing n malinteso m

misuse¹ /mɪsˈjuːz/ vt usare male

misuse² /mɪsˈjuːs/ n cattivo uso m

mite /maɪt/ n (child) piccino, -a mf

mitten /ˈmɪtn/ n manopola f, muffola m

mix /mɪks/ n (combination) mescolanza f; (Culin) miscuglio m; (ready-made) preparato m ● vt mischiare ● vi mischiarsi; (person:) inserirsi; ~ with (associate with) frequentare. □ ~ up vt mescolare (papers); (confuse, mistake for) confondere

mixed /mɪkst/ adj misto; ~ up (person) confuso

mixer /ˈmɪksə(r)/ n (Culin) frullatore m, mixer m inv; he's a good ~ è un tipo socievole

mixture /ˈmɪkstʃə(r)/ n mescolanza f; (medicine) sciroppo m; (Culin) miscela f

'mix-up n (confusion) confusione f; (mistake) pasticcio m

moan /məʊn/ n lamento m ● vi lamentarsi; (complain) lagnarsi

moat /məʊt/ n fossato m

mob /mɒb/ n folla f; (rabble) gentaglia f; (fam: gang) banda f ● vt (pt/pp mobbed) assalire

mobile /ˈməʊbaɪl/ adj mobile ● n composizione f mobile. ~ 'home n casa f roulotte. ~ [phone] n [telefono m] cellulare m, telefonino m

mock /mɒk/ adj finto ● vt canzonare. ~ery n derisione f

model /ˈmɒdl/ n modello m; [fashion] ~ indossatore, -trice mf, modello, -a mf ● adj (yacht, plane) in miniatura; (pupil, husband) esemplare, modello ● vt (pt/pp modelled) ● vt indossare (clothes) ● vi fare l'indossatore, -trice mf; (for artist) posare

modem /ˈməʊdem/ n modem m inv

moderate¹ /ˈmɒdəreɪt/ vt mode-

rare ● vi moderarsi

moderate² /ˈmɒdərət/ adj moderato ● n (Pol) moderato, -a mf. ~ly adv (drink, speak etc) moderatamente; (good, bad etc) relativamente

moderation /mɒdəˈreɪʃn/ n moderazione f; in ~ con moderazione

modern /ˈmɒdn/ adj moderno. ~ize vt modernizzare

modest /ˈmɒdɪst/ adj modesto. ~y n modestia f

modifl|ication /mɒdɪfɪˈkeɪʃn/ n modificazione f. ~y vt (pt/pp -fied) modificare

module /ˈmɒdjuːl/ n modulo m

moist /mɔɪst/ adj umido

moisten /ˈmɔɪsn/ vt inumidire

moistur|e /ˈmɔɪstʃə(r)/ n umidità f. ~izer n [crema f] idratante m

mole¹ /məʊl/ n (on face etc) neo m

mole² n (Zool) talpa f

molecule /ˈmɒlɪkjuːl/ n molecola f

molest /məˈlest/ vt molestare

mollycoddle /ˈmɒlɪkɒdl/ vt tenere nella bambagia

molten /ˈməʊltən/ adj fuso

mom /mɒm/ n Am fam mamma f

moment /ˈməʊmənt/ n momento m; at the ~ in questo momento. ~arily adv momentaneamente. ~ary adj momentaneo

momentous /məˈmentəs/ adj molto importante

momentum /məˈmentəm/ n impeto m

monarch /ˈmɒnək/ n monarca m. ~y n monarchia f

monast|ery /ˈmɒnəstrɪ/ n monastero m. ~ic adj monastico

Monday /ˈmʌndeɪ/ n lunedì m inv

money /ˈmʌnɪ/ n denaro m

money-box n salvadanaio m

mongrel /ˈmʌŋɡrəl/ n bastardo m

monitor /ˈmɒnɪtə(r)/ n (Techn) monitor m inv ● vt controllare

monk /mʌŋk/ n monaco m

monkey /'mʌŋkɪ/ n scimmia f. ∼-nut n nocciolina f americana. ∼-**wrench** n chiave f inglese a rullino

mono /'mɒnəʊ/ n mono m

monologue /'mɒnəlɒg/ n monologo m

monopol|ize /mə'nɒpəlaɪz/ vt monopolizzare. ∼y n monopolio m

monotone /'mɒnətəʊn/ n speak in a ∼ parlare con tono monotono

monoton|ous /mə'nɒtənəs/ adj monotono. ∼y n monotonia f

monsoon /mɒn'su:n/ n monsone m

monster /'mɒnstə(r)/ n mostro m

monstrous /'mɒnstrəs/ adj mostruoso

Montenegro /mɒntɪ'ni:grəʊ/ n Montenegro m

month /mʌnθ/ n mese m. ∼**ly** adj mensile ● adv mensilmente ● n (periodical) mensile m

monument /'mɒnjʊmənt/ n monumento m. ∼**al** adj fig monumentale

moo /mu:/ n muggito m ● vi (pt/pp mooed) muggire

mood /mu:d/ n umore m; be in a good/bad ∼ essere di buon/cattivo umore; be in the ∼ for essere in vena di

moody /'mu:dɪ/ adj (-ier, -iest) (variable) lunatico; (bad-tempered) di malumore

moon /mu:n/ n luna f; over the ∼ 🄵 al settimo cielo

moon: ∼**light** n chiaro m di luna ● vi 🄵 lavorare in nero. ∼**lit** adj illuminato dalla luna

moor[1] /mʊə(r)/ n brughiera f

moor[2] vt (Naut) ormeggiare

mop /mɒp/ n straccio m (per i pavimenti); ∼ of hair zazzera f ● vt (pt/pp mopped) lavare con lo straccio. ⬜ ∼ **up** vt (dry) asciugare con lo

straccio; (clean) pulire con lo straccio

mope /məʊp/ vi essere depresso

moped /'məʊped/ n ciclomotore m

moral /'mɒrəl/ adj morale ● n morale f. ∼**ly** adv moralmente. ∼**s** pl moralità f

morale /mə'rɑ:l/ n morale m

morality /mə'rælətɪ/ n moralità f

more /mɔ:(r)/ adj più; a few ∼ books un po' più di libri; some ∼ tea? ancora un po' di tè?; there's no ∼ bread non c'è più pane; there are no ∼ apples non ci sono più mele; one ∼ word and... ancora una parola e... ● pron di più; would you like some ∼? ne vuoi ancora?; no ∼, thank you non ne voglio più, grazie ● adv più; ∼ interesting più interessante; ∼ and ∼ quickly sempre più veloce; ∼ than più di; I don't love him any ∼ non lo amo più; once ∼ ancora una volta; ∼ or less più o meno; the ∼ I see him, the ∼ I like him più lo vedo, più mi piace

moreover /mɔ:r'əʊvə(r)/ adv inoltre

morgue /mɔ:g/ n obitorio m

morning /'mɔ:nɪŋ/ n mattino m, mattina f; in the ∼ di mattino; (tomorrow) domani mattina

Morocc|o /mə'rɒkəʊ/ n Marocco m ● adj ∼**an** adj & n marocchino, -a mf

moron /'mɔ:rɒn/ n 🄵 deficiente mf

morose /mə'rəʊs/ adj scontroso

Morse /mɔ:s/ n ∼ [**code**] [codice m] Morse m

morsel /'mɔ:sl/ n (food) boccone m

mortal /'mɔ:tl/ adj & n mortale mf. ∼**ity** n mortalità f. ∼**ly** adv (wounded, offended) a morte; (afraid) da morire

mortar /'mɔ:tə(r)/ n mortaio m

mortgage /'mɔ:gɪdʒ/ n mutuo m; (on property) ipoteca f ● vt ipotecare

mortuary /'mɔ:tjʊərɪ/ n camera f mortuaria

m

mosaic /məʊ'zeɪk/ n mosaico m

Moslem /'mʊzlɪm/ adj & n musulmano, -a mf

mosque /mɒsk/ n moschea f

mosquito /mɒs'ki:təʊ/ n (pl -es) zanzara f

moss /mɒs/ n muschio m. ~y adj muschioso

most /məʊst/ adj (majority) la maggior parte di; for the ~ part per lo più ●adv più, maggiormente; (very) estremamente, molto; the ~ interesting day la giornata più interessante; a ~ interesting day una giornata estremamente interessante; the ~ beautiful woman in the world la donna più bella del mondo; ~ unlikely veramente improbabile ●pron ~ of them la maggior parte di loro; at [the] ~ al massimo; make the ~ of sfruttare al massimo; ~ of the time la maggior parte del tempo. ~ly adv per lo più

MOT n revisione f obbligatoria di autoveicoli

motel /məʊ'tel/ n motel m inv

moth /mɒθ/ n falena f; [clothes-] ~ tarma f

mother /'mʌðə(r)/ n madre f; M~'s Day la festa della mamma ●vt fare da madre a

mother: ~-in-law n (pl ~s-in-law) suocera f. ~ly adj materno. ~-of-pearl n madreperla f. ~-to-be n futura mamma f. ~ tongue n madrelingua f

motif /məʊ'ti:f/ n motivo m

motion /'məʊʃn/ n moto m; (proposal) mozione f; (gesture) gesto m ●vt/i ~ [to] sb to come in fare segno a qcno di entrare. ~less adj immobile. ~lessly adv senza alcun movimento

motivat|e /'məʊtɪveɪt/ vt motivare. ~ion n motivazione f

motive /'məʊtɪv/ n motivo m

motley /'mɒtlɪ/ adj disparato

motor /'məʊtə(r)/ n motore m; (car) macchina f ●adj a motore; (Anat) motore ●vi andare in macchina

motor: ~ bike n 🔢 moto f inv. ~ boat n motoscafo m. ~ car n automobile f. ~ cycle n motocicletta f. ~-cyclist n motociclista f. ~ing n automobilismo m. ~ist n automobilista mf. ~way n autostrada f

motto /'mɒtəʊ/ n (pl -es) motto m

mould¹ /məʊld/ n (fungus) muffa f

mould² n stampo m ●vt foggiare; fig formare. ~ing n (Archit) cornice f

mouldy /'məʊldɪ/ adj ammuffito; (🔢: worthless) ridicolo

moult /məʊlt/ vi (bird:) fare la muta; (animal:) perdere il pelo

mound /maʊnd/ n mucchio m; (hill) collinetta f

mount /maʊnt/ n (horse) cavalcatura f; (of jewel, photo, picture) montatura f ●vt montare a (horse); salire su (bicycle); incastonare (jewel); incorniciare (photo, picture) ●vi aumentare. □ ~ up vi aumentare

mountain /'maʊntɪn/ n montagna f; ~ bike n mountain bike f inv

mountaineer /maʊntɪ'nɪə(r)/ n alpinista m. ~ing n alpinismo m

mountainous /'maʊntɪnəs/ adj montagnoso

mourn /mɔːn/ vt lamentare ●vi for piangere la morte di. ~er n persona f che partecipa a un funerale. ~ful adj triste. ~ing n in ~ing in lutto

mouse /maʊs/ n (pl mice) topo m; (Comput) mouse m inv. ~trap n trappola f [per topi]

mousse /mu:s/ n (Culin) mousse f inv

moustache /mə'stɑːʃ/ n baffi mpl

mouth¹ /maʊð/ ~ sth dire qcsa silenziosamente muovendo solamente le labbra

mouth² /maʊθ/ n bocca f; (of river) foce f

mouth: ~ful n boccone m.

~**organ** n armonica f [a bocca].
~**wash** n acqua f dentifricia

move /muːv/ n mossa f; (moving house) trasloco m; **on the** ~ **in** movimento; **get a** ~ **on** 🔲 darsi una mossa • vt muovere; (emotionally) commuovere; spostare (car); (transfer) trasferire; (propose) proporre; ~ **house** traslocare • vi muoversi; (move house) traslocare. □ ~ **along** vi andare avanti • vt muovere in avanti. □ ~ **away** vi allontanarsi; (move house) trasferirsi • vt allontanare. □ ~ **forward** vi avanzare • vt spostare avanti. □ ~ **in** vi (to a house) trasferirsi. □ ~ **off** vi muoversi. □ ~ **out** vi andare via. □ ~ **over** vi spostarsi • vt spostare. □ ~ **up** vi muoversi; (advance) avanzare

movement /'muːvmənt/ n movimento m

movie /'muːvɪ/ n film m inv; **go to the** ~**s** andare al cinema

moving /'muːvɪŋ/ adj mobile; (touching) commovente

mow /məʊ/ vt (pt mowed, pp mown or mowed) tagliare (lawn). □ ~ **down** vt (destroy) sterminare

mower /'məʊə(r)/ n tosaerba m inv

MP n abbr Member of Parliament

MP3 player n lettore m MP3

Mr /'mɪstə(r)/ n (pl Messrs) Signor m

Mrs /'mɪsɪz/ n Signora f

Ms /mɪz/ n (modo m formale di rivolgersi ad una donna quando non si vuole connotarla come sposata o nubile)

much /mʌtʃ/ adj, adv & pron molto; ~ **as** per quanto; **I love you just as** ~ **as before/him** ti amo quanto prima/lui; **as** ~ **as £5 million as** ~ **as** cinque milioni di sterline; **as** ~ **as that** così tanto; **very** ~ **tantissimo**, moltissimo; ~ **the same** quasi uguale

muck /mʌk/ n (dirt) sporcizia f; (farming) letame m; (🔲: filth) porcheria f. □ ~ **about** vi 🔲 perder tempo; ~

about with trafficare con. □ ~ **up** vt 🔲 rovinare; (make dirty) sporcare

mud /mʌd/ n fango m

muddle /'mʌdl/ n disordine m; (mix-up) confusione f • vt ~ [**up**] confondere (dates)

muddy /'mʌdɪ/ adj (-ier, -iest) (path) fangoso; (shoes) infangato

muesli /'muːzlɪ/ n muesli m inv

muffle /'mʌfl/ vt smorzare (sound). **muffle up** vt (for warmth) imbaccuccare

muffler /'mʌflə(r)/ n sciarpa f; Am (Auto) marmitta f

mug[1] /mʌg/ n tazza f; (for beer) boccale m; (🔲: face) muso m; (🔲: simpleton) pollo m

mug[2] vt (pt/pp mugged) aggredire e derubare. ~**ger** n assalitore, -trice mf. ~**ging** n aggressione f per furto

muggy /'mʌgɪ/ adj (-ier, -iest) afoso

mule /mjuːl/ n mulo m

mull /mʌl/ vt ~ **over** rimuginare su

multiple /'mʌltɪpl/ adj multiplo

multiplication /mʌltɪplɪ'keɪʃn/ n moltiplicazione f

multiply /'mʌltɪplaɪ/ v (pt/pp -ied) • vt moltiplicare (by per) • vi moltiplicarsi

mum[1] /mʌm/ adj **keep** ~ 🔲 non aprire bocca

mum[2] n 🔲 mamma f

mumble /'mʌmbl/ vt/i borbottare

mummy[1] /'mʌmɪ/ n 🔲 mamma f

mummy[2] n (Archaeol) mummia f

mumps /mʌmps/ n orecchioni mpl

munch /mʌntʃ/ vt/i sgranocchiare

mundane /mʌn'deɪn/ adj (everyday) banale

municipal /mjʊ'nɪsɪpl/ adj municipale

mural /'mjʊərəl/ n dipinto m murale

murder /'mɜːdə(r)/ n assassinio m • vt assassinare; (🔲: ruin) massacrare. ~**er** n assassino, -a f. ~**ous** adj omicida

m

murky /'mɜːkɪ/ adj (-ier, -iest) oscuro

murmur /'mɜːmə(r)/ n mormorio m ● vt/i mormorare

muscle /'mʌsl/ n muscolo m ● muscle in vi ✗ intromettersi (on in)

muscular /'mʌskjʊlə(r)/ adj muscolare; (strong) muscoloso

muse /mjuːz/ vi meditare (on su)

museum /mjuːˈzɪəm/ n museo m

mushroom /'mʌʃrʊm/ n fungo m ● vi fig spuntare come funghi

music /'mjuːzɪk/ n musica f; (written) spartito m.

musical /'mjuːzɪkl/ adj musicale; (person) dotato di senso musicale ● n commedia f musicale. ~ **box** n carillon m inv. ~ **instrument** n strumento m musicale

musician /mjuːˈzɪʃn/ n musicista mf

Muslim /'mʊzlɪm/ adj & n musulmano, -a mf

mussel /'mʌsl/ n cozza f

must /mʌst/ v aux (solo al presente) dovere; you ~ not be late non devi essere in ritardo; she ~ have finished by now (probability) deve aver finito ormai ● n a ~ 🆃 una cosa da non perdere

mustard /'mʌstəd/ n senape f

musty /'mʌstɪ/ adj (-ier, -iest) stantio

mutation /mjuːˈteɪʃn/ n (Biol) mutazione f

mute /mjuːt/ adj muto

mutilat|e /'mjuːtɪleɪt/ vt mutilare. ~**ion** n mutilazione f

mutter /'mʌtə(r)/ vt/i borbottare

mutton /'mʌtn/ n carne f di montone

mutual /'mjuːtjʊəl/ adj reciproco; (🆃: common) comune. ~**ly** adv reciprocamente

muzzle /'mʌzl/ n (of animal) muso m; (of firearm) bocca f; (for dog) muse-

ruola f ● vt fig mettere il bavaglio a

my /maɪ/ adj il mio m, la mia f, i miei mpl, le mie fpl; **my mother/father** mia madre/mio padre

myself /maɪˈself/ pron (reflexive) mi; (emphatic) me stesso; (after prep) me; **I've seen it** ~ l'ho visto io stesso; **by** ~ da solo; **I thought to** ~ ho pensato tra me e me; **I'm proud of** ~ sono fiero di me

mysterious /mɪˈstɪərɪəs/ adj misterioso. ~**ly** adv misteriosamente

mystery /'mɪstərɪ/ n mistero m; ~ [story] racconto m del mistero

mysti|c[al] /'mɪstɪk[l]/ adj mistico. ~**cism** n misticismo m

mystify /'mɪstɪfaɪ/ vt (pt/pp -ied) disorientare

mystique /mɪˈstiːk/ n mistica f

myth /mɪθ/ n mito m. ~**ical** adj mitico

mythology /mɪˈθɒlədʒɪ/ n mitologia f

Nn

nab /næb/ vt (pt/pp nabbed) 🆃 beccare

nag¹ /næg/ n (horse) ronzino m

nag² (pt/pp nagged) vt assillare ● vi essere insistente ● n (person) brontolone, -a mf. ~**ging** adj (pain) persistente

nail /neɪl/ n chiodo m; (of finger, toe) unghia f ● **nail down** vt inchiodare; ~ **sb down to a time/price** far fissare a qcno un'ora/un prezzo

nail polish n smalto m [per unghie]

naked /'neɪkɪd/ adj nudo; **with the** ~ **eye** a occhio nudo

name /neɪm/ n nome m; **what's**

your ~? come ti chiami?; my ~ is Matthew mi chiamo Matthew; I know her by ~ la conosco di nome; by the ~ of Bates di nome Bates; call sb ~s 🆃 insultare qcno ● vt (to position) nominare; chiamare (baby); (identify) citare; be ~d after essere chiamato col nome di. ~less adj senza nome. ~ly adv cioè

namesake n omonimo, -a mf

nanny /'nænɪ/ n bambinaia f. ~-goat n capra f

nap /næp/ n pisolino m; have a ~ fare un pisolino ● vi (pt/pp napped) catch sb ~ping cogliere qcno alla sprovvista

napkin /'næpkɪn/ n tovagliolo m

Naples /'neɪplz/ n Napoli f

nappy /'næpɪ/ n pannolino m

narcotic /nɑː'kɒtɪk/ adj & n narcotico m

narrat|e /nə'reɪt/ vt narrare. ~ion n narrazione f

narrative /'nærətɪv/ adj narrativo ● n narrazione f

narrator /nə'reɪtə(r)/ n narratore, -trice f

narrow /'nærəʊ/ adj stretto; (fig: views) ristretto; (margin, majority) scarso ● vi restringersi. ~ly adv ~ly escape death evitare la morte per un pelo. ~-minded adj di idee ristrette

nasal /'neɪzl/ adj nasale

nasty /'nɑːstɪ/ adj (-ier, -iest) (smell, person, remark) cattivo; (injury, situation, weather) brutto; turn ~ (person:) diventare cattivo

nation /'neɪʃn/ n nazione f

national /'næʃənl/ adj nazionale ● n cittadino, -a mf

national 'anthem n inno m nazionale

nationalism /'næʃənəlɪzm/ n nazionalismo m

nationality /næʃə'næləti/ n nazionalità f inv

'**nation-wide** adj su scala nazionale

native /'neɪtɪv/ adj nativo; (innate) innato ● n nativo, -a mf; (local inhabitant) abitante mf del posto; (outside Europe) indigeno, -a mf; she's a ~ of Venice è originaria di Venezia

native: ~ '**land** n paese m nativo. ~ '**language** n lingua f madre

Nativity /nə'tɪvəti/ n the ~ la Natività f. ~ **play** n rappresentazione f sulla nascita di Gesù

natter /'nætə(r)/ n 🆅 chiacchierare

natural /'nætʃrəl/ adj naturale

natural 'history n storia f naturale

naturalist /'nætʃ(ə)rəlɪst/ n naturalista mf

naturally /'nætʃ(ə)rəlɪ/ adv (of course) naturalmente; (by nature) per natura

nature /'neɪtʃə(r)/ n natura f; by ~ per natura. ~ **reserve** n riserva f naturale

naughty /'nɔːtɪ/ adj (-ier, -iest) monello; (slightly indecent) spinto

nausea /'nɔːzɪə/ n nausea f

nautical /'nɔːtɪkl/ adj nautico. ~ **mile** n miglio m marino

naval /'neɪvl/ adj navale

nave /neɪv/ n navata f centrale

navel /'neɪvl/ n ombelico m

navigable /'nævɪgəbl/ adj navigabile

navigat|e /'nævɪgeɪt/ vi navigare; (Auto) fare da navigatore ● vt navigare su (river). ~**ion** n navigazione f. ~**or** n navigatore m

navy /'neɪvɪ/ n marina f ● ~ [blue] adj blu marine inv ● n blu m inv marine

Neapolitan /nɪə'pɒlɪtən/ adj & n napoletano, -a mf

near /nɪə(r)/ adj vicino; (future) prossimo; the ~**est** bank la banca più vicina ● adv vicino; draw ~ avvicinarsi; ~ **at hand** a portata di mano ● prep vicino a; he was ~ **to tears** aveva le lacrime agli occhi ● vt avvicinarsi a

near: ~**by** adj & adv vicino. ~**ly** adv quasi; it's not ~**ly enough** non è per niente sufficiente. ~**sighted** adj Am miope

neat /niːt/ adj (tidy) ordinato; (clever) efficace; (undiluted) liscio. ~**ly** adv ordinatamente; (cleverly) efficacemente. ~**ness** n (tidiness) ordine m

necessarily /nesə'serɪlɪ/ adv necessariamente

necessary /'nesəsərɪ/ adj necessario

necessit|ate /nɪ'sesɪteɪt/ vt rendere necessario. ~**y** n necessità f inv

neck /nek/ n collo m; (of dress) colletto m; ~ **and** ~ testa a testa

necklace /'neklɪs/ n collana f

neckline n scollatura f

need /niːd/ n bisogno m; be in ~ of avere bisogno di; if ~ be se ce ne fosse bisogno; there is a ~ for c'è bisogno di; there is no ~ for that non ce n'è bisogno; there is no ~ for you to go non c'è bisogno che tu vada ● vt aver bisogno di; I ~ to know devo saperlo; it ~s to be done bisogna farlo ● v aux you ~ not go non c'è bisogno che tu vada;

~ I come? devo [proprio] venire?

needle /'niːdl/ n ago m; (for knitting) uncinetto m; (of record player) puntina f ● vt (⊞: annoy) punzecchiare

needless /'niːdlɪs/ adj inutile

'needlework n cucito m

needy /'niːdɪ/ adj (-ier, -iest) bisognoso

negative /'negətɪv/ adj negativo ● n negazione f; (Phot) negativo m; in the ~ (Gram) alla forma negativa

neglect /nɪ'glekt/ n trascuratezza f; state of ~ stato m di abbandono ● vt trascurare; he ~**ed** to write non si è curato di scrivere. ~**ed** adj trascurato. ~**ful** adj negligente; be ~**ful** of trascurare

negligen|ce /'neglɪdʒəns/ n negligenza f. ~**t** adj negligente

negligible /'neglɪdʒəbl/ adj trascurabile

negotiable /nɪ'gəʊʃəbl/ adj (road) transitabile; (Comm) negoziabile; not ~ (cheque) non trasferibile

negotiat|e /nɪ'gəʊʃɪeɪt/ vt negoziare; (Auto) prendere (bend) ● vi negoziare. ~**ion** n negoziato m. ~**or** n negoziatore, -trice mf

neigh /neɪ/ vi nitrire

neighbour /'neɪbə(r)/ n vicino, -a mf. ~**hood** n vicinato m; in the ~**hood of** nei dintorni di; fig circa. ~**ing** adj vicino. ~**ly** adj amichevole

neither /'naɪðə(r)/ adj & pron nessuno dei due, né l'uno né l'altro ● adv ~... nor né... né ● conj nemmeno, neanche; ~ **do/did I** nemmeno io

neon /'niːɒn/ n neon m. ~ **light** n luce f al neon

nephew /'nevju:/ n nipote m

nerve /nɜːv/ n nervo m; (⊞: courage) coraggio m; (⊞: impudence) faccia f tosta; lose one's ~ perdersi d'animo. ~**-racking** adj logorante

nervous /'nɜːvəs/ adj nervoso; he makes me ~ mi mette in agitazione; be a ∼ wreck avere i nervi a pezzi. ∼ 'breakdown n esaurimento m nervoso. ∼ly adv nervosamente. ∼ness n nervosismo m; (before important event) tensione f

nervy /'nɜːvɪ/ adj (-ier, -iest) nervoso; (Am: impudent) sfacciato

nest /nest/ n nido m ●vi fare il nido. ∼-egg n gruzzolo m

nestle /'nesl/ vi accoccolarsi

net[1] /net/ n rete f ●vt (pt/pp netted) (catch) prendere (con la rete)

net[2] adj netto ●vt (pt/pp netted) incassare un utile netto di

'netball n sport m inv femminile, simile a pallacanestro

Netherlands /'neðələndz/ npl the ∼ i Paesi mpl Bassi

netting /'netɪŋ/ n [wire] ∼ reticolato m

nettle /'netl/ n ortica f

'network n rete f

neur|osis /njʊə'rəʊsɪs/ n (pl -oses /-siːz/) nevrosi f inv. ∼otic adj nevrotico

neuter /'njuːtə(r)/ adj (Gram) neutro ●n (Gram) neutro m ●vt sterilizzare

neutral /'njuːtrəl/ adj neutro; (country, person) neutrale ●n in ∼ (Auto) in folle. ∼ity n neutralità f. ∼ize vt neutralizzare

never /'nevə(r)/ adv [non...] mai; (🔲: expressing disbelief) ma va; ∼ again mai più; well I ∼! chi l'avrebbe detto!. ∼-ending adj interminabile

nevertheless /nevəðə'les/ adv tuttavia

new /njuː/ adj nuovo

new: ∼born adj neonato. ∼comer n nuovo, -a arrivato, -a mf. ∼fangled /-'fæŋgld/ adj pej modernizzante

'newly adv (recently) di recente; ∼-built costruito di recente. ∼-weds npl sposini mpl

news /njuːz/ n notizie fpl; (TV) tele-

giornale m; (Radio) giornale m radio; piece of ∼ notizia f

news: ∼agent n giornalaio, -a mf. ∼caster n giornalista mf televisivo, -a/radiofonico, -a. ∼flash n notizia f flash. ∼letter n bollettino m d'informazione. ∼paper n giornale m; (material) carta f di giornale. ∼reader n giornalista mf televisivo, -a/radiofonico, -a

next /nekst/ adj prossimo; (adjoining) vicino; who's ∼? a chi tocca?; ∼ door accanto; ∼ to nothing quasi niente; the ∼ day il giorno dopo; ∼ week la settimana prossima; the week after ∼ fra due settimane ●adv dopo; when will you see him ∼? quando lo rivedi la prossima volta?; ∼ to accanto a ●n seguente mf; ∼ of kin parente m prossimo

nib /nɪb/ n pennino m

nibble /'nɪbl/ vt/i mordicchiare

nice /naɪs/ adj (day, weather, holiday) bello; (person) gentile, simpatico; (food) buono; it was ∼ meeting you è stato un piacere conoscerla. ∼ly adv gentilmente; (well) bene. ∼ties n nicchia f

niche /niːʃ/ n nicchia f

nick /nɪk/ n tacca f; (on chin etc) taglietto m; (🔲: prison) galera f; (🔲: police station) centrale f [di polizia]; in the ∼ of time 🔲 appena in tempo ●vt intaccare; (🔲: steal) fregare; (🔲: arrest) beccare; ∼ one's chin farsi un taglietto nel mento

nickel /'nɪkl/ n nichel m; Am moneta f da cinque centesimi

'nickname n soprannome m ●vt soprannominare

nicotine /'nɪkətiːn/ n nicotina f

niece /niːs/ n nipote f

niggling /ˈnɪglɪŋ/ adj (detail) insignificante; (pain) fastidioso; (doubt) persistente

night /naɪt/ n notte f; (evening) sera f; at ~ la notte, di notte; (in the evening) la sera, di sera; Monday ~ lunedì notte/sera • adj di notte

night: ~**cap** n papalina f; (drink) bicchierino m bevuto prima di andare a letto. ~**club** n locale m notturno, night[-club] m inv. ~**dress** n camicia f da notte. ~**fall** n crepuscolo m. ~**gown**, ⊞ ~**ie** /ˈnaɪtɪ/ n camicia f da notte

night: ~**life** n vita f notturna. ~**ly** adj di notte, di sera • adv ogni notte, ogni sera. ~**mare** n incubo m. ~**school** n scuola f serale. ~**time** n at ~-time di notte, la notte. ~**'watchman** n guardiano m notturno

nil /nɪl/ n nulla m; (Sport) zero m

nimbl|e /ˈnɪmbl/ adj agile. ~**y** adv agilmente

nine /naɪn/ adj nove inv • n nove m. ~**teen** adj diciannove inv • n diciannove. ~**teenth** adj & n diciannovesimo, -a mf

ninetieth /ˈnaɪntɪɪθ/ adj & n novantesimo, -a mf

ninety /ˈnaɪntɪ/ adj novanta inv • n novanta m

ninth /naɪnθ/ adj & n nono, -a mf

nip /nɪp/ n pizzicotto m; (bite) morso m • vt pizzicare; (bite) mordere; ~ **in the bud** fig stroncare sul nascere • vi (⊞: run) fare un salto

nipple /ˈnɪpl/ n capezzolo m; (Am: on bottle) tettarella f

nippy /ˈnɪpɪ/ adj (-ier, -iest) ⊞ (cold) pungente; (quick) svelto

nitrogen /ˈnaɪtrədʒn/ n azoto m

no /nəʊ/ adv no • n (pl noes) no m • adj nessuno; I have no time non ho tempo; in no time in un baleno; 'no parking' 'sosta vietata'; 'no smoking' 'vietato fumare'; no one

nessuno v. nobody

noble /ˈnəʊbl/ adj nobile. ~**man** n nobile m

nobody /ˈnəʊbədɪ/ pron nessuno; he knows ~ non conosce nessuno • n he's a ~ non è nessuno

nocturnal /nɒkˈtɜːnl/ adj notturno

nod /nɒd/ n cenno m del capo • vi (pt/pp nodded) fare un cenno col capo; (in agreement) fare di sì col capo • vt ~ **one's head** fare di sì col capo. □ ~ **off** vi assopirsi

noise /nɔɪz/ n rumore m; (loud) rumore m, chiasso m. ~**less** adj silenzioso. ~**lessly** adv silenziosamente

noisy /ˈnɔɪzɪ/ adj (-ier, -iest) rumoroso

nomad /ˈnəʊmæd/ n nomade mf. ~**ic** adj nomade

nominate /ˈnɒmɪneɪt/ vt proporre come candidato; (appoint) designare. ~**ion** n nomina f; (person nominated) candidato, -a f

nonchalant /ˈnɒnʃələnt/ adj disinvolto

non-com'mittal adj che non si sbilancia

nondescript /ˈnɒndɪskrɪpt/ adj qualunque

none /nʌn/ pron (person) nessuno; (thing) niente; ~ **of us** nessuno di noi; ~ **of this** niente di questo; there's ~ **left** non ce n'è più • adv she's ~ **too pleased** non è per niente soddisfatta; I'm ~ **the wiser** non ne so più di prima

nonentity /nɒˈnentətɪ/ n nullità f

non-ex'istent adj inesistente

nonplussed /nɒnˈplʌst/ adj perplesso

nonsens|e /ˈnɒnsəns/ n sciocchezze fpl. ~**ical** adj assurdo

non-'smoker n non fumatore, -trice m/f; (compartment) scompartimento m non fumatori

non-'stop adj ~ **'flight** volo m diretto • adv senza sosta; (fly) senza scalo

noodles /'nu:dlz/ *npl* taglierini *mpl*

nook /nok/ *n* cantuccio *m*

noon /nu:n/ *n* mezzogiorno *m*; at ~ a mezzogiorno

noose /nu:s/ *n* nodo *m* scorsoio

nor /nɔ:(r)/ *adv & conj* né; ~ do I neppure io

norm /nɔ:m/ *n* norma *f*

normal /'nɔ:ml/ *adj* normale. ~ity *n* normalità *f*. ~ly *adv* (*usually*) normalmente

north /nɔ:θ/ *n* nord *m*; to the ~ of a nord di ● *adj* del nord, settentrionale ● *adv* a nord

north: N~ America *n* America *f* del Nord. ~**east** *adj* di nord-est, nordorientale ● *n* nord-est *m* ● *adv* a nord-est; (*travel*) verso nord-est

norther|ly /'nɔ:ðəlɪ/ *adj* (*direction*) nord; (*wind*) verso nord. ~n *adj* del nord, settentrionale. N~n Ireland *n* Irlanda *f* del Nord

north: N~ 'Sea *n* Mare *m* del Nord. ~**ward[s]** /-wəd[z]/ *adv* verso nord. ~**west** *adj* di nord-ovest, nordoccidentale ● *n* nord-ovest *m* ● *adv* a nord-ovest; (*travel*) verso nord-ovest

Nor|way /'nɔ:weɪ/ *n* Norvegia *f*. ~**wegian** *adj & n* norvegese *mf*

nose /nəʊz/ *n* naso *m*

nose: ~bleed *n* emorragia *f* nasale. ~**dive** *n* (Aeron) picchiata *f*

nostalg|ia /nɒ'stældʒɪə/ *n* nostalgia *f*. ~**ic** *adj* nostalgico

nostril /'nɒstrəl/ *n* narice *f*

nosy /'nəʊzɪ/ *adj* (-ier, -iest) 🔲 ficcanaso *inv*

not /nɒt/ *adv* non; he is ~ Italian non è italiano; I hope ~ spero di no; ~ all of us have been invited non siamo stati tutti invitati; if ~ se no; ~ at all niente affatto; ~ a bit per niente; ~ even neanche; ~ yet non ancora; ~ only... but also... non solo... ma anche...

notabl|e /'nəʊtəbl/ *adj* (*remarkable*) notevole. ~**y** *adv* (*in particular*) in particolare

notary /'nəʊtərɪ/ *n* notaio *m*; ~ 'public notaio *m*

notch /nɒtʃ/ *n* tacca *f* ● **notch up** *vt* (*score*) segnare

note /nəʊt/ *n* nota *f*; (*short letter, banknote*) biglietto *m*; (*memo, written comment etc*) appunto *m*; of ~ (*person*) di spicco; (*comments, event*) degno di nota; **make a ~ of** prendere nota di ● *vt* (*notice*) notare; (*write*) annotare. □ ~ **down** *vt* annotare

'notebook *n* taccuino *m*; (*Comput*) notebook *m inv*

noted /'nəʊtɪd/ *adj* noto, celebre (**for** per)

notepaper *n* carta *f* da lettere

nothing /'nʌθɪŋ/ *pron* niente, nulla ● *adv* niente affatto. **for** ~ (*free, in vain*) per niente; (*with no reason*) senza motivo; ~ **but** nient'altro che; ~ **much** poco o nulla; ~ **interesting** niente di interessante; **it's** ~ **to do with you** non ti riguarda

notice /'nəʊtɪs/ *n* (*on board*) avviso *m*; (*review*) recensione *f*; (*termination of employment*) licenziamento *m*; [advance] ~ preavviso *m*; **two months** ~ due mesi di preavviso; **at short** ~ con breve preavviso; **until further** ~ fino nuovo avviso; **hand in one's** ~ (*employee*) dare le dimissioni; **give an employee** ~ dare il preavviso a un impiegato; **take no** ~ **of** non fare caso a; **take no** ~! non farci caso! ● *vt* notare. ~**able** *adj* evidente. ~**ably** *adv* sensibilmente. ~**board** *n* bacheca *f*

noti|fication /nəʊtɪfɪ'keɪʃn/ *n* notifica *f*. ~**fy** *vt* (*pt/pp* -ied) notificare

notion /'nəʊʃn/ *n* idea *f*, nozione *f*; ~ *s pl* (Am: *haberdashery*) merceria *f*

notorious /nəʊ'tɔ:rɪəs/ *adj* famigerato; **be** ~ **for** essere tristemente famoso per

notwith'standing prep malgrado • adv ciononostante

nougat /'nu:gɑ:/ n torrone m

nought /nɔ:t/ n zero m

noun /naʊn/ n nome m, sostantivo m

nourish /'nʌrɪʃ/ vt nutrire. ~ing adj nutriente. ~ment n nutrimento m

novel /'nɒvl/ adj insolito • n romanzo m. ~ist n romanziere, -a mf. ~ty n novità f; ~ties pl (objects) oggettini mpl

November /nəʊ'vembə(r)/ n novembre m

novice /'nɒvɪs/ n novizio, -a mf

now /naʊ/ adv ora, adesso; by ~ ormai; just ~ proprio ora, adesso; ~ and again, ~ and then ogni tanto; ~! su! • conj ~ [that] ora che, adesso che

'nowadays adv oggigiorno

nowhere /'nəʊ-/ adv in nessun posto, da nessuna parte

nozzle /'nɒzl/ n bocchetta f

nuance /'nju:æiɑ.s/ n sfumatura f

nuclear /'nju:klɪə(r)/ adj nucleare

nucleus /'nju:klɪəs/ n (pl -lei /-lɪaɪ/) nucleo m

nude /nju:d/ adj nudo • n nudo m; in the ~ nudo

nudge /nʌdʒ/ n colpetto m di gomito • vt dare un colpetto col gomito a

nudism /'nju:dɪzm/ n nudismo m

nud|ist /'nju:dɪst/ n nudista m. ~ity n nudità f

nuisance /'nju:sns/ n seccatura f; (person) piaga f; what a ~! che seccatura!

null /nʌl/ adj ~ and void nullo

numb /nʌm/ adj intorpidito; ~ with cold intirizzito dal freddo

number /'nʌmbə(r)/ n numero m; a ~ of people un certo numero di persone • vt numerare; (include) annoverare. ~-plate n targa f

numeral /'nju:mərəl/ n numero m, cifra f

numerical /nju:'merɪkl/ adj numerico; in ~ order in ordine numerico

numerous /'nju:mərəs/ adj numeroso

nun /nʌn/ n suora f

nurse /nɜ:s/ n infermiere, -a mf; children's ~ bambinaia f • vt curare

nursery /'nɜ:sərɪ/ n stanza f dei bambini; (for plants) vivaio m; [day] ~ asilo m. ~ rhyme n filastrocca f. ~ school n scuola f materna

nut /nʌt/ n noce f; (Techn) dado m; (🔧: head) zucca f; ~s npl frutta f secca; be ~s 🔧 essere svitato. ~crackers npl schiaccianoci m inv. ~meg n noce f moscata

nutrit|ion /nju:'trɪʃn/ n nutrizione f. ~ious adj nutriente

'nutshell n in a ~ fig in parole povere

nylon /'naɪlɒn/ n nailon m; ~s pl calze fpl di nailon • attrib di nailon

Oo

oaf /əʊf/ n (pl oafs) zoticone, -a mf

oak /əʊk/ n quercia f • attrib di quercia

OAP n abbr (old-age pensioner) pensionato, -a mf

oar /ɔ:(r)/ n remo m. ~sman n vogatore m

oasis /əʊ'eɪsɪs/ n (pl oases /-si:z/) oasi f inv

oath /əʊθ/ n giuramento m; (swearword) bestemmia f

oatmeal /'əʊt-/ n farina f d'avena

oats /əʊts/ npl avena fsg; (Culin) [rolled] ~ fiocchi mpl di avena

obedien|ce /ə'biːdɪəns/ n ubbidienza f. ~**t** adj ubbidiente

obes|e /ə'biːs/ adj obeso. ~**ity** n obesità f

obey /ə'beɪ/ vt ubbidire a; osservare (instructions, rules) • vi ubbidire

obituary /ə'bɪtjʊərɪ/ n necrologio m

object[1] /'ɒbdʒɪkt/ n oggetto m; (Gram) complemento m oggetto; money is no ~ i soldi non sono un problema

object[2] /əb'dʒekt/ vi (be against) opporsi (to a); ~ that... obiettare che...

objection /əb'dʒekʃn/ n obiezione f; have no ~ non avere niente in contrario. ~**able** adj discutibile; (person) sgradevole

objectiv|e /əb'dʒektɪv/ adj oggettivo • n obiettivo m. ~**ely** adv obiettivamente. ~**ity** n oggettività f

obligation /ɒblɪ'geɪʃn/ n obbligo m; be under an ~ avere un obbligo; without ~ senza impegno

obligatory /ə'blɪgətrɪ/ adj obbligatorio

oblig|e /ə'blaɪdʒ/ vt (compel) obbligare; much ~**ed** grazie mille. ~**ing** adj disponibile

oblique /ə'bliːk/ adj obliquo; fig indiretto • n [stroke] barra f

obliterate /ə'blɪtəreɪt/ vt obliterare

oblivion /ə'blɪvɪən/ n oblio m

oblivious /ə'blɪvɪəs/ adj be ~ essere dimentico (of, to di)

oblong /'ɒblɒŋ/ adj oblungo • n rettangolo m

obnoxious /əb'nɒkʃəs/ adj detestabile

oboe /'əʊbəʊ/ n oboe m inv

obscen|e /əb'siːn/ adj osceno; (profits, wealth) vergognoso. ~**ity** n oscenità f inv

obscur|e /əb'skjʊə(r)/ adj oscuro • vt oscurare; (confuse) mettere in ombra. ~**ity** n oscurità f

obsequious /əb'siːkwɪəs/ adj ossequioso

observatory /əb'zɜːvətrɪ/ n osservatorio m

observe /əb'zɜːv/ vt osservare; (notice) notare; (keep, celebrate) celebrare. ~**r** n osservatore, -trice m

obsess /əb'ses/ vt be ~**ed** by essere fissato con. ~**ion** n fissazione f. ~**ive** adj ossessivo

obsolete /'ɒbsəliːt/ adj obsoleto; (word) desueto

obstacle /'ɒbstəkl/ n ostacolo m

obstina|cy /'ɒbstɪnəsɪ/ n ostinazione f. ~**te** adj ostinato

obstruct /əb'strʌkt/ vt ostruire; (hinder) ostacolare. ~**ion** n ostruzione f; (obstacle) ostacolo m. ~**ive** adj be ~**ive** (person:) creare dei problemi

obtain /əb'teɪn/ vt ottenere. ~**able** adj ottenibile

obtrusive /əb'truːsɪv/ adj (object) stonato

obtuse /əb'tjuːs/ adj ottuso

obvious /'ɒbvɪəs/ adj ovvio. ~**ly** adv ovviamente

occasion /ə'keɪʒn/ n occasione f; (event) evento m; on ~ talvolta; on the ~ of in occasione di

occasional /ə'keɪʒənl/ adj saltuario; he has the ~ glass of wine ogni tanto beve un bicchiere di vino. ~**ly** adv ogni tanto

occult /ɒ'kʌlt/ adj occulto

occupant /'ɒkjʊpənt/ n occupante mf; (of vehicle) persona f a bordo

occupation /ɒkjʊ'peɪʃn/ n occupazione f; (job) professione f. ~**al** adj professionale

occupier /'ɒkjʊpaɪə(r)/ n residente mf

occupy /'ɒkjʊpaɪ/ vt (pt/pp occupied) occupare; (keep busy) tenere occupato

occur /ə'kɜː(r)/ vi (pt/pp occurred)

accadere; (*exist*) trovarsi; it ~red to me that mi è venuto in mente che. ~rence *n* (*event*) fatto *m*

ocean /'əʊʃn/ *n* oceano *m*

octave /'ɒktɪv/ *n* (*Mus*) ottava *f*

October /ɒk'təʊbə(r)/ *n* ottobre *m*

octopus /'ɒktəpəs/ *n* (*pl* **-puses**) polpo *m*

odd /ɒd/ *adj* (number) dispari; (*not of set*) scompagnato; (*strange*) strano; forty ~ quaranta e rotti; ~ jobs lavoretti *mpl*; the ~ one out l'eccezione; at ~ moments a tempo perso; have the ~ glass of wine avere un bicchiere di vino ogni tanto

odd|ity /'ɒdɪtɪ/ *n* stranezza *f*. ~ly *adv* stranamente. ~ly enough strana mente. ~ment *n* (*of fabric*) scampolo *m*

odds /ɒdz/ *npl* (chances) probabilità *fpl*; at ~ in disaccordo; ~ and ends cianfrusaglie *fpl*; it makes no ~ non fa alcuna differenza

odour /'əʊdə(r)/ *n* odore *m*. ~less *adj* inodore

of /ɒv/, /əv/ *prep* di; a cup of tea/ coffee una tazza di tè/caffè; the hem of my skirt l'orlo della mia gonna; the summer of 1989 l'estate del 1989; the two of us noi due; that's very kind of you è molto gentile da parte tua; a friend of mine un mio amico; a child of three un bambino di tre anni; the fourth of January il quattro gennaio; within a year of their divorce a circa un anno dal loro divorzio; half of it la metà; the whole of the room tutta la stanza

off /ɒf/ *prep* da; (*distant from*) lontano da; take £10 ~ the price ridurre il prezzo di 10 sterline; ~ the coast presso la costa; a street ~ the main road una traversa della via principale; (*near*) una strada vicino alla via principale; get ~ the ladder scendere dalla scala; get off the bus uscire dall'autobus; leave the lid ~

the saucepan lasciare la pentola senza il coperchio ● *adv* (button, handle) staccato; (light, handle) spento; (brake) tolto; (tap) chiuso; 'off' (*on appliance*) 'off'; 2 kilometres ~ a due chilometri di distanza; a long way ~ molto distante; (*time*) lontano; ~ and on di tanto in tanto; with his hat/coat ~ senza il cappello/cappotto; with the light ~ a luce spenta; 20% ~ 20% di sconto; be ~ (*leave*) andar via; (*Sport*) essere partito; (food): essere andato a male; (*all gone*) essere finito; (wedding, engagement): essere cancellato; I'm ~ alcohol ho smesso di bere; be ~ one's food non avere appetito; she's ~ today (*on holiday*) è in ferie oggi; (*ill*) è malata oggi; I'm ~ home vado a casa; you'd be better ~ doing... faresti meglio a fare...; have a day ~ avere un giorno di vacanza; drive/sail ~ andare via

'off-beat *adj* insolito

'off-chance *n* possibilità *f* remota

offence /ə'fens/ *n* (*illegal act*) reato *m*; give ~ offendere; take ~ offendersi (at per)

offend /ə'fend/ *vt* offendere. ~er *n* (*Jur*) colpevole *mf*

offensive /ə'fensɪv/ *adj* offensivo ● *n* offensiva *f*

offer /'ɒfə(r)/ *n* offerta *f* ● *vt* offrire; opporre (resistance); ~ sb sth offrire qcsa a qcno; ~ to do sth offrirsi di fare qcsa. ~ing *n* offerta *f*

off'hand *adj* (casual) spiccio ● *adv* su due piedi

office /'ɒfɪs/ *n* ufficio *m*; (*post, job*) carica *f*. ~ hours *pl* orario *m* d'ufficio

officer /'ɒfɪsə(r)/ *n* ufficiale *m*; (*police*) agente *m* [di polizia]

official /ə'fɪʃl/ *adj* ufficiale ● *n* funzionario, -a *mf*; (*Sport*) dirigente *m*. ~ly *adv* ufficialmente

'offing *n* in the ~ in vista

'off-licence n negozio m per la vendita di alcolici

'offset vt (pt/pp -set, pres p -setting) controbilanciare

'offshore ● adj (wind) di terra; (company, investment) offshore. ● adv (sail) al largo; (relocate) all'estero (in paesi dove la manodopera costa meno); ~ **rig** piattaforma f petrolifera, off-shore m inv

off'side adj (Sport) [in] fuori gioco; (wheel etc) (left) sinistro; (right) destro

'offspring n prole m

off'stage adv dietro le quinte

often /ˈɒfn/ adv spesso; **how** ~ ogni quanto; **every so** ~ una volta ogni tanto

oh /əʊ/ int oh!; ~ **dear** oh Dio!

oil /ɔɪl/ n olio m; (petroleum) petrolio m; (for heating) nafta f ● vt oliare

oil: ~**field** n giacimento m di petrolio. ~**-painting** n pittura f a olio. ~ **refinery** n raffineria f di petrolio. ~ **rig** piattaforma f per trivellazione subacquea

oily /ˈɔɪlɪ/ adj (-ier, -iest) unto; fig untuoso

ointment /ˈɔɪntmənt/ n pomata f

OK /əʊˈkeɪ/ int va bene, o.k. ● adj if that's OK with you se ti va bene; she's OK (well) sta bene; is the milk still OK? il latte è ancora buono? ● adv (well) bene ● vt (anche okay) (pt/pp okayed) dare l'o.k.

old /əʊld/ adj (vecchio; (girlfriend) ex; how ~ is she? quanti anni ha?; she is ten years ~ ha dieci anni

old: ~ **age** n vecchiaia f. ~**fashioned** adj antiquato

olive /ˈɒlɪv/ n (fruit, colour) oliva f; (tree) olivo m ● adj d'oliva; (colour) olivastro. ~ **branch** n fig ramoscello m d'olivo. ~**oil** n olio m di oliva

Olympic /əˈlɪmpɪk/ adj olimpico; ~**s**, ~ **Games** Olimpiadi fpl

omelette /ˈɒmlɪt/ n omelette f inv

omission /əˈmɪʃn/ n omissione f

omit /əˈmɪt/ vt (pt/pp omitted) omettere

on /ɒn/ prep su; (on horizontal surface) su, sopra; ~ **Monday** lunedì; ~ **Mondays** di lunedì; ~ **the first of May** il primo maggio; ~ **arriving** all'arrivo; ~ **foot** a piedi; ~ **the right/left** a destra/sinistra; ~ **the radio/television** alla radio/televisione; ~ **the bus/train** in autobus/treno ● adv (further on) dopo; (switched on) acceso; (in operation) in funzione; he had his hat/coat ~ portava il cappello/cappotto; be ~ (event:) esserci; ~ **and** ~ senza sosta; go ~ continuare

once /wʌns/ adv una volta; (formerly) un tempo; ~ **upon a time** there was c'era una volta; at ~ subito; (at the same time) contemporaneamente; ~ **and for all** una volta per tutte ● conj [non] appena. ~**-over** n [?] give sb/sth the ~**-over** (look, check) dare un'occhiata veloce a qcno/qcsa

one /wʌn/

● adj one, una; **not** ~ **person** nemmeno una persona

● n uno m

● pron uno; (impersonal) si; ~ **another** l'un l'altro; ~ **by** [a] uno a uno; ~ **never knows** non si sa mai

one: ~**self** pron (reflexive) si; (emphatic) sé, se stesso; **by** ~**self** da solo; **be proud of** ~**self** essere fieri di sé. ~**way** adj (street) a senso unico; (ticket) di sola andata

onion /ˈʌnjən/ n cipolla f

on-line adj/adv su Internet

'onlooker n spettatore, -trice mf

only /ˈəʊnlɪ/ adj solo; ~ **child** figlio, -a m f unico, -a ● adv solo, solamente; ~ **just** appena

'onset n (beginning) inizio m

'onslaught /ˈɒnslɔːt/ n attacco m

ooze /uːz/ vi fluire

opaque /əʊˈpeɪk/ adj opaco

open /ˈəʊpən/ adj aperto; (free to all) pubblico; (job) vacante; in the ~ air all'aperto ● n in the ~ all'aperto; fig alla luce del sole ● vt aprire; (flower:) sbocciare. □ ~ **up** vt aprire ● vi aprirsi

opening /ˈəʊpənɪŋ/ n apertura f; (beginning) inizio m; (job) posto m libero; ~ **hours** npl orario m d'apertura

openly /ˈəʊpənlɪ/ adv apertamente

open: ~-**minded** adj aperto; (broad-minded) di vedute larghe. ~-**plan** adj a pianta aperta

Open University Fondata nel 1969, è il sistema di università a distanza del Regno Unito. L'insegnamento viene impartito con vari mezzi: per corrispondenza, attraverso programmi radiotelevisivi trasmessi dalla BBC e anche via Internet. Gli studenti inviano per posta i compiti svolti a un tutore. Generalmente si seguono corsi part time della durata di quattro o cinque anni, anche se non ci sono limiti di tempo per completare gli studi.

opera /ˈɒpərə/ n opera f

opera-house n teatro m lirico

operate /ˈɒpəreɪt/ vt far funzionare (machine, lift); azionare (lever, brake); mandare avanti (business) ● vi (Techn) funzionare; (be in action) essere in funzione; (Mil, fig) operare; ~ **on** (Med) operare

operatic /ɒpəˈrætɪk/ adj lirico, operistico

operation /ɒpəˈreɪʃn/ n operazione f; (Techn) funzionamento m; in ~ (Techn) in funzione; come into ~ fig entrare in funzione; (law:) entrare in vigore; **have an** ~ (Med) subire un'operazione. ~**al** adj operativo; (law etc) in vigore

operative /ˈɒpərətɪv/ adj operativo

operator /ˈɒpəreɪtə(r)/ n (user) operatore, -trice mf; (Teleph) centralinista mf

opinion /əˈpɪnjən/ n opinione f; in my ~ secondo me. ~**ated** adj dogmatico

opponent /əˈpəʊnənt/ n avversario, -a mf

opportun|e /ˈɒpətjuːn/ adj opportuno. ~**ist** n opportunista mf. ~**istic** adj opportunistico

opportunity /ɒpəˈtjuːnətɪ/ n opportunità f inv

oppos|e /əˈpəʊz/ vt opporsi a; **be ~ed to sth** essere contrario a qcsa; **as ~ed to** al contrario di. ~**ing** adj avversario; (opposite) opposto

opposite /ˈɒpəzɪt/ adj opposto; (house) di fronte; ~ **number** fig controparte f; **the ~ sex** l'altro sesso ● n contrario m ● adv di fronte ● prep di fronte a

opposition /ɒpəˈzɪʃn/ n opposizione f

oppress /əˈpres/ vt opprimere. ~**ion** n oppressione f. ~**ive** adj oppressivo; (heat) opprimente. ~**or** n oppressore m

opt /ɒpt/ vi ~ **for** optare per; ~ **out** dissociarsi (of da)

optical /ˈɒptɪkl/ adj ottico; ~ **illusion** illusione f ottica

optician /ɒpˈtɪʃn/ n ottico, -a mf

optimis|m /ˈɒptɪmɪzm/ n ottimismo m. ~**t** n ottimista mf. ~**tic** adj ottimistico

option /ˈɒpʃn/ n scelta f; (Comm) opzione f. ~**al** adj facoltativo; ~**al extras** pl optional m inv

or /ɔː(r)/ conj o, oppure; (after negative) né; or [**else**] se no; **in a year or two** fra un anno o due

oral /ˈɔːrəl/ adj orale ● n 🄴 esame m orale. ~**ly** adv oralmente

orange /ˈɒrɪndʒ/ n arancia f; (colour) arancione m ● adj arancione. ~**ade** n aranciata f. ~ juice n succo m d'arancia

orbit /'ɔːbɪt/ n orbita f ●vt orbitare. ~al adj ~al road tangenziale f

orchard /'ɔːtʃəd/ n frutteto m

orches|tra /'ɔːkɪstrə/ n orchestra f. ~tral adj orchestrale. ~trate vt orchestrare

orchid /'ɔːkɪd/ n orchidea f

ordain /ɔː'deɪn/ vt decretare; (Relig) ordinare

ordeal /ɔː'diːl/ n fig terribile esperienza f

order /'ɔːdə(r)/ n ordine m; (Comm) ordinazione f; out of ~ (machine) fuori servizio; in ~ that affinché; in ~ to per ●vt ordinare

orderly /'ɔːdəlɪ/ adj ordinato ●n (Mil) attendente m; (Med) inserviente m

ordinary /'ɔːdɪnərɪ/ adj ordinario

ore /ɔː(r)/ n minerale m grezzo

organ /'ɔːgən/ n (Anat, Mus) organo m

organic /ɔː'gænɪk/ adj organico; (without chemicals) biologico. ~ally adv organicamente; ~ally grown coltivato biologicamente

organism /'ɔːgənɪzm/ n organismo m

organist /'ɔːgənɪst/ n organista mf

organization /ɔːgənaɪ'zeɪʃn/ n organizzazione f

organize /'ɔːgənaɪz/ vt organizzare. ~r n organizzatore, -trice mf

orgasm /'ɔːgæzm/ n orgasmo m

orgy /'ɔːdʒɪ/ n orgia f

Orient /'ɔːrɪənt/ n Oriente m. o~al adj orientale ●n orientale mf

orient|ate /'ɔːrɪentert/ vt ~ate oneself orientarsi. ~ation n orientamento m

origin /'ɒrɪdʒɪn/ n origine f

original /ə'rɪdʒɪn(ə)l/ adj originario; (not copied, new) originale ●n originale m; in the ~ in versione originale.

~ity n originalità f. ~ly adv originariamente

originat|e /ə'rɪdʒɪnert/ vi ~e in avere origine in. ~or n ideatore, -trice mf

ornament /'ɔːnəmənt/ n ornamento m; (on mantelpiece etc) soprammobile m. ~al adj ornamentale. ~ation n decorazione f

ornate /ɔː'nert/ adj ornato

orphan /'ɔːfn/ n orfano, -a mf ●vt rendere orfano; be ~ed rimanere orfano. ~age n orfanotrofio m

orthodox /'ɔːθədɒks/ adj ortodosso

oscillate /'ɒsɪlert/ vi oscillare

osteopath /'ɒstɪəpæθ/ n osteopata mf

ostracize /'ɒstrəsaɪz/ vt bandire

ostrich /'ɒstrɪtʃ/ n struzzo m

other /'ʌðə(r)/ adj, pron & n altro, -a mf; the ~ [one] l'altro, -a mf; the ~ two gli altri due; two ~s altri due; ~ people gli altri; any ~ questions? altre domande?; every ~ day (alternate days) a giorni alterni; the ~ day l'altro giorno; the ~ evening l'altra sera; someone/ something or ~ qualcuno/qualcosa ●adv ~ than him tranne lui; somehow or ~ in qualche modo; somewhere or ~ da qualche parte

'otherwise adv altrimenti; (differently) diversamente

otter /'ɒtə(r)/ n lontra f

ouch /autʃ/ int ahi!

ought /ɔːt/ v aux I/we ~ to stay dovrei/dovremmo rimanere; he ~ not to have done it non avrebbe dovuto farlo; that ~ to be enough questo dovrebbe bastare

ounce /auns/ n oncia f (= 28,35 g)

our /'aʊə(r)/ adj il nostro m, la nostra f, i nostri mpl, le nostre fpl; ~ mother/father nostra madre/ nostro padre

ours /'aʊəz/ poss pron il nostro m, la nostra f, i nostri mpl, le nostre fpl; a

o

friend of ~ un nostro amico; friends of ~ dei nostri amici; that is ~ quello è nostro; (as opposed to yours) quello è il nostro

ourselves /auə'selvz/ pron (reflexive) ci; (emphatic) noi, noi stessi; we poured ~ a drink ci siamo versati da bere; we heard it ~ l'abbiamo sentito noi stessi; we are proud of ~ siamo fieri di noi; by ~ da soli

out /aut/ adv fuori; (not alight) spento; be ~ (flower:) essere sbocciato; (workers:) essere in sciopero; (calculation:) essere sbagliato; (Sport) essere fuori; (unconscious) aver perso i sensi; (fig: not feasible) fuori questione; the sun is ~ è uscito il sole; ~ and about in piedi; get ~ 🔲 fuori; you should get ~ more dovresti uscire più spesso; ~ with it! 🔲 sputa il rospo!; ● prep ~ of fuori da; ~ of date non aggiornato; (passport) scaduto; ~ of order guasto; ~ of print/stock esaurito; ~ of bed/the room fuori dal letto/dalla stanza; ~ of breath senza fiato; ~ of danger fuori pericolo; ~ of work disoccupato; nine ~ of ten nove su dieci; be ~ of sugar/bread rimanere senza zucchero/pane; go ~ of the room uscire dalla stanza

outbreak n (of war) scoppio m; (of disease) insorgenza f

'outburst n esplosione f

'outcome n risultato m

'outcry n protesta f

out'dated adj sorpassato

out'do vt (pt -did, pp -done) superare

'outdoor adj (life, sports) all'aperto; ~ clothes pl vestiti per uscire; ~ swimming pool piscina f scoperta

out'doors adv all'aria aperta; go ~ uscire [all'aria aperta]

'outer adj esterno

'outfit n equipaggiamento m; (clothes) completo m; (🔲: organization)

organizzazione. **~ter** n men's ~ter's negozio m di abbigliamento maschile

'outgoing adj (president) uscente; (mail) in partenza; (sociable) estroverso. ~s npl uscite fpl

out'grow vi (pt -grew, pp -grown) diventare troppo grande per

outing /'autɪŋ/ n gita f

outlandish /aut'lændɪʃ/ adj stravagante

'outlaw n fuorilegge mf inv ● vt dichiarare illegale

'outlay n spesa f

'outlet n sbocco m; fig sfogo m; (Comm) punto m [di] vendita

'outline n contorno m; (summary) sommario m ● vt tracciare il contorno di; (describe) descrivere

out'live vt sopravvivere a

'outlook n vista f; (future prospect) prospettiva f; (attitude) visione f

'outlying adj ~ areas pl zone fpl periferiche

out'number vt superare in numero

'out-patient n paziente mf esterno, -a; ~s' department ambulatorio m

'output n produzione f

'outright¹ adj completo; (refusal) netto

out'right² adv completamente; (at once) immediatamente; (frankly) francamente

'outset n inizio m; from the ~ fin dall'inizio

'outside¹ adj esterno ● n esterno m; from the ~ dall'esterno; at the ~ al massimo

out'side² adv all'esterno, fuori; (out of doors) fuori; go ~ andare fuori ● prep fuori da; (in front of) davanti a

'outskirts npl sobborghi mpl

out'spoken adj schietto

out'standing adj eccezionale;

(landmark) prominente; (not settled) in sospeso

out'stretched adj allungato

out'strip vt (pt -stripped) superare

'outward /-wəd/ adj esterno; (journey) di andata ● adv verso l'esterno. **~ly** adv esternamente. **~s** adv verso l'esterno

out'weigh vt aver maggior peso di

out'wit vt (pt/pp -witted) battere in astuzia

oval /'əʊvl/ adj ovale ● n ovale m

ovary /'əʊvərɪ/ n (Anat) ovaia f

ovation /əʊ'veɪʃn/ n ovazione f

oven /'ʌvn/ n forno m. **~-ready** adj pronto da mettere in forno

over /'əʊvə(r)/ prep sopra; (across) al di là di; (during) durante; (more than) più di; **~** the phone al telefono; **~** the page alla pagina seguente; all **~** Italy in tutta [l']Italia; (travel) per l'Italia ● adv (Math) col resto di; (ended) finito; **~** again un'altra volta; **~** and **~** più volte; **~** above oltre a; **~** here there qui/là; all **~** (everywhere) dappertutto; **it's all ~** è tutto finito; **I ache all ~** ho male dappertutto; **come/bring ~** venire/portare; **turn ~** girare

over- pref (too) troppo

overall[1] /'əʊvərɔːl/ n grembiule m; **~s** pl tuta f[sg] [da lavoro]

overall[2] /əʊvər'ɔːl/ adj complessivo; (general) generale ● adv complessivamente

over'balance vi perdere l'equilibrio

over'bearing adj prepotente

'overboard adv (Naut) in mare

'overcast adj coperto

over'charge vt **~** sb far pagare più del dovuto a qcno ● vi far pagare più del dovuto

'overcoat n cappotto m

over'come vt (pt -came, pp -come)

vincere; **be ~ by** essere sopraffatto da

over'crowded adj sovraffollato

over'do vt (pt -did, pp -done) esagerare; (cook too long) stracuocere; **~ it** (丁): do too much) strafare

'overdose n overdose f inv

'overdraft n scoperto m; **have an ~** avere il conto scoperto

over'draw vt (pt -drew, pp -drawn) **~** one's account andare allo scoperto; **be ~n by** (account:) essere [allo] scoperto di

over'due adj in ritardo

over'estimate vt sopravvalutare

'overflow[1] n (water) acqua f che deborda; (people) pubblico m in eccesso; (outlet) scarico m; **~** car park parcheggio m supplementare

over'flow[2] vi debordare

over'grown adj (garden) coperto di erbacce

'overhaul[1] n revisione f

over'haul[2] vt (Techn) revisionare

'overhead[1] adv in alto

'overhead[2] adj aereo; (railway) sopraelevato; (lights) da soffitto. **~s** npl spese fpl generali

over'hear vt (pt/pp -heard) sentire per caso (conversation)

over'joyed adj felicissimo

over'haul vt (Techn) revisionare

over'land adj & adv su terra; **~** route via f terrestre

over'lap v (pt -lapped) ● vi sovrapporsi ● vt sovrapporre

over'leaf adv sul retro

over'load vt sovraccaricare

over'look vt dominare; (fail to see, ignore) lasciarsi sfuggire

over'night[1] adv per la notte; **stay ~** fermarsi a dormire

'overnight[2] adj notturno; **~** bag piccola borsa f da viaggio; **~** stay sosta f per la notte

'overpass n cavalcavia m inv

over'pay vt (pt/pp -paid) strapagare

over'power vt sopraffare. ~ing adj insostenibile

over'priced adj troppo caro

overre'act vi avere una reazione eccessiva. ~ion n reazione f eccessiva

over'rid|e vt (pt -rode, pp -ridden) passare sopra a. ~ing adj prevalente

over'rule vt annullare (decision)

over'run vt (pt -ran, pp -run, pres p -running) invadere; oltrepassare (time); be ~ with essere invaso da

over'seas¹ adv oltremare

'overseas² adj d'oltremare

over'see vt (pt -saw, pp -seen) sorvegliare

over'shadow vt adombrare

over'shoot vt (pt/pp -shot) oltrepassare

'oversight n disattenzione f; an ~ una svista

over'sleep vi (pt/pp -slept) svegliarsi troppo tardi

over'step vt (pt/pp -stepped) ~ the mark oltrepassare ogni limite

overt /əʊˈvɜːt/ adj palese

over'tak|e vt/i (pt -took, pp -taken) sorpassare. ~ing n sorpasso m; no ~ing divieto di sorpasso

'overthrow¹ n (Pol) rovesciamento m

over'throw² vt (pt -threw, pp -thrown) (Pol) rovesciare

'overtime n lavoro m straordinario ●adv work ~ fare lo straordinario

overture /ˈəʊvətjʊə(r)/ n (Mus) preludio m; ~s pl fig approccio msg

over'turn vt ribaltare ●vi ribaltarsi

over'weight adj sovrappeso

overwhelm /-ˈwelm/ vt sommergere (with di); (emotion) confondere. ~ing adj travolgente (victory, majority) schiacciante

over'work n lavoro m eccessivo ●vt far lavorare eccessivamente ●vi lavorare eccessivamente

ow|e /əʊ/ vt also fig dovere ([to] sb a qcno); ~ sb sth dovere qcsa a qcno). ~ing adj be ~ing (money:) essere da pagare ●prep ~ing to a causa di

owl /aʊl/ n gufo m

own¹ /əʊn/ adj proprio ●pron a car of my ~ una macchina per conto mio; on one's ~ da solo; hold one's ~ with tener testa a qcno; get one's ~ back 🇮🇹 prendersi una rivincita

own² vt possedere; (confess) ammettere; I don't ~ it non mi appartiene. □ ~ up vi confessare (to sth qcsa)

owner /ˈəʊnə(r)/ n proprietario, -a mf. ~ship n proprietà f

oxygen /ˈɒksɪdʒən/ n ossigeno m; ~ mask maschera f a ossigeno

oyster /ˈɔɪstə(r)/ n ostrica f

ozone /ˈəʊzəʊn/ n ozono m. ~-'friendly adj che non danneggia l'ozono. ~ layer n fascia f d'ozono

Pp

pace /peɪs/ n passo m; (speed) ritmo m; keep ~ with camminare di pari passo con ●vi ~ up and down camminare avanti e indietro. ~-maker n (Med) pacemaker m; (runner) battistrada m

Pacific /pəˈsɪfɪk/ adj & n the ~ [Ocean] l'oceano m Pacifico, il Pacifico

pacifist /ˈpæsɪfɪst/ n pacifista mf

pacify /ˈpæsɪfaɪ/ vt (pt/pp -ied) placare (person); pacificare (country)

pack /pæk/ n (of cards) mazzo m; (of hounds) muta f; (of wolves, thieves) branco m; (of cigarettes etc) pacchetto m; **a ~ of lies** un mucchio di bugie ● vt impacchettare (article); fare (suitcase); mettere in valigia (swimsuit etc); (press down) comprimere; **~ed [out]** (crowded) pieno zeppo ● vi fare i bagagli; **send sb ~ing** 🔒 mandare qcno a stendere. □ **~ up** vt impacchettare ● vi 🔒 (machine:) piantare in asso

package /'pækɪdʒ/ n pacco ● vt impacchettare. **~ deal** offerta f tutto compreso. **~ holiday** n vacanza f organizzata. **~ tour** viaggio m organizzato

packet /'pækɪt/ n pacchetto m; **cost a ~** 🔒 costare un sacco

pact /pækt/ n patto m

pad¹ /pæd/ n imbottitura f; (for writing) bloc-notes m, taccuino m; (🔒: home) [piccolo] appartamento m (pt/pp **padded**) imbottire. □ **~ out** vt gonfiare

pad² vi (pt/pp **padded**) camminare con passo felpato

paddle¹ /'pæd(ə)l/ n pagaia f ● vt (row) spingere remando

paddle² vi (wade) sguazzare

paddock /'pædək/ n recinto m

padlock /'pædlɒk/ n lucchetto m ● vt chiudere con lucchetto

paediatrician /piːdɪə'trɪʃn/ n pediatra mf

page¹ /peɪdʒ/ n pagina f

page² n (boy) paggetto m; (in hotel) fattorino m ● vt far chiamare (person)

pager /'peɪdʒə(r)/ n cercapersone m inv

paid /peɪd/ ▷ **PAY** ● adj employment lavoro m remunerato; **put ~ to** mettere un termine a

pail /peɪl/ n secchio m

pain /peɪn/ n dolore m; **be in ~** soffrire; **take ~s** darsi un gran d'affare; **~ in the neck** 🔒 spina f nel fianco

pain: **~ful** adj doloroso; (laborious) penoso. **~-killer** n calmante m. **~less** adj indolore

painstaking /'peɪnzteɪkɪŋ/ adj minuzioso

paint /peɪnt/ n pittura f; **~s** colori mpl ● vt/i pitturare; (artist:) dipingere. **~brush** n pennello m. **~er** n pittore, -trice mf; (decorator) imbianchino m. **~ing** n pittura f; (picture) dipinto m. **~work** n pittura f

pair /peə(r)/ n paio m; (of people) coppia f; **~ of trousers** paio m di pantaloni; **~ of scissors** paio m di forbici

pajamas /pə'dʒɑːməz/ npl Am pigiama msg

Pakistan /pɑːkɪ'stɑːn/ n Pakistan m. **~i** adj pakistano ● n pakistano, -a mf

pal /pæl/ n 🔒 amico, -a mf

palace /'pælɪs/ n palazzo m

palatable /'pælətəbl/ adj gradevole (al gusto)

palate /'pælət/ n palato m

pale /peɪl/ adj pallido

Palestin|e /'pælɪstaɪn/ n Palestina f. **~ian** adj palestinese ● n palestinese mf

palette /'pælɪt/ n tavolozza f

palm /pɑːm/ n palmo m; (tree) palma f; **P~ Sunday** n Domenica f delle Palme ● **palm off** vt **~ sth off on sb** rifilare qcsa a qcno

palpable /'pælpəbl/ adj palpabile; (perceptible) tangibile

palpitat|e /'pælpɪteɪt/ vi palpitare. **~ions** npl palpitazioni fpl

pamper /'pæmpə(r)/ vt viziare

pamphlet /'pæmflɪt/ n opuscolo m

pan /pæn/ n tegame m, pentola f; (for frying) padella f; (of scales) piatto m ● vt (pt/pp **panned**) (🔒: criticize) stroncare

pancake n crêpe f inv, frittella f

panda /'pændə/ n panda m inv. **~ car** n macchina f della polizia

pandemonium /pændɪ'məʊnɪəm/ n pandemonio m

pander /'pændə(r)/ vi **~ to sb**

P

compiacere qcno

pane /peɪn/ n ~ [of glass] vetro m

panel /ˈpænl/ n pannello m; (group of people) giuria f; ~ of experts gruppo m di esperti. **~ling** n pannelli mpl

pang /pæŋ/ n ~s of hunger morsi mpl della fame; ~s of conscience rimorsi mpl di coscienza

panic /ˈpænɪk/ n panico m • vi (pt/pp panicked) lasciarsi prendere dal panico. **~-stricken** adj in preda al panico

panoram|a /pænəˈrɑːma/ n panorama m. **~ic** adj panoramico

pansy /ˈpænzɪ/ n viola f del pensiero; (II: effeminate man) finocchio m

pant /pænt/ vi ansimare

panther /ˈpænθə(r)/ n pantera f

panties /ˈpæntɪz/ npl mutandine fpl

pantomime /ˈpæntəmaɪm/ n pantomima f

pantry /ˈpæntrɪ/ n dispensa f

pants /pænts/ npl (underwear) mutande fpl; (woman's) mutandine fpl; (trousers) pantaloni mpl

pantyhose /ˈ.../ n Am collant m inv

paper /ˈpeɪpə(r)/ n carta f; (wallpaper) carta f da parati; (newspaper) giornale m; (exam) esame m; (treatise) saggio m; ~s pl (documents) documenti mpl; (for identification) documento m [d'identità]; on ~ in teoria, per iscritto • attrib di carta • vt tappezzare

paper: **~back** n edizione f economica. **~-clip** n graffetta f. **~weight** n fermacarte m inv. **~work** n lavoro m d'ufficio

parable /ˈpærəbl/ n parabola f

parachut|e /ˈpærəʃuːt/ n paracadute m • vi lanciarsi col paracadute. **~ist** n paracadutista f

parade /pəˈreɪd/ n (military) parata f militare • vi sfilare • vt (show off) far sfoggio di

paradise /ˈpærədaɪs/ n paradiso m

paraffin /ˈpærəfɪn/ n paraffina f

paragraph /ˈpærəgrɑːf/ n paragrafo m

parallel /ˈpærəlel/ adj & adv parallelo. ~ **bars** npl parallele fpl. ~ **port** n (Comput) porta f parallela • n (Geog), fig parallelo m; (line) parallela f • vt essere paragonabile a

Paralympics /pærəˈlɪmpɪks/ npl the P~ le Paraolimpiadi fpl

paralyse /ˈpærəlaɪz/ vt also fig paralizzare

paralysis /pəˈræləsɪs/ n (pl -ses) /-siːz/ paralisi f inv

paramedic /pærəˈmedɪk/ n paramedico, -a mf

parameter /pəˈræmɪtə(r)/ n parametro m

paranoia /pærəˈnɔɪə/ n paranoia f

paraphernalia /pærəfəˈneɪlɪə/ n armamentario m

paraplegic /pærəˈpliːdʒɪk/ adj paraplegico • n paraplegico, -a mf

parasite /ˈpærəsaɪt/ n parassita m

paratrooper /ˈpærətruːpə(r)/ n paracadutista m

parcel /ˈpɑːsl/ n pacco m

parch /pɑːtʃ/ vt disseccare; **be ~ed** (person:) morire dalla sete

pardon /ˈpɑːdn/ n perdono m; (Jur) grazia f; ~? prego?; I beg your ~? fml chiedo scusa?; I do beg your ~ (sorry) chiedo scusa! • vt perdonare; (Jur) graziare

parent /ˈpeərənt/ n genitore, -trice mf; ~s pl genitori mpl. **~al** adj dei genitori

parenthesis /pəˈrenθəsɪs/ n (pl -ses /-siːz/) parentesi f inv

Paris /ˈpærɪs/ n Parigi f

parish /ˈpærɪʃ/ n parrocchia f. **~ioner** n parrocchiano, -a mf

park /pɑːk/ n parco m • vt/i (Auto) posteggiare, parcheggiare; ~ **oneself** II installarsi

park-and-'ride n park

and ride m inv

parking /ˈpɑːkɪŋ/ n parcheggio m, posteggio m; 'no ∼' 'divieto di sosta'. ∼-lot n Am posteggio m, parcheggio m. ∼-meter n parchimetro m. ∼ space n posteggio m, parcheggio m

parliament /ˈpɑːləmənt/ n parlamento m. ∼ary adj parlamentare

---

Parliament Il Parlamento britannico è l'organo legislativo del paese, suddiviso in due Camere: *House of Commons* e *House of Lords*. La prima è composta di 650 parlamentari, o *MPs* (*Members of Parliament*), eletti a suffragio popolare; la seconda è formata da oltre 1000 membri, tra i quali esponenti dell'aristocrazia, ex primi ministri e cittadini che si sono in qualche modo distinti. Ogni anno è il capo della monarchia ad aprire ufficialmente il Parlamento e l'anno legislativo.

---

parlour /ˈpɑːlə(r)/ n salotto m

parochial /pəˈrəʊkɪəl/ adj parrocchiale; fig ristretto

parody /ˈpærədɪ/ n parodia f • vt (pt/pp -ied) parodiare

parole /pəˈrəʊl/ n on ∼ in libertà condizionale • vt mettere in libertà condizionale

parrot /ˈpærət/ n pappagallo m

parsley /ˈpɑːslɪ/ n prezzemolo m

parsnip /ˈpɑːsnɪp/ n pastinaca f

part /pɑːt/ n parte f, (of machine) pezzo m; for my ∼ per quanto mi riguarda; on the ∼ of da parte di; take sb's ∼ prendere le parti di qcno; take ∼ in prendere parte a • adv in parte • vt ∼ one's hair farsi la riga • vi (people:) separarsi; ∼ with separarsi di

partial /ˈpɑːʃl/ adj parziale; be ∼ to aver un debole per. ∼ly adv parzialmente

participant /pɑːˈtɪsɪpənt/ n partecipante mf. ∼ate vi partecipare (in a). ∼ation n partecipazione f

particle /ˈpɑːtɪkl/ n (Gram, Phys) particella f

particular /pəˈtɪkjʊlə(r)/ adj particolare; (precise) meticoloso; (pej noioso; in ∼ in particolare. ∼ly adv particolarmente. ∼s npl particolari mpl

parting /ˈpɑːtɪŋ/ n separazione f; (in hair) scriminatura f • attrib di commiato

partisan /pɑːtɪˈzæn/ n partigiano, -a mf

partition /pɑːˈtɪʃn/ n (wall) parete f divisoria; (Pol) divisione f • vt dividere (in parti). ∼ off vt separare

partly /ˈpɑːtlɪ/ adv in parte

partner /ˈpɑːtnə(r)/ n (Comm) socio, -a mf; (sport, in relationship) compagno, -a mf. ∼ship n (Comm) società f

partridge /ˈpɑːtrɪdʒ/ n pernice f

part-ˈtime adj & adv part time; be or work ∼ lavorare part time

party /ˈpɑːtɪ/ n ricevimento m, festa f; (group) gruppo m; (Pol) partito m; (Jur) parte f (in causa); be ∼ to essere parte attiva in

pass /pɑːs/ n lasciapassare m inv; (in mountains) passo m; (Sport) passaggio m; (Sch: mark) [voto m] sufficiente m; make a ∼ at 🔢 fare delle avances a • vt passare; (overtake) sorpassare; (approve) far passare; fare (remark); (Jur) pronunciare (sentence); ∼ the time passare il tempo • vi passare; (in exam) essere promosso. ∼ away vi mancare. ∼ down vt passare; fig trasmettere. ∼ out vi 🔢 svenire. ∼ round vt far passare. ∼ through vt attraversare. ∼ up vt passare; (🔢 miss) lasciarsi scappare

passable /ˈpɑːsəbl/ adj (road) praticabile; (satisfactory) passabile

passage /ˈpæsɪdʒ/ n passaggio m; (corridor) corridoio m; (voyage) traversata f

passenger /'pæsɪndʒə(r)/ n passeggero, -a mf. ~ **seat** n posto m accanto al guidatore

passer-by /pɑːsə'baɪ/ n (pl ~sby) passante m

passion /'pæʃn/ n passione f. ~ate adj appassionato

passive /'pæsɪv/ adj passivo ● n passivo m. ~ness n passività f

Passover /'pɑːsəʊvə(r)/ n Pasqua f ebraica

pass: ~**port** n passaporto m. ~**word** n parola f d'ordine

past /pɑːst/ adj passato; (former) ex; in the ~ few days nei giorni scorsi; that's all ~ tutto questo è passato; the ~ week la settimana scorsa ● n passato m ● prep oltre; at ten ~ two alle due e dieci ● adv oltre; go/come ~ passare

pasta /'pæstə/ n pasta[sciutta] f

paste /peɪst/ n pasta f; (dough) impasto m; (adhesive) colla f ● vt incollare

pastel /'pæstl/ n pastello m ● attrib pastello

pasteurize /'pɑːstʃəraɪz/ vt pastorizzare

pastime /'pɑːstaɪm/ n passatempo m

pastry /'peɪstrɪ/ n pasta f; ~ies pl pasticcini mpl

pasture /'pɑːstʃə(r)/ n pascolo m

pasty[1] /'pæstɪ/ n ≈ pasticcio m

pasty[2] /'peɪstɪ/ adj smorto

pat /pæt/ n buffetto m; (of butter) pezzetto m ● adv have sth off ~ conoscere qcsa a menadito ● vt (pt/pp patted) dare un buffetto a; ~ sb on the back fig congratularsi per qcno

patch /pætʃ/ n toppa f; (spot) chiazza f; (period) periodo m; not a ~ on [T] molto inferiore a ● vt mettere una toppa su. □ ~ **up** vt riparare alla bell'e meglio; appianare (quarrel)

pâté /'pæteɪ/ n pâté m inv

patent /'peɪtnt/ adj palese ● n brevetto m ● vt brevettare. ~ **leather shoes** npl scarpe fpl di vernice. ~**ly** adv in modo palese

paternal /pə'tɜːnl/ adj paterno. ~**ity** n paternità f

path /pɑːθ/ n (pl ~s /pɑːðz/) sentiero m; (orbit) traiettoria m; fig strada f

pathetic /pə'θetɪk/ adj patetico; ([T]: very bad) penoso

patience /'peɪʃns/ n pazienza f; (game) solitario m

patient /'peɪʃnt/ adj paziente ● n paziente mf. ~**ly** adv pazientemente

patio /'pætɪəʊ/ n terrazza f

patriot /'pætrɪət/ n patriota mf. ~**ic** adj patriottico. ~**ism** n patriottismo m

patrol /pə'trəʊl/ n pattuglia f ● vt/i pattugliare. ~ **car** n autopattuglia f

patron /'peɪtrən/ n patrono m; (of charity) benefattore, -trice mf; (of the arts) mecenate mf; (customer) cliente mf

patronize /'pætrənaɪz/ vt frequentare abitualmente; fig trattare con condiscendenza. ~**ing** adj condiscendente. ~**ingly** adv con condiscendenza

pattern /'pætn/ n disegno m (stampato); (for knitting, sewing) modello m

paunch /pɔːntʃ/ n pancia f

pause /pɔːz/ n pausa f ● vi fare una pausa

pave /peɪv/ vt pavimentare; ~ the way preparare la strada (for a). ~**ment** n marciapiede m

paw /pɔː/ n zampa f ● vt [T] mettere le zampe addosso a

pawn[1] /pɔːn/ n (in chess) pedone m; fig pedina f

pawn[2] vt impegnare ● n in ~ in pegno. ~**broker** n prestatore, -trice mf su pegno. ~**shop** n monte m di pietà

pay /peɪ/ n paga f; **in the ~ of** al soldo di ● v t (pt/pp **paid**) pagare; prestare (attention); fare (compliment, visit); (be profitable) rendere; **it doesn't ~** … fig è fatica sprecata…; **~ for sth** pagare per qcsa. □ **~ back** vt ripagare. □ **~ in** vt versare. □ **~ off** vt saldare (debt) ● vi fig dare dei frutti. □ **~ up** vi pagare

payable /ˈpeɪəbl/ adj pagabile; **make ~ to** intestare a

payment /ˈpeɪmənt/ n pagamento m

PC n abbr (personal computer) PC m inv

pea /piː/ n pisello m

peace /piːs/ n pace f; **~ of mind** tranquillità f

peach /piːtʃ/ n pesca f; (tree) pesco m

peacock /ˈpiːkɒk/ n pavone m

peak /piːk/ n picco m; fig culmine m. **~ed** 'cap n berretto m a punta. **~ hours** npl ore fpl di punta

peal /piːl/ n (of bells) scampanio m; **~s of laughter** fragore m di risate

'**peanut** n nocciolina f [americana]; **~s** ⚠ miseria f

pear /peə(r)/ n pera f; (tree) pero m

pearl /pɜːl/ n perla f

peasant /ˈpeznt/ n contadino, -a mf

pebble /ˈpebl/ n ciottolo m

peck /pek/ n beccata f; (kiss) bacetto m ● vt beccare; (kiss) dare un bacetto a. **~ing order** n gerarchia f. **~ at** vt beccare

peculiar /prˈkjuːlɪə(r)/ adj strano; (special) particolare; **~ to** tipico di. **~ity** n stranezza f; (feature) particolarità f inv

pedal /ˈpedl/ n pedale m ● vi pedalare. **~ bin** n pattumiera f a pedale

pedantic /prˈdæntɪk/ adj pedante

pedestal /ˈpedɪstl/ n piedistallo m

pedestrian /prˈdestrɪən/ n pedone m ● adj fig scadente. **~ 'crossing** n passaggio m pedonale. **~ 'precinct** n zona f pedonale

pedigree /ˈpedɪgriː/ n pedigree m inv; (of person) lignaggio m ● attrib (animal) di razza, con pedigree

peek /piːk/ vi 🔲 sbirciare

peel /piːl/ n buccia f ● vt sbucciare ● vi (nose) etc: spellarsi; (paint): staccarsi

peep /piːp/ n sbirciata f ● vi sbirciare

peer¹ /pɪə(r)/ vi **~ at** scrutare

peer² n nobile m; **his ~s** pl (in rank) i suoi pari mpt; (in age) i suoi coetanei mpl. **~age** n nobiltà f

peg /peg/ n (hook) piolo m; (for tent) picchetto m; (for clothes) molletta f; **off the ~** 🔲 prêt-à-porter

pejorative /prˈdʒɒrətɪv/ adj peggiorativo

pelican /ˈpelɪkən/ n pellicano m

pellet /ˈpelɪt/ n pallottola f

pelt /pelt/ vt bombardare ● vi (🔲: run fast) catapultarsi; **~ down** (rain): venir giù a fiotti

pelvis /ˈpelvɪs/ n (Anat) bacino m

pen¹ /pen/ n (for animals) recinto m

pen² n penna f; (ball-point) penna f a sfera

penal /ˈpiːnl/ adj penale. **~ize** vt penalizzare

penalty /ˈpenltɪ/ n sanzione f; (fine) multa f; (in football) **~ [kick]** [calcio m di] rigore m; **~ area o box area** f di rigore

penance /ˈpenəns/ n penitenza f

pence /pens/ ▷ **PENNY**

pencil /ˈpensl/ n matita f. **~-sharpener** n temperamatite m inv

pendulum /ˈpendjʊləm/ n pendolo m

penetrat|e /ˈpenɪtreɪt/ vt/i penetrare. **~ing** adj acuto; (sound, stare) penetrante. **~ion** n penetrazione f

penguin /ˈpeŋgwɪn/ n pinguino m

penicillin /penɪˈsɪlɪn/ n penicillina f
peninsula /pɪˈnɪnsjʊlə/ n penisola f
penis /ˈpiːnɪs/ n pene m
pen: ∼**knife** n temperino m.
∼**name** n pseudonimo m
penniless /ˈpenɪlɪs/ adj senza
un soldo
penny /ˈpenɪ/ n (pl **pence**; single
coins **pennies**) penny m; Am centesimo m; spend a ∼ 🚻 andare
in bagno
pension /ˈpenʃn/ n pensione f. ∼**er**
n pensionato, -a mf
pensive /ˈpensɪv/ adj pensoso
Pentecost /ˈpentɪkɒst/ n Pentecoste f
pent-up /ˈpentʌp/ adj represso
penultimate /pɪˈnʌltɪmət/ adj penultimo
people /ˈpiːpl/ npl persone fpl, gente
fsg; (citizens) popolo msg; a lot of ∼
una marea di gente; the ∼ la gente;
English ∼ gli inglesi; ∼ say si dice;
for four ∼ per quattro • vt popolare
pepper /ˈpepə(r)/ n pepe m; (vegetable) peperone m • vt (season) pepare
pepper: ∼**corn** n grano m di pepe.
∼ **mill** macinapepe m inv. ∼**mint** n
menta f peperita; (sweet) caramella f
alla menta. ∼**pot** n pepiera f
per /pɜː(r)/ prep per; ∼ **annum** al-
l'anno; ∼ **cent** percento
perceive /pəˈsiːv/ vt percepire; (interpret) interpretare
percentage /pəˈsentɪdʒ/ n percen-
tuale f
perceptible /pəˈseptəbl/ adj per-
cettibile; (difference) sensibile
percept|ion /pəˈsepʃn/ n perce-
zione f. ∼**ive** adj perspicace
perch /pɜːtʃ/ n pertica f • vi (bird:)
appollaiarsi
percolator /ˈpɜːkəleɪtə(r)/ n caffettiera f a filtro
percussion /pəˈkʌʃn/ n percussione f. ∼ **instrument** n strumento

m a percussione
perfect[1] /ˈpɜːfɪkt/ adj perfetto • n
(Gram) passato m prossimo
perfect[2] /pəˈfekt/ vt perfezionare.
∼**ion** n perfezione f; **to** ∼**ion** alla
perfezione. ∼**ionist** n perfezio-
nista mf
perfectly /ˈpɜːfɪktlɪ/ adv perfettamente
perform /pəˈfɔːm/ vt compiere,
fare; eseguire (operation, sonata);
recitare (role); mettere in scena
(play) • vi (Theat) recitare; (Techn) funzionare. ∼**ance** n esecuzione f; (at
theatre, cinema) rappresentazione f;
(Techn) rendimento m. ∼**er** n artista mf
perfume /ˈpɜːfjuːm/ n profumo m
perhaps /pəˈhæps/ adv forse
peril /ˈperɪl/ n pericolo m. ∼**ous** adj
pericoloso
perimeter /pəˈrɪmɪtə(r)/ n perime-
tro m
period /ˈpɪərɪəd/ n periodo m; (men-
struation) mestruazioni fpl; (Sch) ora f
di lezione; (full stop) punto m fermo
• attrib (costume) d'epoca; (furniture)
in stile. ∼**ic** adj periodico. ∼**ical**
n periodico m, rivista f
peripher|al /pəˈrɪfərəl/ adj perife-
rico. ∼**y** n periferia f
perish /ˈperɪʃ/ vi (rot) deteriorarsi;
(die) perire. ∼**able** adj deteriorabile
perjur|e /ˈpɜːdʒə(r)/ vt ∼**e** oneself
spergiurare. ∼**y** n spergiuro f
perk /pɜːk/ n 🅟 vantaggio m
perm /pɜːm/ n permanente f • vt ∼
sb's hair fare la permanente a qno
permanent /ˈpɜːmənənt/ adj permanente; (job, address) stabile. ∼**ly**
adv stabilmente
permissible /pəˈmɪsəbl/ adj am-
missibile
permission /pəˈmɪʃn/ n permesso m
permit[1] /pəˈmɪt/ vt (pt/pp -mitted)
permettere; ∼ sb to do sth permet-

tere a qcno di fare qcsa

permit² /pəˈmɪt/ n autorizzazione f

perpendicular /pɜːpənˈdɪkjʊlə(r)/ adj perpendicolare ● n perpendicolare f

perpetual /pəˈpetjʊəl/ adj perenne. ~ly adv perennemente

perpetuate /pəˈpetjʊeɪt/ vt perpetuare

perplex /pəˈpleks/ vt lasciare perplesso. ~ed adj perplesso. ~ity n perplessità f inv

persecut|e /ˈpɜːsɪkjuːt/ vt perseguitare. ~ion n persecuzione f

perseverance /pɜːsɪˈvɪərəns/ n perseveranza f

persever|e /pɜːsɪˈvɪə(r)/ vi perseverare. ~ing adj assiduo

Persian /ˈpɜːʃn/ adj persiano

persist /pəˈsɪst/ vi persistere; ~ in doing sth persistere nel fare qcsa. ~ence n persistenza f. ~ent adj persistente. ~ently adv persistentemente

person /ˈpɜːsn/ n persona f; in ~ di persona

personal /ˈpɜːsənl/ adj personale. ~ ˈhygiene n igiene f personale. ~ organizer n (Comput) agenda f elettronica. ~ly adv personalmente.

personality /pɜːsəˈnælətɪ/ n personalità f inv; (on TV) personaggio m

personnel /pɜːsəˈnel/ n personale m

perspective /pəˈspektɪv/ n prospettiva f

persp|iration /pɜːspɪˈreɪʃn/ n sudore m. ~ire vi sudare

persua|de /pəˈsweɪd/ vt persuadere. ~sion n persuasione f; (belief) convinzione f

persuasive /pəˈsweɪsɪv/ adj persuasivo. ~ly adv in modo persuasivo

pertinent /ˈpɜːtɪnənt/ adj pertinente (to a)

perturb /pəˈtɜːb/ vt perturbare

peruse /pəˈruːz/ vt leggere

pervers|e /pəˈvɜːs/ adj irragionevole. ~ion n perversione f

pervert /ˈpɜːvɜːt/ n pervertito, -a mf

pessimis|m /ˈpesɪmɪzm/ n pessimismo m. ~t n pessimista mf. ~tic adj pessimistico. ~tically adv in modo pessimistico

pest /pest/ n piaga f; (ɪ: person) peste f

pester /ˈpestə(r)/ vt molestare

pesticide /ˈpestɪsaɪd/ n pesticida m

pet /pet/ n animale m domestico; (favourite) cocco, -a mf ● adj prediletto ● v (pt/pp petted) ● vt coccolare ● vi (couple:) praticare il petting

petal /ˈpetl/ n petalo m

petition /pəˈtɪʃn/ n petizione f

pet ˈname n vezzeggiativo m

petrol /ˈpetrəl/ n benzina f

petroleum /pɪˈtrəʊlɪəm/ n petrolio m

petrol: ~-pump n pompa f di benzina. ~ station n stazione f di servizio. ~ tank n serbatoio m della benzina

petticoat /ˈpetɪkəʊt/ n sottoveste f

petty /ˈpetɪ/ adj (-ier, -iest) insignificante; (mean) meschino. ~ ˈcash n cassa f per piccole spese

petulant /ˈpetjʊlənt/ adj petulante

pew /pjuː/ n banco m (di chiesa)

phantom /ˈfæntəm/ n fantasma m

pharmaceutical /fɑːməˈsjuːtɪkl/ adj farmaceutico

pharmac|ist /ˈfɑːməsɪst/ n farmacista mf. ~y n farmacia f

phase /feɪz/ n fase f ● vt phase in/out introdurre/eliminare gradualmente

pheasant /ˈfeznt/ n fagiano m

phenomen|al /fɪˈnɒmɪnl/ adj fenomenale; (incredible) incredibile. ~ally adv incredibilmente. ~on n (pl -na) fenomeno m

philistine /ˈfɪlɪstaɪn/ n filisteo, -a mf

philosoph|er /fɪˈlɒsəfə(r)/ n filosofo, -a mf. **~ical** adj filosofico. **~ically** adv con filosofia. **~y** n filosofia f

phlegm /flem/ n (Med) flemma f

phlegmatic /fleg'mætɪk/ adj flemmatico

phobia /ˈfəʊbɪə/ n fobia f

phone /fəʊn/ n telefono m; be on the ~ avere il telefono; (be phoning) essere al telefono ● vt telefonare a ● vi telefonare. □~ **back** vt/i richiamare. ~ **book** n guida f del telefono. ~ **box** n cabina f telefonica. ~ **call** telefonata f. ~ **card** n scheda f telefonica. **~-in** n trasmissione f con chiamate in diretta. ~ **number** n numero m telefonico

phonetic /fəˈnetɪk/ adj fonetico. **~s** n fonetica f

phoney /ˈfəʊnɪ/ adj (-ier, -iest) fasullo

phosphorus /ˈfɒsfərəs/ n fosforo m

photo /ˈfəʊtəʊ/ n foto f; ~ **album** album m inv di fotografie. **~copier** n fotocopiatrice f. **~copy** n fotocopia f ● vt fotocopiare

photogenic /fəʊtəʊˈdʒenɪk/ adj fotogenico

photograph /ˈfəʊtəgrɑːf/ n fotografia f ● vt fotografare

photograph|er /fəˈtɒgrəfə(r)/ n fotografo, -a mf. **~ic** adj fotografico. **~y** n fotografia f

phrase /freɪz/ n espressione f ● vt esprimere. **~-book** n libro m di fraseologia

physical /ˈfɪzɪkl/ adj fisico. ~ edu·cation n educazione f fisica. **~ly** adv fisicamente

physician /fɪˈzɪʃn/ n medico m

physic|ist /ˈfɪzɪsɪst/ n fisico, -a mf. **~s** n fisica f

physiology /fɪzɪˈɒlədʒɪ/ n fisiologia f

physio'therap|ist /fɪzɪəʊ-/ n fisioterapista mf. **~y** n fisioterapia f

physique /fɪˈziːk/ n fisico m

pianist /ˈpɪənɪst/ n pianista mf

piano /pɪˈænəʊ/ n piano m

pick¹ /pɪk/ n (tool) piccone m

pick² n scelta f; take your ~ prendi quello che vuoi ● vt (select) scegliere; cogliere (flowers); scassinare (lock); borseggiare (pockets); ~ and choose fare il difficile; ~ one's nose mettersi le dita nel naso; ~ a quarrel attaccar briga; ~ holes in 𝕋 criticare; ~ at one's food spilluzzicare. □~ **on** vt (𝕋: nag) assillare; he always ~s on me ce l'ha con me. □~ **out** vt (identify) individuare. □~ **up** vt sollevare; (off the ground, information) raccogliere; prendere in braccio (baby); (learn) imparare; prendersi (illness); (buy) comprare; captare (signal); (collect) andare/venire a prendere; prendere (passengers, habit); (police:) arrestare (criminal); 𝕋 rimorchiare (girl); ~ oneself up riprendersi ● vi (improve) recuperare; (weather:) rimettersi

'pickaxe n piccone m

picket /ˈpɪkɪt/ n picchettista mf ● vt picchettare. ~ **line** n picchetto m

pickle /ˈpɪkl/ n ~s pl sottaceti mpl; in a ~ fig nei pasticci ● vt mettere sottaceto

pick: ~pocket n borsaiolo m. **~-up** n (truck) furgone m; (on record-player) pickup m

picnic /ˈpɪknɪk/ n picnic m ● vi (pt/pp -nicked) fare un picnic

picture /ˈpɪktʃə(r)/ n (painting) quadro m; (photo) fotografia f; (drawing) disegno m; (film) film m inv; put sb in the ~ fig mettere qcno al corrente; the ~s il cinema ● vt (imagine) immaginare. **~sque** adj pittoresco

pie /paɪ/ n torta f

piece /piːs/ n pezzo m; (in game) pedina f; a ~ of bread/paper un

pezzo di pane/carta; a ∼ of news/
advice una notizia/un consiglio; take
to ∼s smontare. ∼**meal** adj con po'
alla volta. ∼**work** n lavoro m a cottimo ● **piece together** vt montare;
fig ricostruire

pier /pɪə(r)/ n molo m; (pillar) pilastro m

pierc|e /pɪəs/ vt perforare; ∼**e a
hole in** sth fare un buco in qcsa.
∼**ing** n [body] ∼ piercing m inv ● adj
penetrante

pig /pɪg/ n maiale m

pigeon /ˈpɪdʒɪn/ n piccione m.
∼**-hole** n casella f

piggy /ˈpɪgɪ/ ∼**back** n give sb a
∼**back** portare qcno sulle spalle. ∼
bank n salvadanaio m

pig'headed adj 🔢 cocciuto

pigtail n (plait) treccina f

pile n (heap) pila f ● vt ∼ **sth on to**
sth appilare qcsa su qcsa. ▫ ∼ **up** vt
accatastare ● vi ammucchiarsi

piles /paɪlz/ npl emorroidi fpl

'pile-up n tamponamento m a
catena

pilgrim /ˈpɪlgrɪm/ n pellegrino, -a
mf. ∼**age** n pellegrinaggio m

pill /pɪl/ n pillola f

pillar /ˈpɪlə(r)/ n pilastro m. ∼**-box**
n buca f delle lettere

pillow /ˈpɪləʊ/ n guanciale m.
∼**case** n federa f

pilot /ˈpaɪlət/ n pilota mf ● vt pilotare. ∼**-light** n fiamma f di sicurezza

pimple /ˈpɪmpl/ n foruncolo m

pin /pɪn/ n spillo m; (Electr) spinotto
m; (Med) chiodo m; **I have** ∼**s and
needles in my leg** 🔢 mi formicola
una gamba ● vt (pt/pp **pinned**) appuntare (to/on su); (sewing) fissare
con gli spilli; (hold down) immobilizzare; ∼ **sb down to a date** ottenere
un appuntamento da qcno; ∼ **sth
on sb** 🔢 addossare a qcno la colpa
di qcsa. ▫ ∼ **up** vt appuntare; (on
wall) affiggere

pinafore /ˈpɪnəfɔː(r)/ n grembiule
m. ∼ **dress** n scamiciato m

pincers /ˈpɪnsəz/ npl tenaglie fpl

pinch /pɪntʃ/ n pizzicotto m; (of salt)
presa f; **at a** ∼ 🔢 in caso di bisogno ● vt pizzicare; (🔢 steal) fregare
● vi (shoe) stringere

pine[1] /paɪn/ n (tree) pino m

pine[2] vi **she is pining for you** le
manchi molto. ▫ ∼ **away** vi deperire

pineapple /ˈpaɪnæpl/ n ananas m inv

'ping-pong n ping-pong m

pink /pɪŋk/ adj rosa m

pinnacle /ˈpɪnəkl/ n guglia f

PIN number n codice m segreto

pin: ∼**point** vt definire con precisione. ∼**stripe** adj gessato

pint /paɪnt/ n pinta f (= 0,571, Am:
0,47 l); **a** ∼ 🔢 una birra media

pioneer /paɪəˈnɪə(r)/ n pioniere, -a
mf ● vt essere un pioniere di

pious /ˈpaɪəs/ adj pio

pip /pɪp/ n (seed) seme m

pipe /paɪp/ n tubo m; (for smoking)
pipa f; **the** ∼**s** (Mus) la cornamusa
● vt far arrivare con tubature (water,
gas etc). ▫ ∼ **down** vi 🔢 abbassare
la voce

pipe: ∼**dream** n illusione f. ∼**line**
n conduttura f; **in the** ∼**line** 🔢 in
cantiere

piping /ˈpaɪpɪŋ/ adj ∼ **hot** bollente

pirate /ˈpaɪrət/ n pirata m

Pisces /ˈpaɪsiːz/ n (Astr) Pesci mpl

piss /pɪs/ vi ⚠ pisciare

pistol /ˈpɪstl/ n pistola f

piston /ˈpɪstn/ n (Techn) pistone m

pit /pɪt/ n fossa f; (mine) miniera f;
(for orchestra) orchestra f ● vt (pt/pp
pitted) fig opporre (against a)

pitch[1] /pɪtʃ/ n (tone) tono m; (level)
altezza f; (in sport) campo m; (fig: degree) grado m ● vt montare (tent).
▫ ∼ **in** vi 🔢 mettersi sotto

pitch[2] n ∼**-black** adj nero come la
pece. ∼**-dark** adj buio pesto

P

pitfall | plea

'pitfall n fig trabocchetto m

pith /pɪθ/ n (of lemon, orange) interno m della buccia

piti|ful /'pɪtɪfl/ adj pietoso. **~less** adj spietato

pittance /'pɪtns/ n miseria f

pity /'pɪtɪ/ n pietà f; what a ~! che peccato!; take ~ on avere compassione di ● vt aver pietà di

pivot /'pɪvət/ n perno m; fig fulcro m ● vi imperniarsi (on su)

pizza /'piːtsə/ n pizza f

placard /'plækɑːd/ n cartellone m

placate /plə'keɪt/ vt placare

place /pleɪs/ n posto m; (I: house) casa f; (in book) segno m; **feel out of** ~ sentirsi fuori posto; take ~ aver luogo; all over the ~ dappertutto ● vt collocare; (remember) identificare; **an order fare un'ordinazione. be** ~d (in race) piazzarsi. **~mat** n sottopiatto m

placid /'plæsɪd/ adj placido

plague /pleɪg/ n peste f

plaice /pleɪs/ n inv platessa f

plain /pleɪn/ adj chiaro; (simple) semplice; (not pretty) scialbo; (not patterned) normale; (chocolate) fondente; in ~ clothes in borghese ● adv (simply) semplicemente ● n pianura f. **~ly** adv francamente; (simply) semplicemente; (obviously) chiaramente

plaintiff /'pleɪntɪf/ n (Jur) parte f lesa

plait /plæt/ n treccia f ● vt intrecciare

plan /plæn/ n progetto m, piano m ● vt (pt/pp planned) progettare; (intend) prevedere

plane¹ /pleɪn/ n (tree) platano m

plane² n aeroplano m

plane³ /pleɪn/ n (tool) pialla f ● vt piallare

planet /'plænɪt/ n pianeta m

plank /plæŋk/ n asse f

planning /'plænɪŋ/ n pianificazione f. ~ **permission** n licenza f edilizia

plant /plɑːnt/ n pianta f; (machinery) impianto m; (factory) stabilimento m ● vt piantare. **~ation** n piantagione f

plaque /plɑːk/ n placca f

plasma /'plæzmə/ n plasma m

plaster /'plɑːstə(r)/ n intonaco m; (Med) gesso m; (sticking ~) cerotto m; ~ of Paris gesso m ● vt intonacare (wall); (cover) ricoprire. **~ed** adj 🅇 sbronzo. **~er** n intonacatore m

plastic /'plæstɪk/ n plastica f ● adj plastico

plastic surgery n chirurgia f plastica

plate /pleɪt/ n piatto m; (flat sheet) placca f; (gold and silverware) argenteria f; (in book) tavola f [fuori testo] ● vt (cover with metal) placcare

platform /'plætfɔːm/ n (stage) palco m; (Rail) marciapiede m; (Pol) piattaforma f; ~ 5 binario 5

platinum /'plætɪnəm/ n platino m ● attrib di platino

platitude /'plætɪtjuːd/ n luogo m comune

platonic /plə'tɒnɪk/ adj platonico

plausible /'plɔːzəbl/ adj plausibile

play /pleɪ/ n gioco m; (Theat, TV) rappresentazione f; (Radio) sceneggiato m radiofonico; ~ **on words** gioco m di parole ● vt giocare a; (act) recitare; suonare (instrument); giocare (card) ● vi giocare; (Mus) suonare; ~ **safe** non prendere rischi. □ ~ **down** vt minimizzare. □ ~ **up** vi 🅇 fare i capricci

play: **~er** n giocatore, -trice mf. **~ful** adj scherzoso. **~ground** n (Sch) cortile m (per la ricreazione). **~group** n asilo m

playing: **~-card** n carta f da gioco. **~-field** n campo m da gioco

play: **~-pen** n box m inv. **~wright** /-raɪt/ n drammaturgo, -a mf

plc n abbr (public limited company) s.r.l.

plea /pliː/ n richiesta f; make a ~

for fare un appello a

plead /pliːd/ vi fare appello (for a); ~ **guilty** dichiararsi colpevole; ~ **with sb** implorare qcno

pleasant /'plez(ə)nt/ adj piacevole. ~**ly** adv piacevolmente; (say, smile) cordialmente

pleas|e /pliːz/ adv per favore; ~**e do** prego ● vt far contento; ~**e oneself** fare il proprio comodo; ~**e yourself!** come vuoi!; pej fai come ti pare!. ~**ed** adj lieto; ~**ed with/about** contento di. ~**ing** adj gradevole

pleasure /'pleʒə(r)/ n piacere m; **with** ~ con piacere, volentieri

pleat /pliːt/ n piega f ● vt pieghettare. ~**ed 'skirt** n gonna f a pieghe

pledge /pledʒ/ n pegno m; (promise) promessa f ● vt impegnarsi a; (pawn) impegnare

plentiful /'plentɪfl/ adj abbondante

plenty /'plentɪ/ n abbondanza f; ~ **of money** molti soldi; ~ **of people** molta gente; **I've got** ~ ne ho in abbondanza

pliable /'plaɪəbl/ adj flessibile

pliers /'plaɪəz/ npl pinze fpl

plight /plaɪt/ n condizione f

plimsolls /'plɪmsəlz/ npl scarpe fpl da ginnastica

plod /plɒd/ vi (pt/pp **plodded**) trascinarsi; (work hard) sgobbare

plot /plɒt/ n complotto m; (of novel) trama f; ~ **of land** appezzamento m [di terreno] ● vt/i complottare

ploy /plɔɪ/ n 🅸 manovra f

pluck /plʌk/ n fegato m ● vt strappare; depilare (eyebrows); spennare (bird); cogliere (flower). □ ~ **up** vt ~ **up courage** farsi coraggio

plucky /'plʌkɪ/ adj (-ier, -iest) coraggioso

plug /plʌg/ n tappo m; (Electr) spina f; (Auto) candela f; (🅸: advertisement) pubblicità f inv ● vt (pt/pp **plugged**) tappare; (🅸: advertise) pubblicizzare con insistenza. □ ~ **in** vt (Electr) inserire la spina di

plum /plʌm/ n prugna f; (tree) prugno m

plumage /'pluːmɪdʒ/ n piumaggio m

plumb|er /'plʌmə(r)/ n idraulico m. ~**ing** n impianto m idraulico

plume /pluːm/ n piuma f

plump /plʌmp/ adj paffuto ● **plump for** vt scegliere

plunge /plʌndʒ/ n tuffo m; **take the** ~ 🅸 buttarsi ● vt tuffare; fig sprofondare ● vi tuffarsi

plural /'plʊərəl/ adj plurale ● n plurale m

plus /plʌs/ prep più ● adj in più; **500** ~ **più di 500** ● n più m; (advantage) extra m inv

plush /plʌʃ[ɪ]/ adj lussuoso

plutonium /pluˈtəʊnɪəm/ n plutonio m

ply /plaɪ/ vt (pt/pp **plied**) ~ **sb with drink** continuare a offrire da bere a qcno. ~**wood** n compensato m

p.m. abbr (post meridiem) del pomeriggio

PM n abbr Prime Minister

pneumonia /njuːˈməʊnɪə/ n polmonite f

P.O. abbr Post Office

poach /pəʊtʃ/ vt (Culin) bollire; cacciare di frodo (deer); pescare di frodo (salmon); ~**ed egg** uovo m in camicia. ~**er** n bracconiere m

pocket /'pɒkɪt/ n tasca f; **be out of** ~ rimetterci ● vt intascare. ~**-book** n taccuino m; (wallet) portafoglio m. ~**-money** n denaro m per le piccole spese

pod /pɒd/ n baccello m

poem /'pəʊɪm/ n poesia f

poet /'pəʊɪt/ n poeta m. ~ic adj poetico

poetry /'pəʊɪtrɪ/ n poesia f

poignant /'pɔɪnjənt/ adj emozionante

point /pɔɪnt/ n punto m; (sharp end) punta f; (meaning, purpose) senso m; (Electr) presa f [di corrente]; ~s pl (Rail) scambio m; ~ of view punto m di vista; good/bad ~s aspetti mpl positivi/negativi; what is the ~? a che scopo?; the ~ is il fatto è; I don't see the ~ non vedo il senso; up to a ~ fino a un certo punto; be on the ~ of doing sth essere sul punto di fare qcsa ●vt puntare (at verso) ●vi (with finger) puntare il dito; ~ at/to (person): mostrare col dito; (indicator): indicare. □~ out vt far notare (fact); ~ sth out to sb far notare qcsa a qcno

point-'blank adj a bruciapelo

point|ed /'pɔɪntɪd/ adj appuntito; (question) diretto. ~ers npl (advice) consigli mpl. ~less adj inutile

poise /pɔɪz/ n padronanza f. ~d adj in equilibrio; ~d to sul punto di

poison /'pɔɪzn/ n veleno m ●vt avvelenare. ~ous adj velenoso

poke /pəʊk/ n (piccola) spinta f ●vt spingere; (fire) attizzare; (put) ficcare; ~ fun at prendere in giro. □~ about vi frugare

poker[1] /'pəʊkə(r)/ n attizzatoio m

poker[2] n (Cards) poker m

poky /'pəʊkɪ/ adj (-ier, -iest) angusto

Poland /'pəʊlənd/ n Polonia f

polar /'pəʊlə(r)/ adj polare. ~ 'bear n orso m bianco. ~ize vt polarizzare

pole[1] n palo m

pole[2] n (Geog, Electr) polo m

Pole /pəʊl/ n polacco, -a m f

police /pə'liːs/ npl polizia f ●vt pattugliare (area)

police: ~man n poliziotto m. ~ station n commissariato m.

~**woman** n donna f poliziotto

policy[1] /'pɒlɪsɪ/ n politica f

policy[2] n (insurance) polizza f

polio /'pəʊlɪəʊ/ n polio f

polish /'pɒlɪʃ/ n (shine) lucentezza f; (substance) lucido m; (for nails) smalto m; fig raffinatezza f ●vt lucidare; fig smussare. □~ off vt finire in fretta; spazzolare (food)

Polish /'pəʊlɪʃ/ adj polacco ●n (language) polacco m

polished /'pɒlɪʃt/ adj (manner) raffinato; (performance) senza sbavature

polite /pə'laɪt/ adj cortese. ~ly adv cortesemente. ~ness n cortesia f

politic|al /pə'lɪtɪkl/ adj politico. ~ally adv dal punto di vista politico. ~ian n politico m

politics /'pɒlɪtɪks/ n politica f

poll /pəʊl/ n votazione f; (election) elezioni fpl; opinion ~ sondaggio m d'opinione; go to the ~s andare alle urne ●vt ottenere (votes)

pollen /'pɒlən/ n polline m

pollut|e /pə'luːt/ vt inquinare. ~ion n inquinamento m

polo /'pəʊləʊ/ n polo m. ~-neck n collo m alto. ~ shirt n dolcevita f

polythene /'pɒlɪθiːn/ n politene m. ~ bag n sacchetto m di plastica

polyun'saturated adj polinsaturo

pomp /pɒmp/ n pompa f

pompous /'pɒmpəs/ adj pomposo

pond /pɒnd/ n stagno m

ponder /'pɒndə(r)/ vt/i ponderare

pony /'pəʊnɪ/ n pony m. ~-tail n coda f di cavallo. ~-trekking n escursioni fpl col pony

poodle /'puːdl/ n barboncino m

pool[1] /puːl/ n (of water, blood) pozza f; [swimming] ~ piscina f

pool[2] n (common fund) cassa f comune; (in cards) piatto m; (game) biliardo m a buca. ~s npl ≈ totocalcio msg ●vt mettere insieme

poor /pʊə(r)/ adj povero; (not good) scadente; in ~ health in cattiva salute • npl the ~ i poveri. ~ly adj be ~ly non stare bene • adv male

pop¹ /pɒp/ n botto m; (drink) bibita f gasata • v (pt/pp popped) • vt ⨳: put) mettere; (burst) far scoppiare • vi (burst) scoppiare. □ ~ in/out vi ⨳ fare un salto/un salto fuori

pop² n ⨳ musica f pop • attrib pop

'popcorn n popcorn m inv

pope /pəʊp/ n papa m

poplar /ˈpɒplə(r)/ n pioppo m

poppy /ˈpɒpɪ/ n papavero m

popular /ˈpɒpjʊlə(r)/ adj popolare; (belief) diffuso. ~ity n popolarità f inv

populat|e /ˈpɒpjʊleɪt/ vt popolare. ~ion n popolazione f

'pop-up n popup m inv

porcelain /ˈpɔːsəlɪn/ n porcellana f

porch /pɔːtʃ/ n portico m; Am veranda f

porcupine /ˈpɔːkjʊpaɪn/ n porcospino m

pore¹ /pɔː(r)/ n poro m

pore² vi ~ over immergersi in

pork /pɔːk/ n carne f di maiale

porn /pɔːn/ n ⨳ porno m. ~o adj ⨳ porno inv

pornograph|ic /pɔːnəˈɡræfɪk/ adj pornografico. ~y n pornografia f

porpoise /ˈpɔːpəs/ n focena f

porridge /ˈpɒrɪdʒ/ n farinata f di fiocchi d'avena

port¹ /pɔːt/ n porto m

port² n (Naut: side) babordo m

port³ n (wine) porto m

portable /ˈpɔːtəbl/ adj portatile

porter /ˈpɔːtə(r)/ n portiere m; (for luggage) facchino m

'porthole n oblò m inv

portion /ˈpɔːʃn/ n parte f; (of food) porzione f

portrait /ˈpɔːtrɪt/ n ritratto m

portray /pɔːˈtreɪ/ vt ritrarre; (represent) descrivere; (actor:) impersonare. ~al n ritratto m

Portugal /ˈpɔːtjʊgl/ n Portogallo m. ~uese adj portoghese • n portoghese mf

pose /pəʊz/ n posa f • vt porre (problem, question) • vi (for painter) posare; ~ as atteggiarsi a

posh /pɒʃ/ adj ⨳ lussuoso; (people) danaroso

position /pəˈzɪʃn/ n posizione f; (job) posto m; (status) ceto m [sociale] • vt posizionare

positive /ˈpɒzɪtɪv/ adj positivo; (certain) sicuro; (progress) concreto • n positivo m. ~ly adv positivamente; (decidedly) decisamente

possess /pəˈzes/ vt possedere. ~ion n possesso m; ~ions pl beni mpl

possess|ive /pəˈzesɪv/ adj possessivo. ~iveness n carattere m possessivo. ~or n possessore, -ditrice mf

possibility /pɒsəˈbɪlətɪ/ n possibilità f inv

possib|le /ˈpɒsɪbl/ adj possibile. ~ly adv possibilmente; I couldn't ~ly accept non mi è possibile accettare; he can't ~ly be right non è possibile che abbia ragione; could you ~ly...? potrebbe per favore...?

post¹ /pəʊst/ n (pole) palo m • vt affiggere (notice)

post² n (place of duty) posto m • vt appostare; (transfer) assegnare

post³ n (mail) posta f; by ~ per posta • vt spedire; (put in letter-box) imbucare; (as opposed to fax) mandare per posta; keep sb ~ed tenere qcno al corrente

post- pref dopo

postage /ˈpəʊstɪdʒ/ n affrancatura f. ~ stamp n francobollo m

postal /ˈpəʊstl/ adj postale. ~ order n vaglia m postale

post: ~box n cassetta f delle lettere. ~card n cartolina f. ~code n codice m postale

poster /'pəustə(r)/ n poster m inv; (advertising, election) cartellone m

posterity /pɒ'sterətɪ/ n posterità f

posthumous /'pɒstjʊməs/ adj postumo. **~ly** adv dopo la morte

post: **~man** n postino m. **~mark** n timbro m postale

post-mortem /-'mɔːtəm/ n autopsia f

'**post office** n ufficio m postale

postpone /pəust'pəun/ vt rimandare. **~ment** n rinvio m

posture /'pɒstʃə(r)/ n posizione f

pot /pɒt/ n vaso m; (for tea) teiera f; (for coffee) caffettiera f; (for cooking) pentola f; **~s of money** 🗊 un sacco di soldi; **go to ~** 🗊 andare in malora

potato /pə'teɪtəʊ/ n (pl -es) patata f

poten|t /'pəutənt/ adj potente. **~tate** n potentato m

potential /pə'tenʃl/ adj potenziale ●n potenziale m. **~ly** adv potenzialmente

pot: **~hole** n cavità f inv; (in road) buca f. **~shot** n take a **~shot** at sparare a casaccio a

potter[1] /'pɒtə(r)/ vi **~ about** gingillarsi

potter[2] n vasaio, -a mf. **~y** n lavorazione f della ceramica; (articles) ceramiche fpl; (place) laboratorio m di ceramiche

potty /'pɒtɪ/ adj (-ier, -iest) 🗊 matto ●n vasino m

pouch /paʊtʃ/ n marsupio m

poultry /'pəultrɪ/ n pollame m

pounce /paʊns/ vi balzare; **~ on** saltare su

pound[1] /paʊnd/ n libbra f (= 0,454 kg); (money) sterlina f

pound[2] vt battere ●vi (heart:) battere forte; (run heavily) correre pesantemente

pour /pɔː(r)/ vt versare ●vi riversarsi;

(with rain) piovere a dirotto. ◻ **~ out** vi riversarsi fuori ●vt versare (drink); sfogare (troubles)

pout /paʊt/ vi fare il broncio ●n broncio m

poverty /'pɒvətɪ/ n povertà f

powder /'paʊdə(r)/ n polvere f; (cosmetic) cipria f ●vt polverizzare; (face) incipriare. **~y** adj polveroso

power /'paʊə(r)/ n potere m; (Electr) corrente f [elettrica]; (Math) potenza f. **~ cut** n interruzione f di corrente. **~ed** adj **~ed by electricity** dotato di corrente [elettrica]. **~ful** adj potente. **~less** adj impotente. **~-station** n centrale f elettrica

PR n abbr public relations

practicable /'præktɪkəbl/ adj praticabile

practical /'præktɪkl/ adj pratico. **~ 'joke** n burla f. **~ly** adv praticamente

practice /'præktɪs/ n pratica f; (custom) usanza f; (habit) abitudine f; (exercise) esercizio m; (Sport) allenamento m; **in ~** (in reality) in pratica; **out of ~** fuori esercizio; **put into ~** mettere in pratica

practise /'præktɪs/ vt fare pratica in; (carry out) mettere in pratica; esercitare (profession) ●vi esercitarsi; (doctor:) praticare. **~d** adj esperto

praise /preɪz/ n lode f ●vt lodare. **~worthy** adj lodevole

pram /præm/ n carrozzella f

prank /præŋk/ n tiro m

prawn /prɔːn/ n gambero m. **~ 'cocktail** n cocktail m inv di gamberetti

pray /preɪ/ vi pregare. **~er** n preghiera f

preach /priːtʃ/ vt/i predicare. **~er** n predicatore, -trice mf

pre-ar'range /priː-/ vt predisporre

precarious /prɪ'keərɪəs/ adj precario. **~ly** adv in modo precario

precaution /prɪ'kɔːʃn/ n precauzione f; **as a ~** per precauzione.

~ary *adj* preventivo

precede /prɪ'siːd/ *vt* precedere

preceden|ce /'presɪdəns/ *n* precedenza *f*. ~t *n* precedente *m*

preceding /prɪ'siːdɪŋ/ *adj* precedente

precinct /'priːsɪŋkt/ *n* (traffic-free) zona *f* pedonale; (Am: district) circoscrizione *f*

precious /'preʃəs/ *adj* prezioso; (style) ricercato ● *adv* ① ~ **little** ben poco

precipice /'presɪpɪs/ *n* precipizio *m*

precipitate /prɪ'sɪpɪteɪt/ *vt* precipitare

precis|e /prɪ'saɪs/ *adj* preciso. ~ely *adv* precisamente. ~ion *n* precisione *f*

precursor /prɪ'kɜːsə(r)/ *n* precursore *m*

predator /'predətə(r)/ *n* predatore, -trice *mf*. ~y *adj* rapace

predecessor /'priːdɪsesə(r)/ *n* predecessore *m*

predicament /prɪ'dɪkəmənt/ *n* situazione *f* difficile

predict /prɪ'dɪkt/ *vt* predire. ~able *adj* prevedibile. ~ion *n* previsione *f*

preen /priːn/ *vt* lisciarsi; ~ **oneself** *fig* farsi bello

pre|fab /'priːfæb/ *n* ① casa *f* prefabbricata. ~**fabricated** *adj* prefabbricato·

preface /'prefɪs/ *n* prefazione *f*

prefect /'priːfekt/ *n* (Sch) studente, -tessa *mf* della scuola superiore con responsabilità disciplinari, ecc

prefer /prɪ'fɜː(r)/ *vt* (pt/pp preferred) preferire

prefera|ble /'prefərəbl/ *adj* preferibile (to a). ~**bly** *adv* preferibilmente

preferen|ce /'prefərəns/ *n* preferenza *f*. ~**tial** *adj* preferenziale

pregnan|cy /'pregnənsɪ/ *n* gravidanza *f*. ~**t** *adj* incinta

prehi'storic /priː-/ *adj* preistorico

prejudice /'predʒʊdɪs/ *n* pregiudizio *m* ● *vt* influenzare (against contro); (harm) danneggiare. ~**d** *adj* prevenuto

preliminary /prɪ'lɪmɪnərɪ/ *adj* preliminare

prelude /'preljuːd/ *n* preludio *m*

premature /'prematjʊə(r)/ *adj* prematuro

pre'meditated /priː-/ *adj* premeditato

premier /'premɪə(r)/ *adj* primario ● *n* (Pol) primo ministro *m*, premier *m inv*

première /'premɪeə(r)/ *n* prima *f*

premises /'premɪsɪz/ *npl* locali *mpl*; on the ~ sul posto

premium /'priːmɪəm/ *n* premio *m*; be at a ~ essere una cosa rara

premonition /premə'nɪʃn/ *n* presentimento *m*

preoccupied /priː'ɒkjʊpaɪd/ *adj* preoccupato

preparation /prepə'reɪʃn/ *n* preparazione *f*. ~**s** preparativi *mpl*

preparatory /prɪ'pærətrɪ/ *adj* preparatorio ● *adv* ~ **to** per

prepare /prɪ'peə(r)/ *vt* preparare ● *vi* prepararsi (for per); ~**d to** disposto a

preposition /prepə'zɪʃn/ *n* preposizione *f*

preposterous /prɪ'pɒstərəs/ *adj* assurdo

prerequisite /priː'rekwɪzɪt/ *n* condizione *f* sine qua non

prescribe /prɪ'skraɪb/ *vt* prescrivere

prescription /prɪ'skrɪpʃn/ *n* (Med) ricetta *f*

presence /'prezns/ *n* presenza *f*; ~ **of mind** presenza *f* di spirito

present¹ /'preznt/ *adj* presente ● *n* presente *m*; at ~ attualmente

present² *n* (gift) regalo *m*; give sb sth as a ~ regalare qcsa a qcno

P

present³ /prɪˈzent/ vt presentare; ~ sb with an award consegnare un premio a qcno. **~able** adj be ~**able** essere presentabile

presentation /preznˈteɪʃn/ n presentazione f

presently /ˈprezntlɪ/ adv fra poco; (Am: now) attualmente

preservation /prezəˈveɪʃn/ n conservazione f

preservative /prɪˈzɜːvətɪv/ n conservante m

preserve /prɪˈzɜːv/ vt preservare; (maintain, Culin) conservare ● n (in hunting & fig) riserva f; (jam) marmellata f

preside /prɪˈzaɪd/ vi presiedere (over a)

presidency /ˈprezɪdənsɪ/ n presidenza f

president /ˈprezɪdənt/ n presidente m. **~ial** adj presidenziale

press /pres/ n (machine) pressa f; (newspapers) stampa f ● vt premere; pressare (flower); (iron) stirare; (squeeze) stringere ● vi (in) incalzare. □ ~ **for** vi fare pressione per; be ~ed **for** essere a corto di. □ ~ **on** vi andare avanti

press: ~ **conference** n conferenza f stampa. ~ **cutting** n ritaglio m di giornale. **~ing** adj urgente. **~-up** n flessione f

pressure /ˈpreʃə(r)/ n pressione f ● vt = **pressurize**. **~-cooker** n pentola f a pressione. ~ **group** n gruppo m di pressione

pressurize /ˈpreʃəraɪz/ vt far pressione su. **~d** adj pressurizzato

prestige /preˈstiːʒ/ n prestigio m. **~ious** adj prestigioso

presumably /prɪˈzjuːməblɪ/ adv presumibilmente

presume /prɪˈzjuːm/ vt presumere; ~ **to do** sth permettersi di fare qcsa

presup'pose /priː-/ vt presupporre

pretence /prɪˈtens/ n finzione f; (pretext) pretesto m; **it's all** ~ è tutta una scena

pretend /prɪˈtend/ vt fingere; (claim) pretendere ● vi fare finta

pretentious /prɪˈtenʃəs/ adj pretenzioso

pretext /ˈpriːtekst/ n pretesto m

pretty /ˈprɪtɪ/ adj (-ier, -iest) carino ● adv (🔲: fairly) abbastanza

prevail /prɪˈveɪl/ vi prevalere; ~ **on** sb **to do** sth convincere qcno a fare qcsa. **~ing** adj prevalente

prevalen|ce /ˈprevələns/ n diffusione f. **~t** adj diffuso

prevent /prɪˈvent/ vt impedire; ~ sb [from] **doing** sth impedire a qcno di fare qcsa. **~ion** n prevenzione f. **~ive** adj preventivo

preview /ˈpriːvjuː/ n anteprima f

previous /ˈpriːvɪəs/ adj precedente. **~ly** adv precedentemente

prey /preɪ/ n preda f; **bird of** ~ uccello m rapace ● vi ~ **on** far preda di; ~ **on sb's mind** attanagliare qcno

price /praɪs/ n prezzo m ● vt (Comm) fissare il prezzo di. **~less** adj inestimabile; (🔲: amusing) spassosissimo. **~y** adj 🔲 caro

prick /prɪk/ n puntura f ● vt pungere. □ ~ **up** vt ~ **up one's ears** rizzare le orecchie

prick|le /ˈprɪkl/ n spina f; (sensation) formicolio m. **~y** adj pungente; (person) irritabile

pride /praɪd/ n orgoglio m ● vt ~ oneself **on** vantarsi di

priest /priːst/ n prete m

prim /prɪm/ adj (primmer, primmest) perbenino

primarily /ˈpraɪmərɪlɪ/ adv in primo luogo

primary /ˈpraɪmərɪ/ adj primario; (chief) principale. ~ **school** n scuola f elementare

prime¹ /praɪm/ adj principale, primo; (*first-rate*) eccellente ● n be in one's ~ essere nel fiore degli anni

prime² vt preparare (*surface, person*)

Prime Minister n Primo m Ministro

primeval /praɪˈmiːvl/ adj primitivo

primitive /ˈprɪmɪtɪv/ adj primitivo

primrose /ˈprɪmrəʊz/ n primula f

prince /prɪns/ n principe m

princess /prɪnˈses/ n principessa f

principal /ˈprɪnsəpl/ adj principale ● n (*Sch*) preside m

principally /ˈprɪnsəplɪ/ adv principalmente

principle /ˈprɪnsəpl/ n principio m; in ~ in teoria; on ~ per principio

print /prɪnt/ n (*mark, trace*) impronta f; (*Phot*) copia f; (*picture*) stampa f; in ~ (*printed out*) stampato; (*book*) in commercio; out of ~ esaurito ● vt stampare; (*write in capitals*) scrivere in stampatello. ~ed matter n stampe fpl

print|er /ˈprɪntə(r)/ n stampante f; (*Typ*) tipografo, -a mf. ~er port n (*Comput*) porta f per la stampante. ~ing n tipografia f

'printout /ˈprɪntaʊt/ n (*Comput*) stampa f

prior /ˈpraɪə(r)/ adj precedente. ~ to prep prima di

priority /praɪˈɒrɪtɪ/ n precedenza f; (*matter*) priorità f inv

prise /praɪz/ vt ~ open/up forzare

prison /ˈprɪz(ə)n/ n prigione f. ~er n prigioniero, -a mf

privacy /ˈprɪvəsɪ/ n privacy f inv

private /ˈpraɪvət/ adj privato; (*car, secretary, letter*) personale ● n (*Mil*) soldato m semplice; in ~ in privato. ~ly adv (*funded, educated etc*) privatamente; (*in secret*) in segreto; (*confidentially*) in privato; (*inwardly*) interiormente

privation /praɪˈveɪʃn/ n privazione

f; ~s npl stenti mpl

privilege /ˈprɪvəlɪdʒ/ n privilegio m. ~d adj privilegiato

prize /praɪz/ n premio m ● adj (*idiot etc*) perfetto ● vt apprezzare. ~-giving n premiazione f. ~-winner n vincitore, -trice mf. ~-winning adj vincente

pro /prəʊ/ n (🄵: *professional*) professionista mf; the ~s and cons il pro e il contro

probability /prɒbəˈbɪlɪtɪ/ n probabilità f inv

probabl|e /ˈprɒbəbl/ adj probabile. ~y adv probabilmente

probation /prəˈbeɪʃn/ n prova f; (*Jur*) libertà f vigilata. ~ary adj in prova; ~ary period periodo m di prova

probe /prəʊb/ n sonda f; (*fig: investigation*) indagine f ● vt sondare; (*investigate*) esaminare a fondo

problem /ˈprɒbləm/ n problema m ● adj difficile. ~atic adj problematico

procedure /prəˈsiːdʒə(r)/ n procedimento m

proceed /prəˈsiːd/ vi procedere ● vt ~ to do sth proseguire facendo qcsa

proceedings /prəˈsiːdɪŋz/ npl (*report*) atti mpl; (*Jur*) azione fsg legale

proceeds /ˈprəʊsiːdz/ npl ricavato msg

process /ˈprəʊses/ n processo m; (*procedure*) procedimento m; in the ~ nel far ciò ● vt trattare; (*Admin*) occuparsi di; (*Phot*) sviluppare

procession /prəˈseʃn/ n processione f

processor /ˈprəʊsesə(r)/ n (*Comput*) processore m; (*for food*) robot m inv da cucina

proclaim /prəˈkleɪm/ vt proclamare

procure /prəˈkjʊə(r)/ vt ottenere

prod /prɒd/ n colpetto m ● vt (*pt/pp* prodded) punzecchiare; *fig* incitare

p.

produce | Proms

508

produce[1] /ˈprɒdjuːs/ n prodotti mpl; ~ of Italy prodotto in Italia

produce[2] /prəˈdjuːs/ vt produrre; (bring out) tirar fuori; (cause) causare; (🔾: give birth to) fare. ~r n produttore m

product /ˈprɒdʌkt/ n prodotto m. ~ion n produzione f; (Theat) spettacolo m

productive /prəˈdʌktɪv/ adj produttivo. ~ity n produttività f

profession /prəˈfeʃn/ n professione f. ~al adj professionale; (not amateur) professionista; (piece of work) da professionista; (man) di professione ● n professionista mf. ~ally adv professionalmente

professor /prəˈfesə(r)/ n professore m [universitario]

proficien|cy /prəˈfɪʃnsɪ/ n competenza f. ~t adj be ~t in essere competente in

profile /ˈprəʊfaɪl/ n profilo m

profit /ˈprɒfɪt/ n profitto m ● vi ~ from trarre profitto da. ~able adj proficuo. ~ably adv in modo proficuo

profound /prəˈfaʊnd/ adj profondo. ~ly adv profondamente

profus|e /prəˈfjuːs/ adj ~e apologies/flowers una profusione di scuse/fiori. ~ion n profusione f; in ~ion in abbondanza

prognosis /prɒɡˈnəʊsɪs/ n (pl -oses) prognosi f inv

program /ˈprəʊɡræm/ n programma m ● vt (pt/pp programmed) programmare

programme /ˈprəʊɡræm/ n Br programma m. ~r n (Comput) programmatore, -trice m

progress[1] /ˈprəʊɡres/ n progresso m; in ~ in corso; make ~ fig fare progressi

progress[2] /prəˈɡres/ vi progredire; fig fare progressi

progressive /prəˈɡresɪv/ adj progressivo; (reforming) progressista. ~ly adv progressivamente

prohibit /prəˈhɪbɪt/ vt proibire. ~ive adj proibitivo

project[1] /ˈprɒdʒekt/ n progetto m; (Sch) ricerca f

project[2] /prəˈdʒekt/ vt proiettare (film, image) ● vi (jut out) sporgere

projector /prəˈdʒektə(r)/ n proiettore m

prolific /prəˈlɪfɪk/ adj prolifico

prologue /ˈprəʊlɒɡ/ n prologo m

prolong /prəˈlɒŋ/ vt prolungare

promenade /prɒməˈnɑːd/ n lungomare m inv

prominent /ˈprɒmɪnənt/ adj prominente; (conspicuous) di rilievo

promiscu|ity /prɒmɪˈskjuːətɪ/ n promiscuità f. ~ous adj promiscuo

promis|e /ˈprɒmɪs/ n promessa f ● vt promettere; ~e sb that promettere a qcno che; I ~ed to l'ho promesso. ~ing adj promettente

promot|e /prəˈməʊt/ vt promuovere; be ~ed (Sport) essere promosso. ~ion n promozione f

prompt /prɒmpt/ adj immediato; (punctual) puntuale ● adv in punto ● vt incitare (to a); (Theat) suggerire a ● vi suggerire. ~er n suggeritore, -trice mf. ~ly adv puntualmente

Proms /prɒmz/ npl rassegna f di concerti estivi di musica classica presso l'Albert Hall a Londra

Proms I Proms sono una serie di concerti di musica classica che ogni estate, per otto settimane, si tengono giornalmente all'Albert Hall di Londra. Istituiti nel 1895 per iniziativa di Sir Henry Wood, il loro nome è l'abbreviazione di promenade concerts, concerti durante i quali parte del pubblico in sala sono riservati posti in piedi.

prone /prəʊn/ adj be ~ to do sth essere incline a fare qcsa

pronoun /'prəʊnaʊn/ n pronome m

pronounce /prə'naʊns/ vt pronunciare; (declare) dichiarare. ~d adj (noticeable) pronunciato

pronunciation /prənʌnsɪ'eɪʃn/ n pronuncia f

proof /pruːf/ n prova f; (Typ) bozza f, prova f ● adj ~ against a prova di

propaganda /prɒpə'gændə/ n propaganda f

propel /prə'pel/ vt (pt/pp propelled) spingere. ~ler n elica f

proper /'prɒpə(r)/ adj corretto; (suitable) adatto; ([T]: real) vero [e proprio]. ~ly adv correttamente. ~ 'name, ~ 'noun n nome m proprio

property /'prɒpətɪ/ n proprietà f inv. ~ developer n agente m immobiliare. ~ market n mercato m immobiliare

prophecy /'prɒfəsɪ/ n profezia f

prophesy /'prɒfɪsaɪ/ vt (pt/pp -ied) profetizzare

prophet /'prɒfɪt/ n profeta m. ~ic adj profetico

proportion /prə'pɔːʃn/ n proporzione f; (share) parte f; ~s pl (dimensions) proporzioni fpl. ~al adj proporzionale. ~ally adv in proporzione

proposal /prə'pəʊzl/ n proposta f; (of marriage) proposta f di matrimonio

propose /prə'pəʊz/ vt proporre; (intend) proporsi ● vi fare una proposta di matrimonio

proposition /prɒpə'zɪʃn/ n proposta f; ([T]: task) impresa f

proprietor /prə'praɪətə(r)/ n proprietario, -a f

prose /prəʊz/ n prosa f

prosecut|e /'prɒsɪkjuːt/ vt intentare azione contro. ~ion n azione f giudiziaria. ~ion f l'accusa f. ~or n [Public] P~or il Pubblico Ministero m

prospect[1] /'prɒspekt/ n (expectation) prospettiva f

prospect[2] /prə'spekt/ vi ~ for cercare

prospect|ive /prə'spektɪv/ adj (future) futuro; (possible) potenziale. ~or n cercatore f

prospectus /prə'spektəs/ n prospetto m

prosper /'prɒspə(r)/ vi prosperare; (person:) stare bene finanziariamente. ~ity n prosperità f

prosperous /'prɒspərəs/ adj prospero

prostitut|e /'prɒstɪtjuːt/ n prostituta f. ~ion n prostituzione f

prostrate /'prɒstreɪt/ adj prostrato; ~ with grief fig prostrato dal dolore

protagonist /prəʊ'tægənɪst/ n protagonista mf

protect /prə'tekt/ vt proteggere (from da). ~ion n protezione f. ~ive adj protettivo. ~or n protettore, -trice mf

protein /'prəʊtiːn/ n proteina f

protest[1] /'prəʊtest/ n protesta f

protest[2] /prə'test/ vt/i protestare

Protestant /'prɒtɪstənt/ adj protestante ● n protestante mf

protester /prə'testə(r)/ n contestatore, -trice mf

protocol /'prəʊtəkɒl/ n protocollo m

protrude /prə'truːd/ vi sporgere

proud /praʊd/ adj fiero (of di). ~ly adv fieramente

prove /pruːv/ vt provare ● vi ~ to be a lie rivelarsi una bugia. ~n adj dimostrato

proverb /'prɒvɜːb/ n proverbio m. ~ial adj proverbiale

provide /prə'vaɪd/ vt fornire; ~ sb with sth fornire qcsa a qcno ● vi ~ for (law:) prevedere

provided /prə'vaɪdɪd/ conj ~ [that] purché

providen|ce /ˈprovɪdəns/ n provvidenza f. ~**tial** adj provvidenziale

providing /prəˈvaɪdɪŋ/ conj = provided

provin|ce /ˈprovɪns/ n provincia f; fig campo m. ~**ial** adj provinciale

provision /prəˈvɪʒn/ n (of food, water) approvvigionamento m (of di); (of law) disposizione f; ~**s** pl provviste fpl. ~**al** adj provvisorio

provocat|ion /provəˈkeɪʃn/ n provocazione f. ~**ive** adj provocatorio; (sexually) provocante. ~**ively** adv in modo provocatorio

provoke /prəˈvəʊk/ vt provocare

prow /praʊ/ n prua f

prowess /ˈpraʊɪs/ n abilità f inv

prowl /praʊl/ v aggirarsi ●n on the ~ in cerca di preda. ~**er** n tipo m sospetto

proximity /prokˈsɪmətɪ/ n prossimità f

proxy /ˈproksɪ/ n procura f; (person) persona f che agisce per procura

prude /pruːd/ n be a ~ essere eccessivamente pudico

pruden|ce /ˈpruːdəns/ n prudenza f. ~**t** adj prudente; (wise) oculatezza f

prudish /ˈpruːdɪʃ/ adj eccessivamente pudico

prune[1] /pruːn/ n prugna f secca

prune[2] vt potare

pry /praɪ/ vi (pt/pp pried) ficcare il naso

psalm /sɑːm/ n salmo m

psychiatric /saɪkɪˈætrɪk/ adj psichiatrico

psychiatr|ist /saɪˈkaɪətrɪst/ n psichiatra mf. ~**y** n psichiatria f

psychic /ˈsaɪkɪk/ adj psichico; I'm not ~ non sono un indovino

psychological /saɪkəˈlɒdʒɪkl/ adj psicologico

psycholog|ist /saɪˈkɒlədʒɪst/ n psicologo, -a mf. ~**y** n psicologia f

pub /pʌb/ n 🔲 pub m inv

Pub In Gran Bretagna, molti pubs (abbreviazione di public house) fanno parte di catene e sono proprietà di grandi birrerie, altri invece sono indipendenti (free houses). Oltre che per bere, si va al pub per socializzare e giocare a freccette, biliardo, ecc.; alcuni organizzano serate di quiz a gruppi. L'orario di apertura è diverso a seconda della licenza dell'esercizio, ma quello più comune va dalle 11 alle 23.

puberty /ˈpjuːbətɪ/ n pubertà f

public /ˈpʌblɪk/ adj pubblico ●n the ~ il pubblico; in ~ in pubblico. ~**ly** adv pubblicamente

publican /ˈpʌblɪkən/ n gestore, -trice mf/proprietario, -a mf di un pub

publication /pʌblɪˈkeɪʃn/ n pubblicazione f

public: ~ **'holiday** n festa nazionale. ~ **'house** n pub m

publicity /pʌbˈlɪsɪtɪ/ n pubblicità f

publicize /ˈpʌblɪsaɪz/ vt pubblicizzare

public: ~ **relations** pubbliche relazioni fpl. ~ **'school** n scuola f privata; Am scuola f pubblica

public schools In Inghilterra sono, al contrario di quanto il nome farebbe pensare, scuole secondarie private a pagamento, in cui spesso gli allievi risiedono in collegio.

publish /ˈpʌblɪʃ/ vt pubblicare. ~**er** n editore m; (firm) editore m, casa f editrice. ~**ing** n editoria f

pudding /ˈpʊdɪŋ/ n dolce m cotto al vapore; (course) dolce m

puddle /ˈpʌdl/ n pozzanghera f

puff /pʌf/ n (of wind) soffio m; (of

smoke) tirata *f*; (*for powder*) piumino *m*
● *vt* sbuffare. **puff at** *vt* tirare boccate da (pipe). □ **~ out** *vt* lasciare senza fiato (person); spegnere (candle). **~ed** *adj* (*out of breath*) senza fiato. **~ pastry** *n* pasta *f* sfoglia

puffy /'pʌfɪ/ *adj* gonfio

pull /pʊl/ *n* trazione *f*; (*fig: attraction*) attrazione *f*; (🔲: *influence*) influenza *f* ● *vt* tirare; estrarre (tooth); stirarsi (muscle); **~ faces** far boccace; **~ oneself together** controllarsi; **~ one's weight** mettercela tutta; **~ sb's leg** 🔲 prendere in giro qcno. □ **~ down** *vt* (*demolish*) demolire. □ **~ in** *vi* (Auto) accostare. □ **~ off** *vt* togliere; 🔲 azzeccare. □ **~ out** *vt* tirar fuori ● *vi* (Auto) spostarsi; (*of competition*) ritirarsi. □ **~ through** *vi* (*recover*) farcela. □ **~ up** *vt* sradicare (plant); (*reprimand*) rimproverare ● *vi* (Auto) fermarsi

pullover /'pʊləʊvə(r)/ *n* pullover *m*

pulp /pʌlp/ *n* poltiglia *f*; (*of fruit*) polpa *f*; (*for paper*) pasta *f*

pulpit /'pʊlpɪt/ *n* pulpito *m*

pulse /pʌls/ *n* polso *m*

pummel /'pʌml/ *vt* (*pt/pp* **pummelled**) prendere a pugni

pump /pʌmp/ *n* pompa *f* ● *vt* pompare; 🔲 cercare di estrorcere da. □ **~ up** *vt* (*inflate*) gonfiare

pumpkin /'pʌmpkɪn/ *n* zucca *f*

pun /pʌn/ *n* gioco *m* di parole

punch[1] /pʌntʃ/ *n* pugno *m*; (*device*) pinza *f* per forare ● *vt* dare un pugno a; forare (ticket); perforare (hole)

punch[2] *n* (*drink*) ponce *m inv*

punctual /'pʌŋktjʊəl/ *adj* puntuale. **~ity** *n* puntualità *f*. **~ly** *adv* puntualmente

punctuat|e /'pʌŋktjʊeɪt/ *vt* punteggiare. **~ion** *n* punteggiatura *f*. **~ion mark** *n* segno *m* di interpunzione

puncture /'pʌŋktʃə(r)/ *n* foro *m*;

(tyre) foratura *f* ● *vt* forare

punish /'pʌnɪʃ/ *vt* punire. **~able** *adj* punibile. **~ment** *n* punizione *f*.

punk /pʌŋk/ *n* punk *m inv*

punt /pʌnt/ *n* (*boat*) barchino *m*

punter /'pʌntə(r)/ *n* (*gambler*) scommettitore, -trice *mf*; (*client*) consumatore, -trice *mf*

puny /'pju:nɪ/ *adj* (-ier, -iest) striminzito

pup /pʌp/ *n* = **puppy**

pupil /'pju:pl/ *n* alunno, -a *mf*; (*of eye*) pupilla *f*

puppet /'pʌpɪt/ *n* marionetta *f*; (glove ~, *fig*) burattino *m*

puppy /'pʌpɪ/ *n* cucciolo *m*

purchase /'pɜ:tʃəs/ *n* acquisto *m*; (*leverage*) presa *f* ● *vt* acquistare. **~r** *n* acquirente *mf*

pure /pjʊə(r)/ *adj* puro. **~ly** *adv* puramente

purgatory /'pɜ:gətrɪ/ *n* purgatorio *m*

purge /pɜ:dʒ/ (Pol) *n* epurazione *f* ● *vt* epurare

puri|fication /pjʊərɪfɪ'keɪʃn/ *n* purificazione *f*. **~fy** *vt* (*pt/pp* -ied) purificare

puritan /'pjʊərɪtən/ *n* puritano, -a *mf*. **~ical** *adj* puritano

purity /'pjʊərɪtɪ/ *n* purità *f*

purple /'pɜ:pl/ *adj* viola

purpose /'pɜ:pəs/ *n* scopo *m*; (*determination*) fermezza *f*; **on ~** apposta. **~-built** *adj* costruito ad hoc. **~ful** *adj* deciso. **~fully** *adv* con decisione. **~ly** *adv* apposta

purr /pɜ:(r)/ *vi* (cat:) fare le fusa

purse /pɜ:s/ *n* borsellino *m*; (Am: handbag) borsa *f* ● *vt* increspare (lips)

pursue /pə'sju:/ *vt* inseguire; *fig* proseguire. **~r** *n* inseguitore, -trice *mf*

pursuit /pə'sju:t/ *n* inseguimento *m*; (*fig: of happiness*) ricerca *f*; (*pastime*) attività *f inv*; **in ~** all'inseguimento

P

pus /pʌs/ n pus m

push /poʃ/ n spinta f; (*fig: effort*) sforzo m; (*drive*) iniziativa f; at a ~ in caso di bisogno; get the ~ 🅣 essere licenziato ●vt spingere; premere (button); (*pressurize*) far pressione su; be ~ed for time 🅣 non avere tempo ●vi spingere. □ ~ **aside** vt scostare. □ ~ **back** vt respingere. □ ~ **off** vt togliere ●vi (🅣: *leave*) levarsi dai piedi. □ ~ **on** vi (*continue*) continuare. □ ~ **up** vt alzare (price)

push: ~-**chair** n passeggino m. ~-**up** n flessione f

pushy /ˈpoʃi/ adj 🅣 troppo intraprendente

put /pot/ vt (*pt/pp* put, *pres p* putting) mettere; ~ **the** cost of sth at valutare il costo di qcsa ●vi ~ **to** sea salpare. □ ~ **aside** vt mettere da parte. □ ~ **away** vt mettere via. □ ~ **back** vt rimettere; mettere indietro (clock). □ ~ **by** vt mettere da parte. □ ~ **down** vt mettere giù; (*suppress*) reprimere; (*kill*) sopprimere; (*write*) annotare; ~ **one's foot down** 🅣 essere fermo; (*Auto*) dare un'accelerata; ~ **down to** (*attribute*) attribuire. □ ~ **forward** vt avanzare; mettere avanti (clock). □ ~ **in** vt (*insert*) introdurre; (*submit*) presentare ●vi ~ **in** for far domanda di. □ ~ **off** vt spegnere (light); (*postpone*) rimandare; ~ **sb off** tenere a bada qcno; (*deter*) smontare qcno; (*disconcert*) distrarre qcno; ~ **sb off sth** (*disgust*) disgustare qcno di qcsa. □ ~ **on** vt mettersi (clothes); mettere (brake); (*Culin*) mettere su; accendere (light); mettere in scena (play); prendere (accent); ~ **on weight** mettere su qualche chilo. □ ~ **out** vt spegnere (fire, light); tendere (hand); (*inconvenience*) creare degli inconvenienti a. □ ~ **through** vt far passare; (*Teleph*) I'll ~ **you through to** him glielo passo. □ ~ **up** vt alzare; erigere (building); montare (tent); aprire

(umbrella); affiggere (notice); aumentare (price); ospitare (guest); ~ **sb up to sth** mettere qcsa in testa a qcno ●vi (*at hotel*) stare; ~ **up with** sopportare ●adj stay ~-I rimani lì!

puzzle /ˈpʌzl/ n enigma m; (*jigsaw*) puzzle m inv ●vt lasciare perplesso ●vi ~e over scervellarsi su. ~**ing** adj inspiegabile

pygmy /ˈpɪgmi/ n pigmeo, -a mf

pyjamas /pəˈdʒɑːməz/ npl pigiama msg

pylon /ˈpaɪlən/ n pilone m

pyramid /ˈpɪrəmɪd/ n piramide f

python /ˈpaɪθn/ n pitone m

• •

Qq

• •

quack¹ /kwæk/ n qua qua m inv ●vi fare qua qua

quack² n (*doctor*) ciarlatano m

quadrangle /ˈkwɒdræŋgl/ n quadrangolo m; (*court*) cortile m quadrangolare

quadruped /ˈkwɒdruped/ n quadrupede m

quadruple /ˈkwɒdrupl/ adj quadruplo ●vt quadruplicare ●vi quadruplicarsi. ~**ts** npl quattro gemelli mpl

quagmire /ˈkwɒgmaɪə(r)/ n pantano m

quaint /kweɪnt/ adj pittoresco; (*odd*) bizzarro

quake /kweɪk/ n 🅣 terremoto m ●vi tremare

qualification /kwɒlɪfɪˈkeɪʃn/ n qualifica f. ~**ied** adj qualificato; (*limited*) con riserva

qualify /ˈkwɒlɪfaɪ/ v (*pt/pp* -ied) ●vt (*course:*) dare la qualifica a (as di); (*entitle*) dare diritto a; (*limit*) precisare

● *vi* ottenere la qualifica; (*Sport*) qualificarsi

quality /'kwɒlətɪ/ n qualità f inv

qualm /kwɑːm/ n scrupolo m

quandary /'kwɒndərɪ/ n dilemma m

quantity /'kwɒntətɪ/ n quantità f inv; in ∼ in grande quantità

quarantine /'kwɒrəntiːn/ n quarantena f

quarrel /'kwɒrəl/ n lite f ● vi (pt/pp quarrelled) litigare. ∼some adj litigioso

quarry[1] /'kwɒrɪ/ n (prey) preda f

quarry[2] n cava f

quart /kwɔːt/ n 1.14 litro

quarter /'kwɔːtə(r)/ n quarto m; (of year) trimestre m; Am 25 centesimi mpl; ∼s pl (Mil) quartiere msg; at [a] ∼ to six alle sei meno un quarto ● vt dividere in quattro. ∼'final n quarto m di finale

quarterly /'kwɔːtəlɪ/ adj trimestrale ● adv trimestralmente

quartz /kwɔːts/ n quarzo m. ∼ watch n orologio m al quarzo

quay /kiː/ n banchina f

queasy /'kwiːzɪ/ adj I feel ∼ ho la nausea

queen /kwiːn/ n regina f. ∼ mother n regina f madre

queer /kwɪə(r)/ adj strano; (dubious) sospetto; (I: homosexual) finocchio ● n I finocchio m

quench /kwentʃ/ vt ∼ one's thirst dissetarsi

query /'kwɪərɪ/ n domanda f; (question mark) punto m interrogativo ● vt (pt/pp -ied) interrogare; (doubt) mettere in dubbio

quest /kwest/ n ricerca f (for di)

question /'kwestʃn/ n domanda f; (for discussion) questione f; out of the ∼ fuori discussione; without ∼ senza dubbio; in ∼ in questione ● vt

interrogare; (doubt) mettere in dubbio. ∼able /əbl/ adj discutibile. ∼ mark n punto m interrogativo

questionnaire /kwestʃə'neə(r)/ n questionario m

queue /kjuː/ n coda f, fila f ● vi ∼ [up] mettersi in coda (for per)

quick /kwɪk/ adj veloce; be ∼ sbrigati!; have a ∼ meal fare uno spuntino ● adv in fretta ● be cut to the ∼ fig essere punto sul vivo. ∼ly adv in fretta. ∼-tempered adj collerico

quid /kwɪd/ n inv I sterlina f

quiet /'kwaɪət/ adj (calm) tranquillo; (silent) silenzioso; (voice, music) basso; keep ∼ about I non raccontare a nessuno ● n quiete f; on the ∼ di nascosto. ∼ly adv (peacefully) tranquillamente; (say) a bassa voce

quiet|en /'kwaɪətn/ vt calmare. ▫ ∼ down vi calmarsi. ∼ness n quiete f

quilt /kwɪlt/ n piumino m. ∼ed adj trapuntato

quintet /kwɪn'tet/ n quintetto m

quirk /kwɜːk/ n stranezza f

quit /kwɪt/ v (pt/pp quitted, quit) ● vt lasciare; (give up) smettere (doing di fare) ● vi (I: resign) andarsene; (Comput) uscire; give sb notice to ∼ (landlord:) dare a qcno il preavviso di sfratto

quite /kwaɪt/ adv (fairly) abbastanza; (completely) completamente; (really) veramente; ∼ [so]! proprio così!; ∼ a few parecchi

quits /kwɪts/ adj pari

quiver /'kwɪvə(r)/ vi tremare

quiz /kwɪz/ n (game) quiz m inv ● vt (pt/pp quizzed) interrogare

quota /'kwəʊtə/ n quota f

quotation /kwəʊ'teɪʃn/ n citazione f; (price) preventivo m; (of shares) quota f. ∼ marks npl virgolette fpl

quote /kwəʊt/ n I = quotation; in ∼s tra virgolette ● vt citare; quotare (price)

q

Rr

rabbi /'ræbaɪ/ n rabbino m; (title) rabbi

rabbit /'ræbɪt/ n coniglio m

rabies /'reɪbiːz/ n rabbia f

race[1] /reɪs/ n (people) razza f

race[2] n corsa f ● vi correre ● vt gareggiare con; fare correre (horse)

race: ~course n ippodromo m. ~horse n cavallo m da corsa. ~track n pista m

racial /'reɪʃl/ adj razziale. ~ism n razzismo m

racing /'reɪsɪŋ/ n corse fpl; (horse-) corse fpl dei cavalli. ~ car n macchina f da corsa. ~ driver n corridore m automobilistico

racis|m /'reɪsɪzm/ n razzismo m. ~t adj razzista ● n razzista mf

rack[1] /ræk/ n (for bikes) rastrelliera f; (for luggage) portabagagli m inv; (for plates) scolapiatti m inv ● vt ~ one's brains scervellarsi

rack[2] n go to ~ and ruin andare in rovina

racket[1] /'rækɪt/ n (Sport) racchetta f

racket[2] n (din) chiasso m; (swindle) truffa f; (crime) racket m inv, giro m

radar /'reɪdɑː(r)/ n radar m inv

radian|ce /'reɪdɪəns/ n radiosità f inv. ~t adj raggiante

radiat|e /'reɪdɪeɪt/ vt irradiare ● vi (heat:) irradiarsi. ~ion n radiazione f

radiator /'reɪdɪeɪtə(r)/ n radiatore m

radical /'rædɪkl/ adj radicale ● n radicale mf. ~ly adv radicalmente

radio /'reɪdɪəʊ/ n radio f inv

radio|**active** adj radioattivo. ~**activity** n radioattività f

radish /'rædɪʃ/ n ravanello m

radius /'reɪdɪəs/ n (pl -dii /-dɪaɪ/) raggio m

raffle /'ræfl/ n lotteria f

raft /rɑːft/ n zattera f

rafter /'rɑːftə(r)/ n trave f

rag /ræg/ n straccio m; (pej: newspaper) giornalaccio m; in ~s stracciato

rage /reɪdʒ/ n rabbia f; all the ~ ⬚ all'ultima moda ● vi infuriarsi; (storm:) infuriare; (epidemic:) imperversare

ragged /'rægɪd/ adj logoro; (edge) frastagliato

raid /reɪd/ n (by thieves) rapina f; (Mil) incursione f, raid m inv; (police) irruzione f ● vt (Mil) fare un'incursione in; (police, burglars:) fare irruzione in. ~er n (of bank) rapinatore, -trice mf

rail /reɪl/ n ringhiera f; (hand-) ringhiera f; (Naut) parapetto m; by ~ per ferrovia

'railroad n Am = railway

'railway n ferrovia f. ~man n ferroviere m. ~ station n stazione f ferroviaria

rain /reɪn/ n pioggia f ● vi piovere

rain: ~bow n arcobaleno m. ~coat n impermeabile m. ~fall n precipitazione f [atmosferica]

rainy /'reɪnɪ/ adj (-ier, -iest) piovoso

raise /reɪz/ n Am aumento m ● vt alzare; levarsi (hat); allevare (children, animals); sollevare (question); ottenere (money)

raisin /'reɪzn/ n uva f passa

rake /reɪk/ n rastrello m ● vt rastrellare. □ ~ **up** vt raccogliere col rastrello; ⬚ rivangare

rally /'rælɪ/ n raduno m; (Auto) rally m inv; (Tennis) scambio m ● vt (pt/pp -ied) radunare ● vi radunarsi; (recover strength) riprendersi

ram /ræm/ n montone m; (Astr) Ariete m ● vt (pt/pp rammed) cozzare contro

RAM /ræm/ n (memoria f) RAM f

ramble /'ræmbl/ n escursione f ● vi gironzolare; (in speech) divagare. ~er n escursionista mf; (rose) rosa f rampicante. ~ing adj (in speech) sconnesso; (club) escursionistico

ramp /ræmp/ n rampa f; (Aeron) scaletta f mobile (di aerei)

rampage /ræmˈpeɪdʒ/ n be/go on the ~ scatenarsi ● vi scatenarsi through the streets scatenarsi per le strade

ramshackle /'ræmʃækl/ adj sgangherato

ran /ræn/ ▷ RUN

ranch /rɑːntʃ/ n ranch m

random /'rændəm/ adj casuale; ~ sample campione m a caso ● n at ~ a casaccio

rang /ræŋ/ ▷ RING²

range /reɪndʒ/ n serie f; (Comm, Mus) gamma f; (of mountains) catena f; (distance) raggio m; (for shooting) portata f; (stove) cucina f economica; at a ~ of a una distanza di ● vi estendersi; ~ from... to... andare da... a.... ~r n guardia f forestale

rank /ræŋk/ n (row) riga f; (Mil) grado m; (social position) rango m; the ~ and file la base f; the ~s (Mil) i soldati mpl semplici ● vt (place) annoverare (among tra) ● vi (be placed) collocarsi

ransack /'rænsæk/ vt rovistare; (pillage) saccheggiare

ransom /'rænsəm/ n riscatto m; hold sb to ~ tenere qcno in ostaggio (per il riscatto)

rant /rænt/ vi ~ [and rave] inveire; what's he ~ing on about? cosa sta blaterando?

rap /ræp/ n colpo m (secco); (Mus) rap m ● v (pt/pp rapped) ● vt dare colpetti a ● vi ~ at bussare a

rape /reɪp/ n (sexual) stupro m ● vt violentare, stuprare

rapid /'ræpɪd/ adj rapido. ~ity n rapidità f. ~ly adv rapidamente

rapids /'ræpɪdz/ npl rapida fsg

rapist /'reɪpɪst/ n violentatore m

rapture /'ræptʃə(r)/ n estasi f. ~ous adj entusiastico

rare¹ /reə(r)/ adj raro. ~ly adv raramente

rare² adj (Culin) al sangue

rarefied /'reərɪfaɪd/ adj rarefatto

rarity /'reərətɪ/ n rarità f inv

rascal /'rɑːskl/ n mascalzone m

rash¹ /ræʃ/ n (Med) eruzione f

rash² adj avventato. ~ly adv avventatamente

rasher /'ræʃə(r)/ n fetta f di pancetta

rasp /rɑːsp/ n (noise) stridio m. ~ing adj stridente

raspberry /'rɑːzbərɪ/ n lampone m

rat /ræt/ n topo m; (🄵: person) carogna f; smell a ~ 🄵 sentire puzzo di bruciato

rate /reɪt/ n (speed) velocità f; (of payment) tariffa f; (of exchange) tasso m; ~s pl (taxes) imposte fpl comunali sui beni immobili; at any ~ in ogni caso; at this ~ di questo passo ● vt stimare; ~ among annoverare tra ● vi ~ as essere considerato

rather /'rɑːðə(r)/ adv piuttosto; ~! eccome!; ~ too... un po' troppo...

rating /'reɪtɪŋ/ n ~s pl (Radio, TV) indice m d'ascolto, audience f inv

ratio /'reɪʃɪəʊ/ n rapporto m

ration /'ræʃn/ n razione f ● vt razionare

rational /'ræʃənl/ adj razionale. ~ize vt/i razionalizzare

rattle /'rætl/ n tintinnio m; (toy) sonaglio m ● vi tintinnare ● v (shake) scuotere; 🄵 innervosire. □ ~ off vt 🄵 sciorinare

raucous /'rɔːkəs/ adj rauco

rave /reɪv/ vi vaneggiare; ~ about andare in estasi per

raven /'reɪvn/ n corvo m imperiale

ravenous /'rævənəs/ adj (person)

affamato

ravine /rə'viːn/ n gola f

raving /'reɪvɪŋ/ adj ~ **mad** 🔲 matto da legare

ravishing /'rævɪʃɪŋ/ adj incantevole

raw /rɔː/ adj crudo; (not processed) grezzo; (weather) gelido; (inexperienced) inesperto; **get a ~ deal** 🔲 farsi fregare. ● ~ ma'terials npl materie fpl prime

ray /reɪ/ n raggio m; ~ **of hope** barlume m di speranza

raze /reɪz/ vt ~ **to the ground** radere al suolo

razor /'reɪzə(r)/ n rasoio m. ~ **blade** n lametta f da barba

re /riː/ prep con riferimento a

reach /riːtʃ/ n portata f; **within ~** a portata di mano; **out of ~** fuori dalla portata di; **within easy ~** facilmente raggiungibile ● vt arrivare a (place, decision); (contact) contattare; (pass) passare; **I can't ~ it** non ci arrivo ● vi arrivare (to a); ~ **for** allungare la mano per prendere

re'act /rɪ-/ vi reagire

re'action /rɪ-/ n reazione f. ~**ary** adj reazionario, -a mf

reactor /rɪ'æktə(r)/ n reattore m

read /riːd/ vt (pt/pp read /red/) leggere; (Univ) studiare ● vi leggere; (instrument:) indicare. □ ~ **out** vt leggere ad alta voce

readable /'riːdəbl/ adj piacevole a leggersi; (legible) leggibile

reader /'riːdə(r)/ n lettore, -trice mf; (book) antologia f

readily /'redɪlɪ/ adv volentieri; (easily) facilmente. ~**ness** n disponibilità f inv; **in ~ness** pronto

reading /'riːdɪŋ/ n lettura f

rea'djust /riː-/ vt regolare di nuovo ● vi riabituarsi (to a)

ready /'redɪ/ adj (-ier, -iest) pronto; (quick) veloce; **get ~** prepararsi

ready-'made adj confezionato

real /riːl/ adj vero; (increase) reale ● adv Am 🔲 veramente. ~ **estate** n beni mpl immobili

realism /'rɪəlɪzm/ n realismo m. ~**t** n realista mf. ~**tic** adj realistico

reality /rɪ'ælətɪ/ n realtà f inv; ~ **TV** n reality TV f

realization /rɪəlaɪ'zeɪʃn/ n realizzazione f

realize /'rɪələɪz/ vt realizzare

really /'rɪəlɪ/ adv davvero

realm /relm/ n regno m

realtor /'rɪəltə(r)/ n Am agente mf immobiliare

reap /riːp/ vt mietere

reap'pear /riː-/ vi riapparire

rear¹ /rɪə(r)/ adj posteriore; (Auto) di dietro; ~ **end** 🔲 didietro m ● n the ~ (of building) il retro m; (of bus, plane) la parte f posteriore; **from the ~** da dietro

rear² vt allevare ● vi ~ [**up**] (horse:) impennarsi

rear'range /riː-/ vt cambiare la disposizione di

reason /'riːzn/ n ragione f; **within ~** nei limiti del ragionevole ● vi ragionare; ~ **with** cercare di far ragionare. ~**able** adj ragionevole. ~**ably** adv (in reasonable way, fairly) ragionevolmente

reas'surance /riː-/ n rassicurazione f. ~**e** vt rassicurare; ~**e sb of** sth rassicurare qcno su qcsa. ~**ing** adj rassicurante

rebate /'riːbeɪt/ n rimborso m; (discount) deduzione f

rebel¹ /'rebl/ n ribelle mf

rebel² /rɪ'bel/ vi (pt/pp rebelled) ribellarsi. ~**lion** n ribellione f. ~**lious** adj ribelle

re'bound¹ /rɪ-/ vi rimbalzare; fig ricadere

'rebound² /riː-/ n rimbalzo m

rebuff /rɪ'bʌf/ n rifiuto m

re'build /riː-/ vt (pt/pp -built) ricostruire

rebuke /rɪ'bjuːk/ vt rimproverare

re'call /rɪ-/ n richiamo m; beyond ~ irrevocabile ● vt richiamare; riconvocare (diplomat, parliament); (remember) rievocare

recap /'riːkæp/ vt/i 🔲 = recapitulate ● n ricapitolazione f

recapitulate /riːkə'pɪtjʊleɪt/ vt/i ricapitolare

re'capture /riː-/ vt riconquistare; ricatturare (person, animal)

rece|de /rɪ'siːd/ vi allontanarsi. ~ing adj (forehead, chin) sfuggente; have ~ing hair essere stempiato

receipt /rɪ'siːt/ n ricevuta f; (receiving) ricezione f; ~s pl (Comm) entrate fpl

receive /rɪ'siːv/ vt ricevere. ~r n (Teleph) ricevitore m; (Radio, TV) apparecchio m ricevente; (of stolen goods) ricettatore, -trice f

recent /'riːsnt/ adj recente. ~ly adv recentemente

reception /rɪ'sepʃn/ n ricevimento m; (welcome) accoglienza f; (Radio) ricezione f; ~ [desk] (in hotel) reception f inv. ~ist n persona f alla reception

receptive /rɪ'septɪv/ adj ricettivo

recess /rɪ'ses/ n rientranza f; (holiday) vacanza f; Am (Sch) intervallo m

recession /rɪ'seʃn/ n recessione f

re'charge /riː-/ vt ricaricare

recipe /'resəpɪ/ n ricetta f

recipient /rɪ'sɪpɪənt/ n (of letter) destinatario, -a mf; (of money) beneficiario, -a mf

recital /rɪ'saɪtl/ n recital m inv

recite /rɪ'saɪt/ vt recitare; (list) elencare

reckless /'reklɪs/ adj (action, decision) sconsiderato; be a ~ driver guidare in modo spericolato. ~ly adv in modo sconsiderato. ~ness n

reckon /'rekən/ vt calcolare; (consider) pensare. □ ~ on/with vt fare i conti con

re'claim /rɪ-/ vt reclamare; bonificare (land)

reclin|e /rɪ'klaɪn/ vi sdraiarsi. ~ing adj (seat) reclinabile

recluse /rɪ'kluːs/ n recluso, -a mf

recognition /rekəg'nɪʃn/ n riconoscimento m; beyond ~ irriconoscibile

recognize /'rekəgnaɪz/ vt riconoscere

re'coil /rɪ-/ vi (in fear) indietreggiare

recollect /rekə'lekt/ vt ricordare. ~ion n ricordo m

recommend /rekə'mend/ vt raccomandare. ~ation n raccomandazione f

recon|cile /'rekənsaɪl/ vt riconciliare; conciliare (facts); ~cile oneself to rassegnarsi a. ~ciliation n riconciliazione f

reconnaissance /rɪ'kɒnɪsns/ n (Mil) ricognizione f

reconnoitre /rekə'nɔɪtə(r)/ vi (pres p -tring) fare una ricognizione

recon'sider /riː-/ vt riconsiderare

recon'struct /riː-/ vt ricostruire. ~ion n ricostruzione f

record[1] /rɪ'kɔːd/ vt registrare; (make a note of) annotare

record[2] /'rekɔːd/ n (file) documentazione f; (Mus) disco m; (Sport) record m inv; ~s pl (files) schedario msg; keep a ~ of tener nota di; off the ~ in via ufficiosa; have a [criminal] ~ avere la fedina penale sporca

recorder /rɪ'kɔːdə(r)/ n (Mus) flauto m dolce

recording /rɪ'kɔːdɪŋ/ n registrazione f

'record-player n giradischi m inv

recount /rɪ'kaʊnt/ vt raccontare

re-'count[1] /riː-/ vt ricontare

'**re-count**[2] /ˈriː-/ n (Pol) nuovo conteggio m

recover /rɪˈkʌvə(r)/ vt/i recuperare. ~y n recupero m; (of health) guarigione f

re-'cover /riː-/ vt rifoderare

recreation /rekrɪˈeɪʃn/ n ricreazione f. ~al adj ricreativo

recruit /rɪˈkruːt/ n (Mil) recluta f; new ~ (member) nuovo, -a adepto, -a mf; (worker) neoassunto, -a mf ● vt assumere (staff). ~ment n assunzione f

rectangle /ˈrektæŋgl/ n rettangolo m. ~ular adj rettangolare

rectify /ˈrektɪfaɪ/ vt (pt/pp -ied) rettificare

recuperate /rɪˈkuːpəreɪt/ vi ristabilirsi

recur /rɪˈkɜː(r)/ vi (pt/pp recurred) ricorrere; (illness:) ripresentarsi

recurren|ce /rɪˈkʌrəns/ n ricorrenza f; (of illness) ricomparsa f. ~t adj ricorrente

recycle /riːˈsaɪkl/ vt riciclare

red /red/ adj (redder, reddest) rosso ● n rosso m; in the ~ (account) scoperto. R~ Cross n Croce f rossa

redd|en /ˈredn/ vt arrossare ● vi arrossire. ~ish adj rossastro

re'decorate /riː-/ vt (paint) ridipingere; (wallpaper) ritappezzare

redeem /rɪˈdiːm/ vt ~ing quality unico aspetto m positivo

redemption /rɪˈdempʃn/ n riscatto m

red: ~-haired adj con i capelli rossi. ~-handed adj catch sb ~-handed cogliere qcno con le mani nel sacco. ~ herring n diversione f. ~-hot adj rovente

red: ~ light n (Auto) semaforo m rosso

re'double /riː-/ vt raddoppiare

red tape n ⊞ burocrazia f

reduc|e /rɪˈdjuːs/ vt ridurre; (Culin)

far consumare. ~tion n riduzione f

redundan|cy /rɪˈdʌndənsɪ/ n licenziamento m; (payment) cassa f integrazione. ~t adj superfluo; make ~t licenziare; be made ~t essere licenziato

reed /riːd/ n (Bot) canna f

reef /riːf/ n scogliera f

reek /riːk/ vi puzzare (of di)

reel /riːl/ n bobina f ● vi (stagger) vacillare. □ ~ off vt fig snocciolare

refectory /rɪˈfektərɪ/ n refettorio m; (Univ) mensa f universitaria

refer /rɪˈfɜː(r)/ v (pt/pp referred) ● vt rinviare (matter) (to a); indirizzare (person) ● vi ~ to fare allusione a; (consult) rivolgersi a (book)

referee /refəˈriː/ n arbitro m; (for job) garante mf ● vt/i (pt/pp refereed) arbitrare

reference /ˈrefərəns/ n riferimento m; (in book) nota f bibliografica; (for job) referenza f; (Comm) 'your ~' 'riferimento'; with ~ to con riferimento a; make [a] ~ to fare riferimento a. ~ book n libro m di consultazione. ~ number n numero m di riferimento

referendum /refəˈrendəm/ n referendum m inv

re'fill[1] /riː-/ vt riempire di nuovo; ricaricare (pen, lighter)

'**refill**[2] /ˈriː-/ n (for pen) ricambio m

refine /rɪˈfaɪn/ vt raffinare. ~d adj raffinato. ~ment n raffinatezza f; (Techn) raffinazione f. ~ry n raffineria f

reflect /rɪˈflekt/ vt riflettere; be ~ed in essere riflesso in ● vi (think) riflettere (on su); ~ badly on sb fig mettere in cattiva luce qcno. ~ion n riflessione f; (image) riflesso m; on ~ion dopo riflessione. ~ive adj riflessivo. ~or n riflettore m

reflex /ˈriːfleks/ n riflesso m ● attrib di riflesso

reflexive /rɪˈfleksɪv/ adj riflessivo

reform /rɪ'fɔːm/ n riforma f ● vt riformare ● vi correggersi. R∼ation n (Relig) riforma f. ∼er n riformatore, -trice mf

refrain[1] /rɪ'freɪn/ n ritornello m

refrain[2] vi astenersi (from da)

refresh /rɪ'freʃ/ vt rinfrescare. ∼ing adj rinfrescante. ∼ments npl rinfreschi mpl

refrigerat|e /rɪ'frɪdʒəreɪt/ vt conservare in frigo. ∼or n frigorifero m

re'fuel /riː-/ v (pt/pp -fuelled) ● vt rifornire (di carburante) ● vi fare rifornimento

refuge /'refjuːdʒ/ n rifugio m; take ∼ rifugiarsi

refugee /refjʊ'dʒiː/ n rifugiato, -a mf

'refund[1] /'riː-/ n rimborso m

re'fund[2] /rɪ-/ vt rimborsare

refusal /rɪ'fjuːzl/ n rifiuto m

refuse[1] /rɪ'fjuːz/ vt/i rifiutare; ∼ to do sth rifiutare di fare qcsa

refuse[2] /'refjuːs/ n rifiuti mpl. ∼ collection n raccolta f dei rifiuti

refute /rɪ'fjuːt/ vt confutare

re'gain /rɪ-/ vt riconquistare

regal /'riːgl/ adj regale

regard /rɪ'gɑːd/ n (heed) riguardo m; (respect) considerazione f; ∼s pl saluti mpl; send/give my ∼s to your brother salutami tuo fratello ● vt (consider) considerare (as come); as ∼s riguardo a. ∼ing prep riguardo a. ∼less adv lo stesso; ∼less of senza badare a

regatta /rɪ'gætə/ n regata f

regime /reɪ'ʒiːm/ n regime m

regiment /'redʒɪmənt/ n reggimento m. ∼al adj reggimentale. ∼ation n irreggimentazione f

region /'riːdʒən/ n regione f; in the ∼ of fig approssimativamente. ∼al adj regionale

register /'redʒɪstə(r)/ n registro m ● vt registrare; mandare per raccomandata (letter); assicurare (luggage); immatricolare (vehicle); mostrare (feeling) ● vi (instrument:) funzionare; (student:) iscriversi (for a); ∼ with iscriversi nella lista di (doctor)

registrar /redʒɪ'strɑː(r)/ n ufficiale m di stato civile

registration /redʒɪ'streɪʃn/ n (of vehicle) immatricolazione f; (of letter) raccomandazione f; (of luggage) assicurazione f; (for course) iscrizione f. ∼ number n (Auto) targa f

registry office /'redʒɪstrɪ-/ n anagrafe f

regret /rɪ'gret/ n rammarico m ● vt (pt/pp regretted) rimpiangere; I ∼ that mi rincresce che. ∼fully adv con rammarico

regrettab|le /rɪ'gretəbl/ adj spiacevole. ∼ly adv spiacevolmente; (before adjective) deplorevolmente

regular /'regjʊlə(r)/ adj regolare; (usual) abituale ● n cliente mf abituale. ∼ity n regolarità f. ∼ly adv regolarmente

regulat|e /'regjʊleɪt/ vt regolare. ∼ion n (rule) regolamento m

rehears|al /rɪ'hɜːsl/ n (Theat) prova f. ∼e vt/i provare

reign /reɪn/ n regno m ● vi regnare

reinforce /riːɪn'fɔːs/ vt rinforzare. ∼d 'concrete n cemento m armato. ∼ment n rinforzo m

reiterate /riː'ɪtəreɪt/ vt reiterare

reject /rɪ'dʒekt/ vt rifiutare. ∼ion n rifiuto m; (Med) rigetto m

rejoic|e /rɪ'dʒɔɪs/ vi liter rallegrarsi. ∼ing n gioia f

rejuvenate /rɪ'dʒuːvəneɪt/ vt ringiovanire

relapse /rɪ'læps/ n ricaduta f ● vi ricadere

relate /rɪ'leɪt/ vt (tell) riportare; (connect) collegare ● vi ∼ to riferirsi a; identificarsi con (person). ∼d adj imparentato (to a); (ideas etc) affine

r

relation /rɪˈleɪʃn/ n rapporto m; (person) parente mf. ∼ship n rapporto m (blood tie) parentela f; (affair) relazione f

relative /ˈrelətɪv/ n parente mf ●adj relativo. ∼ly adv relativamente

relax /rɪˈlæks/ vt rilassare; allentare (pace, grip) ●vi rilassarsi. ∼ation n rilassamento m, relax m inv; (recreation) svago m. ∼ing adj rilassante

relay[1] /ˈriːleɪ/ vt ritrasmettere; (Radio, TV) trasmettere

relay[2] /ˈriːleɪ/ n (Electr) relais m inv; work in ∼s fare i turni. ∼ [race] n [corsa f a] staffetta f

release /rɪˈliːs/ n rilascio m; (of film) distribuzione f ●vt liberare; lasciare (hand); togliere (brake); distribuire (film); rilasciare (information etc)

relegate /ˈreligeɪt/ vt relegare; be ∼d (Sport) essere retrocesso

relent /rɪˈlent/ vi cedere. ∼less adj inflessibile; (unceasing) incessante. ∼lessly adv incessantemente

relevan|ce /ˈreləvəns/ n pertinenza f. ∼t adj pertinente (to p)

reliab|ility /rɪlaɪəˈbɪlətɪ/ n affidabilità f. ∼le adj affidabile a. ∼ly adv in modo affidabile; be ∼ly informed sapere da fonte certa

relian|ce /rɪˈlaɪəns/ n fiducia f (on in). ∼t adj fiducioso (on in)

relic /ˈrelik/ n (Relig) reliquia f; ∼s npl resti mpl

relief /rɪˈliːf/ n sollievo m; (assistance) soccorso m; (distraction) diversivo m; (replacement) cambio m; (in art) rilievo m; in ∼ in rilievo. ∼ map n carta f in rilievo. ∼ train n treno m supplementare

relieve /rɪˈliːv/ vt alleviare; (take over from) dare il cambio a; ∼ of liberare da (burden)

religion /rɪˈlɪdʒən/ n religione f

religious /rɪˈlɪdʒəs/ adj religioso. ∼ly adv (conscientiously) scrupolosamente

relinquish /rɪˈlɪŋkwɪʃ/ vt abbandonare; ∼ sth to sb rinunciare a qcsa in favore di qcno

relish /ˈrelɪʃ/ n gusto m; (Culin) salsa f ●vt fig apprezzare

reluctan|ce /rɪˈlʌktəns/ n riluttanza f. ∼t adj riluttante. ∼tly adv a malincuore

rely /rɪˈlaɪ/ vi (pt/pp -ied) ∼ on dipendere da; (trust) contare su

remain /rɪˈmeɪn/ vi restare. ∼der n resto m. ∼ing adj restante. ∼s npl (dead body) spoglie fpl

remand /rɪˈmɑːnd/ n on ∼ in custodia cautelare ●vt ∼ in custody rinviare con detenzione provvisoria

remark /rɪˈmɑːk/ n osservazione f ●vt osservare. ∼able adj notevole. ∼ably adv notevolmente

remarry /riːˈ-/ vi risposarsi

remedy /ˈremədɪ/ n rimedio m (for contro) ●vt (pt/pp -ied) rimediare a

remember /rɪˈmembə(r)/ vt ricordare, ricordarsi; ∼ to do sth ricordarsi di fare qcsa; ∼ me to him salutamelo ●vi ricordarsi

remind /rɪˈmaɪnd/ vt ∼ sb of sth ricordare qcsa a qcno. ∼er n ricordo m; (memo) promemoria m; (letter) lettera f di sollecito

reminisce /remɪˈnɪs/ vi rievocare il passato. ∼nces npl reminiscenze fpl. ∼nt adj be ∼ of richiamare alla memoria

remnant /ˈremnənt/ n resto m; (of material) scampolo m; (trace) traccia f

remorse /rɪˈmɔːs/ n rimorso m. ∼ful adj pieno di rimorso. ∼less adj spietato. ∼lessly adv senza pietà

remote /rɪˈməʊt/ adj remoto; (slight) minimo. ∼ access n (Comput) accesso m remoto. ∼ con'trol n telecomando m. ∼con'trolled adj telecomandato. ∼ly adv lontanamente; be not ∼ly... non essere lontanamente...

re'movable /riː-/ adj rimovibile

removal /rɪˈmuːvl/ n rimozione f;

(*from house*) trasloco m. ~ **van** n camion m inv da trasloco

remove /rɪˈmuːv/ vt togliere; togliersi (*clothes*); eliminare (*stain, doubts*)

render /ˈrendə(r)/ vt rendere (*service*)

renegade /ˈrenɪɡeɪd/ n rinnegato, -a mf

renew /rɪˈnjuː/ vt rinnovare (*contract*). ~**al** n rinnovo m

renounce /rɪˈnaʊns/ vt rinunciare a

renovat|e /ˈrenəveɪt/ vt rinnovare. ~**ion** n rinnovo m

renown /rɪˈnaʊn/ n fama f. ~**ed** adj rinomato

rent /rent/ n affitto ● vt affittare; ~ [**out**] dare in affitto. ~**al** n affitto m

renunciation /rɪnʌnsɪˈeɪʃn/ n rinuncia f

re'open /riː-/ vt/i riaprire

re'organize /riː-/ vt riorganizzare

rep /rep/ n (*Comm*) 🔲 rappresentante mf; (*Theat*) ≈ teatro m stabile

repair /rɪˈpeə(r)/ n riparazione f; in good/bad ≈ in cattive/buone condizioni ● vt riparare

repatriat|e /riːˈpætrɪeɪt/ vt rimpatriare. ~**ion** n rimpatrio m

re'pay /riː-/ vt (*pt/pp* -**paid**) ripagare. ~**ment** n rimborso m

repeal /rɪˈpiːl/ n abrogazione f ● vt abrogare

repeat /rɪˈpiːt/ n (*TV*) replica f ● vt/i ripetere; ~ **oneself** ripetersi. ~**ed** adj ripetuto. ~**edly** adv ripetutamente

repel /rɪˈpel/ vt (*pt/pp* repelled) respingere; *fig* ripugnare. ~**lent** adj ripulsivo

repent /rɪˈpent/ vi pentirsi. ~**ance** n pentimento m. ~**ant** adj pentito

repertoire /ˈrepətwɑː(r)/ n repertorio m

repetit|ion /repɪˈtɪʃn/ n ripetizione

f. ~**ive** adj ripetitivo

re'place /rɪ-/ vt (*put back*) rimettere a posto; (*take the place of*) sostituire; ~ **sth with sth** sostituire qcsa con qcsa. ~**ment** n sostituzione m; (*person*) sostituto, -a mf. ~**ment part** n pezzo m di ricambio

'replay /ˈriː-/ n (*Sport*) partita f ripetuta; [*action*] ≈ replay m inv

replenish /rɪˈplenɪʃ/ vt rifornire (*stocks*); (*refill*) riempire di nuovo

replica /ˈreplɪkə/ n copia f

reply /rɪˈplaɪ/ n risposta f (*to* a) ● vt/i (*pt/pp* replied) rispondere

report /rɪˈpɔːt/ n rapporto m; (*TV, Radio*) servizio m; (*Journ*) cronaca f; (*Sch*) pagella f; (*rumour*) diceria f ● vt riportare; ~ **sb to the police** denunciare qcno alla polizia ● vi riportare; (*present oneself*) presentarsi (*to* a). ~**edly** adv secondo quanto si dice. ~**er** n cronista mf, reporter mf inv

reprehensible /reprɪˈhensəbl/ adj riprovevole

represent /reprɪˈzent/ vt rappresentare

representative /reprɪˈzentətɪv/ adj rappresentativo ● n rappresentante mf

repress /rɪˈpres/ vt reprimere. ~**ion** n repressione f. ~**ive** adj repressivo

reprieve /rɪˈpriːv/ n commutazione f della pena capitale; (*postponement*) sospensione f della pena capitale; *fig* tregua f ● vt sospendere la sentenza a; *fig* risparmiare

reprimand /ˈreprɪmɑːnd/ n rimprovero m ● vt rimproverare

reprisal /rɪˈpraɪzl/ n rappresaglia f; in ~ **for** per rappresaglia contro

reproach /rɪˈprəʊtʃ/ n ammonimento m ● vt ammonire. ~**ful** adj riprovevole. ~**fully** adv con aria di rimprovero

repro'duc|e /riː-/ vt riprodurre ● vi

riprodursi. ~tion n riproduzione f.
~tive adj riproduttivo

reprove /rɪ'pruːv/ vt rimproverare

reptile /'reptaɪl/ n rettile m

republic /rɪ'pʌblɪk/ n repubblica f.
~an adj repubblicano ● n repubblicano, -a f

repugnan|ce /rɪ'pʌgnəns/ n ripugnanza f. ~t adj ripugnante

repuls|ion /rɪ'pʌlʃn/ n repulsione f.
~ive adj ripugnante

reputable /'repjʊtəbl/ adj affidabile

reputation /repjʊ'teɪʃn/ n reputazione f

request /rɪ'kwest/ n richiesta f ● vt
richiedere. ~ stop n fermata f a richiesta

require /rɪ'kwaɪə(r)/ vt (need) necessitare di; (demand) esigere. ~d adj
richiesto; I am ~d to do è esige
che io faccia. ~ment n esigenza f;
(condition) requisito m

rescue /'reskjuː/ n salvataggio m
● vt salvare. ~r n salvatore, -trice mf

research /rɪ'sɜːtʃ/ n ricerca f ● vt
fare ricerche su. (Journ) fare un'inchiesta su ● vi ~ into fare ricerche
su. ~er n ricercatore, -trice mf

resem|blance /rɪ'zembləns/ n rassomiglianza f. ~ble vt rassomigliare a

resent /rɪ'zent/ vt risentirsi per.
~ful adj pieno di risentimento.
~fully adv con risentimento. ~ment
n risentimento m

reservation /rezə'veɪʃn/ n (booking) prenotazione f; (doubt, enclosure)
riserva f

reserve /rɪ'zɜːv/ n riserva f; (shyness) riserbo m ● vt riservare; riservarsi (right). ~d adj riservato

reservoir /'rezəvwɑː(r)/ n bacino m
idrico

re'shuffle /riː-/ n (Pol) rimpasto m
● vt (Pol) rimpastare

residence /'rezɪdəns/ n residenza f;
(stay) soggiorno m. ~ permit n permesso m di soggiorno

resident /'rezɪdənt/ adj residente
● n residente mf. ~ial adj residenziale

residue /'rezɪdjuː/ n residuo m

resign /rɪ'zaɪn/ vt dimettersi da; ~
oneself to rassegnarsi a ● vi dare le
dimissioni. ~ation n rassegnazione
f; (from job) dimissioni fpl. ~ed adj
rassegnato

resilient /rɪ'zɪlɪənt/ adj elastico; fig
con buone capacità di ripresa

resin /'rezɪn/ n resina f

resist /rɪ'zɪst/ vt resistere a ● vi resistere. ~ance n resistenza f. ~ant adj
resistente

resolut|e /'rezəluːt/ adj risoluto.
~ely adv con risolutezza. ~ion n risolutezza f

resolve /rɪ'zɒlv/ vt ~ to do decidere di fare

resort /rɪ'zɔːt/ n (place) luogo m di
villeggiatura; **as a last** ~ come ultima risorsa ● vi ~ to ricorrere a

resource /rɪ'sɔːs/ n ~s pl risorse
fpl. ~ful adj pieno di risorse; (solution) ingegnoso. ~fulness n ingegnosità f inv

respect /rɪ'spekt/ n rispetto m; (aspect) aspetto m; **with** ~ **to** per
quanto riguarda ● vt rispettare

respect|able /rɪ'spektəbl/ adj rispettabile. ~ably adv rispettabilmente. ~ful adj rispettoso

respective /rɪ'spektɪv/ adj rispettivo. ~ly adv rispettivamente

respiration /respɪ'reɪʃn/ n respirazione f

respite /'respaɪt/ n respiro m

respond /rɪ'spɒnd/ vi rispondere;
(react) reagire (to a); (patient:) rispondere (to a)

response /rɪ'spɒns/ n risposta f;
(reaction) reazione f

responsibility /rɪspɒnsɪ'bɪlətɪ/ n
responsabilità f inv

responsib|le /rɪ'spɒnsəbl/ adj responsabile; (job) impegnativo

responsive /rɪˈspɒnsɪv/ adj ~ (audience etc:) reagire; (brakes:) essere sensibile

rest¹ /rest/ n riposo m; (Mus) pausa f; have a ~ riposarsi ● vt riposare; (lean) appoggiare (on su); (place) appoggiare ● vi riposarsi; (elbows:) appoggiarsi; (hopes:) riposare

rest² n the ~ il resto m; (people) gli altri mpl ● vi it ~s with you sta a te

restaurant /ˈrestərɒnt/ n ristorante m. ~ car n vagone m ristorante

restful /ˈrestfl/ adj riposante

restive /ˈrestɪv/ adj irrequieto

restless /ˈrestlɪs/ adj nervoso

restoration /restəˈreɪʃn/ n (of building) restauro m

restore /rɪˈstɔː(r)/ vt ristabilire; restaurare (building); (give back) restituire

restrain /rɪˈstreɪn/ vt trattenere; ~ oneself controllarsi. ~ed adj controllato. ~t n restrizione f; (moderation) ritegno m

restrict /rɪˈstrɪkt/ vt limitare; ~ to limitarsi a. ~ion n limite m; (restraint) restrizione f. ~ive adj limitativo

'rest room n Am toilette f inv

result /rɪˈzʌlt/ n risultato m; as a ~ a causa (of di) ● vi ~ from risultare da; ~ in portare a

resume /rɪˈzjuːm/ vt/i riprendere

résumé /ˈrezjʊmeɪ/ n riassunto m; Am curriculum vitae m inv

resurrect /rezəˈrekt/ vt fig risuscitare. ~ion n the R~ion (Relig) la Risurrezione

resuscitat|e /rɪˈsʌsɪteɪt/ vt rianimare. ~ion n rianimazione f

retail /ˈriːteɪl/ n vendita f al minuto o al dettaglio ● adj & adv al minuto ● vt vendere al minuto ● vi ~ at essere venduto al pubblico al prezzo di. ~er n dettagliante mf

retain /rɪˈteɪn/ vt conservare; (hold back) trattenere

retaliat|e /rɪˈtælɪeɪt/ vi vendicarsi. ~ion n rappresaglia f; in ~ion for per rappresaglia contro

retarded /rɪˈtɑːdɪd/ adj ritardato

rethink /riːˈθɪŋk/ vt (pt/pp rethought) ripensare

reticen|ce /ˈretɪsəns/ n reticenza f. ~t adj reticente

retina /ˈretɪnə/ n retina f

retinue /ˈretɪnjuː/ n seguito m

retire /rɪˈtaɪə(r)/ vi andare in pensione; (withdraw) ritirarsi ● vt mandare in pensione (employee). ~d adj in pensione. ~ment n pensione f; since my ~ment da quando sono andato in pensione

retiring /rɪˈtaɪərɪŋ/ adj riservato

retort /rɪˈtɔːt/ n replica f ● vt ribattere

re'trace /riː-/ vt ripercorrere; ~ one's steps ritornare sui propri passi

retract /rɪˈtrækt/ vt ritirare; ritrattare (statement, evidence) ● vi ritrarsi

re'train /riː-/ vt riqualificare ● vi riqualificarsi

retreat /rɪˈtriːt/ n ritirata f; (place) ritiro m ● vi ritirarsi; (Mil) battere in ritirata

re'trial /riː-/ n nuovo processo m

retrieval /rɪˈtriːvl/ n recupero m

retrieve /rɪˈtriːv/ vt recuperare

retrograde /ˈretrəgreɪd/ adj retrogrado

retrospect /ˈretrəspekt/ n in ~ guardando indietro. ~ive adj retrospettivo; (legislation) retroattivo ● n retrospettiva f

return /rɪˈtɜːn/ n ritorno m; (giving back) restituzione f; (Comm) profitto m; (ticket) biglietto m di andata e ritorno; by ~ [of post] a stretto giro di posta; in ~ in cambio (for di); many happy ~s! cento di questi giorni\. ●vi ritornare ●vt (give back) restituire; ricambiare (affection, invitation); (put back) rimettere; (send back) mandare indietro; (elect) eleggere

return: ~ **match** n rivincita f. ~ **ticket** n biglietto m di andata e ritorno

reunion /riːˈjuːnjən/ n riunione f

reunite /riːjuːˈnaɪt/ vt riunire

rev /rev/ n (Auto), 🚗 giro m (di motore) ●v (pt/pp revved) ●vt ~ [up] far andare su di giri ●vi andare su di giri

reveal /rɪˈviːl/ vt rivelare; (dress:) scoprire. ~**ing** adj rivelatore; (dress) osé

revel /ˈrevl/ vi (pt/pp revelled) ~ in sth godere di qcsa

revelation /revəˈleɪʃn/ n rivelazione f

revelry /ˈrevlrɪ/ n baldoria f

revenge /rɪˈvendʒ/ n vendetta f; (Sport) rivincita f; take ~ vendicarsi ●vt vendicare

revenue /ˈrevənjuː/ n reddito m

revere /rɪˈvɪə(r)/ vt riverire. ~**nce** n riverenza f

Reverend /ˈrevərənd/ adj reverendo

reverent /ˈrevərənt/ adj riverente

reverse /rɪˈvɜːs/ adj opposto; in ~ order in ordine inverso ●n contrario m; (back) rovescio m; (Auto) marcia m indietro ●vt invertire; ~ the car into the garage entrare in garage a marcia indietro; ~ the charges (Teleph) fare una telefonata a carico ●vi (Auto) fare marcia indietro

revert /rɪˈvɜːt/ vi ~ to tornare a

review /rɪˈvjuː/ n (survey) rassegna f; (re-examination) riconsiderazione f; (Mil) rivista f; (of book, play) recensione f ●vt riesaminare (situation); (Mil) passare in rivista; recensire (book, play). ~**er** n critico, -a mf

revis|e /rɪˈvaɪz/ vt rivedere; (for exam) ripassare. ~**ion** n revisione f;

(for exam) ripasso m

revive /rɪˈvaɪv/ vt resuscitare; rianimare (person). ●vi riprendersi; (person:) rianimarsi

revolt /rɪˈvəʊlt/ n rivolta f ●vi ribellarsi ●vt rivoltare. ~**ing** adj rivoltante

revolution /revəˈluːʃn/ n rivoluzione f; (Auto) ~s per minute giri mpl al minuto. ~**ary** adj & n rivoluzionario, -a mf. ~**ize** vt rivoluzionare

revolve /rɪˈvɒlv/ vi ruotare; ~ around girare intorno

revolv|er /rɪˈvɒlvə(r)/ n rivoltella f, revolver m inv. ~**ing** adj ruotante

revue /rɪˈvjuː/ n rivista f

revulsion /rɪˈvʌlʃn/ n ripulsione f

reward /rɪˈwɔːd/ n ricompensa f ●vt ricompensare. ~**ing** adj gratificante

re'write /riː-/ vt (pt rewrote, pp rewritten) riscrivere

rhetoric /ˈretərɪk/ n retorica f. ~**al** adj retorico

rhinoceros /raɪˈnɒsərəs/ n rinoceronte m

rhubarb /ˈruːbɑːb/ n rabarbaro m

rhyme /raɪm/ n rima f; (poem) filastrocca f ●vi rimare

rhythm /ˈrɪðm/ n ritmo m. ~**ic[al]** adj ritmico. ~**ically** adv con ritmo

rib /rɪb/ n costola f

ribbon /ˈrɪbən/ n nastro m; in ~s a brandelli

rice /raɪs/ n riso m

rich /rɪtʃ/ adj ricco; (food) pesante ●n the ~ pl i ricchi mpl; ~**es** pl ricchezze fpl. ~**ly** adv riccamente; (deserve) largamente

ricochet /ˈrɪkəʃeɪ/ vi rimbalzare ●n rimbalzo m

rid /rɪd/ vt (pt/pp rid, pres p ridding) sbarazzare (of di); get ~ of sbarazzarsi di

riddance /ˈrɪdns/ n good ~! che liberazione!

ridden /ˈrɪdn/ ▷**RIDE**

riddle /ˈrɪdl/ n enigma m

ride /raɪd/ n (on horse) cavalcata f; (in vehicle) giro m; (journey) viaggio m; **take sb for a** ~ 🗊 prendere qcno in giro ● v (pt rode, pp ridden) ● vt montare (horse); andare su (bicycle) ● vi andare a cavallo; (jockey:) cavalcare; (cyclist:) andare in bicicletta; (in vehicle) viaggiare. ~**r** n cavallerizzo, -a mf; (in race) fantino m; (on bicycle) ciclista mf; (in document) postilla f

ridge /rɪdʒ/ n spigolo m; (on roof) punta f; (of mountain) cresta f

ridicule /'rɪdɪkjuːl/ n ridicolo m ● vt mettere in ridicolo

ridiculous /rɪ'dɪkjʊləs/ adj ridicolo

rife /raɪf/ adj be ~ essere diffuso; ~ **with** pieno di

rifle /'raɪfl/ n fucile m; ~**-range** tiro m al bersaglio ● vt ~ [through] mettere a soqquadro

rift /rɪft/ n fessura f; fig frattura f

rig¹ /rɪg/ n equipaggiamento m; (at sea) piattaforma f per trivellazioni subacquee ● **rig out** vt (pt/pp rigged) equipaggiare. □ ~ **up** vt allestire

rig² (pt/pp rigged) manovrare (election)

right /raɪt/ adj giusto; (not left) destro; be ~ (person:) aver ragione; (clock:) essere giusto; **put** ~ mettere all'ora (clock); correggere (person); rimediare a (situation); **that's** ~! proprio così ● adv (correctly) bene; (not left) a destra; (directly) proprio; (completely) completamente; ~ **away** immediatamente ● n giusto m; (not left) destra f; (what is due) diritto m; **on/to the** ~ a destra; **be in the** ~ essere nel giusto; **know** ~ **from wrong** distinguere il bene dal male; **by** ~**s** secondo giustizia; **the R**~ (Pol) la destra f ● vt raddrizzare; ~ **a wrong** fig riparare a un torto. ~ **angle** n angolo m retto

rightful /'raɪtfl/ adj legittimo

right: ~**-handed** adj che usa la mano destra. ~**-hand 'man** n fig braccio m destro

rightly /'raɪtlɪ/ adv giustamente

right: ~ **of way** n diritto m di transito; (path) passaggio m; (Auto) precedenza f. ~**'wing** adj (Pol) di destra ● n (Sport) ala f destra

rigid /'rɪdʒɪd/ adj rigido. ~**ity** n rigidità f inv

rigorous /'rɪgərəs/ adj rigoroso

rim /rɪm/ n bordo m; (of wheel) cerchione m

rind /raɪnd/ n (on fruit) scorza f; (on cheese) crosta f; (on bacon) cotenna f

ring¹ /rɪŋ/ n (circle) cerchio m; (on finger) anello m; (boxing) ring m inv; (for circus) pista f; **stand in a** ~ essere in cerchio

ring² n suono m; **give sb a** ~ (Teleph) dare un colpo di telefono a qcno ● v (pt rang, pp rung) ● vt suonare; ~ [**up**] (Teleph) telefonare a ● vi suonare; (Teleph) ~ [**up**] telefonare. □ ~ **back** vt/i (Teleph) richiamare. □ ~ **off** vi (Teleph) riattaccare

ring: ~**leader** n capobanda m. ~ **road** n circonvallazione f. ~**tone** n suoneria f

rink /rɪŋk/ n pista f di pattinaggio

rinse /rɪns/ n risciacquo m; (hair colour) cachet m inv ● vt sciacquare

riot /'raɪət/ n rissa f; (of colour) accozzaglia f; ~**s** pl disordini mpl; **run** ~ impazzare ● vi creare disordini. ~**er** n dimostrante mf. ~**ous** adj sfrenato

rip /rɪp/ n strappo m ● vt (pt/pp ripped) strappare; ~ **open** aprire con uno strappo. □ ~ **off** vt 🗊 fregare

ripe /raɪp/ adj maturo; (cheese) stagionato

ripen /'raɪpn/ vi maturare; (cheese:) stagionarsi ● vt far maturare; stagionare (cheese)

'rip-off n 🗊 frode f

ripple /'rɪpl/ n increspatura f; (sound) mormorio m

rise /raɪz/ n (of sun) levata f; (fig: to fame, power) ascesa f; (increase)

r

aumento m; give a ~ to dare adito a
●vi (pt rose, pp risen) alzarsi; (sun:)
sorgere; (dough:) lievitare; (prices,
water level:) aumentare; (to power,
position) arrivare (to a). ~r early
~r persona f mattiniera

rising /'raɪzɪŋ/ adj (sun) levante; ~
generation nuova generazione f ●n
(revolt) sollevazione f

risk /rɪsk/ n rischio m; at one's own
~ a proprio rischio e pericolo ●vt rischiare

risky /'rɪskɪ/ adj (-ier, -iest) rischioso

rite /raɪt/ n rito m; last ~s estrema
unzione f

ritual /'rɪtjʊəl/ adj rituale ●n rituale m

rival /'raɪvl/ adj rivale ●n rivale mf;
~s pl (Comm) concorrenti mpl ●vt (pt/
pp rivalled) rivaleggiare con. ~ry n
rivalità f inv; (Comm) concorrenza f

river /'rɪvə(r)/ n fiume m. ~-bed n
letto m del fiume

rivet /'rɪvɪt/ n rivetto m ●vt rivet-
tare; ~ed by fig inchiodato da

road /rəʊd/ n strada f, via f; be on
the ~ viaggiare

road: ~-map n carta f stradale.
~side n bordo m della strada.
~works npl lavori mpl stradali.
~worthy adj sicuro

roam /rəʊm/ vi girovagare

roar /rɔ:(r)/ n ruggito m; ~s of
laughter scroscio msg di risa ●vi rug-
gire; (lorry, thunder:) rombare; ~
with laughter ridere fragorosa-
mente. ~ing adj do a ~ing trade
⬚ fare affari d'oro

roast /rəʊst/ adj arrosto; ~ pork arrosto m di maiale ●n arrosto m ●vt
arrostire (meat) ●vi arrostirsi

rob /rɒb/ vt (pt/pp robbed) derubare
(of di); svaligiare (bank). ~ber n rapinatore m. ~bery n rapina f

robe /rəʊb/ n tunica f; (Am: bathrobe)
accappatoio m

robin /'rɒbɪn/ n pettirosso m

robot /'rəʊbɒt/ n robot m inv

robust /rəʊ'bʌst/ adj robusto

rock¹ /rɒk/ n roccia f; (in sea) scoglio m; (sweet) zucchero m candito.
on the ~s (ship) incagliato; (marriage) finito; (drink) con ghiaccio

rock² vt cullare (baby); (shake) far
traballare; (shock) scuotere ●vi don-
dolarsi

rock³ n (Mus) rock m inv

rock-'bottom adj bassissimo ●n
livello m più basso

rocket /'rɒkɪt/ n razzo m ●vi salire
alle stelle

rocky /'rɒkɪ/ adj (-ier, -iest) roccioso; fig traballante

rod /rɒd/ n bacchetta f; (for fishing)
canna f

rode /rəʊd/ ▷RIDE

rodent /'rəʊdnt/ n roditore m

rogue /rəʊg/ n farabutto m

role /rəʊl/ n ruolo m

roll /rəʊl/ n rotolo m; (bread) panino
m; (list) lista f; (of ship, drum) rullio m
●vi rotolare; be ~ing in money ⬚
nuotare nell'oro ●vt spianare (lawn,
pastry). □ ~ over vi rigirarsi. □ ~ up
vt arrotolare; rimboccarsi (sleeves)
●vi ⬚ arrivare

'roll-call n appello m

roller /'rəʊlə(r)/ n rullo m; (for hair)
bigodino m. ~ blades npl pattini npl
in linea. ~ blind n tapparella f.
~-coaster n montagne fpl russe.
~-skate n pattino m a rotelle

'rolling-pin n mattarello m

Roman /'rəʊmən/ adj romano ●n
romano, -a mf. ~ Catholic adj cattolico ●n cattolico, -a mf

romance /rəʊ'mæns/ n (love affair)
storia f d'amore; (book) romanzo m
rosa

Romania /rəʊ'meɪnɪə/ n Romania f.
~n adj rumeno ●n rumeno, -a mf

romantic /rəʊ'mæntɪk/ adj roman-

tico. ~**ally** adv romanticamente. ~**ism** n romanticismo m

Rome /rəʊm/ n Roma f

romp /rɒmp/ n gioco m rumoroso ● vi giocare rumorosamente. ~**ers** npl pagliaccetto msg

roof /ruːf/ n tetto m; (of mouth) palato m ● vt mettere un tetto su. ~**rack** n portabagagli m inv. ~**top** n tetto m

rook /rʊk/ n corvo m; (in chess) torre f

room /ruːm/ n stanza f; (bedroom) camera f; (for functions) sala f; (space) spazio m. ~**y** adj spazioso; (clothes) ampio

roost /ruːst/ vi appollaiarsi

root[1] /ruːt/ n radice f; **take** ~ mettere radici ● **root out** vt fig scovare

root[2] vi ~ **about** grufolare; ~ **for** sb Am 🛈 fare il tifo per qcno

rope /rəʊp/ n corda f; **know the** ~**s** 🛈 conoscere i trucchi del mestiere ● **rope in** vt 🛈 coinvolgere

rose[1] /rəʊz/ n rosa f; (of watering-can) bocchetta f

rose[2] ▷RISE

rosé /ˈrəʊzeɪ/ n [vino m] rosé m inv

rot /rɒt/ n marciume m; (🛈: nonsense) sciocchezze fpl ● vi (pt/pp rotted) marcire

rota /ˈrəʊtə/ n tabella f dei turni

rotary /ˈrəʊtərɪ/ adj rotante

rotat|**e** /rəʊˈteɪt/ vt far ruotare; avvicendare (crops) ● vi ruotare. ~**ion** n rotazione f; **in** ~**ion** a turno

rote /rəʊt/ n **by** ~ meccanicamente

rotten /ˈrɒtn/ adj marcio; 🛈 schifoso; (person) penoso

rough /rʌf/ adj (not smooth) ruvido; (ground) accidentato; (behaviour) rozzo; (sport) violento; (area) malfamato; (crossing, time) brutto; (estimate) approssimativo ● adv (play) grossolanamente; **sleep** ~ dormire sotto i

ponti ● vt ~ **it** vivere senza confort. □ ~ **out** vt abbozzare

roughage /ˈrʌfɪdʒ/ n fibre fpl

rough|**ly** /ˈrʌflɪ/ adv rozzamente; (more or less) pressappoco. ~**ness** n ruvidità f; (of behaviour) rozzezza f

roulette /ruːˈlet/ n roulette f inv

round /raʊnd/ adj rotondo ● n tondo m; (slice) fetta f; (of visits, drinks) giro m; (of competition) partita f; (boxing) ripresa f, round m inv; **do one's** ~**s** (doctor:) fare il giro delle visite ● prep intorno a; **open** ~ **the clock** aperto ventiquattr'ore ● adv **all** ~ tutt'intorno; **ask** sb ~ invitare qcno; **go/come** ~ **to** (a friend etc) andare da; **turn/look** ~ girarsi; ~ **about** (approximately) intorno a ● vt arrotondare; girare (corner). □ ~ **down** vt arrotondare (per difetto). □ ~ **off** vt (end) terminare. □ ~ **on** vt aggredire. □ ~ **up** vt radunare; arrotondare (prices)

roundabout /ˈraʊndəbaʊt/ adj indiretto ● n giostra f; (for traffic) rotonda f

round: ~ **trip** n viaggio m di andata e ritorno

rouse /raʊz/ vt svegliare; risvegliare (suspicion, interest). ~**ing** adj incoraggiamento

route /ruːt/ n itinerario m; (Aeron, Naut) rotta f; (of bus) percorso m

routine /ruːˈtiːn/ adj di routine ● n routine f inv; (Theat) numero m

row[1] /rəʊ/ n (line) fila f; **three years in a** ~ tre anni di fila

row[2] vi (in boat) remare

row[3] /raʊ/ n 🛈 (quarrel) litigata f; (noise) baccano m ● vi 🛈 litigare

rowdy /ˈraʊdɪ/ adj (-ier, -iest) chiassoso

rowing boat /ˈrəʊɪŋ-/ n barca f a remi

royal /ˈrɔɪəl/ adj reale

royal|**ty** /ˈrɔɪəltɪ/ n appartenenza f

alla famiglia reale; (persons) i membri mpl della famiglia reale. ~ies npl (payments) diritti mpl d'autore

rub /rʌb/ n give sth a ~ dare una sfregata a qcsa ●vt (pt/pp rubbed) sfregare. □ ~ **in** vt don't ~ it **in** 🔢 non rigirare il coltello nella piaga. □ ~ **off** vt mandar via sfregando (stain); (from blackboard) cancellare ●vi andar via; ~ **off on** essere trasmesso a. □ ~ **out** vt cancellare

rubber /'rʌbə(r)/ n gomma f; (eraser) gomma f [da cancellare]. ~ **band** n elastico m. ~**y** adj gommoso

rubbish /'rʌbɪʃ/ n immondizie fpl; (🔢: nonsense) idiozie fpl; (🔢: junk) robaccia f ●vt 🔢 fare a pezzi. ~ **bin** n pattumiera f. ~ **dump** n discarica f; (official) discarica f comunale

rubble /'rʌbl/ n macerie fpl

ruby /'ru:bɪ/ n rubino m ●attrib di rubini; (lips) scarlatta

rucksack /'rʌksæk/ n zaino m

rudder /'rʌdə(r)/ n timone m

rude /ru:d/ adj scortese; (improper) spinto. ~**ly** adv scortesemente. ~**ness** n scortesia f

ruffian /'rʌfiən/ n farabutto m

ruffle /'rʌfl/ n gala f ●vt scompigliare (hair)

rug /rʌg/ n tappeto m; (blanket) coperta f

rugby /'rʌgbɪ/ n [football] rugby m

rugged /'rʌgɪd/ adj (coastline) roccioso

ruin /'ru:ɪn/ n rovina f; **in** ~**s** in rovina ●vt rovinare. ~**ous** adj estremamente costoso

rule /ru:l/ n regola f; (control) ordinamento m; (for measuring) metro m; ~**s** regolamento msg; **as a** ~ generalmente ●vt governare; dominare (colony, behaviour); ~ **that** stabilire che ●vi governare. □ ~ **out** vt escludere

ruler /'ru:lə(r)/ n capo m di Stato; (sovereign) sovrano, -a mf; (measure) righello m, regolo m

ruling /'ru:lɪŋ/ adj (class) dirigente; (party) di governo ●n decisione f

rum /rʌm/ n rum m inv

rumble /'rʌmbl/ n rombo m; (of stomach) brontolio m ●vi rombare; (stomach:) brontolare

rummage /'rʌmɪdʒ/ vi rovistare (in/through in)

rumour /'ru:mə(r)/ n diceria f ●vt it is ~**ed that** si dice che

run /rʌn/ n (on foot) corsa f; (distance to be covered) tragitto m; (outing) giro m; (Theat) rappresentazioni fpl; (in skiing) pista f; (Am: ladder) smagliatura f (in calze); **at a** ~ di corsa; ~ **of bad luck** periodo m sfortunato; **on the** ~ in fuga; **have the** ~ **of** avere a disposizione; **in the long** ~ a lungo termine ●vi (pt **ran**, pp **run**, pres p **running**) correre; (river:) scorrere; (nose, make-up:) colare; (bus:) fare servizio; (play:) essere in cartellone; (colours:) sbiadire; (in election) presentarsi [come candidato] ●vt (manage) dirigere; tenere (house); (drive) dare un passaggio a; correre (risk); lanciare (Comput); pubblicare (article); (pass) far scorrere (eyes, hand); ~ **a bath** far scorrere l'acqua per il bagno. □ ~ **across** vi (meet, find) imbattersi in. □ ~ **away** vi scappare [via]. □ ~ **down** vi scaricarsi; (clock:) scaricarsi; (stocks:) esaurirsi ●vt (Auto) investire; (reduce) esaurire; (🔢: criticize) denigrare. □ ~ **in** vi entrare di corsa. □ ~ **into** vi (meet) imbattersi in; (knock against) urtare. □ ~ **off** vi andare via di corsa ●vt stampare (copies). □ ~ **out** vi uscire di corsa; (supplies, money:) esaurirsi; ~ **out of** rimanere senza. □ ~ **over** vi (overflow) traboccare ●vt (Auto) investire. □ ~ **through** vi scorrere. □ ~ **up** vi salire di corsa; (towards) arrivare di corsa ●vt accumulare (debts, bill);

(sew) cucire

'runaway n fuggitivo, -a mf

run-'down adj (area) in abbandono; (person) esaurito ●n analisi f

rung¹ /rʌŋ/ n (of ladder) piolo m

rung² ▷RING²

runner /'rʌnə(r)/ n podista mf; (in race) corridore, -trice mf; (on sledge) pattino m. ~ **bean** n fagiolino m. ~-**up** n secondo, -a mf classificato, -a

running /'rʌnɪŋ/ adj in corsa; (water) corrente; **four times** ~ quattro volte di seguito ●n corsa f; (management) direzione f; **be in the** ~ essere in lizza. ~ **'commentary** n cronaca f

runny /'rʌnɪ/ adj semiliquido; ~ **nose** naso che cola

runway n pista f

rupture /'rʌptʃə(r)/ n rottura f; (Med) ernia f ●vt rompere; ~ **one-self** farsi venire l'ernia ●vi rompersi

rural /'rʊərəl/ adj rurale

ruse /ruːz/ n astuzia f

rush¹ /rʌʃ/ n (Bot) giunco m

rush² n fretta f; **in a** ~ di fretta ●vi precipitarsi ●vt far premura a; ~ **sb to hospital** trasportare qcno di corsa all'ospedale. ~-**hour** n ora f di punta

Russia /'rʌʃə/ n Russia f. ~n adj & n russo, -a mf; (language) russo m

rust /rʌst/ n ruggine f ●vi arrugginirsi

rustle /'rʌsl/ vi frusciare ●vt far frusciare; Am rubare (cattle). □ ~ **up** vt 🄣 rimediare

'rustproof adj a prova di ruggine

rusty /'rʌstɪ/ adj (-ier, -iest) arrugginito

rut /rʌt/ n solco m; **in a** ~ 🄣 nella routine

ruthless /'ruːθlɪs/ adj spietato. ~ness n spietatezza f

rye /raɪ/ n segale f

sabot|age /'sæbətɑːʒ/ n sabotaggio m ●vt sabotare. ~**eur** n sabotatore, -trice mf

saccharin /'sæsərɪn/ n saccarina f

sachet /'sæʃeɪ/ n bustina f; (scented) sacchetto m profumato

sack¹ /sæk/ vt (plunder) saccheggiare

sack² n sacco m; **get the** ~ 🄣 essere licenziato ●vt 🄣 licenziare. ~**ing** n tela f per sacchi; (🄣: dismissal) licenziamento m

sacrament /'sækrəmənt/ n sacramento m

sacred /'seɪkrɪd/ adj sacro

sacrifice /'sækrɪfaɪs/ n sacrificio m ●vt sacrificare

sacrilege /'sækrɪlɪdʒ/ n sacrilegio m

sad /sæd/ adj (sadder, saddest) triste. ~**den** vt rattristare

saddle /'sædl/ n sella f ●vt sellare; **I've been ~d with**... fig mi hanno affibbiato...

sad|ly /'sædlɪ/ adv tristemente; (unfortunately) sfortunatamente. ~**ness** n tristezza f

safe /seɪf/ adj sicuro; (out of danger) salvo; (object) al sicuro; ~ **and sound** sano e salvo ●n cassaforte f. ~**guard** n protezione f ●vt proteggere. ~**ly** adv in modo sicuro; (arrive) senza incidenti; (assume) con certezza

safety /'seɪftɪ/ n sicurezza f. ~-**belt** n cintura f di sicurezza. ~-**deposit box** n cassetta f di sicurezza. ~-**pin** n spilla f di sicurezza o da balia. ~-**valve** n valvola f di sicurezza

sag /sæg/ vi (pt/pp sagged) abbassarsi

saga /'sɑːgə/ n saga f

sage /seɪdʒ/ n (herb) salvia f

Sagittarius /sædʒɪˈteərɪəs/ n Sagittario m

said /sed/ ▷ SAY

sail /seɪl/ n vela f; (trip) giro m in barca a vela ● vi navigare; (Sport) praticare la vela; (leave) salpare ● vt pilotare

sailing /ˈseɪlɪŋ/ n vela f. ∼-boat n barca f a vela. ∼-ship n veliero m

sailor /ˈseɪlə(r)/ n marinaio m

saint /seɪnt/ n santo, -a mf. ∼ly adj da santo

sake /seɪk/ n for the ∼ of (person) per il bene di; (peace) per amor di; for the ∼ of it per il gusto di farlo

salad /ˈsæləd/ n insalata f. ∼ bowl n insalatiera f. ∼ cream n salsa f per condire l'insalata. ∼-dressing n condimento m per insalata

salary /ˈsælərɪ/ n stipendio m

sale /seɪl/ n vendita f; (at reduced prices) svendita f; for/on ∼ in vendita

sales|man /ˈseɪlzmən/ n venditore m; (traveller) rappresentante m. ∼woman n venditrice f

saliva /səˈlaɪvə/ n saliva f

salmon /ˈsæmən/ n salmone m

saloon /səˈluːn/ n (Auto) berlina f; (Am: bar) bar m

salt /sɔːlt/ n sale m ● adj salato; (fish, meat) sotto sale ● vt salare; (cure) mettere sotto sale. ∼-cellar n saliera f. ∼ 'water n acqua f di mare. ∼y adj salato

salute /səˈluːt/ (Mil) n saluto m ● vt salutare ● vi fare il saluto

salvage /ˈsælvɪdʒ/ n (Naut) recupero m ● vt recuperare

salvation /sælˈveɪʃn/ n salvezza f. S∼ 'Army n Esercito m della Salvezza

same /seɪm/ adj stesso (as di) ● pron the ∼ lo stesso; all the ∼ essere tutti uguali ● adv the ∼ nello stesso

modo; all the ∼ (however) lo stesso; the ∼ to you altrettanto

sample /ˈsɑːmpl/ n campione m ● vt testare

sanction /ˈsæŋkʃn/ n (approval) autorizzazione f; (penalty) sanzione f ● vt autorizzare

sanctuary /ˈsæŋktjʊərɪ/ n (Relig) santuario m; (refuge) asilo m; (for wildlife) riserva f

sand /sænd/ n sabbia f ● vt ∼ [down] carteggiare

sandal /ˈsændl/ n sandalo m

sandpaper /ˈsændpeɪpə/ n carta f vetrata ● vt cartavetrare

sandwich /ˈsænwɪdʒ/ n tramezzino m ● vt ∼ed between schiacciato tra

sandy /ˈsændɪ/ adj (-ier, -iest) (beach, soil) sabbioso; (hair) biondiccio

sane /seɪn/ adj (not mad) sano di mente; (sensible) sensato

sang /sæŋ/ ▷ SING

sanitary /ˈsænɪtərɪ/ adj igienico; (system) sanitario. ∼ napkin n Am, ∼ towel n assorbente m igienico

sanitation /sænɪˈteɪʃn/ n impianti mpl igienici

sanity /ˈsænɪtɪ/ n sanità f inv di mente; (common sense) buon senso m

sank /sæŋk/ ▷ SINK

sapphire /ˈsæfaɪə(r)/ n zaffiro m ● adj blu zaffiro

sarcas|m /ˈsɑːkæzm/ n sarcasmo m. ∼tic adj sarcastico

sardine /sɑːˈdiːn/ n sardina f

sash /sæʃ/ n fascia f; (for dress) fusciacca f

sat /sæt/ ▷ SIT

satchel /ˈsætʃl/ n cartella f

satellite /ˈsætəlaɪt/ n satellite m. ∼ dish n antenna f parabolica. ∼ television n televisione f via satellite

satin /ˈsætɪn/ n raso m ● attrib di raso

satire /ˈsætaɪə(r)/ n satira f

satirical /səˈtɪrɪkl/ adj satirico

satisfaction /ˌsætɪsˈfækʃn/ n soddisfazione f; **to be to sb's ~** soddisfare qcno

satisfactor|y /sætɪsˈfæktərɪ/ adj soddisfacente. **~ily** adv in modo soddisfacente

satisf|y /ˈsætɪsfaɪ/ vt (pt/pp -fied) soddisfare; (convince) convincere; **be ~ied** essere soddisfatto. **~ying** adj soddisfacente

satphone /ˈsætfəʊn/ n telefono m satellitare

saturat|e /ˈsætʃəreɪt/ vt inzuppare (with di); (Chem), fig saturare (with di). **~ed** adj saturo

Saturday /ˈsætədeɪ/ n sabato m

sauce /sɔːs/ n salsa f; (cheek) impertinenza f. **~pan** n pentola f

saucer /ˈsɔːsə(r)/ n piattino m

saucy /ˈsɔːsɪ/ adj (-ier, -iest) impertinente

Saudi Arabia /saʊdɪəˈreɪbɪə/ n Arabia f Saudita

sauna /ˈsɔːnə/ n sauna f

saunter /ˈsɔːntə(r)/ vi andare a spasso

sausage /ˈsɒsɪdʒ/ n salsiccia f; (dried) salame m

savage /ˈsævɪdʒ/ adj feroce; (tribe, custom) selvaggio ●n selvaggio, -a mf ●vt fare a pezzi. **~ry** n ferocia f

save /seɪv/ n (Sport) parata f ●vt salvare (from da); (keep, collect) tenere; risparmiare (time, money); (avoid) evitare; (Sport) parare (goal); (Comput) salvare, memorizzare ●vi ~ [up] risparmiare ●prep salvo

saver /ˈseɪvə(r)/ n risparmiatore, -trice mf

savings /ˈseɪvɪŋz/ npl (money) risparmi mpl. **~ account** n libretto m di risparmio. **~ bank** n cassa f di risparmio

saviour /ˈseɪvjə(r)/ n salvatore m

savour /ˈseɪvə(r)/ n sapore m ●vt

assaporare. **~y** adj salato; fig rispettabile

saw[1] /sɔː/ see see[1]

saw[2] n sega f ●vt/i (pt sawed, pp sawn or sawed) segare. **~dust** n segatura f

saxophone /ˈsæksəfəʊn/ n sassofono m

say /seɪ/ n **have one's ~** dire la propria; **have a ~** avere voce in capitolo ●vt/i (pt/pp said) dire; **that is to ~** cioè; **that goes without ~ing** questo è ovvio; **when all is said and done** alla fine dei conti. **~ing** n proverbio m

scab /skæb/ n crosta f; pej crumiro m

scald /skɔːld/ vt scottare; (milk) scaldare ●n scottatura f

scale[1] /skeɪl/ n (of fish) scaglia f

scale[2] n scala f; **on a grand ~** su vasta scala ●vt (climb) scalare. □ **~ down** vt diminuire

scales /skeɪlz/ npl (for weighing) bilancia fsg

scalp /skælp/ n cuoio m capelluto

scamper /ˈskæmpə(r)/ vi **~ away** sgattaiolare via

scan /skæn/ n (Med) scanning m inv, scansioscintigrafia f ●vt (pt/pp scanned) scrutare; (quickly) dare una scorsa a; (Med) fare uno scanning di

scandal /ˈskændl/ n scandalo m; (gossip) pettegolezzi mpl. **~ize** vt scandalizzare. **~ous** adj scandaloso

Scandinavia /skændɪˈneɪvɪə/ n Scandinavia f. **~n** adj & n scandinavo, -a mf

scanner /ˈskænə(r)/ n (Comput) scanner m inv

scant /skænt/ adj scarso

scant|y /ˈskæntɪ/ adj (-ier, -iest) scarso; (clothing) succinto. **~ily** adv scarsamente; (clothed) succintamente

scapegoat /ˈskeɪp-/ n capro m

espiatorio

scar /skɑ:(r)/ n cicatrice f ● vt (pt/pp scarred) lasciare una cicatrice a

scarc|e /skeəs/ adj scarso; fig raro; make oneself ~e 🔢 svignarsela. ~ely adv appena; ~ely anything quasi niente. ~ity n scarsezza f

scare /skeə(r)/ n spavento m; (panic) panico m ● vt spaventare; be ~d aver paura (of di)

'**scarecrow** n spaventapasseri m inv

scarf /skɑ:f/ n (pl **scarves**) sciarpa f; (square) foulard m inv

scarlet /ˈskɑ:lət/ adj scarlatto. ~ 'fever n scarlattina f

scary /ˈskeəri/ adj be ~ far paura

scathing /ˈskeɪðɪŋ/ adj mordace

scatter /ˈskætə(r)/ vt spargere; (disperse) disperdere ● vi disperdersi. ~-brained adj 🔢 scervellato. ~ed adj sparso

scavenge /ˈskævɪndʒ/ vi frugare nella spazzatura. ~r n persona f che fruga nella spazzatura

scenario /sɪˈnɑ:rɪəʊ/ n scenario m

scene /si:n/ n scena f; (quarrel) scenata f; behind the ~s dietro le quinte

scenery /ˈsi:nəri/ n scenario m

scenic /ˈsi:nɪk/ adj panoramico

scent /sent/ n odore m; (trail) scia f; (perfume) profumo m. ~ed adj profumato (with di)

sceptic|al /ˈskeptɪkl/ adj scettico. ~ism n scetticismo m

schedule /ˈʃedju:l/ n piano m, programma m; (of work) programma m; (timetable) orario m; behind ~ indietro; on ~ nei tempi previsti; according to ~ secondo i tempi previsti ● vt prevedere. ~d flight n volo m di linea

scheme /ski:m/ n (plan) piano m; (plot) macchinazione f ● vi pej macchinare

scholar /ˈskɒlə(r)/ n studioso, -a mf. ~ly adj erudito. ~ship n erudizione f; (grant) borsa f di studio

school /sku:l/ n scuola f; (in university) facoltà f; (of fish) branco m

school: ~boy n scolaro m. ~girl n scolara f. ~ing n istruzione f. ~-teacher n insegnante mf

sciatica /saɪˈætɪkə/ n sciatica f

scien|ce /ˈsaɪəns/ n scienza f; ~ce fiction fantascienza f. ~tific adj scientifico. ~tist n scienziato, -a mf

scissors /ˈsɪzəz/ npl forbici fpl

scoff¹ /skɒf/ vi ~ at schernire

scoff² vt 🔢 divorare

scold /skəʊld/ vt sgridare. ~ing n sgridata f

scoop /sku:p/ n paletta f; (Journ) scoop m inv ● **scoop out** vt svuotare. □ ~ **up** vt tirar su

scope /skəʊp/ n portata f; (opportunity) opportunità f inv

scorch /skɔ:tʃ/ vt bruciare. ~er n 🔢 giornata f torrida. ~ing adj caldissimo

score /skɔ:(r)/ n punteggio m; (individual) punteggio m; (Mus) partitura f; (for film, play) musica f; a ~ [of] (twenty) una ventina [di]; keep [the] ~ tenere il punteggio; on that ~ a questo proposito ● vt segnare (goal); (cut) incidere ● vi far punti; (in football etc) segnare; (keep score) tenere il punteggio. ~r n segnapunti m inv; (of goals) giocatore, -trice mf che segna

scorn /skɔ:n/ n disprezzo m ● vt disprezzare. ~ful adj sprezzante

Scorpio /ˈskɔ:pɪəʊ/ n Scorpione m

scorpion /ˈskɔ:pɪən/ n scorpione m

Scot /skɒt/ n scozzese mf

scotch /skɒtʃ/ vt far cessare

Scotch /skɒtʃ/ adj scozzese ● n (whisky) whisky m [scozzese]

Scot|land /ˈskɒtlənd/ n Scozia f. ~s, ~tish adj scozzese

Scottish Parliament Istituito nel 1999 con sede a Edimburgo, il Parlamento scozzese ha funzione legislativa e esecutiva riguardo agli affari interni della Scozia. Dei 129 parlamentari o MSPs (*Members of the Scottish Parliament*), 73 sono eletti direttamente dai cittadini scozzesi secondo un sistema di maggioranza relativa; i restanti 56 (*Additional Members*) vengono eletti col sistema proporzionale.

scoundrel /ˈskaʊndrəl/ n mascalzone m

scour[1] /ˈskaʊə(r)/ vt (*search*) perlustrare

scour[2] vt (*clean*) strofinare

scourge /skɜːdʒ/ n flagello m

scout /skaʊt/ n (*Mil*) esploratore m ● vi ~ **for** andare in cerca di

Scout n (*Boy*) ~ [boy]scout m inv

scowl /skaʊl/ n sguardo m torvo ● vi guardare [di] storto

scram /skræm/ vi 🄸 levarsi dai piedi

scramble /ˈskræmbl/ n (*climb*) arrampicata f ● vi (*clamber*) arrampicarsi; ~ **for** azzuffarsi per ● vt (*Teleph*) creare delle interferenze in; (*eggs*) strapazzare

scrap[1] /skræp/ n (🄸: *fight*) litigio m

scrap[2] n pezzetto m; (*metal*) ferraglia f; ~s pl (*of food*) avanzi mpl ● vt (*pt/pp* scrapped) buttare via

'scrap-book n album m inv

scrape /skreɪp/ vt raschiare; (*damage*) graffiare. □ ~ **through** vi passare per un pelo. □ ~ **together** vt racimolare

scraper /ˈskreɪpə(r)/ n raschietto m

'scrap-yard n deposito m di ferraglia; (*for cars*) cimitero m delle macchine

scratch /skrætʃ/ n graffio m; (*to relieve itch*) grattata f; **start from** ~

partire da zero; **up to** ~ (*work*) all'altezza ● vt graffiare; (*to relieve itch*) grattare ● vt/i grattarsi. ~ **card** n gratta e vinci m inv

scrawl /skrɔːl/ n scarabocchio m ● vt/i scarabocchiare

scream /skriːm/ n strillo m ● vt/i strillare

screech /skriːtʃ/ n stridore m ● vi stridere ● vt strillare

screen /skriːn/ n paravento m; (*Cinema, TV*) schermo m ● vt proteggere; (*conceal*) riparare; proiettare (*film*); (*candidates*) passare al setaccio; (*Med*) sottoporre a visita medica. ~**ing** n (*Med*) visita f medica; (*of film*) proiezione f. ~**play** n sceneggiatura f

screw /skruː/ n vite f ● vt avvitare. □ ~ **up** vt (*crumple*) accartocciare; strizzare (*eyes*); storcere (*face*); (🄵: *bungle*) mandare all'aria. ~**driver** n cacciavite m

scribble /ˈskrɪbl/ n scarabocchio m ● vt/i scarabocchiare

script /skrɪpt/ n scrittura f (*a mano*); (*of film*) sceneggiatura f

scroll /skrəʊl/ n rotolo m (*di pergamena*); (*decoration*) voluta f. □ ~ **down** vi scorrere in giù

scrounge /skraʊndʒ/ vt/i scroccare. ~**r** n scroccone, -a mf

scrub[1] /skrʌb/ n (*land*) boscaglia f

scrub[2] vt/i (*pt/pp* scrubbed) strofinare; (🄵: *cancel*) cancellare (*plan*)

scruff /skrʌf/ n **by the** ~ **of the** neck per la collottola

scruffy /ˈskrʌfɪ/ adj (-ier, -iest) trasandato

scruple /ˈskruːpl/ n scrupolo m

scrupulous /ˈskruːpjʊləs/ adj scrupoloso

scrutin|ize /ˈskruːtɪnaɪz/ vt scrutinare. ~**y** n (*look*) esame m minuzioso

scuffle /ˈskʌfl/ n tafferuglio m

sculpt /skʌlpt/ vt/i scolpire. ~**or** n scultore m. ~**ure** n scultura f

scum /skʌm/ n schiuma f; (people) feccia f

scurry /'skʌrɪ/ vi (pt/pp -ied) affrettare il passo

scuttle /'skʌtl/ vi (hurry) ~ away correre via

sea /siː/ n mare m; at ~ in mare; fig confuso; by ~ via mare. ~board n costiera f. ~food n frutti mpl di mare. ~gull n gabbiano m

seal¹ /siːl/ n (Zool) foca f

seal² n sigillo m; (Techn) chiusura f ermetica ●vt sigillare; (Techn) chiudere ermeticamente. □ ~ off vt bloccare (area)

'sea-level n livello m del mare

seam /siːm/ n cucitura f; (of coal) strato m

'seaman n marinaio m

seamy /'siːmɪ/ adj sordido; (area) malfamato

seance /'seɪɑːns/ n seduta f spiritica

search /sɜːtʃ/ n ricerca f; (official) perquisizione f; in ~ of alla ricerca di ●vt frugare (for a ricerca di); perlustrare (area); (officially) perquisire ●vi ~ for cercare. ~ing adj penetrante

search: ~light n riflettore m. ~party n squadra f di ricerca

sea: ~sick adj be/get ~ avere il mal di mare. ~side n at/to the ~side al mare

season /'siːzn/ n stagione f ●vt (flavour) condire. ~able adj, ~al adj stagionale. ~ing n condimento m

'season ticket n abbonamento m

seat /siːt/ n (chair) sedia f; (in car) sedile m; (place to sit) posto m [a sedere]; (bottom) didietro m; (of government) sede f; take a ~ sedersi ●vt mettere a sedere; (have seats for) aver posti [a sedere] per; remain ~ed mantenere il proprio posto. ~-belt n cintura f di sicurezza

sea: ~weed n alga f marina. ~worthy adj in stato di navigare

seclu|ded /sɪ'kluːdɪd/ adj appartato. ~sion n isolamento m

second¹ /sɪ'kɒnd/ vt (transfer) distaccare

second² /'sekənd/ adj secondo; on ~ thoughts ripensandoci meglio ●n secondo m; ~s pl (goods) merce fsg di seconda scelta; have ~s (at meal) fare il bis; John the S~ Giovanni Secondo ●adv (in race) al secondo posto ●vt assistere; appoggiare (proposal)

secondary /'sekəndrɪ/ adj secondario. ~ school n ≈ scuola f media (inferiore e superiore)

second: ~ class adv (travel, send) in seconda classe. ~-class adj di seconda classe

second hand n (on clock) lancetta f dei secondi

second-'hand adj & adv di seconda mano

secondly /'sekəndlɪ/ adv in secondo luogo

second-'rate adj di second'ordine

secrecy /'siːkrəsɪ/ n segretezza f; in ~ in segreto

secret /'siːkrɪt/ adj segreto ●n segreto m

secretarial /sekrə'teərɪəl/ adj (work, staff) di segreteria

secretary /'sekrətrɪ/ n segretario, -a mf

secretive /'siːkrətɪv/ adj riservato. ~ness n riserbo m

sect /sekt/ n setta f. ~arian adj settario

section /'sekʃn/ n sezione f

sector /'sektə(r)/ n settore m

secular /'sekjʊlə(r)/ adj secolare; (education) laico

secure /sɪ'kjʊə(r)/ adj sicuro ●vt proteggere; chiudere bene (door); rendere stabile (ladder); (obtain) assicurarsi. ~ly adv saldamente

security /sɪ'kjʊərɪtɪ/ n sicurezza f;

(for loan) garanzia f. ~ies npl titoli mpl

sedate¹ /sɪˈdeɪt/ adj posato

sedate² vt somministrare sedativi a

sedation /sɪˈdeɪʃn/ n somministrazione f di sedativi; be under ~ essere sotto l'effetto di sedativi

sedative /ˈsedətɪv/ adj sedativo ● n sedativo m

sediment /ˈsedɪmənt/ n sedimento m

seduce /sɪˈdjuːs/ vt sedurre

seduct|ion /sɪˈdʌkʃn/ n seduzione f. ~ive adj seducente

see /siː/ v (pt saw, pp seen) ● vt vedere; (understand) capire; (escort) accompagnare; go and ~ andare a vedere; (visit) andare a trovare; ~ you! ci vediamo!; ~ you later! a più tardi!; ~ing that visto che ● vi vedere; (understand) capire; we'll ~ that (make sure) assicurarsi che; ~ about occuparsi di. □ ~ off vt veder partire; (chase away) mandar via. □ ~ through vi vedere attraverso; fig non farsi ingannare da ● vt portare a buon fine. □ ~ to vi occuparsi di

seed /siːd/ n seme m; (Tennis) testa f di serie; go to ~ fare seme; fig lasciarsi andare. ~ed player n (Tennis) testa f di serie. ~ling n pianticella f

seedy /ˈsiːdɪ/ adj (-ier, -iest) squallido

seek /siːk/ vt (pt/pp sought) cercare

seem /siːm/ vi sembrare. ~ingly adv apparentemente

seen /siːn/ ▷SEE¹

seep /siːp/ vi filtrare

see-saw /ˈsiːsɔː/ n altalena f

seethe /siːð/ vi ~ with anger ribollire di rabbia

'see-through adj trasparente

segment /ˈsegmənt/ n segmento m; (of orange) spicchio m

segregat|e /ˈsegrɪgeɪt/ vt segregare. ~ion n segregazione f

seize /siːz/ vt afferrare; (Jur) confi-

scare. □ ~ up vi (Techn) bloccarsi

seizure /ˈsiːʒə(r)/ n (Jur) confisca f; (Med) colpo m [apoplettico]

seldom /ˈseldəm/ adv raramente

select /sɪˈlekt/ adj scelto; (exclusive) esclusivo ● vt scegliere; selezionare (team). ~ion n selezione f. ~ive adj selettivo. ~or n (Sport) selezionatore, -trice mf

self /self/ n io m

self: ~-a'dressed adj con il proprio indirizzo. ~-'catering adj in appartamento attrezzato di cucina. ~-'centred adj egocentrico. ~-'confidence n fiducia f in se stesso. ~-'confident adj sicuro di sé. ~-'conscious adj impacciato. ~-con'tained adj (flat) con ingresso indipendente. ~-con'trol n autocontrollo m. ~-de'fence n autodifesa f; (Jur) legittima difesa f. ~-em'ployed adj che lavora in proprio. ~-'evident adj ovvio. ~-in'dulgent adj indulgente con se stesso. ~-'interest n interesse m personale

self|ish /ˈselfɪʃ/ adj egoista. ~ishness n egoismo m. ~less adj disinteressato

self: ~-'pity n autocommiserazione f. ~-'portrait n autoritratto m. ~-re'spect n amor m proprio. ~-'righteous adj presuntuoso. ~-'sacrifice n abnegazione f. ~-'satisfied adj compiaciuto di sé. ~-'service n self-service m inv ● attrib self-service. ~-suf'ficient adj autosufficiente

sell /sel/ v (pt/pp sold) ● vt vendere; be sold out essere esaurito ● vi vendersi. □ ~ off vt liquidare

seller /ˈselə(r)/ n venditore, -trice mf

Sellotape® /ˈseləʊ-/ n nastro m adesivo, scotch® m

'sell-out n (🆃: betrayal) tradimento m; be a ~ (concert:) fare il tutto esaurito

S

semblance /'sembləns/ n parvenza f

semester /sɪ'mestə(r)/ n Am semestre m

semi /'semɪ/: ~breve /'semɪbri:v/ n semibreve f. ~circle n semicerchio m. ~circular adj semicircolare. ~colon n punto e virgola m. ~-detached adj gemella: in casa f gemella. ~-final n semifinale f

seminar /'semɪnɑː(r)/ n seminario m. ~y n seminario m

senat|e /'senət/ n senato m. ~or n senatore m

send /send/ vt/i (pt/pp sent) mandare; ~ for mandare a chiamare (person); far venire (thing). ~er n mittente m/f. ~-off n commiato m

senile /'si:naɪl/ adj arteriosclerotico; (Med) senile. ~ity n senilismo m

senior /'si:nɪə(r)/ adj più vecchio; (in rank) superiore ● n (in rank) superiore m/f; (in sport) senior m/f; she's two years my ~ è più vecchia di me di due anni. ~ citizen n anziano, -a mf

seniority /si:nɪ'ɒrətɪ/ n anzianità f inv di servizio

sensation /sen'seɪʃn/ n sensazione f. ~al adj sensazionale. ~ally adv in modo sensazionale

sense /sens/ n senso m; (common ~) buon senso m; in a ~ in un certo senso; make ~ aver senso ● vt sentire. ~less adj insensato; (unconscious) privo di sensi

sensib|le /'sensəbl/ adj sensato; (suitable) appropriato. ~y adv in modo appropriato

sensitiv|e /'sensətɪv/ adj sensibile; (touchy) suscettibile. ~ely adv con sensibilità. ~ity n sensibilità f inv

sensual /'sensjʊəl/ adj sensuale. ~ity n sensualità f inv

sensuous /'sensjʊəs/ adj voluttuoso

sent /sent/ ▷SEND

sentence /'sentəns/ n frase f; (Jur) sentenza f; (punishment) condanna f

● vt ~ to condannare a

sentiment /'sentɪmənt/ n sentimento m; (opinion) opinione f; (sentimentality) sentimentalismo m. ~al adj sentimentale; pej sentimentalista. ~ality n sentimentalità f inv

sentry /'sentrɪ/ n sentinella f

separable /'sepərəbl/ adj separabile

separate[1] /'separət/ adj separato. ~ly adv separatamente

separate[2] /'separeɪt/ vt separare ● vi separarsi. ~ion n separazione f

September /sep'tembə(r)/ n settembre m

septic /'septɪk/ adj settico; go ~ infettarsi. ~ tank n fossa f biologica

sequel /'si:kwəl/ n seguito m

sequence /'si:kwəns/ n sequenza f

Serbia /'sɜ:bɪə/ n Serbia f

serenade /serə'neɪd/ n serenata f ● vt fare una serenata a

seren|e /sɪ'ri:n/ adj sereno. ~ity n serenità f inv

sergeant /'sɑːdʒənt/ n sergente m

serial /'sɪərɪəl/ n racconto m a puntate; (TV) sceneggiato m a puntate; (Radio) commedia f radiofonica. ~ize vt pubblicare a puntate (Radio, TV); trasmettere a puntate. ~ killer n serial killer m inv. ~ number n numero m di serie. ~ port n (Comput) porta f seriale

series /'sɪəri:z/ n serie f inv

serious /'sɪərɪəs/ adj serio; (illness, error) grave. ~ly adv seriamente; (ill) gravemente; take ~ly prendere sul serio. ~ness n serietà f inv; (of situation) gravità f inv

sermon /'sɜ:mən/ n predica f

serum /'sɪərəm/ n siero m

servant /'sɜ:vənt/ n domestico, -a mf

serve /sɜ:v/ n (Tennis) servizio m ● vt servire; scontare (sentence); ~ its purpose servire al proprio scopo; ~s you right! ben ti sta!; ~s two per due persone • *vi* prestare servizio; (*Tennis*) servire; ~ **as** servire da. ~ **r** *n* (*Comput*) server *m inv*

service /'sɜːvɪs/ *n* servizio *m*; (*Relig*) funzione *f*; (*maintenance*) revisione *f*; ~**s** *pl* forze *fpl* armate; (*on motorway*) area *f* di servizio; **in the** ~**s** sotto le armi; **of** ~ **to** utile *a*; **out of** ~ (*machine*) guasto • *vt* (*Techn*) revisionare. ~**able** *adj* utilizzabile; (*hard-wearing*) resistente; (*practical*) pratico

service: ~ **charge** *n* servizio *m*. ~ **station** *n* stazione *f* di servizio

serviette /sɜːvɪ'et/ *n* tovagliolo *m*

servile /'sɜːvaɪl/ *adj* servile

session /'seʃn/ *n* seduta *f*; (*Jur*) sessione *f*; (*Univ*) anno *m* accademico

set /set/ *n* serie *f*, set *m inv*; (*of crockery, cutlery*) servizio *m*; (*Radio, TV*) apparecchio *m*; (*Math*) insieme *m*; (*Theat*) scenario *m*; (*Cinema, Tennis*) set *m inv*; (*of people*) circolo *m*; (*of hair*) messa *f* in piega • *adj* (*ready*) pronto; (*rigid*) fisso; (*book*) in programma; **be** ~ **on doing sth** essere risoluto a fare qcsa; **be** ~ **in one's ways** essere abitudinario • *v* (*pt/pp* **set**, *pres p* **setting**) • *vt* mettere, porre; mettere (*alarm clock*); assegnare (*task, homework*); fissare (*date, limit*); chiedere (*questions*); montare (*gem*); assestare (*bone*); apparecchiare (*table*); ~ **fire to** dare fuoco a; ~ **free** liberare • *vi* (*sun*) tramontare; (*jelly, concrete*) solidificarsi; ~ **about doing sth** mettersi a fare qcsa. □ ~ **back** *vt* mettere indietro; (*hold up*) ritardare; (▯: *cost*) costare a. □ ~ **off** *vi* partire • *vt* avviare; mettere (*alarm*); fare esplodere (*bomb*). □ ~ **out** *vi* partire; ~ **out to do sth** proporsi di fare qcsa • *vt* disporre; (*state*) esporre. □ ~ **to** *vi* mettersi all'opera. □ ~ **up** *vt* fondare (*company*); istituire (*committee*)

'set-back *n* passo *m* indietro

settee /se'tiː/ *n* divano *m*

setting /'setɪŋ/ *n* scenario *m*; (*position*) posizione *f*; (*of sun*) tramonto *m*; (*of jewel*) montatura *f*

settle /'setl/ *vt* (*decide*) definire; risolvere (*argument*); fissare (*date*); calmare (*nerves*); saldare (*bill*) • *vi* (*to live*) stabilirsi; (*snow, dust, bird:*) posarsi; (*subside*) assestarsi; (*sediment:*) depositarsi. □ ~ **down** *vi* sistemarsi; (*stop making noise*) calmarsi. □ ~ **for** *vt* accontentarsi di. □ ~ **up** *vi* regolare i conti

settlement /'setlmənt/ *n* (*agreement*) accordo *m*; (*of bill*) saldo *m*; (*colony*) insediamento *m*

settler /'setlə(r)/ *n* colonizzatore, -trice *mf*

'set-to *n* ▯ zuffa *f*; (*verbal*) battibecco *m*

'set-up *n* situazione *f*

seven /'sevn/ *adj* sette. ~**teen** *adj* diciassette. ~**teenth** *adj* diciassettesimo

seventh /'sevnθ/ *adj* settimo

seventieth /'sevntɪθ/ *adj* settantesimo

seventy /'sevntɪ/ *adj* settanta

sever /'sevə(r)/ *vt* troncare (*relations*)

several /'sevrəl/ *adj & pron* parecchi

severe /sɪ'vɪə(r)/ *adj* severo; (*pain*) violento; (*illness*) grave; (*winter*) rigido. ~**ly** *adv* severamente; (*ill*) gravemente. ~**ity** *n* severità *f inv*; (*of pain*) violenza *f*; (*of illness*) gravità *f*; (*of winter*) rigore *m*

sew /səʊ/ *vt/i* (*pt* **sewed**, *pp* **sewn** or **sewed**) cucire. □ ~ **up** *vt* ricucire

sewage /'suːɪdʒ/ *n* acque *fpl* di scolo

sewer /'suːə(r)/ *n* fogna *f*

sewing /'səʊɪŋ/ *n* cucito *m*; (*work*) lavoro *m* di cucito. ~ **machine** *n* macchina *f* da cucire

sewn /səʊn/ ▸ **SEW**

sex /seks/ *n* sesso *m*; **have** ~ avere rapporti sessuali. ~**ist** *adj* sessista. ~ **offender** *n* colpevole *mf* di delitti

s

a sfondo sessuale

sexual /ˈsɛksjʊəl/ adj sessuale. ∼ 'intercourse n rapporti mpl sessuali. ∼ity n sessualità f inv. ∼ly adv sessualmente

sexy /ˈsɛksɪ/ adj (-ier, -iest) sexy

shabb|y /ˈʃæbɪ/ adj (-ier, -iest) scialbo; (treatment) meschino. ∼iness n trasandatezza f; (of treatment) meschinità f inv

shack /ʃæk/ n catapecchia f • **shack up with** vt 𝄪 vivere con

shade /ʃeɪd/ n ombra f; (of colour) sfumatura f; (for lamp) paralume m; (Am: for window) tapparella f; a ∼ better un tantino meglio • vt riparare dalla luce; (draw lines on) ombreggiare. ∼s npl 𝄪 occhiali mpl da sole

shadow /ˈʃædəʊ/ n ombra f; S∼ Cabinet governo m ombra • vt (follow) pedinare. ∼y adj ombroso

shady /ˈʃeɪdɪ/ adj (-ier, -iest) ombroso; (𝄪: disreputable) losco

shaft /ʃɑːft/ n (Techn) albero m; (of light) raggio m; (of lift, mine) pozzo m; ∼s pl (of cart) stanghe fpl

shaggy /ˈʃægɪ/ adj (-ier, -iest) irsuto; (animal) dal pelo arruffato

shake /ʃeɪk/ n scrollata f • v (pt shook, pp shaken) • vt scuotere; agitare (bottle); far tremare (building); ∼ hands with stringere la mano a • vi tremare. □ ∼ off vt scrollarsi di dosso. ∼-up n (Pol) rimpasto m; (Comm) ristrutturazione f

shaky /ˈʃeɪkɪ/ adj (-ier, -iest) tremante; (table etc) traballante; (unreliable) vacillante

shall /ʃæl/ v aux I ∼ go andrò; we ∼ see vedremo; what ∼ I do? cosa faccio? I'll come too, I ∼? vengo anch'io, no? thou shalt not kill liter non uccidere

shallow /ˈʃæləʊ/ adj basso, poco profondo; (dish) poco profondo; fig superficiale

sham /ʃæm/ adj falso • n finzione f;

(person) spaccone, -a mf • vt (pt/pp shammed) simulare

shambles /ˈʃæmblz/ n baraonda fsg

shame /ʃeɪm/ n vergogna f; it's a ∼ that è un peccato che; what a ∼! che peccato! ∼-faced adj vergognoso

shame|ful /ˈʃeɪmfl/ adj vergognoso. ∼less adj spudorato

shampoo /ʃæmˈpuː/ n shampoo m inv • vt fare uno shampoo a

shape /ʃeɪp/ n forma f; (figure) ombra f; take ∼ prendere forma; get back in ∼ ritornare in forma • vt dar forma a (into di) • vi ∼ [up] mettere la testa a posto; ∼ up nicely mettersi bene. ∼less adj informe

share /ʃeə(r)/ n porzione f; (Comm) azione f • vt dividere; condividere (views) • vi dividere. ∼holder n azionista mf

shark /ʃɑːk/ n squalo m, pescecane m; fig truffatore, -trice mf

sharp /ʃɑːp/ adj (knife etc) tagliente; (pencil) appuntito; (drop) a picco; (reprimand) severo; (outline) marcato; (alert) acuto; (unscrupulous) senza scrupoli; ∼ pain fitta f • adv in punto; (Mus) fuori tono; look ∼! sbrigati! • n (Mus) diesis m inv. ∼en vt affilare (knife); appuntire (pencil)

shatter /ˈʃætə(r)/ vt frantumare; fig mandare in frantumi; ∼ed (𝄪: exhausted) a pezzi • vi frantumarsi

shav|e /ʃeɪv/ n rasatura f; have a ∼e farsi la barba • vt radere • vi radersi. ∼er n rasoio m elettrico. ∼ing-brush n pennello m da barba; ∼ing foam n schiuma f da barba; ∼ing soap n sapone m da barba

shawl /ʃɔːl/ n scialle m

she /ʃiː/ pron lei

sheaf /ʃiːf/ n (pl sheaves) fascio m

shear /ʃɪə(r)/ vt (pt sheared, pp shorn or sheared) tosare

shears /ʃɪəz/ npl (for hedge) cesoie fpl

shed[1] /ʃed/ n baracca f; (for cattle) stalla f

shed[2] vt (pt/pp shed, pres p shedding) perdere; versare (blood, tears); ~ **light on** far luce su

sheep /ʃiːp/ n inv pecora f. ~**-dog** n cane m da pastore

sheepish /ʃiːpɪʃ/ adj imbarazzato. ~**ly** adv con aria imbarazzata

sheer /ʃɪə(r)/ adj puro; (steep) a picco; (transparent) trasparente ● adv a picco

sheet /ʃiːt/ n lenzuolo m; (of paper) foglio m; (of glass, metal) lastra f

shelf /ʃelf/ n (pl shelves) ripiano m; (set of shelves) scaffale m

shell /ʃel/ n conchiglia f; (of egg, snail, tortoise) guscio m; (of crab) corazza f; (of unfinished building) ossatura f; (Mil) granata f ● vt sgusciare (peas); (Mil) bombardare. □ ~ **out** 🔢 sborsare

'shellfish n inv mollusco m; (Culin) frutti mpl di mare

shelter /ʃeltə(r)/ n rifugio m; (air raid ~) rifugio m antiaereo ● vt riparare (from da); (give lodging to) dare asilo a ● vi rifugiarsi. ~**ed** adj (spot) riparato; (life) ritirato

shelve /ʃelv/ vt accantonare (project)

shelving /ʃelvɪŋ/ n (shelves) ripiani mpl

shepherd /ʃepəd/ n pastore m ● vt guidare. ~**'s pie** n pasticcio m di carne tritata e patate

sherry /ʃerɪ/ n sherry m

shield /ʃiːld/ n scudo m; (for eyes) maschera f; (Techn) schermo m ● vt proteggere (from da)

shift /ʃɪft/ n cambiamento m; (in position) spostamento m; (at work) turno m ● vt spostare; (take away) togliere; riversare (blame) ● vi spostarsi; (wind): cambiare; (🔢: move quickly) darsi una mossa

shifty /ʃɪftɪ/ adj (-ier, -iest) pej losco; (eyes) sfuggente

shimmer /ʃɪmə(r)/ n luccichio m ● vi luccicare

shin /ʃɪn/ n stinco m

shine /ʃaɪn/ n lucentezza f; **give sth a ~** dare una lucidata a qcsa ● v (pt/pp shone) ● vi splendere; (reflect light) brillare; (hair, shoes) essere lucido ● vt ~ **a light on** puntare una luce su

shingle /ʃɪŋgl/ n (pebbles) ghiaia f

shiny /ʃaɪnɪ/ adj (-ier, -iest) lucido

ship /ʃɪp/ n nave f ● vt (pt/pp shipped) spedire; (by sea) spedire via mare

ship: ~**ment** n spedizione f; (consignment) carico m. ~**ping** n trasporto m; (traffic) imbarcazioni fpl. ~**shape** adj & adv in perfetto ordine. ~**wreck** n naufragio m. ~**wrecked** adj naufragato. ~**yard** n cantiere m navale

shirk /ʃɜːk/ vt scansare. ~**er** n scansafatiche mf inv

shirt /ʃɜːt/ n camicia f; **in ~-sleeves** in maniche di camicia

shit /ʃɪt/ 🔢 n & int merda f ● vi (pt/pp shit) cagare

shiver /ʃɪvə(r)/ n brivido m ● vi rabbrividire

shoal /ʃəʊl/ n (of fish) banco m

shock /ʃɒk/ n (impact) urto m; (Electr) scossa f [elettrica]; fig colpo m, shock m inv; (Med) shock m inv; **get a ~** (Electr) prendere la scossa ● vt scioccare. ~**ing** adj scioccante; (🔢: weather, handwriting etc) tremendo

shod /ʃɒd/ ▷ SHOE

shoddy /ʃɒdɪ/ adj (-ier, -iest) scadente

shoe /ʃuː/ n scarpa f; (of horse) ferro m ● vt (pt/pp shod, pres p shoeing) ferrare (horse)

shoe: ~**horn** n calzante m. ~**lace** n laccio m da scarpa

shone /ʃɒn/ ▷ SHINE

shoo /ʃuː/ vt ~ away cacciar via
● int sciò

shook /ʃʊk/ ▷ SHAKE

shoot /ʃuːt/ n (Bot) germoglio m; (hunt) battuta f di caccia ● v (pt/pp shot) ● vt sparare; girare (film) ● vi (hunt) andare a caccia. □ ~ **down** vt abbattere. □ ~ **out** vi (rush) precipitarsi fuori. □ ~ **up** vi (grow) crescere in fretta; (prices): salire di colpo

shop /ʃɒp/ n negozio m; (workshop) officina f; **talk** ~ 🔢 parlare di lavoro ● vi (pt/pp shopped) far compere; **go ~ping** andare a fare compere. □ ~ **around** vi confrontare i prezzi

shop- ~ **assistant** n commesso, -a mf. ~**keeper** n negoziante mf. ~**lifter** n taccheggiatore, -trice mf. ~**lifting** n taccheggio m. ~**per** n compratore, -trice mf

shopping /ʃɒpɪŋ/ n compere fpl; (articles) acquisti mpl; **do the** ~ **fare la spesa.** ~ **bag** n borsa f per la spesa. ~ **centre** n centro m commerciale. ~ **trolley** n carrello m

shop- ~**steward** n rappresentante mf sindacale. ~'**window** n vetrina f

shore /ʃɔː(r)/ n riva f

shorn /ʃɔːn/ ▷ SHEAR

short /ʃɔːt/ adj corto; (not lasting) breve; (person) basso; (curt) brusco; **a** ~ **time ago** poco tempo fa; **be** ~ **of essere a corto di; be in** ~ **supply essere scarso; fig essere raro; Mick is** ~ **for Michael Mick è il diminutivo di Michael** ● adv bruscamente; **in** ~ **in breve;** ~ **of doing a meno di fare; go** ~ **essere privato (of di); stop** ~ **of doing sth non arrivare fino a fare qcsa; cut** ~ **interrompere (meeting, holiday); to cut a long story** ~ **per farla breve**

shortage /ʃɔːtɪdʒ/ n scarsità f inv

short- ~**bread** n biscotto m di pasta frolla. ~'**circuit** n corto m circuito. ~**coming** n difetto m. ~'**cut** n scorciatoia f

shorten /ʃɔːtn/ vt abbreviare; accorciare (garment)

shorthand n stenografia f

short|**ly** /ʃɔːtlɪ/ adv presto; ~**ly before/after** poco prima/dopo. ~**ness** n brevità f inv; (of person) bassa statura f

shorts /ʃɔːts/ npl calzoncini mpl corti

short-'sighted adj miope

shot /ʃɒt/ ▷ SHOOT ● n colpo m; (person) tiratore m; (Phot) foto f; (injection) puntura f; (🔢: attempt) prova f; **like a** ~ 🔢 come un razzo. ~**gun** n fucile m da caccia

should /ʃʊd/ v aux **I** ~ **go dovrei andare; I** ~ **have seen him avrei dovuto vederlo; I** ~ **like mi piacerebbe; this** ~ **be enough questo dovrebbe bastare; if he** ~ **come se dovesse venire**

shoulder /ʃəʊldə(r)/ n spalla f ● vt mettersi in spalla; fig accollarsi. ~**bag** n borsa f a tracolla. ~**blade** n scapola f. ~**strap** n spallina f; (of bag) tracolla f

shout /ʃaʊt/ n grido m ● vt/i gridare. □ ~ **at** vi alzar la voce con. □ ~ **down** vt azzittire gridando

shove /ʃʌv/ n spintone m ● vt spingere; (🔢: put) ficcare ● vi spingere. □ ~ **off** vi 🔢 togliersi di torno

shovel /ʃʌvl/ n pala f ● vt (pt/pp shovelled) spalare

show /ʃəʊ/ n (display) manifestazione f; (exhibition) mostra f; (ostentation) ostentazione f; (Theat) (TV) spettacolo m; (programme) programma m; **on** ~ **esposto** ● v (pt showed, pp shown) ● vt mostrare; (put on display) esporre; proiettare (film) ● vi (film): essere proiettato; **your slip is** ~**ing ti si vede la sottoveste.** □ ~ **in** vt fare accomodare. □ ~ **off** vi 🔢 mettersi in mostra ● vt mettere in mostra. □ ~ **up** vi risaltare; (🔢: arrive) farsi vedere ● vt (🔢: embarrass) far fare una brutta figura a '**show-down** n regolamento m dei conti

shower /'ʃaʊə(r)/ n doccia f; (of rain) acquazzone m; have a ~ fare la doccia ●vt ~ **with** coprire di ●vi fare la doccia. □~**proof** adj impermeabile. ~**y** adj di acquazzoni

'**show-jumping** n concorso m ippico

shown /ʃəʊn/ ▷SHOW

'**show-off** n esibizionista mf

showy /'ʃəʊɪ/ adj appariscente

shrank /ʃræŋk/ ▷SHRINK

shred /ʃred/ n brandello m; fig briciolo m ●vt (pt/pp **shredded**) fare a brandelli; (Culin) tagliuzzare. ~**der** n distruttore m di documenti

shrewd /ʃruːd/ adj accorto. ~**ness** n accortezza f

shriek /ʃriːk/ n strillo m ●vt/i strillare

shrift /ʃrɪft/ n **give sb short ~** liquidare qcno rapidamente

shrill /ʃrɪl/ adj penetrante

shrimp /ʃrɪmp/ n gamberetto m

shrine /ʃraɪn/ n (place) santuario m

shrink /ʃrɪŋk/ vi (pt shrank, pp shrunk) restringersi; (draw back) ritrarsi (**from** da)

shrivel /'ʃrɪvl/ vi (pt/pp shrivelled) raggrinzare

shroud /ʃraʊd/ n sudario m; fig manto m

Shrove /ʃrəʊv/ n ~ **Tuesday** martedì m grasso

shrub /ʃrʌb/ n arbusto m

shrug /ʃrʌg/ n scrollata f di spalle ●vt/i (pt/pp shrugged) ~ [**one's shoulders**] scrollare le spalle

shrunk /ʃrʌŋk/ ▷SHRINK. ~**en** adj rimpicciolito

shudder /'ʃʌdə(r)/ n fremito m ●vi fremere

shuffle /'ʃʌfl/ vi strascicare i piedi ●vt mescolare (cards)

shun /ʃʌn/ vt (pt/pp shunned)

rifuggire

shunt /ʃʌnt/ vt smistare

shush /ʃʊʃ/ int zitto!

shut /ʃʌt/ v (pt/pp shut, pres p shutting) ●vt chiudere ●vi chiudersi; (shop:) chiudere. □~ **down** vt/i chiudere. □~ **up** vt chiudere; [I] far tacere ●vi [I] stare zitto; ~ **up!** stai zitto!

shutter /'ʃʌtə(r)/ n serranda f; (Phot) otturatore m

shuttle /'ʃʌtl/ n navetta f ●vi far la spola

shuttle: ~**cock** n volano m. ~ **service** n servizio m pendolare

shy /ʃaɪ/ adj (timid) timido. ~**ness** n timidezza f

Sicily /'sɪsɪlɪ/ n Sicilia f. ~**ian** adj & n siciliano, -a mf

sick /sɪk/ adj ammalato; (humour) macabro; **be** ~ (vomit) vomitare; **be** ~ **of sth** [I] essere stufo di qcsa; **feel** ~ aver la nausea

sick|ly /'sɪklɪ/ adj (-ier, -iest) malaticcio. ~**ness** n malattia f; (vomiting) nausea f. ~**ness benefit** n indennità f di malattia

side /saɪd/ n lato m; (of person, mountain) fianco m; (of road) bordo m; **on the** ~ (as sideline) come attività secondaria; ~ **by** ~ fianco a fianco; **take** ~**s** immischiarsi; **take sb's** ~ prendere le parti di qcno; **be on the safe** ~ andare sul sicuro ●attrib laterale ●vi ~ **with** parteggiare per

side: ~**board** n credenza f. ~**effect** n effetto m collaterale. ~**lights** npl luci fpl di posizione. ~**line** n attività f inv complementare. ~**show** n attrazione f secondaria. ~**step** vt schivare. ~**track** vt sviare. ~**walk** n Am marciapiede m. ~**ways** adv obliquamente

siding /'saɪdɪŋ/ n binario m di raccordo

sidle /'saɪdl/ vi camminare furtivamente (**up to** verso)

siege /siːdʒ/ n assedio m

sieve /sɪv/ n setaccio m • vt setacciare

sift /sɪft/ vt setacciare; ~ [through] fig passare al setaccio

sigh /saɪ/ n sospiro m • vi sospirare

sight /saɪt/ n vista f; (on gun) mirino m; the ~s pl le cose da vedere; at first ~ a prima vista; be within/out of ~ essere/non essere in vista; lose ~ of perdere di vista; know by ~ conoscere di vista. have bad ~ vederci male • vt avvistare

'sightseeing n go ~ andare a visitare posti

sign /saɪn/ n segno m; (notice) insegna f • vt/i firmare. □ ~ **on** vi (as unemployed) presentarsi all'ufficio di collocamento; (Mil) arruolarsi

signal /ˈsɪɡnl/ n segnale m • v (pt/pp signalled) • vt segnalare • vi fare segnali; ~ **to sb** far segno a qcno (to di). ~**box** n cabina f di segnalazione

signature /ˈsɪɡnətʃə(r)/ n firma f. ~ **tune** n sigla f [musicale]

significan|ce /sɪɡˈnɪfɪkəns/ n significato m. ~**t** adj significativo

signify /ˈsɪɡnɪfaɪ/ vt (pt/pp -ied) indicare

signpost /ˈsaɪn-/ n segnalazione f stradale

silence /ˈsaɪləns/ n silenzio m • vt far tacere. ~**r** n (on gun) silenziatore m; (Auto) marmitta f

silent /ˈsaɪlənt/ adj silenzioso; (film) muto; **remain** ~ rimanere in silenzio. ~**ly** adv silenziosamente

silhouette /sɪluˈet/ n sagoma f, silhouette f inv • vt **be** ~**d** profilarsi

silicon /ˈsɪlɪkən/ n silicio m. ~ **chip** n piastrina f di silicio

silk /sɪlk/ n seta f • attrib di seta. ~**worm** n baco m da seta

silky /ˈsɪlkɪ/ adj (-ier, -iest) come la seta

silly /ˈsɪlɪ/ adj (-ier, -iest) sciocco

silt /sɪlt/ n melma f

silver /ˈsɪlvə(r)/ adj d'argento; (paper) argentato • n argento m; (silverware) argenteria f

silver: ~**-plated** adj placcato d'argento. ~**ware** n argenteria f

SIM card /ˈsɪmkɑːd/ n carta f SIM

similar /ˈsɪmɪlə(r)/ adj simile. ~**ity** n somiglianza f. ~**ly** adv in modo simile

simile /ˈsɪmɪlɪ/ n similitudine f

simmer /ˈsɪmə(r)/ vi bollire lentamente • vt far bollire lentamente. □ ~ **down** vi calmarsi

simple /ˈsɪmpl/ adj semplice; (person) semplicotto. ~**-minded** adj sempliciotto

simplicity /sɪmˈplɪsətɪ/ n semplicità f inv

simply /ˈsɪmplɪ/ adv semplicemente

simulat|e /ˈsɪmjʊleɪt/ vt simulare. ~**ion** n simulazione f

simultaneous /sɪmlˈteɪnɪəs/ adj simultaneo

sin /sɪn/ n peccato m • vi (pt/pp sinned) peccare

---

since /sɪns/
● prep da I've been waiting ~ Monday aspetto da lunedì
● adv da allora
● conj da quando; (because) siccome

---

sincere /sɪnˈsɪə(r)/ adj sincero. ~**ly** adv sinceramente; **Yours** ~**ly** distinti saluti

sincerity /sɪnˈserətɪ/ n sincerità f inv

sinful /ˈsɪnfl/ adj peccaminoso

sing /sɪŋ/ vt/i (pt sang, pp sung) cantare

singe /sɪndʒ/ vt (pres p singeing) bruciacchiare

singer /ˈsɪŋə(r)/ n cantante mf

single /ˈsɪŋgl/ adj solo; (not double) semplice; (unmarried) celibe m; (woman) nubile; (room) singolo; (bed) a una piazza ● n (ticket) biglietto m di sola andata; (record) singolo m; ~s pl (Tennis) singolo m ● **single out** vt scegliere; (distinguish) distinguere

single-handed adj & adv da solo

singular /ˈsɪŋɡjʊlə(r)/ adj (Gram) singolare ● n singolare m. ~ly adv singolarmente

sinister /ˈsɪnɪstə(r)/ adj sinistro

sink /sɪŋk/ n lavandino m ● v (pt sank, pp sunk) ● vi affondare ● vt affondare (ship); scavare (shaft); investire (money). □ ~ **in** vi penetrare; it took a while to ~ in (🔲: be understood) c'è voluto un po' a capirlo

sinner /ˈsɪnə(r)/ n peccatore, -trice mf

sip /sɪp/ n sorso m ● vt (pt/pp sipped) sorseggiare

siphon /ˈsaɪfn/ n (bottle) sifone m ● **siphon off** vt travasare (con sifone)

sir /sɜː(r)/ n signore m; S~ (title) Sir m; Dear S~s Spettabile ditta

siren /ˈsaɪrən/ n sirena f

sister /ˈsɪstə(r)/ n sorella f; (nurse) [infermiera f] caposala f. ~-in-law (pl ~s-in-law) cognata f. ~ly adj da sorella

sit /sɪt/ v (pt/pp sat, pres p sitting) ● vi essere seduto; (sit down) sedersi; (committee:) riunirsi ● vt sostenere (exam). □ ~ **back** vi fig starsene con le mani in mano. □ ~ **down** vi mettersi a sedere. □ ~ **up** vi mettersi seduto; (not slouch) star seduto diritto; (stay up) stare alzato

site /saɪt/ n (Archaeol) sito m; (building ~) cantiere m ● vt collocare

sit-in /ˈsɪtɪn/ n occupazione f (di fabbrica)

sitting /ˈsɪtɪŋ/ n seduta f; (for meals) turno m. ~-room n salotto m

situate /ˈsɪtjʊeɪt/ vt situare. ~ed adj situato. ~ion n situazione f; (location) posizione f; (job) posto m

six /sɪks/ adj sei. ~teen adj sedici.

~teenth adj sedicesimo

sixth /sɪksθ/ adj sesto

sixtieth /ˈsɪkstɪɪθ/ adj sessantesimo

sixty /ˈsɪkstɪ/ adj sessanta

size /saɪz/ n dimensioni fpl; (of clothes) taglia f, misura f; (of shoes) numero m; what ~ is the room? che dimensioni ha la stanza? ● **size up** vt 🔲 valutare

sizzle /ˈsɪzl/ vi sfrigolare

skate[1] /skeɪt/ n inv (fish) razza f

skate[2] n pattino m ● vi pattinare

skateboard /ˈskeɪtbɔːd/ n skateboard m inv

skater /ˈskeɪtə(r)/ n pattinatore, -trice mf

skating /ˈskeɪtɪŋ/ n pattinaggio m. ~-rink n pista f di pattinaggio

skeleton /ˈskelɪtn/ n scheletro m. ~ 'key n passe-partout m inv. ~ 'staff n personale m ridotto

sketch /sketʃ/ n schizzo m; (Theat) sketch m inv ● vt fare uno schizzo di

sketch|y /ˈsketʃɪ/ adj (-ier, -iest) abbozzato. ~ily adv in modo abbozzato

ski /skiː/ n sci m inv ● vi (pt/pp skied, pres p skiing) sciare; go ~ing andare a sciare

skid /skɪd/ n slittata f ● vi (pt/pp skidded) slittare

skier /ˈskiːə(r)/ n sciatore, -trice mf

skiing /ˈskiːɪŋ/ n sci m

skilful /ˈskɪlfl/ adj abile

'ski-lift n impianto m di risalita

skill /skɪl/ n abilità f inv. ~ed adj dotato; (worker) specializzato

skim /skɪm/ vt (pt/pp skimmed) schiumare; scremare (milk). □ ~ **off** vt togliere. □ ~ **through** vt scorrere

skimp /skɪmp/ vi ~ **on** lesinare su

skimpy /ˈskɪmpɪ/ adj (-ier, -iest) succinto

skin /skɪn/ n pelle f; (on fruit) buccia f ● vt (pt/pp skinned) spellare

skin: ~-**deep** adj superficiale.

~-diving n nuoto m subacqueo

skinny /ˈskɪnɪ/ adj (-ier, -iest) molto magro

skip[1] /skɪp/ n (container) benna f

skip[2] n salto m • v (pt/pp skipped) • vi saltellare; (with rope) saltare la corda • vt omettere

skipper /ˈskɪpə(r)/ n skipper m inv

skipping-rope /ˈskɪpɪŋrəʊp/ n corda f per saltare

skirmish /ˈskɜːmɪʃ/ n scaramuccia f

skirt /skɜːt/ n gonna f • vt costeggiare

skittle /ˈskɪtl/ n birillo m

skulk /skʌlk/ vi aggirarsi furtivamente

skull /skʌl/ n cranio m

sky /skaɪ/ n cielo m. ~light n lucernario m. ~marshal n guardia f armata a bordo di un aereo. ~scraper n grattacielo m

slab /slæb/ n lastra f; (slice) fetta f; (of chocolate) tavoletta f

slack /slæk/ adj lento; (person) fiacco • vi fare lo scansafatiche. □ ~ off vi rilassarsi

slacken /ˈslækn/ vi allentare; ~ [off] (trade): rallentare; (speed, rain): diminuire • vt allentare; diminuire (speed)

slain /sleɪn/ ▷SLAY

slam /slæm/ n v (pt/pp slammed) • vt sbattere; (fig: criticize) stroncare • vi sbattere

slander /ˈslɑːndə(r)/ n diffamazione f • vt diffamare. ~ous adj diffamatorio

slang /slæŋ/ n gergo m. ~y adj gergale

slant /slɑːnt/ n pendenza f; (point of view) angolazione f; on the ~ in pendenza • vt pendere; fig distorcere (report) • vi pendere

slap /slæp/ n schiaffo m • vt (pt/pp slapped) schiaffeggiare; (put) schiaffare • adv in pieno

slap: ~dash adj fam ① frettoloso

slash /slæʃ/ n taglio m • vt tagliare; ridurre drasticamente (prices)

slat /slæt/ n stecca f

slate /sleɪt/ n ardesia f • vt ① fare a pezzi

slaughter /ˈslɔːtə(r)/ n macello m; (of people) massacro m • vt macellare; massacrare (people). ~house n macello m

slave /sleɪv/ n schiavo, -a mf • vi ~ [away] lavorare come un negro. ~-driver n schiavista mf

slav|ery /ˈsleɪvərɪ/ n schiavitù f inv. ~ish adj servile

slay /sleɪ/ vt (pt slew, pp slain) ammazzare

sleazy /ˈsliːzɪ/ adj (-ier, -iest) sordido

sledge /sledʒ/ n slitta f. ~-hammer n martello m

sleek /sliːk/ adj liscio, lucente; (well-fed) pasciuto

sleep /sliːp/ n sonno m; go to ~ addormentarsi; put to ~ far addormentare • v (pt/pp slept) • vi dormire • vt ~s six ha sei posti letto. ~er n (Rail) treno m con vagoni letto; (compartment) vagone m letto; be a light/heavy ~er avere il sonno leggero/pesante

sleeping: ~-bag n sacco m a pelo. ~-car n vagone m letto. ~-pill n sonnifero m

sleepless adj insonne

sleepy /ˈsliːpɪ/ adj (-ier, -iest) assonnato; be ~ aver sonno

sleet /sliːt/ n nevischio m • vi it is ~ing nevischia

sleeve /sliːv/ n manica f; (for record) copertina f. ~less adj senza maniche

sleigh /sleɪ/ n slitta f

slender /ˈslendə(r)/ adj snello; (fingers, stem) affusolato; fig scarso; (chance) magro

slept /slept/ ▷SLEEP

slew¹ /sluː/ vi girare

slew² ▷SLAY

slice /slaɪs/ n fetta f • vt affettare; ~d bread pane m a cassetta

slick /slɪk/ adj liscio; (cunning) astuto • n (of oil) chiazza f di petrolio

slid|e /slaɪd/ n scivolata f; (in playground) scivolo m; (for hair) fermaglio m (per capelli); (Phot) diapositiva f • v (pt/pp slid) • vi scivolare • vt far scivolare. ~-rule n regolo m calcolatore. ~ing adj scorrevole; (door, seat) scorrevole; ~ing scale scala f mobile

slight /slaɪt/ adj leggero; (importance) poco; (slender) esile. ~est adj minimo; not in the ~est niente affatto • vt offendere • n offesa f. ~ly adv leggermente

slim /slɪm/ adj (slimmer, slimmest) snello; fig scarso; (chance) magro • vi dimagrire

slim|e /slaɪm/ n melma f. ~y adj melmoso; fig viscido

sling /slɪŋ/ n (Med) benda f al collo • vt (pt/pp slung) lanciare

slip /slɪp/ n scivolata f; (mistake) lieve errore m; (petticoat) sottoveste f; (for pillow) federa f; (paper) scontrino m; give sb the ~ ① sbarazzarsi di qcno; ~ of the tongue lapsus m inv • v (pt/pp slipped) • vi scivolare (go quickly) sgattaiolare; (decline) retrocedere • vt ~ped it into his pocket se l'è infilato in tasca; ~ sb's mind sfuggire di mente a qcno. □ ~ away vi sgusciar via; (time:) sfuggire. □ ~ into vi infilarsi (clothes). □ ~ up vi ① sbagliare

slipper /'slɪpə(r)/ n pantofola f

slippery /'slɪpərɪ/ adj scivoloso

slip-road n bretella f

slipshod /'slɪpʃɒd/ adj trascurato

slip-up n ① sbaglio m

slit /slɪt/ n spacco m; (tear) strappo m; (hole) fessura f • vt (pt/pp slit) tagliare

slither /'slɪðə(r)/ vi scivolare

slobber /'slɒbə(r)/ vi sbavare

slog /slɒg/ n [hard] ~ sgobbata f • vi (pt/pp slogged) (work) sgobbare

slogan /'sləʊgən/ n slogan m inv

slop /slɒp/ v (pt/pp slopped) • vt versare. □ ~ over vi versarsi

slop|e /sləʊp/ n pendenza f; (ski ~) pista f • vi essere inclinato, inclinarsi. ~ing adj in pendenza

sloppy /'slɒpɪ/ adj (-ier, -iest) (work) trascurato; (worker) negligente; (in dress) sciatto; (sentimental) sdolcinato

slosh /slɒʃ/ vi ① (person, feet:) sguazzare; (water:) scrosciare • vt (①: hit) colpire

slot /slɒt/ n fessura f; (time~) spazio m • v (pt/pp slotted) • vt infilare. □ ~ in vi incastrarsi

'slot-machine n distributore m automatico; (for gambling) slot-machine f inv

slouch /slaʊtʃ/ vi (in chair) stare scomposto

Slovakia /slə'vækɪə/ n Slovacchia f

Slovenia /slə'viːnɪə/ n Slovenia f

slovenly /'slʌvnlɪ/ adj sciatto. ~iness n sciatteria f

slow /sləʊ/ adj lento; be ~ (clock:) essere indietro; in ~ motion al rallentatore • adv lentamente • ~ down vt/i rallentare

slowly adv lentamente

sludge /slʌdʒ/ n fanghiglia f

slug /slʌg/ n lumacone m; (bullet) pallottola f. ~gish adj lento

slum /slʌm/ n (house) tugurio m; ~s pl bassifondi mpl

slumber /'slʌmbə(r)/ vi dormire

slump /slʌmp/ n crollo m; (economic) depressione f • vi crollare

slung /slʌŋ/ ▷SLING

slur /slɜː(r)/ n (discredit) calunnia f • vt (pt/pp slurred) biascicare

slush /slʌʃ/ n pantano m nevoso; fig sdolcinatezza f. ~ fund n fondi mpl neri. ~y adj fangoso; (sentimental) sdolcinato

sly /slaɪ/ adj (-er, -est) scaltro ● n on the ~ di nascosto

smack¹ /smæk/ n (on face) schiaffo m; (on bottom) sculaccione m ● vt (on face) schiaffeggiare; (on bottom) sculacciare; ~ one's lips far schioccare le labbra ● adv 🗓 in pieno

smack² vi ~ of fig sapere di

small /smɔːl/ adj piccolo; be out of work etc until the ~ hours fare le ore piccole ● adv ~ chop up ~ fare a pezzettini ● n the ~ of the back le reni fpl

small: ~ ads npl annunci mpl (commerciali). ~ 'change n spiccioli mpl. ~pox n vaiolo m. ~ talk n chiacchiere fpl

smart /smɑːt/ adj elegante; (clever) intelligente; (brisk) svelto; be ~ (🗓: cheeky) fare il furbo ● vi (hurt) bruciare

smash /smæʃ/ n fragore m; (collision) scontro m; (Tennis) schiacciata f ● vt spaccare; (Tennis) schiacciare ● vi spaccarsi; (crash) schiantarsi (into contro). ~ [hit] n successo m. ~ing adj 🗓 fantastico

smattering /'smætərɪŋ/ n infarinatura f

smear /smɪə(r)/ n macchia f; (Med) striscio m ● vt imbrattare; (coat) spalmare (with di); fig calunniare

smell /smel/ n odore m; (sense) odorato m ● v (pt/pp smelt or smelled) ● vt odorare; (sniff) annusare ● vi odorare (of di)

smelly /'smelɪ/ adj (-ier, -iest) puzzolente

smelt¹ /smelt/ ▷ SMELL

smelt² vt fondere

smile /smaɪl/ n sorriso m ● vi sorridere; ~ at sorridere a (sb); sorridere di (sth)

smirk /smɜːk/ n sorriso m compiaciuto

smithereens /smɪðə'riːnz/ npl

to/in ~ in mille pezzi

smock /smɒk/ n grembiule m

smog /smɒg/ n smog m inv

smoke /sməʊk/ n fumo m ● vt/i fumare. ~less adj senza fumo; (fuel) che non fa fumo

smoker /'sməʊkə(r)/ n fumatore, -trice mf; (Rail) vagone m fumatori

smoky /'sməʊkɪ/ adj (-ier, -iest) fumoso; (taste) di fumo

smooth /smuːð/ adj liscio; (movement) scorrevole; (sea) calmo; (manners) mellifluo ● vt lisciare. □ ~ out vt lisciare. ~ly adv in modo scorrevole

smother /'smʌðə(r)/ vt soffocare

smoulder /'sməʊldə(r)/ vi fumare; (with rage) consumarsi

smudge /smʌdʒ/ n macchia f ● vt/i imbrattare

smug /smʌg/ adj (smugger, smuggest) compiaciuto. ~ly adv con aria compiaciuta

smuggle /'smʌgl/ vt contrabbandare. ~er n contrabbandiere, a mf. ~ing n contrabbando m

snack /snæk/ n spuntino m. ~-bar n snack bar m inv

snag /snæg/ n (problem) intoppo m

snail /sneɪl/ n lumaca f; at a ~'s pace a passo di lumaca

snake /sneɪk/ n serpente m

snap /snæp/ n colpo m secco; (photo) istantanea f ● attrib (decision) istantaneo ● v (pt/pp snapped) ● vi (break) spezzarsi; ~ at (dog:) cercare di azzannare; (person:) parlare seccamente a ● vt (break) spezzare; (say) dire seccamente; (Phot) fare un'istantanea di. □ ~ up vt afferrare

snappy /'snæpɪ/ adj (-ier, -iest) scorbutico; (smart) elegante; make it ~! sbrigati!

'snapshot n istantanea f

snare /sneə(r)/ n trappola f

snarl /snɑːl/ n ringhio m ● vi

ringhiare

snatch /snætʃ/ n strappo m; (*fragment*) brano m; (*theft*) scippo m; make a ~ at cercare di afferrare qcsa • vt strappare [di mano] (from a); (*steal*) scippare; rapire (child)

sneak /sniːk/ n 🔟 spia mf • vi (🔟: *tell tales*) fare la spia • vt (*take*) rubare; ~ a look at dare una sbirciata a. ▫ ~ **in/out** vi sgattaiolare dentro/fuori

sneakers /ˈsniːkəz/ npl Am scarpe fpl da ginnastica

sneaky /ˈsniːkɪ/ adj sornione

sneer /snɪə(r)/ n ghigno m • vi sogghignare; (*mock*) ridere di

sneeze /sniːz/ n starnuto m • vi starnutire

snide /snaɪd/ adj 🔟 insinuante

sniff /snɪf/ n (of dog) annusata f • vi tirare su col naso • vt odorare (flower); sniffare (glue, cocaine); (dog:) annusare

snigger /ˈsnɪɡə(r)/ n risatina f soffocata • vi ridacchiare

snip /snɪp/ n taglio m; (🔟: *bargain*) affare m • vt/i (pt/pp snipped) ~ [at] tagliare

snippet /ˈsnɪpɪt/ n a ~ of information/news una breve notizia/informazione

snivel /ˈsnɪvl/ vi (pt/pp snivelled) piagnucolare. ~**ling** adj piagnucoloso

snob /snɒb/ n snob mf. ~**bery** n snobismo m. ~**bish** adj snob

snooker /ˈsnuːkə(r)/ n snooker m

snoop /snuːp/ n spia f • vi 🔟 curiosare

snooze /snuːz/ n sonnellino m • vi fare un sonnellino

snore /snɔː(r)/ vi russare

snorkel /ˈsnɔːkl/ n respiratore m

snort /snɔːt/ n sbuffo m • vi sbuffare

snout /snaʊt/ n grugno m

snow /snəʊ/ n neve f • vi nevicare; ~**ed under** with fig sommerso di

snow: ~**ball** n palla f di neve • vi fare a palle di neve. ~**board** n snowboard m. ~**drift** n cumulo m di neve. ~**fall** n nevicata f. ~**flake** n fiocco m di neve. ~**man** n pupazzo m di neve. ~**plough** n spazzaneve m. ~**storm** n tormenta f. ~**y** adj nevoso

snub /snʌb/ n sgarbo m • vt (pt/pp snubbed) snobbare

'snub-nosed adj dal naso all'insù

snug /snʌɡ/ adj (snugger, snuggest) comodo; (tight) aderente

---

so /səʊ/

● adv così; so far finora; so am I anch'io; so long! 🔟 ci vediamo presto!; that is so è così; so much così tanto; so much the better tanto meglio; so it is proprio così; if so se è così; so as to in modo da; so long! 🔟 a presto!

● pron I hope/think/am afraid so spero/penso/temo di sì; I told you so te l'ho detto; because I say so perché lo dico io; I did so! è vero!; so saying/doing,... così dicendo/facendo,...; or so circa; very much so sì, molto; and so forth or on e così via

● conj (therefore) perciò; (in order that) così; so that affinché, so there ecco!; so what! e allora?; so where have you been? allora, dove sei stato?

---

soak /səʊk/ vt mettere a bagno • vi stare a bagno; ~ **into** (liquid:) penetrare. ▫ ~ **up** vt assorbire

soaking /ˈsəʊkɪŋ/ n ammollo m • adj & adv ~ [wet] 🔟 inzuppato

so-and-so /ˈsəʊənsəʊ/ n Tal dei Tali mf; (euphemism) specie f di imbecille

soap /səʊp/ n sapone m. ~ **opera** n telenovela f, soap opera f inv. ~ **powder** n detersivo m in polvere

soapy /ˈsəʊpɪ/ adj (-ier, -iest) insaponato

s

soar /sɔː(r)/ vi elevarsi; (prices:) salire alle stelle

sob /sɒb/ n singhiozzo m ● vi (pt/pp sobbed) singhiozzare

sober /'səʊbə(r)/ adj sobrio; (serious) serio ● **sober up** vi ritornare sobrio

so-called adj cosiddetto

soccer /'sɒkə(r)/ n calcio m

sociable /'səʊʃəbl/ adj socievole

social /'səʊʃl/ adj sociale; (sociable) socievole

socialis|m /'səʊʃəlɪzm/ n socialismo m. ~t adj socialista ● n socialista mf

socialize /'səʊʃəlaɪz/ vi socializzare

social: ~ **se'curity** n previdenza f sociale. ~ **worker** n assistente mf sociale

society /sə'saɪətɪ/ n società f inv

sociolog|ist /səʊsɪ'ɒlədʒɪst/ n sociologo, -a mf. ~y n sociologia f

sock[1] /sɒk/ n calzino m; (kneelength) calza f

sock[2] n 🔢 pugno m ● vt 🔢 dare un pugno a

socket /'sɒkɪt/ n (wall plug) presa f [di corrente]; (for bulb) portalampada m inv

soda /'səʊdə/ n soda f; Am gazzosa f. ~ **water** n seltz m inv

sodium /'səʊdɪəm/ n sodio m

sofa /'səʊfə/ n divano m. ~ **bed** n divano m letto

soft /sɒft/ adj morbido, soffice; (voice) sommesso; (light, colour) tenue; (not strict) indulgente; (🔢: silly) stupido; **have a ~ spot for sb** avere un debole per qcno. ~ **drink** n bibita f analcolica

soften /'sɒfn/ vt ammorbidire; fig attenuare ● vi ammorbidirsi

softly /'sɒftlɪ/ adv (say) sottovoce; (treat) con indulgenza; (play music) in sottofondo

software n software m

soggy /'sɒgɪ/ adj (-ier, -iest) zuppo

soil[1] /sɔɪl/ n suolo m

soil[2] vt sporcare

solar /'səʊlə(r)/ adj solare

sold /səʊld/ ▷ **SELL**

solder /'səʊldə(r)/ n lega f da saldatura ● vt saldare

soldier /'səʊldʒə(r)/ n soldato m ● **soldier on** vi perseverare

sole[1] /səʊl/ n (of foot) pianta f; (of shoe) suola f

sole[2] n (fish) sogliola f

sole[3] adj unico, solo. ~**ly** adv unicamente

solemn /'sɒləm/ adj solenne. ~**ity** n solennità f inv

solicitor /sə'lɪsɪtə(r)/ n avvocato m

solid /'sɒlɪd/ adj solido; (oak, gold) massiccio ● n (figure) solido m; ~**s** pl (food) cibi mpl solidi

solidarity /sɒlɪ'dærətɪ/ n solidarietà f inv

solidify /sə'lɪdɪfaɪ/ vi (pt/pp -ied) solidificarsi

solitary /'sɒlɪtərɪ/ adj solitario; (sole) solo. ~ **con'finement** n cella f di isolamento

solitude /'sɒlɪtjuːd/ n solitudine f

solo /'səʊləʊ/ n (Mus) assolo m ● adj (flight) in solitario ● adv in solitario. ~**ist** n solista mf

solstice /'sɒlstɪs/ n solstizio m

soluble /'sɒljʊbl/ adj solubile

solution /sə'luːʃn/ n soluzione f

solve /sɒlv/ vt risolvere

solvent /'sɒlvənt/ adj solvente ● n solvente m

sombre /'sɒmbə(r)/ adj tetro; (clothes) scuro

some /sʌm/ adj (a certain amount of) del; (a certain number of) qualche, alcuni; ~ **day** un giorno o l'altro; **I need ~ money/books** ho bisogno di soldi/libri; **do ~ shopping** fare qualche acquisto ● pron (a certain amount) un po'; (a certain number) alcuni; **I want ~** ne voglio

some: ~body /-bədɪ/ pron & n qualcuno m. ~how adv in qualche modo; ~how or other in un modo o nell'altro. ~one pron & n = somebody

somersault /'sʌməsɔːlt/ n capriola f; turn a ~ fare una capriola

'**something** pron qualche cosa, qualcosa; ~ different qualcosa di diverso; ~ like un po' come; (approximately) qualcosa come; see ~ of sb vedere qcno un po'

some: ~time adv un giorno o l'altro; ~times adv qualche volta. ~what adv piuttosto. ~where adv da qualche parte ● pron ~where to eat un posto in cui mangiare

son /sʌn/ n figlio m

sonata /sə'nɑːtə/ n sonata f

song /sɒŋ/ n canzone f

sonic /'sɒnɪk/ adj sonico. ~ 'boom n bang m inv sonico

'**son-in-law** n (pl ~s-in-law) genero m

'**sonnet** /'sɒnɪt/ n sonetto m

soon /suːn/ adv presto; (in a short time) tra poco; as ~ as [non] appena; as ~ as possible il più presto possibile; ~er or later prima o poi; the ~er the better prima è, meglio è; no ~er had I arrived than... ero appena arrivato quando...; I would ~er go preferirei andare; ~ after subito dopo

soot /sʊt/ n fuliggine f

sooth|e /suːð/ vt calmare

sooty /'sʊtɪ/ adj fuligginoso

sophisticated /sə'fɪstɪkeɪtɪd/ adj sofisticato

sopping /'sɒpɪŋ/ adj & adv be ~ [wet] essere bagnato fradicio

soppy /'sɒpɪ/ adj (-ier, -iest) 🔟 svenevole

soprano /sə'prɑːnəʊ/ n soprano m

sordid /'sɔːdɪd/ adj sordido

sore /sɔː(r)/ adj dolorante; (Am:

vexed) arrabbiato; it's ~ fa male; have a ~ throat avere mal di gola ● n piaga f. ~ly adv (tempted) seriamente

sorrow /'sɒrəʊ/ n tristezza f. ~ful adj triste

sorry /'sɒrɪ/ adj (-ier, -iest) (sad) spiacente; (wretched) pietoso; you'll be ~! te ne pentirai; I am ~ mi dispiace; be or feel ~ for provare compassione per; ~! scusa!; (more polite) scusi!

sort /sɔːt/ n specie f; (🔟: person) tipo m; it's a ~ of fish è un tipo di pesce; be out of ~s (🔟: unwell) stare poco bene ● vt classificare. □ ~ out vt selezionare (papers); fig risolvere (problem); occuparsi di (person)

'**so-so** adj & adv così così

sought /sɔːt/ ▷SEEK

soul /səʊl/ n anima f

sound[1] /saʊnd/ adj sano; (sensible) saggio; (secure) solido; (thrashing) clamoroso ● adv ~ asleep profondamente addormentato

sound[2] n suono m; (noise) rumore m; I don't like the ~ of it 🔟 non mi suona bene ● vi suonare; (seem) aver l'aria ● vt (pronounce) pronunciare; (Med) auscultare (chest). ~ barrier n muro m del suono. ~ card n (Comput) scheda f sonora. ~less adj silenzioso. □ ~ out vt fig sondare

soundly /'saʊndlɪ/ adv (sleep) profondamente; (defeat) clamorosamente

'**sound:** ~proof adj impenetrabile al suono. ~track n colonna f sonora

soup /suːp/ n minestra f. ~ed-up adj 🔟 (engine) truccato

sour /'saʊə(r)/ adj agro; (not fresh & fig) acido

source /sɔːs/ n fonte f

south /saʊθ/ n sud m; to the ~ of a sud di ● adj del sud, meridionale

● adv verso il sud
south: S∼ **'Africa** n Sudafrica m. S∼ **America** n America f del Sud. S∼ **American** adj e n sudamericano, -a mf. ∼**'east** n sudest m

southerly /'sʌðəlɪ/ adj del sud

southern /'sʌðən/ adj del sud, meridionale; ∼ **Italy** il Mezzogiorno m. ∼**er** n meridionale m

'southward[s] /-wəd[z]/ adv verso sud

souvenir /suːvə'nɪə(r)/ n ricordo m, souvenir m inv

sovereign /'sɒvrɪn/ adj sovrano ● n sovrano, -a mf. ∼**ty** n sovranità f inv

Soviet /'səʊvɪət/ adj sovietico; ∼ **Union** Unione f Sovietica

sow¹ /saʊ/ n scrofa f

sow² /səʊ/ vt (pt sowed, pp sown or sowed) seminare

soya /'sɔɪə/ n ∼ **bean** soia f

spa /spɑː/ n stazione f termale

space /speɪs/ n spazio m ● adj (research etc) spaziale ● vt ∼ [out] distanziare

space: ∼**ship** n astronave f. ∼ **shuttle** n navetta f spaziale

spade /speɪd/ n vanga f; (for child) paletta f; ∼**s** pl (in cards) picche fpl. ∼**work** n lavoro m preparatorio

Spain /speɪn/ n Spagna f

spam /spæm/ n spam m

span¹ /spæn/ n spanna f; (of arch) luce f; (of time) arco m; (of wings) apertura f ● vt (pt/pp spanned) estendersi su

span² ▷ **SPICK**

Spaniard /'spænjəd/ n spagnolo, -a mf. ∼**ish** adj (spanish) spagnolo m (language) spagnolo m; **the** ∼**ish** pl gli spagnoli

spank /spæŋk/ vt sculacciare. ∼**ing** n sculacciata f

spanner /'spænə(r)/ n chiave f inglese

spare /speə(r)/ adj (surplus) in più;

(additional) di riserva ● n (part) ricambio m ● vt risparmiare; (do without) fare a meno di; **can you** ∼ **five minutes?** avresti cinque minuti?; **to** ∼ (surplus) in eccedenza. ∼ **part** n pezzo m di ricambio. ∼ **time** n tempo m libero. ∼ **'wheel** n ruota f di scorta

spark /spɑːk/ n scintilla f. ∼**ing-plug** n (Auto) candela f

sparkle /'spɑːkl/ n scintillio m ● vi scintillare. ∼**ing** adj frizzante; (wine) spumante

sparrow /'spærəʊ/ n passero m

sparse /spɑːs/ adj rado. ∼**ly** adv scarsamente; ∼**ly populated** a bassa densità di popolazione

spasm /'spæzm/ n spasmo m. ∼**odic** adj spasmodico

spat /spæt/ ▷ **SPIT**¹

spate /speɪt/ n (series) successione f; **be in full** ∼ essere in piena

spatial /'speɪʃl/ adj spaziale

spatter /'spætə(r)/ vt schizzare

spawn /spɔːn/ n uova fpl (di pesci, rane, ecc.) ● vi deporre le uova ● vt fig generare

speak /spiːk/ v (pt spoke, pp spoken) ● vi parlare (to a); ∼**ing!** (Teleph) sono io! ● vt dire; ∼ **one's mind** dire quello che si pensa. □ ∼ **for** vi parlare a nome di. □ ∼ **up** vi parlare più forte; ∼ **up for oneself** parlare a favore di

speaker /'spiːkə(r)/ n parlante mf; (in public) oratore, -trice mf; (of stereo) cassa f

spear /spɪə(r)/ n lancia f

special /'speʃl/ adj speciale. ∼**ist** n specialista mf. ∼**ity** n specialità f inv

specialize /'speʃəlaɪz/ vi specializzarsi. ∼**ly** adv specialmente; (particularly) particolarmente

species /'spiːʃiːz/ n specie f inv

specific /spə'sɪfɪk/ adj specifico. ∼**ally** adv in modo specifico

specify /'spesɪfaɪ/ vt (pt/pp -ied)

specificare

specimen /'spesɪmən/ n campione m

speck /spek/ n macchiolina f; (particle) granello m

specs /speks/ npl 🔢 occhiali mpl

spectacle /'spektəkl/ n (show) spettacolo m. ~s npl occhiali mpl

spectacular /spek'tækjʊlə(r)/ adj spettacolare

spectator /spek'teɪtə(r)/ n spettatore, -trice m

spectre /'spektə(r)/ n spettro m

spectrum /'spektrəm/ n (pl -tra) spettro m; fig gamma f

speculat|e /'spekjʊleɪt/ vi speculare. ~ion n speculazione f. ~ive adj speculativo. ~or n speculatore, -trice mf

sped /sped/ ▷ SPEED

speech /spiːtʃ/ n linguaggio m; (address) discorso m. ~less adj senza parole

speed /spiːd/ n velocità f inv; (gear) marcia f; at ~ a tutta velocità ● vi (pt/pp sped) andare veloce; (pt/pp speeded) (go too fast) andare a velocità eccessiva. □ ~ up (pt/pp speeded up) n accelerare

speed: ~boat n motoscafo m. ~ camera n Autovelox® m inv. ~ dating n speed dating m. ~ limit n limite m di velocità

speedometer /spiː'dɒmɪtə(r)/ n tachimetro m

speed|y /'spiːdɪ/ adj (-ier, -iest) rapido. ~ily adv rapidamente

spell[1] /spel/ n (turn) turno m; (of weather) periodo m

spell[2] v (pt/pp spelled, spelt) ● vt how do you ~...? come si scrive...?; could you ~ that for me? me lo può compitare?; ~ disaster essere disastroso ● vi he can't ~ fa molti errori d'ortografia

spell[3] n (magic) incantesimo m. ~bound adj affascinato

spelling /'spelɪŋ/ n ortografia f

spelt /spelt/ ▷ SPELL[2]

spend /spend/ vt/i (pt/pp spent) spendere; passare (time)

sperm /spɜːm/ n spermatozoo m; (semen) sperma m

spew /spjuː/ vt/i vomitare

spher|e /sfɪə(r)/ n sfera f. ~ical adj sferico

spice /spaɪs/ n spezia f; fig pepe m

spick /spɪk/ adj ~ and span lindo

spicy /'spaɪsɪ/ adj piccante

spider /'spaɪdə(r)/ n ragno m

spik|e /spaɪk/ n punta f; (Bot, Zool) spina f; (on shoe) chiodo m. ~y adj (plant) pungente

spill /spɪl/ v (pt/pp spilt or spilled) ● vt versare (blood) ● vi rovesciarsi

spin /spɪn/ v (pt/pp spun, pres p spinning) ● vt far girare; filare (wool); centrifugare (washing) ● vi girare; (washing machine:) centrifugare ● n rotazione f; (short drive) giretto m. □ ~ out vt far durare

spinach /'spɪnɪdʒ/ n spinaci mpl

spin-drier n centrifuga f

spine /spaɪn/ n spina f dorsale; (of book) dorso m; (Bot, Zool) spina f. ~less adj fig smidollato

spin-off n ricaduta f

spiral /'spaɪrəl/ adj a spirale ● n spirale f ● vi (pt/pp spiralled) formare una spirale. ~ staircase n scala f a chiocciola

spire /spaɪə(r)/ n guglia f

spirit /'spɪrɪt/ n spirito m; (courage) ardore m; ~s pl (alcohol) liquori mpl; in good ~s di buon umore; in low ~s abbattuto

spirited /'spɪrɪtɪd/ adj vivace; (courageous) pieno d'ardore

spiritual /'spɪrɪtjʊəl/ adj spirituale ● n spiritual m. ~ism n spiritismo m. ~ist n spiritista mf

spit[1] /spɪt/ n (for roasting) spiedo m

spit[2] n sputo m ● vt/i (pt (pp spat, pres

p spitting) sputare; (cat:) soffiare; (fat:) sfrigolare; it's ~ting [with rain] pioviggina; the ~ting image of il ritratto spiccicato di

spite /spaɪt/ *n* dispetto *m*; **in** ~ **of** malgrado. • *vt* far dispetto a. ~**ful** *adj* indispettito

spittle /ˈspɪtl/ *n* saliva *f*

splash /splæʃ/ *n* schizzo *m*; (*of colour*) macchia *f*; (🅸: *drop*) goccio *m*. • *vt* schizzare; ~ **sb** with schizzare qcno di qcsa • *vi* schizzare. □ ~ **about** *vi* schizzarsi. □ ~ **down** *vi* (spacecraft:) ammarare

splendid /ˈsplendɪd/ *adj* splendido

splendour /ˈsplendə(r)/ *n* splendore *m*

splint /splɪnt/ *n* (*Med*) stecca *f*

splinter /ˈsplɪntə(r)/ *n* scheggia *f*. • *vi* scheggiarsi

split /splɪt/ *n* fessura *f*; (*quarrel*) rottura *f*; (*division*) scissione *f*; (*tear*) strappo *m* • *v* (*pt*/*pp* **split**, *pres p* **splitting**) • *vt* spaccare; (*share, divide*) dividere; (*tear*) strappare • *vi* spaccarsi; (*tear*) strapparsi; (*divide*) dividersi; ~ **on sb** 🅸 denunciare qcno • *adj* a ~ **second** una frazione *f* di secondo. □ ~ **up** *vi* dividersi • *vi* (*couple:*) separarsi

splutter /ˈsplʌtə(r)/ *vi* farfugliare

spoil /spɔɪl/ *n* ~**s** *pl* bottino *msg* • *v* (*pt*/*pp* **spoilt** *or* **spoiled**) • *vt* rovinare; viziare (*person*) • *vi* andare a male. ~**sport** *n* guastafeste *mf inv*

spoke[1] /spəʊk/ *n* raggio *m*

spoke[2], **spoken** /ˈspəʊkn/ ▷**SPEAK**

'**spokesman** *n* portavoce *m inv*

sponge /spʌndʒ/ *n* spugna *f* • *vt* pulire (*con la spugna*) • *vi* ~ **on** scroccare da. ~**-cake** *n* pan *m* di Spagna

sponsor /ˈspɒnsə(r)/ *n* garante *m*; (*Radio, TV*) sponsor *m inv*; (*god-parent*) padrino *m*, madrina *f*; (*for membership*) socio, -a *mf* garante • *vt* sponsorizzare. ~**ship** *n* sponsorizzazione *f*

spontaneous /spɒnˈteɪnɪəs/ *adj* spontaneo

spoof /spuːf/ *n* 🅸 parodia *f*

spooky /ˈspuːkɪ/ *adj* (**-ier, -iest**) 🅸 sinistro

spool /spuːl/ *n* bobina *f*

spoon /spuːn/ *n* cucchiaio *m* • *vt* mettere col cucchiaio. ~**-feed** *vt* (*pt*/*pp* **-fed**) *fig* imboccare. ~**ful** *n* cucchiaiata *f*

sporadic /spəˈrædɪk/ *adj* sporadico

sport /spɔːt/ *n* sport *m inv* • *vt* sfoggiare. ~**ing** *adj* sportivo; ~**ing chance** possibilità *f inv*

sports: ~**car** *n* automobile *f* sportiva. ~**man** *n* sportivo *m*. ~**woman** *n* sportiva *f*

spot /spɒt/ *n* macchia *f*; (*pimple*) brufolo *m*; (*place*) posto *m*; (*in pattern*) pois *m inv*; (*of rain*) goccia *f*; (*of water*) goccio *m*; ~**s** *pl* (*rash*) sfogo *msg*; **a** ~ **of** 🅸 un po' di; **a** ~ **of bother** qualche problema; **on the** ~ sul luogo; (*immediately*) immediatamente; **in a [tight]** ~ 🅸 in difficoltà • *vt* (*pt*/*pp* **spotted**) macchiare; (🅸: *notice*) individuare

spot: ~ **check** *n* (*without warning*) controllo *m* a sorpresa; **do a** ~ **check on sth** dare una controllata a qcsa. ~**less** *adj* immacolato. ~**light** *n* riflettore *m*

spotted /ˈspɒtɪd/ *adj* (*material*) a pois

spotty /ˈspɒtɪ/ *adj* (**-ier, -iest**) (*pimply*) brufoloso

spouse /spaʊz/ *n* consorte *mf*

spout /spaʊt/ *n* becco *m* • *vi* zampillare (*from da*)

sprain /spreɪn/ *n* slogatura *f* • *vt* slogare

sprang /spræŋ/ ▷**SPRING**[2]

spray /spreɪ/ *n* spruzzo *m*; (*preparation*) spray *m inv*; (*container*) spruzzatore *m inv* • *vt* spruzzare. ~**-gun** *n* pistola *f* a spruzzo

spread /spred/ *n* estensione *f*; (*of*

disease) diffusione *f*; (*paste*) crema *f*; (⚠: *feast*) banchetto *m* ● *v* (*pt/pp* spread) ● *vt* spargere; spalmare (butter, jam); stendere (cloth, arms); diffondere (news, disease); dilazionare (payments); ~ sth with spalmare qcsa di ● *vi* spargersi; (butter:) spalmarsi; (disease:) diffondersi. ~sheet *n* (Comput) foglio *m* elettronico. □ ~ out *vt* sparpagliare ● *vi* sparpagliarsi

spree /spriː/ *n* ⚠ go on a ~ far baldoria; go on a shopping ~ fare spese folli

sprightly /ˈspraɪtlɪ/ *adj* (-ier, -iest) vivace

spring[1] /sprɪŋ/ *n* primavera *f* ● *attrib* primaverile

spring[2] *n* (*jump*) balzo *m*; (*water*) sorgente *f*; (*device*) molla *f*; (*elasticity*) elasticità *f* *inv* ● *v* (*pt* sprang, *pp* sprung) ● *vi* balzare; (*arise*) provenire (from da) ● *vt* he just sprang it on me me l'ha detto a cose fatte compiuto. □ ~ up balzare; *fig* spuntare

spring: ~board *n* trampolino *m*. ~time *n* primavera *f*

sprinkle /ˈsprɪŋkl/ *vt* (*scatter*) spruzzare (liquid); spargere (flour, cocoa); ~ sth with spruzzare qcsa di (liquid); cospargere qcsa di (flour, cocoa). ~er *n* sprinkler *m* inv; (for lawn) irrigatore *m*. ~ing *n* (of liquid) spruzzatina *f*; (of pepper, salt) pizzico *m*; (of flour, sugar) spolverizzata *f*; (of knowledge) infarinatura *f*; (of people) pugno *m*

sprint /sprɪnt/ *n* sprint *m* ● *vi* fare uno sprint; (Sport) sprintare. ~er *n* sprinter *mf* inv

sprout /spraʊt/ *n* germoglio *m*; [Brussels] ~s *pl* cavolini *mpl* di Bruxelles ● *vi* germogliare

sprung /sprʌŋ/ ▷SPRING[2] ● *adj* molleggiato

spud /spʌd/ *n* ⚠ patata *f*

spun /spʌn/ ▷SPIN

spur /spɜː(r)/ *n* sperone *m*; (*stimulus*)

stimolo *m*; (*road*) svincolo *m*; **on the ~ of the moment** su due piedi ● *vt* (*pt/pp* spurred) ~ [**on**] *fig* spronare [a]

spurn /spɜːn/ *vt* sdegnare

spurt /spɜːt/ *n* getto *m*; (Sport) scatto *m*; **put on a** ~ fare uno scatto ● *vi* sprizzare; (increase speed) scattare

spy /spaɪ/ *n* spia *f* ● *v* (*pt/pp* spied) ● *vi* spiare ● *vt* (⚠: see) spiare. □ ~ **on** *vi* spiare

squabble /ˈskwɒbl/ *n* bisticcio *m* ● *vi* bisticciare

squad /skwɒd/ *n* squadra *f*; (Sport) squadra

squadron /ˈskwɒdrən/ *n* (Mil) squadrone *m*; (Aeron), (Naut) squadriglia *f*

squalid /ˈskwɒlɪd/ *adj* squallido

squalor /ˈskwɒlə(r)/ *n* squallore *m*

squander /ˈskwɒndə(r)/ *vt* sprecare

square /skweə(r)/ *adj* quadrato; (*meal*) sostanzioso; (⚠: *old-fashioned*) vecchio stampo; **all** ~ ⚠ pari ● *n* quadrato *m*; (in city) piazza *f*; (on chessboard) riquadro *m* ● *vt* (settle) far quadrare; (Math) elevare al quadrato ● *vi* (agree) armonizzare

squash /skwɒʃ/ *n* (drink) spremuta *f*; (sport) squash *m*; (vegetable) zucca *f* ● *vt* schiacciare; soffocare (rebellion)

squat /skwɒt/ *adj* tarchiato ● *n* ⚠ edificio *m* occupato abusivamente ● *vi* (*pt/pp* squatted) accovacciarsi; ~ **in** occupare abusivamente. ~ter *n* occupante *mf* abusivo, -a

squawk /skwɔːk/ *n* gracchio *m* ● *vi* gracchiare

squeak /skwiːk/ *n* squittio *m*; (of hinge, brakes) scricchiolio *m* ● *vi* squittire; (hinge, brakes:) scricchiolare

squeal /skwiːl/ *n* strillo *m*; (of brakes) cigolio *m* ● *vi* strillare; ⚠ spifferare

squeamish /ˈskwiːmɪʃ/ *adj* dallo stomaco delicato

squeeze /skwiːz/ *n* stretta *f*; (crush)

pigia pigia *m inv* • *vt* premere; (*to get juice*) spremere; stringere (hand); (*force*) spingere a forza; (🔲: *extort*) estorcere (out of da). □ ~ **in/out** *vi* sgusciare dentro/fuori. □ ~ **up** *vi* stringersi

squid /skwɪd/ *n* calamaro *m*

squiggle /'skwɪgl/ *n* scarabocchio *m*

squint /skwɪnt/ *n* strabismo *m* • *vi* essere strabico

squirm /skwɜːm/ *vi* contorcersi; (*feel embarrassed*) sentirsi imbarazzato

squirrel /'skwɪrəl/ *n* scoiattolo *m*

squirt /skwɜːt/ *n* spruzzo *m*; (🔲: *person*) presuntuoso *m* • *vt/i* spruzzare

St *abbr* (Saint) S; *abbr* Street

stab /stæb/ *n* pugnalata *f*, coltellata *f*; (*sensation*) fitta *f*; (🔲: *attempt*) tentativo *m* • *vt* (*pt/pp* stabbed) pugnalare, accoltellare

stability /stə'bɪlətɪ/ *n* stabilità *f*

stabilize /'steɪbɪlaɪz/ *vt* stabilizzare • *vi* stabilizzarsi

stable¹ /'steɪbl/ *adj* stabile

stable² /'steɪbl/ *n* stalla *f*; (*establishment*) scuderia *f*

stack /stæk/ *n* catasta *f*; (*of chimney*) comignolo *m*; (*chimney*) ciminiera *f*; (🔲: *large quantity*) montagna *f* • *vt* accatastare

stadium /'steɪdɪəm/ *n* stadio *m*

staff /stɑːf/ *n* (*stick*) bastone *m*; (*employees*) personale *m*; (*teachers*) corpo *m* insegnante; (*Mil*) Stato *m* Maggiore • *vt* fornire di personale. ~**-room** *n* (*Sch*) sala *f* insegnanti

stag /stæg/ *n* cervo *m*

stage /steɪdʒ/ *n* palcoscenico *m*; (*profession*) teatro *m*; (*in journey*) tappa *f*; (*in process*) stadio *m*; by *or* on the ~ darsi al teatro; by *or* in ~s a tappe • *vt* mettere in scena; (*arrange*) organizzare

stagger /'stægə(r)/ *vi* barcollare • *vt* sbalordire; scaglionare (holidays etc); I was ~ed ho sono rimasto sbalordito

• *n* vacillamento *m*. ~**ing** *adj* sbalorditivo

stagnant /'stægnənt/ *adj* stagnante

stagnate /stæg'neɪt/ *vi fig* [ri]stagnare. ~**ion** *n fig* inattività *f*

'**stag party** *n* addio *m* al celibato

staid /steɪd/ *adj* posato

stain /steɪn/ *n* macchia *f*; (*for wood*) mordente *m* • *vt* macchiare; (*wood*) dare il mordente a; ~**ed glass** vetro *m* colorato; ~**ed-glass window** vetrata *f* colorata. ~**less** *adj* senza macchia; (steel) inossidabile. ~ **remover** *n* smacchiatore *m*

stair /steə(r)/ *n* gradino *m*; ~**s** *pl* scale *fpl*. ~**case** *n* scale *fpl*

stake /steɪk/ *n* palo *m*; (*wager*) posta *f*; (*Comm*) partecipazione *f*; **at** ~ **in** gioco *f* • *vt* puntellare; (*wager*) scommettere

stale /steɪl/ *adj* stantio; (air) viziato; (*uninteresting*) trito [e ritrito]. ~**mate** *n* (*in chess*) stallo *m*; (*deadlock*) situazione *f* di stallo

stalk¹ /stɔːk/ *n* gambo *m*

stalk² *vt* inseguire • *vi* camminare impettito

stall /stɔːl/ *n* box *m inv*; (*in market*) bancarella *f*; ~**s** *pl* (*Theat*) platea *f* • *vi* (*engine*) spegnersi; *fig* temporeggiare • *vt* far spegnere (engine); tenere a bada (person)

stallion /'stæljən/ *n* stallone *m*

stalwart /'stɔːlwət/ *adj* fedele

stamina /'stæmɪnə/ *n* [capacità *f inv* di] resistenza *f*

stammer /'stæmə(r)/ *n* balbettio *m* • *vt/i* balbettare

stamp /stæmp/ *n* (*postage* ~) francobollo *m*; (*instrument*) timbro *m*; *fig* impronta *f* • *vt* affrancare (letter); timbrare (bill); battere (feet). □ ~ **out** *vt* spegnere; *fig* soffocare

stampede /stæm'piːd/ *n* fuga *f* precipitosa; 🔲 fuggi-fuggi *m* • *vi* fuggire precipitosamente

stance /stɑːns/ *n* posizione *f*

stand /stænd/ n (*for bikes*) rastrelliera f; (*at exhibition*) stand m inv; (*in market*) bancarella f; (*in stadium*) gradinata f inv; fig posizione f • v (*pt/pp stood*) • vi stare in piedi; (*rise*) alzarsi [in piedi]; (*be*) trovarsi; (*be candidate*) essere candidato (**for** a); (*stay valid*) rimanere valido; ~ **still** non muoversi; **I don't know where I** ~ non so qual'è la mia posizione; ~ **firm** fig tener duro; ~ **together** essere solidali; ~ **to lose/gain** rischiare di perdere/vincere; ~ **to reason** essere logico • vt (*withstand*) resistere a; (*endure*) sopportare; (*place*) mettere; **a chance** avere una possibilità; ~ **one's ground** tener duro; ~ **the test of time** superare la prova del tempo; ~ **sb a beer** offrire una birra a qcno. □ ~ **by** vi stare a guardare; (*be ready*) essere pronto • vt (*support*) appoggiare. □ ~ **down** vi (*retire*) ritirarsi. □ ~ **for** vt (*mean*) significare; (*tolerate*) tollerare. □ ~ **in for** vt sostituire. □ ~ **out** vi spiccare. □ ~ **up** vi alzarsi [in piedi]. □ ~ **up for** vt prendere le difese di; ~ **up for oneself** farsi valere. □ ~ **up to** vt affrontare

standard /'stændəd/ adj standard; **be** ~ **practice** essere pratica corrente • n standard m inv; (Techn) norma f; (*level*) livello m; (*quality*) qualità f inv; (*flag*) stendardo m; ~**s** pl (*morals*) valori mpl; ~ **of living** tenore m di vita. ~**ize** vt standardizzare

'standard lamp n lampada f a stelo

'stand-by n riserva f; **on** ~ (*at airport*) in lista d'attesa

'stand-in n controfigura f

standing /'stændɪŋ/ adj (*erect*) in piedi; (*permanent*) permanente • n posizione f; (*duration*) durata f; ~ **'order** n addebitamento m diretto. ~**-room** n posti mpl in piedi

stand: ~**point** n punto m di vista. ~**still** n come to a ~**still** fermarsi; **at a** ~**still** in un periodo di stasi

stank /stæŋk/ ▷ **STINK**

staple¹ /'steɪpl/ n (*product*) prodotto m principale

staple² n graffa f • vt pinzare. ~**r** n pinzatrice f, cucitrice f

star /stɑ:(r)/ n stella f; (*asterisk*) asterisco m; (Cinema, Sport, Theat) divo, -a mf, stella f • vi (*pt/pp starred*) essere l'interprete principale

starboard /'stɑ:bəd/ n tribordo m

starch /stɑ:tʃ/ n amido m • vt inamidare. ~**y** adj ricco di amido; fig compito

stare /steə(r)/ n sguardo m fisso • vi **it's rude to** ~ **sb** è da maleducati fissare la gente; ~ **at** fissare; ~ **into space** guardare nel vuoto

'starfish n stella f di mare

stark /stɑ:k/ adj austero; (*contrast*) forte • adv completamente; ~ **naked** completamente nudo

starling /'stɑ:lɪŋ/ n storno m

starry /'stɑ:rɪ/ adj stellato

start /stɑ:t/ n inizio m; (*departure*) partenza f; (*jump*) sobbalzo m; **from the** ~ [fin] dall'inizio; **for a** ~ tanto per cominciare; **give sb a** ~ (Sport) dare un vantaggio a qcno • vi [in]cominciare; (*set out*) avviarsi; (*engine, car*) partire; (*jump*) trasalire; **to** **with,...** tanto per cominciare,... • vt [in]cominciare; (*cause*) dare inizio a; (*found*) mettere su; mettere in moto (*car*); mettere in giro (*rumour*). ~**er** n (Culin) primo m [piatto m]; (*in race: giving signal*) starter m inv; (*participant*) concorrente mf; (Auto) motorino m d'avviamento. ~**ing-point** n punto m di partenza

startle /'stɑ:tl/ vt far trasalire; (*news*) sconvolgere

starvation /stɑ:'veɪʃn/ n fame f

starve /stɑ:v/ vi morire di fame • vt far morire di fame

state /steɪt/ n stato m; (*grand style*) pompa f; ~ **of play** punteggio m; **be in a** ~ (*person:*) essere agitato;

stately | step

lie in ~ essere esposto ● attrib di Stato; (Sch) pubblico; (with ceremony) di gala ● vt dichiarare; (specify) precisare. ~less adj apolide

stately /ˈsteɪtlɪ/ adj (-ier, -iest) maestoso. ~ 'home n dimora f signorile

statement /ˈsteɪtmənt/ n dichiarazione f; (Jur) deposizione f; (in banking) estratto m conto; (account) rapporto m

> **state schools** In Gran Bretagna sono le scuole elementari, medie e superiori pubbliche, contrapposte alle *public schools* (scuole private).

'statesman n statista mf

static /ˈstætɪk/ adj statico

station /ˈsteɪʃn/ n stazione f; (police) commissariato m ● vt appostare (guard); be ~ed in Germany essere di stanza in Germania. ~ary adj immobile

'station-wagon n Am familiare f

statistic|al /stəˈtɪstɪkl/ adj statistico. ~s n & pl statistica f

statue /ˈstætjuː/ n statua f

stature /ˈstætʃə(r)/ n statura f

status /ˈsteɪtəs/ n condizione f; (high rank) alto rango m. ~ symbol n status symbol m inv

statut|e /ˈstætjuːt/ n statuto m. ~ory adj statutario

staunch /stɔːntʃ/ adj fedele. ~ly adv fedelmente

stave /steɪv/ vt ~ off tenere lontano

stay /steɪ/ n soggiorno m ● vi restare, rimanere; (reside) alloggiare; ~ the night passare la notte; ~ put non muoversi ● vt ~ the course resistere fino alla fine. □ ~ away vi stare lontano. □ ~ behind vi non andare con gli altri. □ ~ in vi (at home) stare in casa; (Sch) restare a scuola dopo le

lezioni. □ ~ up vi stare su; (person:) stare alzato

stead /sted/ n in his ~ in sua vece; stand sb in good ~ tornare utile a qcno. ~fast adj fedele; (refusal) fermo

steadily /ˈstedɪlɪ/ adv (continually) continuamente

steady /ˈstedɪ/ adj (-ier, -iest) saldo, fermo; (breathing) regolare; (job, boyfriend) fisso; (dependable) serio

steak /steɪk/ n (for stew) spezzatino m; (for grilling, frying) bistecca f

steal /stiːl/ v (pt stole, pp stolen) ● vt rubare (from da). □ ~ in/out vi entrare/uscire furtivamente

stealth /stelθ/ n by ~ di nascosto. ~y adj furtivo

steam /stiːm/ n vapore m; under one's own ~ 🛈 da solo ● vt (Culin) cucinare a vapore ● vi fumare. □ ~ up vi appannarsi

'steam-engine n locomotiva f

steamer /ˈstiːmə(r)/ n piroscafo m; (saucepan) pentola f a vapore

'steamroller n rullo m compressore

steamy /ˈstiːmɪ/ adj appannato

steel /stiːl/ n acciaio m ● vt ~ oneself temprarsi

steep¹ /stiːp/ vt (soak) lasciare a bagno

steep² adj ripido; (🛈: price) esorbitante. ~ly adv ripidamente

steeple /ˈstiːpl/ n campanile m. ~chase n corsa f ippica a ostacoli

steer /stɪə(r)/ vt/i guidare; ~ clear of stare alla larga da. ~ing n (Auto) sterzo m. ~ing-wheel n volante m

stem¹ /stem/ n stelo m; (of glass) gambo m; (of word) radice f ● vi (pt/pp stemmed) ~ from derivare da

stem² vt (pt/pp stemmed) contenere

stench /stentʃ/ n fetore m

step /step/ n passo m; (stair) gradino m; ~s pl (ladder) scala f portatile; in

$\sim$ al passo; **be out of** $\sim$ non stare al passo; $\sim$ **by** $\sim$ un passo alla volta ● vi (*pt/pp* **stepped**) □ **into** entrare in; $\sim$ **out of** uscire da; $\sim$ **out of line** sgarrare. □ $\sim$ **down** vi fig dimettersi. □ $\sim$ **forward** vi farsi avanti. □ $\sim$ **in** vi fig intervenire. □ $\sim$ **up** vt (*increase*) aumentare

step: $\sim$**brother** n fratellastro m. $\sim$**daughter** n figliastra f. $\sim$**father** n patrigno m. $\sim$**ladder** n scala f portatile. $\sim$**mother** n matrigna f

'stepping-stone n pietra f per guadare; fig trampolino m

step: $\sim$**sister** n sorellastra f. $\sim$**son** n figliastro m

stereo /'steriəʊ/ n stereo m; **in** $\sim$ in stereofonia. $\sim$**phonic** adj stereofonico

stereotype /'steriətaɪp/ n stereotipo m. $\sim$**d** adj stereotipato

steril|e /'steraɪl/ adj sterile. $\sim$**ity** n sterilità f inv

sterling /'stɜːlɪŋ/ adj fig apprezzabile; $\sim$ **silver** argento m pregiato ● n sterlina f

stern[1] /stɜːn/ adj severo

stern[2] n (*of boat*) poppa f

stethoscope /'steθəskəʊp/ n stetoscopio m

stew /stjuː/ n stufato m; **in a** $\sim$ 🆃 agitato ● vt/i cuocere in umido; $\sim$**ed fruit** frutta f cotta

steward /'stjuːəd/ n (*at meeting*) organizzatore, -trice mf; (*on ship, aircraft*) steward m inv. $\sim$**ess** n hostess f inv

stick[1] /stɪk/ n bastone m; (*of celery, rhubarb*) gambo m; (*Sport*) mazza f

stick[2] v (*pt/pp* **stuck**) ● vt (*stab*) [con]ficcare; (*glue*) attaccare; (🆃: *put*) mettere; (🆃: *endure*) sopportare ● vi (*adhere*) attaccarsi (to a); (*jam*) bloccarsi; $\sim$ **to** attenersi a (facts); maintain (story); perseverare in (task); $\sim$ **at it** 🆃 tener duro; $\sim$ **at nothing** 🆃 non fermarsi di fronte a niente; **be stuck** (*vehicle, person:*) essere bloccato; (*drawer:*) essere incastrato; **be stuck with sth** 🆃 farsi incastrare con qcsa. □ $\sim$ **out** vi (*project*) sporgere; (🆃: *catch the eye*) risaltare ● vt 🆃 fare (tongue). □ $\sim$ **up for** vt 🆃 difendere

sticker /'stɪkə(r)/ n autoadesivo m

'sticking plaster n cerotto m

stickler /'stɪklə(r)/ n **be a** $\sim$ **for** tenere molto a

sticky /'stɪkɪ/ adj (**-ier, -iest**) appiccicoso; (*adhesive*) adesivo; (*fig: difficult*) difficile

stiff /stɪf/ adj rigido; (brush, task) duro; (person) controllato; (drink) forte; (penalty) severo; (price) alto; **bored** $\sim$ 🆃 annoiato a morte; $\sim$ **neck** torcicollo m. $\sim$**en** vt irrigidire ● vi irrigidirsi. $\sim$**ness** n rigidità f inv

stifl|e /'staɪfl/ vt soffocare. $\sim$**ing** adj soffocante

still[1] /stɪl/ n distilleria f

still[2] adj fermo; (drink) non gasato; **keep/stand** $\sim$ stare fermo ● n quiete f; (*photo*) posa f ● adv ancora; (*nevertheless*) nondimeno, comunque; **I'm** $\sim$ **not sure** non sono ancora sicuro

'stillborn adj nato morto

still 'life n natura f morta

stilted /'stɪltɪd/ adj artificioso

stilts /stɪlts/ npl trampoli mpl

stimulant /'stɪmjʊlənt/ n eccitante m

stimulat|e /'stɪmjʊleɪt/ vt stimolare. $\sim$**ion** n stimolo m

stimulus /'stɪmjʊləs/ n (pl **-li** /-laɪ/) stimolo m

sting /stɪŋ/ n puntura f; (*from nettle, jellyfish*) sostanza f irritante; (*organ*) pungiglione m ● v (*pt/pp* **stung**) ● vt pungere; (jellyfish:) pizzicare ● vi (insect:) pungere. $\sim$**ing nettle** n ortica f

stingy /'stɪndʒɪ/ adj (**-ier, -iest**) tirchio

stink /stɪŋk/ n puzza f ● vi (pt **stank**,

pp stunk) puzzare

stipulat|e /'strpjulert/ *vt* porre come condizione. **~ion** *n* condizione *f*

stir /stɜ:(r)/ *n* mescolata *f*; (*commotion*) trambusto *m* • (*pt/pp* stirred) • *vt* muovere; (*mix*) mescolare • *vi* muoversi

stirrup /'strrəp/ *n* staffa *f*

stitch /strtʃ/ *n* punto *m*; (*in knitting*) maglia *f*; (*pain*) fitta *f*; have sb in ~es 🔢 far ridere qcno a crepapelle • *vt* cucire

stock /stɒk/ *n* (*for use or selling*) scorta *f*, stock *m inv*; (*livestock*) bestiame *m*; (*lineage*) stirpe *f*; (*Fin*) titoli *mpl*; (*Culin*) brodo *m*; in ~ disponibile; out of ~ esaurito; take ~ *fig* fare il punto • *adj* solito • *vt* (*shop*): vendere; approvvigionare (shelves). □ ~ **up** *vi* far scorta (with di)

stock: **~broker** *n* agente *m* di cambio. **S~ Exchange** *n* Borsa *f* Valori

stocking /'stɒkɪŋ/ *n* calza *f*

stock: **~pile** *vt* fare scorta di • *n* riserva *f*. **~still** *adj* immobile. **~taking** *n* (*Comm*) inventario *m*

stocky /'stɒkɪ/ *adj* (-ier, -iest) tarchiato

stodgy /'stɒdʒɪ/ *adj* indigesto

stoke /stəʊk/ *vt* alimentare

stole[1] /stəʊl/ *n* stola *f*

stole[2], stolen /'stəʊln/ ▷ **STEAL**

stomach /'stʌmək/ *n* pancia *f*; (*Anat*) stomaco *m* • *vt* 🔢 reggere. **~ache** *n* mal *m* di pancia

stone /stəʊn/ *n* pietra *f*; (*in fruit*) nocciolo *m*; (*Med*) calcolo *m*; (*weight*) 6,348 *kg* • *adj* di pietra; (wall, Age) della pietra • *vt* snocciolare (fruit). **~cold** *adj* gelido. **~-'deaf** *adj* 🔢 sordo come una campana

stony /'stəʊnɪ/ *adj* pietroso; (glare) glaciale

stood /stʊd/ ▷ **STAND**

stool /stu:l/ *n* sgabello *m*

stoop /stu:p/ *n* curvatura *f* • *vi* stare curvo; (bend down) chinarsi; *fig* abbassarsi

stop /stɒp/ *n* (break) sosta *f*; (*for bus, train*) fermata *f*; (*Gram*) punto *m*; come to a ~ fermarsi; put a ~ to sth mettere fine a qcsa • *v* (*pt/pp* stopped) • *vt* fermare; arrestare (machine); (*prevent*) impedire; ~ sb doing sth impedire a qcno di fare qcsa; ~ doing sth smettere di fare qcsa; ~ that! smettila! • *vi* fermarsi; (rain): smettere • *int* fermo!. □ ~ **off** *vi* fare una sosta. □ ~ **up** *vt* otturare (sink); tappare (hole). □ ~ **with** *vi* (🔢: stay with) fermarsi da

stop: **~gap** *n* palliativo *m*; (*person*) tappabuchi *m inv*. **~over** *n* sosta *f*; (*Aeron*) scalo *m*

stoppage /'stɒpɪdʒ/ *n* ostruzione *f*; (*strike*) interruzione *f*; (*deduction*) trattenute *fpl*

stopper /'stɒpə(r)/ *n* tappo *m*

stop-watch *n* cronometro *m*

storage /'stɔ:rɪdʒ/ *n* deposito *m*; (*in warehouse*) immagazzinaggio *m*; (*Comput*) memoria *f*

store /stɔ:(r)/ *n* (stock) riserva *f*; (shop) grande magazzino *m*; (depot) deposito *m*; in ~ in deposito; what the future has in ~ for me cosa mi riserva il futuro; set great ~ by tenere in gran conto • *vt* tenere; (*in warehouse, Comput*) immagazzinare. **~room** *n* magazzino *m*

storey /'stɔ:rɪ/ *n* piano *m*

stork /stɔ:k/ *n* cicogna *f*

storm /stɔ:m/ *n* temporale *m*; (*with thunder*) tempesta *f* • *vt* prendere d'assalto. **~y** *adj* tempestoso

story /'stɔ:rɪ/ *n* storia *f*; (*in newspaper*) articolo *m*

stout /staʊt/ *adj* (shoes) resistente; (*fat*) robusto; (defence) strenuo

stove /stəʊv/ *n* stufa *f*; (*for cooking*) cucina *f* [economica]

stow /stəʊ/ *vt* metter via. **~away** *n*

passeggero, -a *mf* clandestino, -a

straggl|e /'strægl/ *vi* crescere disordinatamente; (*dawdle*) rimanere indietro. **~er** *n* persona *f* che rimane indietro. **~y** *adj* in disordine

straight /streɪt/ *adj* diritto, dritto; (*answer, question, person*) diretto; (*tidy*) in ordine; (*drink, hair*) liscio ●*adv* diritto, dritto; (*directly*) direttamente; **~ away** immediatamente; **~ on** *or* **ahead** diritto; **~ out** *fig* apertamente; **go ~** 🅵 rigare diritto; **put sth ~** mettere qcsa in ordine; **sit/stand up ~** stare diritto

straighten /'streɪtn/ *vt* raddrizzare ●*vi* raddrizzarsi; **~ [up]** (person:) mettersi diritto. □ **~ out** *vt* fig chiarire (situation)

straight|forward *adj* franco; (*simple*) semplice

strain[1] /streɪn/ *n* (*streak*) vena *f*; (*Bot*) varietà *f inv*; (*of virus*) forma *f*

strain[2] *n* tensione *f*; (*injury*) stiramento *m*; **~s** *pl* (*of music*) note *fpl* ●*vt* tirare; sforzare (eyes, voice); stirarsi (muscle); (*Culin*) scolare ●*vi* sforzarsi. **~ed** *adj* (relations) teso. **~er** *n* colino *m*

strait /streɪt/ *n* stretto *m*; **in dire ~s** in serie difficoltà. **~-jacket** *n* camicia *f* di forza. **~-'laced** *adj* puritano

strand[1] /strænd/ *n* (*of thread*) gugliata *f*; (*of beads*) filo *m*; (*of hair*) capello *m*

strand[2] *vt* **be ~ed** rimanere bloccato

strange /streɪndʒ/ *adj* strano; (*not known*) sconosciuto; (*unaccustomed*) estraneo. **~ly** *adv* stranamente; **~ly enough** curiosamente. **~r** *n* estraneo, -a *mf*

strangle /'stræŋgl/ *vt* strangolare; *fig* reprimere

strap /stræp/ *n* cinghia *f* (*to grasp in vehicle*) maniglia *f*; (*of watch*) cinturino *m*; (*shoulder ~*) bretella *f*, spallina *f* ●*vt*

(*pt/pp* **strapped**) legare; **~ in** *or* **down** assicurare

strategic /strə'tiːdʒɪk/ *adj* strategico

strategy /'strætɪdʒɪ/ *n* strategia *f*

straw /strɔː/ *n* paglia *f*; (*single piece*) fuscello *m*; (*for drinking*) cannuccia *f*; **the last ~** l'ultima goccia

strawberry /'strɔːbərɪ/ *n* fragola *f*

stray /streɪ/ *adj* (*animal*) randagio ●*n* randagio *m* ●*vi* andarsene per conto proprio; (*deviate*) deviare (from da)

streak /striːk/ *n* striatura *f*; (*fig: trait*) vena *f* ●*vi* sfrecciare. **~y** *adj* striato; (bacon) grasso

stream /striːm/ *n* ruscello *m*; (*current*) corrente *f*; (*of blood, people*) flusso *m*; (*Sch*) classe *f* ●*vi* scorrere. □ **~ in/out** *vi* entrare/uscire a fiotti

streamer /'striːmə(r)/ *n* (*paper*) stella filante *f*; (*flag*) pennone *m*

'streamline *vt* rendere aerodinamico; (*simplify*) snellire. **~d** *adj* aerodinamico

street /striːt/ *n* strada *f*. **~car** *n* Am tram *m inv*. **~lamp** *n* lampione *m*

strength /streŋθ/ *n* forza *f*; (*of wall, bridge etc*) solidità *f inv*; **~s** punti *mpl* forti; **on the ~ of** grazie a. **~en** *vt* rinforzare

strenuous /'strenjʊəs/ *adj* faticoso; (*attempt, denial*) energico

stress /stres/ *n* (*emphasis*) insistenza *f*; (*Gram*) accento *m*; (*mental*) stress *m inv*; (*Mech*) spinta *f* ●*vt* (*emphasize*) insistere su; (*Gram*) mettere l'accento [tonico] su. **~ed** *adj* (*mentally*) stressato. **~ful** *adj* stressante

stretch /stretʃ/ *n* stiramento *m*; (*period*) periodo *m* di tempo; (*of road*) estensione *f*; (*elasticity*) elasticità *f inv*; **at a ~** di fila; **have a ~** stirarsi ●*vt* tirare; allargare (shoes, arms etc); (person:) allungare ●*vi* (*become wider*) allargarsi; (*extend*) estendersi; (person:) stirarsi. **~er** *n* barella *f*

strict /strɪkt/ *adj* severo; (*precise*)

s

preciso. ~ly adv severamente; ~ly speaking in senso stretto

stride /straɪd/ n [lungo] passo m; take sth in one's ~ accettare qcsa con facilità ● vi (pt **strode**, pp stridden) andare a gran passi

strident /'straɪdənt/ adj affascinante

strife /straɪf/ n conflitto m

strike /straɪk/ n sciopero m; (Mil) attacco m; on ~ in sciopero ● vt (pt/pp struck) ● vt colpire; accendere (match); trovare (oil, gold); (delete) depennare; (occur to) venire in mente a; (Mil) attaccare ● vi (lightning:) cadere; (clock:) suonare; (Mil) attaccare; (workers:) scioperare; ~ lucky azzeccarla. □ ~ **off**, strike out vt eliminare. □ ~ **up** vt fare (friendship); attaccare (conversation). ~-breaker n persona f che non aderisce a uno sciopero

striker /'straɪkə(r)/ n scioperante mf

striking /'straɪkɪŋ/ adj impressionante; (attractive) affascinante

string /strɪŋ/ n spago m; (of musical instrument, racket) corda f; (of pearls) filo m; (of lies) serie f; the ~s (Mus) gli archi; pull ~s 🔢 usare le proprie conoscenze ● vt (pt/pp strung) (thread) infilare (beads). ~ed adj (instrument) a corda

stringent /'strɪndʒənt/ adj rigido

strip /strɪp/ n striscia f ● vt (pt/pp stripped) ● vt spogliare; togliere le lenzuola da (bed); scrostare (wood, furniture); smontare (machine); (deprive) privare (of di) ● vi (undress) spogliarsi. ~ **cartoon** n fumetto m. ~ club n locale m di strip-tease

stripe /straɪp/ n striscia f; (Mil) gallone m. ~d adj a strisce

strip-'tease n spogliarello m, strip-tease m inv

strive /straɪv/ vi (pt strove, pp striven) sforzarsi (to di); ~ for cercare di ottenere

strode /strəʊd/ ▷ **STRIDE**

stroke[1] /strəʊk/ n colpo m; (of pen) tratto m; (in swimming) bracciata f; (Med) ictus m inv; ~ of luck colpo m di fortuna; put sb off his ~ far perdere il filo a qcno

stroke[2] vt accarezzare

stroll /strəʊl/ n passeggiata f ● vi passeggiare. ~er n (Am: push-chair) passeggino m

strong /strɒŋ/ adj (-er /-gə/, -est /-gɪst/) forte; (argument) valido

strong: ~hold n roccaforte f. ~ly adv fortemente. ~-room n camera f blindata

stroppy /'strɒpɪ/ adj scorbutico

strove /strəʊv/ ▷ **STRIVE**

struck /strʌk/ ▷ **STRIKE**

structural /'strʌktʃərəl/ adj strutturale. ~ly adv strutturalmente

structure /'strʌktʃə(r)/ n struttura f

struggle /'strʌgl/ n lotta f; with a ~ lottare con ● vi lottare; ~ for breath respirare con fatica; ~ to do sth fare fatica a fare qcsa; ~ to one's feet alzarsi con fatica

strum /strʌm/ vt/i (pt/pp strummed) strimpellare

strung /strʌŋ/ ▷ **STRING**

strut[1] /strʌt/ n (component) puntello m

strut[2] vi (pt/pp strutted) camminare impettito

stub /stʌb/ n mozzicone m; (counterfoil) matrice f ● vt (pt/pp stubbed) ~ one's toe sbattere il dito del piede (on contro). □ ~ **out** vt spegnere (cigarette)

stubb|le /'stʌbl/ n barba f ispida. ~ly adj ispido

stubborn /'stʌbən/ adj testardo; (refusal) ostinato

stuck /stʌk/ ▷ **STICK**[2]. ~-'up adj 🔢 snob

stud[1] /stʌd/ n (on boot) tacchetto m;

(on jacket) borchia f; (for ear) orecchino m [a bottone]

stud² /stʌf/ n (of horses) scuderia f

student /'stjuːdənt/ n studente m, studentessa f; (school child) scolaro, -a mf. ~ **nurse** n studente, studentessa infermiere, -a

studio /'stjuːdɪəʊ/ n studio m

studious /'stjuːdɪəs/ adj studioso; (attention) studiato

study /'stʌdɪ/ n studio m • vt/i (pt/pp studied) studiare

stuff /stʌf/ n materiale m; (▣: things) roba f • vt riempire; (with padding) imbottire; (Culin) farcire; ~ **sth into a drawer/one's pocket** ficcare qcsa alla rinfusa in un cassetto/in tasca. ~**ing** n (padding) imbottitura f; (Culin) ripieno m

stuffy /'stʌfɪ/ adj (-ier, -iest) che sa di chiuso; (old-fashioned) antiquato

stumbl|e /'stʌmbl/ vi inciampare; ~**e across** or **on** imbattersi in. ~**ing-block** n ostacolo m

stump /stʌmp/ n ceppo m; (of limb) moncone m. ~**ed** adj ▣ perplesso • **stump up** vt/i ▣ sganciare

stun /stʌn/ vt (pt/pp stunned) stordire; (astonish) sbalordire

stung /stʌŋ/ ▷STING

stunk /stʌŋk/ ▷STINK

stunning /'stʌnɪŋ/ adj ▣ favoloso; (blow, victory) sbalorditivo

stunt¹ /stʌnt/ n ▣ trovata f pubblicitaria

stunt² vt arrestare lo sviluppo di. ~**ed** adj stentato

stupendous /stjuːˈpendəs/ adj stupendo. ~**ly** adv stupendamente

stupid /'stjuːpɪd/ adj stupido. ~**ity** n stupidità f. ~**ly** adv stupidamente

stupor /'stjuːpə(r)/ n torpore m

sturdy /'stɜːdɪ/ adj (-ier, -iest) robusto; (furniture) solido

stutter /'stʌtə(r)/ n balbuzie f • vt/i balbettare

sty, stye /staɪ/ n (pl styes) (Med) orzaiolo m

style /staɪl/ n stile m; (fashion) moda f; (sort) tipo m; (hair~) pettinatura f; in ~ in grande stile

stylish /'staɪlɪʃ/ adj elegante. ~**ly** adv con eleganza

stylist /'staɪlɪst/ n stilista mf; (hair~) parrucchiere, -a mf. ~**ic** adj stilistico

stylus /'staɪləs/ n (on record player) puntina f

suave /swɑːv/ adj dai modi garbati

sub·conscious /sʌb-/ adj subcosciente • n subcosciente m. ~**ly** adv in modo inconscio

'**subdiv|ide** vt suddividere. ~**sion** n suddivisione f

subject¹ /'sʌbdʒɪkt/ adj ~ **to** soggetto a; (depending on) subordinato a; ~ **to availability** nei limiti della disponibilità • n soggetto m; (of ruler) suddito, -a mf; (Sch) materia f

subject² /səb'dʒekt/ vt (to attack, abuse) sottoporre; assoggettare (country)

subjective /səb'dʒektɪv/ adj soggettivo. ~**ly** adv soggettivamente

subjunctive /səb'dʒʌŋktɪv/ adj & n congiuntivo m

sublime /sə'blaɪm/ adj sublime. ~**ly** adv sublimemente

subma·rine /sʌbmə-/ n sommergibile m

submerge /səb'mɜːdʒ/ vt immergere; **be** ~**d** essere sommerso • vi immergersi

submiss|ion /səb'mɪʃn/ n sottomissione f. ~**ive** adj sottomesso

submit /səb'mɪt/ v (pt/pp -mitted, pres p -mitting) • vt sottoporre • vi sottomettersi

subordinate /sə'bɔːdɪneɪt/ vt subordinare (to a)

subscribe /səb'skraɪb/ vi contribuire; ~ **to** abbonarsi a (newspaper); sottoscrivere (fund); fig aderire a. ~**r** n abbonato, -a mf

s

subscription /səb'skrɪpʃn/ n (to club) sottoscrizione f; (to newspaper) abbonamento m

subsequent /'sʌbsɪkwənt/ adj susseguente. ~ly adv in seguito

subside /səb'saɪd/ vi sprofondare; (ground:) avvallarsi; (storm:) placarsi

subsidiary /səb'sɪdɪərɪ/ adj secondario ● n ~ [company] filiale f

subsid|ize /'sʌbsɪdaɪz/ vt sovvenzionare. ~y n sovvenzione f

substance /'sʌbstəns/ n sostanza f

sub'standard adj di qualità inferiore

substantial /səb'stænʃl/ adj solido; (meal) sostanzioso; (considerable) notevole. ~ly adv notevolmente; (essentially) sostanzialmente

substitut|e /'sʌbstɪtjuːt/ n sostituto m ● vt ~e A for B sostituire B con A ● vi ~e for sb sostituire qcno. ~ion n sostituzione f

subterranean /sʌbtə'reɪnɪən/ adj sotterraneo

'subtitle n sottotitolo m

sub|tle /'sʌtl/ adj sottile; (taste, perfume) delicato. ~tlety n sottigliezza f. ~tly adv sottilmente

subtract /səb'trækt/ vt sottrarre. ~ion n sottrazione f

suburb /'sʌbɜːb/ n sobborgo m; in the ~s in periferia. ~an adj suburbano. ~ia n i sobborghi mpl

subversive /səb'vɜːsɪv/ adj sovversivo

'subway n sottopassaggio m; (Am: railway) metropolitana f

succeed /sək'siːd/ vi riuscire; (follow) succedere a; ~ in doing riuscire a fare ● vt succedere a (king). ~ing adj successivo

success /sək'ses/ n successo m; be a ~ (in life) aver successo. ~ful adj riuscito; (businessman, artist etc) di successo. ~fully adv con successo

succession /sək'seʃn/ n successione f; in ~ di seguito

successive /sək'sesɪv/ adj successivo. ~ly adv successivamente

successor /sək'sesə(r)/ n successore m

succulent /'sʌkjʊlənt/ adj succulento

succumb /sə'kʌm/ vi soccombere (to a)

such /sʌtʃ/ adj tale; ~ a book un libro di questo genere; ~ a thing una cosa di questo genere; ~ a long time ago talmente tanto tempo fa; there is no ~ thing non esiste una cosa così; there is no ~ person non esiste una persona così ● pron as ~ come tale; ~ as chi; and ~ e simili; ~ as it is così com'è. ~like pron 🅃 di tal genere

suck /sʌk/ vt succhiare. □ ~ **up** vt assorbire. □ ~ **up to** vt 🅃 fare il lecchino con

sucker /'sʌkə(r)/ n (Bot) pollone m; (🅃: person) credulone, -a mf

suction /'sʌkʃn/ n aspirazione f

sudden /'sʌdn/ adj improvviso ● n all of a ~ all'improvviso. ~ly adv improvvisamente

sue /suː/ vt (pres p suing) fare causa a (for per) ● vi fare causa

suede /sweɪd/ n pelle f scamosciata

suet /'suːɪt/ n grasso m di rognone

suffer /'sʌfə(r)/ vi soffrire (from per) ● vt soffrire; subire (loss etc); (tolerate) subire. ~ing n sofferenza f

suffice /sə'faɪs/ vi bastare

sufficient /sə'fɪʃnt/ adj sufficiente. ~ly adv sufficientemente

suffix /'sʌfɪks/ n suffisso m

suffocat|e /'sʌfəkeɪt/ vt/i soffocare. ~ion n soffocamento m

sugar /'ʃʊɡə(r)/ n zucchero m ● vt zuccherare. ~ **basin**, ~-**bowl** n zuccheriera f. ~y adj zuccheroso; fig sdolcinato

suggest /sə'dʒest/ vt suggerire; (indicate, insinuate) fare pensare a. ~ion n suggerimento m; (trace) traccia f.

~ive adj allusivo. ~ively adv in modo allusivo

suicidal /suːɪˈsaɪdl/ adj suicida

suicide /ˈsuːɪsaɪd/ n suicidio m; (person) suicida mf; commit ~ suicidarsi

suit /suːt/ n vestito m; (woman's) tailleur m inv; (in cards) seme m; (Jur) causa f; follow ~ fig fare lo stesso • vt andar bene a; (adapt) adattare (to a); (be convenient for) andare bene per; be ~ed to or for essere adatto a; ~ yourself! fa come vuoi!

suitabl|e /ˈsuːtəbl/ adj adatto. ~y adv convenientemente

'suitcase n valigia f

suite /swiːt/ n suite f inv; (of furniture) divano m e poltrone fpl assortiti

sulk /sʌlk/ vi fare il broncio. ~y adj imbronciato

sullen /ˈsʌlən/ adj svogliato

sulphur /ˈsʌlfə(r)/ n zolfo m. ~ic acid n acido m solforico

sultana /sʌlˈtɑːnə/ n uva f sultanina

sultry /ˈsʌltrɪ/ adj (-ier, -iest) (weather) afoso; fig sensuale

sum /sʌm/ n somma f; (Sch) addizione f • ~ up (pt/pp summed) vi riassumere • vt valutare

summar|ize /ˈsʌməraɪz/ vt riassumere. ~y n sommario m • adj sommario; (dismissal) sbrigativo

summer /ˈsʌmə(r)/ n estate f. ~house n padiglione m. ~time n (season) estate f

---

Summer camp Negli Stati Uniti indica il campeggio estivo cui moltissimi ragazzi si recano per socializzare e praticare attività ricreative e sportive all'aria aperta; tra queste il nuoto, il canottaggio, l'arrampicata e i corsi di sopravvivenza. ⓘ

---

summery /ˈsʌmərɪ/ adj estivo

summit /ˈsʌmɪt/ n cima f. ~ conference n vertice m

summon /ˈsʌmən/ vt convocare; (Jur) citare. □ ~ up vt raccogliere (strength); rievocare (memory)

summons /ˈsʌmənz/ n (Jur) citazione f • vt citare in giudizio

sumptuous /ˈsʌmptjʊəs/ adj sontuoso. ~ly adv sontuosamente

sun /sʌn/ n sole m • vt (pt/pp sunned) ~ oneself prendere il sole

sun: ~bathe vi prendere il sole. ~burn n scottatura f (solare). ~burnt adj scottato (dal sole)

Sunday /ˈsʌndeɪ/ n domenica f

'sunflower n girasole m

sung /sʌŋ/ ▷SING

'sun-glasses npl occhiali mpl da sole

sunk /sʌŋk/ ▷SINK

sunken /ˈsʌŋkn/ adj incavato

'sunlight n [luce f del] sole m

sunny /ˈsʌnɪ/ adj (-ier, -iest) assolato

sun: ~rise n alba f. ~roof n (Auto) tettuccio m apribile. ~set n tramonto m. ~shine n [luce f del] sole m. ~stroke n insolazione f. ~tan n abbronzatura f. ~tan oil n olio m solare

super /ˈsuːpə(r)/ adj 🔲 fantastico

superb /suˈpɜːb/ adj splendido

supercilious /suːpəˈsɪlɪəs/ adj altezzoso

superficial /suːpəˈfɪʃl/ adj superficiale. ~ly adv superficialmente

superfluous /suˈpɜːfluəs/ adj superfluo

super'human adj sovrumano

superintendent /suːpərɪnˈtendənt/ n (of police) commissario m di polizia

superior /suːˈpɪərɪə(r)/ adj superiore • n superiore, -a mf. ~ity n superiorità f

superlative /suːˈpɜːlətɪv/ adj eccellente • n superlativo m

'supermarket n supermercato m

super'natural adj soprannaturale

'superpower n superpotenza f

supersede /su:pə'si:d/ vt rimpiazzare

super'sonic adj supersonico

superstiti|on /su:pə'stɪʃn/ n superstizione f. **~ous** adj superstizioso

supervis|e /'su:pəvaɪz/ vt supervisionare. **~ion** n supervisione f. **~or** n supervisore m

supper /'sʌpə(r)/ n cena f

supple /'sʌpl/ adj slogato

supplement /'sʌplɪmənt/ n supplemento m ● vt integrare. **~ary** adj supplementare

supplier /sə'plaɪə(r)/ n fornitore, -trice mf

supply /sə'plaɪ/ n fornitura f; (in economics) offerta f; **supplies** pl (Mil) approvvigionamenti mpl ● vt (pt/pp -ied) fornire; **~ sb with sth** fornire qcsa a qcno

support /sə'pɔ:t/ n sostegno m; (base) supporto m; (keep) sostentamento m ● vt sostenere; mantenere (family); (give money to) mantenere per. **~er** n sostenitore, -trice mf; (Sport) tifoso, -a mf. **~ive** adj incoraggiante

suppose /sə'pəʊz/ vt (presume) supporre; (imagine) pensare; **be ~d to do** dover fare; **not be ~d to** 🅣 non avere il permesso di; **I ~ so** suppongo di sì. **~dly** adv presumibilmente

suppress /sə'pres/ vt sopprimere. **~ion** n soppressione f

supremacy /su:'preməsɪ/ n supremazia f

supreme /su:'pri:m/ adj supremo

sure /ʃʊə(r)/ adj sicuro, certo; **make ~** accertarsi; **be ~ to do it** mi raccomando di farlo ● adv Am 🅘 certamente; **~ enough** infatti. **~ly** adv certamente; (Am: gladly) volentieri

surety /'ʃʊərətɪ/ n garanzia f; **stand**

~ for garantire

surf /sɜ:f/ n schiuma f ● vt (Comput) **~ the Net** surfare in Internet

surface /'sɜ:fɪs/ n superficie f; **on the ~** fig in apparenza ● vi (emerge) emergere. **~ mail** n by **~ mail** per posta ordinaria

'surfboard n tavola f da surf

surfing /'sɜ:fɪŋ/ n surf m inv

surge /sɜ:dʒ/ n (of sea) ondata f; (of interest) aumento m; (in demand) impennata f; (of anger, pity) impeto m ● vi riversarsi; **~ forward** buttarsi in avanti

surgeon /'sɜ:dʒən/ n chirurgo m

surgery /'sɜ:dʒərɪ/ n chirurgia f; (place, consulting room) ambulatorio m; (hours) ore fpl di visita; **have ~** subire un'intervento [chirurgico]

surgical /'sɜ:dʒɪkl/ adj chirurgico

surly /'sɜ:lɪ/ adj (-ier, -iest) scontroso

surmise /sə'maɪz/ vt supporre

surmount /sə'maʊnt/ vt sormontare

surname /'sɜ:neɪm/ n cognome m

surpass /sə'pɑ:s/ vt superare

surplus /'sɜ:pləs/ adj d'avanzo ● n sovrappiù m

surpris|e /sə'praɪz/ n sorpresa f ● vt sorprendere; **be ~d** essere sorpreso (at da). **~ing** adj sorprendente. **~ingly** adv sorprendentemente

surrender /sə'rendə(r)/ n resa f ● vi arrendersi ● vt cedere

surreptitious /sʌrəp'tɪʃəs/ adj & adv di nascosto

surround /sə'raʊnd/ vt circondare. **~ing** adj circostante. **~ings** npl dintorni mpl

surveillance /sə'veɪləns/ n sorveglianza f

survey[1] /'sɜ:veɪ/ n sguardo m; (poll) sondaggio m; (investigation) indagine f; (of land) rilevamento m; (of house) perizia f

survey² /sə'veɪ/ vt esaminare; fare un rilevamento di (land); fare una perizia di (building). **~or** n perito m; (of land) topografo, -a mf

survival /sə'vaɪvl/ n sopravvivenza f; (relic) resto m

surviv|e /sə'vaɪv/ vt sopravvivere a ●vi sopravvivere. **~or** n superstite mf; **be a ~or** [i] riuscire sempre a cavarsela

susceptible /sə'septəbl/ adj influenzabile; **~ to** sensibile a

suspect¹ /sə'spekt/ vt sospettare; (assume) supporre

suspect² /'sʌspekt/ adj & n sospetto, -a mf

suspend /sə'spend/ vt appendere; (stop, from duty) sospendere. **~er belt** n reggicalze m inv. **~ders** npl giarrettiere fpl; (Am: braces) bretelle mpl

suspense /sə'spens/ n tensione f; (in book etc) suspense f

suspension /sə'spenʃn/ n (Auto) sospensione f. **~ bridge** n ponte m sospeso

suspici|on /sə'spɪʃn/ n sospetto m; (trace) pizzico m; **under ~on** sospettato. **~ous** adj sospettoso; (arousing suspicion) sospetto. **~ously** adv sospettosamente; (arousing suspicion) in modo sospetto

sustain /sə'steɪn/ vt sostenere; mantenere (life); subire (injury)

swab /swɒb/ n (Med) tampone m

swagger /'swægə(r)/ vi pavoneggiarsi

swallow¹ /'swɒləʊ/ vt/i inghiottire. **□ ~ up** vt divorare; (earth, crowd:) inghiottire

swallow² n (bird) rondine f

swam /swæm/ ▷SWIM

swamp /swɒmp/ n palude f ●vt fig sommergere. **~y** adj paludoso

swan /swɒn/ n cigno m

swap /swɒp/ n [i] scambio m ●vt

(pt/pp swapped) [i] scambiare (for con) ●vi fare cambio

swarm /swɔːm/ n sciame m ●vi sciamare; **be ~ing with** brulicare di

swarthy /'swɔːðɪ/ adj (-ier, -iest) di carnagione scura

swat /swɒt/ vt (pt/pp swatted) schiacciare

sway /sweɪ/ n fig influenza f ●vi oscillare; (person:) ondeggiare ●vt (influence) influenzare

swear /sweə(r)/ v (pt swore, pp sworn) ●vt giurare ●vi giurare; (curse) dire parolacce; **~ at sb** imprecare contro qcno; **~ by** [i] credere ciecamente in. **~-word** n parolaccia f

sweat /swet/ n sudore m ●vi sudare

sweater /'swetə(r)/ n golf m inv

swede /swiːd/ n rapa f svedese

Swed|e n svedese mf. **~en** n Svezia f. **~ish** adj svedese

sweep /swiːp/ n scopata f, spazzata f; (curve) curva f; (movement) movimento m ampio; **make a clean ~** fig fare piazza pulita ● v (pt/pp swept) ●vt scopare, spazzare; (wind:) spazzare ●vi (go swiftly) andare rapidamente; (wind:) soffiare. **□ ~ away** vt fig spazzare via. **□ ~ up** vt spazzare

sweeping /'swiːpɪŋ/ adj (gesture) ampio; (statement) generico; (changes) radicale

sweet /swiːt/ adj dolce; **have a ~ tooth** essere goloso ●n caramella f; (dessert) dolce m. **~ corn** n mais m

sweeten /'swiːtn/ vt addolcire. **~er** n dolcificante m

sweetheart n innamorato, -a mf; **hi, ~** ciao, tesoro

swell /swel/ ●v (pt swelled, pp swollen or swelled) ●vi gonfiarsi; (increase) aumentare ●vt gonfiare; (increase) far salire. **~ing** n gonfiore m

swept /swept/ ▷SWEEP

swerve /swɜːv/ vi deviare bruscamente

swift /swift/ adj rapido. ~ly adv rapidamente

swig /swig/ n 🄵 sorso m ● vt (pt/pp swigged) 🄵 scolarsi

swim /swim/ n have a ~ fare una nuotata ● v (pt swam, pp swum) ● vi nuotare; (room:) girare; my head is ~ming mi gira la testa ● vt percorrere a nuoto. ~mer n nuotatore, -trice mf

swimming /swimiŋ/ n nuoto m. ~-baths npl piscina fsg. ~ costume n costume m da bagno. ~-pool n piscina f. ~ trunks npl calzoncini mpl da bagno

'**swim-suit** n costume m da bagno

swindle /swindl/ n truffa f ● vt truffare. ~r n truffatore, -trice mf

swine /swain/ n 🄵 porco m

swing /swiŋ/ n oscillazione f; (shift) cambiamento m; (seat) altalena f; (Mus) swing m; in full ~ in piena attività ● v (pt/pp swung) ● vi oscillare; (on swing, sway) dondolare; (dangle) penzolare; (turn) girare ● vt oscillare; far deviare (vote). ~-'door n porta f a vento

swipe /swaip/ n 🄵 botta f ● vt 🄵 colpire; (steal) rubare; far passare nella macchinetta (credit card); ~ card n pass m inv magnetico

Swiss /swis/ adj & n svizzero, -a mf; the ~ pl gli svizzeri. ~ 'roll n rotolo m di pan di Spagna ripieno di marmellata

switch /switʃ/ n interruttore m; (change) mutamento m; (exchange) scambiare ● vi cambiare; ~ to passare a. ~ off vt spegnere. ~ on vt accendere

switchboard n centralino m

Switzerland /switsələnd/ n Svizzera f

swivel /swivl/ v (pt/pp swivelled) ● vt girare ● vi girarsi

swollen /swəʊlən/ ▷SWELL ● adj gonfio. ~-headed adj presuntuoso

swoop /swu:p/ n (by police) incur-

sione f ● vi ~ [down] (bird:) piombare; fig fare un'incursione

sword /sɔːd/ n spada f

swore /swɔː(r)/ ▷SWEAR

sworn /swɔːn/ ▷SWEAR

swot /swɒt/ n 🄵 sgobbone, -a mf ● vt (pt/pp swotted) 🄵 sgobbare

swum /swʌm/ ▷SWIM

swung /swʌŋ/ ▷SWING

syllable /sɪləbl/ n sillaba f

syllabus /sɪləbəs/ n programma m [dei corsi]

symbol /sɪmbl/ n simbolo m (of di). ~ic adj simbolico. ~ism n simbolismo m. ~ize vt simboleggiare

symmetr|ical /sɪmetrɪkl/ adj simmetrico. ~y n simmetria f

sympathetic /sɪmpəθetɪk/ adj (understanding) comprensivo; (showing pity) compassionevole. ~ally adv con comprensione/compassione

sympathize /sɪmpəθaɪz/ vi capire; (in grief) solidarizzare; ~ with sb capire qcno/solidarizzare con qcno. ~r n (Pol) simpatizzante mf

sympathy /sɪmpəθɪ/ n comprensione f; (pity) compassione f; (condolences) condoglianze fpl; in ~ with (strike) per solidarietà con

symphony /sɪmfənɪ/ n sinfonia f

symptom /sɪmptəm/ n sintomo m. ~atic adj sintomatico (of di)

synagogue /sɪnəgɒg/ n sinagoga f

synchronize /sɪŋkrənaɪz/ vt sincronizzare

syndicate /sɪndɪkət/ n gruppo m

synonym /sɪnənɪm/ n sinonimo m. ~ous adj sinonimo

syntax /sɪntæks/ n sintassi f inv

synthesize /sɪnθəsaɪz/ vt sintetizzare. ~r n (Mus) sintetizzatore m

synthetic /sɪnθetɪk/ adj sintetico ● n fibra f sintetica

syringe /sɪrɪndʒ/ n siringa f

syrup /sɪrəp/ n sciroppo m; treacle tipo m di melassa

system /ˈsɪstəm/ n sistema m. ~**atic** adj sistematico

Tt

tab /tæb/ n linguetta f; (with name) etichetta f; keep ~s on 🔳 sorvegliare; pick up the ~ 🔳 pagare il conto

table /ˈteɪbl/ n tavolo m; (list) tavola f; at [the] ~ a tavola; ~ of contents tavola f delle materie •vt proporre. ~**cloth** n tovaglia f. ~**spoon** n cucchiaio m da tavola. ~**spoon [ful]** n cucchiaiata f

tablet /ˈtæblɪt/ n pastiglia f; (slab) lastra f; ~ of soap saponetta f

table tennis n tennis m da tavolo; (everyday level) ping pong m

tabloid /ˈtæblɔɪd/ n [giornale m formato] tabloid m inv; pej giornale m scandalistico

taboo /təˈbuː/ adj tabù inv •n tabù m inv

tacit /ˈtæsɪt/ adj tacito

taciturn /ˈtæsɪtɜːn/ adj taciturno

tack /tæk/ n (nail) chiodino m; (stitch) imbastitura f; fig linea f di condotta •vt inchiodare; (sew) imbastire •vi (Naut) virare

tackle /ˈtækl/ n (equipment) attrezzatura f; (football etc) contrasto m, tackle m inv •vt affrontare

tacky /ˈtækɪ/ adj (paint) non ancora asciutto; (glue) appiccicoso; fig pacchiano

tact /tækt/ n tatto m. ~**ful** adj pieno di tatto; (remark) delicato. ~**fully** adv con tatto

tactic|al /ˈtæktɪkl/ adj tattico. ~s npl tattica fsg

tactless /ˈtæktlɪs/ adj privo di tatto.

~**ly** adv senza tatto. ~**ness** n mancanza f di tatto e; (of remark) indelicatezza f

tadpole /ˈtædpəʊl/ n girino m

tag¹ /tæg/ n (label) etichetta f •vt (pt/pp tagged) attaccare l'etichetta a. □ ~ **along** vi seguire passo passo

tag² n (game) acchiapparello m

tail¹ /teɪl/ n coda f; ~s pl (tailcoat) frac m inv •vt (🔳 follow) pedinare. □ ~ **off** vi diminuire

tail light n fanalino m di coda

tailor /ˈteɪlə(r)/ n sarto m. ~**-made** adj fatto su misura

taint /teɪnt/ vt contaminare

take /teɪk/ n (Cinema) ripresa f •v (pt took, pp taken) •vt prendere; (to a place) portare (persona); (contain) contenere (passengers etc); (endure) sopportare; (require) occorrere; (teach) insegnare; (study) studiare (subject); fare (exam, holiday, photograph, walk, bath); sentire (pulse); misurare (sb's temperature); ~ sb prisoner fare prigioniero qcno; be ~n ill ammalarsi; ~ sth calmly prendere con calma qcsa •vi (plant): attecchire. □ ~ **after** vt assomigliare a. □ ~ **away** vt (with one) portare via; (remove) togliere; (subtract) sottrarre; 'to ~ away' da asporto'. □ ~ **back** vt riprendere; ritirare (statement); (return) riportare [indietro]. □ ~ **down** vt portare giù; (remove) tirare giù; (write down) prendere nota di. □ ~ **in** vt (bring indoors) portare dentro; (to one's home) ospitare; (understand) capire; (deceive) ingannare; ri- prendere (garment); (include) includere. □ ~ **off** vt togliersi (clothes); (deduct) togliere; (mimic) imitare; ~ **time off** prendersi delle vacanze; ~ **oneself off** andarsene •vi (Aeron) decollare. □ ~ **on** vt farsi carico di; assumere (employee); (as opponent) prendersela con. □ ~ **out** vt portare fuori; togliere (word, stain); (withdraw) ritirare (money, books); ~

s
t

out a subscription to sth abbonarsi a qcsa; ~ it out on sb ⓘ prendersela con qcno. □ ~ **over** vt assumere il controllo di (firm) • vi ~ over from sb sostituire qcno; (permanently) succedere a qcno. □ ~ **to** vt (as a habit) darsi a; I took to her (liked) mi è piaciuta. □ ~ **up** vt portare su; accettare (offer); intraprendere (profession); dedicarsi a (hobby); prendere (time); occupare (space); tirare su (floor-boards); accorciare (dress); ~ sth up with sb discutere qcsa con qcno • vi ~ up with sb legarsi a qcno

take: ~**-off** n (Aeron) decollo m. ~**-over** n rilevamento m

takings /'teɪkɪŋz/ npl incassi mpl

tale /teɪl/ n storia f; pej fandonia f

talent /'tælənt/ n talento m. ~**ed** adj [ricco] di talento

talk /tɔːk/ n conversazione f; (lecture) conferenza f; (gossip) chiacchiere fpl; make small ~ parlare del più e del meno • vi parlare • vt parlare di (politics etc); ~ sb into sth convincere qcno di qcsa. □ ~ **over** vt discutere

talkative /'tɔːkətɪv/ adj loquace

tall /tɔːl/ adj alto. ~**-boy** n cassettone m. ~ **order** n impresa f difficile. ~ **'story** n frottola f

tally /'tælɪ/ n conteggio m; keep a ~ of tenere il conto di • vi coincidere

tambourine /tæmbə'riːn/ n tamburello m

tame /teɪm/ adj (animal) domestico; (dull) insulso • vt domare. ~**ly** adv docilmente. ~**r** n domatore, -trice m

tamper /'tæmpə(r)/ vi ~ with manomettere

tampon /'tæmpɒn/ n tampone m

tan /tæn/ adj marrone rossiccio • n marrone m rossiccio; (from sun) abbronzatura f • v (pt/pp **tanned**) • vt conciare (hide) • vi abbronzarsi

tang /tæŋ/ n sapore m forte; (smell) odore m penetrante

tangent /'tændʒənt/ n tangente f

tangible /'tændʒɪbl/ adj tangibile

tangle /'tæŋgl/ n groviglio m; (in hair) nodo m • vt ~ [up] aggrovigliare • vi aggrovigliarsi

tango /'tæŋgəʊ/ n tango m inv

tank /tæŋk/ n contenitore m; (for petrol) serbatoio m; (fish ~) acquario m; (Mil) carro m armato

tanker /'tæŋkə(r)/ n nave f cisterna; (lorry) autobotte f

tantrum /'tæntrəm/ n scoppio m d'ira

tap /tæp/ n rubinetto m; (knock) colpo m; on ~ a disposizione • v (pt/pp **tapped**) • vt dare un colpetto a; sfruttare (resources); mettere sotto controllo (telephone) • vi picchiettare. ~**-dance** n tip tap m • vi ballare il tip tap

tape /teɪp/ n nastro m; (recording) cassetta f • vt legare con nastro; (record) registrare

tape-measure n metro m [a nastro]

taper /'teɪpə(r)/ n candela f sottile • **taper off** vi assottigliarsi

tape recorder n registratore m

tapestry /'tæpɪstrɪ/ n arazzo m

tar /tɑː(r)/ n catrame m • vt (pt/pp **tarred**) incatramare

target /'tɑːgɪt/ n bersaglio m; fig obiettivo m

tarnish /'tɑːnɪʃ/ vi ossidarsi • vt ossidare; fig macchiare

tart[1] /tɑːt/ adj aspro; fig acido

tart[2] n crostata f; (individual) crostatina f; (𝕩: prostitute) donnaccia f • **tart up** vt ⓘ ~ oneself up agghindarsi

tartan /'tɑːtn/ n tessuto m scozzese, tartan m inv • attrib di tessuto scozzese

task /tɑːsk/ n compito m; take sb to ~ riprendere qcno. ~ **force** n (Pol) commissione f; (Mil) task-force f inv

tassel /'tæsl/ n nappa f

taste /teɪst/ n gusto m; (sample) assaggio m; get a ~ of sth fig assaporare il gusto di qcsa ● vt sentire il sapore di; (sample) assaggiare ● vi sapere (of di); it ~ lovely è ottimo. ~**ful** adj di [buon] gusto. ~**fully** adv con gusto. ~**less** adj senza gusto. ~**lessly** adv con cattivo gusto

tasty /'teɪstɪ/ adj (-ier, -iest) saporito

tat /tæt/ ▷ **TIT²**

tatter|ed /'tætəd/ adj cencioso; (pages) stracciato. ~**s** npl in ~**s** a brandelli

tattoo¹ /tæ'tu:/ n tatuaggio m ● vt tatuare

tattoo² /tæ'tu:/ (Mil) parata f militare

tatty /'tætɪ/ adj (-ier, -iest) (clothes, person) trasandato; (book) malandato

taught /tɔːt/ ▷ **TEACH**

taunt /tɔːnt/ n scherno m ● vt schernire

Taurus /'tɔːrəs/ n Toro m

taut /tɔːt/ adj teso

tax /tæks/ n tassa f; (on income) imposte fpl; before ~ (price) tasse escluse; (salary) lordo ● vt tassare; fig mettere alla prova; ~ with accusare di. ~**able** adj tassabile. ~**ation** n tasse fpl. ~ **evasion** n evasione f fiscale. ~**-free** adj esentasse. ~ **haven** n paradiso m fiscale

taxi /'tæksɪ/ n taxi m inv ● vi (pt/pp taxied, pres p taxiing) (aircraft:) rullare. ~ **driver** n tassista mf. ~ **rank** n posteggio m per taxi

'taxpayer n contribuente mf

tea /tiː/ n tè m inv. ~**-bag** n bustina f di tè. ~**-break** n intervallo m per il tè

teach /tiːtʃ/ vt/i (pt/pp taught) insegnare; ~ **sb sth** insegnare qcsa a qcno. ~**er** n insegnante mf; (primary)

maestro, -a mf. ~**ing** n insegnamento m

teacup n tazza f da tè

team /tiːm/ n squadra f; fig équipe f inv ● **team up** vi unirsi

'team-work n lavoro m di squadra; fig lavoro m d'équipe

'teapot n teiera f

tear¹ /teə(r)/ n strappo m ● v (pt tore, pp torn) ● vt strappare ● vi strapparsi; (material:) strapparsi; (run) precipitarsi. □ ~ **apart** vt (fig: criticize) fare a pezzi; (separate) dividere. ~ **away** vt ~ oneself away andare via; ~ oneself away from staccarsi da (television). □ ~ **open** vt aprire strappando. □ ~ **up** vt strappare; rompere (agreement)

tear² /tɪə(r)/ n lacrima f. ~**ful** adj (person) in lacrime; (farewell) lacrimevole. ~**fully** adv in lacrime. ~**gas** n gas m lacrimogeno

tease /tiːz/ vt prendere in giro (person); tormentare (animal)

tea: ~**-set** n servizio m da tè. ~**spoon** n cucchiaino m [da tè]

teat /tiːt/ n capezzolo m; (on bottle) tettarella f

'tea-towel n strofinaccio m [per i piatti]

technical /'teknɪkl/ adj tecnico. ~**ity** n tecnicismo m; (Jur) cavillo m giuridico. ~**ly** adv tecnicamente; (strictly) strettamente

technician /tek'nɪʃn/ n tecnico, -a mf

technique /tek'niːk/ n tecnica f

technological /teknə'lɒdʒɪkl/ adj tecnologico

technology /tek'nɒlədʒɪ/ n tecnologia f

tedious /'tiːdɪəs/ adj noioso

tedium /'tiːdɪəm/ n tedio m

teem /tiːm/ vi (rain) piovere a dirotto; be ~**ing with** (full of) pullulare di

t

teenage /'ti:neɪdʒ/ adj per ragazzi; ~ **boy/girl** adolescente mf. ~**r** n adolescente mf

teens /ti:nz/ npl the ~ l'adolescenza fsg; be in one's ~ essere adolescente

teeny /'ti:nɪ/ adj (-ier, -iest) piccolissimo

teeter /'ti:tə(r)/ vi barcollare

teeth /ti:θ/ ▷ TOOTH

teeth|e /ti:ð/ vi mettere i [primi] denti. ~**ing troubles** npl fig difficoltà fpl iniziali

telecommunications /telɪkəmju:nɪ'keɪʃnz/ npl telecomunicazioni fpl

telegram /'telɪgræm/ n telegramma m

telepathy /tɪ'lepəθɪ/ n telepatia f

telephone /'telɪfəʊn/ n telefono m; be on the ~ avere il telefono; (be telephoning) essere al telefono ● vt telefonare a ● vi telefonare

telephone: ~ booth n, ~ **box** n cabina f telefonica. ~ **directory** n elenco m telefonico

telephonist /tɪ'lefənɪst/ n telefonista mf

telescop|e /'telɪskəʊp/ n telescopio m. ~**ic** adj telescopico

televise /'telɪvaɪz/ vt trasmettere per televisione

television /'telɪvɪʒn/ n televisione f; watch ~ guardare la televisione. ~ **set** n televisore m

teleworking /'telɪwɜ:kɪŋ/ n telelavoro m

telex /'teleks/ n telex m inv

tell /tel/ vt (pt/pp told) dire; raccontare (story); (distinguish) distinguere (from da); ~ **sb sth** dire qcsa a qcno; ~ **the time** dire l'ora; I couldn't ~ **why...** non sapevo perché... ● vi (produce an effect) avere effetto; time will ~ il tempo ce lo dirà; his age is beginning to ~ l'età comincia a farsi sentire [per

lui]; you mustn't ~ non devi dire niente. □ ~ **off** vt sgridare

teller /'telə(r)/ n (in bank) cassiere, -a mf

telling /'telɪŋ/ adj significativo; (argument) efficace

telly /'telɪ/ n 🆃 tv f inv

temp /temp/ n 🆃 impiegato, -a mf temporaneo, -a

temper /'tempə(r)/ n (disposition) carattere m; (mood) umore m; (anger) collera f; lose one's ~ arrabbiarsi; be in a ~ essere arrabbiato; keep one's ~ mantenere la calma

temperament /'temprəmənt/ n temperamento m. ~**al** adj (moody) capriccioso

temperate /'tempərət/ adj (climate) temperato

temperature /'temprətʃə(r)/ n temperatura f; have a ~ avere la febbre

temple[1] /'templ/ n tempio m

temple[2] n (Anat) tempia f

tempo /'tempəʊ/ n ritmo m; (Mus) tempo m

temporar|y /'tempərərɪ/ adj temporaneo; (measure, building) provvisorio. ~**ily** adv temporaneamente; (introduced, erected) provvisoriamente

tempt /tempt/ vt tentare; sfidare (fate); ~ **sb to** indurre qcno a; be ~**ed** essere tentato (to do); I am ~**ed by the offer** l'offerta mi tenta. ~**ation** n tentazione f. ~**ing** adj allettante; (food, drink) invitante

ten /ten/ adj dieci

tenaci|ous /tɪ'neɪʃəs/ adj tenace. ~**ty** n tenacia f

tenant /'tenənt/ n inquilino, -a mf; (Comm) locatario, -a mf

tend[1] vi ~ **to do sth** tendere a far qcsa

tendency /'tendənsɪ/ n tendenza f

tender[1] /'tendə(r)/ n (Comm) offerta

f; be legal ~ avere corso legale ● *vt* offrire; presentare (resignation)

tender² /'tendə(r)/ *adj* (*painful*) dolorante. **~ly** *adv* teneramente. **~ness** *n* tenerezza *f*; (*painfulness*) dolore *m*

tendon /'tendən/ *n* tendine *m*

tennis /'tenɪs/ *n* tennis *m*. **~-court** *n* campo *m* da tennis. **~ player** *n* tennista *mf*

tenor /'tenə(r)/ *n* tenore *m*

tense¹ /tens/ *n* (*Gram*) tempo *m*

tense² *adj* teso ● *vt* tendere (muscle). **□ ~ up** *vi* tendersi

tension /'tenʃn/ *n* tensione *f*

tent /tent/ *n* tenda *f*

tentacle /'tentəkl/ *n* tentacolo *m*

tentative /'tentətɪv/ *adj* provvisorio; (smile, gesture) esitante. **~ly** *adv* timidamente; (accept) provvisoriamente

tenterhooks /'tentəhʊks/ *npl* be on ~ essere sulle spine

tenth /tenθ/ *adj* decimo ● *n* decimo, -a *mf*

tenuous /'tenjʊəs/ *adj* fig debole

tepid /'tepɪd/ *adj* tiepido

term /tɜ:m/ *n* periodo *m*; (Sch) (Univ) trimestre *m*; (expression) termine *m*; **~s** *pl* (conditions) condizioni *fpl*; ~ of office carica *f*; in the short/long ~ a breve/lungo termine; in the good/ bad ~s essere in buoni/cattivi rapporti; come to ~s with accettare (past, fact); easy ~s facilità *f* di pagamento

terminal /'tɜ:mɪn(ə)l/ *adj* finale; (Med) terminale *m*; (Aeron) terminal *m inv*; (Rail) stazione *f* di testa; (of bus) capolinea *m*; (on battery) morsetto *m*; (Comput) terminale *m*. **~ly** *adv* be **~ly ill** essere in fase terminale

terminat|e /'tɜ:mɪnet/ *vt* terminare; rescindere (contract); interrompere (pregnancy) ● *vi* terminare; **~e** in finire in. **~ion** *n* termine *m*; (Med) interruzione *f* di gravidanza

terminology /tɜ:mɪ'nɒlədʒɪ/ *n*

terminologia *f*

terrace /'terəs/ *n* terrazza *f*; (houses) fila *f* di case a schiera; the **~s** (Sport) le gradinate. **~d house** *n* casa *f* a schiera

terrain /te'reɪn/ *n* terreno *m*

terrible /'terəbl/ *adj* terribile

terrific /tə'rɪfɪk/ *adj* 🔢 (excellent) fantastico; (huge) enorme. **~ally** *adv* 🔢 terribilmente

terri|fy /'terɪfaɪ/ *vt* (pt/pp -ied) atterrire; be **~fied** essere terrorizzato. **~fying** *adj* terrificante

territorial /terɪ'tɔ:rɪəl/ *adj* territoriale

territory /'terɪtərɪ/ *n* territorio *m*

terror /'terə(r)/ *n* terrore *m*. **~ism** *n* terrorismo *m*. **~ist** *n* terrorista *mf*. **~ize** *vt* terrorizzare

terse /tɜ:s/ *adj* conciso

test /test/ *n* esame *m*; (in laboratory) esperimento *m*; (of friendship, machine) prova *m*; (of intelligence, aptitude) test *m inv*; put to the ~ mettere alla prova ● *vt* esaminare; provare (machine)

testament /'testəmənt/ *n* testamento *m*; Old/New T~ Antico/ Nuovo Testamento *m*

testicle /'testɪkl/ *n* testicolo *m*

testify /'testɪfaɪ/ *vt/i* (pt/pp -ied) testimoniare

testimonial /testɪ'məʊnɪəl/ *n* lettera *f* di referenze

testimony /'testɪmənɪ/ *n* testimonianza *f*

'test: ~ match *n* partita *f* internazionale. **~-tube** *n* provetta *f*

tether /'teðə(r)/ *n* be at the end of one's ~ non poterne più

text /tekst/ *n* testo *m*. **~book** *n* manuale *m*

textile /'tekstaɪl/ *adj* tessile ● *n* stoffa *f*

text message *n* sms *m inv*, breve messaggio *m* di testo

texture /'tekstʃə(r)/ *n* (of skin)

t

grana f; (of food) consistenza f; of a smooth ∼ (to the touch) soffice al tatto

Thames /temz/ n Tamigi m

than /ðæn, accentato /ðæn/ conj che; (with numbers, names) di; older ∼ me più vecchio di me

thank /θæŋk/ vt ringraziare; ∼ you [very much] grazie [mille]. ∼ful adj grato. ∼fully adv con gratitudine; (happily) fortunatamente. ∼less adj ingrato

thanks /θæŋks/ npl ringraziamenti mpl; ∼! 1 grazie!; ∼ to grazie a

that /ðæt/

● adj & pron (pl those) quel, quei pl; (before s + consonant, gn, ps and z) quello, quegli pl; (before vowel) quell' mf, quegli mpl, quelle fpl; ∼ one quello; I don't like those quelli non mi piacciono; ∼ is cioè; is ∼ you? sei tu?; who is ∼? chi è?; what did you do after ∼? cosa hai fatto dopo?; like ∼ in questo modo, così; a man like ∼ un uomo così; ∼ is why ecco perché; ∼'s it! (you've understood) ecco!; (I've finished) ecco fatto!; (I've had enough) basta così!; (there's nothing more) tutto qui!; ∼'s ∼ (with job) ecco fatto!; (with relationship) è tutto finito!; and ∼'s ∼! punto e basta! all ∼ I know tutto quello che so

● adv così; it wasn't ∼ good non era poi così buono

● rel pron che; the man ∼ I spoke to l'uomo con cui ho parlato; the day ∼ I saw him il giorno in cui l'ho visto; all ∼ I know tutto quello che so

● conj che; I think ∼....
penso che...

thaw /θɔː/ n disgelo m ● vt fare scongelare (food) ● vi (food): scon-

gelarsi; it's ∼ing sta sgelando

the /ðə/, di fronte a una vocale /ðiː/

● def art il, la f; i mpl, le fpl; (before s + consonant, gn, ps and z) lo, gli mpl; (before vowel) l' mf, gli mpl, le fpl; at ∼ cinema/station al cinema/alla stazione; from ∼ cinema/station dal cinema/dalla stazione

● adv ∼ more ∼ better più ce n'è meglio è; (with reference to pl) più ce ne sono, meglio è; all ∼ better tanto meglio

theatre /'θɪətə(r)/ n teatro m; (Med) sala f operatoria

theatrical /θɪ'ætrɪkl/ adj teatrale; (showy) melodrammatico

theft /θeft/ n furto m

their /ðeə(r)/ adj il loro m, la loro f, i loro mpl, le loro fpl; ∼ mother/father la loro madre/il loro padre

theirs /ðeəz/ poss pron il loro m, la loro f, i loro mpl, le loro fpl; a friend of ∼ un loro amico; friends of ∼ dei loro amici; those are ∼ quelli sono loro; (as opposed to ours) quelli sono i loro

them /ðem/ pron (direct object) li m, le f; (indirect object) gli, loro fml; (after prep: with people) loro; (after preposition: with things) essi; we haven't seen ∼ non li/le abbiamo visti/viste; give the money dai loro or dagli i soldi; give it to ∼ daglielo; I've spoken to ∼ ho parlato con loro; it's ∼ sono loro

theme /θiːm/ n tema m. ∼ park n parco m a tema. ∼ song n motivo m conduttore

themselves /ðəm'selvz/ pron (reflexive) si; (emphatic) se stessi; they poured a drink si sono versati da bere; they said so lo hanno detto loro stessi; they kept it for ∼ se lo sono tenuti per sé; by ∼ da soli

then /ðen/ adv allora; (next) poi; by

~ (in the past) ormai; (in the future) per allora; **since** ~ sin da allora; **before** ~ prima di allora; **from** ~ on da allora in poi; **now and** ~ ogni tanto; **there and** ~ all'istante ● adj di allora

theoretical /θɪəˈretɪkl/ adj teorico

theory /ˈθɪərɪ/ n teoria f; **in** ~ in teoria

therapeutic /θerəˈpjuːtɪk/ adj terapeutico

therap|ist /ˈθerəpɪst/ n terapista mf. ~**y** n terapia f

there /ðeə/ adv là, lì; **down/up** ~ laggiù/lassù; ~ **is/are** c'è/ci sono; ~ **he/she is** eccolo/eccola ● int ~, ~! dai, su!

there: ~**abouts** adv [or] ~**abouts** (roughly) all'incirca. ~**fore** /-fɔː(r)/ adv perciò

thermometer /θəˈmɒmɪtə(r)/ n termometro m

thermostat /ˈθɜːməstæt/ n termostato m

thesaurus /θɪˈsɔːrəs/ n dizionario m dei sinonimi

these /ðiːz/ ▷ **THIS**

thesis /ˈθiːsɪs/ n (pl -ses /-siːz/) tesi f inv

they /ðeɪ/ pron loro; ~ **are tired** sono stanchi; **we're going, but** ~ **are not** noi andiamo, ma loro no; ~ **say** (generalizing) si dice; ~ **are building a new road** stanno costruendo una nuova strada

thick /θɪk/ adj spesso; (forest) fitto; (liquid) denso; (hair) folto; (☐: stupid) ottuso; (☐: close) molto unito; **be 5 mm** ~ essere 5 mm di spessore ● adv densamente ● n **in the** ~ **of** nel mezzo di. ~**en** vt ispessire (sauce) ● vi ispessirsi; (fog:) infittirsi. ~**ly** adv densamente; (cut) a fette spesse. ~**ness** n spessore m

thief /θiːf/ n (pl **thieves**) ladro, -a mf

thigh /θaɪ/ n coscia f

thimble /ˈθɪmbl/ n ditale m

thin /θɪn/ adj (**thinner, thinnest**) sottile; (shoes, sweater) leggero; (liquid) liquido; (person) magro; (fig: excuse, plot) inconsistente ● adv = **thinly** ● v (pt/pp thinned) ● vt diluire (liquid) ● vi diradarsi. □ ~ **out** vi diradarsi. ~**ly** adv (populated) scarsamente; (disguised) leggermente; (cut) a fette sottili

thing /θɪŋ/ n cosa f; ~**s** pl (belongings) roba fsg; **for one** ~ in primo luogo; **the right** ~ la cosa giusta; **just the** ~! proprio quel che ci vuole!; **how are** ~**s**? come vanno le cose?; **the latest** ~ ☐ l'ultima cosa; **the best** ~ **would be** la cosa migliore sarebbe; **poor** ~! poveretto!

think /θɪŋk/ vt/i (pt/pp **thought**) pensare; (believe) credere; **I** ~ **so** credo di sì; **what do you** ~? (what is your opinion?) cosa ne pensi?; ~ **of/about** pensare a; **what do you** ~ **of it?** cosa ne pensi di questo? □ ~ **over** vt riflettere su. □ ~ **up** vt escogitare

third /θɜːd/ adj & n terzo, -a mf. ~**ly** adv terzo. ~**-rate** adj scadente

thirst /θɜːst/ n sete f. ~**ily** adv con sete. ~**y** adj assetato; **be** ~**y** aver sete

thirteen /θɜːˈtiːn/ adj tredici. ~**th** adj tredicesimo

thirtieth /ˈθɜːtɪɪθ/ adj trentesimo

thirty /ˈθɜːtɪ/ adj trenta

this /ðɪs/ adj (pl these) questo; ~ **man/woman** quest'uomo/questa donna; **these men/women** questi uomini/queste donne; ~ **one** questo; ~ **morning/evening** stamattina/stasera ● pron (pl these) questo; **we talked about** ~ **and that** abbiamo parlato del più e del meno; **like** ~ così; ~ **is Peter** questo è Peter; (Teleph) sono Peter; **who is** ~? (Teleph) chi parla? ● adv così; ~ **big** così grande

thistle /ˈθɪsl/ n cardo m

thorn /θɔːn/ n spina f. ~**y** adj

spinoso

thorough /'θʌrə/ adj completo; (knowledge) profondo; (clean, search, training) a fondo; (person) scrupoloso

thorough: ~**bred** n purosangue m inv. ~**fare** n via f principale; 'no ~**fare**' 'strada non transitabile'

thorough|ly /'θʌrəlɪ/ adv (clean, search, know sth) a fondo; (extremely) estremamente. ~**ness** n completezza f

those /ðəʊz/ ▷THAT

though /ðəʊ/ conj sebbene; as ~ come se • adv tuttavia

thought /θɔːt/ ▷THINK • n pensiero m; (idea) idea f. ~**ful** adj pensieroso; (considerate) premuroso. ~**fully** adv pensierosamente; (considerately) premurosamente. ~**less** adj (inconsiderate) sconsiderato. ~**lessly** adv con noncuranza

thousand /'θaʊznd/ adj one/a ~ mille m inv e mille m inv; ~**s of** migliaia fpl di. ~**th** adj millesimo • n millesimo, -a mf

thrash /θræʃ/ vt picchiare; (defeat) sconfiggere. □ ~ **out** vt mettere a punto

thread /θred/ n filo m; (of screw) filetto m • vt infilare (beads); ~ **one's way through** farsi strada fra. ~**bare** adj logoro

threat /θret/ n minaccia f

threaten /'θretn/ vt minacciare (to do sth) • vi fig incalzare. ~**ing** adj minaccioso; (sky, atmosphere) sinistro

three /θriː/ adj tre. ~**fold** adj & adv triplo. ~**some** n trio m

threshold /'θreʃəʊld/ n soglia f

threw /θruː/ ▷THROW

thrift /θrɪft/ n economia f. ~**y** adj parsimonioso

thrill /θrɪl/ n brivido m • vt entusiasmare; (of fear) brivido m • vt entusiasmare; be ~**ed** with essere entusiasta di. ~**er** n

(book) [romanzo m] giallo m; (film) [film m] giallo m. ~**ing** adj eccitante

thrive /θraɪv/ vi (pt thrived or throve, pp thrived or thriven /'θrɪvn/) (business): prosperare; (child, plant:) crescere bene; I ~ **on pressure** mi piace essere sotto tensione

throat /θrəʊt/ n gola f; **sore** ~ mal m di gola

throb /θrɒb/ n pulsazione f; (of heart) battito m • vi (pt/pp throbbed) (vibrate) pulsare; (heart:) battere

throes /θrəʊz/ npl in the ~ **of** fig alle prese con

throne /θrəʊn/ n trono m

throng /θrɒŋ/ n calca f

throttle /'θrɒtl/ n (on motorbike) manopola f di accelerazione • vt strozzare

through /θruː/ prep attraverso; (during) durante; (by means of) tramite; (thanks to) grazie a; **Saturday** ~ **Tuesday** Am da sabato a martedì incluso • adv attraverso; ~ **and** ~ fino in fondo; **wet** ~ completamente bagnato; **read sth** ~ dare una lettura a qcsa; **let** ~ lasciar passare (sb) • adj (train) diretto; **be** ~ (finished) aver finito; (Teleph) avere la comunicazione

throughout /θruː'aʊt/ prep per tutto • adv completamente; (time) per tutto il tempo

throw /θrəʊ/ n tiro m • vt (pt threw, pp thrown) lanciare; (throw away) gettare; azionare (switch); disarcionare (rider); (🗓: disconcert) disorientare 🗓 dare (party). □ ~ **away** vt gettare via. □ ~ **out** vt gettare via; rigettare (plan); buttare fuori (person). □ ~ **up** vt alzare • vi (vomit) vomitare

thrush /θrʌʃ/ n tordo m

thrust /θrʌst/ n spinta f • vt (pt/pp thrust) (push) spingere; (insert) conficcare; ~ [**up**]**on** imporre a

thud /θʌd/ n tonfo m

thug /θʌɡ/ n delinquente m

thumb /θʌm/ n pollice m; as a rule of ~ come regola generale; under sb's ~ succube di qcno ● vt ~ a lift fare l'autostop. ~**-index** n indice m a rubrica. ~**tack** n Am puntina f da disegno

thump /θʌmp/ n colpo m; (noise) tonfo m ● vt battere su (table, door); battere (fist); colpire (person) ● vi battere (on su); (heart:) battere forte. □ ~ **about** vi camminare pesantemente

thunder /ˈθʌndə(r)/ n tuono m; (loud noise) rimbombo m ● vi tuonare; (make loud noise) rimbombare. ~**clap** n rombo m di tuono. ~**storm** n temporale m. ~**y** adj temporalesco

Thursday /ˈθɜːzdeɪ/ n giovedì m inv

thus /ðʌs/ adv così

thwart /θwɔːt/ vt ostacolare

Tiber /ˈtaɪbə(r)/ n Tevere m

tick /tɪk/ n (sound) ticchettio m; (mark) segno m; ([]: instant) attimo m ● vi ticchettare. □ ~ **off** vt spuntare; ([]: mean) sgridare. □ ~ **over** vi (engine:) andare al minimo

ticket /ˈtɪkɪt/ n biglietto m; (for item deposited, library) tagliando m; (label) cartellino m; (fine) multa f. ~**-collector** n controllore m. ~**-office** n biglietteria f

tick|le /ˈtɪkl/ n solletico m ● vt fare il solletico a; (amuse) divertire ● vi prudere. ~**lish** adj che soffre il solletico

tide /taɪd/ n marea f; (of events) corso m; the ~ is in/out c'è alta/bassa marea ● tide over □ ~ sb over aiutare qcno a andare avanti

tidily /ˈtaɪdɪlɪ/ adv in modo ordinato

tidiness /ˈtaɪdɪnɪs/ n ordine m

tidy /ˈtaɪdɪ/ adj (-ier, -iest) ordinato; ([]: amount) bello ● vt (pt/pp -ied) ~ [up] ordinare; ~ oneself up mettersi in ordine

tie /taɪ/ n cravatta f; (cord) legaccio m; (fig: bond) legame m; (restriction) impedimento m; (Sport) pareggio m ● v (pres p tying) ● vt legare; fare (knot); be ~d (in competition) essere in parità ● vi pareggiare. □ ~ **in with** vi corrispondere a. □ ~ **up** vt legare; vincolare (capital); be ~d up (busy) essere occupato

tier /tɪə(r)/ n fila f; (of cake) piano m; (in stadium) gradinata f

tiger /ˈtaɪgə(r)/ n tigre f

tight /taɪt/ adj stretto; (taut) teso; ([]: drunk) sbronzo; ([]: mean) spilorcio; ~ **corner** [] brutta situazione f ● adv strettamente; (hold) forte; (closed) bene

tighten /ˈtaɪtn/ vt stringere; avvitare (screw); intensificare (control) ● vi stringersi

tight: ~**-fisted** adj tirchio. ~**ly** adv strettamente; (hold) forte; (closed) bene. ~**rope** n fune f (da funamboli)

tights /taɪts/ npl collant m inv

tile /taɪl/ n mattonella f; (on roof) tegola f ● vt rivestire di mattonelle (wall)

till[1] /tɪl/ prep & conj = until

till[2] n cassa f

tilt /tɪlt/ n inclinazione f; at full ~ a tutta velocità ● vt inclinare ● vi inclinarsi

timber /ˈtɪmbə(r)/ n legname m

time /taɪm/ n tempo m; (occasion) volta f; (by clock) ora f; two ~s four due volte quattro; at any ~ in qualsiasi momento; this ~ questa volta; at ~s, from ~ to ~ ogni tanto; ~ and again spesso; two at a ~ due alla volta; on ~ in orario; in ~ in tempo; (eventually) col tempo; in no ~ at all velocemente; in a year's ~ fra un anno; behind ~ in ritardo; behind the ~s antiquato; for the ~ being per il momento; what is the ~? che ora è?; by the ~ we arrive quando arriviamo; did you have a nice ~? ti sei divertito?; have a good ~! divertiti! ● vt scegliere il momento per; cronometrare (race); be well ~d essere ben calcolato

time: ~ **bomb** n bomba f a orologeria. ~**ly** adj opportuno. ~**table** n orario m

timid /'tɪmɪd/ adj (shy) timido; (fearful) timoroso

tin /tɪn/ n stagno m; (container) barattolo m • vt (pt/pp tinned) inscatolare. ~ **foil** n [carta f] stagnola f

tinge /tɪndʒ/ n sfumatura f • vt ~d with fig misto a

tingle /'tɪŋgl/ vi pizzicare

tinker /'tɪŋkə(r)/ vi armeggiare

tinkle /'tɪŋkl/ n tintinnio m; (ፀ: phone call) colpo m di telefono • vi tintinnare

tinned /tɪnd/ adj in scatola

'tin opener n apriscatole m inv

tint /tɪnt/ n tinta f • vt tingersi (hair)

tiny /'taɪnɪ/ adj (-ier, -iest) minuscolo

tip¹ /tɪp/ n punta f

tip² n (money) mancia f; (advice) consiglio m; (for rubbish) discarica f • v (pt/pp tipped) • vt (tilt) inclinare; (overturn) capovolgere; (pour) versare; (reward) dare una mancia a • vi inclinarsi; (overturn) capovolgersi. □ ~ **off** vt ~ sb off (inform) fare una soffiata a qcno. □ ~ **out** vt rovesciare. □ ~ **over** vt capovolgere • vi capovolgersi

tipped /tɪpt/ adj (cigarette) col filtro

tipsy /'tɪpsɪ/ adj ⏸ brillo

tiptoe /'tɪptəʊ/ n **on** ~ in punta di piedi

tiptop /tɪp'tɒp/ adj ⏸ in condizioni perfette

tire /'taɪə(r)/ vt stancare • vi stancarsi. ~**d** adj stanco; ~**d of** stanco di; ~**d out** stanco morto. ~**less** adj instancabile. ~**some** adj fastidioso

tiring /'taɪərɪŋ/ adj stancante

tissue /'tɪʃu:/ n tessuto m; (handkerchief) fazzolettino m di carta.

~**-paper** n carta f velina

tit¹ /tɪt/ n (bird) cincia f

tit² n ~ **for tat** pan per focaccia

title /'taɪtl/ n titolo m. ~**-deed** n atto m di proprietà. ~**-role** n ruolo m principale

---

to /tu:/, atono /tə/

● prep a; (to countries) in; (towards) verso; (up to, until) fino a; I'm going to John's vado da John/dal macellaio; **come/go to** sb venire/andare da qcno; **to Italy/Switzerland** in Italia/Svizzera; I've never been to Rome non sono mai stato a Roma; **go to the market** andare al mercato; **to the toilet/my room** in bagno/camera mia; **to an exhibition** a una mostra; **to university** all'università; **twenty/quarter to eight** le otto meno venti/un quarto; **5 to 6 kilos** da 5 a 6 chili; **to the end** alla fine; **to this day** fino a oggi; **to the best of my recollection** per quanto mi possa ricordare; **give/say sth to** sb dare/dire qcsa a qcno; **give it to me** dammelo; **there's nothing to it** è una cosa da niente

● verbal constructions **to go** andare; **learn to swim** imparare a nuotare; I want to/have to go voglio/devo andare; **it's easy to forget** è facile da dimenticare; **too ill/tired to go** troppo malato/stanco per andare; **you have to devi;** I don't want to non voglio; **live to be 90** vivere fino a 90 anni; **he was the last to arrive** è stato l'ultimo ad arrivare; **to be honest,...** per essere sincero,...

● adv **pull to** chiudere; **to and fro** avanti e indietro

toad /təʊd/ n rospo m. ~**stool** n fungo m velenoso

toast /təʊst/ n pane m tostato; (drink) brindisi m ● vt tostare (bread); (drink a ~ to) brindare a. ~**er** n tostapane m inv

tobacco /təˈbækəʊ/ n tabacco m. ~**nist's** [shop] n tabaccheria f

toboggan /təˈbɒgən/ n toboga m ● vi andare in toboga

today /təˈdeɪ/ adj & adv oggi m; a week ~ una settimana a oggi; ~**'s** paper il giornale di oggi

toddler /ˈtɒdlə(r)/ n bambino, -a mf ai primi passi

toe /təʊ/ n dito m del piede; (of footwear) punta f; **big** ~ alluce m ● vt ~ **the line** rigar diritto. ~**nail** n unghia f del piede

toffee /ˈtɒfɪ/ n caramella f al mou

together /təˈgeðə(r)/ adv insieme; (at the same time) allo stesso tempo; ~ **with** insieme a

toilet /ˈtɔɪlɪt/ n (lavatory) gabinetto m. ~ **paper** n carta f igienica

toiletries /ˈtɔɪlɪtrɪz/ npl articoli mpl da toilette

toilet roll n rotolo m di carta igienica

token /ˈtəʊkən/ n segno m; (counter) gettone m; (voucher) buono m ● attrib simbolico

told /təʊld/ ▷**TELL** ● adj **all** ~ in tutto

tolerab|le /ˈtɒl(ə)rəbl/ adj tollerabile; (not bad) discreto. ~**y** adv discretamente

toleran|ce /ˈtɒl(ə)r(ə)ns/ n tolleranza f. ~**t** adj tollerante. ~**tly** adv con tolleranza

tolerate /ˈtɒləreɪt/ vt tollerare

toll[1] /təʊl/ n pedaggio m; **death** ~ numero m di morti

toll[2] vi suonare a morto

tomato /təˈmɑːtəʊ/ n (pl -es) pomodoro m. ~ **ketchup** n ketchup m.

~ **purée** n concentrato m di pomodoro

tomb /tuːm/ n tomba f

'tombstone n pietra f tombale

tomorrow /təˈmɒrəʊ/ adj & adv domani m; ~ **morning** domani mattina; **the day after** ~ dopodomani; **see you** ~ a domani!

ton /tʌn/ n tonnellata f (= 1.016 kg.); ~**s of** I un sacco di

tone /təʊn/ n tono m; (colour) tonalità f inv ● **tone down** vt attenuare. □ ~ **up** vt tonificare (muscles)

tongs /tɒŋz/ npl pinze fpl

tongue /tʌŋ/ n lingua f; ~ **in cheek** (say) ironicamente. ~**-twister** n scioglilingua m inv

tonic /ˈtɒnɪk/ n tonico m; (for hair) lozione f per i capelli; fig toccasana m inv; ~ [water] acqua f tonica

tonight /təˈnaɪt/ adv stanotte; (evening) stasera ● n questa notte f; (evening) questa sera f

tonne /tʌn/ n tonnellata f metrica

tonsil /ˈtɒnsl/ n (Anat) tonsilla f. ~**litis** n tonsillite f

too /tuː/ adv troppo; (also) anche; ~ **many** troppi; ~ **much** troppo; ~ **little** troppo poco

took /tʊk/ ▷**TAKE**

tool /tuːl/ n attrezzo m

tooth /tuːθ/ n (pl **teeth**) dente m

tooth: ~**ache** n mal m di denti. ~**brush** n spazzolino m da denti. ~**paste** n dentifricio m. ~**pick** n stuzzicadenti m inv

top[1] /tɒp/ n (toy) trottola f

top[2] n cima f; (Sch) primo, -a mf; (upper part or half) parte f superiore; (of page, list, road) inizio m; (upper surface) superficie f; (lid) coperchio m; (of bottle) tappo m; (garment) maglia f; (blouse) camicia f; (Auto) marcia f più alta; **at the** ~ fig al vertice; **at the** ~ **of one's voice** a squarciagola; **on** ~/**on** ~ **of** sopra; **on** ~ **of that** (besides) per di più; **from** ~ **to bottom**

da cima a fondo ● adj in alto; (official, floor) superiore; (pupil, musician etc) migliore; (speed) massimo ● vt (pt/pp topped) essere in testa a (list); (exceed) sorpassare; ~ped with ice-cream ricoperto di gelato. □ ~ up vt riempire

top: ~ '**floor** n ultimo piano m. ~ **hat** n cilindro m. ~**heavy** adj con la parte superiore sovraccarica

topic /'tɒpɪk/ n soggetto m; (of conversation) argomento m. ~al adj d'attualità

topless adj & adv topless

topple /'tɒpl/ vt rovesciare ● vi rovesciarsi. □ ~ **off** vi cadere

top-'secret adj segretissimo, top secret inv

torch /tɔːtʃ/ n torcia f [elettrica]; (flaming) fiaccola f

tore /tɔː(r)/ ▷ **TEAR**[1]

torment[1] /'tɔːment/ n tormento m

torment[2] /tɔː'ment/ vt tormentare

torn /tɔːn/ ▷ **TEAR**[1] ● adj bucato

tornado /tɔː'neɪdəʊ/ n (pl -es) tornado m inv

torpedo /tɔː'piːdəʊ/ n (pl -es) siluro m ● vt silurare

torrent /'tɒrənt/ n torrente m. ~**ial** adj (rain) torrenziale

tortoise /'tɔːtəs/ n tartaruga f

torture /'tɔːtʃə(r)/ n tortura f ● vt torturare

Tory /'tɔːrɪ/ adj & n Ⓝ conservatore, -trice mf

toss /tɒs/ vt gettare; (into the air) lanciare in aria; (shake) scrollare; (horse:) disarcionare; mescolare (salad); rivoltare facendo saltare in aria (pancake); ~ a coin fare testa o croce ● vi ~ and turn (in bed) rigirarsi; let's ~ for it facciamo testa o croce

tot[1] /tɒt/ n bimbetto, -a mf; (Ⓝ: of liquor) goccio m

tot[2] vt (pt/pp totted) ~ **up** Ⓝ fare la somma di

total /'təʊtl/ adj totale ● n totale m ● vt (pt/pp totalled) ammontare a; (add up) sommare

totalitarian /təʊtælɪ'teərɪən/ adj totalitario

totally /'təʊtəlɪ/ adv totalmente

totter /'tɒtə(r)/ vi barcollare; (government:) vacillare

touch /tʌtʃ/ n tocco m; (sense) tatto m; (contact) contatto m; (trace) traccia f; (of irony, humour) tocco m; **get/be in** ~ mettersi/essere in contatto ● vt toccare; (lightly) sfiorare; (equal) eguagliare; (fig: move) commuovere ● vi toccarsi. □ ~ **down** vi (Aeron) atterrare. □ ~ **on** vt fig accennare a. **touch up** vt ritoccare (painting). ~**ing** adj commovente. ~**screen** n touch screen m inv. ~**tone** adj a tastiera. ~**y** adj permaloso; (subject) delicato

tough /tʌf/ adj duro; (severe, harsh) severo; (durable) resistente; (resilient) forte

toughen /'tʌfn/ vt rinforzare. □ ~ **up** vt rendere più forte (person)

tour /tʊə(r)/ n giro m; (of building, town) visita f; (Theat), (Sport) tournée f inv; (of duty) servizio m ● vt visitare ● vi fare un giro turistico; (Theat) essere in tournée

touris|m /'tʊərɪzm/ n turismo m. ~**t** n turista mf ● attrib turistico. ~**t office** n ufficio m turistico

tournament /'tʊənəmənt/ n torneo m

tousle /'taʊzl/ vt spettinare

tout /taʊt/ n (ticket ~) bagarino m; (horse-racing) informatore m ● vi ~ **for** sollecitare

tow /təʊ/ n rimorchio m; 'on ~' 'a rimorchio'; **in** ~ Ⓝ al seguito ● vt rimorchiare. □ ~ **away** vt portare via col carro attrezzi

toward[s] /tə'wɔːd(z)/ prep verso (with respect to) nei riguardi di

towel /'taʊəl/ n asciugamano m.

tower | transfer

~ling n spugna f

tower /'taʊə(r)/ n torre f ∘ vi ~ above dominare. ~ **block** n palazzone m. ~ing adj torreggiante; (rage) violento

town /taʊn/ n città f inv. ~ 'hall n municipio m

toxic /'tɒksɪk/ adj tossico

toy /tɔɪ/ n giocattolo m. ~shop n negozio m di giocattoli. □ ~ **with** vt giocherellare con

trace /treɪs/ n traccia f ∘ vt (find) rintracciare; (draw) tracciare; (with tracing-paper) ricalcare

track /træk/ n traccia f; (path, Sport) pista f; (Rail) binario m; **keep** ~ **of** tenere d'occhio. □ ~ **down** vt scovare

tracksuit n tuta f da ginnastica

tractor /'træktə(r)/ n trattore m

trade /treɪd/ n commercio m; (line of business) settore m; (craft) mestiere m; **by** ~ di mestiere ∘ vt commerciare; ~ **sth for** sth scambiare qcsa per qcsa ∘ vi commerciare. □ ~ **in** vt (give in part exchange) dare in pagamento parziale

'**trade mark** n marchio m di fabbrica

trader /'treɪdə(r)/ n commerciante mf

trades 'union n sindacato m

tradition /trə'dɪʃn/ n tradizione f. ~al adj tradizionale. ~ally adv tradizionalmente

traffic /'træfɪk/ n traffico m ∘ vi (pt/pp trafficked) trafficare

traffic: ~ **circle** n Am isola f rotatoria. ~ **jam** n ingorgo m. ~ **lights** npl semaforo msg. ~ **warden** n vigile m [urbano]; (woman) vigilessa f

tragedy /'trædʒədɪ/ n tragedia f

tragic /'trædʒɪk/ adj tragico. ~ally adv tragicamente

trail /treɪl/ n traccia f; (path) sentiero m ∘ vi strisciare; (plant) arrampicarsi; ~ [**behind**] rimanere indietro; (in competition) essere in svantaggio ∘ vt trascinare

trailer /'treɪlə(r)/ n (Auto) rimorchio m; (Am: caravan) roulotte f inv; (film) presentazione f (di un film)

train /treɪn/ n treno m. ~ **of thought** filo m dei pensieri ∘ vt formare professionalmente; (Sport) allenare; (aim) puntare; educare (child); addestrare (animal, soldier) ∘ vi fare il tirocinio; (Sport) allenarsi. ~**ed** adj (animal) addestrato (to do a fare)

trainee /treɪ'niː/ n apprendista mf

train|er /'treɪnə(r)/ n (Sport) allenatore, -trice mf; (in circus) domatore, -trice mf; (of dog, race-horse) addestratore, -trice mf; ~**ers** pl scarpe fpl da ginnastica. ~**ing** n tirocinio m; (Sport) allenamento m; (of animal, soldier) addestramento m

trait /treɪt/ n caratteristica f

traitor /'treɪtə(r)/ n traditore, -trice mf

tram /træm/ n tram m inv. ~**-lines** npl rotaie fpl del tram

tramp /træmp/ n (hike) camminata f; (vagrant) barbone, -a mf; (of feet) calpestio m ∘ vi camminare con passo pesante; (hike) percorrere a piedi

trample /'træmpl/ vt/i ~ [**on**] calpestare

trampoline /'træmpəliːn/ n trampolino m

trance /trɑːns/ n trance f inv

tranquil /'træŋkwɪl/ adj tranquillo. ~**lity** n tranquillità f

tranquillizer /'træŋkwɪlaɪzə(r)/ n tranquillante m

transatlantic /trænzət'læntɪk/ adj transatlantico

transcend /træn'send/ vt trascendere

transfer[1] /'trænsfɜː(r)/ n trasferimento m; (Sport) cessione f; (design) decalcomania f

transfer[2] /træns'fɜː(r)/ v (pt/pp

transferred ● vt trasferire; (Sport) cedere ● vi trasferirsi; (when travelling) cambiare. ~**able** adj trasferibile

transform /trænsˈfɔːm/ vt trasformare. ~**ation** n trasformazione f. ~**er** n trasformatore m

transfusion /trænsˈfjuːʒn/ n trasfusione f

transient /ˈtrænzɪənt/ adj passeggero

transistor /trænˈzɪstə(r)/ n transistor m inv; (radio) radiolina f a transistor

transit /ˈtrænzɪt/ n transito m; in ~ (goods) in transito

transition /trænˈzɪʒn/ n transizione f. ~**al** adj di transizione

transitive /ˈtrænzɪtɪv/ adj transitivo

translat|e /trænzˈleɪt/ vt tradurre. ~**ion** n traduzione f. ~**or** n traduttore, -trice m f

transmission /trænzˈmɪʃn/ n trasmissione f

transmit /trænzˈmɪt/ vt (pt/pp transmitted) trasmettere. ~**ter** n trasmettitore m

transparen|cy /trænˈspærənsɪ/ n (Phot) diapositiva f. ~**t** adj trasparente

transplant[1] /ˈtrænsplɑːnt/ n trapianto m

transplant[2] /trænsˈplɑːnt/ vt trapiantare

transport[1] /ˈtrænspɔːt/ n trasporto m

transport[2] /trænsˈpɔːt/ vt trasportare. ~**ation** n trasporto m

trap /træp/ n trappola f ● vt (pt/pp trapped) (①: mouth) boccaccia f ● vt (pt/pp trapped) intrappolare; schiacciare (finger in door). ~**door** n botola f

trapeze /trəˈpiːz/ n trapezio m

trash /træʃ/ n robaccia f; (rubbish) spazzatura f; (nonsense) schiocchezze fpl. ~**can** n Am secchio m della spazzatura. ~**y** adj scadente

travel /ˈtrævl/ n viaggi mpl ● v (pt/pp travelled) ● vi viaggiare; (to work) andare ● vt percorrere (distance). ~ **agency** n agenzia f di viaggi. ~ **agent** n agente m f di viaggi

traveller /ˈtrævələ(r)/ n viaggiatore, -trice m f; (Comm) commesso m viaggiatore; ~**s** pl (gypsies) zingari mpl. ~**'s cheque** n traveller's cheque m inv

trawler /ˈtrɔːlə(r)/ n pescereccio m

tray /treɪ/ n vassoio m; (for baking) teglia f; (for documents) vaschetta f sparticarta; (of printer, photocopier) vassoio m

treacher|ous /ˈtretʃərəs/ adj traditore; (weather, currents) pericoloso. ~**y** n tradimento m

treacle /ˈtriːkl/ n melassa f

tread /tred/ n andatura f; (step) gradino m; (of tyre) battistrada m inv ● v (pt trod, pp trodden) ● vi (walk) camminare. □ ~ **on** vt calpestare (grass); pestare (foot)

treason /ˈtriːzn/ n tradimento m

treasure /ˈtreʒə(r)/ n tesoro m ● vt tenere in gran conto. ~**r** n tesoriere, -a m f

treasury /ˈtreʒərɪ/ n the T~ il Ministero del Tesoro

treat /triːt/ n piacere m; (present) regalo m; give sb a ~ fare una sorpresa a qcno ● vt trattare; (Med) curare; ~ sb to sth offrire qcsa a qcno

treatise /ˈtriːtɪz/ n trattato m

treatment /ˈtriːtmənt/ n trattamento m; (Med) cura f

treaty /ˈtriːtɪ/ n trattato m

treble /ˈtrebl/ adj triplo ● n (Mus: voice) voce f bianca ● vt triplicare ● vi triplicarsi. ~ **clef** n chiave f di violino

tree /triː/ n albero m

trek /trek/ n scarpinata f; (as holiday) trekking m inv ● vi (pt/pp trekked) farsi una scarpinata; (on holiday) fare trekking

tremble /'trembl/ vi tremare

tremendous /trɪ'mendəs/ adj (huge) enorme; (fam: excellent) formidabile. **~ly** adv (very) straordinariamente; (fam: a lot) enormemente

tremor /'tremə(r)/ n tremito m; [earth] ~ scossa f [sismica]

trench /trentʃ/ n fosso m; (Mil) trincea f. ~ **coat** n trench m inv

trend /trend/ n tendenza f; (fashion) moda f. **~y** adj (-ier, -iest) fam di o alla moda

trepidation /trepɪ'deɪʃn/ n trepidazione f

trespass /'trespas/ vi ~ **on** introdursi abusivamente in; fig abusare di. **~er** n intruso, -a mf

trial /'traɪəl/ n (Jur) processo m; (test, ordeal) prova f; **on** ~ in prova; (Jur) in giudizio; **by** ~ **and error** per tentativi

triang|le /'traɪæŋgl/ n triangolo m. **~ular** adj triangolare

tribe /traɪb/ n tribù f inv

tribulation /trɪbjʊ'leɪʃn/ n tribolazione f

tribunal /traɪ'bjuːnl/ n tribunale m

tributary /'trɪbjʊtəri/ n affluente m

tribute /'trɪbjuːt/ n tributo m; **pay** ~ rendere omaggio

trick /trɪk/ n trucco m; (joke) scherzo m; (in cards) presa f; **do the** ~ fam funzionare; **play a** ~ **on** fare uno scherzo a ● vt imbrogliare

trickle /'trɪkl/ vi colare

trick|ster /'trɪkstə(r)/ n imbroglione, -a mf. **~y** adj (-ier, -iest) adj (operation) complesso; (situation) delicato

tricycle /'traɪsɪkl/ n triciclo m

tried /traɪd/ ▷TRY

trifl|e /'traɪfl/ n inezia f; (Culin) zuppa f inglese. **~ing** adj insignificante

trigger /'trɪgə(r)/ n grilletto m ● vt ~ **off** scatenare

trim /trɪm/ adj (trimmer, trimmest) curato; (figure) snello ● n (of hair, hedge) spuntata f; (decoration) rifinitura f; **in good** ~ in buono stato; (person) in forma ● vt (pt/pp trimmed) spuntare (hair etc); (decorate) ornare; (Naut) orientare. **~ming** n bordo m; **~mings** pl (decorations) guarnizioni fpl; **with all the ~mings** (Culin) guarnito

trinket /'trɪŋkɪt/ n ninnolo m

trio /'triːəʊ/ n trio m

trip /trɪp/ n (excursion) gita f; (journey) viaggio m; (stumble) passo m falso ● v (pt/pp tripped) ● vt far inciampare ● vi inciampare (on/over in). □ ~ **up** vt far inciampare

tripe /traɪp/ n trippa f; (fam: nonsense) fesserie fpl

triple /'trɪpl/ adj triplo ● vt triplicare ● vi triplicarsi

triplets /'trɪplɪts/ npl tre gemelli mpl

triplicate /'trɪplɪkət/ n **in** ~ in triplice copia

tripod /'traɪpɒd/ n treppiede m inv

trite /traɪt/ adj banale

triumph /'traɪʌmf/ n trionfo m ● vi trionfare (over su). **~ant** adj trionfante. **~antly** adv (exclaim) con tono trionfante

trivial /'trɪvɪəl/ adj insignificante. **~ity** n banalità f inv

trolley /'trɒli/ n carrello m; (Am: tram) tram m inv. ~ **bus** n filobus m inv

trombone /trɒm'bəʊn/ n trombone m

troop /truːp/ n gruppo m; **~s** pl truppe fpl ● vi ~ **in/out** entrare/uscire in gruppo

trophy /'trəʊfi/ n trofeo m

tropic /'trɒpɪk/ n tropico m; **~s** pl tropici mpl. **~al** adj tropicale

trot /trɒt/ n trotto m ● vi (pt/pp trotted) trottare

trouble /'trʌbl/ n guaio m; (difficulties) problemi mpl; (inconvenience, Med) disturbo m; (conflict) conflitto

t

m; be in ∼ essere nei guai; (swimmer, climber:) essere in difficoltà; get into ∼ finire nei guai; get sb into ∼ mettere qcno nei guai; take the ∼ to do sth darsi la pena di far qcsa ● vt (worry) preoccupare; (inconvenience) disturbare; (conscience, old wound:) tormentare ● vi don't ∼! non ti disturbare!. ∼maker n be a ∼-maker seminare zizzania. ∼some adj fastidioso

trough /trɒf/ n trogolo m; (atmospheric) depressione f

troupe /truːp/ n troupe f inv

trousers /ˈtraʊzəz/ npl pantaloni mpl

trout /traʊt/ n inv trota f

trowel /ˈtraʊəl/ n (for gardening) paletta f; (for builder) cazzuola f

truant /ˈtruːənt/ n play ∼ marinare la scuola

truce /truːs/ n tregua f

truck /trʌk/ n (lorry) camion m inv

trudge /trʌdʒ/ n camminata f faticosa ● vi arrancare

true /truː/ adj vero; come ∼ avverarsi

truffle /ˈtrʌfl/ n tartufo m

truly /ˈtruːlɪ/ adv veramente; Yours ∼ distinti saluti

trump /trʌmp/ n (in cards) atout m inv

trumpet /ˈtrʌmpɪt/ n tromba f. ∼er n trombettista mf

truncheon /ˈtrʌntʃən/ n manganello m

trunk /trʌŋk/ n (of tree, body) tronco m; (of elephant) proboscide f; (for travelling, storage) baule m; (Am: of car) bagagliaio m; ∼s pl calzoncini mpl da bagno

truss /trʌs/ n (Med) cinto m erniario

trust /trʌst/ n fiducia f; (group of companies) trust m inv; (organization) associazione f; on ∼ sulla parola ● vt fidarsi di; (hope) augurarsi ● vi ∼ in credere in; ∼ to affidarsi a. ∼ed adj fidato

trustee /trʌsˈtiː/ n amministratore, -trice mf fiduciario, -a

'trust|ful /ˈtrʌstfl/ adj fiducioso. ∼ing adj fiducioso. ∼worthy adj fidato

truth /truːθ/ n (pl -s /truːðz/) verità f inv. ∼ful adj veritiero. ∼fully adv sinceramente

try /traɪ/ n tentativo m, prova f; (in rugby) meta f ● vt (pt/pp tried) ● vt provare; (be a strain on) mettere a dura prova; (Jur) processare (person); discutere (case); ∼ to do sth provare a fare qcsa ● vi provare. □ ∼ on vt provarsi (garment). □ ∼ out vt provare

trying /ˈtraɪɪŋ/ adj duro; (person) irritante

T-shirt /ˈtiː-/ n maglietta f

tub /tʌb/ n tinozza f; (carton) vaschetta f; (bath) vasca f da bagno

tuba /ˈtjuːbə/ n (Mus) tuba f

tubby /ˈtʌbɪ/ adj (-ier, -iest) tozzo

tube /tjuːb/ n tubo m; (of toothpaste) tubetto m; (Rail) metro f

tuberculosis /tjuːbɜːkjʊˈləʊsɪs/ n tubercolosi f

tubular /ˈtjuːbjʊlə(r)/ adj tubolare

tuck /tʌk/ n piega f ● vt (put) infilare. □ ∼ in vt rimboccare; ∼ sb in rimboccare le coperte a qcno ● vi (ⓘ eat) mangiare con appetito. □ ∼ up vt rimboccarsi (sleeves); (in bed) rimboccare le coperte a

Tuesday /ˈtjuːzdeɪ/ n martedì m inv

tuft /tʌft/ n ciuffo m

tug /tʌg/ n strattone m; (Naut) rimorchiatore m ● vt (pt/pp tugged) ● vt tirare ● vi dare uno strattone. ∼ of war n tiro m alla fune

tuition /tjuːˈɪʃn/ n lezioni fpl

tulip /ˈtjuːlɪp/ n tulipano m

tumble /ˈtʌmbl/ n ruzzolone m ● vi ruzzolare. ∼down adj cadente. ∼drier n asciugabiancheria f

tumbler /ˈtʌmblə(r)/ n bicchiere m

(senza stelo)

tummy /'tʌmɪ/ n 🔲 pancia f

tumour /'tjuːmə(r)/ n tumore m

tumult /'tjuːmʌlt/ n tumulto m.
~uous adj tumultuoso

tuna /'tjuːnə/ n tonno m

tune /tjuːn/ n motivo m; out of/in
~ (instrument) scordato/accordato;
(person) stonato/intonato; to the ~
of 🔲 per la modesta somma di ● vt
accordare (instrument); sintonizzare
(radio, TV); mettere a punto (engine). □ ~ **in** vt sintonizzare ● vi sintonizzarsi (to su). □ ~ **up** vi (orchestra:) accordare gli strumenti

tuneful /'tjuːnfl/ adj melodioso

tuner /'tjuːnə(r)/ n accordatore,
-trice mf; (Radio, TV) sintonizzatore m

tunic /'tjuːnɪk/ n tunica f; (Mil)
giacca f; (Sch) ≈ grembiule m

tunnel /'tʌnl/ n tunnel m inv ● vi (pt/
pp tunnelled) scavare un tunnel

turban /'tɜːbən/ n turbante m

turbine /'tɜːbaɪn/ n turbina f

turbulen|ce /'tɜːbjʊləns/ n turbolenza f. **~t** adj turbolento

turf /tɜːf/ n erba f; (segment) zolla f
erbosa ● **turf out** vt 🔲 buttar fuori

Turin /tjuˈrɪn/ n Torino f

Turk /tɜːk/ n turco, -a mf

turkey /'tɜːkɪ/ n tacchino m

Turk|ey n Turchia f. **~ish** adj turco

turmoil /'tɜːmɔɪl/ n tumulto m

turn /tɜːn/ n (rotation, short walk) giro
m; (in road) svolta f, curva f; (development) svolta f; (Theat) numero m; (🔲:
attack) crisi f inv; as a ~ for the better/
worse un miglioramento/
peggioramento; do sb a good ~
rendere un servizio a qcno; take ~s
fare a turno; a turno; out of ~
(speak) a sproposito; it's your ~
tocca a te ● vt girare; voltare (back,
eyes); dirigere (gun, attention) ● vi
girare; (person:) girarsi; (leaves:) ingiallire; (become) diventare; ~ right/

left girare a destra/sinistra; ~ sour
inacidirsi; ~ to sb girarsi verso
qcno; fig rivolgersi a qcno. □ ~
against vi diventare ostile a ● vt
mettere contro. □ ~ **away** vt mandare via (people); girare dall'altra
parte (head) ● vi girare dall'altra
parte. □ ~ **down** vt piegare (collar);
abbassare (heat, gas, sound); respingere (person, proposal). □ ~ **in** vt
piegare in dentro (edges); consegnare (lost object) ● vi (🔲: go to bed)
andare a letto; ~ **into** the drive entrare nel viale. □ ~ **off** vt spegnere;
chiudere (tap, water) ● vi (car:) girare. □ ~ **on** vt accendere; aprire
(tap, water); (🔲: attract) eccitare ● vi
(attack) attaccare. □ ~ **out** vt (expel)
mandar via; spegnere (light, gas);
(produce) produrre; (empty) svuotare
(room, cupboard) ● vi (transpire) risultare; ~ out well/badly (cake,
dress:) riuscire bene/male; (situation:) andare bene/male. □ ~ **over**
vt girare ● vi girarsi; please ~ over
vedi retro. □ ~ **round** vi girarsi;
(car:) girare. □ ~ **up** vt tirare su (collar); alzare (heat, gas, sound, radio)
● vi farsi vedere

turning /'tɜːnɪŋ/ n svolta f.
~-point n svolta f decisiva

turnip /'tɜːnɪp/ n rapa f

turn: **~over** n (Comm) giro m d'affari; (of staff) ricambio m. **~pike** n
Am autostrada f. **~stile** n cancelletto
m girevole. **~table** n piattaforma f
girevole (on record-player) piatto m (di
giradischi). **~-up** n (of trousers) risvolto m

turquoise /'tɜːkwɔɪz/ adj (colour)
turchese ● n turchese m

turret /'tʌrɪt/ n torretta f

turtle /'tɜːtl/ n tartaruga f acquatica

tusk /tʌsk/ n zanna f

tussle /'tʌsl/ n zuffa f ● vi azzuffarsi

tutor /'tjuːtə(r)/ n insegnante mf privato, -a; (Univ) insegnante mf universitario,
-a che segue individualmente un ristretto

numero di studenti. ~ial n discussione f col tutor

tuxedo /tʌk'si:dəʊ/ n Am smoking m inv

TV n abbr (television) tv f inv, tivù f inv

twang /twæŋ/ n (in voice) suono m nasale • vt far vibrare

tweezers /'twi:zəz/ npl pinzette fpl

twelfth /twelfθ/ adj dodicesimo

twelve /twelv/ adj dodici

twentieth /'twentɪɪθ/ adj ventesimo

twenty /'twentɪ/ adj venti

twice /twaɪs/ adv due volte

twiddle /'twɪdl/ vt giocherellare con; ~ one's thumbs fig girarsi i pollici

twig[1] /twɪg/ n ramoscello m

twig[2] /twɪg/ vt/i (pt/pp twigged) 🔲 intuire

twilight /'twaɪ-/ n crepuscolo m

twin /twɪn/ n gemello, -a mf • attrib gemello. ~ beds npl letti mpl gemelli

twine /twaɪn/ n spago m • vi intrecciarsi; (plant:) attorcigliarsi • vt intrecciare

twinge /twɪndʒ/ n fitta f; ~ of conscience rimorso m di coscienza

twinkle /'twɪŋkl/ n scintillio m • vi scintillare

twirl /twɜ:l/ vt far roteare • vi volteggiare • n piroetta f

twist /twɪst/ n torsione f; (curve) curva f; (in rope) attorcigliata f; (in book, plot) colpo m di scena • vt attorcigliare (rope); torcere (metal); girare (knob, cap); (distort) distorcere; ~ one's ankle storcersi la caviglia • vi attorcigliarsi; (road:) essere pieno di curve

twit /twɪt/ n 🔲 cretino, -a mf

twitch /twɪtʃ/ n tic m inv; (jerk) strattone m • vi contrarsi

twitter /'twɪtə(r)/ n cinguettio m • vi cinguettare; (person:) cianciare

two /tu:/ adj due

two: ~-faced adj falso. ~-piece adj

(swimsuit) due pezzi m inv; (suit) completo m. ~-way adj (traffic) a doppio senso di marcia

tycoon /taɪ'ku:n/ n magnate m

tying /'taɪɪŋ/ ▷ TIE

type /taɪp/ n tipo m; (printing) carattere m [tipografico] • vt scrivere a macchina • vi scrivere a macchina. ~writer n macchina f da scrivere. ~written adj dattiloscritto

typical /'tɪpɪkl/ adj tipico. ~ly adv tipicamente; (as usual) come al solito

typify /'tɪpɪfaɪ/ vt (pt/pp -ied) essere tipico di

typing /'taɪpɪŋ/ n dattilografia f

typist /'taɪpɪst/ n dattilografo, -a mf

tyrannical /tɪ'rænɪkl/ adj tirannico

tyranny /'tɪrənɪ/ n tirannia f

tyrant /'taɪrənt/ n tiranno, -a mf

tyre /'taɪə(r)/ n gomma f, pneumatico m

Uu

udder /'ʌdə(r)/ n mammella f (di vacca, capra etc)

ugly /'ʌglɪ/ adj (-ier, -iest) brutto

UK n abbr United Kingdom

ultimate /'ʌltɪmət/ adj definitivo; (final) finale; (fundamental) fondamentale. ~ly adv alla fine

ultimatum /ʌltɪ'meɪtəm/ n ultimatum m inv

ultra'violet adj ultravioletto

umbrella /ʌm'brelə/ n ombrello m

umpire /'ʌmpaɪə(r)/ n arbitro m • vt/i arbitrare

umpteen /ʌmp'ti:n/ adj 🔲 innumerevole. ~th adj 🔲 ennesimo; for the ~th time per l'ennesima volta

UN n abbr (United Nations) ONU f

un'able /ʌn-/ adj be ~ to do sth non potere fare qcsa; (*not know how*) non sapere fare qcsa

unac'companied adj non accompagnato; (*luggage*) incustodito

unac'customed adj insolito; be ~ to non essere abituato a

un'aided adj senza aiuto

unanimous /juːˈnænɪməs/ adj unanime. ~ly adv all'unanimità

un'armed adj disarmato; ~ combat lotta f senza armi

unat'tended adj incustodito

una'voidable adj inevitabile

una'ware adj be ~ of sth non rendersi conto di qcsa. ~s adv catch sb ~s prendere qcno alla sprovvista

un'bearabl|e adj insopportabile. ~y adv insopportabilmente

unbeat|able /ʌnˈbiːtəbl/ adj imbattibile. ~en adj imbattuto

unbe'lievable adj incredibile

un'biased adj obiettivo

un'block vt sbloccare

un'bolt vt togliere il chiavistello di

un'breakable adj infrangibile

un'button vt sbottonare

uncalled-for /ʌnˈkɔːldfɔː(r)/ adj fuori luogo

un'canny adj sorprendente; (*silence, feeling*) inquietante

un'certain adj incerto; (*weather*) instabile; in no ~ terms senza mezzi termini. ~ty n incertezza f

un'charitable adj duro

uncle /ˈʌŋkl/ n zio m

Uncle Sam Personaggio immaginario che rappresenta gli Stati Uniti, il suo governo e i suoi cittadini. Nell'iconografia è tradizionalmente rappresentato con la barba bianca, vestito dei colori nazionali bianco, rosso e azzurro, con un gran cappello a 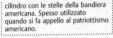 cilindro con le stelle della bandiera americana. Spesso utilizzato quando si fa appello al patriottismo americano.

un'comfortabl|e adj scomodo; imbarazzante (silence, situation); feel ~e fig sentirsi a disagio. ~ly adv (sit) scomodamente; (*causing alarm etc*) spaventosamente

un'common adj insolito

un'compromising adj intransigente

uncon'ditional adj incondizionato. ~ly adv incondizionatamente

un'conscious adj privo di sensi; (*unaware*) inconsapevole; be ~ of sth non rendersi conto di qcsa. ~ly adv inconsapevolmente

uncon'ventional adj poco convenzionale

un'cork vt sturare

uncouth /ʌnˈkuːθ/ adj zotico

un'cover vt scoprire; portare alla luce (buried object)

unde'cided adj indeciso; (*not settled*) incerto

undeniabl|e /ʌndɪˈnaɪəbl/ adj innegabile. ~y adv innegabilmente

under /ˈʌndə(r)/ prep sotto; (*less than*) al di sotto di; ~ there lì sotto; ~ repair/construction in riparazione/costruzione; ~ way fig in corso ● adv (~ water) sott'acqua; (*unconscious*) sotto anestesia

'undercarriage n (Aeron) carrello m

'underclothes npl biancheria fsg intima

under'cover adj clandestino

'undercurrent n corrente f sottomarina; fig sottofondo m

'underdog n perdente m

under'done adj (meat) al sangue

under'estimate vt sottovalutare

under'fed adj denutrito

under'foot adv sotto i piedi; trample ~ calpestare

under'go vt (pt -went, pp -gone) subire (operation, treatment); ~ repair essere in riparazione

under'graduate n studente, -tessa mf universitario, -a

'underground' n sottoterra

underground² adj sotterraneo; (secret) clandestino ● n (railway) metropolitana f. ~ car park n parcheggio m sotterraneo

'undergrowth n sottobosco m

'underhand adj subdolo

under'lie vt (pt -lay, pp -lain, pres p -lying) fig essere alla base di

under'line vt sottolineare

under'lying adj fig fondamentale

under'mine vt fig minare

underneath /ʌndə'niːθ/ prep sotto; ~ it sotto ● adv sotto

under'paid adj mal pagato

'underpants npl mutande fpl

'underpass n sottopassaggio m

under'privileged adj non abbiente

under'rate vt sottovalutare

'undershirt n Am maglia f della pelle

under'stand vt (pt/pp -stood) capire; I ~ that... (have heard) mi risulta che... ● vi capire. ~able adj comprensibile. ~ably adv comprensibilmente

under'standing adj comprensivo ● n comprensione f; (agreement) accordo m; on the ~ that a condizione che

'understatement n understatement m inv

under'take vt (pt -took, pp -taken) intraprendere; ~ to do sth impegnarsi a fare qcsa

'undertaker n impresario m di pompe funebri; (firm of) ~s n impresa f di pompe funebri

'under'taking n impresa f; (promise) promessa f

'undertone n fig sottofondo m; in an ~ sottovoce

under'value vt sottovalutare

'underwater' adj subacqueo

under'water² adv sott'acqua

'underwear n biancheria f intima

under'weight adj sotto peso

'underworld n (criminals) malavita f

unde'sirable adj indesiderato; (person) poco raccomandabile

un'dignified adj non dignitoso

un'do vt (pt -did, pp -done) disfare; slacciare (dress, shoes); sbottonare (shirt); fig, (Comput) annullare

un'doubted adj indubbio. ~ly adv senza dubbio

un'dress vt spogliare; get ~ed spogliarsi ● vi spogliarsi

un'due adj eccessivo

un'duly adv eccessivamente

un'earth vt dissotterrare; fig scovare; scoprire (secret). ~ly adj soprannaturale; at an ~ly hour 🔢 a un'ora impossibile

uneco'nomic adj poco remunerativo

unem'ployed adj disoccupato ● npl the ~ i disoccupati

unem'ployment n disoccupazione f. ~ benefit n sussidio m di disoccupazione

un'ending adj senza fine

un'equal adj disuguale; (struggle) impari; be ~ to a task non essere all'altezza di un compito

unequivocal /ʌnɪ'kwɪvəkl/ adj inequivocabile; (person) esplicito

un'ethical adj immorale

un'even adj irregolare; (distribution) ineguale; (number) dispari

unex'pected adj inaspettato. ~ly adv inaspettatamente

un'fair adj ingiusto. ~ly adv ingiustamente. ~ness n ingiustizia f un'faithful adj infedele

unfa'miliar adj sconosciuto; be ~ with non conoscere

un'fasten vt slacciare; (detach) staccare

un'favourable adj sfavorevole; (impression) negativo

un'feeling adj insensibile

un'fit adj inadatto; (morally) indegno; (Sport) fuori forma; ~ for work non in grado di lavorare

un'fold vt spiegare; (spread out) aprire; fig rivelare • vi (view:) spiegarsi

unfore'seen adj imprevisto

unfor'gettable /ʌnfə'getəbl/ adj indimenticabile

unfor'givable /ʌnfə'gɪvəbl/ adj imperdonabile

unfor'tunate adj sfortunato; (regrettable) spiacevole; (remark, choice) infelice. ~ly adv purtroppo

un'founded adj infondato

un'furl /ʌn'fɜːl/ vt spiegare

un'gainly /ʌn'geɪnlɪ/ adj sgraziato

un'grateful adj ingrato; ~ly adv senza riconoscenza

un'happy adj infelice; (not content) insoddisfatto (with di)

un'harmed adj incolume

un'healthy adj poco sano; (insanitary) malsano

un'hurt adj illeso

unification /juːnɪfɪ'keɪʃn/ n unificazione f

uniform /'juːnɪfɔːm/ adj uniforme • n uniforme f. ~ly adv uniformemente

unify /'juːnɪfaɪ/ vt (pt/pp -ied) unificare

uni'lateral /juːnɪ-/ adj unilaterale

uni'maginable adj inimmaginabile

unim'portant adj irrilevante

unin'habited adj disabitato

unin'tentional adj involontario. ~ly adv involontariamente

union /'juːnɪən/ n unione f; (trade ~) sindacato m. U~ Jack n bandiera f del Regno Unito

unique /juː'niːk/ adj unico. ~ly adv unicamente

unison /'juːnɪsn/ n in ~ all'unisono

unit /'juːnɪt/ n unità f inv; (department) reparto m; (of furniture) elemento m

unite /juː'naɪt/ vt unire • vi unirsi

unity /'juːnətɪ/ n unità f; (agreement) accordo m

universal /juːnɪ'vɜːsl/ adj universale. ~ly adv universalmente

universe /'juːnɪvɜːs/ n universo m

university /juːnɪ'vɜːsətɪ/ n università f • attrib universitario

un'just adj ingiusto

un'kind adj scortese. ~ly adv in modo scortese. ~ness n mancanza f di gentilezza

un'known adj sconosciuto

un'lawful adj illecito, illegale

unleaded /ʌn'ledɪd/ adj senza piombo

un'leash vt fig scatenare

unless /ən'les/ conj a meno che; ~ I am mistaken se non mi sbaglio

un'like adj (not the same) diversi • prep diverso da; that's ~ him non è da lui; ~ me, he... diversamente da me, lui...

un'likely adj improbabile

un'limited adj illimitato

un'load vt scaricare

un'lock vt aprire (con chiave)

un'lucky adj sfortunato; it's ~ to... porta sfortuna...

un'married adj non sposato. ~ 'mother n ragazza f madre

un'mask vt fig smascherare

unmistakab|le /ʌnmɪ'steɪkəbl/ adj inconfondibile. ~y adv chiaramente

u

un'natural adj innaturale; pej anormale. ~ly adv in modo innaturale; pej in modo anormale

un'necessar|y adj inutile. ~ily adv inutilmente

un'noticed adj inosservato

unob'tainable adj (product) introvabile; (phone number) non ottenibile

unob'trusive adj discreto. ~ly adv in modo discreto

unof'ficial adj non ufficiale. ~ly adv ufficiosamente

un'pack vi disfare le valigie ● vt svuotare (parcel); spacchettare (books); ~ one's case disfare la valigia

un'paid adj da pagare; (work) non retribuito

un'pleasant adj sgradevole; (person) maleducato. ~ly adv. sgradevolmente; (behave) maleducatamente. ~ness n (bad feeling) tensioni fpl

un'plug vt (pt/pp -plugged) staccare

un'popular adj impopolare

unprecedented adj senza precedenti

unpre'dictable adj imprevedibile

unpre'pared adj impreparato

unpro'fessional adj non professionale; it's ~ è una mancanza di professionalità

un'profitable adj non redditizio

un'qualified adj non qualificato; (fig: absolute) assoluto

un'questionable adj incontestabile

un'ravel vt (pt/pp -ravelled) districare; (in knitting) disfare

un'real adj irreale; 🔢 inverosimile

un'reasonable adj irragionevole

unre'lated adj (fact) senza rapporto (to con); (person) non imparentato (to con)

unre'liable adj inattendibile; (person) inaffidabile, che non dà affidamento

un'rest n fermenti mpl

un'rivalled adj ineguagliato

un'roll vt srotolare ● vi srotolarsi

un'ruly /ʌnˈruːlɪ/ adj indisciplinato

un'safe adj pericoloso

unsatis'factory adj poco soddisfacente

un'savoury adj equivoco

unscathed /ʌnˈskeɪðd/ adj illeso

un'screw vt svitare

un'scrupulous adj senza scrupoli

un'seemly adj indecoroso

un'selfish adj disinteressato

un'settled adj in agitazione; (weather) variabile; (bill) non saldato

unshakeable /ʌnˈʃeɪkəbl/ adj categorico

unshaven /ʌnˈʃeɪvn/ adj non rasato

un'sightly /ʌnˈsaɪtlɪ/ adj brutto

un'skilled adj non specializzato. ~ worker n manovale m

un'sociable adj scontroso

unso'phisticated adj semplice

un'sound adj (building, reasoning) poco solido; (advice) poco sensato; of ~ mind malato di mente

un'stable adj instabile; (mentally) squilibrato

un'steady adj malsicuro

un'stuck adj come ~ staccarsi; (🔢: project) andare a monte

unsuc'cessful adj fallimentare; be ~ (in attempt) non aver successo. ~ly adv senza successo

un'suitable adj (inappropriate) inadatto; (inconvenient) inopportuno

unthinkable /ʌnˈθɪŋkəbl/ adj impensabile

un'tidiness n disordine m

un'tidy adj disordinato

un'tie vt slegare

until /ʌn'tɪl/ *prep* fino a; not ~ non prima di; ~ **the evening** fino alla sera; ~ **his arrival** fino al suo arrivo ● *conj* finché, fino a quando; not ~ **you've seen it** non prima che tu l'abbia visto

un'told *adj* (wealth) incalcolabile; (suffering) indescrivibile; (story) inedito

un'true *adj* falso; that's ~ non è vero

unused¹ /ʌn'juːzd/ *adj* non [ancora] usato

unused² /ʌn'juːst/ *adj* be ~ to non essere abituato a

un'usual *adj* insolito. ~ly *adv* insolitamente

un'veil *vt* scoprire

un'wanted *adj* indesiderato

un'welcome *adj* sgradito

un'well *adj* indisposto

unwieldy /ʌn'wiːldɪ/ *adj* ingombrante

un'willing *adj* riluttante. ~ly *adv* malvolentieri

un'wind *v* (*pt/pp* unwound) ● *vt* svolgere, srotolare ● *vi* svolgersi, srotolarsi; (🖭: relax) rilassarsi

un'wise *adj* imprudente

un'worthy *adj* non degno

un'wrap *vt* (*pt/pp* -wrapped) scartare (present, parcel)

un'written *adj* tacito

up /ʌp/ *adv* su; (not in bed) alzato; (road) smantellato; (theatre curtain, blinds) alzato; (shelves, tent) montato; (notice) affisso; (building) costruito; prices are up i prezzi sono aumentati; be up for sale essere in vendita; up here/there quassù/lassù; time's up tempo scaduto; what's up? 🖭 cosa è successo?; up to (as far as) fino a; be up to essere all'altezza di (task); what's he up to? 🖭 cosa sta facendo?; (plotting) cosa sta combinando?; I'm up to page 100 sono arrivato a pagina 100; feel up

to it sentirsela; be one up on sb 🖭 essere in vantaggio su qcno; go up salire; lift up alzare; up against *fig* alle prese con ● *prep* su; the cat ran/ is up the tree il gatto è salito di corsa/è sull'albero; further up this road più avanti su questa strada; row up the river risalire il fiume; go up the stairs salire su per le scale; be up the pub 🖭 essere al pub; be up on or in sth essere bene informato su qcsa ● **ups and downs** *npl* alti *mpl* e bassi

'upbringing *n* educazione *f*

up'date¹ *vt* aggiornare

'update² *n* aggiornamento *m*

up'grade *vt* promuovere (person); modernizzare (equipment)

upheaval /ʌp'hiːvl/ *n* scompiglio *m*

up'hill *adj* in salita; *fig* arduo ● *adv* in salita

up'hold *vt* (*pt/pp* upheld) sostenere (principle); confermare (verdict)

upholster /ʌp'həʊlstə(r)/ *vt* tappezzare. ~er *n* tappezziere, -a *mf*. ~y *n* tappezzeria *f*

'upkeep *n* mantenimento *m*

up-'market *adj* di qualità

upon /ə'pɒn/ *prep* su; ~ **arriving home** una volta arrivato a casa

upper /ʌpə(r)/ *adj* superiore ● *n* (of shoe) tomaia *f*

upper class *n* alta borghesia *f*

'upright *adj* dritto; (piano) verticale; (honest) retto ● *n* montante *m*

'uprising *n* rivolta *f*

'uproar *n* tumulto *m*; be in an ~ essere in trambusto

up'set¹ *vt* (*pt/pp* upset, *pres p* upsetting) rovesciare; sconvolgere (plan); (distress) turbare; get ~ about sth prendersela per qcsa; be very ~ essere sconvolto; have an ~ stomach avere l'intestino disturbato

'upset² *n* scombussolamento *m*

'upshot *n* risultato *m*

u

upside 'down adv sottosopra; turn ~ ~ capovolgere

up'stairs¹ adv [al piano] di sopra

'upstairs² adj del piano superiore

'upstart n arrivato, -a mf

up'stream adv controcorrente

'uptake n be slow on the ~ essere lento nel capire; be quick on the ~ capire le cose al volo

up-to-'date adj moderno; (news) ultimo; (records) aggiornato

'upturn n ripresa f

upward /'ʌpwəd/ adj verso l'alto, in su; ~ slope salita f ● adv ~[s] verso l'alto; ~s of oltre

uranium /jʊ'reɪnɪəm/ n uranio m

urban /'ɜːbən/ adj urbano

urge /ɜːdʒ/ n forte desiderio m ● vt esortare (to a). □ ~ **on** vt spronare

urgen|cy /'ɜːdʒənsɪ/ n urgenza f. ~**t** adj urgente

urinate /'jʊərɪneɪt/ vi urinare

urine /'jʊərɪn/ n urina f

us /ʌs/ pron ci; (after prep) noi; they know us ci conoscono; give us the money dateci i soldi; give it to us datecelo; they showed it to us ce l'hanno fatto vedere; they meant us, not you intendevano noi, non voi; it's us siamo noi; she hates us ci odia

US[A] n[pl] abbr (United States [of America]) U.S.A. mpl

usage /'juːsɪdʒ/ n uso m

use¹ /juːs/ n uso m; be of ~ essere utile; be of no ~ essere inutile; make ~ of (exploit) sfruttare; it is no ~ è inutile; what's the ~? a che scopo?

use² /juːz/ vt usare. □ ~ **up** vt consumare

used¹ /juːzd/ adj usato

used² /juːst/ pt be ~ to sth essere abituato a qcsa; get ~ to abituarsi a; he ~ to live here viveva qui

useful /'juːsfl/ adj utile. ~**ness** n

utilità f

useless /'juːslɪs/ adj inutile; (🔲: person) incapace

user /'juːzə(r)/ n utente mf. ~-friendly adj facile da usare

usher /'ʌʃə(r)/ n (Theat) maschera f; (Jur) usciere m; (at wedding) persona f che accompagna gli invitati a un matrimonio ai loro posti in chiesa ● **usher in** vt fare entrare

usherette /ʌʃə'ret/ n maschera f

usual /'juːʒʊəl/ adj usuale; as ~ come al solito. ~**ly** adv di solito

utensil /juː'tensl/ n utensile m

utilize /'juːtɪlaɪz/ vt utilizzare

utmost /'ʌtməʊst/ adj estremo ●n one's ~ tutto il possibile

utter¹ /'ʌtə(r)/ adj totale. ~**ly** adv completamente

utter² vt emettere (sigh, sound); proferire (word). ~**ance** n dichiarazione f

U-turn /'juː-/ n (Auto) inversione f a U; fig marcia f in dietro

Vv

vacan|cy /'veɪk(ə)nsɪ/ n (job) posto m vacante; (room) stanza f disponibile. ~**t** adj libero; (position) vacante; (look) assente

vacate /və'keɪt/ vt lasciare libero

vacation /və'keɪʃn/ n vacanza f

vaccinat|e /'væksɪneɪt/ vt vaccinare. ~**ion** n vaccinazione f

vaccine /'væksiːn/ n vaccino m

vacuum /'vækjʊəm/ n vuoto m ● vt passare l'aspirapolvere in/su. ~ **cleaner** n aspirapolvere m inv. ~ **flask** n thermos® m inv. ~-**packed** adj confezionato sottovuoto

vagina /vəˈdʒaɪnə/ n (Anat) vagina f

vague /veɪɡ/ adj vago; (outline) impreciso; (absent-minded) distratto; I'm still ∼ about it non ho ancora le idee chiare in proposito. ∼ly adv vagamente

vain /veɪn/ adj vanitoso; (hope, attempt) vano; in ∼ invano. ∼ly adv vanamente

valentine /ˈvæləntaɪn/ n (card) biglietto m di San Valentino

valiant /ˈvælɪənt/ adj valoroso

valid /ˈvælɪd/ adj valido. ∼ate vt (confirm) convalidare. ∼ity n validità f

valley /ˈvælɪ/ n valle f

valour /ˈvælə(r)/ n valore m

valuable /ˈvæljʊəbl/ adj di valore; fig prezioso. ∼s npl oggetti mpl di valore

valuation /væljʊˈeɪʃn/ n valutazione f

value /ˈvælju:/ n valore m; (usefulness) utilità f ● vt valutare; (cherish) apprezzare. ∼ 'added tax n imposta f sul valore aggiunto

valve /vælv/ n valvola f

vampire /ˈvæmpaɪə(r)/ n vampiro m

van /væn/ n furgone m

vandal /ˈvændl/ n vandalo. -a mf. ∼ism n vandalismo m. ∼ize vt vandalizzare

vanilla /vəˈnɪlə/ n vaniglia f

vanish /ˈvænɪʃ/ vi svanire

vanity /ˈvænətɪ/ n vanità f. ∼ bag or case n beauty-case m inv

vapour /ˈveɪpə(r)/ n vapore m

variable /ˈveərɪəbl/ adj variabile; (adjustable) regolabile

variance /ˈveərɪəns/ n be at ∼ essere in disaccordo

variant /ˈveərɪənt/ n variante f

variation /veərɪˈeɪʃn/ n variazione f

varied /ˈveərɪd/ adj vario; (diet) diversificato; (life) movimentato

variety /vəˈraɪətɪ/ n varietà f inv

various /ˈveərɪəs/ adj vario

varnish /ˈvɑːnɪʃ/ n vernice f; (for nails) smalto m ● vt verniciare; ∼ one's nails mettersi lo smalto

vary /ˈveərɪ/ vt/i (pt/pp -ied) variare. ∼ing adj variabile; (different) diverso

vase /vɑːz/ n vaso m

vast /vɑːst/ adj vasto; (difference, amusement) enorme. ∼ly adv (superior) di gran lunga; (different, amused) enormemente

vat /væt/ n tino m

VAT /viːeɪˈtiː/, /væt/ n abbr (value added tax) I.V.A. f

vault¹ /vɔːlt/ n (roof) volta f; (in bank) caveau m inv; (tomb) cripta f

vault² n salto m ● vt/i ∼ [over] saltare

VDU n abbr (visual display unit) VDU m

veal /viːl/ n carne f di vitello ● attrib di vitello

veer /vɪə(r)/ vi cambiare direzione; (Auto, Naut) virare

vegetable /ˈvedʒtəbl/ n (food) verdura f; (when growing) ortaggio m ● attrib (oil, fat) vegetale

vegetarian /vedʒɪˈteərɪən/ adj & n vegetariano, -a mf

vehicle /ˈviːɪkl/ n veicolo m; (fig: medium) mezzo m

veil /veɪl/ n velo m ● vt velare

vein /veɪn/ n vena f; (mood) umore m; (manner) tenore m. ∼ed adj venato

velocity /vɪˈlɒsətɪ/ n velocità f

velvet /ˈvelvɪt/ n velluto m. ∼y adj vellutato

vendetta /venˈdetə/ n vendetta f

vending-machine /ˈvendɪŋ-/ n distributore m automatico

veneer /vəˈnɪə(r)/ n impiallacciatura f; fig vernice f. ∼ed adj impiallacciato

venereal /vɪˈnɪərɪəl/ adj ∼ disease malattia f venerea

Venetian /vəˈniːʃn/ adj & n veneziano, -a mf. v∼ blind n persiana f alla veneziana

vengeance /'vendʒəns/ n vendetta f; **with a ~** 🔲 a più non posso

venison /'venɪsn/ n (Culin) carne f di cervo

venom /'venəm/ n veleno m. **~ous** adj velenoso

vent[1] /vent/ n presa f d'aria; **give ~ to** fig dar libero sfogo a ● vt fig sfogare (anger)

vent[2] n (in jacket) spacco m

ventilat|e /'ventɪleɪt/ vt ventilare. **~ion** n ventilazione f; (installation) sistema m di ventilazione. **~or** n ventilatore m

ventriloquist /ven'trɪləkwɪst/ n ventriloquo, -a mf

venture /'ventʃə(r)/ n impresa f ● vt azzardare ● vi avventurarsi

venue /'venju:/ n luogo m (di convegno, concerto, ecc.)

veranda /və'rændə/ n veranda f

verb /vɜ:b/ n verbo m. **~al** adj verbale

verdict /'vɜ:dɪkt/ n verdetto m; (opinion) parere m

verge /vɜ:dʒ/ n orlo m; **be on the ~ of doing** sth essere sul punto di fare qcsa ● **verge on** vt fig rasentare

verify /'verɪfaɪ/ vt (pt/pp -ied) verificare; (confirm) confermare

vermin /'vɜ:mɪn/ n animali mpl nocivi

versatil|e /'vɜ:sətaɪl/ adj versatile. **~ity** n versatilità f

verse /vɜ:s/ n verso m; (of Bible) versetto m; (poetry) versi mpl

versed /vɜ:st/ adj **~ in** versato in

versus /'vɜ:səs/ prep contro

vertebra /'vɜ:tɪbrə/ n (pl -brae /-bri:/) (Anat) vertebra f

vertical /'vɜ:tɪkl/ adj & n verticale m

vertigo /'vɜ:tɪgəʊ/ n (Med) vertigine f

verve /vɜ:v/ n verve f

very /'verɪ/ adv molto; **~ much**

molto; **~ little** pochissimo; **~ many** moltissimi; **~ few** pochissimi; **~ probably** molto probabilmente; **~ well** benissimo; **at the ~ most** tutt'al più; **at the ~ latest** al più tardi ● adj **the ~** first il primissimo; **the ~ thing** proprio ciò che ci vuole; **at the ~ end/beginning** proprio alla fine/all'inizio; **that ~ day** proprio quel giorno; **the ~ thought** la sola idea; **only a ~ little** solo un pochino

vessel /'vesl/ n nave f

vest /vest/ n maglia f della pelle; (Am: waistcoat) gilè m inv. **~ed interest** n interesse m personale

vestige /'vestɪdʒ/ n (of past) vestigio m

vet /vet/ n veterinario, -a mf ● vt (pt/ pp vetted) controllare minuziosamente

veteran /'vetərən/ n veterano, -a mf

veterinary /'vetərɪnərɪ/ adj veterinario. **~ surgeon** n medico m veterinario

veto /'vi:təʊ/ n (pl -es) veto m ● vt proibire

vex /veks/ vt irritare. **~ation** n irritazione f. **~ed** adj irritato; **~ed question** questione f controversa

via /'vaɪə/ prep via; (by means of) attraverso

viable /'vaɪəbl/ adj (life form, relationship, company) in grado di sopravvivere; (proposition) attuabile

viaduct /'vaɪədʌkt/ n viadotto m

vibrat|e /vaɪ'breɪt/ vi vibrare. **~ion** n vibrazione f

vicar /'vɪkə(r)/ n parroco m (protestante). **~age** n casa f parrocchiale

vice[1] /vaɪs/ n vizio m

vice[2] n (Techn) morsa f

vice versa /vaɪsɪ'vɜ:sə/ adv viceversa

vicinity /vɪ'sɪnətɪ/ n vicinanza f; **in the ~ of** nelle vicinanze di

vicious /'vɪʃəs/ adj cattivo; (attack) brutale; (animal) pericoloso. ~ 'circle n circolo m vizioso. ~ly adv (attack) brutalmente

victim /'vɪktɪm/ n vittima f. ~ize vt fare delle rappresaglie contro

victor /'vɪktə(r)/ n vincitore m

victor|ious /vɪk'tɔːrɪəs/ adj vittorioso. ~y n vittoria f

video /'vɪdɪəʊ/ n video m; (cassette) videocassetta f; (recorder) videoregistratore m ● attrib video ● vt registrare

video: ~ recorder n videoregistratore m. ~tape n videocassetta f

vie /vaɪ/ vi (pres p vying) rivaleggiare

view /vjuː/ n vista f; (photographed, painted) veduta f; (opinion) visione f; look at the ~ guardare il panorama; in my ~ secondo me; in ~ of in considerazione di; on ~ esposto; with a ~ to con l'intenzione di ● vt visitare (house); (consider) considerare ● vi (TV) guardare. ~er n (TV) telespettatore, -trice mf; (Phot) visore m

view: ~finder n (Phot) mirino m. ~point n punto m di vista

vigilan|ce /'vɪdʒɪləns/ n vigilanza f. ~t adj vigile

vigorous /'vɪgərəs/ adj vigoroso

vigour /'vɪgə(r)/ n vigore m

vile /vaɪl/ adj disgustoso; (weather) orribile; (temper, mood) pessimo

village /'vɪlɪdʒ/ n paese m. ~r n paesano, -a mf

villain /'vɪlən/ n furfante m; (in story) cattivo m

vindicate /'vɪndɪkeɪt/ vt (from guilt) discolpare; **you are ~d** ti sei dimostrato nel giusto

vindictive /vɪn'dɪktɪv/ adj vendicativo

vine /vaɪn/ n vite f

vinegar /'vɪnɪgə(r)/ n aceto m

vineyard /'vɪnjɑːd/ n vigneto m

vintage /'vɪntɪdʒ/ adj (wine) d'an-

nata ● n (year) annata f

viola /vɪ'əʊlə/ n (Mus) viola f. ~ion n violazione f

violat|e /'vaɪəleɪt/ vt violare. ~ion n violazione f

violen|ce /'vaɪələns/ n violenza f. ~t adj violento

violet /'vaɪələt/ adj violetto ● n (flower) violetta f; (colour) violetto m

violin /vaɪə'lɪn/ n violino m. ~ist n violinista mf

VIP n abbr (very important person) vip mf

virgin /'vɜːdʒɪn/ adj vergine ● n vergine f. ~ity n verginità f

Virgo /'vɜːgəʊ/ n Vergine f

viril|e /'vɪraɪl/ adj virile. ~ity n virilità f

virtual /'vɜːtjʊəl/ adj effettivo. ~ reality n realtà f virtuale. ~ly adv praticamente

virtue /'vɜːtjuː/ n virtù f inv; (advantage) vantaggio f; **by** or **in ~ of** a causa di

virtuous /'vɜːtjʊəs/ adj virtuoso

virulent /'vɪrʊlənt/ adj virulento

virus /'vaɪərəs/ n virus m inv

visa /'viːzə/ n visto m

visibility /vɪzə'bɪlətɪ/ n visibilità f

visibl|e /'vɪzəbl/ adj visibile. ~y adv visibilmente

vision /'vɪʒn/ n visione f; (sight) vista f

visit /'vɪzɪt/ n visita f ● vt andare a trovare (person); andare da (doctor etc); visitare (town, building). ~ing hours npl orario m delle visite. ~or n ospite mf; (of town, museum) visitatore, -trice mf; (in hotel) cliente mf

visor /'vaɪzə(r)/ n visiera f; (Auto) parasole m

visual /'vɪzjʊəl/ adj visivo. ~ aids npl supporto m visivo. ~ dis'play unit n visualizzatore m. ~ly adv visualmente; ~ly handicapped non vedente

visualize /'vɪzjʊəlaɪz/ vt visualizzare

vital /ˈvaɪtl/ adj vitale. **~ity** n vitalità f. **~ly** adv estremamente

vitamin /ˈvɪtəmɪn/ n vitamina f

vivaci|ous /vɪˈveɪʃəs/ adj vivace. **~ty** n vivacità f

vivid /ˈvɪvɪd/ adj vivido. **~ly** adv in modo vivido

vocabulary /vəˈkæbjʊlərɪ/ n vocabolario m; (list) glossario m

vocal /ˈvəʊkl/ adj vocale; (vociferous) eloquente. **~ cords** npl corde fpl vocali

vocalist /ˈvəʊkəlɪst/ n vocalista mf

vocation /vəˈkeɪʃn/ n vocazione f. **~al** adj di orientamento professionale

vociferous /vəˈsɪfərəs/ adj vociante

vogue /vəʊg/ n moda f; **in ~** in voga

voice /vɔɪs/ n voce f ● vt esprimere. **~mail** n posta f elettronica vocale

void /vɔɪd/ adj (not valid) nullo; **~ of** privo di ● n vuoto m

volatile /ˈvɒlətaɪl/ adj volatile; (person) volubile

volcanic /vɒlˈkænɪk/ adj vulcanico

volcano /vɒlˈkeɪnəʊ/ n vulcano m

volley /ˈvɒlɪ/ n (of gunfire) raffica f; (Tennis) volée f inv

volt /vəʊlt/ n volt m inv. **~age** n (Electr) voltaggio m

volume /ˈvɒljuːm/ n volume m; (of work, traffic) quantità f inv. **~ control** n volume m

voluntar|y /ˈvɒləntərɪ/ adj volontario. **~y work** n volontariato m. **~ily** adv volontariamente

volunteer /vɒlənˈtɪə(r)/ n volontario, -a mf ● vt offrire volontariamente (information) ● vi offrirsi volontario; (Mil) arruolarsi come volontario

vomit /ˈvɒmɪt/ n vomito m ● vt/i vomitare

voracious /vəˈreɪʃəs/ adj vorace

vot|e /vəʊt/ n voto m; (ballot) votazione f; (right) diritto m di voto; take

a **~e on** votare su ● vi votare ● vt **~e sb president** eleggere qcno presidente. **~er** n elettore, -trice mf. **~ing** n votazione f

vouch /vaʊtʃ/ vi **~ for** garantire per. **~er** n buono m

vow /vaʊ/ n voto m ● vt giurare

vowel /ˈvaʊəl/ n vocale f

voyage /ˈvɔɪdʒ/ n viaggio m [marittimo]; (in space) viaggio m [nello spazio]

vulgar /ˈvʌlgə(r)/ adj volgare. **~ity** n volgarità f inv

vulnerable /ˈvʌlnərəbl/ adj vulnerabile

vulture /ˈvʌltʃə(r)/ n avvoltoio m

vying /ˈvaɪɪŋ/ ▷VIE

Ww

wad /wɒd/ n batuffolo m; (bundle) rotolo m. **~ding** n ovatta f

waddle /ˈwɒdl/ vi camminare ondeggiando

wade /weɪd/ vi guadare; **~ through** 🔟 procedere faticosamente in (book)

wafer /ˈweɪfə(r)/ n cialda f, wafer m inv; (Relig) ostia f

waffle¹ /ˈwɒfl/ vi 🔟 blaterare

waffle² n (Culin) cialda f

waft /wɒft/ vt trasportare ● vi diffondersi

wag /wæg/ n (vt/pp wagged) ● vt agitare ● vi agitarsi

wage¹ /weɪdʒ/ vt dichiarare (war); lanciare (campaign)

wage² n, **& ~s** pl salario msg. **~ packet** n busta f paga

waggle /ˈwægl/ vt dimenare ● vi dimenarsi

wagon /'wægən/ n carro m; (Rail) vagone m merci

wail /weɪl/ n piagnucolìo m; (of wind) lamento m; (of baby) vagito m ● vi piagnucolare; (wind:) lamentarsi; (baby:) vagire

waist /weɪst/ n vita f. ~coat n gilè m inv; (of man's suit) panciotto m. ~line n vita f

wait /weɪt/ n attesa f; lie in ~ for appostarsi per sorprendere ● vi aspettare; ~ for aspettare ● vt: ~ one's turn aspettare il proprio turno. □ ~ on vt servire

waiter /'weɪtə(r)/ n cameriere m

waiting: ~-list n lista f d'attesa. ~-room n sala f d'aspetto

waitress /'weɪtrɪs/ n cameriera f

waive /weɪv/ vt rinunciare a (claim); non tener conto di (rule)

wake[1] /weɪk/ n veglia f funebre ● v (pt woke, pp woken) ~ [up] ● vt svegliare ● vi svegliarsi

wake[2] n (Naut) scia f; in the ~ of fig nella scia di

Wales /weɪlz/ n Galles m

walk /wɔːk/ n passeggiata f; (gait) andatura f; (path) sentiero m; go for a ~ andare a fare una passeggiata ● vi camminare; (as opposed to drive etc) andare a piedi; (ramble) passeggiare ● vt portare a spasso (dog); percorrere (streets). □ ~ out vi (husband, employee:) andarsene; (workers:) scioperare. □ ~ out on vt lasciare

walker /'wɔːkə(r)/ n camminatore, -trice mf; (rambler) escursionista mf

walk-out n sciopero m

wall /wɔːl/ n muro m; go to the ~ 🔲 fallire; drive sb up the ~ 🔲 far diventare matto qcno ● wall up vt murare

wallet /'wɒlɪt/ n portafoglio m

wallop /'wɒləp/ n 🔲 colpo m ● vt (pt/pp walloped) 🔲 colpire

wallow /'wɒləʊ/ vi sguazzare; (in self-pity) crogiolarsi

'wallpaper n tappezzeria f ● vt tappezzare

walnut /'wɔːlnʌt/ n noce f

waltz /wɔːlts/ n valzer m inv ● vi ballare il valzer

wand /wɒnd/ n (magic ~) bacchetta f [magica]

wander /'wɒndə(r)/ vi girovagare; (fig: digress) divagare. □ ~ about vi andare a spasso

wane /weɪn/ n be on the ~ essere in fase calante ● vi calare

wangle /'wæŋgl/ vt 🔲 rimediare (invitation, holiday)

want /wɒnt/ n (hardship) bisogno m; (lack) mancanza f ● vt volere; (need) aver bisogno di; ~ [to have] sth volere qcsa; ~ to do sth voler fare qcsa; we ~ to stay vogliamo rimanere; I ~ you to go voglio che tu vada; it ~s painting ha bisogno d'essere dipinto; you ~ to learn to swim bisogna che impari a nuotare ● vi ~ for mancare di. ~ed adj ricercato. ~ing adj be ~ing mancare; be ~ing in mancare di

WAP /wæp/ n abbr (wireless application protocol) WAP m inv

war /wɔː(r)/ n guerra f; fig lotta f (on contro); at ~ in guerra

ward /wɔːd/ n (in hospital) reparto m; (child) minore m sotto tutela ● ward off vt evitare; parare (blow)

warden /'wɔːdn/ n guardiano, -a mf

warder /'wɔːdə(r)/ n guardia f carceraria

wardrobe /'wɔːdrəʊb/ n guardaroba m

warehouse /'weəhaʊs/ n

magazzino *m*

war: ~**fare** *n* guerra *f*. ~**head** *n* testata *f*

warm /wɔːm/ *adj* caldo; (welcome) caloroso; **be** ~ (person): aver caldo; it is ~ (weather) fa caldo • *vt* scaldare. □ ~ **up** *vt* scaldare • *vi* scaldarsi; *fig* animarsi. ~**-hearted** *adj* espansivo. ~**ly** *adv* (greet) calorosamente; (dress) in modo pesante. ~**th** *n* calore *m*

warn /wɔːn/ *vt* avvertire. ~**ing** *n* avvertimento *m*; (advance notice) preavviso *m*

warp /wɔːp/ *vt* deformare; *fig* distorcere • *vi* deformarsi

warped /wɔːpt/ *adj fig* contorto; (sexuality) deviato; (view) distorto

warrant /ˈwɒrənt/ *n* (for arrest, search) mandato *m* • *vt* (justify) giustificare; (guarantee) garantire. ~**y** *n* garanzia *f*

warrior /ˈwɒrɪə(r)/ *n* guerriero, -a *mf*

'warship *n* nave *f* da guerra

wart /wɔːt/ *n* porro *m*

'wartime *n* tempo *m* di guerra

war|y /ˈweərɪ/ *adj* (-ier, -iest) (careful) cauto; (suspicious) diffidente

was /wɒz/ ▶BE

wash /wɒʃ/ *n* lavata *f*; (clothes) bucato *m*; (in washing machine) lavaggio *m*; **have a** ~ darsi una lavata • *vt* lavare; (sea): bagnare; ~ **one's hands** lavarsi le mani • *vi* lavarsi. □ ~ **out** *vt* sciacquare (soap); sciacquarsi (mouth). □ ~ **up** *vt* lavare • *vi* lavare i piatti. ~ **away** *vt* lavarsi

washable /ˈwɒʃəbl/ *adj* lavabile

wash-basin *n* lavandino *m*

washer /ˈwɒʃə(r)/ *n* (Techn) guarnizione *f*; (machine) lavatrice *f*

washing /ˈwɒʃɪŋ/ *n* bucato *m*. ~**-machine** *n* lavatrice *f*. ~**-powder** *n* detersivo *m*. ~**-up** *n* do the ~**-up** lavare i piatti. ~**-up liquid** *n* detersivo *m* per i piatti

wash: ~**-out** *n* disastro *m*. ~**-room** *n* bagno *m*

wasp /wɒsp/ *n* vespa *f*

waste /weɪst/ *n* spreco *m*; (rubbish) rifiuti *m*; ~ **of time** perdita *f* di tempo • *adj* (product) di scarto; (land) desolato; **lay** ~ devastare • *vt* sprecare. ~ **away** *vi* deperire

waste: ~**-disposal unit** *n* eliminatore *m* di rifiuti. ~**ful** *adj* dispendioso. ~**'paper basket** *n* cestino *m* per la carta [straccia]

watch /wɒtʃ/ *n* guardia *f*; (period of duty) turno *m* di guardia; (timepiece) orologio *m*; **be on the** ~ stare all'erta • *vt* guardare (film, match, television); (be careful of, look after) stare attento a • *vi* guardare. □ ~ **out** *vi* (be careful) stare attento (**for** a). □ ~ **out for** *vt* (look for) fare attenzione all'arrivo di (person)

watch: ~**-dog** *n* cane *m* da guardia. ~**man** *n* guardiano *m*

water /ˈwɔːtə(r)/ *n* acqua *f* • *vt* annaffiare (garden, plant); (dilute) annacquare • *vi* (eyes): lacrimare; **my mouth was** ~**ing** avevo l'acquolina in bocca. □ ~ **down** *vt* diluire; *fig* attenuare

water: ~**-colour** *n* acquerello *m*. ~**cress** *n* crescione *m*. ~**fall** *n* cascata *f*

'watering-can *n* annaffiatoio *m*

water: ~**-lily** *n* ninfea *f*. ~**logged** *adj* inzuppato. ~**proof** *adj* impermeabile. ~**-skiing** *n* sci *m* nautico. ~**tight** *adj* stagno; *fig* irrefutabile. ~**way** *n* canale *m* navigabile

watery /ˈwɔːtərɪ/ *adj* acquoso; (eyes) lacrimoso

watt /wɒt/ *n* watt *m inv*

wave /weɪv/ *n* onda *f*; (gesture) cenno *m*; *fig* ondata *f* • *vt* agitare; ~ **one's hand** agitare la mano • *vi* far segno; (flag): sventolare. ~**length** *n* lunghezza *f* d'onda

waver /ˈweɪvə(r)/ *vi* vacillare.

(*hesitate*) esitare

wavy /'weɪvɪ/ *adj* ondulato

wax¹ /wæks/ *vi* (moon:) crescere; (*fig* become) diventare

wax² *n* cera *f*; (*in ear*) cerume *m* ● *vt* dare la cera a. **~works** *n* museo *m* delle cere

way /weɪ/ *n* percorso *m*; (*direction*) direzione *f*; (*manner, method*) modo *m*; **~s** *pl* (customs) abitudini *fpl*; **be in the ~** essere in mezzo; **on the ~ to Rome** andando a Roma; **I'll do it on the ~** lo faccio mentre vado; **it's on my ~** è sul mio percorso; **a long ~ off** lontano; **this ~** da questa parte; (*like this*) così; **by the ~** a proposito; **by ~ of** come; (*via*) via; **either ~** (*whatever we do*) in un modo o nell'altro; **in some ~s** sotto certi aspetti; **in a ~** in un certo senso; **in a bad ~** (person) molto grave; **out of the ~** fuori mano; **under ~** in corso; **lead the ~** far strada; *fig* aprire la strada; **make ~** far posto (*for a*); **give ~** (*Auto*) dare la precedenza; **go out of one's ~** *fig* scomodarsi (*to per*); **get one's [own] ~** averla vinta ● *adv* ● **~ behind** molto indietro. **~'in** *n* entrata *f*

way'**lay** *vt* (*pt/pp* -**laid**) aspettare al varco (*person*)

way '**out** *n* uscita *f*; *fig* via *f* d'uscita

way-'**out** *adj* 🔤 eccentrico

we /wi:/ *pron* noi; **we're the last** siamo gli ultimi; **they're going, but we're not** loro vanno, ma noi no

weak /wi:k/ *adj* debole; (liquid) leggero. **~en** *vt* indebolire ● *vi* indebolirsi. **~ling** *n* smidollato, -a *mf*. **~ness** *n* debolezza *f*; (liking) debole *m*

wealth /welθ/ *n* ricchezza *f*; *fig* gran quantità *f*. **~y** *adj* (-ier, -iest) ricco

weapon /'wepən/ *n* arma *f*; **~s of mass destruction** *npl* armi *mpl* di distruzione di massa

wear /weə(r)/ *n* (clothing) abbiglia-

mento *m*; **for everyday ~** da portare tutti i giorni; **~ [and tear]** usura *f* ● *v* (*pt* wore, *pp* worn) ● *vt* portare; (*damage*) consumare; **~ a hole in sth** logorare qcsa fino a fare un buco; **what shall I ~?** cosa mi metto? ● *vi* consumarsi; (*last*) durare. □ **~ off** *vi* scomparire; (effect:) finire. □ **~ out** *vt* consumare [fino in fondo]; (*exhaust*) estenuare ● *vi* estenuarsi

wear|y /'wɪərɪ/ *adj* (-ier, -iest) sfinito ● *v* (*pt/pp* wearied) ● *vt* sfinire ● *vi* **~y of** stancarsi di. **~ily** *adv* stancamente

weather /'weðə(r)/ *n* tempo *m*; **in this ~** con questo tempo; **under the ~** 🔤 giù di corda ● *vt* sopravvivere a (storm)

weather: **~-beaten** *adj* (face) segnato dalle intemperie. **~ forecast** *n* previsioni *fpl* del tempo

weave¹ /wi:v/ *vi* (*pt/pp* weaved) (move) zigzagare

weave² *n* tessuto *m* ● *vt* (*pt* wove, *pp* woven) tessere; intrecciare (flowers etc); intrecciare le fila di (story etc). **~r** *n* tessitore, -trice *mf*

web /web/ *n* rete *f*; (spider's) ragnatela *f*. **W~** (*Comput*) Web *m inv*, Rete *f*. **~bed feet** *npl* piedi *mpl* palmati. **~cam** *n* webcam *f inv*. **~ master** *n* webmaster *m inv*. **~ page** *n* pagina *f* web. **~ site** *n* sito *m* web

wed /wed/ *vt* (*pt/pp* wedded) sposare ● *vi* sposarsi. **~ding** *n* matrimonio *m*

wedding: **~ cake** *n* torta *f* nuziale. **~-ring** *n* fede *f*

wedge /wedʒ/ *n* zeppa *f*; (for splitting wood) cuneo *m*; (of cheese) fetta *f* ● *vt* (fix) fissare

Wednesday /'wenzdeɪ/ *n* mercoledì *m inv*

wee¹ /wi:/ *adj* 🔤 piccolo

wee² *vi* 🔤 fare la pipì

weed /wi:d/ *n* erbaccia *f*; (🔤: person)

mollusco *m* • *vt* estirpare le erbacce da. □ ~ **out** *vt fig* eliminare

'weed-killer *n* erbicida *m*

weedy /'wi:dɪ/ *adj* 🔢 mingherlino

week /wi:k/ *n* settimana *f*. ~**day** *n* giorno *m* feriale. ~**end** *n* fine settimana *m*

weekly /'wi:klɪ/ *adj* settimanale • *n* settimanale *m* • *adv* settimanalmente

weep /wi:p/ *vi* (*pt/pp* wept) piangere

weigh /weɪ/ *vt/i* pesare; ~ **anchor** levare l'ancora. □ ~ **down** *vt fig* piegare. □ ~ **up** *vt fig* soppesare; valutare (person)

weight /weɪt/ *n* peso *m*; **put on/lose** ~ ingrassare/dimagrire. ~**ing** *n* (*allowance*) indennità *f inv*

weight-lifting *n* sollevamento *m* pesi

weir /wɪə(r)/ *n* chiusa *f*

weird /wɪəd/ *adj* misterioso; (*bizarre*) bizzarro

welcome /'welkəm/ *adj* benvenuto; **you're ~!** prego!; **you're ~ to have it/it** ti/le come prendilo/vieni pure • *n* accoglienza *f* • *vt* accogliere; (*appreciate*) gradire

weld /weld/ *vt* saldare. ~**er** *n* saldatore *m*

welfare /'welfeə(r)/ *n* benessere *m*; (*aid*) assistenza *f*. **W~ State** *n* Stato *m* assistenziale

well[1] /wel/ *n* pozzo *m*; (*of staircase*) tromba *f*

well[2] *adv* (better, best) bene; **as ~** anche; **as ~ as** (*in addition*) oltre a; ~ **done!** bravo!; **very ~** benissimo • *adj* **he is ~** non sta bene; **get ~ soon!** guarisci presto! • *int* beh!; ~ **I never!** ma va!

well-behaved *adj* educato

well: ~**-known** *adj* famoso. ~**-off** *adj* benestante. ~**-to-do** *adj* ricco

Welsh /welʃ/ *adj & n* gallese; **the** ~ *pl i* gallesi. ~**man** *n* gallese *m*. ~ **rabbit** *n* toast *m inv* al formaggio

Welsh Assembly Istituita nel 1999 con sede a Cardiff, la *Welsh Assembly* ha poteri legislativi secondari limitati (non ha poteri riguardo al sistema fiscale al contrario dello *Scottish Parliament*). L'Assemblea è composta da 60 rappresentanti, 40 dei quali (*Assembly Members* o *Ams*) eletti a suffragio diretto, i restanti 20 eletti sulla base di liste regionali e col sistema proporzionale.

went /went/ ▷**GO**

wept /wept/ ▷**WEEP**

were /wɜ:(r)/ ▷**BE**

west /west/ *n* ovest *m*; **to the ~ of** a ovest di; **the W~** l'Occidente *m* • *adj* occidentale • *adv* verso occidente; **go ~** 🔢 andare in malora. ~**erly** *adj* verso ovest; occidentale (wind). ~**ern** *adj* occidentale • *n* western *m inv*

West: ~ **'Indian** *adj & n* antillese *mf*. ~ **'Indies** /'ɪndɪz/ *npl* Antille *fpl*

'westward[s] /-wəd[z]/ *adv* verso ovest

wet /wet/ *adj* (wetter, wettest) bagnato; fresco (paint); (*rainy*) piovoso; (🔢: *person*) smidollato; **get** ~ bagnarsi • *vt* (*pt/pp* wet, wetted) bagnare. ~ **'blanket** *n* guastafeste *mf inv*

whack /wæk/ *n* 🔢 colpo *m* • *vt* 🔢 dare un colpo a. ~**ed** *adj* 🔢 stanco morto. ~**ing** *adj* (🔢: *huge*) enorme

whale /weɪl/ *n* balena *f*; **have a** ~ **of a time** 🔢 divertirsi un sacco

wham /wæm/ *int* bum

wharf /wɔ:f/ *n* banchina *f*

what /wɒt/ *pron* che, [che] cosa; for? perché?; ~ **is that for?** a che cosa serve?; ~ **is it?** *che* è?; (*what do you want*) cosa c'è?; ~ **is it like?** com'è?; ~ **is your name?** come ti chiami?; ~ **is the weather like?** com'è il tempo?; ~ **is the film about?** di cosa parla il film?; ~ is he talking about? di cosa sta parlando?; he asked me ~ she had said mi ha chiesto cosa ha detto; ~ about going to the cinema? se ne andassimo al cinema?; ~ about the children? (what will they do) e i bambini?; ~ if it rains? e se piove? ● adj quale, che; take ~ books you want prendi tutti i libri che vuoi; ~ kind of a che tipo di; at ~ time? a che ora? ● adv che; ~ a lovely day! che bella giornata! ● int ~! (that's) cosa!; ~? [che] cosa?

what'ever adj qualunque ● pron qualsiasi cosa; ~ is it? cos'è?; ~ he does qualsiasi cosa faccia; ~ happens qualunque cosa succeda; nothing ~ proprio niente

whatso'ever adj & pron = **whatever**

wheat /wiːt/ n grano m, frumento m

wheel /wiːl/ n ruota f; (steering ~) volante m; at the ~ al volante ● vt (push) spingere ● vi (circle) ruotare; ~ [round] ruotare

wheel: ~barrow n carriola f. **~chair** n sedia f a rotelle. **~-clamp** n ceppo m bloccaruote

wheeze /wiːz/ vi ansimare

when /wen/ adv & conj quando; the day ~ il giorno in cui; ~ swimming/reading nuotando/leggendo

when'ever adv & conj in qualsiasi momento; (every time that) ogni volta che; ~ did it happen? quando è successo?

where /weə(r)/ adv & conj dove; the street ~ I live la via in cui abito; ~ do you come from? da dove vieni?

whereabouts¹ /weərə'baʊts/ adv dove

'whereabouts² n nobody knows his ~ nessuno sa dove si trova

where'as conj dal momento che; (in contrast) mentre

wher'ever adv & conj dovunque; ~

is he? dov'è mai?; ~ possible dovunque sia possibile

whet /wet/ vt (pt/pp whetted) aguzzare (appetite)

whether /'weðə(r)/ conj se; ~ you like it or not che ti piaccia o no

which /wɪtʃ/ adj & pron quale; ~ one? quale?; ~ of you? di voi?; ~ way? (direction) in che direzione? ● rel pron (object) che; ~ he does frequently cosa che fa spesso; after ~ dopo di che; on/in ~ su/in cui

which'ever adj & pron qualunque; ~ it is qualunque sia; ~ one of you chiunque tra voi

while /waɪl/ n a long ~ un bel po'; a little ~ un po' ● conj mentre; (as long as) finché; (although) sebbene ● while away vt passare (time)

whilst /waɪlst/ conj see **while**

whim /wɪm/ n capriccio m

whimper /'wɪmpə(r)/ vi piagnucolare; (dog:) mugolare

whine /waɪn/ n lamento m; (of dog) guaito m ● vi lamentarsi; (dog:) guaire

whip /wɪp/ n frusta f; (Pol: person) parlamentare m incaricato, -a di assicurarsi della presenza dei membri del suo partito alle votazioni ● vt (pt/pp whipped) frustare; (Culin) sbattere; (snatch) afferrare; ([I]: steal) fregare. □ ~ up vt (incite) stimolare; ([I]) improvvisare (meal). **~ped 'cream** n panna f montata

whirl /wɜːl/ n (movement) rotazione f; my mind's in a ~ ho le idee confuse ● vi girare rapidamente ● vt far girare rapidamente. ~ **pool** n vortice m. ~ **wind** n turbine m

whirr /wɜː(r)/ vi ronzare

whisk /wɪsk/ n (Culin) frullino m ● vt (Culin) frullare. ~ **away** vt portare via

whisker /'wɪskə(r)/ n ~s (of cat) baffi mpl; (on man's cheek) basette fpl;

by a ~ per un pelo

whisky /'wɪskɪ/ n whisky m inv

whisper /'wɪspə(r)/ n sussurro m; (rumour) diceria f •vt sussurrare •vi sussurrare

whistle /'wɪsl/ n fischio m; (instrument) fischietto m •vt fischiettare •vi fischiettare; (referee) fischiare

white /waɪt/ adj bianco; **go** ~ (pale) sbiancare •n bianco m; (of egg) albume m; (person) bianco, -a mf

white: ~ **'coffee** n caffè m inv macchiato. ~'**collar worker** n colletto m bianco

white 'lie n bugia f pietosa

whiten /'waɪtn/ vt imbiancare •vi sbiancare

whitewash n intonaco m; fig copertura f •vt dare una mano d'intonaco a; fig coprire

Whitsun /'wɪtsn/ n Pentecoste f

who /huː/ inter pron chi •rel pron che; the children, ~ were all tired,... i bambini, che erano tutti stanchi,...

who'ever pron chiunque; ~ he is chiunque sia; ~ can that be? chi può mai essere?

whole /həʊl/ adj tutto; (not broken) intatto; the ~ truth tutta la verità; the ~ world il mondo intero; the ~ lot (everything) tutto; (pl) tutti; the ~ lot of you tutti voi •n tutto m; as a ~ nell'insieme; on the ~ tutto considerato; the ~ of Italy tutta l'Italia

whole: ~-'**hearted** adj di tutto cuore. ~**meal** adj integrale

wholesale adj & adv all'ingrosso; fig in massa. ~r n grossista mf

wholesome /'həʊlsəm/ adj sano

wholly /'həʊlɪ/ adv completamente

whom /huːm/ rel pron che; the man ~ I saw l'uomo che ho visto; to/with ~ a/con cui •inter pron chi; to ~ did you speak? con chi hai parlato?

whooping cough /'huːpɪŋ/ n pertosse f

whore /hɔː(r)/ n ① puttana f

whose /huːz/ rel pron il cui; people ~ name begins with D le persone i cui nomi cominciano con la D •inter pron di chi; ~ is that? di chi è quello? •adj ~ **car** did you use? di chi è la macchina che hai usato?

why /waɪ/ adv (inter) perché; the reason ~ la ragione per cui; that's ~ per questo •int diamine

wick /wɪk/ n stoppino m

wicked /'wɪkɪd/ adj cattivo; (mischievous) malizioso

wicker /'wɪkə(r)/ n vimini mpl •attrib di vimini

wide /waɪd/ adj largo; (experience, knowledge) vasto; (difference) profondo; (far from target) lontano; **10 cm** ~ largo 10 cm; **how** ~ **is it?** quanto è largo? •adv (off target) lontano dal bersaglio; ~ **awake** del tutto sveglio; ~ **open** spalancato; far and ~ in lungo e in largo. ~**ly** adv largamente; (known, accepted) generalmente; (different) profondamente

widen /'waɪdn/ vt allargare •vi allargarsi

widespread adj diffuso

widow /'wɪdəʊ/ n vedova f. ~**ed** adj vedovo. ~**er** n vedovo m

width /wɪdθ/ n larghezza f; (of material) altezza f

wield /wiːld/ vt maneggiare; esercitare (power)

wife /waɪf/ n (pl **wives**) moglie f

wig /wɪg/ n parrucca f

wiggle /'wɪgl/ vi dimenarsi •vt dimenare

wild /waɪld/ adj selvaggio; (animal, flower) selvatico; (furious) furibondo; (applause) fragoroso; (idea) folle; (with joy) pazzo; (guess) azzardato; be ~ **about** (keen on) andare pazzo per •adv run ~ crescere senza controllo •n in the ~ allo stato naturale; the ~**s** pl le zone fpl sperdute

601

wilderness | wisdom

wilderness /'wɪldənɪs/ n deserto m; (fig: garden) giungla f

'wildfire n spread like ~ allargarsi a macchia d'olio

wild: ~'goose chase n ricerca f inutile. ~life n animali mpl selvatici

will¹ /wɪl/ v aux he ~ arrive tomorrow arriverà domani; I won't tell him non glielo dirò; you ~ be back soon, won't you? tornerai presto, no?; he ~ be there, won't he? sarà là, no?; she ~ be there by now sarà là ormai; ~ you go? (do you intend to go) pensi di andare?; ~ you go to the baker's and buy…? puoi andare dal panettiere a comprare…?; ~ you be quiet! vuoi stare calmo!; ~ you have some wine? vuoi del vino?; the engine won't start la macchina non parte

will² n volontà f inv; (document) testamento m

willing /'wɪlɪŋ/ adj disposto; (eager) volonteroso. ~ly adv volentieri. ~ness n buona volontà f

willow /'wɪləʊ/ n salice m

'will-power n forza f di volontà

wilt /wɪlt/ vi appassire

win /wɪn/ n vittoria f; have a ~ riportare una vittoria ● v (pt/pp won; pres p winning) ● vt vincere; conquistare (fame) ● vi vincere. □ ~ over vt convincere

wince /wɪns/ vi contrarre il viso

winch /wɪntʃ/ n argano m

wind¹ /wɪnd/ n vento m; (breath) fiato m; (□: flatulence) aria f; get/have the ~ up □ aver fifa; get ~ of aver sentore di; in the ~ nell'aria ● vt ~ sb lasciare qcno senza fiato

wind² /waɪnd/ v (pt/pp wound) ● vt (wrap) avvolgere; (move by turning) far girare; (clock) caricare ● vi (road:)

serpeggiare. □ ~ up vt caricare (clock); concludere (proceedings); □ prendere in giro (sb)

windfall /'wɪndfɔːl/ n fig fortuna f inaspettata

'wind farm n centrale f eolica

winding /'waɪndɪŋ/ adj tortuoso

wind: ~ instrument n strumento m a fiato. ~mill n mulino m a vento

window /'wɪndəʊ/ n finestra f; (of car) finestrino m; (of shop) vetrina f

window: ~-box n cassetta f per i fiori. ~-sill n davanzale m

'windscreen, Am **'windshield** n parabrezza m inv. ~ washer n getto m d'acqua. ~-wiper n tergicristallo m

wine /waɪn/ n vino m

wine: ~-glass n bicchiere m da vino. ~-list n carta f dei vini

'wine-tasting n degustazione f di vini

wing /wɪŋ/ n ala f; (Auto) parafango m; ~s pl (Theat) quinte fpl. ~er n (Sport) ala f

wink /wɪŋk/ n strizzata f d'occhio; not sleep a ~ non chiudere occhio ● vi strizzare l'occhio; (light:) lampeggiare

winner /'wɪnə(r)/ n vincitore, -trice mf

wint|er /'wɪntə(r)/ n inverno m. ~ry adj invernale

wipe /waɪp/ n passata f; (to dry) asciugata f ● vt strofinare; (dry) asciugare. □ ~ off vt asciugare; (erase) cancellare. □ ~ out vt annientare; eliminare (village); estinguere (debt). □ ~ up vt asciugare (dishes)

wire /waɪə(r)/ n fil m di ferro; (electrical) filo m elettrico

wiring /'waɪərɪŋ/ n impianto m elettrico

wisdom /'wɪzdəm/ n saggezza f; (of action) sensatezza f. ~ tooth n dente *m* del giudizio

wise /waɪz/ *adj* saggio; (*prudent*) sensato. ~**ly** *adv* saggiamente; (act) sensatamente

wish /wɪʃ/ *n* desiderio *m*; make a ~ esprimere un desiderio; with best ~es con i migliori auguri ● *vt* desiderare; ~ sb well fare tanti auguri a qcno; I ~ you every success to I auguro buona fortuna; I ~ you could stay vorrei che tu potessi rimanere ● *vi* ~ for sth desiderare qcsa. ~**ful** *adj* ~**ful thinking** illusione *f*

wistful /'wɪstfl/ *adj* malinconico

wit /wɪt/ *n* spirito *m*; (*person*) persona *f* di spirito; be at one's ~'s end non saper che pesci pigliare

witch /wɪtʃ/ *n* strega *f*. ~**craft** *n* magia *f*. ~**-hunt** *n* caccia *f* alle streghe

with /wɪð/ *prep* con; (*fear, cold, jealousy etc*) di; I'm not ~ you 🛈 non ti seguo; can I leave it ~ you? (*task*) puoi occupartene tu?; ~ no regrets/money senza rimpianti/soldi; be ~ it 🛈 essere al passo coi tempi; (*alert*) essere concentrato

with'draw *v* (*pt* -drew, *pp* -drawn) ● *vt* ritirare; prelevare (money) ● *vi* ritirarsi. ~**al** *n* ritiro *m*; (*of money*) prelevamento *m*; (*from drugs*) crisi *f inv* di astinenza; (*Psych*) chiusura *f* in se stessi. ~**al symptoms** *npl* sintomi *mpl* da crisi di astinenza

with'drawn ▷ WITHDRAW ● *adj* (*person*) chiuso in se stesso

wither /'wɪðə(r)/ *vi* (*flower:*) appassire

with'hold *vt* (*pt/pp* -held) rifiutare (consent) (from a); nascondere (information) (from a); trattenere (smile)

with'in *prep* in; (*before the end of*) entro; ~ **the law** legale ● *adv* all'interno

with'out *prep* senza; ~ **stopping** senza fermarsi

with'stand *vt* (*pt/pp* -stood) resistere a

witness /'wɪtnɪs/ *n* testimone *mf* ● *vt* autenticare (signature); essere testimone di (accident). ~**-box** *n*, *Am* ~**-stand** *n* banco *m* dei testimoni

witticism /'wɪtɪsɪzm/ *n* spiritosaggine *f*

witty /'wɪtɪ/ *adj* (-ier, -iest) spiritoso

wives /waɪvz/ ▷ WIFE

wizard /'wɪzəd/ *n* mago *m*. ~**ry** *n* stregoneria *f*

wobb|le /'wɒbl/ *vi* traballare. ~**ly** *adj* traballante

woe /wəʊ/ *n* afflizione *f*

woke, woken /wəʊk/, /'wəʊkn/ ▷ WAKE¹

wolf /wʊlf/ *n* (*pl* **wolves** /wʊlvz/) lupo *m*; (🛈: *womanizer*) donnaiolo *m* ● *vt* ~ [down] divorare. ~ **whistle** *n* fischio *m* ● *vi* ~-whistle at sb fischiare dietro a qcno

woman /'wʊmən/ *n* (*pl* **women**) donna *f*. ~**izer** *n* donnaiolo *m*. ~**ly** *adj* femmineo

womb /wuːm/ *n* utero *m*

women /'wɪmɪn/ ▷ WOMAN. W~'s Libber *n* femminista *f*. W~'s Liberation *n* movimento *m* femminista

won /wʌn/ ▷ WIN

wonder /'wʌndə(r)/ *n* meraviglia *f*; (*surprise*) stupore *m*; no ~! non c'è da stupirsi!; it's a ~ that... è incredibile che... ● *vi* restare in ammirazione; (*be surprised*) essere sorpreso; I ~ is quello che mi chiedo; I ~ whether she is ill mi chiedo se è malata?. ~**ful** *adj* meraviglioso. ~**fully** *adv* meravigliosamente

wood /wʊd/ *n* legno *m*; (*for burning*) legna *f*; (*forest*) bosco *m*; out of the ~ *fig* fuori pericolo; touch ~! tocca ferro!

wood: ~**ed** /-ɪd/ *adj* boscoso. ~**en** *adj* di legno, *fig* legnoso. ~ **wind** *n* strumenti *mpl* a fiato. ~**work** *n* (*wooden parts*) parti *fpl* in legno; (*craft*) falegnameria f. **~worm** n tarlo m. **~y** adj legnoso; (hill) boscoso

wool /wʊl/ n lana f ● attrib di lana. **~len** adj di lana. **~lens** npl capi mpl di lana

woolly /ˈwʊlɪ/ adj (-ier, -iest) (sweater) di lana; fig confuso

word /wɜːd/ n parola f; (news) notizia f; **by ~ of mouth** a viva voce; **have a ~ with** dire due parole a; **have ~s** bisticciare; **in other ~s** in altre parole. **~ing** n parole fpl. **~ processor** n programma m di videoscrittura, word processor m inv

wore /wɔː(r)/ ▷ **WEAR**

work /wɜːk/ n lavoro m; (of art) opera f; **~s** pl (factory) fabbrica fsg; (mechanism) meccanismo msg; **at ~** al lavoro; **out of ~** disoccupato ● vi lavorare; (machine, ruse:) funzionare; (study) studiare ● vt far funzionare (machine); far lavorare (employee); far studiare (pupil). □ **~ off** vt sfogare (anger); lavorare per estinguere (debt); fare sport per smaltire (weight). □ **~ out** vt elaborare (plan); risolvere (problem); calcolare (bill); **I ~ed out how he did it** ho capito come l'ha fatto a fare. ● vi evolvere. □ **~ up** vt **I've ~ed up an appetite** mi è venuto appetito; **don't get ~ed up** (anxious) non farti prendere dal panico; (angry) non arrabbiarti

workable /ˈwɜːkəbl/ adj (feasible) fattibile

worker /ˈwɜːkə(r)/ n lavoratore, -trice mf; (manual) operaio, -a mf

working /ˈwɜːkɪŋ/ adj (clothes etc) da lavoro; (day) feriale; **in ~ order** funzionante. **~ class** n classe f operaia. **~-class** adj operaio

work: **~man** n operaio m. **~manship** n lavorazione f. **~shop** n officina f; (discussion) dibattito m

world /wɜːld/ n mondo m; **a ~ of difference** una differenza abissale; **out of this ~** favoloso; **think the ~ of sb** andare matto per qcno. **~ly**

adj materiale; (person) materialista. **~-'wide** adj mondiale ● adv mondialmente

worm /wɜːm/ n verme m ● vt **~ one's way into sb's confidence** conquistarsi la fiducia di qcno in modo subdolo. **~-eaten** adj tarlato

worn /wɔːn/ ▷ **WEAR** ● adj sciupato. **~-out** adj consumato; (person) sfinito

worried /ˈwʌrɪd/ adj preoccupato

worr|y /ˈwʌrɪ/ n preoccupazione f ● v (pt/pp worried) ● vt preoccupare; (bother) disturbare ● vi preoccuparsi. **~ing** adj preoccupante

worse /wɜːs/ adj peggiore ● adv peggio ● n peggio m

worsen /ˈwɜːsn/ vt/i peggiorare

worship /ˈwɜːʃɪp/ n culto m; (service) funzione f; **Your/His ~** (to judge) signor giudice/il giudice ● v (pt/pp -shipped) ● vt venerare ● vi andare a messa

worst /wɜːst/ adj peggiore ● adv peggio [di tutti] ● n **the ~** il peggio; **get the ~ of it** avere la peggio; **if the ~ comes to the ~** nella peggiore delle ipotesi

worth /wɜːθ/ n valore m; **£10 ~ of petrol** 10 sterline di benzina ● adj **be ~** valere; **be ~ it** fig valerne la pena; **it's ~ trying** vale la pena di provare; **it's ~ my while** mi conviene. **~less** adj senza valore. **~while** adj che vale la pena; (cause) lodevole

worthy /ˈwɜːðɪ/ adj degno; (cause, motive) lodevole

---

would /wʊd/ v aux **I ~ do it** lo farei; **~ you go?** andresti?; **~ you mind if I opened the window?** ti dispiace se apro la finestra?; **he ~ come if he could** verrebbe se potesse; **he said he ~n't** ha detto di no; **~ you like a drink?** vuoi qualcosa da bere?; what ∼ you like to drink? cosa prendi da bere?; you ∼n't, ∼ you? non lo faresti, vero?

wound[1] /wuːnd/ n ferita f • vt ferire

wound[2] /waʊnd/ ▷ **WIND**[2]

wrangle /ˈræŋgl/ n litigio m • vi litigare

wrap /ræp/ n (shawl) scialle m • vt (pt/pp wrapped) ∼ [up] avvolgere; (present) incartare; **be** ∼**ped up in** fig essere completamente preso da • vi ∼ **up** warmly coprirsi bene. ∼**per** n (for sweet) carta f [di caramella]. ∼**ping** n materiale m da imballaggio. ∼**ping paper** n carta f da pacchi; (for gift) carta f da regalo

wrath /rɒθ/ n ira f

wreak /riːk/ vt ∼ **havoc** with sth scombussolare qcsa

wreath /riːθ/ n (pl ∼s /-ðz/) corona f

wreck /rek/ n (of ship) relitto m; (of car) carcassa f; (person) rottame m • vt far naufragare; demolire (car). ∼**age** n rottami mpl; fig brandelli mpl

wrench /rentʃ/ n (injury) slogatura f; (tool) chiave f inglese; (pull) strattone m • vt (pull) strappare; slogarsi (wrist, ankle etc)

wrestl|e /ˈresl/ vi lottare corpo a corpo; fig lottare. ∼**er** n lottatore, -trice mf. ∼**ing** n lotta f libera; (all-in) catch m

wretch /retʃ/ n disgraziato, -a mf. ∼**ed** adj odioso; (weather) orribile; **feel** ∼**ed** (unhappy) essere triste; (ill) sentirsi malissimo

wriggle /ˈrɪgl/ n contorsione f • vi contorcersi; (move forward) strisciare; ∼ **out of** sth 🄵 sottrarsi a qcsa

wring /rɪŋ/ vt (pt/pp wrung) torcere (sb's neck); strizzare (clothes); ∼ **one's hands** torcersi le mani; ∼**ing wet** inzuppato

wrinkle /ˈrɪŋkl/ n grinza f; (on skin) ruga f • vt/i raggrinzire. ∼**d** adj (skin,

face) rugoso; (clothes) raggrinzito

wrist /rɪst/ n polso m. ∼**-watch** n orologio m da polso

writ /rɪt/ n (Jur) mandato m

write /raɪt/ vt/i (pt wrote, pp written, pres p writing) scrivere. ∼ **down** vt annotare. ∼ **off** vt cancellare (debt); distruggere (car)

'write-off n (car) rottame m

writer /ˈraɪtə(r)/ n autore, -trice mf; **she's a** ∼ è una scrittrice

writhe /raɪð/ vi contorcersi

writing /ˈraɪtɪŋ/ n (occupation) scrivere m; (words) scritte fpl; (handwriting) scrittura f; **in** ∼ per iscritto. ∼**-paper** n carta f da lettera

written /ˈrɪtn/ ▷ **WRITE**

wrong /rɒŋ/ adj sbagliato; **be** ∼ (person): sbagliare; **what's** ∼? cosa c'è che non va? • adv (spelt) in modo sbagliato; **go** ∼ (person): sbagliare; (machine): funzionare male; (plan): andar male • n ingiustizia f; **in the** ∼ dalla parte del torto; **know right from** ∼ distinguere il bene dal male • vt fare torto a. ∼**ful** adj ingiusto. ∼**ly** adv in modo sbagliato; (accuse, imagine) a torto; (informed) male

wrote /rəʊt/ ▷ **WRITE**

wrought'iron /rɔːt-/ n ferro m battuto • attrib di ferro battuto

wrung /rʌŋ/ ▷ **WRING**

wry /raɪ/ adj (-er, -est) (humour, smile) beffardo

• •

Xx

• •

Xmas /ˈkrɪsməs/ n 🄵 Natale m

'X-ray n (picture) radiografia f; **have an** ∼ farsi fare una radiografia • vt passare ai raggi X

Yy

yacht /jɒt/ n yacht m inv; (for racing) barca f a vela. **~ing** n vela f

yank /jæŋk/ vt 🔢 tirare

Yank n 🔢 americano, -a mf

yap /jæp/ vi (pt/pp yapped) (dog): guaire

yard¹ /jɑːd/ n cortile m; (for storage) deposito m

yard² n iarda f (= 91,44 cm). **~stick** n fig pietra f di paragone

yarn /jɑːn/ n filo m; (🔢: tale) storia f

yawn /jɔːn/ n sbadiglio m ● vi sbadigliare. **~ing** adj **~ing gap** sbadiglio m

yeah /jeə/ adv sì

year /jɪə(r)/ n anno m; (of wine) annata f; **for ~s** 🔢 da secoli. **~book** n annuario m. **~ly** adj annuale ● adv annualmente

yearn /jɜːn/ vi struggersi. **~ing** n desiderio m struggente

yeast /jiːst/ n lievito m

yell /jel/ n urlo m ● vi urlare

yellow /'jeləʊ/ adj & n giallo m

yelp /jelp/ n (of dog) guaito m ● vi (dog): guaire

yes /jes/ adv sì ● n sì m inv

yesterday /'jestədeɪ/ adj & adv ieri m inv; **~'s paper** il giornale di ieri; **the day before ~** l'altroieri

yet /jet/ adv ancora; **as ~** fino ad ora; **not ~** non ancora; **the best ~** il migliore finora ● conj eppure

yield /jiːld/ n produzione f; (profit) reddito m ● vt produrre; fruttare (profit) ● vi cedere; Am (Auto) dare la precedenza

yoga /'jəʊgə/ n yoga m

yoghurt /'jɒgət/ n yogurt m inv

yoke /jəʊk/ n giogo m; (of garment) carré m inv

yokel /'jəʊkl/ n zotico, -a mf

yolk /jəʊk/ n tuorlo m

---

you /juː/ pron (subject) tu, voi pl; (formal) lei, voi pl; (direct/indirect object) ti, vi pl; (formal: direct object) la; (formal: indirect object) le; (after prep) te, voi pl; (formal: after prep) lei;

tu is used when speaking to friends, children and animals. lei is used to speak to someone you do not know. voi is used to speak to more than one person. Note that you is often not translated when it is the subject of the sentence

~ are very kind (sg) sei molto gentile; (formal) è molto gentile; (pl & formal pl) siete molto gentili; **~ can stay, but he has to go** (sg) tu puoi rimanere, ma lui deve andarsene; (pl) voi potete rimanere, ma lui deve andarsene; **all of ~** tutti voi; **I'll give ~ the money** (sg) ti darò i soldi; (pl) vi darò i soldi; **I'll give it to ~** (sg) te/(pl) ve lo darò; **it was ~!** (sg) eri tu!; (pl) eravate voi!; **~ have to be careful** (one) si deve fare attenzione

---

young /jʌŋ/ adj giovane ● npl (animals) piccoli mpl; **the ~** (people) i giovani mpl. **~ lady** n signorina f. **~ man** n giovanotto m. **~ster** n ragazzo, -a mf; (child) bambino, -a mf

your /jɔː(r)/ adj il tuo m, la tua f, i tuoi mpl, le tue fpl; (formal) il suo m, la sua f, i suoi mpl, le sue fpl; (pl & formal pl) il vostro m, la vostra f, i vostri mpl, le vostre fpl; **~ mother/father** tua madre/tuo padre; (formal) sua madre/suo padre; (pl & formal pl) vostra madre/vostro padre

y

yours /jɔːz/ *poss pron* il tuo *m*, la tua *f*, i tuoi *mpl*, le tue *fpl*; (*formal*) il suo *m*, la sua *f*, i suoi *mpl*, le sue *fpl*; (*pl & formal pl*) il vostro *m*, la vostra *f*, i vostri *mpl*, le vostre *fpl*; a friend of ∼ un tuo/suo/vostro amico; friends of ∼ dei tuoi/vostri/suoi amici; that is ∼ quello è il tuo/vostro/suo; (*as opposed to mine*) quello è il tuo/il vostro/il suo

your'self *pron* (*reflexive*) ti; (*formal*) si; (*emphatic*) te stesso; (*formal*) sé, se stesso; do pour ∼ a drink versati da bere; (*formal*) si versi da bere; you said so ∼ lo hai detto tu stesso; (*formal*) lo ha detto lei stesso; you can be proud of ∼ puoi essere fiero di te/di sé; by ∼ da solo

your'selves *pron* (*reflexive*) vi; (*emphatic*) voi stessi; do pour ∼ a drink versatevi da bere; you said so ∼ lo avete detto voi stessi; you can be proud of ∼ potete essere fieri di voi; by ∼ da soli

youth /juːθ/ *n* (*pl* youths /-ðːz/) gioventù *f inv*, (*boy*) giovanetto *m*; the ∼ (*young people*) i giovani *mpl*. ∼ful *adj* giovanile. ∼ hostel *n* ostello *m* [della gioventù]

Yugoslav /ˈjuːɡəslɑːv/ *adj & n* jugoslavo, -a *mf*

Yugoslavia /-ˈslɑːvɪə/ *n* Jugoslavia *f*

Zz

zeal /ziːl/ *n* zelo *m*

zealous /ˈzeləs/ *adj* zelante. ∼ly *adv* con zelo

zebra /ˈzebrə/ *n* zebra *f*. ∼-'crossing *n* passaggio *m* pedonale, zebre *fpl*

zero /ˈzɪərəʊ/ *n* zero *m*

zest /zest/ *n* gusto *m*

zigzag /ˈzɪɡzæɡ/ *n* zigzag *m inv* ●*vi* (*pt/pp* -zagged) zigzagare

zilch /zɪltʃ/ *n* 🗊 zero *m* assoluto

zinc /zɪŋk/ *n* zinco *m*

zip /zɪp/ *n* ∼ [fastener] cerniera *f* [lampo] ●*vt* (*pt/pp* zipped) ∼ [up] chiudere con la cerniera [lampo]

'Zip code *n Am* codice *m* postale

zipper /ˈzɪpə(r)/ *n Am* cerniera *f* [lampo]

zodiac /ˈzəʊdɪæk/ *n* zodiaco *m*

zombie /ˈzɒmbɪ/ *n* 🗊 zombi *mf inv*

zone /zəʊn/ *n* zona *f*

zoo /zuː/ *n* zoo *m inv*

zoolog|ist /zəʊˈɒlədʒɪst/ *n* zoologo, -a *mf*. ∼y zoologia *f*

zoom /zuːm/ *vi* sfrecciare. ∼ lens *n* zoom *m inv*

Verbi inglese irregolari

Infinito	Passato	Participio passato	Infinito	Passato	Participio passato
be	was	been	**drive**	drove	driven
bear	bore	borne	**eat**	ate	eaten
beat	beat	beaten	**fall**	fell	fallen
become	became	become	**feed**	fed	fed
begin	began	begun	**feel**	felt	felt
bend	bent	bent	**fight**	fought	fought
bet	bet, betted	bet, betted	**find**	found	found
			flee	fled	fled
bid	bade, bid	bidden, bid	**fly**	flew	flown
bind	bound	bound	**freeze**	froze	frozen
bite	bit	bitten	**get**	got	got, gotten *US*
bleed	bled	bled	**give**	gave	given
blow	blew	blown	**go**	went	gone
break	broke	broken	**grow**	grew	grown
breed	bred	bred	**hang**	hung, hanged	hung, hanged
bring	brought	brought			
build	built	built	**have**	had	had
burn	burnt, burned	burnt, burned	**hear**	heard	heard
			hide	hid	hidden
burst	burst	burst	**hit**	hit	hit
buy	bought	bought	**hold**	held	held
catch	caught	caught	**hurt**	hurt	hurt
choose	chose	chosen	**keep**	kept	kept
cling	clung	clung	**kneel**	knelt	knelt
come	came	come	**know**	knew	known
cost	cost, costed (*vt*)	cost, costed	**lay**	laid	laid
			lead	led	led
cut	cut	cut	**lean**	leaned, leant	leaned, leant
deal	dealt	dealt			
dig	dug	dug	**learn**	learnt, learned	learnt, learned
do	did	done			
draw	drew	drawn	**leave**	left	left
dream	dreamt, dreamed	dreamt, dreamed	**lend**	lent	lent
			let	let	let
drink	drank	drunk	**lie**	lay	lain

Infinito	Passato	Participio passato	Infinito	Passato	Participio passato
lose	lost	lost	**spend**	spent	spent
make	made	made	**spit**	spat	spat
mean	meant	meant	**spoil**	spoilt,	spoilt,
meet	met	met		spoiled	spoiled
pay	paid	paid	**spread**	spread	spread
put	put	put	**spring**	sprang	sprung
read	read	read	**stand**	stood	stood
ride	rode	ridden	**steal**	stole	stolen
ring	rang	rung	**stick**	stuck	stuck
rise	rose	risen	**sting**	stung	stung
run	ran	run	**stride**	strode	stridden
say	said	said	**strike**	struck	struck
see	saw	seen	**swear**	swore	sworn
seek	sought	sought	**sweep**	swept	swept
sell	sold	sold	**swell**	swelled	swollen,
send	sent	sent			swelled
set	set	set	**swim**	swam	swum
sew	sewed	sewn, sewed	**swing**	swung	swung
shake	shook	shaken	**take**	took	taken
shine	shone	shone	**teach**	taught	taught
shoe	shod	shod	**tear**	tore	torn
shoot	shot	shot	**tell**	told	told
show	showed	shown	**think**	thought	thought
shut	shut	shut	**throw**	threw	thrown
sing	sang	sung	**thrust**	thrust	thrust
sink	sank	sunk	**tread**	trod	trodden
sit	sat	sat	**under-**	under-	understood
sleep	slept	slept	**stand**	stood	
sling	slung	slung	**wake**	woke	woken
smell	smelt,	smelt,	**wear**	wore	worn
	smelled	smelled	**win**	won	won
speak	spoke	spoken	**write**	wrote	written
spell	spelled,	spelled,			
		spelt spelt			

Italian verb tables

1. in -are (eg compr|are)
Present ∼o, ∼i, ∼a, ∼iamo, ∼ate, ∼ano
Imperfect ∼avo, ∼avi, ∼ava, ∼avamo, ∼avate, ∼avano
Past historic ∼ai, ∼asti, ∼ò, ∼ammo, ∼aste, ∼arono
Future ∼erò, ∼erai, ∼erà, ∼eremo, ∼erete, ∼eranno
Present subjunctive ∼i, ∼i, ∼i, ∼iamo, ∼iate, ∼ino
Past subjunctive ∼assi, ∼assi, ∼asse, ∼assimo, ∼aste, ∼assero
Present participle ∼ando
Past participle ∼ato
Imperative ∼a (fml ∼i), ∼iamo, ∼ate
Conditional ∼erei, ∼eresti, ∼erebbe, ∼eremmo, ∼ereste, ∼erebbero

2. in -ere (eg vend|ere)
Pres ∼o, ∼i, ∼e, ∼iamo, ∼ete, ∼ono
Impf ∼evo, ∼evi, ∼eva, ∼evamo, ∼evate, ∼evano
Past hist ∼ei or ∼etti, ∼esti, ∼è or ∼ette, ∼emmo, ∼este, ∼erono or ∼ettero
Fut ∼erò, ∼erai, ∼erà, ∼eremo, ∼erete, ∼eranno
Pres sub ∼a, ∼a, ∼a, ∼iamo, ∼iate, ∼ano
Past sub ∼essi, ∼essi, ∼esse, ∼essimo, ∼este, ∼essero
Pres part ∼endo
Past part ∼uto
Imp ∼i (fml ∼a), ∼iamo, ∼ete
Cond ∼erei, ∼eresti, ∼erebbe, ∼eremmo, ∼ereste, ∼erebbero

3. in -ire (eg dorm|ire)
Pres ∼o, ∼i, ∼e, ∼iamo, ∼ite, ∼ono
Impf ∼ivo, ∼ivi, ∼iva, ∼ivamo, ∼ivate, ∼ivano
Past hist ∼ii, ∼isti, ∼i, ∼immo, ∼iste, ∼irono
Fut ∼irò, ∼irai, ∼irà, ∼iremo, ∼irete, ∼iranno
Pres sub ∼a, ∼a, ∼a, ∼iamo, ∼iate, ∼ano
Past sub ∼issi, ∼issi, ∼isse, ∼issimo, ∼iste, ∼issero
Pres part ∼endo
Past part ∼ito
Imp ∼i (fml ∼a), ∼iamo, ∼ite
Cond ∼irei, ∼iresti, ∼irebbe, ∼iremmo, ∼ireste, ∼irebbero

Notes
• Many verbs in the third conjugation take isc between the stem and the ending in the first, second, and third person singular and in the third person plural of the present, the present subjunctive, and the imperative:
fin|ire *Pres* ∼isco, ∼isci, ∼isce, ∼iamo, ∼ite, ∼iscono. *Pres sub* ∼isca, ∼iscano *Imp* ∼isci.
• The three forms of the imperative are the same as the corresponding forms of the present for the second and third conjugation. In the first conjugation the forms are also the same except for the second person singular: present *compri*, imperative *compra*. The negative form of the second person singular is formed

by putting *non* before the infinitive for all conjugations: *non comprare*. In polite forms the third person of the present subjunctive is used instead for all conjugations: *compri*.

Irregular verbs:

Certain forms of all irregular verbs are regular (except for *essere*). These are: the second person plural of the present, the past subjunctive, and the present participle. All forms not listed below are regular and can be derived from the parts given. Only those irregular verbs considered to be the most useful are shown in the tables.

accadere *as* **cadere**

accendere
Past hist accesi, accendesti
Past part acceso

affliggere
Past hist afflissi, affliggesti
Past part afflitto

ammettere *as* **mettere**

andare
Pres vado, vai, va, andiamo, andate, vanno
Fut andrò *etc*
Pres sub vada, vadano
Imp va', vada, vadano

apparire
Pres appaio *or* apparisco, appari *or* apparisci, appare *or* apparisce, appaiono *or* appariscono
Past hist apparvi *or* apparsi, apparisti, apparve *or* appari *or* apparse,

apparvero *or* apparirono *or* apparsero
Pres sub appaia *or* apparisca

aprire
Pres apro
Past hist aprii, apristi
Pres sub apra
Past part aperto

avere
Pres ho, hai, ha, abbiamo, hanno
Past hist ebbi, avesti, ebbe, avemmo, aveste, ebbero
Fut avrò *etc*
Pres sub abbia *etc*
Imp abbi, abbia, abbiate, abbiano

bere
Pres bevo *etc*
Impf bevevo *etc*
Past hist bevvi *or* bevetti, bevesti
Fut berrò *etc*
Pres sub beva *etc*
Past sub bevessi *etc*
Pres part bevendo
Cond berrei *etc*

cadere
Past hist caddi, cadesti
Fut cadrò *etc*

chiedere
Past hist chiesi, chiedesti
Pres sub chieda *etc*
Past part chiesto *etc*

chiudere
Past hist chiusi, chiudesti
Past part chiuso

cogliere
Pres colgo, colgono
Past hist colsi, cogliesti

Pres sub colga
Past part colto

correre

Past hist corsi, corresti
Past part corso

crascere

Past hist crebbi
Past part cresciuto

cuocere

Pres cuocio, cuociamo, cuociono
Past hist cossi, cocesti
Past part cotto

dare

Pres do, dai, dà, diamo, danno
Past hist diedi or detti, desti
Fut darò *etc*
Pres sub dia *etc*
Past sub dessi *etc*
Imp da' (*fml* dia)

dire

Pres dico, dici, dice, diciamo, dicono
Impf dicevo *etc*
Past hist dissi, dicesti
Fut dirò *etc*
Pres sub dica, diciamo, diciate, dicano
Past sub dicessi *etc*
Pres part dicendo
Past part detto
Imp di' (*fml* dica)

dovere

Pres devo or debbo, devi, deve,
dobbiamo, devono or debbono
Fut dovrò *etc*
Pres sub deva or debba, dobbiamo,
dobbiate, devano or debbano
Cond dovrei *etc*

essere

Pres sono, sei, è, siamo, siete, sono

Impf ero, eri, era, eravamo, eravate,
erano
Past hist fui, fosti, fu, fummo, foste,
furono
Fut sarò *etc*
Pres sub sia *etc*
Past sub fossi, fossi, fosse, fossimo,
foste, fossero
Past part stato
Imp sii (*fml* sia), siate
Cond sarei *etc*

fare

Pres faccio, fai, fa, facciamo, fanno
Impf facevo *etc*
Past hist feci, facesti
Fut farò *etc*
Pres sub faccia *etc*
Past sub facessi *etc*
Pres part facendo
Past part fatto
Imp fa' (*fml* faccia)
Cond farei *etc*

fingere

Past hist finsi, fingesti, finsero
Past part finto

giungere

Past hist giunsi, giungesti, giunsero
Past part giunto

leggere

Past hist lessi, leggesti
Past part letto

mettere

Past hist misi, mettesti
Past part messo

morire

Pres muoio, muori, muore, muoiono
Fut morirò or morrò *etc*

Pres sub muoia
Past part morto

muovere
Past hist mossi, movesti
Past part mosso

nascere
Past hist nacqui, nascesti
Past part nato

offrire
Past hist offersi or offrii, offristi
Pres sub offra
Past part offerto

parere
Pres paio, pari, pare, pariamo, paiono
Past hist parvi *or* parsi, paresti
Fut parrò *etc*
Pres sub paia, paiamo *or* pariamo,
   pariate, paiano
Past part parso

placere
Pres piaccio, piaci, piace, piacciamo,
   piacciono
Past hist piacqui, piacesti, piacque,
   piacemmo, piaceste, piacquero
Pres sub piaccia *etc*
Past part piaciuto

porre
Pres pongo, poni, pone, poniamo,
   ponete, pongono
Impf ponevo *etc*
Past hist posi, ponesti
Fut porrò *etc*
Pres sub ponga, poniamo, poniate,
   pongano
Past sub ponessi *etc*

potere
Pres posso, puoi, può, possiamo,

   possono
Fut potrò *etc*
Pres sub possa, possiamo, possiate,
   possano
Cond potrei *etc*

prendere
Past hist presi, prendesti
Past part preso

ridere
Past hist risi, ridesti
Past part riso

rimanere
Pres rimango, rimani, rimane,
   rimaniamo, rimangono
Past hist rimasi, rimanesti
Fut rimarrò *etc*
Pres sub rimanga
Past part rimasto
Cond rimarrei

salire
Pres salgo, sali, sale, saliamo, salgono
Pres sub salga, saliate, salgano

sapere
Pres so, sai, sa, sappiamo, sanno
Past hist seppi, sapesti
Fut saprò *etc*
Pres sub sappia *etc*
Imp sappi (*fml* sappia), sappiate
Cond saprei *etc*

scegliere
Pres scelgo, scegli, sceglie, scegliamo,
   scelgono
Past hist scelsi, scegliesti *etc*
Past part scelto

scrivere
Past hist scrissi, scrivesti *etc*
Past part scritto

sedere
Pres siedo *or* seggo, siedi, siede, siedono
Pres sub sieda *or* segga

spegnere
Pres spengo, spengono
Past hist spensi, spegnesti
Past part spento

stare
Pres sto, stai, sta, stiamo, stanno
Past hist stetti, stesti
Fut starò *etc*
Pres sub stia *etc*
Past sub stessi *etc*
Past part stato
Imp sta' (*fml* stia)

tacere
Pres taccio, tacciono
Past hist tacqui, tacque, tacquero
Pres sub taccia

tendere
Past hist tesi
Past part teso

tenere
Pres tengo, tieni, tiene, tengono
Past hist tenni, tenesti
Fut terrò *etc*
Pres sub tenga

togliere
Pres tolgo, tolgono
Past hist tolsi, tolse, tolsero
Pres sub tolga, tolgano
Past part tolto
Imp fml tolga

trarre
Pres traggo, trai, trae, traiamo, traete, traggono
Past hist trassi, traesti

Fut trarrò *etc*
Pres sub tragga
Past sub traessi *etc*
Past part tratto

uscire
Pres esco, esci, esce, escono
Pres sub esca
Imp esci (*fml* esca)

valere
Pres valgo, valgono
Past hist valsi, valesti
Fut varrò *etc*
Pres sub valga, valgano
Past part valso
Cond varrei *etc*

vedere
Past hist vidi, vedesti
Fut vedrò *etc*
Past part visto *or* veduto
Cond vedrei *etc*

venire
Pres vengo, vieni, viene, vengono
Past hist venni, venisti
Fut verrò *etc*

vivere
Past hist vissi, vivesti
Fut vivrò *etc*
Past part vissuto
Cond vivrei *etc*

volere
Pres voglio, vuoi, vuole, vogliamo, volete, vogliono
Past hist volli, volesti
Fut vorrò *etc*
Pres sub voglia *etc*
Imp vogliate
Cond vorrei *etc*

Numbers/Numeri

Cardinal numbers/ Numeri cardinali

0	zero **zero**
1	one **uno**
2	two **due**
3	three **tre**
4	four **quattro**
5	five **cinque**
6	six **sei**
7	seven **sette**
8	eight **otto**
9	nine **nove**
10	ten **dieci**
11	eleven **undici**
12	twelve **dodici**
13	thirteen **tredici**
14	fourteen **quattordici**
15	fifteen **quindici**
16	sixteen **sedici**
17	seventeen **diciassette**
18	eighteen **diciotto**
19	nineteen **diciannove**
20	twenty **venti**
21	twenty-one **ventuno**
22	twenty-two **ventidue**
30	thirty **trenta**
40	forty **quaranta**
50	fifty **cinquanta**
60	sixty **sessanta**
70	seventy **settanta**
80	eighty **ottanta**
90	ninety **novanta**

100	a hundred **cento**
101	a hundred and one **centouno**
110	a hundred and ten **centodieci**
200	two hundred **duecento**
1,000	one thousand **mille**
10,000	ten thousand **diecimila**
100,000	a hundred thousand **centomila**
1,000,000	a million **un million**

Ordinal numbers/ Numeri ordinali

1st	first **primo**
2nd	second **secondo**
3rd	third **terzo**
4th	fourth **quarto**
5th	fifth **quinto**
6th	sixth **sesto**
7th	seventh **settimo**
8th	eighth **ottavo**
9th	ninth **nono**
10th	tenth **decimo**
11th	eleventh **undicesimo**
20th	twentieth **ventesimo**
30th	thirtieth **trentesimo**
40th	fortieth **quarantesimo**
50th	fiftieth **cinquantesimo**
100th	hundredth **centesimo**
1,000th	thousandth **millesimo**

Avere = to have | Active
no | I
hai | ya
ha | he/she
abbiamo | we
avete | they
hanno | them

Essere = to be | movement
Sono
Sei
only | è
Ref | siamo
siete
Sono

Andare Andato
Partire Partito
Rimanere Rimasto
Venere Venuto
Uscire Uscito

loro = 2 + people

scrivere
scrivo
Fare = fatto | leggo
Predere → preso | faccio
mettere → messo
Dare → Dato
leggere → lette

Japere = to know | Ato
to so | Vto
Ito

Abbreviations/Abbreviazioni

adjective	*adj*	aggettivo
abbreviation	*abbr*	abbreviazione
administration	*Admin*	amministrazione
adverb	*adv*	avverbio
aeronautics	*Aeron*	aeronautica
American	*Am*	americano
anatomy	*Anat*	anatomia
archaeology	*Archeol*	archeologia
architecture	*Archit*	architettura
astrology	*Astr*	astrologia
attributive	*attrib*	attributo
automobiles	*Auto*	automobile
auxiliary	*aux*	ausiliario
biology	*Biol*	biologia
botany	*Bot*	botanica
British English	*Br*	inglese britannico
chemistry	*Chem*	chimica
commerce	*Comm*	commercio
computers	*Comput*	informatica
conjunction	*conj*	congiunzione
cooking	*Culin*	cucina
definite article	*def art*	articolo determinativo
et cetera	*ecc*	eccetera
electricity	*Electr*	elettricità
et cetera	*etc*	eccetera
feminine	*f*	femminile
figurative	*fig*	figurato
formal	*fml*	formale
geography	*Geog*	geografia
geology	*Geol*	geologia
grammar	*Gram*	grammatica
humorous	*hum*	umoristico
indefinite article	*indef art*	articolo indeterminativo
interjection	*int*	interiezione
interrogative	*inter*	interrogativo
invariable	*inv*	invariabile
law	*Jur*	legge/giuridico
literary	*liter*	letterario
masculine	*m*	maschile
mathematics	*Math*	matematica
mechanics	*Mech*	meccanica
medicine	*Med*	medicina